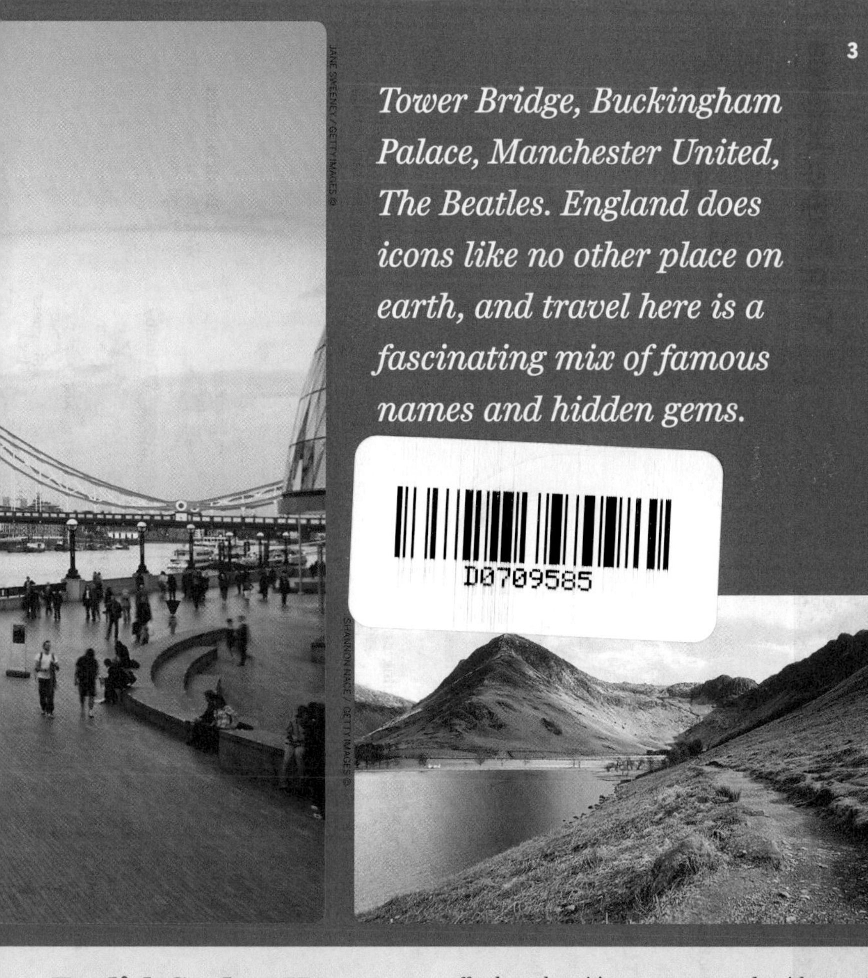

JANE SWEENEY / GETTY IMAGES ©

SHANNON NACE / GETTY IMAGES ©

English Spoken Here

And while England has developed a culture and traditions that may appear complex, on the surface at least it's familiar to many visitors thanks to a vast catalogue of British film and TV exports. The same applies when it comes to communication; this is home turf for the English language. For many visitors this means no need to carry a phrasebook – although you might get a little confused by local accents in places such as Devon or Liverpool.

Easy Does It

A final thing to remember while you're planning a trip to England: travel here is a breeze. Granted, it may not be totally effortless, but it's easy compared with many parts of the world. And although the locals may grumble (in fact, it's a national pastime) public transport is very good, and a train ride through the English landscape can be a highlight in itself. But whichever way you get around, in this compact country you're never far from the next town, the next pub, the next restaurant, the next national park or the next impressive castle on your hit list of highlights. The choice is endless, and we've hand-picked the best places to help steer you from place to place – but don't forget to mix it with making your own discoveries.

England

Top Experiences

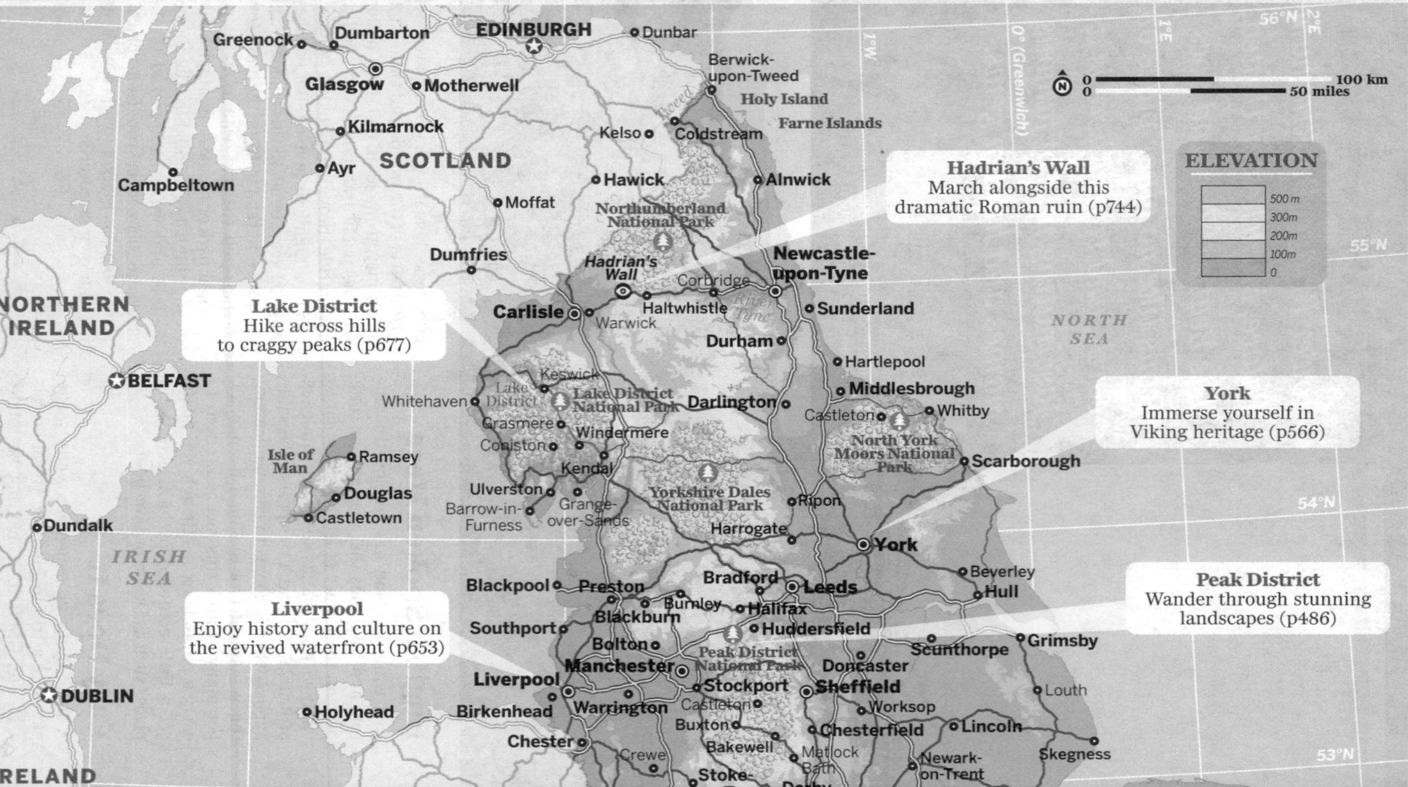

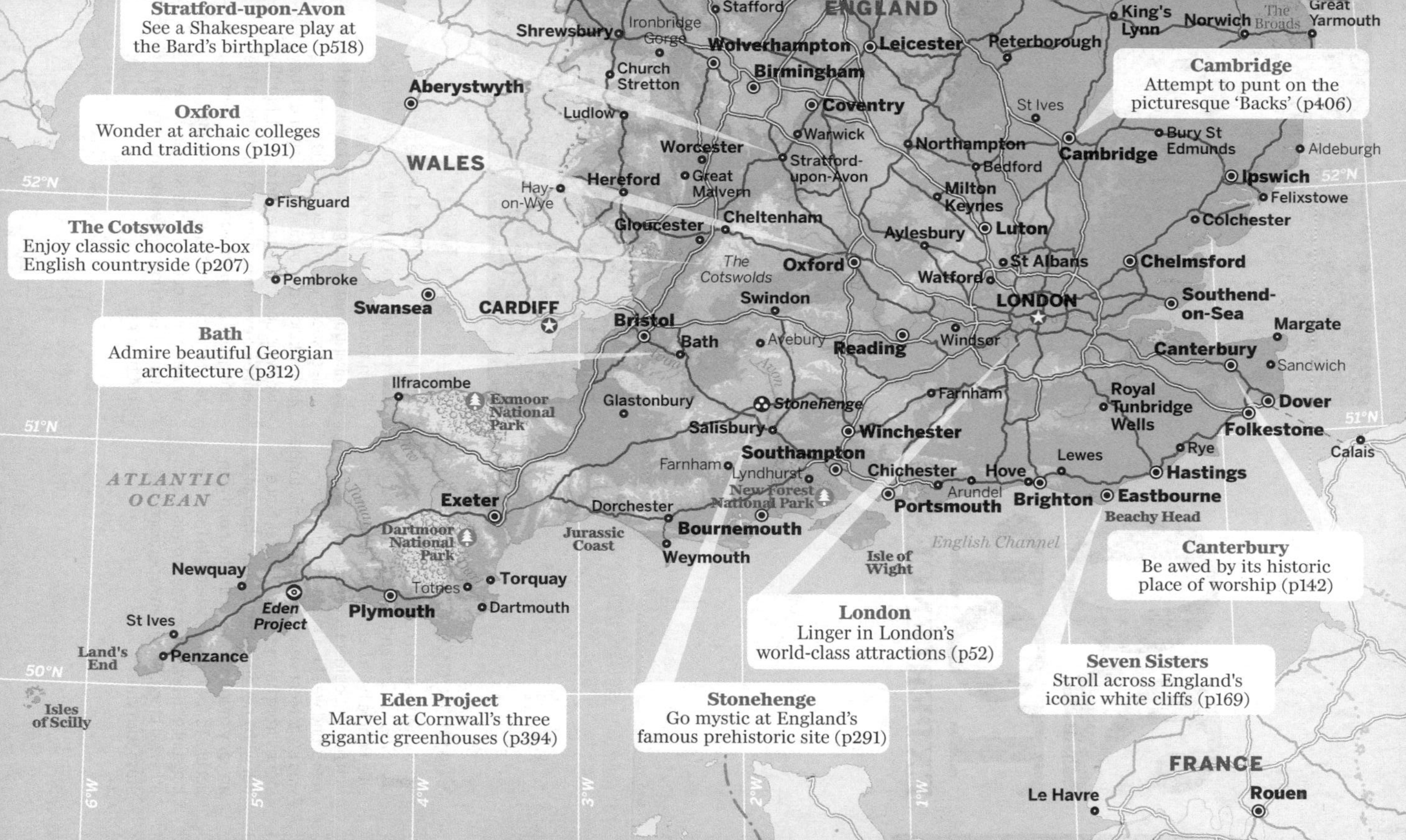
Stratford-upon-Avon
See a Shakespeare play at the Bard's birthplace (p518)
Oxford
Wonder at archaic colleges and traditions (p191)
The Cotswolds
Enjoy classic chocolate-box English countryside (p207)
Bath
Admire beautiful Georgian architecture (p312)
Eden Project
Marvel at Cornwall's three gigantic greenhouses (p394)
Stonehenge
Go mystic at England's famous prehistoric site (p291)
London
Linger in London's world-class attractions (p52)
Seven Sisters
Stroll across England's iconic white cliffs (p169)
Canterbury
Be awed by its historic place of worship (p142)
Cambridge
Attempt to punt on the picturesque 'Backs' (p406)
ENGLAND
WALES
FRANCE
ATLANTIC OCEAN
English Channel
LONDON
CARDIFF
Stafford
Shrewsbury
Ironbridge Gorge
Wolverhampton
Leicester
Peterborough
King's Lynn
Norwich
The Broads
Great Yarmouth
Church Stretton
Birmingham
Aberystwyth
Coventry
Ludlow
St Ives
Warwick
Northampton
Cambridge
Bury St Edmunds
Aldeburgh
Worcester
Stratford-upon-Avon
Bedford
Ipswich
Hereford
Great Malvern
Hay-on-Wye
Milton Keynes
Felixstowe
Fishguard
Cheltenham
Colchester
Gloucester
Aylesbury
Luton
The Cotswolds
Oxford
St Albans
Chelmsford
Pembroke
Watford
Swansea
Swindon
Southend-on-Sea
Bristol
Margate
Bath
Avebury
Reading
Windsor
Canterbury
Sandwich
Ilfracombe
Exmoor National Park
Glastonbury
Farnham
Stonehenge
Royal Tunbridge Wells
Dover
Salisbury
Winchester
Folkestone
Rye
Calais
Southampton
Lewes
Farnham
Lyndhurst
Chichester
Hove
Hastings
New Forest National Park
Arundel
Brighton
Eastbourne
Exeter
Portsmouth
Dorchester
Beachy Head
Bournemouth
Jurassic Coast
Dartmoor National Park
Weymouth
Isle of Wight
Newquay
Torquay
Totnes
Eden Project
Plymouth
Dartmouth
St Ives
Land's End
Penzance
Isles of Scilly
Le Havre
Rouen
52°N
51°N
50°N
6°W
5°W
4°W
3°W
2°W
1°W

20 TOP EXPERIENCES

Stonehenge

1 Mysterious and compelling, Stonehenge (p291) is England's most iconic ancient site. People have been drawn to this myth-rich ring of boulders for more than 5000 years, and we still don't know quite why it was built. Most visitors gaze at the 50-tonne stones from behind the perimeter fence, but with enough planning you can arrange an early morning or evening tour and gain access to the inner ring itself. In the slanting sunlight, away from the crowds, it's an ethereal place. This is an experience that stays with you.

Hadrian's Wall

2 Hadrian's Wall (p744) is one of the country's most revealing and dramatic Roman ruins, its 2000-year-old procession of abandoned forts, garrisons, towers and milecastles marching across the wild and lonely landscape of northern England. The wall was about defence and control, but this edge-of-empire barrier also symbolised the boundary of civilised order – to the north lay the unruly land of the marauding Celts, while to the south was the Roman world of orderly taxpaying, underfloor heating and bathrooms.

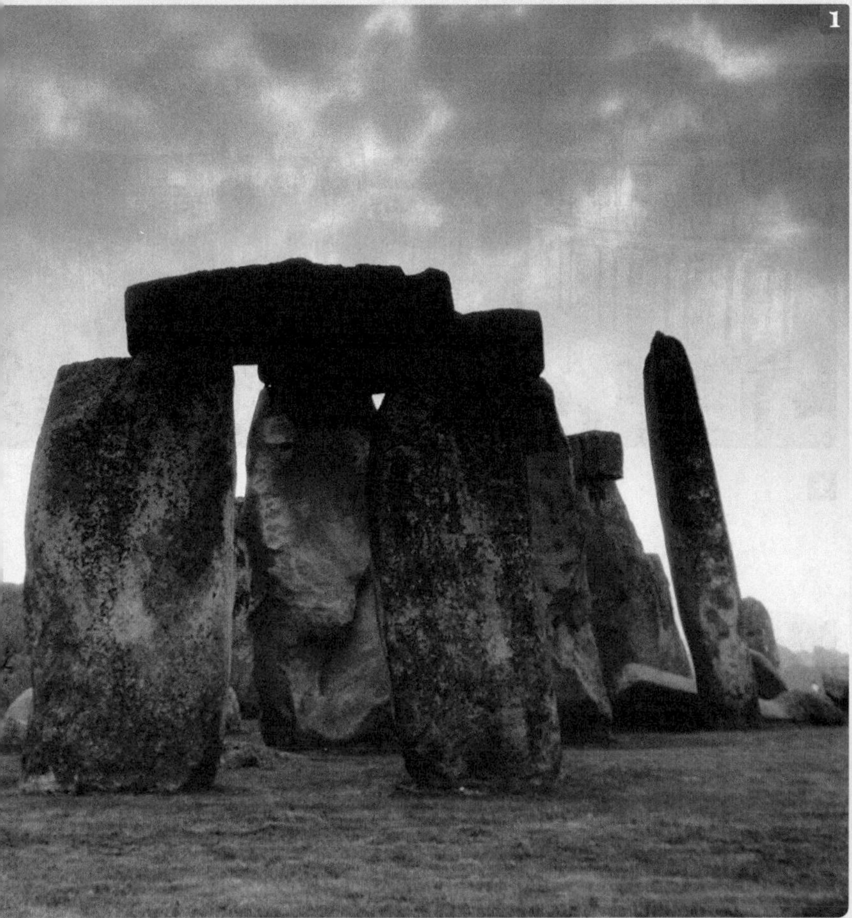

DAVID L. RYAN / GETTY IMAGES ©

DAVID ELSE / GETTY IMAGES ©

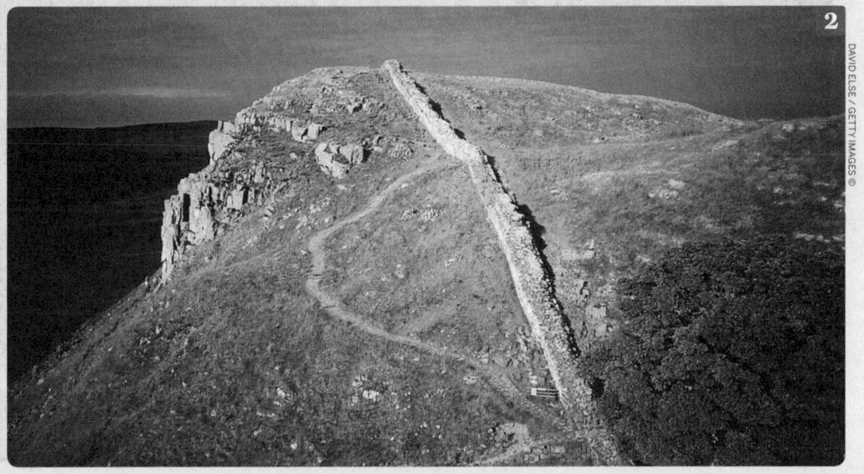

4

NEIL SETCHFIELD / GETTY IMAGES ©

Oxford

3 A visit to Oxford (p191) is as close as most of us will get to the brilliant minds and august institutions that have made this city famous across the globe. But you'll catch a glimpse of this rarefied world in the cobbled lanes and ancient quads where student cyclists and dusty academics roam. The beautiful college buildings, archaic traditions and stunning architecture have changed little over the centuries, leaving the city centre much as Einstein or Tolkien would have found it.

The Lake District

4 William Wordsworth and his Romantic friends were the first to champion the charms of the Lake District (p677) and it's not hard to see what stirred them. The dramatic landscape of whale-backed hills, deep valleys, misty mountain lakes and high peaks (including England's highest summit) makes this craggy corner of the country the spiritual home of English hiking. Strap on the boots, stock up on mint cake and drink in the views: inspiration is sure to follow. Tarn above Elterwater (p695)

York

5 With its Roman and Viking heritage, ancient city walls and maze of cobbled streets, York (p566) is a living showcase for the highlights of English history. Join one of the city's many walking tours and plunge into the network of snickelways (narrow alleys), each one the focus of a ghost story or historical character. Explore the intricacies of York Minster (p566), the biggest medieval cathedral in all of northern Europe, or admire the exhibits from more recent times at the National Railway Museum (p567), the world's largest collection of historic locomotives. The towers of York Minster

Bath

6 In a nation packed with pretty cities, Bath (p312) still stands out as the belle of the ball. Founded by the Romans, who established the spa resort of Aquae Sulis to take advantage of the area's hot springs, Bath hit its stride in the 18th century when the rich industrialist Ralph Allen and architects John Wood the Elder and John Wood the Younger, oversaw the city's reinvention as a model of Georgian architecture. Awash with amber town houses, sweeping crescents and Palladian mansions, Bath demands your undivided attention. Great Bath (p313)

The Cotswolds

7 The most wonderful thing about the Cotswolds (p207) is that no matter where you go or how lost you get, you'll still end up in an impossibly quaint village of rose-clad cottages and honey-coloured stone. There'll be a charming village green, a pub with sloping floors and fine ales, and a view of the lush green hills. It's easy to leave the crowds behind and find your very own slice of medieval England here – and some of the best boutique hotels in the country. Arlington Row (p221)

8

SIMON GREENWOOD / GETTY IMAGES ©

9

CHRISTOPHER FURLONG / GETTY IMAGES ©

Cambridge

8 One of England's two great historic university cities, Cambridge (p406) highlights include a tour of at least one of the ancient colleges, and time spent marvelling at the intricate vaulting of King's College Chapel (p407). But no trip to Cambridge is complete without an attempt to take a punt (flat-bottomed boat) along by the picturesque 'Backs' – the leafy, green lawns behind the city's finest colleges. Polish off the day with a pint in one of the many historic pubs. You'll soon wonder how you could have studied anywhere else. River Cam and Trinity College (p409)

Liverpool Museums

9 After a decade of development, the reborn waterfront is once again the heart of Liverpool (p653). The focal point is Albert Dock, a World Heritage Site of iconic and protected buildings, including a batch of top museums: the Merseyside Maritime Museum (p657) and International Slavery Museum (p656) ensure the good and bad sides of Liverpool's history are not forgotten, while the Tate Liverpool (p657) and the Beatles Story museum (p657) celebrate popular culture and the city's most famous musical sons (still). Tate Liverpool (p657)

Stratford-upon-Avon

10 The pretty town of Stratford-upon-Avon (p518) is where William Shakespeare, the world's most famous playwright, was born and later shuffled off this mortal coil. Today, its tight knot of Tudor streets form a living map of Shakespeare's life and times. Huge crowds of thespians and theatre lovers come to take in a play at the famous theatre. Visit the five historic houses owned by Shakespeare and his relatives, then take a respectful detour to the old stone church where the Bard was laid to rest. Shakespeare's House (p518)

Peak District

11 Curiously, you won't find many peaks in the Peak District (p486), but you will find blissful miles of tumbling moorland, plunging valleys, eroded gritstone crags, lush farmland and ancient pocket-sized villages. This beautiful landscape attracts a veritable army of outdoor enthusiasts – cyclists, hikers, cavers and rock climbers – on summer weekends, while those seeking more relaxing enjoyment can admire the rural market and famous puddings of Bakewell (p496), the Victorian pavilions of spa-town Buxton (p488) and stunning Chatsworth House (p497) – the 'Palace of the Peak'.

10

DAVID ELSE / GETTY IMAGES ©

TIM DRAPER / GETTY IMAGES ©

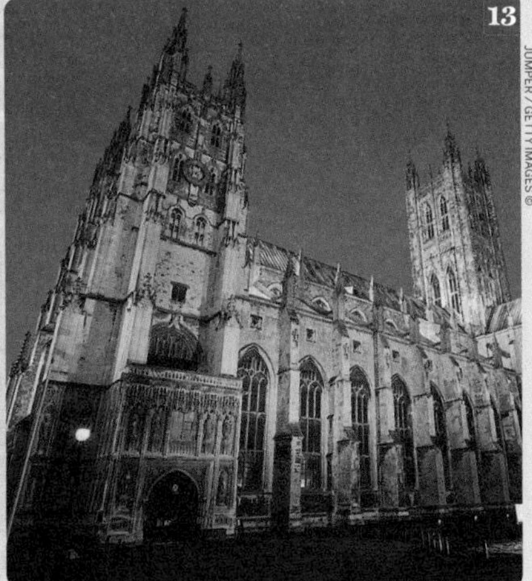

JUMPER / GETTY IMAGES ©

Afternoon Tea

12 Among England's many and varied traditions, afternoon tea is one of the most enticing and certainly one of the tastiest. Central to the ritual is the iconic beverage itself – brewed in a pot, ideally silver-plated, and poured carefully into fine, bone-china cups and saucers. Depending where you are in the country, this hot drink is served with scones and cream, fruitcake or wafer-thin cucumber sandwiches. Fancy city hotels and traditional country cafes are among the best places to sample this epicurean delight.

Canterbury Cathedral

13 Few other English cathedrals come close to Canterbury Cathedral (p142), the very fulcrum of the Anglican Church and a place of worship for over 15 centuries. Its intricate tower dominates the Canterbury city skyline, while at its heart lies a 12th-century crime scene, where Archbishop Thomas Becket was put to the sword on the supposed orders of the king – an event that launched a million pilgrimages and still pulls in the crowds today. A lone candle mourns the gruesome deed, the pink sandstone before it smoothed by 800 years' worth of devout kneeling.

England's Pubs

14 Despite the growth of stylish clubs and designer bars, the traditional neighbourhood or village pub is still the centre of social life in England, and a lunchtime or evening visit can be one of the best ways to get under the skin of the nation. A drink or two may be necessary as well, and ideally that means traditional beer. To outsiders it may be 'warm and flat', but give it a chance and you'll soon learn to savour the complex flavours of the country's many regional varieties.

Football

15 Much of the world may call it 'soccer' but to the English the national sport is definitely 'football'. And despite what the fans may say in Italy or Brazil, the English Premier League has some of the finest football teams in the world, with many of the world's best (and richest) players. The most famous club on the planet is still Manchester United (p636), while other big names include rival Manchester City, Arsenal, Liverpool and Chelsea. Tickets to matches are like gold dust, but most stadiums are open to visitors outside match days.

15

ROGER GAESS / GETTY IMAGES ©

16

TETRA IMAGES / GETTY IMAGES ©

Tower of London

16 The Tower of London (p69) is Europe's best-preserved medieval fortress and one of Britain's best-known attractions. At almost 1000 years old (more if you count the Roman foundations) it's an enduring landmark of the capital, and over the centuries this sturdy fortress has served the nation as a palace, prison, arsenal and mint. Today it's home to the legendary 'Beefeaters' and ravens that are attributed with mythical powers.

CHRISTER FREDRIKSSON / GETTY IMAGES ©

London's Theatre Scene

17 However you budget your time and money in London, make sure you take in a show. For big-names, head for the West End (London's equivalent to Broadway), where famous spots include the National Theatre (p125), Old Vic (p125), Shaftesbury and Theatre Royal at Drury Lane. For new and experimental works, try the Donmar Warehouse (p126) and Royal Court (p125). Either way, you'll see that London's theatre scene easily lives up to its reputation as one of the finest in the world – whatever New Yorkers say.

Seven Sisters Chalk Cliffs

18 Dover's iconic white cliffs grab the most attention, but the colossal chalky walls of the Seven Sisters (p169) are a much more spectacular affair. This 4-mile roller-coaster of sheer white rock rollicks along the Sussex shore overlooking the waters of the English Channel, an impressive southern border to the South Downs National Park (p169) and most dramatic at the towering headland of Beachy Head. Hikes through the grassy clifftop fields provide wide sea views, breathtaking in every sense.

Walking in England

19 Call it hiking or rambling – but most often simply walking – England is the perfect place to explore on two feet, thanks to its compact nature and protected network of 'rights of way'. You can stroll the narrow streets and hidden alleyways of the nation's famous historic towns, then head for the national parks and open countryside where a gentle walk alongside rivers or a serious trek over hills and mountains can be an excellent way to get to know England and the English a little better. South West Coast Path (p40), Cornwall

19

LEANNE WALKER / GETTY IMAGES ©

The Eden Project

20 Looking like a cross between a lunar landing station and a James Bond villain's lair, the three gigantic semispherical greenhouses of the Eden Project (p394) have become a symbol of Cornwall's renaissance. Dreamed up by ex–record producer Tim Smit and built in an abandoned clay pit near St Austell, Eden's three 'biomes' recreate the world's habitats in microcosm, from the lush jungles of the Amazon rainforest to the temperate plains of the African savannah.

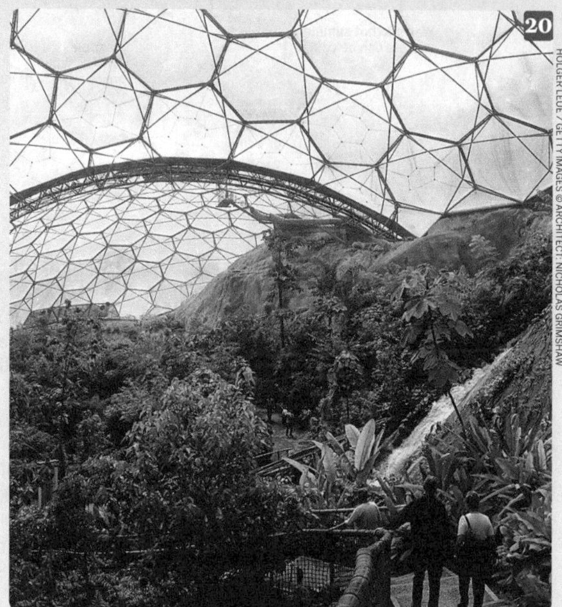

20

HOLGER LEUE / GETTY IMAGES © ARCHITECT: NICHOLAS GRIMSHAW

need to know

Currency

» Pound – also called 'pound sterling' (£)

Language

» English

When to Go

High Season

(Jun–Aug)

» Weather at its best. Accommodation rates high, particularly in August (school holidays).

» Roads busy, especially in seaside areas, national parks and popular cities such as Oxford, Bath and York.

Shoulder

(Easter–May, mid-Sep–Oct)

» Crowds reduce. Prices drop.

» Weather often good: March to May sun mixes with sudden rain; September and October can feature balmy 'Indian summers'.

Low Season

(Dec–Feb)

» Wet and cold is the norm. Snow can fall, especially up north.

» Opening hours reduced October to Easter; some places shut for the winter. Big-city sights (especially London's) operate all year.

Your Daily Budget

Budget less than £50

» Dorm beds £10–25

» Cheap meals in cafes and pubs £5–9

» Long-distance coach £10–30 for 200-mile journey

Midrange £50–100

» Midrange hotel or B&B £60–130 (London £90–180) per double room

» Main course in midrange restaurant £9–18

» Long-distance train £15–50 for 200-mile journey

» Car rental from £30 per day for a small car

Top end more than £100

» Accommodation in a 4-star hotel room from £130 (London £180)

» A three-course meal in a good restaurant £40 plus per person

Money

» Change bureaus and ATMs widely available, especially in cities and major towns.

Visas

» Not required by most citizens of Europe, Australia, NZ, USA and Canada.

Mobile Phones

» Phones from most other countries operate in England, but attract roaming charges. Local SIM cards cost from £10; SIM and basic handset around £30.

Driving

» Traffic drives on the left. Steering wheel on the right. Most rental cars have manual gears (stick-shift).

Websites

» **BBC** (www.bbc.co.uk) News and entertainment.

» **Enjoy England** (www.enjoyengland.com) Official tourism website.

» **Lonely Planet** (www.lonelyplanet.com/england) Destination information, hotel bookings, traveller forums and more.

» **Traveline** (www.traveline.org.uk) Great for all public transport around England.

» **British Arts Festivals** (www.artsfestivals.co.uk) Lists festivals – art, literature, music and more.

Exchange Rates

Australia	A$1	£0.63
Canada	C$1	£0.62
Europe	€1	£0.80
Japan	¥100	£0.77
New Zealand	NZ$1	£0.49
USA	US$1	£0.62

For current exchange rates see www.xe.com

Important Numbers

England (and UK) country code	☎44
International access code	☎00
Emergency (police, fire, ambulance, mountain rescue or coastguard)	☎999

Arriving in England

» **Heathrow Airport**
Train to London Paddington station every 15 minutes (from £18)

» **Gatwick Airport**
Train to London Victoria station every 15 minutes (from £16)

» **Eurostar trains from Paris or Brussels**
Arrive at St Pancras International station in central London

» **Buses from Europe**
Arrive at London Victoria Coach station

» **Taxis from airports**
Taxis cost £40-90 depending on the airport and time of day.

England on a Shoestring

If you're a shoestring traveller, there's no getting around it – England isn't cheap. Public transport, admission fees, restaurants and hotel rooms all tend to be expensive compared to many other European countries. But with some careful planning, a trip to England doesn't have to break the bank. You can save money by staying in B&Bs or hostels instead of hotels. Motels along motorways and outside large towns are soulless but who cares? Most of the time you're in them you'll be asleep.

You can also save considerably by prebooking long-distance travel by coach or train – and by avoiding periods when everyone else is on the move (eg Friday afternoon). Many attractions are free or offer discounts on quiet days (eg Mondays). And you won't have to scrounge up a penny to enjoy England's best assets: the wonderful countryside and coastline.

Everyone needs a helping hand when they visit a country for the first time. There are customs to get used to and etiquette to understand. The following section will help demystify England so your first trip goes as smoothly as your fifth.

Top Tips for Your Trip

» At major London airports, you can buy tickets for the express trains into central London from London Transport staff in the baggage arrivals hall; this saves queuing or dealing with unfamiliar machines.

» The best way to get local currency is usually from an ATM, but this term is rarely used in England; the colloquial term 'cash machine' is more common.

» If staying more than a couple of days in London, get the travel card the locals use, called an Oyster. For more details, see p136.

» Pickpockets and hustlers lurk in the more crowded tourist and transport areas, especially in London. No need to be paranoid, but do be on your guard.

» Britain's electrical plugs are not like those in the rest of Europe, so bring (or buy) a UK-specific plug adaptor.

Booking Ahead

Whatever your budget, book accommodation in advance for the first few nights, especially during high season.

If you're on a longer or more flexible trip, booking in advance is not essential. When arriving in a new area, the local tourist office will usually have a list of local hotels and B&Bs with availability.

Rental car deals are better if you book in advance and avoid peak periods.

Booking ahead is highly recommended for major journeys by public transport, as is avoiding peak periods. For more details, see the Transport chapter.

What to Wear

England's weather is notoriously changeable. A rain jacket is essential, as is a small backpack to carry it when the sun comes out. Bring sunscreen and an umbrella; you're bound to need both. Possibly even on the same day.

For sightseeing at castles, cathedrals, museums and galleries, remember what your granny told you: comfortable shoes can make or break a trip.

If you plan to enjoy England's great outdoors, suitable hiking gear is required in higher or wilder areas, but not for casual strolls in the countryside.

Some smarter pubs, bars and restaurants operate dress codes banning jeans, T-shirts and 'trainers' (sneakers, runners).

What to Pack

» Passport

» Credit card

» Driver's licence

» Phrasebook

» Plug adaptor (UK specific)

» Personal medicines

» Mobile (cell) phone and charger

» Earplugs

» Toiletries

» Sunscreen

» Sunhat

» Sunglasses

» Waterproof jacket

» Umbrella

» Comfortable shoes

» Padlock

» Torch

» Camera, memory cards and charger

» Pen and paper

» Taste for warm beer

Checklist

» Check the validity of your passport

» Check any visa or entry requirements

» Make any necessary bookings (sights, accommodation, travel)

» Check the airline baggage restrictions

» Put all restricted items (eg hair gel, pocket knife) in your hold baggage

» Inform your credit/debit card company

» Organise travel insurance

» Check mobile (cell) phone compatibility

» Check rental car requirements

Etiquette

» Manners

The English have a – sometimes overstated – reputation for being polite, and good manners are considered important in most situations. When asking directions, 'Excuse me, can you tell me the way to...' is a better tactic than 'Hey, where's...'

» Queues

In England, queues ('lines' to Americans) are sacrosanct, whether to board a bus, buy tickets or enter the gates of an attraction. Any attempt to 'jump the queue' will result in an outburst of tutting and hard stares, which is about as angry as most locals get in public.

» Escalators

If you take an escalator (especially at tube stations in London) or a moving walkway (eg at an airport) be sure to stand on the right, so folks can pass on the left.

» Bargaining

If you're in a market, it's OK to haggle over the price of goods (but not food). Politeness is still key though. Haggling in shops is rare.

Tipping

» Restaurants

Around 10% in restaurants and teahouses with table service. Nearer 15% at smarter restaurants. Tips may be added to your bill as a 'service charge'. Paying tips or the service charge is up to you.

» Pubs & Bars

If you order drinks (or food) and pay at the bar, tips are not expected. If you order at the table and your meal is brought to you, then 10% is usual.

» Taxis

Usually 10%, or rounded up to the nearest pound, especially in London.

Money

Paper money comes in £5, £10, £20 and £50 denominations; some shops don't accept £50 notes because fakes circulate. Other currencies are rarely accepted; some gift shops in London may take euros, US dollars and yen.

ATMs (often called 'cash machines') are common in cities and towns. Watch out for tampering; a common ruse is to attach a card reader to the slot. Visa and MasterCard credit and debit cards are widely accepted, except at some small B&Bs. Other credit cards, such as AmEx, are not so widely accepted.

Cities and larger towns have banks and currency-exchange kiosks for changing your money into pounds. Check rates first, as some offer poor rates. You can change money at some post offices. This is very handy in country areas, and exchange rates are fair.

what's new

For this new edition of England, our authors have hunted down the fresh, the transformed, the hot and the happening. Here are some of our favourites. For up-to-the-minute recommendations, see lonelyplanet.com/england.

Olympic Park, London

1 A huge swath of formerly neglected East London was transformed into London's Olympic Park for the 2012 Games, where iconic sporting architecture combined with landscaped grounds and wildlife habitats to create a legacy for the future. (p97)

Emirates Air Line Cable Car, London

2 Initially a public transport solution linking Olympic venues, the spectacular cable car across the River Thames is an attraction in its own right. (p99)

St Pancras Renaissance Hotel, London

3 Renaissance may be a hotel brand, but the name is appropriate here at St Pancras, a famous Victorian Gothic masterpiece now returned to its former glory. (p109)

Turner Contemporary, Margate

4 The landmark Turner Contemporary gallery stands proud on the south coast, bathed in the sea-refracted light so loved by the artist JMW Turner for whom it is named. (p152)

Firstsite, Colchester

5 Contrasting (some say clashing) with surrounding historic buildings, this striking new gallery of curved glass and copper is home to temporary exhibitions of challenging contemporary art. (p423)

Mary Rose Museum, Portsmouth

6 England's most famous shipwreck gets a new home, showing Henry VIII's flagship in a new light, and reuniting the vessel with artefacts raised from the deep. (p252)

River Cottage Canteen, Axminster

7 Chef and TV star Hugh Fearnley-Whittingstall campaigns for food that's local, sustainable, seasonal and organic – and that's exactly what you get at his newest eatery. (p348)

M Shed, Bristol

8 Lodged in a massive old warehouse overlooking the docks, Bristol's new museum is a treasure trove of memorabilia – from reminders of the slave trade to Massive Attack record decks. (p302)

Buxton Baths

9 Built in grand Regency style in 1854, and fronted by a curving facade inspired by the Royal Crescent in Bath, this historic building is due to reopen in 2014 as a five-star hotel and spa. (p489)

Museum of Liverpool

10 Liverpool's storied past is celebrated at this interactive exploration of cultural and historical milestones: poverty, wealth, football, plus – of course – the Beatles. (p658)

National Football Museum, Manchester

11 Football (aka 'soccer') was invented in England, and now the world's most popular game is fittingly celebrated here with exhibitions and events that fans will love. (p631)

Hepworth, Wakefield

12 The 2011 opening of this award-winning gallery of contemporary sculpture, anchored by a world-class collection of works by local lass Barbara Hepworth. (p615)

if you like...

Royal England

Queen Elizabeth II is an English icon, who celebrated her Diamond Jubilee in 2012 after 60 years on the throne. With a monarch at the top for a virtually unbroken 1500-year stretch, it's no surprise that many reminders of England's royal heritage dot the country today.

Buckingham Palace The Queen's official London residence, best known for its royal-waving balcony and the Changing of the Guard (p59)

Westminster Abbey Where English monarchs are crowned and married – most recently William and Kate (p57)

Tower of London A castle and royal palace for centuries, now holding the Crown Jewels; 900 years of history in one iconic building (p69)

Sandringham House The monarch's country residence, with a royal memorabilia museum (p449)

Royal Pavilion Opulent and fantastical palace built for King George IV (p172)

Althorp House Ancestral home and burial place of Diana, Princess of Wales (p473)

Osborne House Royal retreat on the Isle of Wight, built for Queen Victoria (p264)

Castles

England's turbulent history bequeaths a landscape dotted with defensive masterpieces of the medieval era, complete with moats, keeps, battlements, dungeons and all the classic features we know from history books and legends of knights in armour.

Windsor Castle Largest and oldest occupied fortress in the world, and the Queen's weekend retreat (p237)

Warwick Castle One of the finest castles in England; this well-preserved castle is both impressive and romantic (p515)

Tintagel Castle Atmospheric clifftop ruin, and the legendary birthplace of King Arthur (p371)

Bamburgh Castle Spectacularly positioned and largely rebuilt fortress on the Northumberland coast (p758); a sharp contrast to the nearby ruins of Dunstanburgh Castle

Richmond Castle Among England's oldest castles, with fantastic views from the medieval keep (p603)

Skipton Castle Little known, but probably the best-preserved medieval castle in the country (p598)

Cathedrals

The cathedrals of England are impressive and inspiring. Many display an eclectic mix of styles, with solid Norman naves later joined by graceful Gothic arches and, most beautiful of all, epic extents of stained-glass windows.

St Paul's Cathedral Symbol of London for centuries, and still an essential part of the city's skyline (p73)

York Minster One of the largest medieval cathedrals in all of Europe, especially renowned for its windows (p566)

Canterbury Cathedral Mothership of the Anglican Church, still attracting pilgrims and visitors in their thousands (p142)

Salisbury Cathedral Truly majestic cathedral, and English icon, topped by the tallest spire in England (p287)

Ely Visible for miles across the flatlands of eastern England, and locally dubbed the 'Ship of the Fens' (p420)

Liverpool Cathedral Liverpool's is the largest Anglican cathedral in England, and then there's the striking Catholic Cathedral of Christ the King; both are comparatively modern – two for the price of one (p656)

» The village of Castle Combe (p296)

Sporting England

In 2012 the Olympic Games were held in London, but England's sporting heritage goes much deeper, with a long history and passionate fans. Here are some of the best places to be among them.

Olympic Park London's Olympic Stadium has been converted for football, athletics and more, while the Aquatics Centre and Velodrome remain top-class venues (p97)

Old Trafford Home of legendary Manchester United (p636)

Wembley Stadium London home ground for the national football team and the venue for the FA Cup final (p810)

Twickenham Spiritual turf in London for English rugby union (p129)

Wimbledon Iconic London venue for the All England Lawn Tennis Championships (p102)

Epsom Surrey home of horse racing's biggest day, the Derby (p130)

Aintree Liverpool racecourse and site of the Grand National steeplechase (p658)

Lord's Cricket Ground The spot in London to watch cricket 'tests, and major one-day games (p130)

Historic Houses

England boasts a raft of historic houses, or 'stately homes' – vast mansions where the landed gentry have lived for generations and whose doors are now open to the rest of us.

Blenheim Palace Monumental baroque fantasy, Winston Churchill's birthplace and one of England's greatest stately homes (p200)

Castle Howard Another impressive baroque edifice, best-known as the setting for *Brideshead Revisited* (p578)

Harewood House Vast mansion with superb grounds laid out by Capability Brown (p614)

Chatsworth House Quintessential stately home and gardens; a treasure trove of heirlooms and works of art (p497)

Kingston Lacy Smothered with gold and graced by an overwhelming fresco, this is Dorset's must-see stately home (p272)

Wilton House Home for generations of Earls of Pembroke, this house packed with exquisite art and period furniture gives a glimpse into the rarefied existence of British aristocracy (p291)

Quaint Villages

If you want to see the England of your imagination (or period costume dramas), you'll love England's villages. Though different in character from region to region, all are a reminder of a more bucolic age.

Castle Combe Overlooked for centuries, this place in Wessex won the 'Prettiest Village in England' award in the 1960s and then starred in the original *Dr Dolittle* movie. It remains unchanged today, and film crews still stop by (p296)

Lavenham One of England's most beautiful spots: a collection of exquisitely preserved medieval buildings in East Anglia virtually untouched since the 15th century (p430)

Painswick The Cotswold Hills has many pretty villages, with hilltop Painswick an absolute gem, unassuming and gloriously noncommercial (p223)

Hutton-le-Hole One of Yorkshire's loveliest villages, with sheep grazing on a wide green amid a scattering of cottages (p590)

Hawkshead Surrounded by dramatic natural scenery, this maze of cobbled lanes and whitewashed cottages is the Lake District's most handsome village (p690)

If You Like... Weird Stuff
Forbidden Corner is a bizarre labyrinth of miniature castles, caves, temples and gardens. (p584)

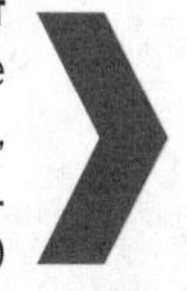

Moors & Mountains

For a crowded country, England has a surprising proportion of countryside, some of it even more surprisingly high and wild – a playground for hikers and other lovers of the great outdoors.

North York Moors National Park Wild and windswept, with whale-back hills stretching all the way to the sea, topped by England's largest expanse of heather (p588)

Lake District A feast of mountains, valleys, views and – of course – lakes; the place to hike the hilltops that inspired William Wordsworth (p677)

Yorkshire Dales National Park With scenic valleys, high hills and deep caves, the Dales are designed for hiking, biking and caving (p597)

Dartmoor Exhilarating wilderness, hidden valleys and southern England's highest hills (p359)

Peak District OK, so it's the most visited national park in Europe, but all those outdoor enthusiasts can't be wrong (p486)

Shopping

For every identikit megastore in England, there's an independent shop with soul and character, whether you're in the market for books, clothes, jewellery, arts and crafts, retro handbags or 1960s vinyl.

Hay-on-Wye Self-proclaimed secondhand book capital of the world, with over 30 bookshops and millions of volumes to attract browsers (p537)

Victoria Quarter In Leeds, lovely arcades of wrought ironwork and stained glass, home to several top fashion boutiques (p612)

Brighton's North Laine The perfect place to pick up vegetarian shoes, Elvis outfits and circus monocycles (p181)

Tetbury An upper-class shopping experience, with stylish shops, and an outlet for goodies from the Prince of Wales' estate at nearby Highgrove (p221)

Ludlow Foodie heaven, where almost everything is organic, artisan, sustainable or locally sourced (p558)

Art Galleries

Fans of the visual arts are spoiled for choice. Galleries abound, from long-standing classics in London and larger cities exhibiting some of the most famous paintings in the world, to quirky locations featuring experimental and up-and-coming artists. Some of the galleries are works of art in themselves.

National Gallery The best-known gallery in London, full to the brim with the finest works (p67)

Tate Modern London's other Tate focuses on modern art in all its wonderful permutations (p76)

BALTIC – Centre for Contemporary Art The 'Tate of the North' in Newcastle features work by some of contemporary art's biggest show-stoppers (p728)

Barber Institute of Fine Arts With works by Rubens, Turner and Picasso, this Birmingham gallery is no lightweight (p507)

Turner Contemporary In seaside Margate, the south coast's newest art space occupies a purpose-built structure next to the sea, named for one of England's finest artists (p152)

If You Like... Clifftop Drama
The **Minack** is a unique theatre, carved into the sheer rocks overlooking the sea in wild west Cornwall. With the Atlantic as a backdrop it's dramatic in every sense. The classic play to see is the theatre's signature piece: *The Tempest*. (p382)

Festivals

Whatever your taste in music or the arts, there's a festival for you somewhere in England.

Notting Hill Carnival London's Caribbean community shows the city how to party (p103)

Glastonbury Thirty years on and still going strong, Britain's biggest and best-loved music festival (p328)

Brighton Festival You know a festival's matured when it grows a fringe, and this gathering of all things arts is now firmly placed on the calendar (p175)

Latitude An eclectic mix of music, literature, dance, drama and comedy, with a stunning location in Southwold and manageable size (p435)

Artsfest Birmingham's cultural extravaganza, featuring ballet and bhangra to rhythm and blues (p508)

Reading Festival Venerable rock gathering that traces its roots back to the 1960s (p237)

Leeds Festival Northern companion to the long-established Reading Festival (p608)

Coastal Beauty

It won't have escaped your notice that England is part of the island of Britain. Surrounded by the sea, the country boasts a nautical heritage and a long coastline with many beautiful spots.

Holkham Bay Pristine 3-mile beach; the vast expanse of sand gives a real sense of isolation with giant skies stretching overhead (p447)

Jurassic Coast Exhilarating 3-D geology lesson, with towering rock stacks, sea-carved arches and fossils aplenty, plus some of the best beaches in the country (p273)

Beachy Head & Seven Sisters Where the South Downs plunge into the sea, these mammoth chalk cliffs provide a dramatic finale (p169)

Spurn Head National nature reserve amid a string of sand dunes, and a paradise for birdwatchers (p624)

Land's End The cliffs and coves at England's far western tip are some of the most dramatic in the country (if you ignore the theme park) (p381)

Seaside Towns

High cliffs and hidden coves are one thing, but for a different view of England's coast you have to sample a traditional seaside resort. This is the place for Victorian piers, buckets and spades, candy floss and a stroll along the prom-prom-prom…

Scarborough The original British seaside resort, where it all began back in the 17th century (p583)

Southwold A genteel seaside town with a lovely sandy beach, charming pier and rows of colourful beach huts (p435)

Bournemouth Seven miles of sandy beach, 3000 deckchairs, 1800 beach huts and a pair of Edwardian cliff lifts (p267)

Brighton Away from the ubercool scene there are still plenty of naughty postcards and kiss-me-quick hats in 'London-by-the-Sea' (p172)

Eastbourne South coast favourite, once known as the nation's retirement home, where new attractions and lively ambience attract a considerably younger crowd (p167)

month by month

Top Events

1 **Brighton Festival**, May

2 **Glastonbury Festival**, Late June

3 **Glyndebourne**, Late May–August

4 **Notting Hill Carnival**, Late August

5 **Trooping the Colour**, Mid-June

January

After the festivities of Christmas and New Year's Eve, the first few weeks of the year can feel a bit of an anticlimax – never helped by the often bad weather.

The London Parade

A ray of light in the gloom, the New Year's Day Parade in London (to use its official title) is one of the biggest events of its kind in the world, featuring marching bands, street performers, classic cars, floats and displays, winding their way through the streets. See www.londonparade.co.uk.

February

February is midwinter in England. The country may be scenic under snow and sunshine, but more likely grey and gloomy. Festivals and events to brighten the mood are still thin on the ground.

Jorvik Viking Festival

In chilly mid-February, the ancient Viking capital of York becomes home once again to invaders and horned helmets galore, with the intriguing addition of longship races (p573).

March

Spring starts to show itself, with daffodil blooms brightening up the month. Some people cling to the winter mood, but hotels and inns offer special weekend rates to tempt them out from under their duvets.

University Boat Race

Annual race down the River Thames in London between rowing teams from Cambridge and Oxford Universities – an institution (since 1856) that still enthrals the country. Late March (p102).

April

The weather is looking up, warmer and drier days bringing out the spring blossoms. Sights and attractions that closed for the low season open up around the middle of the month or at Easter.

Grand National

Half the country has a flutter on the highlight of the three-day horse race meeting at Aintree, a steeplechase with a testing course and high jumps. First Saturday in April (p664).

London Marathon

In early April, super-fit athletes cover 26 miles, 385 yards in just over two hours. Others dress up in daft costumes and take considerably longer (p102).

Camden Crawl

This is your chance to see the next big thing in the music scene or a secret gig by an established act, with 40 of Camden's venues given over to live music for two full days in late April/early May (p102).

May

With sunny spring days, the calendar fills with more events. Two public holidays (the first and last Mondays of May) mean road traffic is very busy over the adjoining long weekends.

FA Cup Final

The highlight of the football season for more than a century. All winter, teams from all of England's football divisions have been battling it out in a knockout tournament, culminating in this heady spectacle at Wembley Stadium – the home of English footy. Held in early May.

Brighton Festival

The lively three-week arts fest takes over the streets of buzzy south-coast resort Brighton during May. Alongside the mainstream performances there's a festival 'fringe' as well (p175).

Chelsea Flower Show

The Royal Horticultural Society flower show in late May is the highlight of the gardener's year. Top garden designers take gold, silver and bronze medals (and TV accolades), while the punters take the plants in the last-day giveaway (p102).

Glyndebourne

From late May til the end of August, this open-air festival of world-class opera enlivens the pastoral surroundings of Glyndebourne House in East Sussex (p172).

Cotswold Food & Farming Festival

A celebration of local food and farming at the Cotswold Farm Park near Cheltenham, with stalls, displays, activities and demonstrating chefs. Main festival in May; others later in the year.

June

Now it's almost summer. You can tell because June sees the music festival season kick off properly, while sporting events – from rowing to racing – fill the calendar.

Derby Week

Horse racing, people-watching and clothes-spotting are on the agenda at this week-long race meeting in Epsom, Surrey, in early June. See www.epsomderby.co.uk.

Cotswold Olimpicks

Welly-wanging, pole-climbing and shin-kicking are the key disciplines at this traditional Gloucestershire sports day in early June (see p214), held each year since 1612.

Isle of Wight Festival

Originally held at the height of the Summer of Love in 1968, this musical extravaganza was resurrected in 2002. Today it attracts top bands, especially from the indie and rock fraternities. Held in mid-June.

Trooping the Colour

Military bands and bearskinned grenadiers march down London's Whitehall in this mid-June martial pageant to mark the monarch's birthday (p102).

Royal Ascot

It's hard to tell which matters more – the fashion or the fillies – at this highlight of the horse-racing year, held in mid-June at Berkshire's Royal Ascot racetrack. Expect top hats, designer frocks and plenty of frantic betting (p239).

Wimbledon Lawn Tennis Championships

Correctly titled the All England Club Championship, and the best-known grass-court tennis tournament in the world, Wimbledon attracts all the big names. Held in late June (p102).

Glastonbury Festival

England's favourite pop and rock fest held (nearly) every year on a dairy farm in Somerset in late June (see p328). Invariably muddy and still a rite of passage for every self-respecting British teenager.

Meltdown Festival

In late June, London's Southbank Centre hands over the curatorial reins to a legend of contemporary music (David Bowie, Morrissey, Patti Smith) to pull together a full program of concerts, talks and films (p102). See www.southbankcentre.co.uk.

Royal Regatta

In late June or early July, boats of every description take to the water for an upper-crust river regatta at Henley-on-Thames (p206).

Rochester Dickens Festival

Charles Dickens is one of England's best-known writers, celebrated at this literary festival in the town where he lived and based many of his novels.

Pride

The big event on the gay-and-lesbian calendar, a technicolour street parade through London's West End, culminating in a concert in Trafalgar Sq (p103). Late June or early July.

July

This is it: summer, with weekly festivals and country shows. Schools break up at the end of the month, so there's a holiday tingle in the air, dulled only by busy Friday-evening roads.

Great Yorkshire Show

In July, the charming town of Harrogate plays host to one of England's largest county shows. Expect Yorkshire grit, Yorkshire tykes, Yorkshire puddings, Yorkshire beef… See www.greatyorkshireshow.co.uk.

International Birdman Competition

In the first weekend in July, competitors dressed as batmen, fairies and flying machines compete in an outlandish celebration of self-powered flight at West Sussex's Bognor Regis. The furthest flight takes home a £30,000 prize. So far no one's got near the hallowed 100m goal. See www.birdman.org.uk.

Latitude Festival

A small but fast-growing art gathering in the lovely Suffolk seaside town of Southwold. There's theatre, cabaret, art, literature and poetry readings, plus top names from the alternative music scene. Held in mid-July.

Cowes Week

The country's biggest yachting spectacular hits the choppy seas around the Isle of Wight in late July.

Womad

In late July, roots and world music take centre stage at this former Reading-based festival, now in a country park near Melmesbury in the south Cotswolds. See www.womad.org.

Truck

Held in late July, this indie music festival in Steventon, Oxfordshire, has a loyal following and is known for its eclectic acts. See www.thisistruck.com.

August

Schools and colleges are closed, parliament is in recess, the sun is shining (hopefully), most people go away for a week or two (some of them abroad), and England is in a holiday mood.

Notting Hill Carnival

A multicultural, Caribbean-style street carnival in late August in London's Notting Hill. Steel drums, dancers, and outrageous costumes (p103).

Reading Festival

England's second-oldest music festival. Originally a rock fest, it veers a bit more towards pop these days, but it's still a good bet for big-name bands. Happens in late August (p237).

Leeds Festival

Leeds' major music festival (p608), and the northern sister of the festival in Reading. The two festivals are the same late-August weekend, with the same line up. If they play Reading on the Friday they'll play Leeds on Saturday, and vice versa.

Manchester Pride

One of England's biggest celebrations of gay, bisexual and transgender life (p637). Happens in late August; see www.manchesterpride.com.

Mathew Street Festival

In last week of August, the world's biggest tribute to the Beatles features six days of music, a convention and a memorabilia auction in Liverpool. See www.mathewstreetfestival.org.

September

The first week of September feels more like August, but then the schools open up again, motorway traffic returns to normal and the summer party's over for another year. Good weather is still a chance.

Bestival

Quirky music festival in early September, with a different fancy-dress theme every year. Held at Robin Hill Country Park on the Isle of Wight (p266).

World Gurning Championships

Gurning is face-pulling, and this has to be one of the weirdest events of the year. Elastic-faced contestants come to Egremont in

Cumbria in mid-September, contorting their features in a bid to pull the most grotesque expressions.

Great North Run

Britain's biggest marathon is in London, but the Great North Run in Tyneside is the biggest half-marathon in the world, with the greatest number of runners of any race over this distance.

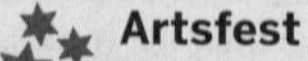

Artsfest

The UK's largest free arts festival features visual arts, dance and musical performances in venues across Birmingham (p508).

October

October means autumn. Leaves turn golden-brown and, unless there's an 'Indian Summer', the weather starts to get cold. Sights and attractions start to shut down for the low season, and accommodation rates drop.

Falmouth Oyster Festival

The westcountry port of Falmouth hosts this event to mark the start of the traditional oyster-catching ('dredging') season, and celebrate of local food from the sea and farmland of Cornwall.

Horse of the Year Show

The country's major indoor horse show, with dressage, show-jumping and other equine activities. Held in early October at the National Exhibition Centre (NEC) near Birmingham.

November

Winter's here, and November is dull. The weather's often cold and damp, summer is a distant memory and Christmas seems far away: suitably sombre for Remembrance Day, while Guy Fawkes Night sparks up some fun.

Guy Fawkes Night

Also called Bonfire Night and Fireworks Night, 5 November sees fireworks filling the country's skies in commemoration of a failed attempt to blow up parliament in 1605. Effigies of Guy Fawkes, the leader of the Gunpowder Plot, often burn on bonfires. See www.bonfirenight.net.

Remembrance Day

On 11 November, red poppies are worn and wreaths are laid in towns and cities around the country. The day commemorates military personnel killed and injured in the line of duty, from the World Wars to modern conflicts. See www.poppy.org.uk.

World's Biggest Liar Contest

Another whacky event, and it's Cumbria again. Fibbers from all walks of life go head-to-head in a battle of mid-November mendacity at the Bridge Inn in Wasdale.

December

Schools break up around mid-December, but most shops and businesses keep going until Christmas Eve. Many towns and cities hold Christmas Markets, ideal places for picking up Christmas presents. Holiday-makers hit the roads on the weekend before Christmas Day, driving to see family or heading for the airports.

New Year Celebrations

On 31 December, fireworks and street parties happen in town squares across the country, lighting up the nation to welcome in the New Year.

itineraries

Whether you've got six days or 60, these itineraries provide a starting point for the trip of a lifetime. Want more inspiration? Head online to lonelyplanet.com/thorntree to chat with other travellers.

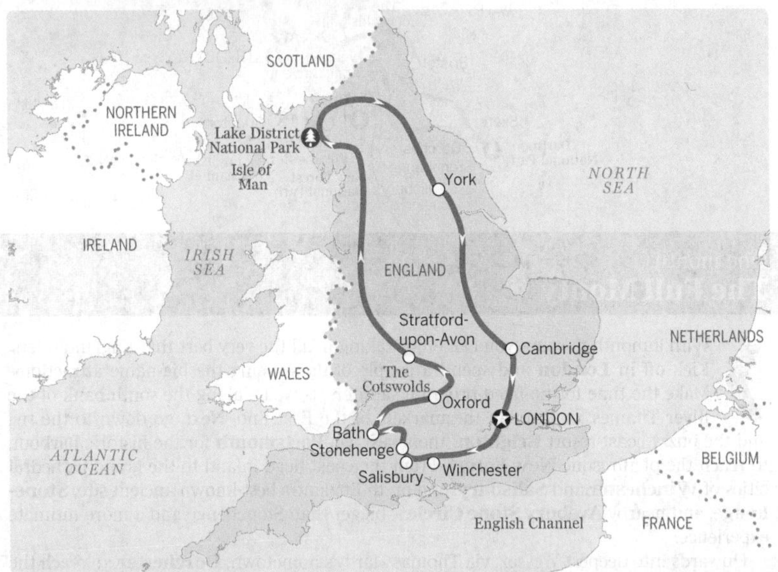

Eight to 10 days

England Express

In just over a week you can still see many of England's highlights. Start with a full day in the capital, **London**, simply walking the streets to admire the world-famous sights: Buckingham Palace, Tower Bridge, Trafalgar Square and more. Then head west for one or both of the grand cathedral cities of **Winchester** and **Salisbury**. Next stop: ancient history – the iconic menhirs of **Stonehenge**.

A short hop northwest is the beautiful historic city of **Bath,** for Roman history and fabulous Georgian architecture. Then cruise across the classic English countryside of the **Cotswolds** to reach that ancient seat of learning, **Oxford**. Not far away is **Stratford-upon-Avon**, for everything Shakespeare.

Next, strike out north for the **Lake District**, one of the country's most scenic areas, then across to **York** for Viking remains and the stunning Minster. End your trip with a visit to **Cambridge**, England's other great university city. Then a final day back in **London**, immersed in galleries, museums, luxury shops, street markets, West End shows or East End cafes – or whatever takes your fancy.

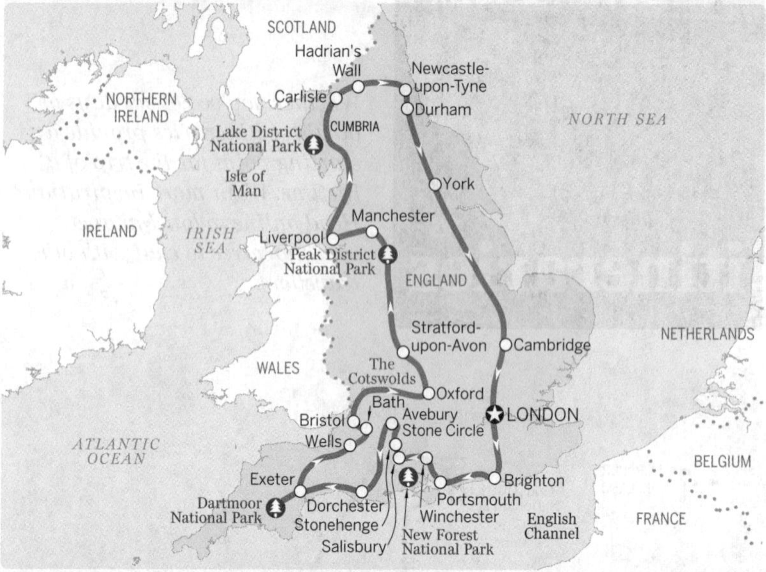

One month

The Full Monty

With a month to spare you can enjoy taking in all the very best that England offers. Kick off in **London** and spend a couple of days seeing the big-name attractions. Make the time for no-fixed-program saunters as well – along the south bank of the River Thames, or through the markets of the East End. Next, go down to the sea and the buzzy coast-resort **Brighton**; then west, via **Portsmouth** for the historic harbour, to reach the picturesque **New Forest**. From the coast head inland to the grand cathedral cities of **Winchester** and **Salisbury**, and on to England's best-known ancient site, **Stonehenge**, and nearby **Avebury Stone Circle** – bigger than Stonehenge and a more intimate experience.

Onwards into deepest Wessex, via Thomas Hardy's hometown, **Dorchester**, to reach the neat little city of **Exeter** and the wide and wild expanse of **Dartmoor National Park**. Then it's time for yet another historic city, **Wells**, with its beautiful cathedral, en route to the Georgian masterpiece of **Bath** and the southwest's big little city, **Bristol**. Next comes the classic English countryside of the **Cotswolds**, with a stop at delightful Stow-on-the-Wold, and maybe Broadway or Chipping Campden, before reaching **Oxford**, England's original seat of learning. Not far away is Shakespeare Central at **Stratford-upon-Avon** – tie in your visit here with seeing a play by the Bard himself. Continue journeying north via the heather-clad moors and tranquil limestone dales of the **Peak District** to reach England's second city, **Manchester**, and neighbouring cultural crossroads **Liverpool**.

Then it's back to the wilds again with a short hop to the scenic wonders of the **Lake District**. From the sturdy border town of **Carlisle**, follow the ancient Roman landmark of **Hadrian's Wall** all the way to revitalised **Newcastle-upon-Tyne**. Then it's into the home stretch, south via **Durham** and its world-class cathedral, and then **York** for its Viking remains and stunning Minster, to reach **Cambridge**, England's other great university city. From here it's a hop back to **London**, to use up the last few days of your grand tour taking in highlights such as Trafalgar Square, the National Gallery, Tate Modern and Tower of London, all polished off with a stroll across Westminster Bridge as Big Ben chimes the hour.

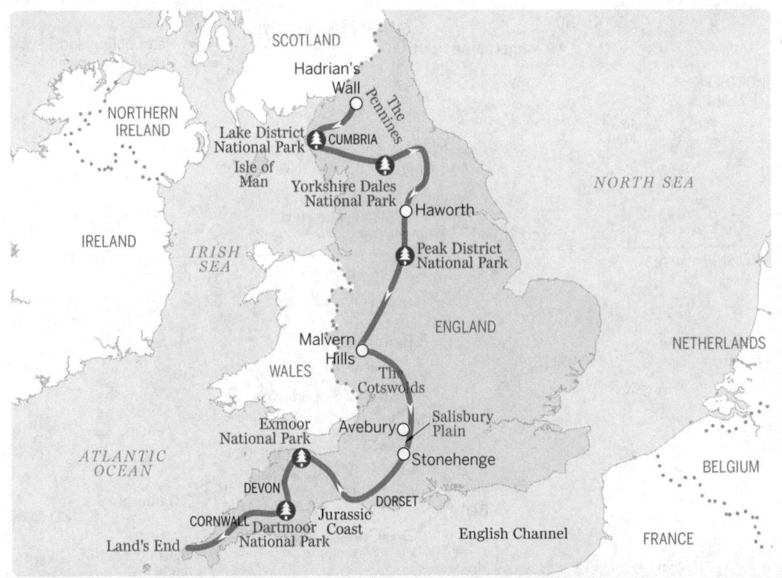

Two to three weeks

The Wild Side

This is a tour through the best of England's natural landscape, the inspiration for generations of poets, writers and composers. So put on your hiking boots, or have a camera at the ready, as we take a northeast–southwest meander through some of the country's finest national parks and stretches of open countryside.

Start at the spectacular Roman remains of **Hadrian's Wall**, one of England's finest reminders of the classical era, where you can explore the ancient forts and stride beside the ramparts centurion-style. Then continue into **Cumbria** for the high peaks of the **Lake District**, once the spiritual home of Wordsworth and the Romantic poets, now a mecca for outdoor fans, with hikes and strolls for all abilities, beautiful vistas of lakes, plus cosy inns and traditional country hotels.

Travelling east from the Lakes carries you across the **Pennines** – the chain of hills known as the backbone of England – to reach the green hills and valleys of the **Yorkshire Dales**. Nearby are the moors around **Haworth** – inspiration for Emily Brontë's *Wuthering Heights*.

Travel south through the hills and dales of the **Peak District**, stopping off to explore the great estate around Chatsworth if time allows, then through central England (via Elgar's beloved **Malvern Hills**) to reach the classic English countryside of the **Cotswolds**. Then continue southwards again to enjoy the epic emptiness of **Salisbury Plain**, home to **Stonehenge** and other archaeological intrigues. Nearby is **Avebury**, England's other great stone circle. A few miles more and you're on Dorset's spectacular fossil-ridden **Jurassic Coast**.

Then head into England's toe, the Westcountry Peninsula, jutting deep into the Atlantic. Take in the lush farmland of Devon and the heathery hills and sandy coves of **Exmoor**, then it's on to the eerie granite tors of **Dartmoor**, offering some of the country's most bleakly beautiful views. Next stop: Cornwall, for pretty ports, gorse-clad cliffs and sparkling bays. Then finish this bucolic excursion at **Land's End**, where the English mainland finally runs out of steam and plunges headlong into the restless ocean.

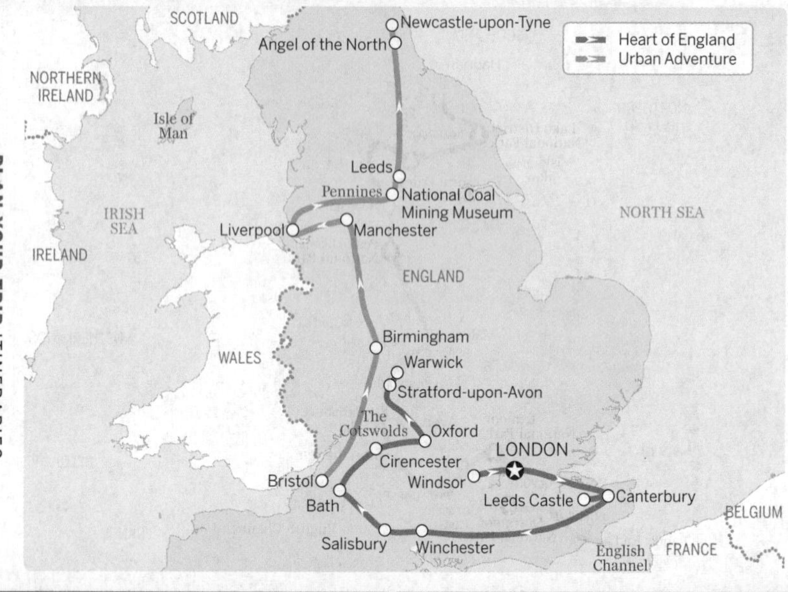

Two to three weeks

Heart of England

This journey through England's central regions starts in **London**, with its biggest landmarks: Trafalgar Square, Westminster Abbey, the Tower of London, St Paul's Cathedral and Buckingham Palace. Out of the centre, the gorgeous gardens at Kew, Eton College and **Windsor Castle** are also must-see sights.

Beyond the capital is old England proper, especially around the market towns of Kent, where **Canterbury Cathedral** and **Leeds Castle** are top architectural spots.

Then loop through Sussex and into Hampshire, where **Winchester**, the ancient capital, boasts another fine cathedral. Jostling for prominence is nearby **Salisbury**, with its famous cathedral spire dominating the landscape for miles around.

Out to the west, **Bath** is crammed with landmark English architecture, while the picture-perfect **Cotswolds** conceal a host of pretty towns and villages, such as Northleach, **Cirencester** and Wantage, as well as the grand stately home of Blenheim Palace. On to **Oxford**, one of the country's great centres of learning, and **Stratford-upon-Avon**, home of Shakespeare. There's just time to top up on English history at stunning **Warwick Castle**.

Eight to 10 days

Urban Adventure

Beyond London, England's cities are a vibrant counterpoint to the tranquil coast and countryside. Start in **Bristol**, a thriving regional capital famed for its engineering heritage and lively cultural scene. Then to **Birmingham**, in the heart of the Midlands, once forlorn and now a byword for successful urban renewal.

Continue north to reach **Manchester**, famous for its music and football team, where architectural highlights include the stunning Imperial War Museum North. Nearby **Liverpool** is reinventing itself as a cultural capital, with the redevelopment most apparent at the historic waterfront, Albert Dock.

Cross the **Pennines** to reach **Leeds**, the 'Knightsbridge of the North' where rundown factories and abandoned warehouses are now loft apartments and ritzy boutiques. But don't forget the past: go underground at the **National Coal Mining Museum**.

Further north is **Newcastle-upon-Tyne** and neighbouring Gateshead, former kings of coal, ships and steel, where heavy industry has given way to art and architecture, most notably the BALTIC contemporary gallery, and the Sage concert hall. Conclude your urban tour with a visit to England's best-known public art, the iconic **Angel of the North**.

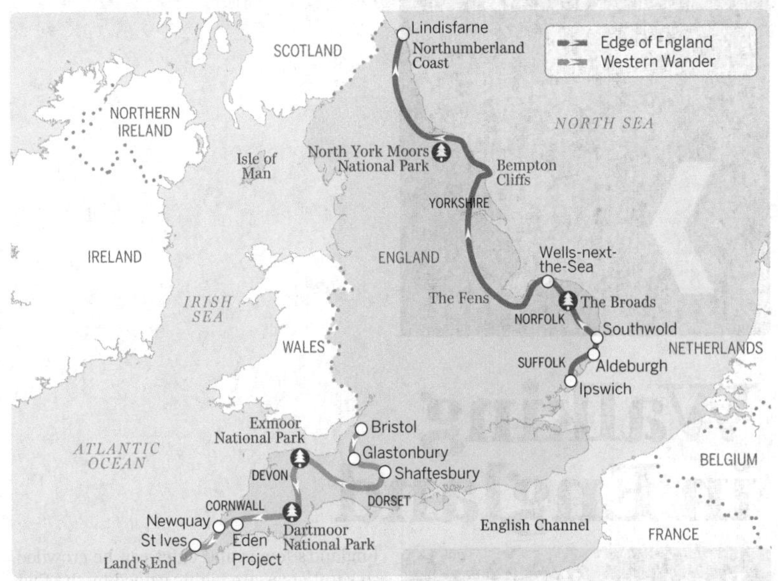

Two weeks

Edge of England

If you like to travel off the main routes, and enjoy less-than-hectic landscapes, try this route.

Start in **Ipswich**, then visit sleepy **Suffolk** county, where quaint villages and market towns like Sudbury and Lavenham dot the landscape, while along the coast are wildlife reserves, shingle beaches, fishing ports such as **Aldeburgh**, and the delightfully retro seaside resort of **Southwold**.

Things get even quieter in **Norfolk**, especially around the misty lakes and windmill-lined rivers of **the Broads**. For beach strolls or historic country pubs head for the coastal villages near **Wells-next-the-Sea**.

North of Norfolk lies the eerie, pan-flat landscape of **the Fens**, now a haven for otters and birdlife. Then it's north again into Yorkshire to one of England's finest wildlife spectacles: the massive breeding seabird colonies at **Bempton Cliffs**.

Continue into the heather-clad **North York Moors** where humpbacked hills roll all the way to the coast to drop dramatically into the choppy waters of the North Sea.

Round things off with a stroll between the castles of Bamburgh and Dunstanburgh on the wild **Northumberland Coast**, finishing your tour at the holy island of **Lindisfarne**.

Two weeks

Western Wander

The southwest of England is characterised by a rich, green landscape surrounded by glistening seas.

Start in **Bristol**, the capital of the Westcountry, then saunter down to **Glastonbury** – famous for its summer music festival and the best place to stock up on candles or crystals at any time of year. South leads into **Dorset**, where highlights include picturesque **Shaftesbury**. West leads to heathery **Exmoor National Park**.

Onwards into **Devon**, where there's a choice of coasts, as well as **Dartmoor**, the highest and wildest hills in southern England.

Cross into **Cornwall** to browse the galleries at **St Ives**, explore **Tintagel Castle**, the legendary birthplace of King Arthur, or wax your board in **Newquay**, epicentre of England's surf scene. Just inland is the **Eden Project**, where giant space-age domes contain habitats from jungle to desert.

Land's End is the natural finish to this wild west meander where the English mainland comes to a final full stop. Sink a drink in the First & Last pub, and promise yourself a return trip some day...

Walking in England

Best Long-distance Walks

Coast-to-Coast (p565), Hadrian's Wall (p745), Cotswold Way (p208), Southwest Coast Path (p243)

Best Areas for Short Walks

Lake District, Yorkshire Dales, Cotswolds, Dartmoor

Best for Coast Walks

Northumberland, Devon & Cornwall, Norfolk & Suffolk, Dorset

Best Time to Go

Summer (June to August) The best time for walking: weather usually warm and hopefully dry; plenty of daylight, too.

Late spring (May) and early autumn (September) The seasons either side of summer can be great for walking: fewer crowds; days often mild and sunny.

Best Maps for Walking

Ordnance Survey (UK's national mapping agency) Explorer series 1:25,000 scale.

Harvey Maps (specially designed for walkers) Superwalker series 1:25,000 scale.

England's towns and cities can be crowded, so rural areas are highly valued by the English, and every weekend millions of locals go walking in the countryside. You could do a lot worse than join them. It might be an hour stroll through tranquil woods and farmland, an all-day hike over moors and mountains, or a week-long trek on a national trail – or anything in between.

Unlike hiking and trekking in some other parts of the world, walking in England is not usually about serious expeditions in vast wilderness areas. The nature of the country means you're rarely more than an hour or so from human habitation – although you can still get a great feeling of peace and solitude.

How much walking you do, and how far you go, is totally your choice. There's something for young and old, and walking is often perfect for families, too.

Whatever option you choose, walking in England will help you appreciate the landscape and understand the country, and maybe even learn a bit about the locals.

Planning

Walking is the most popular outdoor activity in England – for locals and visitors alike – first, because it opens up some beautiful corners of the country, and secondly because it can be done virtually on a whim. In fact, compared to hiking and trekking in some other parts of the world, it doesn't take much planning at all.

Getting Started

A well-established infrastructure for walkers already exists in England, so everything is easy for visitors or first-timers. Most villages and country towns in areas where walking is popular will have shops selling maps and local guidebooks, while the local tourist office can nearly always provide leaflets and other information. In national parks, suggested routes or guided walks are often available. This all means you can arrive in a place for the first time, pick up some info, and within an hour you'll be walking through some of England's finest landscapes. No fees. No permits. No worries. Aside from the actual walking, it really is almost effortless.

England's Footpath Network

England is covered in a vast network of footpaths, many of which are centuries old, dating from the time when walking was the only way to get from farm to village, from village to town, from town to coast, or valley to valley. Any walk you do today will follow these historic paths. Even England's longest walks simply link up these networks of many shorter paths. You'll also sometimes walk along 'bridleways' originally for horse transport, and old unsurfaced roads called 'byways'.

Rights of Way

Nearly all footpaths in England are 'rights of way' – public paths and tracks across private property. Even though most land is privately owned, from tiny cultivated areas to vast mountain ranges, a right of way across the land cannot be overruled by the owner.

If you come from Australia, America or another country where land is jealously guarded with padlocked gates and barbed wire fences, this can be a major revelation.

So if there is a right of way, you can follow it through fields, woods, pastures, paddocks, even farmhouse yards, as long as you keep to the correct route and do no damage.

In some mountain and moorland areas, it gets even better: walkers can move beyond the rights of way, and explore at will. Known as 'freedom to roam', where permitted it's clearly advertised with markers on gates and signposts.

Experience Required?

When deciding which area of England to visit for walking, a lot may depend on your own experience. Generally speaking, the lower and more cultivated the landscape, the easier the walking, with clear paths and signposts – ideal for beginners.

As the landscape gets higher, conditions tend to get more serious. In mountain and moorland areas, if the route is popular there will be a path (although sometimes this is faint), but not many signposts. This option is suitable if you already have a bit of walking or hiking experience.

In the more remote areas, if the route is rarely trodden, there may be no visible path at all, and absolutely no signposts, so you'll need to know what you're doing – and take a detailed map and compass for navigation and wet weather gear in case conditions change.

Best Walking Areas

Although you can walk pretty much anywhere in England, some areas are better than others. Here's a rundown of favourite places, suitable for short walks of a couple of hours, or longer all-day outings. For information on multiday hikes see p40.

Cotswolds

One of the most popular areas for walkers in southern England, the Cotswold Hills offer classic English countryside, where paths meander through neat fields, past pretty villages with cottages of honey-coloured stone. The eastern side of the Cotswolds tends to be a gentler landscape, while the paths undulate more on the western side, especially

THREE STEPS TO HEAVEN

So you've arrived in a new area, and want to know more about local options for walking. Here's what to do.

» Step 1: Read up on the relevant region for an overview of the best options.

» Step 2: Find the local tourist office, where you can pick up leaflets, maps and guidebooks.

» Step 3: Head out, and enjoy!

WALKING WEBSITES

Before you set off, take a look at the comprehensive website of the **Ramblers** (www.ramblers.org.uk), the country's leading organisation for walkers. Also available is the annually updated *Walk Britain* handbook listing walker-friendly accommodation across the country.

Also great for specifics on some longer routes is www.nationaltrail.co.uk.

along the Cotswold Escarpment – although the views are better here.

Dartmoor

In England's southwest, Dartmoor National Park boasts the highest hills for miles around, and a great sense of space on the uplands, where much of the landscape is devoid of trees and surprisingly wild. Meanwhile, below the hills, delightful valleys cut into the edges of the moor, perfect for picnics and riverside strolls in summer.

Exmoor

Just to the north of Dartmoor, and sometimes overshadowed by its larger neighbour, southwest England's other national park is Exmoor. Heather-covered hills cut by deep valleys make it a perfect walking area, edged with the added bonus of a spectacular coastline of cliffs and beaches.

Lake District

If anywhere is the heart and soul of walking in England, it's the Lake District – a wonderful area of soaring peaks, endless views, deep valleys and, of course, beautiful lakes. Protected by the Lake District National Park (and often abbreviated to simply 'The Lakes', but never the 'Lakes District'), it is loved by walkers, partly because of the landscape, and partly because of the history; thanks to poet Wordsworth and his Romantic chums, this is where walking for enjoyment really began.

Isle of Wight

Off the south coast of England this island is a great spot if you're new to walking, or simply not looking for high peaks and wilderness. Many routes are signposted, and there's a range of short and long options.

New Forest

In England's deep south lies the New Forest. Visitors love this name, as the area is more than 1000 years old and there aren't *that* many trees – but the beautiful open areas of gorse and grassland are ideal for easy strolls.

Northumberland

On northern England's frontier, keen walkers love the starkly beautiful moors of Northumberland National Park. For a change of scene, the high cliffs and vast empty beaches on the nearby Northumberland coast are less daunting but just as dramatic – perfect for wild seaside strolls.

Norfolk & Suffolk

In the eastern counties of Norfolk and Suffolk the landscape is generally flat, with quiet paths through farmland and beside rivers and lakes, linking picturesque villages, lakes and welcoming country pubs, while the coastline offers a mix of salt marsh, bird reserves, shingle beaches and holiday resorts.

North Downs & South Downs

Between London and the south coast (and within easy reach of both), the North and South Downs are two parallel ranges of broad chalky hills. On the map, the North Downs appear hemmed-in by motorways and conurbations, and while this area can never be described as wilderness, the walking here is often unexpectedly tranquil. The South Downs are higher, and not so cramped by urban expansion, with more options for walks, and a landscape protected by England's newest national park.

Peak District

Despite the name, the Peak District has very few soaring summits. But there are plenty of hills, valleys and moors, making it a favoured walking area in northern England. Protected as a national park, the landscape falls into two zones: the south is mainly farmland, cut by limestone valleys; in the north are high peaty moors with rocky outcrops, and a more austere character.

Southwest Coast

Westcountry gems Cornwall and Devon enjoy the best of the English climate and some of the finest scenery in the country, especially on the coast. But the rugged landscape means tough days on the trail. Thanks to those beautiful rivers flowing down steep valleys to the sea, you're forever going up or down. The coastline in neighbouring Dorset – known as the Jurassic Coast, thanks to the proliferation of fossils – is less arduous and another great area for seaside walks.

Yorkshire Dales

With rolling hills, wild moors, limestone outcrops and green valleys cut by scenic streams, the Yorkshire Dales National Park is one of the most popular walking areas in England. Paths are a little gentler and conditions a little less serious than in the nearby Lake District, with the happy addition of some delightful villages nestling in the dales – many with pubs and tearooms providing refreshments for walkers.

Long-Distance Walking Tips

As well as enjoying walks that take a few hours, avid hikers savour the chance of completing one of England's famous long-distance routes – many of which are specifically named and signposted as national trails, such as the Pennine Way National Trail and South West Coast Path National Trail.

Most long-distance routes take between one and two weeks to complete, although some are longer. There are so many to choose from you'd easily wear out your boots trying to do them all, but it's easy to pick a route that suits your experience and the time you have available.

Famous Routes

Some long-distance walking routes are well known and well maintained, with signposts and route-markers along the way, as well as being highlighted on Ordnance Survey maps. The most high-profile of these are the national trails, usually very clearly marked on the ground and on the map – ideal for beginners or visitors from overseas (although just because they're easy to follow, it doesn't mean they're necessarily easy underfoot). A downside of these famous routes is that they can be crowded in holiday times, making accommodation harder to find. An upside is the great feeling of camaraderie with other walkers on the trail.

Other Routes

In addition to the national trials and other high-profile routes, England has many other long-distance routes that are 'made up' (by joining many existing paths into a single entity) and exist only in dedicated guidebooks – with no equivalent signposting or markings on maps. This doesn't mean the obscure routes aren't enjoyable or spectacular – one of England's most popular long-distance routes, the Coast-to-Coast Walk, started out as just one man's idea (p40), jotted down and published in a homespun volume – but it does mean you need to be a bit more experienced to follow them.

Where to Stay

Because England just doesn't have the endless tracts of wilderness found in some other countries, you're never more than a few miles from a village – even in the national parks. This means your overnight stops can be at inns or B&Bs, and camping equipment is not required. (In fact, long-distance walkers carrying their own camping kit are relatively rare in England.)

WEATHER WATCH

While enjoying your walking in England, it's always worth remembering the fickle nature of English weather. The countryside can appear gentle and welcoming, and often is, but sometimes conditions can turn nasty – especially on the higher ground. At any time of year, if you're walking on the hills or open moors, it's vital to be well equipped. You should carry warm and waterproof clothing (even in summer), a map and compass (that you know how to use), some water, food and high-energy stuff such as chocolate. If you're really going off the beaten track, leave details of your route with someone.

SAMPLING THE LONG ROUTES

Although England's long-distance trails have official start and finish points, you don't have to do the whole thing end-to-end in one go. Many people walk just a section for a day or two, or use the main route as a basis for loops of just a few hours to explore the surrounding area.

Baggage Transfer

To make your walking in England really easy, you don't even have to carry your pack if you don't want to. Baggage-transfer services operate on most of the main long-distance routes, carrying your kit between each night's accommodation. Some may call it a soft option, but it certainly makes the walking far more enjoyable. Most long routes are served by at least one baggage-transfer service. The main players include the following:

» **Brigantes** (www.brigantesenglishwalks.com)

» **Luggage Transfers** (www.luggagetransfers.co.uk)

» **Sherpa Van** (☎0871-520-0124; www.sherpavan.com)

» **Walkers Bags** (www.walkersbags.co.uk)

Best Long Routes

Many long-distance routes run across England, while many more follow the coastline or traverse national parks and other scenic area. Below is a list of some of the absolute classics.

Cleveland Way

110 miles; 8-10 days; www.nationaltrail.co.uk/clevelandway

A venerable route (England's second-oldest) around the edge of the North York Moors National Park, via wild and empty heather-covered hills and high coastal cliffs, passing ruined abbeys and castles.

Dales Way

85 miles; 6 days; www.dalesway.org.uk

A nonstrenuous walk through the delightful Yorkshire Dales, via some of the most scenic valleys in northern England, to end at Windermere in the Lake District.

Coast to Coast Walk

190 miles; 12-14 days; www.wainwright.org.uk/coasttocoast

Also known as Wainwright's Coast to Coast (after the man who devised it) this is not a national trail, but it is England's number-one favourite long-distance route, for locals and visitors alike – through three national parks via a spectacular mix of valleys, plains, mountains, dales and moors.

Cotswold Way

102 miles; 7-10 days; www.nationaltrail.co.uk/cotswold

A picturesque and dramatic route, delivering England at its most enchanting, from villages in intimate valleys to escarpment ridges with bird's-eye views. It's also a trail through time, passing prehistoric hillforts, Romans reminders and some fine stately homes.

Hadrian's Wall

84 miles; 7-8 days; www.nationaltrail.co.uk/hadrianswall

A new national trail following the world-famous Roman structure across northern England, via forts, castles, ramparts, and battlements and giving the Coast-to-Coast a run for its money in the popularity stakes.

Pennine Way

256 miles; 14-21 days; www.nationaltrail.co.uk/pennineway

The granddaddy of them all, an epic trek on a national trail along the mountainous spine of northern England, via some of the highest, wildest countryside in the country. Even in the summer, the elements can be dire, and many walkers find it an endurance test – but not one without rewards.

South West Coast Path

630 miles; 8-10 weeks; www.southwestcoastpath.com

A roller-coaster romp around England's southwest peninsula, past beaches, bays, shipwrecks, seaside resorts, fishing villages and clifftop castles. Given its length, most walkers do it in sections: the two-week stretch between Padstow and Falmouth around Lands End is most popular.

KIT CHECKLIST

If you're strolling through the lowlands, no special equipment is needed for walking in England – except a small backpack to carry your camera, a snack and a bottle of water, plus a jacket in case the weather turns damp or chilly. If you're heading for the higher ground in wilder areas, or doing a multiday hike on one of England's long-distance national trails, then the following checklist will be useful:

Walking clothes

- ☐ Trekking/hiking shorts or trousers
- ☐ Base-layer shirt or T-shirt
- ☐ Fleece or wool jersey midlayer
- ☐ Warm and windproof jacket
- ☐ Waterproof jacket
- ☐ Sun hat, rain hat, gloves
- ☐ Walking boots or shoes
- ☐ Socks

Equipment

- ☐ Backpack
- ☐ Water bottle
- ☐ Sunglasses
- ☐ Camera

Extra items for multiday routes

- ☐ Spare clothing, underwear etc
- ☐ Training/running shoes or sandals for evenings
- ☐ Swimwear
- ☐ Toiletries
- ☐ Toilet paper
- ☐ Torch (flashlight), spare batteries
- ☐ Penknife
- ☐ Sunscreen
- ☐ Premoistened towelettes ('baby wipes')
- ☐ Medical and first-aid kit

Thames Path

173 miles; 10-14 days; www.nationaltrail.co.uk/thamespath

A journey of contrasts beside England's best-known river, on mainly easy paths from rural Gloucestershire, via the beauties of Henley and Oxford, to the very heart of London and beyond.

South Downs Way

100 miles; 7-9 days; www.nationaltrail.co.uk/southdowns

A sweeping hike through southeast England, from Winchester to the sea, mostly following a line of rolling hills, meaning big skies and wonderful views, plus picture-perfect villages and prehistoric sites.

Ridgeway

87 miles; 6-7 days; www.nationaltrail.co.uk/ridgeway

A route of two halves, starting near Avebury Stone Circle with a three-day section along an ancient route across open grassy downland, then switching to a more wooded environment as the trail meanders through the Chiltern Hills.

Travel with Children

Best Regions for Kids

London
Children's attractions galore – some put a strain on parental purse strings, but many others are free.

Devon, Cornwall & Wessex
Some of the best beaches in England, and fairly reliable holiday weather – though crowded in summer.

East Midlands
Former railways that are now traffic-free cycle routes make the Peak District perfect for family outings by bike; while Sherwood Forest is a no-brainer for Robin Hood games.

Oxford & the Cotswolds
Oxford has kid-friendly museums plus Harry Potter connections; the Cotswold countryside is ideal for little-leg strolls.

West Midlands & the Marches
The historic England–Wales borderland has many castles to explore, plus excellent museums for inquisitive minds.

Lake District & Cumbria
This is Outdoor Activity Central: zip wires and mountain bikes for teenagers; boat rides and Beatrix Potter for the youngsters.

England is great for travel with children because it's compact, with a lot of attractions packed into a small area. So when the kids in the back of the car say, 'Are we there yet?', your answer can often be 'Yes!'. Throughout this book, we've highlighted many kid-friendly attractions. This chapter gives a few more specifics. With a bit of planning ahead and some online research to get the best bargains, having the kids on board can make a trip round England even more enjoyable.

England for Kids

Many places of interest in England cater for kids as much as adults. At the country's historic castles, for example, mum and dad can admire the medieval architecture, while the kids will have great fun striding around the battlements or watching falconry demonstrations. In the same way, many national parks and holiday resorts organise specific activities for children. Everything ramps up in the school holidays.

Bargain Hunting

Most visitor attractions offer family tickets – usually two adults plus two children – for less than the sum of the individual entrance charges. Most offer cheaper rates for solo parents and kids, too. Be sure to ask, as these are not always clearly displayed.

On the Road

If you're going by public transport, trains are great for families: intercity services have plenty of room for luggage and extra stuff like 'buggies' (prams), and the kids can move about a bit if they get bored. In contrast, they need to stay in their seats on long-distance coaches.

If you're hiring a car, most (but not all) rental firms can provide child seats – you'll need to check this in advance. Most will not actually fit the child seats; you must do that yourself, for insurance reasons.

Dining, not Whining

When it's time to refuel, most cafes and tearooms are child-friendly. Restaurants are mixed: some offer highchairs and kiddy portions; others firmly say 'No children after 6pm'.

In some pubs, children under 18 are not allowed, but most pubs in tourist areas serve food, making them 'family-friendly'. If in doubt, simply ask the bar staff.

If you're breastfeeding, some older folks in England may tut-tut a bit if you give junior a top-up in public, but if you're reasonably modest it's usually considered OK.

Children's Highlights

Best Hands-on Action

'Please Do Not Touch'? No chance! Here are some places where grubby fingers and enquiring minds are positively welcomed:

» **Science Museum, London** (p84) Seven floors of educational exhibits at the mother of all science museums.

» **Discovery Museum, Newcastle** (p725) Tyneside's rich history on display; highlights include a buzzers-and-bells science maze.

» **Magna, Yorkshire** (p621) Formerly one of the world's largest steel works, and now a science adventure centre.

» **Action Stations, Portsmouth** (p252) Toys with a military spin; your chance to fly a helicopter, control an aircraft carrier, or up-periscope in a submarine.

» **Enginuity, Ironbridge** (p550) Endless interactive displays at the birthplace of the Industrial Revolution.

» **Roald Dahl Museum, Great Missenden** (p236) Try on costumes, make up stories and explore the writing hut of the much-loved children's author.

PLANNING

Handy Websites

» **Baby Goes 2** (www.babygoes2.com) Advice, tips and encouragement – and a stack of adverts – for families on holiday.

» **Visit England** (www.visitengland.com) Official tourism website for England, with lots of useful info for families.

» **Mums Net** (www.mumsnet.com) No-nonsense advice on travel and more from a gang of UK mothers.

When to Go

The best time for families to visit England is pretty much the best time for everyone else – anytime from April/May till the end of September. It's worth avoiding August – the heart of school summer holidays – when prices go up and the roads are busy, especially near the coast.

Places to Stay

Some hotels welcome kids (with their parents!) and provide cots, toys and babysitting services, while others maintain an adult atmosphere. Many B&Bs offer 'family suites' – two adjoining bedrooms with one bathroom – and an increasing number of hostels (YHA and independent) have family rooms with four or six beds, some even with private bathroom attached. If you want to stay in one place for a while, renting a holiday cottage is ideal. Camping is very popular with English families, and there are lots of fantastic campsites, but you'll usually need all your own equipment.

ALL CHANGE

On the sticky topic of dealing with nappies (diapers), most museums and other attractions in England have good baby-changing facilities. Elsewhere, some city-centre public toilets have baby-changing areas, although these can be a bit grimy; your best bet for clean facilities is an upmarket department store. On the road, baby-changing facilities are usually OK at motorway service stations or out-of-town supermarkets.

Best Fresh-Air Fun

If the kids tire of England's castles and museums, you're never far from a place for outdoor activities to blow away the cobwebs:

» **Conkers, Leicestershire** (p478) Play indoors, outdoors or among the trees in the heart of the National Forest.

» **Puzzle Wood, Forest of Dean** (p231) A wonderful woodland playground with maze-like paths, weird rock formations and eerie passageways to offer a real sense of discovery.

» **Whinlatter Forest Park, Cumbria** (p701) Highlights include a 'Go Ape' adventure park, excellent mountain-bike trails, plus live video feeds from squirrel-cams.

» **Bewilderwood, Norfolk** (p441) Zip wires, jungle bridges, treehouses, marsh walks, boat trips, mazes and all sorts of old-fashioned outdoor adventure.

» **Lyme Regis & the Jurassic Coast, Dorset** (p282) Guided tours show you how to find your very own prehistoric fossil.

» **Tissington Trail, Derbyshire** (p482) Cycling this former railway is fun and almost effortless. You can hire kids' bikes, tandems and trailers. Don't forget to hoot in the tunnels!

Best Rainy-Day Distractions

On those inevitable gloomy days, head for the indoor attractions, including the nation's great collection of museums. Alternatively, try outdoor stuff like coasteering in Cornwall or canyoning (check conditions) in the Lake District – always fun, wet or dry.

» **Cadbury World, Birmingham** (p507) Your dentist may cry, but kids love the story of chocolate. And yes, there are free samples.

» **Eden Project, Cornwall** (p394) It may be raining outside, but inside these gigantic semispherical greenhouses it's forever tropical forest or Mediterranean climate.

» **Cheddar Gorge Caves, Wessex** (p325) Finally nail the difference between stalactites and stalagmites in the Westcountry's deep caverns.

» **Underground Passages, Exeter** (p345) Explore medieval catacombs – the only system of its kind open to the public in England.

Best Stealth Learning

Secretly exercise their minds while the little darlings think they are 'just' having fun.

» **At-Bristol** (p305) One of the best interactive science museums in England, covering space, technology and the human brain.

» **Jorvik Viking Centre, York** (p569) An excellent smells-and-all Viking settlement reconstruction.

» **Natural History Museum, London** (p84) Animals everywhere! Highlights include the life-size blue whale and the animatronics dinosaurs.

» **Thinktank, Birmingham** (p507) Every display comes with a button or a lever at this edu-taining science museum.

» **National Space Centre, Leicester** (p475) Spacesuits, zero-gravity toilets and mini-astronaut training – all guaranteed to fire-up little minds.

regions at a glance

London

Historic Streets ✓✓✓
Entertainment ✓✓✓
Museums ✓✓✓

Historic Streets

London's ancient streets contain many of the nation's most famous and history-steeped landmarks. The echoes of the footfalls of monarchs, poets, whores and saints can still be detected in places like the Tower of London, Westminster Abbey, St Paul's Cathedral, the Houses of Parliament and the capital's many palaces. And away from grand buildings, the humble pubs and coaching inns that once served Dickens, Shelley, Keats and Byron are still pouring pints today.

p52

Entertainment

From West End theatres to East End clubs, from Camden's rock venues to Covent Garden's opera house, from tennis at Wimbledon or cricket at Lords to football at Stamford Bridge, London's world-famous venues and arenas offer a perpetual clamour of entertainment. You can rest assured that you'll never be bored.

Museums & Galleries

While the British Museum is the big crowd-puller, the capital has museums and galleries of every shape and size – and many of the very best are free. Even with London's famously wet weather it's unlikely that your supply of rainy days will ever exhaust the great many collections on offer. Many are geared equally towards children and adults, and some you'll need to dip into again and again just to scratch the surface.

Canterbury & the Southeast

Cathedrals ✓✓✓
Invasion Heritage ✓✓
Food & Drink ✓✓✓

Cathedrals

A major reason to visit southeast England, Canterbury Cathedral is one of the finest in Europe, and one of the most holy places in Christendom. Write your own Canterbury tale as you explore its atmospheric chapels, cloisters and crypts.

Invasion Heritage

The southeast has always been a gateway for arrivals from the Continent, some more welcome than others. Castles and fortresses, the 1066 battlefield and Dover's secret wartime tunnels all tell the region's story of invasion and defence.

Food & Drink

Kent is deservedly known as the Garden of England, long celebrated for its hops, fruit, oysters, fish, lamb and vineyards – yes, vineyards! Sussex isn't far behind, with England's finest sparkling wine giving the French stuff a run for its euro.

p138

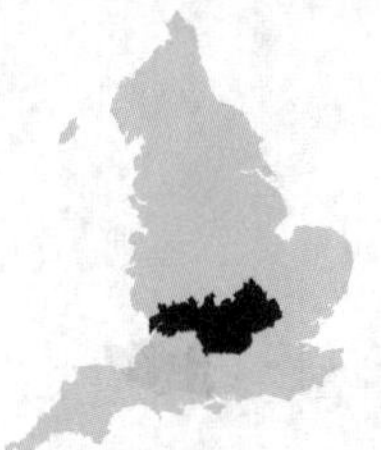

Oxford, Cotswolds & Around

Architecture ✓✓✓
Stately Homes ✓✓✓
Villages ✓✓✓

Architecture
Whether you gaze across the 'dreaming spires' from the top of Carfax Tower, or explore the medieval streets on foot, or simply admire the fantastic gargoyles on college facades, Oxford's architecture will never leave you indifferent.

Stately Homes
Favoured by the rich and powerful for centuries, thanks to its proximity to London and the lush undulating landscape, this region is scattered with some of the finest stately homes and country houses in all of England.

Villages
Littered with picturesque 'chocolate box' scenes of honey-coloured stone cottages, thatched roofs, neat greens and cobbled lanes, the villages of the Cotswolds provide a charming snapshot of rural England.

p188

Wessex

Coastline ✓✓✓
Stone Circles ✓✓✓
Architecture ✓✓

Coastline
The coasts of the rural counties of Hampshire and Dorset together boast beautiful beaches, jolly seaside resorts and wave-sculpted cliffs. Take a dip at Lulworth Cove, search for fossils at Lyme Regis, or go sailing round the Isle of Wight.

Stone Circles
Wessex is an ancient landscape, nowhere more epitomised than the mysterious stone circle of Stonehenge – older than Egypt's Pyramids of Giza and an iconic symbol of England's prehistoric period. Nearby is Avebury Stone Circle, even bigger than Stonehenge.

Architecture
Besides stone circles, Wessex delights with later constructions, too: photogenic ruined castles, impossibly ornate stately homes, quaint villages and handsome country houses. All topped by the grand Georgian crescents of Bath – one of England's most beautiful cities.

p242

Devon & Cornwall

Beaches ✓✓✓
Outdoor Activities ✓✓✓
Food ✓✓✓

Beaches
England's far southwest peninsula juts determinedly into the Atlantic, with a spectacular coast on each side and an endless chain of sandy beaches – some big, some small, some brash, some tranquil.

Outdoor Activities
If you like to take it nice and easy, come to hike on the wilderness moors or tootle along cycle trails. If you prefer life fast and furious, with adrenaline on the side, come to surf the best waves in England, or learn to sail, dive or kitesurf.

Food
Lush fields means fine farm produce, and rich waters mean plenty of seafood, making this region one of England's best foodie hot spots. Tuck into local steak pies in stylish gastropubs, sample Devon cream in friendly teashops or buy super-fresh crab direct from the fishermen.

p339

Cambridge & East Anglia

Historic Buildings ✓✓✓
Coastline ✓✓
The Broads ✓✓

Historic buildings

From the magnificent cathedrals of Ely, Norwich and Peterborough to Cambridge's King's College chapel, Trinity's Great Court and the New Court at St John's, East Anglia's architectural splendour is second to none.

Coastline

With wide sandy beaches, great seafood, delightful old pubs, globally important bird reserves, historic villages still proud of their nautical heritage, and classic seaside resorts like Southwold and Cromer, the coastline of East Anglia is rich and varied.

The Broads

The Norfolk and Suffolk Broads are a tranquil haven of lakes and meandering waterways, a national park, and an ideal spot for boating, birding, canoeing, cycling or walking – perfect for getting back to nature at a leisurely pace.

p402

Nottingham & the East Midlands

Outdoor Activities ✓✓✓
History ✓✓✓
Stately Homes ✓✓✓

Outdoor Activities

The gem of the region is the Peak District National Park: with its high moors and deep valleys, it's a giant adventure playground full of walking trails, cycle routes, cliffs to climb and potholes to explore.

History

You can explore a wide range of historic sites, from the seminal War of the Roses battlefield at Bosworth to the pioneering factories at the Unesco World Heritage Derwent Valley Mills. And if you want to mix in a little myth, head for Nottingham and its Robin Hood connections.

Stately Homes

Stately homes such as Haddon Hall, Burghley House and Chatsworth promise walls dripping with oil paintings, sprawling deer-filled grounds and more priceless heirlooms than you can shake a Chippendale at.

p451

Birmingham, the West Midlands & the Marches

Outdoor Activities ✓✓✓
History ✓✓✓
Food & Drink ✓✓✓

Outdoor Activities

Away from the conurbations, the natural landscape calls fans of the great outdoors, from the long-distance trek along Offa's Dyke National Trail to high-level rambles on the Shropshire and Malvern Hills, via mountain-biking at Cannock Chase or kayaking on the River Wye.

History

Centuries ago, the powerful Marcher Lords sealed their grip on the England–Wales borderlands, leaving us with a legacy of great castles, and giving their name to the region. At the other end of the timeline, England's rich industrial heritage can be savoured at places like Birmingham and Ironbridge.

Food & Drink

Foodies take note – Birmingham is the curry capital of the country (and increasingly, a magnet for Michelin-starred chefs) and the country town of Ludlow is an epicentre of a gastronomic explosion.

p499

Yorkshire

Outdoor Activities ✓✓✓
Food & Drink ✓✓✓
History ✓✓✓

Outdoor Activities
With rolling hills, scenic valleys, high moors and a long, cliff-lined coast, all protected by two national parks, Yorkshire is a natural adventure playground. Come here for some of England's finest hiking, biking, surfing and rock-climbing.

Food & Drink
Lush pastures and a rich farming heritage means Yorkshire beef and lamb are among the most sought after in the country, while the famous twin breweries of Masham turn out some of England's most popular real ales. Where better to enjoy them than one of Yorkshire's many excellent traditional pubs?

History
From York's Viking heritage, and the ancient abbeys of Rievaulx, Fountains and Whitby, to the industrial archaeology of Leeds, Bradford and Sheffield, Yorkshire is steeped in the essence of England's historical narrative.

p561

Manchester, Liverpool & the Northwest

Museums ✓✓✓
Football ✓✓✓
Blackpool ✓✓

Museums
The northwest's collection of heritage sites – from the wonderful People's History Museum in Manchester to the International Slavery Museum in Liverpool's Albert Dock – is testament to the region's rich history and its ability to keep it alive.

Football
Two cities – Liverpool and Manchester – give the world four famous clubs, including the two most successful in English history. The new National Football Museum in Manchester is just another reason for football fans to visit this region.

Blackpool
The queen of England's classic seaside resorts keeps going on the back of the rides of Pleasure Beach, England's best amusement park where adrenaline junkies can always find a fix.

p627

The Lake District & Cumbria

Mountains ✓✓✓
Lakes ✓✓✓
Walking ✓✓✓

Mountains
Cumbria is the most mountainous part of England, a stunningly beautiful region that moved Romantic poet William Wordsworth to write his ode to 'a host of golden daffodils'. Two centuries on, this landscape still inspires and delights.

Lakes
Dotted between the mountains sit numerous lakes. Some are big and famous, such as Windermere, Coniston and Ullswater, while others are small, hidden and little known. Together they give their name to the Lake District National Park that protects this striking and valuable landscape.

Walking
If anywhere is the heart and soul of walking in England, it's the Lake District. Casual strollers find gentle routes through foothills and valleys, while serious hikers hit the high fells and mountains – many heading to the top of Scafell Pike, England's highest point.

p673

Newcastle & the Northeast

Hadrian's Wall ✓✓✓
Big Landscapes ✓✓✓
Castles ✓✓✓

Hadrian's Wall

One of the world's premier Roman Empire sites, this potent symbol of power and defence strides its way for more than 70 miles across the neck of England, from Tyneside to the Solway Firth. You can travel its length – by foot, bike, car, bus or train – stopping off at fascinating museums and forts along the way.

Big Landscapes

If it's widescreen vistas you're after, the northeast never fails to please, with great views from the golden windswept beaches of Northumberland to the high moors and russet dales of the Pennine uplands.

Castles

Vast Northumberland has some of England's finest castles. Some, like Bamburgh and Dunstanburgh stare reflectively out to sea, others stand isolated on the high moors, all reminders of the centuries-long scrap with the Scots over these remote borderlands.

p721

Every listing is recommended by our authors, and their favourite places are listed first

Look out for these icons:

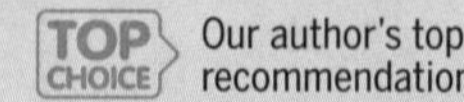

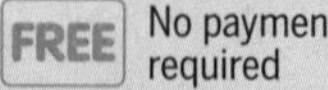

See the Index for a full list of destinations covered in this book.

On the Road

London

☎: 020 / POP: 7.82 MILLION / AREA: 609 SQ MILES

Includes »

Best Places to Eat

» Bistrot Bruno Loubet (p119)
» Gordon Ramsay (p116)
» Hakkasan (p118)
» Laughing Gravy (p115)
» Poppies (p121)

Best Places to Stay

» Haymarket Hotel (p106)
» Hazlitt's (p106)
» Hoxton (p112)
» Zetter Hotel (p112)
» St Pancras Renaissance (p109)

Why Go?

Everyone comes to London with a preconception shaped by a multitude of books, movies, TV shows and songs. Whatever yours is, prepare to have it exploded by this endlessly fascinating, amorphous city. You could spend a lifetime exploring it and find that the slippery thing's gone and changed on you. One thing is constant: that great serpent of a river enfolding the city in its sinuous loops, linking London both to the green heart of England and the world.

From Roman times the world has come to London, put down roots and whinged about the weather. There is no place on earth that is more multicultural; any given street yields a rich harvest of languages, and those narrow streets are also steeped in fascinating history, magnificent art, imposing architecture and popular culture. When you add an endless reserve of cool to this mix, it's hard not to conclude that London is one of the world's great cities, if not the greatest.

When to Go

Spring in the city sees daffodils in bloom, costumed marathon runners and London's edgiest music event, the Camden Crawl. In June you'll find the parks filled with people, Trooping the Colour, summer arts festivals, gay pride and Wimbledon.

London in December is all about Christmas lights on Oxford and Regent Sts, and perhaps a whisper of snow.

That said, London is a place that you can visit any time of the year.

History

London first came into being as a Celtic village near a ford across the River Thames, but the city only really took off after the Roman invasion in AD 43. The Romans enclosed their Londinium in walls that still find refrain in the shape of the City (with a capital 'C') of London today.

By the end of the 3rd century AD, Londinium was almost as multicultural as it is now, with 30,000 people of various ethnic groups and temples dedicated to a host of cults. Internal strife and relentless barbarian attacks took their toll on the Romans, who abandoned Britain in the 5th century, reducing the conurbation to a sparsely populated backwater.

The Saxons then moved in to the area, establishing farmsteads and villages. Their 'Lundenwic' prospered, becoming a large, well-organised town divided into 20 different wards. As the city grew in importance, it caught the eye of Danish Vikings, who launched many invasions and razed the city in the 9th century. The Saxons held on until, finally beaten down in 1016, they were forced to accept the Danish leader Knut (Canute) as King of England, after which London replaced Winchester as its capital. In 1042 the throne reverted to the Saxon Edward the Confessor, whose main contribution to the city was the building of Westminster Abbey.

The Norman Conquest saw William the Conqueror marching into London, where he was crowned king. He built the White Tower (the core of the Tower of London), negotiated taxes with the merchants, and affirmed the city's independence and right to self-government. From then until the late 15th century, London politics were largely taken up by a three-way power struggle between the monarchy, the church and city guilds.

The greatest threat to the burgeoning city was that of disease caused by unsanitary living conditions and impure drinking water. In 1348 rats on ships from continental Europe brought the bubonic plague, which wiped out a third of London's population of 100,000 over the following year.

London was consolidated as the seat of law and government in the kingdom during the 14th century. An uneasy political compromise was reached between the factions, and the city expanded rapidly in the 16th century under the House of Tudor.

The Great Plague struck in 1665 and by the time the winter cold arrested the epidemic, 100,000 Londoners had perished. Just as the population considered a sigh of relief, another disaster struck. The mother of all blazes, the Great Fire of 1666, virtually razed the place. One consequence was that it created a blank canvas upon which master architect Sir Christopher Wren could build his magnificent churches.

London's growth continued unabated, and by 1700 it was Europe's largest city, with 600,000 people. An influx of foreign workers brought expansion to the east and south, while those who could afford it headed to the more salubrious environs of the north and west, divisions that still largely shape London today.

Georgian London saw a surge in artistic creativity, with the likes of Dr Johnson, Handel, Gainsborough and Reynolds enriching the city's culture while its architects fashioned an elegant new metropolis. At the same time the gap between rich and poor grew ever wider, and lawlessness was rife.

In 1837, 18-year-old Victoria ascended the throne. During her long reign (1837–1901), London became the fulcrum of the expanding British Empire, which covered a quarter of the earth's surface. The Industrial Revolution saw the building of new docks and railways (including the first underground line in 1863), while the Great Exhibition of 1851 showcased London to the world. The city's population mushroomed from just over two million to 6.6 million during Victoria's reign.

Although London suffered relatively minor damage during WWI, it was devastated by the Luftwaffe in WWII, when huge swathes of the centre and East End were flattened and 32,000 people were killed. Ugly housing and low-cost developments were hastily erected in postwar London, and immigrants from around the world flocked to the city and once again changed its character. On 6 December 1952 the Great Smog descended, a lethal combination of fog, smoke and pollution caused by residential coal fires, vehicle exhausts and industry, killing some 4000 people.

Prosperity gradually returned, and the creative energy that had been bottled up in the postwar years was suddenly unleashed. London became the capital of cool in fashion and music in the 'Swinging Sixties', a party followed by the hangover of the harsh economic climate of the 1970s. Since then the city has surfed up and down the waves

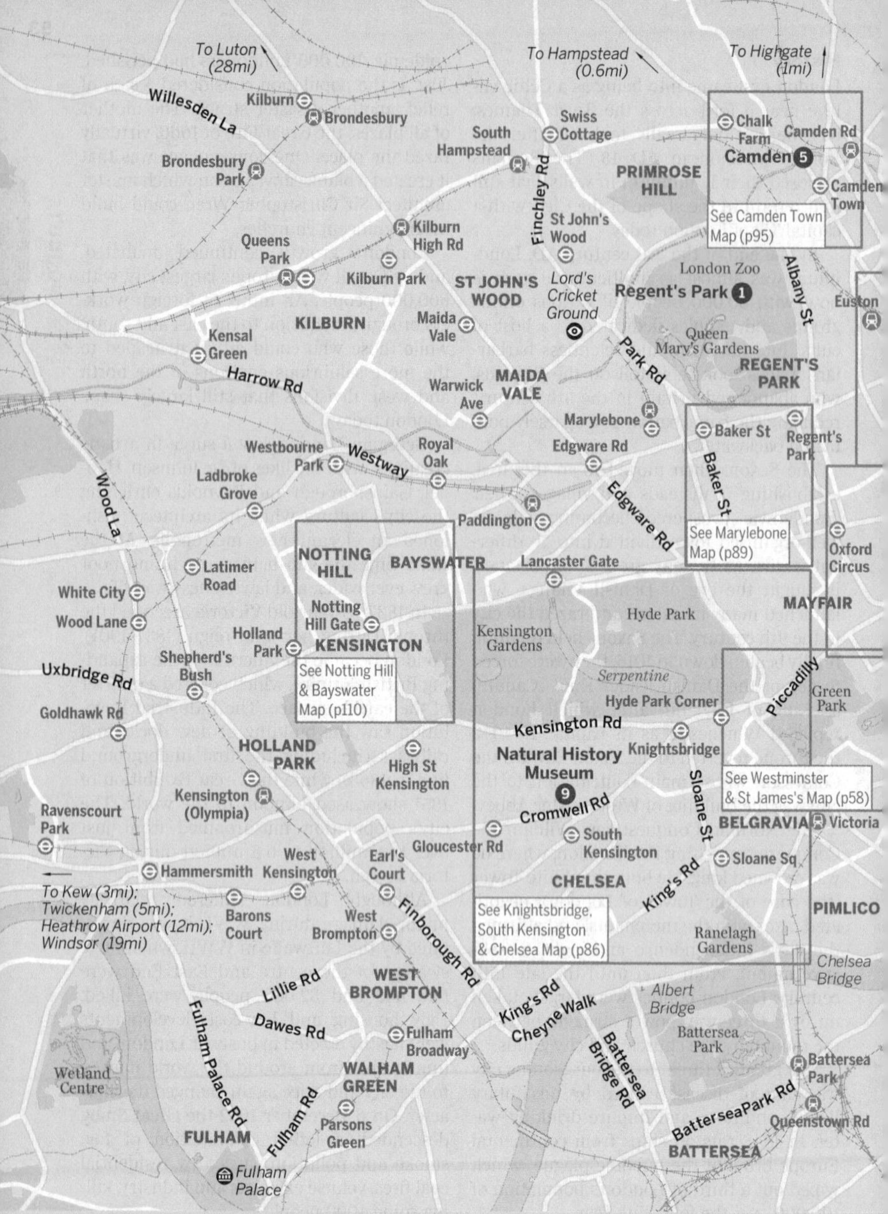

London Highlights

1 Watching the world pass by on a sunny day in **Regent's Park** (p89) or any of London's other green oases

2 Admiring the booty of an empire at the **British Museum** (p91)

3 Losing your head in history at the **Tower of London** (p69)

4 Sizing up the awe-inspiring architecture of **Westminster Abbey** (p57)

5 Discovering the next cool thing in one of Camden's **live music venues** (p127)

6 Seeing the locals through beer goggles on a Hoxton **bar hop** (p124)

7 Getting closer to God at the top of the dome of **St Paul's Cathedral** (p73)

8 Embarking on an eye-opening tour of modern and contemporary art at **Tate Modern** (p76)

9 Revelling in the astounding stonework and displays at the **Natural History Museum** (p84)

of global economics, hanging on to its position as the world's leading financial centre even during the recent international banking crisis.

In 2000, the modern metropolis won its first mayor of London (as distinguished from the Lord Mayor of the City of London), an elected role covering the City and all 32 urban boroughs. Bicycle-riding, shapeless-suit-wearing Boris Johnson, a Conservative with a shock of blond hair and a large, affable persona was elected in 2008 and has proved a popular mayor. In the 2012 mayoral election, he retained his post by defeating arch rival Ken Livingstone.

In August 2011, numerous London boroughs were rocked by riots – characterised by looting and arson – which were initially met by a mild police response. Analysts still debate the causes of the riot, pointing at single-parent families, gang culture, unemployment, criminal opportunism and social moral decay.

Both the Olympics and the Queen's Diamond Jubilee concocted a year of royal pageantry and sporting glory for London in 2012. The countdown to 2012 saw new Overground train lines opening, a cable car flung across the Thames, the massive regeneration of a rundown and once-polluted area of East London for the Olympic Park and a spruce up, tidy and facelift for numerous squares and gardens across town.

Sights

The city's main geographical feature is the murky Thames, which snakes around but roughly divides the city into north and south. The old City of London (note the big 'C') is the capital's financial district, covering roughly a square mile bordered by the river and the many gates of the ancient (long-gone) city walls: Newgate, Moorgate etc. The areas to the east of the City are collectively known as the East End. The West End, on the City's other flank, is effectively the centre of London nowadays. It actually falls within the City of Westminster, which is one of London's 32 boroughs and has long been the centre of government and royalty.

Surrounding these central areas are dozens of former villages (Camden Town, Islington, Clapham etc), each with its own High St, which were long ago swallowed by London's sprawl.

When the sun shines make like a Londoner and head to the parks.

WESTMINSTER & ST JAMES'S

Purposefully positioned outside the old City (London's fiercely independent burghers preferred to keep the monarch and parliament at arm's length), Westminster has been the centre of the nation's political power for nearly a millennium. The area's many landmarks combine to form an awesome display of authority, pomp and gravitas.

LONDON IN...

Two Days

Only two days? Start in **Trafalgar Square** and see at least the outside of all the big-ticket sights – **London Eye**, **Houses of Parliament**, **Westminster Abbey**, **St James's Park Palace**, **Buckingham Palace**, **Green Park**, **Hyde Park**, **Kensington Gardens and Palace** – and then motor around **Tate Modern** until you get booted out. In the evening, explore **Soho**. On day two, race around the **British Museum**, then head to the City. Start with our **walking tour** and finish in the **Tower of London**. Head to the East End for an evening of **foreign food** and **hip bars**.

Four Days

Take the two-day itinerary but stretch it to a comfortable pace, spending extra time in Tate Modern, British Museum and the Tower of London. Stop at the **National Gallery** while you're in Trafalgar Sq and explore inside **Westminster Abbey** and **St Paul's Cathedral**. On your extra evenings, check out **Camden** and **Islington** or enjoy a slap-up dinner in **Kensington** and **Knightsbridge**.

One Week

As above, but add in a day each for **Greenwich**, **Kew Gardens** and **Hampton Court Palace**.

St James's is an aristocratic enclave of palaces, famous hotels, historic shops and elegant buildings, with some 150 historically noteworthy buildings in its 36 hectares.

Westminster Abbey CHURCH

(Map p58; ☎020-7222 5152; www.westminster-abbey.org; 20 Dean's Yard; adult/child £15/6, tours £3; ⏱9.30am-4.30pm Mon, Tue, Thu & Fri, to 7pm Wed, to 2.30pm Sat; ⊖Westminster) Westminster Abbey is simply one of London's most imposing treasures. The abbey is not only a sublime place of worship, but is etched with enough history and architectural detail to fill several days' exploration. The abbey serves up the country's history on cold slabs of stone; for centuries, the country's greatest have been interred here, including most of the monarchs from Henry III (died 1272) to George II (1760).

Westminster Abbey has never been a cathedral (the seat of a bishop). It's what is called a 'royal peculiar' and is administered directly by the Crown. Every monarch since William the Conqueror has been crowned here, with the exception of a couple of unlucky Eds who were murdered (Edward V) or abdicated (Edward VIII) before the magic moment. Look out for the strangely underwhelming **Coronation Chair**.

The building itself is an arresting sight. Though a mixture of architectural styles, it is considered the finest example of Early English Gothic in existence. The original church was built in the 11th century by King (later Saint) Edward the Confessor, who is buried in the chapel behind the main altar. Henry III began work on the new building in 1245 but didn't complete it; the French Gothic nave was finished in 1388. Henry VII's astonishing Late Perpendicular-style **Lady Chapel** was consecrated in 1519 after 16 years of construction.

Apart from the royal graves, keep an eye out for the many famous commoners interred here, especially in **Poets' Corner**, where you'll find the resting places of Chaucer, Dickens, Hardy, Tennyson, Dr Johnson and Kipling as well as memorials to the other greats (Shakespeare, Austen, Brontë etc). Elsewhere you'll find the graves of Handel and Sir Isaac Newton.

The octagonal **Chapter House** dates from the 1250s and was where the monks would meet for daily prayer before Henry VIII's suppression of the monasteries in 1536. Used as a treasury and 'Royal Wardrobe', the cryptlike **Pyx Chamber** dates from about 1070. The neighbouring **Abbey Museum** has as its centrepiece the death masks of generations of royalty.

Parts of the Abbey complex are free to visitors. This includes the **Cloister** and the 900-year-old **College Garden**. Free concerts are held here from 12.30pm to 2pm on Wednesday from mid-July to mid-August. Adjacent to the abbey is **St Margaret's Church** (Map p58; ⏱9.30am-3.30pm Mon-Sat, 2-4.45pm Sun), the House of Commons' place of worship since 1614. There are windows commemorating churchgoers Caxton and Milton, and Sir Walter Raleigh is buried by the altar.

Verger-led tours are held several times a day (except Sunday) and are limited to 25 people per tour; call ahead to secure your place. Of course, admission to the Abbey is free if you wish to attend a service. On weekdays, Matins is at 7.30am, Holy Communion at 8am and 12.30pm, and Choral Evensong at 5pm. There are services throughout the day on Sunday. You can sit and soak in the atmosphere, even if you're not religious.

Houses of Parliament HISTORIC BUILDING

(Map p58; www.parliament.uk; Parliament Sq; ⊖Westminster) Coming face to face with one of the world's most recognisable landmarks is always a surreal moment, but in the case of the Houses of Parliament it's a revelation. Photos just don't do justice to the ornate stonework and golden filigree of Charles Barry and Augustus Pugin's neo-Gothic masterpiece (1840).

Officially called the **Palace of Westminster**, the oldest part is **Westminster Hall** (1097), which is one of only a few sections that survived a catastrophic fire in 1834. Its roof, added between 1394 and 1401, is the earliest known example of a hammerbeam roof and has been described as the greatest surviving achievement of medieval English carpentry.

The palace's most famous feature is its clock tower, aka **Big Ben** (Map p58). Ben is actually the 13-ton bell, named after Benjamin Hall, who was commissioner of works when the tower was completed in 1858.

At the business end, parliament is split into two houses. The green-hued **House of Commons** is the lower house, where the 650 elected Members of Parliament sit. Traditionally the home of hereditary bluebloods, the scarlet-decorated **House of Lords** now has peers appointed through various means. Both houses debate and vote on legislation,

Westminster & St James's

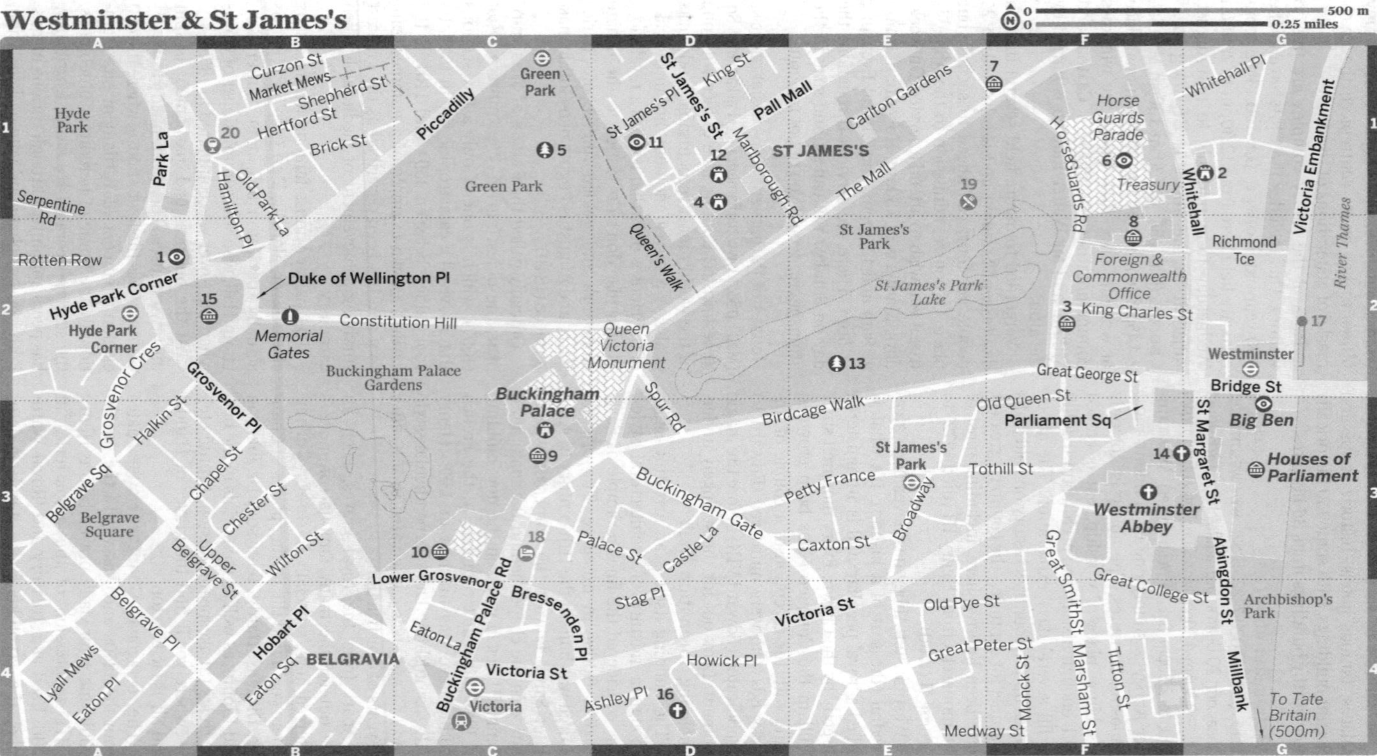

Westminster & St James's

Top Sights
- Big Ben ... G3
- Buckingham Palace ... C3
- Houses of Parliament ... G3
- Westminster Abbey ... F3

Sights
- 1 Apsley House ... A2
- 2 Banqueting House ... G1
- 3 Churchill Museum & Cabinet War Rooms ... F2
- 4 Clarence House ... D1
- 5 Green Park ... C1
- 6 Horse Guards Parade ... F1
- 7 Institute Of Contemporary Arts ... F1
- 8 No 10 Downing Street ... F2
- 9 Queen's Gallery ... C3
- 10 Royal Mews ... C3
- 11 Spencer House ... D1
- 12 St James's Palace ... D1
- 13 St James's Park ... E2
- 14 St Margaret's Church ... F3
- 15 Wellington Arch ... B2
- 16 Westminster Cathedral ... D4

Activities, Courses & Tours
- 17 City Cruises ... G2

Sleeping
- 18 Rubens at the Palace ... C3

Eating
- 19 Inn the Park ... E1

Drinking
- 20 Galvin at Windows ... B1

which is then presented to the Queen for her Royal Assent (in practice, this is a formality; the last time Royal Assent was denied was 1708). At the annual State Opening of Parliament (usually in November), the Queen takes her throne in the House of Lords, having arrived in the gold-trimmed Irish State Coach from Buckingham Palace. It's well worth lining the route for a gawk at the crown jewels sparkling in the sun.

When parliament is in session, visitors are admitted to the **House of Commons Visitors' Gallery**. Expect to queue for at least an hour and possibly longer during Question Time (at the beginning of each day). The **House of Lords Visitors' Gallery** can also be visited.

Parliamentary recesses (ie MP holidays) last for three months over summer and a couple of weeks over Easter and Christmas. When parliament is in recess there are guided **tours** (☎0844 847 1672; www.ticketmaster.co.uk/housesofparliament; 75-min tours adult/child £15/6) of both chambers and other historic areas. UK residents can approach their MPs to arrange a free tour and to climb the clock tower.

Buckingham Palace PALACE
(Map p58; ☎020-7766 7300; www.royalcollection.org.uk; Buckingham Palace Rd; adult/child £17/9.75; ⏲late Jul-Sep, changing of the guard 11.30am May-Jul, alternate days rest of yr; ⊖Victoria) With so many imposing buildings in the capital, the Queen's palatial London pad can come as a bit of an anticlimax. Built in 1703 for the Duke of Buckingham, Buckingham Palace replaced St James's Palace as the monarch's official London residence in 1837. When she's not giving her famous wave to far-flung parts of the Commonwealth, Queen Elizabeth II divides her time between here, Windsor and Balmoral. To know if she's at home, check whether the yellow, red and blue standard is flying.

Nineteen lavishly furnished State Rooms – hung with artworks by the likes of Rembrandt, van Dyck, Canaletto, Poussin and Vermeer – are open to visitors when HRH (Her Royal Highness) takes her holidays. The two-hour tour includes the **Throne Room**, with his-and-hers pink chairs initialed 'ER' and 'P'. Access is by timed tickets with admission every 15 minutes (audio guide included).

Your ticket to Buckingham Palace is good for a return trip if bought direct from the palace ticket office (ask to have it stamped). *A Royal Day Out* is a combined ticket including the State Rooms, Queen's Gallery and Royal Mews (adult/child £31.95/18.20).

Changing of the Guard

At 11.30am daily from May to July (on alternate days, weather permitting, for the rest of the year), the old guard (Foot Guards of the Household Regiment) comes off duty to be replaced by the new guard on the forecourt of Buckingham Palace. Highly popular, the show lasts about half an hour (brace for crowds). If you're here in November, the procession leaving the palace for the State Opening of Parliament is much more impressive.

Queen's Gallery

Originally designed by John Nash as a conservatory, the **gallery** (Map p58; www.royalcollection.org.uk; Buckingham Palace Rd, southern wing, Buckingham Palace; adult/child £9/4.50; ⏲10am-5.30pm) showcases some of the palace's treasures on a rotating basis, through temporary exhibitions. Entrance to the gallery is through Buckingham Gate.

Royal Mews

Indulge your Cinderella fantasies while inspecting the exquisite state coaches in the **Royal Mews** (Map p58; www.royalcollection.org.uk; Buckingham Palace Rd; adult/child £8/5; ⏲10am-5pm Apr-Oct, to 4pm Mon-Sat Nov-Dec), a working stable looking after the immaculately groomed horses and opulent vehicles the royals use for getting from A to B. Highlights include the magnificent gold coach of 1762 and the 1910 Glass Coach (Prince William and Catherine Middleton actually used the 1902 State Landau for their wedding in 2011).

St James's Park & Palace PARK

(⊖St James's Park, Green Park) With its manicured flower beds and ornamental lake, St James's Park is wonderful for strolling and taking in the surrounding palaces. The striking Tudor gatehouse of **St James's Palace** (Map p58; Cleveland Row; Green Park), begun by the palace-mad Henry VIII in 1530, is best approached from St James's St, to the north of the park. This was the residence of Prince Charles and his sons before they shifted next door to **Clarence House** (1828), following the death of its previous occupant, the Queen Mother, in 2002. It's supreme for photo opportunities with one of the resolutely unsmiling royal guards.

Green Park PARK

(Map p58; ⊖Green Park) Green Park's 47-acre expanse of meadows and mature trees links St James's Park to Hyde Park and Kensington Gardens, creating a green corridor from Westminster all the way to Kensington. Once a duelling ground, the park became a vegetable garden during WWII. Although it doesn't have lakes, fountains or formal gardens, it's blanketed with daffodils in spring and seminaked bodies whenever the sun shines.

Westminster Cathedral CATHEDRAL

(Map p58; www.westminstercathedral.org.uk; Victoria St; tower adult/child £5/2.50; ⏲7am-7pm; ⊖Victoria) Begun in 1895, this neo-Byzantine cathedral is still a work in progress, with new sections completed as funds allow. Look out for Eric Gill's highly regarded stone **Stations of the Cross** (1918). The **Chapel of St George and the English Martyrs** displays the body of St John Southwark, a priest who was hanged, drawn and quartered in 1654 for refusing to reject the supremacy of the Pope. The **Chapel of the Blessed Sacrament** and other parts of the interior are ablaze with Eastern Roman mosaics and ornamented with 100 types of marble; other areas are just bare brick. The distinctive 83m red-brick and white-stone **tower** offers splendid views of London and, unlike St Paul's dome, you can take the lift.

Banqueting House PALACE

(Map p58; www.hrp.org.uk/banquetinghouse; Whitehall; adult/child £5/free; ⏲10am-5pm Mon-Sat; ⊖Westminster) The beautiful, classical design of the Banqueting House was conceived by Inigo Jones for James I in 1622. It's the only surviving part of Whitehall Palace after the Tudor bit went skywards in a 1698 conflagration. The chief attraction is the ceiling, painted by Rubens in 1635 at the behest of Charles I. The king didn't get to savour it for long; in 1649 he was frogmarched out of the 1st-floor balcony to lose his head for treason. An audioguide is included in the price.

No 10 Downing Street HISTORIC BUILDING

(Map p58; www.number10.gov.uk; 10 Downing St; ⊖Westminister) It's typically British that the official seat of the prime minister is a nondescript Georgian town house in Whitehall.

THE FOURTH PLINTH

Three of the four plinths located at Trafalgar Square's corners are occupied by notables: King George IV on horseback, and military men General Sir Charles Napier and Major General Sir Henry Havelock. The remaining plinth, originally earmarked for a statue of William IV, has remained largely vacant for the past 150 years. The Royal Society of Arts conceived the **Fourth Plinth Project** (www.london.gov.uk/fourthplinth) in 1999, opting to use the space for works by contemporary artists. The Mayor's office has since taken over the project, continuing with the contemporary art theme.

The street was cordoned off with a rather large iron gate during Margaret Thatcher's tenure, so you can't get up close.

Churchill Museum & Cabinet War Rooms MUSEUM
(Map p58; www.iwm.org.uk/cabinet; Clive Steps, King Charles St; adult/child £15/free; ⏲9.30am-6pm; ⊖Westminster) Winston Churchill co-ordinated the Allied resistance against Nazi Germany on a Bakelite telephone from this underground military HQ during WWII. The Cabinet War Rooms remain much as they were when the lights were flicked off in 1945, capturing the drama and dogged spirit of the time, while the museum affords intriguing insights into the resolute, cigar-smoking wartime leader.

FREE **Institute Of Contemporary Arts** ART GALLERY
(Map p58; www.ica.org.uk; The Mall; ⏲noon-11pm Wed, to 1am Thu-Sat, to 9pm Sun; ⊖Charing Cross) A one-stop contemporary-art bonanza, the excitingly cerebral program at the ICA includes film, photography, theatre, installations, talks, performance art, DJs, digital art and book readings. Stroll around the galleries, watch a film, browse the left-field bookshop, then head to the bar for a beer.

Spencer House HISTORIC HOME
(Map p58; ☎020-7499 8620; www.spencerhouse.co.uk; 27 St James's Pl; adult/child £12/10; ⏲10.30am-5.45pm Sun Feb-Jul & Sep-Dec; ⊖Green Park) The ancestral home of Princess Diana's family, Spencer House was built in the Palladian style between 1756 and 1766. It was converted into offices after the Spencers moved out in 1927, but 60 years later an £18 million restoration returned it to its former glory. Visits are by guided tour.

Apsley House HISTORIC HOME
(Map p58; www.english-heritage.org.uk; 149 Piccadilly; adult/child £6.30/3.80, with Wellington Arch £8.20/4.90; ⏲11am-5pm Wed-Sun Apr-Oct, to 4pm Wed-Sun Nov-Mar; ⊖Hyde Park Corner) This stunning house, containing exhibits devoted to the life and times of the Duke of Wellington, was designed by Robert Adam for Baron Apsley in the late 18th century. It was later sold to the first Duke of Wellington, who cut Napoleon down to size in the Battle of Waterloo and lived here for 35 years until his death in 1852. With 10 of its rooms open to the public, the house has a stairwell dominated by Antonio Canova's staggering 3.4m-high statue of a fig-leafed **Napoleon** with titanic shoulders. Don't miss the elaborate **Portuguese silver service**.

Wellington Arch MUSEUM
(Map p58; www.english-heritage.org.uk; Hyde Park Corner; adult/5-15yr £4/2.40, with Apsley House £8.20/4.90; ⏲10am-5pm Wed-Sun Apr-Oct, 10am-4pm Wed-Sun Nov-Mar; ⊖Hyde Park Corner) Throttled by the Hyde Park Corner roundabout, this is London's answer to the Arc de Triomphe (except this one commemorates France's *defeat* at the hands of the Duke of Wellington). Erected in 1826, the monument is topped with Europe's largest bronze sculpture: *Peace Descending on the Quadriga of War* (1912). Until the 1960s, part of the monument served as the capital's smallest police station (complete with pet moggy); the arch now houses a three-floor exhibition space. The open-air balconies (accessible by lift) afford unforgettable views of Hyde Park, Buckingham Palace and the Houses of Parliament.

WEST END

A strident mix of culture and consumerism but more a concept than a fixed geographical area, the West End is synonymous with roof-raising musicals, bright lights, outstanding restaurants and indefatigable bag-laden shoppers. It casts its net around Piccadilly Circus and Trafalgar Sq to the south, Regent St to the west, Oxford St to the north and Covent Garden to the east and the Strand to the southeast.

Named after the elaborate collars (picadils) that were the sartorial staple of a 17th-century tailor who lived nearby, **Piccadilly** became the fashionable haunt of the well-heeled (and collared), and still boasts establishment icons such as the Ritz hotel and Fortnum & Mason department store. It meets Regent St, Shaftesbury Ave and Haymarket at the neon-lit swirl of **Piccadilly Circus**, home to the ever-popular and ever-misnamed **Eros** statue (really Anteros).

Mayfair, west of Piccadilly Circus, hogs all of the most expensive streets from the Monopoly board, including Park Lane and Bond St, which should give you an idea of what to expect: lots of pricey shops, Michelin-starred restaurants, society hotels and gentlemen's clubs. The elegant bow of **Regent St** and frantic **Oxford St** are the city's main shopping strips. At the heart of the West End lies **Soho**, a boho grid of narrow streets and squares hiding gay bars,

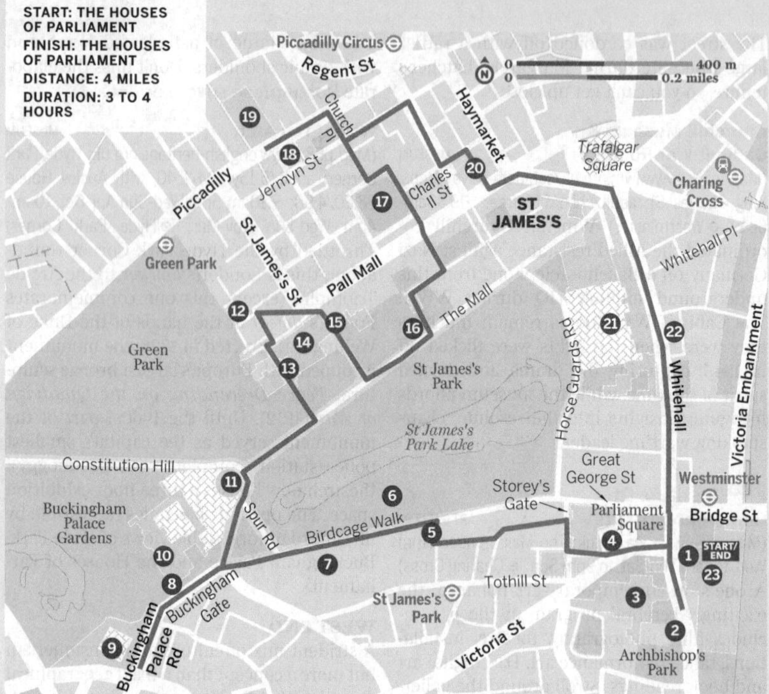

Walking Tour
Royal London Walk

Start at the heart of it all, emerging from Westminster underground station to cross Bridge St to the Palace of Westminster, aka the ❶ **Houses of Parliament**. Originally built in 1097, **Westminster Hall** is the oldest surviving part of the original palace – seat of the English monarchy from the 11th to the 16th century – much of which burned down in October 1834. Note the statue of Oliver Cromwell standing outside, controversially erected in 1899. Following the length of the Houses of Parliament along Abingdon St (which becomes Old Palace Yard) brings you to the ❷ **Jewel Tower**, the only other still-extant chunk of the old palace, built in the 14th century for storing Edward III's royal treasures. Constructed largely from Kentish ragstone, the tower contains intriguing medieval historical features, an exhibition on the history of Parliament and a small cafe.

Exit the Jewel Tower to the breathtaking majesty of ❸ **Westminster Abbey**, London's West Minster (as distinct from the minster in the east – St Paul's Cathedral) and traditional venue of coronation for the English monarchy. Amid great pomp and ceremony, Prince William married Catherine Middleton here on 29 April 2011. Walking around Parliament Sq, note the ❹ **Supreme Court of the United Kingdom**, within the ornate Middlesex Guildhall, dating from 1913. Observe the statue of **Abraham Lincoln**, a copy of an effigy sculpted by Augustus Saint-Gaudens which stands in Lincoln Park, Chicago.

Round the corner and walk west (left) along Great George St, with the **HM Treasury** on the far side of the road. Turn left down Storey's Gate and then right into Old Queen St, before trotting down ❺ **Cockpit Steps** (a surviving part of the former Royal Cockpit, where cockfights were held), said to be haunted by a headless woman dressed in red! The steps lead down to lovely **Birdcage Walk**, named after the royal Aviary, which was once situated here. Cross over the road and walk into ❻ **St James's Park** (which used to be the royal gardens) to walk alongside the lake. As you near the western end of the park, you will pass the 7 **Guards Museum** on the far side of Birdcage Walk. Get here for 10.50am any day from April to August to catch the guards getting into formation outside the museum for their march up to Buckingham Palace.

Walk up Buckingham Gate to the 8 **Queen's Gallery** and the 9 **Royal Mews** before walking back to 10 **Buckingham Palace** and the 11 **Queen Victoria Memorial**, dating from 1911, with its grumpy looking monarch staring down the Mall. Follow the ceremonial route of the Mall (rhymes with 'shall') and cross into **Green Park** (another of London's Royal Parks) to head up Queen's Walk to grand 12 **Spencer House** before retracing your steps back to the Mall and 13 **Clarence House**, residence of Prince Charles and former home of Queen Elizabeth the Queen Mother. Five rooms of the house are usually opened up to the public for pre-booked tours each year between August and October. The unflinching guards on Stable Yard Road are an impressive sight.

Continuing east along the Mall to walk north up Marlborough Road to 14 **St James's Palace** and the 15 **Queen's Chapel** opposite. Open during services only, the church interior has exquisite 17th-century fittings, atmospherically illuminated by light streaming in through the large windows above the altar. Return to the Mall and keep walking east to climb the steps alongside a 16 **bronze statue of Queen Elizabeth II** (unveiled in 2009) with King George VI behind her. On the corner at **No 4 Carlton Gardens** is the house where General Charles de Gaulle set up the headquarters of the Free French Forces in 1940. Ahead you can see the towering **Duke of York Column** rising up in Waterloo Place.

Take the first left and cross over the pedestrian crossing in Pall Mall to walk into 17 **St James's Square**, surrounded by good-looking Georgian architecture. With a statue of King William III at its centre, the private gardens at the heart of the square are open from 10am to 4.30pm on weekdays. **The Naval and Military Club** at No 4 in the northeast corner of the square is known as the 'In and Out', reflected in the words on the entrance; on the northwest corner at No 14 is the **London Library**, established by Thomas Carlyle: a private library with 15 miles of shelving.

Head up Duke of York St towards the side-on form of **St James's Piccadilly**, designed by Christopher Wren, and walk up colonnaded Piccadilly Arcade to exit into Piccadilly. On the far side of the road is the impressive entrance of the 18 **Royal Academy of Arts**, founded by George III in 1768, and located within Burlington House. Explore the impressive stone-paved piazza of the main courtyard. Head back across the road and walk a short distance east to mint-green 19 **Fortnum & Mason**, London's oldest grocery store and holder of many royal warrants.

Walk east along Piccadilly and turn right down Church Pl just west of St James's Piccadilly and onto Jermyn St. Head east and go right to Regent St, turn left onto King Charles II St and walk down 20 **Royal Opera Arcade**, London's oldest shopping arcade. From Pall Mall, walk along Cockspur St to pass Trafalgar Sq and head down Whitehall. Walking past the old Admiralty Building, you will reach 21 **Horse Guards Parade**, where the mounted troopers of the Household Cavalry change guard daily at 11am daily (10am Sunday) and a lite-pomp version takes place at 4pm when the dismounted guards are changed. Open daily, the **Household Cavalry Museum** is here as well. On the far side of Whitehall stands 22 **Banqueting House**, with its bust of Charles I on the corner above the door, while continuing south along Whitehall takes you past **No 10 Downing Street** and returns you to the Houses of Parliament.

West End

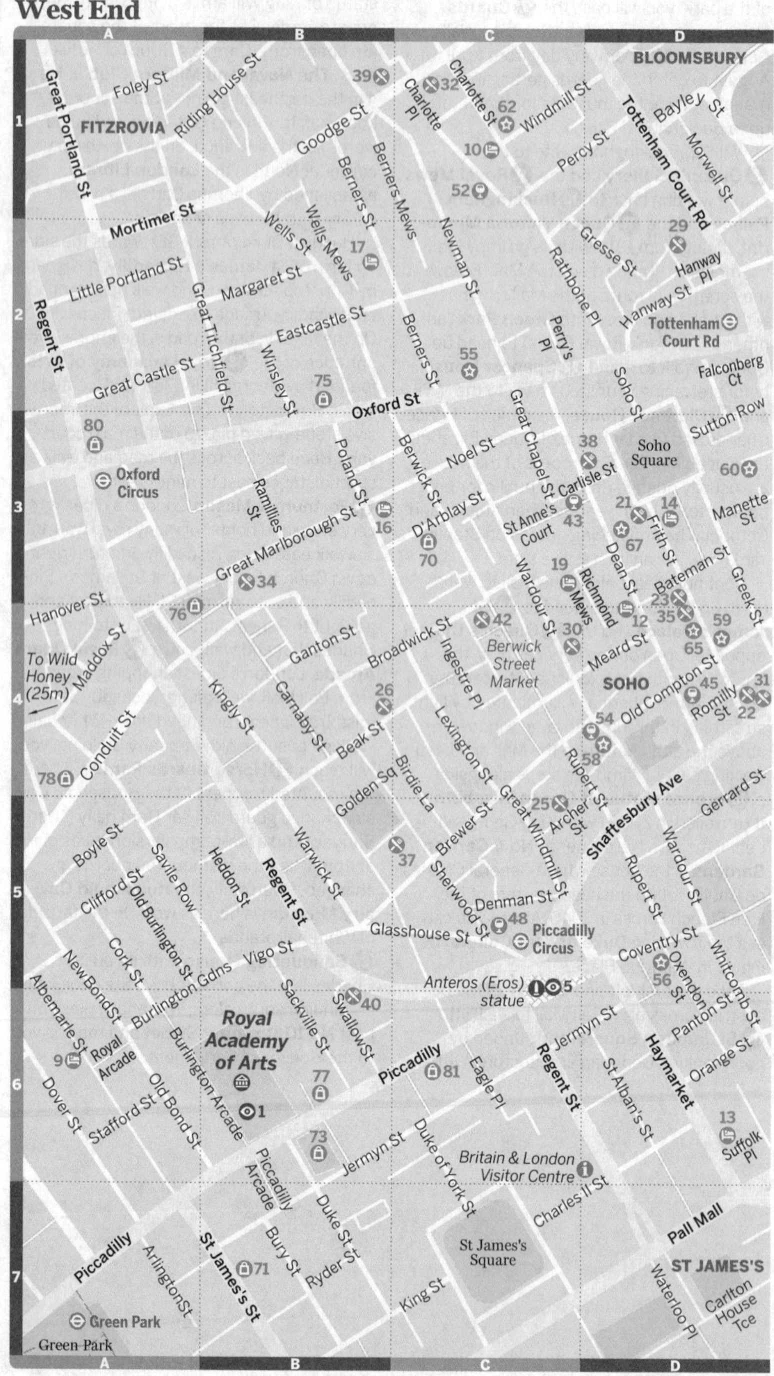
A
B
C
D
1
2
3
4
5
6
7
BLOOMSBURY
FITZROVIA
SOHO
ST JAMES'S
Great Portland St
Foley St
Riding House St
Goodge St
Charlotte Pl
Charlotte St
Windmill St
Tottenham Court Rd
Bayley St
Morwell St
Percy St
Berners St
Berners Mews
Newman St
Rathbone Pl
Gresse St
Hanway Pl
Hanway St
Tottenham Court Rd
Mortimer St
Wells St
Wells Mews
Little Portland St
Margaret St
Great Titchfield St
Eastcastle St
Regent St
Great Castle St
Winsley St
Perry's Pl
Soho St
Falconberg Ct
Sutton Row
Oxford St
Oxford Circus
Poland St
Berwick St
Noel St
Great Chapel St
Soho Square
Carlisle St
Ramillies St
Great Marlborough St
D'Arblay St
St Anne's Court
Frith St
Dean St
Manette St
Greek St
Bateman St
Wardour St
Richmond Mews
Hanover St
Maddox St
To Wild Honey (25m)
Ganton St
Broadwick St
Ingestre Pl
Berwick Street Market
Meard St
Old Compton St
Romilly St
Kingly St
Carnaby St
Beak St
Lexington St
Rupert St
Conduit St
Golden Sq
Birdie La
Great Windmill St
Archer St
Shaftesbury Ave
Gerrard St
Boyle St
Savile Row
Heddon St
Regent St
Warwick St
Brewer St
Sherwood St
Clifford St
Old Burlington St
Denman St
Rupert St
Wardour St
Glasshouse St
Piccadilly Circus
Coventry St
Whitcomb St
Vigo St
Cork St
New Bond St
Burlington Gdns
Sackville St
Swallow St
Anteros (Eros) statue
Oxendon St
Panton St
Albemarle St
Royal Arcade
Burlington Arcade
Royal Academy of Arts
Piccadilly
Eagle Pl
Jermyn St
Regent St
St Alban's St
Haymarket
Orange St
Dover St
Stafford St
Old Bond St
Jermyn St
Duke of York St
Britain & London Visitor Centre
Suffolk Pl
Piccadilly Arcade
Charles II St
Duke St
Bury St
Ryder St
St James's Square
Pall Mall
Piccadilly
Arlington St
St James's St
King St
Waterloo Pl
Carlton House Tce
Green Park
Green Park
1
5
9
10
12
13
14
16
17
19
21
22
23
25
26
29
30
31
32
34
35
37
38
39
40
42
43
45
48
52
54
55
56
58
59
60
62
65
67
70
71
73
75
76
77
78
80
81

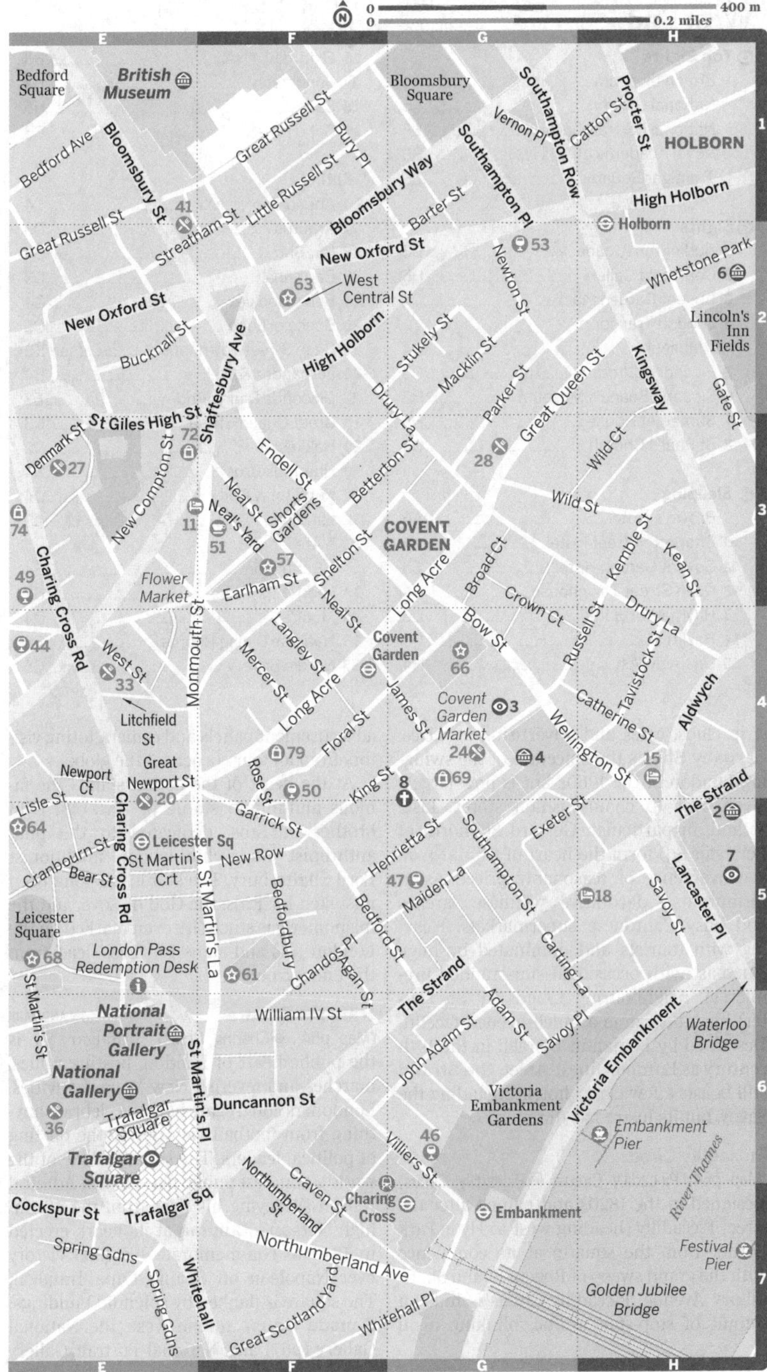

0 400 m
0 0.2 miles
British Museum
Bedford Square
Bloomsbury Square
HOLBORN
Holborn
High Holborn
New Oxford St
Great Russell St
Bloomsbury St
Bloomsbury Way
Southampton Row
Southampton Pl
Shaftesbury Ave
St Giles High St
Charing Cross Rd
COVENT GARDEN
Covent Garden
Covent Garden Market
Long Acre
Neal's Yard
Flower Market
Lincoln's Inn Fields
Kingsway
Aldwych
The Strand
Leicester Sq
Leicester Square
London Pass Redemption Desk
National Portrait Gallery
National Gallery
Trafalgar Square
Charing Cross
Embankment
Victoria Embankment
Victoria Embankment Gardens
Embankment Pier
Waterloo Bridge
Festival Pier
Golden Jubilee Bridge
River Thames
Whitehall
Northumberland Ave
Duncannon St
St Martin's Pl
St Martin's La
Cockspur St
Trafalgar Sq

West End

Top Sights

British Museum ... E1
National Gallery ... E6
National Portrait Gallery ... E6
Royal Academy of Arts ... B6
Trafalgar Square ... E6

Sights

1 Burlington Arcade ... B6
2 Courtauld Gallery ... H5
3 Covent Garden Piazza ... G4
4 London Transport Museum ... G4
5 Piccadilly Circus ... C5
6 Sir John Soane's Museum ... H2
7 Somerset House ... H5
8 St Paul's Church ... G4

Sleeping

9 Brown's Hotel ... A6
10 Charlotte Street Hotel ... C1
11 Covent Garden Hotel ... E3
12 Dean Street Townhouse ... D4
13 Haymarket Hotel ... D6
14 Hazlitt's ... D3
15 One Aldwych ... H4
16 Oxford St YHA ... B3
17 Sanderson ... B2
18 Savoy ... H5
19 Soho Hotel ... C3

Eating

20 Abeno Too ... E4
21 Arbutus ... D3
22 Bar Shu ... D4
23 Barrafina ... D3
24 Ben's Cookies ... G4
25 Bocca di Lupo ... C5
Dean Street Townhouse ... (see 12)
26 Fernandez & Wells ... B4
27 Giaconda Dining Room ... E3
28 Great Queen Street ... G3
29 Hakkasan ... D2
30 Hummus Bros ... C4
31 Konditor & Cook ... D4
32 Lantana ... C1
33 L'Atelier de Joël Robuchon ... E4
34 Leon ... B3
35 Mooli's ... D4
36 National Dining Rooms ... E6
37 Nordic Bakery ... C5

strip clubs, cafes and advertising agencies. **Carnaby St** was the epicentre of the swinging London of the 1960s but is now largely given over to chain fashion stores. Lisle St and, in particular, Gerrard St (north of Leicester Sq) form the heart of **Chinatown**, a convergence of reasonably priced Asian restaurants, decorative Chinese arches and busy Cantonese supermarkets. Heaving with tourists and dominated by huge cinemas (with occasional star-studded premieres), neighbouring **Leicester Sq** (*lester*) has undergone a much-needed facelift. Described by Benjamin Disraeli in the 19th century as Europe's finest street, **the Strand** still boasts a few classy hotels, including the Savoy, but its lustre has dimmed.

Piccadilly Circus SQUARE
(Map p64; Piccadilly Circus; ⊖Piccadilly Circus) Designed in the 1820s and named after the street Piccadilly (heading west to Hyde Park Corner from the square) at its confluence with the grand sweep of Regent St and Shaftesbury Avenue, Piccadilly Circus is today a tumult of stop-start traffic, blinking neon advertisement panels and camera-toting visitors from all four corners of the globe.

At the heart of the action stands the famous aluminium statue of **Anteros**, twin brother of Eros, dedicated to the philanthropist and child-labour abolitionist Lord Shaftesbury. The statue has long been mistaken for Eros, the God of Love, and the misnomer has stuck (it's even marked on the London A-Z and signs for 'Eros' lead from the underground).

Trafalgar Square LANDMARK
(Map p64; ⊖Charing Cross) Trafalgar Sq is the public heart of London, hosting rallies, marches and feverish New Year's festivities. Londoners congregate here to celebrate anything from football victories to the ousting of political leaders. The square is one of the world's grandest public places, with Admiral Nelson surveying his fleet from the 43.5m-high **Nelson's Column** at its heart, erected in 1843 to commemorate his 1805 victory over Napoleon off Spain's Cape Trafalgar. The square is flanked by splendid buildings: **Canada House** to the west, the National Gallery (p67) and National Portrait Gallery

38 Pizza Express D3
39 Salt Yard B1
40 Veeraswamy B6
41 Wagamama E2
42 Yauatcha C4

Drinking
43 Candy Bar C3
44 Coach & Horses E4
45 French House D4
46 Gordon's Wine Bar G6
47 Jewel G5
48 Jewel C5
49 LAB E3
50 Lamb & Flag F4
51 Monmouth Coffee Company F3
52 Newman Arms C1
53 Princess Louise G2
54 Village D4

Entertainment
55 100 Club C2
56 Comedy Store D5
57 Donmar Warehouse F3
58 Friendly Society D4
59 G-A-Y Bar D4
60 G-A-Y Late D3
61 London Coliseum F5
62 Pear Shaped C1
63 Popstarz F2
64 Prince Charles E5
65 Ronnie Scott's D4
66 Royal Opera House G4
67 Soho Theatre D3
68 Tkts E5

Shopping
69 Benjamin Pollock's Toy Shop G4
70 BM Soho C3
71 DR Harris B7
72 Forbidden Planet E3
73 Fortnum & Mason B6
74 Foyle's E3
75 HMV B2
76 Liberty A4
77 Minamoto Kitchoan B6
78 Rigby & Peller A4
79 Stanfords F4
80 Topshop Oxford Circus A3
81 Waterstones C6

(p67) to the north, **South Africa House** and the church of **St Martin-in-the-Fields** to the east. Further south stands **Admiralty Arch**, built in honour of Queen Victoria in 1910 (and with a mysterious stone nose around seven foot up from the ground on one of the northernmost arches), and beyond that, the Mall (rhymes with 'shall', not 'shawl') is the ceremonial route leading to Buckingham Palace.

FREE National Gallery ART GALLERY
(Map p64; www.nationalgallery.org.uk; Trafalgar Sq; 10am-6pm Sat-Thu, to 9pm Fri; Charing Cross)
Gazing grandly over Trafalgar Sq through its Corinthian columns, the National Gallery is the nation's most important repository of largely pre-modern art. Four million visitors flock annually to admire its 2300-plus Western European paintings, spanning the eras from the 13th to the early 20th centuries. Highlights include Turner's *The Fighting Temeraire*, Botticelli's *Venus and Mars* and van Gogh's *Sunflowers*. The medieval religious paintings in the **Sainsbury Wing** are delightful, but for more modern zest, the works by Monet, Cézanne and Renoir are crowd-pullers. The comprehensive audio guides (£3.50) are recommended, as are the free introductory tours, while for sustenance nothing beats the National Dining Rooms (p113) in the Sainsbury Wing.

FREE National Portrait Gallery ART GALLERY
(Map p64; www.npg.org.uk; St Martin's Pl; 10am-6pm Sat-Wed, to 9pm Thu & Fri; Charing Cross)
The fascinating National Portrait Gallery is like stepping into a picture book of English history. Founded in 1856, the permanent collection (around 11,000 works) starts with the Tudors on the 2nd floor and descends to contemporary figures (from pop stars to scientists), including Marc Quinn's *Self*, a frozen self-portrait of the artist's head cast in blood and recreated every five years. An audiovisual guide (£3) will lead you through the gallery's most famous pictures.

Royal Academy of Arts GALLERY
(Map p64; 020-7300 8000; www.royalacademy.org.uk; Burlington House, Piccadilly; admission depending on exhibition £6-20; 10am-6pm Sun-Thu, to midnight Fri, 9am-midnight Sat; Green Park)
Hosting high-profile exhibitions and a small

display from its permanent collection, the crafty academy made it a condition of joining its exclusive club of 80 artists for new members to donate one of their artworks. The collection embraces works from such masters as Constable, Turner and Sir Norman Foster while the Summer Exhibition showcases contemporary art. Free tours of the John Madesjki Fine Rooms are held.

Covent Garden Piazza HISTORIC AREA

(Map p64; ⊖Covent Garden) Hallowed turf – or cobbles – for opera fans descending on the esteemed Royal Opera House, Covent Garden is one of London's biggest tourist hot spots. London's first planned square, Covent Garden Piazza now hosts bands of tourists shopping in quaint old arcades and ringing street entertainers and buskers. On its western flank rises **St Paul's Church** (Map p64; www.actorschurch.org; Bedford St; ⏲8.30am-5.30pm Mon-Fri, 9am-1pm Sun), with a lovely courtyard at the back, ideal for a picnic in the sun.

London Transport Museum MUSEUM

(Map p64; www.ltmuseum.co.uk; Covent Garden Piazza; adult/child £13.50/free; ⏲10am-6pm Sat-Thu, 11am-6pm Fri; ⊖Covent Garden) Kids and adults alike can tick off all manner of vehicles at this refurbished museum, from sedan chairs to train carriages, trams and taxis along with original advertising posters, photos and a fab shop for tube-map boxers shorts or a pair of 'Mind the Gap' socks.

Sir John Soane's Museum MUSEUM

(Map p64; www.soane.org; 13 Lincoln's Inn Fields; tours £5; ⏲10am-5pm Tue-Sat, 6-9pm 1st Tue of month; ⊖Holborn) One of the most atmospheric and intriguing of London's museums, this was the remarkable home of architect and collector extraordinaire Sir John Soane (1753–1837). Now a rewarding museum, the house has been left largely as it was when Sir John was taken out in a box. Among his eclectic acquisitions are an Egyptian sarcophagus, dozens of Greek and Roman antiquities and the original *Rake's Progress,* William Hogarth's set of caricatures telling the story of a late-18th-century London cad. Soane was clearly a bright spark – check out the ingenious folding walls in the picture gallery. Tours (£10) are held at 11am on Saturdays but bookmark the evening of the first Tuesday of each month when the house is candlelit and even more magical (queues are long). The museum is currently undergoing an ambitious expansion.

Somerset House GALLERIES

(Map p64; www.somersethouse.org.uk; Strand; ⏲7.30am-11pm; ⊖Temple) The first Somerset House was built for the Duke of Somerset, brother of Jane Seymour, in 1551. For two centuries it played host to royals (Elizabeth I once lived here), foreign diplomats, wild masked balls, peace treaties, the Parliamentary army (during the Civil War) and Oliver Cromwell's wake. Having fallen into disrepair, it was pulled down in 1775 and rebuilt in 1801 to designs by William Chambers. Among other weighty organisations, it went on to house the Royal Academy of the Arts, the Society of Antiquaries, the Navy Board and, that most popular of institutions, the Inland Revenue.

The tax collectors are still here, but that doesn't dissuade Londoners from attending open-air events in the grand central courtyard, such as films over 12 days in summer and ice skating in winter. The riverside terrace is a popular spot for caffeine with views of the Thames.

Near the Strand entrance, the **Courtauld Gallery** (Map p64; www.courtauld.ac.uk; adult/child £6/free, admission free 10am-2pm Mon; ⏲10am-6pm) displays a wealth of 14th- to 20th-century art, including a room of Rubens and works by van Gogh, Renoir and Cézanne. Downstairs, the **Embankment Galleries** are devoted to temporary exhibitions; prices and hours vary.

Handel House Museum MUSEUM

(Map p89; www.handelhouse.org; 25 Brook St; adult/child £5/2; ⏲10am-6pm Tue, Wed, Fri & Sat, 10am-8pm Thu, noon-6pm Sun; ⊖Bond St) George Frideric Handel's pad from 1723 until his death in 1759 is now a moderately interesting museum dedicated to his life. He wrote some of his greatest works here, including the *Messiah,* and music still fills the house during live recitals (see the website for details).

From songs of praise to *Purple Haze,* Jimi Hendrix lived next door at number 23 many years (and genres) later.

Burlington Arcade SHOPPING ARCADE

(Map p64; 51 Piccadilly; ⊖Green Park) The well-to-do Burlington Arcade, built in 1819, is famously patrolled by the Burlington Beadles, uniformed guards who constitute one of the world's smallest private police forces.

THE CITY

Packed with beguiling churches, intriguing architecture, hidden gardens and atmospher-

LOCAL KNOWLEDGE

ALAN KINGSHOTT: CHIEF YEOMAN WARDER AT THE TOWER

What is the best way to tackle the Tower? To understand the Tower's full history, I suggest visitors take a guided tour (in English) by a Yeoman Warder. With such a vast amount of history within the walls, you should allow at least three hours to fully enjoy your experience.

What of the Crown Jewels? The new presentation of the Crown Jewels is a must-see with a new layout, which will help visitors easily explore our sometimes complex history and ceremonies. Just ask a member of the Jewel House staff about any item: you will be amazed at their wealth of knowledge and it will enhance your visit.

How many Ravens are there in the Tower? We must have six ravens at the Tower at any one time by a Royal Decree put in place by Charles II. According to an old legend, should the birds leave, the Monarchy and the White Tower will crumble and fall. We tend not to provoke legends so generally we have eight birds.

Any ceremonies you can recommend? There are many ceremonies at the Tower of London, most of which can be viewed by visitors. However, many happen around royal events such as the Queen's Birthday and the State Opening of Parliament. Alternatively there is the Ceremony of the Keys (the locking up of the Tower of London), which takes place, as it has done for 700 years, at 9.30pm every night. (Note: attendance is free but requires that you apply by post at least two months in advance and supply a return-address envelope.)

ic lanes, you could spend weeks exploring the City of London, which, for most of its history, *was* London. Its boundaries have changed little since the Romans first founded their gated community here two millennia ago.

It's only in the last 250 years that the City has gone from being the very essence of London and its main population centre to just its central business district. But what a business district it is – despite the hammering its bankers have taken in recent years, the 'square mile' remains at the very heart of world capitalism.

Currently fewer than 10,000 people actually live here, although some 300,000 descend on it each weekday, when they generate almost three-quarters of Britain's entire GDP before squeezing back onto the tube. On Sundays the City becomes a virtual ghost town; it's a good time to poke around but come with a full stomach – most shops and eateries are closed.

Tower of London FORTRESS

(Map p72; ☎0844 482 7777; www.hrp.org.uk; Tower Hill; adult/child £20.90/10.45, audio guides £4/3; ⌚9am-5.30pm Tue-Sat, from 10am Sun & Mon, until 4.30pm Nov-Feb; ⊖Tower Hill) One of London's four World Heritage Sites (joining Westminster Abbey, Kew Gardens and Maritime Greenwich), the Tower offers a window on to a gruesome and quite compelling history.

In the 1070s, William the Conqueror started work on the White Tower to replace the castle he'd previously had built here. By 1285, two walls with towers and a moat were built around it and the defences have barely been altered since. A former royal residence, treasury, mint and arsenal, it became most famous as a prison when Henry VIII moved to Whitehall Palace in 1529 and started meting out his preferred brand of punishment.

The most striking building is the central **White Tower**, with its solid Romanesque architecture and four turrets. Today it houses a collection from the Royal Armouries, including Henry VIII's commodious suit of armour. On the 2nd floor is **St John's Chapel**, dating from 1080 and therefore the oldest church in London. To the north stands **Waterloo Barracks**, which now contains the spectacular and newly redisplayed **Crown Jewels**, including the platinum crown of the late Queen Mother, set with the 105-carat **Koh-i-Noor** (Mountain of Light) diamond and the **Imperial State Crown**. Slow-moving travelators shunt visitors past the collection. On the far side of the White Tower rises the **Bloody Tower**, where the 12-year-old Edward V and his little brother were held 'for their own safety' and later murdered, probably by their uncle, the future Richard III. Sir Walter Raleigh did a 13-year stretch here, when he wrote his *History of the World*.

Tower of London

TACKLING THE TOWER

Although it's usually less busy in the late afternoon, don't leave your assault on the Tower until too late in the day. You could easily spend hours here and not see it all. Start by getting your bearings with the hour-long Yeoman Warder (Beefeater) tours; they are included in the cost of admission, entertaining and the only way to access the **Chapel Royal of St Peter ad Vincula** 1, which is where they finish up.

When you leave the chapel, the **Tower Green scaffold site** 2 is directly in front. The building immediately to your left is Waterloo Barracks, where the **Crown Jewels** 3 are housed. These are the absolute highlight of a Tower visit, so keep an eye on the entrance and pick a time to visit when it looks relatively quiet. Once inside, take things at your own pace. Slow-moving travelators shunt you past the dozen or so crowns that are the treasury's centrepiece, but feel free to double-back for a second or even third pass – particularly if you ended up on the rear travelator the first time around. Allow plenty of time for the **White Tower** 4, the core of the whole complex, starting with the exhibition of royal armour. As you continue onto the 2nd floor, keep an eye out for **St John's Chapel** 5. The famous **ravens** 6 can be seen in the courtyard around the White Tower. Head next through the towers that formed the **Medieval Palace** 7, then take the **East Wall Walk** 8 to get a feel for the castle's mighty battlements. Spend the rest of your time poking around the many, many other fascinating nooks and crannies of the Tower complex.

BEAT THE QUEUES

» **Buy** your fast-track ticket in advance online or at the City of London Information Centre in St Paul's Churchyard.

» **Palacepalooza** An annual Historic Royal Palaces membership allows you to jump the queues and visit the Tower (and four other London palaces) as often as you like.

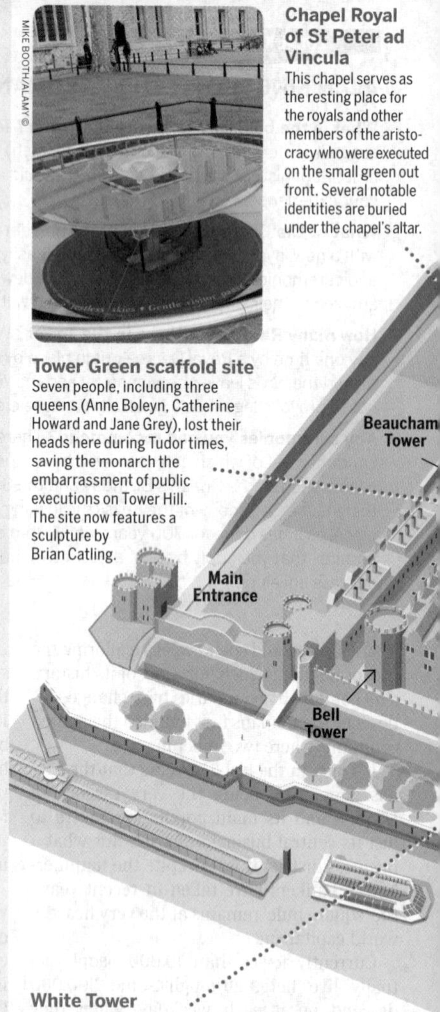

White Tower
Much of the White Tower is taken up with this exhibition of 500 years of royal armour. Look for the virtually cuboid suit made to match Henry VIII's bloated body, complete with an oversized armoured pouch to protect his, ahem, crown jewels.

PAWEL LIBERA IMAGES/ALAMY ©

St John's Chapel

Kept as plain and unadorned as it would have been in Norman times, the White Tower's 2nd-floor chapel is the oldest surviving church in London, dating from 1080.

Crown Jewels

When they're not being worn for affairs of state, Her Majesty's bling is kept here. Among the 23,578 gems, look out for the 530-carat Cullinan diamond at the top of the Royal Sceptre, the largest part of what was (until 1985) the largest diamond ever found.

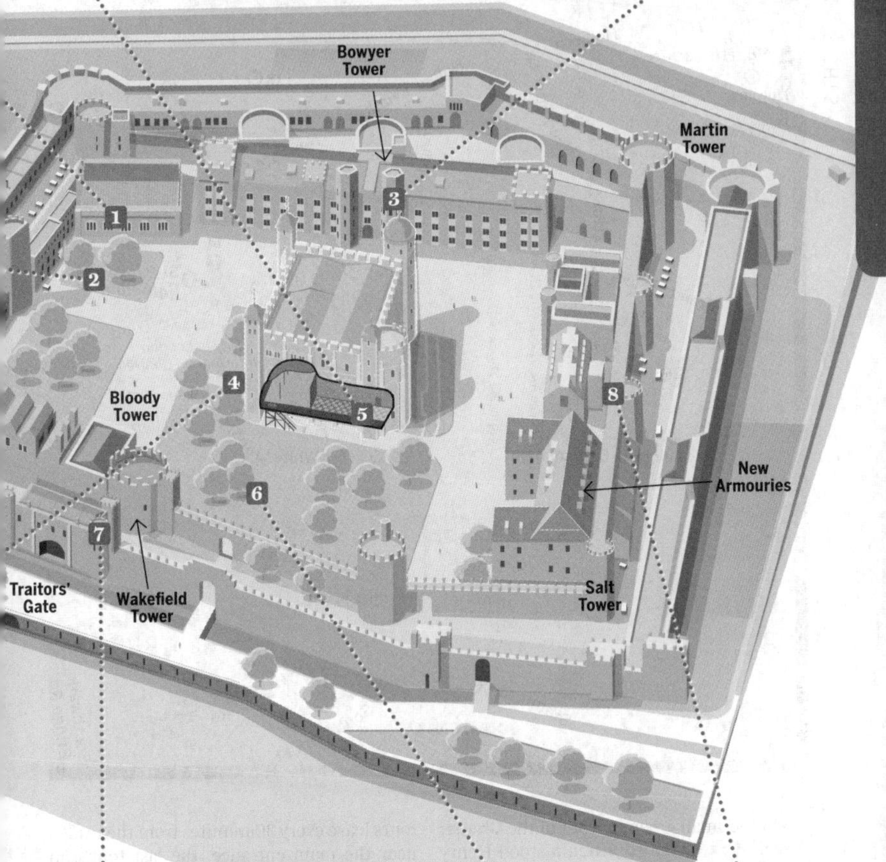

Bowyer Tower

Martin Tower

1

2

3

4

Bloody Tower

5

6

7

8

New Armouries

Traitors' Gate

Wakefield Tower

Salt Tower

Medieval Palace

This part of the Tower complex was commenced around 1220 and was home to England's medieval monarchs. Look for the recreations of the bedchamber of Edward I (1272–1307) in St Thomas' Tower and the throne room on the upper floor of the Wakefield Tower.

Ravens

This stretch of green is where the Tower's famous ravens are kept, fed on raw meat and blood-soaked bird biscuits. According to legend, if the birds were to leave the Tower, the kingdom would fall.

East Wall Walk

Follow the inner ramparts, starting from the 13th-century Salt Tower, passing through the Broad Arrow and Constable Towers, and ending at the Martin Tower, where the Crown Jewels were once stored.

The City

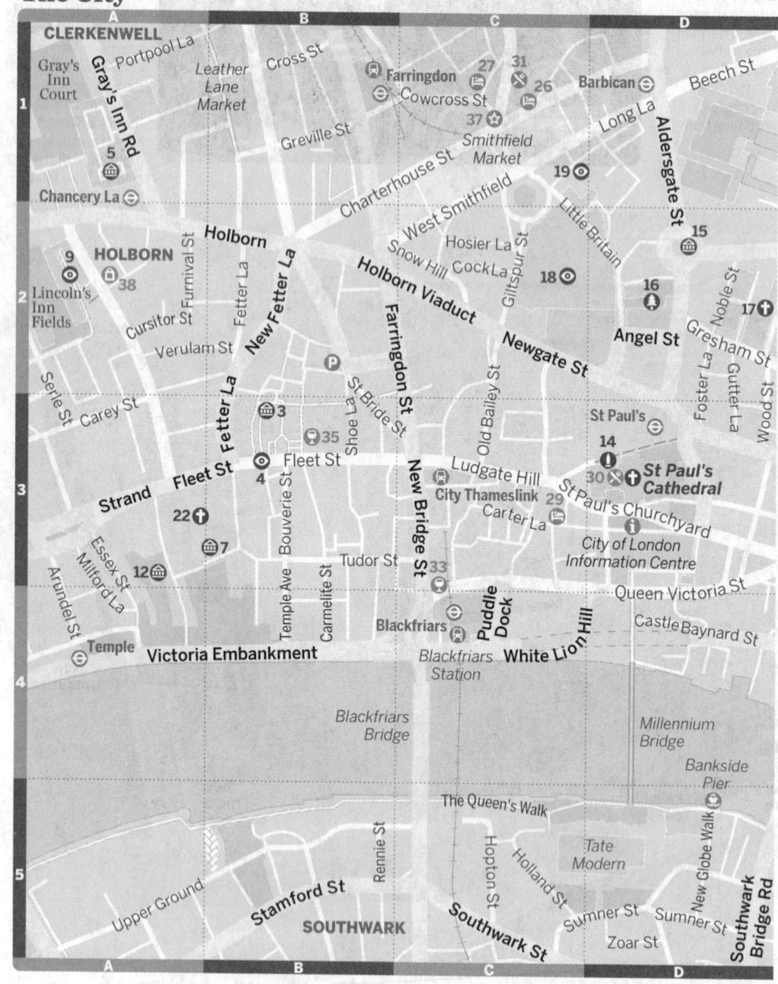

On the small green in front of the **Chapel Royal of St Peter ad Vincula** stood Henry VIII's **scaffold**, where seven people, including Anne Boleyn and her cousin Catherine Howard (Henry's second and fifth wives) were beheaded.

Look out for the latest in the Tower's long line of famous ravens, which legend says could cause the White Tower to collapse should they leave (their wings are clipped in case they get any ideas).

To get your bearings, take the hugely entertaining free guided tour with any of the Beefeaters (Yeoman Warders). Hour-long tours leave every 30 minutes from the bridge near the main entrance; the last tour's an hour before closing. Book online for cheaper rates for the Tower.

Tower Bridge BRIDGE

(Map p72; Tower Hill) London was still a thriving port in 1894 when elegant Tower Bridge was built. Designed to be raised to allow ships to pass (it still lifts around 1000 times a year), electricity has now replaced the original steam power. A lift leads up from the northern tower to the **Tower Bridge Exhibition** (Map p72; www.towerbridge.org.uk;

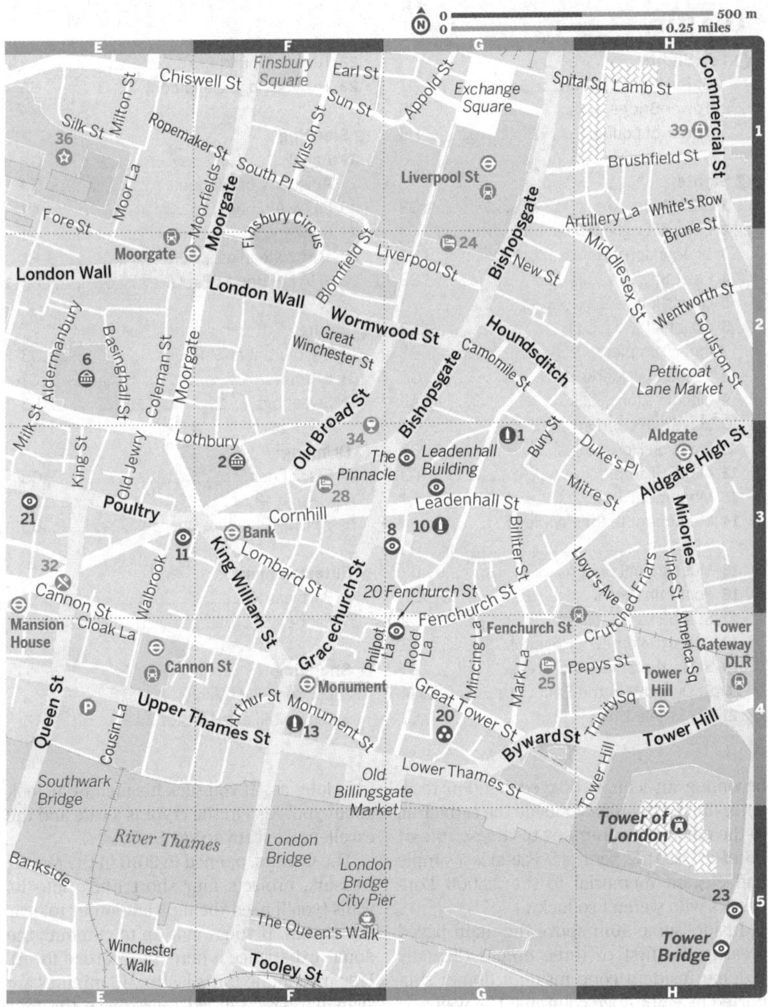

adult/child £7/3; ⏲10am-5.30pm Apr-Sep, 9.30am-5pm Oct-Mar; ⊖Tower Hill) 42m above the water, from where you can walk along the east- and west-facing walkways. The same ticket gets you into the **engine rooms** below the southern tower, for the real mechanical lowdown. Below the bridge on the City side is Dead Man's Hole, where corpses that had made their way into the Thames (through suicide, murder or accident) were regularly retrieved.

St Paul's Cathedral CHURCH
(Map p72; www.stpauls.co.uk; St Paul's Churchyard; adult/child £12.50/4.50; ⏲8.30am-4pm Mon-Sat; ⊖St Paul's) Dominating the City with one of the world's largest church domes (around 65,000 tons worth), St Paul's Cathedral was designed by Christopher Wren after the Great Fire and built between 1675 and 1710. The site is ancient hallowed ground with four other cathedrals preceding Wren's masterpiece here, the first dating from 604. As part of the 300th anniversary celebrations, St Paul's underwent a £40 million renovation project that gave the church a deep clean.

The dome is famed for sidestepping Luftwaffe incendiary bombs in the 'Second Great Fire of London' of December 1940,

The City

Top Sights

St Paul's Cathedral........D3
Tower Bridge........H5
Tower of London........H5

Sights

1 30 St Mary Axe........G3
2 Bank of England Museum........F3
3 Dr Johnson's House........B3
4 Fleet St........B3
5 Gray's Inn........A1
6 Guildhall........E2
7 Inner Temple........B3
8 Leadenhall Market........G3
9 Lincoln's Inn........A2
10 Lloyd's of London........G3
11 Mansion House........E3
12 Middle Temple........A3
13 Monument........F4
14 Monument to the People of London........D3
15 Museum of London........D2
16 Postman's Park........D2
17 St Alban's........D2
18 St Bartholomew's Hospital........C2
19 St Bartholomew-the-Great........C1
20 St Dunstan-in-the-East........G4
21 St Mary-le-Bow........E3
22 Temple Church........A3
23 Tower Bridge Exhibition........H5

Sleeping

24 Andaz........G2
25 Apex City of London........G4
26 Fox & Anchor........C1
27 Rookery........C1
28 Threadneedles........F3
29 YHA London St Paul's........C3

Eating

30 Restaurant at St Paul's........D3
31 St John........C1
32 Sweetings........E3

Drinking

33 Black Friar........C3
34 Vertigo 42........F3
35 Ye Olde Cheshire Cheese........B3

Entertainment

36 Barbican........E1
37 Fabric........C1

Shopping

38 London Silver Vaults........A2
39 Old Spitalfields Market........H1

becoming an icon of dogged London resilience during the Blitz. Outside the cathedral, to the north, a **monument to the people of London** (Map p72; north of St Paul's) is a simple and elegant memorial to the 32,000 Londoners who weren't so lucky.

Inside, some 30m above the main paved area, is the first of three domes (actually a dome inside a cone inside a dome) supported by eight huge columns. The walkway around its base, 257 steps up a staircase on the western side of the southern transept, is called the **Whispering Gallery** because if you talk close to the wall, your words will carry to the opposite side 32m away. A further 119 steps brings you to the **Stone Gallery**, 152 iron steps above which is the **Golden Gallery** at the very top, which rewards you with unforgettable views of London.

The **Crypt** has memorials to up to 300 military demigods, including Wellington, Kitchener and Nelson, whose body lies below the dome. But the most poignant memorial is to Wren himself. On a simple slab bearing his name, a Latin inscription translates as: 'If you seek his memorial, look about you'. Also in the crypt is a cafe and the excellent **Restaurant at St Paul's**.

The **Oculus**, opened in 2010 in the former treasury, projects four short films onto its walls (you'll need the mp3 audiotour to hear the sound). If you're not up to climbing the dome, experience it here (in recorded form). Free mp3 audio tours lasting 45 minutes are available. Free guided tours leave the tour desk four times daily at 10.45am, 11.15am, 1.30pm and 2pm (90 minutes). Evensong takes place at 5pm (3.15pm on Sunday).

FREE **Museum of London** MUSEUM
(Map p72; www.museumoflondon.org.uk; 150 London Wall; ⏲10am-6pm; ⊖Barbican) Catching this riveting museum early on in your stay helps peel back the layers of historical London for valuable perspectives on this great city. The first gallery, **London before London**, illustrates the settlements predating Roman era. The Roman section explores the ancient roots of the modern city as we know it while Saxon, medieval, Tudor and

Stuart London is intriguingly brought to life. The museum's new £20 million **Galleries of Modern London** encompases everything from 1666 (the devastating Great Fire of London) to the present day. While the Lord Mayor's ceremonial coach is the centrepiece, an effort has been made to create an immersive experience: you can enter reconstructions of an 18th-century debtors' prison, a Georgian pleasure garden and a Victorian street.

FREE Guildhall HISTORIC BUILDING
(Map p72; ☎020-7606 3030; www.guildhall.cityoflondon.gov.uk; Gresham St; ⏲9am-5pm unless closed for events, closed Sun Oct-Apr; Clockmakers' Museum 9.30am-4.45pm Mon-Sat, Guildhall Art Gallery 10am-5pm Mon-Sat, noon-4pm Sun; ⊖Bank) Plumb in the middle of the 'square mile', the Guildhall has been the seat of the City's local government for eight centuries. The present building dates from the early 15th century.

Visitors can see the **Great Hall**, where the city's mayor is sworn in and where important fellows such as the Tsar of Russia and the Prince Regent celebrated beating Napoleon. It's an impressive space decorated with the shields and banners of London's 12 principal livery companies, carved galleries (the west of which is protected by disturbing statues of giants Gog and Magog) and a beautiful oak-panelled roof. There's also a lovely bronze statue of Churchill sitting in a comfy chair. Beneath it is London's largest **medieval crypt** (visit by free guided tour only, bookings essential), with 19 stained-glass windows displaying the livery companies' coats of arms.

The **Clockmakers' Museum** charts 500 years of horology with an intriguing collection of more than 700 clocks, including a decimal watch from 1852, with anti-clockwise-sweeping hands, and the **Guildhall Art Gallery** displays around 250 artworks. Included in the art gallery admission is entry to the remains of an ancient **Roman amphitheatre**, which lay forgotten beneath this site until 1988.

FREE Bank of England Museum MUSEUM
(Map p72; www.bankofengland.co.uk/museum; Bartholomew Lane; ⏲10am-5pm Mon-Fri; ⊖Bank) Guardian of the country's current shaky financial system, the Bank of England was established in 1694 when the government needed to raise cash to support a war with France. It was moved here in 1734 and largely renovated by Sir John Soane. The surprisingly interesting museum traces the history of the bank and banking system. Audioguides are free and you even get to pick up (and leave behind) a £230,000 gold bar.

Monument MONUMENT
(Map p72; www.themonument.info; Monument St; adult/child £3/1; ⏲9.30am-5.30pm; ⊖Monument) Designed by Wren to commemorate the Great Fire, the towering Monument is 60.6m high, the exact distance from its base to the bakery on Pudding Lane where the blaze began. Corkscrew your way up the 311 tight spiral steps (claustrophobes beware) for some of London's best wraparound views and twist down again to collect a certificate commemorating your climb.

Dr Johnson's House MUSEUM
(Map p72; www.drjohnsonshouse.org; 17 Gough Sq; adult/child £4.50/1.50; ⏲11am-5pm Mon-Sat; ⊖Chancery Lane) The Georgian house where Samuel Johnson and his assistants compiled the first English dictionary (between 1748 and 1759) is full of prints and portraits of friends and intimates, including the good doctor's Jamaican servant to whom he bequeathed this grand residence.

Inns of Court HISTORIC BUILDINGS
All London barristers work from within one of the four atmospheric Inns of Court, positioned between the walls of the old City and Westminster. It would take a lifetime working here to grasp all the intricacies of their arcane protocols, originating in the 13th century. It's best just to soak up the dreamy ambience of the alleys and open spaces and thank your lucky stars you're not one of the bewigged barristers scurrying about. A roll call of former members would include the likes of Oliver Cromwell, Charles Dickens, Mahatma Gandhi and Margaret Thatcher.

Lincoln's Inn (Map p72; www.lincolnsinn.org.uk; Lincoln's Inn Fields; ⏲grounds 9am-6pm Mon-Fri, chapel & gardens noon-2.30pm Mon-Fri; ⊖Holborn) still has some original 15th-century buildings. It's the oldest and most attractive of the bunch, with a 17th-century chapel and pretty landscaped gardens.

Gray's Inn (Map p72; www.graysinn.org.uk; Gray's Inn Rd; ⏲grounds 10am-4pm Mon-Fri; Chancery Lane) was largely rebuilt after the Luftwaffe levelled it.

Middle Temple (Map p72; www.middletemple.org.uk; Middle Temple Lane; ⏲10-11.30am & 3-4pm Mon-Fri; Temple) and **Inner Temple** (Map p72; www.innertemple.org.uk; King's Bench

Walk; ⌚10am-4pm Mon-Fri; ⊖Temple) both sit between Fleet St and Victoria Embankment. The former is the best preserved, while the latter is home to the intriguing 12th-century **Temple Church** (Map p72; ☎020-7353 8559; www.templechurch.com; ⌚hours vary), built by the Knights Templar and featuring nine stone effigies of knights in its round chapel. Check the church's website or call ahead for opening hours.

Fleet St FAMOUS THOROUGHFARE
(Map p72; ⊖Temple) As 20th-century London's 'Street of Shame', Fleet St was synonymous with the UK's scurrilous tabloids until the mid-1980s, when the press barons embraced computer technology, ditched a load of staff and largely relocated to the Docklands. It's named after the River Fleet, which it once crossed.

St Katharine Docks HARBOUR
(⊖Tower Hill) A centre of trade and commerce for 1000 years, St Katharine Docks is now a buzzing waterside area of pleasure boats, shops and eateries. It was badly damaged during the war, but survivors include the popular **Dickens Inn**, with its original 18th-century timber framework, and **Ivory House** (built 1854) which used to store ivory, perfume and other precious goods.

SOUTH BANK

Londoners once crossed the river to the area controlled by the licentious Bishops of Southwark for all manner of bawdy frolicking frowned upon in the City. It's a much more seemly area now, but the frisson of theatre and entertainment remains. While South Bank only technically refers to the area of river bank between Westminster and Blackfriars Bridges (parts of which are actually on the east bank due to the way the river bends), we've used it as a convenient catch-all for those parts of Southwark and Lambeth that sit closest to the river.

LOCAL KNOWLEDGE

ST DUNSTAN-IN-THE-EAST

For a lovely escape from the hurly-burly of the City's streets, track down this lovely bombed out **church** (Map p72; ⌚7am-dusk; ⊖Monument or Tower Hill) off St Dunstan's Hill, lovingly arranged with a garden and greenery. Overlooked by its surviving Wren-designed steeple, it's a sublime and tranquil spot for a breather.

FREE **Tate Modern** GALLERY
(Map p78; www.tate.org.uk; Queen's Walk; ⌚10am-6pm Sun-Thu, to 10pm Fri & Sat; ⊖Southwark) One of London's most popular attractions, this outstanding modern and contemporary art gallery is housed in the creatively revamped **Bankside Power Station** south of the Millennium Bridge. A spellbinding synthesis of funky modern art and capacious industrial brick design, the eye-catching result is one of London's must-see sights. Tate Modern has also been extraordinarily successful in bringing challenging work to the masses while a stunning extension is under construction, aiming for a 2016 completion date.

The multimedia guides (£3.50) are worthwhile and there are free 45-minute guided tours of the collection's highlights (Level 3 at 11am and midday; Level 5 at 2pm and 3pm). Note the late-night opening hours on Friday and Saturday.

Shakespeare's Globe HISTORIC THEATRE
(Map p78; ☎020-7401 9919; www.shakespeares-globe.org; 21 New Globe Walk; adult/child £11/7; ⌚10am-5pm; ⊖London Bridge) Today's Londoners may flock to Amsterdam to misbehave but back in the bard's day they'd cross London Bridge to Southwark. Free from the city's constraints, men could settle down to a diet of whoring, bear-baiting and heckling of actors. The most famous theatre was the Globe, where a genius playwright was penning box-office hits such as *Macbeth* and *Hamlet*.

The original Globe – known as the 'Wooden O' after its circular shape and roofless centre – was erected in 1599. Rival to the Rose Theatre, all was well but did not end well when the Globe burned down within two hours during a performance in 1613 (a stage cannon ignited the thatched roof). A tiled replacement fell foul of the party-pooping Puritans in 1642, who saw the theatre as the devil's workshop, and it was dismantled two years later. Its present-day incarnation is the vision of American actor and director Sam Wanamaker, who sadly died before the opening night in 1997.
Admission includes the **exhibition hall** and **guided tour** (departing every 15 to 30 minutes) of the theatre, faithfully reconstructed from oak beams, handmade bricks, lime plaster and thatch. Tours shift to the nearby

LONDON'S NEW SKYSCRAPERS

A recent scramble for high-altitude, futuristic towers – given further lift by the Olympics – has shaken up the otherwise rather staid, low-lying London skyline. Most famous is The Shard, rising over London Bridge like a vast glass splinter. The City of London's tallest building, the straight-edged **Heron Tower** (100 Bishopsgate) was completed just up the road from **30 St Mary Axe** (The Gherkin; Map p72; ☎7071 5008; www.30stmaryaxe.co.uk; St Mary Axe; ⊖Aldgate or Bank) (nicknamed the Gherkin) in 2011. Aiming for a 2014 completion date, the top-heavy **20 Fenchurch St** (Walkie Talkie) will be topped with a vast sky garden boasting magnificent views over town. Further construction on the concrete stub of the radical looking **Pinnacle** (22-24 Bishopsgate) – nicknamed the Helter Skelter due to its cork-screwing top – was on hold at the the time of writing. The wedge-shaped 48-storey, 225m-high **Leadenhall Building** (nicknamed the Cheese Grater) is aiming for a 2014 completion date.

Rose Theatre instead when matinees are being staged in season.

Between April and October plays are performed, and while Shakespeare and his contemporaries dominate, modern plays are also occasionally staged (see the website for upcoming performances). As in Elizabethan times, seatless 'groundlings' can watch in all-weather conditions (£5; seats are £15 to £39) for the best views. There is no protection from the elements and you'll have to stand, but it's an unforgettable experience.

London Eye VIEWS

(Map p78; ☎0871 781 3000; www.londoneye.com; adult/child £18/9.50; ⏲10am-8pm; ⊖Waterloo) This 135m-tall, slow-moving Ferris-wheel-like attraction is the tallest in the western hemisphere. Passengers ride in enclosed egg-shaped pods; the wheel takes 30 minutes to rotate completely, offering 25-mile views on clear days. Drawing 3.5 million visitors annually, at peak times (in July and August and school holidays), it can seem like they are all in the queue with you. Save money and shorten queues by buying tickets online, or cough up an extra £10 to show off your fast-track swagger. Alternatively, visit before 11am or after 3pm to avoid peak density. Add sparkle with priority boarding and a glass of champers (£35) and eyeball the huge choice of ticket combinations.

The Shard LANDMARK

(Map p78; www.the-shard.com; 32 London Bridge St; ⊖London Bridge) Puncturing the skies above London, the dramatic splinter-like form of The Shard – the tallest building in Western Europe – has rapidly become an icon of the town. Approaching completion at the time of writing, the tower will boast the rooms-with-a-view, five-star Shangri-La Hotel, restaurants and a 360-degree **viewing gallery** in the clouds, accessible via high-speed lifts.

FREE **Imperial War Museum** MUSEUM

(Map p78; www.iwm.org.uk; Lambeth Rd; ⏲10am-6pm; ⊖Lambeth North) Fronted by a pair of intimidating **15in naval guns** that could lob a 1938lb shell more than 16 miles, this riveting museum is housed in what was once Bethlehem Royal Hospital, known as Bedlam. There's not just Lawrence of Arabia's 1000cc motorbike here, but a **German V-2 rocket**, a **Sherman tank**, a lifelike replica of **Little Boy** (the atom bomb dropped on Hiroshima), a **P-51 Mustang**, a **Focke-Wulf Fw 190** and other classic fighter planes dangling from the ceiling plus a recreated **WWI trench** and WWII bomb shelter as well as a **Holocaust exhibition**.

Old Operating Theatre Museum & Herb Garret MUSEUM

(Map p78; www.thegarret.org.uk; 9A St Thomas St; adult/child £5.80/3.25; ⏲10.30am-4.45pm; ⊖London Bridge) The highlight of this unique museum, 32 steps up the spiral stairway of the Tower of **St Thomas Church** (1703), focuses on the nastiness of 19th-century hospital treatment. A fiendish array of amputation knives presages the operating theatre, where doctors operated in rough-and-ready (pre-ether, pre-chloroform, pre-antiseptic) conditions. Contact the museum for details of their spooky **Surgery by Gaslight** evenings and other events. Also browse the natural remedies in the herb garret, including snail water for venereal disease and bladderwrack for goitre and tuberculosis.

South Bank

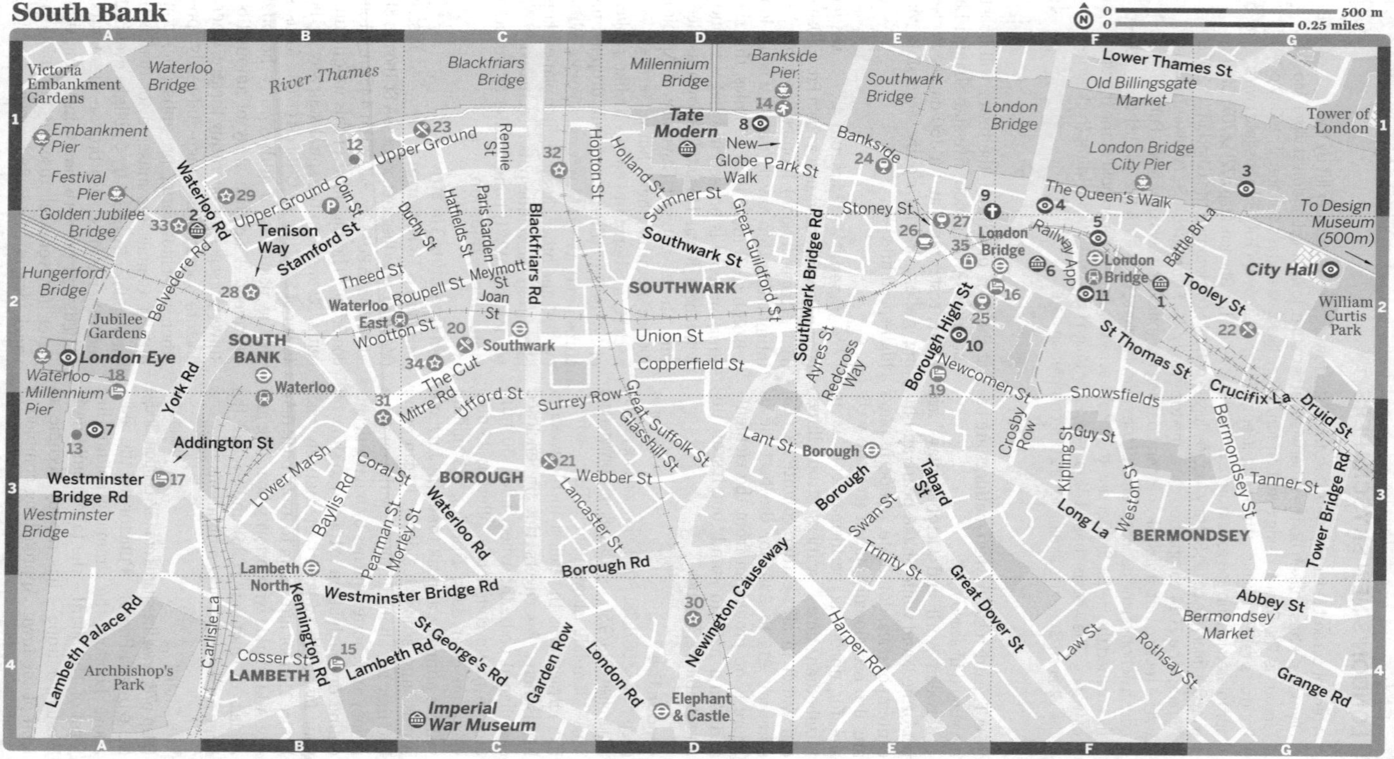
0 500 m
0 0.25 miles
A
B
C
D
E
F
G
1
2
3
4
River Thames
Victoria Embankment Gardens
Waterloo Bridge
Blackfriars Bridge
Millennium Bridge
Bankside Pier
Southwark Bridge
London Bridge
Lower Thames St
Old Billingsgate Market
Tower of London
London Bridge City Pier
Embankment Pier
Festival Pier
Golden Jubilee Bridge
Hungerford Bridge
Jubilee Gardens
London Eye
Waterloo Millennium Pier
Westminster Bridge Rd
Westminster Bridge
Tate Modern
New Globe Walk
Park St
Bankside
Holland St
Sumner St
Hopton St
Rennie St
Upper Ground
Waterloo Rd
Tenison Way
Stamford St
Coin St
Duchy St
Hatfields St
Paris Garden
Blackfriars Rd
Meymott St
Joan St
Theed St
Roupell St
Waterloo East
Wootton St
Southwark
The Cut
Belvedere Rd
SOUTH BANK
Waterloo
York Rd
Addington St
Mitre Rd
Ufford St
Surrey Row
SOUTHWARK
Southwark St
Great Guildford St
Southwark Bridge Rd
Union St
Copperfield St
Ayres St
Redcross Way
Stoney St
London Bridge
Railway App
The Queen's Walk
Battle Br La
Tooley St
City Hall
To Design Museum (500m)
William Curtis Park
St Thomas St
Borough High St
Newcomen St
Snowsfields
Crucifix La
Druid St
Bermondsey St
Tanner St
Tower Bridge Rd
Great Suffolk St
Glasshill St
Lant St
Borough
Crosby Row
Kipling St
Guy St
Weston St
Long La
BERMONDSEY
Lower Marsh
Coral St
BOROUGH
Webber St
Lancaster St
Baylis Rd
Pearman St
Morley St
Waterloo Rd
Borough Rd
Tabard St
Swan St
Trinity St
Lambeth North
Westminster Bridge Rd
Newington Causeway
Harper Rd
Great Dover St
Abbey St
Bermondsey Market
Law St
Rothsay St
Grange Rd
Lambeth Palace Rd
Carlisle La
Archbishop's Park
Cosser St
LAMBETH
Kennington Rd
Lambeth Rd
St George's Rd
Garden Row
London Rd
Elephant & Castle
Imperial War Museum
1
2
3
4
5
6
7
8
9
10
11
12
13
14
15
16
17
18
19
20
21
22
23
24
25
26
27
28
29
30
31
32
33
34
35

South Bank

Top Sights
City Hall G2
Imperial War Museum C4
London Eye A2
Tate Modern D1

Sights
1 Britain at War Experience F2
2 Hayward Gallery A2
3 HMS Belfast G1
4 London Bridge Experience & London Tombs F1
5 London Dungeon F2
6 Old Operating Theatre Museum & Herb Garret F2
7 Sea Life A3
8 Shakespeare's Globe D1
9 Southwark Cathedral E1
10 St Christopher's Inn E2
11 The Shard F2

Activities, Courses & Tours
12 London Bicycle Tour B1
13 London Duck Tours A3
14 Tate Boat D1

Sleeping
15 Captain Bligh House B4
16 The Oasis F2
17 Park Plaza Westminster Bridge A3
18 Premier Inn London County Hall A2
19 St Christopher's Village E2

Eating
20 Anchor & Hope C2
21 Laughing Gravy C3
22 Magdalen G2
23 Oxo Tower Brasserie C1

Drinking
24 Anchor E1
25 George Inn E2
26 Monmouth Coffee Company E2
27 Rake E2

Entertainment
28 BFI IMAX B2
29 BFI Southbank B1
30 Ministry of Sound D4
31 Old Vic B3
32 Pulse C1
33 Southbank Centre A2
34 Young Vic C2

Shopping
35 Borough Market E2

Southwark Cathedral CATHEDRAL
(Map p78; 020-7367 6700; Montague Close; suggested donation £4-6.50; 8am-6pm Mon-Fri, 9am-6pm Sat & Sun, Evensong 5.30pm Tue, Thu & Fri, 4pm Sat, 3pm Sun; London Bridge) The earliest surviving chunks of this relatively small cathedral are the **retrochoir** at the eastern end, some ancient **arcading** by the southwest door, 12th-century wall cores in the north transept and an arch that dates to the original Norman church, although most of the cathedral is Victorian. In the south aisle of the nave, hunt down the green alabaster **monument to William Shakespeare**, next to which is a plaque to Sam Wanamaker (1919–93); nearby hangs a splendid **icon** of Jesus Christ illuminated by devotional candles. Do hunt down the exceedingly fine **Elizabethan sideboard** in the north transept.

City Hall LANDMARK
(Map p78; www.london.gov.uk; Queen's Walk; 8.30am-6pm Mon-Fri; London Bridge) Home to the Mayor of London, bulbous City Hall was designed by Foster and Partners. The 45m, glass-clad building has been compared to a litany of surprising objects, from Darth Vader's helmet to a woodlouse and a 'glass gonad'. Visitors can view the mayor's meeting chamber and attend debates, while the scoop amphitheatre outside is the venue for a variety of free entertainment, from music to theatre in warmer weather.

Design Museum MUSEUM
(www.designmuseum.org; 28 Shad Thames; adult/child £8.50/5; 10am-5.45pm; Tower Hill) Housed in a 1930s-era warehouse, the rectangular galleries here stage a revolving program of special exhibitions devoted to contemporary design, host the annual *Brit Insurance Design Awards* competition for design innovations, and display a permanent collection of modern British design. The museum is moving to a new site in the former **Commonwealth Institute** south of Holland Park in 2014.

HMS Belfast SHIP
(Map p78; http://hmsbelfast.iwm.org.uk; Queen's Walk; adult/child £13/free; 10am-5pm; London Bridge) White ensign flapping on the

The River Thames

A FLOATING TOUR

London's history has always been determined by the Thames. The city was founded as a Roman port nearly 2000 years ago and over the centuries since then many of the capital's landmarks have lined the river's banks. A boat trip is a great way to experience the attractions.

There are piers dotted along both banks at regular intervals where you can hop on and hop off the regular services to visit places of interest. The best place to board is Westminster Pier, from where boats head downstream, taking you from the City of Westminster, the seat of government, to the original City of London, now the financial district and dominated by a growing band of skyscrapers. Across the river, the once shabby and neglected South Bank now bristles with as many top attractions as its northern counterpart.

In our illustration we've concentrated on the top highlights you'll enjoy at a fish's-eye

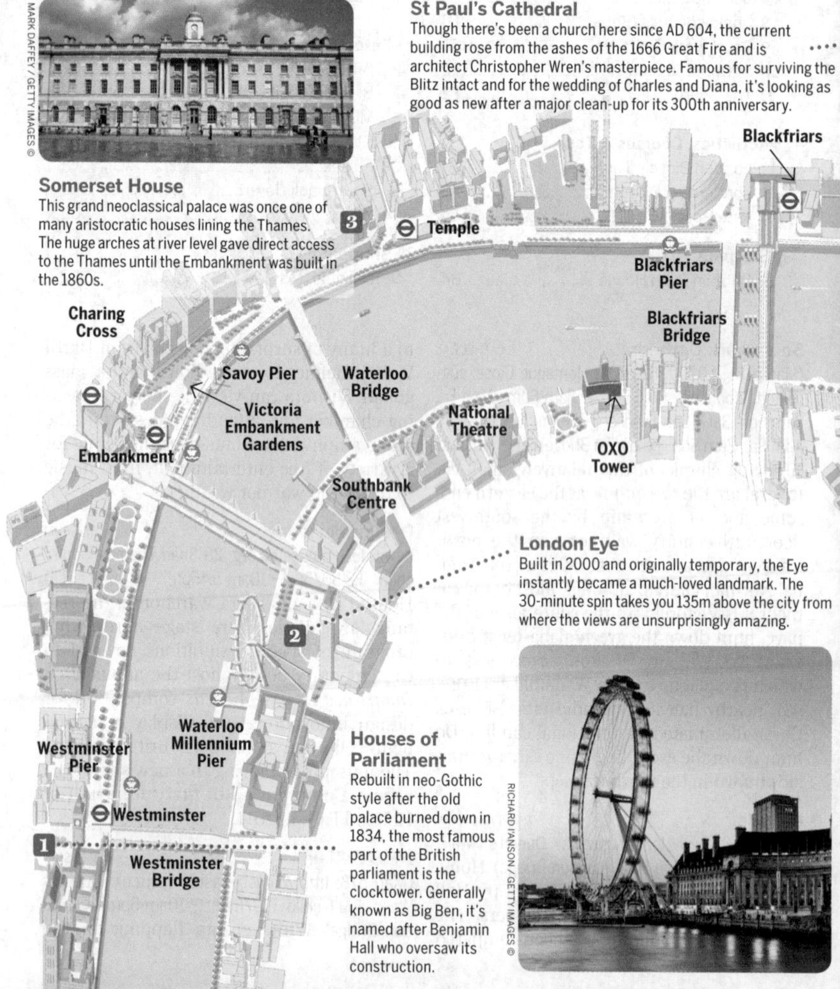

St Paul's Cathedral

Though there's been a church here since AD 604, the current building rose from the ashes of the 1666 Great Fire and is architect Christopher Wren's masterpiece. Famous for surviving the Blitz intact and for the wedding of Charles and Diana, it's looking as good as new after a major clean-up for its 300th anniversary.

Somerset House

This grand neoclassical palace was once one of many aristocratic houses lining the Thames. The huge arches at river level gave direct access to the Thames until the Embankment was built in the 1860s.

London Eye

Built in 2000 and originally temporary, the Eye instantly became a much-loved landmark. The 30-minute spin takes you 135m above the city from where the views are unsurprisingly amazing.

Houses of Parliament

Rebuilt in neo-Gothic style after the old palace burned down in 1834, the most famous part of the British parliament is the clocktower. Generally known as Big Ben, it's named after Benjamin Hall who oversaw its construction.

view as you sail along. These are, from west to east, the **Houses of Parliament** 1, the **London Eye** 2, **Somerset House** 3, **St Paul's Cathedral** 4, **Tate Modern** 5, **Shakespeare's Globe** 6, the **Tower of London** 7 and **Tower Bridge** 8.

Apart from covering this central section of the river, boats can also be taken upstream as far as Kew Gardens and Hampton Court Palace, and downstream to Greenwich and the Thames Barrier.

BOAT HOPPING

Thames Clippers hop-on/hop-off services are aimed at commuters but are equally useful for visitors, operating every 15 minutes on a loop from piers at Embankment, Waterloo, Blackfriars, Bankside, London Bridge and the Tower. Other services also go from Westminster. Oyster cardholders get a discount off the boat ticket price.

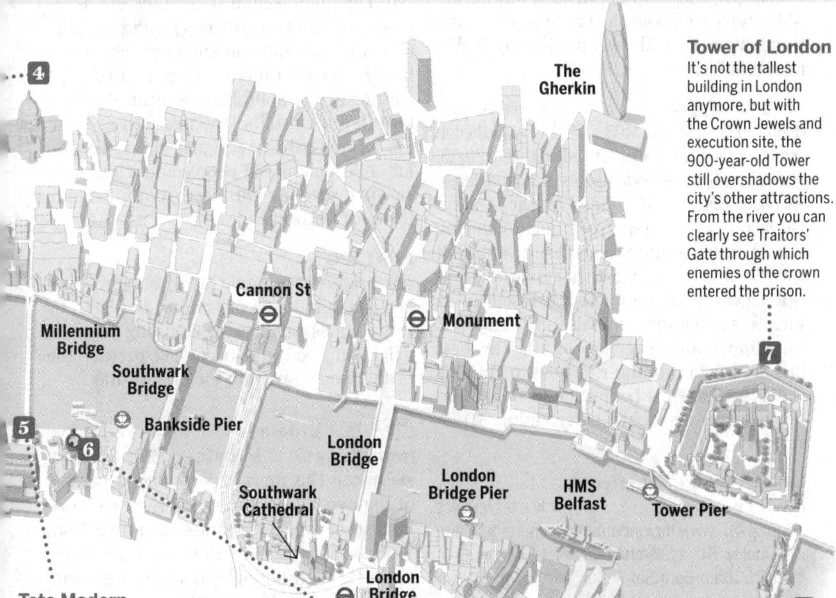

4

The Gherkin

Cannon St

Monument

Millennium Bridge

Southwark Bridge

5

Bankside Pier

6

London Bridge

London Bridge Pier

HMS Belfast

Tower Pier

Southwark Cathedral

London Bridge

City Hall

7

8

Tower of London
It's not the tallest building in London anymore, but with the Crown Jewels and execution site, the 900-year-old Tower still overshadows the city's other attractions. From the river you can clearly see Traitors' Gate through which enemies of the crown entered the prison.

Tate Modern
Directly across the river from St Paul's, this cathedral of modern art is the biggest in the world. Built as a power station in the late 1940s, its industrial architecture is as popular with visitors as the paintings on the walls.

DOUG MCKINLAY / GETTY IMAGES ©

Shakespeare's Globe
The reconstructed Globe stands on the river a few hundred metres from where the original stood (and burnt down in 1613 during a performance). The life's work of American actor Sam Wanamaker, the theatre runs a hugely popular season from April to October each year.

DOUG MCKINLAY / GETTY IMAGES ©

Tower Bridge
It might look as old as its namesake neighbour but one of the world's most iconic bridges was only completed in 1894. Not to be confused with London Bridge upstream, this one's famous raising bascules allowed tall ships to dock at the old wharves to the west and are still lifted up to 1000 times a year.

Thames breeze, HMS *Belfast* is a magnet for naval-gazing kids. This large, light cruiser served in WWII, helping sink the German battleship *Scharnhorst* and shelling the Normandy coast on D-Day. Explore the nine decks and see the engine room, gun decks, galley, chapel, punishment cells, canteen and dental surgery. An audioguide is available.

Britain at War Experience MUSEUM

(Map p78; www.britainatwar.co.uk; 64-66 Tooley St; adult/child £13/5.50; ⏲10am-5pm Apr-Oct, to 4.30pm Nov-Mar; ⊖London Bridge) Here, you can pop down to the London Underground air-raid shelter, look at gas masks and ration books, stroll around Southwark during the Blitz and learn about the battle on the home front. It's crammed with fascinating WWII memorabilia.

London Dungeon FRIGHT EXPERIENCE

(Map p78; ☎020-7403 7221; www.thedungeons.com; 28-34 Tooley St; adult/child £20/15; ⏲10.30am-5pm, extended hours during holidays; ⊖London Bridge) Older kids love the London Dungeon, as the terrifying queues during school holidays and weekends attest. It's all spooky music, macabre hangman's drop-rides, fake blood and actors dressed up as torturers and gory criminals (including Jack the Ripper and Sweeney Todd). The best bits are the fairground-ride boat to Traitor's Gate, the Extremis Drop Ride to Doom and Vengeance – a spookily entertaining '5D laser ride'.

London Bridge Experience & London Tombs FRIGHT EXPERIENCE

(Map p78; www.thelondonbridgeexperience.com; 2-4 Tooley St; adult/child £23/17; ⏲10am-5pm Mon-Fri, 10am-6pm Sat & Sun; ⊖London Bridge) Another coronary-inducing attraction, similar to but not related to nearby London Dungeon. This one starts with the relatively tame London Bridge Experience, where actors bring to life the bridge's history with the assistance of plenty of severed heads. Once the entertaining educational bit is out the way, the London Tombs turns up the terror. Adding to the general creepiness is the knowledge that these were once plague pits and therefore actual tombs. The experience takes about 45 minutes, with the tombs an optional additional 25 minutes. It's all great, occasionally heart-in-the-mouth entertainment and you save up to 50% by buying online.

Sea Life AQUARIUM

(Map p78; ☎0871 663 1678; www.sealife.co.uk/london; County Hall; adult/child £18/13; ⏲10am-6pm; ⊖Waterloo) Within imposing **County Hall**, this is one of the largest aquariums in Europe, with all sorts of aquatic (many endangered) creatures from the briny deep grouped into different zones (coral cave, rainforest, River Thames), culminating with the shark walkway. Check the website for shark-feeding times and book online for a 10% discount.

Hayward Gallery ART MUSEUM

(Map p78; www.southbankcentre.co.uk; Belvedere Rd; ⏲10am-6pm Sat-Thu, to 10pm Fri; ⊖Waterloo) The 1968 Brutalist architecture is as opinion-dividing as you can get but the popular international contemporary art shows held here constitute a further rich seam of culture in the Southbank Centre. Facilities include the upstairs Waterloo Sunset Pavilion, a Dan Graham–designed 'drop-in centre for children and old people and a space for viewing cartoons' with views onto London's Brutalist horizons.

PIMLICO

The origins of its name highly obscure, Pimlico is a grand part of London, bordered by the Thames but lacking a strong sense of neighbourhood and becoming prettier the further you stray from Victoria station.

FREE **Tate Britain** ART MUSEUM

(www.tate.org.uk; Millbank; ⏲10am-5.40pm; ⊖Pimlico) The more elderly and venerable of the two Tate siblings, this riverside Portland stone edifice celebrates paintings from 1500 to the present, with works from Blake, Hogarth, Gainsborough, Barbara Hepworth, Whistler, Constable and Turner – in particular – whose light-infused visions dominate the **Clore Gallery**. It doesn't stop there and vibrant modern and contemporary art finds expression in pieces from Lucian Freud, Francis Bacon and Tracey Emin while the controversial Turner Prize (inviting annual protests outside the gallery) is held here every year between October and January. Free one-hour thematic tours are held at 11am, noon, 2pm and 3pm from Monday to Friday (noon and 3pm on Saturday and Sunday) are eye-opening but don't overlook **Late at Tate** night (first Friday of the month), when the gallery stays open till 10pm.

TATE MODERN HIGHLIGHTS

More than 40 million eager art-goers poured through Tate Modern (p76) in its first decade since opening, making it one of the most-visited of London's sights. The ambitiously run exhibition space is getting even bigger with the recent conversion of two of the former power station's underground oil tanks, while a funky 11-storey extension is slated for a 2016 opening date.

Before tackling Tate Modern, note that special exhibitions are held in levels 2 and 4. Free 45-minute guided highlights tours run on Level 3 (11am and noon) and Level 5 (2pm and 3pm) – no booking is required. Handy multimedia guides are also available. Don't forget that Tate Modern is open till 10pm on Friday and Saturday, so you can make an evening of it.

The collection is in perpetual rotation so while the essential themes of the various galleries remain constant, the paintings and art works that represent each concept may vary.

A major highlight of Tate Modern is the architecture and its splendid conversion into a space housing and displaying art. The 4.2 million bricks of the Sir Gilbert Scott–designed Bankside Power Station – generating its last watt in 1981 when rising oil prices finally switched off its turbines – were ambitiously transformed into this modern and contemporary art gallery in 2000.

You can't exactly miss the cavernous 3300-sq-m **Turbine Hall**, but try to join everyone else streaming down the ramp from Holland St to maximise its impact. Originally housing the power station's colossal turbines, the hall is the jaw-dropping venue for large-scale, temporary exhibitions from October to April. Past exhibits have included Doris Salcedo's dramatic *Shibboleth* fissure cracking the floor and Ai Weiwei's thoughtful and compelling *Sunflower Seeds* – a huge carpet of hand-painted, ceramic seeds.

To give a sense of continuity to the displays, the permanent collection is grouped thematically on levels 3 and 5. For surrealist creations from the lucid minds of Paul Delvaux, Yves Tanguy, Max Ernst and other artists, immerse yourself in **Poetry and Dream** on Level 3. Also on Level 3, **Material Gestures** focuses on European and American painting and sculpture of the 1940s and 1950s, including abstract expressionism and embracing works by Barnett Newman, Victor Pasmore, Alberto Giacometti, Mark Rothko and other artists.

The dramatic pairing of Italian futurist Umberto Boccioni's *Unique Forms of Continuity in Space* and Roy Lichtenstein's pop icon *Whaam!* kicks off **States of Flux** on Level 5. These two pieces are separated by half a century, divided by two World Wars, a Cold War and the arrival of the nuclear age, but both share a common dynamism and iconic power. The gallery proceeds to explore the signature avant-garde art movements of the 20th century, including cubism, futurism, vorticism and pop art, featuring works from Picasso, Georges Braque, Wassily Kandinsky, Piet Mondrian, Juan Gris, Gino Severini and others. Also on Level 5, **Energy and Process** takes Art Povera, the revolutionary art of the 1960s, as its focus.

After you have had your fill of modern art, cap your visit with a trip to the restaurant and bar on Level 7 for sublime views of St Paul's and the River Thames. A popular cafe can be found on Level 2.

CHELSEA & KENSINGTON

Known as the royal borough, Chelsea and Kensington lays claim to the highest income earners in the UK (shops and restaurants will presume you are among them). Kensington High St has a lively mix of chains and boutiques while even the charity shops along King's Rd resemble fashion outlets. If the sun obliges, lie supine on the grass in splendid Hyde Park but don't forget that some of London's most beautiful and fascinating museums, clustered together in South Kensington, are must-sees come rain or shine.

FREE **Victoria & Albert Museum** MUSEUM
(V&A; Map p86; www.vam.ac.uk; Cromwell Rd; ⏲10am-5.45pm Sat-Thu, to 10pm Fri; ⊖South Kensington) This outstanding museum boasts an unparalleled collection specialising in decorative art and design with some 4.5

LONDON'S TOP VIEWPOINTS

Not a predominantly flat city as is Běijīng, for example, London has a host of natural high points and hills yielding long and spectacular views over town. Throw in panoramas from architectural and skyscraping elevations and you've more than enough choice for the wide-angle perspective on London.

London Eye (p77) Does what it says on the packet, but brace for queues.

The Shard (p77) Superb views of London in all directions from the high-altitude viewing platform.

Monument (p75) Wraparound views of London reward climbs to the top.

St Paul's Cathedral (p73) Clamber up to the top of the dome for some divine views.

Parliament Hill (p99) Choose a sunny day, pack a picnic and enjoy the view from this Hampstead Heath highpoint.

Greenwich Park (8858 2608; www.royalparks.gov.uk; King George St; dawn-dusk, cars from 7am; Greenwich or Maze Hill, DLR Cutty Sark) The views from the Royal Observatory are some of London's most supreme.

million objects from Britain and around the globe. The museum setting and gorgeous architecture is as inspiring as the sheer diversity and rarity of its exhibits. Part of Albert's legacy to Londoners in the wake of the Great Exhibition of 1851, the museum is a bit like the nation's attic, spread generously through nearly 150 galleries. Highlights of the world's greatest collection of decorative arts include the **Ardabil Carpet** (Room 42, Level 1), the sumptuous **China Collection** and **Japan Gallery** (Rooms 44 and 47e, Level 1), **Tipu's Tiger** (Room 41, Level 1) the astonishing **Cast Courts** (Room 46a, Level 1), the **Raphael Cartoons** (Rooms 48a, Level 1), the hefty **Great Bed of Ware** (Room 57, Level 2) and the stunning **Jewellery Gallery** (Rooms 91-93, Level 3). You'll need to plan as the museum is epic, but it's open late on Friday evenings, for less crowds. For food and drink, make for the V&A Cafe in the magnificent Refreshment Rooms, dating from the 1860s, or the garden cafe in the John Madesjki Garden in summer.

FREE Natural History Museum — MUSEUM

(Map p86; www.nhm.ac.uk; Cromwell Rd; 10am-5.50pm; South Kensington) This ornate building itself is one of London's finest and a work of art: pale blue and honey-coloured stone, broken by Venetian arches decorated with all manner of carved critters.

A sure-fire hit with kids of all ages, this splendid museum is crammed with fascinating discoveries, starting with the giant **Diplodocus** skeleton that greets you in the main hall. In the **dinosaur gallery**, the fleshless fossils are brought to robotic life with the roaring 4m-high animatronic **Tyrannosaurus Rex**.

The other galleries are equally impressive. An escalator slithers up and into a hollowed-out globe where two exhibits – The Power Within and Restless Surface – explain how wind, water, ice, gravity and life itself impact on the earth. The **mock-up of the Kobe earthquake** is a bone-rattling lesson in plate tectonics.

The **Darwin Centre** houses a team of biologists and a staggering 20-million-plus animal and plant specimens. Take a lift to the top of the Cocoon, a seven-storey egg-shaped structure encased within a glass pavilion, and make your way down through the floors of interactive displays. Glass windows allow you to watch the scientists at work.

Finally, don't overlook **Sensational Butterflies** by the East Lawn and the charming **Wildlife Garden**, a slice of English countryside in SW7.

FREE Science Museum — MUSEUM

(Map p86; www.sciencemuseum.org.uk; Exhibition Rd; 10am-6pm; South Kensington) With seven floors of interactive and educational exhibits, this scientifically spellbinding museum will mesmerise even the most precocious of young Einsteins. Some children head straight for voice warpers, lava lamps, boomerangs, bouncy globes and alien babies in the ground-floor shop, and stay put. Highlights include the **Energy Hall** on the ground floor, the riveting **Flight Gallery** on the 3rd floor and the **flight simulator**. There's also a 450-seat **Imax cinema**. If you've kids under the age of five, pop down to the basement for **The Garden**, where there's a fun-filled play zone, including a water-play area, besieged by tots in red waterproof smocks.

Hyde Park PARK

(Map p86; ⊙5.30am-midnight; ⊖Marble Arch, Hyde Park Corner or Queensway) At 145 hectares, Hyde Park is central London's largest open space. Henry VIII expropriated it from the Church in 1536, when it became a hunting ground and later a venue for duels, executions and horse racing. The 1851 Great Exhibition was held here, and during WWII the park became an enormous potato field. These days, it serves as an occasional concert venue and a full-time green space for fun and frolics. There's boating on the **Serpentine** for the energetic, while **Speakers' Corner** (Map p86; Park Lane; ⊖Marble Arch) is for oratorical acrobats on Sundays, maintaining a tradition begun in 1872 as a response to rioting. Just north of here, **Marble Arch** (Map p89; ⊖Marble Arch) was designed by John Nash in 1828 as the entrance to Buckingham Palace and moved here in 1851; it once served as a police lookout. The infamous Tyburn Tree, a three-legged gallows, once stood nearby. It is estimated that up to 50,000 people were executed here between 1196 and 1783.

Kensington Palace PALACE

(Map p110; www.hrp.org.uk/kensingtonpalace; Kensington Gardens; adult/child £14.50/free; ⊙10am-6pm; ⊖High St Kensington) Kensington Palace (1605) became the favourite royal residence under the joint reign of William and Mary and remained so until the death of George II (in 1762 George III bought Buckingham Palace for his wife, Charlotte). It still contains private apartments where various members of the royal extended family live. In popular imagination it's most associated with three intriguing princesses: Victoria (who was born here in 1819 and lived here with her domineering mother until her accession to the throne), Margaret (sister of the current queen, who lived here until her 2002 death) and, of course, Diana. The building underwent magnificent restoration work totalling £12 million and reopened in early 2012.

Kensington Gardens PARK

(Map p110; ⊙dawn-dusk; ⊖High St Kensington) Blending in with Hyde Park, these royal gardens are part of Kensington Palace and hence popularly associated with Princess Diana. Diana devotees can visit the **Diana, Princess of Wales Memorial Fountain** (Kensington Gardens; Knightsbridge), a soothing structure fashioned from 545 pieces of Cornish granite, channeling a circular stream drawn from chalk aquifers more than 100m underground which cascades gently and flows together in a pool at the bottom; paddling is encouraged. The astonishing **Albert Memorial** (Map p86; ☎7495 0916; 45min tours adult/concession £6/5; ⊙tours 2pm & 3pm 1st Sun of the month Mar-Dec; ⊖Knightsbridge or Gloucester Rd) is a unique chunk of Victorian bombast, a lavish marble, mosaic and gold affair opposite the Royal Albert Hall, built to honour Queen Victoria's husband, Albert (1819–61).

The gardens also house the **Serpentine Gallery** (Map p86; www.serpentinegallery.org; admission free; ⊙10am-6pm), one of London's edgiest contemporary art spaces; the recently opened **Serpentine Sackler Gallery** (Map p86; The Ring) is on the far side of the Serpentine Bridge, in the former Magazine. The **Sunken Garden**, near the palace, is at its prettiest in summer, while tea in the **Orangery** (Map p110; www.hrp.org.uk; Kensington Palace, Kensington Gardens; mains £9.50-14; ⊙10am-6pm Mar-Sep, to 5pm Oct-Feb; ⊖Queensway, Notting Hill Gate or High St Kensington) is a treat any time of the year.

King's Road STREET

(⊖Sloane Square) Named after King Charles II who would return to Hampton Court Palace along a farmer's track here after amorous interludes with Nell Gwyn, this street was almost synonymous with London fashion during the '60s and '70s. The road and surrounding streets are excellent for retail therapy and look-ins on some of the city's best-dressed neighbourhoods. Near the Sloane Sq end, the **Saatchi Gallery** (Map p86; www.saatchi-gallery.co.uk; Duke of York's HQ, King's Rd; ⊙10am-6pm) serves up stimulating temporary exhibitions of contemporary art.

TATE-A-TATE

Whisking art lovers between London's Tate galleries, the colourful **Tate Boat** (Map p78; www.thamesclippers.com) stop en route at the London Eye. Services from Bankside Pier run from 9.57am to 4.44pm daily at 40-minute intervals (10.20am to 4.27pm from Millbank Pier). One-way tickets are £5.50 (children £2.80), with discounts available for Travelcard holders.

Knightsbridge, South Kensington & Chelsea

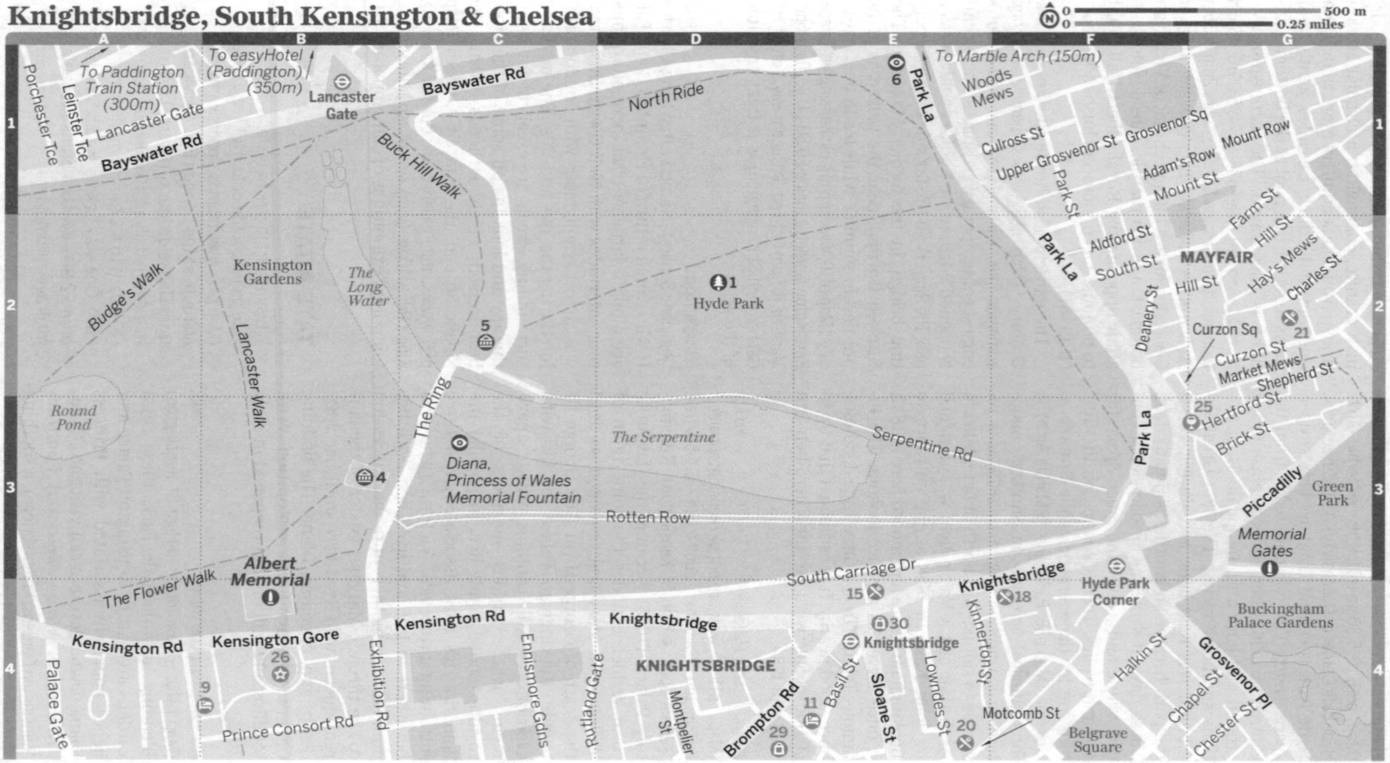

0 — 500 m
0 — 0.25 miles

A B C D E F G
1 2 3 4

To Paddington Train Station (300m)
To easyHotel (Paddington) (350m)
To Marble Arch (150m)
Porchester Tce
Leinster Tce
Lancaster Gate
Bayswater Rd
Lancaster Gate
Bayswater Rd
North Ride
Buck Hill Walk
Park La
6
Woods Mews
Culross St
Upper Grosvenor St
Grosvenor Sq
Mount Row
Adam's Row
Mount St
Park St
Park La
Alford St
South St
Farm St
Hill St
MAYFAIR
Hay's Mews
Charles St
Hill St
Deanery St
Curzon Sq
21
Curzon St
Market Mews
Shepherd St
25
Hertford St
Brick St
Park La
Piccadilly
Green Park
Memorial Gates
Kensington Gardens
The Long Water
Budge's Walk
Lancaster Walk
1
Hyde Park
5
The Ring
Round Pond
The Serpentine
Serpentine Rd
Diana, Princess of Wales Memorial Fountain
4
Rotten Row
Albert Memorial
The Flower Walk
South Carriage Dr
15
Knightsbridge
18
Hyde Park Corner
Buckingham Palace Gardens
Kensington Rd
Kensington Gore
Kensington Rd
Knightsbridge
30
Knightsbridge
26
Palace Gate
9
Prince Consort Rd
Exhibition Rd
Ennismore Gdns
Rutland Gate
KNIGHTSBRIDGE
Montpelier St
Brompton Rd
29
11
Basil St
Sloane St
Lowndes St
Kinnerton St
20
Motcomb St
Belgrave Square
Halkin St
Grosvenor Pl
Chapel St
Chester St

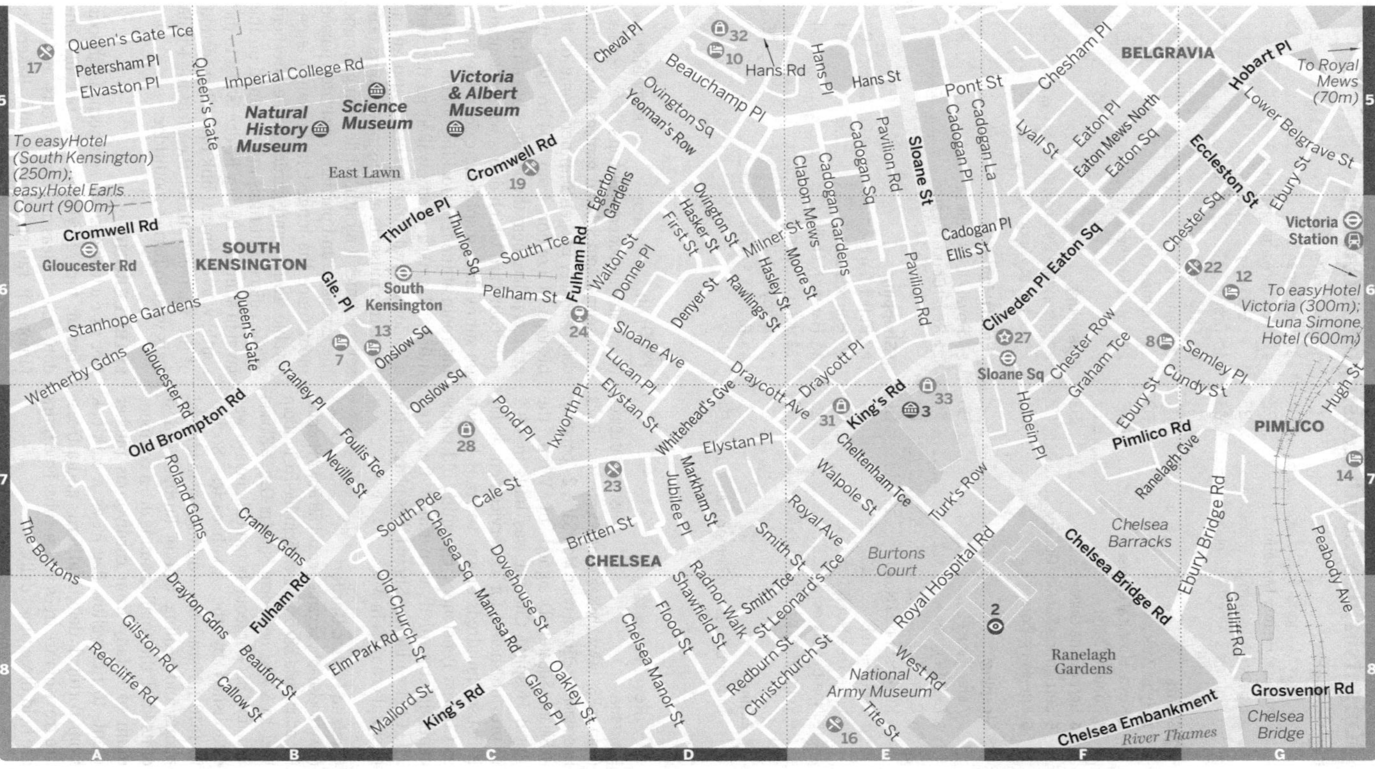
BELGRAVIA
PIMLICO
CHELSEA
SOUTH KENSINGTON
To Royal Mews (70m)
To easyHotel Victoria (300m); Luna Simone Hotel (600m)
To easyHotel (South Kensington) (250m); easyHotel Earls Court (900m)
Victoria Station
Sloane Sq
South Kensington
Gloucester Rd
Victoria & Albert Museum
Science Museum
Natural History Museum
East Lawn
Ranelagh Gardens
Chelsea Barracks
Burtons Court
National Army Museum
Chelsea Bridge
River Thames
Queen's Gate Tce
Petersham Pl
Elvaston Pl
Queen's Gate
Imperial College Rd
Cheval Pl
Beauchamp Pl
Hans Rd
Hans Pl
Hans St
Pont St
Chesham Pl
Hobart Pl
Lower Belgrave St
Ovington Sq
Yeoman's Row
Pavilion Rd
Sloane St
Cadogan Pl
Cadogan La
Lyall St
Eaton Pl
Eaton Mews North
Eaton Sq
Eccleston St
Ebury St
Cromwell Rd
Thurloe Pl
Thurloe Sq
South Tce
Fulham Rd
Egerton Gardens
Walton St
Donne Pl
Ovington St
Hasker St
First St
Milner St
Hasley St
Moore St
Clabon Mews
Cadogan Gardens
Cadogan Sq
Cadogan Pl
Ellis St
Cliveden Pl
Chester Sq
Gle. Pl
Pelham St
Stanhope Gardens
Denyer St
Rawlings St
Onslow Sq
Wetherby Gdns
Gloucester Rd
Old Brompton Rd
Cranley Pl
Sloane Ave
Lucan Pl
Elystan St
Draycott Pl
Draycott Ave
Whitehead's Gve
King's Rd
Chester Row
Graham Tce
Semley Pl
Cundy St
Hugh St
Pond Pl
Ixworth Pl
Elystan Pl
Holbein Pl
Pimlico Rd
Ranelagh Gve
Foulis Tce
Neville St
Roland Gdns
Cale St
Markham St
Jubilee Pl
Cheltenham Tce
Walpole St
Turk's Row
The Boltons
Cranley Gdns
South Pde
Chelsea Sq
Dovehouse St
Britten St
Royal Ave
Smith St
Ebury Bridge Rd
Peabody Ave
Chelsea Bridge Rd
Royal Hospital Rd
Drayton Gdns
Gilston Rd
Redcliffe Rd
Beaufort St
Callow St
Elm Park Rd
Old Church St
Manresa Rd
Oakley St
Glebe Pl
Mallord St
Chelsea Manor St
Flood St
Shawfield St
Radnor Walk
Smith Tce
St Leonard's Tce
Redburn St
Christchurch St
West Rd
Tite St
Gatliff Rd
Grosvenor Rd
Chelsea Embankment
A
B
C
D
E
F
G
5
6
7
8
2
3
7
8
10
12
13
14
16
17
19
22
23
24
27
28
31
32
33

Knightsbridge, South Kensington & Chelsea

Top Sights
- Albert Memorial B4
- Natural History Museum B5
- Science Museum B5
- Victoria & Albert Museum C5

Sights
1 Hyde Park D2
2 Royal Hospital Chelsea F8
3 Saatchi Gallery E7
4 Serpentine Gallery B3
5 Serpentine Sackler Gallery C2
6 Speakers' Corner E1

Sleeping
7 Aster House B6
8 B+B Belgravia F6
9 Gore B4
10 Knightsbridge Hotel D5
11 Levin Hotel E4
12 Lime Tree Hotel G6
13 Number Sixteen B6
14 Windermere Hotel G7

Eating
15 Dinner by Heston Blumenthal E4
16 Gordon Ramsay E8
17 L'Etranger A5
18 Marcus Wareing at the Berkeley F4
19 Orsini C5
20 Ottolenghi E4
21 Tamarind G2
22 Thomas Cubitt G6
23 Tom's Kitchen D7

Drinking
24 Bibendum Oyster Bar C6
25 Galvin at Windows G3

Entertainment
26 Royal Albert Hall B4
27 Royal Court Theatre F6

Shopping
28 Butler & Wilson C7
29 Harrods D4
30 Harvey Nichols E4
31 John Sandoe Books E7
32 Rigby & Peller D5
33 Rigby & Peller E7

FREE Royal Hospital Chelsea HISTORIC BUILDINGS
(Map p86; www.chelsea-pensioners.co.uk; Royal Hospital Rd; 10am-noon Mon-Sat & 2-4pm daily; Sloane Square) Designed by Wren, the Royal Hospital Chelsea was built in 1692 to provide shelter for ex-servicemen. Today it houses hundreds of war veterans known as Chelsea Pensioners, charming old chaps generally regarded as national treasures. The Chelsea Flower Show takes place in the hospital grounds in May.

Chelsea Physic Garden GARDEN
(www.chelseaphysicgarden.co.uk; 66 Royal Hospital Rd; adult/child £8/5; noon-5pm Tue-Fri, to 10pm Wed Jul & Aug, noon-6pm Sun Apr-Oct; Sloane Square) This gorgeous botanical enclave was established by the Apothecaries' Society in 1676 for students working on medicinal plants and healing. One of Europe's oldest of its kind, the small grounds are a compendium of botany from carnivorous pitcher plants to rich yellow flag irises, a cork oak from Portugal, delightful ferns and a treasure trove of rare trees and shrubs. Free tours are held three times daily.

FREE Fulham Palace HISTORIC BUILDING
(www.fulhampalace.org; Bishop's Ave; palace & museum 1-4pm Sat-Wed, gardens dawn to dusk daily; Putney Bridge) Summer home of the bishops of London from 704 to 1975, this genteel palace near the Thames has an adorable courtyard which draws watercolourists on sunny days, a splendid cafe in the drawing room at the rear (looking out on a magnificent lawn), a pretty walled garden and a Tudor Revival chapel. There's also an informative museum and historical tours (£5) several times a month, while hiking around the extensive and partially excavated palace moat (once the longest in England) is enjoyable. Events and garden walks are held at the palace and films are screened on the lawn in summer. Putney Bridge is just to the south, where you can link up with a section of the Thames Path for the pleasant 4-mile walk west to Barnes footbridge.

MARYLEBONE

Not as exclusive as its southern neighbour Mayfair, hip Marylebone has one of London's most pleasant high streets and the famous, if rather disappointing, Baker St, immortalised in the hit song by Gerry Rafferty and strongly associated with Victoria-era sleuth Sherlock Holmes (there's a museum and gift shop at his fictional address, 221b).

Regent's Park PARK
(⊖Regent's Park) A former royal hunting ground, Regent's Park was designed by John Nash early in the 19th century, although what was actually laid out is only a fraction of the celebrated architect's grand plan. Nevertheless, it's one of London's most lovely open spaces – at once serene and lively, cosmopolitan and local – with football pitches, tennis courts, a boating lake, London Zoo, and Regent's canal along its northern side. **Queen Mary's Gardens**, towards the south of the park, are particularly pretty, with spectacular roses in summer. **Open Air Theatre** (☎0844 826 4242; www.openairtheatre.org) hosts performances of Shakespeare and other classics here on summer evenings, along with comedy and concerts.

London Zoo ZOO
(www.londonzoo.co.uk; Outer Circle, Regent's Park; adult/child £18/14; ⏲10am-5.30pm Mar-Oct, to 4pm Nov-Feb; ⊖Camden Town) These famous

Marylebone

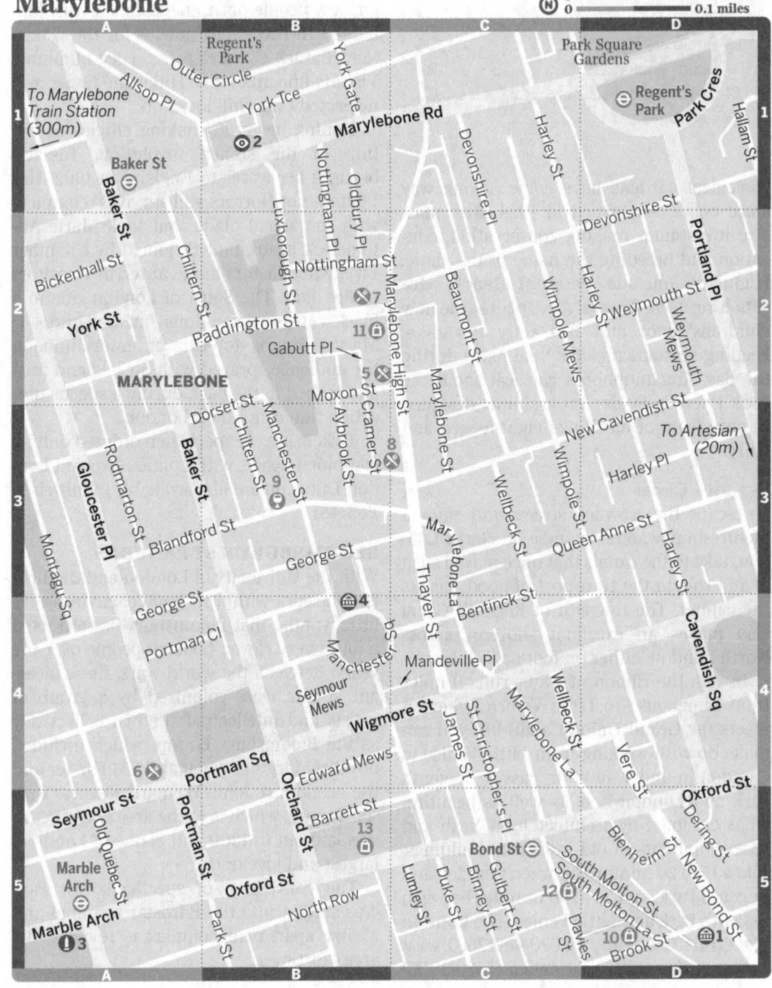

Marylebone

Sights

1 Handel House Museum D5
2 Madame Tussauds B1
3 Marble Arch A5
4 Wellcome Collection B4

Eating

5 La Fromagerie B2
6 Locanda Locatelli A4
7 Ping Pong B2
8 Providores & Tapa Room C3

Drinking

9 Purl B3

Shopping

10 Butler & Wilson D5
11 Daunt Books B2
12 Grays Antiques C5
13 Selfridges B5

zoological gardens have come a long way since being established in 1828, with massive investment making conservation, education and breeding the name of the game. Highlights include **Penguin Beach**, **Gorilla Kingdom**, **Animal Adventure** (the new childrens' zoo) and **Butterfly Paradise**. Feeding sessions or talks take place during the day. Arachnophobes can ask about the zoo's Friendly Spider Programme, designed to cure fears of all things eight-legged and hairy.

Regent's Canal CANAL

To escape the crowded streets and enjoy a picturesque, waterside angle on North London, take to the canals that once played such a vital role in the transport of goods across the capital. The towpath of Regent's Canal also makes an excellent shortcut across North London, either on foot or by bike.

In full, the ribbon of water runs 9 miles from Limehouse to Little Venice (where it meets the Grand Union Canal) but you can make do with walking from Little Venice to Camden in under an hour, passing Regent's Park and London Zoo, as well as beautiful villas designed by architect John Nash and redevelopments of old industrial buildings. Allow 15 to 20 minutes between Camden and Regent's Park, and 25 to 30 minutes between Regent's Park and Little Venice. The **London Waterbus Company** (☎020-7482 2660; www.londonwaterbus.com; single/return £7.20/10.30) and **Jason's Trip** (www.jasons.co.uk; opposite 42 Blomfield Rd; single/return £8/9) run canal boats between Camden Lock and Little Venice.

Madame Tussauds WAXWORKS

(Map p89; ☎0870 400 3000; www.madame-tussauds.co.uk; Marylebone Rd; adult/child £26/22; 9.30am-5.30pm; Baker Street) Tickets may cost a (wax) arm and a (wax) leg and the crowds can be as awesome as the exhibits, but the opportunity to pose beside Posh and Becks has clear-cut kudos. Most of the life-size wax figures – such as Leonardo Di Caprio – are fantastically lifelike and as close to the real thing as most of us will get. It's interesting to see which are the most popular; few people opt to be snapped with Mohamed Al-Fayed, but queues for the Queen (and Barack Obama) can get leg-numbing. Visitors line up to give Hitler the finger as a neglected Churchill looks on.

Honing her craft making effigies of victims of the French revolution, Tussaud brought her wares to England in 1802. Her Chamber of Horrors still survives (complete with the actual blade that took Marie Antoinette's head), but it's joined by Chamber Live, where actors lunge at terrified visitors in the dark. The Spirit of London ride in a black cab is tremendous fun and the 4-D Marvel film is top-drawer entertainment, the audience sprayed with air jets and mist and jabbed in the back during a spectacular action film centred on London.

Tickets are cheaper when ordered online; combined tickets with London Eye and London Dungeon are also available (adult/child £65/48).

BLOOMSBURY & ST PANCRAS

With the University of London and the British Museum within its genteel environs, it's little wonder that Bloomsbury has attracted a lot of very clever, bookish people over the years. Between the world wars, these pleasant streets were colonised by a group of artists and intellectuals known collectively as the Bloomsbury Group, which included novelists Virginia Woolf and EM Forster and the economist John Maynard Keynes. Russell Square, which is at the area's very heart, was laid out in 1800 and is one of London's largest and loveliest.

The conversion of spectacular St Pancras station into the Eurostar terminal and a ritzy apartment complex is reviving the area's fortunes.

TREASURES OF THE BRITISH MUSEUM

The British Museum (p91) is colossal, so it pays to make a judicious selection of the collection's star highlights instead of being laid low by the demands of exploration. Consider joining one of the free Eye Opener tours of individual galleries or 'spotlight' highlight tours, which target individual pieces for a summary lowdown. Don't overlook the big-ticket exhibitions which regularly pitch up (some of which will in future be displayed in the World Conservation and Exhibitions Centre under construction in the northwest corner, due to open in 2014), for which you may need to book tickets in advance.

Covered with a magnificent, Norman Foster–designed glass-and-steel roof, the **Queen Elizabeth II Great Court** is the largest covered public square in Europe. It surrounds the famous **Reading Room**, where users have included Karl Marx, Lenin, Mahatma Gandhi and Bram Stoker (although not simultaneously).

A broken chunk of a larger granite slab found near the village of Rosetta in Egypt, the **Rosetta Stone** in Room 4 on the ground floor west of the Reading Room proved invaluable as the key to deciphering Egyptian hieroglyphics.

Not far away, the **Parthenon Sculptures** (also known as the Elgin Marbles) can be admired in the Ancient Greece gallery (Room 18). The sculptures once decorated the outside of the Parthenon, a temple dedicated to Athena, with events from Greek mythology and a frieze portraying a sacred procession.

Also on the ground floor, the **Feather bonnet of Yellow Calf** is a tremendous headdress from the North America Gallery (Room 26). Next door in the Mexico Gallery (Room 27), the **Mosaic Mask of Tezcatlipoca** (Skull of the Smoking Mirror) – a human skull decorated with bands of turquoise mosaic and black lignite – is an astonishing sight, believed to represent a creator deity. The oldest room in the museum, the 1820 **King's Library** is a marvellous neoclassical space, retracing how such disciplines as biology, archaeology, linguistics and geography emerged during the 18th century Enlightenment.

On the upper floor, the artefacts from the **Sutton Hoo Ship-Burial** (see p428; Room 41) constitute a highly significant Anglo-Saxon hoard from a burial site in Suffolk dating from the 7th century, excavated in 1938. Objects from the largest of the grassy mounds in Suffolk include coins and the highly elaborate and well-known helmet, complete with face mask, eye sockets and eyebrows inlaid with silver wire and garnets; the helmet was painstakingly rebuilt from hundreds of damaged fragments.

The leathery remains of the **Lindow Man** (Room 50) – a 1st-century man aged around 25 at the time of his violent death – were astonishingly well-preserved in a peat bog near Manchester and dug up in the 1980s. The beautiful Oxus chariot model and gold figurines in the Ancient Iran Gallery (Room 52) are glittering highlights of the **Oxus Treasure**, a glorious collection of metalwork from the ancient Persian capital of Persepolis. The artefacts from the **Royal Tombs of Ur** (from modern-day Iraq) are nearby in room 56.

On the upper floor, the **Mummy of Katebet** from Thebes is a tremendous highlight of the Egyptian Death and Afterlife Gallery (Room 63), with its splendidly painted mummy mask. During her lifetime, the mummified woman was an elderly Chantress of Amun (a performer for temple rituals).

When museum fever strikes you down, pop across the way to the lovely **Museum Tavern** (49 Great Russell St) where Karl Marx used to polish off a drink or two after a hard day's graft in the Reading Room of the British Library.

FREE British Museum MUSEUM
(Map p64; ☎020-7323 8000; www.britishmuseum.org; Great Russell St; ⏲10am-5.30pm Sat-Wed, to 8.30pm Thu & Fri; ⊖Russell Square) The country's largest museum and one of the oldest and finest in the world, this famous museum boasts vast Egyptian, Etruscan, Greek, Roman, European and Middle Eastern galleries, among many others.

Begun in 1753 with a 'cabinet of curiosities' bequeathed by Sir Hans Sloane to the nation on his death, the collection mushroomed over the ensuing years partly through plundering the empire. The grand

North Central London

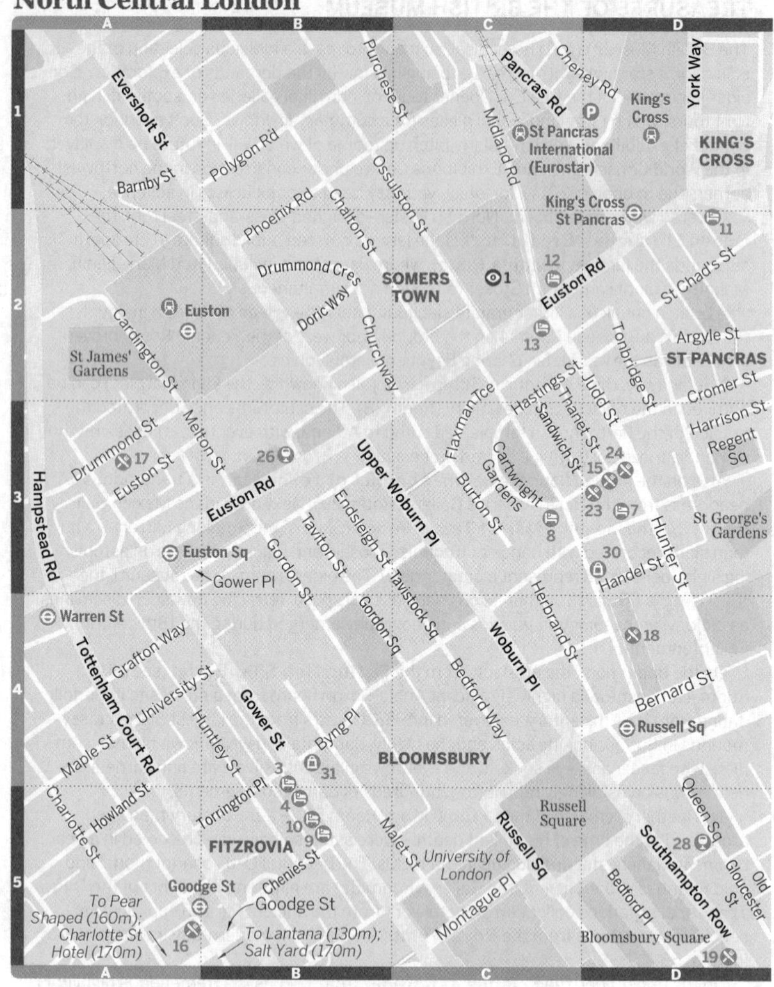

Enlightenment Gallery was the first section of the redesigned museum to be built (in 1820).

Among the must-sees are the **Rosetta Stone**, the key to deciphering Egyptian hieroglyphics, discovered in 1799; the controversial **Parthenon Sculptures**, stripped from the walls of the Parthenon in Athens by Lord Elgin (the British ambassador to the Ottoman Empire), and which Greece wants returned; the stunning **Oxus Treasure** of 7th- to 4th-century-BC Persian gold; and the Anglo-Saxon **Sutton Hoo** burial relics.

The **Great Court** was restored and augmented by Norman Foster in 2000 and now has a spectacular glass-and-steel roof, making it one of the most impressive architectural spaces in the capital. In the centre is the **Reading Room**, with its stunning blue-and-gold domed ceiling, where Karl Marx wrote the *Manifesto of the Communist Party*.

You'll need multiple visits to savour even the highlights here; happily there are 15 half-hour free 'Eye Opener' tours between 11am and 3.45pm daily, focussing on different parts of the collection. Other tours

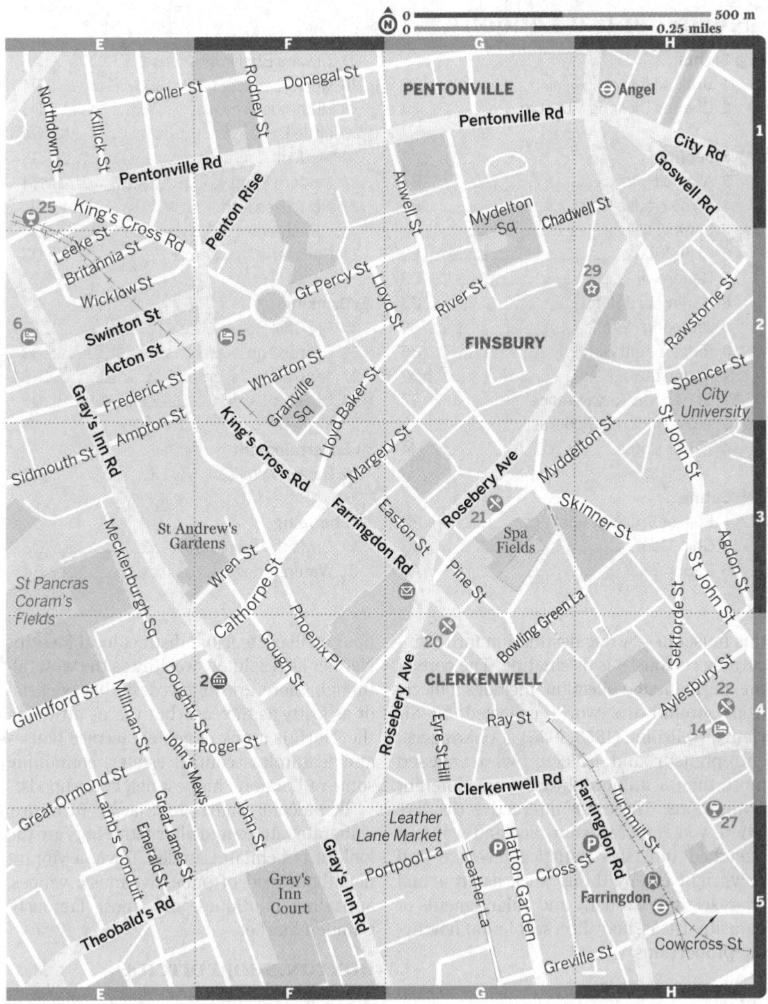

include the 90-minute highlights tour at 10.30am, 1pm and 3pm daily (adult/child £8/5), and audioguides are available (£4.50).

British Library LIBRARY

(Map p92; www.bl.uk; 96 Euston Rd; ⌚9.30am-6pm Mon & Wed-Fri, to 8pm Tue, to 5pm Sat, 11am-5pm Sun; ⊖King's Cross St Pancras) For visitors, the real highlight is a visit to the **Sir John Ritblat Gallery** where the most precious manuscripts, spanning almost three millennia, are held. Here you'll find the *Codex Sinaiticus* (the first complete text of the New Testament), a Gutenberg Bible (1455), the stunningly illustrated Jain sacred texts, Leonardo da Vinci's notebooks, a copy of the *Magna Carta* (1215), explorer Captain Scott's final diary, Shakespeare's First Folio (1623) and the lyrics to 'A Hard Day's Night' (scribbled on the back of Julian Lennon's birthday card) plus original scores by Handel, Mozart and Beethoven.

FREE **Wellcome Collection** MUSEUM

(Map p89; www.wellcomecollection.org; 183 Euston Rd; ⌚10am-6pm Tue, Wed, Fri & Sat, 10am-10pm Thu, 11am-6pm Sun; ⊖Euston Square) Focussing on the interface of art, science and medicine,

North Central London

Sights
1 British Library....C2
2 Charles Dickens Museum....F4

Sleeping
3 Arosfa Hotel....B4
4 Arran House Hotel....B5
5 Clink78....F2
6 Clink261....E2
7 Generator....D3
8 Harlingford Hotel....C3
9 Jesmond Hotel....B5
10 Ridgemount Hotel....B5
11 Rough Luxe....D2
12 St Pancras Renaissance....C2
13 YHA London St Pancras....C2
14 Zetter Hotel....H4

Eating
Bistrot Bruno Loubet....(see 14)
15 Chilli Cool....D3
16 Dabbous....A5
17 Diwana Bhel Poori House....A3
18 GBK....D4
19 Hummus Bros....D5
20 Little Bay....G4
21 Medcalf....G3
22 Modern Pantry....H4
23 North Sea Fish Restaurant....D3
24 Pâtisserie Deux Amis....D3

Drinking
25 Big Chill House....E1
26 Euston Tap....B3
27 Jerusalem Tavern....H5
28 Queen's Larder....D5

Entertainment
29 Sadler's Wells....H2

Shopping
30 Gay's the Word....D3
31 Waterstones....B4

this museum – 'A free destination for the incurably curious' – is fascinating. The core of the permanent collection includes objects from around the world collected by Sir Henry Wellcome (1853–1936), a pharmacist, entrepreneur and collector who amassed more than a million objects from different civilisations. There are interactive displays where you can scan your face and watch it stretched into the statistical average and downright creepy things such as an actual cross-section of a body and enlargements of parasites (fleas, body lice, scabies) at horrifying proportions.

Charles Dickens Museum MUSEUM
(Map p92; www.dickensmuseum.com; 48 Doughty St; adult/child £6/3; 10am-5pm Mon-Sat, 11am-5pm Sun; Russell Square) The handsome four-storey house narrowly escaped demolition and opened as a museum in 1925. Shut for most of 2012 for much-needed refurbishment, Dickens' sole surviving London residence is where his work really flourished – *The Pickwick Papers*, *Nicholas Nickleby* and *Oliver Twist* were all written here.

CAMDEN TOWN

Once well outside the city limits, the former hamlets of North London were long ago gobbled up by the metropolis, yet they still harbour a village feel and distinct local identity. Neither as resolutely wealthy as the west (although there are highly desirable pockets) or as gritty as the east (but there's attitude), the 'Norf' is a mix of genteel terrace houses and featureless council estates, containing some of London's hippest neighbourhoods.

Technicolor hairstyles, facial furniture, elaborate tattoos and alternative togs are the look of bohemian Camden Town, a vibrant neighbourhood of pubs, live-music venues, appealing boutiques and, most famously, Camden Market.

HOXTON, SHOREDITCH & SPITALFIELDS

These revitalised and hip areas northeast of the city have enough sightseeing allure to keep daytime travellers occupied, but things really get going in the evening, when the late-night pubs, clubs and restaurants come into their own. Vibrant Hoxton and Shoreditch form the centre of gravity for nightlife, while Sunday is optimum for strolling at leisure through Spitalfields after a Saturday night out. Over the centuries, waves of immigrants have left their mark here, and it's a great place to come for diverse cuisine and vibrant nightlife.

Camden Town

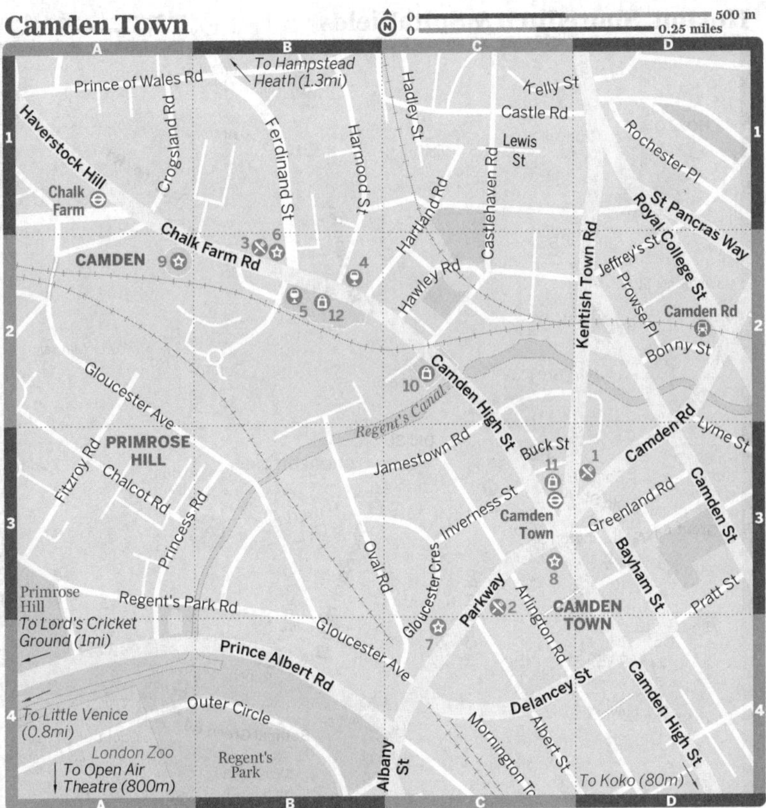

FREE **Dennis Severs' House** MUSEUM

(Map p96; ☎020-7247 4013; www.dennissevershouse.co.uk; 8 Folgate St; ⊖Liverpool St) This extraordinary Georgian house is set up as if its occupants (a family of Huguenot silk weavers) had just walked out the door, with half-drunk cups of tea, lit candles and, with perhaps more detail than we need, a full chamber pot by the bed. More than a museum, it's an opportunity to meditate on the minutiae of everyday Georgian life through silent exploration.

Bookings are required for the Monday evening candlelit sessions (£14; 6pm to 9pm) and the same on Wednesdays (£14; 6pm to 9pm, October to March), but you can just show up on Sundays (£10; noon to 4pm) or Mondays (£7; noon to 2pm) following the first and third Sundays of the month.

Camden Town

Eating

1 Mango Room D3
2 Market Restaurant C3
3 Nando's B2

Drinking

4 Lock Tavern B2
5 Proud Camden B2

Entertainment

6 Barfly B2
7 Dublin Castle C4
8 Jazz Café C3
9 Roundhouse A2

Shopping

10 Camden Lock Market C2
11 Camden Market C3
12 Camden Stables Market B2

Hoxton, Shoreditch & Spitalfields

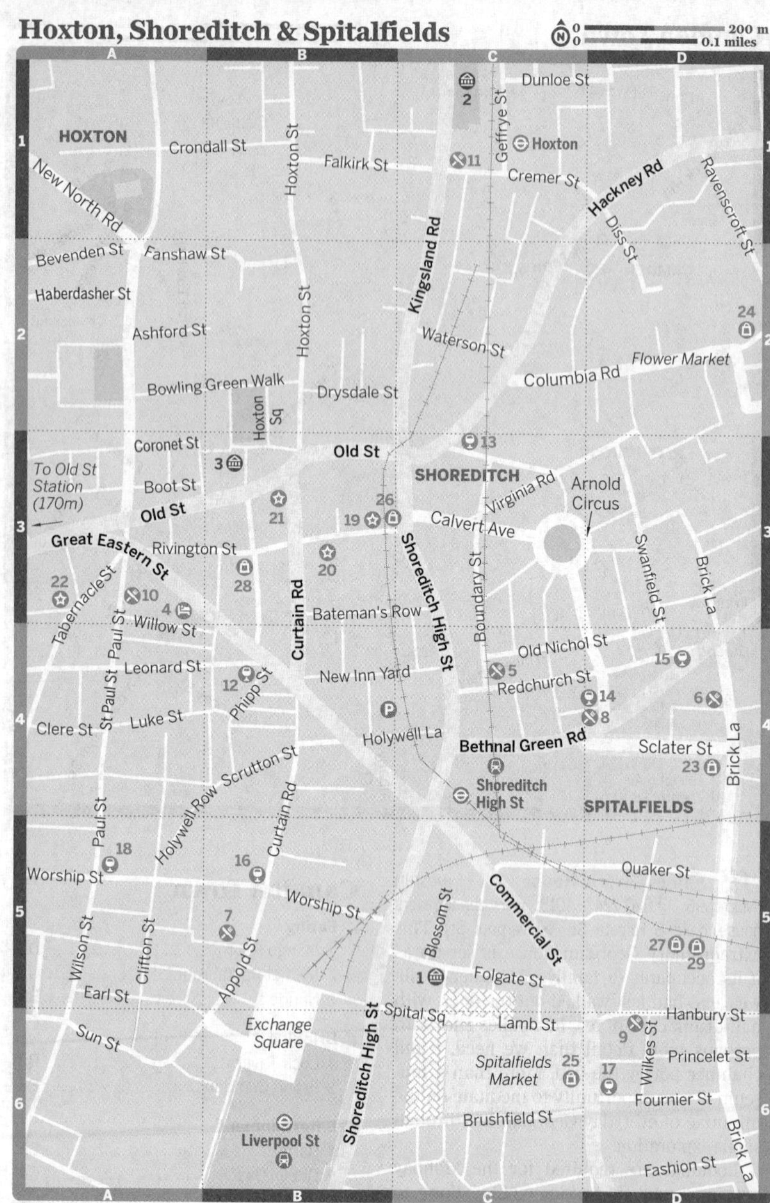

FREE Geffrye Museum MUSEUM

(Map p96; www.geffrye-museum.org.uk; 136 Kingsland Rd; ⏲10am-5pm Tue-Sat, noon-5pm Sun; ⊖Hoxton or Old Street) If you like nosing around other people's homes, you'll love this museum. Devoted to middle-class domestic interiors, these former almshouses (1714) have been converted into a series of living rooms dating from 1630 to the current Ikea generation. On top of the interiors, the back garden has been transformed into period

Hoxton, Shoreditch & Spitalfields

Sights
1 Dennis Severs' House ... C5
2 Geffrye Museum ... C1
3 White Cube Gallery ... B3

Sleeping
4 Hoxton ... A3

Eating
5 Albion ... C4
6 Brick Lane Beigel Bake ... D4
7 L'Anima ... B5
8 Les Trois Garçons ... D4
9 Poppies ... D6
10 Princess of Shoreditch ... A3
11 Sông Que ... C1

Drinking
12 Book Club ... B4
13 George & Dragon ... C3
14 Loungelover ... D4
15 Mason & Taylor ... D4
16 Queen of Hoxton ... B5
17 Ten Bells ... D6
18 Worship St Whistling Shop ... A5

Entertainment
19 Cargo ... B3
20 Comedy Cafe ... B3
21 Plastic People ... B3
22 Xoyo ... A3

Shopping
23 Brick Lane Market ... D4
24 Columbia Road Flower Market ... D2
25 Old Spitalfields Market ... C6
26 Present ... B3
27 Rough Trade East ... D5
28 Start ... B3
29 Sunday (Up) Market ... D5

garden 'rooms' and a lovely walled herb garden (April to October only).

FREE **White Cube Gallery** GALLERY
(Map p96; www.whitecube.com; 48 Hoxton Sq; 10am-6pm Tue-Sat; Old Street) Set in an industrial building with an impressive glazed-roof extension, White Cube hosts an intriguing program of contemporary-art exhibitions, from sculptures to video, installations and painting.

EAST END & DOCKLANDS

A huge area, the East End and Docklands are not rich in sights, but a dramatic new focus has emerged in the Olympic Park, while recently opened Overground lines make transport a breeze.

The Docklands' Canary Wharf and Isle of Dogs are an island of tower blocks, rivalling those of the City itself. London's port was once the world's greatest, the hub of the enormous global trade of the British Empire. Since being pummelled by the unpleasant Luftwaffe in WWII, its fortunes have been topsy-turvy, but massive development of Canary Wharf replaced its crusty seadogs with battalions of dark-suited office workers.

FREE **Museum of London Docklands** MUSEUM
(www.museumoflondon.org.uk/docklands; Hertsmere Rd, West India Quay; 10am-6pm; DLR West India Quay) Housed in a heritage-listed warehouse, this museum uses a combination of artefacts and multimedia to chart the history of the city through its river and docks. There's a lot to see here, including an affecting section on the slave trade. The museum faces West India Quay; head west (towards the city) from the DLR station.

Olympic Park PARK, OLYMPIC VENUE
(www.london2012.com/olympic-park; Stratford) From 2008, a huge, once-contaminated and largely neglected swath of industrial East London was ambitiously regenerated and transformed into London's Olympic Park for the 2012 Games. Complementing its iconic sporting architecture, the Olympic Park was thoughtfully designed with a diverse mix of wetland, woodland, meadow and other wildlife habitats as an environmentally fertile legacy for the future. The signature buildings are the sustainably-built **Olympic Stadium**, the uplifting **Aquatics Centre** and the cutting-edge **Velodrome**. The twisted, abstract tangle of metal overlooking everything is the **ArcelorMittal Orbit**, aka the 'Hubble Bubble Pipe', a 115m-high observation tower which opened during the games. Now that the games are over, the parkland has been renamed the **Queen Elizabeth Olympic Park**. Panoramic views of the Olympic Park can also be had from the **View Tube** (www.theviewtube.co.uk; The

WORTH A TRIP

BRIXTON WINDMILL

Built for one John Ashby in 1816, the lovely **Brixton Windmill** (www.brixtonwindmill.org; Blenheim Gardens; ⊖Brixton, then bus 45 or 59) is the closest one to central London still in existence and a reminder that much of London is made up of once pastoral villages. Recently restored and open for exploration in the afternoons a few weekends a month, it's an astonishing sight.

Greenway; ⊙9am-5pm; Pudding Mill Lane) on the Greenway, next to the park.

Mudchute Park & Farm FARM, SANCTUARY
(www.mudchute.org; Mudchute; ⊙farm 9am-5pm Tue-Sun;) This marvellous and fun-filled inner city farm on the Isle of Dogs has loads of well-kept animals and rare breeds (including the ever-popular llamas), with views of Canary Wharf reinforcing the urban/pastoral context. There's also a neat cafe, serving excellent breakfasts and wholesome lunches.

GREENWICH

Greenwich (*gren*-itch) straddles the hemispheres and the ages, retaining its own sense of identity based on historic associations with the sea and science and possessing an extraordinary cluster of buildings that have earned 'Maritime Greenwich' its place on Unesco's World Heritage list.

Greenwich is easily reached on the DLR or via train from London Bridge. **Thames River Services** (www.thamesriverservices.co.uk; single/return £9.50/12.50) has boats departing from Westminster Pier (single/return £10/13, one hour, every 40 minutes), or alternatively take the cheaper Thames Clippers ferry.

FREE **Old Royal Naval College** HISTORIC BUILDINGS
(www.oldroyalnavalcollege.org; 2 Cutty Sark Gardens; ⊙10am-5pm; DLR Cutty Sark) Designed by Wren, the Old Royal Naval College is a magnificent example of monumental classical architecture. Parts are now used by the University of Greenwich and Trinity College of Music, but you can visit the **chapel** and the extraordinary **Painted Hall**, which took artist Sir James Thornhill 19 years to complete.

The complex was built on the site of the 15th-century Palace of Placentia, the birthplace of Henry VIII and Elizabeth I. This Tudor connection, along with Greenwich's industrial and maritime history, is explored in the **Discover Greenwich** (www.ornc.org; The Pepys Building, King William Walk; ⊙10am-5pm) centre. The tourist office is based here, along with a cafe/restaurant and microbrewery. Yeomen-led tours of the complex leave at 2pm daily, taking in areas not otherwise open to the public (£6, 90 minutes).

FREE **National Maritime Museum** MUSEUM
(020-8858 4422; www.nmm.ac.uk; Romney Rd; ⊙10am-5pm; DLR Cutty Sark) With its newly

LOCAL KNOWLEDGE

RICHARD LIDDLE, LONDON BLACK CABS (TAXI) DRIVER

Celebrity-spotting suggestions? All of London is good for celebrity spotting, but if you want a chance to meet Madonna or see the stars of stage and screen going for workouts or rehearsals then Covent Garden is the main area.

The best-but-least-known part of town? This has to be Southwark. Just across the River Thames over London Bridge you will stumble across the Borough Market, an area you can find food and drink from all over the world. Wander through the market and you enter Southwark. Take a walk along by the Thames, where the shops, restaurants, places of interest and views will amaze you.

The best view of London from a cab? Get the driver to take you over Lambeth Bridge from the north to the south side and as he turns left off of the bridge get him to stop. Look out of the window and there is the Houses of Parliament in all its splendour – the best view in the whole of London

Your favourite part of London and why? Camden Market. The area is huge and you can find every possible type of merchandise. Grab a seat in a cafe, buy a coffee and watch the whole of humanity pass you by. Just fantastic.

opened **Sammy Ofer Wing**, the National Maritime Museum houses a splendid collection of nautical paraphernalia recounting Britain's brine-soaked seafaring history. Exhibits range from **Miss Britain III** (the first boat to top 100mph on open water) from 1933, the 19m-long **golden state barge** built in 1732 for Frederick, Prince of Wales, humdingers such as **Cook's journals** and **Nelson's uniform**, complete with bullet hole and interactive plus educational displays. An ambitious new gallery in the Sammy Ofer Wing narrates the history of Britain partly by way of the Wave, an innovative audio-visual installation.

Royal Observatory HISTORIC BUILDING
(☎0208-858 4422; www.rmg.co.uk; adult/child £7/2; ⏲10am-5pm ; 🚉DLR Cutty Sark) Rising south of Queen's House, idyllic **Greenwich Park** climbs up the hill, affording stunning views of London from the Royal Observatory, which Charles II had built in 1675 to help solve the riddle of longitude.

Success was confirmed in 1884 when Greenwich was designated as the prime meridian of the world, and Greenwich Mean Time (GMT) became the universal measurement of standard time.

In the north of the observatory is lovely **Flamsteed House** and the **Meridian Courtyard** (where you can stand with your feet straddling the western and eastern hemispheres); admission is by ticket. The southern half contains the highly informative and free **Astronomy Centre** and the **Peter Harrison Planetarium** (adult/child £6.50/4.50).

Queen's House HISTORIC BUILDING
(www.rmg.co.uk/queens-house; Romney Rd; ⏲10am-5pm; 🚉DLR Cutty Sark) Looking directly to the Thames between the domes of the Old Royal Naval College (p98), the elegant Palladian Queen's House was designed by Inigo Jones in 1616 for the wife of Charles I. Don't miss the ceremonial Great Hall and the delightful helix-shaped Tulip Staircase.

Greenwich Guided Walks WALKING TOUR
(☎0757-577 2298; www.greenwichtours.co.uk; adult £7; ⏲12.15pm & 2.15pm) Tours leave from the tourist office.

O2 VENUE
(www.theo2.co.uk; Peninsula Sq; ⊖North Greenwich) The world's largest dome (365m in diameter) opened on 1 January 2000, at a cost of £789 million, as the Millennium Dome. Renamed the O2, it's now a 20,000-seat sports and entertainment arena surrounded by shops and restaurants. The Arena also houses the **British Music Experience** (☎0844 847 1761; www.britishmusicexperience.com; Millennium Way; adult/child £12/6; ⏲11am-7.30pm; North Greenwich), which entertainingly traces the history of British popular music from 1945 to the present day. O2 conducts regular guided climbs of the dome's exterior (£22 to £28). There are ferry services from central London on concert nights.

EMIRATES AIR LINE CABLE CAR

Destined to become a sight in its own right and capable of ferrying 2400 people per hour across the Thames in either direction, the new **Emirates Air Line Cable Car** (adult/child single £4.30/2.20, return £8.60/4.40; ⏲7am-9pm Mon-Fri, from 8am Sat, from 9am Sun Apr-Sep, shorter hours rest of the year) links together the Greenwich Peninsula and the Royal Docks in a five- to 10-minute journey. Expected to help regenerate both sides of the river around each embarkation point, the UK's first urban cable car system will have cabins available every half minute; Oyster card and Travelcard holders get a discount for journeys, which are bike-friendly too. Arriving at Royal Docks, you can hop on the DLR at Royal Victoria DLR station while in Greenwich, the underground interchange is with North Greenwich Station.

HAMPSTEAD & HIGHGATE

These quaint and well-heeled villages, perched on hills north of London, are home to a litany of celebrities.

Hampstead Heath PARK
(🚉Gospel Oak or Hampstead Heath) With its 320 hectares of rolling meadows and wild woodlands, Hampstead Heath is a million miles away – well, approximately four – from central London. A walk up **Parliament Hill** affords one of the most spectacular views of the city, and on summer days it's a choice spot for picnickers. Also bewilderingly popular are the murky brown waters of the single-sex and mixed bathing ponds (basically duck ponds with people splashing about in them),

although most folk are content just to sun themselves around London's 'beach'.

FREE **Kenwood House** HISTORIC BUILDING

(www.english-heritage.org.uk; Hampstead Lane; admission free; ⊙11.30am-4pm; ⓡGospel Oak or Hampstead Heath) **Kenwood House** is a magnificent neoclassical mansion (1764) on the northern side of the heath that houses a collection of paintings by English and European masters including Rembrandt, Vermeer, Turner and Gainsborough. Closed for renovations until autumn 2013, the grounds remain accessible.

Highgate Cemetery CEMETERY

(☎020-8340 1834; www.highgate-cemetery.org; Swain's Lane; West Cemetery adult/child £7/3, East Cemetery adult/child £3/2; ⊙West Cemetery tours 2pm Mon-Fri Mar-Nov, hourly 11am-3pm Sat & Sun year-long, East Cemetery 10am-5pm Mon-Fri, 11am-5pm Sat & Sun Mar-Oct, to 4pm Nov-Feb; ⊖Archway) Weaving their Gothic magic, the shrouded urns, obelisks, broken columns, sleeping angels, classical tomb porticoes and overgrown graves make this boneyard a sublime Victorian Valhalla. On the eastern side you can pay your respects to the graves of Karl Marx and George Eliot (Mary Ann Evans), but the highlight is the overgrown West Cemetery, where a maze of winding paths leads to the Circle of Lebanon, rings of tombs flanking a circular path and topped with a majestic cedar of Lebanon tree. Admission to the West Cemetery is by tour only and bookings are essential for weekday tours. From Archway station, walk up Highgate Hill until you reach Waterlow Park on the left. Go through the park; the cemetery gates are opposite the exit.

WORTH A TRIP

ESTORICK COLLECTION OF MODERN ITALIAN ART

The outstanding concentration of art in the **Estorick Collection of Modern Italian Art** (Map p120; ☎7704 9522; www.estorickcollection.com; 39a Canonbury Sq; adult/concession/student £5/3.50/free; ⊙11am-6pm Wed-Sat, noon-5pm Sun; Highbury & Islington) in Islington boasts one of the world's leading collections of futurist painting, from such gifted artists as Umberto Boccioni, Giacomo Balla and Gino Severini.

OUTSIDE CENTRAL LONDON

Kew Gardens BOTANIC GARDENS

(www.kew.org.uk; Kew Rd; adult/child £14/free, Kew Explorer adult/child £4/1; ⊙9.30am-6.30pm Apr-Aug, earlier closing other months; ⓡKew Bridge, ⊖Kew Gardens) In 1759 botanists began rummaging around the world for specimens they could plant in the 3-hectare plot known as the Royal Botanic Gardens. They never stopped collecting, and the gardens, which have bloomed to 120 hectares, provide the most comprehensive botanical collection on earth (including the world's largest collection of orchids). The beautiful gardens are now recognised as a Unesco World Heritage Site.

No worries if you don't know your golden slipper orchid from your fengoky or your quiver tree from your alang-alang; a visit to Kew is a journey of discovery for everyone. You can easily spend a whole day wandering around, but if you're pressed for time, the **Kew Explorer** (adult/child £4/1) is a hop-on/hop-off road train that leaves from Victoria Gate and takes in the gardens' main sights.

Highlights include the enormous early Victorian **Palm House**, a hothouse of metal and curved sheets of glass; the impressive **Princess of Wales Conservatory**; the red-brick, 1631 **Kew Palace** (www.hrp.org.uk/kewpalace; adult/child £5.30/free; ⊙11am-5pm Easter-Sep), formerly King George III's country retreat; the celebrated **Great Pagoda** designed by William Chambers in 1762; the **Temperate House**, the world's largest ornamental glasshouse; and the very enjoyable **Rhizotron and Xstrata Treetop Walkway**, where you can survey the tree canopy from 18m up in the air.

The gardens are easily reached by tube, but you might prefer to take a cruise on a riverboat from the **Westminster Passenger Services Association** (☎020-7930 2062; www.wpsa.co.uk), which runs several daily boats from April to October, departing from Westminster Pier (return adult/child £18/9, 90 minutes).

Hampton Court Palace PALACE

(www.hrp.org.uk/HamptonCourtPalace; adult/child £14/7; ⊙10am-6pm Apr-Oct, to 4.30pm Nov-Mar; ⓡHampton Court) Built by Cardinal Thomas Wolsey in 1514 but coaxed from him by Henry VIII just before Wolsey (as chancellor) fell from favour, Hampton Court Palace is England's largest and grandest Tudor structure. It was already one of the most sophisticated

POUND SAVERS

As many of London's very best sights are free, you can easily spend a busy week without paying much on admission charges. However, if you're hanging around for longer and have particular attractions that you're keen to see, there are options for saving a few pounds.

The **London Pass** (www.londonpass.com; per 1/2/3/6 days £46/61/66/89) is a smart card that gains you fast-track entry to 55 different attractions, including pricier ones such as the Tower of London and St Paul's Cathedral. You'd have to be racing around frantically to get real value from a one-day pass, but you could conceivably save quite a bit with the two- or three-day version. Passes can be booked online and collected from the **London Pass Redemption Desk** (11a Charing Cross Rd; ⊖Leicester Square) (check online for opening hours) opposite the Garrick Theatre. It also sells a version with a preloaded Transport For London (TFL) travel pass, but it's cheaper to buy this separately.

If you're a royalty buff, taking out an annual membership to the **Historic Royal Palaces** (www.hrp.org.uk; individual/joint membership £43/65) allows you to jump the queues and visit the Tower of London, Kensington Palace, Banqueting House, Kew Palace and Hampton Court Palace as often as you like. If you were intending to visit all five anyway, membership will save you more than £18 (£58 for a couple). There can be a lengthy wait for membership cards, but temporary cards are issued immediately.

palaces in Europe when, in the 17th century, Wren was commissioned to build an extension. The result is a beautiful blend of Tudor and 'restrained baroque' architecture.

Take a themed tour led by costumed historians or, if you're in a rush, visit the highlights: **Henry VIII's State Apartments**, including the Great Hall with its spectacular hammer-beamed roof; the **Tudor Kitchens**, staffed by 'servants'; and the **Wolsey Rooms**. You could easily spend a day exploring the palace and its 60 acres of riverside gardens, especially if you get lost in the 300-year-old **maze**.

Hampton Court is 13 miles southwest of central London and is easily reached by train from Waterloo. Alternatively, the riverboats that head from Westminster to Kew continue here (return adult/child £22.50/11.25, three hours).

Richmond Park PARK
(⏲7am-dusk Mar-Sep, from 7.30am Oct-Feb; ⊖Richmond) London's wildest park – and the largest urban parkland in Europe – spans more than 1000 hectares and is home to all sorts of wildlife, most notably herds of red and fallow deer. It's a terrific place for birdwatching, rambling and cycling.

To get there from Richmond tube station, turn left along George St then left at the fork that leads up Richmond Hill.

☞ Tours

One of the best ways to orient yourself when you first arrive in London is with a 24-hour hop-on/hop-off pass for the double-decker bus tours. The buses loop around interconnecting routes throughout the day, providing a commentary as they go, and the price includes a river cruise and three walking tours. Save a few pounds by booking online.

Original Tour BUS TOUR
(www.theoriginaltour.com; adult/child/family £26/13/91; ⏲every 20min 8.30am-5.30pm)

Big Bus Tours BUS TOUR
(☎020-7233 9533; www.bigbustours.com; adult/child £26/10)

Citisights WALKING TOURS
(☎020-8806 3742; www.chr.org.uk/cswalks.htm) Focuses on the academic and the literary.

London Beatles Walks WALKING TOURS
(☎07958 706329; www.beatlesinlondon.com; adult/child £6/free) Following the footsteps of the Fab Four.

London Walks WALKING TOURS
(☎020-7624 3978; www.walks.com) Harry Potter tours, ghost walks and the ever popular Jack the Ripper tours.

London Mystery Walks WALKING TOURS
(☎07957 388280; www.tourguides.org.uk)

WORTH A TRIP

ABBEY ROAD

Beatles aficionados can't possibly visit London without making a pilgrimage to **Abbey Road Studios** (3 Abbey Rd) in St John's Wood. The fence outside is covered with decades of fans' graffiti. Stop-start local traffic is long accustomed to groups of tourists lining up on the zebra crossing to reenact the cover of the fab four's 1969 masterpiece and penultimate swan song *Abbey Road*. In 2010, the crossing received the accolade of Grade II listed status. For an entertaining live view of the crossing and highlights of the day's action, check out the fun webcam at www.abbeyroad.com/crossing. To get here, take the tube to St John's Wood, cross the road, follow Grove End Rd to its end and turn right.

City Cruises FERRY TOURS
(Map p58; ☎020-7740 0400; www.citycruises.com; single/return trips from £8/10.50, day pass £13.50) Ferry service between Westminster, Waterloo, Tower and Greenwich piers.

Capital Taxi Tours TAXI TOURS
(☎020-8590 3621; www.capitaltaxitours.co.uk; two-hour day tour £165 per taxi, by night 2½ hour tour £235 per taxi) Takes up to five people on a variety of tours with Blue Badge, City of London and City of Westminster registered guides/drivers, cheeky Cockney Cabbie option and foreign language availability.

London Bicycle Tour CYCLING TOURS
(Map p78; ☎020-7928 6838; www.londonbicycle.com; 1A Gabriel's Wharf, 56 Upper Ground; tour incl bike from £18.95; ⊖Waterloo) Themed 2½- to 3½-hour tours of the 'West End', 'East', 'Central' or 'Royal West'.

City Jogging Tours JOGGING TOURS
(☎0845 544 0433; www.cityjoggingtours.co.uk; tours £26) Combine sightseeing with keeping fit on a 6km route, graded for 'gentle joggers' or 'recreational runners'.

London Duck Tours AMPHIBIOUS-VEHICLE TOURS
(Map p78; ☎020-7928 3132; www.londonduck tours.co.uk; County Hall ; ⊖Waterloo) Cruise the streets in the same sort of amphibious landing craft used on D-Day before making a dramatic plunge into the Thames.

Festivals & Events

Chinese New Year CULTURAL CELEBRATION
Late January or early February sees Chinatown snap, crackle and pop with fireworks, a colourful street parade, lion dances and *dim sum* aplenty.

University Boat Race BOAT RACE
(www.theboatrace.org) A posh-boy grudge match held annually since 1829 between the rowing crews of Oxford and Cambridge Universities (late March).

London Marathon RUNNING RACE
(www.london-marathon.co.uk) Up to half a million spectators watch the whippet-thin champions and bizarrely clad amateurs take to the streets in late April.

Camden Crawl MUSIC FESTIVAL
(www.thecamdencrawl.com; 1-/2-day pass £39/62) Your chance to spot the next big thing on the music scene or witness a secret gig by an established act, with 40 of Camden's venues given over to live music for two full days (late April/early May).

Chelsea Flower Show HORTICULTURAL SHOW
(www.rhs.org.uk/chelsea; Royal Hospital Chelsea; admission £19-42) Held in May, arguably the world's most renowned horticultural show attracts green fingers from near and far.

Trooping the Colour ROYAL PARADE
Celebrating the Queen's official birthday (in June), this ceremonial procession of troops, marching along the Mall for their monarch's inspection, is a pageantry overload.

Royal Academy Summer Exhibition ART EXHIBITION
(www.royalacademy.org.uk; adult/child £9.50/5) Running from mid-June to mid-August, this is an annual showcase of works submitted by artists from all over Britain, mercifully distilled to 1200 or so pieces.

Meltdown Festival MUSIC FESTIVAL
(www.southbankcentre.co.uk) The Southbank Centre hands over the curatorial reigns to a legend of contemporary music (such as David Bowie, Morrissey or Patti Smith) to pull together a full program of concerts, talks and films in late June.

Wimbledon Lawn Tennis Championships TENNIS TOURNAMENT
(www.wimbledon.org) Held at the end of June, the world's most prestigious tennis event is

as much about strawberries, cream and tradition as smashing balls.

Pride GAY & LESBIAN
(www.pridelondon.org) The big event on the gay and lesbian calendar, a Technicolor street parade heads through the West End in late June or early July, culminating in a concert in Trafalgar Sq.

Lovebox MUSIC FESTIVAL
(www.lovebox.net) London's contribution to the summer music festival circuit, held in Victoria Park in mid-July.

Notting Hill Carnival STREET PARADES
(www.nottinghillcarnival.biz) Held over two days in August, this is Europe's largest and London's most vibrant outdoor carnival, where London's Caribbean community shows the city how to party. Unmissable and truly crazy.

Sleeping

When it comes to finding a place for a good night's kip, London is one of the most expensive places in the world. 'Budget' is pretty much anything below £90 per night for a double; at the top end, how does a £14000-per-night suite on Hyde Park Corner sound? Double rooms ranging between £90 and £180 per night are considered midrange; more expensive options fall into the top-end category.

London, however, has a delightful selection of characterful hotels, whether brimming with history, zany modern decor or all-stops-out charm. Most of the ritzier places offer substantial discounts on the weekends, for advance bookings and at quieter times.

Public transport is good, so you don't need to be sleeping at Buckingham Palace to be at the heart of things.

Budget accommodation is scattered about, with good options in Bloomsbury, St Pancras, Earl's Court and the South Bank. For something a little nicer, check out Bayswater, Notting Hill Gate or Belgravia. To splash the cash, consider the West End, Clerkenwell, Kensington and Knightsbridge. Most budget and midrange places offer free wi-fi (expensive places may charge).

Prices listed here include 20% VAT, when it applies.

WESTMINSTER & ST JAMES'S

A bed in the Queen's own hood can be as ritzy as the Ritz, but won't necessarily cost you a king's ransom.

Rubens at the Palace HOTEL ££
(Map p58; ☎020-7834 6600; www.rubenshotel.com; 39 Buckingham Palace Rd; @📶; ⊖Victoria) Right by Buckingham Palace, Rubens is a firm favourite with US visitors looking for that quintessential royal experience. Rooms are monarchist chic: heavy patterned fabrics, dark wood, thick drapes and crowns above the beds.

WEST END

Like in Monopoly, land on a Mayfair hotel and you may have to sell your house, or at least remortgage. This is the heart of the action, and a couple of hostels cater for would-be Soho hipsters of more modest means.

LONDON FOR CHILDREN

London is terrific for kids. Many of the city's museums – among the best in the world – are free and will fascinate all ages, with bundles of activities on offer, from storytelling at the **National Gallery** to arts and crafts workshops at the **Victoria & Albert Museum** and fun sleepovers at the **British Museum**, **Natural History Museum**, the **Science Museum** and others. Theatre, dance and music performances are perfect for older kids and teens. Playgrounds and parks are ideal for relaxation or wearing the young tykes out. On top of that, Mudchute Park & Farm (p98) and other city farms (see www.london-footprints.co.uk/visitfarms.htm) and the big galleries have activities for children. However, don't expect a warm welcome in swanky restaurants or pubs. **Ice rinks** glisten across London in winter months, at Somerset House, the Natural History Museum, the London Eye, the Tower of London, Kew Gardens and Hampton Court Palace.

All top-range hotels offer in-house babysitting services. Prices vary enormously from hotel to hotel, so ask the concierge about hourly rates. Get a babysitter or nanny at **Greatcare** (www.greatcare.co.uk), a site that provides all manner of childcare options.

Under-16s travel free on buses, under-11s travel free on the tube and under-5s go free on the trains.

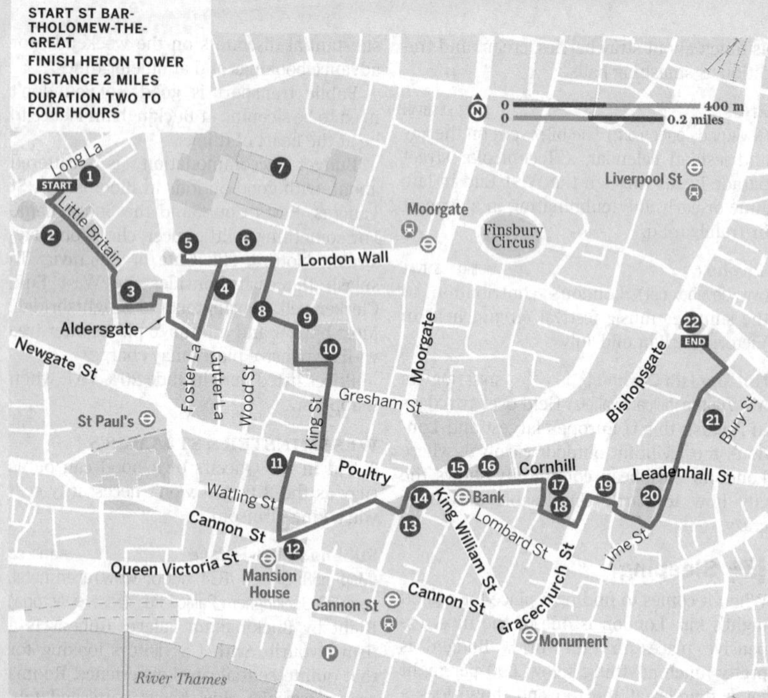

Walking Tour
City of London

The City of London has as much history and intriguing architecture in its square mile as the rest of London put together. This tour traces some of the City's hidden gems (secluded parks, charming churches) in a journey from ancient to ultramodern.

It's fitting to start at ❶ **St Bartholomew-the-Great**, as this fascinating 12th-century church was once a pilgrimage stop for travellers to London. In more recent times, it's been used for scenes in *Four Weddings & A Funeral*, *Shakespeare in Love* and *Sherlock Holmes*.

Head out through the Tudor gatehouse. In the distance you'll see the Victorian arches of Smithfield's meat market, which has occupied this site just north of the old city walls for 800 years. Executions were held here, most famously the torching of Protestants under Mary I and the grisly killing of Scottish hero William Wallace (Braveheart) in 1305; a plaque on the front of ❷ **St Bartholomew's Hospital** commemorates him. Also note the shrapnel damage to the wall – the legacy of an attack in 1916 by a German Zeppelin.

Head back towards the gate and turn right into Little Britain. Follow it as it curves to the right and look out for the large tree marking the entrance to ❸ **Postman's Park**. This lovely space includes a touching legacy of Victorian socialism: a tiled wall celebrating everyday heroes.

Turn right at the end of the park, then left and left again into Noble St. You're now inside what was once the old City's ❹ **walls**, remnants of which you'll pass on your left. Commenced in Roman times, the fortifications were demolished in the 18th and 19th centuries, but the shape of them can be traced in street names such as Newgate, Moorgate, Bishopsgate and Aldgate. This section was only uncovered after WWII bombs destroyed the buildings covering it. Take the stairs up to the footbridge crossing the street called London Wall towards the ❺ **Museum of London**. The museum's Roman section will give you a feel for the layout of the City.

Turn left when leaving the museum and follow the Highwalk. On your left you'll see 6 **ruins** of the barbicans (defensive towers) that once guarded the northwestern corner of the walls, with the 7 **Barbican Centre** behind them. Filling a space bombed out during WWII and once revolutionary, parts of it are extraordinarily ugly, particularly the forbidding high-rise tower blocks (romantically named Shakespeare, Cromwell and Lauderdale). At its heart is an arts centre consisting of concert halls, cinemas, galleries, eateries, a library and a school.

Follow the painted lines on the Highwalk for a closer look, or turn right at Pizza Express, take the escalator down to Wood St and head towards the remaining tower of 8 **St Alban's**, a Wren-designed church destroyed in WWII. Turn left and you'll find a sweet garden on the site of 9 **St Mary Aldermansbury**, capped by a bust of Shakespeare. The 12th-century church was ruined in the war then shipped to Missouri where it was re-erected.

Turn right on to Aldermansbury and head to the 10 **Guildhall**. Take King St down to Cheapside, cross the road and head right to elegant 11 **St Mary-le-Bow**. The church was rebuilt by Wren after the Great Fire, and then rebuilt again after WWII. The term 'Cockney' traditionally refers to someone born within the sound of this church's bell.

Backtrack to Bow Lane and follow this narrow path to beautiful 12 **St Mary Aldermary**, rebuilt in the Perpendicular Gothic style in 1682 following the fire. Turn left on to Queen Victoria St and then right into Bucklersbury, where you'll see 13 **St Stephen's Walbrook** directly in front of you. In the 3rd century, a Roman temple stood here, and in the 7th century a Saxon church. Rebuilt after the Great Fire, the current St Stephen's is one of Wren's greatest masterpieces, with elegant Corinthian columns supporting a beautifully proportioned dome. Henry Moore sculpted the round central altar from travertine marble in 1972.

Leaving the church, you'll pass 14 **Mansion House**, built in 1752 as the official residence of the Lord Mayor. As you approach the busy Bank intersection, lined with neoclassical temples to commerce, you might think you've stumbled into the ancient Roman forum (the actual forum was a couple of blocks east). Head for the 15 **equestrian statue of the Iron Duke**, behind which a metal pyramid details the many significant buildings here. Directly behind you is the 16 **Royal Exchange**; walk through it and exit through the door on the right, then turn left onto Cornhill.

If you're still not churched out, cross the road to 17 **St Michael's**, a 1672 Wren design which still has its box pews. Hidden in the warren of tiny passages behind the church is its 18 **churchyard**. Head through to Gracechurch St, turn left and cross the road to wonderful 19 **Leadenhall Market**. This is roughly where the ancient forum once stood. As you wander out the far end, the famous 20 **Lloyd's of London** displays its metallic innards for all to see.

Once you turn left onto Lime St, you'll see ahead of you Norman Foster's 180m 21 **30 St Mary Axe**. Its dramatic curved shape has given spawned many nicknames (the Crystal Phallus, the Towering Innuendo), but it's as the Gherkin that it is fondly known. Built nearly 900 years after St Bartholomew-the-Great, it's testimony to the City's ability to constantly reinvent itself for the times. A short walk away, the 22 **Heron Tower** was completed in 2011 and is currently the tallest building in the City.

WHEN RIGHT IS RIGHT

Vehicles entering Savoy Ct off the Strand for the Savoy (p106) traditionally drive on the right-hand side of the road, *not* the left. This is the only road in the UK where you can legally drive on the 'wrong' side of the road (Savoy Ct being a private road and not a public thoroughfare).

TOP CHOICE Haymarket Hotel HOTEL £££
(Map p64; 020-7470 4000; www.haymarkethotel.com; 1 Suffolk Pl; r £318-408, ste from £492; @; Piccadilly Circus) An exquisite place to hang your well-trimmed hat, the Tim and Kit Kemp–designed Haymarket is a super-stylish and eye-catching treat, with a knockout swimming pool bathed in serene mood lighting.

Hazlitt's HOTEL £££
(Map p64; 020-7434 1771; www.hazlittshotel.com; 6 Frith St; s £206, d/ste from £259/646; @; Tottenham Court Road) Envelop yourself in Georgian finery at this lovely 1718 house and journey back to the days of four-poster beds, claw-foot baths and panelled walls. Each of the 30 individually-decorated rooms overflows with Georgian antiques and days-gone-by charm (plus up-to-the-minute mod cons).

Dean Street Townhouse BOUTIQUE HOTEL £££
(Map p64; 0207-434 1775; www.deanstreettownhouse.com; 69-71 Dean St; r £160-310; Tottenham Court Road) This Soho gem of a 39-bedroom boutique hotel enjoys a delightful boudoir atmosphere with choice rooms – everything faultlessly in its place – from 'tiny' options upwards.

One Aldwych HOTEL £££
(Map p64; 020-7300 1000; www.onealdwych.com; 1 Aldwych; d/ste from £195/440; @; Covent Garden) Granite bathrooms, long swimming pool with underwater music, majestic bar and restaurant, modern art, and a lift that changes colour to literally lift your mood.

Savoy HOTEL £££
(Map p64; 020-7836 4343; www.fairmont.com/savoy-london; Strand; ; Charing Cross) A night surrounded by the Edwardian and art deco grandeur of the iconic Savoy is never a casual choice, considering the sudden stupefying hole in your bank balance, but as one of life's memorable treats, you can't go wrong. The £100 million refit has injected fizz back into a classic glass of champers and it's all here: river views, sumptuous rooms, pre-eminent restaurants and the much-loved American Bar. There's a charge for parking and wi-fi.

Brown's Hotel HOTEL £££
(Map p64; 020-7493 6020; www.brownshotel.com; 30 Albemarle St; r/ste from £485/915; @; Green Park) A stunner of a five-star number, this 117-room hotel was created in 1837 from 11 houses joined together, where lovely old-world traditional features (Edwardian oak panelling, working fireplaces) complement individually decorated rooms.

Soho Hotel HOTEL £££
(Map p64; 020-7559 3000; www.sohohotel.com; 4 Richmond Mews; r/ste from £354/516; @; Oxford Circus) A converted car park may sound unglamorous, but Kit Kemp's signature touches, bold colours and imagination are all over the place, from the Botero-designed cat in the lobby to the 91 individually-designed rooms, each a modish triumph. Wi-fi costs £20.

Covent Garden Hotel HOTEL £££
(Map p64; 020-7806 1000; www.coventgardenhotel.co.uk; 10 Monmouth St; d/ste from £312/492; @; Covent Garden) Well-positioned and classy Firmdale hotel housed in an old French hospital.

Oxford St YHA HOSTEL £
(Map p64; 0845 371 9133; www.yha.org.uk; 14 Noel St; dm/tw from £18/44; @; Oxford Circus) This recently refurbed hostel is a tip-top choice for its central (albeit noisy) location, bright and colourful complexion, cleanliness and manageable 93-bed size plus decent view over London's rooftops from some rooms.

THE CITY

While it's bristling with bankers during the week, you can often pick up a considerable bargain in the City on weekends.

Threadneedles HOTEL £££
(Map p72; 020-7657 8080; www.theetoncollection.com; 5 Threadneedle St; r weekend/weekday from £175/345; @; Bank) The hand-painted glass dome in the circular lobby recalls Threadneedle's former standing as a bank HQ. It's elegant and chic, with an unruffled air, pleasantly presented rooms and an understated modernity.

Apex City of London HOTEL ££
(Map p72; ☎020-7702 2020; www.apexhotels.co.uk; 1 Seething Lane; r from £100; ; ⊖Tower Hill) Business-focussed but close enough to the Tower to hear the heads roll, the Apex offers particularly enticing weekend rates, a gym, huge TVs, free wi-fi and a rubber ducky in every room.

YHA London St Paul's HOSTEL £
(Map p72; ☎0845 371 9012; www.yha.org.uk; 36 Carter Lane; dm £20-25, d £50; ⊖St Paul's) Perfectly placed for hoovering up the sights of the City and the South Bank, this elegantly housed 208-bed hostel is just down the road from St Paul's (the bells, the bells!). There's no self-catering, no lift and a seven-night maximum stay.

SOUTH BANK

Immediately south of the river is a great spot for reaching the central sights, while gauging the personality of London south of the river.

TOP CHOICE **Kennington B&B** B&B ££
(☎020-7735 7669; www.kenningtonbandb.com; 103 Kennington Park Rd; d £120-150; ⊖Kennington) With gorgeous bed linen and well-preserved Georgian features, this lovely B&B is very tasteful in virtually every regard, from the shining, tiled shower rooms and Georgian shutters to the fireplaces and cast-iron radiators. It's a short walk from Kennington underground station.

Park Plaza Westminster Bridge HOTEL £££
(Map p78; ☎0844-415 6780; www.parkplaza.com; 220 Westminster Bridge Rd; d £159-238; ; ⊖Waterloo) This snazzy fresh hotel offers contemporary, stylish and comfortable rooms. Skimp on it and you'll end up with a room facing into the atrium; splash out and you get a studio or penthouse gazing onto the Thames, Westminster Bridge, Big Ben or the London Eye.

Premier Inn London County Hall HOTEL ££
(Map p78; ☎0871 527 8648; www.premierinn.com; County Hall, Belvedere Rd; rm £112-160; ; ⊖Waterloo) Location, location, location: and a choice positioning within a landmark historic building and a few steps from the London Eye, Westminster and Big Ben. All other crucial boxes come ticked – service is congenial, rooms are decently sized and the tariff is low (but there's a £3 wi-fi charge daily).

Captain Bligh House B&B ££
(Map p78; ☎020-7928 2735; www.captainblighhouse.co.uk; 100 Lambeth Rd; s/d £63-75/85-90; ; ⊖Lambeth North) With helpful but non-intrusive owners, this late-18th-century property opposite the Imperial War Museum has shipshape and quiet rooms with kitchen. The downside is there's a minimum four-night stay policy, no credit cards, one night's nonrefundable deposit and you'll need to book way ahead. No lift.

St Christopher's Village HOSTEL £
(Map p78; ☎020-7939 9710; www.st-christophers.co.uk; 163 Borough High St; dm/r from £14/62; @; ⊖London Bridge) The Village – a huge, up-for-it party hostel, with a club hopping till 4am at weekends and a roof terrace bar – is the main hub of three locations on the same street. It's either heaven or hell, depending on what side of 30 you're on. The other locations are much smaller, quieter and, frankly, more pleasant. **St Christopher's Inn** (Map p78; 121 Borough High St) is above a very nice pub, while **Oasis** (Map p78; 59 Borough High St) is women-only.

PIMLICO & BELGRAVIA

Lime Tree Hotel B&B ££
(Map p86; ☎020-7730 8191; www.limetreehotel.co.uk; 135-137 Ebury St; s £99, d £150-175; @; ⊖Victoria) A smartly renovated Georgian town house hotel with a beautiful back garden to catch the late afternoon rays. The three 'C's: cosy, congenial and clean.

Luna Simone Hotel B&B ££
(☎020-7834 5897; www.lunasimonehotel.com; 47-49 Belgrave Rd; s £70-75, d £95-120; @; ⊖Pimlico) Rooms are quite compact but clean and calming at this central, welcoming hotel; the ones at the back are quieter. Belgrave Rd follows on from Eccleston Bridge, directly behind Victoria Station.

B+B Belgravia B&B ££
(Map p86; ☎020-7259 8570; www.bb-belgravia.com; 64-66 Ebury St; s/d/tw £99/135/145; @; ⊖Victoria) This lovely place marries contemporary chic with Georgian elegance; rooms are neat and although not very spacious, fine studio rooms with compact kitchens are along the road at No 82.

Windermere Hotel B&B ££
(Map p86; ☎020-7834 5163; www.windermere-hotel.co.uk; 142-144 Warwick Way; s £105-155, d £129-165; @; ⊖Victoria) The attractive and newly refurbished Windermere has 19 small,

BOOKING SERVICES

At Home in London (020-8748 1943; www.athomeinlondon.co.uk) For B&Bs.

GKLets (020-7613 2805; www.gklets.co.uk) Apartments.

British Hotel Reservation Centre (020-7592 3055; www.bhrconline.com) Hotels.

London Homestead Services (020-7286 5115; www.lhslondon.com) B&Bs.

LondonTown (020-7437 4370; www.londontown.com) Hotels and B&Bs.

Uptown Reservations (020-7937 2001; www.uptownres.co.uk) Upmarket B&Bs.

Visit London (per min 10p 0871 222 3118; www.visitlondonoffers.com) Hotels.

bright and individually designed rooms in a white mid-Victorian town house, with a recently installed lift and a reasonably priced restaurant.

KNIGHTSBRIDGE

Named after a bridge over the River Westbourne, Knightsbridge is where you'll find some of London's best-known department stores and some top hotels.

Levin Hotel HOTEL £££
(Map p86; 020-7589 6286; www.thelevinhotel.co.uk; 28 Basil St; r from £305; Knightsbridge) As close as you can get to sleeping in Harrods, the 12-room Levin knows its market. Despite the baby-blue colour scheme, there's a subtle femininity to the decor, although it's far too elegant to be flouncy.

Knightsbridge Hotel HOTEL £££
(Map p86; 020-7584 6300; www.knightsbridgehotel.com; 10 Beaufort Gardens; s/d from £235/282; @; Knightsbridge) Another Firmdale property, the six-floor Knightsbridge is on a quiet, tree-lined cul-de-sac very close to Harrods.

CHELSEA & KENSINGTON

Well-turned-out Chelsea and Kensington offer easy access to the museums, natty shopping choices and some of London's best-looking streets.

TOP CHOICE **Number Sixteen** HOTEL £££
(Map p86; 020-7589 5232; www.numbersixteenhotel.co.uk; 16 Sumner Pl; s from £168, d £222-360; @; South Kensington) It's four properties in one delightful whole and a stunning place to stay, with 42 individually designed rooms, a cosy drawing room, a fully stocked library and a simply idyllic back garden.

Gore HOTEL ££
(Map p86; 020-7584 6601; www.gorehotel.com; 190 Queen's Gate; r from £135; @; Gloucester Road) A short stroll from the Royal Albert Hall, the Gore serves up British grandiosity (antiques, carved four-posters, polished mahogany, a secret bathroom in the Tudor room) in 50 individually furnished, magnificent rooms.

Aster House B&B ££
(Map p86; 0207-581 5888; www.asterhouse.com; 3 Sumner Pl; s/d £144/216-300; South Kensington) The Singaporean owners certainly know how to keep things clean and shipshape at this charming and well-priced house hotel with a delightful plant-filled orangerie and ducks in the garden.

Vicarage Private Hotel B&B ££
(Map p110; 020-7229 4030; www.londonvicaragehotel.com; 10 Vicarage Gate; s/d £95/125, without bathroom £56/95; @; High St Kensington) On the corner with Palace Gardens Terrace (with its astonishing cherry trees in spring), this place is all about location (between Notting Hill Gate and Kensington High St) and value for money. Rooms are nothing special, with the cheapest (non–en suite) on floors three and four. Breakfast is included and rates fall in winter.

EARL'S COURT & FULHAM

West London's Earl's Court is lively, cosmopolitan and so popular with travelling Antipodeans it's been nicknamed Kangaroo Valley. There are no real sights, but it has inexpensive digs and an infectious holiday atmosphere.

Barclay House B&B ££
(020-7384 3390; www.barclayhouselondon.com; 21 Barclay Rd; s/d £69/89; @; Fulham Broadway) A proper homestay B&B with a handful of rooms with en suite in a charming Victorian town house. It's so popular there's now a four-night minimum stay requirement, unless they can shoehorn you in between slots. From the tube station head west on

Fulham Broadway and then look out for Barclay Rd on your left.

Twenty Nevern Square HOTEL ££
(020-7565 9555; www.20neverns quare.com; 20 Nevern Sq; r from £95; @; Earl's Court) An Ottoman theme runs through this Victorian town house hotel, where a mix of wooden furniture, luxurious fabrics and natural light helps maximise space – even in the excellent-value cheaper rooms.

Base2stay APARTMENT HOTEL ££
(020-7244 2255; www.base2stay.com; 25 Courtfield Gardens; s/d from £93/99; @; Earl's Court) With comfort, smart decor, power showers, flatscreen TVs with internet access, artfully concealed kitchenettes, neat rooms and a sustainable credo, this boutique establishment feels like a four-star hotel without the wallet-emptying price tag.

easyHotel BUDGET HOTEL £
(www.easyhotel.com; r from £25; @;) Earls Court (44 West Cromwell Rd, Earl's Court; Earl's Court); Paddington (10 Norfolk Pl, Paddington; Paddington); South Kensington (14 Lexham Gardens, South Kensington; Gloucester Rd) This no-frills chain has tiny rooms with even tinier bathrooms, all bedecked in the company's trademark garish orange.

NOTTING HILL, BAYSWATER & PADDINGTON

Don't be fooled by Julia Roberts and Hugh Grant's shenanigans, Notting Hill and the areas immediately north of Hyde Park are as shabby as they are chic. There are some gorgeous gated squares surrounded by Georgian town houses, but the area is better exemplified by the Notting Hill Carnival.

Scruffy Paddington has lots of cheap hotels, with a major strip of unremarkable ones along Sussex Gardens that may be worth checking out if you're short on options.

Vancouver Studios APARTMENT HOTEL ££
(Map p110; 020-7243 1270; www.vancouverstudios.co.uk; 30 Prince's Sq; apt £89-170; @; Bayswater) It's the addition of kitchenettes and a self-service laundry that differentiate these smart, reasonably priced studios and three-bedroom apartment (sleeping from one to six people) from a regular Victorian town house hotel. In spring, the garden is filled with colour and fragrance.

New Linden Hotel HOTEL ££
(Map p110; 020-7221 4321; www.newlinden.co.uk; Herford Rd, near Leinster Sq; s/d from £79/105; @; Bayswater) Cramming in a fair amount of style for little whack, this terrace house hotel exudes a modern and cool feel. The quiet location, helpful staff and monsoon shower heads in the deluxe rooms make this an excellent proposition.

FITZROVIA

Sanderson HOTEL £££
(Map p64; 020-7300 1400; www.sandersonlondon.com; 50 Berners St; r from £253; @; Goodge Street) Liberace meets Philippe Starck in an 18th-century French bordello – and that's just the reception. A 3-D space scene in the lift shuttles you into darkened corridors leading to blindingly white rooms complete with sleigh beds, oil paintings hung on the ceiling, en suites behind glass walls and pink silk curtains.

Charlotte Street Hotel HOTEL £££
(Map p64; 020-7806 2000; www.charlottestreethotel.com; 15-17 Charlotte St; d/ste from £300/492; @; Goodge Street) Another of the Firmdale clan, this one's a favourite with media types, with a small gym and a screening room.

London Central YHA HOSTEL £
(0845 371 9154; www.yha.org.uk; 104-108 Bolsover St; dm £21-32, q from £70; @; Great Portland Street) One of London's new breed of YHA hostels, most of the four- to six-bed rooms have en suites. There's a flash cafe-bar attached to reception and a wheelchair-accessible kitchen downstairs.

BLOOMSBURY & ST PANCRAS

One step from the West End and crammed with Georgian town-house conversions, these are more affordable neighbourhoods. A stretch of lower-priced hotels runs along Gower St and on the pretty Cartwright Gardens crescent. While hardly a salubrious location, St Pancras is handy with some excellent budget options.

TOP CHOICE **St Pancras Renaissance** HOTEL £££
(Map p92; 020-7841 3540; www.marriott.co.uk; Euston Rd; d from £295; P; King's Cross St Pancras) Staying in this iconic George Gilbert Scott–designed Gothic masterpiece is an alluring (but expensive) proposition. The architecture is a redbrick Victorian fantasy, the lobby a magnificent conversion of the former train station taxi rank

Notting Hill & Bayswater

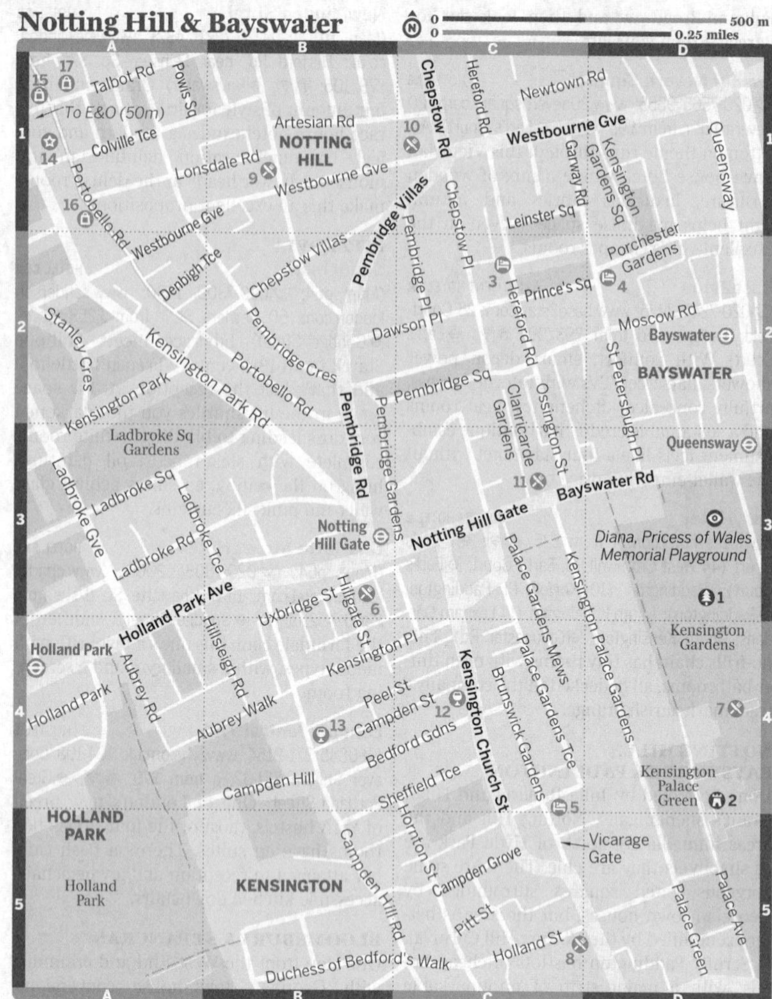

with a splendid double-staircase. Rooms are stylishly modern, dining in the Marcus Wareing–run restaurant is excellent and you can toast the former booking office architecture from the 29m-long bar.

Rough Luxe BOUTIQUE HOTEL £££
(Map p92; ☎0207-837 5338; www.roughluxe.co.uk; 1 Birkenhead St; r £200, with shared bathroom £179; 📶; ⊖King's Cross St Pancras) Half rough, half luxury goes the blurb, and the compelling blend of shabby and chic at this Grade II listed property is a compelling formula. Rooms treat you to the finest quality bed linen, eclectic art works cling to walls, you may get a free-standing copper bath and the service is top-notch, but the wallpaper is fetchingly distressed and the 1970s TV doesn't quite work.

Arran House Hotel B&B ££
(Map p92; ☎020-7636 2186; www.arranhotel-london.com; 77-79 Gower St; s/d/tr/q £70/110/128/132, without bathroom £60/80/105/111; @📶; ⊖Goodge Street) Period features such as cornicing and fireplaces, gorgeous gardens out back for a summer drink and a cosy lounge with two computers pushes this welcom-

Notting Hill & Bayswater

Sights
1 Kensington Gardens....D3
2 Kensington Palace....D4

Sleeping
3 New Linden Hotel....C2
4 Vancouver Studios....D2
5 Vicarage Private Hotel....C4

Eating
Electric Brasserie....(see 14)
6 Geales....B3
7 Orangery....D4
8 Ottolenghi....C5
9 Ottolenghi....B1
10 Taquería....C1
11 Zizzi Italian....C3

Drinking
12 Churchill Arms....C4
13 Windsor Castle....B4

Entertainment
14 Electric Cinema....A1

Shopping
15 Ceramica Blue....A1
16 Portobello Road Market....A1
17 Rough Trade West....A1

ing hotel from the average to the appealing. Squashed en suites or shared bathrooms are the trade-off for these reasonable rates.

Arosfa Hotel B&B ££
(Map p92; ☎020-7636 2115; www.arosfalondon.com; 83 Gower St; s £60-65, d/tr/q £90/102/110; @📶; ⊖Goodge Street) While the decor of the immaculately presented rooms is more understated, Arosfa's guest lounge is blinged up with chandeliers and clear plastic chairs. Recent refurbishments have added en suites to all 15 bedrooms, but they're tiny (putting the 'closet' back into water closet).

Jesmond Hotel B&B £
(Map p92; ☎0207-636 3199; www.jesmonhotel.org.uk; 63 Gower St; s/d/tr/q £60/100/130/145, shared bathroom £50/80/105/135; @📶; ⊖Goodge Street) This family-run B&B in Bloomsbury is a charmer of a place with a very handy location and fab breakfasts. Rooms may be basic and rather small but are clean and everyone is made to feel welcome. Quieter rooms face the pretty garden.

YHA London St Pancras HOSTEL £
(Map p92; ☎020-7388 9998; www.yha.org.uk; 79 Euston Rd; dm/r from £20/61; @📶; ⊖Kings Cross) Recent renovations have made this 185-bed hostel a dependable central London choice – despite the busy road. Rooms range from private doubles to six-bed dorms; most have bathrooms. There's a good bar and cafe but no kitchen.

Ridgemount Hotel B&B ££
(Map p92; ☎020-7636 1141; www.ridgemounthotel.co.uk; 65-67 Gower St; s/d/tr/q £55/78/96/108, without bathroom £43/60/81/96; @📶; ⊖Goodge Street) There's a comfortable, welcoming feel at this old-fashioned, slightly chintzy place that's been in the same family for 40 years.

Harlingford Hotel B&B ££
(Map p92; ☎020-7387 1551; www.harlingfordhotel.com; 61-63 Cartwright Gardens; s/d/tr £86/115/130; @📶; ⊖Russell Square) This family-run Georgian 43-room hotel sports refreshing, upbeat decor: bright-green mosaic-tiled bathrooms (with trendy sinks), fuchsia bedspreads and colourful paintings in a neighbourhood of stiff competition. It's all stairs and no lift; request a 1st-floor room.

Clink78 HOSTEL £
(Map p92; ☎020-7183 9400; www.clinkhostel.com; 78 Kings Cross Rd; dm/r from £12/60; @📶; ⊖Kings Cross) If anyone can think of a more right-on London place to stay than the courthouse where The Clash went on trial, please let us know. You can watch TV from the witness box or sleep in the converted cells, but the majority of the rooms are custom-built and quite comfortable.

Clink261 HOSTEL £
(Map p92; ☎020-7833 9400; www.clinkhostels.com; 261-265 Grays Inn Rd; dm/r £14.60-65; @📶; ⊖Kings Cross) Lacking the history of its sister perhaps, but this brightly refurbished hostel has had a makeover into a funky, welcoming and cheery hostel with very neat dorms, fantastically designed self-catering kitchen, fun TV lounge and internet room.

Generator HOSTEL £
(Map p92; ☎020-7388 7666; www.generatorhostels.com/London; 37 Tavistock Pl; dm/r from

£18/55; @ ; Russell Square) Lashings of primary colours and shiny metal are the hallmarks of this huge hostel. This former police barracks has 820 beds; a bar that stays open until 2am and hosts quizzes, pool competitions, karaoke and DJs; safe-deposit boxes; and a large eating area (but no kitchen). Come to party.

CLERKENWELL & FARRINGDON

In these now fashionable streets, it's hard to find an echo of the notorious 'rookeries' of the 19th century, where families were squeezed into damp, fetid basements, living in possibly the worst conditions in the city's history. This is the London documented so vividly by Dickens.

The availability of accommodation hasn't kept pace with Clerkenwell's revival, but it's still a great area to stay in. The best pickings aren't exactly cheap.

TOP CHOICE Zetter Hotel HOTEL £££
(Map p92; 020-7324 4444; www.thezetter.com; 86-88 Clerkenwell Rd; d from £222, studio £294-438; @ ; Farringdon) Guided by a sustainable ethos (water is supplied by its own bore hole), the 59-room Zetter is lovely, from the fine furnishings to the cutting-edge facilities. The rooftop studios with private patios and long views are the icing on this cake. Bistrot Bruno Loubet (p119) takes care of the fine food end.

Rookery LUXURY HOTEL £££
(Map p72; 020-7336 0931; www.rookeryhotel.com; 12 Peter's Lane, Cowcross St; s £222, d £282-612; @ ; Farringdon) Taking its name from London's notorious slums (Fagin's house in *Oliver Twist* was nearby), this antique-strewn luxury hotel recreates an 18th-century ambience with none of the attendant grime or crime. For a bird's-eye view of St Paul's, book the two-storey Rook's Nest, but be warned: Fagin never had a lift.

Fox & Anchor BOUTIQUE HOTEL
(Map p72; 0121-616 3614; www.foxandanchor.com; 115 Charterhouse St; r £222-246, ste £324, weekend rate r £138-162, ste £234; ; Farringdon or Barbican) Each of the six rooms at this characterful choice above a handsome pub near Smithfield Market is unique: thoughtfully and sumptuously decorated, some with clawfoot baths, but all with up-to-the-minute mod cons and real panache. Rooms are cheaper at weekends.

HOXTON, SHOREDITCH & SPITALFIELDS

Its rough-edged reputation well-smoothed by gentrification and the arrival of moneyed twenty-somethings, this is a knockout area to stay for some of London's best bars and nightlife.

TOP CHOICE Hoxton HOTEL £
(Map p96; 020-7550 1000; www.hoxtonhotels.com; 81 Great Eastern St; d & tw £59-199; @ ; Old Street) A revolutionary pricing structure means that while all the rooms are identical, the hotel aims at constantly full occupancy. Book three months ahead (sign up on the website) and you can, if fortunate, nab a room for £1; you'll also need to book early for £49 to £69 deals. The reasonably sized rooms all have comfy beds, quality linen and TVs that double as computers.

Andaz HOTEL ££
(Map p72; 020-7961 1234; www.london.liverpoolstreet.andaz.com; 40 Liverpool St; r from £145; @ ; Liverpool Street) The former Great Eastern Hotel is now the London flagship for Hyatt's youth-focussed Andaz chain. There's no reception here, just black-clad staff who check you in on laptops. Rooms are a little generic but have free juice, snacks and wi-fi.

EAST END & DOCKLANDS

40 Winks GUESTHOUSE ££
(www.40winks.org; 109 Mile End Rd; s/d £105/175; Stepney Green) This fun Queen Anne town house spills over with charm, eclectic style and whimsy, so much so that the two bedrooms (one single) are devoid of TVs. Fashionistas coming to London make this their first port of call, so book way ahead.

GREENWICH

If you'd rather keep the bustle of central London at arm's length and nightclubbing is your idea of hell, Greenwich offers a village-like ambience and some great old pubs to explore.

Number 16 B&B ££
(020-8853 4337; www.st-alfeges.co.uk; 16 St Alfege Passage; s/d £75/125; @ ; DLR Greenwich) This one-time sweet (candy) shop has two well-appointed doubles and a single, individually decorated in shades of blue, green or yellow and all with bathroom or shower room. The amiable owners make everyone feel at home, with chats and cups of tea in the charming basement kitchen. From the

DLR station head up Greenwich High St and look for St Alfege Passage on your left – it's the lane that skirts the church.

HAMPSTEAD & HIGHGATE

A little further out but still in transport Zone 2, the following are excellent options within walking distance of Hampstead Heath.

Palmers Lodge HOSTEL £

(020-7483 8470; www.palmerslodge.co.uk; 40 College Cres; dm £18-38; Swiss Cottage) Reminiscent of a period murder mystery (in a good way), this former children's hospital has bags of character. Listed by English Heritage, it's stuffed with cornicing, moulded ceilings, original fireplaces and imposing wooden panelling. Ceilings are high, rooms are spacious, and there's a chapel bar with pews, a grand stairway and a roomy lounge. From Swiss Cottage tube station, cross Finchley Rd, turn left and take College Cres, which heads straight up the hill.

Hampstead Village Guesthouse B&B ££

(020-7435 8679; www.hampsteadguesthouse.com; 2 Kemplay Rd; s £55-75, d £80-95, apt £100-175; Hampstead) Eclectic and thoroughly charming, this grand Victorian house has an easygoing hostess, comfy beds and a delightful back garden. There's also a studio flat, which can accommodate up to five people. From the tube station, turn left down Hampstead High St. After a few streets and lanes turn left into Willoughby Rd and then first right into Kemplay Rd.

AIRPORTS

Yotel BUDGET HOTEL £

(020-7100 1100; www.yotel.com; s/d £69/85, or per 4hr £29/45 then per additional hr £8;) Gatwick (South Terminal); Heathrow (Terminal 4) The best news for early-morning flyers since coffee-vending machines, Yotel's smart 'cabins' offer pint-sized luxury: comfy beds, soft lights, internet-connected TVs, monsoon showers and fluffy towels. Swinging cats isn't recommended, but when is it ever?

Eating

Dining out in London has become so fashionable that you can hardly open a menu without banging into some celebrity chef or other. The range and quality of eating options has increased exponentially over the last few decades. Waves of immigrant flavours have deeply infused London cuisine and the expectations of modern-day Londoners are much more demanding.

In this section we have sieved out choice restaurants and cafes noted for their location, value for money, unique character, ambience and, of course, good food. Vegetarians needn't fret; London has a host of dedicated meat-free joints, while most others have veggie offerings. Supermarkets are everywhere in central London. Look out for the big names: Waitrose, Tesco, Sainsbury's, Marks & Spencer, Morrisons and Asda.

WESTMINSTER & ST JAMES'S

Inn the Park BRITISH ££

(Map p58; 0207-451 9999; www.innthepark.com; St James's Park; mains £9.50-18.50; 8am-6pm, till 11pm in spring and summer; Charing Cross or St James's Park) Enjoying a fine location within one of London's best-looking and grandest parks, this Oliver Peyton wooden restaurant rewards diners with fine cuisine and delicious views (especially from the terrace). Book ahead for dinner.

WEST END

Mayfair, Soho and Covent Garden are the gastronomic heart of London, with a blinding choice of restaurants and cuisines at budgets to suit booze hounds, theatre-goers or determined grazers.

Tamarind INDIAN ££

(Map p86; 020-7629 3561; www.tamarindrestaurant.com; 20 Queen St; mains £6.95-28; lunch Sun-Fri, dinner daily; Green Park) A mix of spicy Moghul classics and new creations keep this award-winning Michelin-starred Indian basement restaurant a popular and refreshingly authentic choice.

TOP CHOICE **National Dining Rooms** BRITISH £££

(Map p64; 020-7747 2525; www.peytonandbyrne.co.uk; Sainsbury Wing, National Gallery; mains £14.50-19.50; 10am-5pm Sat-Thu, 10am-8.30pm Fri; Charing Cross) It's fitting that this acclaimed restaurant should celebrate British food, being in the National Gallery and overlooking Trafalgar Sq. For a much cheaper option with the same views, ambience, quality produce and excellent service, try a salad, pie or tart at the adjoining bakery.

Great Queen Street BRITISH ££

(Map p64; 020-7242 0622; 32 Great Queen St; mains £9-19; lunch daily, dinner Mon-Sat; Holborn) Her claret-coloured walls and mismatched wooden chairs convey cosiness and tie-loosening informality, but the daily-changing, seasonal menu is still the very best of British, and booking is a must.

Veeraswamy INDIAN ££
(Map p64; ☎020-7734 1401; www.veeraswamy.com; 99 Regent St, enter Swallow St; mains £15-30, pre- & post-theatre 2-/3-course £18/21; ⊖Piccadilly Circus) Since 1926 Veeraswamy has occupied this prime 1st-floor location, with windows overlooking Regent St – making it Britain's longest-running Indian restaurant. The excellent food, engaging service and exotic, elegant decor make for a memorable eating experience. The entrance is on Swallow St.

Mooli's INDIAN £
(Map p64; www.moolis.com; 50 Frith St; roti wrap £5; ⏲noon-10pm Mon-Wed, to 11.30pm Thu-Sat, closed Sun; ⊖Tottenham Court Road) This snacktastic Soho 'Indian street food' eatery will have you drooling over the homemade rotis packed with scrumptious fillings (meat, paneer, chickpeas), graded through the chilli spectrum.

Wild Honey MODERN EUROPEAN ££
(☎020-7758 9160; www.wildhoneyrestaurant.co.uk; 12 St George St; mains £15-24; ⊖Oxford Circus) If you fancy a relatively affordable meal within the oak-panelled ambience of a top Mayfair restaurant, Wild Honey offers excellent lunch and pre-theatre set menus (respectively, £21.95 and £22.95 for three courses).

L'Atelier de Joël Robuchon FRENCH ££
(Map p64; ☎020-7010 8600; www.joel-robuchon.com; 13 West St; mains £16-34; ⊖Leicester Square) Superchef Robuchon has 25 Michelin stars to his name – and two of them are derived from this, his London flagship. A wall of living foliage adds lushness to the dimly lit dining room, with a sparkling open kitchen as its showcase. Degustation (£125) and set lunch and pre-theatre menus (two/three courses £22/27) are available.

Ben's Cookies BAKERY £
(Map p64; www.benscookies.com; 13a The Piazza, Covent Garden; cookie £1.50; ⏲10am-8pm Mon-Sat, 11am-7pm Sun; ⊖Covent Garden) Simply fantastic – gooey and often warm – freshly baked cookies in 18 delectable varieties. You won't want to leave.

Dean Street Townhouse TEAHOUSE ££
(Map p64; www.deanstreettownhouse.com; 69-71 Dean St; afternoon tea £16.75; ⊖Tottenham Court Road) Serene afternoon tea in the parlour of this fine boutique hotel is the perfect place to unwind on cosy, upholstered furniture with little to occupy you but tea served with finger sandwiches, pastries, scones, crumpets, clotted cream and jam.

Giaconda Dining Room MODERN EUROPEAN ££
(Map p64; ☎020-7240 3334; www.giacondadining.com; 9 Denmark St; mains £13.50-33; ⏲Tue-Fri lunch & dinner, dinner Sat; ⊖Tottenham Court Road) Blink and you'll miss this 10-table restaurant (we did at first). It's well worth hunting down for quality British, French and Italian dishes and attentive service. Pig trotters are a specialty but for those less au fait with offal, there's always a choice of fish dishes.

Abeno Too JAPANESE £
(Map p64; www.abeno.co.uk; 17-18 Great Newport St; mains £8-13; ⊖Leicester Square) This restaurant specialises in soba (noodles) and *okonomiyaki* (Japanese-style pancakes), which are cooked in front of you on a hotplate. Sit at the bar or by the window and feast.

Yauatcha CHINESE ££
(Map p64; ☎020-7494 8888; www.yauatcha.com; 15 Broadwick St; dishes £4-16; ⊖Piccadilly Circus or Oxford Circus) Dim sum restaurants don't come much cooler than this, housed in Richard Rogers–designed Ingeni building, with a choice of light-filled ground-floor tables or hip basement zone. The *dim sum* is outstanding.

Arbutus MODERN EUROPEAN ££
(Map p64; ☎020-7734 4545; www.arbutusrestaurant.co.uk; 63-64 Frith St; mains £14-20; ⊖Tottenham Court Road) Focussing on seasonal produce, inventive dishes and value-for-money set meals, Anthony Demetre's Michelin-starred brainchild just keeps getting better.

Nordic Bakery SCANDINAVIAN £
(Map p64; www.nordicbakery.com; 14a Golden Sq; snacks £4-5; ⏲8am-8pm Mon-Fri, 9am-7pm Sat, 11am-6pm Sun; ⊖Piccadilly Circus) As straightforward and stylish as you'd expect from the Scandinavians, this small cafe has bare wooden walls and uncomplicated Nordic snacks, such as sticky Finnish cinnamon buns, salmon served on dark rye bread and tosca cake.

Fernandez & Wells DELICATESSEN, CAFE £
(Map p64; www.fernandezandwells.com; 73 Beak St; mains £4-5; ⊖Piccadilly Circus) A wonderful West End mini-chain, this is one of the four branches of Fernandez & Wells, each occupying small, friendly and elegant spaces. Both the **cafe** and the **espresso bar** do sandwiches and incredibly good coffee.

Bocca di Lupo ITALIAN ££

(Map p64; ☎020-7734 2223; www.boccadilupo.com; 12 Archer St; mains £11-25; ⊖Piccadilly Circus) Hidden on a dark Soho backstreet, Bocca radiates elegant sophistication, setting taste buds a quiver with a mouth-watering menu spanning Italy's culinary regions.

Barrafina SPANISH ££

(Map p64; ☎020-7813 8016; www.barrafina.co.uk; 54 Frith St; tapas £5-13; ⊖Tottenham Court Road) The tapas here may not be as reasonably priced as you'd get in Spain, but they are simply infused with quality.

Bar Shu CHINESE ££

(Map p64; www.bar-shu.co.uk; 28 Frith St; mains £8-20; ⊖Piccadilly Circus or Leicester Square) Authentic Sìchuān food long eluded the sweet-toothed Cantonese chefs of Chinatown, but Bar Shu concocts all the right flavours with dishes steeped in smoked chillies and the crucial aromatic peppercorn.

Hummus Bros CAFE £

(www.hbros.co.uk; mains £4-8;) Soho (Map p64; 88 Wardour St; Piccadilly Circus); Holborn (Map p92; 37-63 Southampton Row; Holborn); Cheapside (128 Cheapside; St Pauls) Don't come here if you're chickpea-challenged, because this informal place is hummus heaven. It comes in small or regular bowls with a choice of meat or veggie toppings and a side of pita bread.

THE CITY

You'll be sorely dismayed if you've got an empty belly on a Sunday morning in the City. Even during the busy weekdays, the chain eateries are often your best option.

TOP CHOICE Sweetings SEAFOOD ££

(Map p72; www.sweetingsrestaurant.com; 39 Queen Victoria St; mains £12.50-32; lunch Mon-Fri; ⊖Mansion House) Serving customers since 1889, Sweetings is a massively popular fixture on the culinary map of the City, serving delicious and sustainably sourced fish (grilled, fried or poached), fried whitebait, smoked trout and the standout chef's pie (£13.50).

Restaurant at St Paul's MODERN BRITISH £££

(Map p72; www.restaurantatstpauls.co.uk; Crypt, St Paul's Cathedral ; 2/3 course lunch £21.95/24.95; noon-3pm; ⊖St Paul's) Dine in the crypt of St Paul's Cathedral at this choicely located restaurant with a short and simple but regularly changing menu offering two- or three-course lunches and a good-value express lunch, as well as afternoon tea.

SOUTH BANK

Popular restaurants make the most of the iconic riverside views but scouting around turns up gems all over the place. For a feed with a local feel, head to Borough Market (p132) or Bermondsey St.

TOP CHOICE Laughing Gravy BRITISH ££

(Map p78; ☎020-7998 1707; www.thelaughinggravy.co.uk; 154 Blackfriars Rd; mains £8.50-17.50; 11am-late Mon-Fri, 5.30pm-late Sat, noon-6pm Sun; ⊖Southwark) Recently steered in a lucrative fresh direction by new owners, this restaurant is a Southwark gem, with a surefire menu combining locally sourced food and culinary talent, plus splendid roasts on Sunday and attentive service all round.

Oxo Tower Brasserie FUSION £££

(Map p78; ☎020-7803 3888; www.harveynichols.com/restaurants/oxo-tower-london; Barge House St; mains £18-26; ⊖Waterloo) The extravagant views are the big drawcard, so skip the restaurant and head for the slightly less extravagantly priced brasserie, or if you're not hungry, the bar. The food is excellent, combining European and East Asian flavours. Set-price menus (two/three courses £22.50/26.50) are offered at lunchtime, before 6.15pm and after 10pm.

Magdalen MODERN BRITISH ££

(Map p78; ☎020-7403 1342; www.magdalenrestaurant.co.uk; 152 Tooley St; mains £14-18, lunch 2/3 course £16/19; lunch Mon-Fri, dinner Mon-Sat; ⊖London Bridge) This lovely Tooley St restaurant hits the spot for anyone determined to savour some of London's best Modern British fare. With a focus on charcuterie, lovingly cooked and presented, it's not the place to bring a vegetarian or a weight-conscious waif on a date.

Anchor & Hope GASTROPUB ££

(Map p78; 36 The Cut; mains £12-17; lunch Tue-Sun, dinner Mon-Sat; ⊖Southwark) The hope is that you'll get a table without waiting hours because you can't book at this quintessential gastropub, except for Sunday lunch at 2pm. The anchor is gutsy, unashamedly carnivorous British food.

BELGRAVIA

Thomas Cubitt BRITISH ££

(Map p86; ☎020-7730 6060; www.thethomascubitt.co.uk; 44 Elizabeth St; mains £17-23; ⊖Victoria)

WORTH A TRIP

THE BURGERS OF BRIXTON

Honest Burgers (☎020-7733 7963; www.honestburgers.co.uk; Unit 12, Brixton Village; burgers from £6.50; ⏰noon-4pm Sun-Wed, noon-4pm & 6-10pm Thu-Sat; Brixton), an excellent-value burger outfit in the trendy and enterprising Brixton Village, has won serious plaudits for its juicy and tender burgers and glorious rosemary-seasoned triple-cooked chips. It's well worth waiting for a table, which you could well have to do (it's titchy and only seats around 30; no bookings).

The bar below gets rammed to the impressively high rafters with the swanky Belgravia set, and upstairs is this excellent, elegant dining room. The culinary focus is thoroughly British and deftly executed. The downstairs menu is cheaper (£10 to £17).

Kazan TURKISH ££
(www.kazan-restaurant.com; 93-94 Wilton Rd; mains £11.95-15.95; ⊖Victoria) Kazan received repeated accolades for its set *meze* platters, *shish* kebabs and *karniyarik* (lamb-stuffed aubergines). Flavours are rich and full, service attentive and the refreshingly unaffected setting allows diners to concentrate on the culinary aromas. Seafood and vegetarian options also available.

KNIGHTSBRIDGE

Dinner by Heston Blumenthal MODERN BRITISH £££
(Map p86; ☎0207-201 3833; www.dinnerbyheston.com; Mandarin Oriental Hyde Park, 66 Knightsbridge; set lunch £28, mains £32-72; ⊖Knightsbridge) The eagerly awaited opening of sumptuously presented Dinner is a gastronomic tour de force, ushering diners on a tour of British culinary history (with inventive modern inflections). The interior design is a similar triumph, from the glass-walled kitchen and its overhead clock mechanism to the large windows onto the park.

Marcus Wareing at the Berkeley FRENCH £££
(Map p86; ☎020-7235 1200; www.marcus-wareing.com; Berkeley Hotel, Wilton Pl; 3-course lunch/dinner £38/80; ⊖Knightsbridge) Wareing runs this one-time Gordon Ramsay restaurant under his own name, and its reputation for exquisite food and exemplary service has only been enhanced.

CHELSEA & KENSINGTON

These highbrow neighbourhoods harbour some of London's very best (and priciest) restaurants.

Tom's Kitchen MODERN EUROPEAN ££
(Map p86; ☎020-7349 0202; www.tomskitchen.co.uk; 27 Cale St; breakfast £4-15, mains £13.90-30; ⏰breakfast Mon-Fri, lunch & dinner daily; ⊖South Kensington) Celebrity chef Tom Aikens' restaurant keeps the magic flowing through the day, with award-winning breakfasts and pancakes drawing acclaim and crowds to its informal, but engaging, dining setting.

L'Etranger FRENCH, JAPANESE ££
(Map p86; ☎020-7584 1118; www.etranger.co.uk; 36 Gloucester Rd; mains £15-29; ⊖Gloucester Road) A refined grey and burgundy interior (echoed in waitress uniforms that are part kimono, part Parisian runway) sets the tone for a romantic formal dining experience. While most of the menu is French, it's also possible to blow the budget on sashimi and five types of caviar. The two-/three-course weekday set lunch and pre-6.45pm dinner are £17/20.

Orsini ITALIAN ££
(Map p86; www.orsiniristorante.com; 8a Thurloe Pl; snacks £2-6, mains £9-16; ⏰8am-10pm; ⊖South Kensington) Marinated in authentic Italian charm, this tiny family-run eatery serves excellent espresso and deliciously fresh baguettes stuffed with Parma ham and mozzarella. More substantial fare is offered in the evenings.

Gordon Ramsay FRENCH £££
(Map p86; ☎020-7352 4441; www.gordonramsay.com; 68 Royal Hospital Rd; 3-course lunch/dinner £45/90; ⊖Sloane Square) One of Britain's finest restaurants and London's longest-running with three coveted Michelin stars, you'll need to book ahead and hop into your best togs: jeans and T-shirts don't get past the door. And if you've seen the chef in action, you'll know not to argue.

NOTTING HILL, BAYSWATER & PADDINGTON

Notting Hill teems with good places to eat, from cheap takeaways to atmospheric pubs and restaurants worthy of the fine-dining tag. Queensway has the best strip of Asian restaurants this side of Soho.

Taquería MEXICAN £
(Map p110; www.taqueria.co.uk; 139-143 Westbourne Grove; tacos from £4.10; ⏲lunch & dinner; ⊖Notting Hill Gate) Its sustainable credentials are as exacting and appealing as its authentic soft-corn, freshly-made tortillas – this place instantly elbows other Mexican restaurants into the Tex-Mex shade. Fish is all sustainably sourced and the pork, chicken and eggs come free range.

Geales SEAFOOD ££
(Map p110; ☎020-7727 7528; www.geales.com; 2 Farmer St; 2-course lunch £10, mains £10-18; ⏲closed lunch Mon; ⊖Notting Hill Gate) Frying fish since 1939, Geales' fish is highly succulent, although chips disappointingly cost extra (outside of the set lunch) in what should be a classic combination. The corner location, tucked away off energetic Notting Hill Gate, is a big draw, with tables spilling out onto a quiet street.

Electric Brasserie FRENCH ££
(Map p110; ☎020-7908 9696; www.electricbrasserie.com; 191 Portobello Rd; breakfasts £5.50-13.50, mains £9-36; ⊖Ladbroke Grove) The leather-and-cream look is coolly suited to this brasserie attached to the Electric Cinema (p129). And the food's excellent as well, whether it's breakfast, weekend brunches, hearty lunches or dinner. If you're feeling decadent, lobster and chips (£36) is the way to go.

E&O ASIAN ££
(www.rickerrestaurants.com; 14 Blenheim Crescent; mains £9.50-28; ⊖Ladbroke Grove) This splendid-looking restaurant off Portobello Road lures crowds with its ever-popular Japanese-Chinese Pan-Asian fusion fare, sleek black-and-white minimalism and cool bar.

Satay House MALAYSIAN £
(☎020-7723 6763; www.satay-house.co.uk; 13 Sale Pl; mains £5-19; ⊖Edgware Road) Authentic Malaysian cuisine, including some dishes that will blow your head off, have been served here for nearly 40 years. Book ahead for an upstairs table, although the communal tables in the basement can be fun. Sale Pl is one block along Sussex Gardens from Edgware Rd.

MARYLEBONE

You won't go too far wrong planting yourself on a table anywhere along Marylebone's charming High St.

Providores & Tapa Room FUSION £££
(Map p89; ☎020-7935 6175; www.theprovidores.co.uk; 109 Marylebone High St; 2/3/4/5 courses £30/43/53/60; ⊖Baker Street) New Zealand's most distinctive culinary export since kiwi fruit, chef Peter Gordon works his fusion magic here, matching his creations with NZ wines. Downstairs, in a cute play on words, the Tapa Room (as in the Polynesian barkcloth) serves sophisticated tapas, along with excellent breakfasts.

La Fromagerie CAFE £
(Map p89; www.lafromagerie.co.uk; 2-6 Moxon St; mains £6-13; ⊖Baker Street) This deli-cafe has bowls of delectable salads, antipasto, peppers and beans scattered about the long communal table. Huge slabs of bread invite you to tuck in, and all the while the heavenly waft from the cheese room beckons.

Locanda Locatelli ITALIAN ££
(Map p89; ☎020-7935 9088; www.locandalocatelli.com; 8 Seymour St; mains £11-30; ⊖Marble Arch) Known for its sublime but pricey pasta dishes, this dark but quietly glamorous restaurant in an otherwise unremarkable hotel is one of London's hottest tables.

BLOOMSBURY & ST PANCRAS

Dabbous MODERN EUROPEAN ££
(Map p92; ☎0207-323 1544; www.dabbous.co.uk; 39 Whitfield St; mains £11-14, 3/4-course set lunch £21/24; ⊖Goodge Street) An innovative approach to flavour and healthy ingredients lies behind this restaurant's growing popularity. The rather stark and pared down ambience may not suit all tastes, but it's offset by an inventive menu full of surprises and ideas; the basement cocktail bar is just the place for a pre-meal libation.

North Sea Fish Restaurant FISH & CHIPS £
(Map p92; www.northseafishrestaurant.co.uk; 7-8 Leigh St; mains £9-20; ⏲closed Sun; ⊖Russell Square) Every day is fryday except Sunday at the North Sea, a classic chippie for eat-in or takeaway with jumbo-sized plaice or halibut steaks, deep-fried or grilled, and large servings of chips.

Pâtisserie Deux Amis FRENCH £
(Map p92; ☎020-7383 7029; 63 Judd St; baguettes from £2.90; ⊖Russell Square or King's Cross St Pancras) If you crave scrummy croissants, pain au chocolate, fine coffee, filled baguettes and all the gourmand trappings of Gallic breakfasts and snacks, this bijou patisserie is a

delight, with a few tables flung out front and excellent service all round.

Chilli Cool CHINESE £

(Map p92; www.chillicool.com; 15 Leigh St; mains £4.80-19.80; ⊖Russell Square) Don't judge a Chinese book by its cover – what Chilli Cool (Chinese name Lao Chengdu, referring to the capital of Sichuan) lacks in gloss is more than heartily compensated for by its surefire Sichuan menu, which spills forth all the classics: *dan dan* noodles, *ma po tofu* (tofu with nuggets of mince in a spicy sauce) and sliced beef Sicchuan style.

Diwana Bhel Poori House INDIAN £

(Map p92; 121-123 Drummond St; mains £7-9; ; ⊖Euston or Euston Square) This ace Indian vegetarian eatery specialises in *bhel poori* (sweet-and-sour, soft and crunchy 'party mix' snacks), *dosas* (filled rice-flour pancakes), *thali* and the all-you-can-eat, value lunchtime buffet is a legendary blowout.

FITZROVIA

Tucked away behind busy Tottenham Court Rd, Fitzrovia's Charlotte and Goodge Sts form one of central London's most vibrant eating precincts.

TOP CHOICE **Hakkasan** CHINESE £££

(Map p64; 7927 7000; www.hakkasan.com; 8 Hanway Pl; mains £9.50-42; ⊖Tottenham Court Road) Michelin-starred Hakkasan – hidden down a lane like all fashionable haunts should be – elegantly pairs fine Chinese dining with stunning design and some persuasive cocktail chemistry. The low lighting hits all the right romantic notes and the all-embracing menu ranges from Sichuan *ma po doufu* to grilled Shanghai dumplings, Peking duck and beyond.

Salt Yard SPANISH, ITALIAN ££

(Map p64; 020-7637 0657; www.saltyard.co.uk; 54 Goodge St; tapas £4-8; ⊖Goodge Street) Named after the place where cold meats are cured, this softly lit joint serves delicious Spanish and Italian tapas. Try the roasted chicken leg with gnocchi, wild garlic and sorrel, or flex your palate with courgette flowers stuffed with cheese and drizzled with honey.

Lantana CAFE £

(Map p64; www.lantanacafe.co.uk; 13 Charlotte Pl; mains £4-10; breakfast & lunch Mon-Sat; ⊖Goodge Street) Excellent coffee and substantial, inventive brunches induce queues on Saturday mornings outside this Australian-style cafe.

CAMDEN TOWN

Camden's great for cheap eats, while neighbouring Chalk Farm and Primrose Hill are salted with gastropubs and upmarket restaurants.

CHAIN-CHAIN-CHAIN, CHAIN OF FOODS

It's an unnerving, but not uncommon, experience to discover the idiosyncratic cafe or pub you were so proud of finding on your first day in London popping up on every other high street. But among the endless Caffe Neros, Pizza Expresses and All-Bar-Ones are some gems, or, at least, great fallback options. The following are some of the best:

GBK (Map p92; www.gbk.co.uk) Gourmet Burger Kitchens, dishing up creative burger constructions, including lots of vegetarian options.

Konditor & Cook (Map p64; www.konditorandcook.com) London's best bakery chain, serving excellent cakes, pastries, bread and coffee.

Leon (Map p64; www.leonrestaurants.co.uk) Focussing on fresh, seasonal food (salads, wraps and the like).

Nando's (Map p95; 020-7424 9040; www.nandos.co.uk; 57-58 Chalk Farm Rd; Camden Town) Loved by Londoners for fantastic value, mouthwatering spicy chicken *a la portuguesa* – with some blindingly hot peri-peri sauces.

Ping Pong (Map p89; www.pingpongdimsum.com; lunch & dinner) Chinese dumpling joints.

Pizza Express (Map p64; 020-7437 9595; www.pizzaexpress.com; 10 Dean St; mains £6.95-11.50) Excellent pizza, neat ambience and standout locations across London.

Wagamama (Map p64; www.wagamama.com; 4 Streatham St, Bloomsbury) Japanese noodles taking over the world from their London base.

Zizzi (Map p110; www.zizzi.co.uk) Wood-fired pizza.

TOP CHOICE Market Restaurant MODERN BRITISH ££
(Map p95; ☎020-7267 9700; www.marketrestaurant.co.uk; 43 Parkway; 2-course lunch £10, mains £10-14; ⌚lunch & dinner Mon-Sat, lunch Sun; ⊖Camden Town) In a simple, forthright but at the same time appealing setting of bare brick walls and basic wooden chairs, this fantastic and uncomplicated restaurant does a magnificent job of preparing wholesome British cuisine, with the occasional European nod.

Mango Room CARIBBEAN ££
(Map p95; ☎020-7482 5065; www.mangoroom.co.uk; 10-12 Kentish Town Rd; mains £11-14; ⊖Camden Town) Mango Room is an upmarket Caribbean experience serving a mix of modern and traditional dishes: Creole snapper, goat curry, jerk chicken etc set to a ska and reggae musical backdrop.

ISLINGTON

Allow at least an evening to explore Islington's Upper St, along with the lanes leading off it.

TOP CHOICE Le Mercury FRENCH £
(Map p120; ☎020-7354 4088; www.lemercury.co.uk; 140a Upper St; mains £7-10; ⊖Highbury & Islington) A cosy Gallic haunt ideal for cash-strapped Casanovas, given that it appears much more expensive than it is. Sunday lunch by the open fire upstairs is a treat, although you'll have to book.

Ottolenghi BAKERY, MEDITERRANEAN ££
(www.ottolenghi.co.uk; mains £10-15; ✎) Islington (Map p120; ☎020-7288 1454; 287 Upper St; ⌚8am-11pm Mon-Sat, 9am-7pm Sun; ⊖Angel); Belgravia (Map p86; 13 Motcomb St; ⌚8am-8pm Mon-Fri, 8am-7pm Sat, 9am-6pm Sun; ⊖Knightsbridge); Kensington (Map p110; 1 Holland St; ⌚8am-8pm Mon-Fri, 8am-7pm Sat, 9am-6pm Sun; ⊖High St Kensington); Notting Hill (Map p110; 63 Ledbury Rd ; ⌚8am-8pm Mon-Fri, 8am-7pm Sat, 8.30am-6pm Sun; ⊖Notting Hill Gate) Mountains of meringues draw you through the door, where a sumptuous array of bakery treats and salads greets you. Meals are as light and tasty as the lovely white interior design. Vegetarians are well catered for. The Islington branch is open till later – until 11pm, and 7pm on Sundays.

CLERKENWELL & FARRINGDON

Clerkenwell's hidden gems are well worth digging for. Pedestrianised Exmouth Market is a good place to start.

TOP CHOICE Bistrot Bruno Loubet FRENCH ££
(Map p92; ☎020-7324 4455; www.bistrotbrunoloubet.com; 86-88 Clerkenwell Rd; mains £12-17; ⌚breakfast, lunch & dinner; ⊖Farringdon) Facing onto St John's Sq, this elegant restaurant from Bruno Loubet at the Zetter (p112) matches top quality ingredients and inventive taste combinations with impeccable execution, in the food, cocktails and the home-infused aperitifs.

St John BRITISH ££
(Map p72; ☎020-7251 0848; www.stjohnrestaurant.com; 26 St John St; mains £14-22; ⊖Farringdon) Bright whitewashed brick walls, high ceilings and simple wooden furniture keep diners free to concentrate on the world-famous nose-to-tail offerings. Expect chitterlings and ox tongue.

Little Bay EUROPEAN £
(Map p92; ☎020-7278 1234; www.little-bay.co.uk; 171 Farringdon Rd; mains before/after 7pm £6.45/8.45; ⊖Farringdon) The crushed-velvet ceiling, handmade twisted lamps that improve around the room (as their creator got better at making them) and elaborately painted bar and tables showing nymphs frolicking are weird but fun. The hearty food is very good value.

Modern Pantry FUSION ££
(Map p92; ☎020-7553 9210; www.themodernpantry.co.uk; 47-48 St John's Sq; mains £15-22; ⌚breakfast, lunch & dinner; ⊖Farringdon) One of London's most talked-about eateries, this three-floor Georgian town house in the heart of Clerkenwell has a cracking innovative, all-day menu.

Medcalf BRITISH ££
(Map p92; ☎020-7833 3533; www.medcalfbar.co.uk; 40 Exmouth Market; mains £10-16; ⌚closed dinner Sun; ⊖Farringdon) The stylish Medcalf is one of the best value hang-outs right in the heart of Exmouth Market. Housed in a beautifully converted 1912 butcher's shop, it serves up interesting and well-realised British fare.

HOXTON, SHOREDITCH & SPITALFIELDS

From the hit-and-miss Bangladeshi restaurants of Brick Lane to the Vietnamese strip on Kingsland Rd, and the Jewish, Spanish, French, Italian and Greek eateries in between, the East End's cuisine is as multicultural as its residents.

Islington

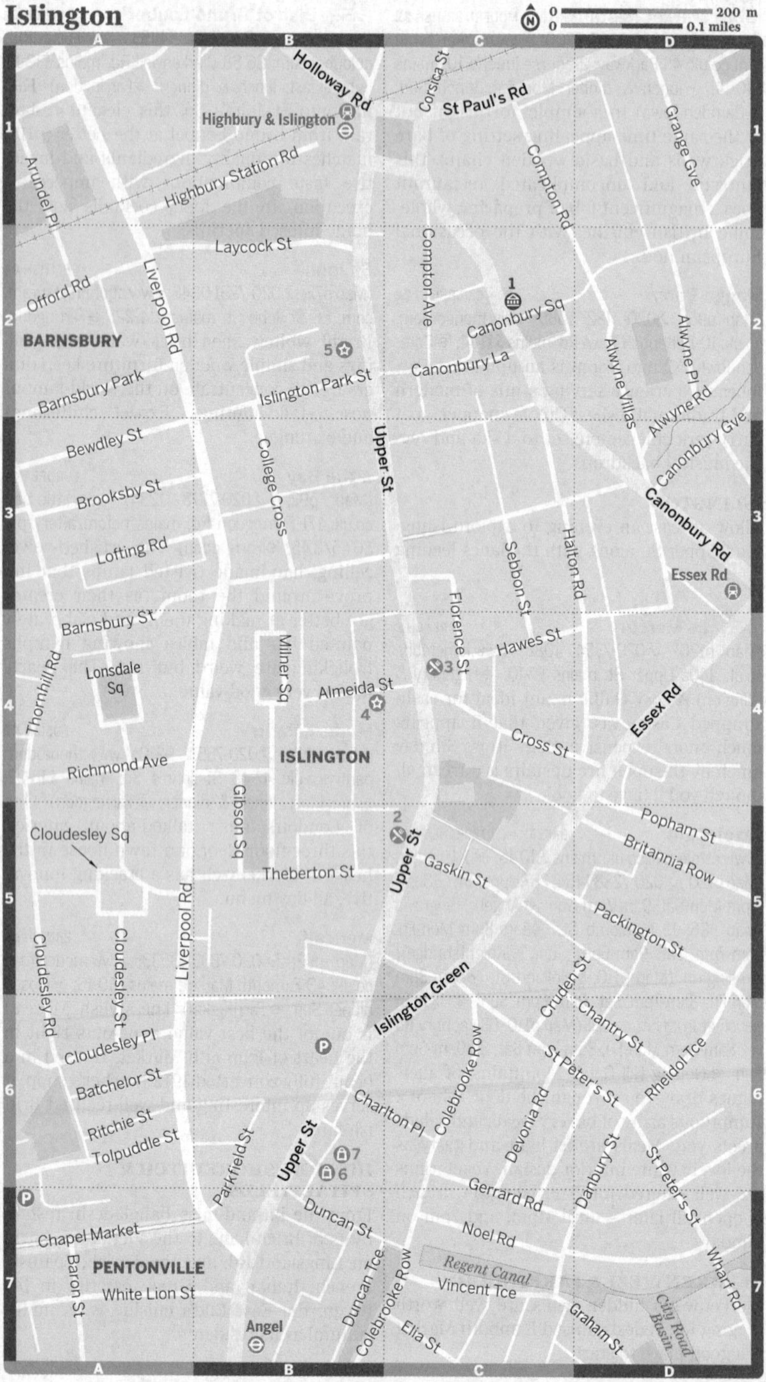

0 — 200 m
0 — 0.1 miles

A B C D
1 2 3 4 5 6 7

Holloway Rd
Highbury & Islington
Corsica St
St Paul's Rd
Grange Gve
Arundel Pl
Highbury Station Rd
Compton Rd
Laycock St
Compton Ave
1
Offord Rd
Liverpool Rd
Canonbury Sq
BARNSBURY
5
Alwyne Villas
Alwyne Pl
Canonbury La
Barnsbury Park
Islington Park St
Alwyne Rd
Bewdley St
Upper St
Canonbury Gve
College Cross
Brooksby St
Canonbury Rd
Lofting Rd
Sebbon St
Halton Rd
Essex Rd
Florence St
Barnsbury St
Milner Sq
Hawes St
3
Lonsdale Sq
Thornhill Rd
Almeida St
4
Essex Rd
Cross St
Richmond Ave
ISLINGTON
Gibson Sq
2
Popham St
Cloudesley Sq
Britannia Row
Theberton St
Gaskin St
Packington St
Cloudesley Rd
Cloudesley St
Liverpool Rd
Islington Green
Cruden St
Chantry St
Cloudesley Pl
Colebrooke Row
St Peter's St
Rheidol Tce
Batchelor St
Charlton Pl
Devonia Rd
Ritchie St
Tolpuddle St
Parkfield St
Upper St
7
6
Danbury St
Gerrard Rd
St Peter's St
Duncan St
Noel Rd
Chapel Market
Regent Canal
Wharf Rd
PENTONVILLE
Duncan Tce
Colebrooke Row
Vincent Tce
Baron St
White Lion St
Graham St
City Road Basin
Angel
Elia St

Islington

Sights

1 Estorick Collection of Modern Italian Art C2

Eating

2 Le Mercury C5
3 Ottolenghi C4

Entertainment

4 Almeida B4
5 Hope & Anchor B2

Shopping

6 Camden Passage Market B6
7 Laura J London B6

TOP CHOICE Poppies FISH & CHIPS £

(Map p96; www.poppiesfishandchips.co.uk; 6-8 Hanbury St; mains £6-11; 11am-11pm, to 10.30pm Sun; Shoreditch High Street, Shoreditch High Street) Frying since 1945, this fantastic Spitalfields chippie is a retro delight, a throwback to the 1950s with iconic jukebox, wall-to-wall memorabilia, waitresses in pinnies and hairnets and classic fish and chips (plus jellied eels).

Fifteen ITALIAN ££

(0871 330 1515; www.fifteen.net; 15 Westland Pl; breakfast £2-8.50, trattoria £6-11, restaurant £11-25; breakfast, lunch & dinner; Old Street) Jamie Oliver's culinary philanthropy started at Fifteen, set up to give unemployed young people a shot at a career. The Italian food is beyond excellent, and, surprisingly, even those on limited budgets can afford a visit. From Old Street tube station, take City Rd and after 300m turn right into Westland Place.

Sông Que VIETNAMESE £

(Map p96; www.songque.co.uk; 134 Kingsland Rd E2; mains £6-9; Hoxton) Arrive after 7.30pm and you can expect to queue: this humble eatery is one of the best Vietnamese restaurants in London and you'll be shunted out shortly after your last bite. Sông Que is 300m along Kingsland Rd, the continuation of Shoreditch High St.

Princess of Shoreditch GASTROPUB ££

(Map p96; 020-7729 9270; www.theprincessofshoreditch.com; 76 Paul St; pub mains £10-18.50; Old Steet) Perfect for a drink or a meal, the Princess can get busy thanks to its excellent gastropub menu, fine wine list, choice ales and particularly good-looking interior. Upstairs is the slightly more expensive dining room.

L'Anima ITALIAN ££

(Map p96; 020-7422 7000; www.lanima.co.uk; 1 Snowden St; mains £15-32.50; lunch Mon-Fri, dinner Mon-Sat; Liverpool Street) Sleek design meets accomplished cooking – what could be more Italian? The capacious space is divided into a formal dining room and a bar/lounge where you can drop in for a quick pasta fix.

Albion BRITISH ££

(Map p96; www.albioncaff.co.uk; 2-4 Boundary St; mains £9-13; Old Street) For those wanting to be taken back to Dear Old Blighty's cuisine but with rather less grease and stodge, this self-consciously retro 'caff' serves up top-quality bangers and mash, steak-and-kidney pies, devilled kidneys and, of course, fish and chips.

Les Trois Garçons MODERN FRENCH £££

(Map p96; 7613 1924; www.lestroisgarcons.com; 1 Club Row; 2/3 courses £39.50/45.50; closed dinner Sun; Shoreditch High Street) A virtual menagerie of stuffed or bronze animals fills every surface, while chandeliers dangle between a set of suspended handbags. The food is great, if overpriced, and the small army of bow-tie-wearing waiters unobtrusively delivers complimentary bread and tasty gifts from the kitchen.

Brick Lane Beigel Bake BAGELS £

(Map p96; 159 Brick Lane; most bagels less than £2; 24hr; Liverpool Street) Always busy, this relic of London's Jewish East End is more takeaway than cafe and sells dirt-cheap bagels, a top late-night snack on a bellyful of booze.

EAST END

TOP CHOICE Formans BRITISH ££

(020-8525 2365; www.formans.co.uk; Stour Rd, Fish Island; mains £11.50-20; dinner Thu & Fri, brunch & dinner Sat, lunch Sun; Hackney) Curing fish since 1905, riverside Formans boasts prime views over the Olympic stadium alongside a delectable choice of smoked salmon (including the signature London cure) and seafood plus a choice of other mouthwatering British dishes. A viewing gallery into the smokery and a lounge bar rounds out an attractive picture.

GREENWICH & SOUTH LONDON

Tai Won Mein NOODLES £

(39 Greenwich Church St; mains from £4.95; ⏲11.30am-11.30pm; DLR Cutty Sark) This busy Cantonese restaurant serves epic portions of steaming noodles to those overcoming Greenwich's titanic sights. Flavours are simple, but fresh, and the namesake *tai won mein* (big bowl of noodles) seafood noodles may have you applauding (but put your chopsticks down first).

Drinking

As long as there's been a city, Londoners have loved to drink – and, as history shows, often immoderately. The pub is the hub of social life and, despite depleting numbers, there's always one near at hand. When the sun shines, drinkers spill out into the streets, parks and squares.

Boho Soho is undoubtedly the heart of bar culture, with enough variety to cater to all tastes. Still great for grungy boozers and rock kids, Camden has lost ground on the bohemian-cool front to Hoxton and Shoreditch.

Neighbourhoods such as Clerkenwell, Islington, Southwark, Notting Hill and Earl's Court are bursting at their beer-addled seams with pub-crawl potential.

Mirroring its worker-base, the City is a Monday to Friday spot and several of its historic pubs shut up shop at weekends or on Sundays. South London has some fine historic pubs near the river.

The price of beer in pubs is enough to drive you to drink – expect to pay upwards of £3.25 per pint of lager.

WEST END

Gordon's Wine Bar BAR

(Map p64; www.gordonswinebar.com; 47 Villiers St; ⊖Embankment) What's not to love about this cavernous, candlelit wine cellar that's been practically unchanged for the last 120 years? Get here before the office crowd (generally around 6pm) or forget about getting a table.

TOP CHOICE **French House** BAR

(Map p64; 49 Dean St; ⊖Leicester Square) French House, the meeting place of the Free French Forces during WWII, is Soho's legendary boho boozer with a history to match: De Gaulle is said to have knocked back shots here, while Dylan Thomas, Peter O'Toole, Brendan Behan and Francis Bacon all conspired to drink the place dry. The no-mobile phones, no-music and no-TV ruling only amplifies the mystique.

LAB COCKTAIL BAR

(Map p64; www.lab-townhouse.com; 12 Old Compton St; ⊖Leicester Square) The decor of the London Academy of Bartending has been left behind, but a frisson of creativity runs through the cocktail menu and LAB's mixologists can have your tastebuds singing.

Princess Louise PUB

(Map p64; 208 High Holborn; ⊖Holborn) This late-19th-century Victorian boozer is arguably London's most beautiful pub. Spectacularly decorated with fine tiles, etched mirrors, plasterwork and a gorgeous central horse-shoe bar, it gets packed with the after-work crowd.

Coach & Horses PUB

(Map p64; www.coachandhorsessoho.co.uk; 29 Greek St; ⊖Leicester Square) Regulars at this no-nonsense Soho institution have included Francis Bacon, Peter O'Toole and Lucien Freud. The Wednesday and Saturday night singalongs are tops.

Lamb & Flag PUB

(Map p64; 33 Rose St; ⊖Covent Garden) Everyone's Covent Garden 'find', this historic pub is often as jammed with punters as it is packed with history. Built in 1623 and formerly (and evocatively) called the 'Bucket of Blood', inside it's all brass fittings and creaky wooden floors.

Galvin at Windows BAR

(Map p58; www.galvinatwindows.com; The Hilton, 22 Park Lane; ⊖Hyde Park Corner) Be stunned by both the views and the cocktail prices at this 28th-floor eyrie at the Hilton, overlooking Hyde Park.

Jewel COCKTAIL BAR

(www.jewelbar.com) Piccadilly Circus (Map p64; 4-6 Glasshouse St; ⊖Piccadilly Circus); Covent Garden (Map p64; 29-30 Maiden Lane; ⊖Covent Garden) Chandeliers, banquettes, cocktails and, in Piccadilly, sunset views.

Monmouth Coffee Company CAFE

(⏲Mon-Sat) Covent Garden (Map p64; 27 Monmouth St; ⊖Covent Garden); Borough (Map p78; 2 Park St; ⊖London Bridge) There's an array of treats on the counter, but it's the coffee that's the star, nay god, here. Chat to a caffeinated stranger on one of the tight tables at the back, or grab a takeaway and slink off to a nearby lane for your fix.

THE CITY

Vertigo 42 BAR

(Map p72; ☎020-7877 7842; www.vertigo42.co.uk; Tower 42, Old Broad St; ⊖Liverpool St) Book a two-hour slot in this 42nd-floor champagne bar (no shorts, caps or flipflops) with stunning vertiginous views across London from the former National Westminster Tower. Reservations only.

Ye Olde Cheshire Cheese PUB

(Map p72; Wine Office Crt, 145 Fleet St; ⊖Holborn) Rebuilt six years after the Great Fire, this hoary pub was popular with Dr Johnson, Thackeray, Dickens and the visiting Mark Twain. Touristy but always atmospheric and enjoyable for a pub meal.

Black Friar PUB

(Map p72; 174 Queen Victoria St; ⊖Blackfriars) With its fabulous Arts and Crafts interior and a strong choice of ales and bitters, this pub is a pleasant surprise, flung up on the site of a Dominican monastery, a theme that finds constant echo throughout.

SOUTH BANK

TOP CHOICE Rake PUB

(Map p78; 14 Winchester Walk; ⏲noon-11pm Mon-Fri, from 10am Sat; ⊖London Bridge) The only pub actually within Borough Market and London's smallest boozer, the Rake crams a superlative choice of bitters and real ales into pea-sized premises. There's valuable elbow space on the bamboo-decorated decking outside.

George Inn PUB

(Map p78; www.nationaltrust.org.uk/main/w-georgeinn; 77 Borough High St; ⊖London Bridge) This glorious old boozer is London's last surviving galleried coaching inn, dating from 1676 and now a National Trust property. Getting a mention in Dickens' *Little Dorrit*, it also stands on the site of the Tabard Inn, where the pilgrims in Chaucer's *Canterbury Tales* gathered before hitting the road to Canterbury.

Anchor PUB

(Map p78; 34 Park St; ⊖London Bridge) This 18th-century riverside boozer replaced the 1615 original where Samuel Pepys witnessed the Great Fire. Trips to the terrace are rewarded with fine views, but brace for a constant deluge of drinkers. Dr Samuel Johnson was once a regular.

CHELSEA & KENSINGTON

Bibendum Oyster Bar BAR

(Map p86; www.bibendum.co.uk; 81 Fulham Rd; ⊖South Kensington) Slurp up some bivalves and knock back a champers in the glorious foyer of the standout art nouveau/deco Michelin House (1911). The Michelin Man is everywhere: in mosaics, stained glass (the originals disappeared in WWII), crockery and the architecture itself.

BLOOMSBURY & ST PANCRAS

TOP CHOICE Newman Arms PUB

(Map p64; www.newmanarms.co.uk; 23 Rathbone St; ⊖Tottenham Court Road) One of the few family-run pubs in central London, this tiny one-room affair with upstairs pie room has a big history; George Orwell and Dylan Thomas drank here and a scene from Michael Powell's *Peeping Tom* was filmed in the passageway alongside the pub in 1960.

Euston Tap BAR

(Map p92; www.eustontap.com; 190 Euston Rd; ⏲from noon; ⊖Euston Square) Housed in a 19th century Portland stone lodge, this small two-floor place squeezes in an impressive range of real ales and bottled beers for specialist drinkers and beer obsessives; if cider is more your calling, head opposite to the Cider Tap for a mouthwatering range.

Queen's Larder PUB

(Map p92; www.queenslarder.co.uk; 1 Queen Sq; ⊖Russell Square) This small and supremely cosy pub in a gorgeous square gets its name from Queen Charlotte, wife of 'Mad' king George III, who rented part of the pub's cellar to store special foods for him while he was undergoing treatment nearby. Poets Sylvia Plath and Ted Hughes married in the church opposite.

Big Chill House BAR, DJS

(Map p92; www.bigchill.net; 257-259 Pentonville Rd; ⊖King's Cross) Come the weekend, the only remotely chilled-out space in this busy bar, split over two levels, is its first-rate and generously proportioned rooftop terrace.

NOTTING HILL, BAYSWATER & PADDINGTON

TOP CHOICE Churchill Arms PUB

(Map p110; 119 Kensington Church St; ⊖Notting Hill Gate) Adorned with a gob-smacking array of flower baskets and Union Jacks, this magnificent old boozer on Kensington Church St is a London classic, famed for its atmosphere,

Winston memorabilia, knick-knacks and attached conservatory serving fine Thai food.

Windsor Castle PUB
(Map p110; www.thewindsorcastlekensington.co.uk; 114 Campden Hill Rd; ⊖Notting Hill Gate) A fine pub with oak partitions separating the original bars at the crest of Campden Hill Rd. One of the loveliest walled gardens of any pub in London is tucked away through the side entrance. The bones of Thomas Paine (*Rights of Man* writer) are rumoured to be in the cellar.

MARYLEBONE

TOP CHOICE **Purl** COCKTAIL BAR
(Map p89; ☎020-7935 0835; www.purl-london.com; 50-54 Blandford St; ⏰5-11.30pm Mon-Thu, till midnight Fri & Sat; ⊖Baker Street) Coined after an old English early morning drink of warm beer, gin, wormwood and spices, Purl is all warm, low lighting, subterranean mellowness and some magnificently presented and unusual cocktails. If you're a group, book an alcove table. On the musical menu is swing and jazz. Book ahead.

Artesian BAR
(www.artesian-bar.co.uk; Langham Hotel, 1c Portland Pl; ⊖Oxford Circus) For doses of colonial glamour with a touch of the Orient, the sumptuous bar at the Langham hits the mark. Rum is the speciality here – award-winning cocktails (from £14) are concocted from the 60 varieties on offer.

CAMDEN TOWN

Lock Tavern PUB, LIVE MUSIC
(Map p95; www.lock-tavern.co.uk; 35 Chalk Farm Rd; ⊖Camden Town) The archetypal Camden pub, the Lock has both a rooftop terrace and a beer garden and attracts an interesting crowd with its mix of ready conviviality and regular live music.

Proud Camden BAR, LIVE MUSIC
(Map p95; www.proudcamden.com; The Horse Hospital, Stables Market; admission free-£10; ⊖Camden Town) Proud occupies a former horse hospital within Stables Market, with booths in the stalls, ice-cool rock photography on the walls and hip locals. Spin around the gallery during the day, enjoy bands at night and hit the terrace in summer.

CLERKENWELL & FARRINGDON

Jerusalem Tavern PUB
(Map p92; www.stpetersbrewery.co.uk; 55 Britton St; ⊖Farringdon) Pick a wood-panelled cubbyhole to park yourself in at this tiny 1720 coffee shop–turned-inn (named after the Priory of St John of Jerusalem) and choose from a selection of St Peter's fantastic beers and ales, brewed in North Suffolk.

HOXTON, SHOREDITCH & SPITALFIELDS

Good stops on a Hoxton hop:

TOP CHOICE **Book Club** BAR, CLUB
(Map p96; ☎020-7684 8618; www.wearebtc.com; 100 Leonard St; ⏰8am-midnight Mon-Wed, 8am-2am Thu & Fri, 10am-2am Sat & Sun; ⊖Old Street) A cerebral/creative vibe animates this fantastic one-time Victorian warehouse in Shoreditch that hosts cultural events (life drawing, workshops, dance lessons) and DJ nights to complement the drinking, enthusiastic ping pong games and pool-playing shenanigans. Early birds can catch breakfast from 8am weekdays and food continues through the day.

TOP CHOICE **Loungelover** COCKTAIL BAR
(Map p96; ☎020-7012 1234; www.lestroisgarcons.com; 1 Whitby St; ⏰6pm-midnight Sun-Thu, to 1am Fri & Sat; ⊖Liverpool Street) Book a table, sip a cocktail and admire the Louis XIV chairs, the huge hippo head, the cage-turned-living room, the jewel-encrusted stag's head and the loopy chandeliers. Utterly fabulous.

Mason & Taylor BAR
(Map p96; www.masonandtaylor.co.uk; 51-55 Bethnal Green Rd; ⏰5pm-midnight Mon-Thu, 5pm-1am Fri, noon-1am Sat, noon-midnight Sun; ⊖Shoreditch High Street) Ale aficionados can migrate to this bar which overflows with a seasoned and expertly selected choice of cask and bottled beers. There's a strong showing of microbrewery beers, including the Camden Town Brewery and the Redchurch Brewery. Sample the range of draught beers in taster flights of three or six one-third pints.

Ten Bells PUB
(Map p96; cnr Commercial & Fournier Sts; ⊖Liverpool Street) The most famous Jack the Ripper pub, Ten Bells was patronised by his last victim before her grisly end, and possibly by the slayer himself. Admire the wonderful 18th-century tiles and ponder the past over a pint.

Queen of Hoxton BAR
(Map p96; www.queenofhoxton.com; 1-5 Curtain Rd; ⏰5pm-midnight Mon-Wed, 5pm-2am Thu & Fri,

6pm-2am Sat; ⊖Liverpool Street) All comers – drinkers, clubbers, film fans – should find things to royally rave about at the graffiti-clad Queen, with its games room, DJ nights and rooftop bar, which comes into its own come summer and open-air film nights (www.rooftopfilmclub.com).

Worship St Whistling Shop COCKTAIL BAR
(Map p96; www.whistlingshop.com; 63 Worship St; ⊖Old Street) The busy master mixologists in this drinking den are content to visit the more unexplored outer regions of cocktail chemistry and aromatic science, concocted within the on-site lab and its rotary evaporators. Many of the ingredients are made in-house.

GREENWICH

TOP CHOICE **Greenwich Union** PUB
(www.greenwichunion.com; 56 Royal Hill; DLR Cutty Sark) The award-winning and handsome Greenwich Union peddles six or seven local microbrewery beers, including raspberry and wheat varieties, and a strong list of ales, bottled international brews, duffed up leather armchairs and a conservatory and beer garden at the rear.

Cutty Sark Tavern PUB
(www.cuttysarktavern.co.uk; 4-6 Ballast Quay; DLR Cutty Sark) Housed in a delightful bow-windowed, wood-beamed Georgian building facing the Thames, this historic gem has half a dozen cask-conditioned ales on tap, and riverside seating outside.

HAMPSTEAD & HIGHGATE

Spaniard's Inn PUB
(www.thespaniardshampstead.co.uk; Spaniards Rd; 11am-11pm; ⊖Hampstead then take bus 21) An enigmatic tavern dating from 1585, complete with dubious claims that Dick Turpin, the dandy highwayman, was born here and used it as a hideout. Literary luminaries such as Dickens, Shelley, Keats and Byron also availed themselves of its charms, which extends to a big, blissful garden and a large choice of specialty beers.

Holly Bush PUB
(22 Holly Mount; ⊖Hampstead) Dating from the early 19th century, this beautiful pub has a secluded hilltop location, open fires in winter and a knack for making you stay a bit longer than you had intended. It's above Heath St, reached via the Holly Bush Steps.

☆ Entertainment

From West End luvvies to East End geezers, Londoners have always loved a spectacle. With bear-baiting and public executions long on the no-no list, they've fallen back on what London does well: some of the world's best theatre, nightclub and live-music scenes.

For a comprehensive list of what to do on any given night, check out *Time Out*. The listings in the free tube papers, *Evening Standard* and *Metro*, are also handy.

Theatre

London is a world capital for theatre across the spectrum from mammoth musicals to thoughtful drama for the highbrow crowd. Blockbuster musicals run and run, with mindboggling longevity. *Les Miserables* and *Phantom of the Opera* lead the pack, with *Mamma Mia!*, *Blood Brothers*, *Chicago* and *The Lion King* in hot pursuit. But the theatrical biscuit goes to Agatha Christie's *The Mousetrap*, keeping audiences guessing since 1952.

On performance days, you can buy half-price tickets for West End productions (cash only) from the official agency **tkts** (Map p64; www.tkts.co.uk; ⊖Leicester Sq; 10am-7pm Mon-Sat, noon-4pm Sun; Leicester Square) on the south side of Leicester Sq. The booth is the one with the clocktower; beware of touts selling dodgy tickets. For a comprehensive look at what's being staged and where, visit www.officiallondontheatre.co.uk, www.theatremonkey.com or http://london.broadway.com.

The term 'West End' – as with Broadway – generally refers to the big-money productions such as musicals, but also includes other heavyweights. Some recommended options:

National Theatre THEATRE
(020-7452 3000; www.nationaltheatre.org.uk; Upper Ground; ⊖Waterloo) Flagship South Bank venue with three theatres and excellent-value tickets for classic and contemporary productions.

Royal Court Theatre THEATRE
(Map p86; 020-7565 5000; www.royalcourttheatre.com; Sloane Sq; ⊖Sloane Square) Progressive theatre and champion of new talent.

Old Vic THEATRE
(Map p78; 0844 871 7628; www.oldvictheatre.com; The Cut; ⊖Waterloo) Kevin Spacey continues his run as artistic director (and

GAY & LESBIAN LONDON

The West End, particularly Soho, is the visible centre of gay and lesbian London, with numerous venues clustered around Old Compton St and its surrounds. However, Soho doesn't hold a monopoly on gay life. Vauxhall is a hub for the hirsute, hefty and generally harder-edged sections of the community. The railway arches are now filled with dance clubs, leather bars and a sauna. Clapham (South London), Earl's Court (West London), Islington (North London) and Limehouse (East End) have their own miniscenes.

Generally, London's a safe place for lesbians and gays. It's rare to encounter any problem with sharing rooms or holding hands in the inner city, although it would pay to keep your wits about you at night and be conscious of your surroundings.

The easiest way to find out what's going on is to pick up the free press from a venue *(Pink Paper, Boyz, QX)*. The gay section of *Time Out* is useful, as are www.gaydarnation.com (for men) and www.gingerbeer.co.uk (for women). The hard-core circuit club nights run on a semiregular basis at a variety of venues: check out **DTPM**, **Fiction** (both at www.dtpmevents.co.uk), **Matinee**, **SuperMartXé** (both at www.loganpresents.com) and **Megawoof!**.

Some venues to get you started:

Candy Bar (Map p64; www.candybarsoho.co.uk; 4 Carlisle St; Tottenham Court Rd) Long-running lesbian hang-out.

Friendly Society (Map p64; 79 Wardour St; Piccadilly Circus) Soho's quirkiest gay bar, this Bohemian basement is bedecked in kid's-room wallpaper and Barbie dolls.

G-A-Y (www.g-a-y.co.uk) Bar (Map p64; 30 Old Compton St; ⊖Leicester Square); G-A-Y Late (Map p64; 5 Goslett Yard; ⏲11pm-3am; ⊖Tottenham Court Rd); G-A-Y Club@Heaven (The Arches, Villiers St; ⏲11pm-4am Thu-Sat; ⊖Charing Cross) Too camp to be restricted to one venue, G-A-Y now operates a pink-lit bar on the strip, a late-night bar a few streets away and club nights at one of gaydom's most internationally famous venues, Heaven.

Gay's the Word (Map p92; 66 Marchmont St; ⊖Russell Square) Books and magazines.

George & Dragon (Map p96; 2 Hackney Rd; ⊖Old St) Appealing corner pub where the crowd is often as eclectically furnished as the venue.

Popstarz (Map p64; www.popstarz.org; The Den, 18 West Central St; ⏲10pm-4am Fri; ⊖Tottenham Court Rd) London's legendary indie pop club night. The online flyer gets you in free.

Royal Vauxhall Tavern (RVT; www.rvt.org.uk; 372 Kennington Lane; admission free-£9; ⊖Vauxhall) Much-loved pub with crazy cabaret and drag acts. Head under the arches from Vauxhall tube station onto Kennington Lane, where you'll see the tavern immediately to your left.

Two Brewers (www.thetwobrewers.com; 114 Clapham High St; admission free-£5; ⊖Clapham Common) Popular bar with regular acts and a nightclub out the back. From the tube station, head north along Clapham High St (away from the common).

Village (Map p64; www.village-soho.co.uk; 81 Wardour St; Piccadilly Circus) Glitzy gay bar with excellent, lengthy happy hours.

occasional performer) at this venue, which features classic, highbrow drama.

Donmar Warehouse THEATRE
(Map p64; ☎0844 871 7624; www.donmarwarehouse.com; 41 Earlham St; ⊖Covent Garden) A not-for-profit company that has forged itself a West End reputation.

Off West End is where you'll generally find the most original works. Some venues to check out:

Almeida THEATRE
(Map p120; ☎020-7359 4404; www.almeida.co.uk; Almeida St; ⊖Highbury & Islington) A plush Islington venue that can be relied on to provide the city with an essential program of imaginative theatre, under its creative artistic director, Michael Attenborough.

Young Vic THEATRE
(Map p78; ☎020-7922 2922; www.youngvic.org; 66 The Cut; ⊖Waterloo) One of the capital's most respected theatre troupes – bold, brave and

talented – the Young Vic stages winning performances. There's a lovely two-level bar-restaurant with an open-air terrace upstairs.

Nightclubs

The volume and variety of venues in today's city is staggering. Clubland is no longer confined to the West End, with megaclubs scattered throughout the city wherever there's a venue big enough, cheap enough or quirky enough to hold them. Some run their own regular weekly schedule, while others host promoters on an ad hoc basis. The big nights are Friday and Saturday, although some of the most cutting-edge sessions are midweek. Admission prices vary widely; it's often cheaper to arrive early or prebook tickets.

Fabric CLUB

(Map p72; www.fabriclondon.com; 77a Charterhouse St; admission £8-18; 10pm-6am Fri, 11pm-8am Sat, 11pm-6am Sun; Farringdon) Consistently rated by DJs as one of the world's greatest, Fabric's three dance floors occupy a converted meat cold-store opposite the Smithfield meat market. Friday's FabricLive offers drum and bass, breakbeat and hip hop, Saturdays see house, techno and electronica, while hedonistic Sundays are delivered by the Wetyourself crew.

Plastic People CLUB

(Map p96; www.plasticpeople.co.uk; 147-149 Curtain Rd; admission £5-10; 10pm-3.30am Fri & Sat, to 2am Sun; Old Street) Taking the directive 'underground club' literally, Plastic People provides a low-ceilinged subterranean den of dubsteppy, wonky, funky, no-frills fun times.

Xoyo CLUB

(Map p96; www.xoyo.co.uk; 32-37 Cowper St; Old Street) This roomy Shoreditch warehouse club throws together a pulsingly popular mix of gigs, club nights and art events.

Pulse CLUB

(Map p78; 020-7261 0981; http://pulseclub.co.uk; 1 Invicta Plaza; Southwark) A siren-call to hedonists city-wide, this vast, superclub just south of Blackfriars Bridge hops with a mind-boggling 4500-clubber capacity.

Ministry of Sound CLUB

(Map p78; www.ministryofsound.com; 103 Gaunt St; admission £13-22; 11pm-6.30am Fri & Sat; Elephant & Castle) Where the global brand started, it's London's most famous club and still packs in a diverse crew with big local and international names.

Cargo CLUB

(Map p96; www.cargo-london.com; 83 Rivington St; admission free-£16; Old Street) A popular club with a courtyard where you can simultaneously enjoy big sounds and the great outdoors. Also hosts live bands.

Rock, Pop & Jazz

It goes without saying that London is a crucible of musical talent, with young bands gigging around venues citywide. Big-name gigs sell out quickly, so check www.seetickets.com before you travel.

Koko CONCERT VENUE

(www.koko.uk.com; 1a Camden High St; 7-11pm Sun-Thu, to 4am Fri & Sat; Mornington Crescent) Occupying the grand Camden Palace theatre, Koko hosts live bands most nights and the regular Club NME (New Musical Express; £5) on Friday.

O2 Academy Brixton LIVE MUSIC

(0844 477 2000; www.o2academybrixton.co.uk; 211 Stockwell Rd; Brixton) This Grade II–listed art deco venue is always winning awards for 'best live venue' (something to do with the artfully sloped floor, perhaps) and hosts big-name acts in a relatively intimate setting (5000 capacity).

Dublin Castle LIVE MUSIC, PUB

(Map p95; 020-7485 1773; www.thedublincastle.com; 94 Parkway; Camden Town) There's live punk or alternative music most nights in this pub's back room (cover usually £6).

Jazz Café LIVE MUSIC

(Map p95; www.jazzcafe.co.uk; 5 Parkway; Camden Town) Jazz is just one part of the picture at this intimate club that stages a full roster of rock, pop, hip hop and dance, including famous names.

Barfly PUB

(Map p95; 0207-691 4245; www.barflyclub.com; 49 Chalk Farm Rd; Chalk Farm) This grungy, indie-rock Camden venue hosts small-time artists looking for their big break. The Killers, Kasabian and Franz Ferdinand have all been on the billing. The lean is clearly towards rock from the US and UK, with alternative-music radio station Xfm hosting regular nights.

Ronnie Scott's JAZZ, CLUB

(Map p64; 020-7439 0747; www.ronniescotts.co.uk; 47 Frith St; Leicester Square) London's legendary jazz club has been pulling in jazz titans since 1959.

100 Club LIVE MUSIC, CLUB
(Map p64; ☎020-7636 0933; www.the100club.co.uk; 100 Oxford St; ⊖Oxford Circus) Hosting live music for 70 years, this legendary London venue once showcased the Stones and was at the centre of the punk revolution. It now divides its time between jazz, rock and even a little swing.

606 Club BLUES, JAZZ
(☎7352 5953; www.606club.co.uk; 90 Lots Rd; Mon-Thu £10, Fri & Sat £12, Sun £10; ⊖Fulham Broadway or Earl's Court) Named after its old address on the King's Road, which cast a spell over jazz lovers London-wide back in the 1980s, this tucked-away basement jazz club and restaurant gives centre stage to contemporary British-based jazz musicians nightly. The club frequently opens until 2am, although at weekends you have to dine to gain admission (booking is advised).

Hope & Anchor LIVE MUSIC, PUB
(Map p120; ☎020-7700 0550; 207 Upper St; admission free-£6; ⊖Angel) There is a scarcity of decent pubs in Islington, where the offerings are overwhelmingly cocktail lounges or DJ bars, but this rough-round-the-edges boozer with a famous musical past (U2, Dire Straits, Joy Division and Keane have all played here) attracts a muso cross-section of the neighbourhood and is a lot of fun.

Roundhouse LIVE MUSIC, THEATRE
(Map p95; ☎0844 482 8008; www.roundhouse.org.uk; Chalk Farm Rd; ⊖Chalk Farm) Built in 1847 as a railway shed, Camden's Roundhouse has been an iconic concert venue since the 1960s (capacity 3300), hosting the likes of the Rolling Stones, Led Zeppelin and The Clash. Theatre and comedy are also staged.

Classical Music

With four world-class symphony orchestras, two opera companies, various smaller ensembles, brilliant venues, reasonable prices and high standards of performance, London is a classical capital. Keep an eye out for the free (or nearly so) lunchtime concerts held in many of the city's churches.

Royal Albert Hall CONCERT HALL
(Map p86; ☎020-7589 8212; www.royalalberthall.com; Kensington Gore; ⊖South Kensington) This landmark elliptical Victorian arena – classically based on a Roman ampitheatre – hosts classical concerts and contemporary artists, but is best known as the venue for the annual classical music festival, the Proms.

Barbican ARTS CENTRE
(Map p72; ☎0845 121 6823; www.barbican.org.uk; Silk St; ⊖Barbican) Home to the excellent **London Symphony Orchestra** (www.lso.co.uk), this famously hulking complex (named after a Roman fortification) has a rich program of film, music, theatre, art and dance including concerts. In the City, the arts centre is well signposted from both the Barbican and Moorgate tube stations.

Southbank Centre CONCERT HALLS
(Map p78; ☎0844 875 0073; www.southbankcentre.co.uk; Belvedere Rd; ⊖Waterloo) Home to the **London Philharmonic Orchestra** (www.lpo.co.uk), **Sinfonietta** (www.londonsinfonietta.org.uk) and the **Philharmonia Orchestra** (www.philharmonia.co.uk), among others, this centre hosts classical, opera, jazz and choral music in three premier venues: the **Royal Festival Hall**, the smaller **Queen Elizabeth Hall** and the **Purcell Room**. Look out for free recitals in the foyer.

Opera & Dance

Royal Opera House OPERA, BALLET
(Map p64; ☎020-7304 4000; www.roh.org.uk; Bow St; tickets £5-195; ⊖Covent Garden) Covent Garden is synonymous with opera thanks to this world-famous venue, which is also the home of the Royal Ballet, Britain's premier classical ballet company. Backstage tours take place three times a day on weekdays and four times on Saturdays (£10.50, book ahead).

Sadler's Wells DANCE
(Map p92; ☎0844 412 4300; www.sadlers-wells.com; Rosebery Ave; tickets £10-49; ⊖Angel) A glittering modern venue that was, in fact, first established in the 17th century, Sadler's Wells has been given much credit for bringing modern dance to the mainstream.

London Coliseum OPERA
(Map p64; ☎0871 911 0200; www.eno.org; St Martin's Lane; tickets £10-87; ⊖Leicester Square) Home of the progressive English National Opera; the English National Ballet also performs here.

Comedy

When London's comics aren't being outrageously funny on TV, you might find them doing stand-up somewhere in your neighbourhood. There are numerous venues to choose from (with pubs in on the act).

Comedy Store CLUB
(Map p64; ☎0844 847 1728; www.thecomedystore.co.uk; 1A Oxendon St; admission from £20; ⊖Piccadilly Circus) One of London's first comedy clubs, featuring the capital's most famous improvisers, the Comedy Store Players, on Wednesdays (8pm) and Sundays (7.30pm).

Comedy Cafe CLUB
(Map p96; ☎020-7739 5706; www.comedycafe.co.uk; 68 Rivington St; admission free-£15; ⏲Wed-Sat; ⊖Old Street) Have dinner and watch comedy; free New Act Night on Wednesday is good for toe-curling entertainment.

99 Club MULTI VENUE CLUB
(☎0776 048 8119; www.the99club.co.uk; admission £10-30) Not quite the famous 100 Club, this virtual venue takes over various bars around town nightly, with three rival clones operating on Saturdays.

Soho Theatre THEATRE
(Map p64; ☎020-7478 0100; www.sohotheatre.com; 21 Dean St; tickets around £10-20; ⊖Tottenham Court Road) This is where grown-up comedians graduate to once crowds start paying attention.

Pear Shaped COMEDY NIGHT
(Map p64; www.pearshapedcomedy.com; Fitzroy Tavern, 16a Charlotte St; admission £5; ⏲8.30pm Wed; ⊖Goodge Street) Advertising themselves as 'London's second-worst comedy club', Pear Shaped has open spots for comic hopefuls.

Cinemas

Glitzy premieres usually take place in one of the mega multiplexes in Leicester Sq.

Electric Cinema CINEMA
(Map p110; ☎020-7908 9696; www.electriccinema.co.uk; 191 Portobello Rd; tickets £8-15; ⊖Ladbroke Grove) Getting Londoners buzzing since 1911, the Electric can help you grab a glass of wine from the bar, head to your leather sofa (£30) and snuggle down for a flick. Check out the Electric Brasserie (p117) next door.

BFI Southbank CINEMA, MEDIATHEQUE
(Map p78; ☎020-7928 3232; www.bfi.org.uk; Belvedere Rd; tickets £9; ⏲11am-11pm; ⊖Waterloo) A film-lover's fantasy, screening some 2000 flicks a year, from classics to foreign art house. There's also the Mediatheque viewing stations, for exploring the British Film Institute's extensive archive of movies and watching whatever you like for free.

BFI IMAX IMAX CINEMA
(Map p78; ☎020-7199 6000; www.bfi.org.uk/imax; Waterloo Rd; tickets £9-16; ⊖Waterloo) Watch 3-D movies and cinema releases on the UK's biggest screen: 20m high (nearly five double-decker buses) and 26m wide.

Prince Charles CINEMA
(Map p64; www.princecharlescinema.com; Leicester Pl; ⊖Leicester Square) West End cinema ticket prices are eye-watering, so wait till the first-runs have finished and come here, central London's cheapest picturehouse. Completing the score are mini-festivals, old classics and sing-along screenings.

Sport

As the capital of a football-mad nation, you can expect London to be brimming over with sporting spectacles during the cooler months. The Wimbledon Lawn Tennis Championships (p102) is one of the biggest events on the city's summer calendar.

FOOTBALL (SOCCER)

The home ground for England's national football team, and the venue for the FA Cup final, is Wembley Stadium (www.wembleystadium.com). Tickets for Premier League football matches are like gold dust, but you could try your luck. Contacts for London's Premier League clubs:

Arsenal Emirates Stadium STADIUM
(☎7704 4040; www.arsenal.com; 75 Drayton Park; self-guided tour £17.50, guided tour £35; ⊖Arsenal, Finsbury Park or Highbury & Islington) Arsenal Emirates Stadium is the third largest in the England. Many were sorry to see the old stadium go, with its old tea ladies and working-class atmosphere, but most have learned to love it. Daily tours available.

Chelsea STADIUM
(www.chelseafc.com; stadium tours adult/child £18/12; ⊖Fulham Broadway)

Fulham STADIUM
(www.fulhamfc.com; Craven Cottage, Stevenage Rd; tours adult/child £10.50/7.50; ⊖Putney Bridge)

Tottenham Hotspur STADIUM
(www.tottenhamhotspur.com; White Hart Lane, 748 High Rd; ⓡWhite Hart Lane)

RUGBY

Twickenham (www.rfu.com; Rugby Rd; Twickenham) is the home of English rugby union, but as with football, tickets for international matches are difficult to get unless you have contacts. The ground also has the **World**

Rugby Museum (☎020-8892 8877; adult/child £7/5; ⏲10am-5pm Tue-Sat, 11am-5pm Sun), which is worth combining with a tour of the stadium (adult/child £15/9, bookings recommended).

CRICKET

Cricket is as popular as ever in the land of its origin. Test matches take place at two venerable grounds: Lord's Cricket Ground (which also hosts tours) and the **Brit Oval** (☎0871 246 1100; www.britoval.com; ⊖Oval). Tickets cost from £20 to £80, but if you're a fan it's worth it. If not, it's an expensive and protracted form of torture.

Lord's Cricket Ground CRICKET GROUND
(☎020-7616 8595; www.lords.org; St John's Wood Rd; tours adult/child £15/9; ⊖St John's Wood) The next best thing to watching a test at Lord's is the absorbingly anecdotal 100-minute tour of the ground and facilities, held when there's no play. It takes in the famous (members only) Long Room and the **MCC Museum**, featuring evocative memorabilia, including the tiny Ashes trophy.

HORSE RACING

Epsom HORSE RACING
(☎01372 470 047; www.epsomderby.co.uk; admission from £7; ⓡEpsom Downs) With much more racing credibility than Ascot, this famous racetrack's star turn is Derby Day in June, but it has meets all year.

Shopping

From world-famous department stores to quirky backstreet retail revelations, London is a mecca for shoppers with an eye for style and a card to exercise.

London's famous department stores are a tourist attraction in themselves and if there's a label worth having, you'll find it in central London. The capital's most famous designers (Paul Smith, Vivienne Westwood, Stella McCartney, the late Alexander McQueen) have their own stores scattered about and are stocked in major department stores. Look out for dress agencies that sell second-hand designer clothes, bags and shoes – there are particularly rich pickings in the wealthier parts of town.

Nick Hornby's book *High Fidelity* may have done for London music-store workers what *Sweeney Todd* did for barbers, but those obsessive types still lurk in wonderful independent stores all over the city.

WEST END

Oxford St is the place for high street fashion, while Regent St cranks it up a notch. Carnaby St is nowhere near the hip hub it was in the 1960s, but the lanes around it still have some interesting boutiques. Bond St has designers galore, Savile Row is all about bespoke tailoring and Jermyn St is the place for smart clobber (particularly shirts). For musical instruments, visit Denmark St (off Charing Cross Rd).

Also check out these stores:

Selfridges DEPARTMENT STORE
(Map p89; www.selfridges.com; 400 Oxford St; ⊖Bond St) Famed for its innovative window displays – especially at yuletide – the funkiest of London's one-stop shops bursts with fashion labels and tempts with an unparalleled food hall and Europe's largest cosmetics department.

Fortnum & Mason DEPARTMENT STORE
(Map p64; www.fortnumandmason.com; 181 Piccadilly; ⊖Piccadilly Circus) It's the byword for quality and service from a bygone era, steeped in 300 years of tradition. The old-world basement food hall is where Britain's elite come for their pantry provisions and epicurean morsels.

Liberty DEPARTMENT STORE
(Map p64; www.liberty.co.uk; Great Marlborough St; ⊖Oxford Circus) An irresistible blend of contemporary styles and indulgent pampering in a mock-Tudor fantasyland of carved dark wood.

Topshop Oxford Circus CLOTHES
(Map p64; www.topshop.com; 216 Oxford St; ⊖Oxford Circus) Billed as the 'world's largest fashion store', the Topshop branch on Oxford Circus is a frenzy of shoppers searching for the latest look at reasonable prices. It's home to a range by London's favourite local supermodel rock chick, Kate Moss. Topman is upstairs.

Grays Antiques ANTIQUES
(Map p89; www.graysantiques.com; 58 Davies St; ⊖Bond St) Top-hatted doormen welcome you to this wonderful building full of specialist stallholders. Make sure you head to the basement where the Tyburn River still runs through a channel in the floor.

HMV MUSIC
(Map p64; www.hmv.com; 150 Oxford St; ⊖Oxford Circus) Giant store selling music, DVDs and magazines.

Foyle's BOOKS
(Map p64; www.foyles.co.uk; 113-119 Charing Cross Rd; ⊖Tottenham Court Road) Flogging books since 1906, Foyles is a bookselling institution and retail landmark. Great to get lost in.

Ray's Jazz JAZZ, BLUES
(www.foyles.co.uk; Foyles, 113-119 Charing Cross Rd; ⊖Tottenham Court Road) Where jazz anoraks find those elusive back catalogues from their favourite jazz and blues artists. It's inside Foyle's.

Stanfords BOOKS, MAPS
(Map p64; www.stanfords.co.uk; 12-14 Long Acre; ⊖Covent Garden) A wonderland of travel titles and maps, with 150 years of experience.

DR Harris BEAUTY PRODUCTS
(Map p64; www.drharris.co.uk; 29 St James's St; ⊙closed Sun; ⊖Green Park) Chemist and perfumer since the 18th century and the Prince of Wales' royal pharmacist, this is the place for moustache wax or the restorative and right royal Dr Harris Pick-me-up, to take the sting out of hangovers.

Minamoto Kitchoan CONFECTIONARY
(Map p64; www.kitchoan.com; 44 Piccadilly; ⊙closed Sun; ⊖Piccadilly Circus) Delectable Japanese Wagashi confectionary made from red beans, rice, sweet potatoes and other natural ingredients, delightfully shaped into tasty morsels and served with a cup of green tea. Charming.

Waterstones BOOKS
(www.waterstones.com) Piccadilly (Map p64; 203-206 Piccadilly; ⊖Piccadilly Circus); Bloomsbury (Map p92; 82 Gower St; ⊖Goodge St) The Piccadilly branch is the largest bookstore in Europe, boasting knowledgeable staff, regular author readings and signings. Check out the 5th View bar in the Piccadilly store; it is well worth a visit.

Benjamin Pollock's Toy Shop TOYS
(Map p64; www.pollocks-coventgarden.co.uk; 1st fl, Covent Garden Market; ⊖Covent Garden) You can turn up all sorts of treasures at this gem of a traditional toy shop selling Victorian paper toy theatres, children's masks, spinning tops, finger puppets, antique teddy bears, dolls and more.

Rigby & Peller LINGERIE
(www.rigbyandpeller.com) Mayfair (Map p64; 22A Conduit St; ⊖Oxford Circus); Knightsbridge (Map p86; 2 Hans Rd; ⊖Knightsbridge); Chelsea (Map p86; 13 Kings Rd; ⊖Sloane Square); Westfield mall (Westfield Mall, Ariel Way; ⊙10am-10pm Mon-Sat, 11am-9pm Sun; ⊖Wood Lane) Get into some right royal knickers with a trip to the Queen's corsetière.

Butler & Wilson JEWELLERY
(www.butlerandwilson.co.uk) Mayfair (Map p89; 20 South Moulton St; ⊖Bond St); Chelsea (Map p86; 189 Fulham Rd; ⊖South Kensington) Camp jewellery, antique baubles and vintage clothing.

BM Soho DANCE MUSIC
(Map p64; www.bm-soho.com; 25 D'Arblay St; ⊖Oxford Circus) Your best bet for dance music – if they haven't got what you're after, they'll know who has.

Forbidden Planet COMICS, SCI-FI
(Map p64; 179 Shaftesbury Ave; ⊖Tottenham Court Rd) Need a set of light sabre chopsticks fast? Forbidden Planet is a mecca for collectors of comics, manga, Star Trek figurines, horror and fantasy literature, sci-fi and Star Wars memorabilia.

KNIGHTSBRIDGE, KENSINGTON & CHELSEA

Knightsbridge draws the hordes with quintessentially English department stores.

Harrods DEPARTMENT STORE
(Map p86; www.harrods.com; 87 Brompton Rd; ⊖Knightsbridge) Simultaneously stylish and garish, Harrods is an obligatory stop for visitors, cash-strapped and big, big spenders alike. The spectacular food hall is a sight in itself.

TOP CHOICE **John Sandoe Books** BOOKS
(Map p86; www.johnsandoe.com; 10 Blacklands Tce; ⊖Sloane Square) This atmospheric little bookshop is a treasure trove of literary gems and hidden surprises. In business for decades, loyal customers swear by it and the knowledgeable booksellers spill forth with well-read pointers.

Harvey Nichols DEPARTMENT STORE
(Map p86; www.harveynichols.com; 109-125 Knightsbridge; ⊖Knightsbridge) London's temple of high fashion, jewellery and perfume.

NOTTING HILL, BAYSWATER & PADDINGTON

Portobello Rd and the lanes surrounding it are the main focus, both for the famous market and the quirky boutiques and gift stores.

ROLL OUT THE BARROW

London has more than 350 markets selling everything from antiques and curios to flowers and fish. Some, such as Camden and Portobello Road, are tourist-packed, while others are just for locals.

Columbia Road Flower Market (Map p96; Columbia Rd; ⏲8am-2pm Sun; ⊖Old St) The best place for East End barrow boy banter ('We got flowers cheap enough for ya muvver-in-law's grave'). Unmissable.

Borough Market (Map p78; Southwark St) A farmers' market sometimes called London's Larder, it has been here in some form since the 13th century. It's wonderfully atmospheric; you'll find everything from organic falafel to boars' heads.

Camden Market (Map p95; www.camdenmarkets.org; Camden High St; ⏲10am-5.30pm; ⊖Camden Town) London's most famous market is actually a series of markets spread along Camden High St and Chalk Farm Rd. Despite a major fire in 2008, the **Camden Lock Market** (Map p95; www.camdenlockmarket.com; 54-56 Camden Lock Pl; ⊖Camden Town, Chalk Farm) and **Camden Stables Market** (Map p95; Camden High St; ⊖Chalk Farm) are still the places for punk fashion, cheap food, hippy chic and a whole lotta craziness.

Portobello Road Market (Map p110; www.portobellomarket.org; Portobello Rd; ⏲8am-6.30pm Mon-Sat, to 1pm Thu; ⊖Notting Hill Gate or Ladbroke Grove) One of London's most famous street markets, in Notting Hill. New and vintage clothes are its main attraction, with antiques at its south end and food at the north.

Old Spitalfields Market (Map p72; www.oldspitalfieldsmarket.com; 105a Commercial St; ⏲10am-4pm Mon-Fri, 11am-5pm Sat, 9am-5pm Sun; ⊖Liverpool St) It's housed in a Victorian warehouse, but the market's been here since 1638. Thursdays are devoted to antiques and vintage clothes, Fridays to fashion and art, but Sunday's the big day, with a bit of everything.

Broadway Market (www.broadwaymarket.co.uk; London Fields; ⏲9am-5pm Sat; ⊖Bethnal Green) Graze from the organic food stalls, choose a cooked meal and then sample one of the 200 beers on offer at the neighbouring Dove Freehouse. It's a bit of a schlep from the tube. Head up Cambridge Heath Rd until you cross the canal. Turn left, following the canal and you'll see the market to the right after a few short blocks.

Brixton Market (www.brixtonmarket.net; Electric Ave; ⏲10.30am-6pm Mon-Wed, to 10pm Thu-Sat, 10.30am-5pm Sun; ⊖Brixton) Immortalised in the Eddie Grant song, Electric Ave is a cosmopolitan treat that mixes everything from reggae music to exotic foods and spices.

Brixton Village (www.brixtonmarket.net; Electric Ave; ⏲10.30am-6pm Mon-Wed, to 10pm Thu-Sat, 10.30am-5pm Sun; ⊖Brixton) Revitalised and hip transformation of Granville Arcade near Brixton Market, with a host of inventively inclined shops and fantastic restaurants and cafes.

Sunday (Up)market (Map p96; www.sundayupmarket.co.uk; The Old Truman Brewery, Brick Lane; ⏲10am-5pm Sun; ⊖Liverpool St) Handmade handbags, jewellery, new and vintage clothes and shoes, plus food if you need refuelling.

Brick Lane Market (Map p96; www.visitbricklane.org; Brick Lane; ⏲8am-2pm Sun; ⊖Liverpool St) An East End pearler, this is a sprawling bazaar featuring everything from fruit and veggies to paintings and bric-a-brac.

Camden Passage Market (Map p120; www.camdenpassageislington.co.uk; Camden Passage; ⏲10am-2pm Wed, to 5pm Sat; ⊖Angel) Get your fill of antiques and trinkets galore. Not in Camden (despite the name).

Greenwich Market (www.greenwichmarket.net; College Approach; ⏲10am-5.30pm Wed-Sun) Rummage through antiques, vintage clothing and collectables (Thursday and Friday) or arts and crafts (Wednesday and weekends), or just chow down in the food section.

Petticoat Lane Market (Wentworth St & Middlesex St; ⏲9am-2pm Sun-Fri; ⊖Aldgate) A cherished East End institution overflowing with cheap consumer durables and jumble-sale ware.

Ceramica Blue HOMEWARES
(Map p110; www.ceramicablue.co.uk; 10 Blenheim Cres; ⊖Ladbroke Grove) A wonderful place for original and eye-catching crockery and coloured glass imported from more than a dozen countries, with Japanese eggshell-glaze teacups, serving plates with traditional South African designs and more.

Rellik VINTAGE THREADS
(www.relliklondon.co.uk; 8 Golborne Rd; ⊖Westbourne Park) Located at the foot of one of London's most notorious Brutalist tower blocks – the 31-storey Ernő Goldfinger–designed shocker called the Trellick Tower – Rellick stocks vintage classic threads for those in the know.

MARYLEBONE

Daunt Books BOOKS
(Map p89; 83 Marylebone High St; ⊖Baker Street) An exquisitely beautiful store, with guidebooks, travel literature, fiction and reference books, all sorted by country.

ISLINGTON

Curios, baubles and period pieces abound along Camden Passage. Upper and Cross Sts have an interesting mix of stores.

Laura J London WOMEN'S SHOES
(Map p120; www.laurajlondon.com; 114 Islington High St; ⊖Angel) A girlie boutique stocking shoes and accessories from a local designer.

CLERKENWELL & FARRINGDON

London Silver Vaults SILVER
(Map p72; www.thesilvervaults.com; 53-63 Chancery Lane; ⊖Chancery Lane) Thirty subterranean shops forming the world's largest retail collection of silver under one roof.

HOXTON, SHOREDITCH & SPITALFIELDS

Rough Trade ALTERNATIVE, PUNK, INDIE
(www.roughtrade.com) East (Map p96; www.roughtrade.com; 91 Brick Lane, Dray Walk, Old Truman Brewery; ⌚8am-8pm Mon-Fri, 11am-7pm Sat & Sun; ⊖Liverpool St); West (Map p110; 130 Talbot Rd; ⊖Ladbroke Grove) At the forefront of the punk explosion of the 1970s, it's the best place to come for anything of an indie or alternative music bent.

Present MEN'S CLOTHES
(Map p96; www.present-london.com; 140 Shoreditch High St; ⊖Old Street) Hip men's designer duds.

Start CLOTHES
(Map p96; www.start-london.com; 42-44 Rivington St; ⊖Old Street) Spilling over three stores on the same lane (womenswear, menswear and men's formal), your quest for designer jeans starts here.

ℹ Information

Dangers & Annoyances

Considering its size and wealth disparities, London is generally safe. That said, keep your wits about you and don't flash your cash unnecessarily. A contagion of youth-on-youth knife crime is cause for concern, so walk away if you sense trouble brewing and take care at night. When travelling by tube, choose a carriage with other people in it and avoid deserted suburban stations. Following reports of robberies and sexual attacks, shun unlicensed or unbooked minicabs.

Nearly every Londoner has a story about a wallet/phone/bag being nicked from under their noses – or arses, in the case of bags on floors in bars. Watch out for pickpockets on crowded tube trains, night buses and streets.

When using ATMs, guard your PIN details carefully. Don't use an ATM that looks like it's been tampered with as there have been incidents of card cloning.

Emergency

Police/Fire/Ambulance (☎999)
Rape & Sexual Abuse Support Centre (☎0808 802 9999)
Samaritans (☎08457 90 90 90)

Internet Access

You'll find free wireless (wi-fi) access at many bars, cafes and hotels. Large tracts of London, notably Canary Wharf and the City, are covered by pay-as-you-go wi-fi services that you can sign up to in situ – and London's mayor has promised blanket wi-fi coverage of this sort for all of London by 2012. You'll usually pay less at the numerous internet cafes (about £2 per hour).

Internet Resources

BBC London (www.bbc.co.uk/london)
Evening Standard (www.thisislondon.com)
Londonist (www.londonist.com)
Time Out (www.timeout.com/london)
Urban Path (www.urbanpath.com)
View London (www.viewlondon.co.uk)
Walk It (www.walkit.com) Enter your destination and get a walking map, time estimate and information on calories burnt and carbon dioxide saved.

Media

Two free newspapers bookend the working day – *Metro* in the morning and the *Evening Standard* in

WANT MORE?

For in-depth information, reviews and recommendations at your fingertips, head to the Apple App Store to purchase Lonely Planet's *London City Guide* iPhone app.

Alternatively, head to **Lonely Planet** (www.lonelyplanet.com/london) for planning advice, author recommendations, traveller reviews and insider tips.

the evening – both available from tube stations. All of the national dailies have plenty of London coverage. Published every Wednesday, *Time Out* (£2.99) is the local listing guide par excellence.

Medical Services

To find a local doctor, pharmacy or hospital, consult the local telephone directory or call ☎0845 46 47.

Hospitals with 24-hour accident and emergency units include the following:

St Thomas' Hospital (☎020-7188 7188; Lambeth Palace Rd; ⊖Waterloo)

University College Hospital (☎0845 155 5000; 235 Euston Rd ; ⊖Euston Square)

Toilets

If you're caught short around London, public toilets can be elusive. Only a handful of tube stations have them, but the bigger National Rail stations usually do (often coin operated). If you can face five floors on an escalator, department stores are a good bet.

Tourist Information

For a list of all tourist offices in London and around Britain, see www.visitmap.info/tic.

Britain & London Visitor Centre (www.visitbritain.com; 1 Regent St; ⊙9am-6.30pm Mon-Fri, 10am-4pm Sat & Sun; ⊖Piccadilly Circus) Books accommodation, theatre and transport tickets; has *bureau de change*, international telephones and internet terminals. Longer hours in summer.

City of London Information Centre (☎020-7332 1456; www.visitthecity.co.uk; St Paul's Churchyard; ⊙9.30am-5.30pm Mon-Sat, 10am-4pm Sun; ⊖St Paul's) Tourist information, fast-track tickets to City attractions and guided walks (adult/child under 12 £7/free).

Greenwich Tourist Office (www.greenwich.gov.uk; Pepys House, 2 Cutty Sark Gardens; ⊙10am-5pm; DLR Cutty Sark) Information plus guided tours.

Getting There & Away

London is the major gateway to England.

AIR There are a number of London airports; see Getting Around for details.

BUS Most long-distance coaches leave London from Victoria Coach Station.

CAR Check reservation numbers of the main car-hire firms, all of which have airport and various city locations. Also see Car & Motorcycle, p822.

TRAIN London's main-line terminals are all linked by the tube and each serves different destinations. Most stations have left-luggage facilities (around £4) and lockers, toilets (20p) with showers (around £3), newsstands and bookshops, and a range of eating and drinking outlets. St Pancras, Victoria and Liverpool St stations all have handy shopping centres attached.

If you can't find your destination in the list of main-line terminals below, consult the journey planner at www.nationalrail.co.uk.

Charing Cross Canterbury.

Euston Manchester, Liverpool, Carlisle, Glasgow.

King's Cross Cambridge, Hull, York, Newcastle, Scotland.

Liverpool Street Stansted airport, Cambridge.

London Bridge Gatwick airport, Brighton.

Marylebone Birmingham.

Paddington Heathrow airport, Oxford, Bath, Bristol, Exeter, Plymouth, Cardiff.

St Pancras Gatwick and Luton airports, Brighton, Nottingham, Sheffield, Leicester, Leeds, Paris.

Victoria Gatwick airport, Brighton and Canterbury.

Waterloo Windsor, Winchester, Exeter, Plymouth.

Getting Around

To/From the Airports

GATWICK There are **National Rail** (www.nationalrail.co.uk) services between Gatwick's South Terminal and Victoria station (from £13.50, 37 minutes), running every 15 minutes during the day and hourly through the night. Other trains head to London St Pancras International (from £10, 66 minutes). Fares are cheaper the earlier you book. If you're racing to make a flight, the **Gatwick Express** (☎0845 850 1530; www.gatwickexpress.com; one way/return £17.90/30.80, 30 minutes, every 15 minutes) departs Victoria every 15 minutes from 5am to 11.45pm (one way/return £18.90/33.20, 30 minutes, first/last train 3.30am/12.32am).

Prices start from £2, depending on when you book, for the **EasyBus** (www.easybus.co.uk)

minibus service between Gatwick and Earls Court (£10, allow 1¼ hours, every 30 minutes from 4.25am to 1am). You'll be charged extra if you have more than one carry-on and one check-in bag. Book online for the cheapest deals.

Gatwick's taxi partner, **Checker Cars** (www.checkercars.com), has a counter in each terminal. Fares are quoted in advance (about £95 for the 65-minute ride to Central London).

HEATHROW The transport connections to Heathrow are excellent, and the journey to and from the city is usually painless. The cheapest option is the Underground (the tube). The Piccadilly line is accessible from every terminal (£5.30, one hour to central London, departing from Heathrow every five minutes from around 5am to 11.30pm). If it's your first time in London, it's a good chance to practice using the tube as it's at the beginning of the line and therefore not too crowded when you get on. If there are vast queues at the ticket office, use the automatic machines instead; some accept credit cards as well as cash. Keep your bags near you and expect a scramble to get off if you're hitting the city at rush hour (7am to 9am and 5pm to 7pm weekdays).

You might save some time on the considerably more expensive Heathrow Express, an ultra-modern train to Paddington station (one way/return £18/34, 15 minutes, every 15 minutes 5.12am to 11.48pm). You can purchase tickets on board (£5 extra), from self-service machines (cash and credit cards accepted) at both stations, or online.

There are taxi ranks for black cabs outside every terminal; a fare to the centre of London will cost between £50 and £85.

LONDON CITY The Docklands Light Railway connects London City Airport to the tube network, taking 22 minutes to reach Bank station (£4.30). A black taxi costs around £25 to/from central London.

LUTON There are regular **National Rail** (www.nationalrail.co.uk) services from St Pancras (£13, 29 to 39 minutes) to Luton Airport Parkway station, where a shuttle bus (£1.50) will get you to the airport within 10 minutes. EasyBus minibuses head from Victoria, Earl's Court and Baker St to Luton (from £2, walk-on £10, allow 1½ hours, every 30 minutes). A taxi costs around £65.

STANSTED The Stansted Express connects with Liverpool Street station (one way/return £21.50/29.50, 46 minutes, every 15 minutes 6am to 12.30am).

EasyBus also has services between Stansted and Baker St (from £2, £10 walk-on, 1¼ hours, every 20 minutes). The Airbus A6 links with Victoria Coach Station (£11, allow 1¾ hours, at least every 30 minutes). National Express also runs buses to Stansted from Liverpool Street Station (£9 one way, 80 mins, every 30 mins).

A taxi cab to/from central London costs about £100.

Bicycle

The central city is flat and relatively compact and the traffic moves slowly – all of which make it surprisingly good for cyclists. It can get terribly congested though, so you'll need to keep your wits about you – and lock your bike (including both wheels) securely. Operating 24 hours a day and already clocking in over 11 million cycle hires, the excellent **Barclays Cycle Hire Scheme** (www.tfl.gov.uk) allows you to hire a bike from one of 400 docking stations around London. The access fee is £1 for 24 hours or £5 per week; after that, the first 30 minutes is free (making the bikes perfect for short hops), or £1/4/6/15 for one hour/90 minutes/two hours/three hours. Cycle as often as you like, but leave five minutes between each trip. Visitors to London can pay either on-line or or using a credit or debit card at a docking station. The minimum age for buying access is 18; the minimum age for riding a Barclays bike is 14.

Car

The M25 ring road encompasses the 609 sq miles that is broadly regarded as Greater London. For motorists it's the first circle of hell; London's streets can be congested beyond belief. Traffic is heavy, roadwork continuous, parking is either impossible or expensive, and wheel-clampers are diligent. If you drive into central London from 7am to 6pm on a weekday, you'll need to pay a £10 per day congestion charge (visit www.tfl.gov.uk for payment options) or face a hefty fine. If you're hiring a car to continue your trip from London, take the tube to Heathrow and pick it up from there.

Public Transport

Although complaining about it is a local sport, London's public transport is excellent, with tubes, trains, buses and boats conspiring to get you anywhere you need to go. **TFL** (www.tfl.gov.uk), the city's public transport provider, is the glue that binds the network together. Its website has a handy journey planner and information on all services, including cabs. As a creature of leisure, you'll hopefully be able to avoid those bits that Londoners hate (especially the sardine

MAPS

No Londoner would be without a pocket-size *London Mini A-Z,* which lists nearly 30,000 streets. Worth getting if you're in London for more than a few weeks.

LONDON'S OYSTER DIET

To get the most out of London, you need to be able to jump on and off public transport like a local, not scramble to buy a ticket at hefty rates each time. The best and cheapest way to do this is with an Oyster card, a reusable smartcard on which you can load either a season ticket (weekly/monthly £29/112) or prepaid credit. The card itself is £5, which is fully refundable when you leave.

London is divided into concentric transport zones, although most places are in Zones 1 and 2. The season tickets will give you unlimited transport on the tube, buses and rail services within these zones. All you need to do is touch your card to the yellow sensors on the station turnstiles or at the front of the bus.

If you opt for pay as you go, the fare will be deducted from the credit on your card at a much lower rate than if you were buying a one-off paper ticket. An Oyster bus trip costs £1.35 as opposed to £2.30 for an individual fare, while a Zone 1 tube journey is £2 as opposed to £4.30. Even better, in any single day your fares will be capped at the equivalent of the Oyster day-pass rate for the zones you've travelled in (Zones 1-2 peak/off-peak £8.40/7).

Assuming you avoid peak hours (6.30am to 9.30am and 4pm to 7pm), this ready reckoner gives the cheapest options for your length of stay:

» **1-4 days**: prepay

» **5-24 days**: weeklies topped up with prepay for any remaining days

» **25-31 days**: monthly

squash of rush-hour tubes), so get yourself an Oyster card and make the most of it.

BOAT

The myriad boats that ply the Thames are a great way to travel, avoiding traffic jams while affording great views. Passengers with daily, weekly or monthly travelcards (including on Oyster) get a third off all fares. London has some 40 miles of inner-city canals, mostly built in the 19th century.

Thames Clippers runs regular commuter services between Embankment, Waterloo, Blackfriars, Bankside, London Bridge, Tower, Canary Wharf, Greenwich, North Greenwich and Woolwich piers (adult/child £6/3) from 7am to midnight (from 9.30am weekends).

Leisure services include the Tate-to-Tate boat and Westminster–Greenwich services. There are also boats to Kew Gardens and Hampton Court Palace.

London Waterbus Company (p90) and Jason's Trip (p90) both run canal boat journeys between Camden Lock and Little Venice; see websites for times.

BUS

Travelling around London by double-decker bus is a great way to get a feel for the city, but it's usually slower than the tube. Heritage 'Routemaster' buses with conductors operate on route 9 (from Aldwych to Royal Albert Hall) and 15 (between Trafalgar Sq and Tower Hill); these are the only buses without wheelchair access. In 2012 a brand new fleet of freshly designed hybrid diesel/electric hop-on/hop-off (and wheelchair-accessible) Routemasters began running on route 38 between Victoria and Hackney.

Buses run regularly during the day, while less frequent night buses (prefixed with the letter 'N') wheel into action when the tube stops. Single-journey bus tickets (valid for two hours) cost £2.30 (£1.35 on Oyster, capped at £4.20 per day); a weekly pass is £18.80. Children ride for free. At stops with yellow signs, you must buy your ticket from the automatic machine (or use an Oyster) before boarding. Buses stop on request, so clearly signal the driver with an outstretched arm.

LONDON UNDERGROUND, DLR & OVERGROUND

'The tube', as it's universally known, extends its subterranean tentacles throughout London and into the surrounding counties, with services running every few minutes from roughly 5.30am to 12.30am (from 7am to 11.30pm Sunday).

It's easy to use. Tickets (or Oyster card top-ups) can be purchased from counters or machines at the entrance to each station using either cash or credit card. They're then inserted into the slot on the turnstiles (or you touch your Oyster card on the yellow reader), and the barrier opens. Once you're through you can jump on and off different lines as often as you need to get to your destination.

Also included within the network are the driverless Docklands Light Railway (DLR), and the train lines shown on tube maps as

'Overground'. The DLR links the City to Docklands, Greenwich and London City Airport.

The tube map itself is an acclaimed graphic design work, using coloured lines to show how the 14 different routes intersect. However, it's not remotely to scale. The distances between stations become greater the further from central London you travel, while Leicester Square and Covent Garden stations are only 250m apart.

TRAIN

Particularly south of the river, where tube lines are in shorter supply, the various rail companies are an important part of the public transport picture. Most stations are now fitted with Oyster readers and accept TFL travelcards. If you travel outside your zone you'll need to have enough prepay credit on your Oyster card to cover the additional charge. As not all stations have turnstiles, it's important to remember to tap-in and tap-out at the Oyster reader at the station or your card will register an unfinished journey and you're likely to be charged extra. You can still buy a paper ticket from machines or counters at train stations.

Taxi

London's famous black cabs are available for hire when the yellow light above the windscreen is lit. To get an all-London licence, cabbies must do 'The Knowledge', which tests them on up to 25,000 streets within a 6-mile radius of Charing Cross and all points of interest from hotels to churches. Fares are metered, with flag fall of £2.20 and the additional rate dependent on time of day, distance travelled and taxi speed. A one-mile trip will cost between £5.20 and £8.40. To order a black cab by phone, try **Dial-a-Cab** (☎020-7253 5000; www.dialacab.co.uk); you must pay by credit card and will be charged a premium.

Licensed minicabs operate via agencies (most busy areas have a walk-in office with drivers waiting). They're a cheaper alternative to black cabs and quote trip fares in advance. To find a local minicab firm, visit www.tfl.gov.uk.

There have been many reports of sexual assault and theft by unlicensed minicab drivers. Only use drivers from proper agencies; licensed minicabs aren't allowed to tout for business or pick you up off the street without a booking, so avoid the shady characters who hang around outside nightclubs or bars.

Canterbury & the Southeast

Includes »

Best Places to Eat

- » Deeson's (p146)
- » Allotment (p159)
- » Eddie Gilbert's (p154)
- » Terre à Terre (p177)
- » Town House (p182)

Best Places to Stay

- » Abode Canterbury (p145)
- » Jeake's House (p163)
- » Wallett's Court (p159)
- » Reading Room (p152)
- » Hotel Una (p176)

Why Go?

Rolling chalk downs (hills), venerable Victorian resorts, fields of hops and grapes sweetening in the sun – welcome to England's southeast, four soothing counties' worth of country houses, fairytale castles and the country's finest food and drink. That fruit-ripening sun shines brightest and longest on the southeast, warming a string of seaside towns wedged between formidable chalk cliffs. There's something for everyone here, from the understated charm of Whitstable to the bohemian spirit of hedonistic Brighton and the more genteel Eastbourne.

But the southeast is also pock-marked with reminders of darker days. From the 1066 battlefield to Dover Castle's secret war tunnels and scattered Roman ruins, the region's position as the frontline against Continental invaders has left a wealth of turbulent history. England's spiritual heart is Canterbury, its cathedral and ancient Unesco-listed attractions are essential viewing for any 21st-century pilgrim.

When to Go

May is a good time to get creative at Great Britain's second-largest arts festival, held in Brighton. During June, don your top hat and breeches to revel in frilly Victoriana at Dickens festivals in Broadstairs and Rochester.

Any time between May and October is ideal for a hike along the South Downs Way, running the length of England's newest national park. In November head to Lewes for one of the most spectacular Guy Fawkes Night celebrations in all of England.

Activities

The southeast of England may be Britain's most densely populated corner, but there are still plenty of off-the-beaten-track walking and cycling routes to enjoy.

Cycling

Finding quiet roads for cycle touring takes a little extra perseverance in England's southeast, but efforts are richly rewarded. Long-distance routes on the **National Cycle Network** (NCN; www.sustrans.org.uk):

Downs & Weald Cycle Route (110 miles; NCN Route 21) London to Eastbourne via Gatwick.

Garden of England Cycle Route (165 miles; NCN Routes 1, 2) London to Dover and then Hastings.

You'll also find information about less-demanding routes on the NCN website. Meanwhile, there are plenty of ups and downs to challenge mountain bikers on national trails, such as the South Downs Way National Trail (100 miles), which takes hard nuts two days, but mere mortals around four.

Walking

Two long-distance trails meander steadily westward through the region, but there are plenty of shorter ambles to fit your schedule, stamina and scenery wish-list.

South Downs Way (p169) This 100-mile National Trail through England's newest national park is a beautiful roller-coaster walk along prehistoric droveways between the ancient capital, Winchester, and the seaside resort of Eastbourne. The SDW100 event sees 200 runners completing the entire route in around 24 hours.

North Downs Way (www.nationaltrail.co.uk/Northdowns) This popular 153-mile walk begins near Farnham in Surrey, but one of its most beautiful sections runs from near Ashford to Dover in Kent; there's also a loop that takes in Canterbury near its end.

Both long-distance routes have sections ideal for shorter walks. History seekers will appreciate the 1066 Country Walk, which connects with the South Downs Way.

Information

Tourism South East (www.visitsoutheastengland.com) The official website for south and southeast England.

Kent Attractions (www.kentattractions.co.uk)

Visit Kent (www.visitkent.co.uk)

Visit Sussex (www.visitsussex.org)

Visit Surrey (www.visitsurrey.com)

Getting There & Around

The southeast is easily explored by train or bus and most attractions can be visited in a day trip from London. Contact **Traveline Southeast** (www.travelinesoutheast.org.uk) for comprehensive information on public transport in the region.

BUS Explorer tickets (adult/child £6.50/4.50) provide day-long unlimited travel on most buses throughout the region; you can buy them at bus stations or on your first bus.

TRAIN The southeast can be reached from either London's Victoria, St Pancras or Charing Cross stations

You can secure 33% discounts on most rail fares in the southeast by purchasing a Network Railcard (p825). Three adults can travel with you and children under 15 save 60%.

KENT

Kent isn't described as the garden of England for nothing. Inside its sea-lined borders you'll find a fragrant landscape of gentle hills, fertile farmland, cultivated country estates and fruit-laden orchards. It could also be described as the beer garden of England, producing the world-renowned Kent hops, some of the country's finest ales and award-winning wines from its numerous vineyards. At its heart is spellbinding Canterbury, crowned by its enthralling cathedral.

WHITE HORSE OF KENT

Forget the *Angel of the North* and any other piece of public art for that matter, the southeast may one day trump them all with the ambitious *White Horse of Kent*. Designed by Turner Prize–winner Mark Wallinger, the gargantuan lifelike stallion will stand more than twice as tall (50m) as Gateshead's angel. Towering above both the Eurostar railway line and the A2 motorway near Ebbsfleet, it will eventually overtake it as the country's most viewed work of public art. However, this proud symbol of Kent must first jump a supersize hurdle – building costs of over £12 million. Don't expect to see it out of your train or car window for some time yet.

Canterbury & the Southeast Highlights

1. Shopping, tanning and partying in **Brighton & Hove** (p172), bustling hedonist capital of the southeast

2. Making a pilgrimage to **Canterbury Cathedral** (p142), among England's most important religious sites

3. Wandering the cobbled lanes of **Rye** (p162), one of England's prettiest towns

4 Kicking back at the moated marvel that is **Leeds Castle** (p149)

5 Scrambling up **Beachy Head** (p169), a spectacular headland in snow-white chalk

6 Shaking out your beach towel for some seaside fun on the **Isle of Thanet** (p154)

7 Packing your thirst for a **vineyard or brewery tour** (p148)

8 Taking a tour of the atmospheric WWII tunnels beneath sprawling **Dover Castle** (p158)

Here, too, are beautiful coastal stretches dotted with beach towns and villages, from old-fashioned Broadstairs to gentrified Whitstable and the aesthetically challenged port town of Dover.

Canterbury

POP 43,400

Canterbury tops the charts when it comes to English cathedral cities and is one of southern England's top attractions. The World Heritage–listed cathedral that dominates its centre is considered by many to be one of Europe's finest, and the town's narrow medieval alleyways, riverside gardens and ancient city walls are a joy to explore. But Canterbury isn't just a showpiece of times past; it's a spirited place with an energetic student population and a wide choice of contemporary bars, restaurants and arts venues. Book ahead for the best hotels and eateries: pilgrims may no longer flock here in their thousands, but tourists certainly do.

The old city centre is enclosed by a bulky medieval city wall that makes a wonderful walk. The Unesco World Heritage Site encompasses the cathedral, St Augustine's Abbey and St Martin's Church. Much of the centre is pedestrianised, but there is parking inside the wall.

History

Canterbury's past is as rich as it comes. From AD 200 there was a Roman town here, which later became the capital of the Saxon kingdom of Kent. When St Augustine arrived in England in 597 to carry the Christian message to the pagan hordes, he chose Canterbury as his *cathedra* (primary seat) and set about building an abbey on the outskirts of town. Following the martyrdom of Thomas Becket, Canterbury became northern Europe's most important centre of pilgrimage, which in turn led to Geoffrey Chaucer's *The Canterbury Tales,* one of the most outstanding poetic works in English literature.

Blasphemous murders and rampant tourism thrown aside, the city of Canterbury still remains the primary seat for the Church of England.

Sights

Canterbury Cathedral CATHEDRAL

(www.canterbury-cathedral.org; adult/concession £8/7, tour adult/child £5/3, audio tour adult/concession £3.50/2.50; ⌚9am-5pm Mon-Sat, 12.30-2.30pm Sun year-round, tour 10.30am, noon & 2.30pm Mon-Fri, 10.30am, noon & 1.30pm Sat Easter-Oct) A rich repository of more than 1400 years of Christian history, the Church of England's mother ship is truly an extraordinary place with an absorbing history. This Gothic cathedral, the highlight of the city's World Heritage Sites, is the southeast's top tourist attraction as well as a pious place of worship. Allow at least two hours to do it justice.

The cathedral is an overwhelming edifice crammed with enthralling stories, striking architecture and a very real and enduring sense of spirituality, although visitors can't help but pick up on the ominous undertones of violence and bloodshed that whisper from its walls.

This ancient structure is packed with monuments commemorating the nation's battles. Also here is the grave and heraldic tunic of one of the nation's most famous warmongers, Edward the Black Prince (1330–76). The spot in the northwest transept where Archbishop Thomas Becket met his grisly end has been drawing pilgrims

KEEP YOUR ENEMIES CLOSE...

Not one to shy away from nepotism, in 1162 King Henry II appointed his good mate Thomas Becket to the highest clerical office in the land, figuring it would be easier to force the increasingly vocal religious lobby to toe the line if he was pally with the archbishop. Unfortunately for Henry, he had underestimated how seriously Thomas would take the job, and the archbishop soon began disagreeing with almost everything the king said or did. By 1170 Henry had become exasperated with his former favourite and, after a few months of sulking, 'suggested' to four of his knights that Thomas was too much to bear. The dirty deed was done on 29 December. Becket's martyrdom – and canonisation in double-quick time (1173) – catapulted Canterbury Cathedral to the top of the premier league of northern European pilgrimage sites. Mindful of the growing criticism of his role in Becket's murder, Henry arrived here in 1174 for a dramatic *mea culpa* and, after allowing himself to be whipped and scolded, was granted absolution.

THE CANTERBURY TALES

If English literature has a father figure, then it must be Geoffrey Chaucer (1342/3–1400). Chaucer was the first English writer to introduce characters – rather than 'types' – into fiction, and he did so to greatest effect in his most popular work, *The Canterbury Tales*.

Written in the now hard-to-decipher Middle English of the day between 1387 and his death, Chaucer's *Tales* is an unfinished series of 24 vivid stories, as told by a party of pilgrims on their journey from London to Canterbury and back. Chaucer successfully created the illusion that the pilgrims, not Chaucer (though he appears in the tales as himself), are telling the stories, which allowed him unprecedented freedom as an author. *The Canterbury Tales* remains one of the pillars of the literary canon but, more than that, it's a collection of rollicking good yarns of adultery, debauchery, crime and edgy romance, and is filled with Chaucer's witty observations regarding human nature.

for more than 800 years and is marked by a flickering candle and striking modern altar.

The doorway to the crypt is beside the altar. This cavernous space is the cathedral's highlight, an entrancing 11th-century survivor from the cathedral's last devastating fire in 1174, which destroyed the rest of the building. Look for original, amazingly well preserved carvings among the forest of pillars.

The wealth of detail in the cathedral is immense and unrelenting, so it's well worth joining a one-hour tour, or you can take a 40-minute self-guided audio tour.

Canterbury Heritage Museum MUSEUM
(www.canterbury-museums.co.uk; Stour St; adult/child £8/free; ⏲10am-5pm daily) A fine 14th-century building – once the Poor Priests' Hospital – now houses the city's absorbing museum, which has a jumble of exhibits from pre-Roman times to the assassination of Becket, and from Joseph Conrad to locally born celebs. The kids' room is excellent, with a memorable glimpse of real medieval poo among other fun activities, and choo-choo fans can admire the Stephensons' *Invicta* loco that ran on the Crab & Winkle line between here and Whitstable (the world's third passenger railway). The building also houses the fun **Rupert Bear Museum** (Rupert's creator, Mary Tourtel, was born in Canterbury) and a gallery celebrating another children's favourite of old, Bagpuss.

St Augustine's Abbey RUIN
(EH; adult/child £4.90/2.90; ⏲10am-6pm Jul & Aug, to 5pm Wed-Sun Apr-Jun) An integral but often overlooked part of the Canterbury World Heritage Site, St Augustine's Abbey was founded in AD 597, marking the rebirth of Christianity in southern England. Later requisitioned as a royal palace, it fell into disrepair and now only stumpy foundations remain. A small museum and a worthwhile audio tour (free) do their best to underline the site's importance and put flesh back on its now humble bones.

FREE **St Martin's Church** CHURCH
(North Holmes Rd; ⏲11am-3pm Tue, Thu & Sat Apr-Sep) This squat little building just off the road out to Sandwich is thought to be England's oldest parish church in continuous use, and is where Queen Bertha (the wife of the Saxon King Ethelbert) welcomed Augustine upon his arrival in the 6th century. The original Saxon church has been swallowed by a medieval refurbishment, but it's still worth the 900m walk east of the abbey.

Eastbridge Hospital HISTORIC BUILDING
(www.eastbridgehospital.org.uk; 25 High St; adult/child £2/1; ⏲10am-5pm Mon-Sat) A 'place of hospitality' for pilgrims, soldiers and the elderly since 1180 and the last of many such buildings in the city still open to the public, Eastbridge Hospital of St Thomas the Martyr is worth a visit for the Romanesque undercroft and historic chapel. The 16th-century almshouses, still in use today, sit astride Britain's oldest road bridge, which dates back over 800 years.

Roman Museum MUSEUM
(Butchery Lane; adult/child £6/free; ⏲10am-5pm) Recently saved from a council ruse to convert it into a restaurant, this fascinating subterranean archaeological site enables visitors to walk around reconstructed Roman rooms, including a kitchen and a market place, as well as view Roman mosaic floors.

Canterbury

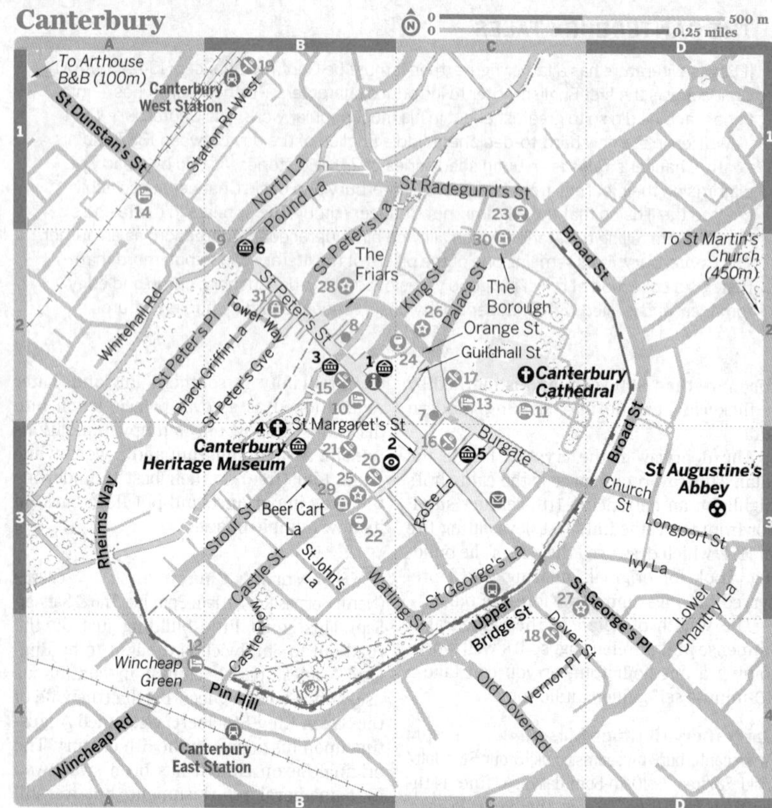

West Gate Towers MUSEUM

(St Peter's St) The city's only remaining medieval gateway has become Canterbury's most discussed sight in recent years. Threatened with closure due to council cuts in 2011, it was taken over by a local businessman who spent large sums turning it into a real family attraction. His sudden death in early 2012 left the towers closed again and their future uncertain. Double-decker buses only ceased edging their way through the narrow 14th-century archway, wing mirrors flattened, in spring 2012.

FREE **Greyfriars Chapel** CHURCH

(⏲2-4pm Mon-Sat Easter-Sep) In serene riverside gardens behind the Eastbridge Hospital you'll find Greyfriars Chapel, the first English monastery built by Franciscan monks in 1267. The grounds are a tranquil spot to unfurl the picnic blanket.

Canterbury Tales INTERPRETATION CENTRE

(www.canterburytales.org.uk; St Margaret's St; adult/child £7.75/5.75; ⏲10am-5pm Mar-Oct) A three-dimensional interpretation of Chaucer's classic tales told through jerky animatronics and audioguides, the ambitious Canterbury Tales show is certainly entertaining but could never do full justice to the original tales. However, it does serve as a light-hearted introduction for the young or uninitiated.

Beaney House of Art & Knowledge MUSEUM

(☎01227-378100; 18 High St; admission free; ⏲9am-5pm Mon-Wed, 9am-7pm Thu, Fri & Sat, 10am-5pm Sun) This mock-Tudor edifice is the grandest on the main shopping thoroughfare, if not the most authentic. It has housed Canterbury's main library, a museum and an art gallery since 1899, but closed in 2009 for major renovation and expansion. The whole caboodle reopened in 2012 with a much larger exhibition space, a much-improved library and a new tenant, the tourist office.

Canterbury

Top Sights

Canterbury Cathedral ... C2
Canterbury Heritage Museum ... B3
St Augustine's Abbey ... D3

Sights

1 Beaney House of Art & Knowledge ... B2
2 Canterbury Tales ... B3
3 Eastbridge Hospital ... B2
4 Greyfriars Chapel ... B3
5 Roman Museum ... C3
6 West Gate Towers ... B2

Activities, Courses & Tours

7 Canterbury Guided Tours ... C2
8 Canterbury Historic River Tours ... B2
9 Canterbury River Navigation Company ... B2
Ghost Tours ... (see 25)

Sleeping

10 Abode Canterbury ... B2
11 Canterbury Cathedral Lodge ... C2
12 Castle House ... A4
13 Cathedral Gate Hotel ... C2
14 House of Agnes ... A1

Eating

15 Boho ... B2
16 Cafe Mauresque ... C3
17 Deeson's ... C2
18 Farmhouse ... C4
19 Goods Shed ... B1
20 Tiny Tim's Tearoom ... B3
21 Veg Box Cafe ... B3

Drinking

22 Loft ... B3
23 Parrot ... C1
24 Thomas Becket ... C2

Entertainment

25 Alberry's Wine Bar ... B3
26 Ballroom ... C2
27 Chill Nightclub ... C3
28 New Marlowe Theatre ... B2

Shopping

29 Chaucer Bookshop ... B3
30 Madame Oiseau ... C2
31 Revivals ... B2

Tours

Canterbury Historic River Tours BOAT TOUR
(07790-534744; www.canterburyrivertours.co.uk; adult/child £8/4.50; 10am-5pm Mar-Oct) Knowledgable guides double up as energetic rowers on these fascinating River Stour minicruises that leave from behind the Old Weaver's House on St Peter's St.

Canterbury River Navigation Company BOAT TOUR
(07816-760869; www.crnc.co.uk; Westgate Gardens; adult/child from £8/4; Apr-Oct) Relaxing punt trips on the River Stour.

Canterbury Guided Tours WALKING TOUR
(01227-459779; www.canterburyguidedtours.com; adult/child/concession £6.50/4.50/6; 11am Feb-Oct, plus 2pm Jul-Sep) These chaperoned walking tours leave from opposite the entrance to Canterbury Cathedral. (Check the website or with the tourist office first as this may change.)

Ghost Tours WALKING TOUR
(0845 519 0267; www.canterburyghosttour.com; adult/child £9/7.50; 8pm Fri & Sat) The award-winning ghost hunts depart from outside Alberry's Wine Bar (p147) on St Margaret's St.

Festivals & Events

Canterbury Festival ARTS
(01227-787787; www.canterburyfestival.co.uk) Myriad musicians, comedians, theatre groups and other artists from around the world come to party for two weeks in mid-October during this festival.

Sleeping

TOP CHOICE **Abode Canterbury** HOTEL £££
(01227-766266; www.abodehotels.co.uk; 30-33 High St; r from £135;) The only boutique hotel in town, the 72 rooms at this supercentral option are graded from 'comfortable' to 'fabulous' and, for the most part, live up to their names. They come with little features such as handmade beds, cashmere throws, velour bathrobes, beautiful modern bathrooms and little tuck boxes of locally produced snacks. There's a splendid Champagne bar, restaurant and tavern here, too.

House of Agnes HOTEL ££
(01227-472185; www.houseofagnes.co.uk; 71 St Dunstan's St; r from £83; @) Situated near the West Gate, this rather wonky 13th-century beamed inn, mentioned in Dickens' *David Copperfield*, has eight themed rooms bearing such names as 'Marrakesh' (Moorish), 'Venice' (inevitable carnival masks), 'Boston' (light and airy) and 'Canterbury' (antiques and heavy fabrics). If you prefer your room to have straight lines and right angles, there are eight less exciting, but no less comfortable, rooms in an annexe in the walled garden.

Arthouse B&B B&B ££
(01227-453032; www.arthousebandb.com; 24 London Rd; r £60-65; P) A night at Canterbury's newest and most laid-back digs, housed in a 19th-century fire station, a bit like staying over at a really cool art student's pad. The theme is funky and eclectic, with furniture by local designers and artwork on the walls by the instantly likeable artist owners, who have their house-studio on-site. The organic continental breakfast is laid out in the guest kitchen with a quite hostel-like vibe. Only one of the three rooms is en suite.

Cathedral Gate Hotel HOTEL ££
(01227-464381; www.cathgate.co.uk; 36 Burgate; s/d £70/105, without bathroom £48/80;) Predating the spectacular cathedral gate that it adjoins, this quaintly dated 15th-century hotel is a medieval warren of steep staircases and narrow passageways providing access to 27 pleasingly old-fashioned rooms with angled floors, low doors and wonky walls. Some have cathedral views, others overlook pretty Buttermarket. There's no lift.

Kipp's Independent Hostel HOSTEL £
(01227-786121; www.kipps-hostel.com; 40 Nunnery Fields; dm/s/d £16/22/36; @) Occupying a red-brick town house in a quietish residential area less than a mile from the city centre, these superb backpacker digs enjoy a homely atmosphere, clean though cramped dorms and rave reviews.

Magnolia House B&B ££
(01227-765121; www.magnoliahousecanterbury.co.uk; 36 St Dunstan's Tce; s/d from £50/95; P@) An alluringly cosy Georgian guesthouse, complete with beautifully appointed if slightly overfilled rooms, lovely gardens and big, cooked-just-for-you breakfasts. Head up St Dunstan's St from the West Gate for around 400m until you reach a roundabout. Turn left and St Dunstan's Terrace is the second turn on the left.

Castle House HOTEL ££
(01227-761897; www.castlehousehotel.co.uk; 28 Castle St; s/d £90/110; P@) This historic guesthouse sits opposite the ruins of Canterbury's Norman castle and incorporates part of the old city walls. The tasteful, high-ceilinged rooms have great views and bags of space and there's a secluded garden out the back.

Canterbury Cathedral Lodge HOTEL ££
(01227-865350; www.canterburycathedrallodge.org; r from £60; @) Located opposite the cathedral within the precinct itself, the position of this purpose-built, circular lodge is pretty special. The 21st-century rooms have excellent facilities but this place is, understandably, full more often than not, so book ahead. If you are watching your budget, the hotel keeps six low-cost rooms for around £60 a night.

Yew Tree Park CAMPSITE £
(01227-700306; www.yewtreepark.com; Stone St; tent & 2 adults £14.50-19.20; Apr-Sep; P@) Set in gentle rolling countryside 5 miles southeast of the city, this lovely family-run campsite has plenty of soft grass to pitch a tent on and a heated swimming pool. Call for directions and transport information.

Eating

TOP CHOICE **Deeson's** BRITISH ££
(01227-767854; 25-27 Sun St; mains £4.50-16) Put the words 'local', 'seasonal' and 'tasty' into a make-believe restaurant search engine and this superb British eatery would magically pop up first under Canterbury. Local fruit and veg, award-winning wines, beers and ciders, fish from Kent's coastal waters and the odd ingredient from the proprietor's very own allotment, all served in a straightforward, contemporary setting a Kentish apple's throw from the cathedral gates. What more do you want? Bookings recommended.

Boho INTERNATIONAL £
(43 St Peter's St; snacks £3-10; 9am-6pm Mon-Sat, 10am-5pm Sun) In a prime spot on the main drag, next to the Eastbridge Hospital, this hip eatery is extraordinarily popular and you'd be lucky to get a table on busy shopping days. The coolest sounds on CD

lilt through the chic retro dining space as chilled-out diners chow down on humungous burgers, full-monty breakfasts and imaginative international mains. Boho doesn't do bookings, so be prepared to queue.

Farmhouse MODERN BRITISH ££
(www.thefarmhousecanterbury.co.uk; 11 Dover St; mains £10-16; ⌚9am-11pm Tue-Thu, to 2am Fri & Sat, 11am-5pm Sun; 📶) This hip, multipurpose venue just outside the city centre is Canterbury's coolest retreat morning, noon and night. The daytime restaurant plates up cooked-to-order mains, all bursting with seasonal Kentish flavour, amid '60s cabinets, old wireless sets and other retro fittings. After dark the focus switches to the moody bar, which at weekends pounds to live bands. The tuned-in owners organise Canterbury's very popular Lounge on the Farm music festival.

Veg Box Cafe VEGETARIAN £
(1 Jewry Lane; soups/specials £4.95/6.95; ⌚breakfast & lunch Mon-Sat; 🌱) Perched above Canterbury's top veggie food store, this welcoming, laid-back spot uses only the freshest, locally sourced organic ingredients in its dishes.

Tiny Tim's Tearoom TEAHOUSE £
(☎01227-450793; 34 St Margaret's St; mains £7-9; ⌚9.30am-5pm Tue-Sat, 10.30am-4pm Sun) Swish 1930s English tearoom offering hungry shoppers big breakfasts bursting with Kentish ingredients and tiers of cakes, crumpets, cucumber sandwiches and scones plastered in clotted cream.

Goods Shed MARKET RESTAURANT ££
(☎01227-459153; Station Rd West; mains £12-20; ⌚market 9am-7pm Tue-Sat, 10am-4pm Sun, restaurant breakfast, lunch & dinner Tue-Sat, lunch Sun) Farmers market, food hall and fabulous restaurant all rolled into one, this converted station warehouse by the Canterbury West train station is a hit with everyone from self-caterers to sit-down gourmets. The chunky wooden tables sit slightly above the market hubbub, but in full view of its appetite-whetting stalls, and country-style daily specials exploit the freshest farm goodies that the garden of England can provide.

Cafe Mauresque NORTH AFRICAN ££
(☎01227-464300; www.cafemauresque.com; 8 Butchery Lane; mains £6.50-18.95) Fun little North African and Spanish spot with a plain cafe upstairs and a noisy basement swathed in exotic fabric, serving up rich tagines, couscous, paella and tapas.

Drinking

Parrot PUB
(1-9 Church Lane) Built in 1370 on Roman foundations, Canterbury's oldest boozer has a snug, beam-rich pub downstairs and a much-lauded dining room upstairs under yet more ageing oak. Needless to say, many a local microbrew ale is pulled in both.

Thomas Becket PUB
(21 Best Lane) This classic English pub has a garden's worth of hops hanging from its timber frame, several quality ales to sample and a traditional decor of copper pots, comfy seating and a fireplace to cosy up to on winter nights. It also serves decent pub grub.

Loft BAR
(5-6 St Margaret's St) Far from Canterbury's quaint ale houses, this slick bar pumps chilled electronic beats into a retro-edged setting with one extremely long couch, a black granite bar and DJs spinning house at the weekend.

☆ Entertainment

Alberry's Wine Bar CLUB
(St Margaret's St) Every night is different at this after-hours music bar, which puts on everything from smooth live jazz to DJ-led drum and bass to commercial pop. It's a two-level place where you can relax over a French kiss (cocktail or otherwise) above, before partying in the basement bar below.

Chill Nightclub NIGHTCLUB
(www.chill-nightclub.com; St George's Pl) Canterbury's most visible nightclub is a large, fun, cheesy place, with a popular student night on Mondays and house anthems and old school–tune at weekends.

Ballroom LIVE MUSIC
(www.theballroom.co; 15 Orange St) The eclectic events calendar features everything from a resident DJ to open-mike nights, and from cabaret to live music, all in a heritage-listed 18th-century ballroom.

Cinema 3 CINEMA
(☎01227-769075; University of Kent) Part of the Gulbenkian Theatre (p148) complex, this cinema shows a mix of mainstream film, arty flicks and old classics. There's a pretty good cafe here, too.

New Marlowe Theatre THEATRE
(☎01227-787787; www.newmarlowetheatre.org.uk; The Friars) The old Marlowe Theatre was bulldozed in 2009 and the spanking new, state-of-the-art building bolted together in its place opened in late 2011. Established from day one as the southeast's premier venue for performing arts, the New Marlowe attracts top companies and quick-selling productions. Check out the bizarre auditorium, with its dark faux veneers contrasting sharply with life-jacket orange seats.

Gulbenkian Theatre THEATRE
(☎01227-769075; www.kent.ac.uk/gulbenkian; University of Kent) Out on the university campus, this large, long-established venue puts on plenty of contemporary plays, modern dance and great live music.

Shopping

Chaucer Bookshop BOOKS
(☎01227-453912; 6-7 Beer Cart Lane) Antiquarian and used books.

Revivals VINTAGE CLOTHING
(42 St Peters St) One of the southeast's best vintage clothing emporia.

Madame Oiseau CHOCOLATE
(8 The Borough) Mouth-watering Belgian chocolates are crafted before your very eyes in this tiny shop.

Information

Kent & Canterbury Hospital (☎01227-766877; Etherbert Rd) Has a minor injuries emergency unit and is a mile from the centre.

PC Repairs Kent (19-21 St Dunstan's St; per hr £3; ⌚10am-6pm Mon-Sat) Nine-machine cybercafe near the Canterbury West train station.

Post Office (19 St George's St) Located in the 1st floor of WH Smiths.

Tourist Office (☎01227-378100; www.canterbury.co.uk; 18 High St; ⌚9am-5.30pm Mon-Sat, 10am-5pm Sun) Recently moved to the Royal Museum & Art Gallery; staff can help book accommodation, excursions and theatre tickets.

Getting There & Away

The city's bus station is just within the city walls on St George's Lane. There are two train stations: Canterbury East for London Victoria and Dover, and Canterbury West for London's Charing Cross and St Pancras stations.

Bus

Canterbury connections:

Dover National Express, £5.40, 40 minutes, hourly

London Victoria National Express, £15.20, two hours, hourly

Margate 50 minutes, three per hour

Ramsgate 45 minutes, hourly

Sandwich 40 minutes, three hourly

Whitstable 30 minutes, every 10 minutes

A SWIG OF KENT & SUSSEX

With booze cruises over to Calais now almost a thing of the past, many Kent and Sussex drinkers are rediscovering their counties' superb home-grown beverages. Both produce some of the most delicious ales in the country and the southeast's wines are even outgunning some traditional continental tipples.

Kent's **Shepherd Neame Brewery** (☎01795-542016; www.shepherdneame.co.uk; 10 Court St, Faversham; tours £11.50; ⌚call ahead or see website for tour times) is Britain's oldest and cooks up aromatic ales brewed from Kent-grown premium hops. Sussex's reply is **Harveys Brewery** (☎01273-480209; www.harveys.org.uk; Bridge Wharf, Lewes; per person £2.50; ⌚evenings three times a week Jun-Jul & Sep-Nov) in Lewes, which perfumes the town centre with a hop-laden scent. Be sure to book in advance for tours of either brewery.

Mention 'English wine' not too long ago and you'd likely hear a snort of derision. Not any more. Thanks to warmer temperatures and determined winemakers, English wine, particularly of the sparkling variety, is developing a fan base of its own.

Award-winning vineyards can be found in both Sussex and Kent, whose chalky soils are likened to France's Champagne region. Many vineyards now offer tours and wine tastings. Some of the most popular are **Biddenden Vineyards** (☎01580-291726; www.biddendenvineyards.com; admission free ; ⌚tours 10am Wed & Sat), 1.5 miles south of Biddenden, and **Chapel Down Vinery** (☎01580-766111; www.englishwinesgroup.com; admission £9; ⌚tours daily Jun-Sep, weekends May & Oct), 2 miles south of Tenterden.

CANTERBURY ATTRACTIONS PASSPORT

The **Canterbury Attractions Passport** (adult/child £19/15.25) gives entry to Canterbury Cathedral (p142), St Augustine's Abbey (p143), Canterbury Tales (p144), Canterbury Heritage Museum (p143) and the Roman Museum (p143), as well as discounts on boat trips and various tours. It's available from the tourist office (p148).

Train

Canterbury connections:

Dover Priory £7.50, 25 minutes, every 30 minutes

London St Pancras High-speed service; £31.80, one hour, hourly

London Victoria/Charing Cross £26.80, 1¾ hours, two to three hourly

Getting Around

Canterbury's centre is mostly pedestrianised. Car parks are dotted along and just within the walls but, due to traffic issues, day trippers may prefer to use one of the three Park & Ride sites, which cost £2.50 per day and are connected to the centre by bus every eight minutes (7am to 7.30pm Monday to Saturday). **Downland Cycles** (☎01227-479643; www.downlandcycles.co.uk; St Stephen's Close) rents bikes from the Malthouse on St Stephen's Crt. Bikes cost £20 per day with helmet.

Taxi companies:

Cabwise (☎01227-712929)

Canterbury Cars (☎01227-453333)

Around Canterbury

HOWLETT'S WILD ANIMAL PARK

This 36-hectare **wildlife park** (www.aspinallfoundation.org/howletts; adult/child £23.95/18.95; ⏲9.30am-6pm) is one of England's best and a superb day out with tots in tow. The animals here live in an environment as close to their natural habitat as possible but are still easily spotted amid the greenery. Tigers, lemurs, African elephants, monkeys, giant anteaters and a very rare snow leopard called Marta are the highlights of the pleasant stroll around the enclosures and, if the kids need a break, there's a rope centre and face painting. The rather hefty admission goes towards funding projects to reintroduce rare and endangered animals to their natural habitat. There's 25% off if you book online.

The park is 4 miles east of Canterbury. By car, take the A257 and turn right at the Anchor Inn in the village of Littlebourne (heading towards Bekesbourne). Regular buses run from Canterbury bus station to Littlebourne, from where it's about a mile's walk.

Leeds Castle

The immense moated **Leeds Castle** (www.leeds-castle.com; adult/child £19.75/12.50; ⏲10am-6pm Apr-Sep, to 5pm Oct-Mar) is for many the world's most romantic castle, and it's certainly one of the most visited in Britain. While it looks formidable enough from the outside – a hefty structure balancing on two islands amid a large lake and sprawling estate – it's actually known as something of a 'ladies castle'. This stems from the fact that, throughout its more than 1000 years of history, it has been home to a who's who of medieval queens, most famously Henry VIII's first wife, Catherine of Aragon.

The castle was transformed from fortress to lavish palace over the centuries, and its last owner, the high-society hostess Lady Baillie, modernised some of the rooms and used them as a princely family home and party pad to entertain the likes of Errol Flynn, Douglas Fairbanks and JFK. Highlights include Queen Eleanor's medieval bathroom, King Henry VIII's ebony-floored banqueting hall and the boardroom where in 1978 Israeli and Egyptian negotiators met for talks about talks prior to the Camp David Accords.

The castle's vast estate offers enough attractions of its own to justify a daytrip: peaceful walks, an aviary, falconry demonstrations and a restaurant. You'll also find plenty of kiddie and toddler attractions and a hedge maze, overseen by a grassy bank where fellow travellers can shout encouragement or misdirections.

Since Lady Baillie's death in 1974, a private trust has managed the property. This means that some parts of the castle are periodically closed for private events.

A tourist train (50p) from the ticket office takes some of the legwork out of a visit.

Leeds Castle is just east of Maidstone. Trains run from London Victoria to Bearsted (£19.60, one hour) where you catch a special shuttle coach to the castle (£5 return; daily March to October, weekends only in winter).

Rochester

POP 27,000

Romans, Saxons and Normans have all occupied this historic riverside town and their architectural remains can be seen to this day, most vividly in a grand cathedral and a ruined Norman castle that loom over the town's medieval walls, cobbled streets and half-timbered buildings. Charles Dickens spent a large chunk of his childhood and the last few years of his life here, and many of the town's streets and buildings feature (albeit disguised) in his books.

Sights

FREE Rochester Cathedral CATHEDRAL
(www.rochestercathedral.org; audioguides £3; ⏲7.30am-6pm Mon-Fri & Sun; to 5pm Sat) Founded in AD 604, this is the second-oldest cathedral in England. Although construction on the present building started in 1080 and remodelling has left a mixture of styles, much of the Norman building remains, including the high-vaulted nave. Sunday afternoons are the best time to visit, when white-robed choristers flood the building with acoustic magic.

Rochester Castle CASTLE
(EH; adult/child £5.65/3.60; ⏲10am-6pm Apr-Sep, to 4pm Oct-Mar) Towering sturdily above the River Medway, Rochester's castle is one of the finest examples of Norman architecture in England and has lived through three sieges and partial demolition. The flooring of the 12th-century, 35m-tall Norman keep is long gone, allowing awesome views of its structure and open roof from the ground. You can also climb to the top of the battlements for panoramic vistas across the town and the vital river crossing it once guarded.

FREE Guildhall Museum MUSEUM
(High St; ⏲10am-4.30pm Tue-Sun) Housed in two splendid 17th-century edifices, this fascinating museum offers an eclectic choice of exhibitions. The highlight of the first building is a dramatic display about life aboard hulks – prison ships used to hold convicts in the 18th century. The second building is a masterpiece of Victoriana with several rooms dedicated to Dickens, a short film exploring the writer's links with Rochester, a display of Victorian toys and a painstakingly re-created late 19th-century drawing room.

Dickens' Swiss Chalet HISTORIC BUILDING
(Eastgate House grounds, Eastgate) Rochester has many Dickens associations, but none so striking as the writer's very own Swiss chalet, brought here from Gads Hill just outside the town where Dickens spent his final years. It's thought he penned his last work in its upper room. Sadly the interior is only accessible on special occasions.

Festivals & Events

Dickens Festival PARADE
(www.rochesterdickensfestival.org.uk) For three days in early June, the streets of Rochester take on an air of Victorian England during the town's annual Dickens Festival. When parades, music and costumed characters make the famous writer's best-loved novels come to life.

Sleeping & Eating

Sovereign B&B B&B ££
(☎01634-400474; www.thesovereignbb.co.uk; 29 Medway Bridge Marina, Manor Lane; s/d £37/75; wi-fi) With all the Medway's naval associations, what could be a more fitting place to stay than aboard a 1930s Rhine cruise ship, permanently docked at Rochester Marina. The six cabins are all different and, as you might expect, quite snug, but the spacious lounge makes up for it.

Riverview Lodge B&B £
(☎01634-842241; www.riverviewlodge-rochester.co.uk; 88 Borstal Rd; s/d from £26/49; P) Less then a mile from the centre, some of the 16 rooms at this homely guesthouse have dramatic Medway views.

Topes INTERNATIONAL ££
(60 High St; mains £10-17.50; ⏲lunch Wed-Sun; dinner Wed-Sat) Deservedly popular, modern European food served in a cosy restaurant with low-beamed slanted ceilings, wood panelling and a large, inviting fireplace. Some windows look out onto the castle.

Shopping

Baggins Book Bazaar SECONDHAND BOOKSHOP
(www.bagginsbooks.co.uk; 19 High St) If Rochester's illustrious literary connections have put you in a bookish mood, this fabulous bookshop claims to stock over half a million secondhand titles, making it one of the largest in the land.

Information

Tourist Office (☎01634-338141; 95 High St; ⏰10am-5pm Mon-Sat year-round, 10.30am-5pm Sun Apr-Sep) Has details of local accommodation, a cafe and a small art gallery. Free town tours leave here at 2.15pm from Easter to September at weekends and on bank holidays and Wednesdays.

Getting There & Away

Rochester train connections:

Canterbury £12.10, 50 minutes, twice hourly

London St Pancras High-speed service; £19.20, 39 minutes, twice hourly

London Victoria £16, 45 minutes, twice hourly

Whitstable

POP 30,195

Perhaps it's for the oysters, harvested since Roman times... Maybe it's for the weatherboard houses and shingle beach... Perhaps it's for the pleasingly old-fashioned main street with its petite galleries, been-there-forever outfitters and emporia of vintage frillies... But, most likely, it's for all of these reasons and more that Whitstable has become a weekend mecca for metropolitans, looking for an easy escape from the city hassle. Between waves of Londoners, the town lapses back into fishing-town mode, with a busy harbour and ice-chilled fish market supplying Kent's restaurants. Steadfast locals also play their part in keeping things authentic, with assorted campaigns in recent years preventing some of the biggest retail names from setting up shop, thus preserving the town's eccentric, artisanal air.

Sights

Whitstable Museum & Gallery MUSEUM
(www.whitstable-museum.co.uk; 5 Oxford St; adult/concession £3/1; ⏰10am-4pm daily) This modest museum has glass cases examining Whitstable's oyster industry, the Crab & Winkle Railway, which once ran from Canterbury, and the local fishing fleet. There's also a corner dedicated to the actor Peter Cushing, the town's most famous resident, and star of several Hammer Horror films, who died in 1994.

Festivals & Events

Whitstable Oyster Festival FOOD
(www.whitstableoysterfestival.co.uk) For a week in late July, the town hosts a seafood, arts and music extravaganza, the Whitstable Oyster Festival. There's a packed schedule of events, from history walks, and crab-catching and oyster-eating competitions, to a beer festival and traditional 'blessing of the waters'.

Sleeping

Pearl Fisher B&B ££
(☎01227-771000; www.thepearlfisher.com; 103 Cromwell Rd; s/d £60/95; P 📶) A few minutes' walk from the high street in a residential area, this B&B has snug rooms themed on places the owners have visited (Windsor, New England, Paris etc). The welcome is warm; the breakfasts substantial.

Hotel Continental HOTEL ££
(☎01227-280280; www.hotelcontinental.co.uk; 29 Beach Walk; r/huts from £80/75; P) The late-'90s quarters in this elegant seaside art-deco building are nothing special – come for the converted clapboard fisherman's cottages (huts) right on the beach. These should be booked well in advance.

Eating & Drinking

It's said Whitstable oysters should only be slurped when the name of the month contains an *r* – hence any available between May and August are imports. EU Protected Geographical Indication status means a Whitstable oyster is just that.

Wheeler's Oyster Bar SEAFOOD £££
(☎01227-273311; 8 High St; mains £18.50-22.50; ⏰lunch & dinner Thu-Tue) Squeeze onto a stool by the bar or into the Victorian four-table dining room of this baby-blue and pink restaurant, choose from a seasonal menu and enjoy the best seafood in Whitstable. Staff know their stuff – they've been serving oysters since 1856. Bookings highly recommended unless you're travelling solo. Cash only.

Samphire MODERN BRITISH ££
(☎01227-770075; 4 High St; mains £10-18; ⏰10am-10pm) The shabby-chic jumble of tables and chairs, big-print wallpaper and black-boarded menus create the perfect stage for meticulously crafted mains containing East Kent's most flavour-packed ingredients. An interesting side dish is its namesake samphire, an asparagus-like plant that grows on seasprayed rocks and cliffs, often found on menus in these parts.

Old Neptune PUB
(www.neppy.co.uk; Marine Tce) A ramshackle pub about as far onto the beach as it's possible to get (it's been washed away several

times by high tides), it has cosy winter window seats and wonky floorboards. Summer sees drinkers tumble out onto the shingle and there's regular live music.

Information

Whitstable has no tourist office, but you can pick up maps and other information at the **library** (31-33 Oxford St; ⏲9am-6pm Mon-Fri, to 5pm Sat, 10am to 4pm Sun), which also lays on free internet access (bring ID).

Getting There & Away

Bus 4 goes to Canterbury (30 minutes) every 10 minutes.

Margate

POP 40,400

A popular resort for over two centuries, Margate's late-20th-century slump was long and bleak as British holidaymakers ditched Victorian frump for the carefree *costas* of Spain. But this grand old seaside dame, with its fine-sand beaches and artistic associations, has bounced off the bottom. Major cultural regeneration projects – including the spectacular new Turner Contemporary art gallery – are slowly reversing the town's fortunes and, on busy days, even the odd non-English speaker can be overheard in the newly minted street cafes and rejuvenated old town.

Sights

TOP CHOICE Turner Contemporary ART GALLERY

(www.turnercontemporary.org; Rendezvous; admission free; ⏲10am-6pm Tue-Sun) This state-of-the-art gallery, bolted together on the site of the seafront guesthouse where Turner used to stay, finally opened in 2011 after much delay. Instantly one of East Kent's top attractions, few fail to be impressed by the strikingly featureless shell and minimalist interior, the only thing distracting the eye, apart from the artwork on display, being the floor-to-ceiling seaview windows. These allow you to appreciate the very thing Turner loved so much about Margate – the sea, sky and refracted light of the north Kent coast. The gallery is attracting top-notch contemporary installations by high-calibre artists such as Tracey Emin (who grew up in Margate) and Alex Katz, so be sure to catch a free gallery tour (11am weekends).

Shell Grotto GROTTO, CAVE

(www.shellgrotto.co.uk; Grotto Hill; adult/child £3/1.50; ⏲10am-5pm Apr-Oct) Margate's unique attraction is this mysterious, subterranean grotto discovered in 1835. It's a claustrophobic collection of rooms and passageways embedded with millions of shells arranged in symbol-rich mosaics. It has inspired feverish speculation over the years, but presents few answers: some think it to be a 2000-year-old pagan temple; others, an elaborate 19th-century hoax. Either way, it's an exquisite place worth seeing.

Tom Thumb Theatre THEATRE

(☎01843-221791; www.tomthumbtheatre.co.uk; Eastern Esplanade) Just over a mile along the seafront heading east into Cliftonville, the tiny Tom Thumb, with its titchy stage and just 58 seats, is thought to be the world's smallest working theatre.

Sleeping & Eating

TOP CHOICE Reading Rooms B&B £££

(☎01843-225166; www.thereadingroomsmargate.co.uk; 31 Hawley Sq; r £180; 📶) Occupying an 18th-century Georgian town house on a tranquil, elegant square just five minutes on foot from the sea, this luxury boutique B&B is as stylish as they come. Generously sized rooms with waxed wooden floors and beautiful French antique reproduction furniture contrast with the 21st-century bathrooms fragrant with posh cosmetics. Breakfast is served in your room. Booking essential.

Walpole Bay Hotel HOTEL ££

(☎01843-221703; www.walpolebayhotel.co.uk; 5th Ave; s/d from £60/85; P) For Margate's most eccentric night's sleep, look no further than this peculiar part-hotel, part-shrine to interwar trinkets. The pink, flouncy rooms are furnished with antiques, while public spaces are lined with glass-cased displays of memorabilia from the early 20th century. The hotel is a mile from central Margate, in Cliftonville.

Mad Hatter CAFE £

(9 Lombard St; mains £4-8; ⏲11am-5.30pm Sat, from noon Sun) Insanely unmissable, this completely cuckoo eatery run by a top-hatted proprietor packs two rooms of a 1690s house with bonkers regalia and miscellaneous knick-knackery from down the ages. Christmas decorations stay up all year and the toilets are original Victorian porcelain. The yummy cakes and snacks are all homemade.

Information

Tourist Office (☎01843-577577; www.visitthanet.co.uk; Droit House, Stone Pier; ⏰10am-5pm daily Easter-Oct, 10am-5pm Tue-Sat, to 4pm Sun Nov-Easter) Serving all of Planet Thanet, this office stands next to the Turner Contemporary. Pick up a copy of *The Isle*, a glossy magazine crammed with listings and Thanet essentials.

Getting There & Away

Margate has good connections with London and East Kent.

BUS Main destinations:

Canterbury Bus 8; 45 minutes, four hourly

London Victoria National Express; £16, 2½ hours, four daily

TRAIN Main destinations:

London St Pancras High-speed service; £37.20, 1½ hours, hourly

London Victoria £31.90, one hour and 50 minutes, twice hourly

Broadstairs

POP 24,370

While its bigger, brasher neighbours seek ways to revive and regenerate, quaint little Broadstairs just quietly gets on with what it's done best for the last 150 years – wowing visitors with its tight sickle of reddish sand and sun-warmed lapping sea. Dickens certainly thought Viking Bay a pretty spot, making several visits between 1837 and 1859. The resort now plays the Victorian nostalgia card at every opportunity and names every second business after the works of its most famous holidaymaker.

Sights

Dickens House Museum MUSEUM

(2 Victoria Pde; adult/child £3.60/2; ⏰2-5pm Easter-May, 10am-5pm Jun-Sep) Given a fresh lick of paint for Dickens' 200th birthday in 2012, Broadstairs' top attraction is this quaint museum, the erstwhile home of Mary Pearson Strong who was Dickens' inspiration for the character of Betsey Trotwood in *David Copperfield*. Diverse Dickensiana on display includes letters from the author.

The large clifftop house dominating the northern end of Viking Bay is where Dickens stayed while in Broadstairs and where he wrote parts of *David Copperfield*. Today it's a private residence and not open to the public.

Festivals & Events

Dickens Festival PARADE, ARTS

(www.broadstairsdickensfestival.co.uk) Broadstairs' biggest bash is this annual, nine-day-long festival held in late June and culminating in a banquet and ball in Victorian fancy dress.

Sleeping & Eating

East Horndon B&B ££

(☎01843-868306; www.easthorndonhotel.com; 4 Eastern Esplanade; s £48, d £80-95; ⏰closed Dec & Jan; 📶) This elegant guesthouse sits on manicured lawns a few yards from the cliff edge. The eight comfortable rooms are decorated in warm colours, the front four enjoying views of the sea and the world's largest offshore wind farm.

Copperfields Guest House B&B ££

(☎01843-601247; www.copperfieldsbb.co.uk; 11 Queen's Rd; s/d £50/75; 📶) This vegetarian B&B has three homely rooms with en suites, and a warm welcome from the owners and pet Yorkie. It also caters for vegans and all products in the bathrooms are cruelty free. It's a short hop away from the seafront and there's space to store muddy bikes.

Oscar's Festival Cafe CAFE £

(www.oscarsfestivalcafe.co.uk; 15 Oscar Rd; snacks £4-6.50; ⏰10.30am-5pm Wed-Sun) Just back from the bandstand at the southern end of Viking Bay, this hidden gem of a cafe successfully re-creates that 1950s nostalgia for buttered-toast-and-railways that the British find so comforting.

Tartar Frigate PUB ££

(42 Harbour St; mains £14.50-18) This 18th-century harbourside pub is a great place in summer when tourists and locals alike spill out onto the beach. It has top-notch local seafood and regular live folk music.

Getting There & Away

BUS The handy Thanet Loop bus runs every eight to 10 minutes to Ramsgate (10 to 15 minutes) and Margate (15 to 25 minutes). Other services:

Canterbury Bus 8A/9; 1½ hours

London Victoria National Express; £14.70, three hours, four daily

TRAIN Main destinations:

London St Pancras High-speed service; £36, 1 hour and 20 minutes, hourly

London Victoria £21, two hours, twice hourly

ISLE OF THANET

Margate, Ramsgate and Broadstairs are all towns on the Isle of Thanet, but you won't need a wetsuit or a ferry to reach them – the 2-mile-wide Wantsum Channel, which divided the island from the mainland, silted up in the 16th century, transforming the East Kent landscape forever. In its island days, Thanet was the springboard of several epoch-making episodes in English history. It was here that the Romans kicked off their invasion in the 1st century AD and where Augustine landed in AD 597 to launch his conversion of the pagans.

Ramsgate

POP 40,000

With a greater variety of things to do compared with other Thanet towns, Ramsgate has a friendlier feel than rival Margate and is more vibrant than quaint little neighbour Broadstairs. A forest of sails whistles serenely in the breeze below the handsomely curved walls of Britain's only royal harbour, surrounded by seafront bars and cosmopolitan street cafes that give things a laid-back feel. One celebrity chef away from being described as 'up and coming', Ramsgate retains a shabbily undiscovered charm, with its sweeping Blue Flag beaches, some spectacular Victorian architecture and a few welcoming places to stay and eat, making it worth the trip.

Sights & Activities

Ramsgate's wide, reddish-sand **beach** is the town's main draw, though it must be said that Thanet has prettier strands. The site of the huge former outdoor swimming pool has been under redevelopment as a beachfront hotel and luxury apartments for years, with no end in sight to the construction work. The timber wall around the site has been turned into an alfresco art gallery, where everyone from local artists and schoolchildren to professionals display their takes on this grand old resort.

FREE **Spitfire Memorial Museum** MUSEUM
(www.spitfiremuseum.org.uk; Manston Rd; ⌚10am-5pm Apr-Oct, to 4pm Nov-Mar) Located around 4 miles northwest of the town centre at Manston Airport (aka Kent International), the main aim at this purpose-built museum is to get up close and personal with two real WWII planes, one a Spitfire, the other a Hurricane. Both look factory fresh, but are surprisingly delicate, so sadly there's no clambering on board. Around the planes are gathered myriad flight-associated exhibits, many relating to Manston's role as an airfield during the Battle of Britain. To get there, take hourly bus 38 from King St and alight at the airport. The museum is around 10 minutes' walk along Manston Rd.

Horizon Sea Safaris BOAT TOUR
(☎07931-744788; www.horizonseasafaris.com; Royal Harbour; tours from £20 per person) This locally recommended company runs rigid inflatable tours to the world's biggest offshore wind farm (just off the Thanet coast), as well as seal-spotting trips to the Goodwin Sands and Pegwell Bay.

Sleeping & Eating

Glendevon Guesthouse B&B ££
(☎01843-570909; www.glendevonguesthouse.co.uk; 8 Truro Rd; s/d from £55/85; P 📶) Run by energetic and outgoing young hosts, this comfy guesthouse takes the whole ecofriendly thing very seriously, with guest recycling facilities, eco-showers and even energy-saving hairdryers. The hallways of this grand Victorian house, a block back from the seafront road, are decorated with watercolours by local artists, and there are bookshelves full of games, books and DVDs to borrow. All the rooms have kitchenettes and breakfast is a convivial affair taken around a communal table.

Royal Harbour Hotel HOTEL ££
(☎01843-591514; www.royalharbourhotel.co.uk; 10-11 Nelson Crescent; s/d from £78/98; 📶) Occupying two regency town houses on a glorious seafront crescent, this boutique hotel feels enveloped in warmth and quirkiness. An eclectic collection of books, magazines, games and artwork line the hotel walls, and there's a gramophone with old records and an honesty bar in the lounge. Rooms range from tiny nautical-inspired 'cabins' to country-house-style, four-poster doubles, and most of them have picture-postcard views over the forest of masts below.

Eddie Gilbert's SEAFOOD ££
(☎01843-852123; 32 King St; mains £8.50-21; ⌚lunch & dinner Mon-Sat, lunch Sun) Indulge

in England's favourite aroma (battered fish and chips) at East Kent's best seafood and gourmet fish-and-chip restaurant above a traditional fishmonger's. The beamed dining space decorated with lobster cages, fish nets and sea charts is the ideal setting for platters of locally caught fish prepared in some very inventive ways by a Michelin-trained chef. There's plenty to choose from even if fish is not your dish.

Bon Appetit BRITISH ££

(4 Westcliff Arcade; mains £7-21) The best of a row of eateries on Westcliff, this first-rate restaurant is the creation of head chef Mark Way, who serves up French-inspired dishes in the simple dining room or with alfresco harbour views. Ingredients on the menu are of the seasonal and locally sourced ilk, with finely crafted mains including such delights as pan-fried Kentish pheasant, line-caught sea bass and lamb rump with rosemary and red-currant preserve.

Information

Tourist Office (☎01843-598751; Customs House, Harbour Parade; ⌚10am-2pm Mon-Sat) Small, municipally run visitors centre with out-of-hours brochure stands.

Getting There & Away

BOAT These companies have daily services:

Euroferries (☎0844 414 5355; www.euroferries.co.uk) High-speed car ferries to Boulogne (from £49 per car, 1¼ hours, four daily).

Transeuropa Ferries (☎01843-595522; www.transeuropaferries.com) Car ferries from Ramsgate to Ostend in Belgium (from £52 per car, five hours, three daily).

BUS Ramsgate is linked to Margate, Broadstairs, Sandwich and Dover by frequent local bus services.

London Victoria National Express; £13.90, three hours, four daily

TRAIN Main destinations:

London Charing Cross £31.20, two hours, hourly

London St Pancras High-speed service; £36.20, 1¼ hours, hourly

Sandwich

POP 4500

As close as you'll get to a living museum, Sandwich was once England's fourth city (after London, Norwich and Ipswich), a fact hard to grasp today as you ponder its drowsy medieval lanes, ancient churches, Dutch gables, crooked peg-tiled roofs and overhanging timber-framed houses. Once a port to rival London, decline set in when the entrance to the harbour silted up in the 16th century, leaving this once vital gateway to and from the Continent to spend the next 400 years retreating into very quaint rural obscurity. Preservation is big here, with huge local interest in period authenticity keeping even the tiny 100-seat cinema as an art-deco museum piece and the local 1920s garage, dealing more in classic cars than modern vehicles. Unlisted buildings are the exception within the historical core.

Of course, though the town makes precious little of it, Sandwich indirectly gave the world its favourite snack when the Fourth Earl of Sandwich called for his meat to be served between two slices of bread, thus freeing him to gamble all night long without leaving the table or smudging his cards. It hence became de rigueur to ask for meat 'like Sandwich' and the rest is fast-food history.

Ageing earls might be interested in another innovation associated with the town – Viagra – developed and produced at the mammoth, but now all-but-defunct, Pfizer pharmaceutical plant on the town's outskirts. However, true-blue conservative Sandwich is understandably a tad shy of its little-blue-pill heritage.

Sights & Activities

Sandwich's web of medieval and Elizabethan streets is perfect for ambling and getting pleasantly lost (many do). **Strand Street** in particular has one of the highest concentrations of half-timbered buildings in the country. Ornate brickwork on some houses betrays the strong influence of 350 Protestant Flemish refugees (the 'Strangers') who settled in the town in the 16th century on the invitation of Elizabeth I.

Guildhall Museum MUSEUM

(adult/child £1/50p; ⌚10.30am-12.30pm & 2-4pm Tue, Wed, Fri & Sat, 2-4pm Thu & Sun Apr-Nov) Sandwich's small but thorough museum is a good place to start. Exhibitions examine the town's rich past as one of the Cinque Ports, its role in various wars and gruesome punishments meted out to felons, fornicators and phoney fishermen.

Sandwich Quay WATERFRONT

Several attractions line the River Stour. First up is a cute little flint-chequered **barbican** toll gate, built by Henry VIII, which controls traffic flow over the only road bridge across the river. Nearby rises the **Fishergate**, built in 1384 and once the main entrance to the town through which passed goods from the Continent and beyond. On fair-weather days, hop aboard the **Sandwich River Bus** (☎07958-376183; www.sandwichriverbus.co.uk; adult/child 30min trip £7/5, 1hr £12/8; ⊙every 30-60min 11am-6pm Thu-Sun Apr-Sep) beside the toll bridge for seal-spotting trips along the River Stour and in Pegwell Bay or just as an interesting way to reach Richborough.

Salutation Gardens GARDENS
(www.the-secretgardens.co.uk; adult/child £6.50/3; ⊙10am-5pm) Just along from Fishergate is Sandwich's top attraction, a set of exquisite gardens laid out by leading early 20th-century garden designers Jekyll and Lutyens behind a 1912 mansion. There's a superb **tearoom** in the grounds.

St Peter's Church CHURCH
(King St) The oldest church in Sandwich is now no longer used for worship. It's a real mixture of styles and years: its tower collapsed in dramatic fashion in 1661 and it was rebuilt with a bulbous cupola by the Flemish 'Strangers'. It houses the town's old horse-drawn fire engine and sparse displays on the often scandalous earls of Sandwich.

St Clement Church & St Mary's Church CHURCHES
Architecture buffs should head for **St Clement's Church** (Church St St Clement's), topped with a handsome Norman tower. **St Mary's** (www.stmarysartscentre.org.uk; cnr Church St St Mary's & Strand St), the town's third church, is now a multipurpose venue hosting some surprisingly big acts, but open during the day for perusal.

Royal St George's GOLF COURSE
(www.royalstgeorges.com) Sandwich is also home to one of the most challenging golf links in England and occasional host to the Open Golf Championships. Ian Fleming of *James Bond* fame was elected captain of St George's in 1964 after setting the famous game of golf between Goldfinger and Bond on the course.

Sleeping & Eating

Sandwich once boasted a brewery and 50 pubs! That number has dropped significantly, but the town is still known for its atmospheric old taverns.

TOP CHOICE **Bell Hotel** HOTEL ££
(☎01304-613388; www.bellhotelsandwich.co.uk; The Quay; s/d from £95/110; P) Today the haunt of celebrity golfers, the Bell Hotel has been sitting on the town's quay since Tudor times, though much of the remaining building is from the 19th century. A splendid, sweeping staircase leads up to luxurious rooms, some with pretty quay views. The **Old Dining Room** restaurant is one of East Kent's poshest nosh spots.

No Name Shop DELI BISTRO ££
(No Name St; snacks £1.60-6.75, meals £6.50-14.50) This far-from-anonymous French-owned deli (downstairs) and bistro (upstairs) near the bus stop is a pleasantly aromatic spot for a quick sandwich in Sandwich or an 'oozy-licious' *croque-monsieur,* as well as more sophisticated dishes, followed by a relaxing glass of something Gallic. Very popular among locals, some of whom seem to regularly prefer it over their own kitchens.

King's Arms INN ££
(☎01304-617330; cnr Church St St Mary's & Strand St; light meals £3-8.50, mains £9.75-21;) This 15th-century inn opposite St Mary's church, serving quality English food and very popular Sunday lunches, has a beamed dining room heated by large fireplaces. There are six B&B rooms upstairs.

George & Dragon PUB ££
(Fisher St; mains £8-17) A short stroll from the quay, this wonderful 15th-century inn has a cosy front bar area, rear dining room and secret walled garden.

Information

Tourist Office (☎01304-613565; www.open-sandwich.co.uk; Guildhall, Cattle Market; ⊙10am-4pm Mon-Sat Apr-Oct) Helpful office situated in the historic Guildhall. In the entrance, take a peek into the impressive wood-panelled Elizabethan courtroom, in use until well into the 1980s.

Getting There & Away

Trains run from Dover Priory train station (22 minutes, hourly), Ramsgate (12 minutes, hourly) and London Charing Cross (£21.20, two hours and 20 minutes, hourly).

Buses also go to Ramsgate (26 minutes, hourly), Dover (41 minutes, hourly) and Canterbury (40 minutes, three hourly).

Around Sandwich

RICHBOROUGH

Roman Britain began here amid the windswept ruins of **Richborough Roman Fort** (EH; adult/child £4.90/2.90; ⏲10am-6pm Apr-Sep, to 4pm Sat & Sun Oct-Mar), two miles north of Sandwich. This is where the successful AD 43 invasion of Britain was launched and, to celebrate their victory, the Romans planted a colossal triumphal arch here, the base of which remains. The fort's clearest features today – high walls and scores of deep defensive ditches that give it the appearance of a vast jelly mould – came later as the Romans were forced to stave off increasingly vicious seaborne attacks.

There's a small on-site museum and an audio tour to steer you through the rise and fall of Roman Richborough. To arrive as the Romans did – by boat – take the Sandwich River Bus from Sandwich quay.

DEAL

Julius Caesar and his armies set foot on Deal's peaceful shingle beach in 55 BC for their first exploratory dip into Britain. Today there's a lovely little 16th-century **castle** (EH; Victoria Rd; adult/child £4.90/2.90; ⏲10am-6pm Apr-Sep) with curvaceous bastions that form petals in a Tudor rose shape. Far from delicate, however, it's the largest and most complete of Henry VIII's defence chain along the south coast.

And hardly a mile south is another link in the 16th-century coastal defences, **Walmer Castle** (EH; Kingsdown Rd; adult/child £7.50/4.50; ⏲10am-6pm Apr-Sep), the much-altered and really rather lavish official residence of the warden of the Cinque Ports. Military hero, the Duke of Wellington, died here.

Dover

POP 39,078

Down-in-the-dumps Dover has certainly seen better days and its derelict, postwar architecture and shabby town centre of vacant shops is a sad introduction to Blighty for travellers arriving from the Continent, most of whom pass through quickly. Lucky, then, that the town has a couple of stellar attractions to redeem it. The port's vital strategic position so close to mainland Europe gave rise to a sprawling hilltop castle, with some 2000 years of history to its credit. The spectacular white cliffs, as much a symbol of English wartime resilience as Winston Churchill or the Battle of Britain, rise in chalky magnificence to the east and west.

A recent development is Dover's rise as a top stopover for cruise ships, with almost 160 vessels calling at the West Docks in 2012 alone.

CINQUE PORTS

Due to their proximity to Europe, southeast England's coastal towns were the front line against raids and invasion during Anglo-Saxon times. In the absence of a professional army and navy, these ports were frequently called upon to defend themselves and the kingdom, on land and at sea.

In 1278 King Edward I formalised this already ancient arrangement by legally defining the Confederation of Cinque Ports. The five original ports – Sandwich, Dover, Hythe, Romney and Hastings – were granted numerous perks and privileges in exchange for providing the king with ships and men. At their peak, the ports were deemed England's most powerful institution after Crown and Church.

Even after shifting coastlines silted up several Cinque Port harbours, a professional navy was established at Portsmouth and the ports' real importance evaporated, the pomp and ceremony remain. The lord warden of the Cinque Ports is a prestigious post now given to faithful servants of the Crown. The Queen Mother was warden until she passed away, and was succeeded by Admiral Lord Boyce. Previous incumbents include the Duke of Wellington and Sir Winston Churchill.

'Who names us "sank" and not "sink" is a foreigner and foe' once went the saying on the south coast, describing a faux pas committed today by just about every unknowing tourist, both foreign and British (*cinque*, as in Cinque Ports, is pronounced 'sink' and not 'sank', as the French would say).

Dover

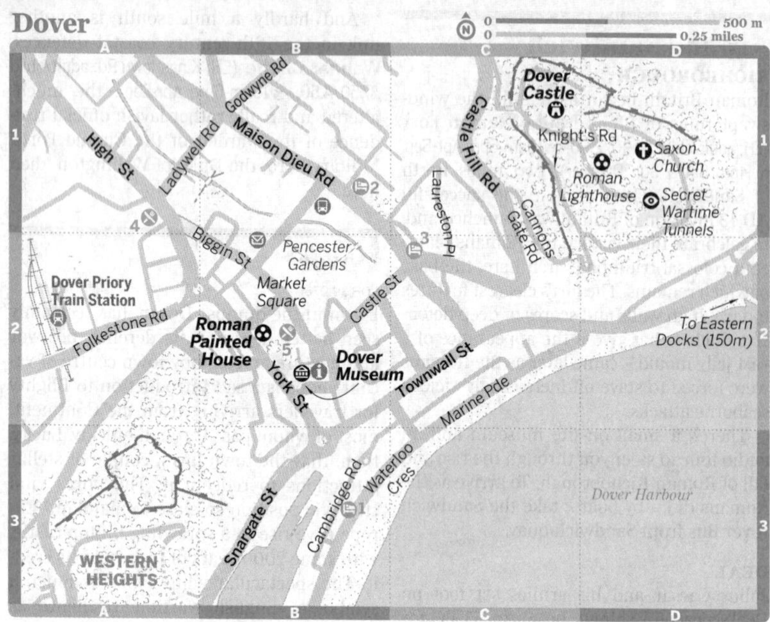

Dover

Sights & Activities

TOP CHOICE Dover Castle CASTLE

(EH; www.english-heritage.org.uk; adult/child £16.50/9.90; 10am-6pm Apr-Jul & Sep, from 9.30am Aug, to 5pm Oct, 10am-4pm weekends only Nov-Mar; P) Occupying top spot, literally and figuratively, on the Dovorian townscape, this most impressive of castles was built to bolster the country's weakest point at this, the shortest sea-crossing to mainland Europe. It sprawls across the city's hilltop, commanding a tremendous view of the English Channel as far as the French coastline. There's lots to see here, so allow yourself at least three hours.

The site has been in use for as many as 2000 years. On the vast grounds are the remains of a **Roman lighthouse**, which date from AD 50 and may be the oldest standing building in Britain. Beside it lies the restored Saxon church of **St Mary in Castro**.

The robust 12th-century **Great Tower**, with walls up to 7m thick, is a medieval warren filled with interactive exhibits and light-and-sound shows that take visitors back to the times of Henry II.

But the biggest draw here is the network of claustrophobic **secret wartime tunnels**. The chalk-hewn passageways were first excavated during the Napoleonic Wars and then expanded to house a command post and hospital in WWII. The new and highly enjoyable 50-minute guided tour (every 20 minutes) tells the story of one of Britain's most famous wartime operations, code-named Dynamo, which was directed from here in 1940 and saw hundreds of thousands of men evacuated from the beaches at Dunkirk. The story is told in a very effective way – video is projected sharply onto the tunnel walls and sounds rumble through the rock. At one point the entire passageway is consumed in flames; at others, visitors are plunged into complete darkness. Simply unmissable.

Dover Museum MUSEUM
(www.dovermuseum.co.uk; Market Sq; adult/child £3.50/2.25; ⏰10am-5pm Mon-Sat year-round, 10am-3pm Sun Apr-Sep) By far the most enthralling exhibit in the town's three-storey museum is an astonishing 3600-year-old Bronze Age boat, discovered here in 1992. Vaunted as the world's oldest-known seagoing vessel, it measures a thumping 9.5m by 2.4m and is kept in a huge, low-lit, climate-controlled glass case.

Roman Painted House RUINS
(New St; adult/child £3/2; ⏰10am-5pm Tue-Sun Jun-Sep) A crumbling 1960s bunker is the unlikely setting for some of the most extensive, if stunted, Roman wall paintings north of the Alps. Several scenes depict Bacchus (the god of wine and revelry), which makes perfect sense as this large villa was built around AD 200 as a *mansio* (hotel) for travellers in need of a little lubrication to unwind.

Sleeping

B&Bs cluster along Castle St, Maison Dieu Rd and Folkestone Rd.

TOP CHOICE **Wallett's Court** HOTEL £££
(☎01304-852424; www.wallettscourt.com; Westcliffe, St Margaret's-at-Cliffe; d from £170; P 📶) The weekend haunt of de-stressing London high-flyers, romantic couples and the odd moneyed cliff walker, this place is just a bit special. Digs at this country house in rolling open country range from spacious Jacobean guest rooms to beamed converted barns and a canvas wigwam in the grounds. Add to that a soothing spa, a first-rate restaurant and perky service, and you have one very relaxing country retreat. Heading towards Deal, turn right off the A258 for Westcliffe after almost 2 miles.

Dover Marina Hotel HOTEL ££
(☎01304-203633; www.dovermarinahotel.co.uk; Waterloo Cres; r £69-107; 📶) Just a few steps from Dover's beach, this newly revamped hotel crams 81 rooms of varying dimensions into a gently curving 1870s crescent edifice. The undulating corridors show the building's age but there's nothing wonky about the rooms with their trendy, ethnic fabrics, big-print wallpaper and contemporary artwork. Half the rooms have unrivalled sea views; 10 boast much-sought balconies.

East Lee Guest House B&B ££
(☎01304-210176; www.eastlee.co.uk; 108 Maison Dieu Rd; d £60; P 📶) This lovely terracotta-shingled town house impresses with its grand, elegantly decorated communal areas, energetic hosts, recently renovated rooms and excellent, varied breakfasts.

Number One Guest House B&B £
(☎01304-202007; www.number1guesthouse.co.uk; 1 Castle St; d from £50; P) Set in a grand Georgian town house at the foot of Dover Castle, rooms are decorated in traditional Victorian style. There's also a quaint walled garden with lovely views, and breakfast is served in bed.

Eating

TOP CHOICE **Allotment** BRITISH ££
(www.theallotmentdover.com; 9 High St; mains £7.50-16; ⏰breakfast, lunch & dinner Tue-Sat) In a relaxed, understated setting, Dover's best dining spot plates up local fish and meat from around Canterbury, seasoned with herbs from the tranquil garden out back. Swab the decks with a Kentish wine as you admire the view of the old town hall directly opposite through the exquisite stained glass frontage.

La Salle Verte CAFE £
(14-15 Cannon St; snacks £2-5.50; ⏰breakfast & lunch Mon-Sat) This much-loved coffee or lunch halt has fascinating black-and-white images of old Dover lining the walls, a rocking jukebox and friendly proprietors. It fills at lunch even on winter Wednesdays.

Information

Post Office (68-72 Pencester Rd)

Tourist Office (☎01304-205108; www.whitecliffscountry.org.uk; Market Sq; ⏰9.30am-5pm Mon-Sat year-round, 10am-3pm Sun Apr-Sep) Located in Dover Museum (p159), staff at this friendly office can book accommodation and ferries for a small fee.

Getting There & Away

Boat

Ferries depart for France from the Eastern Docks below the castle. Fares vary according to season and advance purchase. With the demise of Seafrance, services are in a state of flux.

DFDS (☎0871 574 7235; www.dfdsseaways.co.uk) Services to Dunkirk (two hours, every two hours).

P&O Ferries (☎0871 664 2020; www.poferries.com) Runs to Calais (1½ hours, every 40 minutes to an hour).

Bus

Dover connections:

Canterbury Bus 15; 45 minutes, twice hourly

Deal Bus 15; 40 minutes, twice hourly

London Victoria Coach 007; £14.80, 2½ to 3½ hours, 19 daily

Sandwich Bus 87/88; 45 minutes, hourly

Train

Dover connections:

London Charing Cross £21.10, two hours, twice hourly

London St Pancras High-speed service; £36.20, one hour, hourly

Ramsgate Via Sandwich; £8.70, 35 minutes, hourly

Getting Around

Between 7am and 11pm, a port shuttle bus runs between the Eastern Docks and the train station (£2, five minutes, every 20 minutes) as they're a long walk apart.

Around Dover

THE WHITE CLIFFS

Immortalised in song, film and literature, these iconic cliffs are embedded in the national consciousness, acting as a big, white 'Welcome Home' sign to generations of travellers and soldiers.

The cliffs rise 100m high and extend for 10 miles on either side of Dover, but it is the 6-mile stretch east of town – properly known as the Langdon Cliffs – that particularly captivates visitors' imaginations. The chalk here is about 250m deep, and the cliffs themselves are about half a million years old, formed when the melting ice caps of northern Europe were gouging a channel between France and England.

The Langdon Cliffs are managed by the National Trust, which has a **tourist office** (☎01304-202756; ⊗9.30am-5.30pm Mar-Oct, 10.30am-4pm Nov-Feb) and **car park** (non-members £3). They're 2 miles east of Dover along Castle Hill Rd and the A258 road to Deal or off the A2 past the Eastern Docks.

From the tourist office, follow the stony path east along the clifftops for a bracing 2-mile walk to the stout Victorian **South Foreland Lighthouse** (NT; www.nationaltrust.org.uk; adult/child £4/2; ⊗guided tours 11am-5.30pm Fri-Mon mid-Mar–Oct). This was the first lighthouse to be powered by electricity, and was the site of the first international radio transmissions in 1898.

A mile further on the same trail brings you to delightful **St Margaret's Bay**, a gap in the chalk with a sun-trapping shingle beach and the welcoming **Coastguard Pub** (www.thecoastguard.co.uk; mains £10-20), Britain's closest tavern to the Continent. From the top of the hill, the hourly bus 15 shuttles back to Dover or onwards to Deal.

To see the cliffs in all their full-frontal glory, **Dover White Cliffs Tours** (☎07971-301379; www.doverwhiteclifftours.com; adult/child £8/4; ⊗noon, 2pm & 4pm (5pm in summer) daily Easter-Oct) runs, weather permitting, 40-minute sightseeing trips at least three times a day from the Western Docks.

OCTOBUSSY

Ever wondered why James Bond is known as agent 007? In the 1950s, Bond's creator Ian Fleming lived near Dover and regularly travelled up to London by bus. The number of the service – 007. Yes, the world's most famous secret agent is named after a Kent bus service and, even today, the Dover–London National Express coach still bears the famous three digits.

ROMNEY MARSH

Sparsely populated and echoing with the whistling wind and lonely squawks of sea birds, this eerie landscape of flat reed beds was once a favourite haunt of smugglers and wreckers. The **Romney Marsh Visitor Centre** (www.kentwildlifetrust.org.uk; Dymchurch Rd, New Romney; ⊗9am-5pm Easter-Oct, 10am-4.30pm Nov-Easter) has the low-down if you're up for some detailed exploration of the area's natural habitats and ancient churches. However, the main attraction for most people is the **Romney, Hythe & Dymchurch Railway** (www.rhdr.org.uk; adult/child £15/7.50; ⊗usually daily Apr-Sep, Sat & Sun Nov-Mar), the world's smallest-gauge public railway, which runs 13.5 miles along the coast between Hythe and Dungeness lighthouse (the trip takes roughly an hour each way).

WORTH A TRIP

DOWN HOUSE

Charles Darwin lived the last 40 years of his life (from 1842) at **Down House** (EH; Luxted Road, Downe; adult/child £9.90/5.90; ⏲11am-5pm Wed-Sun mid-April–June & Sep-Oct, daily Jul & Aug), which witnessed the development of Darwin's theory of evolution by natural selection. The house and gardens have been restored to look much as they would have in Darwin's time, including Darwin's study, where he undertook much of his reading and writing; the drawing room, where he tried out some of his indoor experiments; and the gardens and greenhouse, where some of his outdoor experiments are re-created. There are three self-guided trails in the area where you can follow in the great man's footsteps.

The house, Downe village and the surrounding area were put forward by the British government in 2012 for inclusion on Unesco's list of World Heritage Sites.

Down House is in Downe, off the A21. Take bus 146 from Bromley North or Bromley South railway station, or service R8 from Orpington.

DUNGENESS

Sticking out from the western edge of Romney Marsh is a low shingle spit dominated by a brooding nuclear power station. In spite of the apocalyptic desolation, this spot is home to the largest sea-bird colony in the southeast at the **Royal Society for the Protection of Birds Nature Reserve** (☎01797-322588; www.rspb.org.uk; Dungeness Rd; adult/child £3/1; ⏲9am-9pm or sunset, tourist office 10am-5pm Mar-Oct, to 4pm Nov-Feb), which has displays, binocular hire, explorer backpacks for kids and information on birdwatching hides.

Sevenoaks & Around

POP 18,600

A bland commuter town off the M25, Sevenoaks is home to one of England's most celebrated country estates. The gates to **Knole House** (NT; adult/child £10.40/5.20; ⏲house noon-4pm Wed-Sun mid-Mar–Oct) sit on the southern High St, and from there it's a beautiful winding walk or drive through a rolling medieval park dotted with bold deer. The estate was built in the 12th century, but in 1456 the Archbishop of Canterbury, Thomas Bouchier, snapped the property up and set about building a vast and lavish house 'fit for the Princes of the Church'. Its curious calendar design encompasses 365 rooms, 52 staircases and seven courtyards. The house was the childhood home of Vita Sackville-West, whose love affair with Virginia Woolf spawned the novel *Orlando*, set at Knole. The house is 1.5 miles southeast of Sevenoaks train station on London Rd. Trains leave from London Charing Cross (£10.90, 35 minutes, every 15 minutes) and continue to Hastings (£18.60, one hour).

The home of Sir Winston Churchill from 1924 until his death in 1965, delightful **Chartwell** (NT; Westerham; adult/child £11.50/5.80; ⏲11am-5pm Wed-Sun Mar-Oct, plus Tue Jul & Aug), 6 miles west of Sevenoaks, offers a breathtakingly intimate insight into the life of England's famous cigar-chomping bombastic politician. This 19th-century house and its rambling grounds have been preserved much as Winnie left them, full of books, pictures, maps and personal mementos. Churchill was also a prolific painter and his now extremely valuable daubs are scattered throughout the house and fill the garden studio. A couple of rooms have been given over to his uniforms and awards, and an exhibition at the end of the tour route tells the story of his life. Transport options are limited without a car. Bus 236 (20 minutes, four daily) runs from Oxted train station to the nearby village of Crockham Hill, Monday to Friday. A better bet is to get to Westerham, two miles north of Chartwell, from Oxted by regular bus then take a taxi or walk.

Hever Castle

Idyllic little **Hever Castle** (www.hevercastle.co.uk; adult/child £14.50/8.30, gardens only £12/7.80; ⏲noon-6pm Apr-Oct) seems to have leapt right out of a film set. It's encircled by a narrow moat and surrounded by family-friendly gardens, complete with cute topiary of woodland creatures and wandering ducks and swans.

The castle is famous for being the childhood home of Anne Boleyn, mistress to

Henry VIII and, later, his doomed queen. It dates from 1270, with a Tudor house added in 1505 by the Bullen (Boleyn) family. The castle later fell into disrepair until 1903, when American multimillionaire William Waldorf Astor bought it, pouring obscene amounts of money into a massive refurbishment. The exterior is unchanged from Tudor times, but the interior is thick with Edwardian panelling.

From London Bridge trains go direct to Hever (£9.40, 40 minutes, hourly), a one-mile walk from the castle; and to Edenbridge (£9.10, 50 minutes, hourly), from where it's a 4-mile taxi or bike ride. If you're driving, Hever Castle is 3 miles off the B2026 near Edenbridge.

Penshurst

The pretty village of Penshurst, on the B2176, just off the A21, is lined with timber-framed Tudor houses and features a fanciful four-spired church, but most people come for grandiose medieval manor house **Penshurst Place** (www.penshurstplace.com; adult/child £9.80/6.20; ⌚noon-4pm Apr-Oct). Its pride and joy is the splendid **Baron's Hall**, built in 1341, where a number of royal visitors, including Queen Elizabeth I, were entertained beneath its stunning 18m-high chestnut roof. Just outside the main house is a vintage-toy museum, whose empty-eyed dolls, classic rocking horses and mechanical red-eyed bear are enough to give even adults nightmares.

WORTH A TRIP

SISSINGHURST CASTLE GARDEN

One of England's most famous and romantic gardens is at **Sissinghurst** (NT; adult/child £11.50/5.50; ⌚10.30am-5.30pm Fri-Tue Mar-Oct). Though the castle dates to the 12th century, writer Vita Sackville-West crafted the delightful gardens after she bought the estate in 1930. Highlights include the exuberant rose garden and the virginal snowy-bloomed White Garden. Sissinghurst is 2 miles northeast of Cranbrook and 1 mile east of Sissinghurst village off the A262. Hourly bus 5 runs from Staplehurst train station to Sissinghurst village.

Outside, Penshurst's famous **walled gardens** (⌚10.30am-6pm Apr-Oct) were designed in 1346 and have remained virtually unchanged since Elizabethan times. There are also lovely riverside walks in the grounds.

From Edenbridge, buses 231 and 233 leave for Royal Tunbridge Wells via Penshurst every hour (27 minutes).

EAST SUSSEX

Home to rolling countryside, medieval villages and gorgeous coastline, this inspiring corner of England is besieged by weekending Londoners whenever the sun pops out. It's not hard to see why as you explore the cobbled medieval streets of Rye; wander historic Battle, where William the Conqueror first engaged the Saxons in 1066; and peer over the edge of the breathtaking Seven Sisters chalk cliffs and Beachy Head near the gentle seaside town of Eastbourne.

Brighton, a highlight of any visit, offers some kicking nightlife, offbeat shopping and British seaside fun. But you needn't follow the crowds to enjoy East Sussex. It's just as rewarding to get off the beaten track, linger along its winding country lanes and stretch your legs on the South Downs Way, which traverses the South Downs National Park.

Rye

POP 4200

Often described as England's quaintest town, Rye is a little nugget of the past, a medieval settlement that looks like it's been dunked in formaldehyde and left on the shelf for all to admire. Even the most hard-boiled cynic can't fail to be softened by Rye's cobbled lanes, mysterious passageways and crooked half-timbered Tudor buildings. Tales of resident smugglers, ghosts, writers and artists abound.

Rye was once one of the Cinque Ports, occupying a high promontory above the sea. Today the town rises 2 miles from the briny; sheep graze where the Channel's strong tides once swelled.

Sights

A short walk from the Rye Heritage Centre, most start their exploration of Rye in the famous **Mermaid Street**, bristling with 15th-century timber-framed houses with quirky names such as 'The House with Two Front Doors' and 'The House Opposite'.

Church of St Mary the Virgin CHURCH
(Church Sq; tower adult/child £2.50/1; ⏲9.15am-5.30pm Apr-Sep) Rye's church is a hotchpotch of medieval and later styles. Its turret clock is the oldest in England (1561) and still works with its original pendulum, which swings above your head as you enter. Climb the **tower** for panoramic views of the town and surroundings.

Ypres Tower MUSEUM
(www.ryemuseum.co.uk; adult/child £3/free; ⏲10.30am-5pm Apr-Oct, to 4pm Nov-Mar) Just off Church Sq stands the sandcastle-esque Ypres Tower (pronounced 'wipers'), one part of Rye Museum. You can scramble through the 13th-century building to learn about its long history as a fort, prison, mortuary and museum (the last two at overlapping times), but it's the views of Rye Bay, Dungeness nuclear power station and even France on very clear days that will hold your attention longest. The star attraction at the other branch of the **museum** (3 East St; adult/child £1.50/free; ⏲10.30am-5pm Sat & Sun Apr-Oct), a short stroll away on East St, is a well-preserved 18th-century fire engine complete with its leather hoses and lead buckets.

Lamb House MUSEUM
(NT; West St; adult/child £4.60/2.35; ⏲2-6pm Tue & Sat late Mar-Oct) This Georgian town house is a favourite stomping ground for local apparitions, with the exception of its most famous resident, American writer Henry James, who lived here from 1898 to 1916, during which time he wrote *The Wings of the Dove*.

Landgate GATE
At the northeastern edge of the town, this thickset pale-stone tower dating from 1329 is the only remaining gate out of four and is still in use. The name comes from the fact that, when first built, it was the only gate linking the town to the mainland at high tide.

Activities

To combine history and a hearty hike, the well-signposted **1066 Country Walk** meanders 31 miles from Rye to Battle and Pevensey where it connects with the South Downs Way (p169).

Sleeping

Rye boasts an exceptional choice of unique period accommodation.

TOP CHOICE **Jeake's House** HOTEL ££
(☎01797-222828; www.jeakeshouse.com; Mermaid St; s/d from £70/90; P Wi-Fi) Superbly situated on cobbled Mermaid St, this labyrinthine 17th-century town house once belonged to US poet Conrad Aitken. The 11 rooms are named after writers who actually stayed here, though the decor was probably slightly less bold back then, minus the beeswaxed antiques and lavish drapery. You can literally take a pew in the snug book-lined bar and, continuing the theme, breakfast is served in an 18th-century former Quaker chapel.

Mermaid Inn HOTEL ££
(☎01797-223065; www.mermaidinn.com; Mermaid St; d from £90; P) Few inns can claim to be as atmospheric as this ancient hostelry, dating from 1420. Every room is different – but each is thick with dark beams and lit by leaded windows, and some are graced by secret passageways that now act as fire escapes. Small wonder it's such a popular spot – these days you're as likely to spot a celeb or a minor royal as the resident ghost.

George in Rye HOTEL £££
(☎01797-222114; www.thegeorgeinrye.com; 98 High St; d from £135; @ Wi-Fi) This old coaching inn has managed to reinvent itself as a contemporary boutique hotel while staying true to its roots. Downstairs, an old-fashioned wood-panelled lounge is warmed by roaring log fires, while the guest rooms in the main building, created by the set designer from the film *Pride & Prejudice*, are chic and understated. In contrast the two new Scandinavian-styled bedrooms in the courtyard are cosily spartan with their metal free-standing baths and wood cladding. The George's contemporary restaurant can contend with Rye's best and, if you stay here, ask to see the incredible and unexpectedly large 18th-century ballroom.

Windmill Guesthouse B&B ££
(☎01797-224027; www.ryewindmill.co.uk; Mill Lane; d from £70; P Wi-Fi) Visible from the main road, this white windmill, sails still intact, houses perhaps Rye's oddest digs. Due to the shape of the building, room sizes vary, as do standards. The two-storey 'Windmill Suite' is located almost at the top of the mill, enjoying 360-degree views, and is one of the town's most sought-after rooms. Breakfast is served in the former granary and the recently extended octagonal guest lounge occupies the mill's base. Book well ahead.

Old Borough Arms B&B ££
(☎01797-222128; www.oldborougharms.co.uk; Strand Quay; s/d from £73/95;) Very attractively decorated, nine-room B&B located at the foot of Mermaid St.

Eating

Simon the Pieman TEAROOM £
(3 Lion St; snacks £2-9; ⊙9.30am-4.45pm Mon-Fri, to 5.30pm Sat, 11.30am-4pm Sun) Many local cream-tea *cognoscenti* assert that this traditional tearoom – Rye's oldest – does the best scone-cream-jam combo this side of Romney Marsh. Further foes of tooth and waistline tempt from the shop's window.

Apothecary CAFE £
(1 East St; ⊙9am-5pm) With its crammed bookshelves, beat-up leather sofas and antique wood panelling, Rye's most characterful coffee house is a great spot to curl up with a brew and a novel while you watch shoppers scuttle by from the huge old corner windows.

Haydens CAFE £
(108 High St; snacks/meals from £3/9; ⊙10am-5pm) Staunch believers in organic and fair-trade produce, these guys dish up delicious omelettes, ploughman's lunches, salads and bagels in their light, breezy cafe. There's a wonderful elevated terrace at the back with great views over the town and surrounding countryside.

Ypres Castle Inn PUB ££
(Gun Gardens; meals £6.50-18) This traditional family-friendly Sussex inn serves a mix of Mediterranean and British dishes and opens a big beer garden for the summer months.

Information

Post Office (Unit 2, Station Approach)
Rye Heritage Centre (☎01797-226696; www.ryeheritage.co.uk; Strand Quay; ⊙10am-5pm Apr-Oct, reduced hours Nov-Mar) This centre runs a town-model audiovisual history (£3.50) and upstairs has a freaky collection of penny-in-the-slot novelty machines. It also sells a *Rye Town Walk* map (£1.50), rents out multilingual audio tours (adult/child £4/2) and runs occasional wintertime ghost walks (per person £10).
Rye Internet Cafe (46 Ferry Rd; per hr £2; ⊙10am-8pm Tue-Thu, 10am-7pm Fri, 10am-6pm Sat)
Tourist Office (☎01797-229049; www.visit1066country.com; 4/5 Lion St; ⊙10am-5pm Apr-Sep, to 4pm Oct-Mar) Can help with accommodation bookings and train and bus tickets.

Getting There & Away

Dover Bus 100; two hours, hourly
Hastings Bus 344 or 100; 40 minutes, two per hour
London Charing Cross Change trains in Ashford; £29.60, two hours, hourly

Getting Around

Rye Hire (☎01797-223033; 1 Cyprus Pl; ⊙8am-5pm Mon-Fri, to noon Sat) Rents out all-terrain bikes for £15/10 per day/four hours. Call ahead for Sunday hire.

Battle

POP 6000

'If there'd been no battle, there'd be no Battle', goes the saying in this unassuming village, which grew up around the hillside where invading French duke William of Normandy, aka William the Conqueror, scored a decisive victory over local King Harold in 1066. The epicentre of 1066 country, visitors flock here to see the spot where Harold got it in the eye, with the biggest crowd turning up mid-October to witness the annual re-enactment on the original battlefield.

Sights

Battle Abbey HISTORIC SITE
(EH; adult/child £7.50/4.50; ⊙10am-6pm Apr-Sep) Another day, another photogenic ruin? Hardly. On this spot raged *the* pivotal battle in the last successful invasion of England in 1066: an event with unparalleled impact on the country's subsequent social structure, architecture and well – pretty much everything. Four years after, the conquering Normans began constructing an abbey in the middle of the battlefield, a penance ordered by the Pope for the loss of life incurred here.

Only the foundations of the original church remain, the altar's position marked by a **plaque** – also supposedly the spot England's King Harold famously took an arrow in his eye. Other impressive monastic buildings survive and make for atmospheric explorations.

The battlefield's innocently rolling lush hillsides do little to evoke the ferocity of the event, but high-tech interactive presentations and a film at the visitors centre, as well as blow-by-blow audio tours, do their utmost to bring the battle to life.

Yesterday's World MUSEUM
(www.yesterdaysworld.co.uk; 89-90 High St; adult/child £7.25/5.25; ⌚10am-5.30pm Apr-Sep) Overshadowed literally and figuratively by the Battle Abbey, this growing museum is an incredible repository of England's retail past. The first building houses entire streets of quaint old shops, where costumed dummies proffer long-discontinued brands. Every space in between is stuffed with yesteryear products, enamel advertising signs, battered toys, wartime memorabilia and general nostalgia-inducing knick-knackery. The second building is much the same except for the Royalty Room where a cardboard cut-out illustrates just how tiny Queen Victoria was (1.40m).

Sleeping & Eating

Powdermills HOTEL ££
(☎01424-775511; www.powdermillshotel.com; Powdermill Lane; s/d from £100/110; P 📶) Rebuilt in the late 18th century after a gunpowder works saw off the previous manor with a bang, this graceful, ivy-covered country-house hotel has rooms with classic four-poster beds, a wonderful orangery restaurant, and a swimming pool. The 200-acre grounds of tranquil lakes and woodland adjoin Battle Abbey's grounds.

Tollgate Farmhouse B&B ££
(☎01424-777436; www.tollgatefarmhouse.co.uk; 59 North Trade Rd; s/d £40/80; P 🏊) A homely atmosphere can be found 10 minutes' walk from the centre of Battle at this large domestic residence, which has a handful of florid en-suite rooms adorned with embroidery and cut flowers. This must be one of only a handful of B&Bs in the country to have its own outdoor pool. Bookings are essential in summer.

Pilgrim's Restaurant BRITISH £
(1 High St; mains £6-8.50; ⌚lunch & dinner Mon-Sat, lunch Sun) Misshapen beams, rough-plastered walls and a vaulted ceiling make this 15th-century pilgrims' lodging the most spectacular place to eat in Battle. The tasty food is prepared using as much Sussex produce as possible and plated up with panache, but the staff sometimes get flustered when the place is full.

Getting There & Away

Bus 304/305 goes to Hastings (26 minutes, hourly).

There are also trains to Hastings (£3.90, 15 minutes, twice hourly) and to London Charing Cross (£20.90, one hour and 20 minutes, twice hourly).

Around Battle

BODIAM CASTLE

Surrounded by a square moat teeming with oversized goldfish, four-towered archetypal **Bodiam Castle** (NT; adult/child £7/3.50; ⌚10.30am-5pm mid-Feb–Oct) makes you half expect to see a fire-breathing dragon appear or a golden-haired princess lean over its walls. It is the legacy of 14th-century soldier of fortune (the polite term for knights who

THE LAST INVASION OF ENGLAND

The most famous battle in the history of England took place in 1066: a date seared into every English schoolchild's brain. The Battle of Hastings began when Harold's army arrived on the scene on 14 October and created a three-ring defence consisting of archers, then cavalry, with massed infantry at the rear. William marched north from Hastings and took up a position about 400m south of Harold and his troops. He tried repeatedly to break the English cordon, but Harold's men held fast. William's knights then feigned retreat, drawing some of Harold's troops after them. It was a fatal mistake. Seeing the gap in the English wall, William ordered his remaining troops to charge through, and the battle was as good as won. Among the English casualties was King Harold who, as tradition has it, was hit in the eye by an arrow, and struck down by Norman knights as he tried to pull it out. At news of his death, the last English resistance collapsed.

In their wonderfully irreverent *1066 and All That* (1930), WC Sellar and RJ Yeatman wrote of the benefits of the Norman Conquest '...as from this time onward England stopped being conquered and thus was able to become top nation...' When you consider that England hasn't been successfully invaded since, it's hard to disagree.

Interestingly, Kent agreed to a conditional surrender with the Normans, hence its county motto 'Invicta', meaning 'Unconquered'.

slaughtered and pillaged their way around France) Sir Edward Dalyngrigge, who married the local heiress and set about building a castle to make sure everybody knew who was boss.

Parliamentarian forces left the castle in ruins during the English Civil War, but in 1917 Lord Curzon, former viceroy of India, bought it and restored the exterior. Much of the interior remains unrestored, but it's possible to climb to the battlements for some pretty views.

While here, you'll most likely hear the tooting of the nearby **Kent & East Sussex steam railway** (www.kesr.org.uk; day ticket adult/child £15/10), which runs from Tenterden in Kent through 11 miles of gentle hills and woods to Bodiam village, from where a bus takes you to the castle. It operates three to five services on most days from May to September and at the weekend and school holidays in October, December and February.

The castle is in Bodiam, 9 miles northeast of Battle off the B2244, near Robertsbridge. Stagecoach bus 349 from Hastings (40 minutes) stops at Bodiam approximately once every two hours during the day Monday to Saturday, but only four times on a Sunday.

BATEMAN'S

It was love at first sight when Rudyard Kipling, author of *The Jungle Book,* set eyes on **Bateman's** (NT; Bateman's Lane, Burwash; adult/child £9/4.50; ⊙11am-5pm Sat-Wed mid-Mar–Oct), the glorious little 1634 Jacobean mansion he would call home for the last 34 years of his life, and where he would draw inspiration for *The Just So Stories* and other vivid tales.

Even today, the house is pervaded by a sense of Kipling's cosy contentment here. Everything is pretty much just as the writer left it after his death in 1936, even down to the blotting paper on his study desk. Furnishings often reflect his fascination with the East, with many oriental rugs and Indian artefacts adding colour.

The house is surrounded by lovely gardens and a small path leads down to a watermill that grinds corn on Wednesdays and Saturdays at 2pm.

Bateman's is about half a mile south of the town of Burwash along the A259. The nearest railway station is three miles away at Etchingham on the Hastings to London Charing Cross line.

Hastings

POP 86,900

Forever associated with the Norman invasion of 1066, even though the crucial events took place 6 miles away, Hastings thrived as one of the Cinque Ports and, in its Victorian heyday, was one of the country's most fashionable resorts. After a period of steady decline, the town is enjoying a mini renaissance, and these days it's an intriguing mix of tacky resort, fishing port and arty New Age hang-out.

Hastings last hit the news in October 2010 when its Victorian pier burnt down following an alleged arson attack. The ballroom at the end of the pier, where groups such as the Clash, the Sex Pistols and the Rolling Stones once performed, was completely destroyed. Funds to rebuild it are unlikely to be raised any time soon.

Sights

The best place for aimless wandering is the **old town**, a hotchpotch of narrow streets and half-timbered buildings crammed with junk shops, retro boutiques, street cafes, quaint local pubs and galleries.

Stade NEIGHBOURHOOD

(Rock-A-Nore Rd) The seafront area known as the Stade (below the East Hill) is home to distinctive, slender black clapboard structures known as **Net Shops**. These were built to store fishing gear back in the 17th century, but some now house fishmongers who sell the catch brought home by Europe's largest beach-launched fishing fleet, usually hauled up on the shingle behind.

The Stade is very much a working place, where the combined pong of diesel and fish guts 'scent' the air, but there are a couple of attractions here too. Housed in a former church, the **Fishermen's Museum** (www.hastingsfish.co.uk; Rock-A-Nore Rd; ⊙10am-5pm Apr-Oct) has shoals of barnacled exhibits, all swimming around the huge 1912 *Enterprise* fishing boat. Nearby, the fishy theme continues at the **Blue Reef Aquarium** (www.bluereefaquarium.co.uk/hastings; Rock-A-Nore Rd; adult/child £8.20/6.10; ⊙10am-5pm), though the exotically goggle-eyed inhabitants here probably wouldn't taste that great with chips.

Opened in 2012, a controversial addition to the Stade is the **Jerwood Gallery** (www.jerwoodgallery.org; Rock-A-Nore Rd; adult/concession £7/5; ⊙11am-4pm Tue-Fri, to 6pm Sat & Sun), a large, purpose-built exhibition venue used for temporary shows of contemporary British art, as well as housing a permanent display of works from the Jerwood collection. The complex clipped the end off the historic Stade (where coaches used to park), which ignited howls of local disapproval.

Hastings Castle CASTLE RUIN

(www.discoverhastings.co.uk; Castle Hill Rd; adult/child £4.25/3.50; ⊙10am-5pm Easter-Sep) Half the fun of reaching the clifftop ruins of Hastings' Norman castle is the journey up on the **West Hill Cliff Railway** (George St; adult/child £2.50/1.50; ⊙10am-5.30pm Mar-Sep), a late-Victorian funicular. The fortress was built by William the Conquerer and the fun exhibition in the grounds tells the story of the castle and 1066.

Also on West Hill, a short walk east of the castle, is the **Smugglers Adventure** (www.smugglersadventure.co.uk; St Clement Caves; adult/child £7.40/5.40; ⊙10am-5pm Easter-Sep), where you can explore underground caverns and hear smuggling yarns from the Sussex coast.

Hastings Country Park NATURE RESERVE

This 267-hectare clifftop nature reserve, reached by another 19th-century contraption, the **East Hill Cliff Railway** (Rock-A-Nore Rd; adult/child £2.50/1.50; ⊙10am-5.30pm Apr-Sep), is a dog-walkers' and picknickers' paradise.

Sleeping & Eating

The Laindons B&B ££

(☎01424-437710; www.thelaindons.com; 23 High St; s/d from £80/110;) Occupying a Georgian Grade II–listed former coaching inn, this stylish B&B is five minutes' amble from the seafront at the quieter end of High St. The three beautifully appointed rooms are flooded with sea-refracted light from the huge Georgian windows, illuminating the blend of breezy contemporary design and antique furnishings. Owner-cooked breakfasts are taken around a communal table.

Swan House B&B ££

(☎01424-430014; www.swanhousehastings.co.uk; 1 Hill St; s/d from £70/115; @) Inside its ancient, timbered 15th-century shell, this place blends contemporary and vintage chic to perfection. Rooms feature organic toiletries, fresh flowers, hand-painted walls and huge beds. The guest lounge, where pale sofas, painted floorboards and striking modern sculpture sit alongside beams and a huge stone fireplace, is a stunner. The owners run another, equally striking guesthouse called the Old Rectory in Harold Rd.

Dragon Bar BAR, RESTAURANT ££

(71 George St; mains £11.50-21.50; ⊙lunch & dinner Mon-Sat, lunch Sun) Atmospheric, laid-back bar full of dark walls, mismatched furniture and beaten leather sofas, attracting the younger end of the alternative old-town crowds. The eclectic menu features everything from Thai curry and Winchelsea lamb to pizzas.

Information

Tourist Office (☎01424-451111; Queen's Sq; ⊙8.30am-6.15pm Mon-Fri, 9am-5pm Sat, 10.30am-4pm Sun)

Getting There & Away

Bus

Eastbourne Bus 99; one hour and 20 minutes, three per hour

London Victoria National Express; £14.40, 2½ to four hours, twice daily

Rye Buses 100 & 344; 40 minutes, twice hourly

Train

Brighton Via Eastbourne; £13.10, one hour to one hour and 20 minutes, twice hourly

London Charing Cross £21.10, 1½ hours, twice hourly

London Victoria £15.90, two hours, hourly

Eastbourne

POP 97,000

This classic, old-fashioned seaside resort has long brought to mind images of octogenarians dozing in deck chairs. While many of Eastbourne's seafront hotels still have that retirement-home feel, in recent years an influx of students and one of the largest new Polish communities in the southeast have given the town a sprightlier feel.

The creation of the new South Downs National Park to the west also means Eastbourne's pebbly beaches, scrupulously snipped seaside gardens and picturesque, arcade-free promenade are likely to see increasing numbers of walkers and cyclists, finishing or embarking on a trip along the South Downs Way.

Sights & Activities

FREE **Towner Art Gallery** ART GALLERY

(☎01323-434660; www.townereastbourne.org.uk; Devonshire Park, College Rd; ⊙10am-5pm, tours

11.30am Tue-Sun) One of the southeast's most exciting exhibition spaces, this purpose-built, state-of-the-art gallery building has short-term shows of contemporary work on the ground and 2nd floors, while the 1st floor is given over to rotating themed shows created from the 4000-piece-strong Towner collection. Building tours include a peek inside the climate-controlled art store.

Pier WATERFRONT
(www.eastbournepier.com) Eastbourne's quaintly ramshackle pier is a lovable piece of Victoriana jutting out into the chilly Channel. All its tearooms, fish-and-chip counters, twopence machines and fortune-tellers are firmly in place and there's a popular student nightclub at the very tip.

Museum of Shops MUSEUM
(20 Cornfield Tce; adult/child £5/4; ⊙10am-5pm) This small museum is swamped by an obsessive collection of how-we-used-to-live memorabilia.

Eastbourne Heritage Centre MUSEUM
(www.eastbournesociety.co.uk; 2 Carlisle Rd; adult/child £2.50/1; ⊙2-5pm Apr-Oct) Housed in a cute red-brick tower building, this museum livens up exhibits on the town's history with some eccentric asides, such as the ones on Donald McGill, the pioneer of the 'naughty postcard'.

Redoubt Fortress FORTRESS
(www.eastbournemuseums.co.uk; Royal Pde; adult/child £4.50/2.50; ⊙10am-5pm Tue-Sun mid-Apr–mid-Nov) This small military museum occupies one of the 77 strongholds built in the early 19th century to defend the south coast from Napoleon's planned invasion.

Tours

Sussex Voyages BOAT TOUR
(☎01293-888780; www.sussexvoyages.co.uk; Sovereign Harbour Marina Village; tour adult/child/concession £26/23/15) Two-hour Beachy Head and Seven Sisters boat tours aboard rigid-hulled inflatables leave from Sovereign Harbour (take bus 51 or 99). Reservations essential.

City Sightseeing BUS TOUR
(www.city-sightseeing.co.uk; adult/child £7.50/4.50; ⊙tours every 30min 10am-5pm) Open-top bus tours around local sights and up to Beachy Head.

Sleeping

The Big Sleep HOTEL ££
(☎01323-722676; www.thebigsleephotel.com; King Edward's Pde; s/d from £45/59; 📶) Hip, fresh and friendly, this seafront hotel has 50 gob-smacking rooms that really make a strong design statement, from the big-print wallpaper, retro furnishings to the heavy curtains. A trendy bar, a big basement games room and Channel views make this the area's coolest pad.

Albert & Victoria B&B ££
(☎01323-730948; www.albertandvictoria.com; 19 St Aubyns Rd; s/d from £35/75; 📶) Book ahead to stay at this delightful Victorian terraced house with fragrantly opulent rooms, canopied beds, crystal chandeliers and a secluded walled garden for summer breakfasting, mere paces from the seafront promenade. The four rooms are named after Queen Vic's children.

Eastbourne YHA HOSTEL £
(☎0845 371 9316; www.yha.org.uk; 1 East Dean Rd; dm from £16.40) A purpose-built, ecofriendly hostel on the road into the South Downs National Park. To reach it, take bus 12 from the pier.

Eating & Drinking

Eastbourne's dining scene is a tad stuck in the gammon-and-pineapple era, but there are good places to head for honest grub.

Lamb Inn PUB ££
(36 High St; mains £7-13) This Eastbourne institution, located less than a mile northwest of the train station in the undervisited old town, has been plonking Sussex wet ones on the bar for eight centuries. A holidaying Dickens left a few beer rings and smudged napkins here (he stayed across the road). Buses 1 and 1A stop nearby.

Belgian Cafe SEAFOOD ££
(11-23 Grand Pde; mains £11-17) If you've never been to Belgium, you might not know that the national dish there is mussels and chips, Belgian beer can taste of fruit and Tintin hails from Brussels. But you will once you've experienced this popular cafe near the pier.

Little Britain BRITISH £
(5 Motcombe Lane; mains £8-9; ⊙breakfast & lunch Tue-Fri, lunch Sun) Many scenes from the hit British TV series *Little Britain* were shot in Eastbourne, but the theme at this

unassuming Old Town eatery doesn't go past the name. The focus is kept firmly on serving up no-nonsense British comfort food made with Sussex-sourced ingredients.

 Shopping

Camilla's Bookshop SECONDHAND BOOKS (www.camillasbookshop.com; 57 Grove Rd) Packed to the rafters with musty volumes, this incredible book repository, an interesting amble from the train station, fills three floors of a crumbling Victorian town house. The owner claims to have over a million books for sale, making this the best stocked, if not the biggest, secondhand bookstore in England.

 Information

Tourist Office (☎0871 663 0031; www.visiteastbourne.com; Cornfield Rd; ⊙9.15am-5.30pm Mon-Fri, to 5pm Sat Apr-Oct)

 Getting There & Away

Bus

Brighton Bus 12; one hour and 15 minutes, up to four hourly

Hastings Bus 99; one hour and 20 minutes, three per hour

Train

Brighton £9.50, 30 to 40 minutes, twice hourly

London Victoria £27.70, 1½ hours, twice hourly

Around Eastbourne

PEVENSEY CASTLE

The ruins of William the Conqueror's first stronghold, **Pevensey Castle** (EH; adult/child £4.90/2.90; ⊙10am-6pm Apr-Sep), sit 5 miles east of Eastbourne, just off the A259. Picturesquely dissolving into its own moat, the castle marks the point where William the Conqueror landed in 1066, just two weeks before the Battle of Hastings. Shortly afterwards, old Bill wasted no time in building upon sturdy Roman walls to create a castle, which was used time and again through the centuries, right up to WWII. You can roam about its decaying husk with an enlightening audioguide, free with entry.

Regular train services between London Victoria and Hastings via Eastbourne (10 minutes) stop at Westham, half a mile from Pevensey.

ALFRISTON

Eight miles west of Eastbourne lies the twee village of Alfriston, an essential stop for **South Downs Way** (www.nationaltrail.co.uk/southdowns) hikers and south coast explorers.

Most action takes place on boutique- and tavern-lined **High Street**, a crooked hotchpotch of medieval half-timbered houses, some (such as the Star Inn) still supporting their original flagstone roofs. Just off High St, in a bend in the River Cuckmere, stands musty **St Andrew's Church**, a 14th-century creation in flint known as the 'Cathedral of the Downs' due to its size. Notice the rare bell ropes that descend into the chancel crossing (where the nave meets the transepts). The **Clergy House** (NT; adult/child £5/2.55; ⊙10.30am-5pm Sat-Wed) is the church's old vicarage and the first property to be acquired by the National Trust in 1896.

Just across the bridge from the church is the point where the South Downs Way divides, one route heading south to the sea and the Seven Sisters, the other inland to the Long Man.

Where the A27 meets the access road to the village is **Drusillas** (www.drusillas.co.uk; admission £16.50; ⊙10am-5pm), probably the best small zoo in the country. There's heaps of turtle-stroking, cow-milking, dino-hunting fun to be had and the playgrounds and rides are superb.

SOUTH DOWNS NATIONAL PARK & SEVEN SISTERS CHALK CLIFFS

After decades of campaigning, planning and deliberation, the South Downs National Park, stretching west from Eastbourne for around 100 miles, finally came into being in 2010. The sights below fall within the park's boundaries.

The famous cliffs of **Beachy Head** are the highest point in a string of chalky rock faces that slice across this rugged stretch of coast at the southern end of the South Downs. It's a spot of thrilling beauty, at least until you find out that this is also officially one of the world's top suicide spots! From Beachy Head, the stunning, white **Seven Sisters Chalk Cliffs** undulate their way west, a clifftop path (a branch of the South Downs Way (p169)) riding the waves of chalk as far as the picturesque Cuckmere Haven. Along the way, you'll stumble upon the tiny seaside hamlet of **Birling Gap**, where you can stop for a drink, snack or ice cream at the **Birling Gap Hotel**. The secluded suntrap beach here is popular with locals and walkers taking a breather.

Beachy Head is off the A259, then B2103 between Eastbourne and Newhaven.

Eastbourne's City Sightseeing tour bus stops at the clifftop.

If you're travelling along the A27 from Eastbourne towards Lewes, be sure to look southwards, just east of the village of Wilmington, to see the spindly **Long Man of Wilmington**. No one really knows how this leggy 70m-high geoglyph – now marked out with white concrete – arrived here or what he represents, though many assume he's a Victorian hoax. There is a turn-off for the Long Man at Wilmington, 7 miles west of Eastbourne, from where you can get a close-up view. If you're walking this section of the South Downs Way, the path passes right over the figure's head and it's easy to miss.

Five miles west of Eastbourne, **Charleston Farmhouse** (www.charleston.org.uk; off A27; adult/child £9.50/5.50; ⌚1-6pm Wed-Sat, to 5.30pm Sun Apr-Oct) was the bohemian country getaway of the influential Bloomsbury Group. Even now that the joyous frescos and vivid furniture have begun to fade, and the last of its pioneering occupants and visitors have long since passed away, it's still a tangible example of the rich intellectual and aesthetic life that they came to represent. In 1916 Virginia Woolf's sister, painter Vanessa Bell, moved here with her lover Duncan Grant, and they set about redecorating with abandon in a style that owed much to the influence of the post-Impressionists. Hardly a wall, door or piece of furniture was left untouched, and the walls featured paintings by Picasso, Derain, Delacroix and others. There's also a striking garden, interesting Derain works and a medieval dovecote.

Visits to the farmhouse are by guided tour only, except on Sundays. The nearest train station is at Berwick, on the Brighton to Eastbourne line, a stiff 45-minutes' walk from the farmhouse.

Lewes

POP 16,200

Strung out along an undulating High St flanked by elegant Georgian buildings, a part-ruined castle and a traditional brewery perfuming the air with a hoppy aroma, Lewes (pronounced 'Lewis') is a charmingly affluent hillside town with a turbulent past and fiery traditions. Off the main drag, there's a more intimate atmosphere as you descend into twisting narrow streets called 'twittens' – the remainder of the town's original medieval street plan.

One of Lewes' claims to fame is that it straddles the zero degrees line of longitude. An inconspicuous **plaque** in Western Rd marks the meridian, though modern measuring methods have actually placed the line around 100m to the east.

Another claim to fame is the town's wild **Guy Fawkes Night** (5 November); its excellent fireworks display includes the burning of effigies of modern-day figures and the

THE BLOOMSBURY GROUP

The Bloomsbury Group was the most influential artistic and intellectual circle to arise in Britain in the first half of the 20th century. A set of Cambridge graduates, artists and scholars, they all gravitated to London's Bloomsbury area pre-WWI. Its most famous members included Virginia Woolf, Maynard Keynes, Vanessa Bell, Duncan Grant, Lytton Strachey, TS Elliot and EM Forster.

The outspokenly pacifist group gained notoriety for stunts that embarrassed the military forces during WWI, and scandalised London society with their intragroup relationships and, in several cases, bisexuality. Their tastes in post-Impressionist art and avant-garde literature were ahead of their time, and were often savaged by critics only to be later hailed as masterpieces. Woolf, of course, was winning herself acclaim as a novelist and, with her husband Leonard, founded the Hogarth Press. Her artist sister Vanessa and Vanessa's lover Duncan Grant were two of several group members to make a name through the modernist design firm Omega Workshops. Keynes, meanwhile, became one of the foremost economic theorists of the day, and Strachey had several uncompromising biographies under his belt.

Though the group members gradually drifted apart after the war and Woolf committed suicide in 1941, their once-controversial views were steadily accepted into the mainstream and their work has continued to influence generations of new writers, poets, artists and musicians.

rolling of barrels packed with bangers down to the river.

Sights

Lewes Castle CASTLE, MUSEUM

(www.sussexpast.co.uk; 169 High St; adult/child £6.60/3.30; 10am-5.30pm Tue-Sat, from 11am Sun & Mon; P) Now little more than a set of ruins, this castle was built shortly after the 1066 Norman invasion. It never saw warfare, but there were riotous celebrations following the navy's victory over the Spanish Armada in 1588, when happy citizens blew great chunks out of the castle's walls! They left enough standing for it to remain an impressive sight though, and its windy keep, visible for miles around, affords panoramic views across the town and beyond.

The attached **Barbican House Museum** has a good collection of Lewes-related artefacts, but the star attraction is the incredibly accurate town model, glued together by an army of volunteers in the mid-1980s to show how the town looked a century earlier. Viewing is accompanied by a 12-minute film relating the locals' historical advancement from cavemen to Victorians.

Anne of Cleves House Museum MUSEUM

(52 Southover High St; adult/child £4.70/2.40; 10am-5pm Tue-Fri, from 11am Sun & Mon Feb-Oct) When Henry VIII divorced Anne of Cleves in 1541, he gave her this timber-framed house as part of her divorce settlement, although she never moved in. The creak-and-groan floors and spider's-web wooden roof today sandwich an idiosyncratic folk museum, with everything from a witch's effigy complete with pins to a rack of Tudor costumes to try on.

Sleeping

Castle Banks Cottage B&B ££

(01273-476291; www.castlebankscottage.co.uk; 4 Castle Banks; s/d £40/80) Tucked away in a quiet lane near the castle, this tiny B&B has just two rooms. The easygoing travel-writer proprietor is a mine of information about the area's local history. Breakfast is served in the secluded garden in summer.

Berkeley House B&B ££

(01273-476057; www.berkeleyhouselewes.co.uk; 2 Albion St; s from £65, d £80-120;) A favourite with Glyndebourne fans, this delightful Georgian property features opera odds and ends and a roof terrace providing town and country views.

Shelleys HOTEL ££

(01273-472361; www.the-shelleys.co.uk; High St; r from £103; P) Full of old-fashioned charm, this 16th-century manor house was once home to the Earl of Dorset and was owned by the Shelley family (of Percy Bysshe Shelley fame). It has cosy, country rooms and an above-standard restaurant overlooking a lovely walled garden.

Eating & Drinking

Bill's CAFE £

(56 Cliffe High St; meals £3-10; lunch) Part grocers, part delicatessen, part rustic-styled cafe, this insanely popular place envelopes customers in its colours and smells then dishes up melt-in-the-mouth tartlets, gourmet pizzas, salads, desserts and other artisanal snacks. Get here early at meal times, and even in-between times, as it's normally chock-a-block.

Real Eating Company BRITISH ££

(18 Cliffe High St; mains £10-17; 10am-11pm Mon-Fri, from 9am Sat, to 4pm Sun) This large, airy cafe-brasserie stretches back to a lovely outside terrace and serves kick-starting breakfasts, gourmet fish and chips, wild-boar sausages and substantial British meat-and-two-veg combos, all made with Sussex ingredients as much as darn well possible.

Gardener's Arms PUB

(46 Cliffe High St) Unassuming, scrubbed-wood tavern with a large selection of real ales, local Harveys beer and filling pub lunches.

Shopping

Fifteenth Century Bookshop SECONDHAND BOOKSHOP

(99 High St) Rummage through antiquarian treasures and new editions at the fabulous, half-timbered bookshop housed in a former candle factory.

Old Needlemakers SECONDHAND

(www.needlemakers.co.uk; West St) A complex of quaint craft and secondhand shops with a decent cafe.

Information

Post Office (65 High St)

Tourist Office (01273-483448; www.enjoysussex.info; 187 High St; 9am-5pm Mon-Fri, 9.30am-5.30pm Sat & 10am-2pm Sun Apr-Oct) Helps with accommodation bookings.

Getting There & Away

Lewes is 9 miles northeast of Brighton and 16 miles northwest of Eastbourne, just off the A27.

BUS Brighton Bus 28/29; 30 minutes, every 10 minutes

TRAIN Brighton 15 minutes, four times hourly **Eastbourne** £7, 20 minutes, four times hourly **London Victoria** £15.90, 1¼ hours, twice hourly

Around Lewes

GLYNDEBOURNE

In 1934 science teacher John Christie and his opera-singer wife decided to build a 1200-seat opera house in the middle of nowhere. It seemed a magnificent folly at the time, but now **Glyndebourne** (☎01273-812321; www.glyndebourne.com) is one of England's best venues for the lyric arts, with a season that runs from late May to the end of August. Tickets can be like gold dust, so book well ahead. Bring your glad rags (black tie and evening dress), as well as a picnic for the generous interval. Glyndebourne is 4 miles east of Lewes off the B2192.

Brighton & Hove

POP 247,800

Raves on the beach, Graham Greene novels, mods and rockers in bank-holiday fisticuffs, naughty weekends for Mr and Mrs Smith, classic car runs from London, the UK's biggest gay scene and the Channel's best clubbing – this city by the sea evokes many images among the British. One thing is for certain: with its bohemian, cosmopolitan, hedonistic vibe, Brighton is where England's seaside experience goes from cold to cool.

Brighton is without doubt the UK's most colourful and outrageous city and one with many faces. Here bosomy burlesque meets contemporary design, Spanish students leave Starbucks to rub shoulders with stars in Spanish bars, the southeast's grottiest hostels share thin walls with kinky boutique hotels, £4-a-pint microbrew ales occupy bar space with £1 buckets of 'sex on the beach', and stags watch drag. This is a city that returned the UK's first Green Party MP in 2010, and where Valentine's Day is celebrated with more gusto than Christmas, and is the place, according to the 2001 census, with the highest UK population of Jedi.

Brighton rocks all year round, but really comes to life during the summer months, when tourists, language students and revellers from London pour into the city, keen to explore the city's legendary nightlife, summer festivals and quirky shops. The highlight for the sightseeing visitor is, without doubt, the weird and wonderful Royal Pavilion, a 19th-century party palace built by the Prince Regent who kicked off Brighton's love of the outlandish.

Sights

Royal Pavilion PALACE

(www.royalpavilion.org.uk; Royal Pavilion Gardens; adult/child £9.80/5.60; ⏲9.30am-5.45pm Apr-Sep, 10am-5.15pm Oct-Mar) The city's must-see attraction is the Royal Pavilion, the glittering party pad and palace of Prince George, who later became the Prince Regent and then King George IV. It's one of the most opulent buildings in England, certainly the finest example of early 19th-century chinoiserie anywhere in Europe, and is an apt symbol of Brighton's reputation for decadence and high living.

The entire palace is an eye-popping spectacle, but some interiors stand out even amid the riot of decoration. The dragon-themed banqueting hall must be the most incredible in all England; more dragons and snakes writhe in the music room with its ceiling of 26,000 gold scales, and the then state-of-the-art kitchen must have wowed Georgian folk with its automatic spits and hot tables. Prince Albert carted away all its furniture, some of which has been loaned back by the current Queen. An unimpressed Queen Victoria called it 'a strange, odd Chinese place' – for Brighton's visitors it's an unmissable chunk of Sussex history.

Brighton Pier AMUSEMENT PARK

(www.brightonpier.co.uk; Madeira Dr) This grand old centenarian pier is the place to experience Brighton's tackier side. There are plenty of stomach-churning fairground rides and dingy amusement arcades to keep you amused, plus candy floss and Brighton rock to chomp on while you're doing so.

Look west and you'll see the sad remains of the West Pier, a skeletal iron hulk that attracts flocks of starlings at sunset. It's a sad end for a Victorian marvel, upon which the likes of Charlie Chaplin and Stan Laurel once performed.

So far there's no sign of the i360 observation tower ('Hurray!' some may cry), a spectacularly space-age piece of architecture from the creators of the London Eye that may one day loom 150m above the seafront. This would include a West Pier Heritage Centre – a pavilion where audiovisual exhibits will relate the pier's history.

FREE **Brighton Museum & Art Gallery** MUSEUM, GALLERY

(www.brighton-hove-museums.org.uk; Royal Pavilion Gardens; ⏲10am-5pm Tue-Sun) Set in the Royal Pavilion's renovated stable block, this museum and art gallery has a glittering collection of 20th-century art and design, including a crimson Salvador Dalí sofa modelled on Mae West's lips. There's also an enthralling gallery of world art, an impressive collection of Egyptian artefacts and an 'images of Brighton' multimedia exhibit containing a series of oral histories and a model of the defunct West Pier.

Hove Museum & Art Gallery MUSEUM, GALLERY

(19 New Church Rd; ⏲10am-5pm Mon, Tue & Thu-Sat, 2-5pm Sun) Hove can justifiably claim to be the birthplace of British cinema, with the first short film shot here in 1898. You can see it alongside other fascinating films at this attractive Victorian villa. Another highlight is the kids' room, which is full of fairy lights and reverberates to the snores of a wizard and the whirr of an underfloor train. Exhibits include old zoetropes, a magic lantern and a small cupboard with a periscope inside. Take bus 1, 1A, 6 or 49 from Churchill Sq.

Brighton Marina WATERFRONT

(www.brightonmarina.co.uk; Marina Way) Brighton's wave-shaped marina washes ashore 1.5 miles east of the pier. In addition to brand-name shopping and numerous chain eateries, you'll also find Brighton's Hollywood-style **Walk of Fame**, which dedicates a pavement-embedded plaque to anyone rich, famous and with a link to the city, though some associations are tenuous. Big-hitting names honoured include Graham Greene, Winston Churchill and Lewis Carroll.

Reaching the marina is half the fun when you hop aboard the **Volks Electric Railway** (www.volkselectricrailway.co.uk; single/return £2/3.10; ⏲10.15am-5pm). The world's oldest electric railway, opened in 1883, trundles along the seafront from just short of the pier. Otherwise take bus 7.

Brighton Wheel VIEWPOINT

(www.brightonwheel.com; Madeira Dr; adult/child £8/6.50; ⏲10am-8pm Sun-Thu, to 11pm Fri & Sat) Just slightly smaller than the London Eye, Brighton's seafront wheel is best ridden at sunset for gobsmacking views of the Channel, the pier and the town below. Book tickets online during busy times.

FREE **Booth Museum of Natural History** MUSEUM

(194 Dyke Rd; ⏲10am-5pm Mon-Wed, Fri & Sat, 2-5pm Sun) This odd Victorian taxidermy museum has several creepy sights, such as walls full of mammoth butterflies and cabinets of

THE PRINCE'S PARTY PALACE

It's widely known that England's George III was, to be polite, a little nuts. But you'd be forgiven for thinking that the eldest son of 'Mad King George', Prince George (1762–1830), was the eccentric in the family upon visiting his princely pavilion in Brighton. The young prince began drinking with abandon and enjoying the pleasures of women while still a teenager. To daddy's displeasure, he soon started hanging out with his dissolute uncle, the Duke of Cumberland, who was enjoying himself royally by the sea in Brighton.

In 1787 George commissioned Henry Holland to convert a Brighton farmhouse into his personal pleasure palace. While he waited to accede to the throne (when his father was declared officially insane in 1810 he was sworn in as Prince Regent), George whiled away the years with debauched parties for himself, his mistresses and his aristocratic mates.

Ever conscious of what was trendy, George decided in 1815 to convert the Marine Pavilion to reflect the current fascination with all things Eastern. He engaged the services of John Nash, who laboured for eight years to create a Mogul Indian–style palace, complete with the most lavish chinoiserie interior imaginable. George finally had a palace suited to his outlandish tastes and, to boot, he was now the monarch.

His brother and successor William IV (1765–1837) also used the pavilion as a royal residence, as did William's niece Victoria (1819–1901). But the conservative queen never really took to the place and in 1850 sold it to the town.

Brighton & Hove

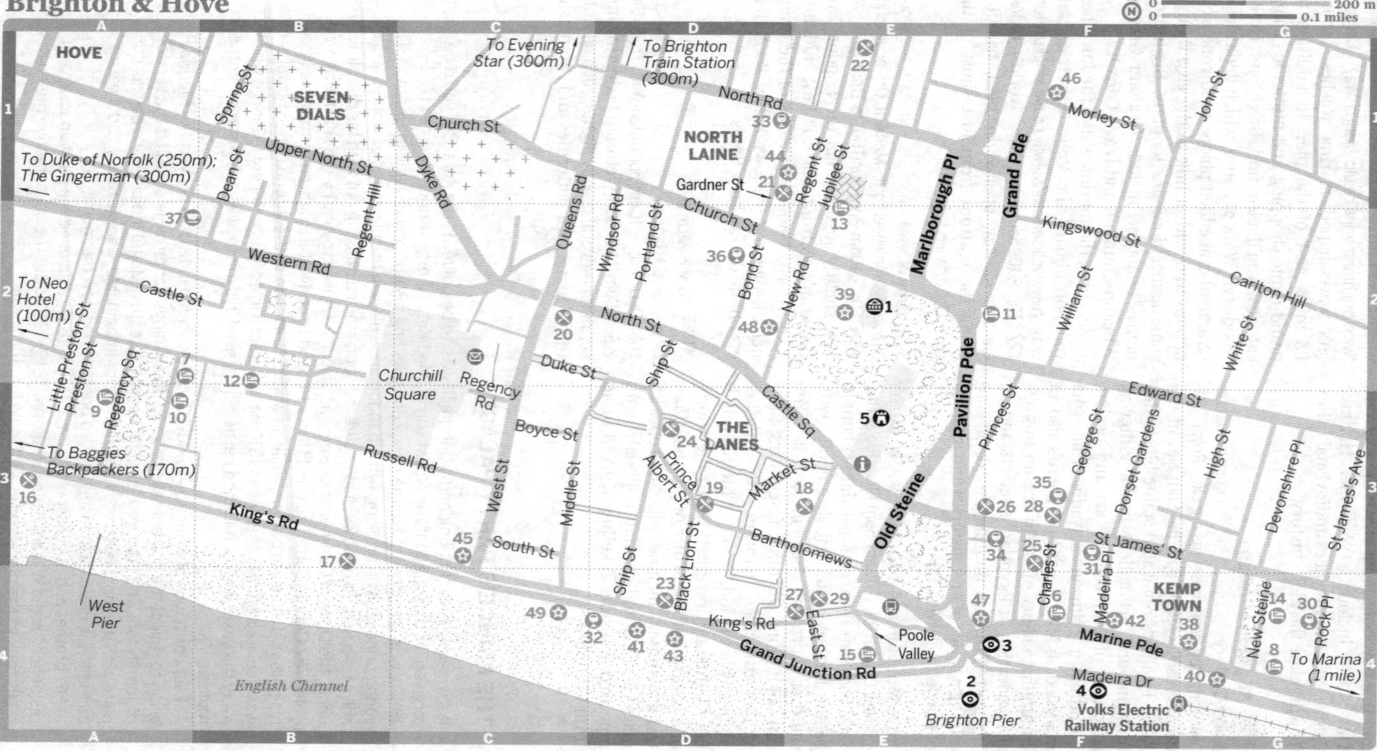

Brighton & Hove

Sights

1 Brighton Museum & Art Gallery ... E2
2 Brighton Pier ... E4
3 Brighton Sea Life Centre ... F4
4 Brighton Wheel ... F4
5 Royal Pavilion ... E3

Sleeping

6 Amsterdam ... F4
7 Brighton House Hotel ... A2
8 Drakes ... G4
9 Hotel Pelirocco ... A3
10 Hotel Una ... A3
11 Kipps Brighton ... F2
12 Motel Schmotel ... B2
13 myhotel ... E2
14 Seaspray ... G4
15 St Christopher's ... E4

Eating

16 Al Fresco ... A3
17 Due South ... B3
18 English's Oyster Bar ... E3
19 Food for Friends ... D3
20 Foodilic ... C2
21 Infinity Foods Cafe ... D1
22 Iydea ... E1
23 JB's American Diner ... D4
24 Piccolo's ... D3
25 Pomegranate ... F3
26 Red Roaster ... F3
27 Scoop & Crumb ... E4
28 Tea Cosy ... F3
29 Terre à Terre ... E4

Drinking

A Bar ... (see 6)
30 Brighton Rocks ... G4
31 Bulldog ... F3
32 Coalition ... D4
33 Dorset ... D1
34 Poison Ivy ... F3
35 Queen's Arms ... F3
36 Riki Tik ... D2
37 Talk of Tea ... A2

Entertainment

Audio ... (see 6)
38 Basement Club ... G4
39 Brighton Dome ... E2
40 Concorde 2 ... G4
41 Digital ... D4
42 Funky Fish Club ... F4
43 Honey Club ... D4
44 Komedia Theatre ... D1
45 Odeon Cinema ... C3
46 Psychosocial ... F1
47 Revenge ... E4
48 Theatre Royal ... D2
49 Tube ... C4

birds poised to tear apart small mammals. The museum is about half a mile north of the train station. Buses 14 and 27 stop nearby on Dyke Rd.

Brighton Sea Life Centre AQUARIUM
(www.visitsealife.com/brighton; Marine Pde; adult/child £16.20/11.40; ⏲10am-6pm Apr-Sep, 10am-5pm Oct-Mar) Dating from Victorian times, the world's oldest operational sea-life centre underwent a major revamp in 2012. Old favourites such as stingrays and giant turtles have been joined by new creatures of the deep, and the general visitor experience has been brought into the 21st century.

Activities

There is a huge range of activities on offer in Brighton, from rollerblading and beach volleyball to skateboarding and paragliding and, of course, myriad water sports. Ask the tourist office for details.

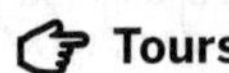

Tours

City Sightseeing BUS TOUR
(www.city-sightseeing.co.uk; adult/child £10/3; ⏲tours every 30min May–mid-Sep) Open-top hop-on/hop-off bus tours leaving from Grand Junction Rd near Brighton Pier.

Tourist Tracks AUDIOGUIDE TOUR
(www.tourist-tracks.com) MP3 audioguides are downloadable from the website (£5) or available on a preloaded MP3 player at the tourist office (£6 per half-day).

Festivals & Events

There's always something fun going on in Brighton, from **Gay Pride** (www.brightonpride.org) to food and drink festivals, but the showpiece is May's three-week-long **Brighton Festival** (☎01273-709 709; www.brightonfestival.org), the biggest arts festival in Britain after Edinburgh, drawing performers from around the globe.

Sleeping

Despite a glut of hotels in Brighton, prices are relatively high and you'd be wise to book well ahead for summer weekends and for the Brighton Festival in May. Expect to pay up to a third more at weekends across the board.

Brighton's hostels are a varied bunch. Several cater to raucous stag and hen nights; others are more traditional and homely. Choose wisely! Brighton is blessed with a wide selection of midrange accommodation.

TOP CHOICE Hotel Una BOUTIQUE HOTEL £££
(01273-820464; www.hotel-una.co.uk; 55-56 Regency Sq; s £55-75, d £115-150;) All the 19 generously cut rooms here wow guests with their bold-patterned fabrics, supersize leather sofas, in-room free-standing bath tubs and vegan/veggie/carnivorous breakfast in bed. But some, such as the two-level suite with its own minicinema, and the under-pavement chambers with their own spa, are truly show-stopping quarters and are not as expensive as you might expect. All this plus a cool cocktail bar and lots of time-warp period features makes the Una our numero uno.

Hotel Pelirocco THEME HOTEL ££
(01273-327055; www.hotelpelirocco.co.uk; 10 Regency Sq; s £59-65, d £99-145, ste from £249;) One of Brighton's sexiest and nuttiest place to stay, the Pelirocco takes the whole theme concept to another level and has become the ultimate venue for a flirty, rock-and-roll weekend in style. Flamboyantly designed rooms – some by artists, some by local sponsors – include the Soviet-chic themed room with vodka bottles frozen into the walls; the Pin-Up Parlour dedicated to Diana Dors; and the Pretty Vacant double, a shrine to the Sex Pistols. But the one everyone wants is the Play Room suite with its 3m circular bed, mirrored ceiling and pole-dancing area.

Neo Hotel BOUTIQUE HOTEL ££
(01273-711104; www.neohotel.com; 19 Oriental Pl; d from £100;) You won't be surprised to learn that the owner of this gorgeous hotel is an interior stylist; the nine rooms could have dropped straight out of the pages of a design magazine, each finished in rich colours and tactile fabrics, with bold floral and Asian motifs and black-tiled bathrooms. Wonderful breakfasts include homemade smoothies and fruit pancakes. Reception not open 24 hours.

Baggies Backpackers HOSTEL £
(01273-733740; www.baggiesbackpackers.com; 33 Oriental Pl; dm/d £13/35;) A warm familial atmosphere, worn-in charm, attentive on-site owners and clean, snug dorms have made this long-established hostel an institution. It's also blessed with a homely kitchen, an inexpensive laundry, a cosy basement music and chill-out room and a TV lounge piled high with video cassettes. The hostel only takes phone bookings and is a stag- and hen-free zone. Cash only.

Snooze HOTEL ££
(01273-605797; www.snoozebrighton.com; 25 St George's Tce; s/d from £55/65;) This eccentric Kemptown pad is fond of retro styling. Rooms feature vintage posters, bright '60s and '70s patterned wallpaper, flying wooden ducks, floral sinks and mad clashes of colour. It's more than just a gimmick though – rooms are comfortable and spotless, and there are great meat-free breakfasts. You'll find it just off St James' St about 500m east of New Steine.

myhotel HOTEL ££
(01273-900 300; www.myhotels.com; 17 Jubilee St; r from £89;) With trend-setting rooms looking like space-age pods full of curved white walls, floor-to-ceiling observation windows and suspended flatscreen TVs, with the odd splash of neon orange or pink, there's nothing square about this place, daddy-o. You can even hook up your iPod and play music through speakers in the ceiling. There's a cocoon-like cocktail bar downstairs and, if you've currency to ignite, a suite with a steam room and harpooned vintage carousel horse.

Motel Schmotel B&B ££
(01273-326129; www.motelschmotel.co.uk; 37 Russell Sq; s/d from £50/60;) If you can overlook the petite rooms and minuscule bathrooms, this 11-room B&B in a Regency town house, a short stroll from virtually anywhere, is a sound, central place to hit the sack. Rooms are accented with colourful oversized prints and an uncluttered design, and guests heap praise on the breakfast cooked by the always-around-to-help couple who run things.

Paskins Town House B&B ££

(☎01273-601203; www.paskins.co.uk; 18-19 Charlotte St; r from £45; @ 🛜) An environmentally friendly B&B spread between two elegant town houses. It prides itself on using eco-friendly products, such as recycled toilet paper, low-energy bulbs and biodegradable cleaning materials. The individually designed rooms are beautifully maintained, and excellent organic and vegetarian breakfasts are served in the art-deco-inspired breakfast room.

Drakes BOUTIQUE HOTEL £££

(☎01273-696934; www.drakesofbrighton.com; 43-44 Marine Pde; r £115-295; P ❄ @ 🛜) This stylishly minimalist boutique hotel oozes understated class – so understated is the entrance, in fact, that you could easily miss it. All rooms have similar decor in bold fabrics and funky European elm panelling, but it's the feature rooms everyone wants with their giant free-standing tubs set in front of full-length bay windows with widescreen Channel views. The basement restaurant is Brighton's best.

Blanch House BOUTIQUE HOTEL ££

(☎01273-603504; www.blanchhouse.co.uk; 17 Atlingworth St; r from £84; @ 🛜) Themed rooms are the name of the game in this boutique hotel, but there's nothing tacky about them – swish art-deco styling rules in the Legacia Room, while the Snowstorm is a frosty vision in white and tinkling ice. The magnificently stylish fine-dining restaurant is all white leather banquettes and space-age swivel chairs and there's a fine cocktail bar. From New Steine, walk for 150m east along St James' St then turn right into Atlingworth St.

Kipps Brighton HOSTEL £

(☎01273-604182; www.kipps-brighton.com; 76 Grand Pde; dm/d from £15/40; @ 🛜) Owners of Canterbury's award-winning hostel have created equally commendable budget digs here in Brighton. There's a real cafe vibe around reception and facilities include a communal kitchen. Free movie, pizza and pub nights are organised to separate guests from their wi-fi-enabled devices.

Seaspray BOUTIQUE HOTEL ££

(☎01273-680332; www.seaspraybrighton.co.uk; 25 New Steine; s/d/ste from £69/69/120; 🛜) A light-hearted theme hotel with boutique touches and attentive owners. We dare you to come down to breakfast in the suit, wig and sunglasses provided in the Elvis Room.

Brighton House Hotel B&B ££

(☎01273-323282; www.brighton-house.co.uk; 52 Regency Sq; s/d from £45/95; 🛜) Honest value is the speciality at this welcoming Regency town-house B&B with immaculate and traditionally styled rooms.

Amsterdam HOTEL ££

(☎01273-688825; www.amsterdam.uk.com; 11-12 Marine Pde; d £85-160) This popular gay-run hotel that also welcomes straights has tastefully decorated, spacious, bright rooms and wonderful sea views. Request a room on higher floors if you're a light sleeper.

Seadragon Backpackers HOSTEL £

(☎01273-711854; www.seadragonbackpackers.co.uk; 36 Waterloo St; dm/tw from £15/50; 🛜) Perched on the edge of Hove, but just a short bus ride from Churchill Sq, this no-frills, uncluttered and well-equipped hostel lacks vibe but is ideal for budget nomads who like to snooze in peace and party outside the hostel. The 20 beds are divided into four-bed dorms and twins, with a bathroom/toilet for each six beds.

St Christopher's HOSTEL £

(☎01273-202035; www.st-christophers.co.uk; 10-12 Grand Junction Rd; dm/tw from £13.50/50; 🛜) If you've come to Brighton to make merry, this is the place to stash your stuff while you do it – sleep lovers should go elsewhere.

Eating

Brighton easily has the best choice of eateries on the south coast, with cafes, diners and restaurants to fulfil every whim. It's also one of the UK's best destinations for vegetarians, and its innovative meat-free menus are also terrific value for anyone on a tight budget. For food from around the former British Empire and beyond, head for **Preston St**, which has an incredible concentration of ethnic eateries.

Terre à Terre VEGETARIAN ££

(☎01273-729051; www.terreaterre.co.uk; 71 East St; mains £14; ⏲noon-10.30pm Tue-Fri, noon-11pm Sat, noon-10pm Sun; ✎) Even staunch meat eaters will come out raving about this legendary vegetarian restaurant. It offers a sublime dining experience, from the vibrant, modern space and the entertaining menus, to the delicious, inventive dishes full of rich robust flavours.

Iydea VEGETARIAN £

(www.iydea.co.uk; 17 Kensington Gardens; mains £5.50-7; ⏲9am-5.30pm Mon-Sat, from 9.30am

Sun;) Even by Brighton's lofty standards, the food at this new vegetarian cafe is a treat. The daily changing menus of curries, lasagnes, felafel, enchiladas and quiches swamp the taste buds with flavour and can be washed down with a selection of vegan wines, organic ales and homemade lemonades. On the hop, you can take any dish away in environmentally friendly packaging; the award-winning veggie breakfast is one of UK's best.

The Gingerman MODERN EUROPEAN £££
(01273-326688; 21a Norfolk Sq; 3-course menu £18; lunch & dinner Tue-Sun) Seafood from Hastings, Sussex beef, Romney Marsh lamb, local sparkling wines and countless other seasonal, local and British treats go into the adroitly flash-fried and slow-cooked dishes at this snug, 32-cover eatery. Reservations advised.

Infinity Foods Cafe VEGETARIAN £
(50 Gardner St; mains £3.50-7.50; 10.30am-5pm Mon-Fri, from 10am Sat, noon-4pm Sun;) The sister establishment of Infinity Foods wholefoods shop, a health-food cooperative and Brighton institution, serves a wide variety of vegetarian and organic food, with many vegan and wheat- or gluten-free options, including tofu burgers, meze plates and felafel.

JB's American Diner BISTRO £
(31 King's Rd; burgers £7, mains £6.50-12) The waft of hot-dog aroma as you push open the door, the shiny red-leather booths, the stars and stripes draped across the wall, the '50s soundtrack twanging in the background and the colossal portions of burgers, fries and milkshakes – in short, it's a hefty slab of authentic Americana teleported to the Brighton seafront.

Food for Friends VEGETARIAN ££
(www.foodforfriends.com; 17-18 Prince Albert St; mains £11-13;) An ever-inventive choice of vegetarian and vegan food keeps locals coming back for seconds and even thirds at this place to see and be seen – literally by every passer-by through the huge street-side windows.

Al Fresco ITALIAN ££
(www.alfresco-brighton.co.uk; Kings Rd Arches; mains £10-23; noon-midnight) Housed in a curved-glass structure with a huge, staggered outdoor terrace, the show-stopping feature here is the expansive vistas out across the Channel and along the seafront. The various pizzas, pastas and Italian meat dishes make a tasty accompaniment to the views.

English's Oyster Bar SEAFOOD ££
(www.englishs.co.uk; 29-31 East St; mains £11-25) An almost 70-year-old institution and celebrity haunt, this Brightonian seafood paradise dishes up everything from Essex oysters to locally caught lobster to Dover sole. It's converted from fishermen's cottages, with echoes of the elegant Edwardian era inside and alfresco dining on the pedestrian square outside.

Pomegranate KURDISH ££
(www.eatpomegranates.com; 10 Manchester St; mains £11.50-15) Take your taste buds to the Middle East at this fascinating Kemptown nosh spot where mains, such as Kurdish-style roast lamb, stuffed aubergine and baked swordfish, are dished up in a cosy setting. There are plenty of veggie choices, as well as such lip-smacking desserts as *revani* (semolina cake) and stuffed figs with pomegranate paste.

Due South INTERNATIONAL £££
(01273-821218; www.duesouth.co.uk; 139 Kings Rd Arches; mains £17-28) Sheltered under a cavernous Victorian arch on the seafront, this refined yet relaxed and convivial restaurant specialises in dishes cooked with seasonal Sussex produce sourced within 35 miles of Brighton beach.

Foodilic BUFFET £
(www.foodilic.com; 60 North St; buffet £6.45; 8am-9.30pm Mon-Sat, to 6pm Sun;) As good for breakfast (£2) as a late dinner, but it's the eat-till-you-burst buffet of scrumptious, healthy fare that packs this funky place all day long.

Scoop & Crumb ICE CREAM £
(5-6 East St; snacks £3-5, sundaes £2.50-6; 10am-6pm Sun-Fri, to 7pm Sat) The sundaes (over 50 types) stacked at this ice-cream parlour, belonging to the city's artisan ice-cream producer, are second to none. Freshly cut sandwiches and monster toasties are also available.

Piccolo's ITALIAN £
(56 Ship St; mains £5-7.50) Cheap, tasty pizza and pasta served in a frantic, friendly restaurant – just what everyone expects from an Italian eatery.

Red Roaster CAFE £

(1d St James' St; light meals £2.40-5; ⏲7am-7pm Mon-Sat, 8am-6.30pm Sun) The aroma of roasting beans draws many a mug hugger to this independent coffee house, which also serves sandwiches, salads and quiche.

Tea Cosy TEAHOUSE £

(www.theteacosy.co.uk; 3 George St; teas £3.50-12; ⏲noon-5pm Wed-Fri & Sun, to 6pm Sat) This bonkers tearoom offers cakes and sandwiches, but you can hardly get in the door for royal family memorabilia, including ample Kate and Wills paraphernalia.

Drinking

Outside London, Brighton's nightlife is the best in the south, with its unique mix of seafront clubs and bars. Drunken stag and hen parties and charmless, tacky nightclubs dominate West St, which is best avoided. For more ideas, visit www.drinkinbrighton.co.uk.

Brighton Rocks BAR

(www.brightonrocksbar.co.uk; 6 Rock Pl; wi-fi) Incongruously located in an alley of garages and used-car lots, this cocktail bar is firmly on the Kemptown gay scene, but welcomes all comers. 'Shocktails' and the 'man wall' aside, there's a damn fine 'grazing' menu and theme parties and other events lure in the punters.

Dorset GASTROPUB

(www.thedorset.co.uk; 28 North Rd; wi-fi) This laid-back Brighton institution throws open its doors and windows in fine weather and spills tables onto the pavement. You'll be just as welcome for a morning coffee as for an evening pint here, and should you not leave between the two, there's a decent gastropub menu.

Talk of Tea TEAHOUSE

(www.talkoftea.co.uk; 26 Spring St; ⏲8.30am-6pm Mon-Sat, 10am-4pm Sun; wi-fi) This sparklingly new teahouse will leave you with a classic black, white, green, herbal or fruit dilemma as it stocks Brighton's biggest selection of teas (almost 60 varieties). Early opening, freshly made sarnies and cakes, and free wi-fi make this a superb spot to start the day.

Evening Star PUB

(www.eveningstarbrighton.co.uk; 55-56 Surrey St) This cosy, unpretentious pub is a beer drinker's nirvana, with a wonderful selection of award-winning real ales, Belgian beers, organic lagers and seasonal brews. Within staggering distance of Brighton train station.

Coalition BAR, CLUB

(171-181 Kings Rd Arches) On a summer's day, there's nowhere better to sit and watch the world go by than at this popular beach bar, diner and club. All sorts of events happen here, from comedy to live music and club nights.

Riki Tik BAR

(18a Bond St) This preclub venue has been pumping out cool cocktails and funky breaks for years. It's stylish, dark and sexy and much bigger than it looks from the outside. DJs play here most nights.

Duke of Norfolk PUB

(113-114 Western Rd) Bookshelf-lined boozer with live music and better-than-average pub grub.

☆ Entertainment

Brighton offers the best entertainment line-up on the south coast, with clubs to rival London and Manchester for cool. Keep tabs on what's hot and what's not by searching out publications such as the *List*, the *Source* and *What's On*.

Nightclubs

When Britain's top DJs aren't plying their trade in London, Ibiza or Ayia Napa, chances are you'll spy them here. All Brighton's clubs open until 2am, and many as late as 5am.

Concorde 2 NIGHTCLUB

(www.concorde2.co.uk; Madeira Dr) Brighton's best-known and best-loved club is a disarmingly unpretentious den, where DJ Fatboy Slim pioneered the Big Beat Boutique and still occasionally graces the decks. There's a huge variety of club nights, live bands and concerts by international names each month.

Audio NIGHTCLUB

(www.audiobrighton.com; 10 Marine Pde) Some of the city's top club nights can be found at this ear-numbing venue where the music's top priority, attracting a young, up-for-it crowd.

Psychosocial NIGHTCLUB

(www.psychosocialbrighton.com; 1-2 Morley St) This club specialises in everything and nothing, from punk to tropical nights, stand-up

GAY & LESBIAN BRIGHTON

For more than a century, the city has been a gay haven. With more than 25,000 gay men and around 15,000 lesbians living here, it is the most vibrant queer community in the country outside London.

Kemptown (aka Camptown), on and off St James' St, is where it's all at. The old Brunswick Town area of Hove is a quieter alternative to the traditionally cruisy (and sometimes seedy) scene in Kemptown.

For up-to-date information on gay Brighton, check out www.gay.brighton.co.uk and www.realbrighton.com, or pick up the free monthly magazine *Gscene* (www.gscene.com) from the tourist office.

For Drinking...

Poison Ivy (129 St James' St) In-your-face pub featuring drag acts and camp karaoke.

Amsterdam (A Bar) (www.amsterdam.uk.com; 11-12 Marine Pde; ⌚noon-2am) Hotel, sauna, restaurant and extremely hip bar above the pier; its sun terrace is a particular hit.

Bulldog (www.bulldogbrighton.com; 31 St James' St) Longest running gay bar in Brighton, mostly frequented by men only.

Queen's Arms (www.queensarmsbrighton.com; 7 George St; ⌚3pm-late) And they don't mean Victoria or Elizabeth! Plenty of camp cabaret and karaoke at this pub.

For Dancing...

Revenge (www.revenge.co.uk; 32-34 Old Steine) Nightly disco with occasional cabaret.

Basement Club (31-34 Marine Pde) Located beneath the Legends Hotel, arguably the best gay hotel in town and winner of the Golden Handbag award 2009.

comedy to live music, and rap to lesbian satire.

Funky Fish Club NIGHTCLUB
(www.funkyfishclub.co.uk; 19-23 Marine Pde) Fun, friendly and unpretentious little club playing soul, funk, jazz, Motown and old-school breaks. No big-name DJs or stringent door policies, just cheap drinks and a rocking atmosphere.

Tube NIGHTCLUB
(Kings Rd Arches) Twin giant, brick, subterranean tunnels have bars at the front and back, playing funky house, '70s, R&B and disco to a stylish and attitude-free crowd.

Digital NIGHTCLUB
(www.yourfutureisdigital.com/brighton; 187-193 Kings Rd Arches) Inconspicuous place on the seafront hosting indie, house and student nights.

Honey Club NIGHTCLUB
(www.thehoneyclub.co.uk; 214 Kings Rd Arches) This cavernous seafront club is almost as popular with DJs as it is with the weekly queues of clubbers.

Cinemas

Odeon Cinema CINEMA
(☎0871 224 4007; West St) Seafront cinema showing mainstream movies.

Duke of York CINEMA
(☎0871 902 5728; Preston Circus) UK's oldest working picture house about a mile north of North Rd.

Theatre

Brighton Dome THEATRE
(☎01273-709709; www.brightondome.org; 29 New Rd) Once the stables and exercise yard of King George IV, this art-deco complex houses three theatre venues within the Royal Pavilion estate. ABBA famously won the 1974 Eurovision Song Contest here.

Theatre Royal THEATRE
(☎08448 717 650; New Rd) Built by decree of the Prince of Wales in 1806, this grand venue hosts musicals, plays and operas.

Komedia Theatre COMEDY
(☎0845 293 8480; www.komedia.co.uk; 44-47 Gardner St) This stylish comedy, theatre and cabaret venue attracts some of the brightest stars on the stand-up circuit.

Shopping

In the market for a pair of vegetarian shoes, a gauche portrait of a Lego man or a letter opener in the shape of a...? Well, whatever item, old or new, you yearn after, you'll probably find it in Brighton. The tightly packed **Lanes** is the most popular shopping district; its every twist and turn jam-packed with jewellers and gift shops, coffee shops and boutiques selling everything from antique firearms to hard-to-find vinyls. There's another, less-claustrophobic shopping district in **North Laine** – a series of partially pedestrianised thoroughfares north of the Lanes, including Bond, Gardner, Kensington and Sydney Sts – which are lined with retro-cool boutiques and bohemian cafes. Mainstream chains gather within the Churchill Square Shopping Centre and along Western Rd.

Information

Brighton City Guide (www.brighton.co.uk)

City Council (www.brighton-hove.gov.uk) A mine of information on every aspect of the city.

Jubilee Library (Jubilee St; ⏲10am-7pm Mon & Tue, to 5pm Wed, Fri & Sat, to 8pm Thu, 11am-4pm Sun) Bring ID to sign up for free web sessions.

Post Office (2-3 Churchill Sq) Located within WH Smiths.

Royal Sussex County Hospital (☎01273-696955; Eastern Rd) Has an accident and emergency department 2 miles east of the centre.

Tourist Office (☎01273-290337; www.visitbrighton.com; Royal Pavilion Shop; ⏲9.30am-5.30pm) Superbly run office with an accommodation booking service (£1.50), train and bus ticketing and a highly recommended (free) greeter scheme.

Getting There & Away

Brighton is 53 miles from London and transport is fast and frequent. If arriving by car, parking is plentiful but pricey; city-centre traffic, bus-clogged; and road layouts, confusing.

Bus

Standard connections:

Arundel Bus 700; two hours, at least hourly

Chichester Bus 700; 2¾ hours, at least hourly

Eastbourne Bus 12; one hour and 10 minutes, up to every 10 minutes

Lewes Bus 28/29; 27 minutes, up to every 10 minutes

London Victoria National Express; £11, 2¼ hours, hourly

Train

All London-bound services pass through Gatwick Airport (£9.50, 30 to 40 minutes, up to five hourly).

Chichester £11.60, 50 minutes, half-hourly

Eastbourne £9.50, 30 to 40 minutes, half-hourly

Hastings £13, one hour and 10 minutes, half-hourly

London St Pancras £15.40, 1¼ hours, half-hourly

London Victoria £16, 50 minutes, three hourly

Portsmouth £15, 1½ hours, hourly

Getting Around

Most of Brighton can be covered on foot. Alternatively, buy a day ticket (£4.40) from the driver for all Brighton and Hove buses, or a £2 PlusBus ticket on top of your rail fare that gives unlimited bus travel for the day.

Parking can be expensive. The city operates a pay-and-display parking scheme. In the town centre, it's usually £3.50 per hour with a maximum stay of two hours. Alternatively, there's a Park & Ride 2.5 miles northwest of the centre at Withdean, from where bus 27 zips into town.

Cab companies include **Brighton Streamline Taxis** (☎01273-747474) and **City Cabs** (☎01273- 205205), and there's a taxi rank on the junction of East and Market Sts. All Brighton taxis have a distinctive white-and-turquoise livery.

WEST SUSSEX

Compared with the fast-paced adventures of Brighton and East Sussex, West Sussex is welcome respite. The serene hills and valleys of the South Downs ripple across the county, fringed by sheltered coastline. Beautiful Arundel and cultured Chichester make good bases from which to explore the county's winding country lanes and remarkable Roman ruins.

Arundel

POP 3408

Arguably West Sussex' prettiest town, Arundel is clustered around a vast fairy-tale castle and its hillside streets overflow with antique emporiums, teashops and a host of eateries. While much of the town appears medieval – the whimsical castle has been home to the dukes of Norfolk for centuries – most of it dates back to Victorian times.

Sights & Activities

Arundel Castle CASTLE
(www.arundelcastle.org; adult/child £17/8; ⏰10am-5pm Tue-Sun Apr-Oct) Originally built in the 11th century, all that's left of the first structure are the modest remains of the keep at its core. Thoroughly ruined during the English Civil War, most of what you see today is the result of passionate reconstruction by the eighth, 11th and 15th Dukes of Norfolk between 1718 and 1900. The current duke still lives in part of the castle. Highlights include the atmospheric keep, the massive Great Hall and the library, which has paintings by Gainsborough and Holbein. The castle does a good impression of Windsor Castle and St James' Palace in the popular 2009 film *The Young Victoria*, and is occasionally closed for other film shoots.

Arundel Cathedral CATHEDRAL
(www.arundelcathedral.org; ⏰9am-6pm Apr-Oct) Arundel's ostentatious 19th-century Catholic cathedral is the other dominating feature of the town's impressive skyline. Commissioned by the 15th Duke of Norfolk in 1868, this impressive structure was designed by Joseph Aloysius Hansom (inventor of the Hansom cab) in the French Gothic style, but marked with much Victorian economy and restraint. Although small for a cathedral – it only holds 500 worshippers – Hansom's clever layout makes the building seem a lot bigger.

A 1970s shrine in the northern transept holds the remains of St Philip Howard, a canonised Catholic martyr who was banged up in the Tower of London by Elizabeth I until his death in 1595 for reverting to Catholicism.

Arundel Ghost Experience HISTORIC BUILDING
(www.arundeljailhouse.co.uk; High St; adult/child £5/3; ⏰noon-6pm Sat & Sun) Hear hair-raising ghost stories and explore supposedly haunted prison cells by candlelight at this kids' attraction. Check the website for opening times as it's often closed.

Wildfowl & Wetlands Centre WILDLIFE RESERVE
(www.wwt.org.uk; Mill Rd; adult/child £9.90/5.45; ⏰9.30am-5.30pm) Bird fanciers will be rewarded by an electric boat safari through this 26-hectare reserve, a mile east of the centre as the duck flies.

Arundel Museum MUSEUM
(www.arundelmuseum.org.uk) Last spotted in a tiny room at the defunct tourist office, poor old Arundel Museum has been waiting for a new home to be erected on a plot by the river for years. The modern structure should have appeared by the time you arrive, but at the time of writing it was still a Lottery-funded hole in the ground.

Sleeping

Arundel House BOUTIQUE B&B ££
(☎01903-882136; www.arundelhouseonline.com; 11 High St; d/ste from £85/110; 📶) The contemporary rooms at this lovely 'restaurant with rooms' may be slightly low-ceilinged but they're clean-cut and very comfortable, with showers big enough for two. The restaurant downstairs serves some of the best food in Arundel, which, happily, extends to breakfast.

Arden Guest House B&B ££
(☎01903-882544; www.ardenguesthouse.net; 4 Queens Lane; s/d £55/75, without bathroom £45/65; P📶) For the classic British B&B experience, head to this eight-room guesthouse just over the river from the historical centre. Rooms are freshly decorated and tick all the boxes, the hosts are amiable and the breakfasts, cooked. No pets or children under 14.

Arundel YHA HOSTEL £
(☎0845 371 9002; www.yha.org.uk; Warningcamp; dm £18; P@) Catering to South Downs walkers and families, this large Georgian hostel has excellent facilities and is set in sprawling grassy grounds on a charming country lane, 20 to 30 minutes' walk from town off the A27 (call for directions).

Eating

TOP CHOICE Town House BRITISH £££
(☎01903-883847; 65 High St; set lunch £15.50-19.50, set dinner £23.50-29; ⏰lunch & dinner Tue-Sat) The only thing that rivals the stunning 16th-century Florentine gilded-walnut ceiling at this compact and very elegant eatery is the acclaimed British cuisine with a European twist and sparkling atmosphere. Book ahead.

Bay Tree INTERNATIONAL ££
(☎01903-883679; 21 Tarrant St; mains lunch £5-11, dinner £16-23) Frequented by famished antique hunters, this uncluttered eatery keeps things surprisingly free of yesteryear knick-knacks. Everything from basic *panini* to sophisticated dishes blending local produce with Mediterranean flavours populates the menu.

Tudor Rose BRITISH £
(49 High St; dishes £3.50-11; ⏲9am-6pm) Decluttered and given a lick of mushroom paint à la 1950s austerity style, this bustlingly popular, wholly English cafe has undergone a much-needed makeover. But the food hasn't changed, with tea and cakes, breakfasts, burgers, Sunday roasts and other substantial meals still served with a smile.

Pallant of Arundel DELI £
(17 High St; ⏲9am-6pm Mon-Sat, 10am-5pm Sun) Set yourself up for an English picnic by the river at this irresistible delicatessen selling crusty loaves, Sussex cheeses and bottles of ale from the Arundel Brewery.

Shopping

Arundel is antiques central as far as West Sussex is concerned and if you've come to splurge on old stuff, **Tarrant Street** must have the highest concentration of antique shops anywhere in the southeast.

Information

At the time of writing Arundel's tourist office had been axed, but museum volunteers were planning to open a new office in the Arundel Museum when it's finally built.

Getting There & Away

Trains run to London Victoria (£15.90, 1½ hours, twice hourly) and to Chichester (20 minutes, twice hourly); change at Barnham. There are also links to Brighton (£8.80, one hour and 20 minutes, twice hourly); again change at Barnham. Bus 700 (two hours, twice hourly) is a slower option to Brighton.

Arriving by car, the most central parking is at Crown Yard (60p per hour).

Around Arundel

BIGNOR ROMAN VILLA

Bignor Roman Villa (www.bignorromanvilla.co.uk; Bignor, Pulborough; adult/child £6/3.50; ⏲10am-5pm Mar-May, Sep & Oct, to 6pm Jun-Aug) is home to an astonishingly fine collection of mosaics preserved within an atmospheric thatched complex that's historic in its own right. Discovered in 1811 by a farmer ploughing his fields, the villa was built around AD 190. The wonderful mosaic floors include vivid scenes of chunky-thighed gladiators, a beautiful Venus and an impressive 24m-long gallery design.

While Bignor is well worth the trip, it's a devil of a place to reach without your own wheels. It's located 6 miles north of Arundel off the A29.

PETWORTH

On the outskirts of its namesake village, the imposing 17th-century stately home **Petworth House** (NT; adult/child £12/6.10; ⏲11am-5pm Sat-Wed Mar-Nov) has an extraordinary art collection, the National Trust's finest. JMW Turner was a regular visitor and the house is still home to the largest collection of his paintings outside London's Tate Gallery. There are also many paintings by Van Dyck, Reynolds, Gainsborough, Titian, Bosch and William Blake. Other highlights are the fabulously theatrical grand staircase and the exquisite Carved Room, which ripples with wooden reliefs by master chiseller Grinling Gibbons.

The surrounding **Petworth Park** (⏲8am-dusk) is the highlight – the fulfilment of Lancelot 'Capability' Brown's romantic natural landscape theory. It's home to herds of deer and becomes an open-air concert venue in summer.

Petworth is 5 miles from the train station at Pulborough, from where hourly bus 1 runs to Petworth's Market Sq (15 minutes). If driving, it's 15 miles northeast of Chichester off the A285.

Chichester

POP 23,700

A lively Georgian market town still almost encircled by its medieval town walls, the administrative capital of West Sussex keeps watch over the plains between the South Downs and the sea. Visitors flock to its splendid cathedral, streets of handsome 18th-century town houses, famous theatre and an annual arts festival, as well as a superb modern art gallery, and nearby Petworth House, a must-visit for culture vultures. A Roman port garrison in its early days, the town is also a launching pad to other fascinating Roman remains as well as Arundel and the coast.

Sights

Chichester Cathedral CATHEDRAL
(www.chichestercathedral.org.uk; West St; ⏲7.15am-7pm) Work on this understated cathedral began in 1075 and it was largely rebuilt in the 13th century. The free-standing church tower, now in fairly bad shape, went

up in the 15th century and the spire dates from the 19th century when its predecessor famously toppled over. Inside, three storeys of beautiful arches sweep upwards, and Romanesque carvings are dotted around. Interesting features to track down include a smudgy stained-glass window added by Marc Chagall in 1978 and a glassed-over section of Roman mosaic flooring. A 50p piece gains you entry into the **treasury**, where ecclesiastical baubles are displayed alongside the weathercock that once topped the spire.

Free guided tours lasting 45 minutes operate at 11.15am and 2.30pm Monday to Saturday, Easter to October, and the excellent cathedral choir is guaranteed to give you goosebumps during the daily evensong (5.30pm).

Novium MUSEUM

(www.thenovium.org; Tower St; adult/concession £7/6; ⏲10am-5pm Mon-Sat, to 4pm Sun Apr-Oct, closed Mon & Tue Nov-Mar) Opened in mid-2012, Chichester's new, purpose-built, cut-busting museum provides a home for the eclectic collections of the now defunct District Museum, as well as many artefacts from Fishbourne and a huge mosaic from the Chilgrove Roman villa. The highlight is the set of Roman baths discovered in the 1970s, around which the £6-million museum was designed.

Pallant House Gallery ART GALLERY

(www.pallant.org.uk; 9 North Pallant; adult/concession £9/5.50; ⏲10am-5pm Tue, Wed, Fri & Sat, to 8pm Thu, from 11am Sun) A Queen Anne mansion built by a local wine merchant, handsome Pallant House, along with a 21st-century wing, hosts this superb gallery that focuses on 20th-century, mostly British, art. Show-stoppers such as Caulfield, Freud, Sutherland, Auerbach and Moore are interspersed with international names such as Filla, Le Corbusier and Kitaj. Most of these older works are in the mansion while the newer wing is packed with pop art and temporary shows of modern and contemporary work.

Fishbourne Palace & Museum RUINS

(www.sussexpast.co.uk; Roman Way; adult/child £8.20/4.20; ⏲10am-5pm daily Mar-Oct, shorter hours & days rest of the year) Mad about mosaics? Then head for Fishbourne Palace, the largest known Roman residence in Britain. Happened upon by labourers in the 1960s, it's thought that this once-luxurious mansion was built around AD 75 for a romanised local king. Housed in a modern pavilion are its foundations, hypocaust and painstakingly re-laid mosaics. The centrepiece is a spectacular floor depicting cupid riding a dolphin flanked by sea horses and panthers. There's also a fascinating little museum and replanted Roman gardens.

Fishbourne Palace is 1½ miles west of Chichester, just off the A259. Bus 700 leaves from outside Chichester Cathedral and stops at the bottom of Salthill Rd (five minutes' walk away; four hourly). The museum is a 10-minute amble from Fishbourne train station.

FREE **Guildhall** CHURCH

(Priory Park; ⏲noon-4pm Sat Jul & Aug) This church building is all that remains of a Franciscan monastery, which didn't survive Henry VIII's 1536 Dissolution of the Monasteries. The church later served as a court of law, where William Blake was tried for sedition in 1804, and then as Chichester's first museum.

Market Cross MARKET

(cnr North, South, East & West Sts) Chichester's epicentre is marked by a cute market building constructed in 1501 by the bishop of the time to enable impoverished locals to sell their wares without paying hefty market fees.

Festivals & Events

For three weeks in June and July, the annual **Chichester Festivities** (☎01243-528356; www.chifest.org.uk) put on an abundance of terrific theatre, art, guest lectures, fireworks and performances of every musical genre.

Sleeping

Accommodation is very thin on the ground in the city centre. Beds fill when there's goings-on at Goodwood racecourse just to the north of Chichester.

Ship Hotel HOTEL ££

(☎01243-778000; www.theshiphotel.net; North St; r from £110; 📶) The grand central staircase in this former Georgian town house climbs to 36 fairly spacious rooms of commandingly clean-cut period chic. It's the most enticing option in the city centre and also boasts an excellent all-day brasserie. Book well ahead.

Trents B&B ££
(☎01243-773714; www.trentschichester.co.uk; 50 South St; s/d from £68/90; 📶) Right in the thick of the city centre, the five snazzy rooms above this trendy bar-restaurant are understandably popular.

Litten House B&B ££
(☎01243-774503; 148 St Pancras St) Freshly home-baked bread and jams are served for breakfast in the garden or conservatory at this disarming central Georgian town house, which has three spacious and gracious old-style rooms. Request room two for an idyllic little balcony overlooking the garden. A car park lies across the way in New St.

Eating

St Martin's Tearooms TEAHOUSE £
(3 St Martins St; mains £4-10; ⏰10am-6pm Mon-Sat) A cocoon of nooks and crannies tucked away in a part-18th-century, part-medieval townhouse, this passionately organic cafe serves freshly ground coffee, wholesome, mostly vegetarian food and a wicked selection of desserts. There's also a guest piano with which to shatter the tranquil scene if you so wish. St Martin's St is off East St.

Comme Ça FRENCH ££
(☎01243-788724; 67 Broyle Rd; mains £9-16; ⏰lunch Wed-Sun, dinner Tue-Sat; Ⓟ) Run by a Franco-English couple, this friendly French place does traditional Normandy cuisine in a converted Georgian inn, with a lovely vine-covered alfresco area. It's a short walk north of the centre.

Wests Bar BAR, RESTAURANT £
(14 West St; mains £5-9.25; ⏰11am-11pm Mon-Sat, to 10.30pm Sun) Occupying every nook and chapel of a large deconsecrated church opposite the entrance to Chichester Cathedral, this daytime temple to tummy-packing and evening ale sanctuary allows you to refuel and kick back in an incongruously ecclesiastical setting. The sinful menu of British pub favourites, pseudo-Italian concoctions and spicy fare is sure to bust your bible belt and invoke a holy thirst.

Cloisters Cafe CAFE £
(Cathedral Cloisters; dishes £5-8; ⏰9am-5pm Mon-Sat, to 4pm Sun) This bright and breezy marble-floored cafe in the cathedral grounds, with a sunny walled garden and airy atmosphere, serves baked potatoes, cakes, salads and fair-trade drinks.

Entertainment

Chichester Festival Theatre THEATRE
(☎01243-781312; www.cft.org.uk; Oakland's Park) This somewhat Soviet-looking playhouse was built in 1962 and has a long and distinguished history. Sir Laurence Olivier was the theatre's first director and Ingrid Bergman, Sir John Gielgud and Sir Anthony Hopkins are a few of the other famous names to have played here.

Information

Post Office (10 West St)

Tourist Office (☎01243-775888; www.visitchichester.org; Novium, Tower St; ⏰10am-5pm Mon-Sat, to 4pm Sun)

Getting There & Around

Bus

Brighton Bus 700; 2½ hours, twice hourly

London Victoria National Express; change at Gatwick Airport; £15.20, every two hours

Portsmouth Bus 700; one hour, twice hourly

Train

Chichester has train connections to the following towns:

Arundel Change at Barnham; £4.30, 20 to 30 minutes, twice hourly

Brighton £12.80, 50 minutes, twice hourly

London Victoria £15.90, 1½ hours, half hourly

Portsmouth £7.50, 30 to 40 minutes, twice hourly

SURREY

Surrey is the heart of Commuterville, chosen by well-off Londoners when they spawn, move out of the city and buy a country pad. For the most part, though, it's made up of uninspiring towns and dull, sprawling suburbs. Further away from the roaring motorways and packed rush-hour trains, the county reveals some inspiring landscapes, made famous by authors Sir Arthur Conan Doyle, Sir Walter Scott and Jane Austen.

Farnham

POP 37,055

Nudging the border with Hampshire and joined at the hip with the garrison settlement of Aldershot, affluent Farnham is Surrey's prettiest town and its most worthwhile destination. Blessed with lively shopping streets of Georgian symmetry, a

12th-century castle and some soothing river walks, this easygoing market town makes for an undemanding day trip just an hour away from the capital.

Farnham has no tourist office, but maps and leaflets are available from the library (28 West St), the museum (38 West St) and the town hall (South St).

Sights

Farnham Castle CASTLE

(☎01252-721194; www.farnhamcastle.com; keep free, palace adult/child £3.50/2.50; ⊙keep 9am-5pm Mon-Fri, 10am-4pm Sat & Sun, closed Jan, palace 2-4pm) Constructed in 1138 by Henry de Blois, the grandson of William the Conqueror, there's not much left of the castle keep today except the beautiful old ramparts. Even if the keep is closed, it's worth walking around the outside for the picturesque views.

A residential palace house, the Bishop's Palace was built in the 13th century for the bishops of Winchester as a stopover on London journeys. From 1926 to the 1950s, it was taken over by the bishops of Guildford. It's now privately owned, but you can visit one afternoon a week with an audioguide.

Farnham Castle is located up the old steps at the top of Castle St.

FREE **Museum of Farnham** MUSEUM

(38 West St; ⊙10am-5pm Tue-Sat) This engaging little museum is located in the splendid Willmer House, a Georgian mansion built for wealthy hop merchant and maltster John Thorne in 1718.

Themed rooms trace Farnham's history from flint tool days to Bakelite nostalgia, with a corner dedicated to William Cobbett, the town's most famous son and 19th-century reformer, radical member of parliament, writer and the journalist who established *Hansard* (the official record of what is said in parliament). Cobbett's bust takes pride of place in the peaceful garden out the back where you'll also find a timber-built gallery housing temporary exhibitions.

Sleeping

Bush Hotel HOTEL ££

(☎01252-715237; www.mercure-uk.com; The Borough; r from £94; P❄📶) You'll like beating about the bush once you've slept at this 17th-century inn right in the heart of the action. Rolling renovation keeps things fresh and there's a snug beamed bar and a highly recommended restaurant that spills out into the pretty courtyard.

Bishop's Table HOTEL ££

(☎01252-710222; www.bishopstable.com; 27 West St; s/d from £65/85) Despite the trendy designer feel of the lobby, clean-cut restaurant and leathery bar, rooms retain as much character as the 17th-century building in which they're housed, and range from scuffed but acceptable to antique-filled and almost luxurious. Rates plummet at weekends.

Eating

Plough Inn PUB £

(74 West St; mains £6-11; ⊙noon-11.30pm) Tasty pub fare with a few nods to vegetarians and the Continent, plus Kentish ale, await at this friendly pub, once popular with a student mob but now a haven for all folks.

Nelson Arms PUB ££

(50 Castle St; mains £7-13) A cosily rustic, low-ceilinged bar with a few modern touches, a small terrace at the back and good-value, locally sourced food.

Entertainment

Farnham Maltings ARTS CENTRE

(☎01252-745444; www.farnhammaltings.com; Bridge Sq) Creative, multipurpose spot with a riverside bar, live music, amateur theatre, exhibitions, workshops and comedy.

Getting There & Away

London Victoria National Express bus; £9.50, two hours, daily

London Waterloo Change trains at Woking; £14.30, one hour, twice hourly

Winchester Change trains at Woking; £18, one hour, twice hourly

Around Farnham

WAVERLEY ABBEY

Said to be the inspiration for Sir Walter Scott's novel, **Waverley Abbey** (EH) sits ruined and forlorn on the banks of the River Wey about 2 miles southeast of Farnham. This was the first Cistercian abbey built in England (construction began in 1128) and was based on a parent abbey at Cîteaux in France.

Across the Wey is the impressive Waverley Abbey House (closed to the public), built in 1783 using bricks from the demolished abbey. In the 19th century it was owned by Florence Nightingale's brother-in-law, and the famous nurse was a regular visitor. Fittingly, the house was used as a hospital in WWI.

The abbey and house are off the B3001.

HINDHEAD

The tiny hamlet of Hindhead, 8 miles south of Farnham off the A287, lies in the middle of the largest area of open heath in Surrey. During the 19th century, a number of prominent Victorians bought up property in the area, including Sir Arthur Conan Doyle (1859–1930). One of the three founders of the National Trust, Sir Robert Hunter, lived in nearby Haslemere, and today much of the area is administered by the foundation.

The most beautiful part of the area is to the northeast, where you'll find a natural depression known as the **Devil's Punchbowl**. There is a number of excellent trails and bridleways here. To get the best view, head for **Gibbet Hill** (280m), which was once an execution ground.

The **Hindhead YHA Hostel** (☎0845 371 9022; www.yha.org.uk; Devil's Punchbowl, Thursley, Godalming; dm £16.95) is a completely secluded cottage run by the National Trust on the northern edge of the Punchbowl – perfect digs for walkers.

Bus 19 runs hourly to Hindhead from Farnham.

Oxford, Cotswolds & Around

Includes »

Best Places to Eat

» Le Champignon Sauvage (p228)

» Prithvi (p228)

» Chef's Table (p221)

» Edamame (p202)

» 5 North St (p217)

Best Places to Stay

» Old Swan & Minster Mill (p210)

» Malmaison (p201)

» Cotswold88 (p223)

» Ellenborough Park (p227)

» Lamb Inn (p211)

Why Go?

Dotted with gorgeous little villages, this part of the country is as close to the old-world English idyll as you'll get. It's a haven of lush rolling hills, rose-clad cottages, graceful stone churches, thatched roofs, cream teas and antique shops. Add to the mix the legendary university city of Oxford, with its splendid architecture and lively student vibe, and it's easy to see why the region is a magnet for visitors.

Although the roads and the most popular villages are busy in summer, it's easy to get off the tourist trail. The Cotswolds are at their best when you find your own romantic refuge and discover the fire-lit inns and grandiose manors that persuade A-list celebrities and the merely moneyed to buy property here.

Most of the area is an easy day-trip from London, but Oxford and the Cotswolds deserve at least a couple of leisurely days.

When to Go

On 1 May you can welcome the dawn with Oxford's Magdalen College Choir, which sings hymns from the college tower. In July you can sip champagne and watch the rowing at Henley's Royal Regatta and Festival. September is the best time to sample England's finest ales at the four-day St Albans Beer Festival.

The Cotswolds are good for a visit at any time of year, though the best time for rambling is in late spring, early summer and September, with the weather in your favour but without the crowds.

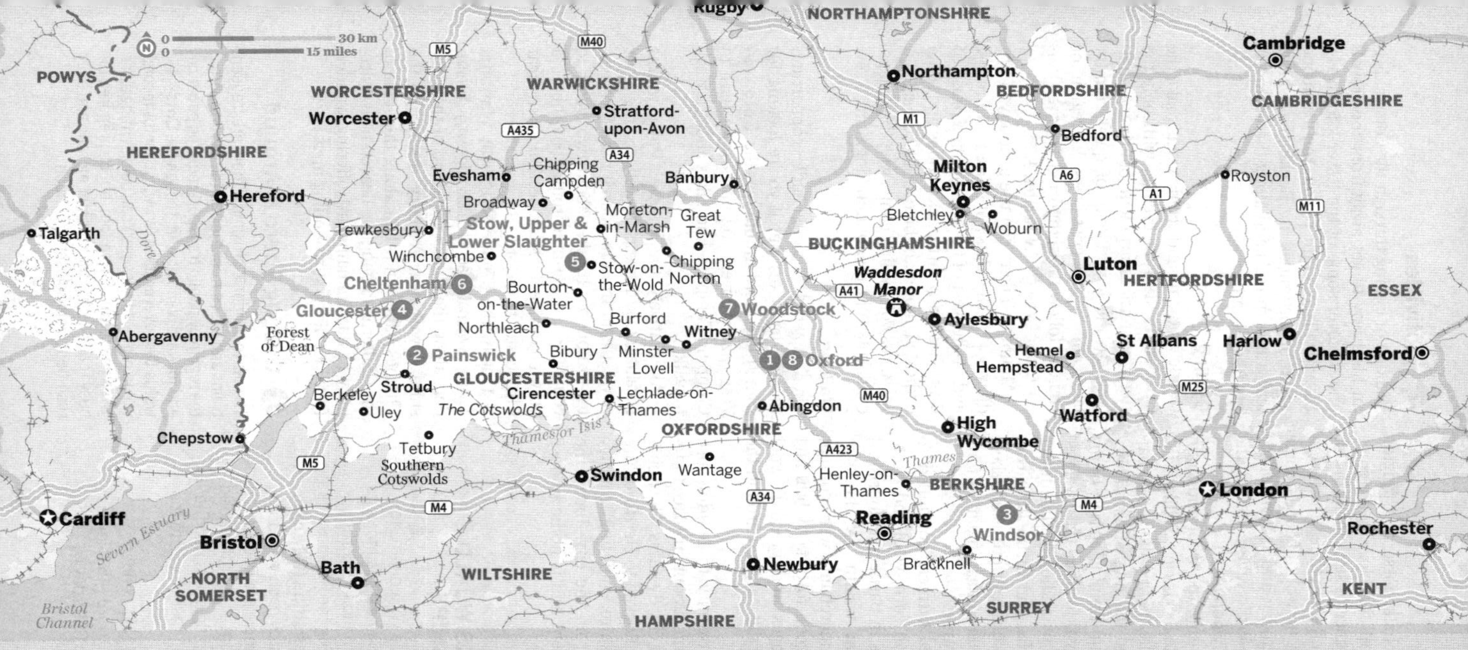

Oxford, Cotswolds & Around Highlights

1. Following in the footsteps of Lyra, Tolkien, CS Lewis and Inspector Morse as you tour the **Oxford colleges** (p194)
2. Meandering around **Painswick** (p223), one of the most beautiful and unspoilt towns in the Cotswolds
3. Getting a glimpse of the high life at the Queen's hideaway, **Windsor Castle** (p237)
4. Touring the elegant cloisters at the magnificent **Gloucester Cathedral** (p230)
5. Driving the pretty country lanes near **Stow-on-the-Wold** (p217)
6. Sampling the superb food at the many fine restaurants in **Cheltenham** (p224)
7. Touring the monumental **Blenheim Palace** in Woodstock (p200), one of the grandest stately homes
8. Exploring the anthropological treasure trove that is the **Pitt Rivers Museum** (p198) in Oxford

History

The Bronze Age chalk horse at Uffington and the Iron Age hill fort close by are some of the earliest evidence of settlement in this part of England. In Roman times, the region was traversed by a network of roads, some of which still exist today, and as word of the good hunting and fertile valleys spread, the area became heavily populated.

By the 11th century, the wool and grain trade had made the locals rich, William the Conqueror had built his first motte and bailey in Windsor, and the Augustinian abbey in Oxford had begun training clerics. In the 12th century, Henry II fortified the royal residence at Windsor by adding a stone tower and protective walls, and in the 13th century, Oxford's first colleges were established, along with its reputation as England's foremost centre of learning.

Meanwhile, local farmers continued to supply London with corn, wool and clothing. The Cotswolds in particular flourished and amassed great wealth. By the 14th century, the wool merchants were content to show off their good fortune by building the beautiful villages and graceful wool churches that are still scattered around the area today.

The region's proximity to London also meant that it became a popular place to retreat to for wealthy city dwellers. The nobility and aristocracy flocked to Hertfordshire and Buckinghamshire, building country piles as retreats from the city. Today, the area remains affluent and is home to busy commuters.

POOH STICKS WORLD CHAMPIONSHIPS

The village of Little Wittenham, near Dorchester-on-Thames, has made its mark on the international sporting calendar by hosting the **Pooh Sticks World Championships** (www.pooh-sticks.com) in March each year. Just like AA Milne's Winnie the Pooh and his friends, teams from all over the world compete by dropping sticks into the river and watching them 'race' to the finish line.

Buses 105 and 114a connect Dorchester with Oxford (45 minutes, hourly Monday to Saturday).

Activities

Walking or cycling through the Cotswolds is an ideal way to get away from the crowds and discover some of the lesser-known vistas and villages of the region. You'll also find great opportunities in Buckinghamshire's leafy Chiltern Hills and along the meandering River Thames.

Cycling

Gentle gradients and scenic vistas make the **Cotswolds** ideal for cycling, with only the steep western escarpment offering a challenge to the legs. Plenty of quiet country lanes and byways criss-cross the region, or you can follow the signposted **Thames Valley Cycle Way** (NCN Routes 4, 5).

Mountain bikers can use a variety of bridleways in the Cotswolds and **Chilterns**, and in the west of the region, the **Forest of Dean** has many dirt-track options and some dedicated mountain-bike trails. Check out www.cotswoldcycling.com, www.bikemaps.co.uk/cotswoldsmountainbiking.htm.

Walking

The **Cotswold Hills** offer endless opportunities for day hikes, but if you're looking for something more ambitious, the **Cotswold Way** (p208) covers 102 miles from Bath to Chipping Campden and takes about a week to walk.

Alternatively, the **Thames Path** (www.nationaltrail.co.uk/thamespath) follows the river downstream from its source near Cirencester to London. It takes about two weeks to complete the 184-mile route, but there's a very enjoyable five-day section from near Cirencester to Oxford.

Finally, the 87-mile **Ridgeway National Trail** (www.nationaltrail.co.uk/ridgeway) meanders along the chalky grassland of the Wiltshire downs near Avebury, down into the Thames Valley and then along the spine of the Chilterns to Ivinghoe Beacon near Aylesbury in Buckinghamshire, offering wonderful views of the surrounding area.

Getting There & Around

Thanks to London's proximity, there are frequent trains and buses from the capital. Getting across the region by public transport requires patience and forward planning and, though the **Cotswolds Discoverer pass** (www.escapetothecotswolds.org.uk/discoverer) can help, renting a car gives you the most freedom, but be prepared for busy roads during the summer months and daily rush-hour traffic closer to London.

Traveline East Anglia (☎0871-200 22 33; www.travelineeastanglia.org.uk) provides timetables for all public transport across the country. Try www.cotswoldsaonb.org.uk for downloadable guides on all bus and rail options in the region.

Bus Major bus routes are run by **Stagecoach** (www.stagecoachbus.com) and **Arriva** (www.arrivabus.co.uk), with smaller companies offering services to local towns and villages. Pick up a copy of Oxfordshire County Council's *Public Transport Map & Guide*, or the *Explore the Cotswolds by Public Transport* brochures in any tourist office.

Train Services in the region are limited, with the exception of the area immediately outside London. For general rail information, try **National Rail** (www.nationalrail.co.uk).

OXFORDSHIRE

The long history of academic achievement and genteel living distinguish Oxfordshire from other parts of the country. Rustic charm and grand attractions are in abundant supply here, with a host of delightful villages surrounding the world-renowned university town.

Oxford is a highlight on any itinerary, with over 1500 listed buildings, a choice of excellent museums and an air of refined sophistication. Between the gorgeous colleges and hushed quads, students cycle along cobbled lanes little changed by time.

Yet there is a lot more to the county. Just to the north is Blenheim Palace, an extravagant baroque pile that's the birthplace of Sir Winston Churchill, while to the south is the elegant riverside town of Henley, famous for its ever-so-posh Royal Regatta.

Activities

Walkers will be delighted in the **Oxfordshire Way**, a scenic, 65-mile signposted trail running from Bourton-on-the-Water to Henley-on-Thames, and the **Wychwood Way**, a historic, 37-mile route from Woodstock, which runs through an ancient royal forest. The routes are divided into manageable sections, described in leaflets available at most local tourist offices.

The quiet roads and gentle gradients also make Oxfordshire good cycling territory. The main signposted route through the county is the **Oxfordshire Cycleway**, which takes in Woodstock, Burford and Henley. If you don't have your own wheels, you can hire bikes in Oxford.

You'll find more information at www.oxfordshire.gov.uk/countryside.

Getting Around

Pick up bus and train timetables for most routes at local tourist offices. The main train stations are in Oxford and Banbury and have frequent connections to London Paddington and London Euston, Hereford, Birmingham, Bristol and Scotland.

The main bus operators are the **Oxford Bus Company** (☎01865-785400; www.oxfordbus.co.uk), **Stagecoach** (☎01865-772250; www.stagecoachbus.com/oxfordshire) and **Swanbrook** (www.swanbrook.co.uk).

Oxford

POP 134,248

Oxford is a privileged place, one of the world's most famous university towns – it's steeped in history, studded with august buildings and yet maintains the feel of a young town, thanks to its large student population. The elegant honey-coloured buildings of the 39 colleges that make up the university wrap around tranquil courtyards along narrow cobbled lanes, and inside their grounds, a studious calm reigns. Just as in Cambridge, the existence of 'town' beside 'gown' makes it more than simply a bookish place of learning.

The city is a wonderful place to ramble: the oldest colleges date back almost 750 years, and little has changed inside the hallowed walls since then. But along with the rich history, tradition and lively academic life, there is a whole other world beyond the college walls. Oxford has a long industrial past and the working majority still outnumber the academic elite.

The university buildings are scattered throughout the city, with the most important and architecturally significant in the centre. Jericho, in the northwest, is the trendy, artsy end of town, with slick bars, restaurants and an art-house cinema, as well as the wonderfully tranquil Port Meadow, while Cowley Rd, southeast of Carfax, is the gritty, ethnically diverse area packed with cheap places to eat and drink. Further out, in the salubrious northern suburb of Summertown, you'll find more upmarket restaurants and bars.

History

Strategically placed at the confluence of the Rivers Cherwell and Thames (called the Isis here, from the Latin *Tamesis*), Oxford was

Oxford

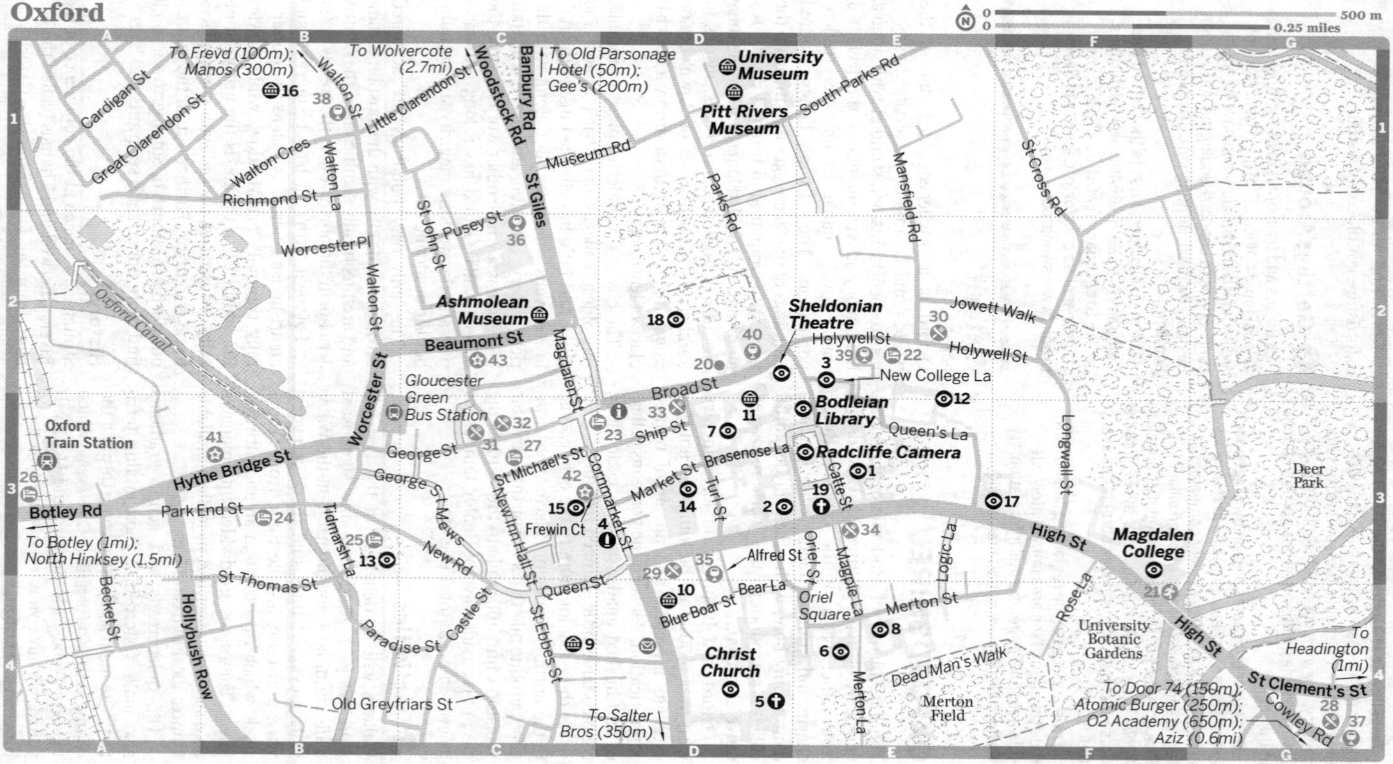

0 500 m
0 0.25 miles
To Frevd (100m); Manos (300m)
To Wolvercote (2.7mi)
To Old Parsonage Hotel (50m); Gee's (200m)
University Museum
Pitt Rivers Museum
South Parks Rd
Cardigan St
Great Clarendon St
Walton St
Little Clarendon St
Woodstock Rd
Banbury Rd
Walton Cres
Walton La
Richmond St
Museum Rd
St Giles
Parks Rd
Mansfield Rd
St Cross Rd
St John St
Pusey St
Worcester Pl
Oxford Canal
Ashmolean Museum
Sheldonian Theatre
Jowett Walk
Holywell St
Beaumont St
Magdalen St
Broad St
New College La
Bodleian Library
Queen's La
Worcester St
Gloucester Green Bus Station
Ship St
Longwall St
Oxford Train Station
George St
Radcliffe Camera
Brasenose La
Catte St
Hythe Bridge St
St Michael's St
Cornmarket St
Market St
Turl St
Deer Park
George St Mews
New Inn Hall St
Botley Rd
Park End St
Frewin Ct
High St
Logic La
Magdalen College
To Botley (1mi); North Hinksey (1.5mi)
Tidmarsh La
New Rd
Alfred St
Oriel St
Magpie La
St Thomas St
Queen St
Bear La
Oriel Square
Merton St
Rose La
Becket St
Hollybush Row
Castle St
Blue Boar St
University Botanic Gardens
Paradise St
St Ebbes St
Christ Church
Dead Man's Walk
To Headington (1mi)
St Clement's St
Old Greyfriars St
To Salter Bros (350m)
Merton La
Merton Field
To Door 74 (150m); Atomic Burger (250m); O2 Academy (650m); Aziz (0.6mi)
Cowley Rd

Oxford

Top Sights

Ashmolean Museum C2
Bodleian Library E3
Christ Church D4
Magdalen College F3
Pitt Rivers Museum D1
Radcliffe Camera E3
Sheldonian Theatre D2
University Museum D1

Sights

1 All Souls College E3
2 Brasenose College D3
3 Bridge of Sighs E2
4 Carfax Tower D3
5 Christ Church Cathedral D4
6 Corpus Christi College E4
7 Exeter College D3
8 Merton College E4
9 Modern Art Oxford C4
10 Museum of Oxford D4
11 Museum of the History of Science D3
12 New College E2
13 Oxford Castle Unlocked B3
14 Oxford Covered Market D3
15 Oxford Union C3
16 Oxford University Press Museum B1
17 St Edmund Hall F3
18 Trinity College D2
19 University Church of St Mary the Virgin E3

Activities, Courses & Tours

20 Blackwell D2
21 Magdalen Bridge Boathouse F4

Sleeping

22 Bath Place Hotel E2
23 Buttery Hotel D3
24 Central Backpackers B3
25 Malmaison B3
26 Oxford YHA A3
27 St Michael's Guest House C3

Eating

28 Café Coco G4
29 Chiang Mai Kitchen D3
30 Edamame E2
31 Fire & Stone C3
32 Jamie's Italian C3
33 Missing Bean D3
34 Quod E3

Drinking

35 Bear D3
36 Eagle & Child C2
37 Kazbar G4
38 Raoul's B1
39 Turf Tavern E2
40 White Horse D2

Entertainment

41 Bridge B3
42 Cellar C3
43 Oxford Playhouse C2

originally a key Saxon town heavily fortified by Alfred the Great during the war against the Danes.

By the 11th century, the Augustinian abbey in Oxford had begun training clerics, and when Anglo-Norman clerical scholars were expelled from the Sorbonne in 1167, the abbey began to attract students in droves. Alongside Oxford's growing prosperity grew the enmity between the new students and the local townspeople, culminating in the St Scholastica's Day Massacre in 1355, which started as an argument over beer. Thereafter, the king ordered that the university be broken up into colleges, each of which then developed its own traditions.

The university – largely a religious entity at the time – was rocked first by the Reformation, and then by the public trials and burning at the stake of Protestant heretics under 'Bloody' Mary. As the Royalist headquarters, Oxford backed the losing side during the Civil War, but flourished after the restoration of the monarchy, with some of its most iconic buildings constructed at that time.

The arrival of the canal system in 1790 had a profound effect on the rest of Oxford. By creating a link with the Midlands' industrial centres, work and trade suddenly expanded beyond the academic core – this development was further strengthened by the construction of the railways. However, the city's real industrial boom came when William Morris began producing cars here in 1913. With the success of his Bullnose Morris and Morris Minor, his Cowley factory went on to become one of the largest motor plants in the world. Although the works have been scaled down since their heyday,

Minis still run off BMW's Cowley production line today.

As for the colleges, the first ones – Balliol, Merton and University – were built in the 13th century, with at least three more being added in each of the following three centuries. Newer colleges, such as Keble, were added in the 19th and 20th centuries to cater for an ever-expanding student population. However, tradition dies hard at Oxford, and it was 1877 before lecturers were allowed to marry, and another year before female students were admitted. Even then, it still took another 42 years before women would be granted a degree. Today, there are 39 colleges that cater for about 20,000 students, and in 2008 the last all-female college, St Hilda's, finally opened its door to male students.

Sights

University Buildings & Colleges

Much of the centre of Oxford is taken up by graceful university buildings and elegant colleges, each one individual in its appearance and academic specialities.

TOP CHOICE **Christ Church** COLLEGE
(www.chch.ox.ac.uk; St Aldate's; adult/child £8/6.50; 9am-5pm Mon-Sat, 2-5pm Sun) The largest of all of Oxford's colleges, and the one with the grandest quad, Christ Church is also its most popular. The magnificent buildings, illustrious history and latter-day fame as a location for the Harry Potter films have tourists coming in droves.

Woe betide you should you display your outsider status by referring to Christ Church as Christ Church College. It's simply Christ Church. Full stop. The Queen's College is not to be confused with Queens' College in Cambridge, and High St and Broad St are referred to as 'the High' and 'the Broad', respectively.

The college was founded in 1524 by Cardinal Thomas Wolsey, who suppressed the monastery existing on the site to acquire the funds for his lavish building project. Over the years numerous luminaries have been educated here, including philosopher John Locke, poet WH Auden, Charles Dodgson (Lewis Carroll), and no less than 13 British prime ministers!

The main entrance is below the imposing **Tom Tower**, the upper part of which was designed by former student Sir Christopher Wren. **Great Tom**, the 7-ton tower bell, still chimes 101 times each evening at 9.05pm (Oxford is five minutes west of Greenwich) to sound the curfew imposed on the original 101 students. Visitors must go further down St Aldate's to the side entrance. Immediately on entering is the 15th-century cloister, a relic of the ancient Priory of St Frideswide, whose shrine was once a focus of pilgrimage. From here, you go up to the **Great Hall**, the college's magnificent dining room, with its hammerbeam roof and imposing portraits of past scholars; it was replicated in the film studios as the dining hall at Hogwarts for

OXFORD ODDITIES

It should not surprise you that a fount of creativity such as Oxford would have more than its fair share of architectural oddities and bizarre rituals. Here are a select few:

The Gandhi roof boss Inside the pleasant but otherwise unremarkable University Church of St Mary the Virgin (p196), you may spot a roof boss in the shape of Mahatma Gandhi. Why Gandhi? No one knows exactly, though he did speak at the church in the 1930s.

The Headington Shark If you happen to be passing along the main street in nearby Headington, you may notice a giant shark sticking out of an ordinary suburban house, apparently having crashed through the roof.

The Tolkien gravestone JRR Tolkien is buried together with his wife Edith at the Wolvercote Cemetery; the names Beren and Lúthien are carved on their gravestone – a reference to the love between a mortal man and an immortal elf maiden who gave up her immortality to be with him.

New College ritual Every three years, the Lord Mayor of Oxford has to walk along the ruins of the city wall which is part of New College (p196) to fulfil a medieval obligation that the wall would be repaired.

Exam attire Oxford students have to wear their formal gowns to take their exams.

the Harry Potter films. The hall often closes between noon and 2pm.

Coming down the grand staircase, you'll enter **Tom Quad**, Oxford's largest and arguably more impressive quadrangle, and from here, **Christ Church Cathedral**, the smallest cathedral in England. Why the smallest? Because it was simply the college chapel that was declared a cathedral by Henry VIII when he broke with the Church of Rome, suppressed more monasteries and convents, and gave the college its current name (it used to be Cardinal's College). Inside, brawny Norman columns are topped by elegant vaulting, and beautiful stained-glass windows illuminate the walls. Look out for the rare depiction of the murder of Thomas Becket, dating from 1320. The cathedral often closes in late afternoon

You can also explore another two quads and the **Picture Gallery**, with its modest collection of Renaissance art. To the south of the college is **Christ Church Meadow**, a leafy expanse bordered by the Rivers Cherwell and Isis, ideal for leisurely walking.

TOP CHOICE Bodleian Library LIBRARY

(www.bodley.ox.ac.uk; Broad St; Divinity School adult/child £1/free, audioguide £2.50; ⌚9am-5pm Mon-Fri, 9am-4.30pm Sat, 11am-5pm Sun) Oxford's Bodleian Library is one of the oldest public libraries in the world, the first of England's three copyright libraries (the other two are the British Library and the Cambridge University Library) and quite possibly the most impressive library you'll ever see. It currently holds over 11 million items, 117 miles of shelving and has seating space for up to 2500 readers, with a staggering 4000 books and articles arriving *every week* – all of which need to be catalogued and stored.

The Bodleian Library has its roots in a 15th century collection of books and its present state is largely due to the efforts of Sir Thomas Bodley, a 16th century Fellow of Merton College who came to the agreement with the Stationers' Company of London that the library would receive a copy of every single book published in the UK – which stands true today.

The oldest part of the library surrounds the stunning Jacobean-Gothic **Old Schools Quadrangle**, which dates from the early 17th century and sports some of Oxford's odder architectural gems. On the eastern side of the quad is the **Tower of Five Orders**, an ornate building depicting the five classical orders of architecture. On the west side is the **Divinity School**, the university's first teaching room. It is renowned as a masterpiece of 15th-century English Gothic architecture and has a superb fan-vaulted ceiling; it featured as the Hogwarts' hospital wing in the Harry Potter films.

Most of the rest of the library is closed to visitors, but **library tours** (library tours £6.50 ; library tours 10.30am, 11.30am, 1pm & 2pm Mon-Sat, 11.30am, 2pm & 3pm Sun) allow access to the medieval **Duke Humfrey's library**, where, the library proudly boasts, no fewer than five kings, 40 Nobel Prize winners, 25 British prime ministers and such writers as Oscar Wilde, CS Lewis and JRR Tolkien studied amid rows filled with grand ancient tomes chained to the shelves. Those wishing to read here (the books may not be borrowed) still have to swear Bodley's Oath, which involves vowing 'not to bring into the Library or kindle therein any fire or flame'. You'll also get to see the 17th-century **Convocation House and Court**, where parliament was held during the Civil War. The tour takes about an hour and it's not suitable for children under 11 years old for fear that they will run amok.

> **VISITING THE COLLEGES**
>
> If you have your heart set on visiting Oxford's iconic buildings, remember that not all are open to the public. For the colleges that are, visiting hours change with the term and exam schedule; check www.ox.ac.uk/colleges for full details of visiting hours and admission before planning your visit.

TOP CHOICE Magdalen College COLLEGE

(www.magd.ox.ac.uk; High St; adult/child £5/4; ⌚noon-7pm) Set amid 40 hectares of lawns, woodlands, river walks and deer park, Magdalen (*mawd*-len), founded in 1458, is one of the wealthiest and most beautiful of Oxford's colleges.

An elegant Victorian gateway leads into a medieval chapel, with its glorious 15th-century tower, and on to the remarkable cloisters – with strange animals perching on the buttresses – some of the finest in Oxford. The fantastic gargoyles and grotesques along the frontage are said to have inspired CS Lewis' stone statues in *The Chronicles of Narnia*. Behind the cloisters, the lovely **Addison's Walk** leads through the grounds and along the banks of the River Cherwell for just under a mile. Were you here in the mid-1870s, you would have encountered Oscar Wilde taking his pet lobster for a walk.

Magdalen has a reputation as an artistic college, and some of its other famous students and fellows have included TE Lawrence 'of Arabia', Poet Laureate Sir John Betjeman, Nobel Laureate Seamus Heaney and explorer Wilfred Thesiger, not to mention seven other Nobel Prize winners.

The college also has a fine choir that sings *Hymnus Eucharisticus* at 6am on May Day (1 May) from the top of the 42m bell tower. The event now marks the culmination of a solid night of drinking for most students as they gather in their glad rags on Magdalen Bridge to listen to the dawn chorus.

Opposite the college and sweeping along the banks of the River Cherwell is the beautiful **Botanic Garden** (www.botanic-garden.ox.ac.uk; adult/child £4/free; ⌚9am-6pm May-Aug), founded in 1621 for the study of medicinal plants. The bench that Lyra and her extra-universal lover Will intend to haunt in Phillip Pullman's *His Dark Materials* is usually well-attended by mooning adolescents.

Radcliffe Camera LIBRARY

(Radcliffe Sq; extended tours £13) The Radcliffe Camera is the quintessential Oxford landmark and one of the city's most photographed buildings. The spectacular circular library/reading room, filled with natural light, was built between 1737 and 1749 in grand Palladian style, and has Britain's third-largest dome. In case you're wondering: no, you cannot enter disguised as a student; the only way to see the inside of the building is to join one of the **extended tours** of the Bodleian Library (p195), which will no longer explore the underground tunnels and passages leading to the library's vast book stacks, as these are to be sealed in 2012 with the rebuilding of the New Bodleian Library. Tours take place on Wednesdays and Saturdays at 9.15am and most Sundays at 11.15am and 1.15pm, and last about an hour and a half.

For excellent views of the Radcliffe Camera and surrounding buildings, climb the 14th-century tower in the beautiful **University Church of St Mary the Virgin** (www.university-church.ox.ac.uk; High St; tower adult/child £3/2.50; ⌚9am-5pm). On Sunday the tower does not open until about noon, after the morning service. At the time of writing, the tower was undergoing restoration, and should reopen again in 2013. Look for a peculiar architectural feature inside (p194).

New College COLLEGE

(www.new.ox.ac.uk; Holywell St; admission £3; ⌚11am-5pm Mar-Sep) From the Bodleian, stroll under the **Bridge of Sighs** (New College Lane), linking the two halves of Hertford College – sometimes erroneously referred to as a copy of the famous bridge in Venice – to New College. (The only thing this bridge has in common with its Venetian namesake is its name.) This 14th-century college was the first in Oxford for undergraduates and is a fine example of the glorious Perpendicular style. The chapel here is full of treasures, including superb stained glass, much of it original, and Sir Jacob Epstein's disturbing statue of Lazarus.

During term time, visitors may attend the beautiful **Evensong**, a choral church service held nightly at 6pm. Access for visitors is through the New College Lane gate from Easter to early October, and through the Holywell St entrance the rest of the year.

William Spooner was once a college warden here, and his habit of transposing the first consonants of words gave rise to the term 'spoonerism'. Local lore suggests that he once reprimanded a student by saying, 'You have deliberately tasted two worms and can leave Oxford by the town drain'. Spooner aside, other famous alumni include Hugh Grant and Kate Beckinsale, and New College is also famous for a bizarre medieval ritual (p194).

Merton College COLLEGE

(www.merton.ox.ac.uk; Merton St; admission £2, guided tour £2; ⌚2-5pm Mon-Fri, 10am-5pm Sat & Sun, guided tour 45min) From High St, follow the wonderfully named Logic Lane to Merton College, one of Oxford's original three colleges. Founded in 1264, Merton is the oldest college and was the first to adopt collegiate planning, bringing scholars and tutors together into a formal community and providing a planned residence for them. Its distinguishing architectural features include the large gargoyles whose expressions suggest that they're about to throw up, and the charming 14th-century **Mob Quad** – the first of the college quads.

Just off the quad is a 13th-century **chapel** and the **Old Library** (admission on guided tour only), the oldest medieval library in use (look for the chained books). It is said that Tolkien spent many hours here writing *The*

Lord of the Rings and that the trees in the Fellows' Garden inspired the walking trees of Middle Earth. Other literary giants associated with the college include TS Eliot and Louis MacNeice.

During the summer months it may be possible to join a **guided tour** of the college grounds. If you're visiting in summer, look out for posters advertising candlelit concerts in the chapel.

Behind Merton College is the ominously named **Dead Man's Walk**, so called because the Jews, who were not allowed to bury their dead within the city, would take the bodies along there to the Jewish cemetery (now the Botanic Garden).

FREE All Souls College COLLEGE

(www.all-souls.ox.ac.uk; High St; 2-4pm Mon-Fri) One of the wealthiest of Oxford's colleges and one of several graduate colleges, though it doesn't accept just any old Oxford graduate. Each year, the university's top finalists sit a fellowship exam, with an average of only two making the grade annually. All Souls was founded in 1438 as a centre of prayer and learning, and today fellowship of the college is one of the highest academic honours in the country.

Much of the college facade dates from the 1440s and, unlike other older colleges, the front quad is largely unchanged in five centuries. It also contains a beautiful 17th-century sundial designed by Christopher Wren. Most obvious, though, are the twin mock-Gothic towers on the north quad. Designed by Nicholas Hawksmoor in 1710, they were lambasted for ruining the Oxford skyline when first erected.

Sheldonian Theatre CEREMONIAL HALL

(www.sheldon.ox.ac.uk; Broad St; adult/child £2.50/1.50; 10am-12.30pm & 2-4.30pm Mon-Sat) The monumental Sheldonian Theatre, built in 1663, was the first major work of Christopher Wren, at that time a professor of astronomy. Inspired by the classical Theatre of Marcellus in Rome, it has a rectangular front end and a semicircular back, while the ceiling of the main hall is blanketed by a fine 17th-century painting of the triumph of truth over ignorance. What's remarkable about the ceiling is its length, made possible by ingenious braces made of shorter timbers for want of trees adequate in length. The Sheldonian is now used for college ceremonies and public concerts, but you can climb to the cupola for good views of the surrounding buildings.

Oxford Union LIBRARY

(www.oxford-union.org; Frewin Crt; admission £1.50; 9.30am-5pm Mon-Fri) Oxford's legendary members' society is famous for its feisty debates, heavyweight international speakers (as well as odder guests, such as Kermit the Frog) and Pre-Raphaelite murals. Although most of the building is off-limits to non-members, you can visit the library to see the murals, which were painted between 1857 and 1859 by Dante Gabriel Rossetti, William Morris and Edward Burne-Jones. The murals depict scenes from the Arthurian legends but are very difficult to see on bright days as they surround the windows.

Brasenose College COLLEGE

(www.bnc.ox.ac.uk; Radcliffe Sq; admission £1.50; noon-4pm) Small and select, this elegant 16th-century college is named after a 'brass nose', or a brass door-knocker, to be precise. The door-knocker in question resides above the high table in the dining hall and is very well travelled: in 1533, it made it all the way to Stamford, Lincolnshire, only to be returned in 1890 along with the house to which it was attached at the time.

Trinity College COLLEGE

(www.trinity.ox.ac.uk; Broad St; adult/child £1.75/1; 10am-noon & 2-4pm Sun-Fri, 2-4pm Sat) This small 16th-century college is worth a visit to see its exquisitely carved chapel, one of the most beautiful in the city, and the lovely garden quad designed by Sir Christopher Wren. An Oxford legend says that the back gates of Trinity will only be opened for a ruler from the previous Stuart dynasty. Not surprisingly, the visitor will find them welded shut.

St Edmund Hall COLLEGE

(www.seh.ox.ac.uk; Queen's Lane; 10am-4pm) St Edmund Hall ('Teddy Hall' to its residents) is the sole survivor of the original medieval halls, the teaching institutions that preceded colleges in Oxford. The Mohawk chief Oronhyatekha studied here in 1862 (and eloped with the principal's daughter) but it's best known for its small chapel decorated by William Morris and Edward Burne-Jones.

FREE Corpus Christi College COLLEGE

(www.ccc.ox.ac.uk; Merton St; 1.30-4.30pm) Reputedly the friendliest and most liberal of Oxford's colleges, Corpus Christi is small but strikingly beautiful. The bizarre pelican

LOCAL KNOWLEDGE

BILL RITCHIE, BILL SPECTRE'S GHOST TRAILS

Although it's a small city, Oxford has no shortage of ghostly goings-on, hidden places and mysteries for a tour guide specialising in spectral sights.

Most Haunted Spots

» The cross in the centre of Broad St, outside Balliol College, is where Nicholas Ridley, Hugh Latimer and Thomas Cranmer were burnt at the stake in the 1500s for heresy.

» Oxford Castle (p199) The Empress Matilda escaped from the castle by abseiling down St George's tower in 1142, and Mary Blandy was hanged there in 1752 for poisoning her father 'by mistake'!

» New College Lane (p196) Royalist cavalrymen would assemble before battle during the Civil War. Listen out for the ghostly echo of horses' hooves.

» Brasenose Lane (p197) The Devil himself is said to have made an appearance here in the 19th century.

Favourite Haunt

A walk along the Oxford Canal from Hythe Bridge St to Jericho.

Oxford Inspires

» The doorway opposite the west entrance of the University Church of St Mary the Virgin inspired CS Lewis to write *The Lion, The Witch and The Wardrobe*.

» Christ Church Meadow is where in 1784 James Sadler, England's first balloonist, took off.

» Christopher Wren, who, although mainly remembered for St Paul's Cathedral, first designed the chapel at Pembroke College and the Sheldonian Theatre (p197) on Broad St.

Hidden Gem

Witch in a bottle and witch's ladder at the Pitt Rivers Museum (p198).

Things the University Would Rather You Didn't Know

In medieval times, Magpie Lane was Oxford's red light district where the 'nymphs of the pavement' would tout for business. Its name in those days – Gropecunt Lane – was indicative of the trade plied there.

sundial in the front quad calculates the time by the sun and the moon, although it is always five minutes fast.

FREE **Exeter College** COLLEGE
(www.exeter.ox.ac.uk; Turl St; ⌚2-5pm) Exeter is known for its elaborate 17th-century dining hall and ornate Victorian Gothic chapel housing *The Adoration of the Magi*, a William Morris tapestry.

Other Sights

TOP CHOICE **University & Pitt Rivers Museums** MUSEUM
(www.oum.ox.ac.uk; Parks Rd; admission free; ⌚University Museum: 10am-5pm; Pitt Rivers Museum: 10am-4.30pm Tue-Sun, noon-4.30pm Mon; 👪) Housed in a glorious Victorian Gothic building with slender, cast-iron columns, ornate capitals and a soaring glass roof, the **University Museum** (www.oum.ox.ac.uk; Parks Rd; entry by donation; ⌚10am-5pm; 👪) is worth a visit for its architecture alone. However, the real draw is the mammoth natural-history collection of more than five million exhibits, ranging from exotic insects and fossils to a towering *T. Rex* skeleton and the remains of the first ever dinosaur ever to be mentioned in a written text (1677).

Hidden away through a door at the back of the main exhibition hall, the wonderful **Pitt Rivers Museum** (www.prm.ox.ac.uk; Parks Rd; admission by donation; ⌚10am-4.30pm Tue-Sun, noon-4.30pm Mon; 👪) is an anthropologist's wet dream – a treasure trove of objects from around the world to satisfy any armchair adventurer and a place where you can spend days on end. The dim light inside the hall lends the glass cases stuffed with Victorian explorers' prized booty an air of mystery, and one of the reasons this museum is so brilliant is because there are no computers here or shiny modern gimmicks; you make your own discoveries. Among this circus of feathered cloaks, necklaces of teeth, blowpipes, magic charms, Noh masks, totem poles, fur parkas, musical instruments and shrunken heads, you may spot ceremonial headgear from Uganda worn during circumcision ceremonies, a Naga skull with buffalo horns surmounted by a German Pickelhaube, blowpipes from South America and Borneo, a porcupine fish helmet from Kiribati, a whalebone ivory war paddle from the South Pacific, an aboriginal cradle made from a single piece of bark, ancient dental implements, ceremonial masks and costume and more, so much more.

Both museums run workshops for children almost every weekend.

TOP CHOICE Ashmolean Museum MUSEUM

(www.ashmolean.org; Beaumont St; admission free; ⏲10am-6pm Tue-Sun;) Britain's oldest public museum, and second only to London's British Museum, the museum was established in 1683 when Elias Ashmole presented the university with the collection of curiosities – which came be to known as Tradescant's Ark – amassed by the well-travelled John Tradescant, gardener to Charles I.

Its collections, displayed in bright, spacious galleries within one of Britain's best examples of neo-Grecian architecture, span the world and include everything from Egyptian mummies and sarcophagi, Islamic and Chinese art, Japan's 'floating world' and examples of the earliest written languages to rare porcelain, tapestries and silverware, priceless musical instruments and extensive displays of European art (including works by Raphael and Michelangelo).

The Ashmolean has recently undergone a makeover, leaving it with new interactive features, a giant atrium, glass walls revealing galleries on different levels, and a beautiful rooftop restaurant. New basement displays include 'Ark to Ashmolean', featuring such gems as the death mask of Oliver Cromwell, Lawrence of Arabia's Arab robes, the lantern Guy Fawkes was carrying when arrested on 5 November 1605, and Powhatan's mantle, said to belong to the father of Pocohontas, and 'Exploring the Past', aimed at younger visitors, as well as the fascinating exhibit focusing on money around the world and what it could have bought in its particular historical period and place.

Oxford Castle Unlocked PRISON

(www.oxfordcastleunlocked.co.uk; 44-46 Oxford Castle; adult/child £9/6; ⏲10am-4.20pm;) Oxford Castle Unlocked explores the 1000-year history of Oxford's castle and prison. Your entertaining costumed guide begins the tour in the 11th-century Crypt of St George's Chapel, possibly the first formal teaching venue in Oxford, and continues into the Victorian prison cells and the 18th-century Debtors' Tower, where you learn about the inmates' grisly lives, daring escapes and cruel punishments. The tour also takes you up the Saxon St George's Tower, which has excellent views of the city, while outside the castle you can clamber up the original medieval motte.

FREE Modern Art Oxford ART GALLERY

(www.modernartoxford.org.uk; 30 Pembroke St; entry by donation; ⏲10am-5pm Tue-Sat, noon-5pm Sun;) Far removed from Oxford's hallowed hallways of history, this is one of the most refreshing contemporary-art museums outside London, with a rota of changing heavyweight exhibitions, a wonderful gallery space and plenty of activities for children.

Museum of the History of Science MUSEUM

(www.mhs.ox.ac.uk; Broad St; admission by donation; ⏲noon-5pm Tue-Fri, 10am-5pm Sat, 2-5pm Sun) Science, art, celebrity and nostalgia come together at this fascinating museum where the exhibits include everything from a blackboard used by Einstein to the world's finest collection of historic scientific instruments, all housed in a beautiful 17th-century building.

Oxford Covered Market MARKET

(www.oxford-covered-market.co.uk; Market St; ⏲9am-5.30pm) A haven of traditional butchers, fishmongers, cobblers, barbers, delis, little eateries and independent shops, this is the place to go for Sicilian sausage, handmade chocolates, traditional pies, funky T-shirts and wacky hats for weddings and/or the Ascot. If you're in Oxford at Christmas, it's a must for its traditional displays of freshly hung deer, wild boar, ostrich and turkey. Otherwise, it's a good spot for lunch.

DON'T MISS

BLENHEIM PALACE

One of the country's greatest stately homes, **Blenheim Palace** (www.blenheimpalace.com; adult/child £20/10; ⏲10.30am-5.30pm mid-Feb–Oct), located in the charming village of Woodstock, is a monumental baroque fantasy designed by Sir John Vanbrugh and Nicholas Hawksmoor between 1705 and 1722. The land and funds to build the house were granted to John Churchill, Duke of Marlborough, by a grateful Queen Anne after his decisive victory at the 1704 Battle of Blenheim. A Unesco World Heritage site, Blenheim (pronounced *blen*-num) is home to the 11th duke and duchess.

Inside, the house is stuffed with statues, tapestries, ostentatious furniture and giant oil paintings. Highlights include the **Great Hall**, a vast space topped by 20m-high ceilings adorned with images of the first duke in battle; the opulent **Saloon**, the grandest and most important public room; the three **state rooms**, with their plush decor and priceless china cabinets; and the magnificent **Long Library**, which is 55m in length.

From the library, you can access the **Churchill Exhibition**, dedicated to the life, work and writings of Sir Winston, who was born at Blenheim in 1874. Particularly moving are the letters written by the young Churchill to his father, whom he clearly revered, apologising profusely for the loss of a watch that his father gave him.

For an insight into life below stairs, the **Untold Story Exhibition** explores the family's history through the eyes of the household staff.

Check out the lavish gardens and vast parklands, parts of which were landscaped by Lancelot 'Capability' Brown. To the front, an artificial lake sports a beautiful bridge by Vanbrugh, and a mini-train takes visitors to a maze, adventure playground and butterfly house.

On a fine day, you couldn't do better than a picnic in the grounds of the palace, and **Hampers deli** (31-33 Oxford St; snacks £1.50-5; ⏲lunch) provides all the essential ingredients: fine cheeses, olives, cold meats, Cotswold smoked salmon and delicious cakes.

Stagecoach bus S3 runs to Blenheim Palace and Woodstock every half-hour (hourly on Sunday) from George St in Oxford (40 minutes). **Cotswold Roaming** (www.cotswoldroaming.co.uk) offers a Cotswolds–Blenheim combination tour (adult £49), with a morning at Blenheim and a half-day Cotswolds tour in the afternoon.

FREE **Museum of Oxford** MUSEUM
(www.museumofoxford.org.uk; St Aldate's; ⏲10am-5pm Tue- Sat) Though it often gets overlooked in favour of Oxford's other museums, this is an absorbing romp through the city's history – from the Roman and Saxon eras to the Victorian era and 20-century industries, such as marmalade-making and car manufacture. The reconstructions of period interiors, such as a 19th-century Jericho kitchen, are particularly good.

Carfax Tower TOWER
(cnr High & Cornmarket Sts; adult/child £2.50/1.30; ⏲10am-5.30pm) Oxford's central landmark, towering over what has been a crossroads for 1000 years, is the sole reminder of medieval St Martin's Church and offers good views over the city centre.

Activities

A quintessential Oxford experience, **punting** is all about sitting back and quaffing Pimms (the quintessential English summer drink) as you watch the city's glorious architecture float by. Which, of course, requires someone else to do the hard work – punting is far more difficult than it appears.

Punts are available from mid-March to mid-October, 10am to dusk, and hold five people including the punter (£16/20 per hour weekdays/weekends, £70 deposit).

The best location to rent punts is **Magdalen Bridge Boathouse** (www.oxfordpunting.co.uk; High St). From here, you can punt downstream around the Botanic Garden and Christ Church Meadow or upstream around Magdalen Deer Park. Alternatively, go to the **Cherwell Boat House** (www.cherwellboathouse.co.uk; Bardwell Rd) for a countryside amble, where the destination of choice is the busy boozer, the **Victoria Arms** (Mill Lane). To get to the boathouse, take bus 2 or 7 from Magdalen St to Bardwell Rd and follow the signs.

Salter Bros (www.salterssteamers.co.uk; Folly Bridge; boat trips adult/child £11.60/6.20; ⏲9.15am & 2.30pm Jun–mid-Sep) offer a range of trips along the Isis from Oxford. The most popular is the scenic journey to the historic market town of Abingdon. The trip takes 1¾ hours and passes the college boathouses and several popular riverside pubs en route.

Tours

The tourist office (p205) runs two-hour walking tours of Oxford city and colleges (adult/child £7.50/4) at 10.45am and 2pm year-round, and at 11am and 1pm in July and August, ultra-popular Inspector Morse tours (adult/child £8/4.50) at 1.30pm on Saturdays, family walking tours (adult/child £6/3.75) at 1.30pm on school holidays, and a bewildering array of themed tours (adult/child £8/4.50) – including an Alice (in Wonderland) tour, a Literary Tour, and a Harry Potter tour; check the website for exact dates. It can also advise on a number of self-guided (brochure or audio) tours of the city and there are themed tours to suit all tastes.

Bill Spectre's Ghost Trails WALKING TOURS
(☎07941 041811; www.ghosttrail.org; adult/child £7/4; ⏲6.30pm Fri & Sat; 👪) For a highly entertaining and informative look at Oxford's dark underbelly, join Victorian undertaker Bill Spectre on a tour of Oxford's most haunted sites. The tour lasts 1¾ hours and departs from Oxford Castle Unlocked and the tourist office. Audience participation likely.

Blackwell WALKING TOURS
(☎01865-333606; oxford@blackwell.co.uk; 48-51 Broad St; adult/child £7/6.50; ⏲mid-Apr–Oct) Oxford's most famous bookshop runs 1½-hour guided walking tours, including a literary tour at 2pm Tuesday and 11am Thursday, a tour devoted to 'The Inklings' – an informal literary group whose membership included CS Lewis and JRR Tolkien – at 11.45am on Wednesday, and a Historic Oxford tour at 2pm on Friday. Book ahead.

Oxon Carts PEDICAB TOURS
(☎07747 024600; www.oxoncarts.com; tour £25) Flexible hour-long tours conducted by a fleet of pedicabs. Passengers receive a copy of a 1904 map of the city and a personal guide to its buildings and history.

City Sightseeing BUS TOUR
(www.citysightseeingoxford.com; 24hr ticket adult/child £13/6; ⏲9.30am-6pm Apr-Oct) Hop-on/hop-off bus tours depart every 10 to 15 minutes from the bus and train stations and the 20 dedicated stops around town.

Sleeping

Book ahead between May and September. If you're stuck, you'll find a string of B&Bs along Iffley, Abingdon, Banbury and Headington Rds.

TOP CHOICE **Malmaison** HOTEL ££
(☎01865-268400; www.malmaison-oxford.com; Oxford Castle; d/ste from £125/275; P@📶) This is the one place where you'll wish they'd lock you up and throw away the key. This former Victorian prison next to Oxford Castle has been converted into a sleek hotel, with plush interiors, sultry lighting, dark woods and giant beds, each room made from three cells knocked together. For a treat, go for the Governor's Suite, complete with four-poster bed and mini-cinema. Great online deals.

TOP CHOICE **Bath Place Hotel** BOUTIQUE HOTEL ££
(☎01865-791812; www.bathplace.co.uk; 4-5 Bath Pl, Holywell St; s/d from £95/120) Comprising several 17th-century weavers' cottages surrounding a tiny, plant-filled courtyard right in the shadow of New College, this is one of Oxford's more unusual hotels. Inside it's all creaky floors, exposed beams and canopied beds. The cheapest doubles are on the small side, but the great service and good buffet breakfast make up for it.

Oxford Rooms STUDENT ROOMS ££
(www.oxfordrooms.co.uk; s/d from £50/90; @) Didn't quite make the cut for a place at Oxford? You can sleep inside the hallowed college grounds and breakfast in a grand college hall by staying overnight in one of their student rooms. Most rooms are functional singles with basic furnishings and shared bathrooms, though there are some en-suite, twin and family rooms available. Some rooms have views over the college quad, while the more modern ones are in a nearby annexe. Available during university holidays.

Old Parsonage Hotel BOUTIQUE HOTEL £££
(☎01865-310210; www.oldparsonage-hotel.co.uk; 1 Banbury Rd; d from £225; P@📶) Wonderfully quirky, the Old Parsonage is a small boutique hotel in a 17th-century stone building covered with wisteria, with just the right blend of period charm and modern luxury. Inside, there's a contemporary-art collection, artfully mismatched furniture and chic bedrooms with handmade beds and marble bathrooms. Oscar Wilde once made it his home.

Ethos Hotel BOUTIQUE HOTEL ££
(☎01865-245800; www.ethoshotels.co.uk; 59 Western Rd; d from £125; @📶) Hidden away off Abingdon Rd, this funky new hotel has bright, spacious rooms with bold, patterned wallpaper, enormous beds and marble bathrooms. It's aimed at independent travellers: you get a minikitchen with a microwave, and breakfast is delivered to your room in a basket. To get here, cross Folly Bridge to Abingdon Rd and take the first right onto Western Rd.

Buttery Hotel HOTEL ££
(☎01865-811950; www.thebutteryhotel.co.uk; 11-12 Broad St; s/d from £65/115; @) Right in the heart of the city with good views, the Buttery is Oxford's most central hotel. The rooms are spacious and rather modest, so it's the location that you're paying for. Ask for a room at the back to avoid being woken up by revellers on weekends.

Oxford YHA HOSTEL £
(☎0845-3719131; www.yha.org.uk; 2a Botley Rd; dm/d from £23/50; @📶) Particularly convenient for budget travellers ridin' the rails, this is Oxford's best budget option, with simple but comfortable four- and six-bed en-suite dorms, private rooms and loads of facilities, including a restaurant, library, garden, laundry and a choice of lounges (though internet is not free).

Burlington House B&B ££
(☎01865-513513; www.burlington-house.co.uk; 374 Banbury Rd, Summertown; s/d from £66/92; P@📶) Twelve big, bright, elegant rooms with brightly patterned wallpaper and bright splashes of colour in a Victorian merchant house. The fittings are luxurious, the service attentive, the bathrooms immaculate and breakfast comes complete with organic eggs and granola. Good public transport links to town.

Remont Guesthouse B&B ££
(☎01865-311020; www.remont-oxford.co.uk; 367 Banbury Rd, Summertown; s/d from £90/120; P📶) All modern style, subtle lighting and plush furnishings, this 25-room guesthouse has rooms decked out in cool neutrals with silky bedspreads and abstract art. Rooms come with huge plasma-screen TVs and a sunny garden. To get here, head up St Giles Street and take Banbury Road branch for 2km when the road branches in two.

St Michael's Guest House B&B £
(☎01865-242101; 26 St Michael's St; s/d from £42/55; 📶) Expect creaky stairs, narrow corridors and spick-and-span rooms with shared bathrooms at this super-central guesthouse, presided over by friendly Margaret. A full English breakfast is included.

Central Backpackers HOSTEL £
(Map p192; ☎01865-242288; www.centralbackpackers.co.uk; 13 Park End St; dm £19-22; @📶) A friendly budget option right in the centre of town, this small hostel has basic, bright and simple rooms that sleep four to 12 people, rooftop terrace and a small lounge with satellite TV – all in a right-on-top-of-a-nightclub location.

Eating

Oxford has plenty of choice when it comes to eating out; head to Walton St in Jericho, to Summertown, St Clements or up Cowley Rd for a good selection of independent restaurants. Look out for local chain G&D's for excellent ice cream and cakes.

TOP CHOICE Edamame JAPANESE £
(www.edamame.co.uk; 15 Holywell St; mains £6-8; ⏲lunch Wed-Sun, dinner Thu-Sat) It may not be the place for a leisurely dinner thanks to its cramped quarters, but the queue out the door speaks volumes about the quality of the food. This tiny joint – all light wood and a friendly bustle of waiters – is the best place in town for genuine Japanese offerings – bento boxes, tempura, noodle dishes and even the love-it-or-hate-it *natto* (fermented soybeans), and the sushi (Thursday night only, £2.70 to £4.30) is divine. Arrive early and be prepared to wait.

Gee's MODERN BRITISH ££
(☎01865-553540; www.gees-restaurant.co.uk; 61 Banbury Rd; mains £12-19) Set in a Victorian conservatory, this top-notch restaurant is popular with the visiting parents of university students, thanks to its creative menu of modern British and European dishes. The two-/three-course lunch menu is a great bet at £17/21 and the setting is stunning, though the atmosphere is rather formal. Book ahead.

Atomic Burger AMERICAN £
(www.atomicburger.co.uk; 96 Cowley Rd; mains £7-11; ⏲closed breakfast Mon-Fri) Atomic comes with the Fallout Challenge, which involves

consuming a triple burger stack complete with fear-inducing ghost chilli hot sauce. Not keen on killing your taste buds? Try the inventive Messy Jessie, Dead Elvis, the barbeque ribs and nachos and curly fries, all washed down with mega shakes. Everything is freshly made; it's fast food, but not as you know it.

Door 74 MODERN BRITISH ££

(☎01865-203374; www.door74.co.uk; 74 Cowley Rd; mains £9-15; ⊙closed Mon & Sun dinner) This cosy little place woos its fans with a rich mix of British and Mediterranean flavours and friendly service. The menu is limited and the tables tightly packed, but the food is consistently good and weekend brunches (full English breakfast, pancakes) supremely filling. Book ahead.

Missing Bean CAFE £

(www.themissingbean.co.uk; 14 Turl St; mains £3-6; ⊙8am-6.30pm Mon-Fri, 10am-6.30pm Sat, 10.30am-5.30pm Sun;) The Brazilian medium roast and cappuccino art at this independent coffee shop is a daily staple for many students, and there are loose-leaf teas, shakes and smoothies for the less caffeine-dependent. The fresh muffins, cakes and ciabatta sandwiches make this a great lunchtime stop.

Quod MODERN BRITISH ££

(www.quod.co.uk; 92 High St; mains £13-17) Bright, buzzing and decked out with modern art and beautiful people, this joint dishes up modern brasserie-style food to the masses. It's always bustling and, at worst, will tempt you to chill by the bar with a cocktail while you wait. The two-course set lunch (£12.95) is great value.

Fishes MODERN BRITISH ££

(☎01865-249796; www.fishesoxford.co.uk; North Hinksey; mains £11-19;) Old and quaint on the outside but sleek and modern inside, this popular summer haunt, a couple of miles west of the city centre, is gastropubbery at its best, with more unusual ingredients such as quinoa sitting comfortably alongside great bangers and mash on the menu. The pub is 3 miles out of town; head south along the A34 and follow the sign after the Botley junction.

THE BRAINS BEHIND THE OED

In 1879, Oxford University Press began an ambitious project: a complete re-examination of the English language. The four-volume work was expected to take 10 years to complete. Recognising the mammoth task ahead, editor James Murray issued a circular appealing for volunteers to pore over their books and make precise notes on word usage. Their contributions were invaluable, but after five years, Murray and his team had still only reached the word 'ant'.

Of the thousands of volunteers who helped out, the most prolific of all was Dr WC Minor, a US Civil War surgeon. Over the next 20 years, he became Murray's most valued contributor, providing tens of thousands of illustrative quotations and notes on word origins and usage. Murray received all of the doctor's contributions by post from Broadmoor, a hospital for the criminally insane. When he decided to visit the doctor in 1891, however, he discovered that Minor was not an employee but the asylum's longest-serving inmate, a schizophrenic committed in 1872 for a motiveless murder. Despite this, Murray was deeply taken by Minor's devotion to his project and continued to work with him, a story told in full in Simon Winchester's book *The Surgeon of Crowthorne*.

Neither Murray nor Minor lived to see the eventual publication of *A New English Dictionary on Historical Principles* in 1928. Almost 40 years behind schedule and 10 volumes long, it was the most comprehensive lexicographical project ever undertaken, and a full second edition did not appear until 1989.

Today, the updating of such a major work is no easier, and the public were again asked for help in 2006. This time, the BBC ran a TV program, *Balderdash and Piffle*, encouraging viewers to contact the publisher with early printed evidence of word use, new definitions and brand-new entries for the dictionary. A second edition of the program was broadcast a year later.

For a full history of the famous dictionary and the development of printing, pay a visit to the **Oxford University Press Museum** (Map p192; ☎01865-267527; Great Clarendon St; ⊙by appointment only).

Chiang Mai Kitchen THAI ££
(www.chiangmaikitchen.co.uk; 138 High St; mains £8.50-10;) Authentic Thai cuisine in the heart of Oxford, complete with tear-jerkingly spicy *som tum* (spicy papaya salad), a range of curries (including, unusually, venison), noodle dishes and standout classics such as chicken with cashew nuts. There's an extensive separate menu for vegetarians.

Fire & Stone PIZZA ££
(www.fireandstone.com; 28 George St; pizza £10) The wood-fired pizzas within this slick, colourful interior take their inspiration from five continents. Try the 'Marrakesh' with ground lamb and mint-and-cucumber yoghurt, the sweet potato and yellow curry 'Koh Samui' or the classic 'New York' with crispy smoked bacon and mozzarella.

Manos GREEK £
(www.manosfoodbar.com; 105 Walton St; mains £6-8;) For delicious home-cooked tastes of the Med, head for this Greek deli and restaurant where you'll find the likes of spinach and feta tart, chicken souvlaki and a great selection of meze. The ground floor has a cafe and deli, serving inexpensive wraps and salads, while downstairs has more style and comfort.

Jamie's Italian ITALIAN ££
(www.jamiesitalian.com; 24-26 George St; mains £9-19) Celebrity chef Jamie Oliver's restaurant serves up some excellent rustic Italian dishes at affordable prices, with the antipasti served on their trademark wooden planks. Decor is modern – all graffitied walls and exposed brick – dishes such as linguini with clams and wild mushroom *panzerotti* are great, and the service efficient.

Café Coco MEDITERRANEAN ££
(www.cafe-coco.co.uk; 23 Cowley Rd; mains £6-10.50) This Cowley Rd institution is a hip hang-out, with classic posters on the walls and a bald plaster-cast clown in an ice bath. The food combines Mediterranean mains with waffles and pecan pie, and most people come for the atmosphere.

Aziz INDIAN £
(www.aziz.uk.com; 230 Cowley Rd; mains £6-9; closed Fri lunch;) Award-winning curry house attracting vegans, vegetarians and curry-lovers in hoards. Standout items on the extensive menu include lamb *razalla* and *murgh kaliya* (black-pepper chicken in creamy sauce), and portions are generous enough to ensure you'll be rolling out the door.

Drinking

Oxford is blessed with some wonderful traditional pubs (www.oxfordpubguide.co.uk) as well as a good selection of funky bars.

TOP CHOICE **Turf Tavern** TRADITIONAL PUB
(4 Bath Pl) Hidden away down a narrow alleyway, this tiny medieval pub is one of the town's best loved and bills itself as 'an education in intoxication' (this is also where president Bill Clinton 'did not inhale'). Home to 11 real ales, it's always packed with a mix of students, professionals and the lucky tourists who manage to find it. One of the few pubs in town with plenty of outdoor seating.

Bear TRADITIONAL PUB
(6 Alfred St) Arguably the oldest pub in Oxford (there's been a pub on this site since 1242), this atmospherically creaky place requires the vertically challenged to duck their heads when passing through doorways. There's a great tie collection on the walls and ceiling (though you can no longer exchange yours for a pint), and there are usually some guest ales worth quaffing.

White Horse TRADITIONAL PUB
(www.whitehorseoxford.co.uk; 52 Broad St) This tiny old-world place – Oxford's smallest pub – was a favourite retreat for TV detective Inspector Morse, and it can get pretty crowded in the evening. It makes a great place for a quiet afternoon pint of Hobgoblin or whatever the guest beer happens to be.

Eagle & Child TRADITIONAL PUB
(49 St Giles) Affectionately known as the 'Bird & Baby', this atmospheric place, dating from 1650, was once the favourite haunt of Tolkien and CS Lewis. Its wood-panelled rooms and good selection of real ales still attract a mellow crowd.

Trout TRADITIONAL PUB
(www.thetroutoxford.co.uk; 195 Godstow Rd, Wolvercote) This charming old-world pub, 2½ miles north of the city centre, has been a favourite haunt of town and gown for many years. Immortalised by Inspector Morse, it's generally crammed with happy diners enjoying the riverside garden, though if you wish to eat, come armed with patience.

Kazbar BAR
(www.kazbar.co.uk; 25-27 Cowley Rd; ⏲5pm-midnight Mon-Fri, noon-midnight Sat & Sun) This Moroccan-themed bar has giant windows, low lighting, warm colours and a cool vibe. It's buzzing most nights with hip young things sipping cocktails and filling up on the Spanish and North African tapas (£4 to £6).

Frevd PUB
(119 Walton St) Cavernous neoclassical church-turned-bar with quirky art and great cocktails, popular with a young style-conscious crowd.

Raoul's COCKTAIL BAR
(www.raoulsbar.co.uk; 32 Walton St; ⏲4pm-midnight) Perfectly mixed cocktails and funky music at Jericho's finest retro-look bar.

☆ Entertainment

Despite its large student population, Oxford's club scene is fairly limited. If you're a fan of classical music, however, you'll be spoilt for choice. See www.dailyinfo.co.uk or www.musicatoxford.com for listings.

Creation Theatre THEATRE
(www.creationtheatre.co.uk) Performing in a variety of nontraditional venues including city parks, the BMW plant and Oxford Castle, this theatre company produces highly original, mostly Shakespearean shows featuring plenty of magic and special effects.

O2 Academy LIVE MUSIC
(www.o2academyoxford.co.uk; 190 Cowley Rd) Oxford's best club and live-music venue hosts everything from big-name DJs and international touring artists to indie bands, hard rock and funk nights across three performance spaces. Expect a mixed crowd of students, professionals and academics.

Bridge CLUB
(www.bridgeoxford.co.uk; 6 Hythe Bridge St; ⏲closed Sun) The three floors of this club heave with revellers almost every night of the week, with resident DJs playing a mix of dance anthems, funk, hip hop and R'n'B, while those needing to rest their feet can retire to the lounge for the signature cocktails.

Cellar LIVE MUSIC
(www.cellaroxford.co.uk; Frewin Crt, off Cornmarket St; 🛜) Live music nightly at this independent venue. From local DJs to indie rock, reggae, funk, hip hop, and drum and bass, to even the odd play, the Cellar's got all angles covered.

Oxford Playhouse THEATRE
(www.oxfordplayhouse.com; Beaumont St) The city's main stage for quality drama also hosts an impressive selection of touring music, dance and theatre performances, and the Burton Taylor Studio has quirky student productions.

ℹ Information

You'll find that every major bank and ATM is handily represented on or close to Cornmarket St.

Daily Info (www.dailyinfo.co.uk) Daily listings for events, gigs, performances and accommodation.

John Radcliffe Hospital (☎01865-231405; Headley Way, Headington) Three miles east of the city centre in Headington.

Oxford City (www.oxfordcity.co.uk) Accommodation and restaurant listings as well as entertainment, activities and shopping.

Oxford Online (www.visitoxford.org) Oxford's official tourism website.

Post Office (102 St Aldate's; ⏲9am-5.30pm Mon-Sat)

Tourist Office (☎01865-252200; www.visitoxford.org; 15-16 Broad St; ⏲9.30am-5pm Mon-Sat, 10am-4pm Sun)

ℹ Getting There & Away

Bus

Oxford's main bus/coach station is at **Gloucester Green**. Services to **London** (£18 return) run up to every 15 minutes, day and night, and take about 90 minutes.

Airline (www.oxfordbus.co.uk) Runs to **Heathrow** (£24, 90 minutes) half-hourly from 4am to 10pm and at midnight and 2am, and **Gatwick** (£29, two hours) hourly 5.15am to 8.15pm, and every two hours from 10pm to 4am.

National Express (www.nationalexpress.com) Runs buses to **Birmingham**, **Bath** and **Bristol**, but all are easier to reach by train.

Stagecoach (www.stagecoachbus.com) Serves most of the small towns in Oxfordshire and runs the X5 service to **Cambridge** (£12, 3½ hours) roughly every half-hour.

Swanbrook (www.swanbrook.co.uk) Services to **Cheltenham** and **Gloucester** via Witney and Burford (£8, three to four daily Monday to Saturday, one daily Sunday, 1½ hours).

Car

Driving and parking in Oxford is a nightmare. Use the five Park & Ride car parks on major routes leading into town. Parking is free and buses (10 to 15 minutes, every 10 minutes) cost £2.50.

Train

Oxford's train station is conveniently placed at the western end of Park End St. There are half-hourly services to **London Paddington** (£23, one hour) and roughly hourly trains to **Birmingham** (£16, 1¼ hours). Hourly services also run to **Bath** (£16, 1¼ hours) and **Bristol** (£22, one to two hours), but require a change at Didcot Parkway.

Getting Around

BICYCLE

Cyclo Analysts (☎01865-424444; 150 Cowley Rd; per day/week £19/55) Rents hybrid bikes.

BUS

Buses 1 and 5 go to Cowley Rd from St Aldate's, 2 and 7 go along Banbury Rd from Magdalen St, and 16 and 35 run along Abingdon Rd from St Aldate's.

A multi-operator **Plus Pass** (per day/week £6/19) allows unlimited travel on Oxford's bus system.

TAXI

There are taxi ranks at the train station and bus station, as well as on St Giles and at Carfax. For a green alternative, call **Oxon Carts** (☎07747 024600), a pedicab service.

Henley-on-Thames

POP 10,646

A well-heeled kind of place, Henley is an attractive commuter town set on the banks of the river, studded with elegant Georgian architecture, and synonymous with the **Henley Royal Regatta** (www.hrr.co.uk), a world-famous rowing tournament which dates back to 1839, and which sees the town bursting into action in July. The five-day regatta has grown into a major fixture in the social calendar of the upwardly mobile, and although rowers of the highest calibre take part, the main event is rather overshadowed by the champagne-fuelled antics of the wealthy who come here to see and be seen. Still, picnicking in the public enclosure (tickets £15 to £19) and watching the rowers' straining muscles as the boats whizz by makes for a very pleasant day out in sunny weather.

The week following the regatta is taken up by the **Henley Festival** (www.henley-festival.co.uk), a vibrant black-tie affair that features everything from big-name international stars to quirky, alternative acts – anything from opera to rock, jazz, comedy and swing, the main events taking place on a floating stage on the Thames.

In keeping with the boat-race theme, the **River & Rowing Museum** (www.rrm.co.uk; Mill Meadows; adult/child £7.50/5.50; ⏰10am-5.30pm; 👪) focuses on the town's relationship with the Thames, the history of rowing, and the wildlife and commerce supported by the river. There are plenty of hands-on activities and interactive displays for kids, and the 'Wind in the Willows' exhibition brings Kenneth Grahame's stories of Ratty, Mole, Badger and Toad to life.

Hobbs & Son (www.hobbs-of-henley.com) runs hour-long afternoon boat trips along the river from April to September (adult/child £8/5).

Sleeping & Eating

Henley has a good choice of accommodation, but is easily doable as a day trip from London. Book way in advance for the regatta. There are decent restaurants just outside Henley, with the centre dominated by chain offerings.

TOP CHOICE Hotel du Vin HOTEL £££

(☎01491-848400; www.hotelduvin.com; New St; d from £130; P📶) Set in the former Brakspears Brewery, this upmarket hotel chain scores high for its blend of industrial chic and designer sophistication, as well as friendly service. The spacious rooms and opulent suites feature supremely comfortable beds, monsoon showers and all the mod cons, while its bistro (mains £13 to £21) is one of the best places to eat in town, complemented as it is by the huge wine cellar.

Old School House B&B ££

(☎01491-573929; www.oldschoolhousehenley.co.uk; 42 Hart St; d £95; P) This small stone cottage in a walled garden in the town centre is a 19th-century schoolhouse. Exposed timber beams and rustic furniture give the two comfortable guest rooms plenty of character, and the central location can't be beat at this price.

Black Boys Inn MODERN BRITISH ££

(☎01628-824212; www.blackboysinn.co.uk; Henley Rd, Hurley; 2-/3-course lunch £12.50/16; ⏰closed Sun dinner) This 16th-century coaching inn is in the nearby village of Hurley, and the deceptively simple dishes, such as mussels mariniere and pancetta-wrapped venison, cooked with passion, are worth the trip. There's an extensive range of fine French wines to choose from, too. The pub is about 4 miles east of Henley just off the A4130.

Crooked Billet INTERNATIONAL ££
(☎01491-681048; www.thecrookedbillet.co.uk; Newlands Lane, Stoke Row; mains £13-27) Atmospheric 17th-century inn with sloping ceilings and creaky floors – once the hideout of notorious highwayman Dick Turpin. You can go for the 'guinea pig' menu (which features newly invented dishes rather than said guinea pig) or else tuck into the likes of John Dory with wild mushrooms, slow-cooked pork belly and a host of dishes with Mediterranean inspiration. Stoke Row is 5 miles west of Henley.

 Getting There & Around

Trains to **London Paddington** (£14.20, hourly) take about one hour though you have to change twice – at Reading/Slough and Twyford.

Wantage

POP 9767

Sleepy but handsome Wantage is a medieval market town of sturdy timber-framed buildings, old coaching inns and crooked cottages. The market square is dominated by a **statue of Alfred the Great**, who was born here in AD 849, and traders still peddle their wares beneath his feet every Wednesday and Saturday. To the west of the square is the beautiful 13th-century **Church of St Peter & St Paul**, with its hammer-beam roof and beautiful corbels.

Wantage also provides easy access to the most attractive part of the **Ridgeway national trail** – which follows a popular Iron Age route – less than 3 miles to the south. There are several hostels along this relatively undemanding walking route, dotted with prehistoric monuments, the most convenient of which is the **Court Hill Centre** (☎01235-760253; www.courthill.org.uk; dm £17), a couple of miles south of Wantage, consisting of five converted barns with 60 bunk beds and a guest kitchen, popular with walkers and cyclists.

Wantage is easily reachable from Oxford by bus X30 from Monday to Saturday (35 minutes, hourly).

THE COTSWOLDS

Glorious villages riddled with beautiful old mansions of honey-coloured stone, thatched cottages, atmospheric churches and rickety almshouses draw crowds of visitors to the Cotswolds. The booming medieval wool trade brought the area its wealth and left it with such a proliferation of beautiful buildings that its place in history is secured for evermore. If you've ever craved 'chocolate box' villages or lusted after a cream tea in the mid-afternoon, there's no finer place to fulfil your fantasies.

Festivals & Events

When the locally sourced, seasonal food movement took off a few years ago, the Cotswolds were already there. Organic, ethically produced produce has long been a staple in the villages. In the delis and independent food shops all over the region, exploring foodies will make many tempting discoveries. Edible goodies to look out for include **Simon Weaver Organic** (www.simonweaver.net) from a farm near Upper Slaughter, organic

WORTH A TRIP

THE WHITE HORSE

Reachable by the Ridgeway national trail from Wantage, the **White Horse** is one of England's oldest chalk carvings, a stylised image cut into a hillside almost 3000 years ago above the present-day village of Uffington. No one is sure why the people of the time went to so much trouble to create the image or what exactly it is supposed to represent, but the mystery only adds to the sense of awe. This huge figure measures 114m long and 49m wide but is best seen from a distance – or, if you're lucky enough, from the air – because of the stylised lines of perspective.

Just below the figure is **Dragon Hill** – so called because it is believed that St George slew the dragon at this location – and above it the grass-covered earthworks of **Uffington Castle**.

The White Horse can also be reached by car. From Uffington, take Broad Way south; it crosses the B4507 and becomes Dragon Hill Road, which leads you to the car park near the White Horse.

Cotswolds

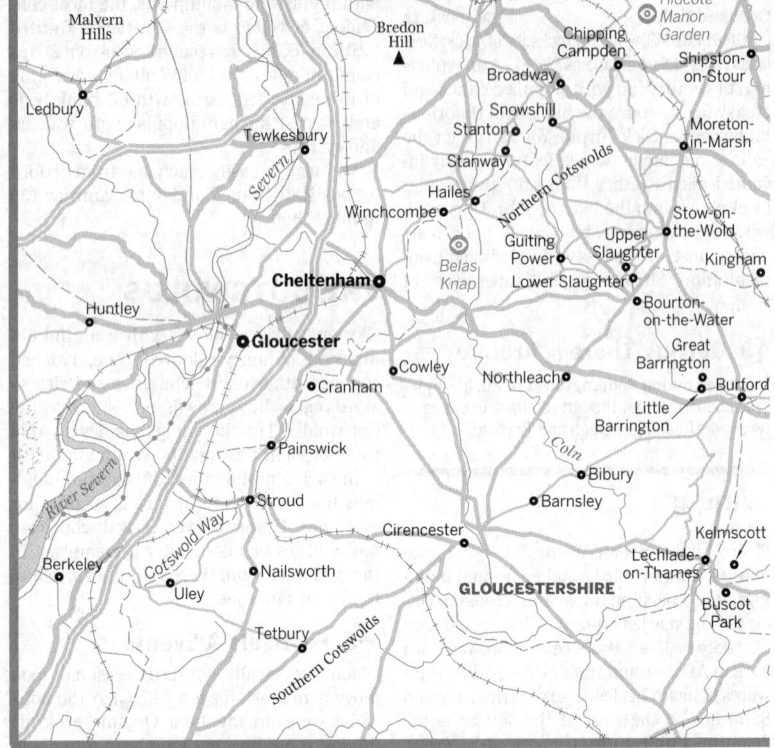

beef from **LoveMyCow** (www.lovemycow.com) in Bourton-on-the-Water, smoked fish and meats from **Upton Smokery** (www.uptonsmokery.co.uk) in Burford and fantastic ice cream from the **Cotswold Ice Cream Company** (www.cotswoldicecream.net).

The feast doesn't stop there. Each calendar year sees a smattering of food festivals all over the Cotswolds, with independent producers bringing their wares, and chefs showing off their stuff. These include the **Stroud Food & Drink Festival** (www.stroudfoodfest.com) in September, the **Wild Thyme Food Festival** (p214) in Chipping Norton in April, and the brand new **Food & Farming Festival** (http://cotswoldfarmpark.co.uk) at Cotswold Farm Park in May.

Finally, **weekly farmers markets** (www.farmersmarkets.net) take place in several villages, with a multitude of local producers selling their seasonal delights to the general public. The biggest ones are held in Stroud, Bourton-on-the-Water, Stow-on-the-Wold, Lechlade and Cirencester. What are you waiting for? Go forth and sample!

Activities

The gentle hills of the Cotswolds are perfect for walking, cycling and riding. The 102-mile **Cotswold Way** (www.nationaltrail.co.uk/cotswold) gives walkers a wonderful overview of the area. The route meanders from Chipping Campden to Bath, passing through some lovely countryside and tiny villages, with no major climbs or difficult stretches, and is easily accessible from many points en route if you fancy tackling a shorter section.

Away from the main roads, the winding lanes of the Cotswolds make fantastic cycling territory. Again, the local tourist offices are invaluable in helping to plot a route.

Information

For information on attractions, accommodation and events:

Cotswolds (www.the-cotswolds.org)

Cotswolds Tourism (www.cotswolds.com)

Oxfordshire Cotswolds (www.oxfordshirecotswolds.org)

Getting Around

The Cotswolds have been well and truly 'discovered', and the most popular villages can be besieged by tourists and traffic in summer. Travel by public transport requires careful planning and patience; for the most flexibility, and the option of getting off the beaten track, your own car is unbeatable. Plan to visit the main centres early in the morning or late in the evening, focus your attention on the south or take to the hills on foot or by bike to avoid the worst of the crowds. Better still, just leave the crowds behind and meander down deserted country lanes and bridleways until you discover your very own bucolic village seemingly undisturbed since medieval times.

Alternatively, **Cotswold Roaming** (01865-308300; www.cotswold-roaming.co.uk) runs guided bus tours from Oxford between April and October. Half-day tours of the Cotswolds (£30) include Minster Lovell, Burford and Bibury, while full-day tours of the North Cotswolds (£45) feature Bourton-on-the-Water, Lower Slaughter, Chipping Campden and Stow-on-the-Wold.

Witney

POP 22,765

The sleepy town of Witney is firmly on Oxford's commuter belt, but make your way through the traffic and new housing developments to the centre of town and you'll find a charming village green flanked by pretty stone houses. At one end is a glorious **wool church** and **18th-century almshouses**, at the other a **17th-century covered market**. Witney built its wealth through blanket production – its main trade from the Iron Age until 2002! – and the mills, wealthy merchants' homes and blanket factories can still be seen today. The baroque, 18th-century **Blanket Hall** dominates genteel High St, while at Wood Green you'll find a second village green and a cluster of stunning old stone cottages.

Pick up a copy of the *Witney Wool & Blanket Trail* from the **tourist office** (01993-775802; www.oxfordshirecotswolds.org; 3 Welch Way; 9am-5.30pm Mon-Thu, 9am-5pm Fri, 9.30am-5pm Sat) to guide you around the town.

Your best bet for a meal is the **Fleece** (01993-892270; www.fleecewitney.co.uk; 11 Church Green; P), a contemporary pub, restaurant and B&B on the main village green. The spacious brasserie has an ambitious seasonal menu, with some wonderful smoked fish, Aberdeenshire steak and a

THE COTSWOLDS DISCOVERER

If you're planning on seeing much of the Cotswolds in a short space of time and don't have your own wheels, your best bet is the **Cotswolds Discoverer** (www.escapetothecotswolds.org.uk/discoverer; 1-/3-day bus pass £10/25, train pass £8.50/20), which gives you unlimited travel on participating bus or train routes.

THE GOOD LIFE

The Cotswolds' mellow charms attract moneyed city folk, A-list celebrities and wealthy downsizers in equal measure, but mere mortals can get a slice of the good life at one of the numerous luxury hotels. Here are just a few to whet your fancy:

Barnsley House (01285-740000; www.barnsleyhouse.com; Barnsley; d £300-525; P@) For funky chic and indulgent sophistication, this hideout for the rich and famous is just the spot for a romantic weekend.

Cowley Manor (01242-870900; www.cowleymanor.com; Cowley; d £180-500; P) Handmade furniture and fabrics by young British designers adorn the simple but elegant rooms at this super-sleek hotel.

Lygon Arms (0800 652 8413; www.barcelo-hotels.co.uk; High St, Broadway; d £152-390; P@) Choose medieval splendour or modern chic at this 16th-century inn in the heart of Broadway.

roast-of-the-day (£12.50). If you wish to stay, the rooms here are sleek and stylish (single/double £80/90).

Stagecoach (www.stagecoachbus.com) bus S1 runs from Oxford to Witney every 20 minutes Monday to Saturday, hourly on Sunday (30 minutes). **Swanbrook** (www.swanbrook.co.uk) runs between Cheltenham (£8, one hour, one to three daily) and Oxford (30 minutes) via Witney.

Minster Lovell

POP 1348

Bet on a gentle slope leading down to the meandering River Windrush, Minster Lovell is a gorgeous village with a cluster of stone cottages nestled beside an ancient pub and riverside mill. One of William Morris' favourite spots, the village has changed little since medieval times; it's divided into two halves – Old Minster, recorded in the Domesday Book (1086) and the rather newer Minster Lovell across the river.

The main sight in Old Minster is **Minster Lovell Hall**, the 15th-century manor house that was home to Viscount Francis Lovell. Lovell fought with Richard III at the Battle of Bosworth in 1485 and joined Lambert Simnel's failed rebellion after the king's defeat and death. Lovell's mysterious disappearance was never explained, and when a skeleton was discovered inside a secret vault in the house in 1708, it was assumed he had died while in hiding. The manor is now in ruins; you can peek past the blackened walls into the roofless great hall and the interior courtyard, the wind whistling eerily through the gaping windows.

The revamped, luxurious **Old Swan & Minster Mill** (01993-774441; www.oldswanandminstermill.com; d from £165-350; P) has charming period-style rooms in the 17th-century Old Swan or sleek, contemporary design in the 19th-century converted mill, covered with creepers. Windrush Spa is due to open alongside the river in late 2012 with full-scale pampering complete with a range of treatments and outdoor pool. The Old Swan serves excellent gastropub food, with doorstep sandwiches for lunch and handmade sausages, daily fish and game for dinner (mains £15 to £23).

Swanbrook coaches stop here on the Oxford to Cheltenham run (one to three daily). Stagecoach bus 233 between Witney and Burford stops here Monday to Saturday (10 minutes each way, 10 daily).

Burford

POP 1340

Slithering down a steep hill to a medieval crossing point on the River Windrush, the classic Cotswold village of Burford made its fortune at the height of the wool trade and is a wonderfully picturesque place with stone cottages, crooked windows, fine townhouses with half-timbered facades and the odd Elizabethan or Georgian gem. Antique shops, tearooms and boutiques peddle nostalgia to the hordes of summer visitors, but you can still wander along quiet side streets seemingly lost in time.

The helpful **tourist office** (01993-823558; www.oxfordshirecotswolds.org; Sheep St; 9.30am-5.30pm Mon-Sat, until 4pm Nov-Feb) provides the Burford Trail leaflet (50p), with information on walking in the local area.

Sights & Activities

Burford's main attraction lies in its incredible collection of buildings, including the 16th-century **Tolsey House** (Toll House; High St; admission free; ⏲2-5pm Mon-Fri, 11am-5pm Sat & Sun Apr-Oct), where the wealthy wool merchants held their meetings. This quaint building perches on sturdy pillars and now houses a small museum on Burford's history.

Just off the main street, you'll find the town's 14th-century **almshouses** and the **Church of St John the Baptist** (www.burfordchurch.org). The Norman tower here is topped by a 15th-century steeple, and inside you'll find a fine fan-vaulted ceiling and several mausoleums that somehow survived the Reformation. Look for a plaque beside the entrance that commemorates the execution of three Levellers – Roundhead soldiers who mutinied due to their leaders' failure to uphold the notion of equality of all men before the law – by Cromwell's army.

Younger visitors will enjoy a visit to the hugely popular **Cotswold Wildlife Park** (☎01993-823006; www.cotswoldwildlifepark.co.uk; adult/child £13/9; ⏲10am-6pm), 3 miles south of Burford and home to a vast menagerie of penguins, zebras, white rhinos, Amur leopards and much more. A miniature train (£1) and petting zoo take the excitement up a notch. Last admission is 1½ hours before closing time.

There are several delightful **walks** (www.escapetothecotswolds.org.uk) from Burford, including the one along the picturesque river path to the untouched and rarely visited village of **Swinbrook** (3 miles), where the 12th-century **Church of St Mary** has the remarkable tombs of the Fettiplace family who dominated the area for 500 years.

Sleeping & Eating

Burford has a wonderful choice of atmospheric, upmarket hotels but far fewer options at more affordable prices.

TOP CHOICE **Lamb Inn** INN £££

(☎01993-823155; www.cotswold-inns-hotels.co.uk/lamb; Sheep St; s/d from £120/160; P 📶) At this atmospheric 15th-century inn, expect flagstone floors, beamed ceilings, creaking stairs, a laid-back vibe downstairs, and luxurious period-style rooms with antique furniture upstairs. The restaurant caters both to vegetarians and the carnivorously inclined with its top-notch modern British food (two-/three-course dinner £32.50/39, eight-course tasting menu £49) there's less formal dining in the bar (mains £11 to £18).

Bull HOTEL ££

(☎01993-822220; www.bullatburford.co.uk; High St; s/d from £70/75) You'll be following in the footsteps of guests as illustrious as Charles II if you stay at this distinguished hotel. The plusher rooms feature four-poster beds and antique furniture, and the restaurant is pure gourmet, with beautifully executed dishes making the most of local ingredients.

Angel MODERN BRITISH ££

(☎01993-822714; www.theangelatburford.co.uk; 14 Witney St; mains £15.50-19) Set in a lovely 16th-century coaching inn, this atmospheric brasserie serves up an innovative menu of modern British and European food. Dine in by roaring fires in winter, or eat alfresco in the lovely walled garden in warmer weather. There are three traditionally decorated rooms (double £100) upstairs if you wish to linger.

PUT THE GUIDEBOOK AWAY

As wonderful as the Cotswolds villages may be, in the summer months you'll encounter camera-wielding crowds and chaotic coach parking.

However, it's easy to get away from the crowds and discover the rarely visited villages lurking in the hills. Stick to the B-roads such as the B4035 between Banbury and Chipping Campden, the B4632 between Uley and Stroud and the B4022 between Witney and Charlbury, and visit places like **Guiting Power** near Bourton, **Broadwell, Maugersbury**, **Adlestrop** and the **Swells** near Stow, **Sheepscombe** and **Slad** near Painswick, **Blockley** near Chipping Campden, **Great Tew** near Chipping Norton, **Taynton**, **Sherborne** and the **Barringtons** near Burford, **Ampney St Mary** and **Ampney Crucis** near Cirencester, or **Coln St Aldwyns** and **Hatherop** near Bibury. Alternatively, join a walking tour with **Cotswold Walking Holidays** (www.cotswoldwalks.com) or a bike tour with **Cotswold Country Cycles** (www.cotswoldcountrycycles.com).

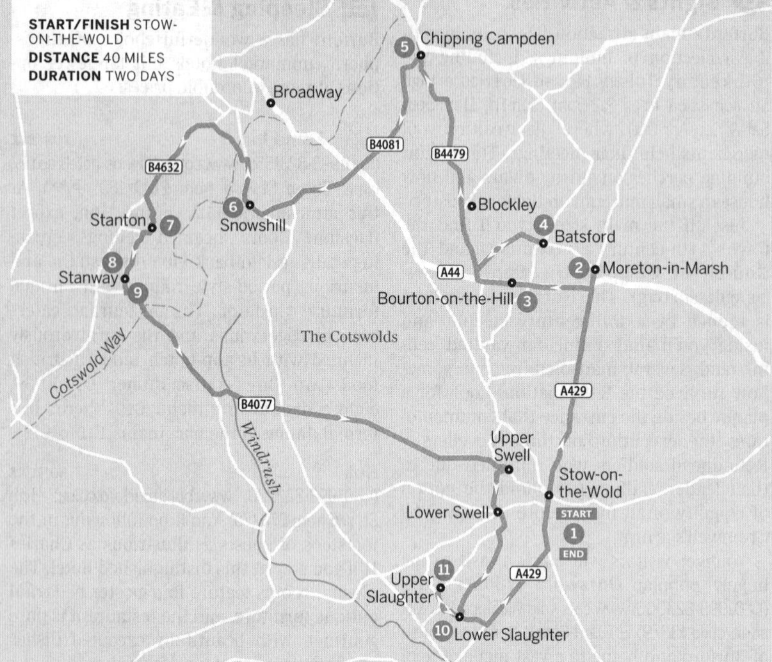

Walking Tour

Cotswolds Highlights

Given its vast network of winding, secluded country lanes, magnificent stately homes, timeless villages with crooked half-timbered houses and independent food markets, it's impossible to cover all of the Cotswold highlights in one go. This circular tour focuses on one of the most picturesque cross-sections of what the Cotswolds has to offer.

Begin your tour at 1 **Stow-on-the-Wold**, the highest of the Cotswold villages at 244m and a market town since the 12th century. Though some feel that its attractive narrow streets, lined with antique stores and bookshops, have a somewhat contrived feel to them, this is still very much a trading centre; in May and October, the village comes alive with the two annual Charter Fairs, with many beautiful equine specimens and Romany Gypsy horse traders camping on the outskirts of town.

In the centre of the village, take your time to admire the Market Square, lined with handsome 17th- and 18th-century houses and dominated by St Edward's Hall with its distinctive Corinthian pilasters.

From Stow, take the A429 4 miles north to 2 **Moreton-in-Marsh**, its wide main street sitting atop what used to be the Roman Fosse Way. Though the town is essentially a busy crossroads, there are appealing coaching inns facing each other across the main street, and the White Hart Royal Hotel is where Charles I stayed on 2 July 1644. Moreton's main street is also known for its excellent local food shops and delis.

From Moreton, take the A44 west, passing through tiny 3 **Bourton-on-the-Hill**, lined with attractive 17th- and 18th-century cottages and famous for two things: the gibbeting cage in which the bodies of dead highwaymen were hung in the 19th century and for horse training, with several stud farms in the vicinity of the village. This is a good spot to pause for lunch before turning north onto the B4479 and taking the first right to 4 **Batsford Park Arboretum**, exotic woodlands unrivalled elsewhere in Britain, with over 3300 labelled trees, bamboos and shrubs from Nepal, China, North America and Japan, as well as bronze statues brought over by Bertie Mitford, Lord Redesdale, who created this enchanted wood in 1880. Highlights here include the vast American redwoods, the flowering Japanese cherries (at their best in spring) and the strangely churchlike 'cathedral' lime.

Follow the signs that will take you back to the B4479 and then head north for 3 miles to 5 **Chipping Campden**. While the village's name derives from the Old English ceapen, meaning 'market', 'Chippy's' visible prosperity derives from its past as a successful wool town, and as you drive down the elegant, S-shaped High St, take in the Jacobean, Georgian and Tudor houses that line it, with their crooked half-timbered facades, bumpy roofs, twisted beams and honey-coloured stone walls. One of the most prominent landmarks here is Grevel House. Dating from the 14th century, it was the home of the highly successful wool merchant William Grevel, and has a splendid Perpendicular-style gabled window.

In the middle of the main street stands the iconic 17th-century Market Hall – an open-sided building where dairy farmers once used to sell their produce – that looks like a cross between a barn and a chapel, with its simple arches and uneven stone floors.

Take Cidermill Lane up from the main street to the church of St James; if you peek through the gates next to it, you'll see the remains of Campden House, a grand 17th-century merchant's pad that was burned down by Royalist soldiers during the Civil War. While one of its pavilions has been restored since, it's not open to the public.

After an overnight stay at Chipping Campden, follow the B4081 south, going straight over the A44 and following the signposts along the unnamed, winding country lane for a couple of miles to the village of 6 **Snowshill**. If the narrow lanes, the church, the gable-windowed houses and slate roofs looks familiar, that's because they featured in part of *Bridget Jones' Diary*, with a local house used as Bridget's parents' house.

Dominating the village is Snowshill Manor – a shrine to the obsessive collecting of its owner, poet and architect Charles Wade, and an absolute delight to wander around. Its rooms are filled with knick-knacks and objects that are 'of interest as records of various vanished handicrafts', be it antique bicycles, wooden toys, Samurai armour and the item which originally inspired the collection – Wade's grandmother's Chinese cabinet covered in black and gold lacquer.

From the manor, take Snowshill Rd towards Broadway for 2miles, but bypass it by taking West End Lane and then the B4632 south towards Cheltenham. Three miles down, take the left turn-off to 7 **Stanton**. A tiny stunner of a village, its houses are crafted out of that golden stone that the Cotswolds are known for, with not a shop or quaint tearoom in sight. The buildings most likely to catch your eye are the Jacobean Stanton Court – belonging to architect Sir Philip Stott, responsible for the restoration of the other Stanton houses, and the fine Perpendicular tower of the church of St Michael, which has an absolutely beguiling medieval interior.

You'll undoubtedly see walkers passing through the village, heading south along the Cotswold Way to the village of 8 **Stanway**, just a mile south; follow the road that runs parallel to the trail. There is little more to Stanway than a few thatched-roofed cottages, a church and the most magnificent Jacobean structure that is Stanway House – the manor belonging to the Lord and Lady Neidpath, hidden behind a triple-gabled gatehouse and home to Britain's tallest fountain which erupts, geyser-like, to a height of 300ft. The manor is a private home and open to the public only on select days.

Just south of Stanway, at a crossroads overlooked by a 9 **war memorial** featuring a bronze *St George and the Dragon* by Alexander Fisher, take the B4077 east for around 8 miles, before turning south at Upper Swell, passing through Lower Swell and following the signs south to 10 **Lower Slaughter**, a picture-perfect village lined with houses made of golden stone. You'll have to leave the car behind for the five-minute stroll to the former village mill – now a museum – set on the River Eye, though it's more a babbling brook. Head 1km west along narrow lanes to 11 **Upper Slaughter**, less visited than its neighbour, but no less attractive, due to its idyllic setting between a small ford and the hills. Stop for lunch at the sumptuous Lords of the Manor, a 17th-century mansion and award-winning restaurant, before following the signposts to the A429 for 4 miles back to Stow.

THE COTSWOLD OLIMPICKS

The medieval sport of shin-kicking lives on in Chipping Campden, where each year the townspeople gather to compete at the **Cotswold Olimpicks** (www.olimpickgames.co.uk), a traditional country sports day first celebrated in 1612. It is one of the most entertaining and bizarre sporting competitions in England, and many of the original events, such as welly wanging (throwing), the sack race and climbing a slippery pole, are still held. It is held annually at the beginning of June.

Huffkins TEAROOM
(www.huffkins.com; 98 High St; afternoon tea £16; ⏲8am-5pm Mon-Sat, 10am-5pm Sun) Superb tearoom serving some of the most memorable scones you're likely to have. Also a great place to stock up on local chutneys and other produce.

Getting There & Away

From Oxford, Swanbrook runs three buses a day (one on Sunday) to Burford (45 minutes) and on to Cheltenham. Stagecoach bus 233 runs between Witney and Burford 10 times a day, Monday to Saturday (20 minutes).

Chipping Norton

POP 5972

The sleepy but attractive town of Chipping Norton ('Chippy' to locals) has plenty of quiet side streets to wander and none of the Cotswold crowds. Handsome Georgian buildings and old coaching inns cluster around the market square, while on Church St you'll find a row of beautiful honey-coloured **almshouses** built in the 17th century. Further on is the secluded **Church of St Mary**, a classic example of the Cotswold wool churches, with a magnificent 15th-century Perpendicular nave and clerestory.

Chippy's most enduring landmark, however, is the arresting **Bliss Mill** on the outskirts of town. This monument to the industrial architecture of the 19th century is more like a stately home than a factory, topped by a domed tower and chimney stack of the Tuscan order.

If you are in town for lunch or dinner your best bet is **Wild Thyme** (☎01608-645060; www.wildthymerestaurant.co.uk; 10 New St; mains £9-19, s/d from £40/60; ⏲Tue-Sat), thrilling the palate with top-notch dishes such as goat's-cheese soufflé with red-onion marmalade and roast pork belly with truffle mash. The desserts are nothing short of sublime, and the three upstairs rooms have feather duvets and Egyptian cotton bedding. Look out for the **Wild Thyme Food Festival** (www.wildthymerestaurant.co.uk) hosted here in May.

Alternatively, head 4 miles southwest of town to the pretty village of Kingham, home of the **Kingham Plough** (☎01608-658327; www.thekinghamplough.co.uk; The Green, Kingham; mains £13-18, s/d from £85/115; ⏲closed Sun dinner) – a city slicker's dream of a country pub, its hearty seasonal dishes cobbled together from very local ingredients, be it pheasant in winter or new season lamb in spring. The three stylish rooms are largely unadorned but comfortable.

Stagecoach bus S3 runs between Chippy and Oxford (55 minutes) roughly every half-hour.

Moreton-in-Marsh

POP 3198

Home to some beautiful buildings but plagued by heavy traffic that clogs up its broad High St – built on top of the Roman Fosse Way – Moreton-in-Marsh is a major transport hub also known for its excellent food shops stocking Cotswold produce; try **Warner's Budgens** (High St) or the **Cotswold Cheese Company** (www.cotswoldcheesecompany.co.uk). On Tuesdays, the town bursts into life for its **weekly market**, and if you're here in September, don't miss the one-day **Moreton Show** (www.moretonshow.co.uk) – the ultimate agricultural extravaganza, attracting up to 20,000 people with the best of local food and gussied-up livestock competitions.

Just east of Moreton, **Chastleton House** (NT; www.nationaltrust.org.uk; adult/child £9.10/4.30; ⏲1-5pm Wed-Fri Mar-Oct) is one of England's finest and most complete Jacobean houses, full of rare tapestries, family portraits and antique furniture, its Long Gallery particularly resplendent. Outside, there's a classic Elizabethan topiary garden.

Pulham's Coaches (www.pulhamscoaches.com) runs hourly bus 801 between Moreton and Cheltenham (1¼ hours, Monday to Saturday) via Stow-on-the-Wold (15 minutes) and Bourton-on-the-Water (20 minutes).

There are trains to Moreton from London Paddington (£30, 1¾ hours, every two hours) via Oxford (£8.90, 35 minutes) and on to Worcester (£11, one hour) and Hereford (£16.90, one hour 45 minutes).

Chipping Campden

POP 2206

An unspoiled gem in an area full of pretty villages, Chipping Campden is a glorious reminder of life in the Cotswolds in medieval times. The graceful curving main street is flanked by a picturesque array of wayward stone cottages, fine terraced houses, ancient inns and historic homes, many made of that honey-coloured stone that the Cotswolds are so famous for. Despite its obvious allure, the town remains relatively unspoiled by tourist crowds, though it is very popular with walkers rambling along the Cotswold Way.

Sights & Activities

Standing out from the splendour of other historic buildings along the High St is the highly photogenic 17th-century **Market Hall**, with multiple gables and an elaborate timber roof; this is where dairy produce used to be sold. Chipping Campden made its fortune during the wool boom, so it's little wonder that one of the most prominent buildings in town is the 14h-century **Grevel House**, former home of successful wool merchant William Grevel. Nearby on Church St is a remarkable row of **almshouses** dating from the 17th century, and the Jacobean lodges and gateways of the now-ruined **Campden House**, a large and lavish 15th-century house, the remains of which you can see clearly from the Shipston Rd. At the western end of the High St, is the 15th-century **St James'** (⏲10am-5pm Mon-Sat, 2-6pm Sun Mar-Oct); built in the Perpendicular style, it has a magnificent tower and some graceful 17th-century monuments.

The surviving **Court Barn Museum** (☎01386-841951; www.courtbarn.org.uk; Church St; adult/child £3.75/free; ⏲10am-5pm Tue-Sun Apr-Sep) is now a craft and design museum featuring work from the Arts and Crafts Movement, such as silverwork, pottery, and hand-dyed cloth. Down Sheep St you'll find the former **Silk Mill**, taken over by galleries of local art, ceramics and silver, with **Hart's silversmithy** (www.hartssilversmiths.co.uk) upstairs.

About 4 miles northeast, **Hidcote Manor Garden** (NT; www.nationaltrust.org.uk; Hidcote Bartrim; adult/child £10/5; ⏲10am-6pm) is one of the finest examples of Arts and Crafts landscaping in Britain, with outdoor 'rooms' filled with flowers and rare plants for the arboreally inclined.

Sleeping & Eating

TOP CHOICE Cotswold House Hotel BOUTIQUE HOTEL £££
(☎01386-840330; www.cotswoldhouse.com; The Square; r £120-670; P @) If you're after a spot of luxury, look no further than this chic Regency townhouse turned boutique hotel. Bespoke furniture, ultra-comfortable king-sized beds, Frette linens, cashmere throws, private gardens and hot tubs are the norm here. You can indulge in some treatments at the Temple Spa, dine in luxuriant style at Juliana's (three-course set dinner, £52) or take a more informal approach at Hick's Brasserie (mains £12 to £20), a slick operation with an ambitious menu.

Eight Bells Inn B&B ££
(☎01386-840371; www.eightbellsinn.co.uk; Church St; s/d from £65/85) This 14th-century inn is also an atmospheric B&B featuring bright, modern rooms with iron bedsteads, soothing neutral decor and warm accents. The pub downstairs wins points for its authentic flagstone floors and good, no-nonsense pub grub (two-/three-course menu £18/22) such as pork medallions with caramelised apples.

Volunteer Inn B&B £
(☎01386-840688; www.thevolunteerinn.net; Lower High St; s/d from £35/50) This is the favourite haunt of walkers and cyclists travelling along the Cotswold Way – a clutch of simple rooms atop a friendly, busy pub.

Majaraja INDIAN £
(www.thevolunteerinn.net; Lower High St; mainc £7-11; ✎) Popular Indian restaurant covering all the classics, as well as the more unusual *shazni* prawns and spiced venison.

Information

Pop into the helpful **tourist office** (☎01386-841206; www.chippingcampdenonline.org; High St; ⏲9.30am-5pm) to pick up a town trail guide (£1) for information on the most historic buildings and to get you off the main drag and down some of the gorgeous back streets. If you're visiting on a Tuesday between July and

September, it's well worth joining a **guided tour** at 2.30pm (suggested donation £3) run by the Cotswold Wardens.

Getting There & Around

Between them, buses 21 and 22 run almost hourly to Stratford-upon-Avon or Moreton-in-Marsh. Bus 21 also stops in Broadway. No Sunday services.

You can hire a bike from **Cotswold Country Cycles** (www.cotswoldcountrycycles.com; Longlands Farm Cottage; per day £15).

Broadway

POP 2496

This pretty village, a quintessentially English place with a smattering of antique shops, tearooms and art galleries, has inspired writers, artists and composers in times past with its graceful, golden-hued cottages set at the foot of a steep escarpment. Take the time to wander down to the lovely 12th-century **Church of St Eadburgha**, a signposted 1-mile walk from town. Near here, a path leads uphill for 2 miles to **Broadway Tower** (www.broadwaytower.co.uk; adult/child £4.50/2.50; 10.30am-5pm), a crenulated, 18th-century Gothic folly on the crest of the escarpment for all-encompassing views from the top.

For a taste of modern comfort set within a 300-year-old exterior, complete with sloped floors, exposed beams and low ceilings, try the wonderfully friendly **Crown & Trumpet** (01386-853202; www.cotswoldholidays.co.uk; Station Rd; d £60; P), the Broadway 'local' with five rooms with en suite above the lively pub. Downstairs is a good bet for real ales and a proper roast dinner. Sleek and stylish **Russells** (01386-853555; www.russellsofbroadway.co.uk; 20 High St; 2-/3-course menu £15/18) is known for its award-winning modern British fare, with everything beautifully executed, from the gnocchi to the saddle of rabbit. Upstairs there are seven spacious, individually designed rooms (doubles £105 to £203) combining exposed beams and four-poster beds with more modern luxuries such as iPod docks.

Bus 21 goes to Moreton-in-Marsh, Chipping Campden and Stratford (50 minutes, four daily Monday to Saturday). Bus 606 goes to Cheltenham (50 minutes, four daily Monday to Saturday).

Around Broadway

About 3 miles south of Broadway is **Snowshill Manor** (NT; www.nationaltrust.org.uk; Snowshill; adult/child £9.70/4.90; noon-5pm Wed-Sun mid-Mar–Oct), a wonderful Cotswold mansion once home to the marvellously eccentric Charles Paget Wade. The house contains Wade's extraordinary collection of crafts and design, inspired by his grandmother's antique lacquered Chinese cabinet, and includes everything from musical instruments to Victorian perambulators and Japanese samurai armour. Outside, the lovely gardens – maintained organically, without any pesticides – were designed as an extension of the house, with pools, terraces and wonderful views.

Nearby is the splendid Jacobean mansion, **Stanway House** (www.stanwayfountain.co.uk; Stanway; adult/child £7.50/2.50; 2-5pm Tue & Thu Jun-Aug). Inhabited by the same family for over 450 years – that of the Earl of Wemyss – it has a delightful, lived-in charm with much of its original furniture and character intact. The house is surrounded by wonderful, baroque water gardens, home to the world's highest gravity fountain.

Winchcombe

POP 4379

Winchcombe is very much a working, living place, with butchers, bakers and small independent shops lining the main street. It was capital of the Saxon kingdom of Mercia and one of the most important towns in the Cotswolds until the Middle Ages, and today the remnants of its illustrious past can still be seen.

The helpful **tourist office** (01242-602925; www.winchcombe.co.uk; High St; 10am-5pm Mon-Sat, 10am-4pm Sun Apr-Oct, 10am-4pm Sat & Sun rest of yr) can assist with planning an itinerary.

Sights & Activities

Don't miss the picturesque cottages on **Vineyard St** and **Dents Tce** and look out for the hideous gargoyles that adorn **St Peter's Church**.

TOP CHOICE **Sudeley Castle** CASTLE

(www.sudeleycastle.co.uk; adult/child £11/4.20; 10.30am-5pm) The town's main attraction, this magnificent castle was once a favoured retreat of Tudor and Stuart monarchs.

It once served as the home of Katherine Parr (Henry VIII's widow) and her second husband, Thomas Seymour, with Princess Elizabeth (before she became Elizabeth I) living in the household for a time until finally, Seymour's inappropriate displays of affection towards Elizabeth prompted Katherine to banish her from the premises. It's worth paying extra to visit the **South Hall exhibition**, detailing the history of the intricate knot garden, and displaying a splendid **portrait of Elizabeth I**. Just outside are the beautiful remains of the banquet hall, covered with creepers. The house is still used as a family home, and much of the interior is off limits to visitors, but you can get a glimpse of its grand proportions while visiting the exhibitions of costumes, memorabilia and paintings and the surrounding gardens. For insight into real life in the castle, join one of the **'Connoisseur Tours'** (£15, Tuesday, Wednesday and Thursday at 11am, 1pm and 3pm).

Walking Trails WALKING
(www.winchecombewelcomeswalkers.com) Winchcombe is ideally situated for walkers, with a spider's web of trails branching out in every direction. The Cotswold Way passes through here, touching on Belas Knap, and there's the Gloucestershire Way to Tewksbury and Stow, the Warden's Way and Windrush Way leading to Bourton-on-the-Water, and the long-distance Worcestershire-bound St Kenelm's Way and Wychavon Way.

Belas Knap BURIAL CHAMBER
There's easy access to the Cotswold Way from Winchcombe, and the 2½-mile hike to Belas Knap is one of the most scenic short walks in the region. Five-thousand-year-old Belas Knap is the best-preserved Neolithic burial chamber in the country. Visitors are not allowed inside, but the views down to Sudeley Castle and across the surrounding countryside are breathtaking.

Hailes Abbey RUINS
(EH; www.english-heritage.org.uk; adult/child £4.40/2.20; 10am-5pm) Just outside the town are the evocative ruins of this Cistercian abbey, once one of the country's main pilgrimage centres due to a long-running medieval scam. The abbey was rumoured to possess a vial of Christ's blood, which turned out to be merely coloured water; before the deception came to light, thousands of credulous pilgrims visited, contributing to the abbey's wealth.

Sleeping & Eating

White Hart Inn HOTEL ££
(01242-602359; www.whitehartwinchcombe.co.uk; r £79-119) An appealing central inn that caters well to walkers; choose one of the three cheaper 'rambler' rooms, with shared bathrooms and iron bedsteads, or go for greater luxury in a superior room. The attached 'wine and sausage' restaurant (mains £10 to £18) serves a good selection of brasserie dishes as well as seven types of the aforementioned sausages.

Westward at Sudeley Lodge B&B ££
(01242-604372; www.westward-sudeley.co.uk; Sudeley; s/d from £45/90; P) At this robust 18th-century hunting lodge that doubles as a warm family home, you get to stay in one of three rooms with sweeping views of the valley. Decor is muted and deliberately dated, the owners hospitable without being intrusive, and the breakfasts ample.

TOP CHOICE **5 North St** MODERN EUROPEAN £££
(01242-604566; www.5northstreetrestaurant.co.uk; 5 North St; 2-/3-course lunch £23/27, 7-course tasting menu £64; lunch Wed-Sun, dinner Tue-Sat) From its splendid 400-year-old timbered exterior to what you find on your plate, this Michelin-starred restaurant is a treat from start to finish. Chef Marcus' cooking is rooted in traditional ingredients but with exotic influences creeping in to create the likes of pigeon with cherry jus or bayleaf-infused rice pudding with Guinness ice cream. Superb.

Getting There & Away

Bus 606 runs from Broadway (65 minutes, four daily Monday to Saturday) to Cheltenham via Winchcombe; bus 559 runs daily (Monday to Saturday only) from Broadway.

Stow-on-the-Wold

POP 2794

The highest town in the Cotswolds (244m), Stow is anchored by a large market square surrounded by handsome buildings and steep-walled alleyways, originally used to funnel the sheep into the fair, and is still an important market town. The town has long held a strategic place in Cotswold history, standing as it does on the Roman Fosse Way and at the junction of six roads. Today, it's famous for its twice-yearly **Stow Horse Fair** (May and October) and attracting a disproportionate number of people from passing coach tours.

Go Stow (www.go-stow.co.uk; 12 Talbot Ct; ⏲10am-5pm Mon-Sat, 11am-4pm Sun) has information on local attractions, makes accommodation bookings, and rents audio tours to the town.

Sleeping & Eating

Number 9 B&B ££
(☎01451-870333; www.number-nine.info; 9 Park St; s/d from £45/65; 📶) Centrally located and wonderfully atmospheric, this friendly B&B is all wonderfully sloping floors and exposed beams. The three rooms are cosy but spacious, and have gleaming bathrooms and low ceilings that somehow manage not to make the rooms seem oppressive. Full English breakfast included.

Stow-on-the-Wold YHA HOSTEL £
(☎0845-371 9540; www.yha.org.uk; The Square; dm £18; P@📶) In a you-can't-get-more-central-than-this location on the market square, the Cotswolds' only hostel is located in a wonderful 16th-century townhouse, with compact dorms, a children's play area and its own on-site cafe, offering inexpensive hot meals.

TOP CHOICE **Old Butchers** MODERN EUROPEAN ££
(☎01451-831700; www.theoldbutchers.com; 7 Park St; mains £15-26; ⏲closed Mon & Sun dinner) Simple, smart and sophisticated, this is Stow's top spot for dining, serving robust, local ingredients whipped up into sublime dishes with big flavours. It's mostly fine modern British cuisine, with chef Peter both drawing inspiration from Continental Europe and not shying away from bone marrow and calves' brains – which make an offally good meal in themselves!

Vine Leaf BRITISH ££
(☎01451-832010; www.thevineleaf.co.uk; 10 Talbot Court; sandwiches £6.50-7.50, 2-/3-course set menu £11/14; ⏲closed alternate Thu) A wonderful little catch-all cafe, serving hearty breakfasts (including pancakes with maple syrup), chunky lunchtime sandwiches with locally baked bread, burgers and more substantial mains crafted from locally sourced produce.

Getting There & Away

Pullhams bus 855 links Stow with Moreton, Bourton, Northleach and Cirencester (eight daily Monday to Saturday). Bus 801 runs to Cheltenham, Moreton and Bourton (four daily Monday to Friday, nine on Saturday).

WORTH A TRIP

COTSWOLD FARM PARK

Cotswold Farm Park (www.cotswoldfarmpark.co.uk; adult/child £7.95/6.50; ⏲10.30am-5pm Mar-Sep; 👪), halfway between Stow and Winchcombe, near Guiting Power, is a wonderful day out for the family. The farm owned by TV presenter Adam Henson is designed to introduce little ones to the world of farm animals. There are milking and shearing demonstrations, an adventure playground and a 2-mile wildlife walk, not to mention the new **food festival** that started in May 2012 and is set to become an annual event.

The Slaughters

POP 400

The picture-postcard villages of Upper and Lower Slaughter manage to maintain their unhurried medieval charm in spite of receiving a multitude of visitors. The village names have nothing to do with abattoirs; they are derived from the Old English 'sloughtre', meaning slough or muddy place, but today the River Eye is contained within limestone banks and meanders peacefully through the village past the 17th-century Lower Slaughter Manor to the **Old Mill** (www.oldmill-lowerslaughter.com; admission £2; ⏲10am-6pm), which houses a small museum and an ice-cream parlour, famous for its fantastic organic ice cream.

Upper Slaughter is less visited than Lower Slaughter, and it's a pleasant stroll between the two villages. Take time to linger in the timeless streets of Upper Slaughter, taking in the peaceful atmosphere, with its own fine manor house and glorious cottages. For eating or sleeping, you can do no better than **Lords of the Manor** (☎01451-820243; www.lordsofthemanor.com; Upper Slaughter; d £199-495; P). 'Countryside splendour' is what comes to mind when you clap your eyes on this 17th-century mansion. The rooms are spacious and tasteful in the traditional sense of the word, the fittings luxurious, but you won't find TV or wi-fi here; the idea is to rest and take in the beautiful countryside and partake in traditional pastimes of horse riding and clay-pigeon shooting. The Michelin-starred restaurant is one of the best around (three-course menu £69), with imaginative, beautifully presented dishes.

To see the Slaughters at their best, arrive in Lower Slaughter on foot from Bourton (a 1-mile walk) across the fields. From here you can continue for another mile across the fields to Upper Slaughter.

Northleach

POP 1855

Little visited and underappreciated, Northleach has been a little market town since 1227 and comprises late-medieval cottages, imposing merchants' stores and half-timbered Tudor houses. A wonderful mix of architectural styles cluster around the market square and the narrow laneways leading off it, but the highlight is the **Church of St Peter & St Paul**, a masterpiece of Cotswold Perpendicular style, its grandeur and architectural complexity testimony to its wool-era wealth. Its large traceried stained-glass windows and collection of memorial brasses are unrivalled in the region.

Near the square is Oak House, a 17th-century wool house that contains **Keith Harding's World of Mechanical Music** (www.mechanicalmusic.co.uk; adult/child £8/3.50; ⌚10am-5pm), a fascinating museum of lovingly restored self-playing musical instruments where you can hear Rachmaninoff's works played on a reproducing piano.

Escape to the Cotswolds (www.cotswoldsaonb.co.uk; ⌚10am-4pm Wed-Sun Apr-Oct; admission free) is an excellent visitors' centre with displays on local conservation efforts and a plethora of tourist info. It's housed in the **Old Prison** – an attraction in itself, its cells initiating you into the world of Gloucestershire's crime and punishment through the ages.

Just outside town is **Chedworth Roman Villa** (NT; www.nationaltrust.org.uk; Yanworth; adult/child £9.40/4.70; ⌚10am-5pm), one of the largest Roman villas in England. Built as a stately home in about AD 120, it contains some wonderful mosaics (some of which were only excavated in 2011) illustrating the seasons, bathhouses and, a short walk away, a temple by the River Coln. It's 3 miles northwest of Fossebridge off the A429.

For overnight stays try **Wheatsheaf** (☎01451-860244; www.cotswoldswheatsheaf.com; West End; d £100-130; @📶), a former coaching inn, is a favourite of those who love hunting, riding and other countryside pursuits. Its 14 rooms blend nice period touches such as free-standing baths with modern comforts, and the restaurant serves an excellent menu of hearty British dishes (£7 to £16).

ℹ Getting There & Away

Swanbrook runs six buses a day Monday to Saturday between Cheltenham (30 minutes) and Northleach, and three to Oxford (one hour). Pullham's bus 855 runs to Stow, Moreton, Bourton and Cirencester (eight daily Monday to Saturday).

Cirencester

POP 18,324

Refreshingly unpretentious, with narrow, winding streets and graceful townhouses, charming Cirencester (siren-sester) is an affluent, elegant town. The lovely market square – the heart of the town – is surrounded by Victorian architecture, and the nearby streets showcase a harmonious medley of buildings from various eras.

It's difficult to believe that under the Romans, Cirencester was second only to London in terms of size and importance and, although little of this period remains, you can still see the grassed-over ruins of one of the largest amphitheatres in the country. The medieval wool trade was also good to the town, with wealthy merchants funding the building of a superb church.

Today, Cirencester is the most important town in the southern Cotswolds, with the lively **Monday and Friday markets** as important as the expensive boutiques and trendy delis that line its narrow streets.

The **tourist office** (☎01285-654180; www.cotswold.gov.uk; Park St; ⌚10am-5pm Mon-Sat, 2-5pm Sun Apr-Oct, until 4pm rest of yr) is in the museum and has a leaflet on a guided walk around the town and its historic buildings.

Sights

TOP CHOICE **Corinium Museum** MUSEUM

(www.cotswold.gov.uk/go/museum; Park St; adult/child £5/2.50; ⌚10am-5pm Mon-Sat, 2-5pm Sun; 👪) This is a romp through Cirencester's (Corinium to the Romans) extensive history up until the 19th century. The largest part of this modern, well-presented, partly interactive museum is, understandably, dedicated to its Roman past and covers everything from Roman forts and armies, daily life in an affluent household, health and beauty according to the Romans and funereal rites and religion – all brought to life through innovative displays and computer reconstructions. You can dress as a Roman soldier, meet an Anglo-Saxon princess and discover what Cirencester was like during its heyday as a wealthy medieval wool town. Highlights of the Roman collection include the beautiful Hunting Dogs and Four Seasons floor mosaics, and a reconstructed Roman kitchen and butcher's shop.

Church of St John the Baptist CHURCH
(www.cirenparish.co.uk; Market Sq; suggested donation £3; ⏲10am-5pm) The cathedral-like St John's, one of England's largest parish churches, boasts an outstanding Perpendicular-style **tower** (open Sat May to September) with wild flying buttresses, but it is the majestic three-storey south porch that is the real highlight. Built as an office by late-15th-century abbots, it subsequently became the medieval town hall.

Soaring arches, magnificent fan vaulting and a Tudor nave adorn the light-filled interior, where you'll also find a 15th- century painted stone pulpit – one of the few surviving pre-Reformation pulpits in Britain. The east window contains fine medieval stained glass, and a wall safe displays the **Boleyn Cup**, made for Anne Boleyn in 1535.

FREE **New Brewery Arts Centre** ARTS CENTRE
(www.newbreweryarts.org.uk; Brewery Ct; ⏲9am-5pm Mon-Sat, 10am-4pm Sun) Home to over a dozen resident craft workers and host to regular exhibitions, workshops and classes, this arts centre is set in a beautifully converted Victorian brewery.

Cirencester Park PARK
(Cecily Hill; ⏲8am-5pm) The extensive baroque-landscaped grounds of the Bathurst Estate, with a lovely walk along Broad Ride. No bicycles allowed.

Sleeping & Eating

Jesse's Bistro MODERN BRITISH ££
(☎01285-641497; www.jessesbistro.co.uk; Blackjack St; mains £14-24; ⏲lunch Tue-Sun, dinner Wed-Sat) Hidden away in a cobbled stable yard with its own fishmonger and cheese shop, Jesse's is a great little place, with flagstone floors, wrought-iron chairs and mosaic tables. The great dishes feature local, seasonal produce, such as Cornish crab and Cotswold beef, but the real treat is the fresh fish and meat cooked in the wood-burning oven.

Made by Bob MODERN BRITISH ££
(www.foodmadebybob.com; 6 Corn Hall, Marketplace; mains £9-18; ⏲7.30am-6.30pm Mon-Sat; ✎) Part deli, part hip brasserie, with a casual atmosphere and inventive, sophisticated fare on the daily changing menu. Lighter bites include doorstop sandwiches, and breakfast is better than in most other cafes – muesli, eggs benedict and, of course, the full English. Bob, you have done well.

Lick the Spoon CAFE £
(www.lickthespoon.co.uk; 3 Black Jack St; drinks £3; ⏲9.30am-5pm Mon-Fri, 9am-5.30pm Sat, 11am-4pm Sun) One word: chocolate. It comes both in award-winning solid form, all boxed up for you to take away, and in glorious liquid form. Coffee is roasted on the premises for those desiring a caffeine kick alongside the sugar rush.

No 12 B&B ££
(☎01285-640232; www.no12cirencester.co.uk; 12 Park St; d £100) This Georgian townhouse right in the centre of Cirencester has four gloriously unfussy rooms kitted out with a tasteful mix of antiques and modern furnishings. Think piles of feather pillows, merino blankets, extra-long beds, slick modern bathrooms and a host of little extras to make you smile.

Old Brewhouse B&B ££
(☎01285-656099; www.theoldbrewhouse.com; 7 London Rd; s/d from £60/75; P) Set in a charming 17th-century townhouse, this lovely B&B has bright, pretty rooms with cast-iron beds and country-style florals or patchwork quilts. The courtyard rooms are newer and larger, with wooden floors, and the beautiful garden room even has its own patio.

Getting There & Away

Stagecoach bus 51 runs to Cheltenham Monday to Saturday (40 minutes, hourly). National Express buses run roughly hourly from Cirencester to the following:

Cheltenham Spa (30 minutes)
Gloucester (one hour)
London (£14, 2½ hours)

Bibury

POP 1235

Once described by William Morris as 'the most beautiful village in England', Bibury is a Cotswold gem with a cluster of gorgeous riverside cottages and tangle of narrow streets flanked by wayward stone buildings. The main attraction is **Arlington Row**, a stunning sweep of cottages, now thought to be the most photographed street in Britain. Also worth a look is the 17th-century **Arlington Mill**, just a short stroll away across Rack Isle, a wildlife refuge once used as a cloth-drying area.

Few visitors make it past these two sights, but for a glimpse of the real Bibury, venture into the village proper behind Arlington Row, where you'll find the Saxon **Church of St Mary**. Although much altered since its original construction, many 8th-century features are still visible among the 12th- and 13th-century additions. You can also fish for your supper at the **Bibury Trout Farm** (www.biburytroutfarm.co.uk; entry £3.75; ⌚9am-7pm Mon-Sat), a fishery with attractive picnic spots and smoked fish for sale.

Bibury's accommodation choices are underwhelming. The best place to stay is in the nearby village of Coln-St-Aldwyns, where the jasmine-clad **New Inn** (☎0844-815 3434; www.new-inn.co.uk; Coln-St-Aldwyns; s/d from £135/145) offers quirky luxury in 16th-century surroundings. It's also the best bet in the area for food, with a particularly imaginative modern British menu (mains £12 to £20).

Buses 860, 865, and 866 pass through Bibury en route to Cirencester (15 minutes) at least once daily from Monday to Saturday.

Kelmscott

POP 101

Three miles east of Lechlade along the A417 lies the gorgeous Tudor pile **Kelmscott Manor** (☎01367 252486; www.kelmscottmanor.org.uk; adult/child £9/4.50; ⌚11am-5pm Wed & Sat Apr-Oct), once the summer home of William Morris, the poet, artist and founder of the Arts and Crafts Movement. The interior is true to his philosophy that one should not own anything that is neither beautiful nor useful and the house contains many of Morris' personal effects, as well as fabrics and furniture designed by him and his associates.

From here it's well worth making a detour to the village of Southrop to dine at the **Swan** (☎01367-850205; www.theswanatsouthrop.co.uk; 2-/3-course menu £15/19; ⌚closed Sun dinner) – a 17th-century inn with stone floors, exposed beams and extremely sophisticated food at reasonable prices.

Tetbury

POP 5250

Once a prosperous wool-trading centre, Tetbury's busy streets are lined with medieval cottages, sturdy old townhouses and Georgian Gothic gems. Prince Charles has an estate near here – Highgrove – as does Princess Anne.

Tetbury is also a great place for antiques fans, with a shop of old curios on almost every corner. A good time to visit is the last Monday in May for the **Woolsack Races** (www.tetburywoolsack.co.uk) – a nod to the town's past – or in August, for the **Festival of British Eventing** (www.gatcombe-horse.co.uk).

Look out for the row of gorgeous medieval weavers' cottages that line the steep hill at **Chipping Steps**, leading up to the **Chipping** (market), surrounded by graceful 17th- and 18th-century townhouses. From here, it's a short stroll to Market Square, where the 17th-century **Market House** stands as if on stilts. Close by, the Georgian Gothic **Church of St Mary the Virgin** has a towering spire and wonderful interior.

If staying overnight, the **Ormond** (☎01666-505690; www.theormond.co.uk; 23 Long St; s/d from £79/110; P📶) is a central, modern hotel with a range of individually styled rooms sporting subtle but striking fabrics and funky wallpapers and with some big, bold flavours served up at the award-winning restaurant. The **Snooty Fox** (☎01666-502436; www.snooty-fox.co.uk; s/d from £70/80), named by a rather sore owner who was snubbed by the local hunting community, is a pleasant old coaching inn with three brightly decorated rooms and a menu of solid Modern British classics (mains £10 to £22). The best place to eat in town is undoubtedly the French-inspired **Chef's Table** (☎01666-504466; www.thechefstable.co.uk; 49 Long St; mains £9-13; ⌚closed dinner Sun-Tue), a fantastic deli and bistro serving up a mouth-watering lunch of local organic ingredients rustled up into hearty rustic dishes, such as bouillabaisse and crispy pork belly.

Cotswold Green bus 29 runs between Tetbury and Stroud (30 minutes, six daily Monday to Saturday). Wessex Connect bus 620 goes to Bath (1¼ hours, six daily Monday to Friday, four on Saturday), stopping at Westonbirt Arboretum en route.

CHEESE OF VICTORY

Cooper's Hill in Cranham, near Painswick, is the location of the Cotswolds' most dangerous sport: the annual **Cheese-Rolling** (www.cheese-rolling.co.uk; ⏲last bank holiday in May). Laugh if you will, but this 200-year-old tradition sees locals running, tumbling and sliding down a steep hill in pursuit of a 7lb block of Double Gloucester cheese; it's only a 90m run, but people get hurt every year. The prize? The cheese itself, and the glory of catching it.

Uley

POP 1100

This lovely little hamlet, with its quaint village green and jumble of pretty houses, sits below the overgrown remains of the largest Iron Age hill fort in England, **Uley Bury**. Dating from about 300 BC, the fort and its 2-mile perimeter walk provide spectacular views over the Severn Vale; follow the steep path that runs from the village church. If you're driving, access to the car park is off the B4066, north of the village.

Virtually untouched since the mid-1870s, **Woodchester Mansion** (www.woodchestermansion.org.uk; adult/child £6.50/free; ⏲11am-4pm Sat & Sun Easter-Oct) is an incredible place, formerly belonging to the Leigh family and abandoned before it was finished, yet amazingly grand and graceful. Doors open to nowhere, fireplaces are stuck halfway up walls, and corridors end at ledges above drops. The house also features an impressive set of gruesome gargoyles and is home to one of England's most important colonies of horseshoe bats and several resident ghosts. It's a mile north of Uley on the B4066.

Bus 20 runs between Uley and Stroud (55 minutes, four times daily Monday to Saturday).

Berkeley

POP 1865

An astounding relic from medieval times, **Berkeley Castle** (www.berkeley-castle.com; adult/child £9.50/5; ⏲11am-5.30pm Thu, Sun & bank holidays Apr-Oct) has remained virtually untouched since it was built as a sturdy fortress in Norman times, though it has been the home of the Berkeleys for nearly 900 years. Edward II was imprisoned and then murdered here in 1327 (allegedly with a hot poker up his rectum) on the order of his wife, Queen Isabella, and her lover, and you can still see the King's Gallery, with its cell and dungeon. You can also visit the castle's **state rooms**, as well as the medieval **Great Hall**, **Picture Gallery** and **kitchen**. Regular jousting events and medieval banquets are held here in summer.

Berkeley is also home to the man who's had a great impact on your life; **Jenner Museum** (www.jennermuseum.com; Church Lane; adult/child £6/3.50, incl Berkeley Castle £14/7.50; ⏲12.30-5.30pm select days Apr-Oct, check website) honours the life and works of Edward Jenner, country doctor who discovered the principle of vaccination. The museum is in the beautiful Queen Anne house, where the doctor performed the first smallpox vaccination in 1796. Follow the path from the castle through St Mary's churchyard.

Bus 207 plies the route between Berkeley and Gloucester (55 minutes, three times daily Monday to Saturday).

Stroud

POP 13,058

Stroud once hummed with the sound of over 150 cloth mills operating around the town, but when the bottom fell out of the market, it fell heavily into decline. Although a handful of the handsome old mills are still operating, the pleasant town has become a bohemian enclave known for its fair-trade shops, delis and independent stores. This is still one of the most important market towns in the Cotswolds, with four dozen or so independent stallholders converging every Saturday on the town for the **farmers' market**. Another great place for organic food, books and more is the **Shambles Market** (www.shamblesmarketstroud.co.uk), which takes place in the historic Shambles on Fridays and Saturdays.

In the centre of town, the Subscription Rooms are home to the **tourist office** (☎01453-760960; www.visitthecotswolds.org.uk; George St; ⏲10am-5pm Mon-Sat).

The main attraction is the diverting **Museum in the Park** (www.stroud.gov.uk/museum; Stratford Pk; free admission; ⏲10am-5pm Tue-Fri, 11am-5pm Sat & Sun; 👪), set in an 18th-century mansion surrounded by parkland. The bright, well-lit museum tells the history of the town and its cloth-making, and there are interactive displays of everything from dinosaurs to Victorian toys and Stroud's female artists. A separate gallery hosts eclectic contemporary-art exhibitions.

The nicest place to stay is in nearby Nailsworth at the 16th-century **Egypt Mill** (☎01453-833449; www.egyptmill.com; s/d £95/105; P), where you can fall asleep to the sound of the water gurgling over the weir. This is also one of the best restaurants in town, serving the likes of great fish and chips and goat's cheese and onion marmalade tart in a lovely waterside location.

For a relaxed meal, head for **Star Anise** (www.staraniseartscafe.com; Gloucester St; mains £6-8; 8am-5pm Mon-Fri, 8.30am-5pm Sat, 10am-2pm Sun;), a vegetarian cafe serving inventive dishes (including a couple of fish ones) featuring local produce and a popular spot for Sunday brunch. It often hosts live music and other community events.

Another good bet is **Woodruffs Organic Cafe** (www.woodruffsorganiccafe.co.uk; 24 High St; mains £5.50-9; 8.30am-5pm Mon-Sat), a small, cheerful place with a schizophrenic menu of salads, soups, tapas, fruit smoothies and even vegan ice cream.

Bus 46 runs hourly to Painswick (10 minutes) and Cheltenham (40 minutes) from Monday to Saturday, while bus 54 serves Cirencester (20 minutes, one to four daily Monday to Saturday). Trains run roughly hourly to London (£18, 1½ to two hours), Gloucester (20 minutes) and Cheltenham (40 minutes).

Painswick

POP 1666

One of the most beautiful and unspoilt towns in the Cotswolds, hilltop Painswick is an absolute gem. Despite its obvious charms, Painswick sees only a trickle of visitors, so you can wander the narrow winding streets and admire the picture-perfect cottages, handsome stone townhouses and medieval inns in your own good time.

Sights & Activities

Running downhill beside and behind the church is a series of gorgeous streetscapes. Look out for **Bisley St**, the original main drag, which was superseded by the now ancient-looking **New St** in medieval times. Just south of the church, rare **iron stocks** stand in the street.

St Mary's Church CHURCH

The village centres on a fine, Perpendicular wool church, its pointy steeple fingering the sky, surrounded by tabletop tombs and exactly 99 clipped yew trees that resemble giant lollipops. Legend has it that if the 100th yew tree were allowed to grow, the devil would appear and shrivel it. They planted it anyway, to celebrate the millennium and – lo and behold! – one of the trees toppled several years later, making the number an odd 99 again. The work of the Horned One, perhaps?

Painswick Rococo Garden ORNAMENTAL GARDEN

(www.rococogarden.co.uk; adult/child £6.50/3; 11am-5pm mid-Jan–Oct;) Just a mile north of town, the ostentatious Painswick Rococo Garden is the area's biggest attraction and the only garden of its type in England, designed by Benjamin Hyett in the 1740s and now restored to its former glory. Winding paths soften the otherwise strict geometrical precision, bringing visitors around the central vegetable garden to the many Gothic follies dotted in the grounds. There's also a children's nature trail and maze.

Sleeping

TOP CHOICE **Cotswolds88** BOUTIQUE HOTEL £££

(☎01452-813688; www.cotswolds88.com; Kemps Lane; d £110-280; P) This is a happy marriage of 18th-century architecture and a thoroughly modern, risqué interior. With avant-garde furnishings that you'd expect to find in a hip London hotel rather than a sleepy village, everything here is over the top – from the wallpaper to the psychedelic lighting. The spacious, individually decorated rooms come with every creature comfort you'd expect, and the suites come with four-poster beds and jacuzzis. The restaurant is one of the region's best, featuring sophisticated yet playful fare.

Cardynham House HOTEL ££

(☎01452-814006; www.cardynham.co.uk; Tibbiwell St; s/d from £65/87; closed Mon & dinner Sun;) Each of the rooms at 15th-century Cardynham House has a different theme, four-poster beds and heavy patterned fabrics. Choose the Shaker-style New England room, the opulent Arabian Nights room, the chintzy Old Tuscany room or for a private pool and garden, the Pool Room. Downstairs, the Bistro (mains £10 to £20) serves modern British cuisine.

Getting There & Away

Bus 46 connects Cheltenham (30 minutes) and Stroud (10 minutes) with Painswick hourly Monday to Saturday.

GLOUCESTERSHIRE

After the crowds and coaches of the Cotswolds, Gloucestershire's languid charms are hard to beat, with its host of mellow stone villages and rustic allure. The county's greatest asset, however, is the elegant Regency town of Cheltenham, with its tree-lined terraces, upmarket boutiques and a tempting collection of dining options.

The county capital, Gloucester, is well worth a visit for its magnificent Gothic cathedral. To the north, Tudor Tewkesbury follows the ecclesiastical splendour with a gracious Norman abbey surrounded by a town full of crooked, half-timbered houses. To the west, the picturesque Forest of Dean is a leafy backwater perfect for cycling and walking.

Cheltenham

POP 110,013

The shining star of the region, Cheltenham is a historic but cosmopolitan hub at the western edge of the rustic Cotswolds. The city oozes an air of gracious refinement, its streetscapes largely left intact since its heyday as a spa resort in the 18th century. At the time, it rivalled Bath as *the* place for the sick, hypochondriac and merely moneyed to go, and today it is still riddled with historic buildings, beautifully proportioned terraces and manicured squares.

Cheltenham is an affluent place, its well-heeled residents attracted by the genteel architecture, leafy crescents, wrought-iron balconies and expansive parks – all of which are kept in pristine condition. Add a slew of festivals of all persuasions and a host of fine hotels, restaurants and shops, and it's easy to conclude that it's the perfect base from which to explore the region.

History

Cheltenham languished in relative obscurity until pigeons were seen eating and thriving on salt crystals from a local spring in the early 18th century. It wasn't long before a pump was bored and Cheltenham began to establish itself as a spa town. Along with the sick, property speculators arrived in droves, and the town started to grow dramatically. Graceful terraced housing was thrown up, parks were laid out and the rich and famous followed.

By the time George III visited in 1788, the town's fate had been sealed and Cheltenham became the most fashionable holiday destination for England's upper crust. Handel, Samuel Johnson and Jane Austen all came here, and by the mid-19th century, the Victorian neo-Gothic Cheltenham College had sprung up, and, soon after, the genteel Cheltenham Ladies' College.

The town retained its period glamour and allure, and in the 20th century became known as the 'Anglo-Indians' Paradise' as so many Empire-serving, ex-military men retired here. Today, the self-styled 'Centre for the Cotswolds' is the most complete Regency town in England, with millions being spent propping up the quick-buck buildings that the Regency entrepreneurs rushed to erect.

Sights

The Promenade BOULEVARD

Famed as one of England's most beautiful streets, the **Promenade** is a wide, tree-lined boulevard flanked by an Art Gallery & Museum and imposing period buildings. The **Municipal Offices**, built as private residences in 1825, are among the most striking on this street and they face a **statue of Edward Wilson** (1872–1912), a local man who joined Captain Scott's ill-fated second expedition to the South Pole.

Continuing on from here, you'll pass the grandiose **Imperial Gardens**, built to service the Imperial Spa (now the Queens Hotel), en route to **Montpellier**, Cheltenham's most fashionable district. Along with the handsome architecture of the area, there's a lively collection of bars, restaurants and independent shops and boutiques. Along Montpellier Walk, **caryatids** (draped female figures based on those on the Acropolis in Athens) act as structural supports between the shops, each balancing an elaborately carved cornice on her head.

FREE **Cheltenham Art Gallery & Museum** MUSEUM

(Map p226; www.cheltenhammuseum.org.uk; Clarence St) Cheltenham's excellent Art Gallery & Museum is well worth a visit for its depiction of Cheltenham life through the ages. It also has wonderful displays on William Morris and the Arts and Crafts Movement, as well as Dutch and British art, rare Chinese and English ceramics and a section on Edward Wilson's expedition to Antarctica. The museum was closed for redevelopment at the time of writing and is due to reopen in spring 2013; the new extension will make a splendid home for the art gallery.

FREE Pittville Pump Room CONCERT HALL

(Off map p226; www.pittvillepumproom.org.uk; Pittville Park; ⌚9am-noon) Built in 1830 as a centrepiece to a vast estate, the Pittville Pump Room is Cheltenham's finest Regency building. Originally used as a spa and social centre, it is now used as a concert hall and wedding venue. You can wander into the main auditorium and sample the pungent spa waters from the fountain when the building is not in use for a private event, or just explore the vast parklands and the lake it overlooks. Phone in advance to check the opening hours.

Holst Birthplace Museum MUSEUM

(Map p226; www.holstmuseum.org.uk; 4 Clarence Rd; adult/child £4.50/4; ⌚10am-5pm Tue-Sat, 1.30-5pm Sun) The composer Gustav Holst was born in Cheltenham in 1874, and his childhood home has been turned into a museum celebrating his life and work. The rooms are laid out in typical period fashion and feature many of Holst's personal possessions, including the piano on which most of *The Planets* was composed, as well as photos of the notoriously camera-shy composer. The Victorian kitchen and other exhibits give you a good idea of what life was like 'below stairs'.

Cheltenham Racecourse RACECOURSE

(Off map p226; www.cheltenham.co.uk) Cheltenham's racecourse can attract up to 40,000 people a day during the **National Hunt Festival**, often simply called 'the Festival', a time of year when the bookies go crazy and huge sums of money are won and lost within four days. Held in mid-March each year, this is England's premier steeplechase event and is attended by droves of breeders, trainers, riders and spectators. The racecourse is about a mile north of the city centre via Evesham Rd.

Tours

Guided 1½-hour **walking tours** of Regency Cheltenham depart from the tourist office (p229). You can also book tickets for a rolling program of day-long **coach tours** to various locations in the Cotswolds here.

Festivals & Events

Cheltenham is renowned as a city of festivals; for more information or to book tickets, visit www.cheltenhamfestivals.com.

WORTH A TRIP

TEWKESBURY ABBEY

Sitting at the confluence of the Rivers Avon and Severn, Tudor-heavy Tewkesbury is all crooked little half-timbered houses, buckled roof lines and narrow alleyways stuck in a medieval time warp. Its highlight is this magnificent **abbey** (☎01684-850959; www.tewkesburyabbey.org.uk; entry by donation; ⌚8.30am-5.30pm Mon, Tue & Sat, 7.30am-5.30pm Wed & Fri, 7.30am-6pm Sun), one of Britain's largest churches, far bigger than many of the country's cathedrals. The Norman abbey, built for the Benedictine monks, was consecrated in 1121 and was one of the last monasteries to be dissolved by Henry VIII. Although many of the monastery buildings were destroyed, the abbey church survived after being bought by the townspeople for the princely sum of £453 in 1542.

The church has a massive 40m-high **tower** (adult/child £3/1; ⌚tours every 30min 1.30-3.30pm Sun Jun-Sep) and some spectacular Norman piers and arches in the nave. The Decorated-style chancel dates from the 14th century, however, and still retains much of its original stained glass. The church also features an organ dating from 1631, originally made for Magdalen College, Oxford, and an extensive collection of medieval tombs. The most interesting is that of John Wakeman, the last abbot, who is shown as a vermin-ridden skeleton.

You can take a **guided tour** (adult £4) of the abbey year-round (call ahead to book) or visit an exhibition on the abbey's history at the **visitor centre** (⌚10am-5.30pm Mon-Sat Apr-Sep) by the main gate. The church also makes a wonderfully atmospheric venue for a range of summer concerts.

Bus 41 runs to Cheltenham (25 minutes) every 15 minutes, hourly on Sunday, and bus 71 (30 minutes) goes to Gloucester hourly.

Cheltenham

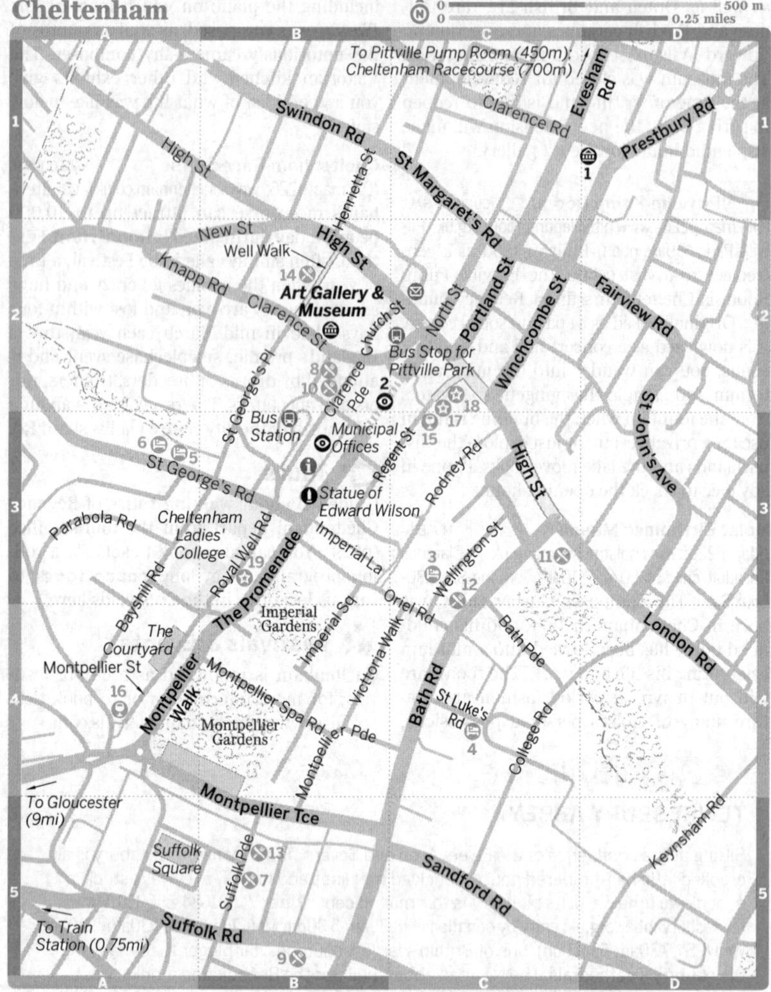

Folk Festival FOLK MUSIC
A showcase of traditional and new-age folk talent in February.

National Hunt Festival HORSE RACING
One of the most prestigious horse races in the world, taking place in March.

Jazz Festival JAZZ
An imaginative program hailed as the UK's finest jazz fest, held in late April/ early May.

Science Festival SCIENCE
Exploring the wonders of the world of science in June.

Food Festival FOOD
A weekend of Cheltenham's best food and wine, with live music, talks and more in mid-June.

Music Festival MUSIC
A celebration of traditional and contemporary sounds with a geographical theme, in July.

Literature Festival LITERATURE
A 10-day celebration of literary celebration in October, attended by authors from all over the world.

Cheltenham

Top Sights

Art Gallery & Museum B2

Sights

1 Holst Birthplace Museum D1
2 The Promenade B2

Sleeping

3 Big Sleep C3
4 Brennan C4
5 George Hotel A3
6 Hanover House A3

Eating

7 Daffodil B5
8 Dfly B2
9 Le Champignon Sauvage B5
10 Lumière B2
11 Marinades Restaurant C3
12 Prithvi C3
13 Suffolk Kitchen B5
14 Well Walk Tea Room B2

Drinking

15 J's Vodka Bar C3
16 Montpellier Wine Bar A4

Entertainment

17 Everyman Theatre C2
18 Fever C2
19 Subtone B3

Sleeping

Book as far in advance as possible if attending the festivals.

TOP CHOICE **Ellenborough Park** BOUTIQUE HOTEL £££
(01242-807541; www.ellenboroughpark.com; Southam Rd; d from £230; P@) If you are someone who likes style in the traditional sense of the word, this majestic country house, sitting amid immaculate landscaped grounds, will undoubtedly appeal. Each of the 62 rooms and suites is individually designed; decorative fireplaces are mixed and matched with modern features, such as iPod docks, while the day spa features a range of relaxing treatments for weary bodies. You can dine on excellent Modern British cuisine either in the formal, wood-panelled Beaufort Dining Room, or else grab a sandwich at the Brasserie. Take Prestbury Road from the city centre; it becomes the B4632 and the hotel is signposted off it.

Beaumont House B&B ££
(01242-223311; www.bhhotel.co.uk; 56 Shurdington Rd; s/d from £75/85; P@) Set in a large garden just a short way from the centre of town, this boutique guesthouse is a memorable place with a range of carefully designed rooms with opulent decor that's fresh and fun without being overly gimmicky. Go for the full-on safari look in Out of Africa, sultry boudoir in Out of Asia or more subtle design in the Prestbury Suite. To get here follow Bath Rd south from the city for about 1 mile.

Brennan B&B £
(Map p226; 01242-525904; www.brennanguesthouse.co.uk; 21 St Luke's Rd; s/d £30/50; P) Just five compact rooms with sinks, all decked out in creams, a convenient central location overlooking St Luke's church, and an attentive, congenial host make this the pick of the budget B&B bunch. Full English breakfast included.

Big Sleep HOTEL ££
(Map p226; 01242-696999; www.thebigsleephotel.com; Wellington St; r £55-300; P@) A luxury budget hotel, this place is all designer looks, thoroughly modern rooms and no-frills minimalism. The family rooms have their own kitchenettes, and breakfast is included. It's an absolute steal, and a brilliant option if you're travelling with family or friends.

George Hotel HOTEL ££
(Map p226; 01242-235751; www.stayatthegeorge.co.uk; St George's Rd; s/d from £115/125; P) Always a favourite, this charming hotel is a converted Georgian house in a wonderful central location. The decor in the sleek doubles is mostly sedate creams and browns with welcome splashes of colour in the deluxe rooms.

Hanover House B&B ££
(Map p226; 01242-541297; www.hanoverhouse.org; 65 St George's Rd; s/d from £70/100; P) This Victorian townhouse has three lovely rooms with high ceilings, big sash windows and quirky, vibrant decor. Blending period details and modern style, the rooms feel lived in, with well-stocked bookcases, colourful throws and a decanter of sherry 'to ease any stress'. Breakfast is organic and consumed around a communal table.

Battledown B&B ££
(01242-233881; www.thebattledown.co.uk; 125 Hales Rd; s/d £55-60; P) If you don't mind staying somewhat out of the centre, this

family-run French colonial-style villa is an especially warm and friendly place with full breakfast cooked from locally sourced produce. Hales Rd branches off London Rd, just southeast of central Cheltenham. The guesthouse is a 10-minute walk from the turnoff.

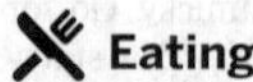

Eating

Cheltenham has a great choice of top-end and midrange places to eat, with new exciting options popping up constantly for those with a smaller budget, too.

TOP CHOICE Le Champignon Sauvage FRENCH £££
(Map p226; 01242-573449; www.lechampignonsauvage.co.uk; 24-26 Suffolk Rd; 2-/3-course set menu £48/59; Tue-Sat) This Cheltenham institution for nearly a quarter of a century has been delighting visitors and locals alike with chef David's finely executed dishes and paring of flavours, such as cured pigeon breast with fig compote, superb bread, and inspired and unlikely sounding desserts that somehow work beautifully, such as the chocolate and olive tart with fennel ice cream. Worth every penny.

TOP CHOICE Prithvi INDIAN ££
(Map p226; 01242-226229; www.prithvirestaurant.com; 37 Bath Rd; 5-course taster menu £25; dinner Tue, lunch & dinner Wed-Sun) A brand new Indian restaurant, Prithvi's top-notch service matches its immaculate dishes, served in semi-formal surroundings. Each mouth-watering offering is presented with great attention to detail, and the superb five-course taster menu is one of the biggest treats in Cheltenham: the sauce that comes with the standout nargil duck has a great depth of flavour to it and the meal leaves you salivating in anticipation of your next visit.

TOP CHOICE Lumière MODERN BRITISH £££
(Map p226; 01242-222200; www.lumiere.cc; Clarence Pde; 2-/3-course lunch £22/26, dinner £42/47; lunch Wed-Sat, dinner Tue-Sat;) Unassuming from the outside, this small, smart restaurant is indeed the shining light of the Cheltenham eating scene. Chef Jon conjurs up inspired dishes, pairing the likes of poached tenderloin with smoked eel truffle and pork belly with cumin caramel – and it all works beautifully. The service is friendly and efficient and the whole experience stands out – even in a town with a lot of competition.

Daffodil MODERN BRITISH ££
(Map p226; 01242-700055; www.thedaffodil.com; 18-20 Suffolk Pde; mains £14.50-19; Mon-Sat) A perennial favourite, the Daffodil is as loved for its top-notch modern British brasserie-style food as for its flamboyant surroundings. Set in a converted art-deco cinema, it harks back to the Roaring Twenties and features live jazz and blues every Monday night. The atmosphere is suitably bubbly and the food consistently good.

Suffolk Kitchen MODERN BRITISH ££
(Map p226; www.thesuffolkkitchen.co.uk; 8 Suffolk Pde; mains £14-18; dinner Tue-Sat, lunch & dinner Fri, lunch Sun;) This brand-new kid on the block has already been winning over fans with its dedication to seasonal ingredients sourced from all over the British isles, transformed by chef Simon into the likes of crisp pork belly with black-pudding mousse, and Cornish monkfish with sweet potato. Even the lighter bites – the homemade burger or the brie and cranberry sandwich – are beautifully prepared, with great attention to detail. A very promising start.

Dfly ASIAN FUSION £
(Map p226; 1a Crescent Pl; mains £7-13; Tue-Sat) Bar, restaurant and hip hang-out rolled into one, Dfly is a friendly place with an eclectic menu of well-executed Thai, Malaysian and Chinese dishes as well as great sushi. Complimentary tap water confusingly arrives in vodka and gin bottles. The decor is a delightful confusion as well: think deep red, oversize cushions, dark woods, Asian carvings and Heath Ledger as the Joker. By night it's a buzzing watering hole with soulful music and monthly live gigs.

Marinades Restaurant CARIBBEAN £
(Map p226; www.marinades.co.uk; 56 High St; mains £8-13; Tue-Sat, lunch Sun;) Think reggae on the stereo, a relaxed vibe and dish after authentic dish from Jamaica and beyond. The pineapple and coconut janga rundown and the guava-glazed pork really stand out, there's Red Stripe, Carib and Dragon Stout to wash them down, and the set menus (£8.95 for a three-course lunch or two-course dinner) are hard to beat for value. Our only request: don't be stingy with the plantain.

Well Walk Tea Room BRITISH £
(Map p226; www.wellwalktearoom.co.uk; 5-6 Well Walk; mains £3-5; lunch) This great local favourite is half family-run tearoom, half antique shop full of curiosities. The home-cooked quiches

and pastas are a steal at £3 and there is no better spot for tea and scones.

Drinking & Entertainment

J's Vodka Bar BAR

(Map p226; www.jsvodkabar.com; 6 Regent St) Ze vodka in zis place vill brink out ze Soviet in you and you vill be saluting Comrade Stalin viz everyone else. Seriously, Russia/vodka jokes aside, this place has plenty of spirit(s). Try the Lemon Meringue Martini or the deceptively mild Kipplin (bakewell tart) shots.

Montpellier Wine Bar WINE BAR

(Map p226; www.montpellierwinebar.com; Bayshill Lodge, Montpellier St) Slick, sophisticated and self-consciously cool, this is where Cheltenham's beautiful people come to hang out. The extensive wine list spans the world (or at least Chile, New Zealand, France, South Africa and Spain) and there's some nice brasserie food to go with it. Not into wine? There are cask ales as well.

Subtone NIGHTCLUB

(Map p226; www.subtone.co.uk; 117 The Promenade) One of the city's most popular venues, Subtone has three floors of DJs, five bars, and live music at its basement club and piano bar. Expect everything from jazz and house to funk and rock. It's a bit rough around the edges, but sweaty, heaving fun at the same time.

Fever NIGHTCLUB

(Map p226; www.fevercheltenham.com; 2 Lower Regent St; ⌚closed Tue & Sun) Take a twin-floored dancing space, throw in some classics from the '70s, '80s and '90s, add a dash of Top 40 'choonz', and sprinkle liberally with cocktails. A winning recipe.

Everyman Theatre THEATRE

(Map p226; www.everymantheatre.org.uk; Regent St) Cheltenham's main stage hosts everything from comedy to panto.

Pittville Pump Room CONCERT HALL

(Off map p226; ☎01242-523852; www.pittvillepumproom.org.uk; Pittville Park) Cheltenham's best bet for classical music.

Information

You'll find all the major banks and the main post office on High St.

Tourist Office (☎01242-522878; www.visitcheltenham.info; 77 The Promenade; ⌚9.30am-5pm Mon-Sat) The tourist office will move into the Cheltenham Art Gallery & Museum once it reopens in 2013.

Getting There & Away

For information on public transport to and from Cheltenham, pick up a free copy of the handy *Getting There by Public Transport* guide, which is available from the tourist office. The bus station is behind the Promenade in the town centre, but the train station is a 20-minute walk west of the centre.

Bus

National Express runs buses to **London** (£8, 2½ hours, hourly). Some of the other bus routes also available are:

Broadway Bus 606 (45 minutes) via **Winchcombe** (20 minutes), four times daily Monday to Friday.

Cirencester Bus 51 (40 minutes, hourly).

Gloucester Bus 94 (30 minutes, every 10 minutes Monday to Saturday, every 20 minutes on Sunday).

Moreton Bus 801 (one hour) via **Bourton** (35 minutes) and **Stow** (50 minutes), seven times daily Monday to Saturday.

Oxford Bus 853 (£8, 1½ hours, three daily Monday to Saturday, one Sunday).

Train

Trains run roughly every half-hour.

Bath (£13, 1¼ hours)

Bristol (£9, 50 minutes)

Gloucester (£4, 11 minutes)

London (£35, 2¼ hours)

Getting Around

Bus D runs to Pittville Park and the train station from Clarence St every 10 minutes.

Gloucester

POP 136,203

Gloucester (*glos*-ter) began life as a settlement for retired Roman soldiers but really came into its own in medieval times, when the pious public brought wealth and prosperity to what was then a prime pilgrimage city. The faithful flocked to see the grave of Edward II and soon financed the building of what remains one of England's most beautiful cathedrals.

In more recent years, Gloucester bore the brunt of hard times and the city fell into decline. But while the centre remains a rather dowdy, workaday place with a glut of greasy-spoon cafes, the historic Gloucester Docks – once Britain's largest inland port – have played a major part in the city's regeneration. Fifteen beautiful Victorian warehouses, many now restored, surround the canal basins and house a series of museums, shops and cafes, and are well worth a wander. Gloucester makes a good day trip from Cheltenham.

Sights

TOP CHOICE **Gloucester Cathedral** CATHEDRAL

(www.gloucestercathedral.org.uk; College Green; suggested donation £5; tower tours: adult/child £4/1.50; ⏲8am-6pm) The main reason to visit Gloucester is to see its magnificent Gothic cathedral, the first and best example of Perpendicular style. It was originally the site of a Saxon abbey, but a Norman church was built here by a group of Benedictine monks in the 12th century, and when Edward II was murdered in 1327, the church was chosen to be his burial place. Edward's tomb proved so popular, however, that Gloucester became a centre of pilgrimage and the income generated from the pious pilgrims was great enough to finance the church's conversion into the magnificent building seen today.

Inside, the cathedral skilfully combines the best of Norman and Gothic design with sturdy columns creating a sense of gracious solidity, and wonderful Norman arcading draped with beautiful mouldings. From the elaborate 14th-century wooden choir stalls, you'll get a good view of the imposing **Great East Window**, one of the largest in England.

To see the window in more detail, head for the **Tribune Gallery**, where you can also see an **exhibition** (admission £2; ⏲10.30am-4pm Mon-Fri, to 3.30pm Sat) on its creation. If you stand at one end of the curving **Whispering Gallery**, a person at the other end should be able to hear your words reverberating across the wonderfully elaborate lierne vaulting. Beneath the window in the northern ambulatory is **Edward II's magnificent tomb**, and nearby is the late-15th-century **Lady Chapel**, a glorious patchwork of stained glass.

There are some modern touches throughout – see if you can spot the late-20th-century stained-glass pieces, as well as the dramatic Iain McKillop take on the crucifixion in the Lady Chapel.

One of the cathedral's greatest treasures is the exquisite **Great Cloister**. Completed in 1367, it is the first example of fan vaulting in England and is only matched in beauty by Henry VIII's Chapel at Westminster Abbey. You (or your children) might recognise the cloister from the first two Harry Potter films: it was used in the corridor scenes at Hogwarts.

A wonderful way to take in the glory of the cathedral is to attend one of the many musical recitals and concerts held here.

Civic Trust volunteers provide free **guided tours** (⏲10.30am-4pm Mon-Sat, noon-2.30pm Sun) of the cathedral. For more insights and a fantastic view of the town, join an hour-long guided **tower tour** (adult/child £4/1.50; ⏲2.30pm Wed-Fri, 1.30pm & 2.30pm Sat).

National Waterways Museum MUSEUM

(www.nwm.org.uk/gloucester; adult/child £4.75/3.25, incl boat trip £10/7; ⏲10.30am-5pm Jul & Aug; 👪) The largest warehouse at the Gloucester Docks, Llanthony, is home to the National Waterways Museum, a hands-on kind of place where you can discover the history of Britain's inland waterways. Among other boat-related topics, exhibitions cover the lives of 'boat people' – workers and their families who lived on narrowboats and moved goods up and down the intricate system of canals and rivers. Interactive hands-on displays include a model of a lock on a river, and you can scramble aboard a restored narrowboat moored outside so that you can pretend that you, too, are a 'boat person'.

Gloucester Folk Museum MUSEUM

(www.gloucester.gov.uk/folkmuseum; 99-103 Westgate St; adult/child £3/2; ⏲10am-5pm Tue-Sat) This creaky-floored folk museum examines Gloucester domestic life, crafts and industries from 1500 to the present. Its exhibits include a variety of Civil War weaponry, a classic retro 1950s kitchen, and Black Dog – a beloved pub mascot. The museum is housed in a wonderful series of 16th- and 17th-century Tudor and Jacobean timber-framed buildings which used to belong to a merchant, an undertaker and a fishmonger.

Gloucester City Museum & Art Gallery MUSEUM

(www.gloucester.gov.uk/citymuseum; Brunswick Rd; adult/child £3/2; ⏲10am-5pm Tue-Sat) The bright, spacious city museum is a jolly romp through everything from dinosaur fossils, interactive natural-history section and Roman artefacts to paintings by the artists Turner and Gainsborough.

Tours

Civic Trust WALKING TOURS
(☎01452-926455; www.gloucestercivictrust.org; adult/child £3/free; ⏲Apr-Sep) Ninety-minute guided tours of the city's most historic buildings leave from St Michael's Tower at 11.30am Monday to Saturday. Tours of the docks depart from the National Waterways Museum at 11.30am Saturday and Sunday (July and August only).

National Waterways Museum BOAT TOURS
(www.nwm.org.uk/gloucester; adult/child £5.50/3.75; ⏲noon, 1.30 & 2.30pm Sat & Sun, daily during school holidays) This 45-minute boat trip runs along the Gloucester and Sharpness Canal – great on sunny days!

Sleeping & Eating

Gloucester's accommodation options are rather limited. You'd be far better off staying in Cheltenham (10 minutes by train) instead.

TOP CHOICE **C & W's African Experience** EAST AFRICAN £
(www.cwsafricanexp.org.uk; 8-10 St Catherine St; meals £10; ⏲dinner Mon-Sat) A short walk from the railway station, this unexpected, cheerful, family-run place delivers some of the best flavours in town. The menu veers from Kenyan goat curry to Ethiopian chicken with fried plantain on the side, and vegetarians are well catered for. Portions are heaped, and your hosts couldn't be friendlier. This place might also be open for lunch in the near future.

Tigers Eye ASIAN ££
(www.theoldbell-tigerseye.co.uk; 9a Southgate St; mains £7-14; ⏲Tue-Sat) Skip the starters and go straight for the Black Rock special – a cook-your-own steak or seafood on a mightily preheated slab of rock. Lighter bites include baguettes, wraps, sushi and noodle soup.

Information

Tourist Office (☎01452-396572; www.visitgloucester.info; 28 Southgate St; ⏲10am-5pm Mon-Sat, 11am-3pm Sun) Pick up a free *Via Sacra* brochure to guide you around the city's most historic buildings.

Getting There & Away

National Express has buses roughly every two hours to **London** (£6, 3¼ hours). Buses 94 and 98 run to **Cheltenham** (30 minutes) every 10 minutes Monday to Saturday, and every 20 minutes on Sunday.

The London-bound train stops at Cheltenham (11 minutes, every 20 minutes).

Forest of Dean

POP 79,982

An ancient woodland with an almost magical character, the Forest of Dean is the oldest oak forest in England and a wonderfully scenic place to walk, cycle or paddle. Its steep, wooded hills, winding, tree-lined roads and glimmering lakes make it a remarkably tranquil place and an excellent spot for outdoor pursuits.

The forest was formerly a royal hunting ground and a centre of iron and coal mining, and its mysterious depths were supposedly the inspiration for Tolkien's forest of Middle Earth in the *Lord of the Rings*, and for JK Rowling's Forbidden Forest in the Harry Potter adventures. Numerous other writers, poets, artists and craftspeople have been inspired by the stunning scenery, designated England's first National Forest Park in 1938.

The Forest of Dean spills over the Gloucestershire border near the village of Goodrich, off the A40 between Ross-on-Wye and Monmouth. The River Wye skirts the forest edge, offering glorious views to canoeists paddling out from the delightful village of Symonds Yat. Covering 42 sq miles between Gloucester, Ross-on-Wye and Chepstow, the forest is in an isolated position, but Coleford, the main population centre, has good transport connections. You'll find information on the area at www.visitforestofdean.co.uk.

Sights & Activities

TOP CHOICE **Puzzle Wood** ADVENTURE PARK
(www.puzzlewood.net; adult/child £6/4.50; ⏲10am-5pm; 👪) If you're travelling with children, this enchanted forest is a must. A pre-Roman, open-cast ore mine, overgrown with eerie lichen-covered trees, it has a maze of paths, weird rock formations, tangled vines and dark passageways, and potential for adventure is immense. If it seems familiar, that's because a recent *Dr Who* episode and the BBC1 *Merlin* series were shot here. Puzzle Wood is 1 mile south of Coleford on the B4228.

Clearwell Caves CAVES
(www.clearwellcaves.com; adult/child £6/4; ⏲10am-5pm) To explore one of the oldest

professions of the residents of the Forest of Dean, descend into a damp subterranean world, mined for iron ore for more than 4000 years, and comprising a warren of dimly lit passageways, caverns and pools – home to several species of bat. Scattered throughout are descriptions of child labour in the mines in the 19th century, with billy-boys as young as seven working 10-hour days. Ye olde miner gear is on display – a *nelly* (tallow candle) and *billy* (backpack) for transporting ore. Deep-level caving can be arranged for small groups. The caves are signposted off the B4228 a mile south of Coleford.

Dean Heritage Centre MUSEUM
(www.deanheritagemuseum.com; Camp Mill, Soudley; adult/child £6/3; ⏲10am-5pm; 🚼) For an insight into the history of the forest (and its people) since the Ice Age, this entertaining museum looks at everything from the forest's geology to Roman occupation, medieval hunting laws, free mining, cottage crafts and coal mining. There is plenty for kids, too, from 'what's that smell?' boxes and other tactile exhibits, to a mini-zoo with pigs, rabbits and weasels, an adventure playground and the current pride and joy – the Gruffalo Trail, featuring life-size wooden carvings from the Julia Donaldson classic.

Dean Forest Railway HERITAGE RAILWAY
(www.deanforestrailway.co.uk; day tickets adult £11-15, child £5-9) This short stretch of rail between Lydney and Parkend is plied by six classic steam engines on select days from March to December, as well as a special treat for children – Thomas the Tank Engine – making the occasional guest appearance. The standard ride is 28 minutes long, but there are lots of special events organised by the railway – from Sunday luncheons in 1st-class carriages to 'drive your own steam engine' experiences; book in advance.

Pedalabikeaway CYCLING
(☎01594-860065; www.pedalabikeaway.co.uk; Cannop Valley, near Coleford; per day £16-26; ⏲9am-6pm) There are a number of excellent cycling trails around the Forest of Dean, varying from tranquil family-friendly jaunts of several miles to longer and more demanding circuits. Pedalabikeaway hires out both leisure bikes – including tandems and buggies for kids – and full suspension mountain bikes, and sells maps and gives advice on cycling routes. Here you'll also find a downhill bike park with nine demanding trails for experienced riders; cycling tours can also be arranged on request.

For more information on cycling in the region, also check out http://deanforestcycles.co.uk/.

Sleeping & Eating

The Forest of Dean can be visited as an easy day trip from Gloucester or Cheltenham, but there are a couple of interesting lodgings if you want to linger overnight.

TOP CHOICE **Dome Garden** GLAMPING ££
(☎01730-261458; www.domegarden.co.uk; Mile End, Coleford; 4-bed dome for 3 nights from £590,

WORTH A TRIP

HATFIELD HOUSE

Hatfield House (www.hatfield-house.co.uk; adult/child £15.50/8.50; ⏲noon-5pm Wed-Sun, West Garden 10am-5.30pm Tue-Sun) For over 400 years Hatfield House has been home to the Cecils, one of England's most influential political families. This magnificent Jacobean mansion was built between 1607 and 1611 for Robert Cecil, first earl of Salisbury and secretary of state to both Elizabeth I and James I. The house is awash with grandiose portraits, tapestries, furnishings and armour. Look out for the grand marble hall, the stunning carved-oak staircase and the stained glass in the chapel.

Outside, the vast grounds were landscaped by 17th-century botanist John Tradescant, and you can see an old oak tree that marks the spot where Elizabeth I, who spent much of her childhood here, first heard of her accession to the throne.

If you'd really like to get into the character of the house, you can attend a four-course **Elizabethan banquet** (☎bookings 01707-262055; £55.50), complete with authentic Elizabethan period music and court jesters, in the atmospheric Great Hall on Friday nights.

The house is opposite Hatfield train station, and there are trains from London King's Cross station (£8, 20 minutes, half-hourly).

B&B d £80) For something completely different why not get back to nature in luxurious style in a cool geodesic dome? Linked by paths of recycled glass and set in glorious gardens, these futuristic-looking domes sleep between two and eight people and have giant bean bags, their own kitchens and showers. Evenings are spent cooking your meals over a campfire; all that's missing is a guitar and singalong!

St Briavels Castle YHA HOSTEL £
(☎01594-530272; www.yha.org.uk; Lydney; dm from £19; P) Live like a king for a night at this unique hostel set in an imposing moated castle once used as King John's hunting lodge. Loaded with character and great value at this price, this 13th-century castle comes complete with round towers, drawbridge and gruesome history. The dorms sleep four to six, and you can even join in the ancient spirit with full-blown medieval banquets on Wednesdays and Saturdays in August.

Severn & Wye Smokery Brasserie SEAFOOD ££
(☎01452-760190; www.severnandwye.co.uk; Chaxhill, Westbury-on-Severn; mains £9-15; ⊙lunch Mon-Sat, dinner Fri) At this celebrated smokery and deli, not only can you pick up a selection of their smoked fish, but you can also sample some of the goodies at the attached restaurant. Your meal is served on a slate, and local produce on offer includes Cornish monkfish, eel and oysters, with Severn Cider and other local tipples to help it down.

Three Choirs Vineyard MODERN BRITISH ££
(☎01531-890223; www.threechoirs.com; Newent; mains £15-17) This bright and airy restaurant serves classic brasserie dishes using locally sourced produce if possible, such as the River Wye salmon. You can also take a guided tour of the working vineyard (£7.50) and try the award-winning wines before departing with a few bottles from the gift shop.

Garden Cafe MODERN BRITISH ££
(www.gardencafe.co.uk; Lower Lydbrook; mains £8-13; ⊙lunch Fri-Sun, dinner Fri, Sat & Mon; ✍) An award-winning organic cafe on the banks of the River Wye, this place is set in a converted malt house and surrounded by a beautiful walled garden. The food is all seasonal and locally sourced, with vegetables from the cafe's garden. Monday night is tapas night.

Getting There & Around

From Gloucester, buses 30 and 31 runs to **Coleford** (one hour, twice hourly) via Cinderford and there are trains to **Lydney** (20 minutes, hourly).

HERTFORDSHIRE

Firmly on the commuter belt and within easy reach of the capital, Hertfordshire is a small county liberally scattered with satellite towns that threaten to overtake the fast-disappearing countryside. However, it is also home to the historic town of St Albans, with its elegant Georgian streetscapes and Roman remains, and to Hatfield House (p232), a spectacular stately home well worth the effort to visit.

St Albans

POP 129,005

A bustling market town with a host of crooked Tudor buildings and elegant Georgian townhouses, St Albans makes a pleasant day trip from London. The town was founded as Verulamium after the Roman invasion of AD 43 but was renamed St Albans in the 3rd century after a Roman soldier, Alban, lost his head in punishment for sheltering a Christian priest. He became England's first Christian martyr, and the small city soon became a site of pilgrimage.

The pilgrims brought business and wealth to the town, and eventually the object of their affection was enshrined in what is now a magnificent cathedral. The town is also home to an excellent Roman museum, which balances out the unprettiness inflicted on the main drag, St Peter's St, by an ugly array of plastic storefronts. Head instead for the quiet back streets or follow George St into Fishpool St, a charming lane that winds its way past old-world pubs to leafy Verulamium Park.

Sights

TOP CHOICE **Verulamium Museum & Roman Ruins** MUSEUM, RUINS
(www.stalbansmuseums.org.uk; St Michael's St; adult/child £3.80/2; ⊙Museum: 10am-5.30pm Mon-Sat, 2-5.30pm Sun; hypocaust: 10am-4.30pm Mon-Sat, 2-4.30pm Sun) A fantastic exposé of everyday life under the Romans, the displays at Verulamium Museum include household objects, legionaries' armour, statuary, jewellery, glassware and grave

ST ALBANS BEER FESTIVAL

Beer is big business in England, and to pint-swilling connoisseurs, real ale is the only brew that matters. To celebrate its key role in national culture, Camra (the Campaign for Real Ale) hosts a four-day **beer festival** (www.hertsale.org.uk/beerfest) in St Albans at the end of September. Over 9000 people converge on the Alban Arena off St Peter's St to sample and talk about the 350-odd real ales on tap and the 500 or so cask and bottled beers, ciders and perries. With food, music and good booze on offer, and tickets a mere £3 to £4, it's a great excuse for a party.

goods. The highlight, however, is the **Mosaic Room**, where five superb mosaic floors, uncovered between 1930 and 1955, are laid out, the most splendid of which is the Shell Mosaic. You can also see re-creations of Roman rooms, and learn about life in the settlement through interactive and audio-visual displays. Every second weekend, the museum is 'invaded' by Roman soldiers who demonstrate the tactics and tools of the Roman army.

Adjacent **Verulamium Park** has remains of a basilica, bathhouse and parts of the city wall, as well as a new building housing the **hypocaust** with an intricate mosaic floor and explaining the wonders of central heating under the Romans.

Across the busy A4147 are the grassy foundations of a **Roman theatre** (www.romantheatre.co.uk; adult/child £2.50/1.50; ⌚10am-5pm), which once seated 2000 spectators.

St Albans Cathedral CATHEDRAL
(www.stalbanscathedral.org.uk; admission by donation; ⌚8.30am-5.45pm; guided tours daily:11.30am & 2.30pm Mon-Fri, 11.30am & 2pm Sat, 2.30pm Sun) Set in tranquil grounds away from the din of the main streets, St Albans' magnificent cathedral began life as a Saxon monastery in 793, built by King Offa of Mercia around the tomb of St Alban. In Norman times, it was completely rebuilt using material from the old Roman town of Verulamium, and then, in the 12th and 13th centuries, Gothic extensions and decorations were added to a structure impressive for its scale alone.

The longest **medieval nave** in the country gives way to ornate ceilings, semi-lost wall paintings, an elaborate nave screen and, of course, the shrine of St Alban, reconstructed after the Reformation and hiding behind a stone reredos. There's also a luminescent rose window from the 20th century. There are free **guided tours** (⌚11.30am & 2.30pm Mon-Fri, 11.30am & 2pm Sat, 2.30pm Sun) daily.

Eating & Drinking

Lussmanns Eatery MODERN BRITISH ££
(☎01727-851941; www.lussmans.com; Waxhouse Gate; mains £12-17) This bright, modern restaurant just off the main street is enduringly popular with locals despite ample competition around town. It serves a changing monthly menu of creative British dishes with Mediterranean touches – from seared Cornish mackerel to wild rabbit and mushroom linguine, all in a bright, modern space with oak, leather and metal decor. Ingredients are ethically and mostly locally sourced, with plenty of information on the menu about where your food has come from. Book ahead.

Singhli INDIAN £
(www.singhli.com; 30 Holywell Hill; mains £5-8.50; ⌚closed Mon; 🌶) This great little newcomer has a short menu, but everything on it is done perfectly – from the tapas-style 'street food' such as amritsari fish and masala peanuts to the filled rotis and the curries.

Ye Olde Fighting Cocks TRADITIONAL PUB
(www.yeoldefightingcocks.co.uk; 16 Abbey Mill Lane) Dating back to the 8th century, this unusual, octagon-shaped former coaching inn is reputedly the oldest pub in England. Oliver Cromwell spent a night here, stabling his horses in what's now the bar, and underground tunnels lead to the cathedral. Drink in the historic atmosphere while you nurse your pint of real ale.

Information

Tourist Office (☎01727-864511; www.stalbans.gov.uk; Market Pl; ⌚10am-4.30pm Mon-Sat) Can book entertaining themed guided walks (adult/child £3/1.50) of the city.

Getting There & Away

Trains run between **London St Pancras** and St Albans (£10.60, 20 minutes) every 10 minutes. The station is on Victoria St, 800m east of St Peter's St.

BEDFORDSHIRE & BUCKINGHAMSHIRE

The sweeping valleys and chalky, forested hills of Bedfordshire and Buckinghamshire once attracted the rich and famous, who used them as a rural hideaway for their majestic stately homes. Today, commuters populate the pretty villages surrounding these vast and magnificent estates and enjoy the quiet woodland walks and mountain-bike trails that criss-cross the undulating Chiltern Hills.

Woburn Abbey & Safari Park

The pretty Georgian village of Woburn is home to Bedfordshire's biggest attractions: a palatial stately home and Europe's largest conservation park.

Built on the foundations of a Cistercian abbey, dissolved by Henry VIII and awarded to the earl of Bedford, **Woburn Abbey** (www.woburn.co.uk; adult/child £13.50/6.50; ⏲11am-4pm Apr-Sep) is a wonderful country pile set within a 1200-hectare deer park. The house is stuffed with 18th-century furniture, porcelain and silver, and displays paintings by Gainsborough, van Dyck and Canaletto. Highlights include the **bedroom of Queen Victoria and Prince Albert**; the beautiful wall hangings and cabinets of the Chinese Room; the imposing *Armada Portrait* of Elizabeth I; the mysterious story of the Flying Duchess; and the gilt-adorned dining room. An **audio tour** brings the history of the house and the people who lived here to life. Outside, the **gardens** are well worth a wander, and host theatre and music events during the summer months.

On an equally grand scale is **Woburn Safari Park** (www.woburn.co.uk/safari; adult/child £20/15; ⏲10am-5pm), the country's largest drive-through animal reserve. Rhinos (including rare African white rhinos), tigers, lions, zebras, bison, monkeys, elephants and giraffes roam the grounds, while in the 'foot safari' area, you can see sea lions, penguins and lemurs. Pick up a timetable on arrival for information on feeding times, keeper talks and animal demonstrations, and visit early on a weekday to avoid the worst of the congestion.

For both attractions, buy a **passport ticket** (adult/child £25/18), which can be used on two separate days within any 12-month period.

The abbey and safari park are easily accessible by car off the M1 motorway. First Capital Connect runs trains from London King's Cross to Flitwick, the nearest station. From here it's a 15-minute taxi journey (£17 to £22) to Woburn.

Waddesdon Manor

A remarkable Renaissance-style chateau, **Waddesdon Manor** (☎01296-653226; www.waddesdon.org.uk; house & gardens adult/child £15/11; ⏲noon-4pm Wed-Fri, 11am-4pm Sat & Sun, gardens 10am-5pm Wed-Sun) was designed by French architect Destailleur and completed in 1889 for the Baron Ferdinand de Rothschild so that he could showcase his collection of French decorative arts and

DON'T MISS

STOWE GARDENS

To call **Stowe Gardens** (NT; www.nationaltrust.org.uk; adult/child £9/5; ⏲10am-5.30pm Wed-Sun Mar-Oct) a 'nice garden' would be a bit like describing the Aya Sofia as 'a cute church'. These are, quite frankly, the most impressive gardens you're ever likely to see – a creation that covers 400 hectares, worked on by the greatest British landscape gardeners, including Charles Bridgeman, William Kent and 'Capability' Brown on behalf of the supremely wealthy Temple family in the 18th century, whose motto, appropriately, was *Templa Quam Delecta* (How Delightful are Your Temples). We're not talking about some adequately pruned bit of shrubbery: the gardens comprise 32 temples and structures, spread throughout the themed landscapes – from the column-studded **Western Garden** with its statuary and the **South Vista** with its symmetrical Lake Pavilions and splendid Corinthian Arch, to the intricately designed temples of **Eastern Garden** and the tranquillity of the **Elysian Fields**, where you can imagine the souls of dead warriors resting in peace for all eternity.

Stowe is 3 miles northwest of Buckingham off the A422.

FANTASTIC MR DAHL

One of the world's most loved children's writers, Roald Dahl, made his home at Great Missenden in Buckinghamshire. The small **Roald Dahl Museum** (www.roalddahlmuseum.org; 81-83 High St, Great Missenden; adult/child £6/4; ⌚10am-5pm Tue-Fri, 11am-5pm Sat & Sun; 👪) explores his writing and the inspiration behind such favourites as *Charlie and the Chocolate Factory* and *The BFG*.

Young and old are encouraged to get dressed up, make up stories, words and poems or get crafty in the art room. There are regular workshops for children, information and memorabilia on Dahl's life, and a chance to explore his writing hut.

In nearby Aylesbury, the award-winning **Roald Dahl Children's Gallery** (www.buckscc.gov.uk; Buckinghamshire County Museum, Church St, Aylesbury; adult/child £6/4; ⌚10am-5pm Mon-Sat Aug & during school holidays; 👪) uses the characters from Dahl's children's stories to illustrate all sorts of scientific wizardry, and kids of all ages can investigate the beasts inside James's Giant Peach, explore Fantastic Mr Fox's tunnel and see the Twit's upside-down bedroom. Opening hours are complicated during term time, so please check the website for details.

Trains to Great Missenden (£9, 40 minutes, hourly) and Aylesbury (£14, one hour, half-hourly) depart from London Marylebone.

throw glamorous parties. Taking in the ostentatious magnificence of the house, it's not difficult to imagine the great and good of the 19th century living it up in the palatial rooms.

Very little space is left unadorned – only the Bachelor's Wing stands out as being noticeably more restrained. On display is the outstanding collection of Dutch Old Masters and English portraits, Sèvres porcelain, ornate furniture and the extensive wine cellar. Don't miss the new exhibition of contemporary art, housed in the Coach House in the Stables. The house hosts a variety of events throughout the year, from Christmas fairs to wine-tasting days, Valentine's dinners and opera and theatre events.

The beautiful **gardens** (gardens only adult/child £6.50/3.50; ⌚10am-5pm Wed-Sun) boast rare flowers, contemporary sculptures and a Rococo-revival aviary filled with exotic birds.

Waddesdon is 6 miles northwest of Aylesbury off the A41. Trains to Aylesbury (£14.40, one hour, half-hourly) depart from London Marylebone. From Aylesbury bus station, take bus 16 (25 minutes, every 30 minutes Monday to Friday, every two hours Saturday).

Bletchley Park

If you have any interest in 20th-century warfare, then coming here is a must. Once England's best-kept secret, **Bletchley Park** (www.bletchleypark.org.uk; The Manor, Bletchley; adult/child £12/6; ⌚9.30am-5pm) was the scene of a huge code-breaking operation during WWII, dramatised in the film *Enigma*. Almost 8500 people worked here in total secrecy intercepting, decrypting, translating and interpreting enemy correspondence. Joining one of the **guided tours** (two daily Monday to Friday, hourly at weekends) gives you a real insight into the complex code-breaking process and the hard work, frustration and successes that shaped this secret war effort. Inside Station X you can also see the Enigma machine itself – crucial to the breaking of the code – as well as a collection of Churchill memorabilia, and a computer museum tracing the development of computers from the early Bletchley model 'Colossus' to the modern day, and get a real appreciation for what life was like for civilians during the war.

Bletchley is just south of Milton Keynes off the B4034. Trains run from London Euston to Bletchley (£15, 40 minutes, hourly).

BERKSHIRE

Long known as the 'Royal County of Berkshire', this rather posh and prosperous part of the world acts as a country getaway for some of England's most influential figures. Within easy reach of London and yet entirely different in character, the pastoral landscape features handsome villages and historic houses as well as some of the top attractions in the country. Few visitors make it past the historic towns of Windsor and Eton, home to the Queen's favourite castle and the world-renowned public school, but wander further afield and you'll be rewarded with tranquil rural countryside and exquisitely maintained villages.

Windsor & Eton

POP 30,568

Dominated by the massive bulk of Windsor Castle, these twin towns have a rather surreal atmosphere, with the morning pomp and ceremony of the changing of the guards in Windsor, and the sight of school boys dressed in formal tailcoats wandering the streets of tiny Eton.

Windsor town centre is full of expensive boutiques, grand cafes and trendy restaurants. Eton, by comparison, is far quieter, its one-street centre lined with antique shops and art galleries. Both are easily doable as a day trip from London.

Sights

Windsor Castle CASTLE

(www.royalcollection.org.uk; adult/child £17/10; ⌚9.45am-5.15pm) The largest and oldest occupied fortress in the world, Windsor Castle is a majestic vision of battlements and towers used for state occasions and as the Queen's weekend retreat.

William the Conqueror first established a royal residence in Windsor in 1070; and since then successive monarchs have rebuilt, remodelled and refurbished the castle complex to create the massive and sumptuous palace that stands here today. Henry II replaced the wooden stockade in 1165 with a stone round tower and built the outer walls to the north, east and south; Charles II gave the state apartments a baroque makeover; George IV swept in with his preference for Gothic style; and Queen Victoria refurbished a beautiful chapel in memory of her beloved Albert.

Join a free **guided tour** (every half-hour) or take a multilingual audio tour of the lavish state rooms and beautiful chapels. The State Apartments and St George's Chapel are closed at times during the year. If the Queen is in residence, you'll see the Royal Standard flying from the Round Tower.

Queen Mary's Dolls' House

Your first sight will be an incredible dolls' house, designed by Sir Edwin Lutyens for Queen Mary in 1924. The attention to detail is spellbinding – there's running water, electricity and lighting, tiny Crown Jewels and vintage wine in the cellar!

State Apartments

The **Grand Staircase** sets the tone for the rooms, and highlights include **St George's Hall**: on the ceiling, the shields of the Knights of the Garter (originally from George IV's time here) were recreated after the fire of 1992. The blank shields indicate knights who had fallen out of favour.

For intimate gatherings (just 60 people), the Queen entertains in the **Waterloo Chamber**, its paintings commemorating the victory over Napoleon. During large parties, this room is used for dancing and the table is tripled in size and set up in St George's Hall.

The **King's Dressing Room** has some of the most important Renaissance paintings in the royal collection. Alongside Sir Anthony van Dyck's magnificent **Triple Portrait of Charles I**, you will see works by Hans Holbein, Rembrandt and Peter Paul Rubens.

St George's Chapel

This elegant chapel, commissioned for the Order of the Garter by Edward IV in 1475, is one of Britain's finest examples of Perpendicular Gothic architecture. The nave and fan-vaulted roof were completed under Henry VII, but the final nail was struck under Henry VIII in 1528.

The chapel – along with Westminster Abbey – serves as a **royal mausoleum**. The most recent royal burial occurred in April 2002, when the body of George VI's widow, the Queen Mother (1900–2002), was transported here in a splendid and sombre procession and interred alongside her husband. And in April 2005, Prince Charles and Camilla Parker-Bowles were blessed here

READING FESTIVAL

Each August Bank Holiday weekend, about 80,000 revellers descend on the industrial town of Reading for one of the country's biggest rock music events. The **Reading Festival** (www.readingfestival.com) is a three-day extravaganza that features the likes of Kasabian, Foo Fighters, the Maccabees, and Florence and the Machine. Tickets will set you back about £85 per day or £198 for a three-day pass.

Windsor & Eton

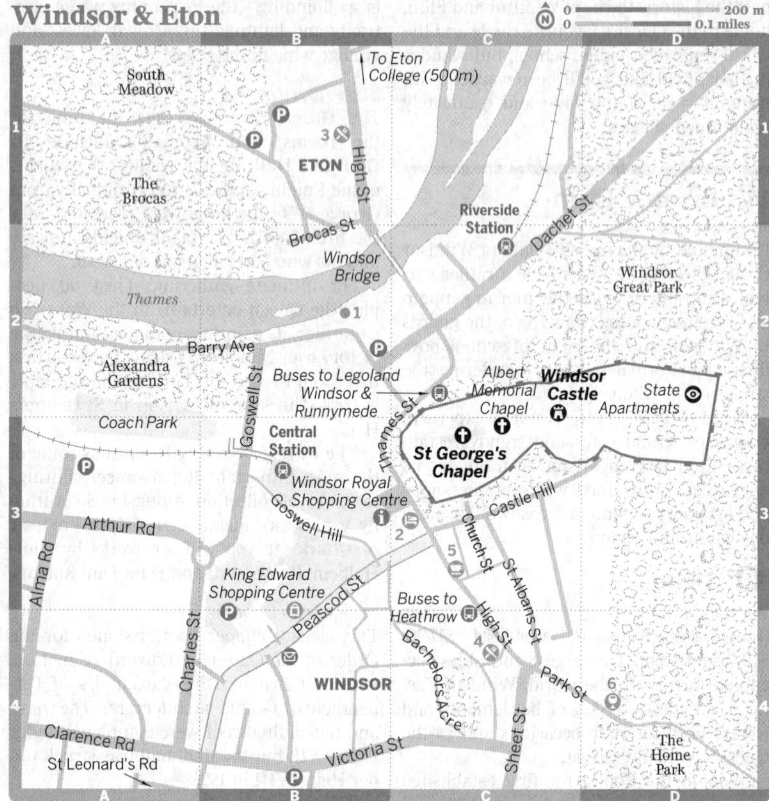

following their civil marriage in the town's Guildhall.

St George's Chapel closes on Sunday, but time your visit well and you can attend **Evensong** at 5.15pm daily except Wednesday.

Albert Memorial Chapel

Originally built in 1240 and dedicated to Edward the Confessor, this small chapel was the place of worship for the Order of the Garter until St George's Chapel snatched that honour. After the death of Prince Albert at Windsor Castle in 1861, Queen Victoria ordered its elaborate redecoration as a tribute to her husband. A major feature of the restoration is the magnificent vaulted roof, whose gold mosaic pieces were crafted in Venice. There's a monument to the prince, although he's actually buried with Queen Victoria in the Frogmore Royal Mausoleum in the castle grounds.

Windsor Great Park

Stretching behind Windsor Castle almost all the way to Ascot, Windsor Great Park covers about 40 sq miles and features a lake, walking tracks, a bridleway and gardens. The **Savill Garden** (www.theroyallandscape.co.uk; adult/child £8.50/3.75; ⌚10am-6pm) is particularly lovely and located about 4 miles south of Windsor Castle. Take the A308 out of town and follow the brown signs.

The **Long Walk** is a 3-mile jaunt along a tree-lined path from King George IV Gate to the Copper Horse statue (of George III) on Snow Hill, the highest point of the park. The Queen can occasionally be spotted driving down the Long Walk, accompanied only by a bodyguard.

Changing of the Guard

A fabulous spectacle, with triumphant tunes from a military band and plenty of stamping of feet, the **changing of the**

Windsor & Eton

guard (11am Mon-Sat Apr-Jul, alternate days Aug-Mar) draws the crowds to the castle gates each day to watch the smartly attired lads in red uniforms and bear-fur hats do their thing. Stay to the right of the crowd for better views.

Eton College BOYS' SCHOOL
(www.etoncollege.com; adult/child £7/5.50; guided tours 2pm & 3.15pm daily during school holidays, Wed, Fri, Sat & Sun during term time) Eton's main street is surprisingly hushed as you make your way down to the most enduring and illustrious symbol of England's class system, Eton College.

Those who have studied here include 18 prime ministers, countless princes, kings and maharajahs, famous explorers, authors, and economists – among them the Duke of Wellington, Princes William and Harry, George Orwell, Ian Fleming, Aldous Huxley, Sir Ranulph Fiennes, John Maynard Keynes and Bear Grylls.

Eton is the largest and most famous public (meaning very private) school in England; it's only under the current headmaster that Eton has begun to accept applicants from state schools rather than just private schools. It was founded by Henry VI in 1440 with a view towards educating 70 highly qualified boys awarded a scholarship from a fund endowed by the king. Every year since then, 70 King's Scholars (aged 12 to 14) have been chosen based on the results of a highly competitive exam; these pupils are housed in separate quarters from the rest of the 1300 or so other students, known as Oppidans.

All the boys are boarders and must wear formal tailcoats, waistcoats and white collars to lessons (though the top hats went out in 1948); fencing, shooting, polo and beagling are on the list of school sporting activities, and Eton very much embodies the old ideal of *mens sana in corpore sano* (A healthy mind in a healthy body).

Tours of Eton take in the **chapel**, the **cloisters**, the **Museum of Eton Life** – with a feature on Eton's star sport: rowing – the **lower school**, with names etched into its ancient desks by bored students, and the **school yard**, with a memorial to Etonians who died in the two world wars. You may recognise some of the buildings, as *Chariots of Fire*, *The Madness of King George*, *Mrs Brown* and *Shakespeare in Love* are just some of the movies that have been filmed here.

You have to buy your tickets in advance at the tourist office as they cannot be purchased at Eton itself.

Legoland Windsor THEME PARK
(www.legoland.co.uk; Winkfield Rd; adult/child £43/34; Complex opening hours: 10am-7, 6 or 5pm, depending on day Mar-Oct) A fun-filled theme park of white-knuckle rides, Legoland is more about the thrills of scaring yourself silly than the joys of building your own castle from the eponymous bricks. The professionals have already done this for you, with

ROYAL ASCOT

Get out your Sunday best and join the glitterati at **Royal Ascot** (www.ascot.co.uk) for the biggest racing meet of the year. The royal family, A-list celebrities and the rich and famous gather here to show off their Jimmy Choos and place the odd bet. The four-day festival takes place in mid-June, and it's essential to book tickets well in advance. You can soak up the atmosphere from the Silver Ring for a mere £20 per day, or head for the Grandstand and Paddock, where you can rub shoulders with the great and the good for £60 per day. Just make sure you dress to impress (ridiculously over-the-top hats are de rigeur for the ladies).

The racecourse is a 10-minute walk from Ascot train station, reached from London Waterloo (50 minutes).

A WORLD FIRST

In June 1215, King John met his barons and bishops in a large field 3 miles southeast of Windsor, and over the next few days they hammered out an agreement on a basic charter of rights guaranteeing the liberties of the king's subjects and restricting the monarch's absolute power. The document they signed was the Magna Carta, the world's first constitution. It formed the basis for statutes and charters throughout the world's democracies. (Both the national and state constitutions of the United States, drawn up more than 500 years later, paraphrase this document.)

Runnymede (9am-5pm) – from the Anglo-Saxon words *ruinige* (take council) and *moed* (meadow) – was chosen because it was the largest piece of open land between the king's residence at Windsor and the bishop's palace at Staines. Today, the field remains pretty much as it was, except that now it features two **lodges** (1930) designed by Sir Edward Lutyens. In the woods behind the field are two **memorials**, the first to the Magna Carta designed by Sir Edward Maufe (1957). The second is to John F Kennedy, and was built by Geoffrey Jellicoe in 1965 on an acre of land granted in perpetuity to the US government following Kennedy's assassination.

Runnymede is on the A308, 3 miles southeast of Windsor. Bus 71 stops near here on the Windsor–Egham route. You can also get there by boat (adult/child £5.20/2.60, 45 minutes) with **French Brothers** (www.frenchbrothers.co.uk; Clewer Court Rd; 11am-5pm Easter-Oct).

almost 40 million Lego bricks transformed into some of the world's greatest landmarks. Book online to save £9 off the ticket prices.

The Legoland shuttle bus departs opposite the Theatre Royal from 10am, with the last bus returning 30 minutes after the park has closed.

Sleeping

Harte & Garter Hotel & Spa HOTEL ££
(01753-863426; www.foliohotels.com/harteandgarter; High St; d from £99;) Right opposite the castle, this Victorian hotel blends period style with modern furnishings. High ceilings, giant fireplaces, decorative cornices and dark woods seamlessly combine with contemporary fabrics, plasma-screen TVs and traditional, cast-iron baths. Some rooms enjoy wonderful views over the castle, and all guests can enjoy the luxurious spa in the converted stable block.

76 Duke Street B&B ££
(01753-620636; www.76dukestreet.co.uk; 76 Duke St; s/d £80/100; P) Two immaculate, centrally located double rooms, presided over by a welcoming hostess who cooks up a superb breakfast. The second bedroom is only available if you book it along with the first – ideal for a family or two couples. Head west along Arthur Rd, turn right into Vansittart Rd, then right, and right again into Duke St.

Eating & Drinking

Windsor and Eton are packed with pubs and brasseries, with a cluster of good sandwich chains situated under the railway arches of the central station.

Gilbey's MODERN BRITISH ££
(01753-854921; www.gilbeygroup.com; 82-83 High St, Eton; 2-/3-course menu £18.50/24) Small but perfectly formed, this restaurant is one of the area's finest. Terracotta tiling and a sunny courtyard garden and conservatory give Gilbey's a Continental cafe feel, complemented by a superb modern British menu. Expect the likes of chicken with wild mushroom risotto, and roast lamb, the dishes almost surpassed by the extensive choice of wines.

Green Olive GREEK £
www.green-olive.co.uk; 10 High St; 2-/3-course lunch £10-13;) A great spot for a light lunch, Green Olive dishes up generous portions of traditional Greek *mezedhes* in bright, simple surroundings, as well as some interesting dessert choices.

Crooked House Tea Rooms TEAROOM
(www.crooked-house.com; 51 High St; afternoon teas from £9.50; 9.30am-5.30pm) Windsor's answer to the Leaning Tower of Pisa, this tiny traditional tearoom comes complete with sloping floors, wooden beams and royal cream teas.

Two Brewers TRADITIONAL PUB

(34 Park St) This 17th-century inn perched on the edge of Windsor Great Park is close to the castle's tradesmen's entrance and supposedly frequented by staff from the castle. Think low-beamed ceilings, dim lighting and royal photographs with irreverent captions on the wall.

Information

Royal Windsor Information Centre (www.windsor.gov.uk; Old Booking Hall, Windsor Royal Shopping Arcade; 9.30am-5pm Mon-Sat, 10am-4pm Sun) Has information on a self-guided heritage walk around town.

Getting There & Away

BUS Bus 702 connects Windsor with **London Victoria** coach station (£9.50, one hour, hourly), and bus 77 connects Windsor with **Heathrow airport** (one hour, hourly).

TRAIN Trains from Windsor Central station go to Slough, with regular connections to **London Paddington** (30 to 45 minutes). Trains from Windsor Riverside station go to **London Waterloo** (one hour). Services run half-hourly from both and tickets cost £8.50.

Wessex

Includes »

Best Places to Eat

» Hix Oyster & Fish House (p283)

» Boathouse (p266)

» Menu Gordon Jones (p320)

» Black Rat (p251)

» Bell's Diner (p308)

Best Places to Stay

» Urban Beach (p268)

» Number 38 (p307)

» The Pig (p259)

» 1 Lyme Townhouse (p282)

» Queensberry Hotel (p318)

Why Go?

With Wessex you get the cream of ancient England. This laid-back corner of the country is packed with some of Britain's best historic sites – here you can encounter iconic stone circles, explore blockbuster stately homes and experience life aboard some of the world's most famous ships. Architectural eye-candy is everywhere; take in Roman remains, romantic castles, serene cathedrals and Bath's sumptuous Georgian cityscape. The rolling, lyrical landscape still echoes with the myths of King Arthur and Alfred the Great, and the writings of Thomas Hardy and Jane Austen.

Wessex also boasts thriving cities, party-hard resorts and the 2012 Olympic sailing venues. Throw in two wildlife-rich national parks, a carefree holiday island and a fossil-packed shoreline studded with bewitching bays and towering rock formations, and you have a bit of a dilemma. With Wessex the question is not so much 'why go', as 'what to do first'.

When to Go

Cliffs, hillsides and formal gardens burst into fragrant blooms during April and May. Most attractions are open, but some may have reduced hours. June brings music festival fever at ultra-cool Glastonbury (alternate years from 2013) and on the funky Isle of Wight.

Coastal areas, big-name sights and key roads can get overwhelmed in July and August. Prices rise, too, but the odds are (fairly) good for better weather. Otherwise wait until September and October when school holidays are over, and expect cheaper sleeping spots, quieter beaches and warmer seas.

History

Wessex's compelling past is visible in the present. Human history here can be traced back as far as the Stone Age; a 9000-year-old skeleton was found at Cheddar Gorge. By 3000 BC a complex tribal society had developed, along with social hierarchies and shared religious beliefs. It's known as the Wessex culture and its peoples built the magnificent stone circles of Stonehenge and Avebury, and the wealth of barrows and processional avenues nearby. Centuries later, Iron Age inhabitants engineered massive forts at Maiden Castle and Old Sarum, before being subjugated by the Romans – their city of Aquae Sulis is now known as Bath.

When the Romans withdrew from here in the 5th century, King Cerdic founded the Anglo-Saxon kingdom of Wessex. At its core was land now covered by Hampshire, Dorset, Wiltshire and Somerset. Borders shifted over the centuries, but at its height the kingdom stretched from Kent in the east to Cornwall in the west. The most famous ruler was King Alfred (r 871–99), who made Winchester his capital and ensured Wessex was the only sizeable Anglo-Saxon territory not overrun by the Danes. Wessex officially became part of England in the mid-9th century.

Dorset novelist Thomas Hardy revived the name of Wessex 1000 years later, using it as the setting for his novels, initially in *Far from the Madding Crowd*. The archaic title Earl of Wessex, last used in the 11th century, was only reintroduced in 1999 when the Queen's youngest son, HRH Prince Edward, was granted it when he married.

Activities

Cycling

Gentle gradients and quiet country lanes make Wessex ideal for pedal-pushers. In the New Forest, hundreds of miles of bike paths snake through a historic, rural environment. Wiltshire is also a highlight – the 160-mile circular **Wiltshire Cycleway** is good for long or short rides. The Isle of Wight has 62 miles of bike-friendly routes and its own cycling festival (p262).

The **West Country Way** is a fabulously varied 240-mile jaunt from Bristol to Padstow in Cornwall. Exmoor provides some superb, and testing, off-road cycling, as do the fields, woods and heathland of the 12-mile-long Quantock Hills, an Area of Outstanding Natural Beauty (AONB) that peaks at 300m. The North Wessex Downs provide gentler terrain and take in the World Heritage site of Avebury, the market towns of Marlborough and Hungerford, and the western part of the Ridgeway National Trail (p243).

Walking

This is a fantastic region for hitting the trail. Top spots include Exmoor, the Mendips, the Quantocks and the Isle of Wight. The 630-mile **South West Coast Path** (www.southwestcoastpath.com) runs along the region's northern and southern shores, taking in some of the main coastal towns en route.

In northeastern Wiltshire, the **Ridgeway National Trail** (www.nationaltrail.co.uk/ridgeway) starts near Avebury and winds 44 miles through chalk hills to the River Thames at Goring in Oxfordshire. The route then continues another 41 miles (another three days' walk) through the Chiltern Hills.

Other Activities

Water sports draw many to Wessex's coasts. Highlights are the 2012 Olympic sailing venues at Weymouth and Portland, the yachting havens of the Isle of Wight, and the watery playgrounds of Poole, where you can try everything from kitesurfing to powerboating. Horse riding, fishing and falconry are available on Exmoor, while beachcombing

WESSEX'S ANCIENT SITES

Avebury Stone Circle (p299) Bigger than Stonehenge in atmosphere and acreage, this huge stone ring encases an entire village.

Stonehenge The world's most famous collection of megaliths – debate still rages over exactly why it was built.

Maiden Castle (p276) Massive and rampart-ringed, this is the biggest Iron Age hill fort in Britain.

Glastonbury Tor (p326) Myth-rich and mighty hard to climb, this iconic mound looks down onto the Vale of Avalon.

Old Sarum (p291) A stunning Iron Age stronghold on Salisbury Plain.

Wessex Highlights

1 Bagging a place on a memorable, early-morning meander inside the massive sarsen ring at **Stonehenge** (p291)

2 Foraging for fossils in Dorset's Lyme Regis on the constantly crumbling **Jurassic Coast** (p273)

3 Strolling along England's most breathtakingly beautiful street, the **Royal Crescent** (p313) in Bath

4 Gazing at the vast, waterlogged hulk of Henry VIII's favourite warship at **Portsmouth** (p252)

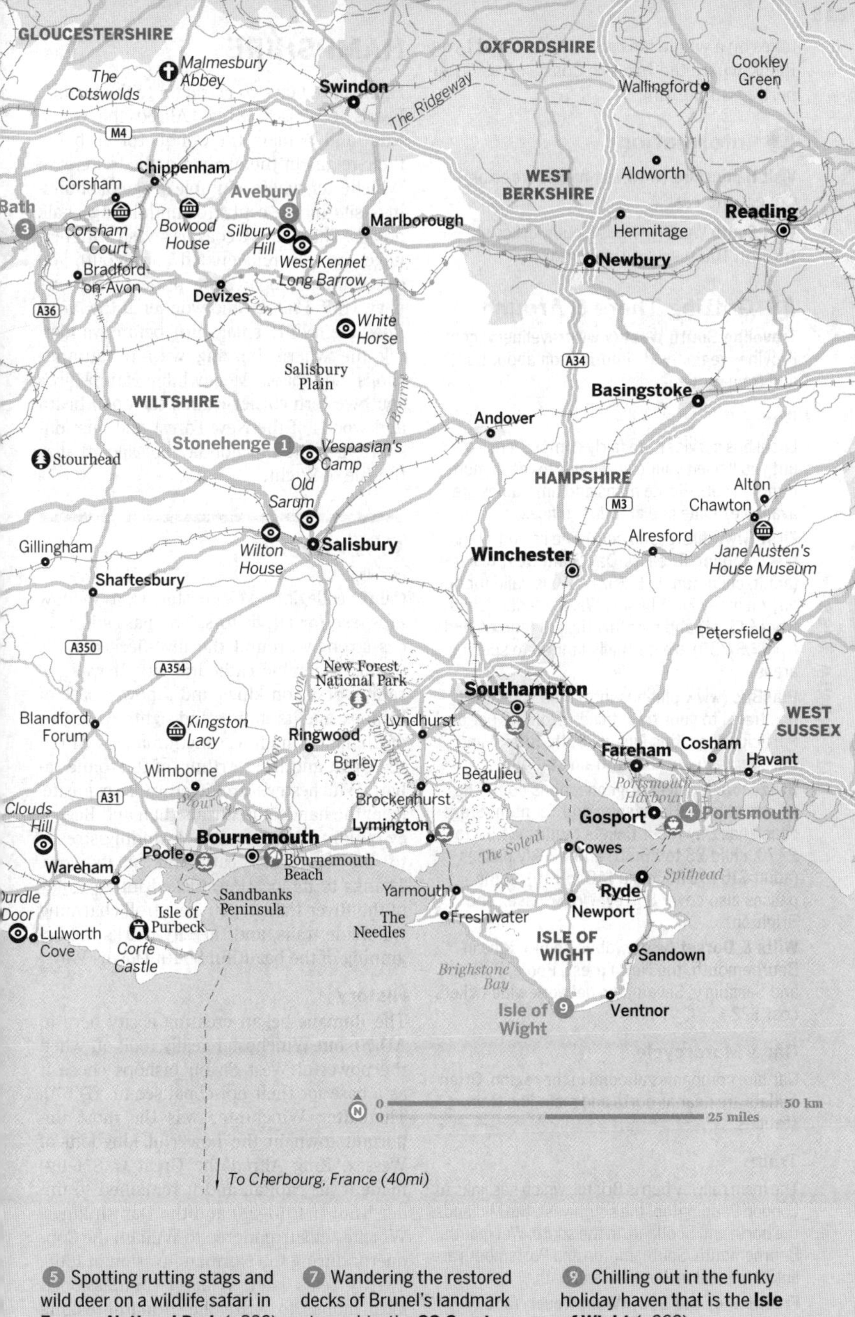

5 Spotting rutting stags and wild deer on a wildlife safari in **Exmoor National Park** (p332)

6 Experiencing sunrise from the summit of **Glastonbury Tor** (p326)

7 Wandering the restored decks of Brunel's landmark steamship, the **SS Great Britain** (p301), in Bristol

8 Sleeping inside the stone circle at **Avebury** (p299)

9 Chilling out in the funky holiday haven that is the **Isle of Wight** (p262)

takes on a whole new meaning around Lyme Regis, where the Jurassic Coast serves up superb fossil hunting.

Information

Visit Hampshire (www.visit-hampshire.co.uk) Covers the east.

Visit South West (www.visitsouthwest.co.uk) Info on the west of the region.

Getting There & Around

Traveline South West (www.travelinesw.com) Provides region-wide information about bus and train routes.

Bus

Local bus services are fairly comprehensive, but you'll need your own wheels to reach more remote spots. Route maps and timetables are available online and at tourist offices.

First (www.firstgroup.com) The region's largest bus company. The FirstDay Southwest ticket (adult/child/family £7/6/17.30) is valid for one day on many First buses. Weekly (adult/child from £15/11) and monthly tickets (adult/child from £37/30) are normally limited to specific areas.

PlusBus (www.plusbus.info) This adds local bus travel to your train ticket (from £2 per day). Participating cities include Bath, Bristol and Salisbury; buy tickets at train stations.

Stagecoach (www.stagecoachbus.com) The key provider in Hampshire and Taunton, Stagecoach has Day Rider tickets (adults £4.50 to £7.70, child £3 to £6.60) and weekly passes (adult £16 to £20, child £10 to £15); some passes also cover Surrey, West Sussex and Brighton.

Wilts & Dorset (www.wdbus.co.uk) Runs in Bournemouth, the New Forest, Poole, Purbeck and Salisbury. Seven-day, network-wide tickets cost £22.

Car & Motorcycle

Car-hire companies abound in the region. Often outlets are near airports and main-line train stations.

Train

The main railway hub is Bristol, which has links to London Paddington, the southwest, the Midlands, the north and Scotland. In the south, Weymouth, Bournemouth, Southampton and Portsmouth are linked to London Waterloo and Bath.

Freedom of the SouthWest Rover (adult/child £100/50) This pass allows eight days' unlimited travel over 15 days in an area including Bath, Bristol, Portsmouth, Salisbury, Taunton and Weymouth.

HAMPSHIRE

Hampshire takes you straight to the historic heart of Wessex. Kings Alfred the Great, Knut and William the Conqueror all based their reigns in the ancient cathedral city of Winchester, where a jumble of age-old buildings sits in the centre of undulating chalk downs. The county's coast is awash with heritage, too – in rejuvenated Portsmouth you can clamber aboard the pride of Nelson's navy, HMS *Victory* and wonder at the *Mary Rose* (Henry VIII's flagship), before wandering the wharfs buzzing with restaurants, shops and bars. Meanwhile, Hampshire's southwestern corner claims the open heath and woods of the New Forest and, just offshore, lies the hip holiday hot spot that is the Isle of Wight.

Winchester

POP 45,000

Calm, collegiate Winchester is a mellow must-see for all visitors. The past still echoes strongly around the flint-flecked walls of this venerable cathedral city. It was the capital of Saxon kings and a power base of bishops, and its statues and sights evoke two of England's mightiest myth-makers: Alfred the Great and King Arthur (of the round table). Winchester's architecture is exquisite, from the handsome Elizabethan and Regency buildings in the narrow winding streets, to the wondrous cathedral at its core. Thanks to its location, tucked into a valley of the River Itchen, you can stroll charming waterside trails, and the city marks the beginning of the beautiful South Downs Way.

History

The Romans began creating a city here in AD 70, but Winchester really took off when the powerful West Saxon bishops chose it as a base for their episcopal see in AD 670. Thereafter, Winchester was the most important town in the powerful kingdom of Wessex. King Alfred the Great (r 871–99) made it his capital, and it remained so under Knut (r 1016–35) and the Danish kings. Winchester surrendered to William the Conqueror during the Norman invasion of 1066. Twenty years later, William commissioned local monks to write the ground-breaking Domesday Book, an administrative survey of the entire country and the most significant clerical accomplishment of the Middle Ages. Winchester thrived until the 12th century,

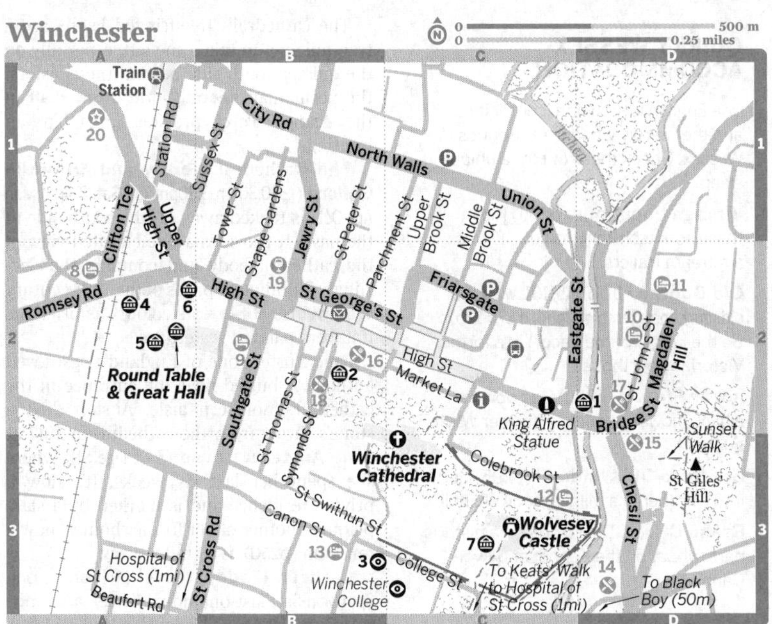

Winchester

Top Sights

Round Table & Great Hall A2
Winchester Cathedral C3
Wolvesey Castle C3

Sights

1 City Mill D2
2 City Museum B2
Gurkha Museum .... (see 5)
3 Jane Austen's House B3
4 Royal Green Jackets Museum A2
5 Horsepower A2
6 Westgate Museum A2
7 Wolvesey Palace C3

Sleeping

8 5 Clifton Terrace A2
9 Hotel du Vin B2
10 No 21 .... D2
11 St John's Croft D2
12 Wolvesey View C3
13 Wykeham Arms B3

Eating

14 Black Rat D3
15 Chesil Rectory D3
16 James Martin at Cadogan B2
17 No 5 .... D2
18 Old Vine B2
Wykeham Arms .... (see 13)

Drinking

19 Plain & Fancy B2
Wykeham Arms .... (see 13)

Entertainment

20 Railway Inn A1

when a fire gutted most of the city – after this, London took its crown.

Sights

Winchester Cathedral CATHEDRAL
(☎01962-857 275; www.winchester-cathedral.org.uk; adult/child £6/free, incl tower tour £9/free; ⊙9am-5pm Sat, 12.30-3pm Sun) Winchester Cathedral is one of southern England's most awe-inspiring buildings. Its walls contain evidence of almost 1000 years of history, best experienced on one of the memorable tours of its sturdy tower. The Cathedral's exterior features a fine Gothic facade, but it's the inside that steals the show with one of the longest **medieval naves** (164m) in Europe,

QUIRKY WESSEX ACCOMMODATION

The English love their eccentricities, and the weirdly wonderful abounds in Wessex. Check these out for a unique sleep.

Vintage Vacations (p265) Kip in these so-kitsch-they're-cool, 1960s airstream trailers.

Old Court (☎01761-451101; www.theoldcourt.com; Temple Cloud; d £70-125) Be the judge (of the decor) in a former Victorian courthouse.

Xoron Floatel (p265) Bed down on a bijou, flower-bedecked, former WWII gunboat.

Bradford Old Windmill (p295) Settle into slumber in a mildly saucy old mill.

Grand Cru (p317) Nod off on a historic narrowboat on the Kennet and Avon Canal.

and a fascinating jumble of features from all eras.

Today's cathedral sits beside foundations that mark the town's original 7th-century minster church. The cathedral was begun in 1070 and completed in 1093, and was subsequently entrusted with the bones of its patron saint, St Swithin (Bishop of Winchester from 852 to 862). He is best known for the proverb stating that if it rains on St Swithin's Day (15 July) it will rain for a further 40 days and 40 nights.

Soggy ground and poor workmanship spelt disaster for the early church; the original tower collapsed in 1107 and major restructuring continued until the mid-15th century. Look out for the monument at the far end of the building to diver William Walker; he saved the cathedral from collapse by delving repeatedly into its waterlogged underbelly from 1906 to 1912 to bolster rotting wooden foundations with vast quantities of concrete and brick.

The intricately carved **medieval choir stalls** are another highlight, sporting everything from mythical beasts to a mischievous green man.

Choral **Evensong** (5.30pm Monday to Saturday, 3.30pm Sunday) is intensely atmospheric; Sunday services also take place at 7.40am, 8am and 10am.

The cathedral's tree-fringed lawns are a tranquil spot to take time out, especially on the quieter south side beyond the cloisters; the permanent **secondhand book stall** in the Deanery Porch provides great bargain hunting.

The Cathedral Library and Triforium Gallery (⏲10.30am-3.30pm Tue-Sat, 2-4pm Mon Apr-Oct) is tucked away on the south side of the nave. It provides a fine elevated view of the cathedral body and contains the dazzlingly illuminated pages of the 12th-century **Winchester Bible** – its colours as bright as if it were painted yesterday.

Jane Austen, one of England's best-loved authors, is buried near the entrance in the cathedral's northern aisle. Austen died a stone's throw from the cathedral in 1817 at **Jane Austen's House** (8 College St), where she spent her last six weeks. It's now a private residence and is marked by a slate plaque. Another of her former homes, now a museum (p250), is 18 miles away.

Cathedral body tours (⏲hourly 10am-3pm Mon-Sat) last one hour. **Tower and roof tours** (tickets £6; ⏲2.15pm Mon, Wed, Fri & Sat, plus 11.30am Sat) see you clambering 213 steps up narrow stairwells, navigating an interior gallery high above the nave, visiting the bell chamber and going onto the roof for views as far as the Isle of Wight. For safety reasons these tours are only open to those aged 12 to 70. They're popular, so book well in advance. **Crypt Tours** (tour free; ⏲10.30am, 12.30pm & 2.30pm Mon-Sat Apr-Oct) aren't always available because of flooding. If the crypt is open, look out for *Sound II*, a poignant sculpture by Anthony Gormley.

FREE Round Table & Great Hall — HISTORIC BUILDING

(☎01962-846476; www.hants.gov.uk/greathall; Castle Ave; suggested donation £2; ⏲10am-5pm) Winchester's cavernous Great Hall is the only part of 11th-century Winchester Castle that Oliver Cromwell spared from destruction. Crowning the wall like a giant-sized dartboard of green and cream spokes is what centuries of mythology have dubbed King Arthur's Round Table. It's actually a 700-year-old copy, but is fascinating nonetheless. It's thought to have been constructed in the late 13th century and then painted during the reign of Henry VIII (King Arthur's image is unsurprisingly reminiscent of Henry's youthful face).

This hall was also the stage for several gripping English courtroom dramas, including the trial of adventurer Sir Walter Raleigh in 1603, who was sentenced to death but received a reprieve at the last minute.

FREE Wolvesey Castle CASTLE
(EH; ☎02392-378291; www.english-heritage.org.uk; ⏲10am-5pm Apr-Sep) The fantastical, crumbling remains of early-12th-century Wolvesey Castle huddle in the protective embrace of the city's walls, despite the building having been partly demolished in the 1680s. It was completed by Henry de Blois, and served as the Bishop of Winchester's residence throughout the medieval era. Queen Mary I and Philip II of Spain celebrated their wedding feast here in 1554. According to legend, its odd name comes from a Saxon king's demand for an annual payment of 300 wolves' heads. Access is via College St. Today the bishop lives in the (private) **Wolvesey Palace** next door.

Hospital of St Cross HISTORIC BUILDING
(☎01962-853525; www.stcrosshospital.co.uk; St Cross Rd; adult/child £3/1; ⏲9.30am-5pm Mon-Sat, 1-5pm Sun) Monk, bishop, knight, politician and grandson of William the Conqueror, Henry de Blois was a busy man. But he found time to establish this still-impressive hospital in 1132. As well as healing the sick and housing the needy, the hospital fed and housed pilgrims and crusaders en route to the Holy Land. It's the oldest charitable institution in England, and is still roamed by 25 elderly black- or red-gowned brothers in pie-shaped trencher hats. Take a peek into the stumpy church, the brethren hall, the kitchen and the peaceful gardens. The best way to arrive is via the 1-mile Keats' Walk. Upon entering, claim the centuries-old Wayfarer's Dole – a crust of bread and horn of ale (now a swig of beer) from the Porter's Gate.

Military Museums MUSEUM
Of Winchester's clutch of army museums, the pick is the **Royal Green Jackets Museum** (The Rifles; ☎01962-877826; www.winchestermilitarymuseums.co.uk; Peninsula Barracks, Romsey Rd; adult/child £3/1.50; ⏲10am-5pm daily), which has a mini rifle-shooting range, a room of 6000 medals and an impressive blow-by-blow diorama of Napoleon's downfall, the Battle of Waterloo. The **Gurkha Museum** (☎01962-843659; www.thegurkhamuseum.co.uk; Peninsula Barracks, Romsey Rd; adult/child £2/free; ⏲10am-5pm Mon-Sat, noon-4pm Sun) features the regiment's history, combining a jungle tableau with a history of Gurkha service to the British crown. **Horsepower** (www.horsepowermuseum.co.uk; Peninsula Barracks, Romsey Rd; admission free; ⏲10am-4pm Tue-Fri, noon-4pm Sat & Sun) gallops through the combat history of the Royal Hussars, from the Charge of the Light Brigade to armour-clad vehicles.

FREE Westgate Museum MUSEUM
(High St; ⏲10am-4pm Sat, noon-4pm Sun) Ideal for fans of the grisly bits of history. Set in a medieval gateway that was once a debtors' prison, it boasts a set of gibbeting irons used to display an executed criminal's body in 1777 and, scrawled all over the interior walls, the 17th-century graffiti of prisoners.

FREE City Museum MUSEUM
(The Square; ⏲10am-4pm Mon-Sat, noon-4pm Sun) This bijou museum whizzes through Winchester's Roman and Saxon history, lingers on its Anglo-Norman golden age, pays homage to Jane Austen, and reconstructs several early-20th-century Winchester shops.

City Mill HISTORIC BUILDING
(NT; ☎01962-870057; www.nationaltrust.co.uk; Bridge St; adult/child £4/2; ⏲10am-5pm Feb-Dec) Seeing the city's 18th-century water-powered mill in action is impressive; you can also buy its stone-ground flour in the shop.

Winchester College SCHOOL
(☎01962-621100; www.winchestercollege.org; College St; tours adult/child £6/5; ⏲10.45am & noon Mon-Sat, plus 2.15pm & 3.30pm Wed, Fri, Sat & Sun) Winchester College gives you a rare chance to nosey around a prestigious English private school. It was set up by William Wykeham, Bishop of Winchester in 1393, 14 years after he founded Oxford's New College. Hour-long guided tours trail through the school's medieval core, taking in the 14th-century Gothic chapel, complete with wooden vaulted roof, the dining room (called College Hall), and a vast 17th-century open classroom (called School), where exams are still held. It's all deeply atmospheric and unshakably affluent; a revealing insight into how the other half learns. Tours start from the Porter's Lodge.

Activities

Winchester has a tempting range of walks. The 1-mile **Keats' Walk** meanders through the water meadows to the Hospital of St Cross (p249). Its beauty is said to have

WORTH A TRIP

JANE AUSTEN'S HOUSE MUSEUM

There's more than a touch of the period dramas she inspired about the former home of Jane Austen (1775–1817). The appealing red-brick house, where the celebrated English novelist lived with her mother and sister in the early 1800s, is now a **museum** (☎01420-83262; www.jane-austens-house-museum.org.uk; Chawton; adult/child £7/2; ⏲10.30am-4.30pm mid-Feb–Dec). While here she wrote *Mansfield Park*, *Emma* and *Persuasion*, and revised *Sense and Sensibility*, *Pride and Prejudice* and *Northanger Abbey*.

The interior depicts a typical well-to-do Georgian family home, complete with elegant furniture and copper pans in the kitchen. Highlights include the occasional table Austen used as a desk, first editions of her novels and the delicate handkerchief she embroidered for her sister.

The museum is 18 miles east of Winchester; take bus 64 from Winchester to Alton Butts (45 minutes, half-hourly Monday to Saturday, five on Sunday) then walk 800m to Chawton village.

prompted the poet to pen the ode *To Autumn* – pick up the trail near Winchester College. Alternatively, head south down Chesil St and head onto Wharf Hill. From here a footpath leads through the water meadows to **St Catherine's Hill** (1 mile). The soothing **Riverside Walk** leads along the bank of the River Itchen from Wolvesey Castle to High St (200m). The stiffer **Sunset Walk** up St Giles' Hill rewards with fine city views, especially at dusk. To get there head up East or Magdalen Hills. St Giles' Hill is also the beginning (or end) of the **South Downs Way**.

Tours

Guided **heritage walks** (adult/child £4.50/free; ⏲11am & 2.30pm Mon-Sat Apr-Oct, 11.30am Sun May-Aug, 11am Sat only Nov-Mar) leave from the tourist office (p252). These 90-minute walks include Kings & Castles, Mitres & Mortarboards, and City Highlights.

Sleeping

Wykeham Arms HISTORIC INN ££
(☎01962-853834; www.fullershotels.com; 75 Kingsgate St; s/d/ste £70/119/150; P wifi) At 250-odd years old, the Wykeham bursts with history – it used to be a brothel and also put Nelson up for a night (some say the events coincided). Creaking stairs lead to plush bedrooms that manage to be both deeply established but also on-trend; brass bedsteads meet jazzy throws, oak dressers sport stylish lights. Each room has its own teddy bear, too.

St John's Croft BOUTIQUE B&B ££
(☎01962-859976; www.st-johns-croft.co.uk; St John's St; s/d £40/70; P wifi) A B&B to fall in love with. Supremely but oh-so-casually stylish, this rambling Queen Anne town house teams rattan carpets with bulging bookcases, and Indian art with shabby-chic antiques. The rooms are vast, the garden is tranquil and breakfast is served beside the Aga in the country-house kitchen.

5 Clifton Terrace BOUTIQUE B&B ££
(☎01962-890053; cliftonterrace@hotmail.co.uk; 5 Clifton Tce; s/d/f £60/75/110; wifi) At this elegant Georgian town house, family heirlooms sit beside candy-striped rugs and peppermint-green claw-footed baths. It's delightful, easy-going and great value.

Hotel du Vin HISTORIC HOTEL £££
(☎01962-841414; www.hotelduvin.com; Southgate St; r £145-230; P @ wifi) A glamorous, gorgeous oasis, boasting luxurious furnishings, ornate chaises longues and extravagant stand-alone baths.

No 21 B&B ££
(☎01962-852989; St John's St; s/d £45/90) Atmospheric cathedral views, a flower-filled cottage garden and rustic rooms (think painted wicker and woven bedspreads) make this art-packed house a peaceful city bolt-hole.

Wolvesey View B&B ££
(☎01962-852082; www.wintonian.co.uk; 10 Colebrook Pl; s/d/f £48/76/90; P @ wifi) Book the simply furnished Yellow Room for captivating views of Wolvesey Castle's storybook tumblings. Rooms share a bathroom.

Eating

TOP CHOICE Black Rat MODERN BRITISH ££
(☎01962-844465; www.theblackrat.co.uk; 88 Chesil St; mains £17-20; ⊙dinner daily, lunch Sat & Sun) The decor here is casually countrified, but the food is something else. Accomplished cooking has won it a Michelin star – partly due to the intense flavours conjured from ingredients such as braised beef cheek, lamb rump and oxtail. Bookings required.

Chesil Rectory BRITISH ££
(☎01962-851555; www.chesilrectory.co.uk; 1 Chesil St; mains £16; ⊙lunch & dinner) Flickering candles and low beams lend this 15th-century restaurant a very romantic feel. Locally sourced delicacies include carpaccio of Hampshire venison with mushrooms, and smoked trout with watercress. The two-course lunch and early-evening menu (£16, served 6pm to 7pm) is a steal. Bookings are recommended.

Wykeham Arms PUB ££
(☎01962-853834; www.wykehamarmswinchester.co.uk; 75 Kingsgate St; mains £14-21; ⊙lunch & dinner Mon-Sat, lunch Sun;) Local fare packs this super-quirky pub's menu. Dishes range from creative to comfort; try salt-baked beetroot with spicy lentils or slow-cooked lamb cassoulet. Their aged Hampshire beef is a carnivore's delight. Bookings recommended.

Old Vine PUB ££
(☎01962-854616; www.oldvinewinchester.com; 8 Great Minster St; mains £11-15) At this mellow old English inn an eclectic menu darts from mushrooms with paprika, to pear and blue cheese tart. It's all best enjoyed at a window table overlooking Cathedral Green. Bookings recommended.

No 5 BISTRO ££
(www.no5bridgestreet.co.uk; 5 Bridge St; mains £13;) This stylish eatery offers new twists on English classics, so expect British charcuterie and cheese, prawns in ink aioli, and quince crumble.

James Martin at Cadogan DELI £
(www.james-martin-at-cadogan.co.uk; 31a The Square; ⊙9.30am-5.30pm Mon-Sat, 10am-4pm Sun) Run by the eponymous celebrity chef, this place exudes aromas of ripe cheese and freshly baked bread – sample some at a tiny table for just £5 per platter.

Drinking & Entertainment

For live music listings, see www.winchestergigguide.co.uk

TOP CHOICE Wykeham Arms PUB
(www.wykehamarmswinchester.co.uk; 75 Kingsgate St;) Somehow reminiscent of an endearingly eccentric old uncle, this is the sort of pub you'd love as your local: thousands of tankards and school canes hang from the ceiling, worn school desks lending pint-supping an illicit air. At 6pm perfect bar snacks emerge: sizzling sausages (75p), served with mustard and a fork.

Black Boy PUB
(www.theblackboypub.com; 1 Wharf Hill) This adorable old boozer is filled with a happy band of drinkers and sometimes-obsessive collections, from pocket watches to wax facial features; bear traps to sawn-in-half paperbacks. The pumps produce five locally brewed real ales.

Railway Inn LIVE MUSIC
(www.railwaylive.co.uk; 3 St Paul's Hill; ⊙5pm-midnight Sun-Thu, to 2am Fri, to 1am Sat) As eclectic and alternative as you get; bands span folk, rock, roots and blues; or there's Dr Strangelove's Burlesque Discotheque every Friday.

Plain & Fancy BAR
(www.plainandfancy.co.uk; 10 Jewry St; ⊙4pm-1am Mon-Sat;) A shocking-pink poseur's paradise, specialising in cocktails and champagne.

Information

Discovery Centre (www3.hants.gov.uk/wdc; Jewry St; ⊙9am-7pm Mon-Fri, 9am-5pm Sat, 10am-3pm Sun;) Free internet access.

A COTTAGE OF YOUR OWN

After a rural bolt-hole far from the madding crowd? Then check out these companies for self-catering cottages.

Dorset Coastal Cottages (www.dorsetcoastalcottages.com)

Dream Cottages (www.dream-cottages.co.uk)

Farm & Cottage Holidays (www.holidaycottages.co.uk)

Hideaways (www.hideaways.co.uk)

Tourist Office (☎01962-840500; www.visitwinchester.co.uk; High St; ⏲10am-5pm Mon-Sat, plus 11am-4pm Sun May-Sep)

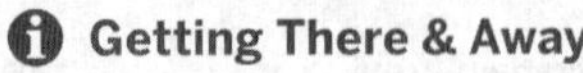

Getting There & Away

Winchester is 65 miles west of London and 14 miles north of Southampton.

Bus

Regular, direct National Express buses shuttle to **London Victoria** (£12, 1¾ hours) and **Southampton** (one hour).

Train

There are fast links to the Midlands. Other train services:

London Waterloo (£30, 1¼ hours, every 30 minutes)

Portsmouth (£10.20, one hour, hourly)

Southampton (£5.80, 20 minutes, every 30 minutes)

Getting Around

PARKING The **Park & Ride** (per day £2 to £3) is signed off junctions 10 and 11 of the M3.

TAXI Try ranks at the train station and outside the tourist office, or phone **Wintax Taxis** (☎01962-878727).

Portsmouth

POP 207,100

Prepare to splice the main brace, hoist the halyard and potter around the poop deck – Portsmouth is one of the principal ports of Britain's Royal Navy, and the sights of its historic dockyard rank alongside London's Greenwich. Here you can jump aboard Lord Nelson's flagship HMS *Victory,* which was in the midst of the fighting at the Battle of Trafalgar, and see the evocative hulk of Henry VIII's flagship, the *Mary Rose.*

Portsmouth was bombed heavily during WWII and chunks of the city feature soulless postwar architecture, but the cobbled streets of the Point still provide a tangible taste of the past. Regeneration at the glitzy shopping enclave of Gunwharf Quays includes the spectacular Spinnaker Tower, which provides jaw-dropping views. Add some superb restaurants and chic sleep spots, and you have plenty of reasons for an overnight stay. The suburb of Southsea, which begins a mile south east of Gunwharf Quays, is rich in good hotels and eateries.

> **HMS VICTORY**
>
> In the summer, tours of Nelson's flagship (p252) are self-guided. But from autumn to spring, hugely popular 40-minute **guided tours** are held. Arrive early to bag a place – you can't book in advance.

Sights & Activities

TOP CHOICE **Portsmouth Historic Dockyard** HISTORIC SHIPS

(☎023-9272 8060; www.historicdockyard.co.uk; adult/child/family £21/16/62; ⏲10am-6pm) Portsmouth's blockbuster attraction features three stunning historic ships and an impressive cluster of museums. They sit in the heart of one of Britain's most important modern-day naval ports in a site peppered with red-brick Georgian warehouses, vast wooden boatsheds, statues and painted ships' figureheads. The ticket price also includes a boat trip around the harbour. Together it all makes for a full day's outing; the last admission is 1½ hours before closing.

As resplendent as it is venerable, the dockyard's star sight is **HMS Victory** (www.hms-victory.com), Lord Nelson's flagship at the Battle of Trafalgar (1805) and the site of his infamous dying words 'Kiss me, Hardy', after victory over the French had been secured. This remarkable ship is topped by a forest of ropes and masts, and weighted by a swollen belly filled with cannon and paraphernalia for an 850-strong crew. Clambering through the low-beamed decks and crew's quarters is an evocative experience.

The raising of the 16th-century warship the **Mary Rose** was an extraordinary feat of marine archaeology. This 700-tonne floating fortress was Henry VIII's favourite vessel, but it sank suddenly off Portsmouth while fighting the French in 1545. It is thought that of a crew of 400, about 360 died. The ship was only raised from its watery grave in 1982. Now the new £35 million, boat-shaped **Mary Rose Museum** (www.maryrose.org) that's been built around it showcases the massive hull. This can be seen from tiered galleries that reconstruct life on each deck, using some of the 19,000 artefacts that were raised with the ship. They range from the military, including scores of cannon and hundreds of longbows, to the touchingly prosaic: water jugs, hair combs and even leather shoes.

Anywhere else, the magnificent warship **HMS Warrior** (www.hmswarrior.org), built in 1860, would grab centre stage. This stately ship was at the cutting edge of technology in its day, riding the transition from wood to iron and sail to steam. The gleaming upper deck, vast gun deck and the dimly lit cable lockers conjure up a vivid picture of life in the Victorian navy.

Expect model ships, battle dioramas, medals and paintings in the **Royal Naval Museum** (www.royalnavalmuseum.org). Audio-visual displays recreate the Battle of Trafalgar, one gallery is devoted to Lord Nelson and others let you take command of a warship – see if you can cure the scurvy and avoid mutiny.

The **Trafalgar Sail Exhibition** is a small museum showcasing the only HMS *Victory* sail to survive the Battle of Trafalgar. Clearly bearing the scars of conflict, it's riddled with the holes made by Napoleonic cannon – a telling illustration of the battle's ferocity.

Stroll into **Action Stations!**, a warehouse full of interactive gadgets, and you'll soon be piloting a replica Merlin helicopter, controlling an aircraft carrier, upping periscope or jumping aboard a ship simulator. The whole set-up is a thinly disguised recruitment drive for the modern navy, but it's fun nonetheless.

The Point HISTORIC AREA

Some 500m south of Gunwharf Quays, the Point (also known as Spice Island) is home to characterful cobbled streets dotted with higgledy-piggledy houses and salty sea-dog pubs; their waterside terraces are top spots to gaze at the passing parade of ferries and navy ships. You can clatter up the steps of the **Round Tower** (originally built by Henry V) and stroll along the old fort walls to the **Square Tower**, which was built in 1494. Underneath, **Sally Ports** are framed by cavernous vaults – openings in the defences that gave historic captains access to the sea, and give modern sun worshippers access to a strip of shingle beach.

To walk to the Point, follow the chain-link design set into the pavement from Gunwharf Quays.

Spinnaker Tower TOWER

(☎023-9285 7520; www.spinnakertower.co.uk; Gunwharf Quays; adult/child £8.50/7; ⏲10am-6pm) The Spinnaker Tower soars 170m above Gunwharf Quays – an unmistakable symbol of Portsmouth's new-found razzle dazzle. Its two sweeping white arcs resemble a billowing sail from some angles, and a sharp skeletal ribcage from others.

It's one of the UK's tallest publicly accessible structures, offering 23-mile views over Portsmouth, the Isle of Wight and the South Downs. **Observation Deck 1** has a hair-raising view through the glass floor, while the roofless **Crow's Nest** on Deck 3 allows you to feel the wind on your face. Tickets are 15% cheaper when booked online.

Royal Navy Submarine Museum MUSEUM

(☎023-9251 0354; www.submarine-museum.co.uk; Haslar Jetty Rd, Gosport; adult/child £12/9; ⏲10am-5.30pm) The tour of this bona-fide ex-service submarine leads from the torpedo compartments via the galley (kitchen) to the heads (toilets), providing a revealing insight into the claustrophobic conditions. To visit, catch the Gosport Passenger Ferry then walk 500m along the waterfront.

D-Day Museum MUSEUM

(☎023-9282 7261; www.ddaymuseum.co.uk; Clarence Esplanade, Southsea; adult/child £6.50/4.50; ⏲10am-5pm) The exhibits here recount the assault mounted by Allied D-Day forces in 1944, and Portsmouth's key role in the operation.

Explosion! MUSEUM

(☎023-9250 5600; www.explosion.org.uk; Priddy's Hard, Gosport; adult/child £10/5; ⏲10am-5pm daily Apr-Oct, 10am-4pm Sat & Sun Nov-Mar) A 1771 powder magazine packed full of ordinance that traces the story of naval munitions from gunpowder to Exocet missiles.

FREE **Cathedral of St Thomas of Canterbury** CATHEDRAL

(☎023-9282 3300; www.portsmouthcathedral.org.uk; High St; ⏲10am-5pm) This airy structure retains fragments of its 12th- and 17th-century incarnations, but a striking modern makeover includes quirky statuettes by Peter Eugene Ball; look for Thomas Becket with a sword through his mitred head.

Blue Reef AQUARIUM

(☎023-92875222; www.bluereefaquarium.co.uk; Clarence Esplanade, Southsea; adult/child £9.75/7.50; ⏲10am-5pm) Open-topped tanks and huge underwater walkways reveal coral reefs, poisonous frogs, otters and rays.

Charles Dickens' Birthplace MUSEUM

(☎023-9282 7261; www.charlesdickensbirthplace.co.uk; 393 Old Commercial Rd; adult/child £4/£3;

Portsmouth

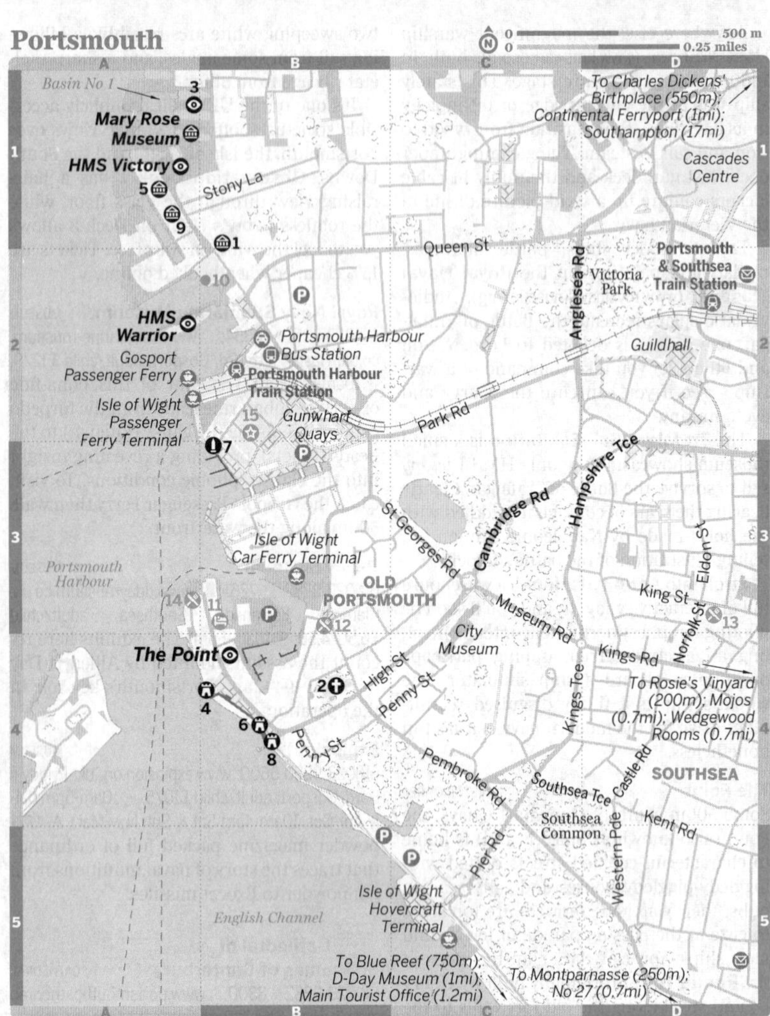

⊙10am-5pm mid-Apr–Sep) The fully furnished bedroom and parlour at this elegant house faithfully recreate the Regency world of Dickens' childhood (look out for the couch he died on, too).

Tours

Boat Trips BOAT TOUR
(☎01983-864602; Historic Dockyard; adult/child £6/3 (incl with dockyard ticket); ⊙10.30am-4pm Apr-Oct, 11am-3pm Nov-Mar) These weather-permitting, 45-minute harbour tours provide salt-sprayed views of *Warrior*, *Victory* and Gunwharf Quays; you'll go past modern warships as well.

Walking Tours HERITAGE WALKS
(adult/child £3/1; ⊙2.30pm Sat & Sun Apr-Oct) Themes for these guided walks include Nelson, Henry VIII and Old Fortifications. They run on some summer weekdays as well – the tourist office (p256) has more information.

Sleeping

TOP CHOICE **Florence House** BOUTIQUE HOTEL ££
(☎023-9275 1666; www.florencehousehotel.co.uk; 2 Malvern Rd, Southsea; d £75-145; P@)

Portsmouth

Definitely in the easy-to-check-into-hard-to-leave category. Enjoy vast beds piled artfully high with bathrobes, and retro-chic bathrooms in black and white tiles. The pamper dial is set to high – they'll even provide picnic baskets on demand.

Fortitude Cottage B&B ££
(☎023-9282 3748; www.fortitudecottage.co.uk; 51 Broad St; s £45, d £65-135; P 🛜) A combination of swish rooms (think dark brown and dull gold), a superb location and thoughtful touches (chocolates on the tea tray) make this a near-perfect B&B. The penthouse is magnificent; its private roof terrace has wicker chairs and binoculars, which make it all the better to experience expansive harbour views.

Somerset House BOUTIQUE HOTEL £££
(☎023-9275 3555; www.somersethousehotel.co.uk; 10 Florence Rd, Southsea; d £100-200; 🛜) An achingly tasteful make-over has turned this late-Victorian townhouse into a haven of designer calm. Stained glass, dark woods and polished floors cosy up to Balinese figurines and the very latest luxury bathrooms.

Oyster Cottage B&B ££
(☎02392-823683; www.theoystercottage.co.uk; 9 Bath Sq; d £70-90; P) A real delight, from the blue-and-white candy-striped bed linen to the warm, funny owner Carol ('I actually *like* guests'). The views, from the Isle of Wight on the left to Portsmouth Harbour on the right, might make you linger longer in your room.

Cecil Cottage B&B ££
(☎07894 072253; www.cecilcottage.co.uk; 45 Broad St; s/d £60/75; P) Luxury smellies in the bathroom, a ferry-view lounge, and tea and biscuits on arrival make this Spice Island B&B a great option. The crisp white and soft grey colour scheme completes the soothing effect.

Southsea Backpackers HOSTEL £
(☎023-9283 2495; www.portsmouthbackpackers.co.uk; 4 Florence Rd, Southsea; dm £15, d £34-38; P @ 🛜) A cheerful if grungy hostel, where a pool table, patio and barbeque compensate for the well-worn rooms.

Eating

Kitsch'n d'or FRENCH ££
(☎023-9286 1519; www.kitschndor.com; 37 Eldon St; mains £15, 4 courses £23; ⊙lunch & dinner Tue-Sat, lunch Mon & Sun) Prepare to be transported to rural Provence. Rustic dishes are rich with hearty flavours, from duck with wild mushrooms and truffle cream, to a meltingly tender shin of beef with red wine sauce. Their *fruits de mer* platter is epic: the mounds of local lobster, scallops and steaming clams are so fresh it needs to be ordered a day in advance.

A Bar BAR, BISTRO ££
(www.abarbistro.co.uk; 58 White Hart Rd; mains £11; ⊙food until 10.30pm; 🛜) A place to sample

local produce and soak up local life: the menu is strong on fish that's been landed just yards away – you may see cider-drinking fishermen from mid-afternoon. Food is served until 10.30pm. The impressive 200-strong wine list includes local Stopham and sparkling Nyetimber; prices span £15 to £1000 a bottle.

No 27 MODERN BRITISH £££
(023-92876272; www.restaurant27.com; 7a South Parade, Southsea; 3-course lunch/dinner £27/40; lunch Sun, dinner Wed-Sat) One of Portsmouth's newest classy eateries, 27 has been impressing local foodies with its creative cuisine. The decor is ultra-smart but discreet; the flavour combinations are surprising: look out for oxtail pudding, and warm rosemary and fig jelly.

Rosie's Vineyard BISTRO ££
(www.rosies-vineyard.co.uk; 87 Elm Grove, Southsea; mains £11; 6-11pm Mon-Sat, noon-11pm Sun) From the rickety cane bar stools to the vast list of vintages chalked up on the wall (from £2.70 a glass), this is the epitome of a snug little wine bar. Bistro classics include chicken and chorizo cassoulet and huge mounds of local sausages and mash.

Montparnasse FRENCH £££
(023-9281 6754; www.bistromontparnasse.co.uk; 103 Palmerston Rd; 2/3 courses £33/38; Tue-Sat) The fine English ingredients here are given a gourmet Gallic twist. Creations include velvety scallop velouté with black pudding, and a rich maple-roasted pheasant with salted caramel walnuts.

Still & West PUB £
(www.fullers.co.uk; 2 Bath Sq; mains £7.50; noon-9pm Mon-Sat, noon-8pm Sun) Genius: two great British institutions in one – a fish and chip shop inside a pub. Your fried delights come wrapped in traditional chippy paper, so buy a pint, bag a window table and tuck in while watching the panorama of passing boats.

Drinking

Rows of bars line Gunwharf Quays; Elm Grove and Albert Rd have a more counterculture vibe.

King St Tavern PUB
(www.thekingstreettavern.co.uk; 70 King St) Just what a British pub should be: friendly and un-messed-about-with. Buffed wood and old mirrors frame long tables around which to share a pint; it's home to jazz and folk sessions, too.

Mojos BAR
(023-9287 3471; 92 Albert Rd, Southsea;) Ready-to-party people of all ages are drawn to this purple and red venue in the heart of Southsea's bar strip.

Entertainment

Southsea is thick with nightclubs and live-music venues.

Wedgewood Rooms LIVE MUSIC
(www.wedgewood-rooms.co.uk; 147b Albert Rd) One of Portsmouth's best live-music venues; also hosts DJs and comedians.

Vue CINEMA
(www.myvue.com; Gunwharf Quays) Big screen multiplex.

Information

Online Cafe (www.online-cafe.co.uk; 163 Elm Grove; per 10min/1hr 50p/£3; 9am-9pm Mon-Fri, 10am-8pm Sat & Sun) Internet access.

Tourist Office (023-9282 6722; www.visitportsmouth.co.uk; Clarence Esplanade; 10am-5pm) Now in the D-Day Museum in Southsea, about 2.5km south of the port area.

Getting There & Away

Boat

You can reach the **Isle of Wight** from Portsmouth; the Wightlink car ferry (p263) goes from the terminal in Old Portsmouth; the Hovertravel passenger ferry (p263) runs from Southsea.

Prices for crossings to **France** vary wildly depending on times and dates of travel – an example fare is £280 return for a car and two adults on the Portsmouth–Cherbourg route. Book online, be prepared to travel off peak and look out for special deals.

Brittany Ferries (www.brittanyferries.co.uk) Services run regularly from Portsmouth to **St Malo** (10¾ hours), **Caen** (four hours) and **Cherbourg** (three hours) in France, and twice-weekly to **Santander** (13 hours) in Spain.

Condor Ferries (www.condorferries.co.uk) Runs a weekly car-and-passenger service from Portsmouth to **Cherbourg** (6½ hours) between June and September.

LD Lines (www.ldlines.co.uk) Shuttles daily to **Le Havre** (five to eight hours) in France.

Bus

There are 13 National Express buses from **London** (£15, 2¼ hours) daily, plus 10 services to **Heathrow Airport** (£16, 3½ hours) which go via **Southampton** (40 minutes). Bus 700 runs to **Chichester** (1¼ hours) and **Brighton** (four hours) at least hourly.

Train

Trains run every 30 minutes from **London Victoria** (£30, 2½ hours) and **Waterloo** (£30, 1¾ hours) stations. For the Historic Dockyard get off at the final stop, Portsmouth Harbour.

Departures include the following:

Brighton (£15, 1½ hours, hourly)

Chichester (£7, 40 minutes, twice an hour)

Southampton (£9, one hour, three per hour)

Winchester (£10, one hour, hourly)

Getting Around

BUS Bus 6 runs every 15 minutes between Portsmouth Harbour bus station and South Parade Pier in Southsea, via Old Portsmouth.

BOAT **Gosport Passenger Ferry** (www.gosportferry.co.uk; adult/child return £2.70/1.80, bicycle £1; ⏲5.30am-midnight) Shuttles from Portsmouth Harbour train station to Gosport every 10 to 15 minutes.

TAXI Ranks near the bus station. Or call **Aquacars** (☎023-9266 6666).

Southampton

POP 239,000

A no-nonsense port city and gateway to the Isle of Wight, Southampton lies deep in the folds of the Solent inlet. Only fragments of the city's medieval core remain, thanks to merciless bombing in WWII. Decades earlier Southampton had waved the *Titanic* off on its ill-fated voyage, and a new museum evoking this extraordinary story, plus the chance to explore more of the city's past, make it well worth a day trip.

Sights & Activities

TOP CHOICE SeaCity Museum MUSEUM
(www.seacitymuseum.co.uk; Havelock Rd; adult/child £8.50/6; ⏲10am-5pm) Southampton's new headline attraction uses innovative exhibits to chart the history of the port and its people. *Titanic* displays include a 1:25 interactive scale model of the vessel, powerful oral testimonies from survivors, and a re-creation of the court room inquiry into the sinking.

Medieval Merchant's House MUSEUM
(EH; www.english-heritage.org.uk; French St; adult/child £4/2; ⏲noon-5pm Sun Apr-Sep) Brightly painted sea chests and replica period furniture dot this French merchant's home, which dates from 1290.

FREE Southampton Art Gallery ART GALLERY
(www.southampton.gov.uk/art; Commercial Rd; ⏲10am-5pm) Features an impressive selection of work by some of the biggest names in British art, including Spencer, Turner and Gainsborough.

FREE Guided Walks HERITAGE TOUR
(www.stga.org.uk; ⏲11am Tue, Thu, Sat & Sun Jun-Sep, Sun only Oct-Mar) Southampton has the third-largest section of 13th-century fortifications in the country; these free, 90-minute guided walks see you strolling beside and on top of the towering walls. Tours leave from Bargate, the city's northern medieval gate.

Information

Tourist Office (☎023-8083 3333; www.visit-southampton.co.uk; 9 Civic Centre Rd; ⏲9.30am-5pm Mon-Fri, to 4pm Sat) Ten minutes' walk east of the central train station, in the main library.

Getting There & Away

Air

Southampton International Airport (www.southamptonairport.com) Connects to more than 50 UK and European destinations, including Amsterdam, Paris and Dublin. Five trains per hour link the airport and the main train station (seven minutes).

Boat

Red Funnel (www.redfunnel.co.uk) Operates regular passenger and car ferries to the Isle of Wight.

Hythe Ferry (www.hytheferry.co.uk; adult/child return £5/3) This passenger vessel shuttles from the Town Quay to Hythe in the New Forest every half-hour.

Bus

Local Bus 6 goes to Lyndhurst, Brockenhurst and Lymington (hourly Monday to Saturday, five on Sunday).

National Express services:

Heathrow Airport (£15, 2½ hours, 10 daily) via Portsmouth.

London (£15, 2¼ hours, 13 daily).

Lymington (40 minutes, one daily) via Lyndhurst (20 minutes) in the New Forest.

Train

Three trains an hour run to **Portsmouth** (£9, one hour) and **Winchester** (£5.80, 20 minutes).

NEW FOREST NATIONAL PARK

With typical, accidental, English irony, the New Forest is anything but new – it was first proclaimed a royal hunting preserve in 1079. It's also not much of a forest, being mostly heathland. Semantics aside, its combined charms make it a delight to explore. Wild ponies mooch around pretty scrub land, deer flicker in the distance, and rare birds flit among the foliage; genteel villages dot the landscape, connected by a web of walking and cycling routes.

Activities

Cycling

The New Forest makes for superb cycling country, with 200 miles of trails linking the main villages and the key railway station at Brockenhurst.

Cycling in the New Forest (£2) shows the approved off-road and quieter 'on-road' routes. The *New Forest Cycle Experience Route Pack* (£4) features seven trips, ranging from a 4-mile glide through the forest to a 24-mile leg test round the cliffs of the Isle of Wight. The *Forest Leisure Cycling Route Pack* (£4) has six circular trails for all abilities – all start from the village of Burley.

Maps and guides can be bought from Lyndhurst tourist office (p259) or via its website.

As applies across the country, to rent bikes you'll need to pay a deposit (usually £20) and provide identification.

AA Bike Hire BIKE RENTAL
(☎023-8028 3349; www.aabikehirenewforest.co.uk; Fern Glen, Gosport Lane, Lyndhurst; adult/child per day £10/5)

Country Lanes BIKE RENTAL
(☎01590-622627; www.countrylanes.co.uk; Train Station, Brockenhurst; adult/child per day £16/9)

Forest Leisure Cycling BIKE RENTAL
(☎01425-403584; www.forestleisurecycling.co.uk; The Cross, Burley; adult/child per day £15/6)

New Forest Cycle Hire BIKE RENTAL
(☎01590-624204; www.newforestcyclehire.co.uk; Train Station, Brockenhurst; adult/child per day £14/7)

Horse Riding

Stables that welcome beginners:

Arniss Equestrian Centre HORSE RIDING
(☎01425-654114; www.arnissequestrian.co.uk; Godshill, Fordingbridge; per hr £35)

Burley Villa HORSE RIDING
(☎01425-610278; www.burleyvilla.co.uk; near New Milton; per hr £32)

Forest Park HORSE RIDING
(☎01590-623429; www.forestparkridingstables.co.uk; Rhienfield Rd, Brockenhurst; per hr £33)

Other Activities

The forest is prime **hiking** territory. Ordnance Survey (OS) produces a detailed, 1:25,000 Explorer map (*New Forest*; No 22, £8); Crimson Publishing's *New Forest National Park Short Walks* (£8) features 20 day-hikes.

MANAGING THE NEW FOREST

The New Forest is one of the few parts of England to remain largely untouched since Norman times, partly because the whole area has been protected ever since William the Conqueror officially named it a royal hunting ground in the 11th century.

The forest was declared a national park in 2005, and while the crown still owns 260 sq km of it, the remaining 130 sq km are owned by commoners and verderers, who traditionally reared ponies as work horses. Today the animals are either schooled for riding stables or left to graze the land at will. The verderers' status is protected by the Commoners' Charter, first laid down in 1077, which guaranteed them six basic rights, the most important being the right to pasture. Every year, the 300-odd verderers gather to elect five agisters, who are responsible for the daily management of the forest's 3000 ponies, 1800 cattle and smaller numbers of donkeys, pigs and sheep.

You can wander freely throughout the forest, but don't feed or touch the wild ponies. For safety, there's a 40mph speed limit – watch out for animals suddenly appearing in the road. If you find an injured pony, contact the **Lyndhurst Police** (☎0845 045 45 45).

Ranger Walks WALKING TOUR
(☎023-8028 6840; www.forestry.gov.uk; per person £5-10) Memorable dusk deer-watching safaris and wild-food foraging trips.

New Forest Activities CANOEING, ARCHERY
(☎01590-612377; www.newforestactivities.co.uk; High St, Beaulieu) Runs canoeing (adult/child per two hours £28/22), kayaking (per two hours £28) and archery (adult/child per 1½ hours £20/15).

Getting There & Around

Bus

Regular services run to Southampton and Bournemouth.

New Forest Tour (www.thenewforesttour.info; 1-day adult/child £10/4, 5-day £20/8; ⌚hourly 10am-5pm mid-Jun–mid-Sep) The hop-on/hop-off bus passes through Lyndhurst's main car park, Brockenhurst station, Lymington, Beaulieu and Exbury.

Train

Trains running to Brockenhurst:

Bournemouth (£7, 25 minutes, twice-hourly)

London Waterloo (£40, two hours, twice-hourly)

Lymington (twice-hourly) Local train.

Winchester (£11, 30 minutes, twice-hourly)

Lyndhurst & Brockenhurst

POP LYNDHURST 3053 / BROCKENHURST 3479

The quaint country villages of Lyndhurst and Brockenhurst are separated by just 4 miles and make for atmospheric bases from which to explore the rest of the national park. Both boast picturesque sleeping spots; Brockenhurst can lay claim to a superb eatery, while Lyndhurst is home to an evocative museum.

The **New Forest Centre**, in Lyndhurst, contains a **tourist office** (☎023-8028 2269; www.thenewforest.co.uk; High St, Lyndhurst; ⌚10am-5pm) with a wealth of information, including camping guides and walking and cycling maps. The centre also houses the **New Forest Museum** (www.newforestcentre.org.uk; High St, Lyndhurst; adult/child £4/free; ⌚10am-4pm), which features a local labourer's cottage (complete with socks drying beside the fire), potato dibbers and a cider press. Listen for recordings of the autumn pony sales, which take place after the annual drifts (roundups).

CAMPING IN THE NEW FOREST

The New Forest is a haven for campers. The **Forestry Commission** (www.campingintheforest.co.uk) runs eight relatively rural sites. Lyndhurst's tourist office (p259) has a free brochure detailing other designated areas; see also www.thenewforest.co.uk.

Just across the car park, the **library** (⌚9.30am-1pm Mon, Wed & Sat, 2-5.30pm Tue & Fri) has free internet access.

Sleeping

TOP CHOICE **The Pig** BOUTIQUE HOTEL £££
(☎01590-622354; www.thepighotel.co.uk; Beaulieu Rd, Brockenhurst; r £125-185; P 📶) What a delight: log baskets, croquet mallets and ranks of guest gumboots give this hotel a country house air; espresso machines and mini-larders lend bedrooms a luxury touch. In fact, all this effortless elegance makes it feel like you're easing into life at a friend's (very stylish) rural retreat. There is an excellent restaurant (p260).

Daisybank Cottage BOUTIQUE B&B ££
(☎01590-622086; www.bedandbreakfast-newforest.co.uk; Sway Rd, Brockenhurst; s £75, d £90-135; P 📶) A wealth of little flourishes make a huge difference here: range-baked cakes on arrival; local goodie-packed breakfasts (think strawberry and Champagne jam); iPod docks in gorgeous bedrooms. Feeling romantic? The Garden Room, apparently, prompts the most proposals.

Crown HOTEL ££
(☎023-8028 2922; www.crownhotel-lyndhurst.co.uk; 9 High St, Lyndhurst; s £65-85 d £95-145; P @ 📶) There's such a deeply established feel to this oak-panelled, old-English coaching inn that you half expect to see a well-trained butler gliding down the grand stairs. The mullioned windows and ancient beams frame polished wardrobes, rich furnishings and a four-poster bed or two.

Little Hayes B&B ££
(☎023-8028 3816; www.littlehayes.co.uk; 43 Romsey Rd, Lyndhurst; d £80-90; P 📶) Moulded ceilings, old oak banisters and the odd chandelier speak of the age of this Edwardian

guesthouse. The breakfasts are full of New Forest produce.

Burwood Lodge B&B ££
(023-8028 2445; www.burwoodlodge.co.uk; 27 Romsey Rd, Lyndhurst; s/d/f £55/75/95; P) The pool table, garden and trampoline make this ideal for families; light rooms and an edge-of-village location make it good for the child-free, too.

Eating

TOP CHOICE **The Pig** MODERN BRITISH ££
(01590-622354; www.thepighotel.co.uk; Beaulieu Rd, Brockenhurst; mains £14-26; lunch & dinner daily, pizzas 2-6pm Fri-Sun;) Add this to your must-do list. Home-grown and own-reared produce packs this hotel's imaginative menu, including rarities like crayfish, quail, and smoked sea salt. Eat inside in style or enjoy a flat-bread pizza on the terrace beside the roaring wood oven – toppings include tomatoes, smoked chilli and home-cured ham. The rooms (p259) here are an excellent place to stay the night.

Waterloo Arms PUB £
(www.waterlooarmsnewforest.co.uk; Pikes Hill, Lyndhurst; mains £11) This cosy 17th-century thatched pub serves hearty grub and excellent ales in a snug, wood-beamed interior.

Getting There & Away

BOAT Hythe Ferry (023-8084 0722; www.hytheferry.co.uk; adult/child return £5/3) carries foot passengers between Southampton and Hythe (12 minutes, every 30 minutes), 13 miles east of Lyndhurst.

BUS Bus 6 shuttles between Lyndhurst, Brockenhurst and Lymington (hourly Monday to Saturday, five on Sunday); so does the New Forest Tour (p259).

TRAIN Trains run twice an hour between Brockenhurst and Lymington.

Around Lyndhurst

Petrol-heads, historians and ghost-hunters all gravitate to **Beaulieu** (www.beaulieu.co.uk; adult/child £19/9.50; 10am-6pm) – pronounced *bew*-lee – an all-in-one vintage car museum, stately home and tourist complex based on the site of what was once England's most important 13th-century Cistercian monastery. Following Henry VIII's monastic land-grab of 1536, the abbey fell to the ancestors of current proprietors, the Montague family.

Car enthusiasts will be in raptures at Lord Montague's **National Motor Museum**, a splendid collection of vehicles that sometimes seem more like strange hybrid boats or planes. It's hard to resist the romance of the early classics, or the oomph of winning F1 cars. Jet-powered vehicles include *Bluebird,* which famously broke the 403mph (649km/h) land-speed record in 1964. Look out, too, for Mr Bean's Austin Mini and James Bond's gadget-packed speed machines.

Beaulieu's grand but indefinably homely **palace** began life as a 14th-century Gothic abbey gatehouse, but received a 19th-century Scottish Baronial makeover from Baron Montague in the 1860s. Don't be surprised if you hear eerie Gregorian chanting or feel the hairs on the back of your neck quiver – the abbey is supposedly one of England's most haunted buildings.

The New Forest Tour (p259) stops directly outside the complex on its circular route via Lyndhurst, Brockenhurst and Lymington.

Buckler's Hard

For such a tiny place, this attractive huddle of 18th-century cottages near the mouth of the River Beaulieu has a big history. It started life in 1722, when one of the dukes of Montague built a port to finance a Caribbean expedition. His dream was never realised, but when the war with France came, this embryonic village with a sheltered gravel waterfront became a secret boatyard where several of Nelson's triumphant Battle of Trafalgar warships were built. It also played its part in 20th-century clandestine wartime manoeuvrings – the preparations for the D-Day landings.

The hamlet is now a fascinating heritage centre – **Buckler's Hard Story** (01590-616203; www.bucklershard.co.uk; Buckler's Hard; adult/child £6.20/4.40; 10am-5pm) – which features immaculately preserved 18th-century labourers' cottages. The **maritime museum** charts the inlet's shipbuilding history and its role in WWII; for a little light relief, seek out Nelson's quaint baby clothes.

Nearby, the luxurious **Master Builder's House** (0844-815 3399; www.themasterbuilders.co.uk; Buckler's Hard; d from £130; P) is a beautifully restored 18th-century hotel with 25 grand rooms featuring soft light-

THREE-DAY CYCLE TRIP

Start your woodland two-wheeled adventure with some research at Lyndhurst's tourist office (p259). Then limber up with an 8-mile, largely off-road jaunt via Denny Wood south to the edge of Brockenhurst, before checking into the gourmet pamper pad that is The Pig (p259). Day two is a 9-mile pedal east via copses and quiet roads to the **National Motor Museum** at Beaulieu (p260). Next comes the 2-mile dash southeast to **Buckler's Hard** and the chance to soothe weary limbs at the super-comfy digs at the Master Builder's House (p260).

The next day it's back to Brockenhurst, via a more southerly route; from there a looping trail takes you 9 miles north and then west past pubs and an arboretum back to Lyndhurst, having explored some of the best cycle routes the New Forest has to offer.

ing, burnished trunks and plush fabrics. The gorgeous restaurant (mains £13 to £19) overlooks the river, while the wood-panelled Yachtsman's Bar serves classy pub grub (mains from £6).

Swiftsure boats operate 30-minute **river cruises** (adult/child £4.50/2.50; ⏲Apr-Oct) from the waterfront between Easter and October.

Buckler's Hard is 2 miles downstream from Beaulieu; a picturesque riverside walking trail links the two.

Lymington

POP 15,383

Yachting haven, New Forest base and jumping-off point to the Isle of Wight – the appealing Georgian harbour town of Lymington has several strings to its tourism bow. This former smugglers' port offers exquisite places to eat and sleep, plenty of nautical shops and, in Quay St, an utterly quaint cobbled lane.

Sights & Activities

St Barbe Museum MUSEUM
(☎01590-676969; www.stbarbe-museum.org.uk; New St; adult/child £4/2; ⏲10am-4pm Mon-Sat) Explores tales of boat-builders, sailing ships, contraband and farming through a mix of models and artefacts.

Puffin Cruises BOAT TOUR
(☎07850 947618; www.puffincruiseslymington.com) Your chance to ride the waves without having to buy a yacht. The best trip is an exhilarating surge across the Solent to the Isle of Wight (adult/child £17/7, Sunday to Friday, May to October), where the Needles lighthouse and towering chalk stacks loom from the water. They also do a two-hour sunset cruise in high summer.

Sleeping

TOP CHOICE **Mill at Gordleton** BOUTIQUE HOTEL £££
(☎01590-682219; www.themillatgordleton.co.uk; Silver St, Hordle; s/d/ste £125/165/245; P wi-fi) Step inside here and know, instantly, you're going to be looked after – beautifully. Wicker, velvet and gingham dot exquisite rooms, while the garden is a magical mix of rushing water, fairy lights and modern sculpture. The acclaimed restaurant (mains £6 to £18) focuses firmly on the homemade and the home-grown. The Mill is 4 miles west of Lymington.

Stanwell House BOUTIQUE HOTEL £££
(☎0844-7046820; www.stanwellhouse.com; 14 High St; s £99, d £140-180, ste £220; @ wi-fi) The epitome of discreet luxury; cane chairs grace the elegant conservatory, and eclectic bedrooms boast stand-alone baths, gently distressed furniture and plush throws. The Drydock bar has nautical touches, while the seafood menu (served noon to 9.30pm) features everything from tapas (£6) to vast shellfish platters for two (£50).

Havenhurst House B&B £
(☎01590-671130; www.havenhurstbedandbreakfast.co.uk; Milford Rd; s/d £35/50; P) Sleep spots this cheap are normally nowhere near this nice. This roomy modern family home has underfloor heating, tasteful bedrooms, stylish bathrooms and top-quality breakfasts. It's a mile from the centre of town.

Bluebird B&B ££
(☎01590-676908; www.bluebirdrestaurant.co.uk; 4 Quay St; d/f £85/115) An ancient cottage of dark beams, white walls and sparkly new bathrooms in the midst of photogenic Quay St.

Eating

Ship Inn PUB ££

(www.theshiplymington.co.uk; The Quay; mains £5-15; ⊙food 11am-10pm) A pub for all seasons: knock back summertime drinks on the waterside terrace, while in winter a toasty log burner will get you warm. Hearty food ranges from French onion soup to slow-roast lamb; drinks totter from tangy real ales to vintage champagne.

Egan's EUROPEAN ££

(☎01590-676165; Gosport St; 2-/3-course lunch £15/18, mains £16-24; ⊙Tue-Sat) The wooden tables here are highly polished and so is the food. Rich local ingredients are transformed by well-travelled flavours – the local cod comes with chorizo, the guinea fowl with porcini mushroom risotto.

Information

The **library** (North Close; ⊙9.30am-5pm Mon, Thu & Sat, to 7pm Tue & Fri, to 1pm Wed) has free internet access.

Getting There & Away

BOAT **Wightlink Ferries** (☎0871 376 1000; www.wightlink.co.uk) runs car and passenger ferries hourly to the Isle of Wight.

BUS The New Forest Tour (p259) stops at Lymington.

TRAIN Lymington has two train stations: Lymington Town and Lymington Pier. Isle of Wight ferries connect with Lymington Pier. Trains run to **Southampton** (£9, 30 minutes, every half-hour) via Brockenhurst.

ISLE OF WIGHT

On the Isle of Wight these days there's something groovy in the air. For decades this slab of rock anchored off Portsmouth has been a magnet for family holidays, and it still has seaside kitsch by the bucket and spade. But now the proms and amusement arcades are framed by pockets of pure funkiness. A brace of music festivals draws the party crowd, you can feast on just-caught seafood in cool fishermen's cafes, and 'glamping' rules – here campsites are dotted with eco-yurts and retro campervans. Yet still the isle's principal appeal remains: a mild climate, myriad outdoorsy activities and a 25-mile shore lined with beaches, dramatic white cliffs and beguiling sand dunes.

CAR FERRY COSTS

The cost of car ferries to the Isle of Wight varies enormously. Make savings by booking ahead, asking about special offers and travelling off-peak. Some deals include admission to island attractions. Booking online can be £20 cheaper.

Activities

Cycling

With 200 miles of cycle routes, the Isle of Wight makes pedal-pushers smile. The island's official visitor **website** (www.islandbreaks.co.uk) has a range of suggested trips, complete with maps. A **Cycling Festival** (☎01983-203891; www.sunseaandcycling.com) is held every September.

Bike rentals start at around £12 per day, or £45 per week. Many firms deliver and collect on orders over £30.

Tavcycles BIKE RENTAL

(☎01983-812989; www.tavcycles.co.uk; 140 High St, Ryde)

Wight Cycle BIKE RENTAL

(☎0800 112 3751; www.thewightcycle.com; Zigzag Rd, Ventnor)

Wight Cycle Hire BIKE RENTAL

(☎01983-761800; www.wightcyclehire.co.uk; Station Rd, Yarmouth)

Walking

This is one of the best spots in southern England for rambling, with 500 miles of well-marked walking paths, including 67 miles of coastal routes. Visit the official visitor website (p262) for maps and routes. The island's two-week **Walking Festival** (www.isleofwightwalkingfestival.co.uk), held in May, is one of the UK's largest.

Water Sports

Water sports are serious business on the Isle of Wight. Cowes is the sailing centre; surfers and wind- and kitesurfers flock to the southwest, especially around Compton Bay. The Yarmouth to Freshwater paddle is popular with kayakers, while power boats run trips (p266) out to the Needles.

Isle of Wight Adventure ACTIVITY CENTRE

(☎01983-755 838; www.isleofwightadventureactivities.co.uk; Freshwater Bay) Runs activities ranging from surfing and kayaking (per two

Isle of Wight

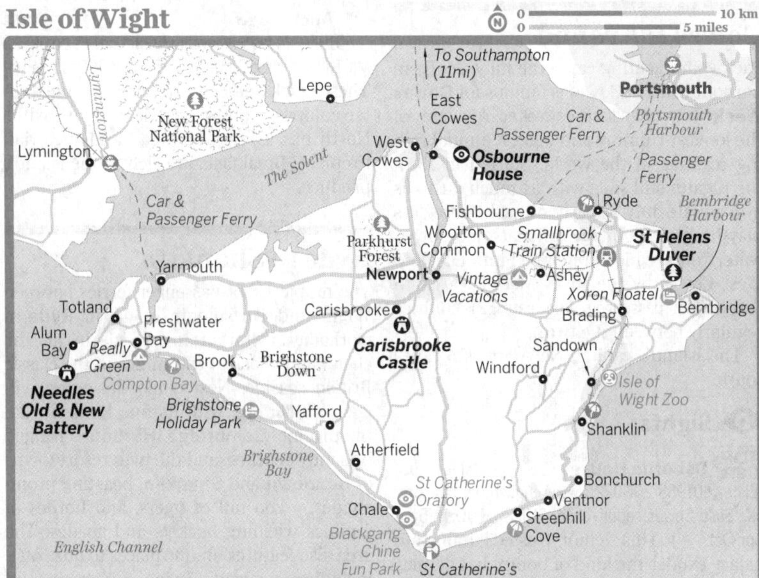

hours/day £30/55) to archery (£10), horse riding (per hour £25) and fossil hunting (adult/child £4/3).

Information

The Isle of Wight closed its tourist offices, as part of spending cuts, and replaced them with a council-run **Tourist Information Call Centre** (☎01983-813813; www.islandbreaks.co.uk; ⊙8am-6pm Mon-Fri, 9am-1pm Sat). There are small-scale info points at the Newport, Ryde and Yarmouth bus stations.

Getting There & Away

Hovertravel (☎08434-87 88 87; www.hovertravel.co.uk; day-return adult/child £18/8; ⊙hourly) Shuttles foot passengers between **Southsea** (a Portsmouth suburb) and **Ryde**.

Red Funnel (☎0844-844 9988; www.redfunnel.co.uk) Operates car-and-passenger ferries between **Southampton** and **East Cowes** (day-return adult/child £15/8, from £45 with car, 55 minutes, hourly) and high-speed passenger ferries between **Southampton** and **West Cowes** (day-return adult/child £21/11, 25 minutes, twice hourly).

Wightlink Ferries (☎0871-376 1000; www.wightlink.co.uk) Operates passenger ferries every half-hour from **Portsmouth** to **Ryde** (day-return adult/child £16/8, 20 minutes). It also runs half-hourly car-and-passenger ferries from **Portsmouth** to **Fishbourne** (40 minutes) and from **Lymington** to **Yarmouth** (30 minutes). For both, an adult/child day-return ticket costs £13/7. Car fares start at around £55 for a short-break return.

Getting Around

Car

1st Call (☎01983-400055; www.1stcallcarsales.com; 15 College Close, Sandown; per day/week from £30/130) Collects and delivers island-wide.

Bus

Southern Vectis (www.islandbuses.info) Runs buses between the eastern towns roughly every 30 minutes; regular services to the remoter southwest, especially sections between Blackgang Chine and Brook, are less frequent. Between April and September the **Island Coaster** makes one return circuit a day along the southern shore from Ryde to Alum Bay in the far southwest. Rover Tickets are available for a day (adult/child £10/5) or a week (£20/12).

Train

Island Line (www.island-line.com) Trains run twice-hourly from **Ryde** to **Shanklin**, via **Sandown**, **Brading** and **Smallbrook Junction** (25 minutes). Day rover tickets are available (adult/family £5.50/14).

Cowes & Around

Pack your yachting cap – the hilly Georgian harbour town of Cowes is famous for **Cowes Week** (www.skandiacowesweek.co.uk), one of the longest-running and biggest annual sailing regattas in the world. Started in 1826, the regatta still sails with as much gusto as ever in late July or early August. Fibreglass playthings and vintage sailboats line Cowes' waterfronts, which are lopped into East and West Cowes by the River Medina; a chain **ferry** (foot passengers free, cars £2) shuttles regularly between the two.

The island's capital, Newport, is 5 miles south.

Sights

TOP CHOICE Osborne House STATELY HOUSE
(EH; ☎01983-200022; www.english-heritage.org.uk; East Cowes; adult/child £13/8; ⊙10am-5pm Apr-Oct; P) This lemon-frosted, Italianate palace exudes the kind of pomp that defines the Victorian era. It was built in the 1840s at the behest of Queen Victoria, and the monarch grieved here for many years after her husband's death, and died here herself in 1901. The extravagant rooms include the opulent Durbar Room; another highlight is a carriage ride to the Swiss Cottage where the royal ankle-biters would play. Between November and March, visits are by booked tours only.

Carisbrooke Castle CASTLE
(EH; ☎01983-522107; www.english-heritage.org.uk; Carisbrooke, near Newport; adult/child £7.50/4.50; ⊙10am-5pm Apr-Oct; P) Charles I was imprisoned here before his execution in 1649. Today you can clamber the sturdy ramparts and play bowls on the very green the doomed monarch used.

Sleeping

Fountain HOTEL ££
(☎01983-292397; www.fountaininn-cowes.co.uk; High St, West Cowes; s £90, d £100-120; ☎) American President Thomas Jefferson and France's King Charles X have both stayed at this cosy harbourside inn. Today it's creaky rather than swish, but sash windows and irregular walls bestow an old-fashioned charm. Enjoy espressos and pastries in the cool cafe; pub grub (mains £9) in the snug bar; and boat-watching from the seafront patio.

Anchorage B&B ££
(☎01983-247975; www.anchoragecowes.co.uk; 23 Mill Hill Rd, West Cowes; s £40-60, d £60-85; P ☎) These spick-and-span rooms are named after compass points: East is spacious, while North has a brass bedstead and Victorian fireplace. Breakfasts are rich in the island's produce.

Ryde to Shanklin

The nippiest foot-passenger ferries between Wight and Portsmouth alight in **Ryde**, a workaday Victorian town rich in all the cheap and cheerful trimmings of the classic British seaside. Next come the cutesy village of **Brading**, with its fine Roman villa; photogenic **Bembridge Harbour**, fringed by sandy beaches; and the twin resort towns of **Sandown** and **Shanklin**, boasting promenades, a zoo full of tigers, and hordes of families wielding buckets and spades. The area also features unique places to doze off – including a decommissioned warship and vintage airstream trailers.

Sights

Brading Roman Villa ROMAN RUINS
(☎01983-406223; www.bradingromanvilla.org.uk; Morton Old Rd, Brading; adult/child £6.50/3.50; ⊙9.30am-4pm) The exquisitely preserved mosaics here (including a famous cockerel-headed man) make this one of the finest Romano-British sites in the UK. Wooden walkways lead over rubble walls and brightly painted tiles, allowing you to gaze right down onto the ruins below.

St Helens Duver NATURE RESERVE
(NT; www.nationaltrust.org.uk; ⊙24hr; P) Head for this idyllic sand and shingle spit bordering the mouth of the River Yar, and walk trails snaking past swathes of sea pink, marram grass and rare clovers. It's signed from the village of St Helens, near Bembridge Harbour.

Isle of Wight Steam Railway HERITAGE RAILWAY
(☎01983-882204; www.iwsteamrailway.co.uk; ⊙Apr-Sep) Chugs regularly from Smallbrook Junction to **Wootton Common** (return adult/child £9.50/5, 1st class £14.50/10, one hour).

Isle of Wight Zoo ZOO
(☎01983-403883; www.isleofwightzoo.com; Yaverland Rd, Sandown; adult/child £10/7.50; ⊙10am-6pm Mar-Oct; P) A conservation-focused

affair, with one of Europe's largest collections of tigers, plus some very cute lemurs.

Sleeping & Eating

TOP CHOICE **Vintage Vacations** CAMPSITE £
(07802-758113; www.vintagevacations.co.uk; Ashey, near Ryde; 4-person caravans per week £450-650; Apr-Oct; P) The bevy of 1960s airstream trailers on this farm are retro chic personified. Their gleaming aluminium shells shelter lovingly selected furnishings ranging from cheerful patchwork blankets to vivid tea cosies. Alternatively, opt for a beach-shack retreat, a 1930s Scout Hut, or the Mission: a late-Victorian tin chapel.

Xoron Floatel FLOATING B&B ££
(01983-874596; www.xoronfloatel.co.uk; Bembridge Harbour; d £60; P) Your chance to go to sleep on a gunboat – this former WWII warship is now a cheery, bunting-draped houseboat. Comfy cabins come complete with snug bathrooms, while the views from the flower-framed sun deck are simply superb.

Kasbah B&B BISTRO ££
(01983-810088; www.kasbahryde.com; 76 Union St, Ryde; d £65-85; @) More North Africa than East Wight, Kasbah brings a funky blast of the Mediterranean to Ryde. Intricate lanterns, stripy throws and furniture fresh from Marrakesh dot the chic rooms; tapas (£3.50; available lunch and dinner) are on offer in the chilled-out bar.

Rijnstroom IV HOUSEBOAT ££
(07563 722846; www.rijnstroomiv.co.uk; Bembridge Harbour; d £58-75; P) Moored amid a community of houseboats, this 92-ft Dutch barge has compact cabins (not all en suite) and long tables on deck for alfresco breakfasts. The water taxi to St Helens Duver pulls up outside.

Crab & Lobster PUB ££
(www.crabandlobsterinn.co.uk; 32 Forelands Field Rd, Bembridge; mains £11) Unsurprisingly, seafood is their speciality – from crab and lobster soup (£6) to shellfish platters to share (£60).

Ventnor & Around

The Victorian town of **Ventnor** slaloms so steeply down the island's southern coast that you'd be forgiven for mistaking it for the south of France. The winding streets are home to a scattering of quirky boutiques, while local hotels, eateries and the atmospheric **Steephill Cove** (p265) are well worth a detour.

To the west, the island's southernmost point is marked by the stocky 19th-century **St Catherine's Lighthouse** and its 14th-century counterpart, **St Catherine's Oratory**. Nearby, kid-friendly **Blackgang Chine Fun Park** (01983-730330; www.blackgangchine.com; admission £10.50; 10.30am-4.30pm Mar-Oct), features water gardens, animated shows and a hedge maze.

Sleeping

Hambrough BOUTIQUE HOTEL £££
(01983-856333; www.thehambrough.com; Hambrough Rd, Ventnor; d £170-280; P) It's very hard to say which views are better: the 180-degree vistas out to sea, or those of super-sleek rooms where espresso machines and heated floors keep luxury levels set sky-high.

St Augustine Villa B&B ££
(Harbour View; 01983-852285; www.harbourviewhotel.co.uk; Esplanade, Ventnor; s £81-94 d £88-103; P) Formerly known as the Harbour View, this delightful Victorian guesthouse offers crisp white linen bedrooms that look

STEEPHILL COVE

You can't drive to Steephill Cove, which makes it all the more special. Its tiny, sandy beach is fringed by buildings that range from stone cottages to rickety-looking shacks. Beach finds festoon porches dotted with driftwood furniture and draped with fishing nets; a tiny clapboard lighthouse presides over the scene. It's let out as a fabulous self-catering **apartment** (07801 899 747; www.theboathouse-steephillcove.co.uk; Steephill Cove; sleeps 6, per week £1100-1800); a couple of other gorgeous options are nearby. Two great places to eat, the Boathouse (p266) and the Crab Shed (p266), add to the appeal.

Steephill Cove is 1 mile west of Ventnor. Walk from the Botanical Gardens, or hike from the hillside car park 200m west of Ventnor Esplanade, then follow the (steep) coast path until you arrive.

onto expansive seascapes – watch the sunset from a sofa, or the waves roll from a four-poster bed. The window-seated Tower Room sees light and views pour in from three sides.

Eating

TOP CHOICE Boathouse SEAFOOD ££
(☎01983-852747; www.theboathouse-steephill-cove.co.uk; Steephill Cove; mains £16-32; ⊙lunch Thu-Tue Jun-early Sep) Arrive early enough, and you'll see Steephill Cove's fishermen (Jimmy and Mark) landing your lunch – the sanded wooden tables here are just steps from the sea. It makes a spellbinding spot to sip some chilled wine, sample succulent lobster and revel in Wight's new-found driftwood chic.

Pond Cafe MODERN BRITISH ££
(☎01983-855666; www.robert-thompson.com; Bonchurch; mains £8-25) This smart little bistro brims with local produce, from the beef carpaccio starter to the island cheeses (soft and blue) for dessert. In-the-know locals book a terrace table for super-value three-course lunches (£18) or early-evening meals (two courses £15).

Crab Shed CAFE £
(Steephill Cove; snacks £4; ⊙noon-3pm Apr-Sep) Lobster pots and fishing boats line the slipway outside a shack that's a riot of sea-smoothed spas, cork floats and faded buoys. Irresistible treats include meaty crab salads, mackerel ciabatta and crumbly crab pasties.

ISLE OF WIGHT FESTIVALS

The isle's festival tradition stretches back to the early 1970s, when 600,000 hippies came to see the Doors, the Who, Joni Mitchell and rock icon Jimi Hendrix's last performance. Decades later the gatherings are still some of England's top musical events.

The **Isle of Wight Festival** (www.isleofwightfestival.org), held in mid-June, has been headlined by the likes of Muse, Pearl Jam, the Foo Fighters and the Rolling Stones, while **Bestival** (www.bestival.net), in early to mid-September, delights in an eclectic, counter-culture feel, drawing the Super Furry Animals, Scissor Sisters, Fatboy Slim and more.

West Wight

Rural and remote, Wight's westerly corner is where the island really comes into its own. Sheer white cliffs rear from a surging sea as the stunning coastline peels west to **Alum Bay** and the most famous chunks of chalk in the region: **the Needles**. These jagged rocks rise shardlike out of the sea, forming a line like the backbone of a prehistoric sea monster. West Wight is also home to arguably the isle's best beach: sandy, windswept **Compton Bay**.

Sights & Activities

Needles Old Battery FORT
(NT; ☎01983-754772; www.nationaltrust.org.uk; adult/child £4.60/2.30; ⊙10.30am-5pm mid-Mar–Oct) Originally established in 1862, this remote gun emplacement was used as an observation post during WWII – today you can explore the Victorian cartridge store, trek down a 60m cliff tunnel to a searchlight lookout and drink in the extraordinary views.

New Battery (⊙11am-4pm Tue, Sat & Sun Apr-Oct) is on the same site. Displays in its vaults outline the clandestine space-rocket testing carried out here in the 1950s.

Walk to the battery along the cliffs from Alum Bay (1 mile) or hop on the tourist **bus** (www.islandbuses.info; adult/child £10/5; ⊙Apr-Sep) that runs twice-hourly between battery and bay.

Needles Pleasure Cruises BOAT TRIPS
(☎01983-761587; www.needlespleasurecruises.co.uk; Alum Bay; adult/child £5/3; ⊙10.30am-4.30pm Apr-Oct) Twenty-minute voyages from Alum Bay beach to the Needles, which provide close-up views of those towering white cliffs.

Sleeping

TOP CHOICE Really Green GLAMPING £
(☎07802 678591; www.thereallygreenholidaycompany.com; Blackbridge Rd, Freshwater Bay; yurt per week £345-595; ⊙Apr-Oct; Ⓟ) The epitome of 'glamping' (glamorous camping), the five-person, fully furnished yurts on this tree-shaded site feature four-poster beds, futons, wood-burning stoves and time-worn antiques. You can even have continental breakfast delivered to your tent flap – roughing it has never been so smooth.

SURF REEF

Bournemouth boasts Europe's first ever artificial surf reef, a clump of 70m long sandbags that's submerged 220m off **Boscombe Pier**. It's designed to create faster, more challenging breaks, but teething troubles and propeller damage have set debate swirling around whether it's delivered on its aims.

The reef itself isn't for beginners, but you can learn nearby. The **Sorted Surf School**, (☎01202-300668; www.bournemouth-surfschool.co.uk; Overstrand Building, Undercliff Dr), right beside Boscombe Pier, does lessons (£30 for two hours) and hires out wetsuits (two/eight hours £10/30), surfboards (two/eight hours £10/30), bodyboards (two/eight hours £5/15) and kayaks (one/four hours £15/45).

Brighstone HOLIDAY PARK £
(☎01983-740244; www.brighstone-holidays.co.uk; tent sites per adult £7, B&B d £65, 2-person cabins per week from £330; P) Perched atop cliffs looking towards the spectacular bluffs at Alum Bay. On the A3055, 6 miles east of Freshwater.

Totland Bay YHA HOSTEL £
(☎0845-371 9348; www.yha.org.uk; Hirst Hill, Totland Bay; dm £17; P) Family-friendly Victorian house overlooking the water, with a maximum of eight beds per room.

DORSET

For many, Dorset conjures up the kind of halcyon holiday memories found in flickering 1970s home movies, and the county does still deliver arcade-loads of seaside kitsch to soak up. But it also offers so much more. Here you can hike, kayak or swim beside the sea-carved bays and rock arches of the stunning Jurassic Coast, then scour fossil-packed beaches for your own prehistoric souvenir. You can also immerse yourself in Thomas Hardy's lyrical landscape, then discover massive Iron Age hill forts, rude chalk figures, must-see stately homes and fairy-tale castles. Hang out in resorts packed with party animals then chill out on beaches beloved by multimillionaires. Or learn to harness the wind in waters that were used for sailing during the 2012 Olympics. These days there's a whole new side of Dorset waiting to be explored.

Information

Jurassic Coast (www.jurassiccoast.com) Official World Heritage site website.

Visit Dorset (www.visit-dorset.com) The county's official tourism website.

Getting Around

BUS A key provider is **First** (www.firstgroup.com). **Wilts & Dorset** (www.wdbus.co.uk) links rural and urban areas in Wiltshire and Dorset.

TRAIN One mainline runs from Bristol and Bath through Dorchester West to Weymouth. The other connects London with Weymouth, via Southampton, Bournemouth, Poole and Dorchester South.

Bournemouth

POP 168,100

If one thing has shaped Bournemouth it's the beach. This glorious, 7-mile strip of soft sand first drew holiday-makers in the Victorian days. Today, as well as grey-haired coach parties, the resort attracts boozed-up stag parties, and on Saturday nights fancy-dress is everywhere; angels in L-plates meet men in mankinis. But Bournemouth is more than just a bright 'n' breezy party town. It also boasts the area's best surf spot, some hip hideaways, great restaurants and boat trips to the start of Dorset's spectacular Jurassic Coast.

Sights & Activities

Bournemouth Beach BEACH
Backed by an impressive array of 3000 deckchairs, Bournemouth's sandy shoreline regularly clocks up seaside awards. It stretches from Southborne in the far east to Alum Chine in the west – an immense promenade backed by ornamental gardens, kids' playgrounds and cafes. The resort also prides itself on two piers (Bournemouth and Boscombe). Around Bournemouth Pier you can hire brightly painted beach **huts** (☎0845-055 0968; per day/week £25/95), deckchairs (per day £2), windbreaks (£2.50) and parasols (£4).

BEACH PODS

The traditional British beach chalet just got funky. Boscombe's attempted rebirth as an oasis of surfer chic includes a range of high-tech **beach pods** (☎0845-0550968; www.boscombeover strand.co.uk; per week £50-300, daytime only). Overlooking Boscombe Pier, each has been individually designed by Wayne and Gerardine Hemingway (of Red or Dead fame), and feature oh-so-stylish murals and furnishings, microwaves and toasted-sandwich makers. So head out onto your own balcony, settle back in your limited-edition director's chair, take in the panoramic views and watch the beachgoers playing in the waves below

At the **East Cliff Lift Railway** (☎01202-451781; Undercliff Dr; adult/child £1.20/80p; ⏰Easter-Oct), cable cars on rails whiz up bracken-covered slopes, cutting out the short, steep hike up the zigzag paths.

Alum Chine GARDEN

(Mountbatten Rd; ⏰24hr) This award-winning subtropical enclave dates from the 1920s, providing a taste of Bournemouth's golden age. Set 1.5 miles west from Bournemouth Pier, its plants come from the Canary Islands, New Zealand, Mexico and the Himalayas; their bright-red bracts, silver thistles and purple flowers frame views of a glittering sea.

In the centre of Bournemouth, the **Pleasure Gardens** stretch back for 1.5 miles from behind Bournemouth Pier in three colourful sweeps.

Russell-Cotes MUSEUM

(☎01202-451858; www.russell-cotes.bournemouth.gov.uk; Russell-Cotes Rd; adult/child £5/4; ⏰10am-5pm Tue-Sun) This ostentatious mix of Italianate villa and Scottish baronial pile was built at the end of the 1800s for Merton and Annie Russell-Cotes as somewhere to showcase the remarkable range of souvenirs gathered on their world travels. Look out for a plaster version of the Parthenon frieze, Maori woodcarvings and Persian tiles. Paintings include those by Rossetti, Edwin Landseer and William Frith.

Oceanarium AQUARIUM

(☎01202-311993; www.oceanarium.co.uk; Pier Approach; adult/child £10/6.50; ⏰10am-6pm) Underwater tunnels bring you eye-to-eye with mean-looking sharks, massive moray eels and giant turtles in watery worlds ranging from Key West and the Ganges to Africa and the Med.

Rib Experience BOAT TRIP

(☎01202-496772; www.bournemouthribexperience.co.uk; Bournemouth Pier; adult/child £25/20) Dorset's extraordinary World Heritage Jurassic Coast starts some 5 miles west of Bournemouth at the Old Harry Rocks. These spray-dashed, 40-minute trips aboard 8m rigid inflatable boats blast past Sandbanks and across the mouth of Poole Harbour, providing up-close views of the chalky columns. The stacks used to be massive arches before erosion brought the tops tumbling down – huge scooped-out sections of cliff clearly show how the sea begins the erosion process.

Sleeping

Bournemouth has huge concentrations of budget B&Bs, especially around the central St Michael's Rd and to the east of the train station.

TOP CHOICE **Urban Beach** BOUTIQUE HOTEL ££

(☎01202-301509; www.urbanbeach.co.uk; 23 Argyll Rd; d £60-180; P@📶) Bournemouth's finest hipster hotel combines a kooky counter-culture vibe with luxury lodgings and top-notch service. Rooms are achingly but casually stylish and you can borrow everything from brightly coloured wellingtons to toothpaste and iPods. There's a cool bistro downstairs and a heated deck for predinner cocktails, and Boscombe Beach is just five minutes' walk away.

Langtry Manor HOTEL ££

(☎01202-553887; www.langtrymanor.com; Derby Rd; s from £102, d £102-240; P📶) Prepare for a delicious whiff of royal indiscretion – this minimansion was built by Edward VII for his mistress Lillie Langtry. Opulent grandeur is everywhere, from the red-carpeted entrance to immense chandeliers. Modern flourishes include artful lighting and Jacuzzis, while the King's Suite is a real jaw-dropper: a monumental, climb-up-to-get-in four-poster bed; the fireplace is big enough to feature a couple of chairs.

Balincourt B&B ££
(☎01202-552962; www.balincourt.co.uk; 58 Christchurch Rd; s £53-60, d £86-120; P 📶) This Victorian guesthouse is a labour of love – even the china on the tea tray is hand painted to match each room's colour scheme. Decor is refined and lightly floral, while elegant umbrella stands and ticking grandfather clocks add to the heritage feel.

Amarillo B&B ££
(☎01202-553884; www.amarillohotel.co.uk; 52 Frances Rd; s £45, d £60-70; P 📶) Minimalist decor, beige throws and clumps of twisted willow make this a real find – an inexpensive Bournemouth sleep spot with style.

Marlins B&B ££
(☎01202-299645; www.marlinshotel.com; 2 West Cliff Rd; s £40, d £60-85) You'll get all the home comforts at Marlins: thick fluffy towels, armchairs and sweet treats on the tea tray. Plus an owner who's more like a friendly concierge – he'll even book you a restaurant table for dinner.

Bournemouth Backpackers HOSTEL £
(☎01202-299491; www.bournemouthbackpackers.co.uk; 3 Frances Rd; dm £14; 📶) Plain dorms in a small (19-bed) suburban house. It's for non-UK citizens only; reservations by email, or by phone between 5.30pm and 6.30pm, Sunday to Friday in summer (5pm to 7pm Sundays only in winter).

Eating

West Beach SEAFOOD ££
(☎01202-587785; www.west-beach.co.uk; Pier Approach; mains £13-20; ⊙breakfast, lunch & dinner) A firm favourite with Bournemouth's foodie crowd, this bustling eatery delivers both award-winning dishes and the best views in town. Try Dorset sea bass with braised fennel or a seafood platter for two (£50) crammed with crab, oysters, langoustines, clams and cockles – best enjoyed on the decked dining terrace that juts out over the sand.

Urban Reef BAR, BISTRO ££
(www.urbanreef.com; Undercliff Dr, Boscombe; mains £10-18; ⊙breakfast, lunch and dinner, closed Sun & Mon dinner Oct-Mar) Join Bournemouth's surf riders and urban trendsetters at this hip haunt, watching the waves pound to a chilled soundtrack on the seafront deck or in the deli-cum-cafe-bar. Alternatively head upstairs for succulent sustainable fish dishes, panoramic views and warming log fires.

Print Room FRENCH ££
(☎01202-789669; www.theprintroom-bournemouth.co.uk; Richmond Hill; mains £14-18; ⊙breakfast, lunch & dinner) This charismatic brasserie exudes Parisian chic, from the black and white tiled floors to the burnished wooden booths. Gallic-influenced dishes include twice-baked gruyère soufflé and a deeply decadent rich chocolate mousse. Or try that most excellent French tradition: the *plat du jour*, including wine, for only £8.

Sixty Million Postcards PUB £
(www.sixtymillionpostcards.com; 19 Exeter Rd; mains £6-11; ⊙breakfast, lunch and dinner; 🖉) Central Bournemouth's top boho pub also dishes up some suitably alternative grub: try the Shroomaloomi (a mushroom and haloumi burger) or the Matador (macaroni cheese and chorizo). Their Sunday roasts (complete with Yorkshire pudding and Bloody Marys) are legendary.

Drinking & Entertainment

Most entertainment venues are clustered around Firvale Rd, St Peter's Rd and Old Christchurch Rd. The gay scene kicks off around the Triangle.

TOP CHOICE **Sixty Million Postcards** PUB
(www.sixtymillionpostcards.com; 19 Exeter Rd) An indie crowd inhabits this quirky drinking den, where worn wooden floors and fringed lampshades frame events ranging from DJ sets (expect '70s vinyl, soul and punk) and cinema screenings, to pub quizzes and pop-up Sunday jumble sales.

Lava Ignite NIGHTCLUB
(www.lavaignite.com; Firvale Rd) Four-room megaclub playing R&B, pop, house, hip hop and dubstep.

O2 Academy LIVE MUSIC
(www.o2academybournemouth.co.uk; 570 Christchurch Rd, Boscombe) Restored Victorian theatre with a wealth of gigs and DJ sets ranging from '80s revival acts to dubstep, hip hop and hardcore.

Information

Cyber Place (☎01202-290099; 25 St Peter's Rd; per 10min/hr 50p/£2; ⊙10am-8pm)

Tourist Office (☎0845-0511700; www.bournemouth.co.uk; Westover Rd; ⊙9.30am-5.30pm Mon-Sat, 11am-3pm Sun)

Getting There & Around

Bus

The **Getting About Card** (adult/child £5/3) gives a day's unlimited bus travel in Poole, Bournemouth and neighbouring Christchurch. National Express routes:

Bristol (£20, four hours, one daily)
London (£23, 2½ hours, half-hourly)
Oxford (£15, three hours, two daily)
Southampton (£6, 50 minutes, half-hourly)

Local buses:

Poole (15 minutes, every 10 minutes) Bus M1/M2.
Salisbury (£6, 1¼ hours, at least hourly) Bus X3.

Train

Dorchester South (£11, 45 minutes, hourly)
London Waterloo (£25, 2¾ hours, half-hourly)
Poole (£4, 11 minutes, half-hourly)
Weymouth (£13, one hour, hourly)

Poole

POP 144,320

Just a few miles west of Bournemouth, Poole was once the preserve of hard-drinking sailors and sunburnt day trippers. But these days you're as likely to encounter super-yachts and Porsches because the town borders the beach-backed Sandbanks district, one of the world's most expensive chunks of real estate. But you don't have to be a millionaire to enjoy this glorious stretch of sand, or Poole's quaint harbour, excellent eateries and nautical pubs. The town is also the springboard for some irresistible boat trips and a tempting array of water sports.

Sights & Activities

Brownsea Island ISLAND

(NT; 01202-707744; www.nationaltrust.org.uk; adult/child £5.60/2.80; 10am-5pm late Mar-Oct) This small, wooded island in the middle of Poole Harbour played a key role in a global movement famous for three-fingered salutes, shorts and toggles – Lord Baden-Powell staged the first ever scout camp here in 1907. Today, trails weave through heath and woods, past peacocks, red squirrels, red deer and a wealth of bird life.

Free **guided walks** (at 11.30am and 2pm) focus on the wartime island, smugglers and pirates.

Half-hourly boats, run by Brownsea Island Ferries (p270), start at 10am, leaving from **Poole Quay** (adult/child return £9.50/6) and **Sandbanks** (adult/child return £5.75/4.50). Services operate when the island is open only; the last boat is at 4.30pm.

Poole Old Town HISTORIC AREA

The attractive historic buildings on Poole Quay range from the 15th to the 19th century, and include the Tudor **King Charles** pub on Thames St; the cream **Old Harbour Office** (1820s) next door; and the impressive red-brick **Custom House** (1813) opposite, complete with Union Jack and gilded coat of arms. The tourist office (p271) sells the *Poole Cockle Trail* guide to the old town (30p).

FREE **Waterfront Museum** MUSEUM

(01202-262600; 4 High St; 10am-5pm Mon-Sat, noon-5pm Sun) This engrossing museum, set in a beautifully restored 15th-century warehouse, is home to a 2300-year-old **Iron Age logboat** dredged up from Poole Harbour. At 10m long and 14 tonnes, it's the largest to be found in southern Britain and probably carried 18 people. It was hand-chiselled from a single tree; millennia later you can still see the blade marks in the wood.

Sandbanks BEACH

A 2-mile, wafer-thin peninsula of land that curls around the expanse of Poole Harbour, Sandbanks is studded with some of the most expensive houses in the world. But the golden beaches that border them are free, and have some of the best water-quality standards in the country. They're also home to a host of water-sport operators.

Brownsea Island Ferries (01929-462383; www.brownseaislandferries.com; Poole Quay) shuttles between Poole Quay and Sandbanks every half-hour (adult/child £8.50/5.50) from 10am to 5pm, between April and October.

Sleeping

TOP CHOICE **Saltings** BOUTIQUE B&B ££

(01202-707349; www.the-saltings.com; 5 Salterns Way; d £85; P) You can almost hear the strains of the Charleston in this utterly delightful 1930s guesthouse. Charming art-deco flourishes include curved windows, arched doorways and decorative uplighters. Immaculate rooms feature dazzling white, spearmint and pastel blue, plus fresh flowers, digital radios and fridges stocked with chocolate bars. Plump for the mini-suite for your own seating area, pocket-sized balcony and view of a blue lagoon. Saltings is halfway between Poole and Sandbanks.

Corkers B&B ££
(☎01202-681393; www.corkers.co.uk; 1 High St; s £61-78, d £83-94;) A superb, central location and cheery rooms (think yellow and blue checks) make this bijou B&B a top hideaway. Rooms 4 and 5 have their own roof terrace with grandstand views over bustling Poole Quay.

Antelope INN ££
(☎01202-672029; www.antelopeinn-poole.co.uk; 8 High St; s £85, d £99-135; P) A creaking old coaching inn with rich colours, dark woods and mini stereos right in the heart of old Poole.

Eating & Drinking

Guildhall Tavern FRENCH ££
(☎01202-671717; www.guildhalltavern.co.uk; 15 Market St; mains £19, 2-course lunch/dinner £12/17; Tue-Sat;) More Provence than Poole, the food at this brasserie is Gallic gourmet charm at its best: unpretentious and first class. Flavour sensations include halibut with Chablis hollandaise, and duck with Grand Marnier. Exquisite aromas fill the dining room, along with the quiet murmur of people enjoying very good food.

Storm SEAFOOD ££
(☎01202-674970; www.stormfish.co.uk; 16 High St; mains £17; lunch & dinner daily Apr-Oct, dinner Mon-Sat Nov-Mar) The superbly cooked seafood served here depends on what Pete, the fisherman-owner, has caught. It might be intense Goan fish curry, whole flounder with herbs, or roast red gurnard with lemon and sea salt.

Poole Arms PUB ££
(www.localbiztoday.com/poole-arms; The Quay; mains £6-17) The grub at this ancient pub is strong on locally landed seafood – try the rich fish soup, herring roe or Lyme Bay cod with pesto. Order some New Forest beer, then settle in the snug wood-lined bar with the locals, or on the terrace overlooking the quay.

Information

Tourist Office (☎0845-234 5560; www.pooletourism.com; Poole Quay; 10am-5pm) Opens to 6pm in July and August.

WATER SPORTS – POOLE HARBOUR

Poole Harbour's sheltered coasts may inspire you to get on the water. Operators cluster near the start of the Sandbanks peninsula. **Pool Harbour Watersports** (☎01202-700503; www.pooleharbour.co.uk; 284 Sandbanks Rd) does lessons in windsurfing (per three hours £45) and kitesurfing (per day £99), as well as kayak tours (per three hours £40).

FC Watersports (☎01202-707757; www.fcwatersports.co.uk; 19 Banks Rd, Sandbanks) provides similarly priced kitesurfing lessons, as does **Watersports Academy** (☎01202-708283; www.thewatersportsacademy.com; Banks Rd), which also runs windsurfer taster sessions (per hour £25), plus sailing courses (per two hours/two days £55/165) and wakeboarding and waterskiing (per 15 minutes £20).

Getting There & Around

Bus

The **Getting About Card** (adult/child £5/3) gives a day's unlimited bus travel in Poole and Bournemouth.

Bournemouth (15 minutes, six per hour) Bus M1/M2.

London (£24, 3¼ hours, twice-hourly) National Express.

Sandbanks (15 minutes, hourly Monday to Saturday) Bus 52.

Boat

Brittany Ferries (www.brittany-ferries.com) Sails between Poole and Cherbourg in France (2½ to 6½ hours, one to three daily May to September). Prices range from around £80 for foot passengers to £250 for a car and two adults.

Sandbanks Ferry (www.sandbanksferry.co.uk; per pedestrian/car £1/3.50; 7am-11pm) Takes cars from Sandbanks to Studland every 20 minutes. It's a short-cut from Poole to Swanage, Wareham and the Isle of Purbeck, but the summer queues can be horrendous.

Taxi

Dial-a-Cab (☎01202-666822)

Train

Rail connections are as for **Bournemouth**; just add 15 minutes travel time to get to **London Waterloo** (£25, three hours).

Wimborne

POP 13,600

Just 10 miles from Bournemouth, but half a world away, Wimborne sits in the middle of a peaceful, pastoral landscape. Its imposing minster, complete with an intriguing chained library, oversees a central array of Georgian houses, sedate tearooms and heritage pubs. With the impressive ancestral pile of Kingston Lacy nearby, it is a soothing antidote to a sometimes cocksure coast.

Sights

TOP CHOICE Kingston Lacy HISTORIC HOME

(NT; ☎01202-883402; www.nationaltrust.org.uk; house adult/child £11.70/5.85, grounds only £6.30/3.15; ⏲house 11am-5pm Wed-Sun, grounds daily mid-Mar–Oct; P) Kingston Lacy is Dorset's must-see stately home. Looking every inch the setting for a classic BBC period drama, it overflows with rich decor, most famously in the Spanish Room, which is smothered with gold and gilt. Other highlights are the hieroglyphics in the Egyptian Room and the elegant marble staircase and loggia. The collection of artworks include the overwhelming ceiling fresco *The Separation of Night and Day*, by Guido Reni in the library, and paintings by Rubens, Titian and Van Dyck.

The house became the home of the aristocratic Bankes family when they were evicted from Corfe Castle by the Roundheads; look out for the bronze statue of Dame Mary Bankes in the loggia – she's shown still holding the keys to her much-loved castle in her hand. In the extensive landscaped grounds, hunt out the restored **Japanese Tea Garden** and the **Iron Age hillfort** of Badbury Rings.

Kingston Lacy is 2.5 miles west of Wimborne off the B3082.

FREE Wimborne Minster CHURCH

(☎01202-884753; www.wimborneminster.org.uk; High St; donation requested; ⏲9.30am-5.30pm Mon-Sat, 2.30-5.30pm Sun) St Cuthburga founded a monastery in Wimborne in around AD 705, but most of the present-day Wimborne Minster was built by the Normans between 1120 and 1180.

The big draw is the famous **chained library** (⏲10.30am-12.30pm & 2-4pm Easter-Oct). Established in 1686, it's stacked with some of the country's oldest medieval books, 12th-century manuscripts written on lambskin, and ancient recipes, including ones for making ink out of oak apples.

The west bell tower has a brightly painted 14th-century **astronomical clock**; note that in this medieval depiction of the solar system, the sun and moon orbit the earth. Outside, the minster's 15th-century west tower features the **Quarter Jack**, a red-coated infantryman, complete with knee-boots and tricorne hat, who strikes the hours and quarters.

Sleeping

Old George B&B ££

(☎01202-888510; www.theoldgeorge.net; 2 Corn Market; s/d £45/70; P) Hidden away in a tiny square beside the minster, this charming 18th-century house has dapper bedrooms decked out in duck-egg blue and cream, topped off by scatterings of cute cushions and elegant armchairs.

Fernhead B&B ££

(☎01202-881248; www.fernheadguesthouse.co.uk; 7 Wimborne Rd; d £70-80, f from £105; P 📶) The light, white rooms in this Edwardian guesthouse have pine bed frames, bay windows and gleaming bathrooms – it's a 10-minute walk into town.

Information

Tourist Office (☎01202-886116; www.visit-dorset.com; 29 High St; ⏲10am-4pm Mon-Sat) Sells a good town trail leaflet (£1).

Getting There & Away

Bournemouth (one hour, half-hourly Monday to Saturday, five on Sunday) Bus 13.

Poole (30 minutes, two to four per hour) Bus 3.

Southeast Dorset

With its string of glittering bays and towering rock formations, the southeast Dorset shoreline is the most beautiful in the county. Also known as the 'Isle' of Purbeck (although it's actually a peninsula), it's the start of the Jurassic Coast, and the scenery and geology, especially around Lulworth Cove, make swimming irresistible and hiking memorable. The hinterland harbours the picture-book ruins of Corfe Castle, while Wareham sheds light on the mysterious figure of Lawrence of Arabia.

WAREHAM & AROUND

POP 5580

Saxons established the sturdy settlement of Wareham on the banks of the River Frome in the 10th century. Their legacy lingers in the remains of their defensive walls and one of Dorset's last remaining Saxon churches. Wareham is also famous for its links to the enigmatic TE Lawrence, the British soldier immortalised in the 1962 David Lean biopic *Lawrence of Arabia*.

Sights

TOP CHOICE Clouds Hill HISTORIC HOME

(NT; ☎01929-405616; www.nationaltrust.org.uk; near Bovington; adult/child £5/2; ⊙11am-5pm Wed-Sun mid-Mar–Oct; P) This tiny cottage was home to TE Lawrence (1888–1935), the British scholar, military strategist and writer made legendary for his role in helping unite Arab tribes against Turkish forces in WWI. The house's four rooms provide a compelling insight into a complex man; they're also much as he left them – he died at the age of 46 after a motorbike accident on a nearby road.

Highlights include the deeply evocative photos taken by Lawrence during his desert campaign, and his sketches of French crusader castles. There's also a surprisingly comfortable cork-lined bathroom, an aluminium-foil-lined bunk room and a heavily beamed music room, which features the desk where Lawrence abridged *Seven Pillars of Wisdom*.

Clouds Hill is 7 miles northeast of Wareham on an unclassified road.

FREE Wareham Museum MUSEUM

(☎01929-553448; www.warehammuseum.fsnet.co.uk; East St; ⊙10am-4pm Mon-Sat Easter-Oct) A good potted history of Lawrence of Arabia's life, plus press cuttings on the speculation surrounding his death.

St Martin's on the Walls CHURCH

(North St; ⊙9am-5pm) This 11th-century church features a 12th-century fresco on the northern wall, and a marble effigy of TE Lawrence. If it's locked during normal shop hours, get the key from Joy's Outfitters in North St.

Tank Museum MUSEUM

(☎01929-462359; www.tankmuseum.org; adult/child £12/7.50; ⊙10am-5pm; P) Lawrence of Arabia's former base is now home to 300 armoured vehicles, ranging from WWI prototypes to tanks used in the first Gulf War.

Monkey World ZOO

(☎01929-462537; www.monkeyworld.co.uk; Longthorns; adult/child £11/7.75; ⊙10am-5pm; P) An appealing sanctuary for rescued chimpanzees, orang-utans, gibbons, marmosets and some utterly adorable ring-tailed lemurs.

JURASSIC COAST

The kind of massive, hands-on geology lesson you wish you had had at school, the Jurassic Coast is England's first natural World Heritage site, putting it on a par with the Great Barrier Reef and the Grand Canyon. This striking shoreline stretches from Exmouth in East Devon to Swanage in Dorset, encompassing 185 million years of the earth's history in just 95 miles. It means you can walk, in just a few hours, many millions of years in geological time.

It began when layers of rocks formed, their varying compositions determined by different climates. Desert conditions gave way to higher then lower sea levels before massive earth movements tilted all the rock layers to the east. Next, erosion exposed the different strata, leaving most of the oldest formations in the west and the youngest in the east.

The differences are very tangible. Rusty-red Triassic rocks in **Devon** are 200 to 250 million years old. **Lyme Regis** has fossil-rich, dark-clay Jurassic cliffs 190 million years old. Pockets of much younger, creamy-coloured Cretaceous rocks (a mere 140 to 65 million years old) also pop up, notably around **Lulworth Cove**, where erosion has sculpted a stunning display of bays, stacks and rock arches.

The coast's **website** (www.jurassiccoast.com) is an excellent information source; also look out locally for the highly readable *Official Guide to the Jurassic Coast* (£4.95), or buy it at www.jurassiccoasttrust.org.

Sleeping

Red Lion INN ££
(☎01929-550099; www.redlionwareham.co.uk; 1 North St; d £120) A supremely stylish makeover of this old inn's vast rooms sees them sporting brass bedsteads, sweet armchairs and wind-up alarm clocks. The locally sourced menu includes home-cured gravlax, while Sunday roast trimmings include Dorset Blue Vinny cauliflower cheese. The pub serves three meals a day.

Trinity B&B ££
(☎01929-556689; www.trinitybnb.co.uk; 32 South St; s/d £45/65; 📶) This 15th-century cottage oozes so much character that you half expect to bump into a chap in doublet and hose. The staircase is a swirl of ancient timber, floors creak under plush rugs, and bathrooms glint with yellow and green tiles and smart new fittings.

Information

Purbeck Tourist Office (☎01929-552740; www.visitswanageandpurbeck.com; Holy Trinity Church, South St; ⏰9.30am-4pm Mon-Sat, plus 10am-4pm Sun Jul & Aug)

Getting There & Away

BUS Bus 40 runs hourly (every two hours on Sunday) between **Poole** (35 minutes) and **Swanage** (30 minutes) via Wareham and Corfe Castle.
TRAIN **London Waterloo** (£20, 2½ hours, hourly)
Weymouth (£9, 30 minutes, hourly)

CORFE CASTLE

The massive, shattered ruins of Corfe Castle loom so dramatically from the landscape it's like blundering into a film set. The defensive fragments tower over an equally photogenic village, which bears the castle's name, and makes for a romantic spot for a meal or an overnight stay.

Sights & Activities

TOP CHOICE **Corfe Castle** CASTLE
(NT; ☎01929-481294; www.nationaltrust.org.uk; adult/child £7.72/3.86; ⏰10am-6pm Apr-Sep, 10am-4pm Oct-Mar) One of Dorset's most iconic landmarks, these towering battlements were once home to Sir John Bankes, right-hand man and attorney general to Charles I. The castle was besieged by Cromwellian forces during the Civil War – for six weeks the plucky Lady Bankes directed the defence and the castle fell only after being betrayed from within. The Bankes family decamped to Kingston Lacy and the Roundheads blew Corfe Castle apart with gunpowder, an action that's still startlingly apparent today: turrets and soaring walls sheer off at precarious angles; the gatehouse splays out as if it's just been blown up. Today you can roam over most of the site, peeping through slit windows and prowling the fractured defences.

Swanage Steam Railway HERITAGE RAILWAY
(☎01929-425800; www.swanagerailway.co.uk; adult/child return £10.50/7; ⏰daily Apr-Oct, Sat & Sun Nov-Mar) Vintage steam trains run (hourly) between Swanage and Norden (25 minutes), stopping at Corfe Castle.

Sleeping & Eating

Mortons House HOTEL £££
(☎01929-480988; www.mortonshouse.co.uk; East St; d £160-215; P📶) This is a place to break open the Bollinger: a romantic, luxurious 16th-century, mini-baronial pile. The rooms are festooned with red brocade and gold tassels; an occasional chaise longue adds to the effect.

Ammonite B&B £
(☎01929-480188; www.ammonite-corfecastle.co.uk; 88 West St; s £50, d £55-75; P📶) The pleasing rooms at this tranquil edge-of-village B&B feature pastels and pine; the Aga-cooked breakfast includes local eggs, homemade jams and crusty bread from Corfe Castle's bakery.

Castle Inn PUB ££
(www.castleinncorfe.com; 63 East St; mains £10-15) With its ancient beams draped with fairy lights and flagstone floors, this is the locals' choice. Prepare for tasty pub classics, plus some surprises: try the Poole Harbour oysters or roast local duck.

Getting There & Away

Bus 40 shuttles hourly (every two hours on Sunday) between Poole, Wareham, Corfe Castle and Swanage.

LULWORTH COVE & AROUND

South of Corfe Castle the coast steals the show. For millions of years the elements have been creating an intricate shoreline of curved bays, caves, stacks and weirdly wonderful rock formations – most notably the massive natural arch at Durdle Door.

At Lulworth Cove, a pleasing jumble of thatched cottages and fishing gear leads down to a perfect circle of white cliffs. It's a charismatic place to stay; inevitably, it draws coach party crowds in the height of summer.

Sights & Activities

TOP CHOICE Durdle Door NATURAL FEATURE
(P) This immense, 150-million-year-old Portland stone arch plunges into the sea near Lulworth Cove. Part of the Jurassic Coast, it was created by a combination of massive earth movements and erosion. Today it's framed by shimmering bays – bring a swimsuit and head down the hundreds of steps for an unforgettable dip.

There's a car park at the top of the cliffs, but it's best to hike along the coast from Lulworth Cove (1 mile), passing the delightfully named **Lulworth Crumple**, where layers of rock have been forced into dramatically zigzagging folds.

Lulworth Castle CASTLE
(EH; ☎0845-4501054; www.lulworth.com; adult/child £5/3; ⏲10.30am-5pm Sun-Fri) A creamy, dreamy white, this baronial pile looks more like a French chateau than a traditional English castle. Built in 1608 as a hunting lodge, it's survived extravagant owners, extensive remodelling and a disastrous fire in 1929. It has now been extensively restored – check out the reconstructed kitchen and cellars, then climb the tower for sweeping coastal views.

Fossil Forest NATURAL FEATURE
A half-mile hike east along the coast path from Lulworth Cove leads to the remains of an ancient Jurassic jungle. Here huge, raised doughnuts of rock (called 'tufa') sprout from the cliff, all that's left of the tree trunks of a 144-million-year-old forest. In the early Purbeck period a wetter climate and flooding killed the trees, and algae gathered round the stumps, preserving them in calcareous sediment.

The forest is at the foot of Bindon Hill, just inside an army live-firing range. The path is normally open weekends and school summer holidays, but check by calling the range **office** (☎01929-404819).

Secondwind Watersports KAYAK TOUR
(☎01305-834951; www.jurassic-kayaking.com; Lulworth Cove; per person £50; ⏲up to 2 tours daily) This three-hour paddle offers jaw-dropping views of Dorset's heavily eroded coast. Starting at Lulworth Cove, you glide through Stair Hole's intricate caves and stacks, across Man O'War Bay then under the massive stone arch at Durdle Door, stopping for swims and picnics along the way.

Sleeping & Eating

Lulworth Cove Inn INN ££
(☎01929-400333; www.lulworth-coveinn.co.uk; Main Rd; d £80-110; P) The decor may be super-simple (think block prints and pine), but the setting is superb – ask for one of the balcony rooms and sit watching seagulls swoop over the cove from your own tiny terrace.

Rose Cottage B&B ££
(☎01929-400253; www.lulworthcove.co.uk; Main Rd; s/d £50/90 ; P) The quintessential 18th-century English Cottage – from the thatched roof to the roses round the door. The aged rooms are truly Lilliputian (some share bathrooms), the doors are hobbit-sized (duck) and you can use the pool of the hotel next door.

Durdle Door Holiday Park CAMPSITE £
(☎01929-400200; www.lulworth.com; sites from £25; ⏲Mar-Oct; P) Clifftop site, just minutes from the famous rock arch.

Lulworth YHA HOSTEL £
(☎0845-371 9331; www.yha.org.uk; School Lane, West Lulworth; dm £16-22; P) A single storey, cabin-style affair.

Cove Fish FISH SHOP £
(☎01929-400807; Lulworth Cove; ⏲10am-4pm Tue-Sun Easter-Oct, Sat & Sun Nov-Easter) Set right beside the path to the beach, this shed is piled high with seafood caught by the owner, ninth-generation fisherman Joe. Bag a fish kebab for the barbeque, or settle at the wobbly table outside and tuck into Lulworth Cove crab – a meal that's travelled food yards, not miles. When weather conditions are bad, and Joe can't fish, the shop doesn't open.

Information

Lulworth Cove Heritage Centre (☎01929-400587; www.lulworth.com; ⏲10am-5pm) Staff can provide a lot of information on the local area. Also has excellent displays that outline how geology and erosion have combined to shape the area's remarkable shoreline.

Dorchester

POP 18,280

With Dorchester, you get two towns in one: a real-life, bustling county town, and Thomas Hardy's fictional Casterbridge. The Victorian writer was born just outside Dorchester and clearly used it to add authenticity to his writing – so much so that his literary locations can still be found amid the town's white

Georgian terraces and red-brick buildings. Dorchester also houses the writer's former homes and his original manuscripts. Add incredibly varied museums (from teddy bears to Tutankhamen) and some attractive places to eat and sleep, and you get an appealing base for a night or two.

Sights

TOP CHOICE **Dorset County Museum** MUSEUM

(01305-262735; www.dorsetcountymuseum.org; High West St; adult/child £6/free; 10am-5pm Mon-Sat) The Thomas Hardy collection here is the biggest in the world, offering extraordinary insights into his creative process – reading his cramped handwriting, it's often possible to spot where he's crossed out one word and substituted another. There's also an atmospheric reconstruction of his study at Max Gate and a letter from Siegfried Sassoon, asking Hardy if Sassoon can dedicate his first book of poems to him.

As well as the superb Hardy exhibits, look out for Jurassic Coast fossils, especially the huge ichthyosaur and the 6ft fore paddle of a plesiosaur. Bronze and Iron Age finds from Maiden Castle include a treasure trove of coins and neck rings, while Roman artefacts include 70 gold coins, nail cleaners and (toe-curlingly) ear picks.

Max Gate HISTORIC BUILDING

(Hardy Country; NT; 01297-489481; www.nationaltrust.org.uk; Alington Ave; adult/child £4/2; 11am-5pm Wed-Sun mid-Mar–Oct; P) Thomas Hardy was a trained architect and designed this attractive house, where he lived from 1885 until his death in 1928. *Tess of the D'Urbervilles* and *Jude the Obscure* were both written here, and the house contains several pieces of original furniture. It's a mile east of Dorchester, on the A352.

Hardy's Birthplace HISTORIC BUILDING

(Hardy Country; NT; 01305-262366; www.nationaltrust.org.uk; adult/child £5/2.20; 11am-5pm Wed-Sun mid-Mar–Oct; P) This picturesque cob-and-thatch house is the birthplace of Thomas Hardy. It's perhaps a little short on attractions, but makes an evocative stop for Hardy completists. It's in Higher Bockhampton, 3 miles northeast of Dorchester.

Hardy Literary Locations NOTABLE BUILDINGS

Mayor of Casterbridge locations hidden among modern Dorchester include **Lucetta's House**, a grand Georgian affair with ornate door posts near the tourist office, while in parallel South St, a red-brick mid-18th-century building (now a bank) is named as the inspiration for the house of the mayor himself. The tourist office sells book location guides.

FREE **Roman Town House** ROMAN VILLA

(www.romantownhouse.org; High West St; 24hr) The flint walls and beautifully preserved mosaics here powerfully conjure up the Roman occupation of Dorchester (then Durnovaria). Peek into the summer dining room to see the underfloor heating system (hypocaust), where charcoal-warmed air circulated around pillars to produce a toasty 18°C.

Tutankhamen MUSEUM

(01305-269571; www.tutankhamun-exhibition.co.uk; High West St; adult/child £8/6; 10am-4pm) Recreates the sounds, smells and sights of ancient Egypt, including a fake-gold mock-up of a pharaoh's tomb.

Teddy Bear Museum MUSEUM

(01305-266040; www.teddybearmuseum.co.uk; East Gate, High East St; adult/child £6/4; 10am-4pm) Populated by historical and famous bears, plus a disconcerting family of human-sized teddies.

MAIDEN CASTLE

Occupying a massive slab of horizon on the southern fringes of Dorchester, **Maiden Castle** (EH; www.english-heritage.org.uk; admission free; 24hr; P) is the largest and most complex Iron Age hill fort in Britain. The huge, steep-sided chalk ramparts flow along the contour lines of the hill and surround 48 hectares – the equivalent of 50 football pitches.

The first hill fort was built on the site around 500 BC and in its heyday was densely populated, with clusters of roundhouses and a network of roads. The Romans besieged and captured it in AD 43 – an ancient Briton skeleton with a Roman crossbow bolt in the spine was found at the site. The sheer scale of the ramparts is awe-inspiring, while the winding complexity of the west entrance reveals just how hard it would be to storm. Finds from the site are displayed at the Dorset County Museum. Maiden Castle is 1½ miles southwest of Dorchester.

Sleeping

TOP CHOICE Beggars Knap BOUTIQUE B&B ££
(☎01305-268191; www.beggarsknap.co.uk; 2 Weymouth Ave; s £50-60, d £65-100, f £75-120; P) Despite the name, this altogether fabulous, vaguely decadent guesthouse is far from impoverished. Opulent rooms drip with chandeliers and gold brocades; beds draped in fine cottons range from French sleigh to four-poster. You could pay much, much more and get something half as nice.

Westwood B&B ££
(☎01305-268018; www.westwoodhouse.co.uk; 29 High West St; s/d/f £70/95/125;) Colours from a Georgian palette grace the walls of this elegant 18th-century townhouse. Plush bedrooms feature wicker furniture and cast-iron bedsteads, while the conservatory is home to a superb breakfast spread.

Slades Farm B&B ££
(☎01305-264032; sladesfm@btinternet.com; North St, Charminster; d £65-75; P) A subtle barn conversion with airy rooms, breakfasts full of farmers-market produce, riverside paddocks and three cute alpacas to befriend. It's 2 miles north of Dorchester.

Casterbridge HOTEL ££
(☎01305-264043; www.casterbridgehotel.co.uk; 49 High East St; s/d £75/130;) Ask for a heritage room for Georgian-style fabrics, dark wood furniture and Thomas Hardy books on the shelf.

Eating

Surf & Turf at Shelley's Plaice SEAFOOD ££
(☎01305-757428; Trinity St; mains £12-18; lunch Tue-Sat, dinner Thu-Sat) Lobster pots and life belts dangle from the rafters at this kooky bistro, where the chalked-up menu depends entirely on what local fishermen have caught. Flavoursome delights range from fish soup to perfectly cooked cod, monkfish or lemon sole; or get cracking on a whole Portland crab.

Sienna MODERN BRITISH £££
(☎01305-250022; www.siennarestaurant.co.uk; 36 High West St; 2-course lunch/dinner £26/37; lunch Wed-Sat, dinner Tue-Sat) Dorchester's Michelin-starred eatery casts a culinary spell over seasonal produce. Look out for wild garlic and pungent truffles; duck might be teamed with spiced blackberry purée. The cheeseboard bears the very best of the west, served with apple chutney and home-made digestives. Booking is required.

No 6 FRENCH ££
(☎01305-267679; www.no6-restaurant.co.uk; 6 North Sq; mains £13-20; lunch & dinner Tue-Fri, dinner Sat) Much of the fish at this cosmopolitan bistro comes straight off a Weymouth trawler. The French chef specialises in giving local produce a Gallic makeover – look out for lamb's kidney on brioche, and crab baked Creole-style.

Information

Tourist Office (☎01305-267992; www.visit-dorset.com; Antelope Walk; 9am-5pm Mon-Sat)

Getting There & Around

Bicycle

Dorchester Cycles (☎01305-268787; 31 Great Western Rd; adult/child per day £12/8; 9am-5pm Mon-Sat)

Bus

Most buses into and out of Dorchester stop at either Dorchester South train station or the more central Trinity St.

London (£24, four hours, one daily) National Express.

Lyme Regis (1¾ hours, hourly) Bus 31.

Poole (1¼ hours, three daily Monday to Saturday) Bus 347/387.

Sherborne (one hour, four to seven daily Monday to Saturday) Bus 216; via Cerne Abbas.

Weymouth (35 minutes, three per hour Monday to Saturday, six on Sunday) Bus 10/210.

Train

Hourly trains from Dorchester South:

Bournemouth (£11, 45 minutes)

London Waterloo (£25, 2¾ hours)

Southampton (£22, 1½ hours)

Weymouth (11 minutes)

Services, every two hours, from Dorchester West:

Bath (£16, two hours)

Bristol (£17, 2½ hours)

Around Dorchester

CERNE ABBAS & THE CERNE GIANT

If you had to describe an archetypal sleepy Dorset village, you'd come up with something a lot like Cerne Abbas: its houses run the gamut of England's architectural styles, roses climb countless doorways, and half-timbered houses frame a honey-coloured, 12th-century church.

But this village also packs one heck of a surprise – a real nudge-nudge, wink-wink tourist attraction in the form of the **Cerne Giant** (admission free; ⏲24hr; 🅿). Nude, full frontal and notoriously well endowed, this chalk figure is revealed in all his glory on a hill on the edge of town. And he's in a stage of excitement that wouldn't be allowed in most magazines. The giant is around 60m high and 51m wide and his age remains a mystery; some claim he's Roman but the first historical reference comes in 1694, when three shillings were set aside for his repair. The Victorians found it all deeply embarrassing and allowed grass to grow over his most outstanding feature. Today the hill is grazed by sheep and cattle, though only the sheep are allowed to do their nibbling over the giant – the cows would do too much damage to his lines.

The village has the swish **New Inn** (www.newinncerneabbas.com; 14 Long St), plus **Abbots** (☎01300-341349; www.abbotsbedandbreakfast.co.uk; 7 Long St; s/d/f £45/85/120; ⏲cafe 10am-5pm; 📶), a B&B-cum-cafe, where atmospheric rooms are either stone, lemon or blue, and wooden attic ceilings slope just above head-height. The cafe's cakes are real diet-busters.

Dorchester is 8 miles to the south. Bus 216 (four to seven daily Monday to Saturday) connects Cerne Abbas with **Dorchester** (30 minutes) and **Sherborne** (30 minutes).

Weymouth, Portland & Around

A 3-mile sandy beach and an immense harbour ensured this strip of Dorset coast was the 2012 Olympic sailing venue – a state-of-the-art water-sports centre and a soaring viewing tower are among the legacies. Otherwise, the area's core character remains: Weymouth's billowing deckchairs and candy-striped beach kiosks signal a sometimes faded Georgian resort, while the pock-marked central plateau of the neighbouring Isle of Portland still proudly proclaims a rugged, quarrying past. Portland also offers jaw-dropping views down on to 17-mile Chesil Beach, which is backed by the Fleet, Britain's biggest tidal lagoon – a home to 600 nesting swans.

WEYMOUTH

POP 51,130

King George III (the one with a 'nervous disorder') took an impromptu dip here in 1789, prompting the start of Weymouth's life as a classic British seaside resort. Some 220-plus years later, the town is still popular with holidaymakers, drawn by a curling golden beach, a revitalised historic harbour and swathes of seaside kitsch.

Sights & Activities

Weymouth Beach BEACH

Weymouth's fine sandy shore is perfect for a stroll down seaside memory lane. Here you can rent a deckchair, sun-lounger or pedalo (per hour £6), watch Punch and Judy shows and take a donkey ride. Alternatively, go all Californian and join a volleyball game.

FREE **Sand Sculptures** PUBLIC ART

(www.sculpturesinsand.com; Seafront; ⏲24hr) This tarpaulin-framed patch of beach holds some truly remarkable art. Professional sand-sculptor Mark learnt his trade from his grandfather, who worked here in the 1920s. Today he carves intricate designs from the golden grains – look out for full-sized dragons, trains and dinosaurs. There are even top tips for creating your own beautiful beach-based creations.

Sea Life Tower OBSERVATION TOWER

(☎0871-423 2110; www.weymouth-tower.com; The Quay; admission £8; ⏲10am-dusk) This £3.5 million tower was put up just in time for the 2012 Olympic Games. Its doughnut-shaped viewing platform lifts 70 passengers up the 53m shaft for Jurassic Coast views, before gliding back down. Get cheaper rates by buying online.

Nothe Fort FORT

(☎01305-766626; www.nothefort.org.uk; Barrack Rd; adult/child £6/1; ⏲10.30am-5.30pm Apr-Oct) Crowning the headland beside Weymouth Harbour, these photogenic 19th-century defences are studded with cannon, searchlights and 12in coastal guns. Exhibits detail the Roman invasion of Dorset, a Victorian soldier's drill, and Weymouth in WWII. Commanding an armoured car and clambering around the magazine prove popular with regiments of children.

Tudor House MUSEUM

(☎01305-779711; Trinity St; adult/child £3.50/1; ⏲1-3.45pm Tue-Fri May-Oct) A late-16th-century,

WATER SPORTS – PORTLAND HARBOUR

The 890-hectare Portland Harbour, just south of Weymouth, lets you glide in the wake of sailors at the 2012 Olympics. The new Weymouth & Portland National Sailing Academy is home to **SailLaser** (☎0845-337 3214; www.sail-laser.com; Osprey Quay, Portland), which runs lessons (two/four days £190/330) and hires lasers (two hours/day £45/95). **Windtek** (☎01305-787900; www.windtek.co.uk; 109 Portland Rd, Wyke Regis; ⏲Thu-Mon) runs lessons in windsurfing (four hours/day £45/80) and kitesurfing (per day £95).

Local waters offer superb diving, with a huge variety of depths, seascapes and wrecks. Operators include **Underwater Explorers** (☎01305-824555; www.underwaterexplorers.co.uk; 15 Castletown, Portland) and **Fathom & Blues** (☎01305-766220; www.fathomandblues.co.uk; 262 Portland Rd, Wyke Regis). Lessons start at around £95 a day; some operators shuttle qualified divers to a site (around £20) and rent equipment sets (from £60).

furnished home that recreates the atmosphere of Elizabethan England.

Sea Life AQUARIUM
(☎01305-761070; www.sealife.co.uk; Lodmoor Country Park; admission £20; ⏲10am-5pm; P) Profiles sharks, penguins and seahorses in a 3-hectare aquatic park. To save £8 per ticket, buy online, 24 hours in advance.

White Motor Boats BOAT TRIP
(☎01305-785000; www.whitemotorboat.freeuk.com; adult/child return £8/6; ⏲3-4 boats daily Apr-Oct) This wind-blown, 40-minute jaunt crosses Portland Harbour's vast Olympic sailing waters, before dropping you off at Portland Castle. Boats leave from Cove Row on Weymouth Harbour.

Sleeping

B+B B&B ££
(☎01305-761190; www.bb-weymouth.com; 68 The Esplanade; s £60, d £75-115; P 📶) Cool, sleek B+B deposits a dollop of boutique glamour amid Weymouth's B&B scene. Minimalist lines, monogrammed bed linen and own-brand toiletries grace the bedrooms, while the 1st-floor lounge sports espresso machines, leather sofas and panoramic views of the bay.

Old Harbour View B&B ££
(☎01305-774633; www.oldharbourviewweymouth.co.uk; 12 Trinity Rd; s/d £76/96; P 📶) In this spruce Georgian terrace you get boating themes in the fresh, white bedrooms and boats right outside the front door – one room overlooks the busy quay, the other faces the back.

Chatsworth B&B ££
(☎01305-785012; www.thechatsworth.co.uk; 14 The Esplanade; s £35-50, d £80-120; P 📶) A sunny waterside terrace lets you watch yachts cast off just metres away while you eat breakfast. Inside, crisp colours define compact rooms, with either a harbour or sea view.

Eating & Drinking

Clusters of bars line the old harbour; ice-cream kiosks dot the prom.

Perry's EUROPEAN ££
(☎01305-785799; www.perrysrestaurant.co.uk; 4 Trinity Rd; mains £13-24) Weymouth's top table is a genteel, relaxed Georgian townhouse that consistently delivers irresistible dishes – try the locally landed whole grilled fish of the day. The cognoscenti book the 1st-floor window table (complete with fabulous harbour view) for a two-course set lunch; a bargain at £14.

Mallams MODERN BRITISH ££
(☎01305-776757; www.mallamsrestaurant.co.uk; 5 Trinity Rd; 2-courses £25; ⏲dinner daily May-Sep, Mon-Sat Oct-Apr) With its subdued lighting and old stone walls this romantic harbourside eatery has been a feature of Weymouth's restaurant scene for more than 20 years. Find out why it's lasted so long by sampling tasty, often organic, fare – it might be a risotto-style, saffron-infused speltotto or lemon sole with crab and ginger butter.

Marlboro CAFE £
(46 St Thomas St; mains £8; ⏲noon-9.45pm) This traditional chippy is just yards from Weymouth's quay so the seafood is super-fresh. Order to take away, or tuck into mounds of crisp chips and succulent fish in the bay-windowed, licensed cafe (open till 8pm).

Information

Tourist Office (☎01305-785747; www.visitweymouth.co.uk; Pavilion Theatre, The Esplanade; ⏲9.30am-5pm)

Getting There & Away

BOAT

Condor Ferries (www.condorferries.co.uk) Shuttles daily between Weymouth and the Channel Islands. At time of writing, ferries between Weymouth and the Channel Islands had been re-located to Poole; check the website for updates.

BUS

The Jurassic Coast Bus X53 (two to six daily) travels from Weymouth to **Wareham** (50 minutes), **Poole** (1½ hours), **Abbotsbury** (35 minutes) and **Lyme Regis** (1¾ hours). Between Monday and Saturday it goes on to **Exeter** (three hours).

Axminster (two hours, hourly) Bus 31.

Dorchester (35 minutes, three per hour to six daily) Bus 10/210.

Fortuneswell (Isle of Portland; 30 minutes,half-hourly) Bus 1.

London (£21,4¼ hours, one daily) National Express.

Lyme Regis (1¾ hours, hourly) Bus 31.

Portland Bill (Isle of Portland; 45 minutes, four daily to one per hour May to September only) Bus 501.

TRAIN

Hourly services:

Bournemouth (£13, one hour)

Dorchester South (11 minutes)

London Waterloo (£56, 3½ hours)

Services every two hours:

Bath (£15.60, two hours)

Bristol (£17.40, 2½ hours)

ISLE OF PORTLAND

POP 12,400

The 'Isle' of Portland is really a hard, high comma of rock fused to the rest of Dorset by the ridge of Chesil Beach. Its strip of waste waterfront land now features a **new sailing centre** (p279) and a glitzy apartment block. But inland, on the 500ft central plateau, a quarrying past still holds sway, evidenced by huge craters and large slabs of limestone. Proud, and at times bleak and rough around the edges, Portland is decidedly different from the rest of Dorset, and is all the more compelling because of it. Its industrial heritage, water-sport facilities, rich bird life and starkly beautiful cliffs make it worth at least a day trip.

The key population clusters of **Fortuneswell** and **Chiswell** are towards the north of the isle; **Portland Bill** is 4 miles south at the tip.

Sights

TOP CHOICE Tout Quarry PUBLIC ART

(24hr) Portland's unique white limestone has been quarried for centuries, and has been used in some of the world's finest buildings, such as the British Museum, St Paul's Cathedral and Buckingham Palace. The disused workings at Tout Quarry now house 53 sculptures that have been carved into the rock in situ. The result is a fascinating combination of the raw material, the detritus of the quarrying process and the beauty of chiselled works. Labyrinthine paths snake through hacked-out gullies and around jumbled piles of rock, revealing the half-formed bears, bison and lizards that emerge out of stone cliffs. Highlights include *Still Falling* by Antony Gormley, *Woman on Rock* by Dhruva Mistry and the well-hidden *Green Man*. Tout Quarry is signed off the main road, just south of Fortuneswell.

Portland Lighthouse LIGHTHOUSE

(01255-245156; www.trinityhouse.co.uk; Portland Bill; adult/child £4/3; 11am-5pm Sun-Thu Apr-Sep; P) For a real sense of the isle's remote nature, head to its southern tip, Portland Bill. Then climb the 13m-high, candy-striped lighthouse for breathtaking views of rugged cliffs and the Race, a surging vortex of conflicting tides.

Portland Castle CASTLE

(EH; 01305-820539; www.english-heritage.org.uk; Liberty Rd, near Chiswell; adult/child £5/3; 10am-5pm Apr-Oct) A particularly fine product of Henry VIII's castle-building spree, with expansive views over Portland harbour. Open until 6pm in July and August.

Eating & Drinking

Crab House Cafe SEAFOOD ££

(01305-788867; www.crabhousecafe.co.uk; Portland Rd, Wyke Regis; mains £16-21; lunch & dinner Wed-Sat, lunch Sun) This is the place to come for as-fresh-as-it-gets seafood and beach-shack chic. The funky cabin has views onto its own oyster beds in the Fleet Lagoon, and the waterside terrace makes a top spot to enjoy dishes like clam and cockle spaghetti or cracked whole crab, best washed down with a glass of lip-smacking Somerset cider from Bridge Farm.

Cove House PUB £

(Chiswell Seafront; mains £10) Extraordinary Chesil Beach views, memorable sunsets and

ABBOTSBURY SWANNERY

Every May some 600 free-flying swans choose to nest at the **Abbotsbury Swannery** (☎01305-871858; www.abbotsbury-tourism.co.uk; New Barn Rd, Abbotsbury; adult/child £10.50/7.50; ⏲10am-5pm late Mar–Oct), which shelters in the Fleet lagoon, protected by the ridge of Chesil Beach. The swannery was founded by local monks about 600 years ago, and feathers from today's birds are still used in the helmets of the Gentlemen at Arms (the Queen's official bodyguard). Wandering the network of trails that wind between the swans' nests is an awe-inspiring experience that is punctuated by occasional territorial displays (think snuffling cough and stand-up flapping), ensuring that even the liveliest children are stilled.

The swannery is at the picturesque village of Abbotsbury, 10 miles from Weymouth off the B3157.

great grub (try the Lyme Bay scallops) in a history-rich fishermen's inn.

Information

Tourist Office (☎01305-861233; www.visitweymouth.co.uk; Portland Bill; ⏲11am-5pm Easter-Sep)

Getting There & Away

BUS

Bus 1 runs from Weymouth to Fortuneswell (half-hourly, 20 minutes). Between May and September bus 501 goes from Weymouth to Portland Bill (four daily to one per hour).

BOAT

White Motor Boats (p279) runs ferries to Portland Castle from Weymouth.

CHESIL BEACH

One of the most breathtaking beaches in Britain, Chesil is 17 miles long, 15m high and moving inland at the rate of 5m a century. This mind-boggling, 100-million-tonne pebble ridge is the baby of the Jurassic Coast. A mere 6000 years old, its stones range from pea-sized in the west to hand-sized in the east.

Chesil Beach Visitors Centre (☎01305-759692; www.chesilbeach.org; Ferrybridge; admission free; ⏲10am-4pm) Just over the bridge to Portland is a great gateway to one of the best parts of the beach. The pebble ridge is at its highest around this point – 15m high compared to 7m at Abbotsbury. From the car park an energy-sapping hike up sliding pebbles leads to the sound of the constant surge and rattle of water on stones, and dazzling views of the sea, with the thin pebble line and the expanse of the Fleet behind. The visitors centre details an ecosystem that includes ringed plovers, redshanks and oyster catchers, as well as drifts of thrift and sea campion. There is also a sustainable seafood **cafe** (⏲9am-5pm, plus dinner Thu-Sat Jul & Aug), plus glass-bottom-boat trips run by **Fleet Observer** (☎01305-759692; adult/child £7/4) on the Fleet lagoon.

Lyme Regis

POP 3570

Fantastically fossiliferous Lyme Regis packs a heavyweight historical punch. Rock-hard relics of the past pop out repeatedly from the surrounding cliffs – exposed by the landslides of a retreating shore. Now a pivot point of the Unesco-listed Jurassic Coast, fossil fever is definitely in the air and everyone, from proper palaeontologists to those out for a bit of fun, can engage in a spot of coastal rummaging.

Lyme was also famously the setting for *The French Lieutenant's Woman*, the film version, starring Meryl Streep, which immortalised the iconic Cobb harbour defences in movie history. Add sandy beaches and some delightful places to sleep and eat, and you end up with a charming base for explorations.

Sights & Activities

Lyme Regis Museum MUSEUM

(☎01297-443370; www.lymeregismuseum.co.uk; Bridge St; adult/child £3.75/free; ⏲10am-5pm Mon-Sat 11am-5pm Sun Apr-Oct, 11am-4pm Wed-Sun Nov-Mar) In 1814 a local teenager called Mary Anning found the first full ichthyosaurus skeleton near Lyme Regis, propelling the town onto the world stage. An incredibly famous fossilist in her day, Miss Anning did much to pioneer the science of modern-day palaeontology. The museum, on the site of

FOSSIL HUNTING

Fossil fever is catching. Lyme Regis sits in one of the most unstable sections of Britain's coast, and regular landslips mean nuggets of prehistory constantly tumble from the cliffs. If you are bitten by the bug, the best cure is one of the regular fossil walks staged locally.

In the village of Charmouth, 3 miles east of Lyme, the **Charmouth Heritage Coast Centre** (☎01297-560772; www.charmouth.org; adult/child £7/3) runs one to seven trips a week. Or, in Lyme itself, **Lyme Regis Museum** (☎01297-443370; adult/child £10/5) offers three to seven walks a week; local expert **Brandon Lennon** (☎07944 664757; www.lymeregisfossilwalks.com; adult/child £7/5; ⏲Sat-Mon) also leads expeditions. Book early – places fill up weeks in advance.

For the best chances of a find, time your trip to Lyme to within two hours of low water. If you choose to hunt by yourself, official advice is to check tide times and collect on a falling tide, observe warning signs, keep away from the cliffs, only pick up from the beach and always leave some behind for others. Oh, and tell the experts if you find a stunner.

her former home, tells her story and exhibits its spectacular fossils and other prehistoric finds.

Dinosaurland FOSSIL MUSEUM
(☎01297-443541; www.dinosaurland.co.uk; Coombe St; adult/child £5/4; ⏲10am-5pm mid-Feb–Nov) This joyful, mini, indoor Jurassic Park overflows with fossilised remains – look out for belemnites, plesiosaurus and an impressive locally found ichthyosaur. Lifelike dinosaur models will thrill youngsters – the rock-hard tyrannosaurus eggs and 73kg dinosaur dung will have them in raptures.

Cobb HARBOUR WALL
(⏲24hr) First built in the 13th century, this curling, protective barrier has been strengthened and extended over the years, so it doesn't present the elegant line it once did, but it's still hard to resist wandering its length for a wistful, sea-gazing Meryl Streep moment at the tip.

Undercliff NATURE RESERVE
This wildly undulating, 304-hectare nature reserve just west of Lyme was formed by massive landslides. One, in 1839, saw an immense section of cliffs weighing 8 million tonnes slide part-way towards the sea, creating a deep chasm. Today the reserve's slipped cliffs, fissures and ridges are smothered in dense vegetation, exposed tree roots and tangles of brambles.

The 8-mile hike between Lyme Regis and Axmouth takes an arduous four hours; alternatively walk the first mile of the reserve from the Lyme Regis end; the chalk-white bulk of Pinhay Cliffs makes a handy point at which to double back.

The Undercliff starts a mile west of central Lyme Regis; follow footpath signs from Holmbush Car Park.

Sleeping

TOP CHOICE **1 Lyme Townhouse** BOUTIQUE B&B ££
(☎01297-442499; www.1lymetownhouse.co.uk; 1 Pound St; d £100-110, ste £135; 📶) With its witty designer decor, luxury flourishes and in-town location, this 18th-century terrace is hard to resist. Swanky wrought-iron beds, coffee machines and Molton Brown toiletries dot the bedrooms, while breakfast is a gourmet hamper delivered directly to your door. Book room 5 for a don't-want-to-leave double with gorgeous sea views.

Coombe House B&B ££
(☎01297-443849; www.coombe-house.co.uk; 41 Coombe St; s/d £36/68, 5-person flat per week £350-610; P) Easygoing and stylish with airy bedrooms, this fabulous value guesthouse is full of bay windows, wicker and white wood. Breakfast is delivered to your room on a trolley, complete with homemade bread and a toaster – perfect for a lazy lie-in in Lyme.

Old Lyme B&B ££
(☎01297-442929; www.oldlymeguesthouse.co.uk; 29 Coombe St; d £82-90, tr £120; P) Simple, blue and yellow rooms, patterned curtains and china trinkets define this quaint, 17th-century cottage.

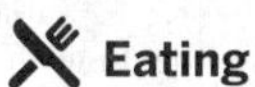

Eating

TOP CHOICE **Hix Oyster & Fish House** SEAFOOD ££

(☎01297-446910; www.hixoysterandfishhouse.co.uk; Cobb Rd; mains £12-21; ⊙noon-10pm Tue-Sun) Expect sweeping views of the Cobb and dazzling food at this super-stylish open-plan cabin. Ink-cooked spelt comes with Devon squid, scallops with black pudding, and steak with scrumpy-fried onions. Perhaps start by slurping some oysters: Brownsea Island or Falmouth molluscs come at £2.25 to £3.50 a pop.

Town Mill CAFE, BAKERY £

(www.townmillbakery.com; 2 Coombe St; mains £5; ⊙8.30am-3.30pm Mon-Sat, from 10am Sun) More like a friend's front room than a cafe, this is Lyme's top snacking spot. Brunch sees you carving slices off huge loaves to toast, before asking the stranger sitting next to you to please pass the jam. Lunch tempts with soups and flans, while the pizza suppers (5pm to 8pm) in the summer holidays are worth arriving early for.

Alexandra TEAROOM

(www.hotelalexandra.co.uk; Pound St; afternoon tea £5-21; ⊙2.30-5.30pm) Head to this grand, 18th-century hotel's sea-view lawns for the ultimate English experience: afternoon tea, complete with scones, clotted cream and cucumber sandwiches.

Harbour Inn PUB £

(Marine Pde; mains £9-14) Stone walls, wooden settles, a harbourside beer garden and the best pub grub in town.

Information

Tourist Office (☎01297-442138; www.westdorset.com; Church St; ⊙10am-5pm Mon-Sat, 10am-4pm Sun)

Getting There & Away

Bus 31 runs to **Dorchester** (1¼ hours) and **Weymouth** (1¾ hours) hourly. Bus X53 (two to six daily) goes west to **Exeter** (1¾ hours) and east to **Weymouth** (1¾ hours).

Sherborne

POP 9590

Sherborne gleams with a mellow, orangey-yellow stone – it's been used to build a central cluster of 15th-century buildings and the impressive abbey church at their core. This serene town exudes wealth. The five local fee-paying schools include the famous Sherborne School, and its pupils are a frequent sight as they head off to lessons around the town. Ranks of clothing boutiques and shops selling antiques reinforce the well-heeled feel. Evidence of splashing the cash 16th- and 18th-century style lies on the edge of town with two castles: one a crumbling ruin, the other a marvellous manor house, complete with a Capability Brown lake.

Sights & Activities

FREE **Sherborne Abbey** CHURCH

(☎01935-812452; www.sherborneabbey.com; suggested donation £3.50; ⊙8am-6pm) At the height of its influence, the magnificent Abbey

LOCAL KNOWLEDGE

STEVE DAVIES: OWNER OF DINOSAURLAND FOSSIL MUSEUM

Steve Davies is a man with weathered legs and a gleam in his eye. And that gleam's never brighter than when, in his trademark shorts and running shoes, he's heading off to the beach on a fossil-hunting foray.

Why is it addictive? It's hunting and gathering, collecting booty off the beach. To look down and see a tiny, gold ammonite lying there waiting to be picked up is mind-blowing.

Best spot? Black Ven, a mud flow between Lyme and Charmouth. The rocks tumble down, the tides wash the silt away and the fossils just drop onto the beach. Every day there's a new crop. But it's very easy to get cut off there. You must only search within 1½ hours of low tide, and take local advice on conditions first.

Top tip? Don't use a fossil-hunting hammer. You'll get much better results by just looking closely at the gravel around the mudflows: then you could find bucket loads.

Don't Miss! The Ammonite Pavement about 400m west of the Cobb. It has hundreds of fossilised, swirling sea creatures embedded in layers of rock. There's something to see at all stages of the tide, but for the best displays visit at low water; then it's truly extraordinary.

FORDE ABBEY

A former Cistercian monastery, **Forde Abbey** (☎01460-220231; www.fordeabbey.co.uk; Chard; abbey adult/child £10.50/free, gardens £8.50/free; ⌚abbey noon-4pm Tue-Fri & Sun Apr-Oct, gardens 10am-4.30pm) was built in the 12th century, updated in the 17th century, and has been a private home since 1649. The building boasts magnificent plasterwork ceilings and fine tapestries, but it's the gardens that are the main attraction: 12 hectares of lawns, ponds, shrubberies and flower beds packed with bamboo, rhododendron and asters – though the 160ft fountain can steal the show.

It's 10 miles north of Lyme Regis; public transport is a nonstarter.

Church of St Mary the Virgin was the central cathedral of the 26 Saxon bishops of Wessex. Established early in the 8th century, it became a Benedictine abbey in 998 and functioned as a cathedral until 1075. The church has mesmerising fan vaulting that's the oldest in the country; a central tower supported by Saxon-Norman piers; and an 1180 Norman porch. Its tombs include the elaborate marble effigy belonging to John Lord Digby, Earl of Bristol, and those of the elder brothers of Alfred the Great, Ethelred and Ethelbert.

On the edge of the abbey lie the beautiful 15th-century **St John's Almshouses** (admission £2; ⌚2-4pm Tue & Thu-Sat May-Sep); look out, too, for the six-sided **conduit** now at the foot of Cheap St. This arched structure used to be the monks' lavatorium (washhouse), but was moved to provide the townsfolk with water when the abbey was disbanded.

Sherborne Old Castle CASTLE

(EH; ☎01935-812730; www.english-heritage.org.uk; adult/child £3.40/2; ⌚10am-5pm Apr-Oct) These days the epitome of a picturesque ruin, Sherborne's Old Castle was built by Roger, Bishop of Salisbury, in around 1120. Elizabeth I gave it to her one-time favourite Sir Walter Raleigh in the late 16th century. He spent large sums of money modernising it before opting for a new-build instead, moving across the River Yeo to start work on Sherborne New Castle. The old one became a Royalist stronghold during the English Civil War, but Cromwell reduced the 'malicious and mischievous castle' to rubble after a 16-day siege in 1645, leaving just the fractured southwest gatehouse, great tower and north range.

Sherborne New Castle CASTLE

(☎01935-812072; www.sherbornecastle.com; house adult/child £10/free, gardens only £5/free; ⌚11am-4.30pm Tue-Thu & weekends Apr-Oct; P) Having had enough of the then 400-year-old Sherborne Old Castle, Sir Walter Raleigh began building the New Castle in 1594. Raleigh got as far as the central block before falling out of favour with the royals and ending up back in prison – this time at the hands of James I. In 1617 James sold the castle to Sir John Digby, Earl of Bristol, who added the wings we see today. Some 130 years later, the grounds received a mega-makeover by landscape-gardener extraordinaire Capability Brown; visit today and marvel at the massive lake he added, along with the remarkable 12-hectare waterside gardens.

Sherborne Museum MUSEUM

(☎01935-812252; www.sherbornemuseum.co.uk; Church Lane; adult/child £1/free; ⌚10.30am-4.30pm Tue-Sat Apr-Nov, 10.30am-12.30pm Tue & Thu Nov-Mar) Contains an interactive digital version of the *Sherborne Missal*, an exquisite illuminated manuscript dating from the Middle Ages.

Walking Tours HERITAGE TOURS

(tour £4; ⌚11am Fri Jul-Sep) These 90-minute trips explore the photogenic old town, leaving from the tourist office.

Sleeping

Cumberland House B&B ££

(☎01935-817554; www.bandbdorset.co.uk; Green Hill; s £50-65, d £65-85; P 📶) There are few straight lines in this 17th-century cottage; instead, walls undulate towards each other in charming rooms done in oatmeal, fresh lemon and terracotta colours. Breakfast is either continental (expect tangy homemade compote) or full English – there's freshly squeezed orange juice either way.

Stoneleigh Barn B&B ££

(☎01935-389288; www.stoneleighbarn.co.uk; North Wootton; s/d/f £60/80/90; P 📶) Outside, this gorgeous 18th-century barn delights the senses – it's smothered in bright, fragrant flowers. Inside, exposed trusses frame spacious rooms delicately decorated in lilac and turquoise. Stoneleigh is 3 miles southeast of Sherborne.

Eastbury HOTEL £££
(☎01935-813131; www.theeastburyhotel.co.uk; Long St; s £70, d £140-190; P 📶) The best rooms here have real 'wow' factor – black and gold lacquer screens frame minimalist free-standing baths; shimmering fabrics swathe French sleigh beds. The standard rooms are less exotic but still swish, boasting fresh-baked biscuits, luxury smellies and linen bathrobes.

Eating

Green MODERN BRITISH ££
(☎01935-813821; www.greenrestaurant.co.uk; 3 The Green; mains £7-14; ⊙Tue-Sat) The contented chatter of Sherborne's food fans lends this restaurant a vibrant air, while creative flavour combos keep taste buds tingling: pheasant breast is teamed with mulled wine; local scallops are paired with blood-orange butter. On Friday and Saturday there's a sumptuous set dinner (2/3 courses £32/37).

Three Wishes CAFE BISTRO ££
(www.thethreewishes.co.uk; 78 Cheap St; mains £6-12; ⊙9.30am-5.30pm Mon-Thu, dinner Fri & Sat, lunch Sun) Imaginative uses of Dorset produce keeps customers happy at this buzzing eatery – favourites include the flavoursome seared beef and blue-cheese salad, or the fragrant kiln-roasted local salmon risotto.

Information

Tourist Office (☎01935-815341; www.visit-dorset.com; Digby Rd; ⊙9am-5pm Mon-Sat) Stocks the free *Sherborne: Famous Abbey Town* leaflet, which has a map and town trail.

Getting There & Away

Bus

Dorchester (one hour, two-hourly Monday to Saturday) Bus 216, via **Cerne Abbas** (30 minutes).

Shaftesbury (£5.30, 30 minutes, daily) National Express.

Yeovil (30 minutes, hourly Monday to Saturday) Buses 57 and 58.

Train

Hourly services:

Exeter (£17, one hour)

London Waterloo (£30, 2½ hours)

Salisbury (£12, 40 minutes).

Shaftesbury & Around

POP 6640

Crowning a ridge of hog-backed hills and overlooking pastoral meadows, the agreeable market town of Shaftesbury circles around its historic abbey ruins. The medieval faith community that lived here was nationally significant, and the names of its key players – Kings Alfred and Knut – still evoke a rich heritage. Shaftesbury's other big landmark is Gold Hill. This often-photographed, painfully steep, quaint cobbled slope is lined by chocolate-box cottages and starred in a famous TV advert for Hovis bread.

Sights

Shaftesbury Abbey RUINS
(☎01747-852910; www.shaftesburyabbey.org.uk; Park Walk; adult/child £3/free; ⊙10am-5pm Apr-Oct) These hilltop ruins mark the site of what was England's largest and richest nunnery. It was founded in 888 by King Alfred the Great, and was the first religious house in Britain built solely for women; Alfred's daughter, Aethelgifu, was its first abbess. St Edward is thought to have been buried here, and King Knut died at the abbey in 1035. Most of the buildings were dismantled by Henry VIII in the Dissolution of 1539, but you can still wander around its foundations with a well-devised audioguide and hunt out statuary and illuminated manuscripts in the museum.

Old Wardour Castle CASTLE
(EH; ☎01747-870487; www.english-heritage.org.uk; adult/child £4/2.40; ⊙10am-5pm Apr-Oct, 10am-4pm Sat & Sun Nov-Mar; P) The six-sided Old Wardour Castle was built around 1393 and suffered severe damage during the English Civil War, leaving these imposing remains. The views from the upper levels are fabulous while its grassy lawns make a fine spot for a picnic. It's open until 6pm in July and August and is 4 miles west of Shaftesbury.

FREE **Gold Hill Museum** MUSEUM
(☎01747-852157; www.goldhillmuseum.org.uk; Gold Hill; ⊙10.30am-4.30pm) Combines an 18th-century fire engine, a collection of decorative Dorset buttons and the ornamental 'Byzant', used during the town's ancient water ceremony.

Sleeping & Eating

Fleur de Lys HOTEL £££

(☎01747-853717; www.lafleurdelys.co.uk; Bleke St; s £80-90, d £110-150; P@☎) For a delicious dollop of luxury, immerse yourself in the world of Fleur de Lys. Fluffy bathrobes, mini-fridges and laptops ensure you click into pamper mode. The **restaurant** (book lunch Wednesday to Sunday, dinner Monday to Saturday, two/three courses £27/33) rustles up elegant dishes such as crab consommé, and local Dover sole with caviar.

Updown COTTAGE £

(☎07710 307202; www.updowncottage.co.uk; 12 Gold Hill; per week from £500; P☎) This whitewashed, four-bedroom cottage clinging to Gold Hill is a supremely picturesque place to sleep. Snug, beam-lined rooms, open fires and a hillside garden make it one to remember; the boutique bathrooms make it hard to leave.

Mitre PUB ££

(23 High St; mains £6-10) Expect drink-them-in views over Blackmore Vale from this atmospheric old inn's decked terrace, and a menu crammed with classy pub classics – try the Cumberland bangers 'n' mash, or pork and cider casserole.

Information

Tourist Office (☎01747-853514; www.shaftesburydorset.com; 8 Bell St; ⊙10am-5pm)

Getting There & Away

London Victoria (£20, four hours, one daily) National Express, goes via Heathrow.

Salisbury (one hour, three to four Monday to Saturday) Bus 26/27.

Sherborne (£5.30, 30 minutes, one daily) National Express.

WILTSHIRE

Wiltshire is rich in the reminders of ritual and packed with not-to-be-missed sights. Its verdant landscape is littered with more mysterious stone circles, processional avenues and ancient barrows than anywhere else in Britain. It's a place that teases and tantalises the imagination – here you'll experience the prehistoric majesty of Stonehenge and the atmospheric stone ring at Avebury. Then there's the serene 800-year-old cathedral at Salisbury – a relatively modern religious monument. Add the supremely stately homes at Stourhead and Longleat and the impossibly pretty villages of Castle Combe and Lacock, and you have a county crammed full of English charm waiting to be explored.

Activities

Walking

Wiltshire is great walking country, much of it flat or rolling farmland that's interspersed with steep-sided valleys, edged with grassy hills and dotted with ancient monuments.

The 87-mile Ridgeway National Trail (p243) starts near Avebury shorter walks include hikes around Stonehenge, Old Sarum and the Stourhead Estate.

Visit Wiltshire has scores of downloadable guides to both shorter walks (3 to 10 miles) and long distance routes – a highlight is the White Horse Trail, a 90-mile route which takes in all eight of the historic horse figures that are cut into Wiltshire's chalk hills. Tourist offices stock leaflets too.

Foot Trails (☎01747-820626; www.foottrails.co.uk; 2-days from £300) leads guided walks and can help you plan your own self-guided route.

Cycling

The 160 mile **Wiltshire Cycleway** traces an oval around the county, taking in Salisbury, Bradford-on-Avon and Malmesbury; look out for route guides in tourist offices. Visit Wiltshire has links to downloadable maps of sections of the trail, as well as five other cycling routes, ranging from 16 to 33 miles; it also details off-road trails.

Dedicated cycling tours are offered by several operators, including **History on Your Handlebars** (☎01249-730013; www.historyonyourhandlebars.co.uk; per day from £35).

Canal Trips

The 87-mile-long **Kennet & Avon Canal** (www.katrust.org) runs all the way from Bristol to Reading. **Sally Boats** (☎01225-864923; www.sallyboats.ltd.uk) and **Foxhangers** (☎01380-828795; www.foxhangers.co.uk) both have narrow boats for hire. Weekly rates for a four-berth boat range from around £630 in the winter to £1200 in high summer.

Information

There are tourist offices in Salisbury (p290) and Bradford-on-Avon (p295), but council-run offices in Devizes and Avebury have been closed.

Visit Wiltshire (www.visitwiltshire.co.uk)

Getting Around

BUS Bus coverage in Wiltshire can be patchy, especially in the county's northwest. The two main operators:

First (www.firstgroup.com) Serves west Wiltshire.

Wilts & Dorset Buses (www.wdbus.co.uk) Covers Salisbury and many rural areas. It sells one-day **Explorer Tickets** (£8) and seven-day **Passes** (Salisbury area £13, network-wide £22).

TRAIN Rail lines run from London to Salisbury and beyond to Exeter and Plymouth, branching off north to Bradford-on-Avon, Bath and Bristol. Most of the smaller towns and villages aren't served by trains.

Salisbury

POP 39,730

Centred on a majestic cathedral that's topped by the tallest spire in England, the city of Salisbury makes a charismatic base for forays into the rest of Wiltshire. It's been an important city for more than 800 years, and its streets form an architectural timeline stretching from medieval walls and half-timbered Tudor houses, to Georgian mansions and Victorian villas. Beautiful buildings aside, Salisbury is also a lively, modern town, boasting plenty of bars and terraced cafes, as well as a concentrated cluster of excellent museums, some with key Stonehenge finds.

Sights

FREE Salisbury Cathedral CATHEDRAL

(☎01722-555120; www.salisburycathedral.org.uk; requested donation adult/child £5/3; ⏰7.15am-6.15pm) England is endowed with countless stunning churches, but few can hold a candle to the grandeur and sheer spectacle of Salisbury Cathedral. Built between 1220 and 1258, the structure bears all the hallmarks of the early English Gothic style, with an elaborate exterior decorated with pointed arches and flying buttresses, and a sombre, austere interior designed to keep its congregation suitably pious.

Beyond the highly decorative **West Front**, a small passageway leads into the 70m-long nave, lined with handsome pillars of Purbeck stone. In the north aisle look out for a fascinating **medieval clock** dating from 1386, probably the oldest working timepiece in the world. At the eastern end of the ambulatory the glorious **Prisoners of Conscience** stained-glass window (1980) hovers above the ornate tomb of Edward Seymour (1539–1621) and Lady Catherine Grey. Other monuments and tombs line the sides of the nave, including that of William Longespée, son of Henry II and half-brother of King John. When the tomb was excavated a well-preserved rat was found inside Longespée's skull.

The cathedral really comes into its own during **Evensong**, which takes place at 5.30pm Monday to Saturday and 3pm on Sunday, during term time only.

Salisbury's 123m crowning glory, its **spire**, was added in the mid-14th century, and is the tallest one in Britain. It represented an enormous technical challenge for its medieval builders; it weighs around 6500 tons and required an elaborate system of cross-bracing, scissor arches and supporting buttresses to keep it upright. Look closely and you'll see that the additional weight has buckled the four central piers of the nave.

Sir Christopher Wren surveyed the cathedral in 1668 and calculated that the spire was leaning by 75cm. A brass plate in the floor of the nave is used to measure any shift, but no further lean was recorded in 1951 or 1970. Despite this, reinforcement of the notoriously 'wonky spire' continues to this day.

Salisbury Cathedral's **Chapter House** (⏰10am-4.30pm Mon-Sat, 12.45-4.30pm Sun) is home to one of only four surviving original copies of the **Magna Carta**, the historic agreement made between King John and his barons in 1215 that acknowledged the fundamental principle that the monarch was not above the law. It's still a powerful document; beautifully written and remarkably well preserved.

The best way to experience the cathedral is on a 90-minute **tower tour** (☎01722-555156; adult/child £8.50/6.50; ⏰11am-2.30pm Apr-Sep, 1 per day Mon-Sat Nov-Mar); these see you climbing 332 vertigo-inducing steps to the base of the spire for jaw-dropping views across the city and the surrounding countryside. Bookings are required.

Cathedral Close HISTORIC AREA

Salisbury's medieval cathedral close, a hushed enclave surrounded by beautiful houses, has an otherworldly feel. Many of the buildings date from the same period as the cathedral, although the area was heavily restored during an 18th-century clean-up by James Wyatt.

Salisbury

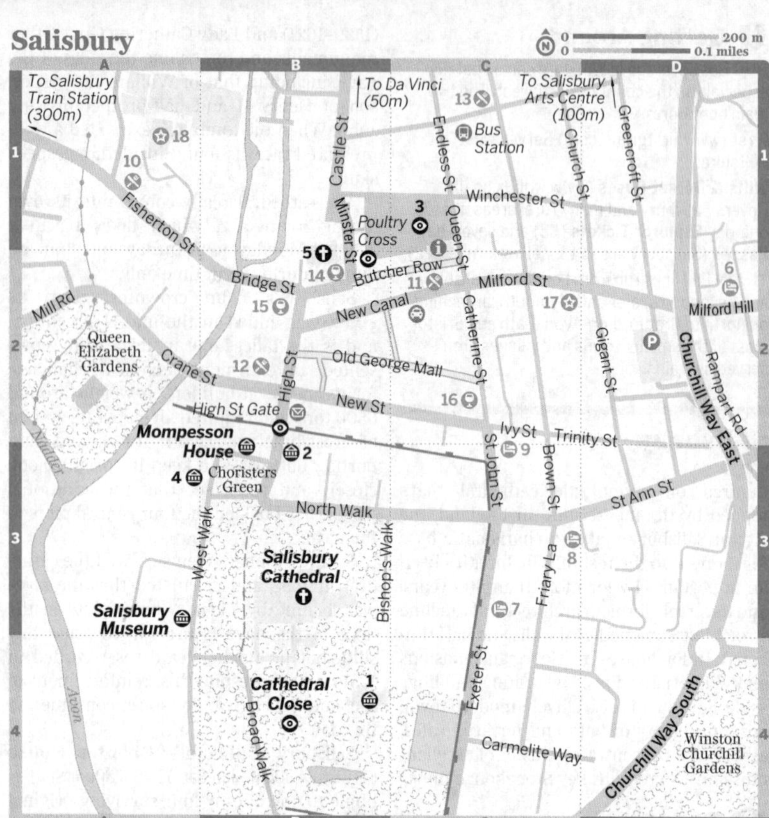

The close is encircled by a sturdy outer wall, constructed in 1333; the stout gates leading into the complex are still locked every night. Just inside the narrow High St Gate is the **College of Matrons**, founded in 1682 for widows and unmarried daughters of clergymen. South of the cathedral is the **Bishop's Palace**, now the private Cathedral School, parts of which date back to 1220. The close is also home to three museums and historic buildings – **Salisbury Museum**, **Mompesson House**, and the **Rifles**.

Salisbury Museum MUSEUM

(☎01722-332151; www.salisburymuseum.org.uk; 65 Cathedral Close; adult/child £5.40/1.80; ⏲10am-5pm Mon-Sat year-round, plus noon-5pm Sun Jun-Sep) The hugely important archaeological finds here include the Stonehenge Archer: the bones of a man found in the ditch surrounding the stone circle – one of the arrows found alongside probably killed him. Add gold coins dating from 100 BC and a Bronze Age gold necklace, and it's a great introduction to Wiltshire's prehistory.

Mompesson House HISTORIC BUILDING

(NT; ☎01722-335659; www.nationaltrust.org.uk; Cathedral Close; adult/child £5.30/2.65; ⏲11am-5pm Sat-Wed mid-Mar–Oct) Built in 1701, this fine Queen Anne building boasts magnificent plasterwork ceilings, exceptional period furnishings and a wonderful carved staircase. All that made it the perfect location for the 1995 film *Sense and Sensibility*.

Rifles MUSEUM

(The Wardrobe; ☎01722-419419; www.thewardrobe.org.uk; 58 Cathedral Close; adult/child £4/1; ⏲10am-5pm Mon-Sat, noon-4.30pm Sun, closed Dec & Jan) Collections include a cannonball from the American War of Independence, Victorian redcoat uniforms and displays on 19th- and 21st-century conflicts in Afghanistan.

Salisbury

Top Sights

- Cathedral Close B4
- Mompesson House B3
- Salisbury Cathedral B3
- Salisbury Museum A3

Sights

1 Bishop's Palace B4
2 College of Matrons B3
3 Market Square C1
4 Rifles A3
5 St Thomas's Church B2

Sleeping

6 Salisbury YHA D2
7 Spire House C3
8 St Ann's House C3
9 White Hart C3

Eating

10 Anokaa A1
11 Bird & Carter C2
12 Lemon Tree B2
13 Pheasant C1

Drinking

14 Haunch of Venison B2
15 Moloko B2
16 Spirit C2

Entertainment

17 Chapel C2
18 Salisbury Playhouse A1

St Thomas's Church CHURCH
(☎01722-322537; www.stthomassalisbury.co.uk; Minster St; ⏲9am-5pm) This stately church was built for cathedral workmen in 1219 and named after St Thomas Becket. Its most famous feature is the amazing **doom painting** above the chancel arch, painted in 1475, which depicts Christ on the Day of Judgement, sitting astride a rainbow flanked by visions of Heaven and Hell. On the Hell side, look out for two naked kings, a nude bishop, a miser with his moneybags, and a female alehouse owner – the only person allowed to hang on to her clothes.

Market Square HISTORIC AREA
Markets were first held here in 1219, and the square still bustles with traders every Tuesday and Saturday (from 8am to 4pm), when you can pick up anything from fresh fish to discount watches. The narrow lanes surrounding the square reveal their medieval specialities: Oatmeal Row, Fish Row and Silver St. The 15th-century **Poultry Cross** is the last of four market crosses that once stood on the square.

Tours

Salisbury Guides HERITAGE TOURS
(☎07873 212941; www.salisburycityguides.co.uk; adult/child £4/2; ⏲11am daily Apr-Oct, 11am Sat & Sun Nov-Mar) These 90-minute walking trips leave from the tourist office (p290). There's an 8pm ghost walk on Fridays from May to September.

Festivals

Salisbury Festival ARTS FESTIVAL
(www.salisburyfestival.co.uk) A prestigious, eclectic event running from late May to early June, encompassing classical, world and pop music, plus theatre, literature and art.

Sleeping

TOP CHOICE **St Ann's House** BOUTIQUE B&B ££
(☎01722-335657; www.stannshouse.co.uk; 32 St Ann St; s/d £60/110) For some perfectly priced indulgence, head to this sumptuous Georgian terrace, which overflows with antiques, fine silk and linen direct from Istanbul. The gourmet breakfast buffet includes *ashera* (a cinnamon-scented Turkish pudding), roll mops and baked goat's cheese. The chef-proprietor has spent decades cooking for the rich and famous – ask about former clients and prepare for some great stories.

Spire House B&B ££
(☎01722-339213; www.salisbury-bedandbreakfast.com; 84 Exeter St; s £65-75, d £80, f £95-100; P) Breakfast tables here groan with homemade goodies: Dorset apple cakes, muffins, bread and jam. The comfy rooms have four-poster beds, Georgian-themed wallpaper and, at the front, excellent cathedral views.

Old Rectory B&B ££
(☎01722-502702; www.theoldrectory-bb.co.uk; 75 Belle Vue Rd; s £45-55, d £70-85; P Wi-Fi) This B&B's serene, airy rooms are decked out in cream and shades of blue, the delightful walled garden is framed by roses and the Australian owner, Trish, will make you feel right at home. The Old Rectory is a mile north of the cathedral.

Rokeby B&B ££
(☎01722-329800; www.rokebyguesthouse.co.uk; 3 Wain-a-long Rd; s £40-70, d £60-95; P Wi-Fi)

Glinting bathrooms, satin cushions and gauzy throws lift this late-Victorian B&B above the rest. Stand-alone baths, wrought-iron fireplaces and the decking overlooking the lawn help, too. Rokeby is a mile north-east of the cathedral.

Salisbury YHA HOSTEL £
(☎0845-371 9537; www.yha.org.uk; Milford Hill; dm £18; P@) A real gem: neat rooms in a rambling, listed Victorian building. Choose from doubles or dorms; a cafe-bar, laundry and dappled gardens add to the appeal.

White Hart HOTEL ££
(☎01722-327476; www.mercure-uk.com; St John St; s from £90, d £122-142; P🛜) In this old-school coaching inn expect muted conversation, swish rooms and attentive service.

Eating

Anokaa INDIAN
(☎01722-414142; www.anokaa.com; 60 Fisherton St; mains £11-32; ⊙lunch & dinner; ✎) Sophisticated, contemporary Indian cuisine makes this the top table in town. Expect char-grilled halibut to be flavoured with curry leaves, and asparagus to come with cheese and roast strawberries. Wise locals head for the bargain buffet lunches (£9 per person).

Da Vinci ITALIAN ££
(☎01722-328402; www.davinciofsalisbury.co.uk; 68 Castle St; mains £8-26; ⊙lunch & dinner Mon-Sat) The Da Vinci *ristorante* brings a dash of southern Europe to south Wiltshire. Here risottos come infused with saffron, meats are wrapped in rich hams and cheese, and the pasta comes laced with flavour-packed sauces.

Pheasant GASTROPUB ££
(☎01722-322866; www.restaurant-salisbury.com; 19 Salt La; mains £7-15; ⊙food noon-9.30pm) Flying the flag for great British bar food, this chilled-out gastropub does the basics well; try the pheasant stuffed with bacon and leeks, and the gooey, crumbly Eton mess. To drink? Perhaps a pint of Pigswill (honestly – it's a local ale).

Bird & Carter DELI, CAFE £
(3 Fish Row, Market Sq; snacks from £5; ⊙8.30am-6pm Mon-Sat, 10am-4pm Sun) This heavily beamed deli-cafe is piled high with local meats and cheeses – the New Forest Blue, Old Sarum and Nanny Williams come from just a few miles away. Grab a wedge of quiche and chunky potato salad to go, or duck upstairs to eat surrounded by weathered wood, stained glass and old church pews.

Lemon Tree BRITISH ££
(☎01722-333471; www.thelemontree.co.uk; 92 Crane St; mains £10; ⊙Mon-Sat) A bijou bistro with a menu that combines English classics with the unexpected; the pork is roasted with rosemary, but the ham comes with buffalo liver.

Drinking

Haunch of Venison PUB
(www.haunchofvenison.uk.com; 1 Minster St) Featuring wood-panelled snugs, spiral staircases and wonky ceilings, this 14th-century drinking den is packed with atmosphere – and ghosts. One is a cheating whist player whose hand was severed in a game – look out for his mummified bones on display inside.

Spirit BAR
(46 Catherine St) Hip hang-out with a multi-coloured light-up floor, crowd-pleasing tunes on the decks and a choice of vivid cocktails.

Moloko BAR
(www.themolokobar.co.uk; 5 Bridge St) Black and red decor, Soviet stars and hot-coloured vodkas create a Cold War theme.

Entertainment

Salisbury Arts Centre ARTS CENTRE
(www.salisburyartscentre.co.uk; Bedwin St) Housed in the converted St Edmund's church some 800m northeast of the cathedral, this innovative arts centre showcases cutting-edge theatre, indie films, dance and live gigs.

Salisbury Playhouse THEATRE
(www.salisburyplayhouse.com; Malthouse Lane) A major producing theatre that also hosts top touring shows and musicals.

Chapel NIGHTCLUB
(www.chapelnightclub.com; 34 Milford St) Buzzing bar with adjoining club where the DJ sets range from urban to chart and cheese.

Information

Library (Market Pl; ⊙10am-7pm Mon,Tue & Fri, to 5pm Wed, Thu & Sat) Internet access.

Tourist Office (☎01722-334956; www.visitwiltshire.co.uk/salisbury; Fish Row, Market Sq; ⊙9.30am-6pm Mon-Sat, 10am-4pm Sun Jun-Sep, Mon-Sat Oct-Apr)

Getting There & Away

Bus

National Express services:

Bath (£11, 1¼ hours, one daily)
Bristol (£10, 2¼ hours, daily)
London (£10, three hours, three daily) via **Heathrow**

Local services include:

Shaftesbury (1 hour, three to four Monday to Saturday) Bus 26/27
Devizes (1 hour, hourly Monday to Saturday) Bus 2

Tour buses leave Salisbury for Stonehenge regularly.

Train

Trains run half-hourly from **London Waterloo** (£35,1½ hours).

Hourly connections include the following:

Bath (£9, one hour)
Bradford-on-Avon (£11.60, 40 minutes)
Bristol (£11, 1¼ hours)
Exeter (£30, two hours)
Portsmouth (£17, 1½ hours)
Southampton (£8.40, 30 minutes)

Around Salisbury

Old Sarum HISTORIC SITE

(EH; ☎01722-335398; www.english-heritage.org.uk; adult/child £3.50/1.80; ⏲10am-5pm; P) The huge ramparts of Old Sarum sit on a grassy rise 2 miles north of Salisbury. It began life as a hill fort during the Iron Age, and was later occupied by both the Romans and the Saxons. By the mid-11th century it was one of the most important towns in the west of England; William the Conqueror convened one of his earliest councils here. The first cathedral was built in 1092, snatching the bishopric from nearby Sherborne Abbey. But Old Sarum always had problems: it was short on water and exposed to the elements, and in 1219 the bishop was given permission to move the cathedral to a new location beside the River Avon, founding the modern-day city of Salisbury. By 1331 Old Sarum's cathedral had been demolished for building materials and the settlement was practically abandoned.

Today you can wander the grassy ramparts, see the stone foundations of the original cathedral, and look across the Wiltshire countryside to the soaring spire of Salisbury's new cathedral. Medieval tournaments, open-air plays and mock battles are held on selected days. There are free guided tours at 3pm in June, July and August. Old Sarum stays open longer in July and August: from 9am to 6pm.

Between them, buses 5 and 8 run twice an hour from Salisbury to Old Sarum (hourly on Sundays).

TOP CHOICE **Wilton House** HISTORIC BUILDING

(☎01722-746700; www.wiltonhouse.com; house adult/child £14/7.50; ⏲11.30am-4.30pm Sun-Thu May-Aug; P) Stately Wilton House provides an insight into the exquisite, rarefied world of the British aristocracy. The Earls of Pembroke have lived here, in one of the finest stately homes in England, since 1542, and it's been expanded, improved and embellished by successive generations since a devastating fire in 1647. The result is a staggering whistle-stop tour of the history of European art and architecture: magnificent period furniture, frescoed ceilings and elaborate plasterwork frame paintings by Van Dyck, Rembrandt and Joshua Reynolds. Highlights are the **Single** and **Double Cube Rooms**, designed by the pioneering 17th-century architect Inigo Jones. The fine landscaped **grounds** (adult/child £5.50/4; ⏲11am-5pm daily May-Aug) were largely laid out by Capability Brown.

All that architectural eye candy makes the house a favoured film location: *The Madness of King George, Sense and Sensibility* and *Pride and Prejudice* were all shot here. But Wilton was serving as an artistic haven long before the movies – famous guests include Ben Jonson, Edmund Spenser, Christopher Marlowe and John Donne. Shakespeare's *As You Like It* was performed here in 1603, shortly after being penned.

Wilton House is 2½ miles west of Salisbury; bus R3 runs from Salisbury (10 minutes, two hourly).

Stonehenge

This compelling ring of monolithic stones has been attracting a steady stream of pilgrims, poets and philosophers for the last 5000 years and is easily Britain's most iconic archaeological site.

The landscape around Stonehenge is undergoing a two-year revamp which should improve the experience of those visiting. But even before the changes, and despite the huge numbers of tourists who traipse around the perimeter, Stonehenge still

Stonehenge

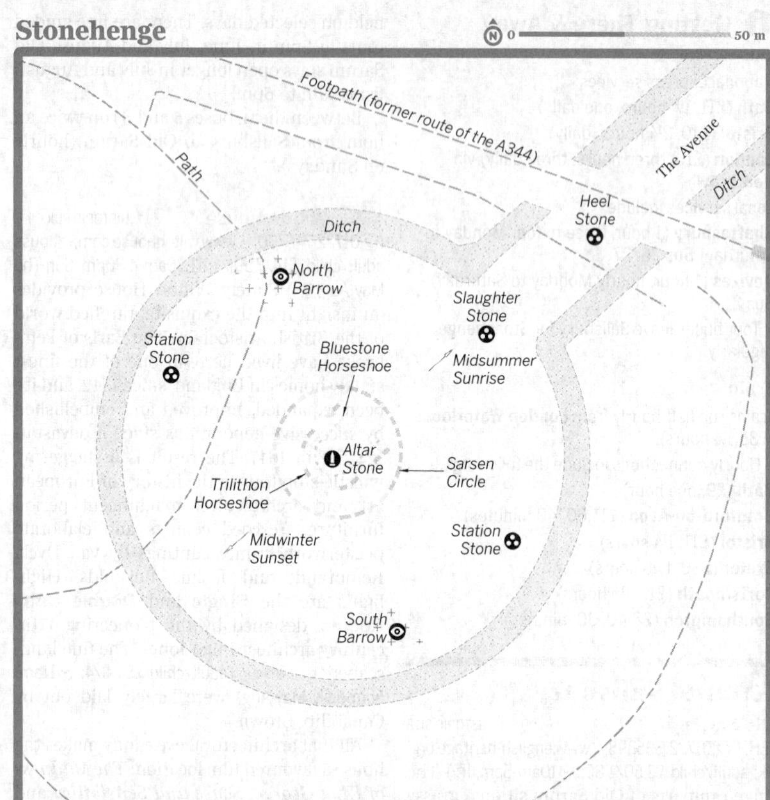

manages to be a mystical, ethereal place – a haunting echo from Britain's forgotten past, and a reminder of the people who once walked the many ceremonial avenues across Salisbury Plain. Even more intriguingly, it's still one of Britain's great archaeological mysteries: despite countless theories about what the site was used for, ranging from a sacrificial centre to a celestial timepiece, in truth, no one knows for sure what drove prehistoric Britons to expend so much time and effort on its construction.

TOP CHOICE Stone Circle Access Visits WALKING TOUR
(☎01722-343830; www.english-heritage.org.uk; adult/child £14.50/7.50) Access visits are an unforgettable experience. Visitors normally have to stay outside the stone circle itself, but on these self-guided walks, you get to wander around the core of the site, getting up-close views of the iconic bluestones and trilithons. They take place in the evening or early morning so the quieter atmosphere and the slanting sunlight add to the effect. Each visit only takes 26 people; to secure a place book at least two months in advance.

THE SITE

The first phase of construction at Stonehenge started around 3000 BC, when the outer circular bank and ditch were erected. A thousand years later, an inner circle of granite stones, known as bluestones, was added. It's thought these mammoth 4-ton blocks were hauled from the Preseli Mountains in South Wales, some 250 miles away – an almost inexplicable feat for Stone Age builders equipped with only the simplest tools. Although no one is entirely sure how the stones were transported so far, it's thought a system of ropes, sledges and rollers fashioned from tree trunks was used –

Salisbury Plain was still covered by forest during Stonehenge's construction.

Around 1500 BC, Stonehenge's main stones were dragged to the site, erected in a circle and crowned by massive lintels to make the trilithons (two vertical stones topped by a horizontal one). The sarsen (sandstone) stones were cut from rock found on the Marlborough Downs, 20 miles from the site. It's estimated dragging one of these 50-ton stones across the countryside would require about 600 people.

Also around this time, the bluestones from 500 years earlier were rearranged as an inner **bluestone horseshoe** with an **altar stone** at the centre. Outside this the **trilithon horseshoe** of five massive sets of stones was erected. Three of these are intact; the other two have just a single upright. Then came the major **sarsen circle** of 30 massive vertical stones, of which 17 uprights and six lintels remain.

Much further out, another circle was delineated by the 58 **Aubrey Holes**, named after John Aubrey, who discovered them in the 1600s. Just inside this circle are the **South and North Barrows**, each originally topped by a stone.

Like many stone circles in Britain (including Avebury, 22 miles away), the inner horseshoes are aligned to coincide with sunrise at the midsummer solstice, which some claim supports the theory that the site was some kind of astronomical calendar. Prehistoric pilgrims would have entered the site via the **Avenue**, whose entrance to the circle is marked by the **Slaughter Stone** and the **Heel Stone**, located slightly further out on one side.

A marked pathway leads around the henge, and although you can't walk freely in the circle itself, it's possible to see the stones fairly close up. An audioguide (in 10 languages) is included in the admission price.

Tours

The **Stonehenge Tour** (01722-336855; www.thestonehengetour.info; return adult/child £11/5) leaves Salisbury's railway and bus stations half-hourly from June to August, and hourly between September and May. Tickets last all day, so you can hop off at Old Sarum (p291) on the way back. If you're going into both sites the bus-plus-entry ticket (adult/child £20/12) produces big savings. For guided tours, try **Salisbury Guided Tours** (0777 5674816; www.salisburyguidedtours.com; per person from £72).

Getting There & Around

Taxis charge £40 from Salisbury to Stonehenge, wait for an hour and come back. Tour buses aside, no regular buses go to the site.

Around Stonehenge

Stonehenge actually forms part of a huge complex of ancient monuments. North of Stonehenge and running roughly east–west is the **Cursus**, an elongated embanked oval; the slightly smaller **Lesser Cursus** is nearby. Theories abound as to what these sites were used for, ranging from ancient sporting arenas to processional avenues for the dead. Two clusters of burial mounds, the **Old** and **New Kings Barrows**, sit beside the ceremonial pathway the **Avenue**, which originally linked Stonehenge with the River Avon, 2 miles away.

CHANGING STONEHENGE

Ancient Stonehenge is undergoing significant change. For decades, debate has raged over the impact of the modern world on the jewel in Britain's archaeological crown. Framed by busy roads, bound by wire fences, crowded with visitors and underscored by traffic noise, it's been a long way from the haven of spiritual tranquillity some expected to find.

But work is now underway to reconnect this stirring monument with its surrounding ritual landscape. The busy A344, which cut the henge off from its processional Avenue, is being closed (from April 2013) and turned into a grassy footpath which will provide the main access to the site. Close to the stones, the visitor centre and car park are being removed and the land returned to grassland. A new visitor centre, due for completion in October 2013, is being built 1.5 miles to the west. It'll have an archaeology gallery with Stonehenge finds, plus a cluster of recreated Neolithic houses. The desired result? Dignity and mystery returned to an archaeological gem in a much more fitting setting.

The website of the National Trust (www.nationaltrust.org.uk) has a downloadable 3.5-mile circular walk that traces tracks across the chalk downland from Stonehenge, past the Cursus and Kings Barrows and along a section of the Avenue itself. The **Stonehenge visitor centre** (EH; ☎0870-333 1181; www.english-heritage.org.uk; adult/child £6.90/3.50; ⏲9am-7pm) also has leaflets detailing walking routes.

Some 1.5 miles east of Stonehenge, near Amesbury, is **Woodhenge** (EH; ☎0870 3331181; www.english-heritage.org.uk; admission free; ⏲dawn-dusk), a series of concentric rings that would once have been marked by wooden posts. It's thought there might be some correlation between the use of wood and stone in both henges. Excavations in the 1970s at Woodhenge revealed the skeleton of a child with a cloven skull, buried near the centre.

Stourhead HISTORIC BUILDING

(NT; ☎01747-841152; www.nationaltrust.org.uk; house or garden adult/child £7.50/4.10, house & garden £12.50/6.20; ⏲house 11am-5pm Fri-Tue mid-Mar–Sep; P) Overflowing with vistas, temples and follies, Stourhead is landscape gardening at its finest. The Palladian house has some fine Chippendale furniture and paintings by Claude and Gaspard Poussin, but it's a sideshow to the magnificent 18th-century **gardens** (⏲9am-dusk), which spread out across the valley. A picturesque 2-mile circuit takes you past the most ornate follies, around the lake and to the **Temple of Apollo**; a 3.5-mile side trip can be made from near the Pantheon to **King Alfred's Tower** (adult/child £3/1.50; ⏲noon-4pm school holidays only), a 50m-high folly with wonderful views.

Stourhead is off the B3092, 8 miles south of Frome (in Somerset).

Longleat HISTORIC HOME

(☎01985-844400; www.longleat.co.uk; all-inclusive ticket adult/child £27/20, house & grounds £13.50/8.50; ⏲10am-7.30pm Jul & Aug, to 5pm Apr-Jun, to 4pm Mar, Sep & Oct; P) Today Longleat is half safari park and half ancestral mansion, but in 1946 it was the first stately home in England to open its doors to the public. It was prompted by finance: heavy taxes and mounting post-WWII bills meant the house had to earn its keep. The estate was transformed into Britain's first safari park in 1966, turning Capability Brown's landscaped grounds into an amazing drive-through zoo, populated by a menagerie of animals more at home in the African wilderness than the fields of Wiltshire. Longleat also has a throng of attractions, including a narrow-gauge railway, a Dr Who exhibit, a Postman Pat village, pets' corner and a butterfly garden.

Under all these tourist trimmings it's easy to forget the house itself, which contains fine tapestries, furniture and decorated ceilings, as well as seven libraries containing around 40,000 tomes. The highlight, though, is an extraordinary series of paintings and psychedelic murals by the present-day marquess, who was an art student in the '60s and upholds the long-standing tradition of eccentricity among the English aristocracy – check out his **website** (www.lordbath.co.uk).

Longleat House is just off the A362, 3 miles from both Frome and Warminster.

Bradford-on-Avon

POP 9370

Tumbling down the slopes of a wooded hillside towards the banks of the River Avon, the beautiful amber-coloured town of Bradford-on-Avon is one of Wiltshire's prettiest – a handsome jumble of Georgian townhouses and riverside buildings that makes a pleasant day trip from Bath, just 8 miles away.

Sights & Activities

Old Town HISTORIC AREA

Bradford grew rich in the 17th and 18th centuries as a thriving centre for the weaving industry, and the town's elegant architecture is a reminder of its former wealth. To the north of the river, former warehouses line the banks, while rows of honey-yellow weavers' cottages stack up in the hills behind; hunt them out in **Middle Rank** and **Tory**.

Westbury House (St Margaret's St), near the river, is where a riot against the introduction of factory machinery in 1791 led to three deaths; the machinery was subsequently burnt on **Town Bridge**.

FREE **Bradford-on-Avon Musuem** MUSUEM

(www.bradfordonavonmuseum.co.uk; Bridge St; ⏲10.30am-12.30pm & 2-4pm Wed-Sat, 2-4pm Sun) Evidence of Bradford's weaving heritage fills this tiny exhibition space above the library. As well as bobbins, reels of wool and evocative late-Victorian photos, there are some formidable ladies' undergarments.

FREE **Tithe Barn** HISTORIC BUILDING
(EH; www.english-heritage.org.uk; ⌚10.30am-4pm Apr-Mar) Tucked away 400m southwest of the town's train station, this vast 14th-century stone structure originally belonged to monks from nearby Shaftesbury Abbey, and was used to store tithes (a 10% produce tax) during the Middle Ages. It's worth visiting for its beautiful wood-vaulted interior and stone-tiled roof. The barn is half a mile south of the town centre, off the B3109.

St Laurence Church CHURCH
(Church St) One of the last surviving Saxon churches in Britain, this was built in the early 11th century. Look out for the twin angels carved above the chancel arch.

Sleeping & Eating

Priory Steps B&B ££
(☎01225-862230; www.priorysteps.co.uk; Newtown; d £98-110) This cosy little hillside hideaway has been created by knocking six weavers' cottages together. Now the charming rooms house antique wooden furniture and sparkling bathrooms – all have captivating views down onto the River Avon.

Bradford Old Windmill B&B ££
(☎01225-866842; www.bradfordoldwindmill.co.uk; 4 Masons Lane; d £110-125; P) One for the 'places-I-have-stayed' photo album: a circular, three-storey former windmill boasting eyebrow-raising features. Queen-sized waterbeds and satin sheets cosy up to conical ceilings and spiral staircases. The whole slightly saucy affair clings to a hill overlooking town.

Beeches FARM B&B ££
(☎01225-865170; www.beeches-farmhouse.co.uk; Holt Rd; d £85; P) Exposed beams, rustic charm and a dollop of luxury in a honey-coloured converted barn – the Buff Orpington chickens clucking around outside will probably lay your breakfast eggs.

Bear INN ££
(☎01225-862356; www.thebearinn.vpweb.co.uk; 26 Silver St; d £85) The natty rooms here are housed in an ancient inn – expect swathes of exposed stone, heritage wallpaper and slatted blinds. The stylish restaurant dishes up gastropub-style food (mains £13).

Fat Fowl EUROPEAN ££
(www.fatfowl.com; Silver St; dinner mains £13; ⌚breakfast, lunch & dinner, closed dinner Sun) Head here for crumbly breakfast pastries, leisurely lunches (mains from £6), tasty tapas (£4) and dinners strong on comfort food: think calves' liver and French beans, and hake with creamed potatoes. There's jazz on some Sundays, too.

Information

Tourist Office (☎01225-865797; www.bradfordonavon.co.uk; 50 St Margaret's St; ⌚10am-5pm)

Getting There & Away

BUS Buses 264 and 265 run from **Bath** (30 minutes, half-hourly, five hourly on Sunday) en route to **Warminster** (40 minutes).

TRAIN Trains go roughly half-hourly to **Bath** (15 minutes), and hourly to **Warminster** (£5, 30 minutes) and **Salisbury** (£11.40, 40 minutes).

Malmesbury

The mellow hilltop town of Malmesbury is peppered with ancient buildings constructed out of orangey-yellow Cotswold stone. It's the oldest borough in England, having been awarded that civic status in 880 AD, and boasts one of the county's finest market crosses – a 15th-century crown-like structure built to shelter the poor from the rain.

The town's big draw is **Malmesbury Abbey** (☎01666-826666; www.malmesburyabbey.info; suggested donation £2; ⌚10am-5pm), a vibrant blend of ruin and living church. Its turbulent history began in the 7th century when a monastery was founded, later to be replaced by a Norman church. By the mid-15th century the abbey had been embellished with a spire and two towers, but in 1479 a storm toppled the east tower and spire, devastating the eastern end of the church. The west tower followed suit in 1662, destroying much of the nave. The present-day church is about a third of its original size, and is flanked by ruins at either end. Notable features include the **Norman doorway** decorated with biblical figures, the Romanesque **Apostle carvings** and a four-volume **illuminated bible** dating from 1407. A window at the western end of the church depicts Elmer the Flying Monk, who in 1010 strapped on wings and jumped from the tower. Although he broke both legs during this leap of faith, he survived and became a local hero.

Just below the abbey are the **Abbey House Gardens** (☎01666-822212; www.abbeyhousegardens.co.uk; adult/child £8/3; ⌚11am-5.30pm mid-Mar–Oct), which include a herb garden, river, waterfall and 2 hectares of colourful blooms.

Bus 31 runs to Swindon (45 minutes, hourly Monday to Saturday); bus 91 heads to Chippenham (35 minutes, hourly Monday to Saturday).

Castle Combe

Proudly trumpeting itself as the 'prettiest village in England', the little hamlet of Castle Combe presents a picture-perfect image of old England – so much so that its quiet streets and stone-walled cottages have appeard in a number of films; most recently it doubled as the Dartmoor village at the centre of Steven Spielberg's WWI epic *War Horse*.

The village grew up around a medieval castle (which no longer exists) and later became an important centre for the local wool trade: old weavers' cottages still huddle around the 18th-century bridge, where the riverbanks were once lined with 20 clattering mills. The village centre has a 13th-century **market cross**, while the medieval **church of St Andrew** contains the carved tomb of Sir Walter de Dunstanville, a 13th-century lord of the manor who fought in the Crusades and was killed in 1270.

The best place to stay in the village is the 12th-century **Castle Inn** (☎01249-783030; www.castle-inn.info; s £85-165, d £115-195), where sumptuous fabrics frame well-worn beams, and atmospheric lights illuminate whirlpool baths. The restaurant (mains £6 to £20) serves up time-honoured British fare including home-baked ham, egg and chips, and a smashing Sunday lunch.

Head to the **White Hart** (☎01249-782295; mains £7-14) for real ales, cheap eats and country atmosphere.

Bus 35/35A runs from Chippenham bus station (40 minutes, four daily Monday to Friday) to Castle Combe.

Lacock

With its geranium-covered cottages, higgledy-piggledy rooftops and idyllic location beside a rushing brook, pockets of the medieval village of Lacock seem to have been preserved in aspic since the mid-19th century. The village has been in the hands of the National Trust since 1944, and in many places it's remarkably free of modern development – there are no telephone poles or electric street lights, and although villagers drive to and fro, the main car park on the outskirts keeps it largely traffic-free. Unsurprisingly, it's also a popular location for movie makers – the village and its abbey pop up in the Harry Potter films, *The Other Boleyn Girl* and BBC adaptations of *Moll Flanders* and *Pride and Prejudice*.

Sights

Lacock Abbey ABBEY

(NT; ☎01249-730459; www.nationaltrust.org.uk; adult/child £10.70/5.30; ⊙10.30am-5.30pm Mar-Oct, 11am-4pm Nov-Feb) Lacock Abbey was founded as an Augustinian nunnery in 1232 by Ela, Countess of Salisbury. After the Dissolution of the Monasteries, the abbey was sold to Sir William Sharington in 1539, who converted the nunnery into a home, demolished the church, built a tower and added a brewery. Highlights are the deeply atmospheric medieval rooms, while the stunning Gothic entrance hall is lined with bizarre terracotta figures; spot the scapegoat with a lump of sugar on its nose. Some of the original 13th-century structure is evident in the cloisters and there are traces of medieval wall paintings. The recently restored botanic garden is also worth a visit.

On Tuesdays year-round and on winter weekdays, access to the abbey is limited to the cloisters. A cheaper ticket (adult/child £7.90/4) will get you into the grounds, museum and abbey cloisters, but not the abbey building itself.

CORSHAM COURT

Three miles northwest of Lacock in Corsham, the Elizabethan mansion of **Corsham Court** (☎01249-712214; www.corsham-court.co.uk; adult/child £7/3; ⊙2-5.30pm Tue-Thu, Sat & Sun late Mar–Sep, Sat & Sun only Oct–late Mar) dates from 1582, although the property was later improved by John Nash and Capability Brown. The opulent house is renowned for its outstanding art collection, which features works by Reynolds, Caravaggio, Rubens and Van Dyck. It's also known for its fragrance-filled formal gardens, which contain a bewitching ruined folly, stunning ornamental box hedges and a Gothic bathhouse.

The ticket into the abbey also includes admission to the **Fox Talbot Museum of Photography**, which profiles the man who pioneered the photographic negative: William Henry Fox Talbot (1800–77). A prolific inventor, he began developing the system in 1834 while working at the abbey. The museum details his ground-breaking work and displays a superb collection of his images.

Sleeping & Eating

Sign of the Angel B&B £££
(☎01249-730230; www.lacock.co.uk; 6 Church St; s £85, d £130-165; P) If you want to slumber amid a superb slice of history, check into this 15th-century beamed bolt-hole. Packed with antique beds, tapestries and buffed chests, comfort levels are brought up to date with free-standing sinks and slipper baths. The restaurant (mains from £14) revels in English classics – try the pigeon, Stilton and walnut paté, then squeeze in treacle tart with clotted cream.

King John's Hunting Lodge B&B ££
(☎01249-730313; www.kingjohnslodge.2day.ws; 21 Church St; s/d/f £80/100/130; P) Lacock's oldest building is a picturesque venue for a quintessentially English afternoon tea (£7 to £16 served from 11am to 5.30pm) of cucumber sandwiches, scones, clotted cream and homemade jam. Upstairs, snug, resolutely old-fashioned bedrooms are crammed with creaky furniture and Tudor touches.

Lacock Pottery B&B ££
(☎01249-730266; www.lacockbedandbreakfast.com; d £84-94; P 🛜) A serene, airy former workhouse featuring peat fires, organic breakfasts and, appropriately, fine ceramics.

George Inn PUB £
(4 West St; mains from £10) A 14th-century, horse brass–hung pub dispensing good grub and local ales.

Getting There & Away

Bus 234 runs hourly, Monday to Saturday, from **Chippenham** (15 minutes).

Devizes

POP 31,330

The busy market town of Devizes is famous for its grand oval marketplace, which is the largest anywhere in England. It also offers a superb collection of archaeological finds from Stonehenge and Avebury, a historic brewery and the chance to connect with age-old means of transport, ranging from shire horses to canal boats.

Sights & Activities

Wiltshire Heritage Museum MUSEUM
(☎01380-727369; www.wiltshireheritage.org.uk; 41 Long St; adult/child £5/4; ⏲10am-5pm Mon-Sat, noon-4pm Sun) The prehistoric finds here are some of Britain's finest, and include the Bush Barrow hoard – the country's richest Bronze Age burial, often dubbed the 'crown jewels of the king of Stonehenge'. This treasure trove was discovered just south of the famous stone circle and includes two exquisitely worked gold plaques, ornate belt hooks and a gold-studded dagger.

Wadworth Brewery BREWERY
(☎01380-732277; www.wadworthvisitorcentre.co.uk; New Park St; adult/child £10/6; ⏲11am & 2pm Mon-Sat, plus 12.30pm Sun Apr-Oct; P) A must for ale aficionados, this Victorian brewery has been producing the tawny elixir since 1875. During a two-hour **tour** you get to smell the hops, see the signwriter's studio and sample the product at the end. There's also a visit to the brewery's shire horse stables. These colossal creatures still stop traffic in Devizes each day, when they deliver beer to the local pubs by cart. Book your tour in advance.

Kennet & Avon Canal MUSEUM
(☎01380-721279; www.katrust.org.uk; The Wharf; adult/child £3.30/1; ⏲10am-4pm) Just west of Devizes, at Caen Hill, 29 locks raise the water level 72m in just 2½ miles. They're part of an 18th- and 19th-century inland waterway network that's brought vividly to life at this museum. For more on the canal, see the boxed text, p317.

Kenavon Venture BOAT TRIPS
(☎0800 028 3707; www.katrust.org.uk; The Wharf; adult/child from £6/3; ⏲2.30pm Wed, Sat & Sun Apr-Oct) Two-hour cruises on a 60ft, wide-beam canal boat, which beautifully conjure up a slower-paced past.

Sleeping & Eating

TOP CHOICE **Blounts Court** FARM B&B ££
(☎01380-727180; www.blountscourtfarm.co.uk; Coxhill La; s/d £45/75; P) In this adorable rural oasis the only sounds you'll hear are birdsong, whinnying horses and the occasional cluck of the now free-roaming, rescued

battery hens. Super-comfy bedrooms effortlessly carry off the unusual combo of old English beams and Ancient Greek figurines. The village cricket green is next door; it's a five-minute walk to the local pub and Devizes is 2 miles away.

Rosemundy Cottage B&B ££
(☎01380-727122; www.rosemundycottage.co.uk; London Rd; s/d £45/75; P@☎≋) There can't be many guesthouses that can match this one's canalside terrace and heated pool. The cheerful owners delight in going the extra mile, providing plunger coffee and DVD players in the bedrooms, and local honey, sausages and free-range duck eggs for breakfast.

Bear HOTEL ££
(☎01380-734669; www.thebearhotel.net; Market Pl; s £95, d £135-165; P☎) A rambling 16th-century coaching inn with spacious rooms, subdued checks and a well-established, old-English feel. The four-poster rooms are gorgeous.

Bistro MODERN BRITISH ££
(☎01380-720043; www.thebistrodevizes.co.uk; 7 Little Brittox; mains £10-18; ⏲Tue-Sat; ✎) The head chef at this foodies' favourite is a passionate champion of local producers. Wiltshire ingredients are laced with exotic flavours; expect the rillette of game to sit beside garlic toast, and the mushroom and herb soufflé to come with chilli jam.

Getting There & Away

Avebury (25 minutes, hourly) Bus 49.
Bath (50 minutes, hourly Monday to Saturday, two-hourly Sunday) Buses X72/271-3.
Salisbury (1¼ hours, hourly Monday to Saturday) Bus 2.

Avebury

While the tour buses head straight for Stonehenge, prehistoric purists make for the massive stone circle at Avebury. Though it undoubtedly lacks the dramatic trilithons of its sister site across the plain, Avebury is arguably a more rewarding place to visit. It's bigger, older and a great deal quieter, and a large section of the village is actually inside the stones – footpaths wind around them, allowing you to really soak up the extraordinary atmosphere. Avebury also boasts a surrounding landscape that's rich in prehistoric sites, and a unique attraction: a manor house where extensively restored rooms span five completely different eras.

Sights

TOP CHOICE **Avebury Stone Circle** MONUMENT
(NT; ☎01672-539250; www.nationaltrust.org.uk; ⏲24hr) With a diameter of about 348m, Avebury is the largest stone circle in the world. It's also one of the oldest, dating from around 2500 to 2200 BC, between the first and second phase of construction at Stonehenge. The site originally consisted of an outer circle of 98 standing stones of up to 6m in length, many weighing 20 tons, which had been carefully selected for their shape and size. The stones were surrounded by another circle delineated by a 5m-high earth bank and ditch up to 9m deep. Inside were smaller stone circles to the north (27 stones) and south (29 stones).

In the Middle Ages, when Britain's pagan past was an embarrassment to the church, many of the stones were buried, removed or broken up. In 1934, wealthy businessman and archaeologist Alexander Keiller supervised the re-erection of the stones, and planted markers to indicate those that had disappeared; he later bought the site for posterity using funds from his family's marmalade fortune.

Self-Guided Tour

Modern roads into Avebury neatly divide the circle into four sectors. Starting at High St, near the Henge Shop, and walking round the circle in an anticlockwise direction, you'll encounter 11 standing stones in the southwest sector. They include the **Barber Surgeon Stone**, named after the skeleton of a man found under it – the equipment buried with him suggests he was a travelling barber-cum-surgeon.

The southeast sector starts with the huge portal stones marking the entry to the circle from the West Kennet Avenue. The **southern inner circle** stood in this sector and within this ring was the **obelisk** and a group of stones known as the **Z Feature**. Just outside this smaller circle, only the base of the **Ring Stone** remains.

In the **northern inner circle** in the northeast sector, three sarsens remain of what would have been a rectangular **cove**. The northwest sector has the most complete collection of standing stones, including the

Avebury

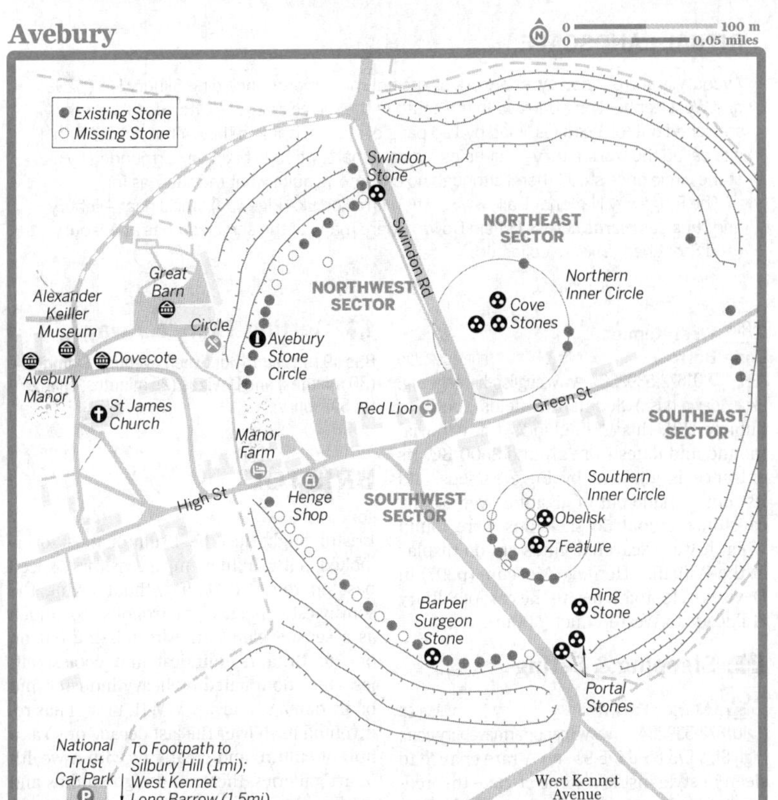

massive 65-ton **Swindon Stone**, one of the few never to have been toppled.

Avebury Manor HISTORIC BUILDING

(NT; ☎01672-539250; www.nationaltrust.org.uk; adult/child £9/4.50; ⊙11am-5pm Thu-Tue Apr-Oct) This 16th-century manor house had the mother of all heritage make-overs as part of the BBC TV series *The Manor Reborn*. It used original techniques and materials to recreate interiors spanning five eras, so now you can sit on beds, play billiards and listen to the gramophone in rooms that range from Tudor, through Georgian to the 1930s. In the garden, the topiary and box hedges create a series of rooms that inspired Vita Sackville-West, creator of Sissinghurst gardens in Kent. Visits are by timed tickets only; arrive early to bag a slot.

Alexander Keiller Museum MUSEUM

(NT; ☎01672-539250; www.nationaltrust.org.uk; adult/child £4.50/2.20; ⊙10am-5.30pm Apr-Oct, to 3.30pm Nov-Mar) Explores the archaeological history of Avebury Stone Circle and traces the story of the archaeologist who dedicated his life to unlocking the secret of the stones.

Silbury Hill PREHISTORIC SITE

(www.english-heritage.org.uk) This huge mound rises abruptly from the surrounding fields just west of Avebury. At more than 40m high, it's the largest artificial earthwork in Europe, and was built in stages from around 2500 BC. No significant artefacts have been found at the site, and the reason for its construction remains unclear. A massive project to stabilise the hill took place in 2008 after a combination of erosion and damage caused by earlier excavations caused part of the top to collapse. Direct access to the hill isn't allowed, but you can view it from a lay-by on the A4. For more atmospheric views though, take the footpath across the fields from Avebury (1½ miles each way) to the hill's north side.

RITUAL LANDSCAPE

Avebury is surrounded by a network of ancient monuments, including Silbury Hill (p299) and West Kennet Long Barrow. To the south of the village, the **West Kennet Avenue** stretched out for 1½ miles, lined by 100 pairs of stones. It linked the Avebury circle with a site called the **Sanctuary**. Post holes indicate that a wooden building surrounded by a stone circle once stood there, although no one knows quite what the site was for.

The Ridgeway National Trail (www.nationaltrail.co.uk/ridgeway) starts near Avebury and runs eastwards across Fyfield Down, where many of the sarsen stones at Avebury (and Stonehenge) were collected.

FREE **West Kennet Long Barrow** BURIAL MOUND
(EH; ☎01672-539250; www.english-heritage.org.uk; ⊙dawn-dusk) Set in the fields south of Silbury Hill, this is England's finest burial mound and dates from around 3500 BC. Its entrance is guarded by huge sarsens and its roof is made out of gigantic overlapping capstones. About 50 skeletons were found when it was excavated; finds are on display at the Wiltshire Heritage Museum (p297) in Devizes. A footpath just to the east of Silbury Hill leads to West Kennet (500m).

Sleeping & Eating

TOP CHOICE **Manor Farm** B&B ££
(☎01672-539294; www.manorfarmavebury.com; High St; s £75-85, d £75-95; P) A rare chance to sleep in style inside a stone circle – this red-brick farmhouse snuggles just inside Avebury henge. The elegant, comfy rooms blend old woods with bright furnishings, there's a splendid free-standing claw-foot bath, and the windows provide spine-tingling views of those 4000-year-old standing stones.

Circle CAFE £
(mains from £7; ⊙10am-6pm;) Veggie and wholefood cafe beside the Great Barn serving homemade quiches and cakes, chunky sandwiches and afternoon teas.

Drinking

Red Lion PUB
(Swindon Rd; mains from £7) Having a pint here means downing a drink at the only pub in the world inside a stone circle. It's also haunted by Flori, who was killed during the Civil War when her husband threw her down a well – it now forms the centrepiece of the dining room.

Getting There & Away

Bus 49 runs hourly between Avebury, **Swindon** (30 minutes) and **Devizes** (25 minutes; change for Salisbury).

BRISTOL

POP 393,300

Bristol might just be Britain's most overlooked city. While most visitors speed past en route to Bath without giving the southwest's biggest metropolis so much as a second glance, they're missing out on one of Britain's quirkiest and coolest cities. Once dominated by heavy industry and badly damaged during WWII, Bristol has reinvented itself over the last decade or so as a hub of culture and creativity, with a wealth of art galleries, theatres, design studios and media companies dotted around the much-revitalised centre. With a revamped waterfront, a flashy new shopping centre at Cabot Circus and a landmark new history museum at M Shed – not to mention its status as the UK's first-ever Bike City – there's a definite buzz about Brizzle these days.

History

The city began as a small Saxon village and the medieval river-port of Brigstow. Bristol later developed as a trading centre for cloth and wine, before 'local hero' John Cabot (actually a Genoese sailor called Giovanni Caboto) really put the city on the map, when he set sail from Bristol to discover Newfoundland in 1497. Over the following centuries, Bristol became one of Britain's major ports, and grew rich on the proceeds of the transatlantic slave trade, and from dealing in cocoa, sugar and tobacco.

By the 18th century, Bristol was suffering from competition from other UK ports, especially London and Liverpool. The city itself was an industrial centre, becoming an important hub for shipbuilding and the terminus for the pioneering Great Western Railway line from London.

During WWII the city's heavy industry became a key target for German bombing, and much of the city centre was reduced to rubble. The postwar rush for reconstruction left Bristol with plenty of concrete eyesores, but over the last decade the city has undergone extensive redevelopment, especially around the dockside. During the 20th century, Bristol also played a key role in Britain's burgeoning aeronautics industry: many key components of Concorde were developed in the nearby suburb of Filton.

In 2006, the city celebrated the bicentenary of the birth of Isambard Kingdom Brunel, the pioneering Victorian engineer responsible for developing (among many other things) the Great Western Railway, the Clifton Suspension Bridge and the SS *Great Britain*.

Sights

TOP CHOICE **SS Great Britain** SHIP

(www.ssgreatbritain.org; Great Western Dock, Gas Ferry Rd; adult/child/family £12.50/6.25/33.50; 10am-5.30pm Apr-Oct) Bristol's pride and joy is the mighty steamship SS *Great Britain*, designed by the genius engineer Isambard Kingdom Brunel in 1843. Built from iron and driven by a revolutionary screw propeller, this massive vessel was one of the largest and most technologically advanced steamships ever built, measuring a mighty 322ft (98m) from stern to tip, and capable of completing the transatlantic crossing between Bristol and New York in just 14 days. It served as a luxury liner until 1886, but enormous running costs and mounting debts eventually led it towards an ignominious end: it was sold off and served variously as a troop vessel, quarantine ship, emigration transport and coal-hulk, before finally being scuttled near Port Stanley in the Falklands in 1937.

Happily, that wasn't the end for the SS *Great Britain*. The ship was towed back to Bristol in 1970, and a painstaking 30-year restoration program has since brought it back to stunning life. You can wander around the ship's impeccably refurbished interior, including the galley, surgeon's quarters, dining saloon and the great engine room, but the highlight is the amazing 'glass sea' on which the ship sits, enclosing an airtight dry dock that preserves the delicate hull and allows visitors to see the groundbreaking screw propeller up close.

Tickets also allow admission to the neighbouring **Maritime Heritage Centre** (0117-927 9856; Great Western Dockyard, Gas Ferry Rd; 10am-5.30pm), which has exhibits relating to the ship's illustrious past and the city's boat-building heritage.

During autumn and winter, a replica of John Cabot's ship, the **Matthew** (0117-927 6868; www.matthew.co.uk), is moored nearby, the same design of ship in which the explorer made his landmark voyage from Bristol to Newfoundland in 1497. When the ship's docked in Bristol, it runs regular cruises around the harbour (adult/child £10/8); see the website for the next sailing dates.

BRISTOL IN...

Two Days

Begin your time in Bristol by exploring the city's historic **Floating Harbour**. Devote a morning to the magnificent **SS Great Britain**, followed by lunch at **Bordeaux Quay**. In the afternoon, check out the latest exhibition at the **Arnolfini Art Gallery**, and then spend some time exploring Bristol's history at its excellent new city museum, **M Shed**. Finish up with a bit of shopping at **St Nicholas Market** and the huge **Cabot Circus** shopping centre. Finish up with dinner at **Riverstation**, and indulge yourself with a night at the swanky **Hotel du Vin**.

On day two, head up the hill to stately Clifton. Factor in a walk across the **Suspension Bridge**, a stroll across the **Downs**, and lunch at one of the area's many cafes and restaurants – we particularly like **Fishers**, the **Clifton Sausage** and the **Thali Café**. Spend the afternoon talking to the animals at **Bristol Zoo** or swimming at the **Bristol Lido**, then catch a cab to **Bell's Diner** or **The Muset by Ronnie** for supper before retiring to bed at **Number 38**.

Bristol

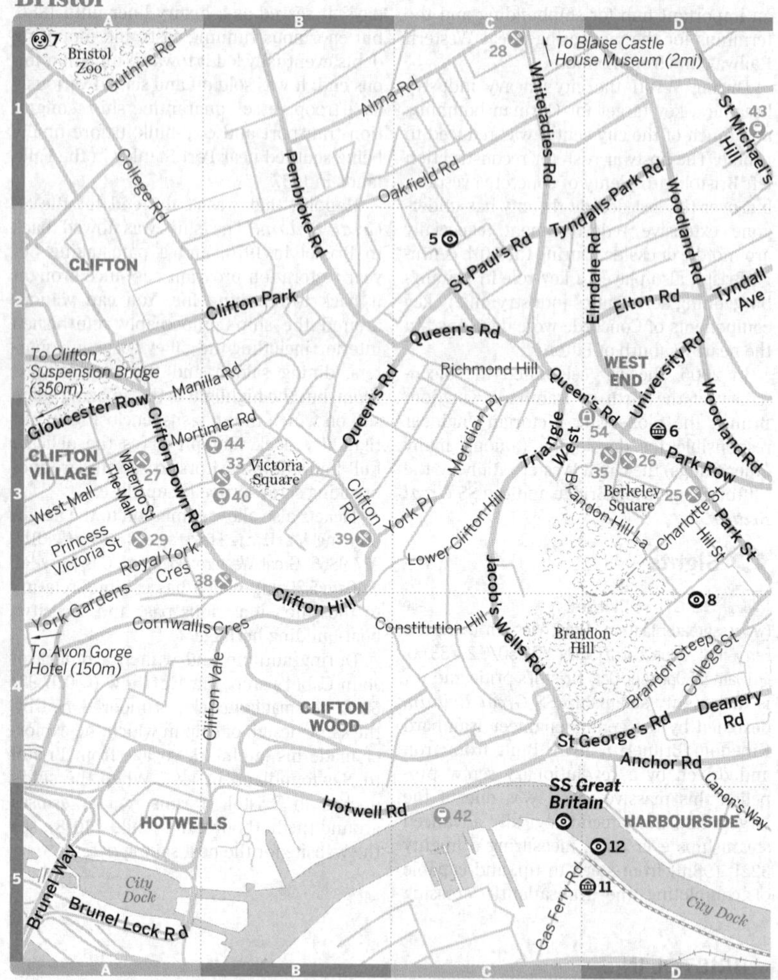

FREE M Shed MUSEUM

(www.mshed.org; Princes Wharf; 10am-5pm Tue-Fri, 10am-6pm Sat & Sun;) It's taken four years and £27m to build, but Bristol's brand-new museum is finally open – and it's really rather brilliant. Lodged in a massive old warehouse overlooking the docks, it's a treasure trove of weird-and-wonderful memorabilia rummaging through the city's past. The 3000-odd exhibits are divided into three sections (People, Place and Life), and provide a panoramic overview of Bristol's history – from slaves' possessions and vintage double-decker buses to Wallace and Gromit figurines and a set of bright-pink decks once used by Massive Attack. Multimedia displays and background panels make everything enormously accessible, and you're absolutely guaranteed to walk away with a deeper understanding of the city. Best of all, it's free – although well worth the £2 suggested donation.

Clifton Village HISTORIC AREA

During the 18th and 19th centuries, wealthy Bristol merchants transformed the former spa resort of Clifton into an elegant hilltop suburb packed with impressive Georgian

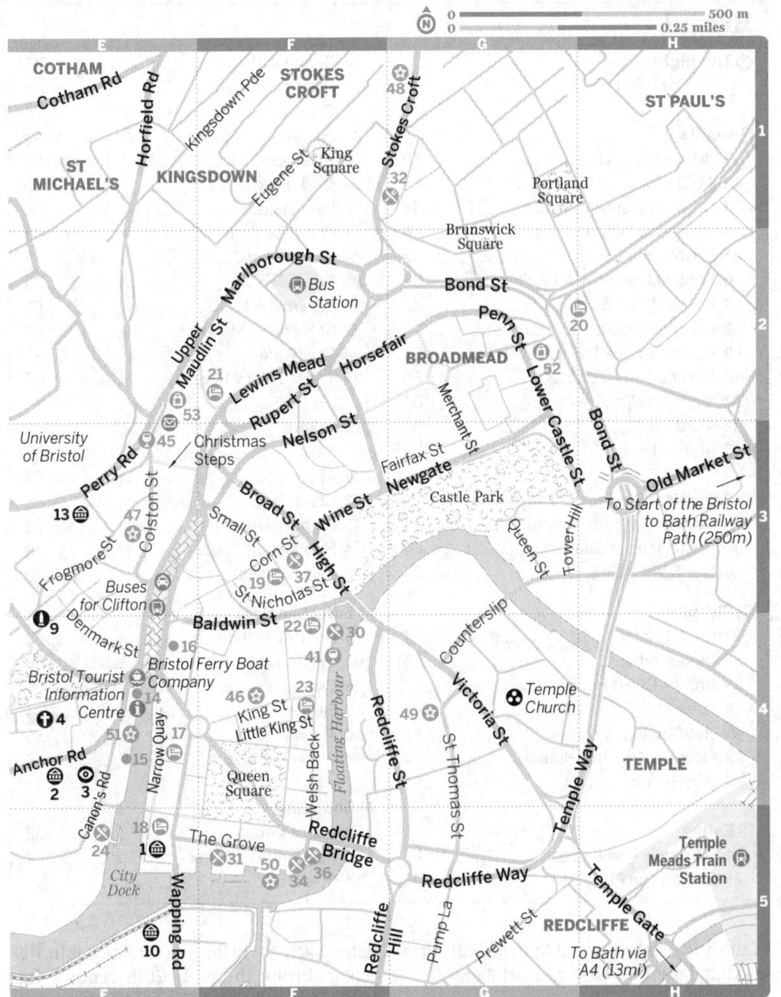

mansions. Some of the finest examples can be seen along **Cornwallis Crescent** and **Royal York Crescent**. These days, Clifton is still the poshest postcode in Bristol, with a wealth of streetside cafes and designer shops, and a villagey atmosphere that's far removed from the rest of the city.

Clifton Suspension Bridge BRIDGE

(www.cliftonbridge.org.uk) Clifton's most famous (and photographed) landmark is a Brunel masterpiece, the 76m-high Clifton Suspension Bridge, which spans the Avon Gorge from Clifton over to Leigh Woods in northern Somerset. Construction began in 1836, but sadly Brunel died before the bridge's completion in 1864. It was mainly designed to carry light horse-drawn traffic and foot passengers, but these days around 12,000 cars cross it every day – testament to the quality of the construction and the vision of Brunel's design.

It's free to walk or cycle across the bridge; car drivers pay a 50p toll. There's a **visitor information point** (visitinfo@clifton-suspension-bridge.org; ⏲10am-5pm) near the tower on the Leigh Woods side. Free guided tours (£3)

Bristol

Top Sights

SS Great Britain ... C5

Sights

1 Arnolfini ... E5
2 At-Bristol ... E4
3 Bristol Aquarium ... E4
4 Bristol Cathedral ... E4
5 Bristol Lido ... C2
6 Bristol Museum & Art Gallery ... D3
7 Bristol Zoo ... A1
8 Georgian House ... D4
9 Banksy's Love Triangle Stencil ... E4
10 M Shed ... E5
11 Maritime Heritage Centre ... D5
12 Matthew ... D5
13 Red Lodge ... E3

Activities, Courses & Tours

14 Bristol Highlights Walk ... E4
15 Bristol Packet Boat Trips ... E4
16 City Sightseeing ... E4

Sleeping

17 Bristol Hotel ... E4
18 Bristol YHA ... E5
19 Brooks Guest House ... F3
20 Future Inn Cabot Circus ... H2
21 Hotel du Vin ... F2
22 Mercure Brigstow Hotel ... F4
23 Premier Inn, King St ... F4

Eating

24 Bordeaux Quay ... E5
25 Boston Tea Party ... D3
26 Chandos Deli ... D3
27 Clifton Sausage ... A3
28 Cowshed ... C1
29 Fishers ... A3
30 Glassboat ... F4
31 Mud Dock ... F5
32 Pieminister ... G1
33 Primrose Café ... B3
34 Riverstation ... F5
35 Rocotillo's ... D3
36 Severnshed ... F5
37 St Nicholas Market ... F3
38 Thali Café ... B3
39 The Muset by Ronnie ... B3

Drinking

40 Albion ... B3
41 Apple ... F4
42 Grain Barge ... C5
43 Highbury Vaults ... D1
44 Hophouse ... B3
45 Zerodegrees ... E3

Entertainment

46 Bristol Old Vic ... F4
47 Colston Hall ... E3
48 Croft ... G1
49 Fleece ... G4
50 Thekla ... F5
51 Watershed ... E4

Shopping

52 Cabot Circus ... G2
53 Rag Trade Boutique ... E2
54 Rise Music ... D3

of the bridge take place at 3pm on Saturdays and Sundays from Easter to October.

The Downs PARKS

Near the bridge, the grassy parks of Clifton Down and Durdham Down (often referred to as just the Downs) make a fine spot for a picnic. Nearby, a well-worn observatory houses a **camera obscura** (adult/child £2/1; ⏰10.30am-5.30pm) and a tunnel leading down to the **Giant's Cave** (adult/child £1.50/50p), a natural cavern that emerges halfway down the cliff with dizzying views across the Avon Gorge.

Bristol Lido BATHS

(☎0117-933-9530; www.lidobristol.com; Oakfield Pl; pool adult/child £20/7.50; ⏰nonmembers sessions 1-4pm Mon-Fri) Bristol's public hot tub dates back to 1849. Since falling into disrepair during the early 20th century, this lovely naturally heated pool has been fully restored and is back to its steamy best (with a balmy water temperature of around 24°C). Spa treatments and massage sessions are also available, and there's a rather good bar and restaurant where you can relax once you're done. Priority is given to members; on weekends and busy days the lido is closed for day visitors, so phone ahead to make sure there's space.

Bristol Zoo ZOO

(www.bristolzoo.org.uk; £14.50/8.75; ⏰9am-5.30pm) The city's award-winning zoo occupies a huge site on the north side of Clifton. Highlights include gorilla and gibbon islands, a reptile and bug house, a butterfly forest, a lion enclosure, a monkey jungle and the new **Zooropia** (adult/child £7.70/6.70), a treetop adventure park strung with net ramps, rope bridges, hanging logs and a zip-line. There's a 10% discount for tickets purchased online.

At-Bristol MUSEUM
(www.at-bristol.org.uk; Anchor Rd; adult/child/family £12.50/8/35.50; ⏲10am-5pm Mon-Fri, to 6pm Sat & Sun) Bristol's interactive science museum has several zones spanning space, technology and the human brain. In the Curiosity Zone you get to walk through a tornado, spin on a human gyroscope and strum the strings of a virtual harp. It's fun, imaginative and interactive, and should keep kids entertained for a few hours.

Bristol Aquarium AQUARIUM
(www.bristolaquarium.co.uk; Harbourside; adult/child/family £12.50/8.75/38.50; ⏲10am-5pm Mon-Fri, to 6pm Sat & Sun) Bristol's harbourside aquarium has been newly renovated, with underwater habitats including a Bay of Rays, a Coral Sea, a Shark Tank and an Amazon River Zone. There's also an informative section about Britain's native habitats and an impressive underwater tunnel, as well as a new star resident, Velcro the Pacific Octopus. There's a £2 discount if you buy tickets online.

Arnolfini ART GALLERY
(www.arnolfini.org.uk; 16 Narrow Quay; ⏲10am-6pm Tue-Sun) The city's avant-garde art gallery occupies a hulking red-brick warehouse by the river, and remains the top venue in town for modern art, as well as occasional exhibitions of dance, film and photography.

FREE **Bristol Museum & Art Gallery** MUSEUM
(Queen's Rd; ⏲10am-5pm) Housed in a stunning Edwardian baroque building, the city Museum & Art Gallery has an excellent collection of British and French art; galleries dedicated to ceramics and decorative arts; and archaeological, geological and natural history wings. Renovation works are currently in progress, so some galleries may be closed.

FREE **Georgian House** HISTORIC BUILDING
(7 Great George St; ⏲10am-4pm Tue-Sun Apr-Aug) This 18th-century house provides an evocative illustration of aristocratic life in Bristol during the Georgian era. The six-storeyed house belonged to West India merchant John Pinney, along with his slave Pero (after whom Pero's Bridge across the harbour is named). It's decorated throughout in period style, typified by the huge kitchen (complete with cast-iron roasting spit), the book-lined library and the grand drawing rooms. Look out for Pinney's cold-water plunge-pool in the basement.

FREE **Red Lodge** HISTORIC BUILDING
(Park Row; ⏲10am-4pm Tue-Sun Apr-Aug) Built in 1590 but remodelled in 1730, this red-brick house is a mix of Elizabethan, Stuart and Georgian architecture. The highlight is the Great Oak Room, which still features its original Elizabethan oak panelling, plasterwork ceiling and carved chimneypiece.

FREE **Ashton Court Estate** PARK
(www.ashtoncourtestate.com; ⏲8am-9.15pm) Two miles from the city centre, this huge estate is Bristol's 'green lung', with 850 sprawling acres of oak woodland, trails and public park. It hosts many of Bristol's key events, including the Balloon and Kite festivals. There are also 6.5km of bike trails, two 18-hole golf courses and a miniature railway – and if you're really lucky, you might even spot a roe or fallow deer.

FREE **Blaise Castle House Museum** MUSEUM
(Henbury Rd; ⏲10am-5pm Wed-Sat) In the northern suburb of Henbury is this late-18th-century house and social-history museum. Displays include vintage toys, costumes and other Victorian ephemera. Bus 42/42A (45 minutes, every 15 minutes) passes the castle from Colston Ave; bus 1 (20 minutes, every 10 minutes) from the station and St Augustine's Pde doesn't stop quite as close, but is quicker.

Bristol Cathedral CATHEDRAL
(www.bristol-cathedral.co.uk; College Green; ⏲8am-6pm) Originally founded as a 12th-century monastery church, Bristol Cathedral was heavily remodelled during the 19th century. It's one of Britain's best examples of a 'Hall Church' (meaning the nave, chapels and choir are the same height). Although the nave and west towers are Victorian, parts of the choir are medieval, and the south transept contains a rare Saxon carving of the *Harrowing of Hell,* discovered under the chapter-house floor after a 19th-century fire.

THE TRIANGULAR TRADE

It's a sobering thought that much of Bristol's 18th-century wealth was founded on the proceeds of slavery.

During the 17th and 18th centuries, Bristol was one of Britain's three major slave ports, alongside Liverpool and London. The first slave ship set sail from Bristol Harbour in the early 1600s, heralding the beginning of the so-called **triangular trade**, in which Africans were kidnapped (or traded, usually for munitions) before being shipped across the Atlantic and sold into a life of slavery in the New World. Their human cargo unloaded, the merchants stocked their vessels with luxury goods such as sugar, rum, indigo, tobacco and cotton, and sailed back to Britain.

Conditions on the boats were horrific; it was expected that one in 10 of those captured would die en route – although in reality, the number was usually much higher. By the time the slave trade (not slavery itself) was finally abolished in the British Empire in 1807, it's thought that 500,000 Africans had been enslaved by Bristol merchants – a fifth of all people sold into slavery by British vessels.

The financial profits were immense, and Bristol's slave traders and shipping merchants became enormously wealthy as a result: many of Clifton's grandest terraces were built on the proceeds of the 'trade', and several of the city's most important buildings – such as the Bristol Old Vic – were partly financed by slave-trading investors.

For further insights, download the excellent MP3 audio tour from the **Visit Bristol website** (www.visitbristol.co.uk), or pick up the Slave Trade Trail leaflet (£3) from the tourist office.

Tours

Bristol Highlights Walk WALKING TOUR
(www.bristolwalks.co.uk; adult/under 12yr £3.50/free; ⏲11am Sat Apr-Sep) Tours the old town, city centre and Harbourside. It's run every Saturday at 11am; just turn up outside the tourist office (p311). Themed tours for groups exploring Clifton, Brunel and the history of Bristol traders are run on request.

FREE **MP3 Tours** WALKING TOUR
(www.visitbristol.co.uk/about-bristol/video-and-audio/audio-tours) Free downloadable MP3 guides covering the slave trade, Brunel, pirates, heritage architecture, historic churches and the city's literary connections.

City Sightseeing BUS TOUR
(www.bristolvisitor.co.uk; 24hr ticket adult/child £10/5; ⏲10am-4pm Easter-Sep) Open-topped hop-on/hop-off bus visiting all the major attractions. Buses leave Broad Quay hourly (every 30 minutes from July to September). Single trips cost adult/child £1/50p.

Bristol Packet Boat Trips BOAT TOUR
(www.bristolpacket.co.uk; ⏲11am-4.15pm Sat & Sun) This boat company runs regular cruises around the harbour area (adult/child £5.50/3.50, departures every 45 minutes, daily during school holidays). There are also weekly cruises along the Avon from May to October (adult/child £15/13) and a regular Sunday afternoon trip to Beese's Tea Gardens (£9.90/6.25). Cruises to Bath (£26/15) run once a month from May to September.

Festivals & Events

Bristol Shakespeare Festival THEATRE
(www.bristolshakespeare.org.uk) Britain's biggest outdoor festival devoted to the Bard, held between May and September.

St Paul's Carnival COMMUNITY FESTIVAL
(www.stpaulscarnival.co.uk) Community knees-up on the first Saturday of July.

Bristol Harbour Festival COMMUNITY FESTIVAL
(www.bristolharbourfestival.co.uk) Bands, events and historic ships take over the city's docks in early August.

International Balloon Fiesta HOT-AIR BALLOONS
(www.bristolballoonfiesta.co.uk) Hot-air balloons fill the skies at Ashton Court in August.

International Kite Festival KITES
(www.kite-festival.org.uk) Held in September, also at Ashton Court.

Encounters FILM FESTIVAL
(www.encounters-festival.org.uk) Bristol's largest film fest is in November.

Christmas Markets CHRISTMAS
Late-night shopping around St Nicholas Market in December.

Sleeping

Bristol's hotels tend to be geared towards the business crowd, but there are a couple of great-value chains and a handful of intriguing new B&Bs dotted around the city centre.

TOP CHOICE **Number 38** B&B £££
(☎0117-946 6905; www.number38clifton.com; 38 Upper Belgrave Rd, Clifton; d £138; P 📶) Perched on the edge of the Downs, this super new B&B puts most of the city's hotels to shame in terms of designer decor. The 10 rooms are huge, contemporary and very cool – sombre greys and smooth blues dictate the colour palette, while waffle bath robes and REN bath goodies await in the power showers, and city views unfold from the roof terrace. The two suites even have old-fashioned tin baths. It's really handy for Clifton and Whiteladies Rd, but a long walk from the centre, so it might not be ideal for everyone.

TOP CHOICE **Hotel du Vin** HOTEL £££
(☎0117-925 5577; www.hotelduvin.com; Narrow Lewins Mead; r £145-215; P 📶) If expense is no object, there's only one choice in Bristol, and that's this indulgently elegant warehouse conversion. Occupying an old sugar store, it's a mix of industrial chic and sleek minimalism, complete with giant futon beds, claw-foot baths and frying-pan showerheads. All the rooms are named after vintage champagnes; the best are the split-level suites with mezzanines. The bistro is a beaut, too.

Brooks Guest House B&B ££
(☎0117-930 0066; www.brooksguesthousebristol.com; Exchange Ave; d £70-99; 📶) Bristol has been crying out for a smart, modern B&B near the city centre for years – and at long last it has one, and in a fantastic spot right next door to St Nick's Market too. Rooms are a tad boxy, but pleasantly finished with flock wallpaper, John Lewis bed linen and Hansgröhe power showers. Downstairs, there's a contemporary lounge with leather chairs and wood floors, and a cute city garden for breakfast or afternoon tea. Parking is available for £9.50 at the nearby Queen Charlotte St car park.

Future Inn Cabot Circus HOTEL ££
(☎0845-094 5588; www.futureinns.co.uk/bristol-hotels; Bond St South; d £59-99; P 📶) This hotel mini-chain has outlets in Plymouth, Cardiff and Bristol. It's modern, functional and businessy, and the concrete skin is charmless, but the rooms are clean in beige, white and

BANKSY

Bristol's artistic anti-hero, **Banksy**, may be a world-famous name these days, but his heart's still very much rooted in the city. Known for his guerrilla graffiti and stencil street art, Banksy's true identity is a closely guarded secret, but it's generally believed he was born in 1974 in Yate, 12 miles from Bristol, and cut his artistic teeth in a graffiti outfit.

He's since become known across the globe for his anti-establishment, anti-authoritarian artworks, which frequently take a wry view of 21st-century culture (especially capitalism, consumerism and the cult of celebrity). Banksy's most notorious works include the production of spoof banknotes (featuring Princess Diana's head instead of the Queen's), a series of murals on Israel's West Bank barrier (depicting people digging holes and climbing ladders over the wall) and a painting of a caveman pushing a shopping trolley at the British Museum (which the museum promptly claimed for their permanent collection). More recently, Banksy has made forays into the film world: his documentary *Exit Through The Gift Shop*, about an LA street artist, was nominated for an Oscar in 2011.

Long despised by the city's authorities, Banksy's become a real tourist magnet for Bristol. Though many of his works have been washed away, a few still survive: look out for the **love triangle stencil** (Frogmore St, visible from Park St), featuring an angry husband, a two-timing wife, and a naked man dangling from a window; stencils of the **Grim Reaper** on the side of the Thekla (p311) and a **SWAT Marksman** opposite the Children's Hospital on Kingsdown; and the **Mild Mild West** mural (featuring a Molotov cocktail–wielding teddy bear) on Cheltenham Rd.

For more on the artist's latest antics, check out www.banksy.co.uk.

pine, and the rates are fantastic this close to the centre. Room prices include parking at the Cabot Circus car park.

Premier Inn, King St HOTEL ££

(☎0871-527 8158; www.premiertravelinn.com; King St; r £59-89; ❄📶) Yes, we realise this is a Premier Inn, but stop being snobby and just appreciate the cheap rates and riverside spot. Rooms have big beds, desk and wi-fi, and some even have glimpses of the harbour. Worth considering – although the Llangoger Trow pub next door gets rowdy at weekends. Discounted parking is available at the NCP on Queen Charlotte St (although it's still pretty expensive).

Greenhouse B&B ££

(☎0117-902 9166; www.thegreenhousebristol.co.uk; 61 Greenbank Rd, Southville; s/d £60/99; P📶) No bells and whistles here – just a lovely, friendly, quiet B&B in Southville, a few minutes' stride to the river and the centre of town. Cream rooms, white sheets and an excellent all-organic breakfast make it well worth considering.

Bristol Hotel HOTEL ££

(☎0117-923 0333; www.doylecollection.com/locations/bristol_hotels/the_bristol_hotel.aspx; Prince St; d £95-155; 📶) This newly redone hotel (formerly the Jury's Inn) has lots in its favour – riverside location, luxurious rooms, bistro – but it's pretty pricey and frequented by a businessy crowd. The downstairs River Grille restaurant is a popular spot for dinner with the city's suits. No car park, but there's an NCP next door.

Mercure Brigstow Hotel HOTEL ££

(☎0117-929 1030; H6548@accor.com; Welsh Back; d £63-125; 📶) Despite the concrete-and-glass facade, this Mercure hotel is surprisingly cool inside. Bedrooms boast floating beds, curved panel walls and tiny TVs set into bathroom tiles (gimmicky, yes, but fun).

Bristol YHA HOSTEL ££

(bristol@yha.org.uk; 14 Narrow Quay; dm £22, s £37, d £74; @) Few hostels can boast a position as good as this one, right beside the river in a red-brick warehouse. Facilities are great, including kitchens, cycle store, games room and the excellent Grainshed coffee lounge – but the dorms are pretty basic, and the doubles are not such good value.

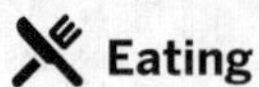

Eating

Bristol has a really vibrant dining scene, with choices to suit all budgets – from fine-dining emporia to budget curry houses, and pretty much everything in between.

TOP CHOICE Bell's Diner BRITISH ££

(☎0117-924 0357; www.bellsdiner.com; 1-3 York Rd; dinner mains £14.50-21, tasting menu £49.50; ⏰lunch Wed-Fri, dinner Tue-Sat) Run by one of the city's most respected chefs, Christopher Wicks, Bell's is very probably Bristol's best – and certainly most adventurous – bistro. Wicks is known for his adventurous flavour combinations, and the menu is full of exotic-sounding ingredients (pink fur potato, onion soubise, seaweed, toasted hay). But at its core, his food is all about celebrating the very best of British – best experienced with the eight-course tasting menu – an ethos that seems perfectly suited to the restaurant's setting in a converted grocer's shop in lively Montpelier. Bookings are essential.

The Muset by Ronnie BRITISH ££

(☎0117-973 7248; www.ronnies-restaurant.co.uk; 12-16 Clifton Rd; 2-/3-course lunch menu £13/16, dinner menu £19/22, mains £13-21) Chef Ron Faulkner has a new Clifton establishment, in addition to his original, much-vaunted address in Thornbury. Faulkner trained under big names including Anton Mosimann and Ed Baines, and his Brit-meets-Mediterranean blend has earned him local fans as well as critical acclaim. Expect rich, hearty fare such as smoked eel, lamb shank and roast duck, served with a contemporary side of steamed kohlrabi or brown shrimp butter.

Riverstation BRITISH ££

(☎0117-914 4434; www.riverstation.co.uk; 2-/3-course lunch £12.75/15.50; dinner mains £14.50-19.75) It's been around for many years now, but this riverside bistro is as reliable as ever, turning out some of the city's best European cuisine. Head upstairs for dining, downstairs for coffee – and ask for a window table to make the most of the harbour views.

Cowshed BRITISH ££

(☎0117-973 3550; www.thecowshedbristol.com; 46 Whiteladies Rd; 3-course lunch £10, dinner mains £12.95-21.50) Country dining in a city setting. The feel's half-rustic, half-contemporary –

big windows and modern murals contrast with exposed stone and pine furniture – and the menu's all about hearty flavours: lamb shoulder with root veg mash, or roast quail and pigeon with bubble-and-squeak. The Sunday roast is an institution.

Cafe Maitreya VEGETARIAN ££

(0117-951 0100; www.cafemaitreya.co.uk; 89 St Marks Rd; mains £8.95-10.95; 10am-11.30pm Tue-Sat, 10am-4pm Sun;) This Easton eatery has won a raft of awards for its innovative veggie food, and it's recently branched out with a funky new arts space–cum–music venue. The vibe is deliberately casual, and the all-veggie food is universally good, whether you choose the nettle risotto or the root veg *tarte tatin*.

Thali Café INDIAN £

(0117-974 3793; www.thethalicafe.co.uk; 1 Regent St; meals £7.95-10.50) Bristol has some great Indian restaurants, but few are as beloved as this mini-chain of canteens, which now has four outlets, including this one in Clifton. It specialises in fresh, authentic thalis (multicourse Indian meals), as well as regional dishes ranging from Goan fish fries to Chompatti beach snacks. For dining on a budget, there's really nowhere better in Bristol.

Glassboat FRENCH ££

(0117-929 0704; www.glassboat.co.uk; Welsh Back; 2-/3-course lunch menu £15/20, dinner mains £15.50-22; lunch Tue-Fri & Sun, dinner Mon-Sat) You couldn't ask for a more romantic place for dinner than this double-decked river barge, with its candlelit tables and watery views. The food is solid rather than spectacular, revolving around French standards such as fish soup, rabbit hotpot and tarragon chicken with *pommes dauphinoises*.

Primrose Café BISTRO ££

(0117-946 6577; www.primrosecafe.co.uk; 1/2 Boyce's Ave; dinner mains £13.50-17.50; breakfast & lunch Mon-Sat, dinner Tue-Sat) A Clifton classic, perfect for morning coffee spent with the papers, a quick lunchtime snack or a proper sit-down dinner. The food is British with a French accent, served up in a cosy candle-lit dining room full of wooden furniture and chalkboard menus, and if the weather's sunny, the pavement tables are perfect for watching Clifton life mosey by. It's right next door to one of Bristol's oldest shopping arcades.

Pieminister PIES £

(24 Stokes Croft; pies around £4.50; 10am-7pm Sat, 11am-4pm Sun) Bristol's beloved pie shop turns out imaginative creations such as Thai Chook (chicken with green curry sauce) and Chicken of Aragon (chicken, bacon, garlic and vermouth), all drowned in lashings of gravy (meat-free if you wish). The main shop is on Stokes Croft, but there's another outlet in St Nick's market.

Bordeaux Quay BRITISH ££

(0117-943 1200; www.bordeaux-quay.co.uk; Canon's Way; brasserie mains £8.50-13.50, dinner mains £13.50-25) This ecoconscious restaurant is housed in a converted dock warehouse, and offers a choice of settings: a downstairs cafe for cake, coffee and bistro lunches, and a more formal upstairs for Mediterranean-style dining. The same open-plan industrial feel runs throughout, but standards can be variable, especially considering the prices and 12.5% service charge. There's a cookery school if you'd like to brush up your own skills.

Fishers SEAFOOD ££

(0117-974 7044; www.fishers-restaurant.com; 35 Princess Victoria St; mains £14.25-21.50) This sophisticated seafooderie originally opened in Oxford, but has had a Bristol outpost for over a decade. It's one of the city's top choices for a fish supper, from baked bream to fresh British lobster; the hot shellfish platter (£42 for two people) is made for sharing. The simple setting, with its stripy table cloths, whitewashed walls and ships' lanterns, adds to the maritime vibe.

Clifton Sausage GASTROPUB ££

(0117-973 1192; www.cliftonsausage.co.uk; 7-9 Portland St; sausage & mash £9.95, other mains £14-18) At least six different bangers grace the menu at this refined gastropub, from Gloucester Old Spot to Beef and Spitfire Ale (there's always a veggie version, too). It's a popular lunch spot for the Clifton trendies, especially at weekends.

Severnshed FUSION ££

(0117-925 1212; www.shedrestaurants.co.uk; The Grove; mains £10.95-15.95) A waterside bistro in a Brunel-built boathouse, offering standard grub (fajitas, steaks, pizzas, risottos) served with a side of river views.

Rocotillo's CAFE £

(1 Queens Row; mains £6-10; breakfast & lunch) American-style diner serving gourmet

burgers, crispy fries and the best milkshakes in town.

Mud Dock CAFE £
(40 The Grove; mains £8-14; ⏲lunch & dinner Mon-Sat, 10am-4.30pm Sun) Upstairs, a cool urban cafe; downstairs, Bristol's best bike shop.

St Nicholas Market MARKET
(Corn St; ⏲9.30am-5pm Mon-Sat) The city's lively street market has a bevy of food stalls selling everything from artisan bread to cheese toasties. Look out for local **farmers markets** on Wednesdays and a **slow-food market** on the first Sunday of each month.

Chandos Deli DELI £
(www.chandosdeli.com) Popular deli serving gourmet goodies. Branches can be found on Whiteladies Rd, Princess Victoria St and Quaker's Friars.

Boston Tea Party CAFE £
(www.bostonteaparty.co.uk; Park St; sandwiches & salads £4-6) This southwest deli chain serves great sandwiches, wraps, salads and fresh juices. It also has branches on Princess Victoria St and Whiteladies Rd.

Drinking

Apple THEME BAR
(Welsh Back) Cider-lovers won't want to miss this converted barge on Welsh Back, which offers more than 40 varieties, including raspberry and strawberry, and six different perries (pear ciders).

Grain Barge PUB
(www.grainbarge.com; Mardyke Wharf, Hotwell Rd) Built in 1936, overhauled in 2007, this barge near SS *Great Britain* is owned by the city's renowned microbrewery, the Bristol Beer Factory. Gaze across the harbour while downing a pint of traditional No. 7 Bitter or dark Exhibition ale.

Highbury Vaults PUB
(164 St Michaels Hill) This endearingly scruffy boozer has a warren of wood-panelled rooms and hallways, and a choice of at least eight real ales on tap. There's a delightful little beer garden, too – look out for the little train running through the greenery.

Albion PUB
(Boyce's Ave) Lovely old-fashioned place that's popular with evening drinkers from Clifton's well-heeled streets.

Pipe & Slippers PUB
(www.barwarsltd.com/the-pipe-and-slippers; 118 Cheltenham Rd) Top-notch community boozer on Cheltenham Rd, with a proper pub feel thanks to its lofty ceilings, burnished wood and hand-pulled beers. It's good for food and gets lively at weekends with DJs and a 1am licence.

Hophouse PUB
(16 Kings Rd; 👪) This venerable Clifton local looks fresh from a recent refit, and now serves grub, too, in addition to its Cask Marque approved ales.

Zerodegrees PUB
(www.zerodegrees.co.uk; 53 Colston St) Plentiful glass, chrome and steel set the metropolitan tone for this modern microbrewery. Options range from fruit beers and pale wheat ale to Czech-style Black and Pilsner lagers.

Avon Gorge Hotel PUB
(Sion Hill) The clifftop beer patio at this old Victorian hotel has a truly knockout view across Avon Gorge and the Suspension Bridge – hard to beat on a sunny summer's day.

Entertainment

The Bristol club scene moves fast; check the latest listings at www.venue.co.uk or www.whatsonbristol.co.uk. The freebie mag *Folio* is published monthly.

Watershed CINEMA, MEDIA CENTRE
(www.watershed.co.uk; 1 Canon's Rd) Bristol's digital media centre hosts regular art-house programs and film-related events, including the Encounters Festival in November.

Bristol Old Vic THEATRE
(www.bristololdvic.org.uk; 103 The Cut) Bristol's stately theatre (one of England's oldest) hosts big touring productions in its ornate auditorium, plus more experimental work in its smaller studio.

Colston Hall LIVE MUSIC
(www.colstonhall.org; Colston St) Bristol's historic concert hall tends to attract the best bands and big-name comedy acts.

Tobacco Factory THEATRE
(www.tobaccofactory.com; Raleigh Rd) This small-scale theatre venue is across the river in Southville. Catch bus 24 or 25 from Broadmead to the Raleigh Rd stop.

Thekla CLUB
(www.thekla.co.uk; The Grove) Bristol's venerable club-boat has nights for all moods: electro-punk, indie, disco and new wave, plus regular live gigs.

Croft LIVE MUSIC
(www.the-croft.com; 117-119 Stokes Croft) Chilled pub venue with a policy of supporting new names and Bristol-based artists.

Fleece PUB, LIVE MUSIC
(www.fleecegigs.co.uk; St Thomas St) Another gig pub much favoured by indie artists.

Shopping

Cabot Circus SHOPPING CENTRE
(www.cabotcircus.com; Cabot Circus) The city's multimillion-pound new shopping centre hosts all the big names, selling everything from new threads to boxes of chocolates. High-end fashion boutiques and designer brands tend to cluster around Quakers Friars.

Rag Trade Boutique VINTAGE CLOTHES
(www.ragtradeboutique.co.uk; 2 Upper Maudlin St; ⌚noon-6pm Mon, 10am-6pm Tue-Sat) Vintage threads with a bring-and-buy ethos.

Rise Music MUSIC
(bristol@rise-music.co.uk; 70 Queens Rd; ⌚10am-7pm Mon-Sat, noon-6pm Sun) Bristol's top independent record shop.

Beast Clothing CLOTHING, SOUVENIRS
(www.beast-clothing.com; 224 Cheltenham Rd; ⌚9.30-5pm Mon-Sat) T-shirts and souvenirs emblazoned with slogans such as 'Gert Lush' and 'Proper Job', all inspired by local Brizzle lingo. Cheesy, but fun. The main shop is on Cheltenham Rd, but there's a concession stall at St Nick's Market.

Information

Bridewell Police Station (☎101; 1-2 Bridewell St; ⌚8.30am-4.30pm Mon-Sat)

Bristol Royal Infirmary (Marlborough St; ⌚24hr)

Bristol Tourist Information Centre (☎0333-321 0101; www.visitbristol.co.uk; E-Shed, 1 Canons Rd; ⌚10am-6pm)

Trinity Road Police Station (☎101; Trinity Rd; ⌚24hr)

Getting There & Away

The useful **Travel Bristol** (www.travelbristol.org) website lists comprehensive information on public transport in and around Bristol city.

Air

Bristol International Airport (☎0871-334-4344; www.bristolairport.co.uk) Bristol airport is 8 is eight miles southwest of the city. UK destinations include London Gatwick, Leeds, Manchester, Edinburgh and Glasgow (mainly handled by Ryanair and Easyjet) as well as direct flights to many European cities (handled by many different carriers).

Bus

Bristol has excellent bus and coach connections. Timetables are available from the bus station on Marlborough Rd.

National Express coach destinations:

Birmingham (£21.30, two hours, six to eight daily)

Cardiff (£8.70, 1¼ hours, every two hours)

Exeter (£15, two hours, four daily)

London (£21, 2½ hours, hourly)

Useful local buses:

Bath (50 minutes, several per hour) Express bus X39/339.

Wells (one hour, half-hourly Monday to Saturday, hourly on Sunday) Bus 376, with onward connections to Glastonbury (1¼ hours).

Weston-super-Mare (one hour, every half-hour Monday to Saturday) Bus X1.

Train

Bristol is an important rail hub in the southwest of England, and there are regular services to London provided by **First Great Western** (www.firstgreatwestern.co.uk), while services to northern England and Scotland are mainly covered by **Cross Country** (www.crosscountrytrains.co.uk).

DESTINATION	DETAILS
Penzance	£42, 5½ hr, hourly
Truro	£42, 5 hr, hourly
Exeter	£25, 1 hr, hourly
London Paddington	£39, 1¾ hr, hourly
Birmingham	£47, 1½ hr, hourly
Glasgow	£136.50, 6½ hr, hourly
Edinburgh	£136.50, 6½ hr, hourly

Getting Around

To/From the Airport

Bristol International Flyer (http://flyer.bristolairport.co.uk) Runs shuttle buses (one way/return £10/7, 30 minutes, every 10 minutes at peak times) from the bus station and Temple Meads.

Parking at the airport is very expensive (starting at around £30 in the cheapest Silver Zone), but, if you have the time, substantial discounts are available online.

Boat

Bristol Ferry Boat Company (☎0117-927 3416; www.bristolferry.com; adult/child return £3.80/3.20, day pass £7/5) Regular ferry service around the harbour that runs from its city centre base near the tourist office. There are two hourly routes: the red route runs west towards Hotwells, with stops including Millennium Square and the SS *Great Britain;* the blue route runs east to Temple Meads, with stops including Castle Park (for Cabot Circus), Welsh Back, Millennium Square, the SS *Great Britain* and Bathurst Basin. Single hops from the city centre to M Shed and Temple Meads to Castle Park cost £1.

Bus

Useful buses around the city:

Bus 8/9 To Clifton (10 minutes), Whiteladies Rd and Bristol Zoo Gardens every 15 minutes from St Augustine's Pde. Add another 10 minutes from Temple Meads.

Bus 73 Runs from Bristol Parkway train station, 5 miles to reach the city centre (30 minutes).

Car

Heavy traffic and pricey parking make driving in Bristol a headache. If you do decide to drive, make sure your hotel has parking, or use the **Park & Ride buses** (☎0117-922-2910; return before 10am Mon-Fri £3.50, after 10am Mon-Fri £2.50, Sat £2.50; ⊙every 10min Mon-Sat) from Portway, Bath Rd and Long Ashton. Note that overnight parking is not permitted at the Park & Ride car parks.

Taxi

The taxi rank on St Augustine's Pde is a central but rowdy place on weekend nights. There are plenty of companies; try **Streamline Taxis** (☎0117-926 4001). If you're taking a nonmetered cab, agree on the fare in advance.

BATH

POP 90,144

Britain is littered with beautiful cities, but precious few can hold a candle to Bath. Home to some of the nation's finest Georgian architecture and grandest streets – not to mention one of the world's best-preserved Roman bathhouses – this slinky, sophisticated, snooty city has been a tourist draw for nigh-on 2000 years.

Though the city sometimes seems like it's been pickled in time, beneath the stately surface, Bath is very much a cosmopolitan, 21st-century city. Cafes, bistros and boutiques line streets, and the innovative new SouthGate shopping centre has been seamlessly blended in with the rest of the city's period buildings.

Bath certainly has its drawbacks – it's pricey, ostentatious and plagued by teeth-grindingly awful traffic – but you'll find yourself falling for it just the same.

History

Prehistoric people probably knew about Bath's natural hot springs; legend has it King Bladud, a Trojan refugee and father of King Lear, founded Bath some 2800 years ago when his pigs were cured of leprosy by a dip in the muddy swamps. The Romans established the town of Aquae Sulis in AD 44 and built the extensive baths complex and a temple to the goddess Sulis-Minerva.

Long after the Romans decamped, the Anglo-Saxons arrived, and in 944 a monastery was founded on the site of the present abbey. Throughout the Middle Ages, Bath

WORTH A TRIP

TYNTESFIELD

The ridiculously extravagant stately home of **Tyntesfield** (NT; ☎01275-461900; www.nationaltrust.org.uk/tyntesfield; adult/child £12.60/6.20, gardens only £7.50/4.10; ⊙11am-5pm Sat-Wed Mar-Oct) was built by the Victorian entrepreneur William Gibbs, who made his fortune from selling fertiliser. It's a classic piece of 19th century showmanship, pricked with spiky turrets and Gothic-inspired towers designed by its architect John Norton. Owned by the National Trust since 2002, the house has since been lavishly restored at a cost of around £24m. Major renovation work finished in 2012, and the house's antiques, furniture and artworks are slowly being taken out of storage and returned to their rightful positions around the house. Elsewhere, there's a working kitchen garden, private chapel, farm shop and restaurant inside the old cow barn. The house is 7 miles southwest of Bristol, off the B3128.

was an ecclesiastical centre and a wool-trading town, but it wasn't until the early 18th century that Ralph Allen and the celebrated dandy Richard 'Beau' Nash made Bath the centre of fashionable society by constructing fabulous landmarks such as the Circus and Royal Crescent.

Allen developed the quarries at Coombe Down, constructed Prior Park and employed the two John Woods (father and son) to create many of Bath's buildings, while Nash organised the city's social calendar and laid down strict edicts concerning social etiquette (including a ban on the wearing of sabres and swearing in public).

During WWII, Bath was hit by the Luftwaffe during the so-called Baedeker raids, which deliberately targeted historic cities in an effort to sap British morale. Several houses on the Royal Crescent and the Circus were badly damaged, and the city's Assembly Rooms were gutted by fire, although all have since been carefully restored.

In 1987, Bath became the only city in Britain to be declared a World Heritage Site by Unesco in its entirety, leading to many subsequent wrangles over construction and development, most recently concerning the design of the redeveloped Thermae Bath Spa and SouthGate shopping centre.

Sights

Roman Baths MUSEUM

(www.romanbaths.co.uk; Abbey Churchyard; adult/child £12/7.80; 9am-6pm) Ever since the Romans arrived in Bath, life in the city has revolved around the three geothermal springs that bubble up near the abbey. In typically ostentatious style, the Romans constructed a glorious complex of bathhouses above these thermal waters to take advantage of their natural temperature, which is a constant 46°C. Situated alongside an important temple dedicated to the healing goddess Sulis-Minerva, the baths are believed to have attracted tourists from right across the Empire, and now form one of the best-preserved ancient Roman spas in the world.

The heart of the complex is the **Great Bath**, a large lead-lined pool filled with steaming, geothermally heated water from the so-called 'Sacred Spring' to a depth of 1.6m. Though it's now open to the air, the bath would originally have been covered by a vast 45m-high barrel-vaulted roof. Further bathing pools and changing rooms are situated to the east and west, with excavated sections revealing the hypocaust system that would have kept the bathing rooms balmy.

One of the most picturesque corners of the complex is the 12th-century **King's Bath**, built around the original sacred spring; 1.5 million litres of hot water still pour into the pool every day. Beneath the Pump Room are the remains of the **Temple of Sulis-Minerva**; look out for the famous gilded head of Minerva herself and the engraved Haruspex stone on which the statue would originally have stood.

Even though the baths are off-limits to modern-day bathers, they remain a fascinating window into everyday Roman life, and unsurprisingly get very busy. You can usually avoid the worst crowds by buying tickets in advance online, visiting early on a midweek morning, and avoiding July and August. Admission includes an audioguide in a choice of eight languages, featuring a special commentary by the bestselling author Bill Bryson.

Joint tickets are available with the Fashion Museum (p316).

Bath Abbey CHURCH

(www.bathabbey.org; requested donation £2.50; 9am-6pm Mon-Sat, 1-2.30pm & 4.30-5.30pm Sun) Looming above the centre of the city, Bath's huge abbey church was built between 1499 and 1616, making it the last great medieval church raised in England. Its most striking feature is the west facade, where angels climb up and down stone ladders, commemorating a dream of the founder, Bishop Oliver King. Among those buried here are Sir Isaac Pitman (who devised the Pitman method of shorthand) and the celebrated *bon viveur* Beau Nash.

On the abbey's southern side, the small **Vaults Heritage Museum** (10am-4pm Mon-Sat) explores the abbey's history and its links with the nearby baths.

Royal Crescent HISTORIC AREA

(Royal Crescent) Bath is rightly celebrated for its glorious Georgian architecture, and it doesn't get any grander than on Royal Crescent, a semicircular terrace of majestic townhouses overlooking the green sweep of Royal Victoria Park. Designed by John Wood the Younger (1728–82) and built between 1767 and 1775, the houses were designed to appear perfectly symmetrical from the outside, but the original owners were allowed

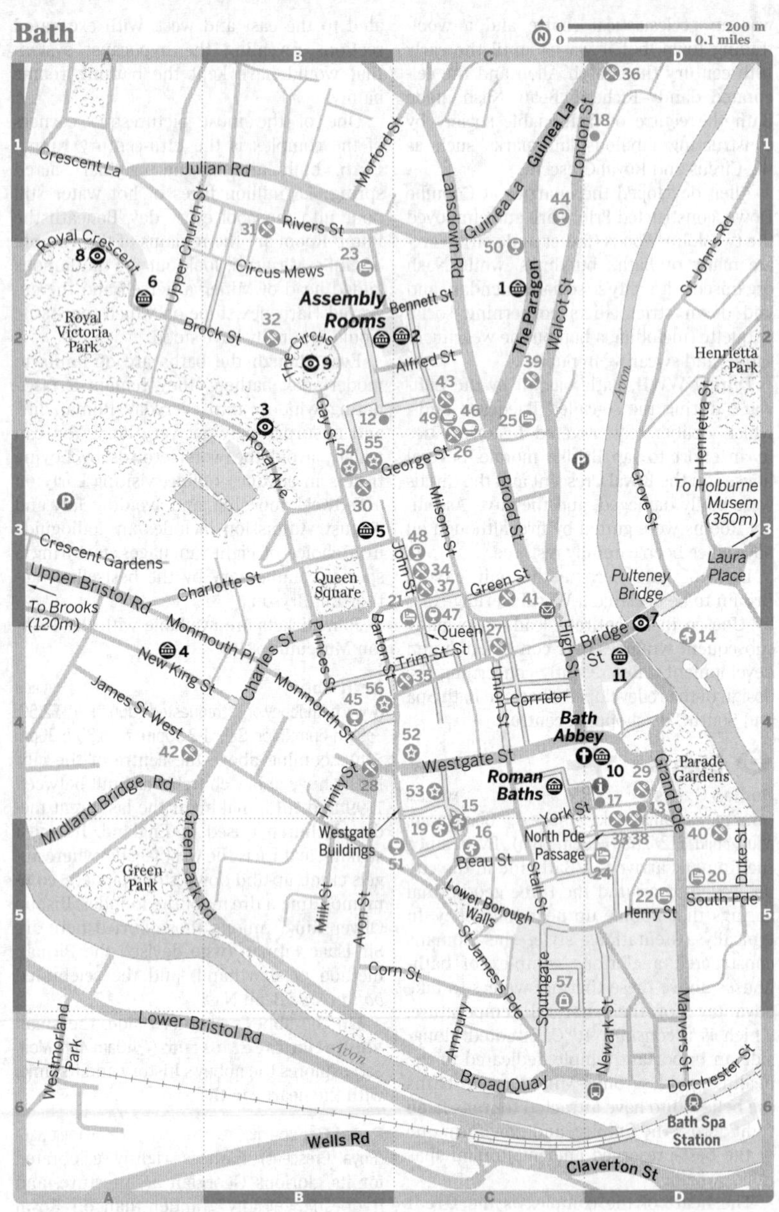

to design the interiors to their own specifications; consequently no two houses on the Crescent are quite the same. They would originally have been rented for the summer season by wealthy socialites, who descended on Bath to indulge in a whirlwind program of masquerades, dances, concerts and tea parties.

For a glimpse into the splendour and razzle-dazzle of Georgian life, head for the beautifully restored house at **No 1 Royal Crescent** (www.bath-preservation-trust.org.uk;

Bath

Top Sights

	Assembly Rooms	B2
	Bath Abbey	C4
	Roman Baths	C4

Sights

1	Building of Bath Museum	C2
2	Fashion Museum	C2
3	Georgian Garden	B2
4	Herschel Museum of Astronomy	A4
5	Jane Austen Centre	B3
6	No 1 Royal Crescent	A2
7	Pulteney Bridge	D3
8	Royal Crescent	A2
9	The Circus	B2
10	Vaults Heritage Museum	D4
11	Victoria Art Gallery	D4

Activities, Courses & Tours

12	Bertinet Kitchen	B2
13	Bizarre Bath Comedy Walk	D4
14	Boat Trips	D4
15	Cross Bath	C5
16	Hot Bath	C5
17	Jane Austen's Bath Walking Tours	D4
18	Makery Workshop	D1
19	Thermae Bath Spa	C5

Sleeping

20	Halcyon	D5
21	Haringtons Hotel	C3
22	Henry	D5
23	Queensberry Hotel	B2
24	Three Abbey Green	D5
25	YMCA	C2

Eating

26	Adventure Cafe	C3
27	Bertinet Bakery	C4
28	Boston Tea Party	B4
29	Café Retro	D4
30	Chandos Deli	B3
31	Chequers	B1
32	Circus	B2
33	Demuth's	D5
34	Firehouse Rotisserie	C3
35	Gascoyne Place	C4
36	Hudson Steakhouse	D1
37	Paxton & Whitfield	C3
38	Sally Lunn's	D5
39	Sam's Kitchen Deli	C2
40	Sotto Sotto	D5
41	Tasting Room	C3
42	Thoughtful Bread Company	A4
43	Yen Sushi	C2

Drinking

44	Bell	C1
45	Door 34	B4
46	Jika Jika	C2
47	Raven	C3
48	Salamander	C3
49	Same Same But Different	C2
50	Star Inn	C2
51	The Cork	C5

Entertainment

52	Komedia	C4
53	Little Theatre Cinema	C4
54	Moles	B3
55	Porter Cellar Bar	B3
56	Theatre Royal	B4

Shopping

57	SouthGate	C5

1 Royal Cres; adult/child £6.50/2.50; 10.30am-5pm Tue-Sun late Feb–mid-Dec), given to the city by the shipping magnate Major Bernard Cayzer, and since restored using only 18th-century materials. Among the rooms on display are the drawing room, several bedrooms and the huge kitchen, complete with massive hearth, roasting spit and mousetraps.

The Circus HISTORIC AREA

(Union St) Inspired by the Roman Colosseum, the Circus is a Georgian masterpiece of John Wood the Elder's design. Arranged over three equal terraces, the 33 mansions overlook a garden populated by plane trees; a German bomb fell into the square in 1942 and demolished several houses, although they've since been rebuilt in seamless style. Look out for plaques to Thomas Gainsborough, Clive of India and David Livingstone, all former Circus residents.

To the south along Gravel Walk is the **Georgian Garden**, restored to resemble a typical 18th-century townhouse garden.

FREE **Holburne Museum** ART GALLERY

(www.holburne.org; Great Pulteney St; temporary exhibitions incur fee; 10am-5pm) Sir William

Holburne, the 18th-century aristocrat, aesthete and art fanatic, amassed a huge collection which now forms the core of the Holburne Museum, in a lavish mansion at the end of Great Pulteney St. Fresh from a three-year refit, the museum houses an impressive roll call of works by artists including Turner, Stubbs, William Hoare and Thomas Gainsborough, as well as a fine collection of 18th-century majollica and porcelain.

Pulteney Bridge BRIDGE
Hovering gracefully above the rushing waters of Pulteney Weir, this elegant bridge is one of only a handful in the world to be lined with shops (the most famous other example is the Ponte Vecchio in Florence). It was built in 1773 and is now Grade-I listed.

Jane Austen Centre MUSEUM
(www.janeausten.co.uk; 40 Gay St; adult/child £7.45/4.25; ⌚9.45am-5.30pm) Bath is known to many as a location in Jane Austen's novels, including *Persuasion* and *Northanger Abbey*. Though Austen only lived in Bath for five years from 1801 to 1806, she remained a regular visitor throughout her life, as well as a keen student of the city's social scene. This museum houses a small collection of memorabilia relating to the writer's life in Bath, and costumed guides bring the era to life. There's also a Regency tearoom that serves crumpets and cream teas in suitably frilly surrounds.

Assembly Rooms HISTORIC BUILDING
(NT; www.nationaltrust.org.uk/main/w-bathassemblyrooms; 19 Bennett St; adult/child £2/free; ⌚10.30am-6pm) Opened in 1771, the city's glorious Assembly Rooms were where fashionable Bath socialites once gathered to waltz, play cards and listen to the latest chamber music. You're free to wander around the rooms, as long as they haven't been reserved for a special function; rooms open to the public include the card room, tearoom and the truly splendid ballroom, all of which are lit by their original 18th-century chandeliers. The Assembly Rooms were all but gutted by incendiary bombs during WWII but have since been carefully restored.

Fashion Museum MUSEUM
(www.fashionmuseum.co.uk; Assembly Rooms, Bennett St; adult/child £7.25/5.25; ⌚10.30am-5pm) In the basement of the Assembly Rooms, this museum contains a wonderful collection of costumes worn from the 16th to late 20th centuries. Exhibitions are changed annually, so check the website for the latest shows.

American Museum in Britain MUSEUM
(www.americanmuseum.org; Claverton Manor; adult/child £8/4.50; ⌚noon-5pm) Britain's largest collection of American folk art, including Native American textiles, patchwork quilts and historic maps, is housed in a fine mansion a couple of miles from the city centre. Several rooms have been recreated in period style, including a 17th-century Puritan house, an 18th-century tavern and a New Orleans boudoir c 1860. Catch bus 18/418/U18 from the bus station.

Building of Bath Museum MUSEUM
(www.bath-preservation-trust.org.uk; The Vineyards, The Paragon; adult/child £4/2; ⌚10.30am-5pm Tue-Sun mid-Feb–Nov) This museum explores the story of Bath's architecture, with antique tools, displays on Georgian construction methods and a 1:500 scale model of Bath.

Herschel Museum of Astronomy MUSEUM
(19 New King St; adult/child £5/2.50; ⌚1-5pm Mon, Tue, Thu & Fri, from 11am Sat & Sun) In 1781 astronomer William Herschel discovered Uranus from the garden of his home, now converted into an intriguing museum. The house is decorated as it would have been in the 18th century; an astrolabe in the garden marks where Herschel would have placed his telescope.

FREE **Victoria Art Gallery** ART GALLERY
(www.victoriagal.org.uk; Pulteney Bridge; ⌚10am-5pm Tue-Sat, 1.30-5pm Sun) This excellent art museum houses some fine canvases by Gainsborough, Turner and Sickert, as well as a wonderful series of Georgian caricatures from the wicked pens of artists such as James Gillray and Thomas Rowlandson.

Prior Park GARDEN
(NT; ☎01225-833422; www.nationaltrust.org.uk/priorpark; Ralph Allen Dr; adult/child £5.40/3; ⌚10am-5.30pm Feb-Nov) This 18th-century estate on Bath's southern fringe was built by the entrepreneur Ralph Allen, who made his fortune founding Britain's first postal service, and owned many of the local quarries from which the city's amber-coloured Bath stone was mined. The famous landscape architect Capability Brown and the satirical poet Alexander Pope both had a hand in laying out the grounds, which feature cascading lakes and a graceful Palladian

bridge, one of only four such structures in the world – look out for the period graffiti, some of which dates back to the 1800s.

The house itself is now occupied by a private school, but there are several lovely pathways around the estate, including the **Bath Skyline**, a 6-mile circular trail offering truly inspirational views.

The park is a mile south of Bath's centre. Bus 2 (every 10 minutes) and the City Skyline tour both stop nearby.

Activities

Boat Trips CRUISES

Various cruise operators offer trips up and down the River Avon from the landing station underneath Pulteney Bridge, including:

Bath City Boat Trips (07974-560197; www.bathcityboattrips.com; adult/child £6.95/4.95)

Pulteney Cruisers (01225-312900; www.bathboating.com; adult/child £8/4)

Pulteney Princess (07791-910650; www.pulteneyprincess.co.uk; adult/child £8/3).

You can pilot your own vessel down the Avon from the **Bathwick Boating Station** (01225-312900; www.bathboating.co.uk; Forrester Rd; 1st hr per adult/child £7/3.50, additional hr £3/1.50; 10am-6pm Easter-Oct), which rents out traditional skiffs, rowboats and Canadian canoes. The jetty is in the suburb of Bathwick, a 20-minute walk southeast from the city centre.

Makery Workshop CRAFTS

(01225-421175; www.themakeryonline.co.uk; 146 Walcot St) This innovative craft centre hosts regular workshops in sewing, patchwork, upholstery and other handicrafts. Check out the calendar for forthcoming sessions.

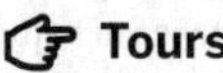

Tours

FREE **Mayor's Guide Tours** WALKING TOUR

(01225-477411; www.bathguides.co.uk; 10.30am & 2pm Sun-Fri, 10.30am Sat) Excellent historical tours provided free by the Mayors Corp of Honorary Guides. Tours leave from outside the Pump Rooms. There are extra tours at 7pm on Tuesdays and Thursdays May to September. They cover about 2 miles and are wheelchair-friendly.

Jane Austen's Bath Walking Tours WALKING TOUR

(01225-443000; adult/child £6/5; 11am Sat & Sun) A guided tour of the Georgian city, organised by the Jane Austen Centre. Tours leave from the Abbey Churchyard.

Bath City Sightseeing BUS TOUR

(01225-330444; www.city-sightseeing.com; adult/child £12.50/7.50; 9.30am-6.30pm Mar-Nov) Hop-on/hop-off city tour on an open-topped bus, with a commentary in seven

THE KENNET & AVON CANAL

Tracing a languid 87-mile course between Bath and Newbury, the Kennet & Avon Canal was built in the early 19th century as a link for industrial traffic between the River Avon and the River Kennet, a tributary of the River Thames, although its commercial viability was quickly eclipsed by the railway.

After decades in disrepair, the canal has been thoroughly restored, and its tow-paths now make the perfect place for a leisurely stroll or bike ride.

There are several impressive **locks** to see in the city, including the **Bath Deep Lock** (just to the east of Bath Spa station), England's second-deepest canal lock. Several miles east of the city, other landmarks include the three-arched Dundas Aqueduct, completed in 1805 and now Grade I listed, and the **Claverton Pumping Station**, which still has its 19th-century waterwheel (currently undergoing restoration). A useful guide to the Kennet & Avon Trail can be downloaded from the Sustrans website at www.sustrans.org.uk/assets/files/leaflets/KAcycleguide.pdf.

If you want to get out on the water, the **Kennet & Avon Canal Trust** (www.katrust.co.uk) operates narrowboat cruises from Bradford-on-Avon, Devizes, Hungerford, and Newbury. Alternatively, if you'd prefer to be your own captain, vessels can be hired from **Moonraker Boats** (01672-851550; www.moonboats.co.uk) and **Bath Canal Boats** (01225-312935; www.bathcanalboats.co.uk) starting from around £1100 per week.

Bath Canal Boats also offers two-night B&B breaks on its **Grand Cru** (www.bedandbreakfastonaboat.co.uk; 2-nights for 4/6 people £379/429) houseboat, including a 90-minute cruise.

DON'T MISS

THERMAE BATH SPA

You simply couldn't come to Bath and not take a bath, now could you? The Roman Baths may be off-limits, but you can still sample the city's curative waters thanks to the flashy **Thermae Bath Spa** (☎0844-888 0844; www.thermaebathspa.com; Bath St; ⏰9am-10pm, last entry 7.30pm), an ultra-modern complex of steel and glass lodged among Georgian buildings.

The main **New Royal Bath** (spa per two/four hours £25/35) houses aromatherapy steam rooms, saunas and a choice of bathing venues – including the jaw-dropping open-air rooftop pool, where you can swim in the thermal waters against a backdrop of Bath's stunning cityscape. Incurable romantics can even book in for a twilight dip (£80), which includes a meal and drinks at the spa's restaurant.

Across the street are treatment rooms above the old **Hot Bath**. There's also another open-air pool in the nearby **Cross Bath** (1½hr £16), which is served by its own hot spring and is often quieter than the main complex.

Note that towels, robes and slippers aren't included in spa prices, but you can hire all three for £9 – or better still, bring your own.

languages. Buses stop several times an hour at various points around town. A second route, the **Skyline tour**, also travels out to Prior Park; the same tickets are valid on both routes.

Bizarre Bath Comedy Walk WALKING TOUR
(☎01225-335124; www.bizarrebath.co.uk; adult/student £8/5; ⏰8pm Mar-Oct) This daft city tour entertainingly mixes street theatre and live performance. It leaves from outside the Huntsman Inn on North Parade Passage. The walk is usually entirely wheelchair-accessible, but construction work has made access to one area impossible, so they're not currently charging wheelchair visitors.

FREE **Jane Austen Audio Tour** WALKING TOUR
(www.visitbath.co.uk/janeausten/audio-tour) This specially recorded MP3 tour guides listeners to various locations around Bath connected with Jane Austen, and also covers some of the city's other highlights. It can be downloaded free from the Visit Bath website.

Festivals & Events

Bath has lots of festivals. All bookings are handled by **Bath Festivals** (☎01225-463362; www.bathfestivals.org.uk; 2 Church St; ⏰9.30am-5.30pm Mon-Sat).

Bath Literature Festival BOOK FESTIVAL
(www.bathlitfest.org.uk) Annual book festival in late February or early March.

Bath International Music Festival MUSIC
(www.bathmusicfest.org.uk) Mainly classical and opera, plus smaller gigs of jazz, folk and world. Mid-May to early June.

Bath Fringe Festival THEATRE
(www.bathfringe.co.uk) Major theatre festival around mid-May to early June.

Jane Austen Festival STREET FESTIVAL
(www.janeausten.co.uk/festival) The highlight of this September festival is a costumed parade through the city's streets.

Bath Film Festival FILM
(www.bathfilmfestival.org.uk) Early November.

Sleeping

Bath gets incredibly busy, especially in the height of summer and at weekends, when prices are at a premium. Very few hotels have parking, although some offer discounted rates at municipal car parks.

TOP CHOICE **Queensberry Hotel** HOTEL £££
(☎01225-447928; www.thequeensberry.co.uk; 4 Russell St; d £150-270, ste £460; 📶) It's a budget-buster, but the quirky Queensberry is undoubtedly one of Bath's best boutique spoils. Four Georgian townhouses have been combined into one seamlessly stylish whole, but all the rooms are subtly different: some are cosy in gingham checks and country creams; others feature zesty upholstery, original fireplaces and free-standing tubs. The basement Olive Tree Restaurant is one of the town's top tables, too. Parking is available at a nearby private garage. Rates don't include breakfast.

TOP CHOICE **Halcyon** HOTEL ££

(☎01225-444100; www.thehalcyon.com; 2/3 South Pde; d £125-145; 📶) Just what Bath needed: a smart, stylish city-centre hotel that doesn't break the bank. Situated in a listed terrace off Manvers St, the heavily renovated Halcyon is all about style on a budget: white-washed rooms, bright bed linen, Philippe Starck bath fittings and White Company smellies, along with a smart basement breakfast room and the brand new Circo cocktail bar. The drawbacks? Rooms are spread out over three floors and there's no lift. They're also very variable in size. Front rooms have the views, and the ones on the top-floor avoid late-night bar noise.

Henry B&B ££

(☎01225-424052; www.thehenry.com; 6 Henry St; d £80-120, f £145-165) This tall, slim townhouse has an absolutely superb position, literally steps from the centre, and offers a good choice of clean, uncluttered rooms finished in crisp whites and smooth beiges. It's decent value considering the location, but there's no parking and it can feel very cramped when it's full. More space is available at the 'Below Stairs' self-catering apartment nearby. Two-night minimum stay at weekends.

139 Bath B&B ££

(☎01225-314769; www.139bath.co.uk; 139 Wells Rd; r £120-195; P📶) It's a bit out of the centre, but this swish B&B really sets the pace. It's been throughtfully designed throughout, with swirly fabrics, contemporary colour schemes and supremely comfy beds, plus lots of little spoils such as cafetière coffee, Molton Brown bath products and a generous buffet breakfast (two four-poster rooms even have Jacuzzis). Posh it certainly is, but it's still a touch pricey for a B&B.

Brooks HOTEL ££

(☎01225-425543; www.brooksguesthouse.com; 1 & 1a Crescent Gardens; s £59-89, d £80-150, f £120-160; 📶) On the west side of Bath, this townhouse blends heritage fixtures with snazzy finishes. The owners have focused on the details: goose-down duvets, pocket-sprung mattresses, DAB radios and breakfast choices including smoked-salmon brioche and homemade muesli. Parking is problematic.

Haringtons Hotel HOTEL ££

(☎01225-461278; www.haringtonshotel.co.uk; Queen St; d £88-168) Bath's classical trappings aren't to everyone's taste, so things are kept modern and minimal at this city-centre crash pad: clean lines, crisp colour schemes and LCD TVs, although some of the rooms are shoebox-sized.

Three Abbey Green B&B ££

(☎01225-428558; www.threeabbeygreen.com; 3 Abbey Green; d £90-140, f £140-220; 📶) Considering the location, this place is a steal – tumble out of the front door and you'll find yourself practically on the abbey's doorstep. It's on a leafy square, and though the rooms lack sparkle, the suites have adjoining singles – ideal for family travellers.

Georgian Stables APARTMENT ££

(☎01225-465956; 41 Sydney Buildings; d £85) This deliciously quirky apartment is a find: it's in a lovely canalside location 10 minutes' walk from the city, and offers unusual accommodation inside a converted stable block, accessed by the original cobbled ramp. The apartment itself is all clean lines and white walls, but patches of exposed stone in the bedroom and shower room provide reminders of its heritage.

Paradise House B&B ££

(☎01225-317723; www.paradise-house.co.uk; 88 Holloway; d £130-195; P) If it's classic English trappings you're after, this hilltop beauty is the place. Set among a landscaped garden with views over Bath's rooftops, it's awash with vintage interest: gilded mirrors, flouncy beds, claw-foot baths and an old-fashioned sitting room complete with roaring hearth. It's a long, long walk from town, though.

Appletree Guest House B&B ££

(☎01225-337642; www.appletreeguesthouse.co.uk; 7 Pulteney Gardens; s £55-66, d £85-110, f £135-149; 📶) It's tiny, but this welcoming B&B is worth recommending for the sunny disposition of its husband-and-wife owners, Les and Lynsay. Rooms are straightforward and simple, and street parking is free if you can find a space.

Bath YHA HOSTEL £

(www.yha.org.uk; Bathwick Hill; dm £20.40, d from £59; P@) Lodged inside an Italianate mansion and a more modern annexe, a steep climb (or a short hop on bus 18) from the city centre, this hostel offers decent rooms, spacious kitchens and lovely grounds.

Oldfields B&B ££

(☎01225-317984; www.oldfields.co.uk; 102 Wells Rd; d £115-175; P) Luxurious B&B in a quiet area on Wells Rd.

YMCA HOSTEL £
(☎01225-325900; www.bathymca.co.uk; International House, Broad St Pl; dm £20-22, s £31-35, d & tw £54-60; @) Institutional, yes, but bright, clean and bang in the centre – it's even got a health suite and cafe.

Eating

TOP CHOICE **Menu Gordon Jones** GOURMET BRITISH ££
(☎01225-480871; www.menugordonjones.co.uk; 2 Wellsway; 5-course lunch £30, 6-course dinner £40) Gordon Jones is the name to watch in Bath. Previously head honcho at the uber-expensive Royal Crescent Hotel, he's since branched out with his own pocket-sized restaurant, which has already earned him critical plaudits aplenty. The multicourse 'surprise menus' are dreamt up by Jones on the day, and showcase his taste for experimentation, both in terms of ingredients (smoked eel, seagull's eggs, samphire) and presentation (test-tubes, edible cups, slate plates). The pop soundtrack and minuscule dining room won't please everyone, but the menus are incredible value considering the skill. Jones is destined for big things: book now while you can.

Circus MODERN BRITISH ££
(☎01225-466020; www.thecircuscafeandrestaurant.co.uk; 34 Brock St; mains lunch £5.50-10, dinner £11-14; ⏰10am-midnight Mon-Sat) It's not quite the locals' secret it once was, but the Circus is still one of Bath's best. Installed in a converted townhouse between the Circus and Royal Crescent, it's the model of a modern Brit bistro: chef Ali Golden has a taste for hearty dishes such as rabbit pie and roast guinea-fowl, all seasonally inspired, impeccably presented and reassuringly generous. The dining room's cellar feels cramped when it's full, so aim for an upstairs table and reserve ahead.

Marlborough Tavern GASTROPUB ££
(☎01225-423731; www.marlborough-tavern.com; 35 Marlborough Buildings; mains £12-17) Bath certainly isn't short on gastropubs, but the Marlborough is still very much top of the class. It's half cosy boozer, half contemporary bistro, with big wooden tables, deep seats, and a crackling fire on winter nights. Chef Richard Knighting previously worked in Michelin-starred restaurants, and it shows: his menu is a mix of heart-warming classics and cheffy showiness, and rarely fails to hit the mark.

Chequers GASTROPUB
(☎01225-360017; www.thechequersbar.com; 50 Rivers St; £10.50-£19) Big, bold flavours are the order of the day at the Chequers: chunky pork chops, venison bangers and braised beef cheek, dished up perhaps with a classy champ mash or a rich red wine jus. It's scooped multiple awards for its food, and it's usually packed out for Sunday lunch. The pub is 18th-century, but feels designer-modern.

Demuth's VEGETARIAN ££
(☎01225-446059; www.demuths.co.uk; 2 North Pde Passage; lunch £4.95-11, dinner £14.50-17; 🅥) Even the most committed of carnivores can't fail to fall for this long-established veggie restaurant, which consistently turns out some of the city's most creative food – from cheddar soufflé served with figs, walnut purée and spring greens, to a port-poached pear baked with fennel seeds and sheep's cheese.

Sotto Sotto ITALIAN ££
(☎01225-330236; 10a North Pde; pasta £9, mains £13-17) Authentic Italian food served in a lovely cellar setting complete with barrel-brick roof. Ingredients are shipped in directly and everything's just like mama made, from the osso bucco (veal shank) to the *orecchiette mare e monti* (top-hat pasta with seafood, beans and pancetta).

Hudson Steakhouse STEAK HOUSE £££
(☎01225-332323; www.hudsonbars.com; 14 London St; steaks £22-34; ⏰dinner Mon-Sat) Steak, steak and more steak is this place's raison d'être. Top-quality cuts take in everything from porterhouse to prime fillet, all sourced from a Staffordshire farmers' co-op.

Sam's Kitchen Deli CAFE £
(www.samskitchendeli.co.uk; 61 Walcot St; lunch £8-10; ⏰8am-6pm Mon-Sat, every 2nd Fri 8am-10pm) This eclectic cafe is a fantastic place for lunch, offering a choice of set dishes (including a daily roast), served straight from the pans on the counter. With its dilapidated piano, cast-iron staircase and reclaimed furniture, it's vintage shabby-chic Bath, and very popular. Look out for supper clubs and live gigs every other Friday.

Yen Sushi JAPANESE ££
(11-12 Bartlett St; sushi £4-6) Bath's very own *kaiten* (conveyor-belt) restaurant, with colour-coded dishes of nigiri, sushi and sashimi. Look out for unusual options such

BAKED TO PERFECTION

If you've always yearned to know how to bake the perfect sourdough or craft the lightest choux bun, you're in luck – one of the nation's top bakers, Richard Bertinet, runs his very own **Bertinet Kitchen Cookery School** (☎01225-445531; www.thebertinetkitchen.com; 12 St Andrews Tce) in Bath. The school organises regular courses in everything from cake-making to bread-making, some of which are conducted by the great Frenchman himself. Alternatively, if you'd prefer to sample his pastry without putting in the effort, you can pop into his brand new city-centre cafe, the **Bertinet Bakery** (www.bertinet.com/bertinetbakery; 6 New Bond St Place; ⏰8am-6pm Mon-Sat, 10.30am-4pm Sun), where the shelves are stocked with a heavenly choice of quiches, croissants, tarts and vienoisseries. Just don't expect to walk out empty-handed...

as *hirame* (turbot), *suzuki* (sea bass) and *unagi* (eel).

Café Retro CAFE £
(18 York St; mains £5-11; ⏰breakfast, lunch & dinner Tue-Sat, breakfast & lunch Mon) This place is a poke in the eye for the corporate coffee chains. The paint job's scruffy, the crockery's ancient and none of the furniture matches, but that's all part of the charm: this is a cafe from the old school, and there's nowhere better for a burger, cake or hot mug of tea. Takeaways available from Retro to Go next door.

Tasting Room TAPAS
(☎01225-483070; www.tastingroom.co.uk; 6 Green St; 3-course tapas £10; ⏰10am-4.30pm Sun & Mon, 9.30am-11pm Tue-Sat) Plates of tapas to share partnered with high-class vintages are the *modus operandi* of this slinky cafe-bar, located on the top floor of Bath's top wine merchant.

Firehouse Rotisserie AMERICAN ££
(2 John St; mains £11-15; ⏰Mon-Sat) Californian flavours such as achiote lamb, Pacific crab cakes and spicy Baja chicken take centre stage at this popular bistro run by a couple of ex-LA chefs. The brick-fired pizzas are enormous, too.

Sally Lunn's TEAROOM £
(4 North Pde Passage; lunch mains £5-6, dinner mains from £8) This fabulously frilly tearoom occupies one of Bath's oldest houses, and makes the perfect venue for classic cream tea (served in proper bone china), accompanied by finger sandwiches, dainty cakes and the trademark Sally Lunn's Bun.

Adventure Cafe CAFE £
(5 Princes Buildings, George St; mains £4-8; ⏰breakfast, lunch & dinner; 📶) This cool cafe is equally suited to morning cappuccino, lunchtime ciabatta and late night beer.

Gascoyne Place GASTROPUB ££
(www.gascoyneplace.co.uk; 1 Sawclose; mains £9-17) Another quality gastropub opposite the Theatre Royal.

Self-Catering

For a quick lunchtime salad or wrap, try **Chandos Deli** (George St; ⏰Mon-Sat) and the **Boston Tea Party** (19 Kingsmead Sq; mains from £4; ⏰7.30am-7pm Mon-Sat, from 8.30am Sun).

Paxton & Whitfield CHEESE £
(1 John St; ⏰Mon-Sat) Renowned fromagerie that specialises in locally made cheeses.

Thoughtful Bread Company BAKERY £
(www.thethoughtfulbreadcompany.com; Green Park Railway Station; ⏰9am-6pm Tue-Sat) Handmade pastries and breads, based in the old Green Park Station.

Drinking

Jika Jika CAFE
(www.jikajika.co.uk; 4a Princes Buildings, George St; ⏰8am-6.30pm Mon-Thu, 8am-7pm Fri, 8.30am-7pm Sat, 9am-5.30pm Sun) If you're serious about your caffeine, this award-winning cafe serves the city's best espresso, roasted by hand and sourced from rare estates.

Same Same But Different CAFE, BAR
(7a Prince's Buildings, Bartlett St; ⏰8am-6pm Mon-Wed, 8am-11pm Thu-Sat, 10am-5pm Sun) Boho hang-out for the town's trendies, tucked down an alley off George St. Savour wine by the glass, snack on a plate of tapas or sip a cappuccino with the Sunday papers.

Door 34 COCKTAIL BAR
(www.door34.co.uk; 34 Monmouth St; cocktails from around £8; ⏰from 7pm) This cocktail bar

touts itself as a 'liquid alhemist's lounge', and it certainly mixes a mean martini. The townhouse decor and paperback menus add a touch of class, and the mixologists will happily give you some cocktail tips if you smile sweetly. Look out for the weekly rum club.

Raven PUB
(Queen St) This traditional pub commands a devoted following for its well-kept real ales and trad atmosphere, complete with beer mats, bar and brass trinkets.

Salamander PUB
(3 John St) Run by local brewer Bath Ales, this modern pub offers a range of bespoke ales. At the lighter end are amber-coloured Gem and Golden Hare, while the strongest is dark Rare Hare at a punchy 5.2%. Takeaway kegs are available if you develop a taste for the amber nectar.

Star Inn PUB
(www.star-inn-bath.co.uk; 23 The Vineyards, off the Paragon) Not many pubs are registered relics, but the Star is – it still has many of its 19th-century bar fittings. It's the brewery tap for Bath-based Abbey Ales; some ales are served in traditional jugs, and you can even ask for a pinch of snuff in the 'smaller bar'.

The Cork PUB
(www.thecork.co.uk; 11-12 Westgate Buildings) Lively and very central pub, with a gleaming wood interior and a fine outside terrace. There's a good choice of ales, and the cocktail menu is temptingly good too.

Bell PUB
(Walcot St;) Scruffy pub on boho Walcot St, with a good beer garden and regular bands.

☆ Entertainment

Venue (www.venue.co.uk) has listings for Bath's theatre, music and gig scenes.

Moles LIVE MUSIC
(www.moles.co.uk; 14 George St) Bath's historic music club is the place to catch live gigs by big-name bands.

Porter Cellar Bar LIVE MUSIC
(George St) Run by the folk at Moles, this student favourite lays on the acts who aren't yet big enough to play the main venue; it's Bath's only veggie pub, too.

Theatre Royal THEATRE
(www.theatreroyal.org.uk; Sawclose) This is one of the southwest's classiest regional theatres. Major touring productions go in the main auditorium, while smaller shows appear in the Ustinov Studio.

Komedia CABARET, COMEDY
(www.komedia.co.uk; 22-23 Westgate St) Live comedy and cabaret at this Bath offshoot of the Brighton-based original.

Little Theatre Cinema CINEMA
(St Michael's Pl) Bath's excellent art-house cinema screens fringe films and foreign-language flicks.

Shopping

Bath's multimillion-pound new shopping district, **SouthGate** (www.southgatebath.com), occupies much of the south side of town, with flagship stores for all the major retail names.

High-end fashion stores and upmarket boutiques tend to cluster around Milsom St, Milsom Pl and Broad St.

Funky Walcot St is the place for quirky design, vintage clothes and retro furniture.

Information

Bath Visitor Centre (www.visitbath.co.uk; Abbey Churchyard; 9.30am-5pm Mon-Sat, 10am-4pm Sun) Sells the Bath City Card (£3), which is valid for three weeks and offers discounts at many local shops, restaurants and attractions.

Main Post Office (27 Northgate St)

Police Station (Manvers St; 7am-midnight)

Royal United Hospital (01225-428331; Combe Park)

What's On (www.whatsonbath.co.uk) City listings.

Getting There & Away

Bus

Bath's **bus and coach station** (9am-5pm Mon-Sat) is on Dorchester St near the train station.

National Express coaches run directly to **London** (£20.70, 3½ hours, eight to 10 daily) via **Heathrow** (£20.70, 2¾ hours). Services to most other destinations require a change at Bristol or Heathrow.

Local bus services:

Bath (50 minutes, four per hour Monday to Saturday, half-hourly on Sunday) Bus X39/339.

Bradford-on-Avon (30 minutes, half-hourly, eight on Sunday) Bus 264/265.

Frome (hourly Monday to Saturday) Bus 184.
Wells (one hour 10 minutes, hourly Monday to Saturday, five on Sunday) Bus 173.

Train

Bath Spa station is at the end of Manvers St. Many services connect through **Bristol** (£9.90, 20 minutes, two or three per hour), especially to the north of England.

Direct services:

Bradford-on-Avon (£3.90, 11 to 15 minutes, two per hour)
Cardiff Central (£18, one hour, hourly)
Exeter (£27.50, 1¼ hours, hourly)
London Paddington or **London Waterloo** (£39, 1½ hours, half-hourly)
Salisbury (£15.70, one hour, hourly)

Getting Around

Bicycle

Bath's hills are a challenge; for easier cycling, try the tow paths along the **Kennet & Avon Canal** (www.kennetandavontrust.co.uk) or the 13-mile **Bristol & Bath Railway Path** (www.bristolbathrailwaypath.org.uk).

Bus

Bus 18 runs from the bus station, High St and Great Pulteney St up Bathwick Hill past the YHA to the university every 10 minutes. Bus 4 runs every 20 minutes to Bathampton from the same places.

Car & Motorcycle

Bath has serious traffic problems (especially at rush hour). **Park & Ride buses** (☎01225-464446; return Mon-Fri £3, Sat £2.50; ⌚6.15am-7.30pm Mon-Sat) operate from Lansdown to the north, Newbridge to the west and Odd Down to the south. It takes about 10 minutes to the centre; buses leave every 10 to 15 minutes.

If you brave the city, the best value car park is underneath the SouthGate shopping centre (up to two hours £3.10, over eight hours £12.50, after 6.30pm £2).

SOMERSET

Beyond the big cities of Bath and Bristol, the rest of Somerset harks back to a simpler, quieter world. This is still a deeply rural corner of England, where cider's brewed in the time-honoured way, thatch still graces many a rooftop, and the landscape unfurls across a varied panorama of meadows, mumps, hamlets and hills.

Information

Somerset Visitor Centre (☎01934-750833; www.visitsomerset.co.uk; Sedgemoor Services M5 South; ⌚9.15am-5pm daily Easter-Oct, 9.15am-5pm Mon-Fri Nov-Easter)
Visit South Somerset (www.visitsouthsomerset.co.uk)

Getting Around

Most buses in Somerset are operated by **First** (☎0845-606-4446; www.firstgroup.com), supplemented by smaller operators. For timetables and general information contact **Traveline South West** (☎0871-200 2233; www.travelinesw.com).

Key train services link Bath, Bristol, Bridgwater, Taunton and Weston-super-Mare. The M5 heads south past Bristol, to Bridgwater and Taunton, with the A39 leading west across the Quantocks to Exmoor.

Wells

POP 10,406

With Wells, small is beautiful. This tiny, picturesque metropolis is England's smallest city, and only qualifies for the 'city' title thanks to a magnificent medieval cathedral, which sits in the centre beside the grand Bishop's Palace. Wells has been the main seat of ecclesiastical power in this part of Britain since the 12th century, and is still the official residence of the Bishop of Bath and Wells. Medieval buildings and cobbled streets radiate out from the cathedral green to a marketplace that has been the bustling heart of Wells for some nine centuries (Wednesday and Saturday are market days). A quiet provincial city, Wells' excellent restaurants and busy shops help make it a good launching pad for exploring the Mendip Hills and northern Somerset.

Sights

Wells Cathedral CATHEDRAL
(www.wellscathedral.org.uk; Cathedral Green; requested donation adult/child £6/3; ⌚7am-7pm)
Wells' gargantuan Gothic cathedral (officially known as the Cathedral Church of St Andrew) sits plumb in the centre of the city, surrounded by one of the largest cathedral closes anywhere in England. It was built in several stages between 1180 and 1508, and consequently showcases a range of different Gothic styles.

Dominated by its squat towers, the cathedral's most famous asset is its **west front**, an immense sculpture gallery decorated with more than 300 figures, built in the 13th century and restored in 1986. The facade would once have been painted in vivid colours, but has long since reverted to its original sandy hue. Apart from the figure of Christ, installed in 1985 in the uppermost niche, all the figures are original.

Inside, the cathedral's famous **scissor arches** separate the nave from the choir. Though they appear purely decorative, they were actually built to counter the subsidence of the central tower.

High up in the north transept is a **mechanical clock** dating from 1392 – the second-oldest in England after the one at Salisbury Cathedral – which shows the position of the planets and the phases of the moon.

Other highlights include the elegant **Lady Chapel** (1326), the fan-vaulted **Chapter House** (1306) and the celebrated **chained library**, which contains books and manuscripts dating back to 1472. Outside, the cathedral's **Chain Bridge** enabled clerics to reach the cathedral without getting their robes wet.

Free guided tours usually run every hour from Monday to Saturday, but you'll need a photography permit (£3) to take pictures.

Cathedral Close HISTORIC AREA

Wells Cathedral forms the centrepiece of a cluster of ecclesiastical buildings dating back to the Middle Ages. Facing the west front, on the left are the 15th-century **Old Deanery** and the **Wells & Mendip Museum** (www.wellsmuseum.org.uk; 8 Cathedral Green; adult/child £3/1; ⏲10am-5.30pm Easter-Oct, 11am-4pm Wed-Mon Nov-Easter), with exhibits on local life, cathedral architecture and the infamous Witch of Wookey Hole.

Further along, **Vicars' Close** is a stunning 14th-century cobbled street, with a chapel at the end; members of the cathedral choir still live here. It is thought to be the oldest complete medieval street in Europe.

Penniless Porch, a corner gate leading onto Market Sq, is so-called because beggars asked for alms here.

Bishop's Palace HISTORIC BUILDING

(www.bishopspalacewells.co.uk; adult/child £6.35/2.70; ⏲palace 10am-6pm Apr-Dec, gardens Feb-Dec) Built for the bishop in the 13th century, this moat-ringed palace is purportedly the oldest inhabited building in England. Inside, the palace's state rooms and ruined great hall are worth a look, but it's the shady gardens that are the real draw. The natural springs after which Wells is named bubble up in the palace's grounds. The swans in the moat have been trained to ring a bell outside one of the windows when they want to be fed.

Sleeping

TOP CHOICE **Babington House** LUXURY HOTEL £££

(☎01373-812266; www.babingtonhouse.co.uk; near Frome; r £340-530; P W ☒) It's eye-poppingly pricey, but this lauded design hotel is without doubt one of Britain's most luxurious places to stay. It's somewhere between *Homes & Gardens* and *Wallpaper*: heritage beds, antique dressers and period fireplaces sit side-by-side with minimalist furniture, sanded wood floors and retro lamps. There's a top-class restaurant, cool library, private 45-seat cinema and, of course, a spa in the old cow-shed.

Beryl B&B ££

(☎01749-678738; www.beryl-wells.co.uk; Hawkers Lane; d £100-150; P ☒) This grand gabled mansion offers a delicious taste of English eccentricity. Every inch of the house is crammed with antique atmosphere, and the rooms boast grandfather clocks, chaises longues and four-posters galore. It's about a mile from Wells.

Ancient Gate House Hotel HOTEL ££

(☎01749-672029; www.ancientgatehouse.co.uk; Browne's Gate; d £106-131; W) This old hostelry is as central as you can get – it's partly built right into the cathedral's west gate. Rooms are prettily decorated in regal reds and duck-egg blues; the best have four-poster beds and knockout views of the cathedral through their latticed windows.

Number Twelve B&B ££

(☎01749-679406; www.numbertwelve.info; 12 North Rd; d £80-95; P W) Arts and Crafts house offering two pleasant bedrooms. Number 1 is the nicest, with free-standing bath and a small balcony with cathedral views. You'll be treated to tea and cake on arrival.

Stoberry House B&B ££

(☎01749-672906; www.stoberry-park.co.uk; Stoberry Park; d £75-115; P W) Just outside the city outskirts, this refined B&B offers four fancy rooms equipped with plush throws and silky cushions. One-night stays incur a £10 to £20 surcharge.

Eating

TOP CHOICE **Goodfellows** BISTRO, CAFE ££
(☎01749-673866; www.goodfellows.co.uk; 5 Sadler St; 3-course dinner in bistro £39) Two eateries in one, both excellent. The continental-style **cafe** (menus £10-17; ⊙8.30am-4pm Mon & Tue, 8.30am-5pm & 6-10pm Wed-Sat) serves quick lunch food and pastries made by the inhouse pastry chef. For something more sophisticated, the seafood **bistro** (mains £11.50-23; ⊙noon-2pm Tue-Sat, 6.30-9.30pm Wed-Sat) offers a full line-up of fishy delights plus a choice of settings (downstairs for open-plan dining, upstairs for intimacy); hard-core fish-fans should plump for the six-course tasting menu (£55).

Old Spot BRITISH ££
(☎01749-689099; www.theoldspot.co.uk; 12 Sadler St; 2-/3-course lunch $15.50/18.50, dinner mains £14-18.50; ⊙lunch Wed-Sun, dinner Tue-Sat) Hale and hearty classics form the core of Ian Bates's bistro. It's heavy on rich, meaty dishes such as duck terrine, pork fillet with lentils and black pudding, or guinea-fowl with mushroom pithivier. The interior is attractive, too: rough wood tables, and big glass windows.

Cafe Romna INDIAN ££
(☎01749-670240; 13 Sadler St; mains £5-16) Some unusual flavours are on offer alongside classic curries at this Bangladeshi fusion restaurant.

Information

Tourist Office (☎01749-672552; www.wellstourism.com; Market Pl; ⊙9.30am-5.30pm Apr-Oct, 10am-4pm Nov-Mar) Stocks the *Wells City Trail* leaflet (30p) and sells discount tickets to Wookey Hole and Cheddar Gorge.

Getting There & Away

The bus station is south of Cuthbert St, on Princes Rd. Useful services:

Bath (1¼ hours, hourly Monday to Saturday, five on Sunday) Bus 173.

Bristol (one hour, half-hourly Monday to Saturday, hourly on Sunday) Bus 376.

Cheddar (25 minutes, hourly Monday to Saturday, four on Sunday) Bus 126; continues to **Weston-Super-Mare** (1½ hours).

Glastonbury (15 minutes, several per hour) Bus 377.

Taunton (1¼ hours, hourly Monday to Saturday) Bus 29, stops in **Glastonbury** (15 minutes).

Wookey Hole & Cheddar Gorge

Wookey Hole CAVE
(www.wookey.co.uk; adult/child £16/11; ⊙10am-5pm Apr-Oct, 10.30am-4pm Nov-Mar) Two miles from Wells on the southern edge of the Mendip Hills, the River Axe has carved out a series of deep limestone caverns collectively known as Wookey Hole. They're famous for their ornate stalagmites and stalactites, one of which is supposedly the legendary Witch of Wookey Hole, who was turned to stone by a local priest. There are also many subterranean lakes and rivers, some of which are astonishingly deep – Britain's deepest cave dive was made here in September 2004, when divers descended more than 45m.

Admission to the caves is by guided tour. The rest of the complex is disappointingly tacky, with attractions including a mirror maze, an Edwardian penny arcade, a paper mill and a valley populated by giant plastic dinosaurs. During weekends, you might even be greeted by the witch herself, Carla Calamity (real name Carole Bonahan, a former estate agent).

Tickets remain valid for the whole day, and there's a 15% discount for booking online.

Cheddar Gorge CAVES
(www.cheddarcaves.co.uk; Explorer Ticket adult/child £18.50/12, 10% discount for online booking; ⊙10am-5.30pm) Only marginally less touristy than their Wookey cousins, the massive cliffs of Cheddar Gorge are nonetheless a dramatic sight. This is England's deepest natural canyon, and in places the limestone cliffs tower 138m above the twisting road.

The gorge is famous for its bewildering network of subterranean caves, a few of which are open to the public. **Cox's Cave** and **Gough's Cave**, both lined with stalactites and stalagmites, are subtly illuminated to bring out the spectrum of colours in the rock. To explore the more remote caverns, you'll need to organise a caving trip with **X-Treme** (☎01934-742343; www.cheddargorge.co.uk/x-treme; 1½-hr trip adult/child £21/19); be prepared to get cold, wet and very muddy. Rock-climbing sessions are also available.

The Cheddar caves have been inhabited by prehistoric people since the last ice age; a 9000-year-old skeleton (imaginatively named Cheddar Man) was discovered here in 1903, although carbon dating has suggested Gough's Cave was inhabited several thousand years earlier. Rumours of prehistoric cannibalism also seem to have been confirmed by recent discoveries of polished human skulls that are believed to have been used as drinking vessels.

Cheddar gets extremely busy during summer and school holidays, when the gorge road turns into one long traffic jam. You can normally escape the worst crowds by climbing the 274-step staircase known as **Jacob's Ladder**, which leads to a spectacular viewpoint and a 3-mile cliff trail.

Cheddar Gorge Cheese Company CHEESEMAKER

(☎01934-742810; www.cheddargorgecheeseco.co.uk; adult/child £2.25/free; ⏱10am-5pm Easter-Oct) Along with its caves, Cheddar is also famous as the home of the nation's favourite cheese, which has been produced here since the 12th century (Henry II considered it 'the best cheese in Britain', and the king's accounts from 1170 record that he purchased 10,240lb of the stuff). You can take a guided tour of this traditional cheesemaker's factory and purchase top-quality cheddars and other cheesy goods at its excellent on-site shop.

Mendip Hills

The Mendip Hills (often known simply as the Mendips) are a range of limestone ridges stretching from the coast near Weston-Super-Mare to Frome in eastern Somerset. Their highest point is **Black Down** (326m) to the northwest – but because they rise sharply, there are panoramic views towards Exmoor and across northwest Wiltshire.

Historically, the hills provided perfect natural fortifications, and the area is littered with neolithic earthworks, Bronze Age barrows and Iron Age forts. More recently, mining and quarrying both left their mark, although the Mendips have been protected as an AONB (Area of Outstanding Natural Beauty) since 1972.

The landscape is peppered with pretty hamlets and half-timbered houses, as well as several historic church towers, most notably at **Chewton Mendip** and **Compton Martin**. Nearby Priddy, the highest village in the Mendips, is renowned for its huge annual sheep fair, held on the green in mid-August. The remains of the Norman castle of Richmont can also be seen near the village of East Harptree.

The **Mendips AONB office** (☎01761-462338; www.mendiphillsaonb.org.uk) in Blagdon offers lots of information on hiking, cycling and other activities in the Mendips area.

Glastonbury

POP 8429

Ley-lines converge, white witches convene and every shop is filled with the aroma of smouldering joss-sticks in good old Glastonbury, the southwest's undisputed capital of alternative culture. Now famous for its annual musical mudfest held on Michael Eavis' farm in nearby Pilton, Glastonbury has a much older and more mysterious past: the town's iconic Tor was an important pagan site, and is rumoured by some to be the mythical Isle of Avalon, King Arthur's last resting place. It's also allegedly one of the world's great spiritual nodes, marking the meeting point of many mystical lines of power – so if you feel the need to get your chakras realigned, this is definitely the place. Whatever the truth of the various legends swirling round Glastonbury, one thing's for certain – watching the sunrise from the top of the Tor is an experience you definitely won't forget in a hurry.

Sights

TOP CHOICE **Glastonbury Tor** LANDMARK

(NT; www.nationaltrust.org.uk) The iconic hump of Glastonbury Tor looms up from flat fields to the northwest of town. This 160m-high grassy mound provides glorious views over the surrounding countryside, and a focal point for a bewildering array of myths. According to some it's the home of a faery king, while an old Celtic legend identifies it as the stronghold of Gwyn ap Nudd (ruler of Annwyn, the Underworld) – but the most famous legend identifies the tor as the mythic Isle of Avalon, where King Arthur was taken after being mortally wounded in battle by his nephew Mordred, and where Britain's 'once and future king' sleeps until his country calls again.

Whatever the truth of the legends, the tor has been a site of pilgrimage for many years, and was once topped by the medieval chapel of **St Michael**, although today only the tower remains.

It takes about 45 minutes to walk up and down the tor, plus an extra half-hour to walk

Glastonbury

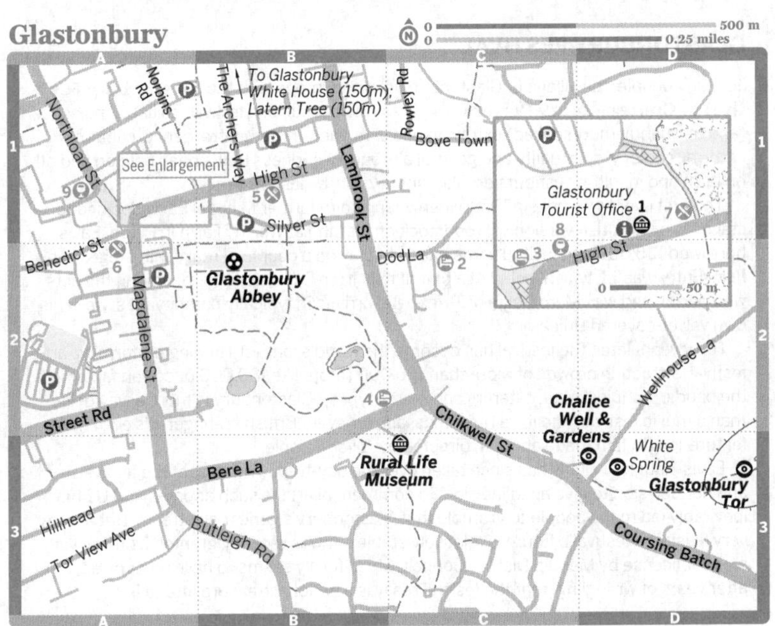

from town. The regular Tor Bus (adult/child £3/1.50, half-hourly April to September) from Dunstan's car park stops at Chalice Well, near the start of the main trail on Well House Lane.

Glastonbury Abbey RUINS

(www.glastonburyabbey.com; Magdalene St; adult/child £6/4; ⏲9am-8pm) The scattered ruins of Glastonbury Abbey give little hint that this was once one of England's great seats of ecclesiastical power. Legend has it that the first abbey here was founded by Joseph of Arimathea, Jesus' great uncle, although the present-day ruins largely date from the 12th century.

The abbey was torn down following Henry VIII's Dissolution of the Monasteries in 1539, when the last abbot, Richard Whiting, was hung, drawn and quartered on the tor. Precious little remains of the original building, except for the nave walls, the ruined St Mary's chapel, and the remains of the crossing arches, which may have been scissor-shaped like those in Wells Cathedral. The grounds also contain a museum, cider orchard and herb garden, as well as the Holy Thorn tree, which supposedly sprung from Joseph's staff and mysteriously blooms twice a year, at Christmas and Easter.

Glastonbury

Top Sights

- Chalice Well & Gardens D3
- Glastonbury Abbey B2
- Glastonbury Tor D3
- Rural Life Museum C3

Sights

1. Lake Village Museum D1

Sleeping

2. Chalice Hill C2
3. Crown Glastonbury Backpackers C2
4. Parsnips B2

Eating

5. Hundred Monkeys Cafe B1
6. Mocha Berry A2
7. Rainbow's End D1

Drinking

8. George & Pilgrim C2
9. Who'd a Thought It Inn A1

In the 12th century, monks supposedly uncovered a tomb in the abbey grounds inscribed *Hic iacet sepultus inclitus rex arturius in insula avalonia*, or 'Here lies buried the renowned King Arthur in the Isle of

GLASTONBURY FESTIVAL

To many people, the village of Glastonbury is synonymous with the **Glastonbury Festival of Contemporary Performing Arts** (www.glastonburyfestivals.co.uk), a majestic (and frequently mud-soaked) extravaganza of music, street theatre, dance, cabaret, carnival, ecology, spirituality and general all-round weirdness that's been held on and off on farmland in Pilton, just outside Glastonbury, for the last 40 years.

The first event was held in 1970, when young dairy farmer Michael Eavis decided to stage his own British version of Woodstock on his land at Worthy Farm in Pilton. Eavis borrowed £15,000 and invited some bands to play on a couple of makeshift stages in his field. Entry was £1, which included a pint of milk from Eavis' dairy herd; among the acts who performed was Marc Bolan of T-Rex, who arrived in typically flamboyant style in his own velvet-covered Buick.

Forty years later, the festival has become the world's longest-running performing-arts festival, attracting crowds of more than 120,000 (more like 180,000 once you factor in the bands, technical staff, caterers and media types). Glastonbury is more a way of life than a music festival, and it's a rite of passage for every British teenager. It's even had a feature-length film made about it, directed by Julien Temple.

Eavis' daughter Emily has since taken over the day-to-day running of the festival, and her decision to give headline slots to commercial artists such as Jay-Z and U2 have inevitably led many people to grumble that Glastonbury's gone mainstream. But at the very least, the festival's future is relatively stable – it was recently granted its first-ever six-year licence by Mendip District Council, which finally seems to have recognised, after years of wrangling, that the festival really is a national treasure after all.

Avalon'. Inside the tomb were two entwined skeletons, supposedly those of Arthur and his wife Guinevere; the bones were reburied beneath the altar in 1278, but were lost following the abbey's destruction.

Chalice Well & Gardens GARDENS
(www.chalicewell.org.uk; adult/child £3.70/1.90; ⌚10am-6pm) Shaded by yew trees and criss-crossed by quiet paths, the Chalice Well and Gardens have been sites of pilgrimage since the days of the Celts. The iron-red waters from the 800-year-old well are rumoured to have healing properties, good for everything from eczema to smelly feet; some legends also identify the well as the hiding place of the Holy Grail. In fact, the reddish waters are caused by iron deposits in the soil. You can drink the water from a lion's-head spout, or rest your feet in basins surrounded by flowers.

The Chalice Well is also known as the 'Red Spring' or 'Blood Spring'; its sister, **White Spring**, surfaces across Wellhouse Lane.

FREE **Rural Life Museum** MUSEUM
(Abbey Farm, Chilkwell St; ⌚10am-5pm Tue-Sat) This modest museum explores Somerset's agricultural heritage, with a restored farmhouse detailing the life of local farmer John Hodges, and a wonderful barn containing vintage tools relating to local industries such as willow growing, peat digging, cider making and cheese making. Try to time your visit with one of the regular craft displays.

Lake Village Museum MUSEUM
(The Tribunal, 9 High St; adult/child £2/1.50; ⌚10am-5pm) Upstairs from Glastonbury's tourist office, the Lake Village Museum displays finds from a prehistoric bog village discovered in nearby Godney. The houses were clustered in about six groups and built from reeds, hazel and willow. It's thought they were occupied by summer traders who lived the rest of the year around Glastonbury Tor.

Sleeping

Chalice Hill B&B **££**
(☎01458-838828; www.chalicehill.co.uk; Dod Lane; d £100; P) This grand Georgian B&B has been renovated with flair by its artistic owner Fay Hutchcroft. A sweeping staircase circles up through the house, leading to three spacious rooms: try Phoenix for its modern art, or Sun & Moon for its handsome cast-iron bed. Breakfast is served communally in the book-lined lounge.

Lantern Tree B&B ££

(☎01458-833455; www.thelanterntree.co.uk; 19 Manor House Rd; s/d/tr £55/65/85) Lovely B&B offering a brace of rooms: Amethyst has a brass bedstead and fluffy pillows, while the Green Room has a roll-top bath and two-bed layout (ideal for families). Fridges, fruit teas and memory-foam mattresses are nice additions. There is a £10 supplement for one-night stays.

Glastonbury White House B&B ££

(☎01458-830886; www.theglastonburywhitehouse.com; 21 Manor House Rd; d £50-60; P) There are only two rooms here, but owner Carey has made them super-cosy, with extra touches such as fridges, fresh milk and bottles of White Spring water. Breakfast is extra (£5 continental, £7.50 cooked). It's about five minutes' walk from High St.

Parsnips B&B ££

(☎01458-835599; www.parsnips-glastonbury.co.uk; 99 Bere Lane; s/d £55/70; P@) Modern it may be, but this red-brick B&B is a solid bet, with bright rooms in gingham and cream, complimentary coffee on arrival, and a range of holistic treatments by arrangement.

Crown Glastonbury Backpackers HOSTEL £

(☎01458-833353; www.glastonburybackpackers.com; 4 Market Pl; dm £16.50, d £35-60; P@) Basic hostel above the old Crown pub. Rooms are spartan, and the pub's proximity can make things noisy. Kitchen and laundry available.

Eating & Drinking

Rainbow's End CAFE £

(17a High St; mains £4-8; ⌚breakfast & lunch; ✎) This psychedelic cafe sums up the spirit of Glastonbury, with its all-veggie food, potted plants and mix-and-match furniture. Tuck into homity pie or a hot quiche, and follow up with a scrumptious homemade cake. There's a small patio out back.

Hundred Monkeys Cafe BISTRO ££

(52 High St; mains £8-15; ⌚lunch Mon-Wed & Sun, lunch & dinner Thu-Sat) Surprisingly sleek bistro, decked out with leather sofas, pine tables and a big blackboard listing fresh pastas, salads and mains. If you've a spare half-hour ask about the origin of the name – the original 100th monkey.

Mocha Berry CAFE £

(14 Market Pl; mains £4-8; ⌚Sun-Wed) Ideal for a quick cappuccino, sandwich or stack of pancakes.

Who'd a Thought It Inn PUB

(17 Northload St) In keeping with Glastonbury's outsider spirit, this town pub is brimming with wacky character, from the vintage signs and upside-down bike on the ceiling to the reclaimed red telephone box tucked in one corner. Locals pack in for its superior ales and food (mains £10 to £15); Glastonbury kingpin Michael Eavis has even been known to pop in for a pint.

George & Pilgrim PUB

(1 High St; mains £7-15) Partly-15th-century inn with one of the town's most convincingly historic interiors: timbers, flagstones and all. There's a wide choice of southwest ales, and a solid if unremarkable pub menu (lunch daily, dinner Monday to Saturday).

Information

Glastonbury Tourist Office (☎01458-832954; www.glastonburytic.co.uk; The Tribunal, 9 High St; ⌚10am-5pm)

Getting There & Away

There is no train station in Glastonbury, so buses are the only public transport option. The frequent Bus 377 (several times per hour) travels north to **Wells** (15 minutes) and south to **Street** (10 minutes) and **Yeovil** (50 minutes). Bus 29 travels to **Taunton** (50 minutes, hourly Monday to Saturday).

Quantock Hills

The range of red sandstone hills known as the **Quantocks** traces a graceful 12-mile curve across Somerset's northern reaches. A mix of high moors, slender valleys and ancient oak woodland, these little-visited hills offer truly stirring views across the Bristol Channel: when the weather's fine, the Gower coastline shimmers along the horizon, birds of prey hover in the skies overhead, and the hedgerows buzz with rare insects and butterflies.

Though a designated AONB (Area of Outstanding Natural Beauty), the Quantocks receive far fewer visitors than the nearby national parks of Exmoor and Dartmoor, making them perfect for hikers and mountain bikers in search of quiet trails. The **AONB Service** (www.quantockhills.com; ⌚9am-5pm Mon-Fri) runs an excellent program of guided walks from its base at Fyne Court, a National Trust reserve at Broomfield, in the south Quantocks.

Literary buffs might also like to make a stop at the village of **Nether Stowey**, best known for its association with the poet Samuel Taylor Coleridge, who moved to the village with his wife Sara and son Hartley in 1796. His **cottage** (NT; ☎01278-732662; 35 Lime St, Nether Stowey; adult £5/2.50; ⊙11am-5pm Thu-Mon) is now owned by the National Trust; the poet is thought to have composed some of his greatest works during his three-year stay here, including *The Rime of the Ancient Mariner, Kubla Khan* and *This Lime Tree Bower My Prison.*

Sleeping & Eating

TOP CHOICE Blue Ball Inn B&B ££
(☎01984-618242; www.blueballinn.info; Triscombe; r £75-105) Cracking gastropub in tiny Triscombe, 5 miles from Watchet and 8 miles from Taunton. It's housed in a converted barn with lashings of country character, and serves top-class food (mains £11 to £18) with plenty of local provenance: it's especially good for game such as wood pigeon, rabbit, duck and venison, and the Sunday roast deserves legendary status. Three cute cottages can be rented on a B&B basis.

Hood Arms PUB ££
(☎01278-741210; www.thehoodarms.com; mains £11-17) This Kilve coaching inn is known for its generous grub. Inside, it's full of hunting memorabilia, wonky beams and deep armchairs, and if you overindulge, there are 12 rooms (single/double/family £75/95/125) plus a self-catering cottage, the Stag Lodge.

Carew Arms PUB ££
(☎01984-618631; www.thecarewarms.co.uk; mains £10-16) Partly 16th-century, this convivial inn (single rooms £49 to £59, double £64 to £84) in titchy Crowcombe oozes period character with its stags' horns and inglenook fireplace. Several local ales are always on tap, including Tawny Bitter, Otter Bright and Exmoor Ale, best savoured in its grassy beer garden.

Getting There & Away

Bus services around the Quantocks are very limited.

Nether Stowey, Holford, Kilve and **West Quantoxhead** (four daily Monday to Saturday) Bus 14; runs from Bridgwater to Williton.

Crowcombe and **Bicknoller** (half-hourly Monday to Saturday, nine on Sunday) Bus 28; runs from Taunton to Minehead. Sunday buses only stop at Bicknoller.

Taunton

POP 58,241

There's not a great deal to keep you long in Somerset's main county town, but it's a useful transport hub and the main gateway for the Quantocks. It's also well worth stopping in at the spanking new Museum of Somerset, recently reopened after a £6.93m overhaul.

Sights

FREE Museum of Somerset MUSEUM
(☎01823-255088; Castle Green; ⊙10am-5pm Mon-Sat) Somerset's main county museum is housed in the great hall of the town's 12th-century **castle**. The highlight of the collection is the Frome Hoard, an enormous haul of 52,503 Roman coins that was discovered in a Somerset field in 2010. Also look out for the Low Ham Mosaic, a beautiful mosaic depicting the story of Dido and Aeneas that was found in a nearby Roman villa, and the specially commissioned *Tree of Somerset*, an oak sculpture depicting local historical events.

There are also various exhibits relating to the Bloody Assizes, a series of trials held at the Castle in the wake of the Monmouth Rebellion against James II. Presided over by the infamously taciturn lawman Judge Jeffreys, it resulted in the bloodthirsty execution of over 300 rebels, 144 of whom were displayed around Taunton's streets as a warning of the consequences of treason.

The castle also houses the **Somerset Military Museum**, which houses a collection of vintage weapons, uniforms, flags and other ephemera relating to the county's various military regiments.

Church of St Mary Magdalene CHURCH
(www.stmarymagdalenechurch.org.uk; Church Sq; entry by donation; ⊙10am-4pm Mon-Fri, to 1pm Sat) Built in 1308, Taunton's impressive parish church is notable for its 50m-high tower, carved from crimson Quantock rock.

Sleeping & Eating

Corner House Hotel HOTEL ££
(☎01823-284683; www.corner-house.co.uk; Park St; d £65-85, f £105; P 📶) This modern hotel is just outside the town centre, perched above

WORTH A TRIP

HAM HILL

Looming above the village of Stoke-sub-Hamdon, the viewpoint of **Ham Hill** (www.southsomerset.gov.uk/hamhill; near Stoke-sub-Hamdon) provides an unparalleled panorama across southern Somerset. It's served a variety of purposes over the years – Iron Age hillfort, medieval village, Victorian stone quarry – but it now makes a wonderful spot for a blustery picnic and a bracing stroll. Stoke-sub-Hamdon is about 7 miles west of Yeovil off the A303; just follow the brown signs.

the popular Wine & Sausage restaurant. The upstairs rooms are plain and functional, but the rates are excellent value. The three-course dinner costs £25.

Frog St Farmhouse B&B
(☎01823-481883; www.frogstreet.co.uk; Hatch Beauchamp; d £90-120) The name of this amber-stoned longhouse in nearby Hatch Beauchamp apparently derives from the Anglo-Saxon for 'meeting place'. It's a beauty, with three rooms mixing rusticity (beams, stone, wonky doors) with luxurious furnishings (roll-top baths, cotton linen, wood floors).

Augustus BISTRO ££
(☎01823-324354; 3 The Courtyard, St James St; mains £12-16) Taunton's town restaurants leave a bit to be desired, but this tucked-away bistro is a treat, with Med-style plates of sea bream, stuffed peppers or garlicky mussels, served in light, bright surrounds. Owner Richard Guest has worked at Michelin-level, so he certainly knows how to turn out a quality plate.

Information

Taunton Tourist Office (☎01823-336344; www.heartofsomerset.com; Paul St; ⌚9.30am-5pm Mon-Sat) Inside the library.

Getting There & Away

Bus

Useful local services:

Minehead (1¼ hours, half-hourly Monday to Saturday, nine on Sunday) Bus 28; crosses the Quantocks.

Wells (1¼ hours, hourly Monday to Saturday) Bus 29 via **Glastonbury** (one hour).

Train

Regular services east to **London** (£50.50, 2½ hours) and west to **Exeter** (£10.40, 30 minutes) and **Plymouth** (£16.90, 1½ hours).

Around Taunton

Montacute House HISTORIC BUILDING
(NT; ☎01935-823289; montacute@nationaltrust.org.uk; house adult/child £10/5, garden only £5/2.50; ⌚house 11am-4pm, gardens 10am-5pm Wed-Mon) This stunning manor was built in the 1590s for Sir Edward Phelips, a Speaker of the House of Commons, and contains some of the finest 16th- and 17th-century interiors in the country. The house is particularly renowned for its plasterwork, chimney pieces and tapestries, but the highlight is the Long Gallery, the longest such hall in England. It's decorated with Elizabethan portraits on loan from the National Portrait Gallery in London. It's also surrounded by glorious parkland, with trails leading to the wonderful viewpoint of St Michael's Hill.

Haynes Motor Museum MUSEUM
(☎01963-440804; www.haynesmotormuseum.com; adult/child £10/5; ⌚9.30am-5.30pm Apr-Oct, 10am-4.30pm Nov-Mar) The 300-strong collection at this car museum includes an array of outstanding and outlandish motors, from Aston Martins and Ferraris to oddities such as the Sinclair C5. Don't miss the Red Room, famous for its collection of scarlet cars. And yes, it is *that* Haynes, publisher of Britain's ubiquitous car-repair manuals. The museum is near Sparkford, off the A303 northwest of Yeovil.

West Somerset Railway HERITAGE RAILWAY
(☎01643-704996; www.west-somerset-railway.co.uk; 24hr rover ticket adult/child £17/8.50) The chuffing steam trains of this vintage railway are one of the best ways to see the Somerset countryside. The 20-mile route runs from Bishops Lydeard to Minehead, stopping at Dunster, Watchet, Williton, Crowcombe Heathfield and several other stations en route. There are four to eight trains daily from March to October, with a much more limited service for the rest of the year. Bikes can be carried on board for £2.

Fleet Air Arm Museum MUSEUM
(☎01963-840565; www.fleetairarm.com; adult/child £10.50/7.50; ⏲10am-5.30pm daily Apr-Oct, 10am-4.30pm Wed-Sun Nov-Mar) This aviation museum houses hundreds of naval aircraft from Sopwiths to Phantom fighters. You can walk onto the flight deck of the first British-built Concorde and take a simulated flight onto the aircraft carrier HMS *Ark Royal*. The museum is 4 miles north of Somerset, near Yeovilton.

Hestercombe GARDENS
(☎01823-413923; www.hestercombe.com; adult/child £9.70/3.70; ⏲10am-6pm) Designed by the architect Sir Edward Lutyens and the garden designer Gertrude Jekyll, this trio of gardens was laid out to reflect the prevailing tastes of the Georgian, Victorian and Edwardian ages. Work is currently underway to restore its 17th-century watermill. The gardens are 3 miles north of Taunton.

Sleeping & Eating

TOP CHOICE **Queen's Arms** INN ££
(☎01963-220317; www.thequeensarms.com; Corton Denham; d £100-165) Somerset's certainly not short on lovely pubs, but this one in Corton Denham is definitely worth the trip. Rugs, reclaimed pews and slate flagstones nod to its 18th-century heritage, but the first-rate gastropub menu (mains £15.50 to £24.50) and rustic-chic rooms are altogether modern. It's scooped numerous awards, most recently CAMRA's Somerset Cider Pub of the Year. It's 8 miles northeast of Yeovil.

Lord Poulett Arms GASTROPUB ££
(☎01460-73149; www.lordpoulettarms.com; Hinton St George; mains £11-20) The tiny village of Hinton St George is a devil to find, but you'll be very glad you made the effort. This deliciously olde-worlde pub is always packed out with well-heeled punters thanks to its great food and cask ales, tapped straight from the barrels behind the bar. Upstairs rooms (£60 to £95) are really quirky, too, with exposed stone, creaky floorboards and ornate headboards. It's halfway between Yeovil and Taunton, 15 miles from each.

EXMOOR NATIONAL PARK

Barely 21 miles across and 12 miles north to south, Exmoor might be the little sister of England's national parks, but what she lacks in scale she more than makes up in scenery. Part wilderness expanse, part rolling fields, dotted with bottle-green meadows, wooded combes and crumbling cliffs, Exmoor National Park seems to sum up everything that's green and pleasant about the English landscape. Waymarked paths criss-cross the moor, and a dramatic section of the South West Coast Path runs from Minehead (a family-fun resort just outside the park) all the way to Padstow in Cornwall.

It's a haven for ramblers, mountain-bikers and horse-riders, and it's also home to lots of rare wildlife, including some of England's largest herds of wild red deer.

THE SOMERSET LEVELS

Pan-flat, mostly sub-sea-level and criss-crossed with canals (known locally as *rhynes*), the Somerset Levels are one of England's largest and most unspoilt native wetlands. Covering over 160,000 acres between the Quantock and Mendip Hills, they're brilliant for bird-spotters – particularly in October and November, when huge flocks of starlings (properly known as 'murmurations') descend on the area. Nature reserves have been established at Ham Wall, Shapwick Heath, Sedgemoor and Westhay, complete with bird hides.

In previous centuries, the Levels were notoriously flood-prone, and still would be without the assistance of the complex system of rhynes and pump stations, but the moist ground is ideal for several traditional industries, especially peat digging, reed harvesting and willow growing. At the **Willows & Wetlands Visitor Centre** (☎01823-490249; www.englishwillowbaskets.co.uk; ⏲9.30am-5pm Mon-Sat) near Stoke St Gregory, you can buy wicker artefacts, from pigeon panniers to picnic baskets, or take a guided tour of the willow beds (£3). Regular willowcraft courses are held throughout the year.

Exmoor National Park

0 — 10 km
0 — 5 miles

Activities

Active Exmoor OUTDOORS
(☎01398-324599; www.activeexmoor.com) Comprehensive info on outdoor activities.

Bush Craft

Mountains+Moor (☎01643-841610; www.mountainsandmoor.co.uk) offers navigation lessons (from £80 per two days) and summer mountain-craft courses (two/five days £110/270), which include camping skills, rope work and river crossings.

Cycling

Cycling is popular on Exmoor, despite the formidable hills. Several sections of the **National Cycle Network** (NCN; www.sustrans.org.uk) cross the park, including the **West Country Way** (NCN route 3) from Bristol to Padstow, and the Devon **Coast to Coast Cycle Route** (NCN route 27) between Exmoor and Dartmoor.

For off-road cycling, popular trails travel through the Brendon Hills, the Crown Estate woodland and along the old Barnstaple railway line. **Exmoor & Quantocks MTB Experiences** (☎01643-705079; www.exqumtb.co.uk) runs weekend mountain-biking courses from £75 to £150.

For bike hire, try one of the following companies:

Fremington Quay BICYCLE HIRE
(☎01271-372586; www.biketrail.co.uk; per day adult/child £16.75/8.50; ⏲10am-5pm Wed-Sun) Delivers bikes to your door, including tandems, tag-a-longs, choppers and dog trailers.

Pompys BICYCLE HIRE
(☎01643-704077; www.pompyscycles.co.uk; ⏲9am-5pm Mon-Sat) Standard bikes £14 per day, full-suspension £30.

Pony Trekking & Horse Riding

Exmoor is a popular riding area, and lots of stables offer pony and horse treks from around £40 to £45 for a two-hour hack – see the *Exmoor Visitor* for full details.

Brendan Manor Stables HORSE RIDING
(☎01598-741246) Near Lynton.

Burrowhayes Farm HORSE RIDING
(☎01643-862463; www.burrowhayes.co.uk)

Knowle Riding Centre HORSE RIDING
(☎01643-841342; www.knowleridingcentre.co.uk)

Outovercott Stables HORSE RIDING
(☎01598-753341; www.outovercott.co.uk)

Walking

The open moors and plentiful footpaths make Exmoor ideal for hiking. The best-known routes are the **Somerset & North Devon Coast Path**, which is part of the **South West Coast Path** (www.southwestcoastpath.com), and the Exmoor section of the **Two Moors Way**, which starts in Lynmouth and travels south to Dartmoor and beyond.

Other routes include the **Coleridge Way** (www.coleridgeway.co.uk), which winds for 36 miles through Exmoor, the Brendon Hills and the Quantocks. Part of the 180-mile **Tarka Trail** also cuts through the park; join it at Combe Martin, hike along the cliffs to

EXMOOR SAFARIS

If you're a nature-lover or keen photographer, you definitely won't want to miss taking your very own **wildlife safari**. The national park is home to a wonderful range of unusual birds and beasts, from endangered bats to stubby Exmoor ponies, but it's best known for its large populations of wild red deer. These skittish creatures are very elusive, however, so if you want to see them, your best bet is to rely on the skills of a local guide (and, of course, get up nice and early).

Several companies offer 4WD 'safari' trips across the moor: the best season to visit is autumn, especially from October onwards, when the annual autumn 'rutting' season begins, and stags can be seen bellowing, charging and clashing horns in an attempt to impress their prospective mates.

Standard 2½-hour safari trips cost around £25, although longer expeditions can usually be arranged with plenty of advance notice. Experienced companies include the following:

Barle Valley Safaris (☎01643-851386; www.exmoorwildlifesafaris.co.uk; £30)

Discovery Safaris (☎01643-863080; www.discoverysafaris.com; £20)

Exmoor Safari (☎01643-831229; www.exmoorsafari.co.uk; £30)

Red Stag Safari (☎01643-841831; www.redstagsafari.co.uk; £25-38)

Lynton/Lynmouth, then head across the moor towards Barnstaple.

The National Parks Authority (NPA) organises walks throughout the year. Its autumn dawn safaris to see rutting stags are superb, as are its summertime evening deer-watching hikes. Pick up the *Exmoor Visitor* for full details – NPA walks are highlighted in green.

Sleeping

The only YHA hostel inside the national park is at **Exford** (☎0845-371 9634; exford@yha.org.uk; dm £13), although for more basic accommodation, there's also **Pinkery Bunkhouse** (☎01643-831437; pinkery@exmoor-nationalpark.gov.uk) near Simonsbath and camping barns at **Mullacott Farm** (☎01629-592700) near Ilfracombe and **Northcombe Farm** (☎01629-592700) near Dulverton. Prices start at around £8.50 per night, and you'll need all the usual camping supplies.

Information

Tourist Offices

There are three NPA tourist offices around the park – the main one is in Dulverton. All are open from 10am to 5pm daily.

Dulverton (☎01398-323841; NPCDulverton@exmoor-nationalpark.gov.uk; 7-9 Fore St)

Dunster (☎01643-821835; NPCDunster@exmoor-nationalpark.gov.uk)

Lynmouth (☎01598-752509; NPCLynmouth@exmoor-nationalpark.gov.uk)

Websites

Exmoor National Park (www.exmoor-nationalpark.gov.uk) The official NPA site.

Exmoor Tourist Association (www.exmoor.com) Accommodation and activities.

Visit Exmoor (www.visit-exmoor.info) Useful advice on activities, events, accommodation and eating out.

What's On Exmoor (www.whatsonexmoor.com) Local event listings.

Getting Around

Various buses serve Exmoor's main towns and villages, all of which are listed at the useful **ExploreMoor** (www.exploremoor.co.uk) website. Other useful services:

300 Coastal Link Runs along the coast from Minehead to Lynmouth via Allerford and Porlock.

400 Exmoor Explorer Cross-moor bus via Minehead, Allerford, Porlock, Exford, Wheddon Cross and Dunster.

MoorRover (☎01643-709701; moorrover@aol.com) On-demand minibus that can take you anywhere on Exmoor for £6; they'll also carry bikes and provide a luggage transfer service. You need to book at least a day ahead.

Dulverton

Dulverton is the southern gateway to Exmoor National Park, and sits at the base of the Barle Valley near the confluence of two key rivers: the Exe and Barle. It's a no-

nonsense sort of country town, home to a collection of gun-sellers, fishing-tackle stores and gift shops.

There's a lovely 12-mile circular walk that's well worth doing; it goes along the river from Dulverton to **Tarr Steps** – an ancient stone clapper bridge haphazardly placed across the River Barle and shaded by gnarled old trees. The bridge was supposedly built by the devil for sunbathing. It's a four- to five-hour trek for the average speed walker. You can add another three or four hours to the walk by continuing from Tarr Steps up Winsford Hill for distant views over Devon.

Eating

Woods BISTRO ££
(☎01398-324007; 4 Bank Sq; mains £11-16.50) This cute bistro is a far more sophisticated affair than you'd expect to find in out-of-the-way Dulverton. Generous portions of corn-fed chicken, confit duck and stuffed sea bream are served up in a cosy dining room, full of wooden furniture and black-and-white photos. But it's the 'Famous Steak-And-Chips' that really pulls in the punters – don't be surprised if you need a friend to finish yours.

Lewis' Tea Rooms CAFE ££
(☎01398-323850; 13 High St; mains £5-18; ⌚breakfast & lunch Mon-Sat, plus dinner Thu-Sat Jul & Aug) Top-class teas (including many rare estate varieties) are the order of the day at this delightful tearoom, but it's definitely worth leaving room for the Welsh rarebits and crumbly cakes, too. It's charmingly frilly and floral, and it opens late for suppers in summer.

Tantivy CAFE £
(☎01398-323465; www.tantivyexmoor.co.uk; ⌚9am-5pm Mon-Sat) Dulverton's answer to a cappuccino cafe, usually full of locals enjoying the proper frothy coffee and lovely cakes – especially on a sunny day, when the patio is often full.

Farthings Farm Shop DELI £
(☎01398-323878; www.exmoor-farm-shop.co.uk; 5 Bridge St; ⌚9am-5pm Mon-Sat) The place to stock up on moor goodies, from big slabs of Exmoor Blue Cheese to locally made jams and chutneys. There's a great choice of meat cuts, too.

Sleeping

Tarr Farm HOTEL £
(☎01643-851507; www.tarrfarm.co.uk; s/d £90/150, restaurant mains £11-20; P) This is the place to really lose yourself: a charming farmhouse nested among the woods near Tarr Steps, 7 miles from Dulverton. The nine rooms are spacious and luxurious, with nice extras such as organic bath goodies and homemade biscuits. The restaurant is especially good on game, fish and local lamb.

Town Mills B&B ££
(☎01398-323124; www.townmillsdulverton.co.uk; High St; s/d £65/90; P wi-fi) The top choice if you want to stay within walking distance of town. It's in a riverside mill, and the rooms are thoroughly contemporary, with creamy carpets, magnolia walls and bits of floral artwork.

Three Acres B&B ££
(☎01398-323730; www.threeacrescountryhouse.co.uk; d £90-120; P) If you don't mind a drive, this sweet farmhouse is lost among the narrow lanes around Dulverton. It has scooped lots of B&B awards, and with good reason: the six prim rooms overlook rolling Exmoor hills, and there's a different daily special for breakfast, from Exe trout to homemade bangers. Lovely.

Exford & Wheddon Cross

Nestled on the banks of the River Exe at the heart of the moor, Exford is a delightful muddle of cottages and slate-roofed houses clustered around a village green. The village is the base of Devon and Somerset Staghounds, and meets are still an important part of life here, despite the hunting ban.

Exmoor's highest point is 4 miles northeast of the village at **Dunkery Beacon** (519m). The best route up is from the village of Wheddon Cross, about 3 miles east of Exford. The round trip is 8 miles, and steep in places; wear good boots and take a picnic.

Another popular walk from Wheddon Cross is to the local beauty spot of **Snowdrop Valley**, which as its name suggests is carpeted by snow-white blossoms in spring. A Park & Ride scheme operates during the peak season – see www.wheddoncross.org.uk/snowdropvalley.htm for details.

The village pubs are your best bet for country nosh – try the solid old **Crown**

(☎01643-831554; www.crownhotelexmoor.co.uk; Chapel St; mains £13-18; P) or the more upmarket **Exmoor White Horse** (☎01643-831229; www.exmoor-whitehorse.co.uk; d £170-250, mains £14-22).

Lynton & Lynmouth

Nestled on the northern edge of the moor, these twin coastal towns are quite different in feel: bustling Lynmouth is a busy harbour lined with pubs, souvenir sellers and fudge shops, while its clifftop cousin of Lynton feels much more genteel and well-to-do. The two areas are linked by a cliffside railway that's powered by the rushing waters of the West Lyn River, which feeds numerous cascades and waterfalls nearby.

Sights & Activities

Cliff Railway HERITAGE RAILWAY
(www.cliffrailwaylynton.co.uk; single/return adult £2.25/3, child £1.40/2; 10am-6pm Easter-Oct) This extraordinary piece of Victorian engineering was designed by George Marks, believed to be a pupil of Brunel. Two cars linked by a steel cable descend or ascend the slope according to the amount of water in the cars' tanks. It's been running like clockwork since 1890, and certainly makes an interesting way to commute between Lynton and Lynmouth.

Glen Lyn Gorge GORGE
(☎01598-753207; adult/child £5/3; 10am-5pm Easter-Oct) Halfway between the two towns, this shady gorge offers some delightful riverside walks and a small exhibition centre devoted to hydroelectric power.

Lyn & Exmoor Museum MUSEUM
(St Vincent's Cottage, Market St; adult/child £1/20p; 10am-12.30pm & 2-5pm Mon-Fri, 2-5pm Sun Apr-Oct) This small harbourside museum contains background on the Lynmouth Flood, a devastating flash flood that swept through the town in 1952 and claimed 34 lives.

Valley of the Rocks WALKING
This rocky valley is about a mile's walk west of Lynton, and is well known for its dramatic rock formations, which poet Robert Southey memorably described as 'rock reeling upon rock, stone piled upon stone, a huge terrifying reeling mass'. Many of the rocks have evocative names such as Devil's Cheesewring and Ragged Jack, and you might even spy a feral goat or two wandering along the banks.

Other popular walking trails wind up to the lighthouse at **Foreland Point** and the riverside glade of **Watersmeet**, 2 miles upriver from Lynmouth.

Sleeping & Eating

There's no shortage of B&Bs and hotels round these parts, but most are heavy on the chintz.

North Walk House B&B ££
(☎01598-753372; www.northwalkhouse.co.uk; Lynton; d £50-78; P) This smart cliffside house is refreshingly frill-free, with five colour-themed rooms decked out with stripy bedspreads, wood floors, pine furniture and the odd sea view. Ecofriendly toiletries and an all-organic breakfast ensure the green factor stays high, too.

Castle Hill B&B ££
(☎01598-752291; www.castlehill.biz; Castle Hill, Lynton; d £60-95, f £120-130) This slender Victorian house occupies a prime position in Lynton, literally steps from the shops and clifftops. It's a trad, value-focused B&B, with six decent rooms in tones of cream and beige: go for one of the two balcony suites if you prefer to sleep with a view.

St Vincent House B&B ££
(☎01598-752244; www.st-vincent-hotel.co.uk; Castle Hill, Lynton; d £75-80; P) Grade-II listed and built by a compatriot of Nelson, this sea-captain's house has history by the bucket-load. All the rooms are named after famous battleships and, though the decor is a touch flouncy, they're very comfortable. Top-floor Victory feels suspiciously like a ship's cabin, with its low ceiling and tiny windows.

Old Rectory HOTEL £££
(☎01598-763368; www.oldrectoryhotel.co.uk; Martinhoe; d £215-250) Cheap it most certainly isn't, but this swish hotel along the coast in Martinhoe beats seven bells out of Lynton's B&Bs in terms of style. Rooms are supremely plush (elegant baths, silky fabrics) and the hotel hosts regular wine-tasting sessions in its *table d'hôte* restaurant.

Rising Sun PUB ££
(☎01598-753223; www.risingsunlynmouth.co.uk; mains £11.25-18) It's only a quick walk uphill from the touristy Lynmouth seafront, but this thatched pub is a world away from pasties-from-a-bag. Head chef Paul Sage has

turned this into the town's most enticing eatery, making maximum use of the meat, seafood and game on his doorstep – try the lobster for an absolute treat. The building itself has plenty of smugglers' character, with higgledy-piggledy floors and hefty beams.

Information

Lynton Tourist Office (☎01598-752225; info@lyntourism.co.uk; Lynton Town Hall, Lee Rd; ⏰10am-4pm Mon-Sat, to 2pm Sun)

Porlock & Around

The coastal village of Porlock is one of the prettiest on the north Exmoor coast; the huddle of thatched cottages lining its main street is framed on one side by the sea, and on the other by a jumble of houses that cling to the steeply sloping hills behind. Winding lanes lead to the picturesque breakwater of **Porlock Weir**, 2 miles to the west, with a fine shingly beach and lovely coastal views.

The village of **Selworthy**, 2½ miles southeast of Porlock, forms part of the 50-sq-km **Holnicote Estate** (NT; www.nationaltrust.org.uk/holnicote-estate), the largest area of National Trust land on Exmoor. Though its cob-and-thatch cottages look ancient, the village was almost completely rebuilt in the 19th century by local philanthropist Thomas Acland to provide housing for elderly workers on his estate.

Eating

Culbone PUB
(☎01643-862259; www.theculbone.com; mains £12.50-22) On the A39 between Porlock and Lynmouth, this smart pub-with-rooms offers 28-day aged steaks (there's a choice of five different cuts, as well as a huge *côte de boeuf* for two), but the seafood and veggie choices are both good, too. It's in a country location but the setting is contemporary, with slate floors and black leather chairs, a vibe which runs into the upstairs rooms. Chef Jack Scarterfield also runs cooking courses.

Cafe Porlock Weir RESTAURANT,HOTEL £££
(☎01643-863300; www.thecafeporlockweir.co.uk; Porlock Weir; mains £11.50-14.50) Chef Andrew Dixon has renamed his seaside establishment, but its selling points are the same: classic dishes and a sea-blown spot beside Porlock Weir. The restaurant is more about good value than gourmet these days, so while the flavours are still rich, the price tag is much leaner. The upstairs rooms (£110) are looking tired, though.

Ship Inn PUB £
(www.shipinnporlock.co.uk; High St; mains £8.50-12.50; Ⓟ) Coleridge and pal Robert Southey both downed pints in this thatched Porlock pub – you can even sit in 'Southey's Corner'. Substantial pub food – mainly steaks, roasts and stews – are served in the bar, and there are 10 surprisingly light rooms (d £60) in pine and cream.

Information

Porlock Tourist Office (☎01643-863150; www.porlock.co.uk; West End, High St; ⏰10am-5pm Mon-Sat, 10am-1pm Sun)

Getting There & Away

If you're driving, the most scenic route to Porlock is the steep, twisting **toll-road** (car/motorbike/bicycle £2.50/1.50/1) that hugs the coast all the way from Lynmouth. Better still, you get to avoid the 1:4 gradient on Porlock Hill.

Dunster

Centred around a scarlet-walled castle and a medieval yarn market, Dunster is one of Exmoor's oldest villages, an attractive muddle of bubbling brooks, packhorse bridges and cobbled streets.

Sights

Dunster Castle CASTLE
(NT; www.nationaltrust.org.uk/dunstercastle; castle adult/child £8.80/4.40, garden & park only £4.80/2.20; ⏰11am-5pm Mar-Oct) This impressive red-brick castle was originally owned by the Luttrell family, whose manor encompassed much of northern Exmoor. Although it served as a fortress for around 1000 years, the present castle was heavily remodelled during Victorian times, so little remains of the original Norman stronghold, save for the 13th-century gateway. Its grand rooms are full of Tudor furnishings, ornate plasterwork and ancestral portraits, and the terraced gardens offer sweeping coastal views, as well as an important collection of strawberry trees.

St George's Church CHURCH
This beautiful church dates mostly from the 15th century and boasts a wonderfully carved fan-vaulted rood screen. Just behind

the church is a 16th-century dovecote, which would have housed squab pigeons destined for the Luttrell's dinner table.

Watermill MILL

(www.dunsterwatermill.co.uk; Mill Lane; adult/child £3.50/2; ⏲11am-4.45pm Apr-Oct) Further down the road is this working 18th-century mill, which still has most of its original cogs, wheels and grinding stones. There's also a sweet riverside tearoom.

Sleeping & Eating

Dunster Castle Hotel HOTEL ££

(☎01643-823030; www.thedunstercastlehotel.co.uk; 5 High St; r £90-125; 📶) Right in the heart of the village, this former coaching inn has been expensively refurbished and now has a good choice of light, uncluttered rooms – the Superior Kingsize are definitely worth the extra outlay, especially rococo-style Grabbist and spacious Conyger. The restaurant specialises in rich, chunky fare: belly pork with lyonnaise potatoes, or rump of lamb with minted jelly (mains £15 to £18).

Spears Cross B&B ££

(☎01643-821439; www.spearscross.co.uk; 1 West St; d £89-99) If you like your floral fabrics, puffy armchairs and china crockery, you'll be throughly happy at this four-room B&B, which is still flying the flag for the old-fashioned style of British B&B. The house is 15th century, and the rooms are squeezed into all kinds of awkward spaces, but luxuries such as Penhaligon's toiletries are a welcome surprise. Savour rare-breed bangers and traditional 'Dunster Toast' at the brekkie table.

Luttrell Arms PUB ££

(☎01643-821555; www.luttrellarms.co.uk; High St; d £120-150; Ⓟ) In medieval times this glorious old coaching inn was the guesthouse of the Abbots of Cleeve. Huge flagstones, heavy armchairs and faded tapestries dot the lounge – a perfect fit for the hearty bar food. The rooms have period curios too: four-poster beds, brass plates, beams or perhaps a plaster fireplace.

Reeve's BRITISH ££

(☎01643-821414; www.reevesrestaurantdunster.co.uk; dinner £12.25-16.25; ⏲lunch Sat & Sun, dinner Tue-Sat) This surprisingly swanky restaurant dishes up Dunster's best food in an attractive dining room full of fairy lights and stripped-wood floors. Its dishes are complex and satisfying: think delicate stacks of monkfish, venison marinated in port and juniper or Exmouth scallops in chive butter.

Cobblestones Cafe CAFE ££

(High St; mains £5-14; ⏲lunch daily, dinner Wed-Sat) Plump for the daily roast or potted shrimps on toast at this village cafe, or better still just drop in for a superior cream tea.

Getting There & Away

Bus 29 stops at Dunster on its way between Taunton and Minehead (half-hourly Monday to Saturday, hourly on Sunday).

The West Somerset Railway (p331) stops at Dunster during the summer.

Devon & Cornwall

Includes »

Best Places to Eat

» Paul Ainsworth at No 6 (p373)

» Seagrass (p379)

» Gurnard's Head (p381)

» Riverford Field Kitchen (p354)

» Seahorse (p352)

Best Places to Stay

» The Scarlet (p375)

» Artist Residence Penzance (p383)

» Cove (p382)

» Gidleigh Park (p365)

» St Elizabeth's House (p357)

Why Go?

Dipping into the Atlantic like a toe testing the water, Britain's westernmost counties stand one step removed from the rest of the nation. The world just feels different out west: fields are greener, cliffs are craggier, beaches are whiter and skies are wider. Every road reveals another postcard panorama: whitewashed lighthouses on blustery clifftops, rocky tors on empty moors, golden beaches washed by surf.

Dig a little deeper and these neighbours reveal subtle differences in character. Devon is still a deeply rural county, a land of hamlets, hedgerows, moors and meadows: next-door Cornwall feels starker, emptier and wilder, a land hewn by the wind and the tides, where the elements still very much hold sway. They're more than just pretty pictures, though: in recent years both counties have become culinary innovators, cultural hotspots and eco-pioneers; and the days when the Westcountry could be dismissed as a backwater are well and truly over.

When to Go

Padstow hosts the 'Obby 'Oss ceremony over the town's streets around May Day; the Port Eliot Festival in mid-July has music, theatre, dance and literary events, and in August bursts of colour fill Plymouth's skies during the British Fireworks Championships. The Cornish coastal town of Mousehole is famous for its Christmas lights in December.

Crowds are inevitable in July and August, and around Easter, so avoid these times if you can. Spring and autumn often have the best weather, too.

Devon & Cornwall Highlights

1 Wandering round the futuristic biomes of the **Eden Project** (p394)

2 Cracking the clues at **Greenway** (p351), Agatha Christie's enchanting holiday home

3 Exploring the southwest's very own pocket wilderness, **Dartmoor** (p359)

4 Climbing to the roof for awe-inspiring views from **Exeter Cathedral** (p343)

5 Escaping the 21st century on the **Isles of Scilly** (p397)

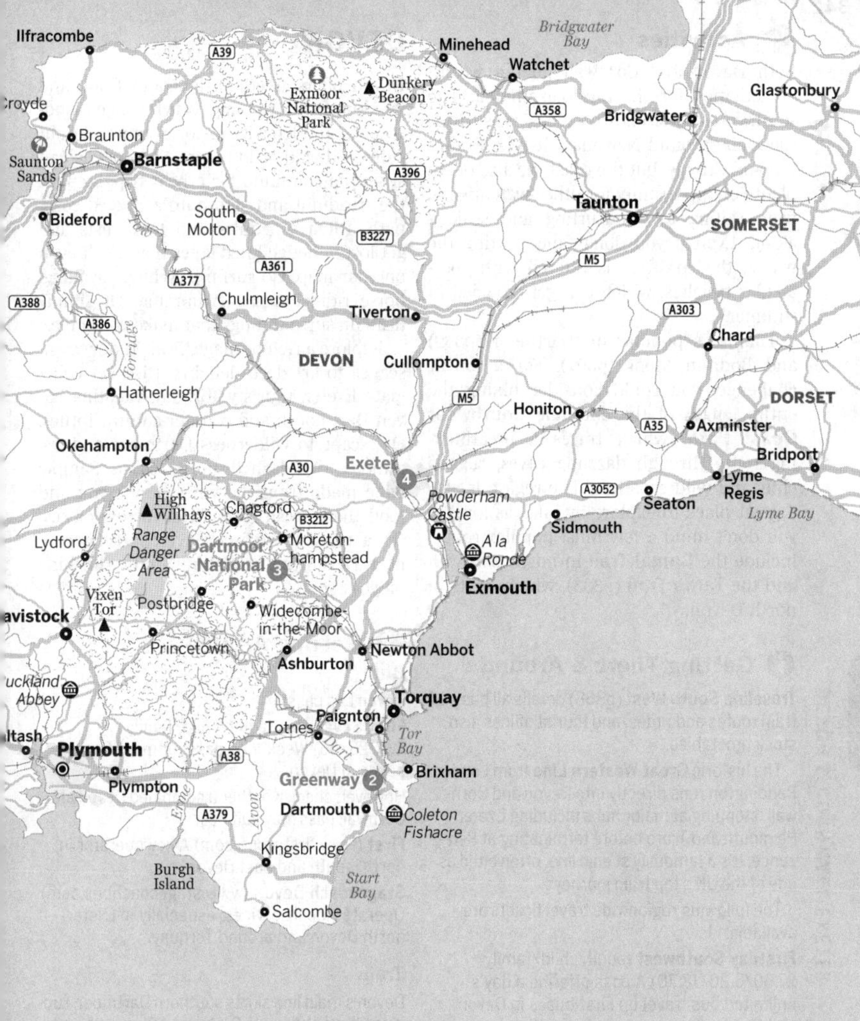

6 Crossing the cobbled causeway over to **St Michael's Mount** (p385)

7 Standing at the southernmost point of England, **Lizard Point** (p386)

8 Catching a clifftop play at the **Minack Theatre** (p382), near Porthcurno

Activities

Both Devon and Cornwall offer a wealth of activities for the outdoor-minded. The southwest's best-known sport is surfing, especially around Newquay, St Ives, Braunton and Croyde, but the coastline also offers plenty of opportunity for other watersports, from sailing to windsurfing and seakayaking. Even if you don't fancy hitting the waves, the coastline is littered with spectacular beaches, which can get crowded in summer.

Hiking is popular on Dartmoor (p359) and Bodmin Moor (p397). For a longer challenge, you could consider hiking the entire length of the 630-mile **Southwest Coast Path**, which traces a breathtaking route through dazzling coves, rugged cliffs and wild coastline. The region is also a great place to explore by bike, as long as you don't mind a few hills: popular routes include the **Camel Trail** in north Cornwall and the **Tarka Trail** (p333), which starts in north Devon.

Getting There & Around

Traveline South West (p368) details all bus and train routes and times, and tourist offices also stock timetables.

The historic **Great Western Line** from London Paddington runs directly into Devon and Cornwall, stopping at major hubs including Exeter, Plymouth and Truro before terminating at Penzance. It's a famously scenic line. often cited as one of the UK's top train journeys.

The following regionwide travel tickets are available:

Firstday Southwest (adult/child/family £7.60/6.20/18.70) A pass offering a day's unlimited bus travel on First buses in Devon and Cornwall.

Freedom of Devon & Cornwall Rover This train pass allows unlimited train travel in Devon and Cornwall for three days out of seven (adult/child £42/21), or 8 days out of 15 (£64/32).

Freedom of the SouthWest Rover Covers trains west of Bath, Bristol and Bournemouth (including Devon & Cornwall). Three days' off-peak travel in 7 days (adult/child £74/36.50) or 8 days in 15 (adult/child £100.50/50.25).

Stagecoach Explorer One day's bus travel on Stagecoach's southwest network (adult/child/family £7/5/15).

DEVON

Devon offers freedom. Freedom from, and freedom to. Its rippling, beach-fringed landscape is studded with historic homes, vibrant cities and wild, wild moors. So here you can swap the commute for a boat trip. Step off the treadmill and step onto a rugged coast path. Ditch schedules and to-do lists and get lost in hedge-lined lanes that aren't even on your map. Go surfing, cycling, kayaking, horse riding or sea swimming. Or simply drink in surroundings that make you smile.

Explore a rich heritage, from Tudor townscapes to art deco delights. Discover collegiate Exeter, touristy Torquay, yachting haven Dartmouth and counter-culture Totnes. Or escape to wilderness Dartmoor and the remote, surf-dashed north coast. Sample wine made from the vines beside you and food that's fresh from field, furrow or sea. It's a place to rediscover, recharge, reconnect. Devon can help shine a little sunshine on your soul.

Getting Around

Bus

Devon bus pass:

First Seven Day (adult/child/family £37/23/56) Week-long pass for most First buses in Devon.

However, check whether a combined Devon and Cornwall pass may suit best.

First (www.firstgroup.com) A key operator in north, south and east Devon.

Stagecoach Devon (www.stagecoachbus.com) Operates local services, especially in Exeter, north Devon and around Torquay.

Train

Devon's main line skirts southern Dartmoor, running from London via Exeter and Plymouth and on to Cornwall. Trains from London Paddington cover the region, though Exeter is also served by London Waterloo station.

Branch lines include the 39-mile Exeter–Barnstaple Tarka Line; the 15-mile Plymouth–Gunnislake Tamar Valley Line and the scenic Exeter–Torquay and Paignton line.

Exeter

POP 119,600

Well heeled and comfortable, Exeter bears evidence of its centuries-old role as the spiritual and administrative heart of Devon. The city's Gothic cathedral presides over stretches of cobbled streets, fragments of the terracotta Roman city wall and a tumbling of medieval and Georgian buildings. A snazzy new shopping centre brings bursts of the modern, thousands of university students ensure a buzzing nightlife and the vibrant quayside acts as a launch pad for cycling or kayaking trips. Throw in some stylish places to stay and eat and you have a relaxed but lively base for explorations.

History

Exeter's past can be read in its buildings. The Romans marched in around AD 55 – their 17-hectare fortress included a 2-mile defensive wall, crumbling sections of which remain, especially in **Rougemont** and **Northernhay Gardens**. Saxon and Norman times saw growth: a castle went up in 1068, the cathedral 40 years later. The Tudor wool boom brought Exeter an export trade, riches and half-timbered houses; prosperity continued into the Georgian era when hundreds of merchants built genteel homes. The Blitz of WWII brought devastation: in just one night in 1942, 156 people died and 12 hectares of the city were flattened. In the 21st century the £220-million **Princesshay Shopping Centre** added shimmering glass and steel to the architectural mix.

Sights

Exeter Cathedral CATHEDRAL

(01392-285983; www.exeter-cathedral.org.uk; The Close; adult/child £5/free; 9.30am-4.45pm Mon-Sat) Magnificent in warm, honey-coloured stone, Exeter's **Cathedral Church of St Peter** is framed by lawns and wonky half-timbered buildings – a quintessentially English scene peopled by picnickers snacking to the sound of the bells.

The site has been a religious one since at least the 5th century but the Normans started the current building in 1114; the towers of today's cathedral date from that period. In 1270 a 90-year remodelling process began, introducing a mix of Early English and Decorated Gothic styles.

Above the **Great West Front** scores of weather-worn figures line a once brightly painted screen that now forms England's largest collection of 14th-century sculpture. Inside, the ceiling is mesmerising – the longest unbroken Gothic vaulting in the world, it sweeps up to meet ornate ceiling bosses in gilt and vibrant colours. Look out for the 15th-century **Exeter Clock** in the north transept: in keeping with medieval astronomy it shows the earth as a golden ball at the centre of the universe with the sun, a fleur-de-lys, travelling round. Still ticking and whirring, it chimes on the hour.

The huge oak canopy over the **Bishop's Throne** was carved in 1312, while the 1350 **minstrels' gallery** is decorated with 12 angels playing musical instruments. Cathedral staff will point out the famous sculpture of the lady with two left feet and the tiny **St James Chapel**, built to repair the one destroyed in the Blitz. Look out for its unusual carvings: a cat, a mouse and, oddly, a rugby player.

In the **Refectory** (mains £6; 10am-5pm Mon-Sat) you can tuck into cakes, quiches and soups at trestle tables surrounded by vaulted ceilings, stained glass and busts of the great, the good and the dead.

Free **guided tours** (11am & 12.30pm Mon-Sat, plus 2.30pm Mon-Fri) last 45 minutes. Evocative **Evensong** services are held at 5.30pm Monday to Friday, and 3pm on Saturday, with **Choral Evensong** on Sunday at 3pm.

FREE **Bill Douglas Centre** MUSEUM

(01392-724321; www.billdouglas.org; Old Library, Prince of Wales Rd; 10am-5pm Mon-Fri) A delightful homage to film and fun, the Bill Douglas Centre is a compact collection of all things celluloid, from magic lanterns to Mickey Mouse. Inside discover just what the butler did see and why the flicks are called the flicks. Among the mass of movie memorabilia are Charlie Chaplin bottle stoppers, Ginger Rogers playing cards, James Bond board games and Star Wars toys.

St Nicholas Priory MONASTERY, MUSEUM

(01392-665858; www.exeter.gov.uk/priory; The Mint; adult/child £3/1; 10am-5pm Sat, plus Mon-Fri school holidays) This 900-year-old former Benedictine monastery is built of beautiful russet stone and vividly recreates life inside a late-Elizabethan town house. Expect

CATHEDRAL ROOF TOURS

For a sensational view of Exeter Cathedral, book one of these high-rise **guided walks** (01392-285983; www.exeter-cathedral.org.uk; adult/child £10/5; 2pm Tue-Thu, 11am Sat Apr-Sep). Climb 251 steps up a spiral staircase, head out onto the sweeping roof to stroll its length, then gaze down on the city from the top of the North Tower. The tours are popular so book two weeks ahead.

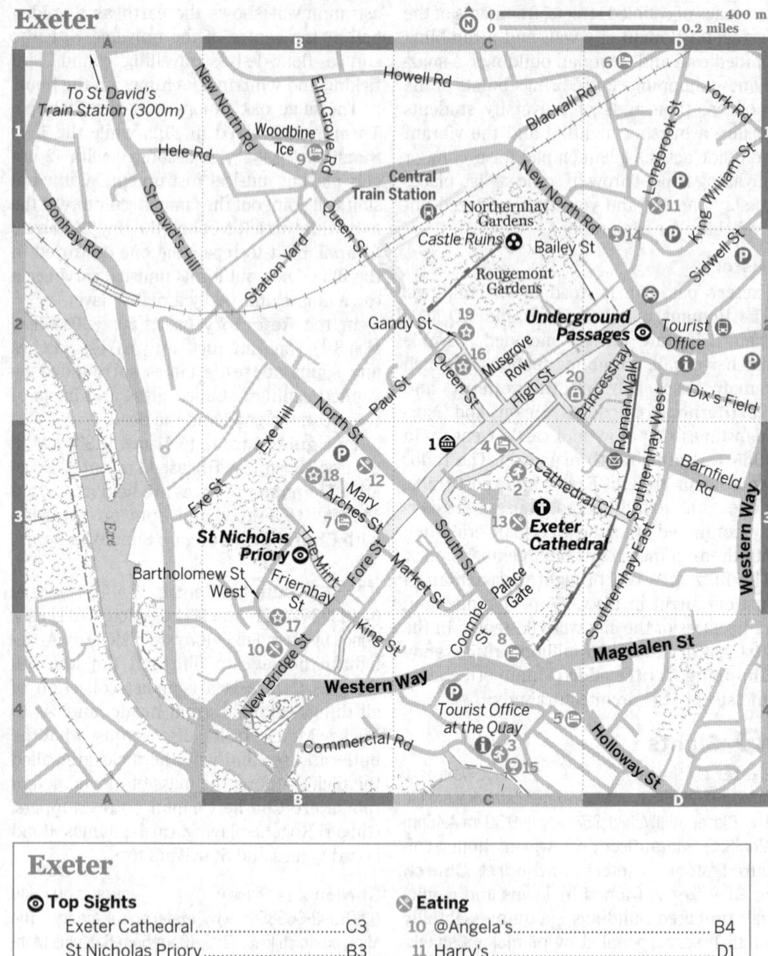

Exeter

Top Sights

Exeter Cathedral C3
St Nicholas Priory B3
Underground Passages D2

Sights

1 Guildhall C3

Activities, Courses & Tours

2 Redcoat Tours C3
3 Saddles & Paddles C4

Sleeping

4 Abode at the Royal Clarence C3
5 Globe Backpackers C4
6 Raffles D1
7 St Olaves B3
8 White Hart C4
9 Woodbine B1

Eating

10 @Angela's B4
11 Harry's D1
12 Herbies B3
MC Cafe, Bar & Grill .... (see 4)
Michael Caines .... (see 4)
13 Refectory C3

Drinking

14 Old Firehouse D2
15 On the Waterfront C4

Entertainment

16 Cavern Club C2
17 Exeter Picturehouse B4
18 Mamma Stone's B3
19 Phoenix C2

Shopping

20 Princesshay Shopping Centre C2

brightly coloured furnishings, elaborate plaster ceilings and intricate oak panelling.

FREE **Guildhall** HISTORIC BUILDING
(☎01392-665500; High St) The earliest parts of Exeter's Guildhall date from 1330, making it the oldest municipal building still in use in the country. An ornate barrel roof arches above wooden benches and crests of dignitaries – the mayor still sits in the huge throne-like chair at the end. It's often open on weekdays, but it depends on civic functions; call first to check.

TOP CHOICE **Underground Passages** TUNNELS
(☎01392-665887; www.exeter.gov.uk/passages; Paris St; adult/child £5.50/4; ⊙9.30am-5.30pm Mon-Sat, 10am-4pm Sun Jun-Sep, 11.30am-4pm Tue-Sun Oct-May) Prepare to crouch down, don a hard hat and possibly get spooked in what is the only publically accessible system of its kind in England. These medieval vaulted passages were built to house pipes bringing fresh water to the city. Unlike modern utility companies, the authorities opted to have permanent access for repairs, rather than dig up the streets each time – genius. Guides lead you on a scramble through the network telling tales of ghosts, escape routes and cholera. The last tour is an hour before closing; they're popular – book ahead.

Activities

The River Exe and the Exeter Canal are framed by foot and cycle paths that wind south from the Quay, past pubs, beside an ever-broadening estuary towards the sea, 10 miles away.

Saddles & Paddles BIKE HIRE, CANOE HIRE
(☎01392-424241; www.sadpad.com; Exeter Quay; ⊙9.30am-5.30pm) Rents out **bikes** (adult per hour/day £6/15), **kayaks** (per hour/day £10/35) and Canadian **canoes** (per hour/day £15/50); the tourist office stocks maps.

Tours

FREE **Redcoat Tours** WALKING TOURS
(☎01392-265203; www.exeter.gov.uk/visiting; ⊙2-4pm daily Apr-Oct, 2-3pm daily Nov-Mar) For an informed and entertaining introduction to Exeter's history, tag along on one of these 1½ hour tours. Themes range from murder and trade to Romans and religion – there are even torch-lit prowls through the catacombs and night-time ghost walks. Tours leave from Cathedral Yard or the Quay; pick up a program from the tourist office.

Sleeping

TOP CHOICE **Abode at the Royal Clarence** HOTEL ££
(☎01392-319955; www.abodehotels.co.uk/exeter; Cathedral Yard; r not incl breakfast £120-300; 📶) This is the epitome of sink-into-it luxury. Exquisite room are categorised as Comfortable, Desirable, Enviable or Fabulous – whichever way they're a drop-dead gorgeous blend of Georgian grandeur and minimalist chic. Expect bespoke beds, roll-topped baths and a complimentary tuckbox of local treats.

Raffles B&B ££
(☎01392-270200; www.raffles-exeter.co.uk; 11 Blackall Rd; s/d £42/72; P) The antique dealer owner has peppered each room of this late-Victorian town house with heritage features – look out for Bakelite radios, wooden plant stands and creaking trunks. Largely organic breakfasts and a walled garden add to the appeal.

White Hart INN ££
(☎01392-279897; www.whitehartpubexeter.co.uk; 66 South St; s £50-70, d £50-80; P📶) They've been putting people up here since the Plantagenets were on the throne in the 1300s. The courtyard is a wisteria-fringed bobble of cobbles and the bar is book-lined and beamed. Rooms are tasteful modern affairs with suede chairs, honey and gold hues and glinting bathrooms. Their Sunday night doubles (£50) are a steal.

St Olaves HOTEL ££
(☎01392-217736; www.olaves.co.uk; Mary Arches St; d £80-125, ste £95-155, f £165; P📶) This hotel's swirling spiral staircase is so beautiful it's tempting to sleep beside it. But if you did, you'd miss out on the 18th-century-with-contemporary-twist bedrooms: think rococo mirrors, brass bedsteads and plush furnishings.

Globe Backpackers HOSTEL £
(☎01392-215521; www.exeterbackpackers.co.uk; 71 Holloway St; dm/d £16.50/42; 📶) Rightly a firm favourite among budget travellers, this spotlessly clean, relaxed, rambling house boasts three doubles, roomy dorms and wet room showers that are positively luxurious.

The Wood Life CAMPSITE £
(☎01392-832509; www.thewoodlife.org; The Linhay, near Kenn; 5/7 nights from £550/730; ⊙Apr-Oct; P)

Your chance to get back to nature without getting grubby, this cavernous, 6-person tent has decked floors, wicker chairs and brass bedsteads; the highlights though are the wood-burning stove and campfire – you can even chop your own logs. Exeter, Dartmoor and the beach are each about 5 miles away.

Woodbine B&B ££
(☎01392-203302; www.woodbineguesthouse.co.uk; 1 Woodbine Tce; s/d £38/66; 📶) A surprise sits behind this archetypal flower-framed terrace: fresh, modish rooms with low beds and burgundy flashes – there's even underfloor heating in the bathrooms.

Eating

Michael Caines FINE DINING ££
(☎01392-223638; www.michaelcaines.com; Cathedral Yard; mains £25) Run by the eponymous, double-Michelin starred chef, the food here is a complex blend of prime Westcountry ingredients and full-bodied French flavours. Gastronomes linger over the seven-course tasting menu (£72), and the three-course set lunches (£23) are a comparative bargain.

MC Cafe, Bar & Grill CAFE, BISTRO ££
(Cathedral Yard; mains £12, 2-course lunch/dinner £10/11; ⏰9am-10pm) The MC in the title stands for TV chef Michael Caines, so prepare for bistro classics with creative twists: beef burgers with onion confit; fish encased in a local Otter Ale batter. Leave room though for the devilishly dark chocolate tart.

@Angela's MODERN BRITISH £££
(☎01392-499038; www.angelasrestaurant.co.uk; 38 New Bridge St; dinner mains £19; ⏰lunch Wed-Sat, dinner Tue-Sat) Dedication to sourcing local ingredients sometimes sees the chef at this smart bistro rising before dawn to bag the best fish at Brixham Market; his steamed John Dory with seared scallops is worth the trip alone. The beef has grazed Devon fields, while local duck is made memorable by a rich Grand Marnier sauce. Wise foodies opt for the pre-booked lunch (2-/3-courses £19/23).

Herbies VEGETARIAN £
(15 North St; mains £5-9; ⏰lunch Mon-Sat, dinner Tue-Sat; 🌿) Cosy and gently groovy, Herbies has been cheerfully feeding Exeter's veggies for more than 20 years. It's *the* place in town to tuck into delicious sundried tomato and mushroom risotto or a hearty Greek vegetable pie. They're strong on vegan dishes too.

Harry's BISTRO ££
(www.harrys-exeter.co.uk; 86 Longbrook St; mains £8-12; ⏰closed Sun) Harry's is the kind of welcoming neighbourhood eatery you wish was on your own doorstep but rarely is. The decor is all wooden chairs, blackboard menus and gilt mirrors; the food includes seared tuna, Spanish ham with marinated figs, and a hearty three-bean chilli.

BLACKDOWN YURTS

Organic bedding, fresh spring water, thick rugs and blazing log burners make these **yurts** (☎01884-266699; www.blackdownyurts.co.uk; nr Exeter; four person yurt per week £375-460; Ⓟ) the epitome of cushy camping. There's a field kitchen, a fire pit and an endless supply of logs, too. The four cosy, ecofriendly yurts are tucked away on a sleepy smallholding around 15 miles east of Exeter.

Drinking

On the Waterfront BAR
(www.waterfrontexeter.co.uk; The Quay) In 1835 this was a warehouse; now its redbrick, barrel-vaulted ceilings stretch back from a thoroughly modern bar. The tables outside are a popular spot for a riverside pint.

Old Firehouse PUB
(www.oldfirehouseexeter.co.uk; 50 New North Rd) A candle-lit Exeter institution, often crowded with students and famous for its buzzing atmosphere, sunny terrace and impressive range of real ales and ciders.

Entertainment

Mamma Stone's LIVE MUSIC
(www.mamastones.com; 1 Mary Arches St; ⏰6pm-midnight, 9pm-3am when bands play) This boho hangout is a riot of painted wood and showcases everything from acoustic sets to pop, folk and jam nights. Mamma Stone's daughter, Joss (yes, *the* Joss Stone), plays sometimes too. Roll up about 11pm and see them pull back the tables so the crowd can groove away.

Phoenix ARTS CENTRE
(www.exeterphoenix.org.uk; Gandy St; ⏰closed Sun; 📶) The city's art and soul; Phoenix is a hub of exhibitions, performance, music,

dance, film, classes and workshops. There's a buzzing cafe-bar too.

Exeter Picturehouse CINEMA
(www.picturehouses.co.uk; 51 Bartholomew St West) An intimate, independent cinema, screening mainstream and art-house movies.

Cavern Club LIVE MUSIC
(www.cavernclub.co.uk; 83 Queen St; ⌚11am-5pm Mon-Sat, 8pm-1am Sun-Thu, 11am-2am Fri & Sat) Prepare for a sweaty, hectic melee when bands take to the stage at this long-standing indie club, famous for big-name DJs and breaking acts from the counter-culture scene.

Information

Exeter Library (Castle St; ⌚9am-6pm Mon, Tue, Thu & Fri, 10am-5pm Wed, 9am-4pm Sat;) Internet (per 30 minutes £2.20), plus free wi-fi.

Police Station (☎08452-777444; Heavitree Rd; ⌚24hr)

Royal Devon & Exeter Hospital (Barrack Rd) Accident and Emergency.

Tourist Office (☎01392-665700; www.heartofdevon.com; Dix's Field; ⌚9am-5pm Mon-Sat Apr-Sep, 9.30am-4.30pm Oct-Mar)

Tourist Office at the Quay (☎01392-271611; www.heartofdevon.com; The Quay; ⌚10am-5pm Apr-Sep, 11am-4pm Sat & Sun Oct-Mar)

Getting There & Away

Air

Exeter's key airline is **Flybe** (www.flybe.com).

Exeter International Airport (www.exeter-airport.co.uk) Flights connect with cities in Europe and the UK, including Glasgow, Manchester and Newcastle, plus the Channel Islands and the Isles of Scilly.

Bus

On Sundays between June and mid-September Bus 82, the **Transmoor Link**, makes five trips from Exeter to Plymouth via Moretonhampstead, Postbridge, Princetown and Yelverton.

Bude (£6.50, two hours, five Monday to Saturday) Bus X9; runs via Okehampton.

Jurassic Coastlinx (Bus X53) runs three to seven services daily to Lyme Regis, Weymouth and Poole.

Moretonhampstead (one hour, six daily Monday to Saturday) Bus 359.

Plymouth (£6.50, 1¼ hours, every two-hours Monday to Saturday, three on Sunday) Bus X38.

Sidmouth (one hour, one to three per hour) Bus 52A/B.

Totnes (50 minutes, seven daily Monday to Saturday, two on Sunday) Bus X64.

Train

Main-line and branch-line trains run from Exeter St David's and Exeter Central stations:

Barnstaple (£9, 1¼ hours, one to two every hour)

Bristol (£15, 1¼ hours, half-hourly)

Exmouth (£4, 40 minutes, hourly)

London Paddington (£35, 2½ hours, half-hourly)

Paignton (£6, 50 minutes, half-hourly) via **Torquay** (£6, 45 minutes, services every half hour)

Penzance (£15, three hours, hourly) via **Totnes** (£5, 35 minutes) and **Plymouth** (£6, one hour)

Getting Around

TO/FROM THE AIRPORT Bus 56 runs from the bus station and Exeter St David's train station to Exeter Airport (30 minutes, hourly 7am-6pm).

BICYCLE Saddles & Paddles (p345) hires out rental bikes

BUS Bus H links St David's train station with Central Station and the High St, passing near the bus station.

CAR Hire options include Europcar (www.europcar.co.uk). **Park & Ride** buses (adult/child £2.25/1.50) operate every ten minutes, running from **Sowton** (near M5, junction 30) and **Matford** (near M5, junction 31) Monday to Saturday, and from **Honiton Rd** (near M5, junction 29) daily.

TAXI Ranks are at St David's train station and on High and Sidwell St.

Capital Taxis (☎01392-434343; ⌚24hrs)

Club Cars (☎01392-213030; ⌚24hrs)

Gemini (☎01392-666666; ⌚24hr)

Around Exeter

Powderham Castle HISTORIC BUILDING
(☎01626-890243; www.powderham.co.uk; adult/child £10.50/8.50; ⌚11am-4.30pm Sun-Fri Apr-Oct; P) The historic home of the Earl of Devon, **Powderham** is a stately but still friendly place. Built in 1391, it was damaged in the Civil War and remodelled in the Victorian era. A visit takes in a fine wood-panelled Great Hall, parkland with 650 deer and glimpses of life 'below stairs' in the kitchen. The earl and family are still resident and, despite the grandeur of the place, for disarming, fleeting moments it feels like you're actually wandering through someone's sitting room.

Powderham is on the River Exe near Kenton, 8 miles south of Exeter. Bus 2 runs from Exeter (30 minutes, every 20 minutes Monday to Saturday).

A La Ronde HISTORIC BUILDING
(NT; ☎01395-265514; www.nationaltrust.org.uk; Summer Lane; adult/child £7.20/3.70; ⏰11am-5pm Sat-Wed Feb-Jun & Sep-Oct, 11am-5pm daily Jul & Aug; Ⓟ) This quirky 16-sided **cottage** was built in 1796 so two spinster cousins could display a mass of curiosities acquired on their 10-year European grand tour. Its glass alcoves, low lintels and tiny doorways mean it's like clambering through a doll's house – highlights are a delicate feather frieze in the drawing room and a gallery smothered with a thousand seashells. In a fabulous collision of old and new, the seashells can only be seen via remote control CCTV from the butler's pantry. The house is 10 miles south of Exeter, near Exmouth; bus 57 (30 minutes, every 15 minutes) runs close by.

Torquay & Around

POP 110,370

It may be south Devon, not the south of France, but Torquay has long been dubbed the English Riviera, thanks to palm trees, plentiful beaches and steep hills. The town is the quintessential, sometimes faded, English resort, torn between targeting elderly vacationers and young party animals. But an azure circle of bay and a mild microclimate have also drawn a smarter set, and the bay now competes with Devon's finest foodie hubs in terms of top eateries. Add an intriguing Agatha Christie connection and attractions ranging from an immense aviary to an impressive eco-zoo, and it all adds up to some grand days out beside the sea.

Torquay's neighbouring resort, Paignton, sits 3 miles south; the fishing port of Brixham (p350) is 5 miles further south again.

Sights & Activities

Beaches BEACH
Torquay boasts no fewer than 20 beaches and a surprising 22 miles of coast. Holidaymakers flock to the central (but tidal) **Torre Abbey Sands**; locals head for the sand-and-shingle beaches beside the 240ft red-clay cliffs around **Babbacombe**. A steep, narrow road leads to the beach (there's a car park at the bottom). Better still, take a glorious 1920s **funicular railway** (☎01803-328750; www.babbacombecliffrailway.co.uk; adult/child return £1.90/1.30; ⏰9.30am-5pm Feb-Oct, to 6pm Jun-Sep); a memorable trip in a tiny wooden carriage that shuttles up and down rails set into the cliff.

Paignton Zoo ZOO
(☎0844-474 2222; www.paigntonzoo.org.uk; Totnes Rd, Paignton; adult/child £13/9; ⏰10am-5pm; Ⓟ) This 80-acre site is dotted with spacious enclosures recreating habitats as varied as savannah, wetland, tropical forest and desert. Highlights are the crocodile swamp, orangutan island, a huge glass-walled lion enclosure and a lemur wood, where you walk over a plank suspension bridge as the primates leap around in surrounding trees. Buses 81 and 12A run at least hourly from Torquay (25 minutes).

Living Coasts ZOO
(☎0844-474 3366; www.livingcoasts.org.uk; Beacon Quay; adult/child £10/7.45; ⏰10am-5pm) An enormous open-plan aviary bringing you up close to free-roaming penguins, punk-rocker

WORTH A TRIP

RIVER COTTAGE

TV chef Hugh Fearnley-Whittingstall campaigns hard on sustainable food, so it's fitting that his east Devon **canteen** (☎01297-631862; www.rivercottage.net; Trinity Sq, Axminster; mains £5-16; ⏰9am-5pm daily, dinner Tue-Sat; ✎) champions local, seasonal and organic ingredients. Hearty flavours include pollock with bacon, and a deeply satisfying Dorset mushroom and Ticklemoor goat's cheese risotto; try the Stinger Beer, brewed from (carefully) handpicked Dorset nettles; it's spicy with just a hint of tingle. Alternatively, book a four-course gastronomic delight at the nearby **River Cottage HQ** (☎01297-630313; www.rivercottage.net; 4 courses £60-70; ⏰lunch Sun, dinner Fri & Sat, booking required). There's another River Cottage Canteen in Plymouth (p358).

Axminster is 30 miles east of Exeter. Trains (£8.40, 40 minutes, hourly) leave from Exeter's St David's station.

AGATHA CHRISTIE

Torquay is the birthplace of the 'Queen of Crime', Agatha Christie (1890–1976), author of 75 novels and 33 plays, and creator of Hercule Poirot, the moustachioed, immodest Belgian detective, and Miss Marple, the surprisingly perceptive busybody spinster. Born Agatha Miller, she grew up, courted and honeymooned in Torquay and also worked as a hospital dispenser here during WWI, thus acquiring her famous knowledge of poisons.

The tourist office stocks the free *Agatha Christie Mile* leaflet, which guides you round significant local sites, while **Torquay Museum** (☎01803-293975; www.torquaymuseum.org; 529 Babbacombe Rd; adult/child £5.15/3.25; ⏲10am-5pm Mon-Sat, 1.30-5pm Sun Jul-Sep) has a huge collection of photos, handwritten notes and displays devoted to her famous detectives. The highlight, though, is Greenway (p351), her summer home near Dartmouth. The **Agatha Christie Cruise** (☎01803-882811; www.greenwayferry.co.uk; adult/child £14/10; ⏲daily Wed-Sun Apr-Oct) sails there from Torquay's Princess Pier – it's best to book. Boats also go from Dartmouth (p351) and Totnes; a steam train runs from Paignton (p350).

style tufted puffins and disarmingly cute bank cormorants.

Babbacombe Model Village ATTRACTION
(☎01803-315315; www.model-village.co.uk; Hampton Ave; adult/child £9.50/7.50; ⏲10am-dusk) Prepare for a fabulously eccentric, 4-acre world in miniature, complete with tiny Stonehenge, football stadium, beach and Lilliputian population.

Ferry to Brixham FERRY
(☎01803-882811; www.greenwayferry.co.uk; Princess Pier; adult/child return £5/3; ⏲12 sailings daily April-Oct) This blast across Tor Bay offers spray-dashed views of beaches, crumbling cliffs and grand Victorian hotels.

Sleeping

TOP CHOICE **Cary Arms** BOUTIQUE HOTEL £££
(☎01803-327110; www.caryarms.co.uk; Babbacombe Beach; d £230-270, ste £370) The great British seaside goes seriously stylish at this oh-so-chic bolthole. Neutral tones are jazzed up by candy-striped cushions, balconies directly overlook the beach and there's even a stick of rock with the hotel's name running through it on your pillow.

Headland View B&B ££
(☎01803-312612; www.headlandview.com; Babbacombe Downs; s/d £57/72; P ᯤ) Set high on the cliffs at Babbacombe, this charming terrace is peppered with subtle nautical flourishes, from jaunty model lighthouses to boat motifs on the curtains. The wicker chairs on the tiny balconies have five-star views of a cracking stretch of sea.

Lanscombe House B&B ££
(☎01803-606938; www.lanscombe house.co.uk; Cockington Lane; d £70-115; P) Laura Ashley herself would love the lashings of tasteful fabrics, four-poster beds and free-standing slipper baths on show here. This serene hideaway is in a country park a mile southwest of central Torquay – in its English cottage garden you can hear owls hoot at night.

Torquay Backpackers HOSTEL £
(☎01803-299924; www.torquaybackpackers.co.uk; 119 Abbey Rd; dm/d £16/34; @ ᯤ) Photos of grinning past guests plaster noticeboards and flags of all nations drape the walls at this budget stalwart. There are luxuries too: great showers, a DVD den and a decked, alfresco pool-table terrace.

Hillcroft B&B ££
(☎01803-297247; www.thehillcroft.co.uk; 9 St Lukes Rd; s £75-80, d £75-90, ste £115-130; P @ ᯤ) The swish rooms range from boutique Bali to Moroccan chic; the top-floor suite (think exposed stone, beams and antique beds) is smashing.

Eating & Drinking

Room in the Elephant FINE DINING £££
(☎01803-200044; www.elephantrestaurant.co.uk; 3 Beacon Tce; 2/3/7 courses £46/56/70; ⏲dinner Tue-Sat) A restaurant to remember. Torquay's Michelin-starred eatery is defined by imaginative cuisine: smoked beef tartare, pickled turnips, wild garlic and quail eggs dot the menu. Dessert might be bitter chocolate fondant topped by salted caramel ice cream or a raid on a platter packed with prime West-country cheeses. Book ahead.

Number 7 SEAFOOD ££
(☎01803-295055; www.no7-fish.com; 7 Beacon Tce; mains £14; ⊙lunch Wed-Sat, dinner daily Jul-Sep, Tue-Sat Oct-Jun) Fabulous smells fill the air at this bustling harbourside bistro, where the chalked-up menus are packed with crab, lobster and fish fresh from the boats. Try it grilled or baked; accompaniments range from oil and herbs through garlic and brandy to Moroccan spices.

Elephant Brasserie MODERN BRITISH ££
(☎01803-200044; www.elephantrestaurant.co.uk; 3 Beacon Tce; 2/3 courses £23/27; ⊙Tue-Sat) The setting may be less formal, but the bistro below Torquay's Michelin-starred Room in the Elephant is still super-stylish. Innovative treatments include lovage and apple vichyssoise, and a squid and mackerel burger with sea-salted fries.

Orange Tree EUROPEAN ££
(☎01803-213936; www.orangetreerestaurant.co.uk; 14 Park Hill Rd; mains £17; ⊙dinner Mon-Sat) This award-winning brasserie adds a dash of Continental flair to local fish, meat and game. Ingredients and flavours are rich; in the vein of pan-seared Devon beef laced with Madeira, mushrooms and white truffle oil.

Gemelli ITALIAN ££
(☎01803-294183; www.gemellirestaurant.co.uk; 172 Union St; pizzas £8, mains £7-18; ⊙Wed-Mon) There's a welcome feeling of eating in someone's home at this snug, family-run restaurant. Goodies range from authentic pizzas and golden pasta, to dishes where local produce gets a dash of the Med – look out for Devon fillet steak with gorgonzola, and Brixham mussels steamed in white wine.

Hole in the Wall PUB
(6 Park Lane) A heavily beamed, Tardis-like boozer with a tiny terrace; an atmospheric spot for a pint.

Information

Tourist Office (☎0844 474 2233; www.theenglishriviera.co.uk; Vaughan Pde, the Harbour; ⊙9.30am-5pm Mon-Sat, daily Jun-Sep)

Getting There & Away

Bus

Brixham via Paignton (50 minutes, every 15 minutes) Bus 12.

Totnes (one hour, hourly to four a day) Bus X80.

Dartmouth (1¼ hours, hourly Monday to Friday) Bus X81.

Ferry

Regular ferries shuttle between Torquay and Brixham (p349).

Train

Trains run from Exeter via Torquay (£6, 50 minutes, hourly) to **Paignton** (£6, 52 minutes).

Dartmouth Steam Railway & Riverboat Co (www.dartmouthrailriver.co.uk; Paignton Station; adult/child return £10.50/7.50; ⊙Mar-Nov) These steam trains puff from Paignton via Greenway Halt to Kingswear (30 minutes, four to nine trains a day). Kingswear is linked by ferry to Dartmouth (p353).

Brixham

POP 17,460

An appealing, pastel-painted tumbling of fishermen's cottages leads down to Brixham's horseshoe harbour, signalling a very different place from Torquay. Here arcades and gift shops coexist with winding streets, brightly coloured boats and one of England's busiest fishing ports. Although picturesque, Brixham is far from a neatly packaged resort, and its brand of gritty charm offers an insight into work-a-day life along Devon's coast.

Sights

Golden Hind SAILING SHIP
(☎01803-856223; www.goldenhind.co.uk; The Quay; adult/child £4/3; ⊙10am-4pm Mar-Sep) Devon explorer Sir Francis Drake carried out a treasure-seeking circumnavigation of the globe aboard the *Golden Hind*, in the late 1500s. This replica is full-sized, but it's a remarkably small vessel for such a voyage. Cross the gangplank and see how 60 men crammed in below decks, before peering into the captain's cabin and prowling around the poop deck.

Brixham Heritage Museum MUSEUM
(☎01803-856267; www.brixhamheritage.org.uk; Bolton Cross; adult/child £2/free; ⊙10am-4pm Tue-Sat Apr-Oct, till 1pm Nov-Mar) The town's salty history is explored here, with an eclectic collection of exhibits on sail boats, smuggling, ship-building and sea rescues.

Eating & Drinking

Beamers BISTRO ££
(☎01803-854777; www.beamersrestaurant.co.uk; 19 The Quay; mains £12-23; ⊙dinner Wed-Mon; ☑) The superbly cooked fish is from the market just round the corner, the meat and veg

comes from Devon's rolling hills. Samphire, saffron and Pernod spring some menu surprises, while bagging a window table secures an absorbing harbour view.

Maritime PUB
(79 King St) Eccentric old boozer smothered in thousands of key rings, stone jugs and chamber pots, presided over by a chatty parrot called Mr Tibbs.

David Walker FISH MARKET £
(Unit B, Fish Market; 9am-3pm Mon-Fri, to 1pm Sat) *The* place to connect with Brixham's fishing industry and stock up for your BBQ – the counters are piled high with the day's catch. Picnic goodies include huge, cooked shell-on prawns (per 500g £8) and dressed crab (from £5 each).

Information

Tourist Office (0844-474 2233; www.theenglishriviera.co.uk; The Quay; 9.30am-5pm Mon-Sat Apr-Oct, plus Sun late Jul to Sep)

Getting There & Away

BUS Bus 22 shuttles to **Kingswear** (20 minutes, three-per-hour to hourly); where you can catch the ferry to Dartmouth (p353). Bus 12 (every 15 minutes) runs to Torquay via Paignton.

FERRY Regular ferries (p349) link Brixham and Torquay.

Dartmouth & Around

POP 9555

A bewitching blend of primary-coloured boats and delicately shaded houses, Dartmouth is hard to resist. Buildings cascade down steep, wooded slopes towards the River Dart while 17th-century shops with splendidly carved and gilded fronts line narrow lanes. Its popularity with a trendy sailing set brings ranks of boutiques and upmarket restaurants, but Dartmouth is also a busy port and the constant traffic of working boats ensures an authentic tang of the sea. Agatha Christie's summer home and a captivating art deco house that belonged to the D'Oyly Carte family are both nearby, adding to the town's appeal.

Dartmouth hugs the quay on the west side of the Dart estuary. It's linked to the village of Kingswear on the east bank by car- and foot ferries, providing key transport links to Torquay.

Sights & Activities

TOP CHOICE **Greenway** HISTORIC BUILDING
(NT; 01803-842382; www.nationaltrust.org.uk; Greenway Rd, Galmpton; adult/child £9/5; 10.30am-5pm Wed-Sun Mar-Oct, plus Tue Aug) The enchanting summer home of crime writer **Agatha Christie** (p349) sits beside the River Dart near Dartmouth. Here you wander between rooms where the furnishings and knick-knacks are much as she left them; check out her hats in the lobby; the books in her library and the clothes in her wardrobe; and listen to her speak (via replica radio) in the drawing room.

Woods speckled with splashes of magnolias, daffodils and hydrangeas frame the water, while the planting creates intimate, secret spaces – the boathouse provides not-to-be-missed views over the river. In Christie's book *Dead Man's Folly,* Greenway doubles as Nasse House, with the boathouse making an appearance in a murder scene.

Greenway's few parking spaces have to be pre-booked. It's more fun to go by the **Greenway Ferry** (01803-882811; www.greenwayferry.co.uk), which runs from Dartmouth (adult/child return £7/4.50, eight daily), Totnes (adult/child return £12/9, one daily) and Torquay (p349). It only operates when the house is open – booking is advised. Alternatively, take the Dartmouth Steam Railway (p353) from Paignton to Greenway Halt (adult/child £7.50/5) then walk a mile through the woods, or hike along the picturesque **Dart Valley Trail** from Kingswear (4 miles).

Coleton Fishacre HISTORIC BUILDING
(NT; 01803-752466; www.nationaltrust.org.uk; Brownstone Rd, near Kingswear; adult/child £9/5; 10.30am-5pm Sat-Thu Apr-Sep, Sat-Wed Mar & Oct; P) For an evocative glimpse of Jazz Age glamour, drop by this former home of the D'Oyly Carte family of theatre impresarios. Built in the 1920s, its faultless art deco embellishments include original Lalique tulip uplighters, comic bathroom tiles and a stunning saloon – complete with tinkling piano. The croquet terrace leads to deeply shelved subtropical gardens and suddenly revealed vistas of the sea. Hike the 4 miles along the cliffs from Kingswear, or drive.

Dartmouth Castle CASTLE
(EH; 01803-833588; www.english-heritage.org.uk; adult/child £5/3; 10am-5pm Apr-Sep, to 4pm Oct, 10am-4pm Sat & Sun Nov-Mar) Encounter mazy

ON THE WATER

The River Dart is so beautiful it's hard to resist the urge to get out onto the water. **Totnes Kayaks** (☎07799 403788; www.totneskayaks.co.uk; The Quay, Stoke Gabriel; per 1/3/6 hrs £10/23/35; ⏲9am-5pm Apr-Oct), in the placid village of Stoke Gabriel offers you the chance to do just that with their sit-on-top boats. Owner Tom can give you good advice on the best routes depending on the tide – going with the flow might take you up river to Sharpham Wine & Cheese (p353) and Totnes, or down river to Greenway (p351) and Dartmouth. The village of Stoke Gabriel is 9 miles up river from Dartmouth, on the Kingswear side.

TV marine biologist **Monty Halls** (☎01803-431858; www.montyhalls.co.uk/great-escapes/trips/boat-trips; per person £30) is also setting up boat trips from a new Dartmouth base.

passages, atmospheric guard rooms and great views from the battlements. Get there via the tiny, open-top **Castle Ferry** (return ticket £1.40; ⏲10am-4.45pm Apr-Oct).

Blackpool Sands BEACH

Sun-loving locals head 3 miles south of Dartmouth to this long curl of coarse sand, lured by beautiful views, **kayaking** (per hour/day £15/40) and a licensed **cafe** (⏲8am-5pm, later in Jul & Aug) stacked with organic, local produce. Take bus 93 from Dartmouth (25 minutes, hourly Monday to Saturday).

Sleeping

Brown's BOUTIQUE HOTEL ££

(☎01803-832572; www.brownshoteldartmouth.co.uk; 29 Victoria Rd; s £75, d £95-165; P) With leather armchairs and white painted shutters, Browns somehow conjures the feel of a contemporary, unstuffy London club. Rooms are snug but luxurious, designer smellies dot the bathrooms and sketches by local cartoonist Simon Drew line the walls. The cocktail bar is casually cool and the free Friday tapas (5pm to 7pm) draw the crowds – nonguests are welcome.

Just B GUESTHOUSE £

(☎01803-834311; www.justbdartmouth.com; reception 17 Fosse St; r £62-90) The 11 chichi options here range from bedrooms with bathrooms to mini-apartments, all featuring snazzy furnishings, crisp cottons and comfy beds. They're scattered over three central properties, and the 'just B' policy (no '&B' means no breakfast) keeps the price down.

Charity House B&B ££

(☎01803-832176; Collaford Ln; s/d £60/80) Quirky collectibles pepper this 17th century guesthouse in an artful array of driftwood, Panama hats and gleaming bits of boats. Classy bedrooms team stylish fabrics and modern bathrooms with views of a historic church – it's right in the heart of town too.

Eating

TOP CHOICE **Seahorse** SEAFOOD £££

(☎01803-835147; www.seahorserestaurant.co.uk; 5 South Embankment; mains £17-28; ⏲lunch Wed-Sun, dinner Tue-Sat) Only when chefs really know their stuff do they dare to cook food this simply. The house speciality is revelatory – fish grilled over a charcoal fire, and finished with herbs and oil. Superfresh seafood comes largely from Brixham (7 miles away) or Dartmouth Embankment (10 paces), the atmosphere is relaxed; definitely one not to miss. Canny locals opt for the set lunch (2/3 courses £15/20).

Rockfish SEAFOOD ££

(☎01803-832800; www.rockfishdevon.co.uk; 8 South Embankment; mains £9-17; ⏲noon-9.30pm) Weathered boarding and a chilled soundtrack lend this award-winning fish n' chip shop the air of a beatnik boathouse. The menu is a cut above your average chippy; along with cod and haddock there's also monkfish, scallops, oysters and good wine. Eat in (enjoy the atmosphere) or take away (fight the seagulls).

Annabelles Kitchen MODERN BRITISH ££

(☎01803-833540; www.annabelleskitchen.co.uk; 24 South Embankment; mains £16; ⏲lunch Thu-Sat, dinner Tue-Sat) Top-notch local produce combines with creative treatments at this smart restaurant. The scallops come with black pudding, the catch of the day comes with brown shrimp, and a table at the picture window comes with views of a river lined with pastel-painted houses.

Alf Resco CAFE, B&B £
(☎01803-835880; www.cafealfresco.co.uk; Lower St; mains from £6; ⏰7am-2pm ; 📶) Tucked under a huge canvas awning, this hip hangout brings a dash of cosmopolitan charm to town. Rickety wooden chairs and old street signs are scattered around the front terrace, making a great place for brunch alongside the riverboat crews. The B&B rooms (£75) are pure shabby-chic.

Information

Tourist Office (☎01803-834224; www.discoverdartmouth.com; Mayor's Ave; ⏰10am-5pm Mon-Sat, to 2pm Sun Apr-Oct, 10am-4.30pm Mon, Tue, Thu-Sat Nov-Mar)

Getting There & Away

Boat

Dartmouth-Kingswear Ferries (www.dartmouthhigherferry.com; car/pedestrian £4/1; ⏰7am-10.20pm) Dartmouth's Higher and Lower Ferries both take cars and foot passengers, shuttling across the river to Kingswear every six minutes. The slightly bigger Higher Ferry crosses the river 300m north (upstream) of the town centre, but both services connect to the main road in Kingswear, on the east bank.

Dartmouth Steam Railway & River Boat Co (☎01803-555872; www.dartmouthrailriver.co.uk; adult/child £12/7.50) Cruises along the River Dart to Totnes (1¼ hours, two to four daily April to September).

Bus

Plymouth (£6.25, two hours, hourly Monday to Saturday) via Kingsbridge (one hour) Bus 93

Torquay (1¼ hours, hourly Monday to Friday) Bus X81

Totnes (50 minutes, hourly, Monday to Saturday) Bus 81

Train

Regular steam trains (p350) link **Kingswear** with Paignton.

Totnes & Around

POP 8336

Totnes has such a reputation for being alternative that local jokers wrote 'twinned with Narnia' under the town sign. Famous as Devon's hippie haven, for decades eco-conscious Totnes also became Britain's first 'transition town' in 2005, when it began trying to wean itself off a dependence on oil. Sustainability aside, Totnes boasts a tempting vineyard, an important Modernist-era house, a gracious Norman castle and a mass of fine Tudor buildings.

Sights & Activities

High Cross House HISTORIC BUILDING
(NT; ☎01803-842382; www.nationaltrust.org.uk; Dartington Estate; adult/child £7.20/3.70; ⏰10.30am-5pm Mar-Dec; Ⓟ) This exquisite blue and white creation is one of the most important Modernist-era houses in England. Designed by William Lescaze in 1932, its rectilinear and curved lines are deeply evocative of the period, as is the interior of pared-down furniture and smooth wood. It was created as a 'machine for living' and mirroring that, today you're encouraged to experience the space: play the piano, sit on the chairs and browse the art books. But be warned, having settled into one of the streamlined 1930s sofas, it is rather hard to leave. It's all tucked away on the Dartington Estate (p354).

Totnes Castle CASTLE
(EH; ☎01803-864406; www.english-heritage.org.uk; Castle St; adult/child £3.50/2.10; ⏰10am-5pm Apr-Sep, to 6pm July & Aug, to 4pm Oct) The outer keep of Totnes' Norman motte-and-bailey fortress crowns a hill at the top of town, providing engrossing views over higgledy-piggledy rooftops and the river valley. Hunt out the medieval loo, too.

TOP CHOICE **Sharpham Wine & Cheese** VINEYARD
(☎01803-732203; www.sharpham.com; ⏰10am-5pm Apr-Sep) Row upon row of vines line up on sloping hills more reminiscent of Chablis than south Devon. Tours and tastings range from self-guided rambles (£2.50), to a tasting of wines and cheeses (£7-10), right up to full blown tours and tutored tastings (£15-55). The award-winning alfresco **cafe** (☎01803-732178; www.vineyardcafe.co.uk; Sharpham Estate, nr Totnes; mains £10-15; snacks £4-7; ⏰10am-5pm Apr-Oct) dishes up gourmet air-dried hams, smoked fish and (inevitably) superb cheese and wine – book ahead. The vineyard is 3 miles south of Totnes, signed off the A381. A more atmospheric option is to hike from town along the Dart Valley Trail.

Canoe Adventures CANOEING
(☎01803-865301; www.canoeadventures.co.uk; adult/child £22/17) Voyages in 12-seater Canadian canoes – the monthly moonlit paddles are a treat.

Sleeping

Dartington Hall (TOP CHOICE) B&B ££
(☎01803-847000; www.dartington.org; Dartington Estate; s £39-104 d £99-209; P) The wings of this idyllic, ancient manor house have been carefully converted into rooms that range from heritage-themed to deluxe-modern. Ask for one overlooking the grassy, cobble-fringed courtyard and settle back for a truly tranquil night's sleep.

Steam Packet INN ££
(☎01803-863880; www.steampacketinn.co.uk; St Peters Quay, Totnes; s/d/f £60/80/95; P) It's almost as if the minimalist bedrooms of this wharf-side former warehouse have been plucked from the pages of a design magazine; expect painted wood panels, willow arrangements and neutral tones. Opt for a river-view room, then watch the world float by.

Old Forge B&B ££
(☎01803-862174; www.oldforgetotnes.com; Seymour Pl; s £60, d £72-92, f £105; P📶) This 600-year-old B&B used to be a smithy and the town jail – thankfully comfort has now replaced incarceration: deep red and sky blue furnishings cosy up to bright throws and spa baths. The family room has its own decked sun terrace and there's a hot tub and a walled garden too.

Eating & Drinking

Riverford Field Kitchen (TOP CHOICE) BRITISH ££
(☎01803-762074; www.riverford.co.uk; Wash Barn; 2/3 courses £20/27; ⊙lunch daily, dinner Mon-Sat; ✎) At this futuristic farm-bistro, vegetables are plucked to order from the fields in front of you and the meats are organic and locally-sourced. Eating is a convivial affair – sitting at trestle tables you pass platters laden with food to your neighbours. Rich flavours and creative treatments might include garlic char-grilled chicken plus British veg that's transformed by saffron, cumin, pistachio and pecan. To eat here, you need to book in advance, and take a free tour (guided or self-led) of the fields. The farm is 3 miles west of Totnes.

DARTINGTON ESTATE

Henry VIII gave this beguiling 800-acre **estate** (☎01803-847000; www.dartington.org; Dartington, near Totnes) to two of his wives (Catherines Howard and Parr), now it's home to a B&B (p354), the 1930s High Cross House (p353), the Barn art-house cinema, a mellow pub (p354), landscaped grounds and a medieval great hall that hosts events ranging from classical music to literature festivals. The estate is 1½ miles northwest of Totnes.

Rumour PUB, RESTAURANT ££
(☎01803-864682; www.rumourtotnes.com; 30 High St; mains £7-15; ⊙dinner daily, lunch Mon-Sat) It's so friendly here it's almost like dining in a friend's front room. The menu includes favourites like sea bass with samphire, south Devon steak, and roast beetroot and goats' cheese, as well as seriously good pizzas and irresistible puds.

White Hart GASTROPUB ££
(☎01803-847111; www.dartingtonhall.com; Dartington Estate; mains £12-17; ✎) Head here for lawn-side tables, real fires and a quality selection of local meats, fish and veggie options. Liquid delights include cloudy Devon cider, fragrant Sharpham wine and tangy local Otter Ale.

Willow VEGETARIAN £
(87 High St; mains £8; ⊙lunch Mon-Sat, dinner Wed, Fri & Sat; ✎) A long-time hangout for Totnes' New Agers. Tuck into couscous, quiches, hotpots and homemade cakes – look out for the curry nights, too.

Information

Tourist Office (☎01803-863168; www.totnesinformation.co.uk; Coronation Rd; ⊙9am-5pm Mon-Fri & 10am-4pm Sat Apr-Oct, 10am-4pm Mon-Fri & to 1pm Sat Nov-Mar)

Getting There & Away

BOAT Boats shuttle down river to Dartmouth (p353).

BUS **Torquay** (one hour, hourly Monday to Saturday, four on Sunday) Bus X80.

Dartmouth (50 minutes, hourly, Monday to Saturday) Bus X81.

TRAIN Trains go at least hourly to **Exeter** (£6, 35 minutes) and **Plymouth** (£6, 30 minutes). The privately run **South Devon Steam Railway** (www.southdevonrailway.org; adult/child return £12/7; ⊙4-9 trains daily Apr-Oct) chuffs to **Buckfastleigh**, on the edge of Dartmoor.

Plymouth

POP 258,700

Plymouth is decidedly different from the rest of Devon. The county's biggest city is an important Royal Navy port, thanks to its location beside a vast, sheltered bay. For decades, some have dismissed Plymouth as sprawling and ugly, pointing to architectural eyesores and sometimes palpable poverty. But the arrival of two celebrity chefs and ongoing waterfront regeneration begs a rethink. Plymouth is also packed with possibilities: swim in an art deco lido; tour a gin distillery; learn to kayak; roam an aquarium; take a boat trip across the bay; then see a show and party till dawn. And the ace in the pack? Plymouth Hoe – a cafe-dotted, wide grassy headland offering captivating views of a boat-studded bay.

History

Plymouth's history is dominated by the sea. The first recorded cargo left in 1211 and by the late 16th century it was the port of choice for explorers and adventurers. It's waved off Sir Francis Drake, Sir Walter Raleigh, the fleet that defeated the Spanish Armada, the pilgrims who founded America, Charles Darwin, Captain Cook and countless boats carrying emigrants to Australia and New Zealand.

During WWII Plymouth suffered horrendously at the hands of the Luftwaffe – more than 1000 civilians died in the Blitz, which reduced the city centre to rubble. The 21st century has brought regeneration to waterfront areas, a £200-million Drake Circus shopping centre and a growing university sector, bringing a burst of new buildings and 30,000 students to the heart of town.

Sights

Plymouth Hoe HEADLAND

Francis Drake supposedly spied the Spanish fleet from this grassy headland overlooking **Plymouth Sound** (the city's wide bay); the fabled bowling green where he finished his game was probably where his **statue** now stands. Later the Hoe became a Victorian-era holiday spot and the wide promenade is backed by an array of multistoreyed villas and once-grand hotels.

The red-and-white-striped former lighthouse, **Smeaton's Tower** (☎01752-304774; The Hoe; adult/child £2.50/1; ⏰10am-noon & 1-3pm Tue-Sat Apr-Oct), was built 14 miles offshore on the Eddystone Rocks in 1759, then moved to the Hoe in 1882. Climbing its 93 steps provides an illuminating insight into lighthouse keepers' lives and stunning views of the city, Dartmoor and the sea. Evidence of Plymouth's martial past comes in the form of the **Citadel**, a huge 17th-century fortress (still an army base), and scores of **war memorials**; the largest bears the names of 23,186 Commonwealth sailors who were lost at sea during WWI and WWII.

Barbican NEIGHBOURHOOD

(www.plymouthbarbican.com) To get an idea of what Plymouth was like before the Blitz, head for the Barbican, a district of cobbled streets and Tudor and Jacobean buildings, many now converted into galleries, antiques shops and restaurants.

The Pilgrim Fathers' *Mayflower* set sail for America from here on 16 September 1620. The **Mayflower Steps** mark the approximate embarkation point – track down the passenger list displayed on the side of **Island House** nearby. Scores of other famous departures are also commemorated at the steps, including Captain James Cook's 1768 voyage of discovery, and the first emigrant ships to New Zealand.

National Marine Aquarium AQUARIUM

(☎0844 893 7938; www.national-aquarium.co.uk; Rope Walk; adult/child £12/8; ⏰10am-5pm daily, to 6pm Apr-Sep) The sharks here swim in coral seas that teem with moray eels and vividly coloured fish – there's even a loggerhead turtle called Snorkel who was rescued from a Cornish beach. Walk-through glass arches and see huge rays glide over your head, while the gigantic Atlantic Reef tank reveals what's lurking a few miles offshore.

FREE **City Museum & Art Gallery** MUSEUM

(☎01752-304774; Drake Circus; ⏰10am-5pm Tue-Sat) Imaginative displays conjure up Plymouth's rich history – look out for Napoleonic-era bone model ships and the skis of doomed Antarctic explorer Captain Robert Falcon Scott – a Plymouth man.

Plymouth Gin Distillery DISTILLERY

(☎01752-665292; www.plymouthgin.com; 60 Southside St; tours £6; ⏰half-hourly 10.30am-4.30pm Mon-Sat, 11.30am-3.30pm Sun) They've been making gin here since 1793, making it the world's oldest producer. The Royal Navy ferried it round the world in countless officers' messes and the brand was specified in the first recorded recipe for a dry martini

Plymouth

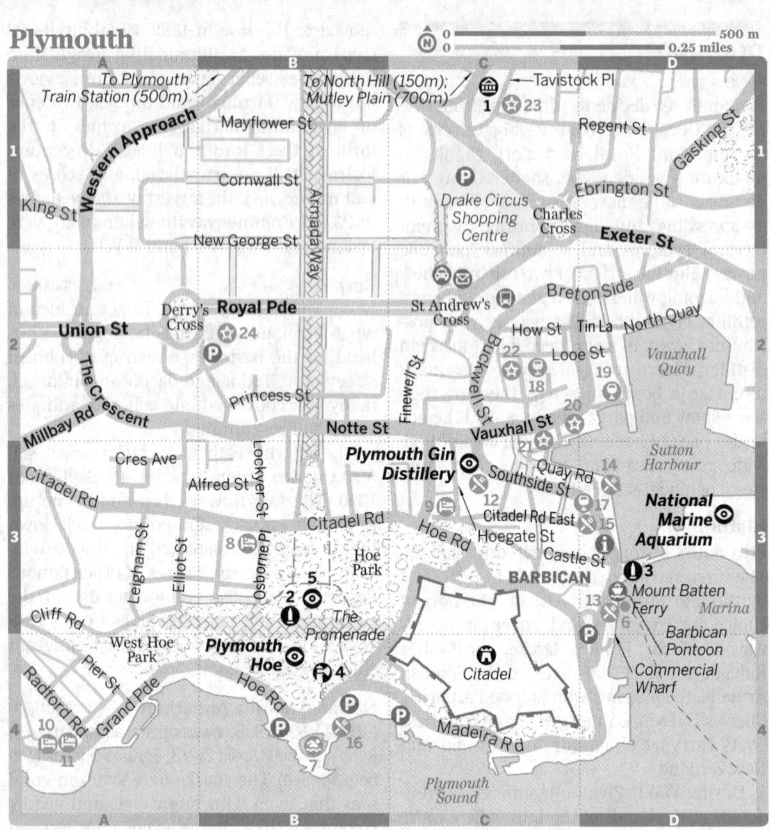

in the 1930s. Tours wind past the stills and take in a tutored tasting before depositing you in the heavily beamed medieval bar for a free tipple.

Activities

TOP CHOICE **Tinside Lido** SWIMING POOL
(☎01752-261915; www.everyoneactive.com; Hoe Rd; adult/child £3.65/2.40; ⏲10am-6pm Jun-Sep) Taking a dip at this Jazz Age, open-air swimspot is an unforgettable experience. Its 1935, art-deco design sees cream curves and light-and-dark blue tiles sweep gracefully out from the foot of the Hoe. Plunge into the chilly salt water to join the regulars doing laps and the youngsters larking around beside the fountains.

Boat Trips BOAT TOUR, FERRY
Plymouth Boat Trips (☎01752-253153; www.plymouthboattrips.co.uk; Barbican Pontoon) offers a wide range of options – the pick is a 30-minute blast-across-the-bay to the quaint, pub-packed Cornish fishing villages of **Kingsand** and **Cawsand** (adult/child £8/4, four daily April to October). They also do one-hour **harbour cruises** (adult/child £6.50/3.50, four daily) to the warships at Plymouth's naval base, and **fishing trips** (per 3 hours £20) – have your catch turned into a meal at their funky **Boathouse Cafe** (2 Commercial Wharf; dishes £2-8; ⏲9am-5pm Sun-Thu, 8am-9pm Fri & Sat) for £10 extra.

The little yellow **Mount Batten Ferry** (www.mountbattenferry.com; adult/child return £3/2) shuttles from the Barbican Pontoon across to the Mount Batten Peninsula (10 minutes, half hourly).

Mount Batten Centre BOATING
(☎01752-404567; www.mount-batten-centre.com; 70 Lawrence Rd, Mount Batten Peninsula) Two-hour taster sessions include those in sailing dinghies (£20) and sit-on-top kayaks (£17).

Plymouth

Top Sights

	National Marine Aquarium	D3
	Plymouth Gin Distillery	C3
	Plymouth Hoe	B4

Sights

1	City Museum & Art Gallery	C1
2	Drake Statue	B3
	Island House	(see 15)
3	Mayflower Steps	D3
4	Smeaton's Tower	B4
5	War Memorial	B3

Activities, Courses & Tours

6	Plymouth Boat Trips	D3
7	Tinside Lido	B4

Sleeping

8	Bowling Green	B3
9	Four Seasons	C3
10	Rusty Anchor	A4
11	Sea Breezes	A4

Eating

12	Barbican Kitchen	C3
13	Boathouse Cafe	D3
14	Cap'n Jaspers	D3
15	Platters	D3
16	Terrace	B4

Drinking

17	Dolpin	D3
18	Minerva	C2
19	View 2	D2

Entertainment

20	Annabel's	C2
21	Barbican Live Lounge	C2
22	Plymouth Arts Centre	C2
23	Ride	C1
24	Theatre Royal	B2

Two-day courses include kayaking (£86), sailing (£160) and windsurfing (£136).

Sleeping

Fertile B&B hunting grounds are just back from the Hoe, especially around Citadel Rd.

TOP CHOICE St Elizabeth's House BOUTIQUE HOTEL £££
(☎01752-344840; www.stelizabeths.co.uk; Longbrook St; d £90-199; P wi-fi) This pamper palace overflows with jaw-dropping bathrooms, from free-standing tubs and wetrooms, to waterfall baths with a TV above your toes. The bedrooms are the size of suites while the suites are the size of apartments. It's all set amid sloping lawns in the suburb-village of Plympton St Maurice, 5 miles east of Plymouth.

Sea Breezes B&B ££
(☎01752-667205; www.plymouth-bedandbreakfast.co.uk; 28 Grand Pde; s/d/f £40/70/95) At this deeply comfortable guesthouse, fresh decor ranges from subtle gingham to groovy swirls. The bathrooms gleam, the towels are fluffy and the breakfasts feature melon, strawberries and hand-cut toast. Bag a front-facing bedroom (go for the one with the window seat) for smashing sea views.

Bowling Green HOTEL ££
(☎01752-209090; www.thebowlinggreenplymouth.com; 10 Osborne Pl; s/d/f £50/70/80; P wi-fi) Some of the airy cream-and-white rooms in this family-run hotel look out onto the modern incarnation of Drake's famous bowling green. If you tire of watching people throw woods after jacks you can play chess in the conservatory.

Four Seasons B&B £
(☎01752-223591; www.fourseasonsguesthouse.co.uk; 207 Citadel Rd East; s £32-8, d £48-64) Treats are everywhere at this B&B, from the big bowls of free sweets to the mounds of Devon bacon for breakfast. They've got the basics right, too: tasteful rooms decorated in gold and cream.

Rusty Anchor B&B ££
(☎01752-663924; www.therustyanchor-plymouth.co.uk; 30 Grand Pde; s/d/ £35/70) Decorative driftwood and shells lend this relaxed B&B a flavour of the sea; four rooms have views of Plymouth Sound's wide waters. Owner Jan will try to meet your breakfast requests – be they kippers, pancakes or home-made rolls.

Eating

The arrival of two celebrity chefs is changing Plymouth's eating scene. As well as Hugh Fearnley-Whittingstall's new gaff, Gary

ROYAL WILLIAM YARD

This cluster of 1830s waterfront warehouses once supplied stores for countless Royal Navy vessels. Today it's home to sleek apartments, a couple of **art galleries**, a relaxed **pub** and a string of **eateries**; the best being River Cottage Canteen and the Royal William Bakery. A simple **exhibition** (⏲9am-4pm Mon-Thurs, to noon Fri) outlines the yard's history; roaming past the former slaughterhouse, bakery, brewery and cooperage underlines just how big this victualling operation was. The yard is 2 miles west of the city centre, hop on bus 34 (8 minutes, one-to-two hourly), better still catch the **ferry** (www.royalwilliamyardharbour.co.uk; adult/child single £2.50/1.50; ⏲10.30am-6pm Apr-Sep) that runs from the Barbican Pontoon.

Rhodes' Hoe-side **eatery** (www.rhodesatthedome.co.uk) is due to open in 2012.

TOP CHOICE River Cottage Canteen & Deli MODERN BRITISH ££
(☎01752-252702; www.rivercottage.net; Royal William Yard; mains £7-15; ⏲breakfast, lunch & dinner Tue-Sat, breakfast & lunch Sun; ✎) Television-chef Hugh Fearnley-Whittingstall has long campaigned for local, sustainable, seasonal, organic produce, and that's exactly what you get here. Expect meats roasted in front of an open fire, fish simply grilled and familiar veg given a revelatory makeover.

Barbican Kitchen MODERN BRITISH ££
(☎01752-604448; www.barbicankitchen.com; 60 Southside St; mains £5-18; ✎) In this busy bistro the stone interior fizzes with bursts of shocking pink and lime. The food is attention grabbing, too – try the confit duck salad or the herb gnocchi with mushrooms, garlic and pine nuts. The beef medallions, with Devon blue cheese sauce, are divine.

Royal William Bakery CAFE, BAKERY £
(www.royalwilliambakery.com; Royal William Yard; mains £5; ⏲8.30am-4.30pm Tue-Sun) Piles of huge, just-cooked loaves, tureens full of soup, crumbly pastries and irresistible cakes – this is a bakery like few others. The serve-yourself style is so laidback you don't get a bill – just tell them what you've eaten and they'll tot it up at the end.

Platters SEAFOOD ££
(www.platters-restaurant.co.uk; 12 The Barbican; mains £16) A down-to-earth eatery with fish so fresh it's just stopped flapping – try the scallops sautéed in garlic butter or the grilled mackerel.

Rock Salt MODERN BRITISH ££
(☎01752-225522; www.rocksaltcafe.co.uk; 31 Stonehouse St; mains £7-20 ; ⏲breakfast, lunch & dinner Tue-Sat; 📶) They bill it as good honest food, and it is: great ingredients and creative flavour combos delivered with flair in a chilled-out brasserie. It's set slightly south of Plymouth's edgy nightclub strip, Union St.

Cap'n Jaspers CAFE £
(www.capn-jaspers.co.uk; Whitehouse Pier, Quay Rd; snacks £3-5; ⏲7.30am-midnight) Unique and slightly insane, this cabin-kiosk has been delighting bikers, tourists, locals and fishermen for decades with motorised gadgets and teaspoons attached to the counter by chains. Try the crab rolls, the filling could have been caught by the bloke sitting next to you.

Terrace CAFE, BAR £
(www.theterracecafebar.co.uk; Hoe Rd; snacks £3-6; ⏲breakfast & lunch) With Plymouth Sound stretching out below and chilled tunes on the sound system this is the perfect spot to sip a glass of wine, watch the boats, and tuck into huge jacket potatoes. On fine summer evenings they keep the bar open till late.

Drinking

Like any naval city, Plymouth has a more than lively nightlife. Union St is club-land; Mutley Plain and North Hill have a studenty vibe, while the Barbican has more restaurants amid the bars. All three areas get rowdy, especially at weekends.

Dolpin PUB
(14 The Barbican) This wonderfully unreconstructed Barbican boozer is all scuffed tables, padded bench seats and an authentic, no-nonsense atmosphere. Feeling peckish? Get a fish n' chip takeaway from next-door-but-one, then settle down with your pint.

View 2 BAR
(www.view2barbican.co.uk; Vauxhall Quay; ⏲10am-midnight Sun-Thu, 10am-3am Fri, 10am-2am Sat)

Just round from the heart of the Barbican, this cool venue's flagstone terrace is ideal for a waterside drink. Expect comedy, quiz nights, soul, funk and R&B.

Minerva PUB
(www.minervainn.co.uk; 31 Looe St) Stone walls, wooden benches, chunks of sailing ships, real ales, live music and Thursday night jam sessions make this 16th-century drinking den a local favourite.

✩ Entertainment

Annabel's CABARET, CLUB
(www.annabelscabaret.co.uk; 88 Vauxhall St; ⌚8.30am-2am Thu-Sat) The stage spots in this quirky venue are filled by an eclectic collection of acts (expect anything from comedy to burlesque). Crowd-pleasing tunes fill the dance floor while classy cocktails fill your glass.

Barbican Live Lounge NIGHTCLUB
(www.barbicanlivelounge.com; 11 The Parade; ⌚8pm-4am Wed-Sat) The live music in this buzzing, barrel-roofed club ranges from rock and jazz, to indie, blues and soul.

Ride NIGHTCLUB
(www.ridecafe.co.uk; 46 Tavistock Pl; ⌚9pm-2am Tue-Sun, 11am-2am Mon) Student hangout with a tented, outdoor music stage that hosts DJs, bands, open mic and acoustic Sundays.

Plymouth Arts Centre CINEMA, CAFE
(www.plymouthac.org.uk; 38 Looe Street; ⌚10am-8.30pm Tue-Sat, 4-8.30pm Sun) This cultural hot-spot combines an independent cinema, modern-art exhibitions, and a licensed, vegetarian-friendly cafe.

Theatre Royal THEATRE
(www.theatreroyal.com; Royal Pde) Plymouth's main theatre stages large-scale touring and home-grown productions; its studio space, the Drum, is renowned for featuring new writing.

ℹ Information

Plymouth Library (Drake Circus; per 30 min £2; ⌚9am-7pm Mon & Fri, to 5pm Tue-Thu & Sat) Internet access.

Police Station (Charles Cross; ⌚24hr)

Tourist Office (☎01752-306330; www.visitplymouth.co.uk; 3 The Barbican; ⌚9am-5pm Mon-Sat, 10am-4pm Sun Apr-Oct, 9am-5pm Mon-Fri, 10am-4pm Sat Nov-Mar)

ℹ Getting There & Away

Bus

Birmingham (£53, 5½ hours, four daily)
Bristol (£31, three hours, four daily)
Exeter (£6.50, 1¼ hours, two-hourly Monday to Saturday, three on Sunday) Bus X38.
London (£33, five to six hours, four daily)
Penzance (£9, 3½ hours, four daily)

On Sundays between June and mid-September the **Transmoor Link**, bus 82, makes five cross-Dartmoor trips from Plymouth to Exeter, via Yelverton, Princetown, Postbridge and Moretonhampstead

Train

Bristol (£25, two hours, two or three per hour)
Exeter (£8, one hour, two or three per hour)
London Paddington (£45, 3¼ hours, half-hourly)
Penzance (£8, two hours, half-hourly)
Totnes (£5, 30 minutes, half-hourly)

Around Plymouth

Buckland Abbey HISTORIC BUILDING
(NT; ☎01822-853607; www.nationaltrust.org.uk; near Yelverton; adult/child £8/4; ⌚10.30am-5.30pm Mar-Oct, 11am-4.30pm Fri-Sun Nov-Dec & Feb; Ⓟ) Buckland Abbey was originally a Cistercian monastery and 13th-century abbey church, but was transformed into a family residence by Sir Richard Grenville before being purchased in 1581 by his cousin and nautical rival Sir Francis Drake. Its displays include **Drake's Drum**, said to beat by itself when Britain is in danger of being invaded. Look out for the fine Elizabethan garden and estate walks too.

Buckland Abbey is 11 miles north of Plymouth. You'll need your own transport to get here.

Dartmoor National Park

Dartmoor is an ancient, compelling landscape, so different from the rest of Devon that a visit feels like falling straight into Tolkien's *Return of the King*. Exposed granite hills (called tors) crest on the horizon, linked by swathes of honey-tinged moors. On the fringes, streams tumble over moss-smothered boulders in woods of twisted trees. The centre of this 368-sq-mile wilderness is the higher moor; an elemental, treeless expanse. Moody and utterly empty, you'll either find its remote

Dartmoor National Park

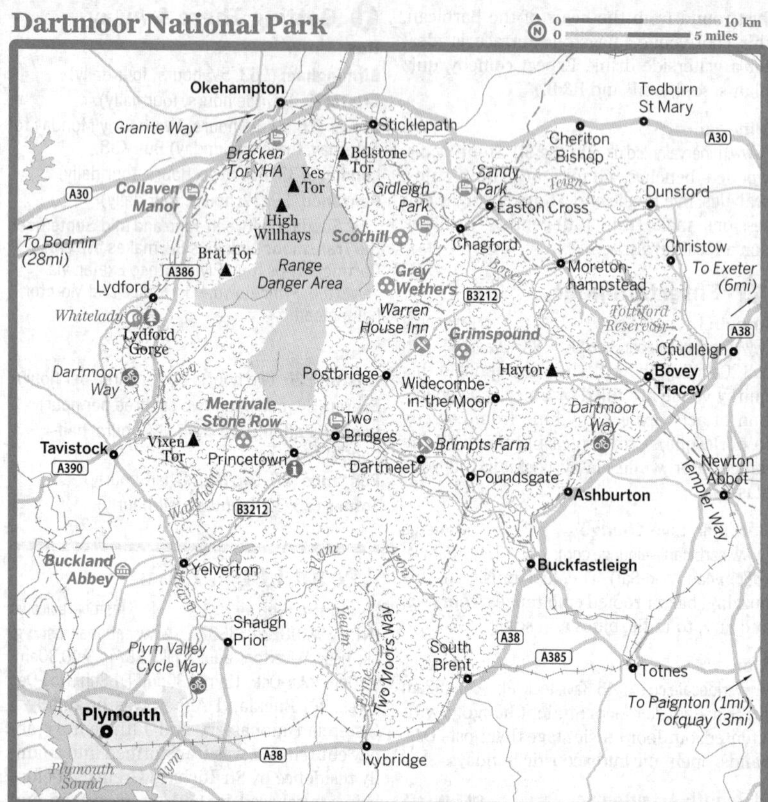

beauty exhilarating or chilling, or quite possibly a bit of both.

Dartmoor can be picture-postcard pretty, and on sunny summer days it's idyllic; ponies wander at will and sheep graze beside the road. But peel back the picturesque and there's a core of hard reality – stock prices mean many farmers struggle to make a profit. In this mercurial place the urban illusion of control over our surroundings is stripped away and the elements are in charge. Steven Spielberg chose to film part of Michael Morpurgo's WWI epic *War Horse* in this landscape; a century earlier it inspired Sir Arthur Conan Doyle to write *The Hound of the Baskervilles*. In sleeting rain and swirling mists you suddenly see why – the moor morphs into a bleak wilderness where tales of a phantom hound can seem very real indeed

Dartmoor is also a natural breakout zone with a checklist of charms: superb walking, cycling, horse riding, climbing and white-water kayaking; rustic pubs and fancy restaurants; wild camping nooks and country-house hotels – perfect boltholes when the fog rolls in. It is administered by the Dartmoor National Park Authority (p361).

Activities

Walking

Some 730 miles of public footpath snake across Dartmoor's open heaths and rocky tors. Crimson's *Dartmoor Walks* (£12) has 28 hikes of up to 9 miles, its *Dartmoor Short Walks* (£8) focuses on family-friendly treks. Tourist offices can advise on trails and **guided walks** (www.dartmoor.gov.uk/visiting; £4) – themes include *War Horse*, Sherlock Holmes, myths, geology, industry and archaeology; highlights are the memorable moonlit rambles amid stone rows.

Cycling

Routes include the 11-mile **Granite Way**, which runs along a former railway line between Okehampton and Lydford. The 13-mile **Princetown & Burrator Mountain Bike Route** is a challenging moorland circuit along tracks and bridleways taking in Princetown, Sheepstor village and Burrator Reservoir. Tourist offices also sell the *Dartmoor Cycling Map* (£13).

Devon Cycle Hire BIKE HIRE
(☎01837-861141; www.devoncyclehire.co.uk; Sourton Down, near Okehampton; per half/full day £12/14; ⏰9am-5pm Apr-Sep) On the Granite Way.

Horse Riding

Horse riding costs around £20/36 per hour/half-day.

Babeny Farm HORSE RIDING
(☎01364-631296; Poundsgate, nr Ashburton) All experience levels.

Cholwell HORSE RIDING
(☎01822-810526; www.cholwellridingstables.co.uk; nr Mary Tavy) Caters for novices and experts.

Shilstone Rocks HORSE RIDING
(☎01364-621281; www.dartmoorstables.com; Widecombe-in-the-Moor) Beginners welcome.

Tor Royal HORSE RIDING
(☎01822-890189; www.torroyal.co.uk; nr Yelverton) Riders need some previous experience.

White Water

The raging River Dart makes Dartmoor a top spot for thrill-seekers. Experienced kayakers can get access advice from the **Dartmoor National Park Authority** (DNPA; ☎01822-890414; www.dartmoor.gov.uk), and **CRS Adventures** (☎01364-653444; www.crsadventures.co.uk) near Widecombe-in-the-Moor runs white-water rafting (per 4 people £180). Rivers are only open between October and March.

Climbing

Adventure Okehampton ACTIVITY CENTRE
(☎01837-53916; www.adventureokehampton.com; Klondyke Rd, Okehampton; per half day £15; ⏰school holidays only) Runs both indoor and outdoor climbing sessions, plus activities including archery, abseiling and bushcraft.

Rock Centre ROCK CLIMBING
(☎01626-852717; www.rockcentre.co.uk; Rock House, Chudleigh; per hr £40)

Sleeping

From spoil-yourself-silly luxury – Gidleigh Park (p365) and 22 Mill St (p365) – to snoozing under the stars, with some lovely thatched cottages in between, Dartmoor has a wide range of sleeping options.

The **YHA** (www.yha.org.uk) has hostels near Postbridge (p363) and Okehampton (p366), plus three bare-bones camping barns, including one near Postbridge (p363). Independent hostels and bunkhouses include those at Moretonhampstead (p364) and Princetown (p362).

Dartmoor is also perfect for 'wild camping'; pitching a tent on some sections of open moor is allowed provided simple but strict rules are followed; tourist offices can advise.

Eating & Drinking

Dartmoor caters for all tastes and budgets. Chagford boasts the double-Michelin starred Gidleigh Park (p365) and the polished 22 Mill St (p365). Then there's stylish bar food at Widecombe's Rugglestone Inn (p364), hiker-friendly grub and authentic atmosphere at the Warren House Inn (p363) near Postbridge, and some of Devon's best cream teas at Brimpts Farm (p363).

Information

The free *Enjoy Dartmoor* magazine is packed with details of activities, attractions, campsites

WARNING

The military uses three adjoining areas of Dartmoor as training ranges where live ammunition is used. Tourist offices can explain their locations; they're also marked on OS maps. You're advised to check if the route you're planning falls within a range; if it does, find out if firing is taking place from the **Firing Information Service** (☎0800 458 4868; www.dartmoor-ranges.co.uk). During the day red flags fly at the edges of in-use ranges, while red flares burn at night. Even when there's no firing, beware of unidentified metal objects lying in the grass. Don't touch anything you find: note its position and report it to the **Commandant** (☎01837-650010).

DARTMOOR HIKES

The 18-mile **Templer Way** is a two- to three-day leg stretch from Haytor to Teignmouth, while the **West Devon Way** forms a 36-mile trek linking Okehampton and Plymouth. The 90-mile **Dartmoor Way** circles from Buckfastleigh in the south, through Moretonhampstead, northwest to Okehampton and south through Lydford to Tavistock. The 102-mile **Two Moors Way** runs from Ivybridge, across Dartmoor and Exmoor to Lynmouth, on the north Devon coast.

Be prepared for Dartmoor's notoriously fickle weather and carry a map and compass as many trails are not waymarked. The Ordnance Survey (OS) Explorer 1:25,000 map No 28, *Dartmoor* (£7.99), is the most comprehensive and shows park boundaries and MOD firing-range areas (p361).

and the full diary of guided walks. Pick it up at tourist offices and venues across the moor.

Dartmoor's official visitor website is www.dartmoor.co.uk.

Higher Moorland Tourist Office (DNPA Princetown; ☎01822-890414; www.dartmoor.gov.uk; ⊙10am-5pm Apr-Sep, to 4pm Mar & Oct, 10.30am-3.30pm Thu-Sun Nov-Feb) Dartmoor's main tourist office in Princetown also stocks walking guides, maps and clothes.

DNPA Haytor (☎01364-661520; ⊙10am-4pm Apr-Oct, 10.30am-3.30pm Thur-Sun Nov-Mar)

DNPA Postbridge (☎01822-880272; ⊙10am-5pm Apr-Sep, to 4pm Oct)

ℹ Getting There & Around

Public transport is an option, but planning is needed. Tourist offices stock bus timetables; see also www.journeydevon.co.uk.

Bus

For unlimited Sunday travel on most moorland bus routes, try the **Dartmoor Sunday Rover** (adult/child/family £7.50/5/16). Available from drivers or at Plymouth train station.

Key routes onto the moor:

» Plymouth to Tavistock, via Yelverton (hourly) Bus 83/84/86.

» Barnstaple to Tavistock (2¼ hours), via Lydford and Okehampton (one to four daily). Bus 118.

» Exeter to Moretonhampstead (two hourly Monday to Saturday). Bus 35.

There are several key routes around the Moor, be warned: some are seasonal.

» Tavistock to Merrivale and Princetown (three daily, Monday to Saturday, year-round) one bus a day goes onto Two Bridges and Postbridge. Bus 98

» Plymouth to Exeter (2½ hours) via Yelverton, Princetown, Two Bridges, Postbridge, Warren House Inn and Moretonhampstead. Runs on summer Sundays only (June to mid-September, five buses). Transmoor Link (bus 82)/Bus 8.

» Newton Abbot to Haytor, Widecombe-in-the-Moor and Bovey Tracey. Runs on summer Saturdays only (April to October, four buses). Haytor Hoppa.

PRINCETOWN

POP 1767

Set in the heart of the remote, higher moor, Princetown is dominated by the grey, foreboding bulk of Dartmoor Prison. When the jail stopped housing American and French prisoners of war in the early 1800s, the town fell into decline and on bad weather days it can still have a bleak feel. But it's also a useful insight into the harsh realities of moorland life and makes an atmospheric base for some excellent walks.

The prison reopened as a convict jail in 1850 and just up from its looming gates the **Dartmoor Prison Heritage Centre** (☎01822-322130; www.dartmoor-prison.co.uk; adult/child £3/2; ⊙9.30am-12.30pm & 1.30-4pm) provides a chilling glimpse of life inside – look out for straitjackets, manacles and mock-up cells, and the escape tale of Frankie 'the mad axeman' Mitchell, supposedly sprung by 1960s gangster twins the Krays. The centre also sells the bizarrely cheery garden ornaments made by today's inmates.

The **tourist office** (p362) has displays worth seeing; it also used to be Princetown's main hotel and is where Arthur Conan Doyle began *The Hound of the Baskervilles*. Staff can point you towards the real-life locations that inspired the book, such as nearby Foxtor Mires, which appear as Grimpen Mire.

The **Prince of Wales** (☎01822-890219; www.theprinceofwalesprincetown.co.uk; Tavistock Rd; dm £12, breakfast £5) pub runs the pick of Dartmoor's bunk-houses, boasting central heating and double glazing (on the moor, this matters), snazzy showers, a cool communal lounge and (joy of joys) a drying room. The bar is famous for its three open fires, mixed grill platters the size of tea trays and pints of full-bodied, Princetown-brewed Jail Ale.

Getting There & Away

Key bus routes:

» Tavistock to Princetown, one service a day goes onto Two Bridges and Postbridge. Bus 98 (3 daily, Monday to Saturday).

» Plymouth to Exeter (2½ hours) via Yelverton, Princetown, Two Bridges, Postbridge, Warren House Inn and Moretonhampstead. Transmoor Link (Sunday only, June to mid-September, five buses).

POSTBRIDGE

There's not much to the quaint village of Postbridge apart from a cluster of shops, pubs and whitewashed houses. It's best known for its 13th-century **clapper bridge** across the East Dart, made of large granite slabs supported by stone pillars.

There's a **tourist office** (p362) in the car park, and a post office and shop nearby.

Sleeping & Eating

Two Bridges HOTEL, RESTAURANT £££

(01822-890581; www.twobridges.co.uk; Two Bridges; s £95-125, d £140-190; P) Polished wood panels, hand-hewn furniture and the sense of entering a cocoon-like country house define this elegant moorland hotel. Squishy leather sofas frame huge inglenook fireplaces in the bar, former guests Wallis Simpson, Winston Churchill and Vivien Leigh probably enjoyed sitting here, too. The elegant restaurant serves dishes packed with rich local ingredients: lunch mains cost around £12 and a three-course dinner £28. It's 3 miles southwest of Postbridge.

Brimpts Farm B&B, CAFE £

(0845-0345968; www.brimptsfarm.co.uk; campsite per person £2.50, s/d £30/55; cafe: 11.30am-5.30pm weekends & school holidays; P) The brightly painted, country-cottage bedrooms above this farmhouse have views over *War Horse* location, Combestone Tor. Converted barns provide another batch of rooms and there's back-to-nature camping too. Brimpts is also one of the best moorland cream tea venues, offering freshly baked scones, home-made jams and utterly gooey clotted cream (£4.50). The farm is signed off the B3357, Two Bridges–Dartmeet road.

Runnage YHA CAMPING BARN £

(0800 0191 700; www.yha.org.uk; dm £9; P) Set in a working farm, this converted hayloft sees you rolling out your sleeping bag to a soundtrack of bleating sheep. It's 1.5 miles east of Postbridge: take the 'Widecombe' turning off the Moretonhampstead road.

Bellever YHA HOSTEL £

(0845-371 9622; www.yha.org.uk; dm £18; P) A characterful former farm on the edge of a conifer plantation, with a huge kitchen, lots of rustic stone walls and cosy dorms. It's a mile south of Postbridge.

TOP CHOICE **Warren House Inn** PUB £

(www.warrenhouseinn.co.uk; mains £6-12; bar: 11am-11pm; food: noon–8.30pm) Marooned amid miles of open moor, this former tin miners' haunt exudes the kind of hospitality you only get in a pub in the middle of nowhere. A Dartmoor institution, its stone floors, trestle tables and hearty food are warmed by a fire that's reputedly been crackling since 1845. The Warreners' Pie (local rabbit) is legendary. Between November and March the pub closes at 5pm on Monday and Tuesday. It's on the B3212, 2 miles northeast of Postbridge.

Getting There & Away

Bus 98 runs to Princetown (one per day Monday to Saturday).

Postbridge is also served by the **Transmoor Link** (Sunday only, June to mid-September) service from Plymouth to Exeter via Yelverton, Princetown, Two Bridges, Postbridge, Warren House Inn and Moretonhampstead.

WIDECOMBE-IN-THE-MOOR

POP 566

This is archetypal Dartmoor, down to the ponies grazing on the village green. Widecombe's honey-grey 15th-century buildings

> **DRIVING ON DARTMOOR**
>
> Dartmoor's roads are exciting to drive, but large stretches are unfenced grazing so you'll come across Dartmoor ponies, sheep and even cows in the middle of the road. Many sections have a 40mph speed limit. Car parks on the moor can be little more than lay-bys; their surface can be rough to very rough.

PREHISTORIC DARTMOOR

With an estimated 11,000 monuments, Dartmoor is ripe for archaeological explorations. It has the largest concentration of Bronze Age (c 2300-700 BC) remains in the country, 75 stone rows (half the national total), 18 stone circles and 5000 huts.

The **Merrivale Stone Rows**, near Princetown, are a handy one-stop shop for most monument types. The site has a parallel stone row, a stone circle, a menhir, burial chambers and dozens of hut circles. To the northeast, near Chagford, the **Grey Wethers** stone circles stand side by side on a stretch of open moor; another stone circle is 400m away near Fernworthy. Also nearby, at Gidleigh, **Scorhill** stone circle is sometimes called the Stonehenge of Dartmoor, although only half of the original stones remain. The biggest site is the Bronze Age village of **Grimspound**, just off the B3212, where you can wander inside the circular stone wall that once surrounded an entire village, and the ruins of several granite round houses.

You can buy guides to some sites (£4), while the Dartmoor National Park Authority runs archaeology-themed walks (p362).

circle a church whose 40m tower has seen it dubbed the Cathedral of the Moor. Inside search out the boards telling the fire-and-brimstone tale of the violent storm of 1638 – it knocked a pinnacle from the roof, killing several parishioners. As ever on Dartmoor, the devil was blamed, said to be in search of souls.

The village is commemorated in the traditional English folksong of 'Widecombe Fair'; the event itself takes place on the second Tuesday of September.

Sleeping & Eating

Higher Venton Farm B&B ££

(01364-621235; www.ventonfarm.com; Widecombe; s/d £32/65; P) This 16th-century farmhouse could be used to define the architectural style 'picture-postcard thatch'. With low lintels and a tightly winding staircase, there's not a straight line in the place.

Rugglestone Inn PUB £

(www.rugglestoneinn.co.uk; mains £5-9) You'll find plenty of locals in front of this intimate old pub's wood-burning stove. Its stone floor and low beams set the scene for hearty dishes; pies are a speciality, including fishermen's, beef in ale, and a rich steak and stilton.

Getting There & Away

Bus connections to Widecombe are not good. Year-round, bus 672 stops once a week (Wednesdays) en route to **Buckfastleigh** (40 minutes) and **Newton Abbot** (one hour).

On summer Saturdays the **Haytor Hoppa** runs four services, linking Widecome with Newton Abbot, Haytor and Bovey Tracey.

MORETONHAMPSTEAD

POP 1786

The small market town of Moretonhampstead stands at an old crossroads where two of the main routes across Dartmoor meet. With welcoming accommodation and eating options, it makes a likeable base for exploring the eastern moor.

Sleeping & Eating

Sparrowhawk HOSTEL £

(01647-440318; www.sparrowhawkbackpackers.co.uk; 45 Ford St; dm/d/f £17/38/46) At this longstanding backpacker favourite, primary colours meet beams, exposed stone and hand-painted lampshades. Light dorms overlook a central courtyard that's ringed by rickety outbuildings – a great spot to swap travellers' tales.

Walled Garden B&B ££

(01647-441353; www.moretonwalledgarden.co.uk; Mount Pleasant; s/d £45/65; P) In-vogue bathrooms, snazzy furnishings (think burgundy, blue, or chocolate and gold) and a large, tranquil garden with an outdoor chess set, make this an agreeable sleep spot.

White Horse PUB ££

(01647-440242; www.whitehorsedevon.co.uk; 7 George St; dishes £5-19; bar noon-midnight; food lunch & dinner Tue-Sun) With a style somewhere between boho-chic and casual country house, this funky gastropub makes for a chilled-out hangout. Mediterranean goodies crowd a menu which ranges from posh snacks and pizzas to worth-forking-out-for a la carte. Between November and March the bar is open 5pm to midnight, and only dinner is served (Tuesday to Saturday).

Getting There & Away

Bus 359 goes to **Exeter** (50 minutes, two hourly, Monday to Saturday).

On Sundays only between June and mid-September, five **Transmoor Link** (no 82) services run west to Warren House Inn, Postbridge, Two Bridges, Princetown, Yelverton and Plymouth, and east to Exeter.

CHAGFORD

POP 1479

With its wonky thatches and cream and white-fronted buildings, Chagford gathers round a busy square, apparently every inch a timeless moorland town. But the purveyors of waxed jackets and hip flasks have also been joined by health-food shops, contemporary pottery galleries, and some supremely stylish places to eat and sleep.

In a steep gorge 4 miles northeast of Chagford, hunt out an enchanting architectural oddity: the stately but cosy, Lutyens-designed **Castle Drogo** (NT; 01647-433306; www.nationaltrust.org.uk; nr Drewsteignton; adult/child £8.40/4.20; mid-Mar to Oct 11am-5pm; P).

Sleeping & Eating

Gidleigh Park HOTEL, RESTAURANT £££

(01647-432367; www.gidleigh.com; near Gidleigh; d £325-1175; P) This sumptuous oasis of ultimate luxury brings together crests, crenellations and roaring fires with shimmering sanctuaries of blue marble, waterproof TVs and private saunas. Culinary alchemy occurs in the double-Michelin starred **restaurant**, where a three-course dinner costs £105 – thrifty cognoscenti opt for the £40 two-course lunch instead. This dollop of utter extravagance is 2 miles west of Chagford.

22 Mill Street B&B, RESTAURANT ££

(01647-432 244; www.22millst.com; 22 Mill St; d £89-109, 2-course lunch/dinner £17/36; Tue-Sun) The elegant rooms of this sleek retreat feature exposed stone walls, wooden floorboards, satin cushions and bursts of modern art. Its intimate restaurant delivers creative dishes packed with produce from the moors and the shores – look out for wild garlic-infused Dartmoor lamb, and hand-harvested local scallops.

Sandy Park INN, RESTAURANT ££

(01647-433267; www.sandyparkinn.co.uk; Sandy Park; s/d £59/79, mains £8-12; P) Part pub, part chic place to stay, at this 17th-century thatch you can sip a pint of real ale in a comfy, exposed-beam bar, sample cracking Dartmoor fare in the restaurant, then totter upstairs to sleep amid plump pillows and bright furnishings.

Easton Court B&B ££

(01647-433469; www.easton.co.uk; Easton Cross; s/d £65/80; P) Rooms dotted with cast-iron beds and soft sofas look out onto wooded hills; breakfast options include fresh fish or soufflé omelette.

Getting There & Away

Bus 178 runs to **Okehampton** and **Newton Abbot** (one daily Monday to Saturday). Between Monday and Saturday bus 173 runs from Chagford to **Moretonhampstead** (twice daily) and **Exeter** (five daily).

OKEHAMPTON & LYDFORD

POP 7831

Okehampton huddles on the edge of an uninhabited tract of bracken-covered slopes and granite tors – the mind-expanding landscape known as the higher moor. The town has a staging-post feel, and its traditional shops and pubs are good places to prepare for a foray into the wilderness.

Some 9 miles southwest, the village of Lydford has an archetypal inn, a string of weathered granite cottages, castle ruins and a stunning gorge.

Sights & Activities

Lydford Gorge WATERFALL

(NT; 01822-820320; www.nationaltrust.org.uk; Lydford; adult/child £6/3; 10am-5pm mid-Mar to Sep, to 4pm Oct) The 1½-mile rugged riverside hike into this gorge snakes past a series of bubbling whirlpools (including the fearsome 'Devil's Cauldron') to the thundering, 30m-high White Lady waterfall.

Okehampton Castle CASTLE

(EH; 01837-52844; www.english-heritage.org.uk; Castle Lodge, Okehampton; adult/child £3.80/2.30; 10am-5pm Apr-Jun & Sep, to 6pm Jul & Aug) Clinging to a wooded spur, the ruined Norman motte and keep of what was once Devon's largest castle set the scene for some picturesque rampart clambering.

Finch Foundry HISTORIC SITE

(NT; 01837-840046; www.nationaltrust.org.uk; Sticklepath; adult/child £4.70/2.40; 11am-5pm mid-Mar to Oct; P) The last working water-powered forge in England sits at the end of a 3½-hour walk east along the Tarka Trail from Okehampton.

Sleeping & Eating

Collaven Manor B&B ££
(01837-861522; www.collavenmanor.co.uk; Sourton; s £55-65, d £98-146; P) For a delightful dollop of old England, head to this exquisite, 15th-century mini-manor house. A baronial hall, ancient beams and sumptuous furnishings reinforce the heritage-meets-modern comforts feel. It's 5 miles southwest of Okehampton.

Bracken Tor YHA HOSTEL £
(0844 293 0555; www.yha.org.uk; Saxongate; dm £19; P@) A perfect base for hikes or an adventurous break – this 100-year-old country house sits in four acres of grounds on the fringe of the higher moor. It's a mile south of Okehampton, and is also a YHA activity centre, offering climbing, canoeing and bike hire.

Castle INN ££
(01822-820241; www.castleinndartmoor.co.uk; Lydford; d £60-95, mains £9; P) This Elizabethan inn's bedrooms range from small-ish and simple to spacious and luxurious – bag room one for a double shower, private deck and 13th-century castle views. The bar is the ultimate snug: lamp-light bathes bow ceilings and high-backed benches, while the food is hearty Dartmoor pub fare.

Information

Tourist Office (01837-53020; www.okehamptondevon.co.uk; 3 West St, Okehampton; 10am-5pm Mon-Sat Easter-Oct, 10am-4.30pm Mon & Fri-Sat Nov-Easter)

Getting There & Away

Key bus routes:

» **Exeter** and **Bude** via Okehampton. Bus X9 (five daily Monday to Saturday).

» Okehampton to **Chagford** (30 minutes) and **Moretonhampstead** (one hour). Bus 178 (one daily Monday to Saturday).

» Tavistock to **Barnstaple** via Lydford and Okehampton. Bus 118 (two to five daily).

Croyde & Braunton

POP 8360

The cheerful, chilled village of Croyde is Devon's surf central. Here olde-worlde meets new wave: thatched roofs peep out over racks of wetsuits; crowds of cool guys in boardshorts sip beer outside 17th-century inns. Inland, Braunton boasts Britain's first surf museum and a **tourist office** (01271-816400; www.brauntontic.co.uk; Caen St, Braunton; 10am-3pm Mon-Fri, 10am-2pm Sat).

Sights & Activities

Surfing SURFING
The water's hard to resist. **Ralph's** (01271-890147; Hobbs Hill, Croyde; surfboard & wetsuit per 4/24hrs £12/18, bodyboard & wetsuit per 4/24 hours £10/15; mid-Mar to Dec 9am-dusk) is among those hiring equipment. Lessons are provided by **Surf South West** (01271-890400; www.surfsouthwest.com; Croyde Beach; per half/full day £28/54; Mar-Nov) and **Surfing Croyde Bay** (01271-891200; www.surfingcroydebay.co.uk; 8 Hobbs Hill; per half day adult/child £40/35).

Museum of British Surfing MUSEUM
(01271-815155; www.museumofbritishsurfing.org.uk; Caen St, Braunton; adult/child £3.75/2.75; 10am-5pm Tue-Sun) Few museums are quite this cool. Vibrant surfboards and vintage wetsuits line the walls, sepia images catch your eye. The stories are compelling: 18th-century British sailors riding Hawaiian waves; England's home-grown surf pioneers of the 1920s; the wetsuit innovators of the 1960s – here heritage meets hanging ten.

Sleeping & Eating

Croyde gets very busy in the summer – book ahead, even for campsites.

Thatch B&B ££
(01271-890349; www.thethatchcroyde.com; 14 Hobbs Hill, Croyde; d £50-110, f £130) This cavernous, thatched pub is a legendary surfers' hang out. Its trendy bedrooms feature delicate creams, browns and subtle checks; the owners also run similar rooms above another wave-riders' pub and in the cottage opposite. The pick though are at the nearby (quieter) Priory, where elegant beams frame exposed stone.

Chapel Farm B&B ££
(01271-890429; www.chapelfarmcroyde.co.uk; Hobbs Hill, Croyde; s/d/tr £35/70/90; P) Walls and ceilings shoot off at atmospherically random angles in this thatched cob farmhouse. It used to be a home to monks – now it's a study in light, pretty bedrooms, finished with bursts of pine.

Bay View Farm CAMPSITE £
(01271-890501; www.bayviewfarm.co.uk; Croyde; campsites per two adults £24; P) One of the area's best campsites, with laundry, showers

and surf-view pitches. Often requires a week's minimum booking in summer.

Mitchum's CAMPSITE £
(☎07875 406473; www.croydebay.co.uk; sites per two adults £29-63; ⊙Jun–Aug; P) Mitchum's has superb facilities at two sites, one next to Croyde village, the other overlooking the sandy beach. There's a two-night minimum booking in July and August.

Hobb's BISTRO ££
(☎01271-890256; www.hobbsincroyde.co.uk; 10 Hobb's Hill, Croyde; mains £15-19; ⊙dinner Wed-Sun) Heavily beamed eatery rustling up bistro standards – specialities include sizzling steaks, local scallops, mussels and sea bass.

Getting There & Away

Bus 308 (hourly Monday to Saturday, five on Sunday) goes from Barnstaple to Braunton, Saunton Sands and Croyde (40 minutes).

Bus 3 (half-hourly Monday to Saturday, hourly Sunday) runs between Ilfracombe and Barnstaple (40 minutes), via Braunton.

Ilfracombe

POP 19,136

Ilfracombe's geology is startling. Precipitous headlands plunge down to pint-sized beaches; waterfront walkways cling to the sides of sheer cliffs. It seems at first a classic, well-worn Victorian watering hole. Steep streets slope to a historic harbour lined with touristy shops; formal gardens, crazy golf and ropes of twinkling lights line the promenade. But the resort also has a snazzier side, as evidenced by a string of smart eateries and places to sleep, some artistic allure with a Damien Hirst connection and an utterly unusual heritage swim spot.

Sights & Activities

Ilfracombe Aquarium AQUARIUM
(☎01271-864533; www.ilfracombeaquarium.co.uk; The Pier; adult/child £3.50/2.50; ⊙10am-4.30pm, to 5.45pm late-Jul & Aug) This bijou but beautifully executed aquarium recreates aquatic environments stretching from Exmoor to the Atlantic, via estuary, rock pool and harbour (hunt out the fearsome lobster and graceful rays).

TOP CHOICE **Tunnelsbeaches** SWIMMING
(☎01271-879882; www.tunnelsbeaches.co.uk; Granville Rd; adult/child £2.50/1.95; ⊙10am-5pm or 6pm Easter-Oct, to 7pm Jul & Aug) These Victorian tidal swimming pools beautifully evoke Ilfracombe's heyday. Passageways hacked out of solid rock lead to a strip of beach where you can still plunge into the sea. Sepia photos depict the pools in the 19th century, conveying a world of woollen bathing suits, segregated swimming and boating etiquette ('Gentlemen who cannot swim should never take ladies upon the water').

Sleeping & Eating

TOP CHOICE **Westwood** B&B ££
(☎01271-867443; www.west-wood.co.uk; Torrs Park; d £80-125; P 📶) Modern, minimal and marvellous; this ultrachic guesthouse is a study of neutral tones and dashes of vivid colour. It's graced by ponyskin chaises longues and stand-alone baths; some rooms have sea glimpses.

Olive Branch & Room B&B, BISTRO ££
(☎01271-879005; www.olivebranchguesthouse.co.uk; 56 Fore St; s £42-75 d £70-95, mains £14; 📶) Artful decor, ritzy bathrooms and bay windows with armchairs and sea views, make this a swish in-town retreat. Its bistro echoes to cool tunes and the chatter of happy diners. Try the squash, spinach and pine-nut lasagne, or sea bream with salsa verde – either way there's prosecco by the glass.

Ocean Backpackers HOSTEL £
(☎01271-867835; www.oceanbackpackers.co.uk; 29 St James Pl; dm/d £15/38; P @ 📶) Brightly painted en suite dorms, a convivial kitchen

NORTH DEVON'S BEACHES

North Devon's 80-mile coast boasts some of the region's most tempting beaches. Five miles south of Ilfracombe, **Woolacombe** is a traditional family resort with 3 miles of sand. A jaw-dropping coast road (and path) winds down from Croyde to **Saunton Sands**, 3 miles away. This 3-mile stretch of beach is backed by **Braunton Burrows**, a 2000-acre Unesco World Biosphere Reserve. Paths snake past sandy hummocks, salt marshes and rich plant life, as well as occasional WWII mock landing craft – poignantly the Burrows were the main training area for American troops before D-Day.

and free coffee lend this long-established indie hostel a laid-back vibe, the giant world map in the lounge is a real travel conversation kick-starter.

11 The Quay EUROPEAN ££

(☎01271-868090; www.11thequay.com; 11 The Quay; mains £6-25; ⊙lunch & dinner daily Apr-Oct, Wed-Sun Nov-Mar) Ilfracombe's hippest harbourside hangout by far is owned by the glamour boy of British art, Damien Hirst (he of the cut-in-half cows). His creations line the walls, so you get to tuck into risotto nero, shellfish bisque and Lundy Island lobster while gazing at his dot paintings, *Pharmacy* installation and, with delicious irony, fish in formaldehyde.

ℹ Information

Tourist Office (☎01271-863001; www.visitilfracombe.co.uk; Landmark Theatre, the Seafront; ⊙9am-5pm Mon-Fri, 10.30am-4.30pm Sat & Sun Apr-Oct, closed Sun Nov-Mar)

ℹ Getting There & Away

Key bus routes:

Barnstaple, via Braunton. Bus 3 (40 minutes, every half-hour Monday to Saturday, hourly Sunday).

Lynton (45 minutes) with connections on to Minehead. Bus 300 (one to two daily).

Clovelly

POP 450

Clovelly is the quintessential, picture-postcard pretty Devon village. Its white cottages cascade down cliffs to meet a curving crab claw of a harbour, which is lined with lobster pots and set against a deep-blue sea. Clovelly's cobbled streets are so steep that cars can't negotiate them, so supplies are still brought in by sledge – you'll see these big bread baskets on runners leaning outside homes. Clovelly is often branded artificial, but this is a real community – 98% of the houses are occupied; in some Westcountry villages more than half the properties are holiday homes.

Entry to the privately owned village is via the **visitor centre** (☎01237-431781; www.clovelly.co.uk; adult/child £6.50/4; ⊙9am-6.30pm Jun-Sep, 9.30am-5pm Apr-May & Oct, 10am-4pm Nov-Mar).

Charles Kingsley, author of the children's classic *The Water Babies,* spent much of his early life in Clovelly. You can visit his former house, as well as a highly atmospheric fisherman's cottage and the village's twin chapels. Right on the waterfront, the **Red Lion** (☎01237-431237; www.clovelly.co.uk; d £145-75, bar mains £8, restaurant 2/3 courses £25/30) has gorgeous bedrooms with either harbour or sea views, a quality restaurant, and a welcoming bar. Half way up the hill, **Donkey Shoe Cottage** (☎01237-431601; www.donkeyshoecottage.co.uk; 21 High St; s/d £30/60) has country-style B&B rooms, with stripped floorboards and raspberry-red walls.

Bus 319 (four to six Monday to Saturday) runs between Clovelly, Hartland Village, Bideford (40 minutes) and Barnstaple (one hour).

Hartland Abbey HISTORIC BUILDING

(☎01237-441234; www.hartlandabbey.com; adult/child £10.50/4; ⊙11.30am-5pm, house Sun-Thu Jun-Sep, Wed-Thu & Sun Apr-May, gardens Sun-Fri Apr-Sep; Ⓟ) This 12th-century former monastery was a post-Dissolution handout, given to the sergeant of Henry VIII's wine cellar in 1539. Now a stately home, it boasts fine murals, ancient documents, paintings by English masters, Victorian photos, and bewitching gardens.

Hartland Abbey is 5 miles west of Clovelly, off the A39 between Hartland and Hartland Quay.

CORNWALL

You can't get further west than the ancient Celtic kingdom of Cornwall (or Kernow, as it's known around these parts). Blessed with the wildest coastline and most breathtakingly beautiful beaches in England, this proudly independent land has always been determined to march to its own tune.

While the staple industries of old – mining, fishing and farming – have all but disappeared, Cornwall has since reinvented itself as one of the nation's creative corners. Whether it's exploring the space-age domes of the Eden Project, sampling the culinary creations of a celebrity chef or chilling out on the faraway Isles of Scilly, this is one place where you're guaranteed to feel the itch of inspiration. Time to let a little Kernow into your soul.

ℹ Getting Around

Bus, train and ferry timetables can be found on the **Traveline South West** (☎0871-200-2233; www.travelinesw.com) website. Also useful is the website of **Cornwall Public Transport** (www.cornwallpublictransport.info).

Air

Flights to London, Manchester and the Isles of Scilly are available year-round from **Newquay Airport** (p376), 5 miles from Newquay town centre.

Bus

Buses connect Cornwall's main towns, but rural services are much patchier. The two main operators are:

First (☎customer services 0845-600 1420, timetables 0871-200 2233; www.firstgroup.com/ukbus/devon_cornwall)

Western Greyhound (☎01637-871871; www.westerngreyhound.com)

Public Transport Passes

Western Greyhound Day Explorer (adult/child/family £8.50/5.50/17) All Western Greyhound buses in Cornwall, plus Stagecoach buses in Devon. Available from bus drivers.

Ride Cornwall Ranger (adult/child/family £10/7.50/20) One days' travel on all trains and buses in Cornwall. Valid after 9am Monday to Friday and weekends. Available from stations, train conductors and bus drivers.

Train

Devon and Cornwall's main railway line follows the coast as far as Penzance, with branch lines to Barnstaple, Paignton, Torquay, Gunnislake, Looe, Falmouth, Newquay and St Ives.

CrossCountry (☎0844-811 0124; www.crosscountrytrains.co.uk) Operates services to the north of England, the Midlands and Scotland.

First Great Western (☎08457-000125; www.firstgreatwestern.co.uk) Operates the main line from London Paddington via Exeter, Plymouth, St Austell, Truro and Penzance, as well as the regional branch lines.

South West Trains (☎0845-6000 650; www.southwesttrains.co.uk) Runs services between London Waterloo and Axminster and Exeter.

Bude

POP 9242

Just a scant few miles across the Devon border, Bude might not be the prettiest town on the north Cornish coast, but it has a bevy of impressive beaches.

Sights & Activities

Beaches BEACH

Bude's beaches are definitely its main asset. Closest is **Summerleaze**, a bucket-and-spade affair with lots of space at low tide, as well as a 1930s saltwater **sea pool**. North across Summerleaze Down is **Crooklets**, offering golden sand and rockpools at low tide.

To reach Bude's other beaches requires either a car or a hike along the coast path. 3 miles south of town is **Widemouth Bay** (pronounced *widmouth*), a broad, sandy beach good for both families and surfers. Two miles further is the shingly beach of **Millook**, followed by cliff-backed **Crackington Haven**.

Three miles north of town are the National Trust–owned **Northcott Mouth** and **Sandymouth**. A mile further on is pebbly **Duckpool**, often quiet even in summer.

Bude Castle MUSEUM

(www.thecastlebude.org.uk; The Castle; adult/child £3.50/2.50; ⊙10am-5pm Easter-Oct, 10am-4pm Nov-Easter) Housed in a peculiar folly behind Summerleaze Beach, Bude Castle was built by local inventor Sir Goldsworth Gurney, whose creations included theatrical limelight and steam carriages. The building now houses the Castle Restaurant and a small **heritage centre** that roves through Bude's maritime, geological and social history.

Bude Canal CANAL

Bude's 19th-century canal was built to carry mineral-rich sand from the coastline into the countryside, but fell into disuse following the arrival of the railway. Its tow-paths make for a lovely stroll or bike ride. The Bude Tourist Office (p370) has leaflets detailing several routes.

Sleeping

Dylan's Guesthouse B&B £

(☎01288-354705; www.dylansguesthouseinbude.co.uk; Downs View; s £40-50, d £50-70; P) This snazzy B&B has rooms decked out in white linen, chocolate throws, pine throws and quirky curios. Most look across the town's golf course and downlands.

Elements Hotel HOTEL ££

(☎01288-275066; www.elements-life.co.uk; Marine Dr; s £52.50, d £89-109; P) Smart clifftop hotel with 11 rooms in whites and creams, big views from the outdoor deck, a gym and Finholme sauna, and surf packages courtesy of nearby Raven Surf School.

Bangor's Organic B&B ££

(☎01288-361297; www.bangorsorganic.co.uk; Poundstock, Bude; d £110; P) Ecofriendly B&B near

Poundstock, 7 miles from Bude. The house is elegantly Victorian, but the draw is the rural location; it's set amongst 5 acres, and you'll find fresh-picked veg and just-laid eggs on the breakfast table. Evening meals are available too.

Eating

Life's a Beach CAFE ££
(www.lifesabeach.info; Summerleaze; lunch mains £4-6, dinner mains £16-21.50; ⏲Mon-Sat) This beachside bistro overlooking Summerleaze has a split personality: by day it's a beach cafe serving coffees, panini and ice-creams, by night it's a smart seafood restaurant.

The Castle Restaurant EUROPEAN ££
(☎01288-355222; www.thecastlerestaurantbude.co.uk; Bude Castle; lunch mains £8.50-10, dinner mains £14.50-18; ⏲lunch & dinner) Inside the town's 'castle', Kit Davis's restaurant serves European-style food taking in everything from roast ling to rack of lamb. Aim for one of the balcony tables if the weather's good.

Information

Bude Tourist Office (☎01288-354240; www.visitbude.info; The Crescent; ⏲10am-5pm Mon-Sat, plus 10am-4pm Sun summer) Beside the main car park near the Castle.

Getting There & Away

Boscastle via Widemouth and Crackington Haven. Bus 594/595 (six daily Monday to Saturday, four on Sunday in summer).

Boscastle

Precious few Cornish harbours can match Boscastle in the beauty stakes. Nestled in the crook of a steeply wooded coombe (valley) at the confluence of three rivers, Boscastle's seagoing heritage stretches back to Elizabethan times, and with its quaint cottages, steep cliffs, tinkling streams and sturdy quay, it's an almost impossibly photogenic spot.

But the peaceful setting belies some turbulent history: in 2004 Boscastle was devastated by one of Britain's largest-ever flash floods, which carried away cars, bridges and buildings. The village has since been rebuilt, but look closely and you'll still spot reminders of the floods dotted around.

Sights

Museum of Witchcraft MUSEUM
(☎01840-250111; www.museumofwitchcraft.com; The Harbour; adult/child £4/3; ⏲10.30am-6pm Mon-Sat, 11.30am-6pm Sun Mar-Nov) This oddball museum claims to house the world's largest collection of witchy memorabilia, from haunted skulls to hags' bridles and voodoo dolls. It's half-tacky, half-spooky, and some of the more 'controversial' exhibits definitely aren't suitable for kids of a sensitive disposition (or adults, for that matter).

St Juliot Church CHURCH
From Boscastle's harbour, a 3-mile trail leads along the wooded banks of the River Valency to two historic churches: pint-sized **Minster**, which partly dates from the 12th century, and nearby **St Juliot**, where author Thomas Hardy famously met his future wife Emma Lavinia Gifford while training as a young architect.

Sleeping & Eating

Boscastle's dining scene is limited to the village pubs: try the cosy **Cobweb** (☎01840-250278; www.cobwebinn.co.uk; The Bridge; mains £5-14) and the old-time **Napoleon** (☎01840-250204; High Street; mains £6-12).

Boscastle House B&B ££
(☎01840-250654; www.boscastlehouse.com; Tintagel Rd; s/d £55/120; P 📶) This is the fanciest of the Boscastle B&Bs, set in a Victorian house overlooking the valley, with six rooms named after Cornish legends. Charlotte has bay window views, Nine Windows has his-and-hers sinks and a freestanding bath, Trelawney has ample space and its own sofa.

Orchard Lodge B&B £
(☎01840-250418; www.orchardlodgeboscastle.co.uk; Gunpool Ln; d £75-104; P 📶) A short walk uphill, this is a thoroughly modern B&B, crisply finished in slinky fabrics and cool colours and run with efficiency by owners Geoff and Shirley Barratt. Rates get cheaper the longer you stay.

Boscastle YHA HOSTEL £
(boscastle@yha.org.uk; dm £14; ⏲Apr-Nov) Boscastle's shoebox-sized hostel was all but washed away by the floods, but it's been completely renovated. It's in one of the village's oldest buildings beside the harbour, but be prepared for small dorms.

QUIRKY CAMPING

Tired of saggy tents and unwieldy flysheets? Don't fret – just try one of these offbeat campsites out for size.

» Blackdown Yurts (p346)
» The Wood Life (p345)
» Lovelane Caravans (p387)
» Cornish Tipi Holidays (p373)
» St Martin's Campsite (p400)

Information

Boscastle Tourist Office (☎01840-250010; www.visitboscastleandtintagel.com; The Harbour; ⏱10am-5pm Mar-Oct, 10.30-4pm Nov-Feb)

Getting There & Away

Stopping in Boscastle en route from Bude and Newquay is bus 594/595 (six daily Monday to Saturday, four on Sundays in summer)

Tintagel

POP 1822

The spectre of King Arthur looms large over Tintagel and its spectacular clifftop **castle** (EH; ☎01840-770328; adult/child £5.20/2.60; ⏱10am-6pm Apr-Sep, 10am-5pm Oct, 10am-4pm Nov-Mar). Though the present-day ruins mostly date from the 13th century, archaeological digs have revealed the foundations of a much earlier fortress, fuelling speculation that Arthur may indeed have been born at the castle as locals like to claim.

Whatever the truth of the legend, it's certainly a fine spot for a fortress. Though much of the structure has crumbled away, it's still possible to make out several walls and much of the original layout. Part of the castle stands on a rocky outcrop cut off from the mainland, and is accessed via a wooden bridge and a very steep staircase (vertigo sufferers beware).

The village itself is a bit of a letdown in comparison. Its touristy shops and tearooms make the most of the King Arthur connection, but the only worthwhile sight is the **Old Post Office** (NT; ☎01840-770024; Fore St; adult/child £3.20/1.60; ⏱11am-5.30pm mid-Mar–Sep, 11am-4pm Oct), a 16th-century longhouse that was used as a post office during the 19th century.

Getting There & Away

There are several car parks in the village, from where it's a steep walk of about 600m to the castle entrance. A Landrover shuttle service runs from April to October.

Tintagel is on the route for the 594/595 bus (six daily Monday to Saturday), with connections to Bude, Boscastle and Newquay.

Port Isaac

A few miles along the coast from Tintagel is Port Isaac, another picturesque fishing village composed of narrow lanes, seafront cottages and slender opes (alleyways). In recent years it has provided the backdrop for the popular TV series *Doc Martin* (a sign points to Doc Martin's Cottage near the quay).

Port Isaac's summer crowds can be a headache, but peace and quiet can usually be found at the neighbouring coves of **Port Gaverne** and **Port Quin**.

The narrow streets here are a drivers' nightmare, so ditch the wheels in the car park at the top of the village.

Stopping at Port Gaverne, Port Isaac, Port Quin and Polzeath en route between Camelford and Wadebridge is bus 584 (seven daily Monday to Saturday, four on Sundays in summer).

Padstow

POP 3162

If anywhere symbolises Cornwall's recent renaissance, it's Padstow. This once-sleepy fishing port has been transformed into one of the county's most cosmopolitan corners thanks to celebrity chef Rick Stein, whose property portfolio encompasses several restaurants, shops and hotels around town, as well as a seafood school and fish-and-chip outlet.

The 'Stein Effect' has certainly changed the place: Padstow feels more Kensington-chic than Cornish-quaint these days, with a rash of fancy restaurants, fashion boutiques and chichi shops sitting alongside the old pubs and pasty shops.

Whether the town's managed to hold on to its soul in the process is debatable, but it's still hard not to be charmed by the quayside setting – especially once the summer crowds have left for home.

WORTH A TRIP

ROCK & THE CAMEL ESTUARY

West of Port Isaac, a patchwork of fields and lanes unfurls to the Camel Estuary, where the bluffs and sandbars of the River Camel meld into the blue Atlantic.

This was famously John Betjeman's favourite corner of Cornwall, and the former Poet Laureate commemorated the area in some of his most classic poems (especially *Trebetherick* and its immortal lines 'Sand in the sandwiches, wasps in the tea').

More recently, the area has become one of Cornwall's poshest (and priciest) corners, especially around the village of Rock, now home to many a millionaire's getaway and celebrity second home – as well as one of Cornwall's most renowned gourmet addresses, the double–Michelin starred **Nathan Outlaw Restaurant** (www.nathan-outlaw.com; tasting menu £85).

It's certainly no longer the quiet backwater commemorated by Betjeman, but the area around Rock is still worth exploring. It's home to some beautiful beaches, especially around **Polzeath** and the shifting dunes of **Daymer Bay**. The coast path around **Pentire Headland** is brilliant for walks, and literary types will want to visit **St Enodoc Church**, where Betjeman was buried in 1984.

The Black Tor Ferry (p374) putters regularly across the estuary from Padstow.

Sights & Activities

National Lobster Hatchery NATURE DISPLAY
(www.nationallobsterhatchery.co.uk; adult/child £3.50/1.50; 10am-7.30pm Jul & Aug, 10am-5pm Apr-Jun & Sep-Oct, earlier closing Nov-Mar) To combat falling lobster stocks, this harbourside hatchery rears baby lobsters in special tanks before returning them to the wild. Displays detail the crustaceans' life cycle, and there are viewing tanks where you can watch the residents.

Prideaux Place HISTORIC HOME
(www.prideauxplace.co.uk; house & grounds adult £7.50, grounds only £2; 1.30-4pm Sun-Thu, grounds & tearoom 12.30-5.30pm Apr-Oct) Much favoured by directors of costume dramas, this stately manor house above town was built by the Prideaux-Brune family (who still reside here). The house can be visited on a guided tour.

Beaches BEACH
Padstow is surrounded by fine beaches, including the so-called **Seven Bays**: Trevone, Harlyn, Mother Ivey's, Booby's, Constantine, Treyarnon and Porthcothan. Bus 556 runs close to most of them.

Camel Trail CYCLING
The old Padstow–Bodmin railway was closed in the 1950s, and has now been turned into Cornwall's most popular bike trail. The main section starts in Padstow and runs east through Wadebridge (5.75 miles), but the trail runs on all the way to Poley Bridge on Bodmin Moor (18.3 miles). The views of coast and countryside are grand, but it gets busy – book bikes well in advance, or bring your own.

Bikes can be hired from **Padstow Cycle Hire** (01841-533533; www.padstowcyclehire.com; South Quay; 9am-5pm, plus 5pm-9pm in summer) or **Trail Bike Hire** (01841 532594; www.trailbikehire.co.uk; Unit 6, South Quay; 9am-6pm) at the Padstow end, or from **Bridge Bike Hire** (01208-813050; www.bridgebikehire.co.uk) at the Wadebridge end, for around £12 to £15 per day. Tagalongs, tandems and kids' trailers cost extra.

Boat Trips BOAT TOUR
Between Easter and October, cruise boats including the **Jubilee Queen** (07836-798457; adult/child £10/5) and **Padstow Sealife Safaris** (01841-521613; www.padstowsealifesafaris.co.uk; 2-hour cruise adult/child £39/£25) run trips to local seal and seabird colonies.

Padstow Boat Trips (www.padstowboattrips.com) keeps listings of all the local operators.

Sleeping

Prices in Padstow are higher than in other parts of Cornwall.

Treann House B&B ££
(01841-553855; www.treannhousepadstow.com; 24 Dennis Rd; d £95-125) This stylish number makes a fancy place to stay. The three rooms are finished with stripped floors, crisp sheets and antique beds, and the Estuary

Room has its own balcony with a panorama over Padstow's rooftops.

Treverbyn House B&B ££
(☎01841-532855; www.treverbynhouse.com; Station Rd; d £85-120; P) This townhouse offers four colour-themed rooms (pink, green, lilac or yellow) plus an extra-romantic turret hideaway. The style is classic – oriental rugs, brass bedsteads, traditional tea trays – but the rooms are huge, and breakfast includes home-made jams and smoked kippers.

Treyarnon Bay YHA HOSTEL £
(treyarnon@yha.org.uk; Tregonnan; dm £14; P@) A super 1930s beach hostel on the bluffs above Treyarnon Bay. Rooms are big and there's a good cafe, plus barbecues in summer. Bus 556 stops nearby at Constantine.

Cornish Tipi Holidays CAMPSITE ££
(☎01208-880781; www.cornishtipiholidays.co.uk; Pendoggett; per week £485-1100) Camp Sioux-style in a secluded valley near St Kew. Tipis are in communal 'village' fields, or you can pay extra for a private area. All come with camp lanterns, stoves and coolboxes.

Eating

TOP CHOICE Paul Ainsworth at No 6 BRITISH £££
(☎01840-532093; www.number6inpadstow.co.uk; 6 Middle St; dinner mains £22-27) Paul Ainsworth is the name to watch in Padstow – partly thanks to his recent TV appearances, but mainly because he's one of Cornwall's most talented young chefs. His flagship restaurant blends classic British and modern European, focusing on local goodies such as just-landed seafood, ham knuckle, squab pigeon and Cornish lamb. Don't miss his signature dessert, 'A Trip to the Fairground', which scooped top honours on BBC2's *Great British Menu* in 2011.

TOP CHOICE Seafood Restaurant SEAFOOD £££
(☎01841-532700; www.rickstein.com; Riverside; £22.50-62.50; ⊙lunch & dinner) Rick Stein's much-vaunted seafooderie needs no introduction – it's one of Britain's foremost fish addresses, with offerings that can be expensive; the menu has treats such as fresh Padstow lobster and sumptuous *fruits de mer*. You'll generally need to book months in advance – although last-minute lunch tables sometimes crop up, so it might be worth trying your luck.

Margot's Bistro BRITISH ££
(☎01840-533441; margotspadstow.blogspot.com; 11 Duke St; mains £14.50-17.50; ⊙dinner Tue-Sat year-round, lunch Wed-Sat in summer) While the food snobs head for Stein's, Margot's is where you'll be sent by the locals. Run by madcap chef Adrian Oliver, known for his chaotic style and homely, seasonal food, it's a fantastically convivial place – but it's tiny and the tables are packed in sardine-tight.

Rick Stein's Cafe EUROPEAN ££
(☎01841-532700; Middle St; mains £10-18; ⊙closed Sun) Stein's backstreet bistro offers stripped-down samples of his trademark cuisine (you'll probably need to book, though).

Rojano's in the Square ITALIAN ££
(www.rojanos.co.uk; 9 Mill Sq; pizzas & pastas £6.95-10.95) Authentic pizza and pasta joint, with a tiny streetside terrace and a buzzy modern dining room. It's now run by Paul Ainsworth, a talented local chef, so standards are high.

Basement CAFE ££
(☎01841-532846; 11 Broad St; lunch mains £5-10, dinner mains £10-14; ⊙all day) Continental cafe covering all the bases, from doorstep sandwiches to steaming bowls of mussels.

THE 'OBBY 'OSS CEREMONY

Padstow's raucous annual street party, the 'Obby 'Oss Ceremony, is an ancient May Day festival that's believed to derive from the ancient spring rite of Beltane.

The ritual begins at 10am, when the Blue (or Peace) 'Oss – a man garbed in a hooped sailcloth and snapping horse headdress – emerges from its 'stable' at the Market Institute, followed an hour later by the Red (or Original) 'Oss from the Golden Lion pub. Both 'Osses dance around town accompanied by their own baton-wielding 'teazer' and musicians, singing the traditional May Day and dressed in white with coloured ribbons denoting their 'loyalty' to each 'Oss. After a day of revelling, the 'Osses end up at the town's Maypole, where they dance together before being 'stabled' for another year.

Unsurprisingly, May Day is one of Padstow's most popular events. Parking is problematic, so it's best to arrive by public transport if you can.

BEDRUTHAN STEPS

A few miles east of Watergate Bay are the majestic towers known as **Bedruthan Steps** (Carnewas; www.nationaltrust.org.uk/carnewas-and-bedruthan-steps), a string of rocky pinnacles cut off from the cliffs by eons of natural erosion. It's a stirring spot for a stroll, especially at sunset, although the beach itself is reached via a steep path and disappears at high tide. Tea and cake is served in the National Trust cafe beside the car park. Bus 556 stops nearby.

Information

Padstow Tourist Office (☎01841-533449; www.padstowlive.com; North Quay; ⊙10am-5pm Mon-Sat)

Getting There & Away

Bus

Newquay runs via Padstow's main beaches and Newquay Airport before following the coast road to Newquay. Bus 556 (hourly Monday to Saturday, five on Sunday).

Bude via Wadebridge, Boscastle and Tintagel. Bus 594/595 (six daily Monday to Saturday).

Ferry

Black Tor Ferry (www.padstow-harbour.co.uk/phc_ferry.html; adult/child return £3/2, bikes £2, dogs £1) Runs Padstow to Rock year-round (pick-up/drop-off points depend on the tides). The first ferry is at 8am year-round. The last ferry is at 7.30pm in mid-July and August; 6.30pm June and September; 5.30pm April, May & October; 4.30pm November to March.

Newquay

POP 19,423

Bright, breezy and brash: that's Newquay, Cornwall's premier party town and the spiritual home of British surfing. Perched above a cluster of golden beaches, Newquay's clifftop setting is fabulous, but the town's become better known for its after-dark antics – it's a favourite summer getaway for surfers, clubbers and stag parties, creating a drink-till-dawn atmosphere that's more Costa del Sol than Cornwall. The drab, concrete-heavy town centre doesn't do it any favours – but if it's white sand and wild nights you're after, Newquay definitely fits the bill.

Sights & Activities

Newquay Beaches BEACH

Newquay is set amid some of North Cornwall's finest beaches. The best-known is **Fistral**, England's most famous surfing beach and the venue for the annual **Boardmasters surfing festival**. It's nestled on the west side of Towan Head, a 10-minute walk from the town centre.

To the east of Towan Head are Newquay's other main beaches. Just below town are **Towan**, **Great Western** and **Tolcarne**, followed by nearby **Lusty Glaze**. All offer good swimming and lifeguard supervision throughout the summer.

You'll need transport to reach Newquay's other beaches. North of Lusty Glaze is **Porth**, a long, narrow beach that's popular with families, followed a couple of miles later by the massive curve of **Watergate Bay**, home to Jamie Oliver's much-vaunted restaurant, Fifteen Cornwall (p375). Two miles north brings you to **Mawgan Porth**, a horseshoe-shaped bay which often stays quieter than its neighbours.

You'll find even more beaches to the southwest of Newquay, including the large, sandy beaches of **Crantock** (about 3 miles from town) and **Holywell Bay** (6 miles from town).

Blue Reef Aquarium AQUARIUM

(☎01637-878134; www.bluereefaquarium.co.uk/newquay.htm; Towan Promenade; adult/child/family £9.75/7.50/32.50; ⊙10am-5pm) On Towan Beach, Newquay's aquarium displays aquatic characters including jellyfish, seahorses, octopi and rays. Touch pools allow you to get up close and personal with the residents.

Newquay Zoo ZOO

(☎01637-873342; www.newquayzoo.co.uk; Trenance Gardens; adult/child/family £10.95/8.45/35; ⊙9:30am-5pm Apr-Sep, 10am-5pm Oct-Mar) Red pandas, sloths, penguins, great horned owls and a python called Monty (get it?) are on show at Newquay's small zoo, 10 minutes walk from town.

Trerice HISTORIC BUILDING

(NT; ☎01637-875404; www.nationaltrust.org.uk/trerice; adult/child £7.20/3.60; ⊙house 11am-5pm, gardens 10.30-5pm mid-FebOct) Three miles southeast of Newquay, the Elizabethan manor of

Trerice is notable for the barrel-roofed ceiling of the Great Chamber, as well as ornate fireplaces, original plasterwork and period furniture. There's also an amusing lawnmower museum in the barn, with over 100 grass-cutters going back more than a century.

Adventure Sports ADVENTURE SPORTS
Newquay has several outdoor activity centres where you can try out sports such as kitebuggying, paddle surfing and coasteering (a mix of rock climbing, scrambling and wild swimming).

Two of the best are **Adventure Centre** (☎01637-872444; www.adventure-centre.org) on Lusty Glaze, and **EboAdventure** (☎0800-781-6861; www.penhaleadventure.com) on Holywell Bay.

Sleeping

TOP CHOICE **The Scarlet** HOTEL £££
(☎01637-861600; www.scarlethotel.co.uk; r from £195 in winter, £295 in summer; P) For out-and-out luxury, Cornwall's fabulously chic new eco-hotel takes the crown. In a regal location above Mawgan Porth, it screams designer style, from the huge seaview rooms with their funky furniture and minimalist decor to the luxurious spa, complete with meditation lounge, outdoor hot tubs and wild swimming pool. The restaurant's a beauty, too.

Carnmarth Hotel HOTEL ££
(☎01637-872519; www.carnmarth.com; Headland Rd; r £95-130; P) This decent midrange hotel is a short walk uphill from Fistral Beach, overlooking the golf course. Rooms aren't spectacular, but neutral tones, plain furniture and distant coast views make the prices seem reasonable, even in season.

Newquay Townhouse B&B £
(☎01637-620009; www.newquaytownhouse.co.uk; 6 Tower Rd; d £50-70; P) Near the town centre, with bright rooms livened up with stripy cushions and wicker furniture. Some have window seats, but only one has bay views.

Eating

TOP CHOICE **Fifteen Cornwall** ITALIAN £££
(☎01637-861000; www.fifteencornwall.com; lunch/dinner menu £28/60; ⊙lunch & dinner) Jamie Oliver's social enterprise restaurant on Watergate Bay is where everyone wants to eat. Underprivileged youngsters learn their trade in the kitchen preparing Oliver's trademark zesty, Italian-influenced food, while diners soak up the views and the buzzy, beachy vibe. It's a red-hot ticket: bookings essential.

Beach Hut BISTRO ££
(☎01637-860877; Watergate Bay; mains £9.75-19.95; ⊙breakfast, lunch & dinner) This bistro by the sand has a beachy feel, and the menu's simple surf 'n' turf: sticky pork ribs, 'extreme' burgers and a different fish every day.

Lewinnick Lodge BISTRO, BAR ££
(☎01637-878117; Pentire Headland; lunch mains £10-14, dinner mains £12-18; ⊙breakfast, lunch & dinner) Out of town on Pentire Head, this

LEARNING TO SURF

With its sparkling beaches and reliable swells, Cornwall is the best place in Britain to learn to surf. It's best to go with a small dedicated school rather than a multiactivity company; most charge around £25-30 per hour for lessons.

Recommended schools:

GB Surf School (☎01736-711289; www.gbsurfschool.com) Based in Marazion, but travels all over in search of the best waves.

Gwithian Academy of Surfing (p376) Small school certified by the ASI (Academy of Surfing Instructors).

Harlyn Surf School (☎01841-533076; www.harlynsurfschool.co.uk) Experienced school on Harlyn Bay, near Padstow. Also offers paddle boarding and sea kayaking.

O'Neill Surf Academy (☎01841-520052; www.oneillsurfacademy.co.uk/) Organised school on Watergate Bay, affiliated with the O'Neill surfing brand.

Raven Surf School (☎01288-353693; www.ravensurf.co.uk) Bude-based school run by ex-pro Mike Raven.

Wavehunters (☎01208-880617; www.wavehunters.co.uk) Polzeath-based outfit, with options including female-only lessons and pro-instructor sessions.

bistro-bar wins the prize for views – there are panoramic coastal vistas from nearly every window. The food's eclectic, veering from spicy Chinese duck to fishcakes.

Café Irie CAFE £
(☎01637-859200; www.cafeirie.co.uk; 38 Fore St; lunch £3-8; ⊙breakfast & lunch Mon-Sat) A surfer's favourite in the centre of Newquay, perfect for hot chocolate, sticky cakes and jacket spuds before hitting the waves. The decor's cool too, with mix-and-match furniture, a psychedelic piano and surfy murals.

Drinking & Entertainment

The town centre gets very rowdy at weekends.

Chy BAR
(www.thekoola.com/the-chy-bar; 12 Beach Rd) Chrome, wood and leather dominate this cafe-bar overlooking Towan Beach. The action continues till late at the Koola nightclub downstairs.

Central PUB
(11 Central Sq) As its name suggests, this rowdy pre-club pub is in the heart of town, and the outside patio is always packed on summer nights.

Information

Newquay Tourist Office (☎01637-854020; www.visitnewquay.com; Marcus Hill; ⊙9.30am-5.30pm Mon-Sat, 9.30am-12.30pm Sun)

Getting There & Away

Air

Newquay Airport (☎01637-860600; www.newquaycornwallairport.com) Regular flights to London, Belfast, Birmingham, Cardiff, Edinburgh and the Isles of Scilly.

Bus 556 (22 minutes, hourly Monday to Saturday, five on Sunday) runs to the airport from the bus station.

Bus

Newquay's bus station is on Manor Rd.

Bus 585/586 (twice hourly Monday to Saturday) is the fastest service to Truro, while the slower 587 runs along the coast via Crantock, Holywell Bay and Perranporth. For the Padstow area, catch the 556.

Train

There are trains every couple of hours on the branch line between Newquay and Par (£4.30, 45 minutes), on the London–Penzance line.

Perranporth

West of Newquay, the craggy North Coast cliffs run through a string of white-sand beaches. Largest of all is the mile-long crescent of Perranporth, one of the county's largest bays, backed by rolling, grass-fringed dunes.

The town itself is of limited interest, but Perranporth's venerable beach bar the **Watering Hole** (www.the-wateringhole.co.uk; Perranporth Beach) is a popular place for a sundowner.

Bus 587 runs hourly to Newquay and Truro. The 583 (hourly Monday to Saturday) also stops in St Agnes.

Gwithian & Godrevy

For golden sand (and acres of it), the beaches of Gwithian and Godrevy Towans are impossible to top. Stretching for almost 2 miles southwest of Hayle, at low tide they join together to form a vast expanse of sparkling sand, framed by deep rockpools and marram-pocked dunes.

Of the two, Gwithian offers the most sand, while neighbouring Godrevy is rockier and wilder. The lighthouse offshore famously inspired Virginia Woolf's iconic stream-of-consciousness novel *To the Lighthouse*, and you can usually spot the local seal colony in one of the coves tucked in around Godrevy Point.

The neighbouring beach of **Porth Kidney** sits further west across the mouth of the Hayle estuary. It's the quietest of all the Hayle beaches, but you'll need to drive round to Lelant, on the way to St Ives, to get there.

For drinks and light lunches, the timber-clad **Godrevy Cafe** (☎01736-757999; www.godrevycafe.com; lunch £6-10; ⊙10am-5pm) and the **Sandsifter** (☎01736-757809; www.sandsiftercornwall.com; mains £4-16; ⊙breakfast, lunch & dinner) bar are both beside Godrevy's main car park, while the relaxed **Sunset Surf Cafe** (☎01736-752575; www.sunset-surf.com; mains £4-8; ⊙breakfast & lunch) is just behind the Gwithian dunes, and also hires wetsuits and surf gear. The **Gwithian Academy of Surfing** (☎01736-757579; www.surfacademy.co.uk) gives surfing lessons.

Bus 515 (three daily Monday to Saturday) stops near Gwithian and Godrevy en route from Hayle.

DON'T MISS

CHAPEL PORTH

The rugged cliffs around St Agnes and Porthtowan were once a mining heartland, and the coastline is littered with the remains of crumbling minestacks and engine houses.

One of the most famous (and photogenic) is above the rocky cove of Chapel Porth, a National Trust–owned beach 2 miles from St Agnes. From the NT car park, it's a steep, mile-long walk to the ruined engine stack of **Wheal Coates**, which teeters above the cliffs and still boasts its original chimney and winding house.

From here, the coast path winds along the cliffs around **Tubby's Head** and **St Agnes Head**, both offering wonderfully wild views.

After the walk, you can reward yourself with fresh flapjacks, hot chocolates and bacon butties at the **Chapel Porth Cafe** (10am-5pm), where the house special is a 'hedgehog' ice-cream (vanilla covered in clotted cream and hazelnuts).

St Ives

POP 9870

Even if you've seen St Ives several times before, it's still hard not to be dazzled as you gaze across its jumble of slate roofs, church towers and turquoise bays. Once a busy pilchard harbour, St Ives later became the centre of Cornwall's arts scene in the 1920s and 30s, and the town's cobbled streets are crammed with quirky galleries and crafts shops – although the town's outsider edge has been somewhat dulled by the steady dribble of chain stores and generic restaurants.

A ghost town in winter, St Ives is one of Cornwall's crown jewels, despite the crowds and traffic jams in summer.

Sights & Activities

Tate St Ives ART MUSEUM
(01736-796226; www.tate.org.uk/stives; Porthmeor Beach; adult/child £5.75/3.25; 10am-5pm Mar-Oct, to 4pm Tue-Sun Nov-Feb) Hovering like a concrete curl above Porthmeor Beach, this far-westerly outpost of the Tate focuses mainly on the work of the artists of the so-called 'St Ives School'. Key works by Terry Frost, Patrick Heron, Naum Gabo, Ben Nicholson and Barbara Hepworth are all on show, as well as the naive paintings of fisherman-turned-artist Alfred Wallis, who didn't start painting until the ripe old age of 67. On the top floor there's a stylish cafe-bar which has a memorable panorama across St Ives.

A joint ticket with the Barbara Hepworth Museum costs adult/child £10/5.50.

Barbara Hepworth Museum MUSEUM
(01736-796226; Barnoon Hill; adult/child £5.50/3.25; 10am-5pm Mar-Oct, 10am-4pm Tue-Sun Nov-Feb) Barbara Hepworth (1903–75) was one of the leading abstract sculptors of the 20th century, and a key figure in the St Ives art scene. Her studio on Barnoon Hill has remained almost untouched since her death, and the adjoining garden contains several of her most notable sculptures. Hepworth's work is scattered throughout St Ives; look for works outside the Guildhall and inside the 15th-century parish church of St Ia.

Leach Pottery GALLERY
(01736-796398; www.leachpottery.com; adult/child £5.50/4.50; 10am-5pm Mon-Sat, 11am-4pm Sun) Another of St Ives' best-known artists was the potter Bernard Leach, who founded his studio here in 1920. Known for his fusion of Eastern and Western ceramics, Leach's studio is now a gallery and museum, and you can often watch contemporary potters in action in the attached workshop. It's a mile uphill along Higher Stennack.

Beaches BEACH
The largest town beaches are **Porthmeor** and **Porthminster**, both of which have sand aplenty and good cafes.

Between them juts the grassy promontory known as **The Island**, topped by the tiny pre-14th century Chapel of St Nicholas. On the peninsula's east side is the little cove of **Porthgwidden**, which is often a good place to escape the crowds.

For more space, you'll need to head a mile east to the sandy crescent of **Carbis Bay**.

Boat Trips BOAT TOUR
From the harbourfront, several operators including **St Ives Boats** (0777-300 8000;

St Ives

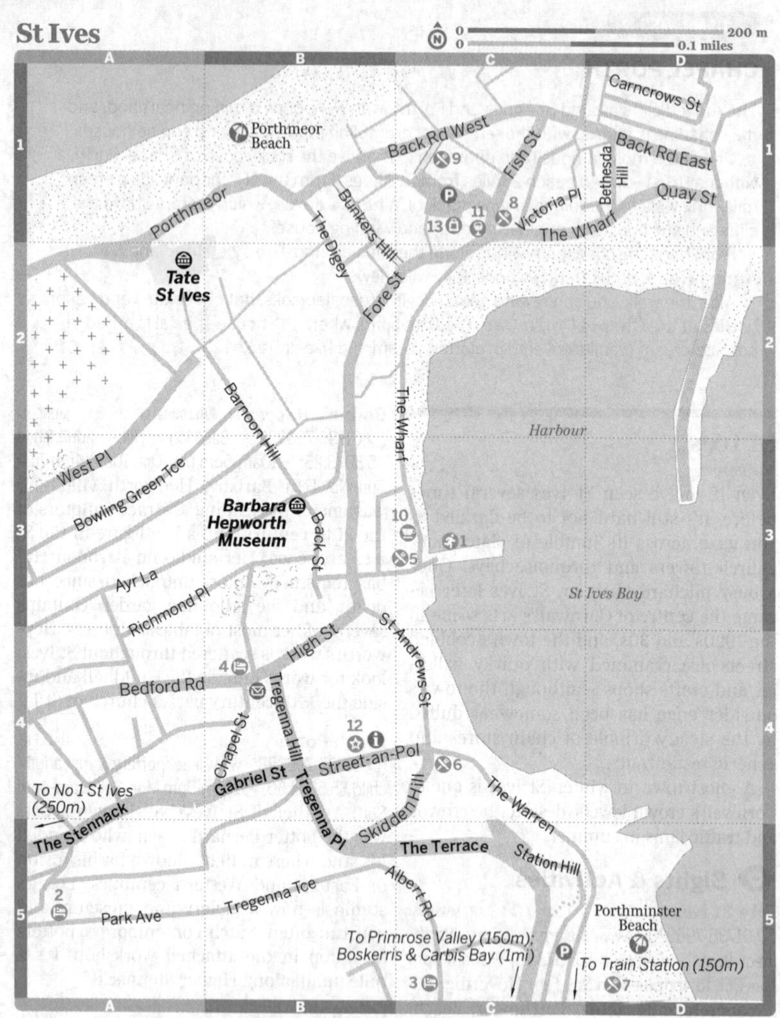

www.stivesboats.co.uk; adult/child £10/8) offer fishing trips and scenic cruises, including to the grey seal colony on Seal Island. If you're really lucky, you might even spot a porpoise or a basking shark in summer.

Sleeping

TOP CHOICE Boskerris HOTEL £££
(☎01736-795295; www.boskerrishotel.co.uk; Boskerris Rd; d £130-195; P 📶) It's a bit out of St Ives in nearby Carbis Bay, but this flashy guesthouse is worth the trip. It's a favourite with the weekend supplements: cool monotones contrast with bespoke wallpaper, scatter cushions, shell-shaped chandeliers and curvy lamps, and bay views extend in grandstand style from the floaty patio.

No 1 St Ives B&B ££
(☎01736-799047; www.no1stives.co.uk; 1 Fern Glen; d £85-125; P 📶) This renovated granite cottage bills itself as 'shabby chic', but it's nothing of the sort. It's a model of a modern B&B, and full of spoils – filtered water, goose-down duvets, iPod docks and White Company bathstuffs. Rooms vary in size, but

St Ives

Top Sights

Barbara Hepworth Museum B3
Tate St Ives A2

Activities, Courses & Tours

1 St Ives Boats C3

Sleeping

2 Little Leaf Guest House A5
3 Organic Panda C5
4 Treliska B4

Eating

5 Alba C3
6 Blas Burgerworks C4
7 Porthminster Beach Café D5
8 Seagrass C1
9 The Loft C1

Drinking

10 Hub C3
11 Sloop Inn C1

Entertainment

12 Guildhall B4

Shopping

13 Sloop Craft Market C1

all sport the same palette of white, cream and cappuccino.

Primrose Valley HOTEL £££
(01736-794939; www.primroseonline.co.uk; Porthminster Beach; d £105-155, ste £175-225; P) An Edwardian house with a mixed bag of rooms – some with pale pine and soothing blues, others exposed brick and stripped-wood floors. Extras include a REN therapy room and a stylish bar, and it's dead handy for Porthminster Beach.

Blue Hayes HOTEL £££
(01736-797129; www.bluehayes.co.uk; Trelyon Ave; r £110-240) Riviera luxury in a St Ives stunner, with manicured grounds, a balustraded breakfast terrace and five suite-sized rooms, most of which provide a memorable perspective along the St Ives coastline.

Treliska B&B ££
(01736-797678; www.treliska.com; 3 Bedford Rd; d £60-80;) The smooth decor at this B&B is attractive – chrome taps, wooden furniture, cool sinks – but it's the position that sells it, just steps from the town centre.

Little Leaf Guest House B&B ££
(01736-795427; www.littleleafguesthouse.co.uk; Park Ave; r £80-115;) This five-room B&B is on a hill uphill from town. Rooms are sweet and simple, finished in creamy colours and pine furniture. Ask for Room 2 or 5 if you're a sucker for a sea view.

Organic Panda B&B ££
(01736-793890; www.organicpanda.co.uk; 1 Pednolver Tce; d £100-40;) This eco-conscious B&B has four rooms, all with reclaimed timber beds, allergen-free duvets and local art. Room 1's the best, with a huge window overlooking the bay. The all-organic breakfast is a treat, too.

Eating

St Ives' harbourside has no shortage of restaurants (including the controversial addition of a Pizza Express), and the back lanes conceal tempting options too.

TOP CHOICE **Seagrass** RESTAURANT ££
(01736-793763; www.seagrass-stives.com; Fish St; dinner mains £13.25-19.95; Tue-Fri) This vaunted restaurant on the 'front is overseen by Lee Groves, who was a semifinalist on *Masterchef: The Professionals*. His elegant food and flavours have earned him plenty of plaudits: seafood and Cornish game figure heavily, often with an adventurous twist. The 2-/3-course menu (served from Sunday to Thursday) is fab value at £15.95/19.95.

TOP CHOICE **Porthminster Beach Café** BISTRO ££
(01736-795352; www.porthminstercafe.co.uk; Porthminster Beach; lunch £10.50-16.50, dinner £10-22; 9am-10pm) For a seaside lunch there's nowhere better than this designer beach cafe, with its gorgeous suntrap terrace and Mediterranean-influenced menu. Tuck into rich bouillabaisse or Provençal fish soup, accompanied by beachy vistas.

Alba SEAFOOD ££
(01736-797222; Old Lifeboat House; mains £11-18) Split-level sophistication next to the lifeboat house, serving top-quality seafood. With its banquette seats and sharp decor, it's stylish – especially if you get one of the prime tables next to the panoramic window.

The Loft RESTAURANT ££
(01736-794204; www.theloftrestaurantandterrace.co.uk; Norway Ln; dinner £12.95-22.95) Tucked away in the old artists' quarter and housed in a converted net loft, this relaxed

bistro is a good bet. The menu has a choice of meat, seafood and veggie options, although the standard is solid rather than spectacular.

Blas Burgerworks CAFE £

(The Warren; burgers £5-10; ⊙dinner Tue-Sun) Imaginative burger-joint with an ecofriendly, Fair Trade, home-made manifesto. Traditionalists go for the 6oz, 100%-beef Blasburger, while veggies could plump for a halloumi stack or a ginger, coriander and chilli tofuburger.

Drinking & Entertainment

Hub CAFE, BAR

(www.hub-stives.co.uk; The Wharf) The open-plan Hub is the heart of St Ives' (limited) nightlife: frothy lattes by day, cocktails after dark, concertina doors onto the harbour.

Sloop Inn PUB

(The Wharf) A classic fishermen's boozer, complete with tankards behind the bar and a comprehensive selection of Cornish ales. The quayside tables go fast, so arrive early if it's sunny.

Guildhall CONCERT VENUE

(1 Street-an-Pol) Hosts regular music and theatre, especially during the annual **St Ives September Festival** (www.stivesseptemberfestival.co.uk).

Shopping

Sloop Craft Market ARTS & CRAFTS

Just off the harbourfront, this miniscule craft centre houses 11 artists' studios, selling offbeat souvenirs such as handmade jewellery and driftwood furniture.

Information

St Ives Tourist Office (☎01736-796297; www.stivestic.co.uk; Street-an-Pol; ⊙9am-5.30pm Mon-Fri, 9am-5pm Sat, 10am-4pm Sun) Inside the Guildhall.

Getting There & Away

BUS The quickest bus to **Penzance** is bus 17 (30 minutes, twice hourly Monday to Saturday, hourly on Sunday). In summer the open-top 300 takes the scenic route via Zennor, Land's End and St Just.

CAR There are several large car parks dotted around the edge of St Ives, but parking can be a nightmare in summer. You might find it easier to park at St Erth and catch the train.

TRAIN The gorgeous branch line from St Ives is worth taking just for the views. Trains run to **St Erth** (£3, 14 minutes, half-hourly) on the main Penzance–Paddington main line.

Zennor

POP 217

The twisting B3306 from St Ives to the windswept village of Zennor is a coastal rollercoaster of a road, winding through a landscape of ancient drystone walls, barren moorland and rocky bluffs.

The village itself clusters around the medieval church of **St Senara**. Inside, a famous carved chair depicts the legendary Mermaid of Zennor, who is said to have fallen in love with the singing voice of local lad Matthew Trewhella. Locals say you can still sometimes hear them singing down at nearby Pendour Cove – and even if you don't, the coast path here is gloriously wild.

Downhill from the church, the **Wayside Folk Museum** (admission £3; ⊙10.30am-5pm Sun-Fri May-Sep, 11am-5pm Sun-Fri Apr & Oct) houses a treasure trove of artefacts gathered by inveterate collector Colonel 'Freddie' Hirst in the 1930s. The displays range from blacksmiths' hammers and cobblers' tools to an 18th-century kitchen and two reclaimed watermills.

Between the church and museum is the marvellous **Tinner's Arms** (☎01736-792697; www.tinnersarms.com; s/d £55/95, mains £10.50-16.50), a classic Cornish inn with a rambling bar, roaring hearth and a refreshing lack of TVs and fruit-machines. Four rooms are available at the nearby White House (run by the owners of the inn) if you feel like prolonging your visit.

The village also has an attractive **hostel** (☎01736-798307; zennorbackpackers@btinternet.com; dm/f £12/50; P) housed in a converted chapel, with four- to six-bed dorms and a cafe serving sandwiches and cream teas.

St Just-in-Penwith

Beyond Zennor, the Penwith landscape starts to feel big, wild and empty. Blustery cliffs, lonely fields and heather-clad hills unfurl along the horizon en route to the stern granite mining town of St Just and the rocky promontory of **Cape Cornwall**, a notorious shipwreck spot, now guarded by the blinking lighthouse at **Pendeen Watch**.

WORTH A TRIP

GURNARD'S HEAD

Pubs don't get much more remote than the **Gurnard's Head** (☎01736-796928; www.gurnardshead.co.uk; lunch £5.50-12, dinner £12.50-16.50). It's 6 miles out along the Zennor coast road, but don't fret about missing it – it's the only building for miles and has its name spelled out in huge white letters on the roof. Having been taken over by renowned hoteliers the Inkin brothers (who also run the Old Coastguard near Mousehole), it's now one of Cornwall's loveliest rural retreats.

Book-lined shelves, sepia prints, scruffy wood and rough stone walls create a reassuringly lived-in feel, and the menu's crammed with comfort food – pheasant, braised beef, or beetroot risotto, followed perhaps by figgy tart or cinammon sponge. Upstairs rooms are simple and stylish, with checked throws and sunny colours: standard rates are £97.50 to £167.50, but the dinner–B&B rates (£142.50 to £212.50 for two people) offer the best value.

Sights

TOP CHOICE **Geevor Tin Mine** MINE
(www.geevor.com; adult/child £9.95/6; 9am-5pm Sun-Fri Mar-Oct, to 4pm Nov-Feb) Just north of St Just near Pendeen, this historic mine closed in 1990 and now provides a memorable insight into the dark, dingy and dangerous conditions in which Cornwall's miners worked. Above ground, you can view the dressing floors and the original machinery used to sort the minerals and ores, before taking a guided tour into some of the underground shafts. Claustrophobes need not apply.

Levant Mine & Beam Engine INDUSTRIAL HERITAGE
(www.nationaltrust.org.uk/main/w-levantmineandbeamengine; adult/child £6.30/3.10; 11am-5pm Sun-Thu) At this National Trust-owned site, one of the world's only working beam engines is still in thunderous action. Built in 1840, this great engine design was the powerhouse behind the Cornish mining boom, powering mineral trains and pumping water from the shafts. Lovingly restored by a team of enthusiasts, it's a sight to behold when it's in full steam.

Botallack Mine RUIN, MINE
Clinging to the cliffs near Levant, this dramatic engine house has abandoned mine shafts extending right out beneath the raging Atlantic waves. It's a treacherous climb down, so it's best viewed from a distance from nearby Botallack Head.

Getting There & Away

St Just is 6 miles north of Land's End. Bus 17/17A/17B travel from **St Ives** (1¼ hours) via **Penzance** (half-hourly Monday to Saturday, five on Sunday).

Sennen & Land's End

Further west, the coastline peaks and plunges all the way into the sandy scoop of Sennen, which overlooks one of Penwith's most stunning stretches of sand at **Whitesand Bay** (pronounced Whitsand).

From here, there's a wonderful stretch of coast path that leads for a mile-and-a-half along the clifftops all the way to Land's End, the westernmost point of mainland England, where the coal-black cliffs plunge dramatically down into the pounding surf, and the views stretch all the way to the Isles of Scilly on a clear day.

Sadly, the criminal decision to build the **Legendary Land's End** (www.landsend-landmark.co.uk; adult/child £10/7; 10am-5pm Mar-Oct) theme park just behind the headland in the 1980s has done nothing to enhance the view. It's home to a few uninspired multimedia shows (including Arthur's Quest, Air-Sea Rescue and a '4D' Film Experience) and a small petting zoo, all of which pale into insignificance compared to the scenery – so just pay for the car park and opt for an exhilarating clifftop stroll instead.

Land's End is 9 miles from Penzance. Bus 1/1A travels from Penzance (one hour, six daily Monday to Saturday) to Land's End; half the buses go via Sennen, the other half via Treen and Porthcurno.

In summer, the open-top 300 bus runs five times daily via Penzance, Land's End, Sennen and St Ives.

DON'T MISS

MINACK THEATRE

In terms of theatrical settings, the **Minack** (01736-810181; www.minack.com) has to take top billing. Carved into the crags overlooking the azure-blue Atlantic, this clifftop amphitheatre was the lifelong passion of local lady Rowena Cade, who dreamt up the idea in the 1930s and oversaw the theatre until her death in 1983.

The Minack's season runs from mid-May to mid-September. Seasoned regulars bring wine, picnic supplies, wet-weather gear and (most importantly of all, considering the seats are carved out of granite) a comfy cushion.

Above the theatre, the **visitor centre** (adult/child £3.50/1.40; 9.30am-5.30pm Apr-Sep, 10am-4pm Oct-Mar) recounts the theatre's history; it's closed when there's a matinée. Half-a-mile below the theatre, the golden crescent of **Porthcurno** makes a glorious place for a swim. Several secluded bays can be reached via the cliff path, as well as the dramatic promontory of **Logan's Rock**, about a mile to the east.

The Minack is 3 miles from Land's End and 9 miles from Penzance. Bus 1/1A from Penzance stops several times daily.

Mousehole

With a tight tangle of slate-roofed cottages and alleyways gathered behind the granite breakwater, Mousehole (pronounced Mowzle) looks like something from a children's storybook. In centuries past this was Cornwall's busiest pilchard port, but the fish dried up at the turn of the century, and the village now survives almost entirely on tourist traffic.

Packed in summer and deserted in winter, the village is ripe for a wander, with a maze of tiny sloops, slips, netlofts and courtyards. It's also famous for its annual display of Christmas lights, and as the home of 'stargazey pie', a pilchard pie in which the fishheads are left poking up through the pie's crust. It's traditionally eaten on Tom Bawcock's Eve (23 December), named after a local lad who reputedly rescued the town from a famine by braving stormy seas to land a bumper haul of pilchards.

The stretch of coast path between Mousehole and Porthcurno is another wonderfully rewarding walk, zig-zagging for around 9 miles via the picturesque coves of **Lamorna** and **Penberth**.

Sleeping & Eating

TOP CHOICE Cove APARTMENTS £££
(01736-731411; www.thecovecornwall.com; Lamorna Cove; £115-375 per night, £1470-2625 per week) If it's style you want, it's style you'll find in abundance at the Cove. These lavish seaside apartments above Lamorna Cove are straight out of a glossy design magazine: gleaming wood, razor-sharp furniture, minimalist bathrooms and picture windows opening onto coastal vistas. The 16 apartments share a lavish pool, and slap-up meals are served in the Fireside Restaurant. All in all, this is as sexy as seaside boltholes get.

Old Coastguard Hotel HOTEL ££
(01736-731222; www.oldcoastguardhotel.co.uk; d £110-195; P) Now run by the owners of the Gurnard's Head, this coastal beauty has a much more relaxed atmosphere than it used to. Rooms are still classic – restrained colour schemes, stately beds – and the best ones obviously have a sea view. Seafood takes prominence in the restaurant, and there's a cliff garden for soaking up the rays.

TOP CHOICE 2 Fore St FRENCH ££
(01736-731164; www.2forestreet.co.uk; Fore St; mains £15-20) Chic French food is the watchword at Joe Wardell's harbourfront diner: plates of pan-fried fish and lightly grilled lobster, served in a light-filled dining room or a little garden patio. The sleek decor and unfussy style mean it's popular: bookings are advisable at any time, but essential in summer.

Ship Inn PUB
(01736-731234; www.shipmousehole.co.uk; South Cliff; mains £8.95-13.95, d £80-110) The old Ship dates (at least in parts) back to the 1700s and has lashings of period charm, with hefty fireplaces and leaded glass windows. Food is standard pub grub – steak pie, veggie chilli – and there are St Austell ales on tap.

Getting There & Away

Bus 6 makes the 20-minute journey to Penzance half-hourly.

Penzance

POP 21,168

Overlooking the sweep of Mount's Bay, the old harbour of Penzance has a salty, sea-blown charm that feels altogether more authentic than many of Cornwall's polished-up ports.

It's resisted the urge to prettify itself simply to cater to the summer trade, and feels all the better for it: its streets and shopping arcades still feel real and a touch ramshackle, and there's nowhere better for a windy-day walk than the town's stately seafront prom.

Sights

Despite what you may have heard from Messrs Gilbert and Sullivan, Penzance was never renowned for its pirates – but it was known for trading in tin, grain and pilchards.

The export trade brought riches and the old town is littered with Georgian and Regency houses, especially along Chapel St; look out for the 19th-century **Egyptian House** (Chapel St), which looks like a bizarre cross between a Georgian townhouse and an Egyptian sarcophagus.

Penlee House Gallery & Museum GALLERY
(www.penleehouse.org.uk; Morrab Rd; adult/child £4.50/3; ⊙10am-5pm Mon-Sat Easter-Sep, 10.30am-4.30pm Mon-Sat Oct-Easter) Penzance's historic art gallery displays paintings by artists of the Newlyn School (including Stanhope Forbes) and hosts regular exhibitions. Admission is free on Saturday.

FREE **The Exchange** GALLERY
(www.theexchangegallery.co.uk; Princes Street; ⊙10am-5pm Mon-Sat Easter-Sep, Wed-Sat Oct-Easter) Housed in Penzance's old telecoms building, this cool gallery hosts regular exhibitions of contemporary art. The pulsating light installation outside is by the artist Peter Freeman. It's the sister gallery to the **Newlyn Art Gallery** (www.newlynartgallery.co.uk; ⊙10am-5pm Mon-Sat Easter-Sep, Wed-Sat Oct-Easter), a mile west along Penzance's prom.

Jubilee Pool SWIMMING
(www.jubileepool.co.uk; adult/child £4.30/3.20, family day-ticket £14; ⊙10.30am-6pm May-Sep) At the eastern end of the town's 19th-century promenade, this 1930s lido is open throughout the summer – just don't expect the water to be warm. Entry is half-price after 3.30pm.

Sleeping

Penzance has lots of cheap B&Bs along Alexandra Rd and Morrab Rd.

TOP CHOICE **Artist Residence Penzance** B&B ££
(☎01736-365664; www.arthotelcornwall.co.uk; Chapel St; d £80-120; ⓦ) This deliciously different new hotel on Chapel St is like sleeping inside an art gallery. All the rooms have their own bespoke design courtesy of a local artist: cartoony murals by Matt MacIvor, pop-art doves by Pinky Vision, butterfly wallpapers by Dolly Divine. They're furnished with hand-picked bits of retro furniture, and most peep across Penzance's rooftops. Bold, imaginative and brilliant fun.

Hotel Penzance HOTEL ££
(☎01736-363117; www.hotelpenzance.com; Briton's Hill; d £109-125; ⓦ) Perched on a hill with views across Mount's Bay, this townhouse hotel makes a pleasant Penzance base. Bedrooms are staid in style, with cream-and-magnolia colours, varnished desks and vintage lamps: the best have bay windows looking out to sea. The hotel's restaurant, the Bay, serves quality food. It is about 400m northeast of the train station.

Summer House B&B ££
(☎01736-363744; www.summerhouse-cornwall.com; Cornwall Tce; s £105, d £120-150; Ⓟ) For a touch of Chelsea-on-Sea, check into this elegant Regency house. Checks, pinstripes and cheery colours characterise the five bedrooms, and breakfast is sometimes served on an alfresco terrace.

Abbey Hotel HOTEL £££
(☎01736-366906; www.theabbeyonline.co.uk; Abbey St; d £90-200; ⓦ🐾) A creaky sea-captain's house off Chapel Street, reminiscent of Penzance in its 18th-century heyday. It's awash with architectural quirks – antique dressers, wonky corridors, cupboard bathrooms – and there's a sweet garden for twilight drinks.

Camilla House B&B ££
(☎01736-363771; www.camillahouse.co.uk; 12 Regent Tce; s £35, d £75-85; Ⓟ) The pick of the heritage B&Bs on Regent's Tce, worth

Penzance

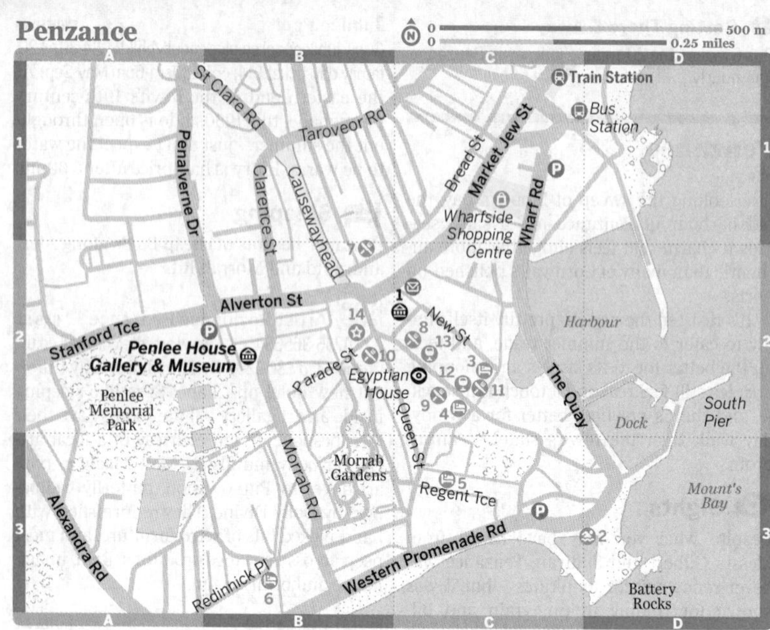

considering for its period architecture and views over the prom. Hardly cutting-edge, but cosy.

Penzance YHA HOSTEL £

(☎0845-371 9653; penzance@yha.org.uk; Castle Horneck, Alverton; dm from £14; P@) Penzance's YHA is inside an 18th-century house on the edge of town. It's a rambling place, with a cafe, laundry and four- to 10-bed dorms. It's a 15-minute walk from the front; buses 5 and 6 stop nearby.

Bodrifty Farm GLAMPING £££

(☎07887-522788; www.bodriftyfarm.com; £190 per night, 2-night minimum) This remote farm on the Penwith Moors offers camping with a difference: you get to sleep in a full-sized replica of a thatched Neolithic roundhouse (admittedly, with mod-cons including a bathroom, woodburner and bed). For more luxury, there's snazzy self-catering in the Swallow Barn.

Eating

TOP CHOICE **Untitled by Robert Wright** BRITISH ££

(☎01736-448022; www.untitledbyrobertwright.com; Abbey St; mains £14.50-18.95; ⊙lunch Tue-Sat) Penzance's classiest dining can be found at Robert Wright's curiously named restaurant on Abbey St. The menu makes maximum use of the fish and meat on the restaurant's doorstep, but gives it a spicy spin: oysters with merguez sausage, or red mullet escabeche. The upstairs dining room is light and inviting, with modern art arranged over white walls, and the downstairs lounge makes a chilled space for Cornish tapas. Altogether, a treat.

Bakehouse MEDITERRANEAN ££

(☎01736-331331; www.bakehouserestaurant.co.uk; Chapel St; mains £8.95-19.50; ⊙lunch Wed-Sat, dinner daily) This attractive double-floored diner is tucked down an alley off Chapel St. Food is filling and unpretentious: fish served with Med-style marinades, or steaks with a choice of sauces or spicy rubs. The dining room has A-frame beams and art, or there's a small palm-filled courtyard.

Archie Brown's CAFE £

(☎01736-362828; Bread St; mains £4-10; ⊙breakfast & lunch Mon-Sat) Archie Brown's has long been a favourite lunch-spot for Penzance's artists and earth-mothers: it's perched above a health shop, and serves quiches, salads and homebaked cakes with a wholefood ethos.

Assay House BISTRO ££

(☎01736-369729; 12-13 Chapel St; mains £14-17; ⊙breakfast & lunch daily, dinner Fri & Sat) This

Penzance

Top Sights

Sights

Activities, Courses & Tours

Sleeping

Eating

Drinking

Entertainment

glass-fronted establishment keeps changing hands, but its current guise is this streetside bistro, serving crispy fish goujons and tapas-style platters.

Honey Pot CAFE £

(☎01736-368686; 5 Parade St; mains £4-10; ⊙9am-5pm Mon-Sat) A popular and friendly local's cafe, serving no-nonsense jacket spuds and homity pies.

Drinking & Entertainment

Turk's Head PUB

(Chapel St) They pull a fine pint of ale at Penzance's oldest boozer. The bar's covered in maritime memorabilia, and it's said a secret smugglers' tunnel still links the pub to the harbour.

Zero Lounge BAR

(Chapel St) More urban chic than olde worlde, this open-plan bar also boasts the town's best beer garden.

Acorn Arts Centre THEATRE

(www.acornartscentre.co.uk; Parade St) The town's arts centre has been through troubled times, but it's now up and running again. Check the website for film, theatre, comedy and gigs.

Getting There & Away

Bus

Helston & Falmouth Bus 2/2A (hourly Monday to Saturday, six on Sunday) via Marazion, Praa Sands.

St Ives (30 minutes, half-hourly Monday to Saturday, hourly on Sunday) Buses 17/17A/17B.

Truro (one hour, three or four daily Monday to Saturday) Bus X18. The slower Bus 18 runs hourly via Camborne and Redruth.

Train

Penzance is the last stop on the line from London Paddington. Trains run roughly hourly. Sample fares:

Exeter (£39.50, three hours)

London Paddington (£56, hourly, 5½ hours)

St Ives (£3.80, 30 minutes)

Truro (£9.50, 30 minutes)

Marazion

Looming from the waters of Mount's Bay is the unmistakeable silhouette of **St Michael's Mount** (NT; ☎01736-710507; www.stmichaelsmount.co.uk; castle & gardens adult/child £8.75/4.25; ⊙house 10.30am-5.30pm Sun-Fri late Mar-Oct, gardens open Mon-Fri Apr-Jun, Thu & Fri Jul-Sep), a dreamy abbey set on a rocky island that's connected to the small seaside town of Marazion by a cobbled causeway.

There's been a monastery on the island since at least the 5th century, but the present abbey was mostly built during the 12th century by the Benedictine monks of Mont St Michel. The abbey later became the family seat of the St Aubyns (who still reside here), and is now under the stewardship of the National Trust.

Highlights include the rococo drawing room, the original armoury, the 14th-century priory church and the abbey's subtropical cliff gardens. Recent excavations have also uncovered important Bronze Age finds, including an axe-head, dagger and metal clasp, now on display inside the castle. You can also see one of the island's three remaining pillboxes, built during WWII when fears of German invasion were at their height.

Marazion is about 3 miles from Penzance. You can catch a ferry (adult/child £2/1) at high tide, but it's worth timing your arrival for low tide so you can walk across on the causeway, just as the monks and pilgrims did centuries ago. The 513 bus runs three times daily from Penzance.

If you're driving, it's well worth stopping in at the **Victoria Inn** (☎01736-710309; www.victoriainn-penzance.co.uk; Perranuthnoe; mains £11.50-18.95; ⊙lunch daily, dinner Mon-Sat) just outside Marazion, which has made a name for itself thanks to its top-quality posh-pub food, created by a talented young chef who trained under Raymond Blanc and Michael Caines.

The Lizard

For a taste of Cornwall's stormier side, there's nowhere finer than the Lizard Peninsula. Wind-lashed in winter, in summer it bristles with wildflowers and butterflies, and boasts countless inviting coves that are perfect for a secluded swim.

The Lizard used to be at the centre of Cornwall's smuggling industry and is still alive with tales of Cornish 'free-traders' (otherwise known as smugglers). The most notorious excise dodger was John Carter, the so-called King of Prussia – Prussia Cove near Marazion is named after him. It was also an ill-famed graveyard for ships – more vessels have come to grief on the Lizard's treacherous reefs than almost anywhere else in Britain.

Getting There & Away

Buses are the only public transport.

» Penzance to Falmouth, with stops at Porthleven and Helston. Bus 2 (eight to ten Monday to Saturday, six on Sunday).

» Helston to Gunwalloe, Gweek, Coverack and St Keverne. Bus 32 (two on Sundays only).

» Helston to Poldhu, Mullion and the Lizard. Bus 33 (three daily Monday to Friday).

» Helston to Truro. Bus 82 (hourly Monday to Saturday, five on Sunday).

HELSTON & PORTHLEVEN

The only town of size on the Lizard is Helston, one of Cornwall's five Stannary towns, where local tin was assayed and stamped before being shipped out across the world. The town stages a lively festival on **Flora Day** (www.helstonfloraday.org.uk) (8th May), an ancient spring celebration in which locals process through the town dressed in all their finery, dancing the traditional twirls and reels of the 'Furry Dance'.

Three miles from Helston is the attractive harbour of Porthleven, which still has a small fleet of working fishing boats, as well as an increasing number of artists' studios, cafes and restaurants, including Jude Kereama's fantastic Pacific-fusion fine-diner, **Kota** (☎01326-562407; www.kotarestaurant.co.uk; mains £12-20; ⊙lunch & dinner Tue-Sat).

A mile south of Porthleven is the treacherous sandbank known as **Loe Bar** and Cornwall's largest freshwater lake, **Loe Pool**, said to be the resting place of King Arthur's magical blade, Excalibur. It's now circled by walking trails.

Further south is the tucked-away cove of **Gunwalloe**, where the tiny church of St Winwaloe is quite literally lost amongst the dunes. Don't miss a pint and a plate at the clifftop **Halzephron Inn** (☎01326-240406; www.halzephron-inn.co.uk; mains £10.95-18.50) nearby.

LIZARD POINT

Five miles south of Mullion, Britain reaches its southernmost tip at Lizard Point, one of Britain's deadliest headlands and the last resting place of countless shipwrecks. It's a wild spot, with a rugged panorama of

DON'T MISS

KYNANCE COVE

Cornwall's littered with photogenic coves, but it's hard to find a more picture-perfect spot than Kynance Cove, a National Trust (NT)–owned beach just north of Lizard Point. It's a showstopper, studded with offshore islands and blessed with some of the most dazzlingly turquoise water in Cornwall. It's also known for its unusual geology: the cliffs around the cove are rich in serpentine, a red-green rock popular with Victorian trinket-makers.

The cove is a mile north of Lizard Point. There's a large NT car park on the cliffs (free for NT members), about half a mile uphill. Light lunches, coffees and cream teas are available at the **Kynance Cove Cafe** (www.kynancecovecafe.co.uk; mains £8-14), right beside the beach.

ROSKILLY FARM & LOVELANE CARAVANS

Let's face it, caravanning has never been cool – but the retro beauties on offer at **Lovelane Caravans** (www.lovelanecaravans.com; Tregallast Barton; caravan per week £340-475) near Helston might just change your mind. These vintage caravans have been lovingly restored and come complete with lino floors, charity-shop china, antique kettles and period furnishings. There's no electricity, so the only light comes from paraffin lamps and wood-stoves (ideal for star-spotting), and there's space for pitching your own tent if you'd prefer.

The campsite sits on the same land as **Roskilly's** (☎01326-280479; www.roskillys.co.uk; meals £6-12; ⏰10am-6pm), one of Cornwall's top organic ice-cream makers, which also has farm trails to explore and the charming Croust House cafe for lunch. It's near St Keverne, about 12 miles from Helston.

heather-clad cliffs, and the remains of an old lifeboat station hidden beneath the point.

Inland is the **Lizard Lighthouse Heritage Centre** (www.lizardlighthouse.co.uk; adult/child £6/3; ⏰11am-5pm Mon-Fri Mar-Oct), housed in a landmark lighthouse built in 1751. It contains exhibits on local seafaring and shipwrecks, and you can take a guided tour into the tower to see the lamp room.

Needless to say, the best way to appreciate the scenery is by striking out along the coast path. The nearby beaches of **Housel Bay** and **Church Cove** and the thatched fishing village of **Cadgwith** make ideal targets: plan on a round-trip of about 8 miles from Lizard Point.

Stock up for the walk with a takeaway lunch from **Ann's Pasties** (☎01326-290889; www.annspasties.co.uk; pasties £2.85; ⏰Mon-Sat 9am-3pm), one of the county's top pasty-makers, and a favourite of Rick Stein's.

THE RIVER HELFORD

Cutting across the northern Lizard, the River Helford is Cornwall's most beautiful (and biologically important) tidal estuary. The rich tidal mudflats support many rare bird and marine species, not to mention the county's largest oyster farm at Porth Navas, and the **Cornish Seal Sanctuary** (☎0871-423-2110; www.sealsanctuary.co.uk; adult/child £14.40/12; ⏰10am-5pm May-Sep, 9am-4pm Oct-Apr) near Gweek rescues sick and injured seals before returning them to the wild.

It's a glorious area to explore on foot, with numerous pebble beaches and hidden inlets to discover – including the famous **Frenchman's Creek**, which inspired one of Daphne du Maurier's most famous smuggling yarns. Helford village makes a handy base, and has a charming thatched pub called the **Shipwright Arms** (☎01326-231235; mains £7-14).

To see the river at its best, though, you'll need to get out on the water. Falmouth-based **Helford River Expeditions** (☎01326-250258) and **Aberfal Outdoor Pursuits** (☎07968-770756; www.aberfaloutdoorpursuits.co.uk) run guided kayaking trips along the estuary.

There's a useful summer passenger ferry (p390) which shuttles between Helford village and the Helford Passage, 4 miles from Falmouth.

Falmouth

POP 20,775

Nestled at the head of the Fal River, the harbour town of Falmouth made its fortune during the 18th and 19th centuries, when clippers, trading vessels and mail packets from across the world stopped off to unload their cargoes. The town is still an important centre for shipbuilding and repairs, although these days it's also a lively student hangout thanks to the nearby campus of University College Falmouth.

It's also a great base for venturing along Cornwall's south coast, with a wealth of bars and bistros, a trio of beaches and the nation's foremost maritime museum on its doorstep.

⊙ Sights & Activities

National Maritime Museum MUSEUM
(www.nmmc.co.uk; Discovery Quay; adult/child £10.50/7.20; ⏰10am-5pm) This is an outpost of the National Maritime Museum in Greenwich, London. It focuses on Falmouth's history as a seafaring port, with varied exhibitions exploring everything from the

underwater environment of the Fal Estuary to the town's groundbreaking nautical mail service, the Falmouth Packet.

At the heart of the complex is the Flotilla Gallery, where a collection of important vessels are suspended from the ceiling on steel wires. From the top floor of the Look Out tower, there's a 360-degree panorama right across Falmouth Bay.

Pendennis Castle CASTLE
(EH; ☎01326-316594; adult/child £5.40/2.70; ⏱10am-6pm Jul & Aug, 10am-5pm Apr-Jun & Sep, 10am-4pm Oct-Mar) Falmouth's been an important port since the Middle Ages. This Tudor castle on the promontory of Pendennis Point was built by Henry VIII to protect the harbour in tandem with its sister fortress at St Mawes, on the opposite side of the estuary.

Highlights include the atmospheric Tudor gun deck, a WWI guard house and the WWII-era Half-Moon Battery. The Noonday Gun rings out at noon sharp daily in July and August.

Beaches BEACH
Falmouth has three lovely beaches. Nearest to town is busy **Gyllyngvase**, a short walk from the town centre, where there's lots of sand and the lively Gylly Beach Café. Just around the headland is little **Swanpool**, while **Maenporth** is another mile further west. The 500 bus stops at all three in season.

Sleeping

Falmouth Townhouse HOTEL ££
(☎01326-312009; www.falmouthtownhouse.co.uk; d £85-120; 📶) The choice for the design-conscious, in a townhouse halfway between the high street and Discovery Quay. Despite the heritage building, the feel is studiously modernist: slate greys, retro furniture and minimal clutter throughout. Go for a top-floor room to avoid bar noise.

Highcliffe Contemporary B&B B&B ££
(☎01326-314466; www.falmouth-hotel.co.uk; 22 Melvill Rd; d £92-130) Does what it says on the tin – contemporary B&B rooms, all with their own different decorative touch, and luxuries such as iPod docks, retro radios and pocket-sprung mattresses. Go for spacious Room 2 or the light, white Attic Suite (Room 7).

St Michael's Hotel HOTEL £££
(☎01326-312707; www.stmichaelshotel.co.uk; r £118-248; P📶🏊) The pick of the seafront hotels, with checks, stripes and slatted wood for that essential maritime feel. It's not worth skimping here: go for the biggest room you can afford, and indulge at the spa, swimming pool and the smart Flying Fish Restaurant (2/3 courses £25/29).

Falmouth Backpacker's HOSTEL £
(☎01326-319996; www.falmouthbackpackers.co.uk; 9 Gyllyngvase Tce; dm/s £19/25, d £50-60) This indie hostel has been brightened up with primary colours and the odd funky print. There's an Aga in the kitchen and a DVD lounge, and owner Judi is full of fun and activity ideas.

Greenbank HOTEL £££
(☎01326-312440; www.greenbank-hotel.co.uk; Harbourside; s £99-129, d £185-225; P📶) A Falmouth classic, and still a good choice for heritage and harbour views. Public rooms have maritime touches – nautical knick-knacks and ships in cabinets – but the rooms stick to safe beiges and creams. 'Executive Harbour' rooms offer the most space and the choicest sea views.

Eating

TOP CHOICE **Wheelhouse** SEAFOOD ££
(☎01326 318050; Upton Slip; ⏱dinner Wed-Sat) This backstreet shellfish bar has become a red-hot recommendation since opening in 2011. Tables are crammed into the tiny dining room, and the chalkboard menu's deliberately simple: fresh crab, scallops, mussels or lobsters, all eaten hands-on and served with either matchstick fries or crusty bread. It's only open four nights a week, and always packed out – book well ahead.

Cove BRITISH ££
(☎01326-251136; www.thecovemaenporth.co.uk; Maenporth; 3-course menu £20, mains £13.95-24.50) Maenporth's beach-view restaurant is run by chef Arty Williams, who's stock-in-trade is giving a zesty fusion spin to traditional Brit cuisine. It's a bit of a trek, but worth the journey – and the 3-course *prix fixe* menu is super value.

Oliver's BISTRO ££
(☎01326-218138; www.oliverstheeatery.com; 33 High St; mains £12.95-19.95; ⏱lunch Tue-Sat, dinner Tue-Sun) The decor feels stark at this streetside diner – plain white walls, plain wood furniture – but the food is simple and reliable. The menu has a strong French in-

fluence, with a surfeit of meaty dishes, seafood and foraged ingredients.

Gylly Beach Café CAFE ££

(01326-312884; www.gyllybeach.com; Gyllyngvase Beach; mains £10.95-15.95; breakfast, lunch & dinner) The Gylly Beach is definitely the choice for a sundowner – it has a lovely patio deck overlooking the sands, and serves cold beers and killer cocktails. The menu's great too: quality steak, seafood and pasta after dark, and fry-ups and pancakes for brekkie.

Indaba on the Beach SEAFOOD £££

(01326-311886; www.indabafish.co.uk; Swanpool; mains £11-18; lunch daily, dinner Mon-Sat) Seafood-specific restaurant, perched on a rock above Swanpool. Go for classic mussels or splash out on a full-blown *fruits de mer* platter.

Stein's Fish & Chips FISH & CHIPS ££

(01841-532700; Discovery Quay; fish £7.85-9.25; 12-2.30pm & 5-9pm, oyster bar 5-9pm) Rick Stein's posh Falmouth fish-and-chips shop batters unusual species including lemon sole and sea bream alongside the usual cod and hake – be prepared to pay the premium. Sit-down dishes are served at the oyster bar upstairs.

Provedore CAFE £

(www.provedore.co.uk; 43 Trelawney Rd; Mon-Sun) Cool continental cafe serving choice coffee and pastries.

Boathouse GASTROPUB ££

(Trevethan Hill; mains £6-12) This groovy gastropub has the atmosphere of a ship's galley, with a deck overlooking the river to Flushing. There's usually a good choice of mains chalked on the blackboard.

Harbour Lights FISH & CHIPS £

(Arwenack St; fish & chips £4-6) Falmouth's classic chippie, sustainably sourced and very reasonably priced.

Drinking

Espressini CAFE

(39 Killigrew St; coffee from £2; 9am-5pm Mon-Sat) Indecisive drinkers beware: the vast choice of blends, roasts and coffee concoctions here are enough to fill a 6-foot long blackboard. Literally.

The Front PUB

(Arwenack St) The place for boutique beers, named CAMRA's Kernow Pub of the Year in 2011. It's off Arwenack St by the seafront.

FAL RIVER FERRIES

Fal River Links (tel, info 861914; www.falriverlinks.co.uk) operates a network of ferries up, down and across the Fal Estuary. The **Fal Mussel Card** (adult/child £16/11) buys a day's unlimited travel, and discounts on other boat trips.

St Mawes Ferry (p393) Cross-river service that runs every 20 minutes in summer to St Mawes.

Flushing Ferry (adult/child £2.50/1) Half-hourly boat from Falmouth to Flushing.

King Harry Ferry (p393) Cross-river service that carrries vehicles and pedestrians between Trelissick and Philleigh on the Roseland Peninsula.

Place Ferry (p393) St Mawes to Place Creek.

Falmouth Water Taxi (www.falmouthwatertaxi.co.uk) On-demand shuttle service stopping at Penryn Quay, St Mawes, the Pandora Inn, Trelissick and Malpas (near Truro).

Quayside PUB

(Arwenack St) Harbourside pub with tables on the quays.

Chain Locker PUB

(Quay St) A proper old sea-dog of a pub, complete with head-scraping rafters and a hugger-mugger atmosphere.

Getting There & Away

BUS Glendurgan, Gweek & the Helford Passage (hourly Monday to Saturday, four to seven on Sunday) Bus 500 only runs as far as the Helford Passage; Bus 35 continues to Helston.

Truro (hourly) Bus 88 is the fastest; Bus 88A continues to Newquay.

TRAIN Falmouth is at the end of the branch line from **Truro** (£3.80, 20 minutes), which also stops at **Penryn**.

Around Falmouth

GLENDURGAN & TREBAH GARDENS

Two of Cornwall's great gardens sit side by side along the northern bank of the Helford River. They're about 4 miles' drive from Falmouth: head for Mawnan Smith and follow the signs.

WORTH A TRIP

PANDORA INN

One of Cornwall's oldest and loveliest creekside pubs, the **Pandora Inn** (☎01326-372678; www.pandorainn.com; Restronguet Creek; mains £10-16) is nestled in a beautiful river setting. Inside, blazing hearths, snug alcoves and ships in cabinets; outside, thatched roof, cob walls and a pontoon snaking out onto Restronguet Creek. The location really has the wow factor, but the pub hit the headlines in 2011 when a stray ember set fire to the roof and burned it to the ground – not that you'd ever know it, as it has since been impeccably rebuilt.

The Pandora sits at the bottom of a steep hill near the village of Mylor, roughly equidistant from Truro and Falmouth. It's signed off the A39, but it's still tricky to find, so a decent map will come in handy.

First planted in 1840, **Trebah** (☎01326-252200; www.trebahgarden.co.uk; adult/child £8.50/2.50 Mar-Oct; ⊙10.30am-4.30pm) is one of Cornwall's finest subtropical gardens, dramatically situated in a steep ravine filled with giant rhododendrons, huge Brazilian rhubarb plants and jungle ferns.

Next-door **Glendurgan** (NT; ☎01326-250906; www.nationaltrust.org.uk/glendurgan-garden; adult/child £6.80/3.50; ⊙10.30am-5.30pm Tue-Sat) was established around the same time by the wealthy Fox family, and is now owned by the National Trust. It's known for stunning views of the River Helford, as well as an impressive maze and secluded beach near Durgan village.

A mile further on from the gardens is the fantastic **Ferryboat Inn** (☎01326-250625; mains £8-18; ⊙lunch & dinner), a picture-perfect spot for a creekside pint and a plate of something filling. Now owned by the Wright Brothers, who also run the nearby Porth Navas Oyster Farm, its gastropub menu is first rate, and the pub sits opposite its own beach, which is made for post-pint paddling.

The **Helford Ferry** (☎01326-250770; www.helford-river-boats.co.uk; adult/child £5.50/4; ⊙9.30am-9.30pm Jun-Aug, to 5.30pm Apr-May & Sep-Oct) leaves directly opposite the pub.

TRELISSICK GARDENS

At the head of the Fal estuary, 4 miles from Truro, **Trelissick** (NT; www.nationaltrust.org.uk/trelissick-garden; adult/child £7.20/3.60; ⊙10.30am-5.30pm Feb-Oct, 11am-4pm Nov-Jan) is another of Cornwall's landmark estates, and is particularly known for its magnolias and hydrangeas. Outside the formal gardens, trails wind out across the parkland and riverbanks: big tankers can often be seen moored up along the deep creeks nearby.

The gardens are now managed by the National Trust, and have a small tea room and shop.

Just downhill from the garden entrance, the King Harry Ferry (p393) shuttles across the Fal River to the Roseland Peninsula.

Truro

POP 17,431

Cornwall's capital has been at the centre of the county's fortunes for eight centuries. Truro grew up around a now vanished hilltop castle, and later became rich as a busy river port and one of Cornwall's five stannary towns. The town was granted its own bishop in 1877, and the soaring three-spired cathedral followed soon after.

These days it's a busy commercial city, with a selection of shops, galleries and restaurants, as well as Cornwall's main county museum.

⊙ Sights & Activities

FREE **Royal Cornwall Museum** MUSEUM
(☎01872-272205; www.royalcornwallmuseum.org.uk; River St; ⊙10am-5pm Mon-Sat) Collections at the county's archaeological museum encompass everything from geological specimens to Celtic torques and a ceremonial carriage. Upstairs there's an Egyptian section and a little gallery with some surprising finds: a Turner here, a van Dyck there, and several works by Stanhope Forbes.

Truro Cathedral CHURCH
(www.trurocathedral.org.uk; High Cross; suggested donation £4; ⊙7.30am-6pm Mon-Sat, 9am-7pm Sun) Built on the site of a 16th-century parish church in soaring Gothic Revival style, Truro Cathedral was completed in 1910, making it the first cathedral built in England since St

Paul's. Inside, the vast nave contains some fine Victorian stained glass and the impressive Father Willis Organ.

Lemon St Market MARKET
(www.lemonstreetmarket.co.uk; Lemon St; ⏲10.30am-5.30pm Mon-Sat) A covered market housing craft shops, cafes, delis and an upstairs gallery. The willow-and-paper lanterns hanging from the ceiling were built for Truro's Christmas street parade, the City of Lights, held in early December.

Enterprise Boats BOAT TOUR
(☎01326-374241; www.enterprise-boats.co.uk; adult/child return £13/8) This boat company runs scenic boat trips up and down the Fal, stopping at Trelissick Gardens, the **Smuggler's Restaurant** (☎01872-580309; www.tregothnan.co.uk/smugglers; dinner mains £11-15; ⏲noon-5pm, dinner by booking only) beside the King Harry Ferry, and finally Falmouth.

Depending on the tides, boats run from Truro or further down the river at Malpas; connecting shuttle buses leave from outside the harbour-master's office.

Sleeping

Considering this is Cornwall's capital, Truro's paucity of accommodation is rather bewildering.

Mannings Hotel HOTEL ££
(☎01872-270345; www.manningshotels.co.uk; Lemon St; s £79, d £99-109; P 📶) The city's best option is this efficient city-centre pad (formerly the Royal Hotel), geared heavily towards the business crowd. Bold colours, wall-mounted TVs and sleek furniture keep things uncluttered, and there are 'aparthotels' for longer stays (£129).

Townhouse B&B ££
(☎01872-277374; www.trurotownhouse.com; 20 Falmouth Rd; s £59-69, d £69-79) A practical, businessy B&B uphill from the town centre. Snug rooms feature colourful throws, workdesks and angle-poise lamps; some have four-posters. They're all on the small side.

Eating

Saffron BRITISH ££
(☎01872-263771; www.saffronrestauranttruro.co.uk; 5 Quay St; mains £13.50-16.50; ⏲lunch Mon-Fri, dinner Tue-Sat) This stalwart restaurant remains as reliable as ever. Its generous menu is Cornish-meets-Mediterranean – spider crab bisque, seared cod with saffron potatoes – and the dining room's sunny tones make it feel warm and inviting.

Bustopher's BISTRO ££
(☎01872-279029; www.bustophersbarbistro.com; 62 Lemon St; mains £10-18) Another long-stander that's been modernised to cater for the city's changing tastes. Cosy candles, sash windows and stripped-wood floors give things an intimate ambience, ideal for bistro fare such as creamy cider mussels or Toulouse sausage with pomme purée.

Indaba Fish SEAFOOD ££
(☎01872-274700; Tabernacle St; mains £14-18; ⏲dinner) The 'city' sister to Indaba's beachside establishment at Swanpool. Again, the emphasis is on classic seafood – Falmouth oysters, Newlyn lobsters, North Coast fish – although the backstreet location is nothing like as sexy as its sister.

Blend 71 CAFE £
(☎01872-279686; www.blend71.co.uk; 71 Lemon St; ⏲10am-5pm Mon-Sat) The city's top coffee stop, next door to the Plaza cinema.

Archie Brown's CAFE £
(☎01872-278622; www.archiebrowns.co.uk; 105-106 Kenwyn St; mains £4-12; ⏲9am-5pm Mon-Sat) Penzance's wholefood original comes to the big city.

Duke St Sandwich Deli CAFE £
(10 Duke St; sandwiches £2.50-5; ⏲9am-5.30pm Mon-Sat) Gourmet sandwiches and handmade ciabattas.

Fodder's CAFE £
(☎01872-271384; Pannier Market, Lemon Quay; mains £6-9; ⏲9am-5.30pm Mon-Sat) Chaotic cafe hidden away above Truro's Pannier Market.

Drinking & Entertainment

Old Ale House PUB
(Quay St) Burnished wood 'n' beer mats sum up the vibe at the OAH – there's a different choice of daily ales chalked up behind the bar, and live jazz at weekends. You're even encouraged to throw your peanut shells on the floor.

Old Grammar School PUB
(19 St Mary St; ⏲10am-late) Open-plan drinking den with big tables and soft sofas to sink into. Lunch is served from noon to 3pm; later it's cocktails, candles and imported Belgian and Japanese beers.

CORNISH MINING SITES

Since 2006, Cornwall and West Devon's mining areas have formed part of the UK's newest Unesco World Heritage Site, the **Cornwall & West Devon Mining Landscape** (www.cornish-mining.org.uk).

The **Cornish Mines & Engines** (☎01209-315027; cornishmines@nationaltrust.org.uk; adult/child £6.30/3.10) centre in Pool, near Redruth, is the best place to get acquainted with this once-great industry. At the heart of the complex are two working beam engines, both once powered by steam boilers designed by genius engineer (and local lad) Richard Trevithick. Films, photos and artefacts trace the area's mining history, and you can see more mining gear in action at **King Edward Mine.** (☎01209-614681; www.kingedwardmine.co.uk; adult/child £6/1.50; ⊙10am-5pm May-Sep) Other unmissable mining sites include the historic beam engine at Levant (p381) and the mine at Geevor (p381).

For a modern perspective, the massive £35m regeneration project known as **Heartlands** (www.heartlandscornwall.com) has breathed new life into 19 acres of derelict mining land near Pool. The site is now home to a cultural centre, outdoor adventure playground and art exhibition space, and you can take regular guided tours of the old engine house at Robinson's Shaft.

Vertigo BAR
(15 St Marys St; ⊙10am-late) Stylish late-night bar, worth a look for its metro decor and sweet walled garden.

Heron PUB
(Malpas) Two miles along the river from Truro, this Malpas pub can't be bettered for a riverside pint.

Hall for Cornwall THEATRE
(☎01872-262466; www.hallforcornwall.co.uk; Lemon Quay) The county's main venue for touring theatre and music.

Information

Tourist Office (☎01872-274555; tic@truro.gov.uk; Boscawen St; ⊙9am-5.30pm Mon-Fri, 9am-5pm Sat)

Getting There & Away

Bus

Truro's bus station is beside Lemon Quay. Useful lines:

Falmouth (40 minutes to one hour, hourly) Bus 88.

Penzance (one hour, hourly Monday to Saturday, six on Sunday) Bus X18. Express service via Redruth and Camborne.

Helston (one hour, hourly, five on Sunday) Bus 82.

St Agnes (30 to 40 minutes, hourly Monday to Saturday) Bus 85/85A.

St Ives (1½ hours, hourly Monday to Saturday) Bus 14/14A.

Train

Truro is on the main Paddington-Penzance line and the branch line to Falmouth. Destinations:

Bristol (£42, 3½ hours)

Exeter (£16.90, 2¼ hours)

Falmouth (£3.80, 30 minutes)

London Paddington (£56, 4½ hours)

Penzance (£9.50, 30 minutes)

The Roseland

Stretching into the sea southwest of Truro, this rural peninsula gets its name not from flowers but from the Cornish word *ros*, meaning promontory. Highlights include the old fishing harbour of **Portloe** and **Veryan**, a quiet village framed by two thatched roundhouses.

Nearby are the beaches of **Carne** and **Pendower**, which join together at low tide to form the longest stretch of sand on Cornwall's south coast.

Around the point of St Anthony's Head sits the swish town of **St Mawes**, best known for its clover-shaped Elizabethan **castle** (EH; ☎01326-270526; adult/child £4.60/2.40; ⊙10am-6pm Sun-Fri Jul-Aug, 10am-5pm Sun-Fri Apr-June & Sep, earlier closing at other times), the sister fortress to Pendennis across the estuary.

The town is home to some pleasant pubs and hotels, and there are several sparkling beaches nearby, including **Great** and **Little Molunan**: you can explore them under your own steam with **St Mawes Kayaks** (☎07971-846786; www.stmaweskayaks.co.uk; 2 hr £15), or catch the regular **Place Ferry** (adult/child return £6/4; ⌚half-hourly Apr-Oct) from St Mawes.

The shortest way to get to the Roseland is by ferry. The **St Mawes Ferry** (adult/child return £8/4.50) shuttles pedestrians across from Falmouth several times an hour, while the **King Harry Ferry** (per car single/return £5/8, free for bicycles and pedestrians) carries cars, cyclists and pedestrians from the landing near Trelissick.

St Austell & Around

While tin mining was once the staple industry for much of Cornwall, the area around St Austell was dominated by china clay, used in everything from medicines to porcelain manufacture. Its legacy lingers on in the form of huge spoil heaps, mica dams and turquoise pools on the horizon around St Austell (known locally as the 'Cornish Alps').

St Austell itself is a pretty workaday place, although it's looking better since the multi-million-pound spruce-up of the town centre. Decent accommodation and restaurants are still thin on the ground.

Sights

TOP CHOICE Lost Gardens of Heligan GARDENS
(☎01726-845100; www.heligan.com; adult/child £10/6; ⌚10am-6pm Mar-Oct, 10am-5pm Nov-Feb) This is Cornwall's real-life secret garden. Formerly the family estate of the Tremaynes, Heligan's magnificent 19th-century gardens fell into disrepair following WWI, and have since been restored to their former splendour by the brains behind the Eden Project, Tim Smit, and a huge army of gardeners, horticulturalists and volunteers.

It's a horticultural wonderland: wandering round the grounds you'll discover formal lawns, working kitchen gardens, fruit-filled greenhouses, a secret grotto and a rhododendron that's said to be the world's largest at a mighty 82ft from root to tip. For many people, though, it's the jungle valley which really steals the show – a Lost World landscape of gigantic ferns, towering palms and tropical blooms.

Heligan is 7 miles from St Austell. Bus 526 (30 minutes, hourly, ten on Sunday) links Heligan with Mevagissey and St Austell train station.

Charlestown Shipwreck & Heritage MUSEUM
(☎01726-69897; www.shipwreckcharlestown.com; adult/child £5.95/2.95; ⌚10am-5pm Mar-Oct) Charlestown was a key china clay port, and is now a favourite location for film crews: many blockbusters and costume dramas have used its quays as a ready-made backdrop.

The town's heritage is explored at this intriguing museum, which houses artefacts collected from 150 shipwrecks, including a few pieces from the *Titanic* and *Lusitania*.

Restormel Castle CASTLE
(EH; adult/child £3.50/2.10; ⌚10am-6pm Jul & Aug, 10am-5pm Apr-Jun & Sep, 10am-4pm Oct) Squatting on a hill 1½ miles north of Lostwithiel, this 13th-century castle is one of the best-preserved circular keeps in England. The interior has long since crumbled, but you can still climb the battlements for evocative views over the Fowey River.

Getting There & Around

Bus

Western Greyhound buses from St Austell:

Charlestown (15 minutes, 10 daily Monday to Saturday) Bus 525.

Fowey (40 minutes, 10 daily) Bus 524.

Mevagissey, Heligan and Gorran Haven Bus 526 runs to Mevagissey and Heligan hourly in summer; five or six buses a day continue to Gorran Haven.

Newquay & the Eden Project (hourly Monday to Saturday, five on Sunday) Bus 527 travels from Newquay to St Austell, then on to the Eden Project.

Truro (70 minutes, hourly Monday to Saturday) Bus 522.

Train

St Austell and Lostwithiel are on the main Paddington–Penzance line.

Mevagissey

Sturdy cottages and a small fishing fleet shelter behind a double-walled breakwater in Mevagissey, another of Cornwall's quintessential fishing ports. It won't take you too long to exhaust the town's meandering alleys, and the town has several atmospheric pubs, including the supremely snug **Fountain Inn** (☎01726-842320; St George's Sq; pub meals £8-12). The quay also makes a great spot for crab-lining.

Beyond town, there's a popular holiday beach at Pentewan, and several tucked-away coves around Gorran Haven and Dodman Point.

DON'T MISS

THE EDEN PROJECT

Lodged at the base of a disused clay-pit 3 miles from St Austell, the gigantic biomes of the **Eden Project** (www.edenproject.com) look like something out of a science-fiction film. Since being built in 2001, they've become both an ecological *cause célèbre* and one of Cornwall's most iconic landmarks.

The brainchild of ex–record producer turned environmental pioneer Tim Smit, these vast domed greenhouses recreate the world's key microclimates in miniature – including the steamy **Rainforest Biome**, populated with huge palms, tropical mangroves and soaring banana trees, and the **Mediterranean Biome**, filled with species all the way from the Californian desert to the African savannah. Other areas of the site illustrate the vital roles of plants in medicine, industry, food production and even perfume-manufacture – as well as their crucial role in regulating the global climate and ensuring our own species' survival.

It's informative, educational and enormous fun, but it gets busy: booking online avoids the queues and gets a discount of 10-15%. Arriving by bike or bus entitles you to £4 off standard admission.

The biomes also host a series of events throughout the year, including a series of summer gigs during the **Eden Sessions** (www.edensessions.com), and the winter **Time of Gifts** festival, complete with a full-size ice rink.

There are regular buses from St Austell; if you're driving, just follow signs from the A38.

Mevagissey is 8 miles from St Austell. The 526 bus (hourly in summer) stops nearby.

Looe

POP 5280

Perched on the long curve of south coast between the Fowey River and Plymouth Sound, Looe is a breezy blend of historic fishing port and bucket-and-spade resort. Split into East and West Looe, and divided by the broad river, it's a pleasant base for exploring Cornwall's southeastern reaches, and has some good beaches nearby.

Sights & Activities

Boat Trips BOAT TOUR

Half a mile offshore is tiny **Looe Island**, a 22-acre nature reserve run by the Cornwall Wildlife Trust. The boat **Islander** (07814-139223; adult/child return £6/4, plus £2.50/1 landing fee) crosses to the island in summer.

Other boats set out from Buller Quay for destinations along the coast, including Polperro (£19) and Fowey (£12). Check the signs on the quayside for the next sailings.

Wild Futures Monkey Sanctuary WILDLIFE RESERVE

(01503-262532; www.monkeysanctuary.org; St Martins; adult/child £8/5; 11am-4.30pm Sun-Thu Easter-Sep) Half a mile west of town, this wildlife centre is guaranteed to raise some 'aaahhhhs' over its woolly and capuchin monkeys, many of which were rescued from illegal captivity.

Sleeping

Barclay House B&B £££

(01503-262929; www.barclayhouse.co.uk; St Martins Rd; d £125-165; P) This detached Victorian villa sits in 2.5-hectare gardens and has the best bedrooms in East Looe, with wraparound river views and graceful shades of peach, pistachio and aquamarine.

Beach House B&B ££

(01503-262598; www.thebeachhouselooe.co.uk; Hannafore Point; d £100-130; P) Smart B&B in a modern house overlooking Hannafore Point. The compact rooms are named after Cornish bays: top of the pile is Kynance, with a massive bed and private balcony.

Information

Looe Tourist Office (01503-262072; www.visit-southeastcornwall.co.uk; Fore St; 10am-5pm Easter-Oct, plus occasional days Nov-Easter) In the Guildhall.

Getting There & Away

Bus 572 goes to **Plymouth** (1¼ hours, seven daily Monday to Saturday).

A scenic train trundles to Liskeard on the London–Penzance line. Looe Valley Line (every two hours Monday to Saturday, eight on Sunday, day ranger adult/child £3.90/1.95).

Polperro

The fishing village of Polperro is a postcard muddle of lanes, quays and cottages set around a tiny harbour. It's always jammed in summer, so arrive in the evening or out of season if possible.

Apart from the town itself, there's not that much to see, although the small **Heritage Museum** (☎01503-272423; The Warren; adult/child £1.75/50p; ⏲10am-6pm Mar-Oct) has eclectic displays on the village's smuggling and seagoing heritage.

Bus 573 runs from Fowey (30 minutes, hourly in summer).

Fowey

POP 2273

Pastel-coloured houses tumble down the steep hillsides of Fowey (pronounced Foy), an old port with a long history as a miltary harbour, ship-building centre and industrial port.

During the 14th century Fowey was the base for raids on France and Spain; to guard against reprisals Henry VIII constructed **St Catherine's Castle** above Readymoney Cove, south of town.

It later became the area's key port for transporting china-clay, although the heavy industry is long gone, and these days Fowey has become another of Cornwall's swish seaside getaways.

The author Daphne du Maurier lived in Fowey, and every May the town hosts the **Daphne du Maurier Literary Festival** (www.dumaurier.org) in her honour.

Sleeping

TOP CHOICE Upton House B&B £££
(☎01726-832732; www.upton-house.com; 2 Esplanade; d £140-180) An utterly bonkers B&B that's gone all-out for decorative overload: the four rooms are full of tongue-in-cheek touches, from neon pink flamingos and catskin mats to skull-meets-fleur-de-lys wallpaper. Owner Angelique holds regular soirées, too: supper clubs, craftwork sessions and parties. Mad, but marvellous.

Coriander Cottages B&B ££
(☎01726-834998; www.foweyaccommodation.co.uk; Penventinue Ln; r £90-120; P 📶) A delightfully rural complex on the outskirts of Fowey, with ecofriendly accommodation in a choice of open-plan self-catering barns, all with quiet country views. Unusually, nightly and weekly rates are available.

Old Quay House HOTEL £££
(☎01726-833302; www.theoldquayhouse.com; 28 Fore St; d £255-395; 📶) The epitome of Fowey's upmarket trend, this exclusive quayside hotel is all natural fabrics, rattan chairs and tasteful tones, and the rooms are a mix of estuary-view suites and attic penthouses. Very Kensington; not very Cornish.

Golant YHA HOSTEL £
(☎0845-371 9019; golant@yha.org.uk; Penquite House; dm from £14; P @) A few miles north of Fowey, this rural hostel sits amongst 16 hectares and is reached by its own kilometre-long drive. The architecture's Georgian, and many rooms have estuary views.

Eating

The Bistro FRENCH ££
(☎01726-832322; www.thebistrofowey.co.uk; 24 Fore St; 2-/3-course menu £15.95/18.95)

CORNWALL'S BIKE TRAILS

Many cyclists have heard of the Camel Trail (p372), but there are several other dedicated bike routes criss-crossing Cornwall, including the 25-mile **First-and-Last Trail** from Land's End to Hayle, the 45-mile **Coast & Clay Trail** around St Austell's clay-pits and the popular 11-mile **Coast-to-Coast Trail** between Devoran and Portreath, which forms part of a larger **Mineral Tramways** network through the rugged mining country around Camborne and Redruth. Each individual route makes a great day ride, or you can link them together into an epic 200-mile route known collectively as the **Cornish Way** (the western half of NCN3).

Maps and route guides are available from local tourist offices or can be downloaded from the Cornwall Council website (www.cornwall.gov.uk). **Sustrans** (www.sustrans.org.uk) also publishes a dedicated route map covering the entire Cornish Way.

Sparkling bistro dining on Fowey's main street, with a seasonal menu offering Cornish interpretations of Gallic classics: bouillabaisse, fish soup, roast cod loin, sole menunière. Mosaic floors and monochrome prints keep the dining area sleek and chic.

Sam's BISTRO ££
(www.samsfowey.co.uk; 20 Fore St; mains £9.95-14.95) Comfortable as an old pair of flip-flops, this Fowey diner just keeps pulling in the punters. It's deliberately laid-back – booth seats, day-glo menus, sauce bottles on the tables – and offers solid seafood and burgers in starter or main sizes. There's a beachside outpost beside Polkerris Beach. No bookings.

Pinky Murphy's Café CAFE £
(☎01726-832512; www.pinkymurphys.com; 19 North St; ⏰9am-5pm Mon-Sat, 9.30am-4pm Sun) Mismatched crockery and colourful bean-bags make this cafe a quirky spot for lunch or tea. Our tip: go for a Pinky's Cream Tease, which includes homemade scones, clotted cream and fresh strawberries.

Dwelling House CAFE £
(☎01726-833662; 6 Fore St; tea £3-6; ⏰10am-6.30pm summer, 10am-5.30pm Wed-Sun winter) Top spot for tea (20-plus varieties) and dainty cupcakes (decorated with sprinkles and icing swirls, and served on a proper cake stand).

Drinking

Fowey's awash with pubs: try the pastel-pink **King of Prussia** (www.kingofprussia.co.uk; Town Quay) for a harbour view, or the tiny **Lugger** (Fore St) for shipshape atmosphere: both serve St Austell Ales.

Getting There & Away

BUS Buses to Fowey all stop at Par Station, with onward connections on the Penzance–London Paddington mainline.

St Austell First's 25 (45 minutes, hourly Monday to Saturday) and Western Greyhound's 525 (45 minutes, 10 or 11 daily in summer) both serve Fowey.

FERRY Bodinnick Ferry (car with 2 passengers/pedestrian/bicycle £4.50/1.30/1.60; ⏰last ferry around 8.45pm Apr-Oct, 7pm Nov-Mar) Car ferry crossing the river to Bodinnick.

Polruan Ferry (adult/child/bicycle £1.60/80p/1) Foot passenger ferry across the estuary to Polruan village, starting point for some lovely coastal walks. Depending on the time of year, boats leave from either Town Quay or Whitehouse slip, just off the Esplanade.

Around Looe

Lanhydrock HISTORIC BUILDING
(NT; ☎01208-265950; www.nationaltrust.org.uk/lanhydrock; adult/child £10.70/5.30, grounds only £6.30/3.40; ⏰house 11am-5pm Tue-Sat, grounds 10am-6pm daily) This huge house provides a fascinating insight into the 'upstairs, downstairs' lives of the Cornish gentry, namely the Robartes family. Extensively rebuilt after a fire in 1881, it's the quintessential Victorian manor, complete with gentlemen's smoking room, toy-strewn nursery and antique-filled dining room – as well as a network of enormous kitchens where the family's lavish dinner parties would have been prepared.

Also look out for the impressive plasterwork ceiling of the Long Gallery, which was created by 17th-century Italian artists and miraculously escaped the great fire.

The house is situated 2½ miles southeast of Bodmin.

Cotehele HISTORIC BUILDING
(NT; ☎01579-351346; St Dominick; adult/child £9/4.50, grounds only £5.40/2.70; ⏰house 11am-4pm Sat-Thu, gardens dawn-dusk daily) Seven miles from Tavistock, this Tudor manor served as the family seat of the Edgcumbe dynasty for some 400 years. It's stocked with Tudor interiors, best seen in the great hall, and many impressive tapestries and suits of armour. It's also notoriously haunted – several ghostly figures are said to wander through the house, accompanied by music and a peculiar herbal smell.

Outside, the terraced **gardens** feature a medieval dovecote, a working mill and a heavily restored quay.

Antony House HISTORIC BUILDING
(☎01752-812191; www.nationaltrust.org.uk/antony; adult/child £8.10/5.10, grounds only £4.10/2.10; ⏰house 1-5pm Tue-Thu & Sun Jun-Aug, gardens open from midday) Owned by the National Trust and occupied by the Carew-Pole family, this house's main claim to fame are its decorative gardens, designed by the 18th-century landscape architect Humphry Repton and filled with outlandish topiary, some of which featured in Tim Burton's big-screen adaptation of *Alice in Wonderland*.

The house is 9 miles east of Looe or 6 miles west from Plymouth – the **Torpoint Ferry** (www.tamarcrossings.org.uk/index.

aspx?articleid=36386; cars £2.50, pedestrians & cyclists free; ⌚24hr) stops a couple of miles away. Opening days vary through the year, so phone ahead or check the website.

Port Eliot HISTORIC BUILDING
(☎01503-230211; www.porteliot.co.uk; house & grounds adult/child £8/4, grounds only £4/2; ⌚2-6pm Sat-Thu Mar-Jun) Stretching across the eastern end of Cornwall is the 6000-acre estate of Port Eliot, the seat of the Earl of St Germans. Since March 2008 the house and grounds have been opened to the public for a hundred days every year, and every July the estate hosts a major outdoor bash, the **Port Eliot Festival** (www.porteliotfestival.com), which began life as a literary festival but has now branched out into live music, theatre and outdoor art.

Occasional trains from Plymouth stop at the tiny station of St Germans; otherwise you'll need your own transport to get to the estate.

Bodmin Moor

It can't quite boast the wild majesty of Dartmoor, but Bodmin Moor has a bleak beauty all of its own.

Cornwall's 'roof' is a high heath pockmarked with bogs, ancient remains and lonely granite hills, including **Rough Tor** (pronounced *row-tor*, 400m) and **Brown Willy** (419m), Cornwall's highest points. It's a desolate place that works on the imagination; for years there have been reported sightings of the Beast of Bodmin, a large, black cat-like creature, although no one's ever managed to snap a decent picture.

The wild landscape offers some superb walking, and there are some great trails suitable for hikers and mountain-bikers around **Cardinham Woods** (www.forestry.gov.uk/cardinham) on the moor's eastern edge. Other landmarks to look out for are **Dozmary Pool**, at the centre of the moor said to have been where Arthur's sword, Excalibur, was thrown after his death. Nearby is **Jamaica Inn** (☎01566-86250; www.jamaicainn.co.uk; s £65, d £80-110; P), made famous by Daphne du Maurier's novel of the same name (although it's been modernised since du Maurier's day).

The **Bodmin & Wenford Railway** (www.bodminandwenfordrailway.co.uk; rover pass adult/child £11.50/6; ⌚Mar-Oct) is the last standard-gauge railway in Cornwall plied by steam locomotives. Trains are still decked out in original 1950s livery and chug from Bodmin Parkway and Bodmin General station to Boscarne Junction, where you can join the Camel Trail cycle route. There are two to four return trips daily depending on the season.

For general information on the moor, contact **Bodmin tourist office** (☎01208-76616; www.bodminlive.com; Mount Folly; ⌚10am-5pm Mon-Sat).

ISLES OF SCILLY

Twenty-eight miles southwest of mainland Cornwall lie the tiny Isles of Scilly, an archipelago of over 140 islands, five of which are inhabited. Nurtured by the Gulf Stream and blessed with a balmy subtropical climate, the Scillys have long survived on the traditional industries of farming, fishing and flower-growing, but these days tourism is by far the biggest money spinner. St Mary's is the largest and busiest island, closely followed by Tresco, while only a few hardy souls remain on Bryher, St Martin's and St Agnes.

With a laid-back island lifestyle, a strong community spirit and some of the most glorious beaches anywhere in England, it's hardly surprising that many visitors find themselves drawn back to the Scillys year after year. While life moves on at breakneck speed in the outside world, time in the Scillys seems happy to stand still.

The islands get very busy in summer, while many businesses shut down completely in winter. Hotels are expensive, so most people choose to stay in self-catering cottages – the two main companies are **Island Properties** (☎01720-422082; www.scillyhols.com) and **Sibley's Island Homes** (☎01720-422431; www.sibleysonscilly.co.uk). All of the islands (except Tresco) have a basic campsite.

Information

There's a locally run website, www.scillyonline.co.uk, and the official tourist site is www.simplyscilly.co.uk.

Isles of Scilly Tourist Board (☎01720-422536; tic@scilly.gov.uk; St Mary's; ⌚8.30am-6pm Mon-Fri, 9am-5pm Sat, 9am-2pm Sun May-Sep, shorter hrs in winter)

Getting There & Away

Air

British International (☎01736-363871; www.islesofscillyhelicopter.com) Helicopters fly to

St Mary's and Tresco from **Penzance heliport**. Full return fares are adult/child £190/110. Saver fares (for travel Monday to Friday) and day-trip fares are much cheaper.

Isles of Scilly Skybus (☎0845-710-5555; www.islesofscilly-travel.co.uk) Several daily flights from Land's End (adult/child return £120/93) and Newquay (£150/118), plus at least one from Exeter, Bristol and Southampton daily in summer.

Boat

Scillonian III (☎0845-710-5555; www.islesofscilly-travel.co.uk; ⊙Mar-Oct) Scilly's ferry plies the notoriously choppy waters between Penzance and St Mary's (2¾ hours, adult/child return £95/43). There's at least one daily crossing in summer (except on Sundays), dropping to four a week in the shoulder months.

Getting Around

BOAT Inter-island launches run by the **St Mary's Boatmen Association** (☎01720-423999; scillyboating.co.uk) sail regularly from St Mary's to the other islands. Trips cost a flat rate adult/child £8.20/4.10, or you can take a 'circular' return via another island for £12/6. Make sure your luggage is labelled with your destination island.

BUS The only bus services are on St Mary's. The airport bus (£3) departs from Hugh Town 40 minutes before each flight, while the **Island Rover** (☎01720-422131; www.islandrover.co.uk; £8) offers a twice-daily sightseeing trip in a vintage bus in summer.

TAXI For taxis, try **Island Taxis** (☎01720-422126), **Scilly Cabs** (☎01720-422901) or **St Mary's Taxis** (☎01720-422555).

St Mary's

The main island of St Mary's is the closest the Scillys get to a metropolis – which is to say, not very close at all. While it's certainly the most populous island, even in the height of summer it never feels too crowded – especially once you get outside the main settlement of Hugh Town.

Sights

Hugh Town NEIGHBOURHOOD

About a mile west of the airport is the main settlement of Hugh Town, home to most of the island's hotels, shops and guesthouses, as well as the main harbour. The small **Isles of Scilly Museum** (Church St; adult/child £3.50/1; ⊙10am-4.30pm Mon-Fri, 10am-noon Sat Easter-Sep, 10am-noon Mon-Sat Oct-Easter or by arrangement) explores the islands' history, with a collection of artefacts recovered from shipwrecks (including muskets, a cannon and a ship's bell), Romano-British finds and a fully rigged 1877 pilot gig.

A little way east of Hugh Town is **Old Town**, once the island's main harbour but now home to a few small cafes, a village pub and a curve of beach. Look out for the minuscule **Old Town Church**, which contains the graves of Augustus Smith, founder of the Abbey Garden, and former British prime minister Harold Wilson, who often holidayed here.

Beaches BEACH

The small inlets scattered around the island's coastline are best reached on foot or by bike. Porth Hellick, Watermill Cove and the remote Pelistry Bay are particularly worth seeking out.

Ancient Ruins RUIN

St Mary's prehistoric sites include the Iron Age village at **Halangy Down**, a mile north of Hugh Town, and the barrows at **Bant's Carn** and **Innisidgen**.

Activities

Scilly Walks WALKING TOUR

(☎01720-423326; www.scillywalks.co.uk; tour per adult/child £5/2.50) Katharine Sawyer runs three-hour archaeological and historical tours, as well as visits to the off-islands.

Island Wildlife Tours WALKING TOUR

(☎01720-422212; www.islandwildlifetours.co.uk) Regular birdwatching and wildlife walks with local boy Will Wagstaff. A full-day walk costs £12 per person, or you can book for just the morning or afternoon for £6.

Island Sea Safaris BOAT TOUR

(☎01720-422732; www.islandseasafaris.co.uk) Offers trips to see local seabird and seal colonies (adult/child £32/22) and one-hour 'island taster' cruises (£22 per person). Also rents wesuits and snorkelling gear.

Sleeping

Isles of Scilly Country Guesthouse B&B **££**

(☎01720-422440; www.scillyguesthouse.co.uk; High Lanes; d £88-100; 🛜) Set back from the Hugh Town hustle, this charming rural guesthouse is one of the comfiest on St Mary's. The large rooms are completely chintz-free and look out across St Mary's fields, and there's an onsite conservatory Kaffeehaus serving Bavarian goodies such

GIG RACING

The traditional sport of gig racing is still hugely popular in the Scillys. These six-oared wooden boats were originally used to race out to secure valuable pilotage of sailing ships, but these days the boats are raced purely for pride.

You can often see gig racing around the shores of St Mary's between May and September, and every May the island hosts the **World Pilot Gig Championships** (www.worldgigs.co.uk), which attracts teams from as far away as Holland and the USA.

as *apfelstrudel* and German breads baked by owner Sabine.

Wingletang B&B ££
(☎01720-422381; www.wingletangguesthouse.co.uk; s £32-42, d £72-88) This granite-fronted cottage in the heart of Hugh Town is well over 200 years old, but the accommodation is surprisingly light inside. Sea-blue curtains, magnolia walls and simple furnishings make it feel like a family home, and you're welcome to browse the little library of nature books.

Star Castle Hotel HOTEL £££
(☎01720-422317; www.star-castle.co.uk; The Garrison; r incl dinner £198-394;) Shaped like an eight-pointed star, this former fort on Garrison Point is one of Scilly's star hotels, with a choice of castle rooms or more modern garden suites. Considering the price, you'd expect a bit more style than the furnishings on offer – but rates include dinner in the castle's heavily beamed restaurant.

St Mary's Hall Hotel HOTEL £££
(☎01720-422316; www.stmaryshallhotel.co.uk; Church St; r £186-256) Built as a private house for Count Leon Ferrari, this wood-panelled beauty is awash with stately staircases, chandeliers and grand rooms. Rooms are either flowery or stripy, and the suites also have their own galley kitchens.

Garrison Campsite CAMPSITE £
(☎01720-422670; tedmoulson@aol.com; Tower Cottage, Garrison; campsites £8.15-11;) This 4-hectare site sits on the garrison above Hugh Town. Facilities are surprisingly good, including electrical hook-ups, wifi and a laundry-cum-shower block – but as ever on Scilly, the sea-views are the main sell.

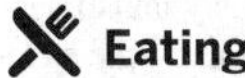

Eating

Juliet's Garden Restaurant RESTAURANT, CAFE ££
(☎01720-422228; www.julietsgardenrestaurant.co.uk; mains £8-16; ⏲lunch & dinner summer) Apart from a couple of pubs, cafes and a deli around Hugh Town, eating choices are limited on St Mary's, which makes this converted barn 15 minutes' walk from town extra-special. Light lunches by day, candle-lit fare by night, all treated with loving care and attention. Try and bag a garden table if the weather's fine.

Tresco

Once owned by Tavistock Abbey, Tresco is the second-largest island, and the second most visited after St Mary's. The main attraction is the magical **Tresco Abbey Garden** (☎01720-424105; www.tresco.co.uk/stay/abbey-garden; adult/child £12/free; ⏲10am-4pm), first laid out in 1834 on the site of a 10th-century Benedictine abbey. The terraced gardens feature more than 5000 subtropical plants, including species from Brazil, New Zealand and South Africa, and the intriguing Valhalla collection made up of figureheads and nameplates salvaged from the many ships that have foundered off Tresco's shores.

Sleeping & Eating

Apart from self-catering cottages, there are now three places to stay on the island, but unfortunately the two hotels are eye-poppingly expensive.

New Inn PUB, HOTEL £££
(☎01720-422849; contactus@tresco.co.uk; d £110-240) The island's popular pub-hotel has pleasant pastel rooms, some of which have views over the channel to Bryher.

Sea Garden Cottages HOTEL COTTAGES £££
(☎01720-422849; contactus@tresco.co.uk; £185-235 per night;) This newly finished complex of self-contained cottages at the Island Hotel has nine properties available on a nightly basis. Checked tiles, wood and nautical pictures give them a suitably seaside feel, and rates include breakfast and dinner at the Ruin Bay Café.

Flying Boat Club APARTMENTS £££
(☎01720-422849; contactus@tresco.co.uk; apts £4500-5000;) Ludicrously lavish sea-view houses with indoor pool and spa; prices drop to a mere £1475 to £2000 in winter.

Bryher & Samson

Only around 70 people live on Bryher, Scilly's smallest and wildest inhabited island. Covered by rough bracken and heather, this chunk of rock takes the full force of Atlantic storms; **Hell Bay** in a winter gale is a truly powerful sight.

Watch Hill provides cracking view over the islands, and **Rushy Bay** is one of the finest beaches in the Scillys. From the quay, occasional boats visit local seal and bird colonies and deserted Samson Island, where abandoned settlers' cottages tell a story of hard subsistence living.

Sleeping & Eating

Hell Bay HOTEL £££
(☎01720-422947; www.hellbay.co.uk; d £190-320) From the outside, Bryher's only hotel looks rather like an upmarket beach shack. Inside, the 25 rooms showcase the same taste for sunny checks, Lloyd Loom furniture and cornflower-and-cream colour schemes: a balcony room is essential to make the most of the coastal setting. The restaurant specialises in rich dishes: braised lamb shoulder, or monkfish with crab risotto.

Fraggle Rock CAFE, PUB £
(☎01720-422222; ⌚10.30am-4.30pm & 7-11pm;) This cheery pub-cafe is one of the few places to eat on Bryher. Pizzas and burgers are the mainstay, and you're pretty much guaranteed to meet most of Bryher's residents at the teeny bar.

Bryher Campsite CAMPSITE £
(☎01720-422886; www.bryhercampsite.co.uk; sites from £10) Bare-bones camping near the quay. Hot showers and transport from the boat are included in the rates.

St Martin's

The northernmost of the main islands, St Martin's is renowned for its beaches. Worth hunting out are **Lawrence's Bay** on the south coast, which becomes a broad sweep of sand at low tide; **Great Bay** on the north, arguably Scilly's finest beach; **White Island** in the northwest, which you can cross to (with care) at low tide; and the secluded cove of **Perpitch** in the southeast.

The largest settlement is **Higher Town** where you'll find a small village shop and **Scilly Diving** (☎01720-422848; www.scillydiving.com; Higher Town), which offers snorkelling trips and diving courses.

Sleeping & Eating

Accommodation options on the island are almost non-existent, apart from one super-expensive hotel, **St Martin's on the Isle** (☎01720-422090; www.stmartinshotel.co.uk; d £300-560), a campsite and a handful of B&Bs.

Polreath B&B £
(☎01720-422046; Higher Town; d £100-110, weekly stays only May-Sep) This granite cottage is one of the few B&Bs on the island, offering titchy rooms, a bright conservatory cafe and home-cooked meals three times a week.

St Martin's Campsite CAMPSITE £
(☎01720-422888; www.stmartinscampsite.co.uk; campsites £9-10.50; ⌚Mar-Oct) Towards the western end of Lawrence's Bay, this site has 50 pitches spread across three fields, so it never feels crowded. Coin-operated laundry and showers are available, and water comes from the campsite's own bore-hole. Eggs and veg are even available for your morning fry-up.

St Martin's Bakery BAKERY £
(☎01720-423444; www.stmartinsbakery.co.uk; ⌚9am-6pm Mon-Sat, 9am-2pm Sun) Fresh bread, pastries and cakes.

Shopping

Little Arthur Farm FOOD
(☎01720-422457; www.littlearthur.co.uk; ⌚10.30am-4pm daily, 6.30-8.30pm Mon-Fri) Wonderful little organic farm where you can buy fresh eggs, milk, homemade cakes and other goodies.

St Agnes

England's southernmost community somehow transcends even the tranquillity of the other islands in the Isles of Scilly; with its cloistered coves, coastal walks and a scattering of prehistoric sites, it's an ideal spot to stroll, unwind and reflect.

Visitors disembark at Porth Conger, near the decommissioned **Old Lighthouse** – one of the oldest lighthouses in the country. Other points of interest include the 200-year-old stone **Troy Town Maze** and the inlets of Periglis Cove and St Warna's Cove (dedicated to the patron saint of shipwrecks). At low tide you can cross over to the island of **Gugh**, where you'll find intriguing standing stones and Bronze Age remains.

Sleeping & Eating

Covean Cottage B&B ££
(☎01720-422620; http://st-agnes-scilly.org/covean.htm; d £60-80) A little stone-walled cottage, with four sea-view rooms and meals cooked up by friendly owner Mark Sedgman.

Troytown Farm CAMPSITE £
(☎01720-422360; www.troytown.co.uk; Troy Town Farm; campsites £7.50-8.50, tents £1-7 depending on size) At the southwestern corner of the island. Originally a flower farm, it's now home to Scillys' only dairy herd.

Turk's Head PUB £
(☎01720-422434; mains £7-12) The most southwesterly pub in England is a communal beauty, with pints and pasties served in the atmospheric bar, tables in the outside garden, and regular sea shanty sessions courtesy of the local boys.

Cambridge & East Anglia

Includes »

Best Places to Eat

» Midsummer House (p417)

» Great House (p430)

» Company Shed (p424)

» Pea Porridge (p432)

» Roger Hickman's (p443)

Best Places to Stay

» Lavenham Priory (p430)

» Cley Windmill (p446)

» The Varsity Hotel & Spa (p416)

» Angel Hotel (p432)

» Sutherland House (p436)

Why Go?

Unfurling gently eastwards to the sea, the vast flatlands of East Anglia are a rich web of lush farmland, melancholy fens and sparkling rivers. The area is justly popular for its sweeping sandy beaches, big skies and the bucolic landscape that inspired Constable and Gainsborough.

It's not all rural idyll, though: rising out of the Fens is the famous university town of Cambridge, with its iconic classical architecture and relaxed vibe, and to the east is the cosmopolitan city of Norwich, with its magnificent cathedral. Around them, splendid cathedral cities, busy market towns and picturesque villages are testament to the wealth amassed here during medieval times, when the wool and weaving industries flourished.

Meanwhile, the meandering coastline is peppered with appealing fishing villages, seafood restaurants and traditional bucket-and-spade resorts, while inland is the languid, hypnotic charm of the Norfolk Broads.

When to Go

Aldeburgh swings into action with its classical music festival in June. You can chill out and tune in at the Latitude Festival in Southwold in July. On 24 December the King's College Chapel is at its best at the Festival of Nine Lessons and Carols.

East Anglia is at its best between late spring and early autumn, though during the months of July and August, the Norfolk coast beaches and seaside towns tend to be busiest with visitors. If visiting Cambridge, bear in mind that many colleges are closed to visitors during the exams in May and June.

History

East Anglia was a major Saxon kingdom, and the treasures unearthed in the Sutton Hoo burial ship proved that they enjoyed something of the good life here.

The region's heyday, however, was in the Middle Ages, during the wool and weaving boom, when Flemish weavers settled in the area and the grand churches and the world-famous university began to be established.

By the 17th century much of the region's marshland and bog had been drained and converted into arable land, and the good times rolled. The emergence of a work-happy urban bourgeoisie coupled with a strong sense of religious duty resulted in the parliamentarianism and Puritanism that would climax in the Civil War. Oliver Cromwell, the uncrowned king of the parliamentarians, was a small-time merchant residing in Ely when he took up arms against the fattened and corrupt monarchy of Charles I.

East Anglia's fortunes waned in the 18th century, however, when the Industrial Revolution got under way up north. The cottage industries dwindled, and today crops have replaced sheep as the rural mainstay. During WWII East Anglia became central to the fight against Nazi Germany. With plenty of flat open land and its proximity to mainland Europe, it was an ideal base for the Royal Air Force (RAF) and the United States Air Force. The remains of these bases can still be seen today.

Activities

East Anglia is a great destination for walking and cycling enthusiasts, with miles of coastline to discover, vast expanses of flat land for leisurely touring and plenty of inland waterways for quiet boating. Try www.visiteastofengland.com for information, or visit local tourist offices for maps and guides.

Cycling

East Anglia is famously flat, and all four counties boast networks of quiet country lanes. There's gorgeous riding to be had along the Suffolk and Norfolk coastlines and in the Fens. Mountain bikers should head for Thetford Forest, near Thetford, while much of the popular on- and off-road Peddars Way walking route is also open to cyclists.

Walking

Gentle rambles through farmland, beside rivers and lakes and along the wildlife-rich coastline are in ample supply.

The **Peddars Way and Norfolk Coast Path** (www.nationaltrail.co.uk/peddarsway) is a six-day, 93-mile national trail from Knettishall Heath near Thetford to Cromer on the coast. The first half follows along an ancient Roman road, then finishes by meandering along the beaches, sea walls, salt marshes and fishing villages of the coast. Day-trippers and weekend walkers tend to dip into its coastal stretches, which also cover some of the best birdwatching country in England.

Further south, the 50-mile **Suffolk Coast Path** (www.suffolkcoastandheaths.org) wanders between Felixstowe and Lowestoft, via Snape Maltings, Aldeburgh, Dunwich and Southwold, but is also good for shorter rambles.

Other Activities

With wind and water so abundant here, it's a popular destination for **sailing**, both along

ANGLIAN ANTICS

Ah, the English; stiflingly proper, embarrassingly prudish and impeccably reserved. And just a little bit eccentric. Where else could you see laser technology employed to shoot peas, watch Elvis roll a wooden blue cheese down a village main street or find grown adults painting snails with racing stripes? East Anglia, of course.

Here you can enter your own pet invertebrate in the **World Snail Racing Championships** (www.snailracing.net) in Congham, about 7 miles east of King's Lynn. Each year more than 300 racing snails gather here in mid-July to battle it out for a tankard full of juicy lettuce leaves.

In Witcham, about 8 miles west of Ely, it's the **World Pea Shooting Championships** (www.witcham.org.uk) that draws contestants from far and wide. The schoolroom prank of blasting dried peas through a tube at a target is alive and well, with shooters gathering in early July on the Village Green.

And in the village of Stilton, a few miles south of Peterborough, every May Day Bank Holiday teams in fancy dress scramble along the main street to become **Stilton cheese rolling champions** (www.stilton.org).

Cambridge & East Anglia Highlights

1. Dreaming of your student days as you **punt** past Cambridge's historic colleges (p414)
2. Wallowing in the heavenly sounds of evensong at **King's College Chapel** (p407)
3. Soaking up the medieval atmosphere in topsy-turvy **Lavenham** (p430)
4. Walking on the prom, dining on sublime food and just chilling out in understated **Aldeburgh** (p433)
5. Canoeing your way through the tranquil waterways of the **Norfolk Broads** (p441)
6. Marvelling at the exquisite rib vaulting at **Norwich Cathedral** (p438)
7. Wandering aimlessly along the pristine sands of **Holkham beach** (p447)

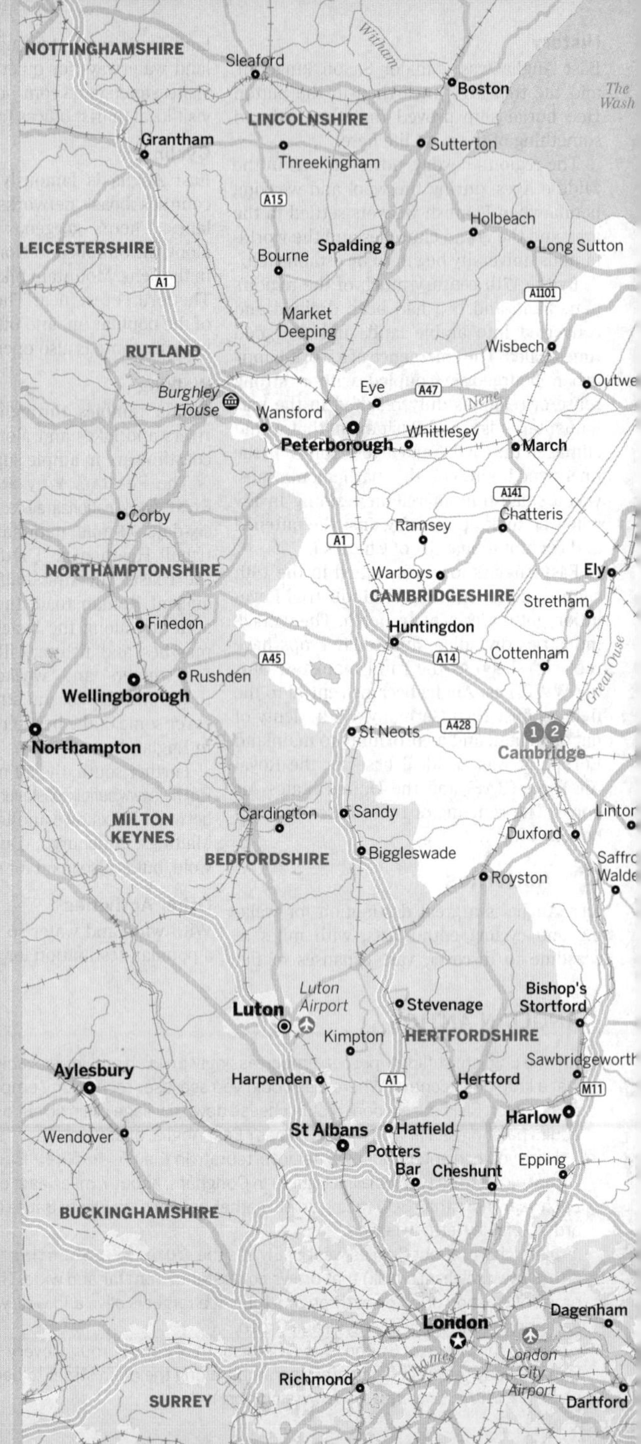

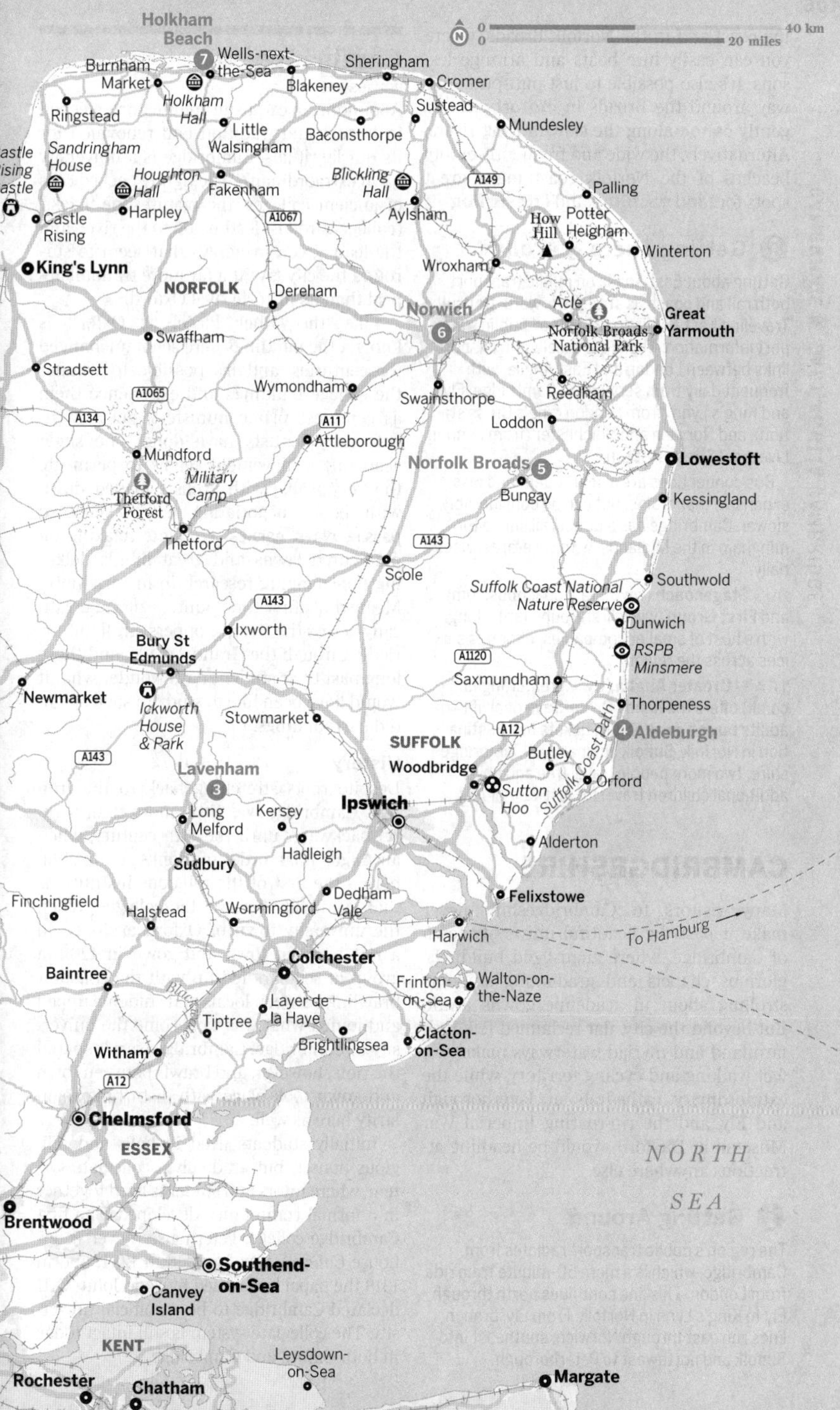

0
0
40 km
20 miles
Holkham Beach
7
Wells-next-the-Sea
Burnham Market
Holkham Hall
Sheringham
Blakeney
Cromer
Sustead
Ringstead
Little Walsingham
Baconsthorpe
Mundesley
Sandringham House
Houghton Hall
Fakenham
Blickling Hall
A149
Palling
Castle Rising
Harpley
A1067
Aylsham
How Hill
Potter Heigham
Winterton
King's Lynn
Wroxham
NORFOLK
Dereham
Norwich
6
Acle
Great Yarmouth
Norfolk Broads National Park
Swaffham
Stradsett
Wymondham
Swainsthorpe
Reedham
A1065
A134
A11
Loddon
Mundford
Attleborough
Norfolk Broads
5
Lowestoft
Thetford Forest
Military Camp
Bungay
Kessingland
Thetford
A143
Scole
Southwold
Suffolk Coast National Nature Reserve
A143
Dunwich
Ixworth
RSPB Minsmere
Bury St Edmunds
A1120
Newmarket
Saxmundham
Ickworth House & Park
Stowmarket
Thorpeness
Suffolk Coast Path
4
Aldeburgh
A12
SUFFOLK
A143
Butley
Woodbridge
Lavenham
3
Orford
Sutton Hoo
Ipswich
Long Melford
Kersey
Hadleigh
Alderton
Sudbury
Felixstowe
Finchingfield
Dedham Vale
Halstead
Wormingford
Harwich
To Hamburg
Colchester
Baintree
Frinton-on-Sea
Walton-on-the-Naze
Layer de la Haye
Tiptree
Brightlingsea
Clacton-on-Sea
Witham
A12
Chelmsford
ESSEX
NORTH SEA
Brentwood
Southend-on-Sea
Canvey Island
KENT
Leysdown-on-Sea
Rochester
Chatham
Margate

the coast and in the Norfolk Broads, where you can easily hire boats and arrange lessons. It's also possible to just putt-putt your way around the Broads in **motorboats** or gently **canoe** along the slow-moving rivers. Alternatively, the wide and frequently empty beaches of the Norfolk coast make great spots for **land yachting** and **kitesurfing**.

ℹ Getting There & Around

Getting about East Anglia on public transport, both rail and coach, is straightforward. Consult Traveline East Anglia (p428) for all public transport information. There are excellent transport links between London and East Anglia, with frequent daily train services to Cambridge, Ely and King's Lynn (from London King's Cross station), and Norwich and Colchester (from London Liverpool Street station).

Bus connections are also frequent and less expensive than trains, but can be considerably slower. Cambridge has a direct rail link to Birmingham in the Midlands, with several services daily.

BUS Stagecoach (www.stagecoachbus.com) and **First Group** (www.firstgroup.com), along with a host of smaller companies, offer bus services across the region.

TRAIN Greater Anglia (www.greateranglia.co.uk) offers the handy **GroupSave** deal: if two adults buy off-peak return tickets to a destination in Norfolk, Suffolk and parts of Cambridgeshire, two more people travel free and any additional children travel for just £1.

CAMBRIDGESHIRE

Many visitors to Cambridgeshire never make it past the beautiful university town of Cambridge, where august old buildings, glorious chapels and graduating students strolling about in academic gowns await. But beyond the city, flat reclaimed fen, lush farmland and myriad waterways make perfect walking and cycling territory, while the extraordinary cathedrals at Peterborough and Ely, and the rip-roaring Imperial War Museum at Duxford, would be headline attractions anywhere else.

ℹ Getting Around

The region's public transport radiates from Cambridge, which is a mere 50-minute train ride from London. This line continues north through Ely to King's Lynn in Norfolk. From Ely, branch lines run east through Norwich, southeast into Suffolk and northwest to Peterborough.

Cambridge

POP 108,863

Abounding in exquisite architecture, steeped in history and tradition and renowned for its quirky rituals, Cambridge is a university town extraordinaire. The tightly packed core of ancient colleges, the picturesque 'Backs' (college gardens) leading on to the river, and the leafy green meadows that seem to surround the city give it a far more tranquil appeal than its historic rival Oxford.

Like 'the Other Place', as Oxford is known, the buildings here seem unchanged for centuries, and it's possible to wander the college buildings and experience them as countless prime ministers, poets, writers and scientists have done. The sheer academic achievement seems to permeate the very walls, with cyclists loaded down with books negotiating narrow cobbled passageways, earnest students relaxing on manicured lawns and great minds debating life-changing research in historic pubs. Meanwhile, first-time punters zigzag erratically across the river, shoppers stroll unhurriedly through the Grand Arcade, and those long past their student days wonder what it would have been like to study in such splendid surroundings.

History

Despite roots stretching back to the Iron Age, Cambridge was little more than a rural backwater until the 11th century, when an Augustinian order of monks set up shop here – the first of the religious institutions that eventually became the colleges. When the university town of Oxford exploded in a riot between town and gown in 1209, a group of scholars fed up with the constant brawling between locals and students upped and joined what was to become the university of Cambridge. Cambridge wasn't spared the riots, however, and brawls between town and gown took place with disturbing regularity here as well.

Initially students lived in halls and religious houses, but gradually a collegiate system, where tutors and students lived together in a formal community, developed. The first Cambridge college, Peterhouse (never Peterhouse *College*), was founded in 1284, and in 1318 the papal bull issued by Pope John XXII declared Cambridge to be an official university. The collegiate system is still intact today in both Oxford and Cambridge.

PETERBOROUGH CATHEDRAL

Few of England's cathedrals can rival the instant 'wow' factor of Peterborough's unique early-13th-century western front, with its three cavernous Gothic arches.

Visitors enter the **cathedral** (www.peterborough-cathedral.org.uk; requested donation £3; ⏲9am-5.15pm Mon-Fri, to 3pm Sat, noon-3.15pm Sun), founded in AD 1118 on the site of a 7th-century Saxon monastery, through an odd 14th-century porch that peeks out between the arches. Inside, you're immediately struck by the height of the magnificent three-storey Norman nave and by its lightness, created by the mellow local stone and fine clerestory windows. The nave is topped by a breathtaking early-13th-century painted-timber ceiling, which is one of the earliest and most important of its kind in Europe and still sports much of its original diamond-pattern paintwork.

Press on below the Gothic tower, which was painstakingly reconstructed in the 19th century, to the northern choir aisle and you'll find the rather plain tombstone of Henry VIII's first wife, the tragic Catherine of Aragon, buried here in 1536. Her divorce, engineered by the king because she could not produce a male heir, led to the Reformation in England. Just beyond this is the cathedral's wonderful 15th-century eastern tip, which has superb fan vaulting thought to be the work of master mason John Wastell, who worked on King's College Chapel in Cambridge.

Loop around into the southern aisle, and you'll find gold lettering marking the spot where the ill-fated Mary, Queen of Scots, was once buried. On the accession of her son, James, to the throne, her body was moved to Westminster Abbey.

The cathedral makes a good day trip from Cambridge or London, and the hour-long **tours** (£4; ⏲2pm Mon, Tue & Thu-Sat, 11.30am Wed) are worth it.

The train station is an easy walk from the cathedral. Trains run to Cambridge (£9, 50 minutes, hourly) and London Kings Cross (£25, 45 minutes, every 15 minutes).

By the 14th century, royalty, nobility, churches, trade guilds and anyone rich enough could court prestige by founding their own colleges, though the system was shaken up during the Reformation with the dissolution of the monasteries. It was 500 years before female students were allowed into the hallowed grounds, though, and even then they were only allowed into women-only colleges Girton and Newnham, founded in 1869 and 1871 respectively. By 1948 Cambridge minds had broadened sufficiently to allow the women to actually graduate.

The honour roll of famous Cambridge graduates reads like an international who's who of high achievers: 87 Nobel Prize winners (more than any other institution in the world), 13 British prime ministers, nine archbishops of Canterbury, an immense number of scientists, and a healthy host of poets and authors. This is the town where Newton refined his theory of gravity, Whittle invented the jet engine, Crick and Watson discovered DNA, and Stephen Hawking was, until 2009, a professor of mathematics. William Wordsworth, Lord Byron, Vladimir Nabokov and John Cleese all studied here.

Today the university remains one of the best for research worldwide. Thanks to some of the earth-shaking discoveries made here, Cambridge is inextricably linked to the history of learning.

Sights

Cambridge University

Cambridge University comprises 31 colleges, though not all are open to the public.

King's College Chapel CHAPEL

(www.kings.cam.ac.uk/chapel; King's Pde; adult/child £7.50/free, evensong free; ⏲9.45am-4.30pm Mon, from 9.30am Tue-Sun, evensong 5.30pm Mon-Sat & choral services 10.30am & 3.30pm Sun, term time only) In a city crammed with show-stopping architecture, this is the show stealer. Chances are you will already have seen it on a thousand postcards, tea towels and choral CDs before you catch your first glimpse of the grandiose King's College Chapel, but still it inspires awe. It's one of the most extraordinary examples of Gothic architecture in England, begun in 1446 as an act of piety by Henry VI and finished by Henry VIII around 1516. Its steeples have long been a magnet for night climbers (p414).

While you can enjoy stunning front and back views of the chapel from King's Pde and the river, the real drama is within.

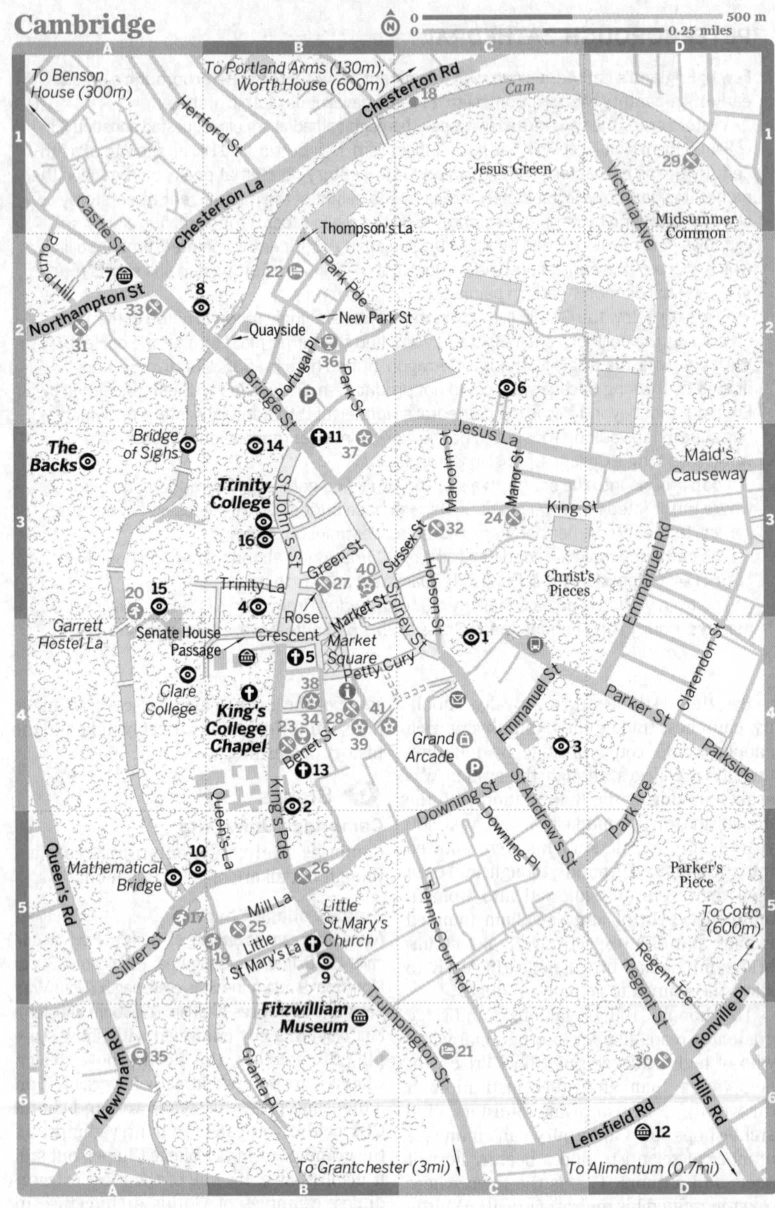

Mouths drop open upon first glimpse of the inspirational **fan-vaulted ceiling**, its intricate tracery soaring upwards before exploding into a series of stone fireworks. This vast 80m-long canopy is the work of John Wastell and is the largest expanse of fan vaulting in the world.

The chapel is also remarkably light, its sides flanked by lofty **stained-glass windows** that retain their original glass – rare survivors of the excesses of the Civil War

Cambridge

Top Sights
- Fitzwilliam Museum ... B6
- King's College Chapel ... B4
- The Backs ... A3
- Trinity College ... B3

Sights
- Cambridge & County Folk Museum ... (see 7)
- 1 Christ's College ... C4
- 2 Corpus Christi College ... B4
- 3 Emmanuel College ... C4
- 4 Gonville & Caius College ... B3
- 5 Great St Mary's Church ... B4
- 6 Jesus College ... C2
- 7 Kettle's Yard ... A2
- 8 Magdalene College ... A2
- 9 Peterhouse ... B5
- 10 Queens' College ... A5
- 11 Round Church ... B3
- 12 Scott Polar Research Institute ... D6
- 13 St Bene't's Church ... B4
- 14 St John's College ... B3
- 15 Trinity Hall College ... A3
- 16 Wren Library ... B3

Activities, Courses & Tours
- 17 Cambridge Chauffer Punts ... A5
- Cambridge Revisited ... (see 28)
- Granta ... (see 35)
- 18 Riverboat Georgina ... C1
- 19 Scudamore's ... B5
- 20 Trinity Punt Hire ... A3

Sleeping
- 21 Hotel du Vin ... C6
- 22 Varsity Hotel & Spa ... B2

Eating
- 23 Chop House ... B4
- 24 Clowns ... C3
- 25 Dojo ... B5
- 26 Fitzbillies ... B5
- 27 Gardenia ... B3
- 28 Jamie's Italian ... B4
- 29 Midsummer House ... D1
- 30 Oak Bistro ... D6
- 31 St John's Chop House ... A2
- 32 Stickybeaks ... C3
- 33 Thanh Binh ... A2

Drinking
- 34 Eagle ... B4
- 35 Granta ... A6
- 36 Maypole ... B2

Entertainment
- 37 ADC ... B3
- 38 Arts Theatre ... B4
- 39 Corn Exchange ... B4
- 40 Fez ... B3
- 41 Lola Lo ... B4

in this region. It's said that these windows were ordered to be spared by Cromwell himself, who knew of their beauty from his own studies in Cambridge.

The antechapel and the choir are divided by a superbly carved **wooden screen**, designed and executed by Peter Stockton for Henry VIII. The screen bears his master's initials entwined with those of Anne Boleyn. Look closely and you may find an angry human face – possibly Stockton's – amid the elaborate jungle of mythical beasts and symbolic flowers. Above is the magnificent batwing organ, originally constructed in 1686 though much altered since.

The thickly carved wooden stalls just beyond the screen are a stage for the chapel's world-famous **choir**. You can hear them in full voice during the magnificent **evensong**. If you happen to be visiting at Christmas, it is also worth queuing for admission to the incredibly popular **Festival of Nine Lessons and Carols** on Christmas Eve.

Beyond the dark-wood choir, light suffuses the **high altar**, which is framed by Rubens' masterpiece *Adoration of the Magi* (1634) and the magnificent east window. To the left of the altar in the side chapels, an **exhibition** charts the stages and methods of building the chapel.

The chapel is open for reduced hours during term time, and charges an entry fee for nonmembers of the university.

Trinity College COLLEGE

(www.trin.cam.ac.uk; Trinity St; adult/child £1.50/1; ⏲10.30am-4.30pm) The largest of Cambridge's colleges, Trinity is entered through an impressive Tudor gateway first created in 1546. As you walk through, have a look at the statue of the college's founder, Henry VIII, that adorns it. His left hand holds a golden orb, while his right grips not the original

SOMETHING FOR THE WEEKEND

Start your weekend in style with a night of romance and fine dining at Cambridge's **Hotel du Vin**, and venture out for a nightcap at the friendly local pub, the **Maypole**. Next morning, go **punting** along the Backs to beat the afternoon crowds and then reward yourself with lunch at swanky **Midsummer House**. Spend the afternoon checking out Cambridge's prettiest college grounds and dip into the sublime **King's College Chapel** before bidding farewell to the glorious college architecture and breezing east to the **Stour Valley**. Install yourself in the spectacular **Lavenham Priory** and explore the time-transcending streets of gorgeous **Lavenham**, lined with picturesque crooked houses, to work up an appetite for slick French cuisine at the **Great House**.

On Sunday morning roll west to check out the twin stately homes of **Long Melford**, then east for the picture-postcard hamlet of **Kersey**, where you can toast the weekend with a pint and pub lunch at the medieval **Bell Inn**.

sceptre but a table leg, put there by student pranksters and never replaced. It's a wonderful introduction to one of Cambridge's most venerable colleges, and a reminder of who really rules the roost.

As you enter the **Great Court**, scholastic humour gives way to wonderment, for it is the largest of its kind in the world. To the right of the entrance is a small tree, planted in the 1950s and reputed to be a descendant of the apple tree made famous by Trinity alumnus Sir Isaac Newton. Other alumni include Alfred Tennyson, Francis Bacon, Lord Byron, HRH Prince Charles (legend has it that his bodyguard scored higher in the exams than he did) and at least nine prime ministers, British and international. And 32 Nobel Prize winners besides.

The college's vast hall has a dramatic hammerbeam roof and lantern, and beyond this are the dignified cloisters of Nevile's Court and the renowned **Wren Library** (⏲noon-2pm Mon-Fri). It contains 55,000 books dated before 1820 and more than 2500 manuscripts, including AA Milne's original *Winnie the Pooh*. Both Milne and his son, Christopher Robin, were graduates.

Henry VIII would have been proud to note, too, that his college would eventually come to throw the best party in town, the lavish May Ball in June, though you will need a fat purse, and a friend on the inside, to get an invitation.

St John's College COLLEGE

(www.joh.cam.ac.uk; St John's St; adult/child £4/free; ⏲10am-5.30pm) Alma mater of six prime ministers, three saints and Douglas Adams (author of *The Hitchhiker's Guide to the Galaxy*), St John's is one of the city's most photogenic colleges, and is also the second-biggest after Trinity. Founded in 1511 by Henry VII's mother, Lady Margaret Beaufort, it sprawls along both banks of the river, joined by the **Bridge of Sighs** (Map p408), a masterpiece of stone tracery and a focus for student pranks. Over the bridge is the 19th-century **New Court**, an extravagant neo-Gothic creation, and out to the left are stunning views of the **Backs**. Parts of the college are much older and the chapel, though smaller than King's, is one of Cambridge's hidden gems.

Christ's College COLLEGE

(www.christs.cam.ac.uk; St Andrew's St; admission free, Darwin room £2.50; ⏲9.30am-noon, Darwin room 10am-noon & 2-4pm) Over 500 years old and a grand old institution, Christ's is worth visiting if only for its gleaming Great Gate emblazoned with heraldic carving of spotted Beaufort yale (antelope-like creatures), Tudor roses and portcullis. Its founder, Lady Margaret Beaufort, hovers above like a guiding spirit. A stout oak door leads into First Court – one of Cambridge's more picturesque front courts and the only circular one. Pressing on through the Second Court there is a gate to the Fellows' Garden, which contains a mulberry tree under which 17th-century poet John Milton reputedly wrote *Lycidas*. Charles Darwin also studied here, and his room has been restored as it would have been when he lived in it. You can buy a guided-walk brochure (£1.20) to Darwin-related sites in the college from the porter's lodge. Other controversy-generating alumni include Sacha Baron Cohen (aka Ali G and Borat) and historian Simon Schama.

Corpus Christi College COLLEGE

(www.corpus.cam.ac.uk; King's Pde; admission £2.50; ⏲10am-4.30) Entry to this illustrious college is via the so-called New Court, which dates back a mere 200 years. To your right is the door to the Parker Library, which holds the finest collection of Anglo-Saxon manuscripts in the world. As you enter, take a look at the statue on the right of the eponymous Matthew Parker, who was college master in 1544 and Archbishop of Canterbury to Elizabeth I. Mr Parker was known for his curiosity, and his endless questioning gave rise to the term 'nosy parker'. Meanwhile, a monastic atmosphere still oozes from the inner Old Court, which retains its medieval form. Look out for the fascinating sundial and plaque to playwright and past student Christopher Marlowe (1564–93), author of *Dr Faustus* and *Tamburlaine*.

On the corner of Bene't St you'll find the college's new **Corpus Clock**. Made from 24-carat gold, it displays the time through a series of concentric LED lights. A hideous-looking insect 'time-eater' crawls across the top. The clock is only accurate once every five minutes. At other times it slows or stops and then speeds up, which, according to its creator, JC Taylor, reflects life's irregularity.

Trinity Hall College COLLEGE

(www.trinhall.cam.ac.uk; Trinity Lane; admission by donation) Henry James once wrote of the delightfully diminutive Trinity Hall ('Tit Hall' to students), 'If I were called upon to mention the prettiest corner of the world, I should draw a thoughtful sigh and point the way to the gardens of Trinity Hall'. Wedged cosily among the great and the famous, but unconnected to better-known Trinity, it was founded in 1350 as a refuge for lawyers and clerics escaping the ravages of the Black Death, thus earning it the nickname, the 'Lawyers' College'. The college's 16th-century library has original Jacobean reading desks and chained books (an early antitheft device) on the shelves, while the chapel is one of the most beautiful of the colleges. You can attend **evensong** here on Thursdays (6.30pm) and Sundays (6pm) during term time. Writer JB Priestley, astrophysicist Stephen Hawking and actor Rachel Weisz are among Trinity Hall's graduates.

FREE **Gonville & Caius College** COLLEGE

(www.cai.cam.ac.uk; Trinity St) Known locally as Caius (pronounced 'keys'), Gonville and Caius was founded twice, first by a priest called Gonville in 1348, and then again in 1557 by Dr Caius (his given name was Keys – it was common for academics to use the Latin form of their names), a brilliant physician who supposedly spoilt his legacy by insisting in the statutes that the college admit no 'deaf, dumb, deformed, lame, chronic invalids, or Welshmen'! Fortunately for the college, his policy didn't last long, and the megastar of astrophysics, Stephen Hawking, was a fellow here until 2009. Other notable ex-students include Francis Crick, of Crick & Watson, who discovered DNA, and Edward Wilson of the tragic Scott expedition to the Antarctic.

The college is of particular interest thanks to its three fascinating gates: Virtue, Humility and Honour. They symbolise the progress of the good student, since the third gate (the *Porta Honoris,* a fabulous domed and sundial-sided confection) leads to the Senate House and thus graduation.

FREE **Peterhouse** COLLEGE

(www.pet.cam.ac.uk; Trumpington St) The oldest and smallest college, Peterhouse is a charming place founded in 1284. Much of the college was rebuilt or added to over the years, including the exceptional little chapel built in 1632, but the main hall is bona-fide 13th century and has been beautifully restored. Just to the north is **Little St Mary's Church**, which has a memorial to Peterhouse student Godfrey Washington, great-uncle of George. His family coat of arms was the stars and stripes, the inspiration for the US flag. Rumours among undergrads – vigorously denied by college authorities – abound with tales of hauntings and spectral happenings on the site. Three Nobel Prize winners count themselves among Peterhouse's alumni.

Queens' College COLLEGE

(www.queens.cam.ac.uk; Silver St; adult/child £2.50/free; ⌚10am-4.30pm) The lovely 15th-century

CHARIOTS OF FIRE

The Trinity College Great Court is the scene of the run made famous by the film *Chariots of Fire* – a 350m-sprint around the quadrangle in 43 seconds (the time it takes the clock to strike 12). Although many students attempt it, Harold Abrahams (the hero of the film) never did, and the run in the movie was filmed at Eton. If you fancy your chances, remember that you'll need Olympian speed to even come close.

VISITING THE COLLEGES

Most colleges close to visitors for the Easter term (April to June) and all are closed for exams from mid-May to mid-June. Also, opening hours vary from day to day, so if you have your heart set on visiting a particular college, contact it for information in advance to avoid disappointment.

Queens' College sits elegantly astride the river and has two enchanting medieval courtyards: Old Court and Cloister Court. Here, too, is the beautiful half-timbered President's Lodge and the tower in which famous Dutch scholar and reformer Desiderius Erasmus resided from 1510 to 1514. He had plenty to say about Cambridge: the wine tasted like vinegar, the beer was slop and the place was too expensive, but he did note that the local women were good kissers. Don't forget to have a look at the Mathematical Bridge.

FREE Magdalene College COLLEGE

(www.magd.cam.ac.uk; Magdalene St) Originally a Benedictine hostel, riverside Magdalene has the dubious honour of being the last college to allow women students; when they were finally admitted in 1988, male students wore black armbands and flew the college flag at half-mast. Its greatest asset is the Pepys Library, housing the magnificent collection of books bequeathed by the famous mid-17th-century diarist to his old college.

FREE Emmanuel College COLLEGE

(www.emma.cam.ac.uk; St Andrew's St) The 16th-century Emmanuel College ('Emma' to students) is famous for its exquisite chapel designed by Sir Christopher Wren. The college features a prodigious collection of ducks, who roam the area freely and in early spring produce armies of bright yellow ducklings. Here, too, is a plaque commemorating John Harvard (BA 1632), a scholar here who later settled in New England and left his money to a certain Cambridge College in Massachusetts – now Harvard University.

FREE Jesus College COLLEGE

(www.jesus.cam.ac.uk; Jesus Lane) This tranquil 15th-century college was once a nunnery of St Radegund before the Bishop of Ely, John Alcock, expelled the nuns for 'improvidence, extravagance and incontinence'. Highlights include a Norman arched gallery, a 13th-century chancel, and art-nouveau features by Pugin, William Morris (ceilings), Burne-Jones (stained glass) and Ford Madox Brown. Illustrious alumni include Thomas Cranmer, burnt for his faith in Oxford during the Reformation, and long-running (58 years!) BBC radio journalist Alistair Cook. And no, in spite of what some tour guides may tell you, Jesus did not attend Jesus College.

Other Sights

TOP CHOICE The Backs PARKLANDS

Behind the grandiose facades, stately courts and manicured lawns of the city's central colleges lies a series of gardens and parklands butting up against the river. Collectively known as the Backs, these tranquil green spaces and shimmering waters offer unparalleled views of the colleges and are often the most enduring image of Cambridge for visitors. The picture-postcard snapshots of college life, graceful bridges and weeping willows can be seen from the pathways that cross the Backs, from the comfort of a chauffeur-driven punt or from the lovely pedestrian bridges that criss-cross the river.

The fanciful Bridge of Sighs (built in 1831) at St John's is best observed from the stylish bridge designed by Christopher Wren just to the south. The oldest crossing is at **Clare College**, built in 1639 and ornamented with decorative balls. Its architect was paid a grand total of 15p for his design and, feeling aggrieved at such a measly fee, it's said he cut a chunk out of one of the balls adorning the balustrade so the bridge would never be complete. Most curious of all is the flimsy-looking wooden construction joining the two halves of Queen's College, known as the **Mathematical Bridge**, first built in 1749. Despite what unscrupulous guides may tell you, it wasn't the handiwork of Sir Isaac Newton (he died in 1727), originally built without nails, or taken apart by academics who then couldn't figure how to put it back together.

TOP CHOICE Fitzwilliam Museum MUSEUM

(www.fitzmuseum.cam.ac.uk; Trumpington St; entry by donation, guided tour £5; ⏲10am-5pm Tue-Sat, noon-5pm Sun) Fondly dubbed 'the Fitz' by locals, this colossal neoclassical pile was one of the first public art museums in Britain, built to house the fabulous treasures that the seventh Viscount Fitzwilliam had bequeathed to his old university. An unabashedly over-the-top building, it sets out to mirror its contents in an ostentatious jumble of styles that mixes mosaic with marble, Greek with Egyptian and more. It was begun by George Basevi in 1837, but he did not live to see its completion: while working on Ely Cathedral he stepped back to admire his handiwork, slipped and fell to his death.

The lower galleries are filled with priceless treasures spanning the ancient world; look out for a Roman funerary couch, an inscribed copper votive plaque from Yemen (c AD 150), a figurine of the Egyptian cat goddess Bastet, some splendid Egyptian sarcophagi and mummified animals – a cat, and an ibis – and some dazzling illuminated manuscripts. The Chinese ceramics section was closed at the time of writing due to a robbery. The upper galleries showcase works by Leonardo da Vinci, Titian, Rubens, Rembrandt, the Impressionists, Gainsborough and Constable, right through to Picasso; standout works include the tender *Pietà* by Giovanni del Ponte and Salvator Rosa's dark and intensely personal *L'Umana Fragilita*. You can join a one-hour **guided tour** of the museum on Saturdays at 2.30pm.

FREE Kettle's Yard — ART GALLERY

(www.kettlesyard.co.uk; cnr Northampton & Castle Sts; ⏲house 2-4pm Tue-Sun, gallery 11.30am-5pm Tue-Sun) If you like snooping around other people's houses (let's face it, most of us do!), you'll love this very personal glimpse into the incredible home of HS 'Jim' Ede, a former curator at the Tate Gallery in London. Ring the bell of this deceptively small cottage (which turns out to be much bigger on the inside, like the Tardis) and then wander around the rooms at your leisure, where all the furniture, ceramics and art – such as the collection of 20th-century works by the likes of Miró, Henry Moore and others – is arranged just so, and you get a real sense of the man's personality. Look out for the pebble spiral and don't forget to peek into the attic. There are also exhibitions of contemporary art in the modern **gallery** next door.

Cambridge & County Folk Museum — MUSEUM

(www.folkmuseum.org.uk; 2/3 Castle St; adult/child £3.50/2; ⏲10.30am-5pm Tue-Sat, 2-5pm Sun) Next door to Kettle's Yard, this 300-year-old former inn is now cluttered with a wonderfully diverse collection of domestic tools and equipment from 1700 onwards.

FREE Scott Polar Research Institute — MUSEUM

(www.spri.cam.ac.uk/museum; Lensfield Rd; ⏲10am-4pm Tue-Sat) The Scott Polar Institute was founded with part of the relief fund set up in the wake of the ill-fated Scott expedition to the South Pole. These days it takes a lead role in climate change research and has an excellent museum that focuses on polar exploration, charting the feats of the likes of Amundsen, Nansen and Scott himself. Regardless of whether you see Scott as a valiant explorer or a vain, poorly prepared expedition leader whose bad decisions led to the demise of his team, it's difficult not to be moved by the collection of artefacts, including paintings, photographs, clothing, equipment and maps, journals and last messages left for loved ones by Scott's polar crew.

Other engaging exhibits include models of ships that ventured into the frigid Arctic and Antarctic waters, innovative equipment such as the 'Nansen cooker' and interactive displays on ice and climate change. In the section devoted to the people of the Arctic, you can examine Inuit carvings and scrimshaw (etched bones), a Sámi knife with a carved reindeer-horn sheath, a walrus tusk with walrus hunt scenes etched on it, and particularly fine examples of *tupilaat* (carved caribou horn figures with ancestor souls captured inside) from Greenland. For an entertaining free guided tour, contact independent tour guide Kay Smith (01223-336 573) in advance.

Great St Mary's Church — CHURCH

(www.gsm.cam.ac.uk; Senate House Hill; tower adult/child £3.50/2; ⏲9am-5pm Mon-Sat, 12.30-5pm Sun) Cambridge's staunch university church was built between 1478 and 1519 in the late-Gothic Perpendicular style and is one of few churches to boast two organs. Climb the 123 steps of the tower for superb vistas of the dreamy spires, albeit marred by wire fencing.

The beautiful classical building directly across King's Pde is the **Senate House**, designed in 1730 by James Gibbs; graduations are held here in summer, when gowned and mortar-boarded students parade the streets.

Round Church — CHURCH

(www.christianheritageuk.org.uk; Bridge St; adult/child £2.20/free; ⏲10am-5pm Tue-Sat, 1-5pm Sun)

The beautiful Round Church is another of Cambridge's gems and one of only four such structures in England. It was built by the mysterious Knights Templar in 1130 and shelters an unusual circular nave ringed by chunky Norman pillars. Its proximity to Bridge St reminds you of its original role – a chapel for pilgrims crossing the river.

Cambridge University Botanic Garden BOTANIC GARDEN
(www.botanic.cam.ac.uk; entrance Bateman St; adult/child £4.50/free, with guided tour £7; ⌚10am-6pm) Founded by Charles Darwin's mentor, Professor John Henslow, the beautiful Botanic Garden is home to 8000 plant species, a wonderful arboretum and glasshouses – which house carnivorous pitcher plants as well as the delicate slipper orchid – a winter garden and flamboyant herbaceous borders. You can take an hour-long **guided tour** of the garden on the first Saturday of the month at 11am and on some Wednesdays. The gardens are 1200m south of the city centre via Trumpington St.

St Bene't's Church CHURCH
(http://stbenetschurch.org; Bene't St) The oldest structure in the county, the Saxon tower of this Franciscan church was built around 1025. The round holes above the belfry windows were designed to offer owls nesting privileges: they were valued as mouse killers.

Activities

Punting

Gliding a self-propelled punt along the Backs is an entertaining experience once you've got the knack – particularly on a warm and sunny day – though it can also be a manic challenge to begin with. If you wish to be propelled along by someone else while getting the potted history of the colleges at the same time, opt for a chauffeured punt.

Punt hire costs £14 to £18 per hour (cash deposit £40 to £50); chauffeured trips of the Backs cost £12 to £14, and a return trip to Grantchester will set you back £27 to £30. Book online for discounts. These are some recommended operators.

Cambridge Chauffer Punts PUNTING
(www.punting-in-cambridge.co.uk; Silver St Bridge) One of the biggest punting companies in Cambridge, with regular chauffered punting tours.

Granta PUNTING
(www.puntingincambridge.com; Newnham Rd) Conveniently located punt rental company for those looking to head towards Grantchester.

Scudamore's PUNTING
(www.scudamores.com; Silver St) Also hires rowboats, kayaks and canoes.

Trinity Punt Hire PUNTING
(☎01223-338800; www.trin.cam.ac.uk; Garret Hostel Lane; punts per hr £12) Has punts for hire and chauffeured rides.

Walking & Cycling

For an easy stroll into the countryside, follow the meandering River Cam southwest through flower-flecked meadows for 3 miles to Grantchester.

PRANKSTERS, NIGHT CLIMBERS & CUBES

In a city with so much concentrated mental prowess, it is perhaps inevitable that the student community would excel at all kinds of mischief. The most impressive prank ever to take place in Cambridge – lifting an Austin Seven van onto the roof of the landmark Senate House in 1958 – involved a great deal of planning from four Mechanical Sciences students and spawned a number of copycat pranks, including suspending another Austin Seven from the Bridge of Sighs.

King's College has long been a target of night climbers – students who get their thrills be scaling the lofty heights of out-of-bounds buildings at night. The sport is taken very seriously, to the point where a Trinity College student, Geoffrey Winthrop Young, wrote the *Roof Climber's Guide to Trinity* in 1900. If you're in Cambridge after a particularly spectacular climber excursion, you may find some out-of-place object atop the pinnacles of King's College Chapel – anything from a traffic cone to a Santa hat.

Finally, we have the Cubes (Cambridge University Breaking and Entering Society) whose objective is to get someplace where they shouldn't be and leave a distinctive calling card – the most famous being the wooden mallard in the rafters of Trinity's Great Hall.

HOW TO PUNT

Punting looks pretty straightforward but, believe us, it's not. We thought we'd share a few tips with you to prevent you from zigzagging wildly across the river, losing your pole and falling in.

» Standing at the back end of the punt, lift the pole out of the water at the side of the punt.

» Let the pole slide through your hands to touch the bottom of the river.

» Tilt the pole forward (that is, in the direction of travel of the punt) and push down to propel the punt forward.

» Twist the pole to free the end from the mud at the bottom of the river, and let it float up and trail behind the punt. You can then use it as a rudder to steer.

» If you haven't fallen in yet, raise the pole out of the water and into the vertical position to begin the cycle again.

» Hold on to the pole particularly when passing under Clare Bridge as students sometimes snatch them for a giggle.

Scooting around town on a bike is easy thanks to the pancake-flat landscape; the Cambridge tourist office stocks info on cycling routes.

Tours

Check out **Visit Cambridge** (www.visitcambridge.org) for information on self-guided walking and audio tours.

The Tourist Office conducts two-hour city **walking tours** (adult/child £13.50/6.50, 11am & 1pm Mon-Thu, 11am, noon, 1pm & 2pm Fri-Sun), **ghost tours** (adult/child £7/5, 6pm Fri) and **bike tours** of the city and/or Grantchester (adult/child £20/18, 10.30am, 1.30pm & 7pm daily except Tue). Book in advance.

Cambridge Revisited SELF-GUIDED TOUR
(Peas Hill; adult/child £3.50/2.50; ⏲11.30am-4pm) Set in the former Cambridge courts, this light-hearted attraction, consisting of an introductory video and self-guided walk, follows the trial and punishment of fictional Mr Tymins, found guilty of the heinous crime of using the word 'Oxford' while in Cambridge. The show aims to be a virtual educational tour of Cambridge and its colleges.

Riverboat Georgina BOAT TOUR
(☎01223-307694; www.georgina.co.uk) One-/two-hour cruises £6/12, with the option of including lunch or a cream tea. Tailor-made tours possible.

City Sightseeing BUS TOUR
(www.city-sightseeing.com; adult/child £13/7; ⏲every 20min 10am-4.40pm) Hop-on/hop-off bus tours around Cambridge.

Festivals & Events

Cambridge has a jam-packed schedule of almost continual events of which the tourist office has exhaustive listings; also, check the notices on the fence around St Mary's church for more information about what's happening.

Bumps BOAT RACE
(www.cucbc.org/bumps; ⏲Mar & May) Traditional rowing races along the Cam (or the Granta as the Cambridge stretch is called), in which college boat clubs compete to 'bump' the crew in front.

Beer Festival BEER FESTIVAL
(www.cambridgebeerfestival.com; ⏲May) Hugely popular week-long beer and cider extravaganza on Jesus Green, featuring brews from all over the country as well as a great range of British cheeses.

May Balls FORMAL BALLS
(⏲early Jun) These formal balls are the biggest student event of the year; the Trinity College Ball is the biggest and most prestigious. Why *May* Ball in June? Because they were originally held in May until the college authorities decided that booze-fuelled revelry just before the exams was not a great idea, so now they take place after the exams.

Strawberry Fair FAIR
(www.strawberry-fair.org.uk; ⏲early Jun) Cambridge's best-loved summer fair, complete with live bands, hippie clothing stalls, great food and barely legal substances.

Folk Festival MUSIC FESTIVAL
(www.cambridgefolkfestival.co.uk; ⏲late Jul) Popular three-day music fest in neighbouring Cherry Hinton, which has hosted the likes of Elvis Costello, Paul Simon, kd lang and Joan Armatrading in recent years.

Cambridge Shakespeare Festival THEATRE
(www.cambridgeshakespeare.com; ⏲Jul & Aug) The famous playwright's best-loved works played out in outdoor settings.

Sleeping

Some of Cambridge's most central B&Bs use their convenient location as an excuse not to upgrade. Some of the better places are a bit of a hike from town but well worth the effort.

TOP CHOICE **Varsity Hotel & Spa** HOTEL £££
(01223-306030; www.thevarsityhotel.co.uk; Thompson's Lane; d/ste from £225/385;) A celebration of Cambridge's august intellectual heritage, this hotel has an unparalleled location. The decor is understated, with lovely touches such as four-poster beds, floor-to-ceiling glass windows, monsoon showers and MP3 docks. From the roof terrace there's a splendid view of the city, and though it's too large to call itself a boutique hotel, it certainly doesn't want for amenities.

TOP CHOICE **Hotel du Vin** HOTEL £££
(01223-227330; www.hotelduvin.com; Trumpington St; d from £150; @) This hotel chain really knows how to do things right. Its Cambridge offering has all the usual trademarks, from quirky but incredibly stylish rooms with monsoon showers and luxurious Egyptian cotton sheets to the atmospheric vaulted cellar bar and the French-style bistro (mains £15 to £22). The central location, character-laden building and top-notch service make it a great deal at this price.

Cambridge Rooms COLLEGE ROOMS ££
(www.cambridgerooms.co.uk; s/d from £41/78) If you wish to experience life inside the hallowed college grounds, you can stay in a student room in one of several colleges. Accommodation varies from functional singles (with shared bathroom) overlooking college quads to more modern, en-suite rooms in nearby annexes. There's a good choice of rooms during university holidays.

Hotel Felix BOUTIQUE HOTEL £££
(01223-277977; www.hotelfelix.co.uk; Whitehouse Lane, Huntingdon Rd; s/d from £165/200; P@) This luxurious boutique hotel occupies a lovely grey-brick Victorian villa in landscaped grounds a mile from the city centre. Its 52 rooms embody designer chic with minimalist style and wonderful touches such as Egyptian cotton bedding and monsoon showers in many rooms. The slick restaurant serves Mediterranean cuisine with a modern twist (mains £13 to £23). Follow Castle St and then Huntingdon Rd out of the city for about 1.5 miles.

Alexander B&B £
(01223-525725; www.beesley-schuster.co.uk; 56 St Barnabas Rd; s/d from £40/60; P) Set in a Victorian house in a quiet residential area, the Alexander has two cream-and-blue rooms with period fireplaces, big windows and lots of light. The location off Mill Rd – Cambridge's pub-and-eatery-central – is a bonus. The B&B is about 1 mile from the corner of Parker's Piece.

Worth House B&B £
(01223-316074; www.worth-house.co.uk; 152 Chesterton Rd; s/d from £44/55; P) A pleasant 20-minute walk from the centre across Jesus Green, this warm and welcoming B&B has five spacious, carpeted rooms with all the comforts and placid decor. Full English breakfast is included, and the owners go out of their way to be helpful.

Rosa's Bed and Breakfast B&B £
(01223-512596; www.rosasbedandbreakfast.co.uk; 53 Roseford Rd; s £45-60;) Ideal for solo travellers, this friendly family-run B&B has four cosy en-suite singles – all creams and pale wood – and the hosts are engaging without being intrusive. Well connected to the centre by the Citi 7 bus. Head up Castle St for 300m, turn right into Histon Rd, follow it for 1.2km and turn right into Roseford Rd.

Benson House B&B ££
(01223-311594; www.bensonhouse.co.uk; 24 Huntingdon Rd; d from £90; P) Just a 15-minute walk from the city centre, the rooms at this B&B range from monochrome minimalism to muted classical elegance, and breakfast includes the less usual addition of kippers. To get here follow Castle St north of the city centre into Huntingdon Rd.

City Roomz HOTEL ££

(☎01223-304050; www.cityroomz.co.uk; Station Rd; s/d from £52.50/67.50; @📶) This converted-granary-cum-budget-hotel features compact en suites with exposed brick walls and bunk beds in the twins. Avoid like the proverbial plague on Friday and Saturday nights when last-minute guests, too drunk to catch the last train home, raise the roof.

Cambridge YHA HOSTEL £

(☎0845-371 9728; www.yha.org.uk; 97 Tenison Rd; dm/tw £19/45; @📶) Busy, popular hostel with compact dorms and good facilities near the train station.

Eating

Cambridge is packed with chain restaurants, particularly around the city centre. You'll find upmarket chains such as Browns and Loch Fyne on Trumpington St and plenty of Asian eateries on Regent St. If you're looking for something more independent you'll have to search a little harder.

TOP CHOICE **Midsummer House** MODERN BRITISH £££

(☎01223-369299; www.midsummerhouse.co.uk; Midsummer Common; 3-/4-/5-course set menu £40/50/60, tasting menu £95; ⏲lunch Wed-Sat, dinner Tue-Sat) In a wonderful Victorian villa backing onto the river, this sophisticated place is a sheer gastronomic delight. Chef Daniel's creations, rightly justifying the two Michelin stars, are distinguished by their depth of flavour, great technical skill and expert pairings of ingredients. Expect the likes of slow-roast duck with sweet potato and grapefruit, and sea bass with truffle. The service is exemplary, with none of the pretension you'd expect of a restaurant of its calibre.

Cotto INTERNATIONAL ££

(www.cottocambridge.co.uk; 183 East Rd; lunch mains £9-23, 3-course dinner £45; ⏲9am-3pm Tue-Fri, dinner Thu-Sat; ✍) The popularity of this busy spot is due to chef Hans' ability to coax wonderful flavours out of simple ingredients, most of them seasonal and locally sourced. For lunch you can expect risotto with mushrooms and seasonal veggies, and hearty soup, whereas the evening menu is more sophisticated, giving you veal kidneys à la dijonaise, salt marsh lamb and beautiful desserts – all executed with great flair.

Oak Bistro MODERN BRITISH ££

(☎01223-323361; www.theoakbistro.co.uk; 6 Lensfield Rd; mains £12-20, 2-/3-course set lunch £12/15; ⏲Mon-Sat) This great local favourite serves up simple, classic dishes with modern flair, such as tuna nicoise salad and slow-roasted lamb. The atmosphere is relaxed and welcoming, the decor minimalist and there's even a hidden walled garden for alfresco dining. Reservations are essential even for lunch due to its size and popularity.

Hakka CHINESE ££

(☎01223-568988; www.hak-ka.co.uk; 24 Milton Rd; mains £7.50-11.50; ⏲closed lunch; ✍) Chef Daniel's mother has taught him the secrets of Hakka cooking and once you've tasted his signature salt and chilli chicken, you'll be inclined to give her a hug and a kiss. The menu is extensive but the sizzling dishes stand out. Service can be slow on busy nights.

Thanh Binh VIETNAMESE ££

(☎01223-362456; www.thanhbinh.co.uk; 17 Magdalene St; mains £11-14, 2-course lunch menu £9) Cambridge's only Vietnamese restaurant has some wonderfully flavourful dishes on the menu – from the sublime pork balls to beef *pho* (spicy noodle soup) and fish steamed in lemongrass. Dinner on weekends requires a reservation and can feel a bit rushed, but it's perfect for lunch.

Stickybeaks CAFE £

(www.stickybeakscafe.co.uk; 42 Hobson St; mains £3-7; ⏲8am-5.30pm Mon-Fri, 9am-5.30pm Sat, 10am-5pm Sun; ✍) Sip creamy hot chocolate, nibble on a wide array of cakes or tuck into some imaginative salads (couscous with pomegranate, puy lentils with goat's cheese) and sausage rolls with unusual chutney at this popular new cafe.

Chop House TRADITIONAL BRITISH ££

(http://www.cambscuisine.com/cambridge-chop-house; 1 Kings Pde; mains £9.50-24) Set on the busy corner of Kings Pde and Bene't St, this place has wooden floors, giant windows overlooking the street, and – true to the name – a menu of classic, meat-heavy English cuisine. If you're craving sausage and mash, a sizzling steak, suet pudding, fish pie or potted ham, look no further. Sister restaurant **St John's Chop House** (http://www.cambscuisine.com/st-johns-chop-house; 21-24 Northampton St) has the same menu and is located near the rear entrance to St John's College.

Alimentum MODERN EUROPEAN £££
(01223-413001; www.restaurantalimentum.co.uk; 152-154 Hills Rd; 2-/3-course lunch £16.50/22.50, dinner £32.50/45; closed dinner Sun) Slick, stylish and eager to impress, this place aims to wow with its ambitious menu and attentive service. The emphasis is on slow cooking and ethically sourced local produce, and the dishes are imaginative and well presented, but somehow lack the 'wow' factor. It's a short bus ride out of the centre.

Jamie's Italian ITALIAN ££
(www.jamieoliver.com/italian; Old Library, Wheeler St; mains £9-19) Set in the city's Guildhall, the celebrity chef's 'neighbourhood Italian' is popular with the city's young trendsters. The building itself has loads of character, the antipasti arrives on the signature wooden planks and the mains are simple, filling, unpretentious dishes.

Dojo ASIAN £
(www.dojonoodlebar.co.uk; 1-2 Miller's Yard, Mill Lane; mains £5-8.50) Favoured by students from Queens and noodle lovers in general, this brisk spot serves generous portions of Chinese, Thai, Japanese, Vietnamese and Malaysian noodle and rice dishes within a compact, bright interior.

Fitzbillies BAKERY, CAFE ££
(www.fitzbillies.co.uk; 52 Trumpington St; cafe mains £8-19; closed dinner Mon) Cambridge's oldest bakery, beloved by generations of students for its ultrasticky buns and quaint wood shopfront, makes a good stop for breakfast, while its cafe next door serves good British food in simple surroundings.

Gardenia GREEK £
(2 Rose Cres; mains £4-6.50) 'Gardi's' is responsible for the late-night nutrition of a large chunk of the student population, its walls plastered with photos of happy customers munching on the lamb souvlaki and doner kebabs.

Clowns CAFE £
(54 King St; coffee £1.70, mains £4.50-8; 8am-11pm) A Cambridge institution, run by a friendly Italian family, decked out with pictures of clowns. Great for a cooked breakfast, homemade lasagne, or simply lingering over a good coffee and a newspaper.

Drinking

Cambridge has a lively drinking scene, with watering holes running the gamut from independent pubs serving real ale to chains such as Wetherspoons and a few cocktail bars. King St, Regent St and Mitchum's Corner (the Chesterton Rd/Milton Rd junction) are good places to start.

Maypole PUB
(www.maypolefreehouse.co.uk; 20a Portugal Pl) This friendly, locally popular traditional pub has hit a winning formula: serve a good selection of real ales, not forgetting lesser-known beers from smaller breweries, throw in some great cocktails, and then, when it seemed that things couldn't get any better, throw a successful beer festival in 2012 (set to become an annual event).

Eagle PUB
(Bene't St) Cambridge's most famous pub has loosened the tongues and pickled the grey cells of many an illustrious academic in its day; among them are Nobel Prize–winning scientists Crick and Watson, who discussed their research into DNA here. It's a traditional 17th-century pub with five cluttered, cosy rooms and good pub grub. The back room was once popular with WWII airmen, who left their signatures on the ceiling.

Portland Arms PUB
(www.theportlandarms.co.uk; 129 Chesterton Rd) The best spot in town to catch a gig and see the pick of up-and-coming bands, the Portland is a popular student haunt and music venue. Its wood-panelled interior and spacious terrace make it a good bet any day of the week, and there's a monthly comedy night as well.

Granta PUB
(01223-505016; Newnham Rd) If the exterior of this picturesque waterside pub, overhanging a pretty mill pond, looks strangely familiar, it could well be because it is the darling of many a TV director. Its terrace sits directly beside the water, and when your courage has been sufficiently fuelled, there are punts for hire alongside the terrace.

Entertainment

Thanks to a steady stream of students and tourists there's always something on in Cambridge. You'll find all the railings in the city centre laden with posters advertising classical concerts, theatre shows, academic lectures and live music. Despite the huge student population, Cambridge isn't blessed with the best nightclubs in the country.

PsychoCandy NIGHTCLUB
(www.clubpsychocandy.com; Station Rd; ⌚bi-monthly) This quirky basement club is by no means mainstream and you won't find any rowdy townies here. It's a wonderful gamer-nerdfest-meets-club-heaven and you're guaranteed a fun night with the likes of Legend of Zelda techno, and club remixes of the Teenage Mutant Ninja Turtles theme tune. It's on the corner of Hills and Station Rds.

Fez NIGHTCLUB
(www.cambridgefez.com; 15 Market Passage) Hip-hop, dance, R&B, techno, funk, top-name DJs and club nights – you'll find it at Cambridge's most popular club, the Moroccan-themed Fez, strewn with Turkish rugs and cushions.

Lola Lo NIGHTCLUB
(www.lolalocambridge.com; 1-6 Guildhall Chambers, Corn Exchange St; ⌚8pm-3am Thu-Mon) Bringing a South Pacific vibe to the centre of Cambridge, Lola Lo specialises in cocktails and themed nights, featuring disco, current hits, club anthems and not-so-big-name DJs. Grass skirts are de rigueur for ladies (though we might be lying).

Corn Exchange THEATRE
(www.cornex.co.uk; Wheeler St) The city's main centre for arts and entertainment. It attracts all kinds of acts, the top names in pop and rock to ballet.

Junction ARTS CENTRE
(www.junction.co.uk; Cambridge Leisure Park, Clifton Way) Theatre, dance, comedy, live bands and club nights at Cambridge's youth venue near the railway station. To get here follow Regent St, then Hills Rd south out of the city for about a mile before turning left onto Clifton Way.

Arts Theatre THEATRE
(www.cambridgeartstheatre.com; 6 St Edward's Passage) Cambridge's biggest bona-fide theatre puts on everything from pantomime to drama fresh from London's West End.

ADC THEATRE
(www.adctheatre.com; Park St) Students' theatre and home to the university's Footlights comedy troupe, which jump-started the careers of scores of England's comedy legends.

Information

You'll find all the major banks and a host of ATMs around St Andrew's St and Sidney St. The going rate for internet access is about £1 per hour and some cafes offer wi-fi.

Addenbrooke's Hospital (☎01223-245151; Hills Rd) Southeast of the centre.

Budget Internet Cafe (30 Hills Rd; ⌚10am-9pm Mon-Sat, 11am-7pm Sun)

Police Station (☎01223-358966; Parkside)

Post Office (St Andrew's St)

Tourist Office (☎0871-266 8006; www.visitcambridge.org; Old Library, Wheeler St; ⌚10am-5.30pm Mon-Fri, to 5pm Sat, 11am-3pm Sun) Pick up a guide to the Cambridge colleges (£4.99) in the gift shop or a leaflet (£1.20) outlining two city walks. Download audio tours from the website or book slots on a plethora of tours. Rudimentary Cambridge maps costs £1.

Getting There & Away

BUS From Parkside there are regular National Express (www.nationalexpress.co.uk) buses to the following destinations:

Gatwick (£37, 3½ to four hours)

Heathrow (£31, 2½ to three hours)

Luton (£15, 1½ hours, every two hours)

Oxford (£11, 3¼ to 3½ hours, twice-hourly)

Stansted (£13, 50 minutes)

CAR Cambridge's centre is largely pedestrianised and the car parks are expensive. Use one of the five free **Park & Ride** car parks on major routes into town. Buses (tickets £2.70) serve the city centre every 10 minutes between 7am and 7pm daily, then every 20 minutes until 10pm.

TRAIN The train station is off Station Rd, which is off Hills Rd. Destinations:

Birmingham New Street (£30, three hours, hourly)

Bury St Edmunds (£9, 40 minutes, every two hours)

Ely (£4, 15 minutes, three hourly)

King's Lynn (£9, 45 minutes, hourly)

London Kings Cross (£19, 50 minutes to 1¼ hours)

Stansted (£11, 30 minutes, hourly)

Getting Around

BICYCLE Cambridge is very bike-friendly, and two wheels provide a great way of getting about town.

Cambridge Station Cycles (www.stationcycles.co.uk; Station Building, Station Rd; per half-day/day/week £7/10/25) Near the train station.

City Cycle Hire (www.citycyclehire.com; 61 Newnham Rd; per half-day/day from £6/10, per week £17-22)

BUS A free gas-powered City Circle bus runs around the centre. It stops every 15 minutes from 9am to 5pm on Downing St, King's Pde and Jesus Lane. City bus lines run around town from Drummer St bus station; C1, C3, C7 and C8 stop at the train station. Dayrider passes (£3.70) offer unlimited travel on all buses within Cambridge for one day, while Dayrider Plus (£5.70) is valid for all of Cambridgeshire.

Around Cambridge

GRANTCHESTER

Old thatched cottages with gardens covered in flowers, breezy meadows and some classic cream teas aren't the only reason to make the pilgrimage along the river to the picture-postcard village of Grantchester that the poet Rupert Brooke waxed lyrical about. You'll also be following in the footsteps of some of the world's greatest minds on a 3-mile walk, cycle or punt that has changed little since Edwardian times.

The journey here is idyllic on a sunny day, and once you arrive you can flop into a deck chair under a leafy apple tree and wolf down calorific cakes or light lunches at the quintessentially English **Orchard Tea Garden** (www.orchard-grantchester.com; Mill Way; lunch mains £6-8; ⌚9.30am-7pm). This was the favourite haunt of the Bloomsbury Group and other cultural icons who came to camp, picnic, swim and discuss their work.

IMPERIAL WAR MUSEUM

The romance of the winged war machine is alive and well at Europe's biggest **aviation museum** (http://aam.iwm.org.uk/; Duxford; adult/child £17/free; ⌚10am-6pm; 👪) where almost 200 lovingly waxed vintage aircraft are housed in several enormous hangars. The vast airfield, a frontline fighter station in WWII, showcases everything from dive bombers to biplanes, a Spitfire and Concorde, and you can poke your head inside several of the planes (including said Concorde). Be prepared to make this a day trip, especially if you're bringing your kids, who'll want to try their hand at the interactive rocket launchers and flight simulators.

The awe-inspiring **American Air Museum** hangar, designed by Norman Foster, pays homage to the daring of the American servicemen in WWII and hosts the largest collection of American civil and military aircraft outside the USA, while the slick **AirSpace hangar** houses an exhibition on British and Commonwealth aviation.

The winged machines are not here just to look pretty; a number of the lovingly restored planes, such as the legendary 'Flying Fortress', take to the skies during the ultra-popular June/July **Winged Legends airshow** – an exhilarating spectacle not least because there's considerable risk involved for the pilot.

The 20th-century's major battles are also well covered – from the Normandy landing and the Battle of Britain to the latest desert warfare in Afghanistan and Iraq, complete with an assortment of tanks and artillery from WWII onwards.

Regardless of how you may feel about warfare, it's difficult not to be impressed by the extent of human ingenuity.

Duxford is 9 miles south of Cambridge at Junction 10 of the M11. Bus C7 runs from Emmanuel St in Cambridge to Duxford (45 minutes, every half-hour, less frequently on Sundays). The last bus back from the museum leaves at 5.30pm.

Ely

POP 15,102

A small but charming city dominated by a jaw-dropping cathedral, Ely (*ee*-lee) makes an excellent day trip from Cambridge. Beyond the dizzying heights of the cathedral towers lie medieval streets, pretty Georgian houses and riverside walks reaching out into the eerie fens that surround the town, while traditional tearooms and antiques shops vie for attention. The abundance of eels that once inhabited the undrained fens when Ely was an island gave the town its unusual name, and you can still sample eel stew or eel pie in some local restaurants.

Sights & Activities

TOP CHOICE **Ely Cathedral** CATHEDRAL

(www.elycathedral.org; tower tour Mon-Sat £6, Sun £8.50; ⌚7am-6.30pm, evensong 5.30pm Mon-Sat, 4pm Sun, choral service 10.30am Sun) Dominating the town, the stunning silhouette of Ely Cathedral is locally dubbed the 'Ship of the Fens' due to its visibility across the flat fenland for vast distances.

Just in front of the entrance, the floor of the West Tower has a maze on it symbolising a Christian's convoluted path through life; the same message is conveyed by the aluminium 'The Way of Life' sculpture on the wall to the left of the entrance.

Walking into the early-12th-century Romanesque nave (with some Gothic arches added later to support the weight of the mighty walls) you're immediately struck by its clean, uncluttered lines and lofty sense of space. The cathedral is renowned for its entrancing ceiling, painted by two artists: Henry Le Strange and Thomas Gambier (can you spot the difference in style?), the masterly 14th-century Octagon – the most impressive in all of England's churches – and lantern towers, which soar upwards in shimmering colours.

The vast 14th-century Lady Chapel is the biggest in England; it's filled with eerily empty niches that once held statues of saints and martyrs. They were hacked out unceremoniously by iconoclasts during the English Civil War. However, the astonishingly delicate tracery and carving remain, overseen by a rather controversial **statue of Holy Mary** by David Wynne, unveiled in 2000 to mixed reviews. With a bright blue dress, golden hair and her arms raised high to praise the Lord, she seems more X Factor hopeful than mother of Christ.

The cathedral's incredible architecture and light have made it a popular film location: you may recognise some of its fine details from scenes in *Elizabeth: The Golden Age* and *The Other Boleyn Girl*.

Ely has been a place of worship and pilgrimage since at least 673, when Etheldreda, daughter of the king of East Anglia, founded a nunnery here. In her determination to be a nun, she shrugged off the fact that she had been twice married, and was canonised shortly after her death. The nunnery was sacked by the Danes, rebuilt as a monastery, demolished and then resurrected as a church after the Norman Conquest. In 1109 Ely became a cathedral, leaving mere mortals in no doubt about the power of the church.

For more insight into the fascinating history of the cathedral join a free **guided tour**, or a **tower tour** of the Octagon Tower or the West Tower. Try to time your visit to attend the spine-tingling evensong or choral service.

Near the entrance a **stained-glass museum** (www.stainedglassmuseum.com; adult/child £4/3; ⏲10.30am-5pm Mon-Fri, to 5.30pm Sat, noon-6pm Sun Easter-Oct) tells the history of decorated glasswork from the 14th century onwards.

Oliver Cromwell's House MUSEUM
(www.olivercromwellshouse.co.uk; adult/child £4.50/4, joint ticket with Ely Museum £6.80; ⏲10am-5pm; 👪) By St Mary's Green is the attractive half-timbered house where England's only dictator (p422) lived with his family from 1636 to 1647, when he was the local tithe collector. From the introductory video and the audio-guided tour of the living quarters, to exhibits on the Civil War and Cromwell's posthumous execution, this entertaining museum challenges you to answer one question: was this complex character (who executed a king and fought a bloody Civil War that killed 185,000 people) a hero or a villain? The interactive exhibits keep children (and your inner child) happily occupied throughout.

Ely Museum MUSEUM
(www.elymuseum.org.uk; Market St; adult/child £3.50/1; ⏲10.30am-5pm Mon-Sat, 1-5pm Sun; 👪) Housed in the Old Gaol House, this quirky little museum appropriately features gruesome prison tableaux inside prisoners' cells, as well as historical displays on Romans, Anglo-Saxons, the Long Barrow burial ground at nearby Haddlington and the formation of the Fens. It also has a hands-on 'feel that fossil' and 'mystery objects' exhibit for kids. You are also initiated into the mysteries of old Ely trades such as eel catching and leatherwork, as well as the local role in the world wars. One thing you *won't* learn here is that from the Middle Ages onwards, Ely was one of the biggest opium-producing centres in Britain, with high-class ladies holding 'poppy parties', and mothers in the Fens sedating their children with 'poppy tea', lest they fall in the water and drown.

Waterside Antiques Centre ANTIQUES
(www.ely.org.uk/waterside.html; The Wharf; ⏲9.30am-5.30pm Mon-Sat, 11.30am-5.30pm Sun) The largest place in East Anglia for antiques and collectables.

Great Ouse WALKING
From the antiques centre, this charming riverside walk ambles east with the Fens stretching to the horizon.

Sleeping & Eating

Cathedral House B&B ££
(☎01353-662124; www.cathedralhouse.co.uk; 17 St Mary's St; s/d £80/100; P 📶) Set in a lovely Georgian house bursting with antiques and curios, this elegant B&B offers three

OLIVER CROMWELL – THE SCOURGE OF KINGS

Well, one king, at any rate. Though some believe that the enigmatic Cromwell was a regicidal dictator, while others hail him as a hero of liberty, the truth is much more complex than that.

East Anglia's most notorious son was born in Huntingdon in 1599, and though his first 40 years or so as a smallholder were spent in obscurity, after he'd undergone a religious conversion and became a militant Puritan there was no stopping him, driven as he was by ambition and clarity of purpose before God. After a spell as a Member of Parliament for Huntingdon and then Cambridge, 'Old Ironsides' excelled as a military commander during the English Civil War, fighting on the side of the victorious Republicans; though he was only one of several signatories of the death warrant of Charles I, he is the one largely held responsible.

Controversy followed controversy. Though modern interpretation suggests that Cromwell allowed Jews back into Britain to 'stimulate the economy', the fact that he used the full weight of his office as Lord Protector to force through this unpopular decision shows how firmly he believed that the conversion of the Jews to Christianity was the essential precondition to the establishment of Christ's rule on earth: 'Was it not our duty in particular to encourage them to settle here, where alone they could be taught the truth?'

His other major achievements were the conquests of Ireland and Scotland, acts that – together with the death of Charles I – won him widespread posthumous animosity, to the point where his body was exhumed from Westminster Abbey after Restoration and then treated as if he had been a live rebel: hanged at Tyburn and decapitated. The body was almost certainly thrown into the common pit at Tyburn (the present-day site of Marble Arch), while the head was stuck on Westminster Hall and remained there for several decades, blowing down in a storm in the early 18th century. Picked up, it passed into private ownership and was occasionally exhibited as a curiosity. A descendant of its last owner deeded it to Sidney Sussex College in 1960 – Cromwell's alma mater – and it was buried in the chapel. There is a plaque on the wall by the door but the exact location is kept secret, lest self-proclaimed Royalists dig it up and defile it.

individually decorated rooms, all with period features and cast-iron baths. Outside there's a beautiful walled garden and views of the cathedral. Two-night minimum booking on weekends.

Riverside Inn B&B ££

(☎01353-661667; www.riversideinn-ely.co.uk; 8 Annesdale; s/d £65/90; P) You'll get great views of the river from this elegant house right on the waterfront. It has just three spacious rooms with king-size beds, silky, brocade bedspreads, dark furniture and sparkling new bathrooms.

TOP CHOICE Peacocks Tearoom TEAROOM ££

(www.peacockstearoom.co.uk; 65 Waterside; cream teas £7; ⏲10.30am-4.30pm Wed-Sun;) Consistently voted one of Britain's top teashops, this award-winning, family-run, wisteria-clad place serves a vast selection of leaf teas (from black-tea mixes named after characters out of Sherlock Holmes to delicate, citrus-infused green teas), as well as luscious homemade cakes, scones, soups, salads and sandwiches – try the brie and bacon with homemade blueberry chutney.

Old Fire Engine House BRITISH ££

(☎01353-662582; www.theoldfireenginehouse.co.uk; 25 St Mary's St; 2-/3-course set lunch £15/20, mains £15-18; ⏲closed dinner Sun) Backed by beautiful gardens and showcasing a variety of artwork, this delightfully homey place – which has been run by the same husband-and-wife team for over 40 years – serves classic English food, prepared from seasonal local ingredients, and excellent afternoon teas. Expect the likes of steak-and-kidney pie or rabbit with prunes and bacon, washed down with a carefully chosen wine.

Boathouse MODERN BRITISH ££

(☎01353-664388; www.cambscuisine.com/the-boathouse-ely; 5 Annesdale; 2-/3-course set lunch £15/19.50, mains £10-18.50) This sleek riverside restaurant with wonderful patio dining overlooking the water serves up excellent modern English food, such as venison with braised cabbage and thyme mash, and goat's cheese and red onion tagliatelle.

Information

Tourist Office (☎01353-662062; www.visitely.org.uk; 29 St Mary's St; ⏲10am-5pm) Inside Oliver Cromwell's House, it stocks leaflets on the 'Eel Trail' town walk (50p) and organises guided walking tours of the city, as well as ghost tours and other events.

Getting There & Away

The easiest way to get to Ely is by train:

Cambridge (£4, 20 minutes, every 20 minutes)

King's Lynn (£6, 30 minutes, hourly)

Norwich (£18, one hour, every 20 minutes)

Following the **Fen Rivers Way** (map available from tourist offices), it's a lovely 17-mile towpath walk from Cambridge to Ely.

ESSEX

The county's inhabitants have been the butt of some of England's cruellest jokes and snobbery for years due to the chav stereotypes – young people who favour designer sportswear and gold bling – but beyond the fake Burberry bags, bleached hair and slots 'n' bumper car resorts, there's a rural idyll of sleepy medieval villages and rolling countryside. One of England's best-loved painters, John Constable, found inspiration here, and the rural Essex of his time remains hidden down winding lanes little changed for centuries. Here, too, is the historic town of Colchester, Britain's oldest, with a castle and vibrant arts scene. Even Southend-on-Sea, the area's most popular resort, has a softer side in the traditional cockle-sellers and cobbled lanes of sleepy suburb Leigh.

Colchester

POP 104,390

Dominated by its sturdy castle and ancient walls, Colchester is Britain's oldest recorded city, with settlement noted here as early as the 5th century BC. Centuries later, in AD 43, the Romans came, saw, conquered and constructed their capital, Camulodunum, here, which was razed by Boudica in AD 60. A thousand years later, the invading Normans saw Colchester's potential and built the monstrous war machine that is the castle, though its mighty walls were not enough to withstand the three-month siege during the Civil War, when Colchester found itself allied to the losing side.

Today the city has a rather dowdy atmosphere, but amid the maze of narrow streets in the city centre you'll find a few half-timbered gems, the fine castle and a striking new art space.

Sights

TOP CHOICE firstsite ARTS CENTRE

(www.firstsite.uk.net; St Botolph's; free entry; ⏲10am-5pm Tue, Wed, Sat & Sun, to 7pm Thu & Fri; 👪) Opinion has been divided about Colchester's newest attraction – a new arts centre housed inside a stunning curved-glass and copper building. Inside, it's also visually striking – lots of space, lots of light, installations flowing seamlessly into one another, and seats to perch on if you wish to leaf through some art books. The contemporary visual art on display is carefully chosen to be presented alongside historical works for context, and most exhibitions are temporary, with the exception of the magnificent Berryfield Mosaic – a Roman artefact found on firstsite's location in 1923, and now under glass in the centre of the gallery space. There's an interactive element to firstsite as well: besides the works on display and the Arts Picturehouse cinema, there are also art courses for young people, as well as creative sessions for young children and their parents. Love it or hate it, firstsite will not leave you indifferent.

TOP CHOICE Colchester Castle CASTLE

(www.colchestermuseums.org.uk; adult/child £6.25/4; ⏲10am-5pm Mon-Sat, from 11am Sun; 👪) Built upon the foundations of the Roman Temple of Claudius, England's largest surviving Norman keep (bigger even than that of the Tower of London) was first established in 1076 and now houses an exceptional interactive museum that brings the Romano-British archaeological exhibits to life through a combination of artefacts, videos and hands-on displays. Standout exhibits focus on the Iceni revolt against the Romans, the Siege of Colchester and the Essex witch hunts. There are **guided tours** (adult/child £2.20/1; ⏲hourly noon-3pm) of the Roman vaults, Norman rooftop chapel and castle walls. The museum will be closed for redevelopment between January 2013 and Easter 2014.

FREE **Hollytrees Museum** MUSEUM
(www.colchestermuseums.org.uk; High St; ⏲10am-5pm Mon-Sat, from 11am Sun;) Housed in a graceful Georgian town house beside the castle, this museum trawls through 300 years of domestic life of the wealthy and their servants, with quirky exhibits that include a shipwright's baby carriage in the shape of a boat, a make-your-own-Victorian-silhouette feature and an intricate, envy-inducing dolls' house. One room is dedicated to the art of clock making – a prestigious trade that Colchester was once famous for.

Colchester Zoo ZOO
(www.colchester-zoo.co.uk; Maldon Rd, Stanway; adult/child £17/11; ⏲9.30am-5.30pm) With its world-class animal enclosures, Colchester Zoo is particularly well known for its successful breeding programs and conservation efforts. The zoo is 5 miles northeast of the castle, reachable by bus 75.

Dutch Quarter NEIGHBOURHOOD
The best of the city's half-timbered houses and rickety roof lines are clustered together in this Tudor enclave just a short stroll north of High St. The area remains as a testament to the 16th-century Protestant weavers who fled here from Holland.

Sleeping & Eating

Colchester is easily doable as a day trip from London, but if you're staying, there are some excellent B&Bs that give the town's ancient hotels a run for their money.

Charlie Browns B&B £
(☎01206-517541; www.charliebrownsbedandbreakfast.co.uk; 60 East St; s/d from £35/50;) A former hardware shop turned boutique B&B, this place offers incredible value, with a couple of stunning rooms blending 14th-century character with 21st-century style. Antique and modern furniture mix seamlessly with the half-timbered walls, limestone bathrooms and rich fabrics to create an intimate, luxurious feel. Dogs welcome, including Snoopy.

Trinity Townhouse B&B ££
(☎01206-575955; www.trinitytownhouse.co.uk; 6 Trinity St; s/d from £85/100;) This central Tudor town house has five lovely rooms, each with its own character. Go for four-poster Wilbye, cottage-style Darcy or the more modern Furley. Each has period features, king-size bed, flatscreen TV and a designer bathroom. No children under five.

TOP CHOICE **Company Shed** SEAFOOD £
(☎01206-382700; www.the-company-shed.co.uk; 129 Coast Rd, West Mersea; mains £4-12; ⏲9am-5pm Tue-Sat, 10am-5pm Sun) It's a simple idea: bring your own bread and wine, perch on one of the seats inside this seaside shack, and tuck into the mussels, Colchester oysters, prawns and smoked fish, courtesy of the Howard family – eighth-generation oystermen. The seafood platter (£11.95) lets you sample a good cross-section. West Mersea is on Mersea Island, 9 miles south of town.

Green Room MODERN BRITISH ££
(☎01206-574001; 50-51 North Hill; lunch mains £7-9, dinner mains £14-17) Relaxed, friendly and down to earth, this easygoing bistro has simple wooden tables, bright artwork and some of the best food in town. Locally sourced meats, fish and oysters feature heavily on the seasonal menu, and it buzzes with happy diners lapping up the likes of seared cod cheeks, and pork belly and black-pudding salad.

Information

Tourist Office (☎01206-282920; www.visitcolchester.com; 1 Queen St; ⏲9.30am-5pm Mon-Sat)

Getting There & Away

The bus station is on Queen St. There are three daily National Express buses to **London Victoria** (£15, 2½ hours).

Mainline services stop at Colchester North, about half a mile north of the centre. Trains run to **London Liverpool Street** (£25, one hour, every 15 minutes).

Dedham Vale

I love every stile and stump and lane...
these scenes made me a painter
John Constable (1776–1837)

Born and bred in East Bergholt, John Constable's romantic visions of country lanes, springtime fields and babbling creeks were inspired by and painted in this serene vale. The area has hung on to its rural charm despite the intervening centuries, and although you may not see the rickety old cart pictured in his renowned painting *The Hay Wain,* the background of picturesque cottages, rolling countryside and languid charm remains.

Now known as Constable country, Dedham Vale centres on the picturesque villages of Dedham, East Bergholt and Flatford. With leafy lanes, arresting pastoral views and graceful old churches, it's a glorious area to explore on foot or by bike. There's a **tourist office** (01206-299460; www.dedhamvalestourvalley.org; Flatford Lane, East Bergholt; 10am-5pm Easter-Oct, 11am-4pm Sat & Sun Nov-mid-Mar) beside the vale's top attraction, the riverside **Flatford Mill** once owned by the artist's family and now used as an education centre. Constable fans will recognise the picturesque red-brick mill immediately as it features in many of his paintings and remains as idyllic a setting today.

Near the mill is thatched **Bridge Cottage** (NT; 01206-298260; www.nationaltrust.org.uk; Flatford Lane, East Bergholt; parking £3, admission free; 10.30am-5.30pm May-Sep), which has an exhibition on the artist but none of his works. Call ahead about the organised tours (£6), which feature the Flatford Mill, Willy Lott's Cottage (which features in *The Hay Wain*) and other sites of Constable's paintings.

If you'd like to base yourself here, try **Dedham Hall** (01206-323027; www.dedhamhall.co.uk; Dedham; s/d £65/110), an atmospheric 15th-century manor house where you can also take **painting courses** (nonresidential rate three-/seven-days £245/310) if you wish to follow in Constable's footsteps.

Alternatively, pamper yourself at the luxurious **Maison Talbooth** (01206-322367; www.milsomhotels.com; Stratford Rd, Dedham; ste £235-350; P), with its individually decorated suites and outdoor hot tub, and chow on down at the **Sun Inn** (www.thesuninndedham.com; mains £13-19), featuring a changing seasonal menu of expertly prepared British and Italian dishes, as well as a good selection of real ales.

Buses 247 and 87A run regularly from Colchester to Dedham (40 minutes); buses 93 and 93A run to East Bergholt (35 minutes). If coming by train, the mill is a lovely 2-mile walk from Manningtree.

Saffron Walden

POP 14,313

The little market town of Saffron Walden, around since 1141, is a delightful knot of half-timbered houses, narrow lanes, crooked roofs and ancient buildings. It's a really lovely place to wander, with a host of antique shops, galleries and secondhand bookshops to catch your eye. The town gets its curious title from the saffron crocus – the purple flower responsible for the most expensive spice on earth – which was cultivated in the surrounding fields from the 15th century until 1717.

Sights

The town's most famous building is the 14th-century **Old Sun Inn** (Church St), an ornate wooden structure once used as Cromwell's HQ. Don't miss the stunning 17th-century pargeting (decorative plasterwork).

Nearby is the **Church of St Mary the Virgin** (www.stmaryssaffronwalden.org; Church St) with a 59m-tall tower, its oldest parts dating back to 1250. A symbol of the town's saffron-inspired golden age, it is one of the largest churches in the county and sports some impressive Gothic arches and Lord Audley's tomb.

In the excellent **museum** (www.saffronwaldenmuseum.org; Museum St; adult/child £1.50/free; 10am-5pm Mon-Sat, 2-5pm Sun;), itself dating from 1835, you'll find an eclectic collection of artefacts covering everything from local history and 18th- and 19th-century costume to geology, a partially interactive natural-history exhibit, Victorian toys and ancient Egyptian items. There's a sand pit for young archaeologists and a fascinating 'Worlds of Man' collection, ranging from West African carvings and weaponry to Inuit bone harpoons. The bramble-covered ruins of **Walden Castle Keep**, built about 1125, lie in the grounds.

Tucked down at the end of quiet lanes off Bridge St and Castle St is the restored Victorian **Bridge End Garden** (www.bridgeendgarden.org; admission free; dawn-dusk), with a proliferation of fruit trees and roses; one exit leads to the **Fry Gallery** (www.fryartgallery.org; admission free; 2-5pm Tue, Thu & Fri, 11am-5pm Sat, 2.15-5pm Sun), dedicated to the 20th-century paintings, ceramics and prints by local artists.

On the eastern side of the town, across the common, is the **Turf Maze**, thought to be 800 years old and the largest of its kind.

Sleeping & Eating

Accommodation options in Saffron are limited, and it's easily doable as a day trip from Cambridge.

DON'T MISS

AUDLEY END HOUSE

Positively palatial in its scale, style and the all-too-apparent ambition of its creator, the first earl of Suffolk, the fabulous early-Jacobean **Audley End House** (EH; www.english-heritage.org.uk; adult/child £13/7.80; ⌚house noon-5pm Wed-Sun) eventually did become a royal palace when it was bought by Charles II in 1668.

Although it's hard to believe, the enormous building today is only one-third of its original size, but it's still magnificent. The lavishly decorated rooms glitter with silverware, priceless furniture and paintings, making it one of England's grandest country homes. The sumptuous interior was remodelled in Gothic style by the third Baron Braybrooke in the 19th century, and much of his creations are what remain today. You can also visit the service wing, where a new exhibition explores the lives of those who worked in the house in Victorian times.

Outside, the house is surrounded by a landscaped **park** (⌚10am-6pm Wed-Sun) designed by Lancelot 'Capability' Brown and host to a series of concerts throughout the summer months.

Audley End House is 1 mile west of Saffron Walden off the B1383. Audley End train station is 1.25 miles from the house. Taxis will ferry you here from the town marketplace for around £5.

TOP CHOICE **Chaff House** B&B ££
(☎01763-836278; Ash Grove Barns, Littlebury Green; d £60) Though not the easiest to find, this countryside guesthouse certainly separates the wheat from the chaff. A delightful converted barn, this one has just three rooms – all with high-beamed ceilings, and two sharing a kitchen. Freshly cooked breakfast is included in the price, and the hostess can provide dinner on request.

Old Forge B&B B&B £
(☎01799-521494; 23 Fairycroft Rd; s/d £30/50) Hospitable John and Cindy preside over eight rooms, tastefully decorated in muted colours and a dining room full of Beatles and Queen memorabilia. Full English breakfast included and there's a hot tub in the garden that guests may use.

Eight Bells PUB ££
(www.8bells-pub.co.uk; 18 Bridge St; mains £12-18; ⌚closed dinner Sun; 🖉) A warm mix of medieval character and contemporary style, this 16th-century gastropub serves up the likes of roast pork tenderloin with sage-infused apple and home-cured gravadlax. Scrubbed wooden floors, half-timbered walls, abstract art, deep leather sofas and roaring fires make it a great place to sip on a pint or enjoy a top-notch meal.

Cafe Coucou CAFE £
(17 George St; mains £7-10; ⌚9am-5pm Mon-Sat) Delicious homemade quiches, huge scones, chunky doorstop sandwiches and salads sell like hotcakes at this cheerful family-run cafe.

ℹ Information

Tourist office (☎01799-524002; www.visitsaffronwalden.gov.uk; 1 Market Pl; ⌚9.30am-5pm Mon-Sat Apr-Oct) Ultra helpful and provides a useful town trail leaflet with information on the town's historic buildings.

ℹ Getting There & Around

BUS The C7 bus runs into **Cambridge** (one hour, hourly). Buses 301 and 59 run from Audley End station into **Saffron Walden** (15 minutes) regularly on weekdays, less often on weekends.

TRAIN Audley End station is 2.5 miles west of town.

Cambridge (£6, 20 minutes, services every 20 minutes)

London Liverpool Street (£19, one hour, twice hourly Monday to Saturday, hourly Sunday)

Southend-on-Sea

POP 160,257

Full of flashing lights and fairground rides, Southend is London's weekend playground, with gaudy amusements and nightclubs that border on the seedy. But beyond the tourist shops, roller coasters and slot machines there's a glorious stretch of sandy beach, an absurdly long pier and in the suburb of Old Leigh, a traditional fishing village. Incidentally, neither Southend nor Leigh are actually 'on sea'; they are both on the Thames estuary.

Sights & Activities

Southend's main attraction is the world's longest **pier** (☎01702-215620; pier train adult/child £3.50/2, pier walk & ride £2.50/1.50; ⏰8.15am-8pm), a staggering 1.34 miles to be precise, built in 1830 – and a magnet for boat crashes, storms and fires, the last of which ravaged its tip in 2005. In spite of that, at the time of writing, a new **cultural centre** had just been lowered onto the end of the pier. It houses a cafe, artists' studios and an auditorium. It's a peaceful if windy stroll to the head of the pier, and you can hop on the **Pier Railway** to save the long slog back.

Afterwards, dip beneath the pier's entrance to see the antique slot machines at the **museum** (www.southendpiermuseum.co.uk; adult/child £1.50/free; ⏰11am-5pm Sun-Wed).

Also right by the pier, the colourful metal ribbons of roller coasters at **Adventure Island** (www.adventureisland.co.uk; admission £12-24; ⏰approximately 11am-6pm) tend to be packed with happily shrieking revellers on sunny days.

Just west along the seafront, Southend morphs seamlessly into the suburbs of Westcliff-on-Sea, Chalkwell and Leigh-on-Sea, reachable by a long stroll or short hops on the local train. Wander the cobbled streets, cockle sheds, art galleries and craft shops of **Old Leigh** for a taste of life before the amusement arcades took over (not to mention a taste of the cockles themselves). The **Leigh Heritage Centre** (☎01702-470834; High St, Old Leigh) offers an insight into the history and heritage of the village and its buildings. The centre is run by volunteers so call in advance to check opening times.

Sleeping

Roslin Beach Hotel HOTEL ££

(☎01702-586375; www.roslinhotel.com; Thorpe Esplanade; s/d from £87/115; P 📶 🐾) This delightful, low-key hotel is a little out of the way – a 30-minute walk from the pier – but its location right on the waterfront and its bright, unfussy rooms decked out in subtle pastel shades make it worthwhile. The adjoining restaurant is a sure bet for well-executed Modern British dishes, too.

Pebbles B&B ££

(☎01702-582329; www.mypebbles.co.uk; 190 Eastern Esplanade; s/d from £45/65; 📶) Subtle, contemporary style is a real winner at this lovely B&B on the waterfront. The rooms here still retain their Victorian features, but the decor is modern, with funky wallpapers, plenty of cushions, big, comfy beds and great cooked breakfast to boot.

Beaches B&B ££

(☎01702-586124; www.beachesguesthouse.co.uk; 192 Eastern Esplanade; s/d from £40/70; 📶) A welcome respite from violent florals and heavy swag curtains, rooms at Beaches are bright, simple and tasteful, with white Egyptian cotton bed linen, feather duvets and subtle individual colour schemes.

Eating

TOP CHOICE **Simply Seafood** SEAFOOD ££

(☎01702-716645; www.simplyseafood.co.uk; High St, Leigh-on-Sea; lunch mains £8-13, dinner mains £11-20; ✎) Tucked away under a flyover just east of the heart of Old Leigh, the strength of this light, bright little restaurant is undoubtedly seafood. The crispy whitebait is so fresh it may as well have leapt out of the sea onto your plate, the scallops are perfectly seared and the emperor's seafood platter is fit for royalty. The service is wonderfully attentive and there's even an extensive vegetarian menu.

Azurro ITALIAN ££

(☎01702-435845; www.azzurrosouthend.com; 326 London Rd, Westcliff-on-Sea; 2-course early dinner £9.95; ✎) The guys at this fabulous Italian joint know their stuff: their professional pride won't allow them to grill a fine piece of meat to oblivion, so don't ask for your venison to be 'well done'. Apart from the grilled carnivorous offerings and the likes of swordfish with *salsa picante*, the array of pizzas and pastas is simple, but very nicely done.

Mews FUSION ££

(☎01702-393626; www.clarencegroup.co.uk; 2 Nelson Mews; lunch mains £8-15, dinner mains £9-25) Tucked away near the train station, this relaxed, modern restaurant and bar with a stone fireplace and stuffed leather sofas is filled with a low hum of contented diners tucking into some playful fusion dishes (jerk pork loin with sweet potato mash, wild mushroom risotto) or sandwiches at lunchtime.

Information

Tourist Office (☎01702-618747; www.visitsouthend.co.uk; Southend Pier, Western Esplanade; ⏰8.15am-8pm) At the entrance to the pier.

Getting There & Around

The easiest way to arrive is by train. There are trains roughly every 15 minutes from **London Liverpool St** to Southend Victoria, and from **London Fenchurch St** to Southend Central (£10.60, 55 minutes). Southend Central is a 10-minute walk from the sea, whereas Southend Victoria is a 15-minute walk away. Trains leave Southend Central for **Leigh-on-Sea** (10 minutes, every 10 to 15 minutes).

SUFFOLK

Dotted with quaint seaside resorts and picturesque villages seemingly lost in time, this charming county makes a delightfully tranquil destination. Suffolk built its wealth and reputation on the back of the medieval wool trade, and although the once-busy coastal ports little resemble their former selves, the inland villages remain largely untouched, with magnificent wool churches and lavish medieval homes attesting to the once-great might of the area. To the west are the picture-postcard villages of Lavenham and Long Melford; further north the languid charm and historic buildings attract visitors to Bury St Edmunds; and along the coast the genteel seaside resorts of Aldeburgh and Southwold seem miles away from their more brash neighbours to the north and south.

Getting There & Around

Consult **Suffolk County Tourism** (www.suffolkonboard.com) or **Traveline East Anglia** (www.travelineeastanglia.org.uk) for local transport information. The two main bus operators in rural areas are **Constable** (www.constablecoachesltd.co.uk) and **Chambers** (www.chamberscoaches.co.uk).

Ipswich is the main transport hub of the region but is not of great interest to visitors. Trains from Ipswich:

Bury St Edmunds (£8, 35 minutes, twice hourly)

London Liverpool St (£26, 1¼ hours, every 20 minutes)

Norwich (£13.40, 45 minutes, twice every hour)

Stour Valley

The soft, pastoral landscape and comely villages of the Stour Valley have provided inspiration for some of England's best-loved painters. Both Constable and Gainsborough grew up or worked here, and the timber-framed houses and elegant churches that date all the way back to the region's

DON'T MISS

SUTTON HOO – A KING'S RESTING PLACE

Somehow missed by plundering grave robbers and left undisturbed for 1300 years, the hull of an enormous Anglo-Saxon ship was discovered buried under a mound of earth in a field near Sutton Hoo in 1939 – arguably the most important archaeological discovery in East Anglia. The ship was the final resting place of Raedwald, king of East Anglia until AD 625, who was buried alongside his most prized possessions; his helmet alone has iconic status and you'll undoubtedly recognise it on sight.

Many of the original finds and a full-scale reconstruction of his burial chamber can be seen in the **visitors centre** (NT; www.nationaltrust.org.uk/suttonhoo; Woodbridge; adult/child £7.50/3.90; ⊙10.30am-5pm; 👪). The finest treasures, which underline Raedwald's importance in life, include an exquisitely crafted helmet, shield, intricate gold buckle aswirl with dragons, and Byzantine silver. These are all displayed in London's British Museum. However, replicas are on show here and they raise all sorts of unanswered questions, such as why were there only Frankish coins found with the bones (and not English ones)? Modest original finds are also on display: a sword, a bowl, parts of horse harness.

Join a one-hour **guided tour** (adult/child £2.50/1.25; ⊙11.30am & 12.30pm) to be initiated into the world of Anglo-Saxons, their lifestyle and death rites. If you wish to go it alone, there's a path that meanders through a copse to the original burial mounds where the ship was found, and where you can contemplate this ancient graveyard at your leisure. There are also activity packs for kids and hands-on digging fun for budding archaeologists.

Sutton Hoo is 2 miles east of Woodbridge and 10 miles northeast of Ipswich off the B1083.

15th-century boom in the weaving trade are still very much as they were then. This now-quiet backwater once produced more cloth than anywhere else in England, but in the 16th century production gradually shifted elsewhere and the valley reverted to a rustic idyll.

LONG MELFORD

POP 3675

Strung out along a winding road, the village of Long Melford, dating back to the Domesday Book, is home to a clutch of historic buildings and two impressive country piles. The 2-mile High St is supposedly the longest in England; it's flanked by some stunning timber-framed houses, Georgian gems and Victorian terraces.

Sights

At one end is a sprawling village green lorded over by the magnificent **Holy Trinity Church** (9am-6pm) – more cathedral-sized than church-sized. Though its present incarnation is a spectacular example of a 15th-century wool church, its roots date back to the 11th century and its defining features are its stained-glass windows and distinctive flushwork.

From outside, the romantic Elizabethan mansion of **Melford Hall** (NT; www.nationaltrust.org.uk/melfordhall; adult/child £7/3.50; 1-5pm Wed-Sun May-Oct) seems little changed since the queen was entertained here in 1578. Inside, there's a panelled banqueting hall, much Regency and Victorian finery, and a display on Beatrix Potter, who was a cousin of the Parker family, which owned the house from 1786 to 1960.

There's a noticeably different atmosphere at Long Melford's other red-brick Elizabethan mansion, **Kentwell Hall** (www.kentwell.co.uk; adult/child £9.95/6.50; noon-4pm Apr-Sep;). Despite dating back to the Domesday Book and being full of Tudor pomp and centuries-old ghosts, it is still used as a private home by the Phillips family and has a wonderfully lived-in feel. It's surrounded by a rectangular moat, and there's a Tudor-rose maze and a rare-breeds farm that'll keep the kids happy. Kentwell hosts special events throughout the year, including several full Tudor re-creations when the whole estate bristles with bodices and hose, and Scaresville – a costumed Halloween extravaganza.

Sleeping & Eating

Black Lion Hotel & Restaurant HOTEL ££
(01787-312356; www.blacklionhotel.net; The Green; s/d from £102/125; P) Discover your favourite vintage at this small hotel on the village green, with flamboyant rooms named after different types of wine. The decor – serious swag curtains, four-poster and half-tester beds and rich fabrics – is a creative combination of contemporary style and traditional elegance, and the same can be said of the dishes served at its restaurant (mains £13 to £21).

High Street Farmhouse B&B ££
(01787-375765; www.highstreetfarmhouse.co.uk; High St; d £70; P) This 16th-century farmhouse offers a choice of cosy (read: room to swing only a small cat) but bright rooms full of rustic charm. Expect patchwork quilts, pretty florals, knotty pine and cast-iron bedsteads. There's a lovely mature garden outside and cooked breakfast included.

Scutcher's Bistro BRITISH ££
(01787-310200; www.scutchers.com; Westgate St; mains £19-22; Tue-Sat) With its rather mismatched decor, this unpretentious place is renowned throughout the Stour Valley for its beautiful takes on traditional dishes such as fish and chips and roast lamb (though the prices are a tad high) that leave locals coming back regularly for more. It's just off the Green.

Tiffin's Tea Emporium TEAROOM £
(Hall St, Drury House; tea £2.50; 9am-5pm) A great favourite for its extensive range of cakes, perfectly brewed tea, and savoury pies and sandwiches.

Getting There & Away

Buses from High St outside the post office run to **Bury St Edmunds** (50 minutes, hourly Monday to Saturday) and **Sudbury** (10 minutes, twice hourly Monday to Saturday).

SUDBURY

POP 11,933

Besides giving us the celebrated portrait and landscape painter Thomas Gainsborough (1727–88) and being the model for Charles Dickens' fictional town Eatanswill in *The Pickwick Papers* (written from 1836 to 1837), Sudbury is a bustling market town that prospered during the wool trade – small-scale silk weaving survives here to this day.

Most visitors come to see the birthplace of the town's most famous export – **Gainsborough's House** (www.gainsborough.org; 46

Gainsborough St; adult/child £5/2; ⏲10am-5pm Mon-Sat) – which showcases the largest collection of his work in the world. The 16th-century house and gardens feature a Georgian facade built by Thomas Gainsborough's own father in the 18th century. Inside, look for his earliest surviving portrait, *A Boy and a Girl in a Landscape,* the exquisite *Portrait of Harriett, Viscountess Tracy,* celebrated for its delicate portrayal of drapery, and the landscapes that were his passion.

Sudbury has a train station with an hourly service to **London** (£24, 1¼ hours). There are regular buses to **Ipswich** (one hour), Long Melford, Lavenham, Bury St Edmunds and Colchester.

LAVENHAM

POP 1738

One of East Anglia's most beautiful and rewarding towns, the former wool trade centre of Lavenham is home to a wonderful collection of exquisitely preserved medieval buildings that lean and lurch to dramatic effect. Lavenham's 300 half-timbered and pargeted houses and thatched cottages have been left virtually untouched since the town's heyday in the 15th century due to the zealous preservation efforts of the locals. Curiosity shops, art galleries, quaint tearooms and ancient inns line the streets, where the predominant colour is 'Suffolk pink', a traditional finish of whitewash mixed with red ochre.

Sights & Activities

Lavenham's most enchanting buildings cluster along High St, Water St and around the unusually triangular Market Pl, dominated by the early-16th-century whitewashed **Guildhall of Corpus Christi** (NT; www.nationaltrust.org.uk/lavenham; adult/child £4.30/1.80; ⏲11am-5pm), a superb example of a close-studded, timber-framed building. It is now a local-history museum with displays on the wool trade and medieval guilds, and in its tranquil garden you can see dye plants that produced the typical medieval colours.

Also on Market Pl, the caramel-coloured 14th-century **Little Hall** (www.littlehall.org.uk; Market Pl; adult/child £3/free; ⏲2-5.30pm Wed, Thu, Sat & Sun Apr-Oct) was once home to a successful wool merchant. Inside, the rooms of this medieval gem had been restored to period splendour through the efforts of the Gayer-Anderson twins who made it their home in the 1920s and 1930s.

At the village's high southern end rises the **Church of St Peter & St Paul** (⏲8.30am-5.30pm), a late Perpendicular edifice that seems to lift into the sky, with its beautifully proportioned windows, soaring flint tower and gargoyle water spouts. Built between 1485 and 1530, it was one of Suffolk's last great wool churches, completed on the eve of the Reformation, and is now a lofty testament to Lavenham's past prosperity.

If you're visiting at a weekend it's well worth joining a guided village **walk** (£3; ⏲2.30pm Sat, 11am Sun) run by the **tourist office** (☎01787-248207; www.discoverlavenham.co.uk; Lady St; ⏲10am-4.45pm mid-Mar–Oct, Sat & Sun only Nov–mid-Mar).

Sleeping & Eating

TOP CHOICE **Lavenham Priory** B&B ££

(☎01787-247404; www.lavenhampriory.co.uk; Water St; s/d from £87/120; P 📶) A rare treat, this sumptuously restored 15th-century B&B steals your heart as soon as you walk in the door. Each of the six Elizabethan rooms is a classic in its own right, with cavernous fireplaces, leaded windows, oak floors, original wall paintings, canopied four-poster beds (and even a sleigh bed) and exquisite period features throughout. Book well in advance.

Swan Hotel HOTEL £££

(☎01787-247477; www.theswanatlavenham.co.uk; High St; d from £195; P 📶) A warren of stunning timber-beamed 15th-century buildings now shelters one of the region's best-known hotels. Rooms are suitably spectacular – some with immense fireplaces, colossal beams and magnificent four-poster beds – without eschewing the very modern plasma-screen TVs. The Great Hall is an atmospheric place to try the modern English cuisine (three-course set dinner £38).

Guinea House B&B ££

(☎01787-249046; www.guineahouse.co.uk; 16 Bolton St; d from £75) Wonderfully snug, salmon-coloured B&B with just two en-suite doubles with sloped ceilings and floral patterns. Full English breakfast included and credit cards are not accepted.

TOP CHOICE **Great House** FRENCH ££

(☎01787-247431; www.greathouse.co.uk; Market Pl; 3-course lunch/dinner £21/32; ⏲lunch Wed-Sat, dinner Tue-Fri; 📶) Chic design blends effortlessly with 15th-century character at this much-loved restaurant in the centre of town. The decor in the five rooms (d from £95 to

£195) is an effortless marriage between classic period features and contemporary design, with funky wallpaper, sleek furniture and plasma-screen TVs. The restaurant – one of Britain's Top 100 restaurants according to the *Sunday Times* in 2011 – serves classic French dishes with a modern flourish.

Getting There & Away

Regular bus 743 connects Lavenham with **Bury St Edmunds** (30 minutes) and **Sudbury** (20 minutes) hourly until 6pm Monday to Saturday.

KERSEY

Slithering down either side of a steep slope to a shallow ford, picture-perfect Kersey is a pocket-sized hamlet lined with handsome timber-framed houses. Strolling the length of the street takes all of five minutes, after which there is little to do here save snap photos, visit the village's unadorned centrepiece – the **Church of St Mary** at the top of the hill, check out the stoneware at the **Kersey Pottery** (01473-822092; www.kerseypottery.com; The Street; 10am-5pm Sat, call ahead if visiting on a different day) by the ford, and grab some lunch and a pint at the 14th-century, oak-timbered **Bell Inn** (£9-14).

Kersey is 8 miles southeast of Lavenham off the A1141.

Bury St Edmunds

POP 36,218

Once home to one of the most powerful monasteries of medieval Europe, Bury has long attracted travellers for its powerful history, atmospheric ruins, handsome Georgian architecture and bustling agricultural markets. It's a genteel kind of place with tranquil gardens, a newly completed cathedral and the famous Greene King brewery.

History

Bury's slogan, 'Shrine of a King, Cradle of the Law' recalls two defining events in the town's history. St Edmund, last Saxon king of East Anglia, was decapitated by the Danes in 869, and in 903 the martyr's body was reburied here. Soon a series of ghostly miracles emanated from his grave, and the shrine became a centre of pilgrimage and the core of a new Benedictine monastery. In the 11th century, King Knut built a new abbey that soon became one of the wealthiest and most famous in the country. Meanwhile, the town thrived on the flocks of visiting pilgrims, and with the creation of a planned town surrounding the abbey came an influx of craftspeople.

In 1214 the English barons chose the abbey to draw up a petition that would form the basis of the Magna Carta, making it a 'Cradle of the Law' and setting the country on the road to a constitutional government. In medieval times the town grew rich on the wool trade and prospered until Henry VIII closed the abbey down in 1539 as part of the Dissolution of the Monasteries.

Sights

Abbey & Park RUINS

(dawn-dusk) Now a picturesque ruin residing in beautiful gardens behind the cathedral, the once all-powerful abbey still impresses despite the townspeople having made off with much of the stone after the Dissolution in 1539. The Reformation also meant an end to the veneration of relics, and St Edmund's grave and bones have long since disappeared.

You enter the park via one of two well-preserved old gates: opposite the tourist office, the staunch mid-14th-century **Great Gate** is intricately decorated and ominously defensive, complete with battlements, portcullis and arrow slits. The other entrance sits further up Angel Hill, where a gargoyle-studded early-12th-century **Norman Tower** looms.

Just beyond the Great Gate is a peaceful garden where the **Great Court** was once a hive of activity, and further on a dovecote marks the only remains of the **Abbot's Palace**. Most impressive, however, are the remains of the **western front**, where the original abbey walls were burrowed into in the 18th century to make way for houses. The houses are still in use and look as if they have been carved out of the stone-like caves. Nearby is **Samson Tower** and in front of it is a beautiful **statue of St Edmund** by Dame Elisabeth Frink (1976). The rest of the abbey spreads eastward like a ragged skeleton, with various lumps and pillars hinting at its immense size.

St Edmundsbury Cathedral CATHEDRAL

(www.stedscathedral.co.uk; St James, Angel Hill; requested donation £3; 8.30am-6pm) Completed in 2005, the 45m-high Millennium Tower of St Edmundsbury Cathedral is a vision in Lincolnshire limestone, and its traditional Gothic-style construction gives a good idea of how the towers of many other English cathedrals must have looked fresh from the stonemason's chisel.

Most of the rest of the building dates from the early 16th century, though the eastern end is postwar 20th century, and the northern side was completed in 1990. The overall effect is light and lofty, with a gorgeous hammerbeam roof and a striking sculpture of the crucified Christ by Dame Elisabeth Frink in the north transept. The impressive entrance porch has a tangible Spanish influence, a tribute to Abbot Anselm (1121–48), who opted against pilgrimage to Santiago de Compostela in favour of building a church dedicated to St James (Santiago in Spanish) right here.

Stop by the **Treasury** (⏲10am-4pm) in the cellar for a glimpse of church silver and ornate medieval Bibles.

For a more in-depth insight into the church's history and heritage join one of the **guided tours** (⏲1.30am Mon-Sat Apr-Sep) of the cathedral.

St Mary's Church CHURCH
(www.stmarystpeter.net/stmaryschurch; Honey Hill; entry by donation; ⏲10am-4pm) With the longest nave of any parish church in England, St Mary's contains the tomb of Mary Tudor (Henry VIII's sister and a one-time queen of France). Built around 1430, it also has a host of vampire-like angels swooping from its roof, and a bell is still rung to mark curfew, as it was in the Middle Ages.

Greene King Brewery BREWERY
(www.greeneking.co.uk; Crown St; tours day/evening £8/10, museum free; ⏲museum 10.30am-4.30pm Mon-Sat) Churning out some of England's favourite booze since Victorian times, this famous brewery runs popular daily tours, after which you can appreciate what all the fuss is about in its brewery bar. Even if you don't make the tour, you can check out the scale model of the brewery at the on-site museum, and learn about the history of beer.

Moyse's Hall Museum MUSEUM
(www.stedmundsbury.gov.uk/moyseshall; Cornhill; adult/child £7.30/5.30; ⏲10am-5pm Mon-Sat, noon-4pm Sun;) In an impressive 12th-century undercroft, this enjoyable museum covers the important episodes in Bury's history, such as the Bury witch trials, which preceded (and encouraged) the witch trials in Salem, Massachusetts. There are also medieval dressing-up clothes to engage the kids. The ticket also allows entry to the **West Stow Anglo-Saxon Village** (Icklingham Rd; ⏲10am-5pm), complete with actors in period costume.

FREE **Smith's Row** ART GALLERY
(www.smithsrow.org; Cornhill; ⏲10.30am-5pm Tue-Sat) Temporary exhibitions of contemporary art in a beautiful 18th-century theatre.

Sleeping

TOP CHOICE **Angel Hotel** HOTEL ££
(☎01284-714000; www.theangel.co.uk; 3 Angel Hill; r from £100; P) Peeking out from behind a shaggy mane of vines, this famous old coaching inn has hosted many a dignitary, such as Charles Dickens – the 'Dickens room' remains as it was, complete with four-poster bed. Rooms are split between a slick contemporary wing, featuring the new funky retro 'Impression' rooms, and a traditional Georgian building, its 'Classic' rooms boasting exposed beams. The modern restaurant has bright artwork, high ceilings and a stylish menu (mains £14 to £18), complemented by organic and biodynamic wines.

Fox Inn HOTEL ££
(☎01284-705562; www.thefoxinnbury.co.uk; 1 Eastgate St; s/d from £89/95;) Set in an old courtyard barn attached to Bury's oldest inn, the six luxurious rooms here blend the warmth of exposed brick and beams with minimalist contemporary styling. You'll find trendy but subtle wallpapers and tasteful furniture. The restaurant serves a good selection of modern British food (mains £10 to £18). The Fox is about 600m from the cathedral. Head up Angel Hill, bearing right at the end into Mustow St and on to Eastgate St.

Eating & Drinking

TOP CHOICE **Pea Porridge** MODERN BRITISH ££
(☎01284-700200; www.peaporridge.co.uk; 28-29 Cannon St; mains £13-20; ⏲Tue-Sat) Set in a 19th-century former bakery, this exciting newcomer on the Bury scene is responsible for some of the most memorable dishes in town, executed with imagination and flair. Expect the likes of curried sweetbreads with sweet potato, and grilled mackerel with Yorkshire champagne rhubarb, with attentive service to boot and beautiful presentation. All mains £11.95 at lunchtime.

WORTH A TRIP

ICKWORTH HOUSE & PARK

The puffed-up pomposity of stately home **Ickworth House** (NT; www.nationaltrust.org.uk/ickworth; adult/child £10.40/5, gardens only £4.50/1.80; ⌚house 11am-5pm Fri-Tue Mar-Oct, gardens 10am-5pm) is palpable from the minute you catch sight of its immense oval rotunda and wide outspread wings. The building is the whimsical creation of fourth earl of Bristol and Bishop of Derry, Frederick Hervey (1730–1803), and contains fine paintings by Titian, Gainsborough and Velázquez. There's also a lovely Italian garden, parkland bearing the landscaping eye of Lancelot 'Capability' Brown, a deer enclosure and a hide to explore.

Ickworth is 3 miles southwest of Bury on the A143. Haverhill-bound buses 14 and 15 from Bury bus station (eight minutes, hourly) can drop you nearby.

TOP CHOICE **Maison Bleue** FRENCH £££
(☎01284-760623; www.maisonbleue.co.uk; 31 Churchgate St; mains £16-22; ⌚Tue-Sat) Muted colours, pale leather banquettes, white linens and contemporary style merge with a fish-heavy menu of imaginative dishes in this excellent French restaurant. The food – from the Colchester oysters to the Gressingham duck – is superb but not fussy, the service impeccable and the setting very stylish yet relaxed. The three-course set lunch/dinner menu (£21/32) is a great way to sample everything that's good about this place.

Old Cannon MODERN BRITISH ££
(www.oldcannonbrewery.co.uk; 86 Cannon St; mains £8-13) This working brewery serves some fantastic ales, such as the award-winning Black Pig and Gunner's Daughter, and 'cannon fodder' to accompany your brew comprises brasserie dishes such as deep-fried whitebait, poached smoked haddock and sausages with colcannon – the ingredients are sourced locally. There are seven comfortable rooms upstairs (singles/doubles £85/110).

Nutshell PUB
(The Traverse) See how many of your friends you can squeeze into this thimble-sized timber-framed pub, recognised by the *Guinness Book of Records* as Britain's smallest (we think probably six people or so).

Information

Tourist Office (☎01284-764667; tic@stedsbc.gov.uk; 6 Angel Hill; ⌚9.30am-5pm Mon-Sat, 10am-3pm Sun)

Getting There & Around

BUS The central bus station is on St Andrew's St North.

Cambridge (Stagecoach; bus 11, 65 minutes, hourly Monday to Saturday)

London (National Express; £16, 2½ hours, daily)

TRAIN The train station is 900m north of the tourist office, with frequent buses to the centre.

Cambridge (£9, 45 minutes, hourly)

Ely (£9, 30 minutes, every two hours)

Aldeburgh

POP 2790

One of the region's most charming, time-warped towns, the small fishing and boat-building village of Aldeburgh has an understated charm. Handsome pastel-coloured houses, independent shops, art galleries and ramshackle fishing huts selling fresh catch line the High St, while a sweeping shingle beach stretches along the shore offering tranquil big-sky views.

Aldeburgh also has a lively cultural scene. Composer Benjamin Britten and lesser-known poet George Crabbe both lived and worked here. Britten founded East Anglia's primary arts and music festival, the **Aldeburgh Festival** (www.aldeburgh.co.uk; ⌚Jun), which has been going for over 60 years and takes place at the **Snape Maltings** (www.snapemaltings.co.uk) – a former malthouse turned concert hall 5 miles west of town. Britten's legacy is commemorated by Maggi Hambling's controversial 13ft-high steel *Scallop* sculpture, a short stroll north along the seashore.

In late September/early October, the **Aldeburgh Food & Drink Festival** (www.aldeburghfoodanddrink.co.uk) celebrates the best of Suffolk cooking at nearby Snape Maltings.

Aldeburgh's other photogenic gem is the intricately carved and timber-framed 16th-century **Moot Hall** (www.aldeburghmuseum.org.uk; adult/child £1/free; ⏲2.30-5pm), which now houses a local history museum.

Sleeping

Most places in Aldeburgh ask for a two-night minimum stay at weekends.

TOP CHOICE Ocean House B&B ££
(☎01728-452094; www.oceanhousealdeburgh.co.uk; 25 Crag Path; s/d £70/90) Right on the seafront and with only the sound of the waves to lull you to sleep at night, this beautiful Victorian guesthouse has three wonderfully cosy, period-style rooms. Expect pale pastels, subtle florals and tasteful furniture. There's a baby grand piano on the top floor, a gaily painted rocking horse and bikes to borrow.

Martello Tower B&B ££
(☎01728-454226; www.landmarktrust.org.uk; Slaughden Rd; d £95; P) Guests can stay on the self-contained 2nd floor of this New England–style home, where you'll find a spacious bedroom, kitchenette and a private lounge with balcony and sea views. There's also an option of a second 'secret' adjoining room for children or friends. The decor is cosy contemporary with lots of attention to detail and loads of space.

Dunan House B&B ££
(☎01728-452486; www.dunanhouse.co.uk; 41 Park Rd; d from £75; P 📶) Set well back off the street in lovely gardens, this charming B&B has a range of individually styled rooms mixing contemporary and traditional elements to surprisingly good effect. With friendly hosts, and breakfast assembled from local, wild and home-grown produce, it's a real treat.

Blaxhall YHA HOSTEL £
(☎0845-3719305; www.yha.org.uk; Heath Walk, Blaxhall; dm/d £18/40; P) Well-run hostel with fully equipped guest kitchen in the nearby village of Blaxhall. No internet or wi-fi.

Eating

TOP CHOICE Lighthouse MODERN EUROPEAN ££
(☎01728-453377; www.lighthouserestaurant.co.uk; 77 High St; mains £11-16; 👪) Rightly deserving the accolade of Aldeburgh's best restaurant, this unassuming bistro with casual decor welcomes you with friendly and knowledgeable service, and a menu looking to the sea for inspiration. Catch-of-the-day is always a good bet, but the likes of slow-cooked pork belly with chilli jam and lentils don't lag far behind.

Regatta Restaurant SEAFOOD ££
(☎01728-452011; www.regattaaldeburgh.com; 171 High St; mains £13-21; ⏲noon-2pm & 6-10pm) Sleek, contemporary restaurant where local fish is the main attraction. The celebrated owner-chef supplements his wonderful seafood with meat and vegetarian options and regular gourmet nights. Book ahead.

Aldeburgh Market Cafe CAFE £
(www.thealdeburghmarket.co.uk; 170-172 High St; dishes £3-7; ⏲8am-5pm) The good people of Lighthouse bring you this delightful little cafe, its eclectic menu featuring anything from kedgeree to Malay-style noodles, as well as imaginative desserts.

Fish & Chip Shop FISH & CHIPS £
(226 High Street; fish & chips £5-6; ⏲noon-2pm & 5-8pm Mon-Sat, noon-7pm Sun) Aldeburgh has a reputation for the finest fish and chips in the area, and this is the place that kick-started it.

Information

Tourist office (☎01728-453637; www.suffolkcoastal.gov.uk/tourism; 152 High St; ⏲9am-5.30pm Mon-Sat, 10am-4pm Sun)

Getting There & Away

There are frequent bus services to **Ipswich** (1¼ hours), where you can make connections to the rest of the country.

Orford

Secluded and seductive, the gorgeous village of Orford, 6 miles south of Snape Maltings, is dominated by the odd polygonal keep of **Orford Castle** (EH; www.english-heritage.org.uk; adult/child £5.80/3.50; ⏲10am-6pm Apr-Oct, Sat & Sun only Nov-Mar), constructed for Henry II. The keep of the 12th-century castle is remarkably intact and has an innovative, 18-sided drum design with three square turrets, as well as displays on the history of the place. From the roof there are glorious views of **Orford Ness** (NT; www.nationaltrust.org.uk/orfordness; incl ferry crossing adult/child £7.50/4; ⏲10am-2pm Tue-Sat Jul-Sep), the largest vegetated shingle spit in Europe. Once a secret military testing ground, it is now a nature reserve, its bogs and mud flats attract-

WORTH A TRIP

DUNWICH & MINSMERE NATURE RESERVE

Strung along the coastline north of Aldeburgh is a poignant trail of serene and little-visited coastal heritage towns that are gradually succumbing to the sea. Most dramatically, the once-thriving port town of **Dunwich** is now an eerie village, its 12 medieval churches lost under the waves.

The region is a favourite haunt of the binocular-wielding birdwatcher brigade, and **RSPB Minsmere** (www.rspb.org.uk; Westleton; adult/child £5/1.50; ⏲9am-dusk) flickers with feathered activity year-round. The reserve is home to one of England's rarest birds, the bittern, with hundreds of migrant birds paying a visit in autumn. Binoculars are available for rent and there are hides along the trails to facilitate bird-spotting.

With public transport lacking you'll need your own wheels, or the will to walk or bike this stretch of peaceful and varied coastline.

ing rare wading birds and wildfowl. Ferries run from Orford Quay; the last ferry departs at 2pm and returns from the reserve at 5pm.

On your return make a beeline for the **Butley Orford Oysterage** (www.butleyorfordoysterage.co.uk; mains £8-13), lauded locally for the fish and seafood it catches and smoke. Get some goodies to take home with you from Pinney's, their shop by the harbour.

For overnight stays, the **Crown & Castle** (☎01394-450205; www.crownandcastle.co.uk; r from £130; Ⓟ) offers bright, modestly stylish rooms and excellent service. Their brasserie-style restaurant **Trinity** (mains £17-22) is renowned for its fine, internationally inspired dishes.

Southwold

POP 3858

Southwold's reputation as a well-heeled holiday getaway has earned it the nickname 'Kensington-on-Sea' after the upmarket London borough, and its lovely sandy beach, pebble-walled cottages, cannon-dotted clifftop and rows of beachfront bathing huts are all undeniably picturesque. Over the years the town has attracted many artists, including JMW Turner, Charles Rennie Mackintosh, Lucian Freud and Damien Hirst.

For most visitors Southwold's shorefront is the main attraction. Take time to amble along its promenade and admire the squat 19th-century **lighthouse** before ending up at the little **pier** (www.southwoldpier.co.uk), first built in 1899 but recently reconstructed. In the 'under the pier' show you'll find a quirky collection of slot machines, the likes of which you're not likely to have seen elsewhere; in the current recession climate, how about having a satisfying go at Whack-a-Banker?

The **Coastal Voyager** (www.coastalvoyager.co.uk) is on hand to whisk you off on a range of boat trips, including a 30-minute high-speed fun trip (adult/child £22/12), a leisurely river cruise to nearby Blythburgh and a three-hour trip to Scroby Sands to see a seal colony and wind farm.

Inland, the **Church of St Edmund** (Church St; admission free; ⏲9am-6pm) is worth a peek for its fabulous medieval screen and 15th-century bloodshot-eyed 'Southwold Jack' effigy, grumpily overlooking the church's rear – purpose unknown, though believed to be part of a clock. A mere stone's throw away is an old weavers' cottage that now houses the **Southwold Museum** (www.southwoldmuseum.org; 9-11 Victoria St; requested donation £3; ⏲10.30am-noon & 2-4pm Aug, 2-4pm Apr-Jul & Sep-Oct), which explores Southwold's 1000-year-old fishing industry, the explosive 132-ship and 50,000-men Battle of Solebay (1672) fought just off the coast, and the role of the sea – Southwold's livelihood and its destroyer.

You can also take an hour-long tour (£10) of the town's very own **Adnams Brewery** (www.adnams.co.uk; Adnams Pl) – producer of six types of beer, as well as vodka and gin – followed by a 30-minute tutored beer tasting.

Southwold's liveliest event is the **Latitude Festival** (www.latitudefestival.co.uk; ⏲Jul) held in Henham Park (5 miles west of town), combining an eclectic mix of music, literature, dance, drama and comedy with a stunning location.

The **tourist office** (☎01502-724729; www.visit-sunrisecoast.co.uk; 69 High St; ⏲10am-5pm Mon-Sat, 11am-4pm Sun) has extensive accommodation listings.

Sleeping & Eating

TOP CHOICE Sutherland House HOTEL £££

(☎01502-724544; www.sutherlandhouse.co.uk; 56 High St; d £140-180; P 📶) Each of the three individually styled boudoirs at this 15th-century house has its own unforgettable feature – be it pargeted ceilings, exposed beams or a free-standing bath-tub. In contrast to the decor, all the gadgets are ultramodern, and the top-notch restaurant (mains £11 to £19) – reputedly the best in town – specialises in fish, with catch-of-the-day dishes reinvented daily.

Swan HOTEL £££

(☎01502-722186; www.adnams.co.uk; Market Sq; s/d from £110/165; 🐾) There's a timeless elegance to the public rooms at the Swan, where large fireplaces, grandfather clocks and old-fashioned lamps induce a kind of soporific calm within a splendid Georgian exterior. You can choose between similarly period-style rooms or the newly refurbished Lighthouse Rooms with garden views. The atmospheric restaurant serves a mainly fishy menu (mains £15 to £22).

Home@21 B&B ££

(☎01502-722573; www.homeat21northparade.co.uk; 21 North Pde; d from £80; 📶) This well-kept Victorian house near the pier has just three rooms – two with sea views – and some appealing period features. One has an antique half-tester bed, another has a four-poster. As the name suggests, the atmosphere is more 'home' than 'hotel'.

Coasters MODERN BRITISH ££

(☎01502-724734; www.coastersofsouthwold.co.uk; 12 Queen St; mains £8-15; ⏲closed Mon) Right on the main drag, this unassuming restaurant has a great reputation and a loyal local following. The menu is short but sweet, and every dish – from Thai green curry mussels to braised pork belly – is memorable. There is also a range of sandwiches and cakes for a light lunch. Book ahead for dinner.

Getting There & Away

Bus connections are limited: catch one of the hourly services to **Lowestoft** (45 minutes) or **Halesworth train station** (30 minutes) and continue from there.

Around Southwold

WALBERSWICK

These days it requires an interstellar leap of the imagination to picture the sleepy seaside village of Walberswick as the thriving medieval port it once was. A mile south of Southwold, it's an arty little place popular with

THE HAUNTING OF BLICKLING HALL

The Fens – formerly the land of eerie waterways, mist and unexplained occurrences – has its share of ghosts and haunted places, but **Blickling Hall** (NT; www.nationaltrust.org.uk/blickling; Blickling; adult/child £10.95/5.35, garden only £7.65/3.85; ⏲house noon-5pm Wed-Mon, gardens 10am-5pm) takes the cake. Largely remodelled in the 17th century for Sir Henry Hobart, James I's chief justice, the manor began life in the 11th century as a manor house and bishop's palace. Today it is a grand Jacobean mansion set in vast parklands and as famous for its ghostly sightings as its spectacular Long Gallery.

In 1437 the isolated house was claimed by the Boleyn family and passed through the generations to Thomas, father of Anne Boleyn. Poor old Anne was executed by her husband Henry VIII in 1536, and it's said that on the anniversary of her death – 19th May – a coach drives up to the house, drawn by headless horses, driven by a headless coachman and containing the queen with her head on her lap. Some motorists who have driven past Blickling Hall on that day also claim that they felt an irresistible urge to swerve off the road, as if to avoid an oncoming vehicle, even though the road was clear.

If you don't happen to witness the spectral goings-on, there's still quite a lot to see. The grand state rooms are stuffed with fine Georgian furniture, pictures and tapestries, and the Long Gallery has an impressive Jacobean plaster ceiling. There's also an exhibition describing life below stairs, with stories from those who lived and worked at Blickling over the centuries.

Blickling Hall is 15 miles north of Norwich off the A140. Buses run twice hourly from Castle Meadow and Tombland in Norwich. Aylsham is the nearest train station, 1.5 miles away.

well-heeled holidaymakers, reachable either by pedestrian bridge or the summer **ferry** (80p; ⏲10am-12.30pm & 2-5pm Easter & Jun-Sep, 10am-5pm Sat & Sun May & Oct), which crosses the River Blyth at half-hourly intervals.

Just south of the village is the largest block of freshwater reedbed in Britain, incorporated into the **Suffolk Coast National Nature Reserve** (www.naturalengland.org.uk) and home to otters, deer and rare butterflies. It's accessed by a web of public footpaths.

Oak beams, open fires and flagstone floors make the 600-year-old warrenlike **Bell Inn** (☎01502-723109; www.adnams.co.uk; Ferry Rd; mains £12-17, r from £110) your best bet by far for a pint of Adnams beer and a bed, with award-winning seafood served in the bar downstairs.

NORFOLK

Big skies, sweeping beaches, windswept marshes, meandering inland waterways and pretty flint houses make up the county of Norfolk, a handsome rural getaway with a thriving regional capital. They say the locals have 'one foot on the land, and one in the sea' and you're never far from water here, whether it's the tranquil setting of rivers and windmills in the Norfolk Broads or the wide sandy beaches, fishing boats and nature reserves along the coast. Twitchers flock here too, for some of the country's best birdwatching. Meanwhile, in Norwich, the county's bustling capital, you'll find a remarkable cathedral and castle, medieval churches, a lively market and an excellent choice of pubs, clubs and restaurants.

Activities

Signposted walking trails include the well-known Peddars Way and Norfolk Coast Path. Other long-distance paths include the **Weavers Way**, a 57-mile trail from Cromer to Great Yarmouth, and the **Angles Way** (www.eastsuffolklinewalks.co.uk/anglesway), which negotiates the valleys of the Rivers Waveney and Little Ouse for 70 miles. Meanwhile the **Wherryman's Way** (www.wherrymansway.net) is a 35-mile walking and cycling route through the Broads, following the River Yare from Norwich to Great Yarmouth.

For a real challenge, the **Around Norfolk Walk** is a 220-mile circuit that combines most of the above.

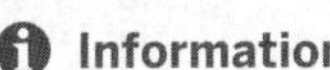

Information

Some handy websites:

Backpack East (www.backpackeast.co.uk)

Norfolk Tourist Attractions (www.norfolktouristattractions.co.uk)

Tour Norfolk (www.tournorfolk.co.uk)

Visit Norfolk (www.visitnorfolk.co.uk)

Norwich

POP 121,550

The affluent and easygoing city of Norwich (pronounced 'nor-ritch') is a rich tapestry of meandering laneways liberally sprinkled with architectural gems – spoils of the city's heyday at the height of the medieval wool boom. A magnificent cathedral lords over it all from one end of the city centre and a sturdy Norman castle from the other. Around these two landmarks a series of leafy greens, grand squares, quiet lanes, crooked half-timbered buildings and a host of medieval churches pan out across this compact and artsy city.

Meanwhile thriving markets, modern shopping centres, contemporary-art galleries and a young student population give the city an easygoing vibe that makes it one of the most appealing cities in East Anglia. Add easy access to the Broads and sweeping beaches along the coast and you have an excellent base to use for touring the area.

History

Though Norwich's history stretches back well over 1000 years, the city's golden age was during the Middle Ages, when it was England's most important city after London. Its relative isolation meant that it traditionally had stronger ties to the Low Countries than to London, and when Edward III encouraged Flemish weavers to settle here in the 14th century, this connection was sealed. The arrival of the immigrants helped establish the wool industry that fattened the city and sustained it right through to the 18th century.

Mass immigration from the Low Countries peaked in the troubled 16th century. In 1579 more than a third of the town's citizens were foreigners of a staunch Protestant stock, which proved beneficial during the Civil War when the Protestant parliamentarians caused Norwich little strife.

Sights

Norwich is a fantastic city to see on foot, with winding laneways and narrow passageways

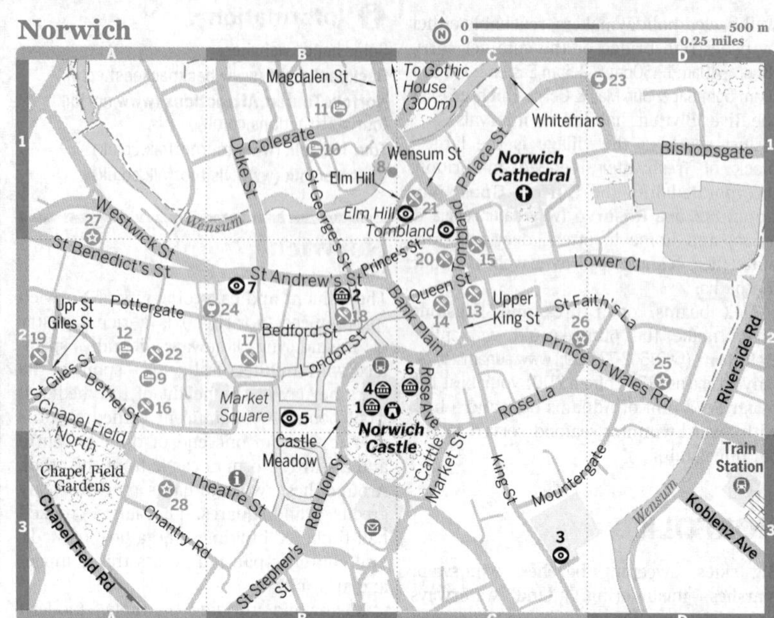

criss-crossing the centre of town. Most radiate from the candy-stripe canopied **Market Square** (⏲8am-4.30pm), one of the biggest and oldest markets in England, which has been running since 1025. As you walk it's impossible to miss the huge number of **medieval churches** (www.norwich-churches.org) in the city. There are 36, to be precise – a testament to the city's wealth during the Middle Ages – as well as two cathedrals.

TOP CHOICE **Norwich Cathedral** CATHEDRAL
(www.cathedral.org.uk; admission by donation; ⏲7.30am-6pm, Hostry 9.30am-4.30pm Mon-Sat) Norwich's most stunning landmark is the magnificent Anglican cathedral, its barbed spire soaring higher than any in England except Salisbury, while the size of its cloisters is second to none.

Begun in 1096, the cathedral is one of the finest Anglo-Norman abbey churches in the country, rivalled only perhaps by Durham. The sheer size of its nave is impressive, but its most renowned feature is the superb **Gothic rib vaulting** added in 1463. Among the spidery stonework are 1200 sculpted roof bosses depicting Bible stories. Together they represent one of the finest achievements of English medieval masonry.

Similar bosses can be seen in closer detail in the cathedral's remarkable cloisters. Built between 1297 and 1430, the **two-storey cloisters** are unique in England today and were originally built to house a community of about 100 monks.

Some features that perhaps you won't have been expecting: in the centre of the nave, above the bronze font (which came from a nearby chocolate factory), you'll find a 21st-century touch – **Censing Angel** (2012) – a suspended celestial figure woven out of willow branches by sculptor Joy Whiddett, trailing the words 'peace', 'hope' and 'love'.

Outside the cathedral's eastern end is the grave of the WWI heroine Edith Cavell, a Norfolk-born nurse who was executed for helping hundreds of Allied soldiers escape from German-occupied Belgium. The **cathedral close** also contains handsome houses and the old chapel of King Edward VI School (where English hero Admiral Nelson was educated). Its current students make up the choir, which performs in at least one of the three services held daily.

The visitor entrance to the cathedral is through the stunning new **Hostry** building – all glass and light – which rises within the walls of its original equivalent. Inside

Norwich

Top Sights
Norwich Castle ... B2
Norwich Cathedral ... C1

Sights
1 Art Gallery ... B2
2 Bridewell Museum ... B2
3 Dragon Hall ... C3
4 Museum ... B2
5 Mustard Shop ... B2
6 Royal Norfolk Regimental Museum ... C2
7 Strangers' Hall ... B2

Activities, Courses & Tours
8 Broads Boatrains ... B1
Ghost Walks ... (see 23)

Sleeping
9 38 St Giles ... A2
10 By Appointment ... B1
11 Number 17 ... B1
12 St Giles House Hotel ... A2

Eating
13 BamBam ... C2
14 Beluga ... C2
15 Farmer Browns ... C2
16 Greenhouse ... A2
17 Library ... B2
18 Mustard ... B2
19 Roger Hickman's ... A2
20 Shiki ... C2
21 Tea House ... C1
22 Waffle House ... A2

Drinking
23 Adam & Eve ... D1
24 Birdcage ... B2

Entertainment
25 Mercy ... D2
26 Mojo's ... C2
27 Norwich Arts Centre ... A1
28 Theatre Royal ... A3

you can learn about the history and role of the cathedral. For a deeper insight join one of the **guided tours** (10.45am, 12.30pm & 2.15pm); the tours are free but a donation is expected.

Tombland & Elm Hill HISTORIC SITE
In the heart of the city, near the cathedral, lies leafy Tombland, where the market was originally located. Despite its ominous overtones, 'tomb' is an old Norse word for 'empty', hence the space for a market. Cross over and follow Princes St to reach Elm Hill – Norwich's prettiest street, with its medieval cobblestones, crooked timber beams and doors, intriguing shops and tucked-away cafes. It's one of the oldest intact streets in the city and now the centre of the local antiques business.

TOP CHOICE **Norwich Castle** CASTLE
(www.museums.norfolk.gov.uk; castle & exhibitions adult/child £7/5; 10am-5pm Mon-Sat, 1-5pm Sun;) Perched on a hilltop overlooking central Norwich, this massive Norman castle keep is a sturdy example of 12th-century aristocratic living. The castle is one of the best-preserved examples of Anglo-Norman military architecture in the country, despite a gigantic shopping centre grafted to one side.

A jail for five centuries, it's now home to an art gallery and superb interactive museum, approached across a bridge on which hangings were staged throughout Norwich's existence. The **museum** crams in a wealth of history, including lively exhibits on Boudica and the Iceni, the Anglo-Saxons and Vikings, natural history displays and even an Egyptian gallery. Every room is enlivened with plenty of fun for kids, but best of all is the atmospheric keep itself, which sends shivers down the spine, with graphic displays on grisly punishments meted out in its days as a medieval prison. **Guided tours** (adult/child £2.40/1.80) also run around the battlements (minimum age eight) and the creepy dungeons.

Meanwhile the **art gallery** houses paintings of the acclaimed 19th-century Norwich School of landscape painting founded by John Crome, and even if displays of ceramics normally make you glaze over, don't miss the world's largest collection of novelty teapots.

The **Royal Norfolk Regimental Museum** (www.rnrm.org.uk; Shirehall, Market Ave), which details the history of the local regiment since 1830, was in the process of being refurbished and moved at the time of writing.

EXPLORING THE NORFOLK BROADS

What Are the Norfolk Broads & Where Are They?

The Broads are vast wetlands, formed when the slow-moving rivers Wensum, Bure, Waveney and Yare flooded the big gaping holes in the land dug by 12th-century crofters looking for peat. They comprise fragile ecosystems and, protected as a national park, are home to some of the UK's rarest plants and birds, so the appeal to twitchers and naturalists is obvious. Apart from that, if you've ever envisioned yourself captaining your own boat and living as a 'boat person', there are 125 miles of lock-free waterways to explore. And if you enjoy paddling a solitary canoe and losing yourself in the hypnotic lapping of the water away from the rest of humanity, there's plenty of scope for that, too. The **Broads Authority** (www.broads-authority.gov.uk) can wax eloquently about the Broads.

What Is There to See & Do that Doesn't Involve Water?

The **Museum of the Broads** (www.northnorfolk.org/museumofthebroads; Staithe; adult/child £4/3.50; ⌚10.30am-5pm Easter-Oct), 5 miles north of Potter Heigham off the A149, teaches you about the marshdwellers who lived in the area, their traditional lifestyles, peat extraction and modern conservation.

If you want to delve deeper into the life of a fen dweller, the tiny **Toad Hole Cottage** (How Hill; free admission; ⌚9.30am-6pm Jun-Sep, 10.30am-1pm & 1.30-5pm Apr, May & Oct) is restored in period style, showing how the eel-catcher's family lived and the tools they used to work the marshes around them.

The more frivolous **Bewilderwood** (www.bewilderwood.co.uk; Hornig Rd, Hoveton; adult/child £13.50/10.50; ⌚10am-5.30pm Mar-Oct) is a forest playground for children and adults alike, with zip wires, jungle bridges, tree houses and all sorts of old-fashioned outdoor adventure involving plenty of mud, mazes and marsh walks.

The Broads' most impressive eccelesiastical attraction is the 14th-century **St Helen's Church** (Ranworth; ⌚8am-7pm), known locally as the 'Cathedral of the Broads', dominating the pretty village of Ranworth and featuring a magnificent painted medieval rood screen and, in a bulletproof cabinet by the main door, a 15th-century antiphoner (a rare illustrated book of prayers).

Finally, train enthusiasts will love the **Bure Valley Steam Railway** (www.bvrw.co.uk; adult/child £8.50/6; ⌚Feb-Oct) – a narrow-gauge steam train that runs between Aylsham and Wroxham.

How Do I Get There?

Driving around the Broads is missing the point and pretty useless. The main centres in the Broads – Wroxham, on the A1151 from Norwich, and Potter Heigham, on the A1062 from Wroxham – are reachable by bus from Norwich and Great Yarmouth, respectively, and from there you can either take to the water or to the trails.

Exploring by Boat

Taking to the water gives you the most freedom and you'll find numerous boat rental outlets.

You can hire a variety of launches (full tuition given), from large cabin cruisers to little craft with outboards, for anything from a couple of hours' gentle messing about on the water to a weeklong trip. Depending on boat size, facilities and season, a boat costs from around £65 for four hours, £110 for one day and from £650 to £1300 for a week, including

FREE Sainsbury Centre for Visual Arts GALLERY
(www.scva.org.uk; University of East Anglia; ⌚10am-5pm Tue-Sun) Housed in the first major building designed by Norman Foster – now the darling of Britain's architectural set – in the university grounds, the Sainsbury Centre is the most important centre for the arts in East Anglia. It is filled with an eclectic collection of works by Picasso, Moore, Degas and Bacon, displayed beside an extensive collection of

fuel and insurance. If you don't want to drive your own, you can choose anything from hour-long jaunts on the water to multiday boat holidays. **Broads Tours** (www.broads.co.uk) takes care of both, while **Boats for the Broads** (www.dayboathire.com) and **Barnes Brinkcraft** (www.barnesbrinkcraft.co.uk) arrange short-term rental from Wroxham, and **Blakes** (www.blakes.co.uk) arranges all manner of boating holidays.

Exploring by Canoe

Solitary paddlers can find canoes for hire in different spots around the Broads for around £38 per day; **Rowan Craft** (www.rowancraft.com; Geldeston) and **Waveney River Centre** (www.waveneyriver centre.co.uk; Burgh St Peter) come recommended. **Mark the Canoe Man** (www.thecanoeman.com; half-day trip £25-45) knows the secrets of the Broads and arranges day and overnight guided trips to areas the cruisers can't reach, as well as canoe and kayak hire, weekend camping canoe trails (two nights £70), bushcraft courses (two days £140) and the paddle steamer – paddling one way, then taking the steam train back (from £50).

Exploring by Foot/Bike

Walkers and cyclists will also find a web of trails crossing the region, including the 56-mile Weavers' Way that stretches from Cromer to Great Yarmouth, taking in some choice parts of the landscape along the way. The Broads' highest point, How Hill, is just 12m above sea level, so superhero levels of fitness are not required. There are numerous bike rental points along the way; these include **Broadland Cycle Hire** (www.norfolkbroadscycling.co.uk; Bewilderwood, Hoveton) and **Clippesby** (www.clippesby.com; Clippesby). Bikes cost about £16 per day (you can also hire child seats and tandems).

Mark 'Canoe Man' Wilkinson's Highlights

Best paddle The Buxton to Coltishall stretch of the River Bure. It's really beautiful and you'll see kingfishers, otters, marsh harriers and a very tame barn owl here. You start in the wide open fields with their big skies and great views, then there's a tree-lined section that is like a different world – totally calm even when there's a gale howling elsewhere – the water's crystal clear and you can just meander along at a slow pace. There are no other people here – sometimes another canoeist but even that is quite unusual. At Horstead Mill there's a lovely open lock and weir; a great place for picnics and for families. Then you paddle on to Coltishall Green, where there are some lovely pubs.

Secret spot It's very difficult to access the River Wensum, but the stretches you can paddle are simply stunning.

Favourite time of year Late September. The holidaymakers are gone, the colours are gorgeous and there's lots of wildlife scurrying about preparing for winter.

A spot of history At Bargate you can see the remains of 14 wherries (sailing barges traditionally used on the Broads). It's known as the 'wherry graveyard' and you can see the ribs sticking up out of the water.

Getting Around

Norwich is well connected by train and bus to Cambridge, Ely and Bury St Edmunds, while Coasthopper buses connect it to all the seaside towns and villages along the Norfolk coast in summer. For comprehensive travel advice and timetables, contact **Traveline East Anglia** (☎0871-200 22 33; www.travelineeastanglia.co.uk).

curios from Africa, the Pacific and the Americas; keep an eye out for walrus-ivory snow goggles, an elaborately carved ceremonial staff from Zaïre, and an intricate warrior's pendant from the Admiralty Islands. Equally worthwhile are the temporary offerings, which range from local heritage to international art movements. These have recently included photography by Avi Gupta and the fantastic 'Japan: Kingdom of Characters' exhibition, which focused on the significance of manga creations in Japanese everyday life.

The gallery is about 2 miles west of the city centre. To get here take bus 25, 26 or 35 from Castle Meadow (20 minutes).

Strangers' Hall HISTORIC BUILDING
(www.museums.norfolk.gov.uk; Charing Cross; adult/child £3.50/2; ⌚10.30am-4pm Wed & Sat) A maze of atmospheric rooms furnished in different medieval styles is on view in this early-14th-century town house. You can see the Great Hall set for a banquet, examine historic toys or try your hand making a bed Tudor style. Outside is a pretty 17th-century knot garden. Last visitors admitted at 3.30pm.

Bridewell Museum MUSEUM
(www.museums.norfolk.gov.uk; Bridewell Alley;) The 14th-century Bridewell, or 'prison for women, beggars and tramps', housed in a former merchant's house, has reopened after a grand facelift in July 2012. The museum focuses on key points in the city's history, such as its prominence as England's second city in the Middle Ages and its 19th-century industrial heritage. The displays include some wonderfully eccentric objects, such as the snake-proof boot, and the interactive displays in the pharmacy are proving a hit with younger visitors.

Dragon Hall HISTORIC BUILDING
(www.dragonhall.org; 115-123 King St; adult/child £4.50/3.50; ⌚10am-4pm Tue-Thu, noon-4pm Sun Apr-Oct) A remarkable medieval building, this magnificent trading hall dates from 1430 and is the only building of its kind to have belonged to one man – Robert Toppes – rather than a guild, suggesting that he was a successful 15th-century entrepreneur. The 1st-floor great hall has a stunning crown-post roof with a carved dragon figure, which gave the building its name, and the displays in the cellars, together with the audioguide, introduce you to the building's various incarnations. Guided tours are available on Tuesdays at 2pm.

Mustard Shop HISTORIC BUILDING
(www.colmansmustardshop.com; 15 Royal Arcade; ⌚9.30am-5pm Mon-Sat, 11am-4pm Sun) Though it's more shop than museum, this replica Victorian shop tells the 200-year story of Colman's Mustard, a famous local product, and sells every type of mustard you can think of. It's in the lavish art-nouveau Royal Arcade, which has been a shopping gallery since the late 19th century.

Tours

The tourist office organises a dizzying array of guided tours, departing from outside the Forum, and has free downloadable pdf and audio city tours on its website.

Ghost Walks WALKING TOUR
(07831-189985; www.ghostwalksnorwich.co.uk; adult/child £6/4; ⌚7.30pm Mon, Tue & Thu) A wonderful immersion in Norwich's haunted history; tours depart from the Adam & Eve pub.

Olde Norwich HISTORICAL TOUR
(07917-664472; www.oldenorwich.co.uk; adult/child £6/3; ⌚2pm May-Oct) A 12-seater open-top charabanc drives you around town, taking in all 12 of Norwich's iconic buildings (www.norwich12.co.uk). Tours depart from Castle Meadow, outside Waterstones.

City Sightseeing BUS TOUR
(www.city-sightseeing.com; adult/child £9/5; ⌚hourly 10am-4pm Apr-Oct) Hop-on/hop-off bus service stopping at nine destinations around the city centre, including by the tourist office.

Broads Boatrains BOAT TOUR
(www.cityboats.co.uk; 1hr city cruise adult/child £9/5) Runs a variety of cruises from Griffin Lane, Station Quay and Elm Hill Quay.

Sleeping

Gothic House B&B ££
(01603-631879; www.gothic-house-norwich.com; Magdalen St, King's Head Yard; s/d £65/95; P) This faithfully restored Grade II Regency house hidden away in a quiet courtyard in the heart of the city has just two rooms, but if period style is your thing, they are *the* place to be. From the fabrics and furnishings to the ornaments and mirrors, it's flush with character and charm. The rooms are bright, spacious and immaculately kept, and each private bathroom is stocked with Molton Brown toiletries.

38 St Giles B&B ££
(01603-662944; www.38stgiles.co.uk; 38 St Giles St; s/d from £90/130; P) Ideally located, beautifully styled and reassuringly friendly, this boutique B&B is a real gem. There are no airs and graces here – just three handsome, individually decorated rooms with wooden floors, hand-made rugs, original fireplaces and a contemporary feel. Your gracious hosts prepare what is a sure contender for

the best breakfast in Norwich – featuring granola, local and organic meats and eggs, and cinnamon pancakes.

St Giles House Hotel HOTEL ££

(☎01603-275180; www.stgileshousehotel.com; 41-45 St Giles St; d incl breakfast £120-210; 📶) Right in the heart of the city in a stunning 19th-century building, you'll find this large hotel with individually styled rooms. There's a grandiose air to the whole place, but the rooms range from fashionably art deco in style to less personal modern decor. There's a good restaurant serving a modern British menu (mains £13.50 to £22), a spa and a lovely terrace for sipping cocktails. If you're a light sleeper, ask for a room away from the road.

By Appointment HOTEL ££

(☎01603-630730; www.byappointmentnorwich.co.uk; 25-29 St George's St; s/d incl breakfast from £95/125; @) This fabulously theatrical and delightfully eccentric B&B occupies three heavy-beamed 15th-century merchants' houses, and is also home to a labyrinthine restaurant well known for its classic English fare. Its antique furniture, creaky charm and superb breakfasts make this well worth booking in advance.

No 15 B&B ££

(☎01603-250283; www.number15bedandbreakfast.co.uk; 15 Grange Rd; s/d £50/70; 📶) There are just two cosy but uncluttered bedrooms at this serene B&B in a leafy residential street. The pastel-shade rooms have period satinwood furniture, white linens and good bathrooms; breakfasts are ample, vegetarian, organic and local; holistic massage is on offer; and your congenial host Ian makes the whole experience a home away from home. No 15 is about a mile west of the city centre. Bus 25 passes nearby.

Caversham House B&B ££

(☎01603-412726; www.caversham-house.co.uk; 108 Constitution Hill; s/d £42/75; 📶) Though this friendly, understated guesthouse is a brisk 20-minute walk north of the centre, it's worth it for the warm welcome from June and Don who are glad to share their knowledge of Norwich. The three rooms are snug en suites decked out in neutral shades, and a continental breakfast is included. Follow Magdalen St north of the centre and keep going straight.

Arthouse B&B B&B ££

(☎07870 188714; www.arthousebnb.com; 13 Grange Rd; s/d £55/70; 📶) Just two rooms on offer here – one retro and one with oriental rugs and sumptuous wallpaper – and with all the artwork about the place, you feel as if you're living in your hostess' studio. The ample breakfasts here are above par, with vegetarians well-catered for. Take Chapel Field North west to the roundabout, then follow Unthank Rd for 1.2km, turn right into Christchurch Rd, then right again into Grange Rd.

Number 17 B&B ££

(☎01603-764486; www.number17norwich.co.uk; 17 Colegate; s/d from £52/80; 📶) The location couldn't be more central and the full English breakfasts are vast, though served with a side of ill grace.

Eating

TOP CHOICE **Roger Hickman's** MODERN BRITISH £££

(☎01603-633522; www.rogerhickmansrestaurant.com; 79 Upper St Giles St; 2-/3-course set menu lunch £18/21, dinner £33/38; ⏰Tue-Sat) Understated, classic elegance is what this place is all about: pale floorboards, white linen, bare walls and professional, unobtrusive service. In fact, there's nothing to distract you from the top-quality dishes such as smoked venison with fig chutney or spring lamb with sweetbreads, made with flair, imagination and a simple dedication to quality.

TOP CHOICE **Farmer Browns** MODERN BRITISH ££

(☎01603-628542; www.farmerbrowns.co.uk; 22 Tombland; mains £10-18) This excellent newcomer is making quite a reputation for itself, thanks to its commitment to Norfolk ingredients and an ever-changing, creative menu. The lunchtime menu is a bargain, the service is friendly and efficient, and you can expect the likes of Bingham blue and apricot gnocchi, pigeon breast with Turkish delight, or anything else that Stuart the chef concocts.

Library MODERN EUROPEAN ££

(www.thelibraryrestaurant.co.uk; 1a Guildhall Hill; mains £10-15; ⏰closed dinner Sun) We don't normally encourage people to eat in a library, but for this 19th-century library, housing a chilled-out brasserie, we'll make an exception. The menu is heavy on imaginative meat and fish dishes using locally sourced produce, such as Lowestoft haddock and oysters, but there are few dishes to tempt vegetarians, and no one should skip out on the Eton Mess.

BamBam ASIAN ££
(☎01603-665660; www.mybambam.co.uk; 27-28 Tombland; mains £12-15; ⊙dinner Tue-Sat) Part glam bar, part innovative Asian restaurant, BamBam still seems to be trying to establish its identity. The eccentric menu sounds like a concoction of a mad genius: how about a 16-course spoon-tasting menu of bite-sized delights? Or sweetcorn soup with tuna terrine and ice cream? Whatever you pick, it's guaranteed to be memorable.

Shiki JAPANESE ££
(6 Tombland; sushi £1.70-3, mains £10-13; ⊙Mon-Sat) This minimalist Japanese restaurant has a stylish, contemporary interior and a reputation for some of the best Asian food in town. From delicate sushi to superb teppanyaki, it's a firm local favourite with a particularly friendly vibe.

Greenhouse VEGETARIAN £
(www.greenhousetrust.co.uk; 42-48 Bethel St; snacks & mains £4-7.50; ⊙10am-5pm Tue-Sat) This organic, free-trade, vegetarian/vegan cafe is bound to leave you feeling wholesome, with a menu of simple dishes such as hearty soups, notice boards crammed with posters for community events, and a lovely vine-covered, herb-planted terrace.

Mustard CAFE £
(Bridewell Alley; breakfast £4.50-6; ⊙9am-6pm Tue-Sat) On the very spot where the original Colman's Mustard shop once stood, this funky little cafe proudly carries on with the theme, with flashes of bright yellow throughout. The coffees are decent, the breakfast menu features some unusual items, such as *huevos rancheros* (Mexican-style eggs with salsa), and the changing daily lunch items include the likes of hearty lasagne.

Beluga INTERNATIONAL ££
(www.mybeluga.co.uk; 11 Queen St; mains £7-15; ⊙Thu-Sat) American-ish staples such as rack of ribs with Jack Daniels sauce, heaped nacho platters and mega burgers seem out of place in these sumptuous, formal surroundings, but in the evenings, Beluga lets its hair down when the weekly music events kick in: soul on Thursdays, Motown classics on Fridays and disco during Saturday's Floorplay.

Waffle House WAFFLES £
(www.wafflehouse.co.uk; 39 St Giles St; waffles £3.50-9.50; ⊙10am-10pm Mon-Sat, from 11am Sun) Pop in for a crisp and light Belgian waffle with sweet or savoury toppings at this down-to-earth and friendly cafe beloved by Norwich families, students and professionals.

Tea House TEAROOM £
(5 Wrights Crt, Elm Hill; tea £2.50; ⊙9am-5pm Mon-Sat) This compact, friendly tearoom in a tiny courtyard makes a great stop for tea and scones.

Drinking

It was once said that Norwich had a pub for every day of the year, and you'll find hip and trendy or quaint and traditional pubs all across the city centre. Start your quest in Tombland or St Benedict's St.

Adam & Eve PUB
(www.adamandevenorwich.co.uk; Bishopsgate) Norwich's oldest surviving pub, Adam & Eve has been on that same spot since biblical times (OK, since at least 1249, when it was built to quench the thirst of the cathedral builders). It's a tiny place with a sunken floor and a mixed clientele of regulars, choristers and ghost hunters. There's even a 'spooky' meal-and-ghost-walk deal, to top the already enticing selection of ales, bitters and malt whiskies.

Fat Cat PUB
(49 West End St) If you're a true connoisseur of real ales, don't miss Norwich's mecca for ale lovers. The decor is Any Pubblington, Wherever, but it's what is behind the bar that counts: 32 – count 'em! – real ales, including their own Marmalade Cat and lesser-known gems such as Spectrum Trip Hazard and Burton Bridge Stairway to Heaven. A chirpy crowd of locals and outdoor seating seal the deal. Head west from the centre along St Benedict's St, which merges into Dereham Rd at the junction. Follow the road for another 600m, then turn right into Nelson St and right again into West End St.

Birdcage BAR
(www.thebirdcagenorwich.co.uk; 22 Pottergate; 📶) A bohemian hang-out with kitsch decor that includes strips of bunting, mismatched furniture and a much-loved juke box. There's eclectic music in the back room, plenty of board games, free wi-fi, cupcakes on the menu, cabaret nights and a lovely outside deck area.

☆ Entertainment

Norwich has a flourishing arts scene and pulsating weekend nightlife.

Mercy NIGHTCLUB
(www.mercynightclub.com; 86 Prince of Wales Rd; ⏲Thu-Sat) A massive club set in a former cinema, with DJs that favour R&B and club classics. Its offshoot, **Über**, is a new psychedelic-stylish spot for cocktails.

Mojo's NIGHTCLUB
(www.mojosnightclub.com; 60-62 Prince of Wales Rd; ⏲Thu-Sat) Newly refurbished favourite with resident DJ, R & B and hip hop on Saturdays, and Jaegerbomb deals to fuel the festivities.

Theatre Royal THEATRE
(www.theatreroyalnorwich.co.uk; Theatre St) Features programs by touring drama, opera and ballet companies.

Norwich Arts Centre ARTS CENTRE
(www.norwichartscentre.co.uk; St Benedict's St) A wide-ranging program of alternative drama, concerts, dance and jazz set in a medieval church.

ℹ Information

Norfolk & Norwich University Hospital (☎01603-286286; Colney Lane) Four miles west of the centre.

Post Office (84-85 Castle Mall)

Tourist Office (☎01603-213999; www.visitnorwich.co.uk; The Forum; ⏲9.30am-6pm Mon-Sat, to 2.30pm Sun) Just inside the Forum.

ℹ Getting There & Around

Norwich has convenient free parking at six Park & Ride locations. Buses (£2.30) run to the city centre up to every 15 minutes from 6.40am to 7.50pm.

Air

Norwich International Airport (www.norwichinternational.com) is 4 miles north of town; there are cheap flights to Europe and several British destinations.

Bus

The bus station is on Queen's Rd 400m south of the castle. Follow Red Lion St into Stephen's St and then turn left onto Surrey St. **National Express** (www.nationalexpress.com) and **First Eastern Counties** (www.firstgroup.com) run services:

Cromer (£5, one hour, hourly)

King's Lynn (£8.60, 1½ hours, hourly)

London (£18, three hours, seven services daily)

Train

The train station is off Thorpe Rd 600m east of the castle.

Cambridge (£21, 1¼ hours, twice every hour)

Ely (£15, one hour, twice hourly)

London Liverpool Street (£30, two hours, twice hourly)

North Coast Norfolk

The north coast of Norfolk has something of a split personality, with a string of busy seaside towns with brash attractions and hordes of people clustering along the eastern end, and a collection of small villages with trendy gastropubs and boutique hotels scattered about the western end. In between sit vast sandy beaches and the marshy coast that attracts numerous bird species, including oystercatchers, plovers, curlews and brent geese.

The **Coast Hopper bus** (www.coasthopper.co.uk) runs from Cromer to Hunstanton, serving Cley, Blakeney, Wells, Holkham, Burnham Deepdale and (with a connection) King's Lynn.

CROMER

POP 3800

Once a thriving medieval port, having taken the place of the village of Shipden after it was claimed by the sea (ships have been wrecked here on underwater church spires!), and then a fashionable Victorian coastal resort, Cromer is slowly becoming gentrified again after years of degeneration into a glut of fish-and-chip shops and trashy amusement arcades. Its main attractions are Cromer crabs, the atmospheric pier and its appealing stretch of sandy beachfront.

THE LEGEND OF BLACK SHUCK

The stretch of Norfolk coast has long been known for the ghostly appearances of Black Shuck – a malevolent-looking black dog the size of a calf with flaming eyes that prowls lonesome paths at night. The inspiration behind Arthur Conan Doyle's *The Hound of the Baskervilles*, Black Shuck is said to be an omen of bad luck to those who spot him.

The **Rocket Cafe** (The Gangway; mains £4-10; ⌚10am-5pm daily, dinner Sat), which shares the new Royal National Lifeboat Institution (RNLI) building on the waterfront with the **Lifeboat Museum**, has an airy interior and outdoor terrace overlooking the water, nicely complementing the heaped Cromer crab platters, soups and sandwiches.

Just 2 miles southwest of town off the B1436 is **Felbrigg Hall** (NT; www.nationaltrust.org.uk; adult/child £7.80/3.65; ⌚11am-5pm Sat-Wed Mar-Oct), an elegant Jacobean mansion that once belonged to the Windham family, with a fine Georgian interior and splendid facade. The walled gardens and orangery are particularly lovely, with access to the **Weavers Way** running through the estate.

Cromer has direct trains to Norwich hourly Monday to Saturday and services every two hours on Sunday (£6, 45 minutes). The Coasthopper bus runs from Cromer west along the coast roughly every half-hour in summer.

SHERINGHAM

POP 7143

Sheringham is the quintessential English seaside town with distinctive pebbled houses, an easygoing atmosphere and a relative absence of tat, making its shingled beach popular with day trippers. The sea wall may be an unappealing concrete reinforcement, but the view of the waves, crashing loudly against the rocks below, is still thoroughly atmospheric.

The Mo (www.sheringhammuseum.co.uk; adult £3.50; ⌚10am-4.30pm Tue-Sat, noon-4pm Sun mid-Mar–Nov; 👪) explores the town's seafaring history. Those who enjoy ridin' the rails will be thrilled by Sheringham's other noteworthy attraction: the **North Norfolk Railway** (www.nnrailway.co.uk; adult/child return £10.50/7), with steam and diesel trains chugging their way up the 5-mile track to the nearby market town of Holt.

A proper seaside town is not complete without a decent fish-and-chip outlet, and Sheringham has several lining the main street, all comparable in quality. Just down the street towards the sea, Ronaldo's ice cream at **Ellie's** features some unusual flavours, such as Christmas pudding.

Regular trains run from Sheringham's main train station (across the road from the North Norfolk Railway) to Norwich (£6.40, one hour, hourly).

CLEY MARSHES

One of England's premier birdwatching sites, the **Cley Marshes Nature Reserve** (pronounced 'cly') is a mecca for twitchers, with over 300 bird species recorded here – numerous waders, as well as plentiful migrant species passing through – and a network of walking trails leading to a series of hides hidden amid the golden reed beds. There's a **visitors centre** (www.norfolkwildlifetrust.org.uk; adult/child £5/free; ⌚10am-5pm) built on high ground across the A149 where you pay the entrance fee, pick up trail maps and rent binoculars.

You can pick up some fantastic picnic food in the village of Cley, just west of the reserve. The renowned **Cley Smokehouse** (☎01263-740282; ⌚9am-5pm) is the place for all manner of locally smoked fish and meats, while the **Picnic Fayre** (⌚9am-5pm) across the road, is a superb deli featuring great breads, cheeses, homemade pork pies and cakes, Norfolk ice cream and all manner of jams and chutneys. If you don't suffer from the Don Quixote syndrome, a substantial dinner is to be had at the impressive 17th-century **Cley Windmill** (☎01263-740209; www.cleymill.co.uk; set dinner menu £32, d £89-189), where the chef works wonders with seasonal produce. One of the most unique places to sleep in East Anglia, it has nine bedrooms with four-poster, half-tester or cast-iron beds (the room at the top reached by ladder alone), a circular living room, and far-reaching views across the marshes.

BLAKENEY POINT

The pretty village of Blakeney was once a busy fishing and trading port before its harbour silted up. These days it has an inviting seafront walk lined with yachts, and is a good place to jump aboard boat trips out to a 500-strong colony of common and grey seals that live, bask and breed on nearby Blakeney Point. Several companies, including **Bishop's Boats** (www.norfolksealtrips.co.uk; Blakeney Harbour), and **Beans Boat Trips** (www.beansboattrips.co.uk; Morston) run hour-long trips (adult/child £9/5) daily from April to October, but the best time to come is between June and August when the common seals pup.

The best place to eat in town is the **Moorings** (www.themoorings.co.uk; High St; sandwiches £6, dinner mains £14-20; ⌚closed dinner Sun & Mon), with cheery decor suggestive of summer and beaches, wonderfully attentive service and a menu featuring Poseidon's subjects (though the likes of seared pigeon breast sneak in too); don't miss the puddings. The **Kings Arms** (☎01263-740341; www.blakeneykingsarms.co.uk; Westgate St; d £75), a traditional pub, sits just back from the quay, and its seven modest en-suite rooms with low, beamed ceilings make for a peaceful stay.

WELLS-NEXT-THE-SEA

POP 2451

Thronged with crowds on holiday weekends, what used to be an important port in the 16th and 17th centuries is now a tranquil old town a mile or so from the water. Curio shops line its tiny main drag, Staithe St, attractive Georgian houses and flint cottages surround a large green, and a long stretch of beach is flanked by pine-covered dunes.

The steam train that plies this 10¼-inch **narrow-gauge railway** (www.wellswalsinghamrailway.co.uk; adult/child return £8.50/7; ⏲3-5pm daily Apr-Oct) – the longest of its kind in the world – huffs its way for 5 miles to **Little Walsingham**, where there are shrines and a ruined abbey that used to rival Canterbury and Bury St Edmunds as the most important pilgrimage site in England due to the popularity of its **Chapel of Our Lady of Walsingham**. The picturesque journey takes 45 minutes.

If staying overnight, the **Wells YHA** (☎0845-371 9544; www.yha.org.uk; Church Plains; dm £17; Ⓟ) has simple rooms in an ornately gabled early-20th-century church hall. If you prefer to rough it right by the beach, **Pinewoods Holiday Park** (☎01328-710439; www.pinewoods.co.uk; per tent site £20; 4-bed lodge per week £1290; Ⓟ) has attractive tent sites, rudimentary beach huts for storage and lodges scattered among the pines and assorted shrubbery. Bike hire and water sports are available and a tiny railway connects the site to Wells. In Wells proper, the **Crown** (www.thecrownhotelwells.co.uk), a former coaching inn, is renowned locally for its robust dishes made from locally sourced ingredients.

The small **tourist office** (☎01328-710885; www.visitnorthnorfolk.com; Staithe St; ⏲10am-5pm Mon-Sat, to 1pm Sun Apr-Oct) can help with all inquiries.

The Coasthopper bus goes through Wells roughly half-hourly in summer on its way between Cromer (one hour) and King's Lynn (1½ hours).

HOLKHAM

The pretty village of Holkham is dominated by **Holkham Hall and Estate** (www.holkham.co.uk; adult/child £12/6, parking £2.50; ⏲noon-4pm Sun, Mon & Thu Apr-Oct), a somewhat severe Palladian mansion, largely unadorned on the outside, set in a vast deer park designed by William Kent. This is the ancestral seat of the original Earl of Leicester and still belongs to his descendants.

The interior is sumptuous but nevertheless restrained by the standards of the day, though 'restrained' may not be the first word that comes to mind when you glimpse the red-velvet-lined saloon, the copies of Greek and Roman statues, the fluted columns of the Marble Hall (it's actually Derbyshire alabaster) or the unrestrained luxury of the Green State Bedroom where various kings and queens have stayed. The public entrance brings you to the rear of the building; for the best views continue along the road around the house and past the ice house to see the building as originally intended. You can also visit the **Bygones Museum** (museum only adult/child £7/3.50; ⏲10am-5pm Apr-Oct) in the stable block. It has over 4000 exhibits – everything from mechanical toys to agricultural equipment, vintage cars and steam engines.

For many, Holkham's true delight is the other part of the estate – the **Holkham National Nature Reserve**, comprising the vast expanse of almost pristine beach of **Holkham Bay**, its air permeated with the aroma of pine forest, and a chunk of woodland with ribboning pathways leading to hides where you can spot some of the shy wildlife. Regularly voted one of England's best, the reserve is a popular spot with walkers and you can reach nearby villages by following the signposted seafront paths. The only place to park for access to the beach is **Lady Anne's Drive** (parking per hr from £2).

The Coasthopper bus goes through Holkham roughly half-hourly in summer.

BURNHAM DEEPDALE

In-the-know backpackers and walkers flock to this lovely coastal spot, with its tiny twin villages of **Burnham Deepdale** and **Brancaster Staithe** strung along a rural road. Stroked by the beautiful Norfolk Coastal Path, surrounded by beaches and reedy marshes, alive with bird life and criss-crossed by cycling routes, Burnham Deepdale is also a base for a whole host of water sports.

WORTH A TRIP

TITCHWELL MARSH NATURE RESERVE

Just west of Burnham Deepdale is tiny Titchwell, whose primary attraction is the **Titchwell Marsh Nature Reserve** (parking £4; ⏲dawn-dusk), comprising some choice marshland, sandbars and lagoons that attract numerous sea birds and waders. If you wish to linger, **Titchwell Manor** (☎01485-210221; www.titchwellmanor.com; Titchwell; d £130-250, mains £10-18; P@) is a slick contemporary hotel set in a grand Victorian house with modern British cuisine served in the conservatory restaurant. Its large garden is popular with children.

Ecofriendly, well-run **Deepdale Farm** (☎01485-210256; www.deepdalefarm.co.uk; site per adult/child £9/5, dm/d £15/60, 2-person tepees/yurts £80/95; P@) is a backpacker haven. It has spotless en suite rooms set in converted 17th-century stables, as well as camping space and glamping options in the form of Native American–style tepees and Mongolian yurts. There's a large kitchen and lounge area, picnic tables, a barbecue and a laundry and cafe next door.

The hostel also operates a **tourist office** (☎01485-210256; ⏲10am-4pm), the best place to go to organise kitesurfing or windsurfing on nearby beaches. Bike hire is also available (half-day/full day £10/16).

Just west of the hostel is the award-winning **White Horse** (☎01485-210262; www.whitehorsebrancaster.co.uk; mains £10-14, s/d from £95/150; P), a gastropub with a menu strong on seafood; the tapas-style dishes, featuring brown potted shrimp, seared tuna, tempura mackerel and more set it apart from its competitors. The guest rooms upstairs embody the seaside with their subtle colour scheme.

The Coasthopper bus stops outside Deepdale Farm roughly half-hourly in summer.

King's Lynn

POP 34,565

Once one of England's most important ports, King's Lynn was long known as 'the Warehouse on the Wash'. It was said that in the town's heyday you could cross from one side of the River Great Ouse to the other by simply stepping from boat to boat. Something of the salty port-town tang can still be felt in old King's Lynn, with its cobbled lanes and narrow streets flanked by old merchants' houses. Unfortunately, the rest of the town is not so pretty, but King's Lynn is redeemed by the vibrant open-air **markets** – the Saturday one at the Saturday Market Place, and the Tuesday and Friday markets on the Tuesday Market Place.

Sights

Old Lynn huddles along the eastern bank of the river. Walk between the two market places to take in the most handsome buildings in town, or pick up a heritage trail leaflet from the tourist office.

St Margaret's Church CHURCH
(www.stmargaretskingslynn.org.uk; Margaret Plain) A patchwork of architectural styles, this church is worth a look for its two extraordinarily elaborate Flemish brasses. You can also see a remarkable 17th-century moon dial, which tells the tide, not the time. You'll find historic flood-level markings by the west door. Opposite is the 1421 **Trinity Guildhall**, with an attractive stone facade.

Old Gaol House MUSEUM
(Saturday Market Pl; adult/child £3.20/2.20, Regalia Room free; ⏲10am-4pm Wed-Sat Apr-Oct;) Explore the old cells and hear grisly tales of smugglers, witches and highwaymen in the town's old jail. Also here is the **Regalia Room**, which houses the town's civic treasures, including the 650-year-old King John Cup, exquisitely decorated with scenes of hunting and hawking.

Lynn Museum MUSEUM
(www.museums.norfolk.gov.uk; Market St; adult/child £3.60/2; ⏲10am-5pm Tue-Sat;) The town's main museum features displays on maritime life in Lynn and West Norfolk history. Highlights include a large hoard of Iceni gold coins and the Seahenge gallery, which showcases a 4000-year-old timber circle that has miraculously survived intact, and explores the lives of the Bronze Age people who created it.

Green Quay MUSEUM
(www.thegreenquay.co.uk; South Quay; admission free; 9am-5pm;) This fantastic interactive museum introduces you to the wildlife, flora and fauna of the area through a mix of displays, videos and freshwater tank holding some denizens of the Wash (the estuary). There are sensitive exhibitions on the effects of climate change and how to preserve the fragile local ecosystems.

True's Yard MUSEUM
(www.truesyard.co.uk; North St; adult/child £3/1.50; 10am-4pm Tue-Sat) Housed in two restored fishermen's cottages – the only remainder of the bustling, fiercely independent fishing community that once lived in this part of the city – this museum looks at the traditions and difficult lives of the fishers and their families, who were packed into such cottages like sardines.

Festivals & Events

King's Lynn Festival CULTURE
(www.kingslynnfestival.org.uk; Jul) East Anglia's most important cultural gathering, with a diverse program of concerts and recitals of all kinds, from medieval ballads to opera, as well as literary talks.

Festival Too MUSIC
(www.festivaltoo.co.uk; Jul) A free rock-and-pop bash featuring the likes of Lemar, The Stranglers and Atomic Kitten, and attracting upwards of 10,000 people.

Sleeping & Eating

Bank House B&B ££
(01553-660492; www.thebankhouse.co.uk; Kings Staithe Sq; s/d from £80/100;) Overlooking the water, the 18th-century former bank is now an elegantly furnished town house with five luxurious rooms, mixing exposed beams with modern furnishings and nice touches, such as Molton Brown toiletries. There's also a lovely, modern brasserie (mains £8 to £17) serving seriously good British food – including hefty lunchtime sandwiches (£5) – made from locally sourced ingredients.

Market Bistro MODERN BRITISH ££
(01553-771483; www.marketbistro.co.uk; 11 Saturday Market Pl; 2-/3-course lunch menu £12/15; Mon-Sat) This friendly, family-run place has been winning a lot of fans with its commitment to Norfolk ingredients such as Cromer crab, locally smoked fish and samphire from

DON'T MISS

SANDRINGHAM HOUSE

Royalists and those bemused by the English sovereigns will have plenty to mull over at the Queen's **country estate** (www.sandringhamestate.co.uk; adult/child £11.50/5.50, gardens & museum only £8.50/4.50; 11am-4.30pm Apr-Oct), set in 25 hectares of beautifully landscaped gardens and lakes. It is open to the general public when the royal family is not in residence.

Queen Victoria bought the estate in 1862 for her son, the Prince of Wales (later Edward VII), but he promptly had it overhauled in the style later named Edwardian. Half of the surrounding 8000 hectares is leased to farm tenants, while the rest is managed by the Crown Estate as forestry.

Visitors can wander around the ground-floor rooms – all regularly used by the royal family – from the sumptuous dining room and the royal rifle room, to the Big Game Room and the hall, with its superb collection of swords, sabres, dirks and chainmail adorning the walls. Head out to the old stables, which house a flag-waving museum filled with diverse royal memorabilia, such as the royal family tree and engaging family photos of British monarchs. The superb royal vintage-car collection includes the very first royal motor from 1900, darling electrical toy cars driven by various royal children, and the buggy in which the now deceased Queen Mother would bounce around race tracks. For another oddity, look for the pet cemetery just outside the museum.

There are **guided tours** (11am & 2pm Wed & Sat) of the gardens. The shop is also worth a visit for the organic goodies produced on the sprawling estate.

Sandringham is 6 miles northeast of King's Lynn off the B1440. Take Hunstanton-bound bus 10 or 11 from the bus station (30 minutes, hourly).

the marshes, not to mention inventive seasonal dishes. These all-rounders make their own ice cream, too.

Information

Tourist Office (☎01553-763044; www.visitwestnorfolk.com; Purfleet Quay; ⏰10am-5pm Mon-Sat, noon-5pm Sun) Housed in the lovely 17th-century Custom House, the tourist office arranges guided walks (adult/child £4.50/1.50) at 2pm on Tuesdays, Fridays and Saturdays in high season. There's an engaging exhibition (£1.50) here on King's Lynn's maritime days.

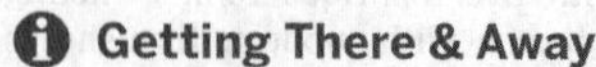

Getting There & Away

There are hourly trains from Cambridge (£9, 50 minutes) via Ely and London Kings Cross (£31, 1¾ hours). Coasthopper 1 (www.coasthopper.co.uk) bus runs to Hunstanton (35 minutes, hourly) and connects with the Coasthopper 2 service, which runs along the north Norfolk coast. Services are frequent from April to September, less so the rest of the year.

Around King's Lynn

CASTLE RISING CASTLE

There's something bordering on ecclesiastical about the beautifully embellished keep of this well reserved, compact **castle** (www.castlerising.co.uk; adult/child £4/2.50; ⏰10am-6pm Apr-Nov), built in 1138 and set in the middle of a massive earthwork. So extravagant is the stonework that it's no surprise to learn that it may well have shared stonemasons with some of East Anglia's finest cathedrals. It was once the home of Queen Isabella, who (allegedly) arranged the gruesome murder of her husband, Edward II. As you wander about the deserted keep with its green-tinted stone, keep an eye out for the gargoyles adorning the Great Hall – one pensive, another possibly throwing up.

Castle Rising Castle is 4 miles northeast of King's Lynn off the A149. Hunstanton-bound buses 10 and 11 run here (15 minutes, hourly) from the King's Lynn bus station.

HOUGHTON HALL

Built for Britain's first de facto Prime Minister Sir Robert Walpole in 1730, the grand Palladian-style **Houghton Hall** (www.houghtonhall.com; adult/child £10/3.50; ⏰house 1.30-5pm, grounds 11.30am-5.30pm Wed, Thu & Sun Easter-Sep) is worth seeing for the ornate staterooms alone; you could build another half-dozen houses with the amount of swirling decorative plasterwork here. The sumptuous interiors are overflowing with gilt, tapestries, velvets and period furniture, but the most remarkable thing about Houghton Hall is not actually there: Sir Robert Walpole's grandson sold the estate's splendid art collection to Catherine the Great of Russia as part of the estate's accumulated debt, and those paintings formed part of the basis for the world-renowned collection at the State Hermitage in St Petersburg.

Even when the house is closed, the surrounding grounds, home to 600 deer, make for pleasant rambling. Houghton Hall is just off the A148 on the way from Kings Lynn to Cromer.

Nottingham & the East Midlands

Includes »

Best Places to Eat

» Chequers Inn (p468)
» Hammer & Pincers (p479)
» Reform (p465)
» Piedaniel's (p497)
» The Old Bakery Tea Rooms (p461)

Best Places to Stay

» Hart's (p455)
» Hotel Maiyango (p476)
» Hambleton Hall (p480)
» George Hotel (p468)

Why Go?

Postcard-perfect villages and rugged hiking trails of the Peak District aside, this peaceful corner of the country lies largely off the tourist radar. Away from the vibrant cities of Nottingham, Leicester and Derby (and their sprawling suburbs), the East Midlands is a rolling carpet of farmland, strewn with historic market towns, ruined castles, spellbinding cathedrals and the lavish stately homes you were expecting after reading all those Jane Austen novels.

Where you go in the region will depend on your temperament. City slickers are drawn to Nottingham, with its lively nightlife and Robin Hood connections, while foodies head to Leicester to sample the imported culinary delights of the Indian subcontinent. Fans of the great outdoors make for the Peak District in their hundreds of thousands. However, you may find more peace and quiet in the backwaters of Rutland and Lincolnshire.

When to Go

The East Midlands is at its best in summer, when the countryside comes alive with village fetes and festivals. For walkers and cyclists, June through September is the high season in the Peak District.

May brings flowers, parades and pagan goings-on to Castleton's Garland Festival, while February and March bring the wonderful chaos of Shrovetide football to Ashbourne.

Nottingham & the East Midlands Highlights

1 Walking or cycling the rugged trails of the **Peak District National Park** (p486)

2 Contemplating the apple tree that inspired Isaac Newton's theories on gravity at his birthplace, **Woolsthorpe Manor** (p467)

3 Discovering how the spire of Chesterfield's **St Mary & All Saints Church** (p485) came to be crooked on a tour or at the town museum

4 Being awed by the mighty **Minster** (p460) dominating the story-book-pretty village of Southwell

5 Drinking in the history of **Ye Olde Trip to Jerusalem** (p457), allegedly England's oldest inn, carved into the cliff below Nottingham's castle

6 Stepping back into Jane Austen's England in the stone-lined streets of **Stamford** (p468)

7 Getting lost in the grandeur of **Chatsworth House** (p497), one of the nation's stateliest homes

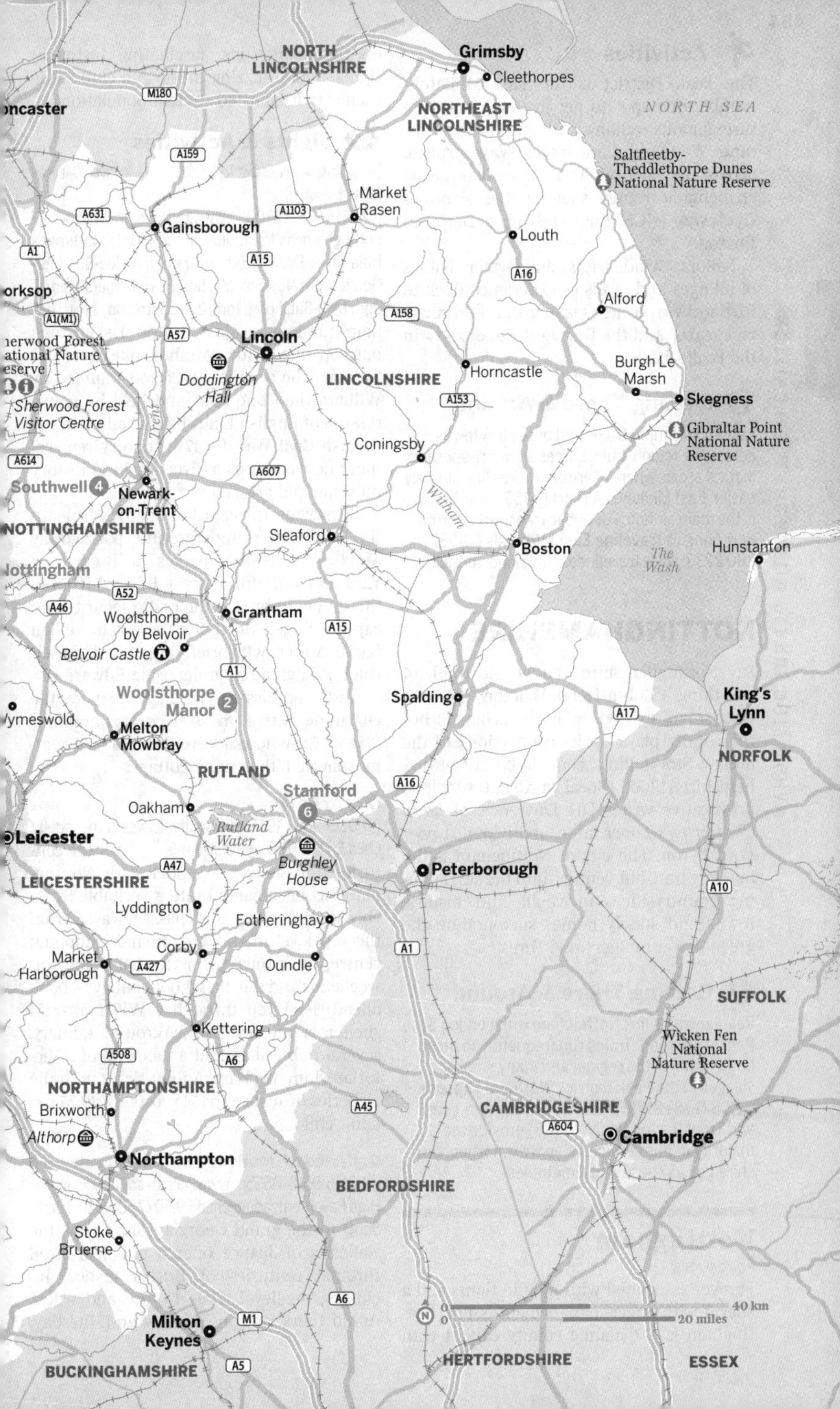

NORTH SEA
NORTH LINCOLNSHIRE
Grimsby
Cleethorpes
NORTHEAST LINCOLNSHIRE
M180
A159
A631
A1103
A1
A15
A1(M1)
A57
A158
A16
A153
A614
A607
A52
A46
A1
A17
A16
A47
A427
A508
A6
A45
A604
A10
A6
M1
A5
Saltfleetby-Theddlethorpe Dunes National Nature Reserve
Market Rasen
Gainsborough
Louth
Alford
Lincoln
Doddington Hall
LINCOLNSHIRE
Horncastle
Burgh Le Marsh
Skegness
Gibraltar Point National Nature Reserve
Sherwood Forest Visitor Centre
Trent
Coningsby
Witham
Southwell 4
Newark-on-Trent
NOTTINGHAMSHIRE
Sleaford
Boston
The Wash
Hunstanton
Grantham
Woolsthorpe by Belvoir
Belvoir Castle
Woolsthorpe Manor 2
Melton Mowbray
RUTLAND
Spalding
King's Lynn
NORFOLK
Stamford 6
Oakham
Rutland Water
Leicester
Burghley House
Peterborough
LEICESTERSHIRE
Lyddington
Fotheringhay
Corby
Market Harborough
Oundle
SUFFOLK
Kettering
Wicken Fen National Nature Reserve
NORTHAMPTONSHIRE
Brixworth
CAMBRIDGESHIRE
Althorp
Cambridge
Northampton
BEDFORDSHIRE
Stoke Bruerne
0 40 km
0 20 miles
Milton Keynes
HERTFORDSHIRE
ESSEX
BUCKINGHAMSHIRE

Activities

The Peak District is the East Midlands' number-one spot to get in touch with nature: famous walking trails such as the **Pennine Way** and **Limestone Way** struggle across the hills, while road cyclists tackle challenging routes such as the **Pennine Cycleway** (NCN Route 68) from Derby to Buxton.

Sailors, windsurfers and water babies of all ages and levels of experience flock to **Rutland Water** near Oakham, and **Carsington Water** and the **Derwent Reservoirs** in the Peak District.

Getting There & Around

Fast and frequent trains and buses link towns across the region, but services are more sporadic in rural areas, where a hire car makes life infinitely easier. East Midlands Airport (p459) near Derby is the main air hub. For public transport information, consult **Traveline East Midlands** (☎0871 200 2233; www.travelineeastmidlands.org.uk).

NOTTINGHAMSHIRE

Say Nottinghamshire and people think of one thing – Robin Hood. Whether the hero woodsman existed is hotly debated, but the county plays up its connections to the outlaw. Storytelling seems to be in Nottinghamshire's blood – local wordsmiths include provocative writer DH Lawrence, of *Lady Chatterley's Lover* fame, and hedonist poet Lord Byron. The city of Nottingham is the bustling hub, but venture into the surrounding countryside and you'll find historic towns and stately homes surrounding the green bower of Sherwood Forest.

Getting There & Around

Regular trains link Nottingham with London St Pancras station. Trains run frequently to most large towns in the region, and many smaller villages in the Peak District. **National Express** (☎0871 781 8178; www.nationalexpress.com) and Trent Barton Buses (p488) provide the majority of bus services. See www.nottinghamshire.gov.uk/buses for timetables.

Nottingham

POP 266,988

Forever associated with men in tights and a sheriff with anger-management issues, Nottingham is a dynamic county capital with big-city aspirations, fascinating historical sights, and a buzzing music and club scene thanks to its spirited student population.

Sights & Activities

Nottingham Castle & Art Gallery CASTLE, GALLERY

(☎0115-915 3700; www.nottinghamcity.gov.uk/nottinghamcastle; adult/child £5.50/4, Mortimer's Hole tours £2.50/1.50; ⊙10am-5pm Tue-Sun Mar-Oct, to 4pm Nov-Feb, Mortimer's Hole tours 11am & 2pm Mon-Sat, noon, 1pm, 2pm, 3pm Sun) Nottingham's famous castle sits atop a sandstone outcrop, filled with wormhole-like caves and tunnels. The original castle was founded by William the Conqueror and held by a succession of English kings before falling in the English Civil War. Its 17th-century replacement now contains a diverting local history museum and art gallery.

Burrowing through the bedrock beneath the castle, the underground passageway **Mortimer's Hole** emerges at Brewhouse Yard. In 1330, supporters of Edward III used the tunnel to breach the castle security and capture Roger Mortimer, the machiavellian Earl of March, who briefly appointed himself ruler of England after deposing Edward II.

Castle admission includes entry to the charming **Museum of Nottinghamshire Life at Brewhouse Yard**, housed in five atmospheric 17th-century cottages.

City of Caves CAVE

(☎0115-988 1955; www.cityofcaves.com; adult/child £6.50/5.50; ⊙10.30am-5pm) Over the centuries, the sandstone underneath Nottingham has been carved into a veritable Swiss cheese of caverns and passageways. From the top level of the Broadmarsh shopping centre, audio tours (or performance tours at weekends and during school holidays – book ahead) lead you through a WWII air-raid shelter, a medieval underground tannery, several pub cellars and a mock-up of a Victorian slum dwelling. A joint ticket with the Galleries of Justice (p454) costs £12/9.75 per adult/child.

Galleries of Justice MUSEUM

(☎0115-952 0555; www.galleriesofjustice.org.uk; High Pavement; adult/child £9.50/7.50; ⊙10.30am-5pm) In the grand Georgian Shire Hall, the Galleries of Justice offer a ghoulish stroll through centuries of British justice, including medieval trials by fire and water. Audio tours run on Monday and Tuesday;

live-action tours with 'gaolers' run Wednesday to Sunday (daily during school holidays).

FREE **Nottingham Contemporary** GALLERY
(☎0115-948 9750; www.nottinghamcontemporary.org; Weekday Cross; ⏱10am-7pm Tue-Fri, 10am-6pm Sat, 11am-5pm Sun) Behind its lace-patterned concrete facade, this sleek gallery mounts edgy, design-oriented exhibitions of paintings, prints, photography and sculpture.

National Ice Centre SKATING
(☎0843 373 3000; www.national-ice-centre.com; Bolero Square; skating £6, skate hire £2) On Bolero Square – named for local skaters Torvill and Dean's iconic 1984 gold-medal-winning routine – is the UK's first ice centre with twin Olympic-sized rinks (60m by 30m). The complex incorporates the East Midlands' premier entertainment venue, the **Capital FM Arena**, which hosts sporting fixtures, competitions and performances. Daily skating session times are posted online.

Tours

Ezekial Bone Tours WALKING TOUR
(☎07941 210986; www.bonecorporation.co.uk; tours adult/child £8/4; ⏱Sat May-Sep) Entertaining history tours are led by Nottingham's 'modern day Robin Hood' **Ezekial Bone aka Ade Andrews** (p458). In addition to two-hour Robin Hood town tours, Ezekial/Ade runs Robin Hood Sherwood Forest tours and various other walks year-round by request.

Nottingham Princess CRUISE
(☎0115-910 0400; www.princessrivercruises.co.uk) Lunch and dinner (and dance) cruises along the River Trent.

Original Nottingham Ghost Walk WALKING TOUR
(www.ghost-walks.co.uk; adult/child £5/3; ⏱7pm Sat Jan-Nov) Tours lasting 1¼ hours depart from **Ye Olde Salutation Inn** (Maid Marian Way). Descend into the medieval caves if you dare…

Festivals & Events

Nottingham hosts an intriguing selection of festivals – search for events online at www.nottinghamcity.gov.uk.

The city's biggest live music festival, **Splendour**, takes place in July, while the Caribbean community celebrates its **Carnival** in August. October's medieval **Goose Fair** has evolved from a travelling market to a modern funfair; the **Robin Hood Beer Festival**, featuring over 1000 beers and 200 ciders, and the family-friendly **Robin Hood Pageant** take place the same month.

Sleeping

TOP CHOICE **Hart's** BOUTIQUE HOTEL ££
(☎0115-988 1900; www.hartsnottingham.co.uk; Standard Hill, Park Row; d from £125; P@☎) Within the Nottingham General Hospital compound, the ultracontemporary rooms of the city's swishest hotel are in a striking modernist building, while its renowned restaurant (p456) is housed in a historic red-brick wing. Work out in the small gym or unwind in the private garden.

Lace Market Hotel BOUTIQUE HOTEL ££
(☎0115-852 3232; www.lacemarkethotel.co.uk; 29-31 High Pavement; s/d incl breakfast from £59/79; P☎) This elegant Georgian town house in the heart of the trendy Lace Market offers sleek rooms that have state-of-the-art furnishings and amenities. Its fine-dining restaurant, **Merchants**, and adjoining genteel pub, the **Cock & Hoop** (☎0115-852 3231; 25 High Pavement), are both excellent.

Greenwood Lodge City Guest House B&B ££
(☎0115-962 1206; www.greenwoodlodgecityguesthouse.co.uk; Third Ave, Sherwood Rise; s/d incl breakfast from £51.50/86.50; P☎) A gorgeous B&B set in a large Victorian house north of the centre. The location is quiet, the house and frilly rooms are full of period character, and there's a pretty courtyard garden. Children under 10 aren't permitted.

Igloo Backpackers Hostel HOSTEL £
(☎0115-947 5250; www.igloohostel.co.uk; 110 Mansfield Rd; dm/s/d £16/38/48; ☎) A favourite with international backpackers, this independent hostel is situated opposite the Golden Fleece pub and a 24-hour supermarket.

Park Hotel HOTEL £
(☎0115-978 6299; www.parkhotelnottingham.co.uk; 5-7 Waverley St; s/d from £30/50; @☎) Comfortable rooms in this imposing turn-of-the-century mansion are decked out in warms reds, creams and browns. Follow Goldsmith St northwest from the centre.

Eating

Nottingham reputedly has more restaurants, pubs and bars per square mile than anywhere else in Europe.

Nottingham

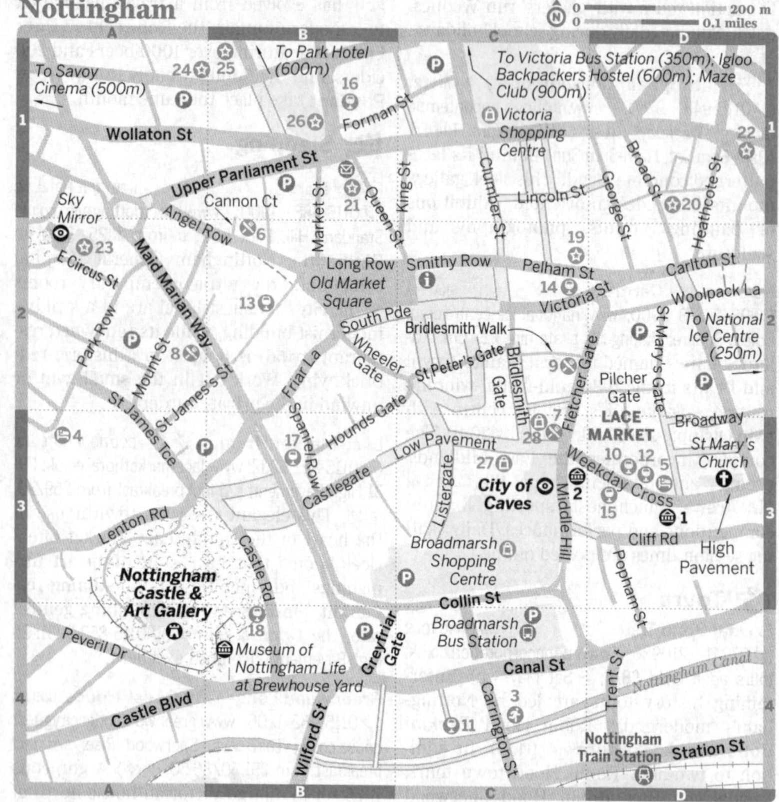

TOP CHOICE Hart's Restaurant MODERN BRITISH £££
(☎0115-988 1900; www.hartsnottingham.co.uk; Standard Hill, Park Row; mains £17.50-29;) Adjacent to Hart's (p455) boutique hotel, this contemporary restaurant has plush booths, extremely attentive service and surprisingly affordable prices, considering it offers central Nottingham's finest cuisine (deconstructed prawn cocktail, bacon-wrapped monkfish and so on).

Delilah Fine Foods DELI, CAFE £
(www.delilahfinefoods.co.uk; 15 Middle Pavement; dishes £3.95-8.95; 8am-7pm Mon-Fri, 9am-7pm Sat, 11am-5pm Sun) Impeccably selected cheeses, pâtés, meats and more from artisan producers are available to sample, take away or eat on-site at this gourmand's dream.

Restaurant Sat Bains MODERN EUROPEAN £££
(www.restaurantsatbains.com; Lenton Lane; tasting menus £75-99; dinner Tue-Sat;) Two miles southwest of the centre off the A52, Nottingham's top table recently gained a second Michelin star for its wildly inventive modern European cooking. Book well in advance and beware of hefty cancellation charges. It also has eight chic guest rooms.

The Walk Cafe CAFE ££
(☎0115-950 1502; www.thewalkcafe.co.uk; 12 Bridlesmith Walk; mains £7.20-11.90; 11am-6pm Sun-Wed, to 10pm Thu-Sat) Hidden off a pedestrian walkway, this local secret serves some of the best seafood around, including premium fish and triple-cooked chips, and succulent crab platters.

Memsaab INDIAN ££
(☎0115-9570009; www.mem-saab.co.uk; 12-14 Maid Marian Way; mains £7.50-17.50; dinner) The best of the glamorous modern Indian eateries on Maid Marian Way, serving fabulous regional specialities in dinner-date-friendly surroundings.

Nottingham

Top Sights

City of Caves ... C3
Nottingham Castle & Art Gallery ... A4

Sights

1 Galleries of Justice ... D3
2 Nottingham Contemporary ... C3

Activities, Courses & Tours

3 Bunneys Bikes ... C4

Sleeping

4 Hart's ... A3
5 Lace Market Hotel ... D3

Eating

6 Alley Cafe Bar ... B2
7 Delilah Fine Foods ... C3
8 Memsaab ... A2
9 The Walk Cafe ... C2

Drinking

10 Brass Monkey ... D3
11 Canal House ... C4
12 Cock & Hoop ... D3
13 Malt Cross ... B2
14 Pit & Pendulum ... C2
15 Pitcher & Piano ... D3
16 Rocket @ Saltwater ... B1
17 Ye Olde Salutation Inn ... B3
18 Ye Olde Trip to Jerusalem ... B4

Entertainment

19 Bodega Social Club ... C2
20 Broadway Cinema ... D1
21 Gatecrasher ... B1
22 NG1 ... D1
23 Nottingham Playhouse ... A2
24 Rock City ... A1
25 Stealth ... B1
26 Theatre Royal Concert Hall Booking Office ... B1

Shopping

27 Paul Smith ... C3
28 Paul Smith ... C3

Alley Cafe Bar VEGETARIAN £
(☎01159-551013; www.alleycafe.co.uk; Cannon Ct; mains £5.50-6.85; ⏲11am-9pm Mon & Tue, 11am-late Wed-Sat, noon-5pm Sun; ✍) Down a narrow alleyway, this beat-spinning hippie haven serves dishes such as tofu, tempeh and hemp-seed burgers, and organic beers, wines and ciders. It also hosts events, like open-mic nights and creative competitions, and exhibits local art.

Drinking

Weekends in Nottingham are boisterous affairs, when the streets throng with lads on stag nights, girls on hen parties, student revellers and various other intoxicated grown-ups who should really know better. There are also plenty of low-key alternatives.

TOP CHOICE **Ye Olde Trip to Jerusalem** PUB
(☎0115-947 3171; www.triptojerusalem.com; Brewhouse Yard, Castle Rd) Wedged into the cliff below the castle, this fantastically atmospheric alehouse claims to be England's oldest pub. Founded in 1189, it supposedly slaked the thirst of departing crusaders and its low-ceilinged rooms and cobbled courtyards are still the most ambient place in Nottingham for a pint. Informal tours (per person £2.50) of its ancient cellars can be arranged by booking at least two weeks ahead.

Pitcher & Piano BAR, RESTAURANT
(www.pitcherandpiano.com; Unitarian Church, High Pavement) A deconsecrated 19th century church, complete with soaring ceilings, glorious stained glass and flickering candles, makes this branch of a chain bar and restaurant one of a kind.

Pit & Pendulum PUB
(http://www.eerie-pubs.co.uk/pit-pendulum; 17 Victoria St; 📶) Local goths flock to this dimly lit pub for the vampire vibe and theatrical decor (push the floor-to-ceiling basement 'bookcase' to reach the toilets), as well as 'seven deadly sins' cocktails and occasional live music.

Brass Monkey BAR
(www.brassmonkeybar.co.uk; High Pavement; ⏲4pm-1am Mon-Sat, till midnight Sun) Nottingham's original cocktail bar rocks the Lace Market with DJ sets and quirky takes on favourites, like elderflower mojitos. The roof terrace gets packed on summer evenings.

Rocket @ Saltwater BAR
(☎0115-924 2664; www.rocketrestaurants.co.uk; The Cornerhouse, Forman St) Slick hipster rooftop bar and restaurant.

LOCAL KNOWLEDGE

EZEKIAL BONE AKA ADE ANDREWS

What is your background? I did a history degree and worked as a Heritage Ranger at Sherwood Forest, then set up Ezekial Bone Tours (p455) to deconstruct the Robin Hood myths and focus on the historic building blocks.

Did Robin Hood actually exist? He's a composite hero: many real outlaws in the medieval period were woven together over time by minstrels and storytellers. **St Mary's Church** (guided tours 0115-948 3658; www.stmarysnottingham.org; High Pavement; 10.30am-2.30pm Tue-Sat) is mentioned in the 1450 *Ballad of Robin Hood and the Monk*, and (Old) Market Sq in *Robin Hood and the Potter* c 1500. It was only at the end of the 16th century that playwright Antony Munday elevated Robin Hood from a yeoman to a displaced Saxon earl as a symbol of the gentry's dissatisfaction with the crown.

What is Robin Hood's relevance in the 21st century? Robin Hood was an original eco-warrior in harmony with the land. I want to put him on the pedestal he deserves – as a figurehead of culture and the environment.

What are the best places to experience Nottingham's history? The Lace Market area, the caves (p454), Nottingham Castle (p454) and Ye Olde Trip to Jerusalem (p457).

Ade Andrews is a writer, actor, producer and tour guide.

Canal House PUB
(0115-955 5060; http://thecanalhouse.co.uk; 48-52 Canal St) The best of the sprawling canal-front pubs, run by the independent Castle Rock Brewery and split in two by a watery inlet.

Malt Cross PUB
(www.maltcross.com; 16 St James's St) A fine place for a pint in a stately old Victorian music hall.

☆ Entertainment

Musicals, touring theatre shows and veteran music acts at the **Royal Concert Hall** and **Theatre Royal** share a **booking office** (0115-989 5555; www.royalcentre-nottingham.co.uk; Theatre Sq) and arrange 90-minute backstage tours (£5.50).

Rock City LIVE MUSIC
(0115-950 6547; www.rock-city.co.uk; 8 Talbot St) This monster venue hosts everything from goth rock and Midlands metal to northern soul.

Nottingham Playhouse THEATRE
(0115-941 9419; www.nottinghamplayhouse.co.uk; Wellington Circus) Beside Anish Kapoor's enormous Sky Mirror dish, the Playhouse puts on serious theatre, from stage classics to the avant-garde. Arty types hang out at its attached restaurant and bar.

Stealth CLUB
(0845 413 4444; www.stealthattack.co.uk; Masonic Pl, Goldsmith St) An underground club for those who like their bass heavy and their drums supercharged. The attached **Rescue Rooms** (0115-828 3173; www.rescuerooms.com) has a varied line-up of live bands and DJs.

Gatecrasher CLUB
(0115-910 1101; www.gatecrasher.com; Elite Bldg, Queen St) Spread over numerous rooms, this mainstream club throbs to the sound of house, R&B, hip hop and international guest DJs.

NG1 CLUB
(0115-958 8440; www.ng1club.co.uk; 76-80 Lower Parliament St; 11pm-4am Wed, 10pm-5am Fri, to 6am Sat, 11pm-4am Sun) Nottingham's favourite gay club is unpretentious, hedonistic fun, with two dance floors belting out funky house, pop and '80s classics.

Bodega Social Club LIVE MUSIC
(0845 413 4444; www.thebodegasocialclub.co.uk; 23 Pelham St) Bands of the calibre of the Strokes, Arctic Monkeys and Coldplay perform at this agreeably grungy venue.

Broadway Cinema CINEMA
(www.broadway.org.uk; 14-18 Broad St) Artistic hub with an independent cinema, media-arts gallery and a cafe-bar where you can actually hear yourself talk.

Savoy Cinema CINEMA
(www.savoycinemas.co.uk; 233 Derby Rd) Family-friendly independent cinema west of the city.

Shopping

Pedestrian Bridlesmith Gate has upmarket boutiques. Local fashion designer Sir Paul Smith's first, 1970-opened boutique **Byard Lane** is on Byard Lane while his flagship store is in **Willoughby House** (20 Low Pavement).

Information

Post Office (Queen St) Has a currency exchange service.

Tourist Office (☎0844 477 5678; www.experiencenottinghamshire.com; The Exchange, 1-4 Smithy Row; ⊙9.30am-5.30pm Mon-Sat year-round, 11am-5pm Sun late Jul-Aug & mid-late Dec) Friendly office with racks of info and Robin Hood merchandise.

Getting There & Away

Air

East Midlands Airport (☎0871 919 9000; www.eastmidlandsairport.com) is about 18 miles south of Nottingham; Skylink buses, running 24 hours a day, pass the airport (one hour, at least hourly). Buses leave from Broadmarsh bus station, and from Friar Lane, off Old Market Sq.

Bus

Local services run from the Victoria bus station on Milton St, behind the Victoria Shopping Centre. Bus 100 runs to Southwell (50 minutes, every 20 minutes Monday to Saturday, four Sunday services) and bus 90 to Newark (55 minutes, hourly Monday to Saturday, every two hours Sunday).

Long-distance buses operate from the dingy Broadmarsh bus station. For the Peaks, the hourly Transpeak service runs to Derby (40 minutes), Matlock Bath (1¼ hours), Bakewell (two hours) and Buxton (2½ hours).

Frequent National Express services:

Birmingham £9.90, 1¼ hours, seven daily

Leicester £3.80, 45 minutes, 10 daily

London St Pancras £6.50, 3½ hours, 10 daily

Sheffield £7.90, one hour and 20 minutes, hourly

Train

The train station is just south of the town centre. Useful services:

Derby £6.30, 25 minutes, three hourly

Lincoln £10.20, one hour, hourly

London St Pancras £27, two hours, three hourly

Manchester £20.60, two hours, every 40 minutes

Newark-on-Trent £5.60, 30 minutes, hourly

Sheffield £8, one hour, half-hourly

Getting Around

For information on buses within Nottingham, call **Nottingham City Transport** (☎0115-950 6070; www.nctx.co.uk). A Kangaroo ticket gives you unlimited travel on buses and trams within the city for £4.

The single tram line operated by **Nottingham Express Transit** (www.thetram.net; single/day from £1.90/3.50) runs from Nottingham train station to Hucknall, passing close to Broadmarsh bus station, the tourist office (p459) and **Theatre Royal**.

Bunneys Bikes (☎0115-947 2713; www.bunneysbikes.com; 97 Carrington St; bike hire per day £12.99; ⊙9am-5.30pm Mon, Thu & Fri, 8am-5.30pm Tue, 9am-7pm Wed, 10am-5pm Sat) is near the train station.

Around Nottingham

NEWSTEAD ABBEY

The evocative lakeside ruins of **Newstead Abbey** (☎01623-455900; www.newsteadabbey.org.uk; adult/child £10/8, gardens only £4/3; ⊙house noon-5pm Fri-Mon Apr-Sep, garden 9am-dusk year-round) are inextricably associated with the original tortured romantic, Lord Byron (1788–1824), who owned the house until 1817. Founded as an Augustinian priory around 1170, the building was converted into a residence in 1539. Byron's old living quarters are full of suitably eccentric memorabilia, and the landscaped grounds include a monument to his yappy dog, Boatswain.

DON'T MISS

WOLLATON HALL

Built in 1588 for land owner and coal mogul, Sir Francis Willoughby, **Wollaton Hall** (www.nottinghamcity.gov.uk; Wollaton Park, Derby Rd; admission free, parking per 3hr/day £2/4, tours adult/child £5/3; ⊙11am-5pm Mar-Oct, to 4pm Nov-Feb) has more frills and ruffs than an Elizabethan banquet hall. This fabulous manor was created by avant-garde architect Robert Smythson. As well as extravagant rooms from the Tudor, Regency and Victorian periods, the hall incorporates a natural history museum, and sits within 500 acres of grounds roamed by herds of fallow and red deer.

Wollaton Hall is 2.5 miles west of the city centre; take bus 30 or 2 from Victoria bus station (15 minutes).

Newstead Abbey is 12 miles north of Nottingham, off the A60. **Pronto** (www.pronto.co.uk) buses run from Victoria bus station, stopping at Newstead Abbey gates (30 minutes, every 20 minutes Monday to Saturday, half-hourly on Sunday), a mile from the house and gardens. Trains run to Newstead station, 2.5 miles from the abbey.

EASTWOOD

POP 18,000

About 10 miles northwest of Nottingham, Eastwood has a handful of sights linked to the author DH Lawrence (1885–1930), who rose to fame, and then notoriety, for the graphic depictions of sexuality in such novels as *Lady Chatterley's Lover,* which was only published unexpurgated in 1960.

Set in the modest terrace house where Lawrence was born, the **DH Lawrence Birthplace Museum** (☎01773-717353; www.broxtowe.gov.uk; 8a Victoria St; adult/child £5/3.50; ⊙11am-4pm) has been restored to what it would have been like in his childhood. Book ahead for guided tours (three to five per day by reservation). Tickets also provide entrance to the **Durban House Heritage Centre** (Mansfield Rd; ⊙10am-5pm Tue-Sun) down the road, which provides context for Lawrence's writing by recreating life in a Nottinghamshire mining community at the turn of the 20th century.

Rainbow bus 1 runs from Nottingham's Victoria bus station to Eastwood (20 minutes, half-hourly), or follow the A610.

SHERWOOD FOREST NATIONAL NATURE RESERVE

If Robin Hood wanted to hide out in Sherwood Forest today, he'd have to disguise himself and the Merry Men as day trippers on mountain bikes. Now covering just 182 hectares of old growth forest, it's nevertheless a major destination for Nottingham city dwellers.

The **Sherwood Forest visitor centre** (www.sherwoodforest.org.uk; Swinecote Rd, Edwinstowe; parking £3; ⊙10am-5pm), on the B6034, is an uninspiring collection of faded late-20th-century buildings housing cafes, gift shops and 'Robyn Hode's Sherwode', with wooden cut-outs, murals and mannequins telling the tale of the famous woodsman. It's the departure point for walking trails passing such Sherwood Forest landmarks as the **Major Oak** (1 mile return), a broad-boughed oak tree (propped up by supporting rods) alleged to have sheltered Robin of Locksley. For informative guided walks, contact Ezekial Bone Tours (p455). The week-long **Robin Hood Festival** is a massive medieval re-enactment that takes place here every August.

Sherwood Pines Cycles (☎01623-822855; adult/child per hr £8/7, per day £20/17; ⊙9am-5pm Tue-Sun), at Sherwood Pines Forest Park (3.8 miles southwest of Sherwood Forest, just off the B6030), has bikes for hire.

An arrow's flight from the visitor centre, **Sherwood Forest YHA** (☎0845 371 9139; www.yha.org.uk; Forest Corner; dm £12.40-24.90; P) is a modern hostel with comfortable dorms, a bar, self-catering kitchen and meals.

From Nottingham, take the Sherwood Arrow (bus 33, 30 minutes, four daily Monday to Saturday, two Sunday).

Southwell

POP 6285

A graceful scattering of grand, wisteria-draped country houses, Southwell is straight out of the pages of an English Romantic novel. Rising from the village centre, the awe-inspiring **Southwell Minster** (www.southwellminster.org; suggested donation £3, photo permit £5; ⊙8am-7pm), built over Saxon and Roman foundations, blends 12th- and 13th-century features including zigzag door frames and curved arches. Its chapter house features some unusual stained glass and detailed carvings of faces, animals and leaves of forest trees.

On the road to Newark, **Southwell Workhouse** (NT; Upton Rd; adult/child £7/3.50; ⊙noon-5pm Wed-Sun Mar-Oct, closed Nov-Feb) is a sobering reminder of the tough life faced by paupers in the 19th century. You can explore the factory floors and workers' chambers accompanied by an audioguide narrated by 'inmates' and 'officials'.

By the main junction, the rambling, timbered coaching inn **Saracen's Head Hotel** (☎01636-812701; www.saracensheadhotel.net; s/d incl breakfast from £75/95, 2-/3-course menus £15.95/19.95; Wi-Fi) has 27 beautifully refurbished rooms and an oak-panelled restaurant. Enticing gourmet delis and tearooms line the village streets.

Bus 100 runs from Nottingham (50 minutes, every 20 minutes Monday to Saturday, four Sunday). For Newark-on-Trent, take bus 28 or 29 (30 minutes, at least hourly) or the less frequent bus 3.

Newark-on-Trent

POP 25,376

Dominated by its ruined castle, the delightful riverside town of Newark paid the price for backing the wrong side in the English Civil War. After surviving four sieges by Cromwell's men, the town was ransacked by Roundheads when Charles I surrendered in 1646.

Sights

Newark's large, cobbled square is overlooked by the fine, timber-framed, 14th-century **Olde White Hart Inn** (now a building society), and the **Clinton Arms Hotel** (today a shopping precinct), from where former prime minister Gladstone made his first political speech and where Lord Byron stayed while his first volume of poetry was published.

FREE **Newark Castle** CASTLE

(Castlegate; 9am-6pm) Set in a pretty park overlooking the River Trent, the ruins include an impressive Norman gate and a series of underground passages and chambers. The real King John, portrayed as a villain in the Robin Hood legend, died here in 1216. Contact the tourist office (p461) about tours.

FREE **Millgate Museum** MUSEUM

(01636-655730; 48 Millgate; 10.30am-4.30pm) Southwest of Newark Castle along the river, this family-friendly place is packed with old agricultural and industrial machinery, but the highlight is the walk-through re-creation of a Victorian shopping street.

Newark Air Museum MUSEUM

(01636-707170; www.newarkairmuseum.org; adult/child £7/4; 10am-5pm) About 2 miles east of Newark by the Winthorpe Showground, this air museum has an impressive collection of aircraft, including a fearsome Vulcan bomber.

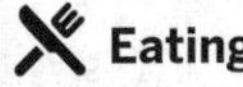

Eating

TOP CHOICE **The Old Bakery Tea Rooms** TEAHOUSE £

(01636-611501; www.oldbakerytearooms.co.uk; 4 Queens Head Court; mains £5.95-8.95; 9.30am-5pm Mon-Sat;) A Hansel-and-Gretel-like timber-framed Tudor building dating from the 15th century houses this enchanting tearoom. Cakes are tantalisingly displayed in the windows, and everything is baked fresh on the premises. Lunch specials include soups, frittata, bruschetta, and smoked salmon brioche.

Cafe Bleu MODERN EUROPEAN ££

(01636-610141; www.cafebleu.co.uk; 14 Castlegate; mains £11.95-18.95; lunch daily, dinner Mon-Sat) The riverside setting is part of the allure at this sophisticated restaurant serving Mediterranean-inspired cuisine. Live classical and jazz musicians perform on Tuesdays and Wednesdays, and the art-filled dining room has open fires. In fine weather, head to the courtyard garden.

Information

Tourist Office (01636-655765; www.visitnewarkandsherwood.co.uk; Gilstrap Centre, Castlegate; 10am-4pm) Runs castle tours and has a small Civil War museum.

Getting There & Away

BUS Useful bus services:

Nottingham Bus 90; 55 minutes, hourly (every two hours on Sunday).

Southwell Bus 28 or 29 (30 minutes, at least hourly) or the less frequent bus 3.

TRAIN Newark has two train stations. Trains on the East Coast Main Line between London and the north stop at **Newark North Gate**, while East Midlands trains between Leicester, Nottingham and Lincoln stop at **Newark Castle** station.

LINCOLNSHIRE

One of the most sparsely populated corners of England, Lincolnshire's farmland unfolds over low hills and the pancake-flat Fens, and is dotted with windmills and, more recently, wind turbines. Surrounding its charming county town of Lincoln, you'll find seaside resorts, scenic waterways, serene nature reserves, and stone-built towns tailor-made for English period dramas.

Activities

The 140-mile **Viking Way** walking trail snakes across the gentle hills of the Lincolnshire Wolds from the banks of the River Humber to Oakham in Leicestershire.

Cyclists can find information on routes across the county in any of the local tourist offices; the **Water Rail Way** is a sculpture-lined, flat on-road cycling route that follows the River Witham through classic Fens countryside between Lincoln and Boston.

Information

South West Lincs (www.southwestlincs.com) Also covers Rutland.

Visit Lincolnshire (www.visitlincolnshire.com)

Visit North Lincolnshire (www.visitnorthlincolnshire.com)

Getting There & Around

East Midlands trains connect Lincoln, Newark Castle and Nottingham, and Newark North Gate and Grantham lie on the East Coast Main Line between London and Edinburgh. Local buses link Lincolnshire's towns, but services are slow and infrequent. Check the transport pages at www.lincolnshire.gov.uk, which also has cycling route info.

Lincoln

POP 85,595

A bustling metropolis by Lincolnshire standards, but a sleepy backwater compared with almost anywhere else, Lincolnshire's county town is a tangle of cobbled medieval streets surrounding its colossal 12th-century cathedral. This is one of the Midlands' most beautiful cities – the lanes that topple over the edge of Lincoln Cliff are lined with Tudor town houses, ancient pubs and quirky independent stores. Flanking the River Witham at the base of the hill, the new town is less absorbing, but the revitalised Brayford Waterfront development by the university is an idyllic spot to watch the boats go by.

Sights

Lincoln Cathedral CHURCH

(http://lincolncathedral.com; Minster Yard; adult/child £6/1; ⏱7.15am-8pm Mon-Fri, to 6pm Sat & Sun) Towering over Lincoln like a medieval skyscraper, Lincoln's magnificent cathedral is a breathtaking representation of divine power on earth. The great tower rising above the crossing is the third-highest in England at 83m, but in medieval times, a lead-encased wooden spire added a further

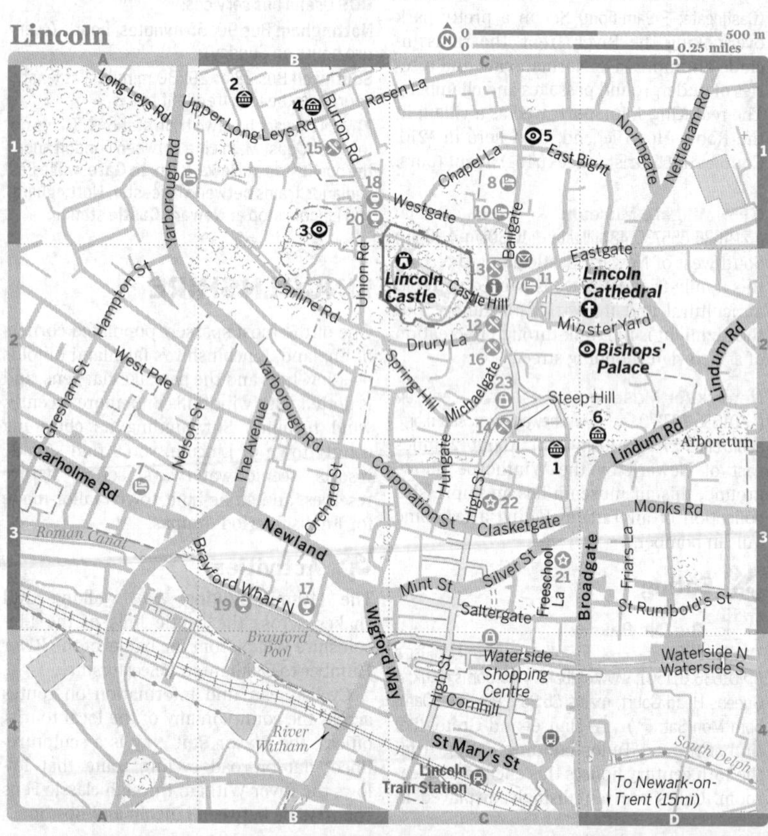

79m, topping even the great pyramids of Giza.

The first Lincoln cathedral was constructed between 1072 and 1092, but it fell in a devastating fire in 1141, and the second cathedral was destroyed by an earthquake in 1185. Bishop Hugh of Avalon (St Hugh) rebuilt and massively expanded the cathedral, creating one of the largest Gothic buildings in Europe.

On the fabulous exterior, restored Norman friezes show Adam and Eve bringing sin into the world, and Jesus making the ultimate sacrifice to undo the damage.

The vast interior of the church is too large for modern congregations – services take place in **St Hugh's Choir**, a church within a church running east from the crossing. The choir stalls are accessed through a magnificent carved stone screen; look north to see the stunning rose window known as the Dean's Eye (from 1192), mirrored to the south by the floral flourishes of the Bishop's Eye (1330). There's more stained glass in the three Services Chapels in the North Transept.

The glory of Lincoln cathedral is in the detail. Beyond St Hugh's Choir, the **Angel Choir** is supported by 28 columns topped by carvings of angels and foliate scrollwork. Tucked atop one of the columns is the official emblem of Lincoln, the tiny Lincoln Imp – a cheeky horned pixie, allegedly turned to stone by the angels after being sent by the devil to vandalise the church.

Other interesting details include the 10-sided **chapter house** – where Edward I held his parliament, and where the climax of *The Da Vinci Code* was filmed in 2005.

Don't miss the one-hour **guided tours**, which take place at least twice a day, plus less-frequent tours of the roof and the tower. All are included in the admission price. The best time to hear the organ resounding through the cathedral is during evensong (5.30pm Monday to Saturday, 3.45pm Sunday).

Lincoln Castle CASTLE
(www.lincolnshire.gov.uk/lincolncastle; adult/child £6/4; ⏲10am-6pm) One of the first castles erected by the victorious William the Conqueror to keep his new kingdom in line, Lincoln Castle offers awesome views over the city and miles of surrounding countryside. Highlights include the chance to view one of the four surviving copies of the **Magna Carta** (dated 1215), and the grim **Victorian prison chapel**, dating back to the days when this was the county jailhouse and execution ground.

Free **guided tours** of the castle run once or twice daily (weekends only in December and January).

Bishops' Palace HISTORIC SITE
(EH; ☎01522-527468; www.english-heritage.org.uk; adult/child £4.50/2.70; ⏲10am-5pm Thu-Mon

Lincoln

Top Sights

Bishops' Palace	D2
Lincoln Castle	C2
Lincoln Cathedral	D2

Sights

1 Collection	C3
2 Ellis Mill	B1
3 Lawn	B1
4 Museum of Lincolnshire Life	B1
5 Newport Arch	C1
6 Usher Gallery	D2

Sleeping

7 Admiral Guest House	A3
8 Bail House	C1
9 Carline Guest House	A1
10 The Castle Hotel	C1
11 White Hart Hotel	C2

Eating

12 Brown's Pie Shop	C2
13 Gino's	C2
14 Jew's House	C2
15 Old Bakery	B1
Reform	(see 10)
16 Wig & Mitre	C2

Drinking

17 Royal William IV	B3
18 Strugglers Inn	B1
19 The Electric Bar & Restaurant	B3
20 Victoria	B1

Entertainment

21 Lincoln Drill Hall	C3
22 Lola Lo	C3

Shopping

23 Readers Rest	C2

TOP LINCOLN TIPS

Walking between Lincoln's old and new towns can feel like an Everest expedition. Fortunately, Lincoln's 'Little Green Bus', the **Walk & Ride** (all-day pass adult/child £3/1.60) service runs every 20 minutes from the Stonebow at the corner of High St and Saltergate to the cathedral and Newport Arch, then back via Brayford Waterfront and the train station.

To tour the city in comfort, hop aboard the new Tour Lincoln bus. Tickets are sold at the tourist office; tours last one hour and tickets are valid all day. The tourist office also sells the three-day **Visit Lincoln Pass** (adult/family £12/35), giving access to several heritage sites, including the castle, cathedral and Bishops' Palace; and the three-day **Explore Lincoln Pass** (adult/family £20/50), which includes both the Tour Lincoln bus and the Visit Lincoln Pass.

Apr-Oct, 10am-4pm Sat & Sun Nov-Mar) Beside Lincoln Cathedral are the time-ravaged but still imposing ruins of the 12th-century Bishops' Palace, gutted by parliamentary forces during the Civil War. From here, the local bishops once controlled a diocese stretching from the Humber to the Thames. Entertaining audioguides are included in admission.

FREE **Collection** MUSEUM
(www.thecollectionlincoln.org; Danes Tce; ⏲10am-4pm daily, from 10.45am 1st Sun of month) Archaeology bursts into life with loads of hands-on displays where kids can handle artefacts and dress up in period costume. Check out the crushed skull of a 4000-year-old 'yellowbelly' (the local term for, well, the locals), pulled from a Neolithic burial site near Sleaford.

FREE **Usher Gallery** GALLERY
(www.thecollectionlincoln.org; Lindum Rd; ⏲10am-5pm Tue-Sat, 1-5pm Sun) A handsome Edwardian building, decorated with carvings of cow skulls, houses the town gallery's impressive collection of works by such greats as Turner, Lowry and English watercolourist, Peter de Wint (1784–1849).

FREE **Museum of Lincolnshire Life** MUSEUM
(Old Barracks, Burton Rd; ⏲10am-4pm daily Apr-Sep, closed Sun Oct-Mar) In an old Victorian barracks, displays at this charming community museum span everything from Victorian farm implements to the tin-can tank built in Lincoln for WWI. Around the corner from the museum is the cute little **Ellis Mill** (Mill Rd; admission free; ⏲2-5pm Sat & Sun Apr-Sep, 2pm-dusk Sun Oct-Mar), the windmill that ground the town's flour in the 18th century.

Lawn GARDENS
(www.thelawninlincoln.co.uk; Union Rd; ⏲10am-5pm Mon-Sat, 10.30am-5pm Sun) The lush grounds of the town's former lunatic asylum contain the ornamental **Dawber Gardens** and the **Sir Joseph Banks Conservatory**, containing descendants of some of the plants brought back by the botanist who accompanied Captain Cook to Australia.

Tours

History-focused 90-minute guided **walking tours** (☎01522-521256; www.lincolnguidedtours.co.uk; adult/child £4/free; ⏲tours 11am daily Jul & Aug, Sat & Sun Jun, Sep & Oct) run from outside the tourist office (p467). Genuinely spooky 75-minute **ghost walks** (☎01522-874056; adult/child £4/2; ⏲7pm Wed-Sat year-round) depart adjacent to the tourist office in Castle Sq.

Boat trips along the River Witham and Fossdyke Navigation, a canal system dating back to Roman times, start from Brayford Waterfront. The **Brayford Belle** (☎01522-881200; www.lincolnboattrips.com; adult/child £6.50/4) runs five times daily from Easter to September, and weekends only in October. No credit cards.

See **Tour Lincoln** (adult/child/family £10/4/25) for bus tours.

Sleeping

TOP CHOICE **The Castle Hotel** BOUTIQUE HOTEL ££
(☎01522-538801; www.castlehotel.net; Westgate; s incl breakfast £90, d £110-120; P 📶) Each of the 18 rooms at this boutique hotel have been exquisitely refurbished in olive, truffle and oyster tones. Built on the site of Lincoln's Roman forum in 1852, the redbrick building's incarnations variously include a school and WWII lookout station. Take advantage of the great-value dinner, bed and breakfast deals at its award-winning new restaurant, Reform.

Bail House B&B ££
(☎01522-541000; www.bailhouse.co.uk; 34 Bailgate; r from £89; P@) Stone walls, worn flagstones, secluded gardens and one room with an extraordinary timber-vaulted ceiling are just some of the charms of this lovingly restored Georgian town house in central Lincoln. There's even a seasonal heated outdoor swimming pool.

White Hart Hotel HOTEL ££
(☎01522-526222; www.whitehart-lincoln.co.uk; Bailgate; s/d from £70/90; P@) You can't get more venerable than this grand dame of Lincoln hotels, sandwiched between castle and cathedral with a history dating back 600 years and flowing countrified rooms.

Carline Guest House B&B ££
(☎01522-530422; www.carlineguesthouse.co.uk; 1-3 Carline Rd; s/d/f from £40/60/80; P) An elegant Edwardian brick house, in a stylish residential part of town, with big, flowery rooms.

Admiral Guest House B&B £
(☎01522-544467; www.admiralguesthouse.co.uk; 16-18 Nelson St; s/d £30/55; P) A hike from the old town in the industrial terraces northwest of Brayford Wharf, the Admiral mainly scores points for its prices.

Eating

Tearooms are dotted along Steep Hill. Unless otherwise stated, restaurant reservations are recommended in the evenings.

TOP CHOICE **Reform** MODERN BRITISH ££
(☎01522 538801; www.castlehotel.net; The Castle Hotel, Westgate; mains £11.95-22.95; ⊙breakfast, lunch & dinner) Inside the stylised Castle Hotel, the menu of its sophisticated restaurant, Reform, is inspired by local, seasonal produce. Starters such as Stilton mousse or crispy pig cheeks with polenta are followed by mains such as *confit* of pork belly or seared scallops and pigeon, but the real showstoppers are desserts such as warm plum and raspberry crumble tart with white chocolate ice cream and quince purée.

Brown's Pie Shop BRITISH ££
(☎01522-527330; www.brownspieshop.co.uk; 33 Steep Hill; takeaway pies £1.50-3, lunch mains £8.95-11.95, dinner mains £9.95-24.95; ⊙lunch & dinner Mon-Sat, noon-8pm Sun) This long-established pie shop is one of Lincoln's top tables, encompassing a smart upstairs dining room and cosy brick-lined basement. Its hearty pies are stuffed with locally sourced beef, rabbit and game.

Jew's House MODERN EUROPEAN ££
(☎01522-524851; www.jewshouserestaurant.co.uk; 15 The Strait (Steep Hill); 2-/3-course lunch menus £13.50-17.50, mains £14.75-26; ⊙lunch & dinner Tue-Sat) Set in one of England's oldest houses, the Romanesque Jew's House, constructed in around 1160, this local favourite serves up gourmet fare in atmospheric surrounds. For the ultimate indulgence, go for the six-course tasting menu (£49.50).

Gino's ITALIAN ££
(☎01522-513770; www.ginoslincoln.co.uk; 7 Gordon Rd, Bailgate; mains £12.95-24.95) The heavenly aromas that greet you outside attest to Gino's high quality cuisine. In addition to a long list of fish, chicken and meat dishes, there's a stellar selection of pizzas and pastas.

Wig & Mitre PUB ££
(www.wigandmitre.com; 30 Steep Hill; mains £10-15; ⊙breakfast, lunch & dinner) Civilised pub-restaurant the Wig & Mitre has an excellent menu yet retains the ambience of a friendly local. Food is served throughout the day, from morning fry-ups to lunchtime sandwiches and filling evening roasts. Bookings not necessary.

DON'T MISS

LINCOLN CITY GATES

Lincoln is ringed by historic city gates. Starting at the north end of the city, the **Newport Arch** (Bailgate) is a relic from the original Roman settlement; traffic has been passing beneath this arch for at least 1500 years. A short walk south, the 13th-century **Exchequergate** leads from Castle Hill to the courtyard of Lincoln Cathedral, marking the spot where tenant farmers gathered to pay rent to the land-owning Bishops of Lincoln.

Behind the cathedral, Pottergate is bookended by the free-standing Victorian **Priory Gate**, and the ancient **Pottergate**, part of the fortifications that once protected the Bishops' Palace. At the bottom of the hill, by the junction of High St and Saltergate, the 1520-constructed Gothic gatehouse **Stonebow** marks the southern entrance to the medieval city and contains the **Lincoln Guildhall**.

 **Old Bakery** MODERN BRITISH ££
(📞01522-576057; www.theold-bakery.co.uk; 26-28 Burton Rd; mains £14-20.95; ⏰lunch Tue-Sun, dinner Tue-Sat) The menu at this eccentric foodie haven is built around impeccably presented local produce and, appropriately, freshly baked bread. It also has a deli, offers regular four-and-a-half-hour **cookery lessons** (£90), and has four quaint **guest rooms** upstairs.

Drinking

Bland chain pubs crowd the High St, but there are a few worthy independent public houses.

Strugglers Inn PUB
(83 Westgate) A sunny walled courtyard beer garden out back, a cosy interior and a superb selection of real ales on tap make this the pick of Lincoln's independent pubs.

The Electric Bar & Restaurant BAR
(📞01522-565182; www.electricbarandrestaurant.co.uk; 5th fl, DoubleTree by Hilton Lincoln, Brayford Wharf North; 📶) Opened in 2012 on the top floor of Lincoln's snazzy new four-star DoubleTree by Hilton hotel, this swish spot has twin glass balconies with glittering river views, streamlined decor, a great cocktail list, regular live jazz, and a restaurant serving sophisticated British dishes with a retro twist (eg ham hock terrine, and iced peanut butter parfait).

Victoria PUB
(6 Union Rd) A serious beer-drinker's pub with a pleasant patio looking up at the castle's western walls, the Victoria has a huge selection of guest brews, cask ales, thick stouts and superb ciders.

Royal William IV PUB
(Brayford Wharf North) Part of the regenerated Brayford Waterfront development, this student-friendly stone pub offers a more intimate drinking environment than the brash chain restaurants on all sides.

Entertainment

Ask at the tourist office to find our more information about theatre venues.

Lincoln Drill Hall ARTS CENTRE
(www.lincolndrillhall.com; Freeschool Lane) Downhill near the station, this stern-looking building hosts bands, orchestras, stage shows, comedy and daytime festivals.

Lola Lo CLUB
(www.lolalolincoln.com; 280-281 High St; ⏰10pm-3am Mon-Thu, from 8pm Fri & Sat) Lincoln might be a long way from the Pacific, but this Tiki bar and club goes all out to convince revellers otherwise, with tropical cocktails and themed nights such as Tuesday's millionaire-style Decorus night, Wednesday's Naughty Disko and Thursday's Kitsch night.

Shopping

Steep Hill is packed with bijou shops selling quirky gifts, antiques and bric-a-brac.

Readers Rest BOOKS
(13-14 Steep Hill; ⏰closed Sun) A delightfully chaotic secondhand bookshop with stacks of local history and children's titles.

LINCOLNSHIRE: BOMBER COUNTY

Following WWI, the Royal Air Force (RAF) was formed in 1918 and two years later its college was established in Lincolnshire. During WWII, England's 'Bomber County' was home to numerous squadrons and by 1945 had more airfields (49) than any other county in the country. US Navy flying boats flew anti-submarine patrols along the coast and B-29 bombers were based here.

Lincoln's tourist office has details of the county's aviation legacies, including Spitfires and the Avro Lancaster *City of Lincoln* at the **Battle of Britain Memorial Flight Visitor Centre** (📞01522-782040; www.lincolnshire.gov.uk/bbmf; Dogdyke Rd, Coningsby; admission free, hangar tours adult/child £6/4; ⏰10am-5pm Mon-Fri), and the **Lincolnshire Aviation Heritage Centre** (📞01790-763207; www.lincsaviation.co.uk; East Kirkby, near Spilsby; adult/child £7/3; ⏰10am-5pm Mon-Sat Easter-Oct, to 4pm Mon-Sat Nov-Easter), on a WWII Bomber Command airfield complete with its original wartime control tower. The RAF's **Waddington Air Show** (www.waddingtonairshow.co.uk) takes place 3 miles south of Lincoln on the first weekend in July.

WORTH A TRIP

DODDINGTON HALL

About 5 miles west of Lincoln on the B1190, peaceful **Doddington Hall** (☎01522-694308; www.doddingtonhall.com; adult/child £9.50/4.75, garden only £5/2.75; ⊙11am-5pm Wed, Sun & bank holidays Apr-Sep, house open from 1pm) was a creation of the talented Robert Smythson, who also designed Longleat (p294) and Hardwick Hall (p480). Completed in 1600 and inhabited by the same family ever since, this handsome Elizabethan pile has hectares of gorgeous ornamental gardens and all the tapestries, oil paintings and heirlooms you could ask for. It's best reached by your own wheels; a taxi from Lincoln costs around £12 one-way.

Information

Check out www.lovelincoln.co.uk or www.visitlincolnshire.com for events listings.

County Hospital (☎01522-512512; off Greetwell Rd)

Post Office (90 Bailgate) Has a currency exchange service.

Tourist Office (☎01522-545458; www.visitlincoln.com; 9 Castle Hill; ⊙10.30am-4pm Mon-Sat) Friendly office in a handsome 16th-century building by the castle.

Getting There & Away

Bus

National Express (p819) runs direct bus services from Lincoln to London (£24.90, 5¼ hours, daily) and Birmingham (£6.60, three hours, daily). Local **Stagecoach** (☎0845 605 0605; www.stagecoach.com) buses mainly run Monday to Saturday; useful services include the following:

Grantham Bus 1; 1¼ hours, half-hourly (five on Sundays)

Louth Bus 10; one hour, six daily

Newark Bus 46; 1¼ hours, four to five daily

Skegness Bus 6; 1½ hours, hourly

Train

Getting to and from Lincoln by rail usually involves changing trains.

Boston Change at Sleaford; £12.30, 1¼ hours, every two hours

Peterborough £14.50, 1½ hours, hourly

Sheffield £13.10, one hour and 20 minutes, hourly

Grantham & Around

POP 34,592

Grantham would be just another country town were it not for two famous 'yellow-bellies' (as Lincolnshire locals call themselves) – Isaac Newton and former prime minister Margaret Thatcher, the daughter of a humble Grantham greengrocer, who plied his trade at 2 North Pde. The town itself has just a few sights, but there are some fascinating country houses in the surrounding countryside, including Newton's birthplace.

Sights

St Wulfram's CHURCH

(☎01476-561342; www.stwulframs.org.uk; ⊙9am-4pm Mon-Sat) You can easily spot the parish church of St Wulfram's thanks to its pin-sharp 85m spire, which provides a nesting site for peregrine falcons. Inside are an interesting crypt chapel and a 16th-century chained library, where Newton once pored over his study.

Belton House HISTORIC BUILDING

(NT; A607; adult/child £11.50/7.50, grounds only £9.50/6.30; ⊙house 12.30-5pm Wed-Sun, grounds 10.30am-5.30pm daily) About 3 miles northeast of Grantham, Belton House is a dream location for English period dramas – indeed, the mansion crops up in numerous period romps from the BBC, including *Jane Eyre, Tom Jones* and the Colin Firth version of *Pride and Prejudice*. Built in 1688 in classic Restoration style, the house features some stunning period details, including ornate woodcarvings attributed to the master Dutch carver Grinling Gibbons, as well as elegant formal gardens. Centrebus 9 (15 minutes) and Stagecoach bus 1 run here from near Grantham train station.

Woolsthorpe Manor HISTORIC BUILDING

(NT; Water Lane; adult/child £6.65/3.35; ⊙11am-5pm Wed-Sun) Newton fans may feel the gravitational pull of the great man's former home, about 8 miles south of Grantham. The 17th-century house contains reconstructions of Newton's rooms; the apple that inspired the theory of gravity allegedly fell from the tree in the garden. There's a nifty kids science room and a cafe. Take Centrebus 9 from Grantham (20 minutes, five to six Monday to Saturday).

Belvoir Castle CASTLE

(☎01476-871002; www.belvoircastle.com; adult/child £15/8, gardens only £8/5; ⏲castle tours generally 11.15am, 1.15pm & 3.15pm, gardens 11am-5pm Sun & Mon May-Aug, generally closed rest of year) The ancestral home of the Duke and Duchess of Rutland, Belvoir (pronounced 'beaver') is a magnificent baroque and Gothic fantasy constructed in the 19th century over the ruins of three previous castles. Still inhabited by the Manners family, it overflows with tapestries, priceless furniture and ancient oil paintings (including a magnificent portrait of Henry VIII by Holbein). Hours can vary.

Although Belvoir Castle is technically in Leicestershire, Grantham, 6 miles east, is the nearest town.

Sleeping & Eating

TOP CHOICE **Chequers Inn** INN ££

(☎01476-870701; www.chequersinn.net; Main St, Woolsthorpe by Belvoir; mains £10.50-19.50) Some 7 miles southwest of Grantham, you can dine on the sunny patio overlooking Belvoir Castle, the open-fire-warmed interior or the rambling garden bordering a sheep-filled paddock at this enchanting country inn. Some of the finest food in the Midlands spans starters such as fried brie or warm crab salad, followed by mains such as escalopes of English rose veal and desserts including baked white chocolate cheesecake with pistachio ice cream. A fabulous range of ciders and real ales are on tap. Across the lane, the former stables house four simple but stylish guest rooms.

Red House B&B £

(☎01476-579869; www.red-house.com; 74 North Pde; s/d from £35/53; P@🛜) This handsome Georgian town house has large, spick-and-span rooms. The welcome is very friendly and rooms have big TVs, minifridges and microwaves.

Angel & Royal Hotel HOTEL ££

(☎01476-565816; www.angelandroyal.com; High St; bistro mains £9.75-13.95; d from £80; P@🛜) In the centre of town, this courtyard hotel has played host to no fewer than seven kings of England since 1200. These days, commoners are just as welcome, and the rooms have all the anticipated olde-English touches. In addition to the classy **Berties Bistro** (open lunch and dinner daily), there's a regal 1st-floor restaurant, the **King's Room** (open according to demand).

Blue Pig PUB

(9 Vine St) A cosy nook of a pub in a half-timbered Tudor building, serving a fine selection of thirst-quenching real ales.

Information

Tourist Office (☎01476-406166; www.guildhallartscentre.com; St Peter's Hill; ⏲9.30am-4.30pm Mon-Fri, 9.30am-2pm Sat) In the Guildhall Arts Centre.

Getting There & Away

Lincoln Bus 1; one hour and 20 minutes, hourly (four services Sunday)

Stamford Bus 4; 1¼ hours, three daily Monday to Saturday

TRAIN Change at Newark North Gate (£7.30, 15 minutes, hourly) to get to Lincoln (£10, 1¼ hours). Direct trains run to and from London King's Cross (£24, 1¼ hours, twice hourly).

Stamford

POP 19,525

One of England's prettiest towns, Stamford seems frozen in time, with elegant streets lined with honey-coloured limestone buildings and hidden alleyways dotted with hearty alehouses, interesting eateries and small independent boutiques. A forest of historic church spires rises overhead and the gently gurgling River Welland meanders through the town centre. Unsurprisingly, the town is favourite with film-makers looking for the quintessential vision of England, appearing in everything from *Pride and Prejudice* to *The Da Vinci Code*.

Sights

The town's top attraction is nearby Burghley House (p469), but just strolling the streets is a delight. Drop in on **St Mary's Church** (St Mary's St), with its charmingly wonky broach spire, or explore the 15th-century chapel and chambers of the **William Browne Hospital** (Broad St; adult/child £2.50/1; ⏲11am-4pm Sat & Sun May-Sep).

Sleeping

TOP CHOICE **George Hotel** HISTORIC HOTEL £££

(☎01780-750750; www.georgehotelofstamford.com; 71 St Martin's; s/d from £95/175, 4-poster d £230; P@🛜) Stamford's luxurious landmark

DON'T MISS

BURGHLEY HOUSE

Lying just a mile south of Stamford, flamboyant **Burghley House** (www.burghley.co.uk; adult/child incl sculpture garden £13.80/7; ⏲11am-5pm Sat-Thu mid-Mar–late Oct, closed late Oct–mid-Mar) (pronounced 'bur-lee') was built by Queen Elizabeth's chief adviser William Cecil, whose descendants have lived here ever since.

Set in more than 810 hectares of grounds, landscaped by the famous Lancelot 'Capability' Brown, the house bristles with cupolas, pavilions, belvederes and chimneys. The staterooms are a treasure trove of ormolu clocks, priceless oil paintings, Louis XIV furniture and magnificent murals painted by the 17th-century Italian master Antonio Verrio.

The renowned **Burghley Horse Trials** take place here in early September. Follow the marked path for 15 minutes through the park by Stamford train station.

inn opened its doors in 1597 and its rooms impeccably blend period charm and modern elegance, while its restaurant serves superior Modern British cuisine.

The William Cecil at Stamford HISTORIC HOTEL £££
(☎01780-750070; www.thewilliamcecil.co.uk; High St, St Martins; s/d midweek £100/110, weekends £120/130; P wifi) Within the Burghley Estate, rooms at this stunningly renovated hotel are inspired by Burghley House, with period furnishings and luxuries like in-room claw-foot baths. The smart restaurant opens to a wicker-chair-strewn patio.

Stamford Lodge B&B ££
(☎01780-482932; www.stamfordlodge.co.uk; 66 Scotgate; s/d £65/85; wifi) Centrally situated, this 18th-century former bakehouse has five fresh, modern rooms and excellent breakfasts.

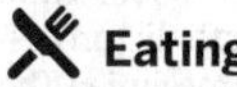

Eating

The finest meals in town are served at the George Hotel (p468) and The William Cecil at Stamford (p469).

Tobie Norris PUB ££
(www.tobienorris.com; 12 St Pauls St; mains £9.95-15.95; ⏲lunch daily, dinner Mon-Sat) A wonderful stone-walled, flagstone-floored pub with a warren of rooms and a sunny courtyard, serving international dishes like wasabi chicken with crushed plum potatoes and wholesome ales from the Ufford microbrewery.

Jim's Yard MODERN BRITISH ££
(☎01780-756080; www.jimsyard.biz; 3 Ironmonger St; mains £13-19; ⏲lunch & dinner Tue-Sat) Tucked in a courtyard off a narrow laneway, Jim's upmarket fare is sourced from local producers.

Voujon INDIAN ££
(☎01780-757030; www.voujonrestaurant.co.uk; 26 Broad St; mains £6.85-12.95) Well-prepared Indian favourites are served up in stylish surroundings.

☆ Entertainment

Stamford Arts Centre ARTS CENTRE
(☎01780-763203; www.stamfordartscentre.com; 27 St Mary's St) Hosts everything from live jazz and art-house cinema to stand-up comedy.

ℹ Information

Tourist Office (☎01780-755611; www.southwestlincs.com; 27 St Mary's St; ⏲9.30am-5pm Mon-Sat) In the Stamford Arts Centre.

ℹ Getting There & Away

Grantham Kimes bus 4; 1¼ hours, three daily Monday to Saturday

London National Express (p819); £15.30, three hours, one daily

Peterborough Delaine Buses 201; one hour, hourly Monday to Saturday

TRAIN Cross-country trains run to Birmingham (£14, 1½ hours, hourly) and Stansted Airport (£17, 1¾ hours, hourly) via Cambridge (£9, 1¼ hours) and Peterborough (£7.30, 15 minutes).

Boston

POP 35,124

It's hard to believe that sleepy Boston was the inspiration for its larger and more famous American cousin. Although no Boston citizens sailed on the *Mayflower*, the town became a conduit for persecuted Puritans fleeing for religious freedom to the Netherlands and America. In the 1630s, the fiery sermons of Boston vicar John Cotton inspired many locals to follow their lead, among them the ancestors of John Quincy Adams, the sixth American president. These pioneers founded a namesake town in the new colony of Massachusetts, and the rest, as they say, is history.

Sights

St Botolph's Church CHURCH
(church free, tower adult/child £3/1; ⊙church 8am-4.30pm daily, tower 10am-4pm Mon-Sat, last climb 3pm) Built in the early 14th century, St Botolph's Church (the name Boston is a corruption of 'St Botolph's Stone') is known locally as the Stump in reference to the truncated appearance of its 88m-high tower. Puff your way up the 365 steps on a clear day and you'll see to Lincoln, 32 miles away.

FREE **Guildhall** MUSEUM
(☎01205-365954;www.bostonguildhall.co.uk;South St; ⊙10.30am-3.30pm Wed-Sat) Before escaping to the New World, the Pilgrim Fathers were briefly imprisoned in the 14th-century Guildhall, one of Lincolnshire's oldest brick buildings, dating from the 1390s and situated close to the River Witham. Inside are fun, interactive exhibits, as well as a restored 16th-century courtroom, and a recreated Georgian kitchen.

Maud Foster Windmill HISTORIC BUILDING
(☎01205-352188; www.maudfoster.co.uk; adult/child £4/2; ⊙10am-5pm Wed & Sat) About 800m northeast of Market Pl, England's tallest working windmill has seven floors that creak and tremble with every turn of the sails, and sells bags of flour milled on site.

Sleeping & Eating

White Hart PUB ££
(☎01205-311900; www.whitehartboston.com; 1-5 High St; s/d £78/98, mains £6.95-16.95; P@) Right in the middle of town, this handsome pub-hotel has tastefully modernised rooms and a decent menu in the Modern British mould.

Information

Tourist Office (☎01205-365954; www.boston guildhall.co.uk; South St; ⊙10.30am-3.30pm Wed-Sat) Inside the Guildhall.

Getting There & Away

Trains connect Boston with Skegness (£6.60, 30 minutes, hourly Monday to Saturday, nine on Sunday), and Lincoln (£12.30, 1¼ hours) via a change at Sleaford. Bus services include the Interconnect 7 to Skegness (one hour, hourly; reduced service Sunday).

Skegness

POP 16,806

Spread out along the sandy beach at Skegness (or 'Skeggy', as it is known to the locals), you'll find the ABC of the English seaside – amusements, bingo and candyfloss – accompanied by a soundtrack of klaxons and bells from the slot machines and fairground rides. Wind turbines resembling supersize daisies provide a surreal backdrop to thousands of mobile homes. Culture vultures will probably run a mile screaming, but the tacky spectacle has to be seen to be believed.

You can escape the beeps and flashing lights in the National Nature Reserve at **Gibraltar Point**, a pristine area of dunes and marshes 5km south of Skegness. The plentiful bird species include terns, skylarks and redshanks.

There are plenty of faded seaside hotels and cheap and cheerful B&Bs – the **tourist office** (☎0845 674 0505; www.embassythe atre.co.uk; Grand Pde; ⊙9.30am-4pm Sun-Wed, 9.30am-7pm Thu, 9.30am-7.30pm Fri & Sat) has listings and leaflets on local walks. It's located inside the **Embassy Centre** (www.em bassytheatre.co.uk), the centre of the Skeggy cabaret scene.

Trains run between Skegness and Boston (£6.60, 30 minutes, hourly Monday to Saturday, nine on Sunday). Bus services include the Interconnect 7 to Boston (one hour, hourly Monday to Saturday, reduced service Sunday) and the Interconnect 6 to Lincoln (1½ hours, hourly).

Louth

POP 15,930

About 23 miles northeast of Lincoln, straddling the line of zero longitude, the charming town of Louth was the starting point for a short-lived uprising against the Dissolution of the Monasteries in 1536. At the height of the revolt, 40,000 Catholic protestors marched on Lincoln and occupied the cathedral, before being driven back by the forces of Henry VIII.

THE FENS

The low-lying Fens were pulled from the desolate marshlands that once lined the east coast of Norfolk, Cambridgeshire and Lincolnshire. Dutch engineer Sir Cornelius Vermuyden was commissioned to hold back the waters with giant dykes and wind-powered pumps in the 17th century, creating new tracts of farmland. The spooky, windswept landscape is brilliantly captured in Graham Swift's haunting novel *Waterland*.

Visit while you can – with changing weather patterns and rising sea levels, it's estimated that up to 1544 sq miles could vanish beneath the still, black waters by the year 2030.

The best way to see the Fens today is to follow the **Water Rail Way** road cycle path between Boston and Lincoln, or to swing by one of its most attractive reserves, **Saltfleetby-Theddlethorpe Dunes National Nature Reserve** (www.naturalengland.org.uk; admission free; ⌚dawn-dusk), which erupts with orchids in early summer and attracts vast flocks of migratory wildfowl in spring and autumn. Dozens of short and long trails keep your feet dry as you negotiate the myriad lagoons. The reserve is 10 miles east of Louth at the end of the B1200; you'll need your own transport.

Sights

St James' Church CHURCH

(spire £1.50; ⌚10.30am-4pm Mon-Sat Easter-Christmas, 8am-noon Mon, Wed, Fri & Sat Christmas-Easter) Louth's top attraction – the tallest parish church spire in England – rises atop St James' Church, propped up by dramatic buttresses. The elbow-scraping climb up 198 steps to the top is rewarded by stellar views over the town and surrounding countryside. Captain John Smith, of Pocahontas fame, once worshipped here.

Opposite the churchyard at 47 Westgate, an archway leads to **Westgate Pl** and a row of impossibly cute terraced cottages, one of which bears a plaque commemorating the four years that Alfred Lord Tennyson spent here.

Louth Museum MUSEUM

(www.louthmuseum.co.uk; 4 Broadbank; adult/child £2.50/1.50; ⌚10am-4pm Tue-Sat Apr-Oct, closed Nov-Mar) A short walk north from the centre, the 100-year-old Louth Museum has displays on local history, including a reproduction of William Brown's *Panorama*, painted from the spire of St James' in 1844. You can view the original inside the **Sessions House** (Eastgate; ⌚10am-1pm Mon, Wed & Fri).

Sleeping & Eating

Priory HOTEL ££

(☎01507-602930; www.theprioryhotel.com; 149 Eastgate; s/d from £59/79; P 📶) This is a glorious, whitewashed Gothic-style building from 1818, set in gardens sprawling down to old ruins and a lake. Its nine rooms have beautiful period-style furnishings and its restaurant serves dinner (from £29.50; Monday to Saturday by reservation).

TOP CHOICE **The Cheese Shop** DELI £

(www.thecheeseshoplouth.com; 110 Eastgate; ⌚8am-5pm daily) Pack a delectable picnic at this aromatic artisan deli stocking dozens of cheeses, homemade chutneys and luscious quiches, like wild mushroom and garlic, as well as fine wines.

Chuzzlewits CAFE £

(20 Mercer Row; dishes £2.10-6.95; ⌚8am-4.30pm Tue-Sat) Gourmet sandwiches made with freshly baked bread and its locally famous Earl Grey teacake can be eaten inside this delightful cafe, or taken away to enjoy elsewhere.

Mad Hatter's Tearooms CAFE £

(117 Eastgate; dishes £1.40-5; ⌚9.30am-4pm Mon-Sat) This cute, flower-drenched place serves up a good selection of cakes, sandwiches and soups.

Information

Tourist Office (☎01507-609289; www.louth.org; cnr Eastgate & Cannon St; ⌚9am-5pm Mon, Tue, Thu & Fri, 9am-4pm Wed year-round, 10am-4pm Sat Easter-Oct) At the town hall.

Getting There & Away

Louth is best reached from Lincoln – take bus 10 (one hour, six daily).

NORTHAMPTONSHIRE

Dotted with villages full of pincushion cottages with thatched roofs and Tudor timbers, Northamptonshire also has a string of stately manors, including the ancestral homes of George Washington and Diana, Princess of Wales.

Getting Around

Northampton is the hub for bus services around the county – see the 'Transport & Streets' pages at www.northamptonshire.gov.uk for routes and timetables. Trains run by London Midland are useful for getting to/from Northampton; Corby and Kettering are on the East Midlands line.

Northampton

POP 194,458

Rebuilt after a devastating fire in 1675, Northamptonshire's county town was one of the prettiest in the Midlands, but WWII bombers and postwar town planners wreaked their usual havoc. Today navigating the one-way road system is a nightmare, not helped by poor signage, but the city's heart retains some grand architecture. Northampton played a significant role in the Wars of the Roses and the English Civil War, before shifting its attention to manufacturing shoes.

Sights & Activities

For more fine architecture, take a peek at the handsome **Sessions House** (containing the tourist office) and the **Guildhall** on George Row.

All Saints' Church CHURCH
(www.allsaintsnorthampton.com; George Row; ⌚9am-6pm) Constructed after the 1675 fire, All Saints' Church owes an obvious debt to the churches built by Sir Christopher Wren after the Great Fire of London, with an ornate barrel-vaulted ceiling and dark-wood organ and reredos.

Northampton Museum & Art Gallery MUSEUM, GALLERY
(www.northampton.gov.uk/museums; Guildhall Rd; ⌚10am-5pm Tue-Sat, 2-5pm Sun) Even those without a shoe fetish will get a kick out of the impressive displays, where you can learn about the history of shoemaking and footwear fashions.

St Peter's Church CHURCH
West of the central Market Sq, St Peter's Church – collect the key from the nearby **Ibis Hotel** (☎01604-608900; www.ibishotel.com; Sol Central, Marefair) – is a marvellous Norman edifice built in 1150 and adorned with ancient carvings.

Church of the Holy Sepulchre CHURCH
(⌚2-4pm Wed, 11am-3pm Sat May-Sep) North of the centre, beyond the eyesore bus station, the Church of the Holy Sepulchre is one of the few surviving round churches in the country, founded when the first Earl of Northampton returned from the Crusades in 1100.

Sleeping & Eating

The tourist office can advise on B&Bs in the area.

Church Bar & Restaurant MODERN EUROPEAN ££
(☎01604-603800; www.thechurchrestaurant.com; 67-83 Bridge St; mains £13-15; ⌚lunch & dinner Mon-Sat) At this superbly converted old church, you can feast on modern European cooking (bookings recommended), or sip a cocktail under the stained-glass windows in the bar.

Information

Tourist Office (☎01604-367997; www.explorenorthamptonshire.co.uk; Sessions House, George Row; ⌚8am-5.30pm Mon-Fri year-round, 10am-2pm Sat Apr-Sep)

Getting There & Away

BUS Greyfriars bus station is on Lady's Lane, just north of the Grosvenor shopping centre. National Express coach services:

Birmingham £7.40, one hour and 40 minutes, three daily

London £6.50, 2¼ hours, five daily

Nottingham £13.20, 2½ hours, one daily

TRAIN Northampton has good rail links with Birmingham (£12, one hour, half-hourly) and London Euston (£13, one hour, three hourly). The train station is about half a mile west of town along Gold St.

Around Northampton

Northamptonshire has a cache of ancient churches, some dating back to Saxon times. Many open only from May to September; Northhampton's tourist office has information, including bus schedules.

WORTH A TRIP

SULGRAVE MANOR

Sulgrave Manor (www.sulgravemanor.org.uk; adult/child £8.25/4; ⏲11am-4pm Tue-Sun May-Oct, closed Nov-Apr), an impressively preserved Tudor mansion, was built by Lawrence Washington in 1539 and the Washington family lived here for almost 120 years before Colonel John Washington, the great-grandfather of America's first president George Washington, sailed to Virginia in 1656.

Sulgrave Manor is southwest of Northampton, just off the B4525 near Banbury. Trains run to Banbury, from where you can take a taxi.

ALTHORP

The ancestral home of the Spencer family, **Althorp House** (☎bookings 01604-770107; www.althorp.com; adult/child £13/6, upper floors extra £2.50; ⏲11am-5pm Jul & Aug, last entry 4pm, closed Sep-Jun) – pronounced 'al-trup' – is the final resting place of Diana, Princess of Wales, who is commemorated by a memorial and museum. You don't have to be a Di devotee to enjoy the outstanding art collection, with works by Rubens, Gainsborough and Van Dyck. Tickets are limited and must be booked by phone or online; profits go to charities supported by the Princess Diana Memorial Fund.

Althorp is off the A428, 5.5 miles northwest of Northampton. Stagecoach bus 96 (hourly, not Sundays) runs from Northampton to Rugby, passing the gates to the Althorp estate, where you can call to arrange a pick up.

STOKE BRUERNE

POP 395

About 8 miles south of Northampton, brightly-painted barges frequent this charming little village nestled against the Grand Union Canal, the main drag of England's canal network. From here, you can follow the waterways all the way to Leicester, Birmingham or London. Set in a converted corn mill, the entertaining **National Waterways Museum** (www.nwm.org.uk/stoke; adult/child £4.75/3.10; ⏲11am-3pm Wed-Fri, 11am-5pm Sat & Sun) charts the history of the canal network and its bargemen, lock keepers and pit workers.

Several other boat owners offer summertime cruises and charters including 25-minute trips aboard the Boat Inn's **Indian Chief** (☎01604-862428; adult/child £3/2.50; ⏲Sun & bank holiday weekends).

For overnight stays, try **Waterways Cottage** (☎01604-863865; www.waterwayscottage.co.uk; Bridge Rd; d incl breakfast £75), an adorable thatched cottage right off the front of a biscuit box.

Meals and brews are served up at the canalside **Boat Inn** (☎01604-862428; www.boatinn.co.uk; mains £6.75-17.95; ⏲lunch & dinner).

Buses 86 and 87 both run between Stoke Bruerne and Northampton (30 minutes, six daily Monday to Saturday).

LEICESTERSHIRE & RUTLAND

Leicestershire was a vital creative hub during the Industrial Revolution, but its factories were a major target for German air raids in WWII and most towns in the county still bear the scars of wartime bombing. Nevertheless, there are some impressive remains, from Elizabethan castles to Roman ruins, while the busy capital, Leicester, offers a taste of India, with its temples and curry houses.

Centred on the water-sports playground Rutland Water, tiny Rutland was merged with Leicestershire in 1974, but in 1997 regained its 'independence' as England's smallest county.

Information

Leicestershire Tourism (www.goleicestershire.com)

Discover Rutland (www.discover-rutland.co.uk)

Getting There & Around

Leicester is well served by buses and trains. For bus routes and timetables, visit the 'Roads & Transport' pages at www.leics.gov.uk. Frequent buses connect Rutland to Leicester, Stamford and other surrounding towns.

Leicester

POP 279,923

Built over the buried ruins of two millenniums of history, Leicester (*les*-ter) suffered at the hands of the Luftwaffe and some ill-conceived postwar town planning. However, since the 1960s a massive influx of textile workers from India and Pakistan has established dozens of mosques and temples, transforming the city into a bustling global melting pot. Modern Leicester is alive with the sights, sounds and flavours of the subcontinent. Historical treasures include one of England's finest medieval guildhalls.

Sights

Apart from the National Space Centre, all of Leicester's **museums** (www.leicester.gov.uk/museums) are free.

FREE New Walk Museum & Art Gallery MUSEUM, GALLERY

(New Walk; ⌚10am-5pm Mon-Sat, from 11am Sun) Highlights of this grand Victorian museum include the revamped dinosaur galleries, the painting collection (with works by Francis Bacon, TS Lowry and Stanley Spencer), and the Egyptian gallery, where real mummies rub shoulders with displays on Boris Karloff's *The Mummy*.

FREE Guildhall HISTORIC BUILDING

(Guildhall Lane; ⌚11am-4.30pm Mon-Wed & Sat, 1-4.30pm Sun Feb-Nov, closed Dec & Jan) Leicester's perfectly preserved 14th-century guildhall is reputed to be the most haunted building in Leicester. You can search for spooks in the magnificent Great Hall, the wood-panelled Mayor's Parlour and the old police cells, which contain a reconstruction of a 19th-century gibbet.

Leicester

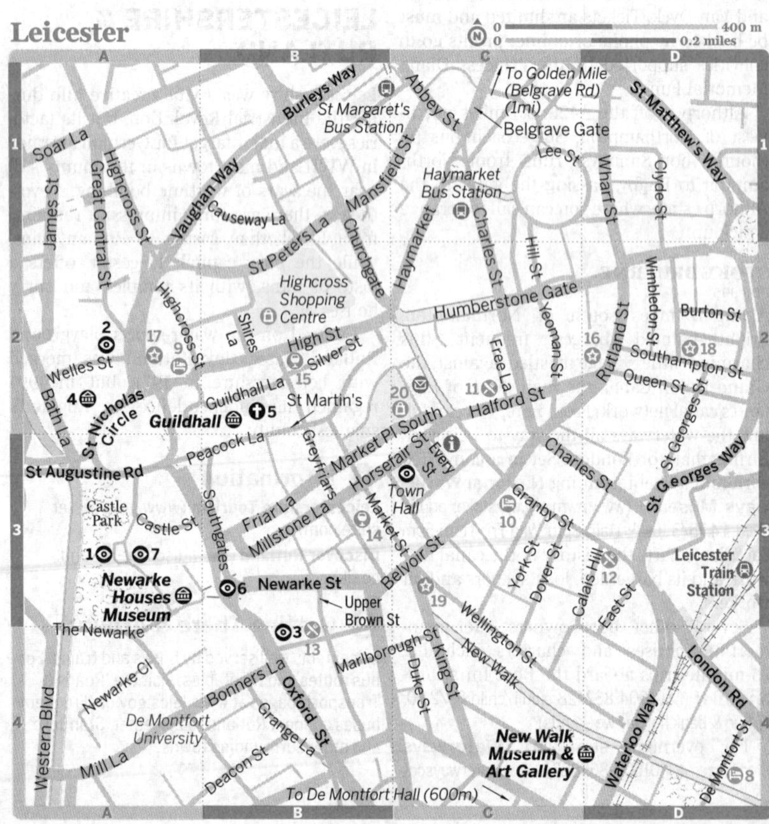

National Space Centre MUSEUM
(www.spacecentre.co.uk; adult/child £13/11; 10am-5pm Tue-Sun, last entry 3.30pm) Although British space missions usually launch from French Guiana or Kazakhstan, Leicester's space museum is still a fascinating introduction to the mysteries of the spheres. The ill-fated Beagle 2 mission to Mars was controlled from here and fun, kid-friendly displays cover everything from astronomy to the status of current space missions. The centre is off the A6 about 1.5 miles north of the city centre. Take bus 54 from Charles St in the centre.

FREE **Newarke Houses Museum** MUSEUM
(The Newarke; 10am-5pm Mon-Sat, from 11am Sun) Sprawling over two 16th-century mansions, this entertaining museum has exhibits detailing the lifestyles of local people through the centuries. Don't miss the walk-through recreation of a WWI trench, and the trophies of the Royal Leicestershire Regiment, including an outrageous snuff box made from a tiger's head.

Leicester Castle CASTLE
Scattered around the Newarke Houses Museum are the ruins of Leicester's medieval castle, where Richard III spent his final days before the Battle of Bosworth. The most impressive chunk of masonry is the monumental gateway known as the **Magazine** (Newarke St), once a storehouse for cannonballs and gunpowder. Clad in Georgian brickwork, the 12th-century **Great Hall** (Castle Yard) stands behind a 15th-century gate near the church of **St Mary de Castro** (Castle St), where Geoffrey Chaucer was married in 1336. The hall was closed at the time of writing due to structural damage; contact the tourist office for more details.

FREE **Jewry Wall Museum** MUSEUM
(St Nicholas Circle; 11am-4.30pm Feb-Oct, closed Nov-Jan) You can see fine Roman mosaics and frescos in this museum exploring the history of Leicester from Roman times to the modern day. In front of the museum is the **Jewry Wall**, part of Leicester's Roman baths. Tiles and masonry from the baths were incorporated in the walls of neighbouring **St Nicholas' Church**.

FREE **Leicester Cathedral** CHURCH
(www.cathedral.leicester.anglican.org; 21 St Martin's; 8am-6pm Mon-Sat, 7am-5pm Sun) In the midst of the shopping district on Guildhall Lane, this substantial medieval church features some striking carvings on its roof supports. Inside, you can see a memorial to Richard III, who rode out from Leicester to fatal defeat at the Battle of Bosworth.

Jain Centre TEMPLE
(www.jaincentre.com; 32 Oxford St; 8.30am-8.30pm Mon-Sat, to 6.30pm Sun) Housed in a converted church, the Jain Centre caters to followers of Jainism, the ancient religion that arose in India at the same time as Buddhism. Fronted with gleaming white marble, the lavish interior recalls the ancient

Leicester

Top Sights
Guildhall ... B2
New Walk Museum & Art Gallery ... D4
Newarke Houses Museum ... A3

Sights
1 Great Hall ... A3
2 Guru Nanak Gurdwara ... A2
3 Jain Centre ... B4
4 Jewry Wall Museum ... A2
5 Leicester Cathedral ... B2
6 Magazine ... B3
7 St Mary de Castro ... A3

Sleeping
8 Belmont House Hotel ... D4
9 Hotel Maiyango ... A2
10 Mercure Hotel ... C3

Eating
11 Good Earth ... C2
12 Kayal ... D3
13 Tinseltown Diner ... B4

Drinking
14 Firebug ... B3
15 The Globe ... B2

Entertainment
16 Curve Theatre ... D2
17 Mosh ... A2
18 Phoenix Square ... D2
19 Superfly ... C3

Shopping
20 Leicester Market ... C2

sandstone temples at Jaisalmer in Rajasthan. Remove your shoes before entering.

Guru Nanak Gurdwara TEMPLE
(9 Holy Bones; ⊙1-4pm Thu, 7-8.30pm Sat) Although outwardly plain, the Guru Nanak Gurdwara contains an engaging museum dedicated to Sikh culture and history, with an impressive model of the Golden Temple in Amritsar.

Festivals & Events

Leicester Comedy Festival COMEDY
(☎0116-261 6812; www.comedy-festival.co.uk; ⊙Feb) England's longest-running comedy festival draws big names as well as fresh talent.

Leicester Caribbean Carnival CULTURE
(www.leicestercarnival.com; ⊙1st Sat Aug) The biggest Caribbean celebration in the country after London's Notting Hill Carnival has colourful costumes galore.

Diwali RELIGION
(⊙Oct or Nov) Leicester's Hindu community celebrates the Festival of Lights with fireworks, parades and ornate street lights on Belgrave Rd. Dates vary according to the Hindu calendar.

Sleeping

TOP CHOICE **Hotel Maiyango** HOTEL ££
(☎0116-251 8898; www.maiyango.com; 13-21 St Nicholas Pl; d incl breakfast from £99; @☰) Attached to Leicester's funkiest bar at the end of the pedestrian High St, this sophisticated pad has spacious rooms decorated with handmade Asian furniture, contemporary art and massive plasma TVs. In addition to its lantern- and candle-lit **Maiyango Restaurant & Bar**, it also has a fabulous new **Kitchen Deli** gourmet shop-cafe.

Belmont House Hotel HOTEL ££
(☎0116-254 4773; www.belmonthotel.co.uk; De Montfort St; s/d from £59/79; P@☰) In a quiet location near De Montfort Hall, the 19th-century Belmont has been owned and run by the same family for four generations and recently received a stylish contemporary makeover.

Mercure Hotel HOTEL ££
(☎0844 815 9012; www.mercure.com; Granby St; d from £69; P@☰) Set in a listed Victorian building, this central, upmarket hotel spills out onto a noisy street that gets even noisier on weekend evenings.

Eating

A visit to Leicester isn't complete without singeing your taste buds on a curry along the **Golden Mile** (p477). Self-caterers should head to the fabulous Leicester Market (p477). The glitzy High Cross shopping centre on Shires Lane has upmarket chain restaurants.

Tinseltown Diner AMERICAN £
(www.tinseltown.co.uk; 5-9 Upper Brown St; mains £6.99-14.99; ⊙11.30am-2am Sun-Thu, 11.30am-3.30am Fri & Sat; ♿) Craving a triple-decker chilli burger or an Oreo cookie and peanut butter milkshake? This being Leicester, Tinseltown's effect is more Bollywood than Hollywood, but kids will love the menu and razzmatazz.

Kayal INDIAN ££
(☎0116-255 4667; www.kayalrestaurant.com; 153 Granby St; mains £8.99-14.99; ⊙lunch & dinner Mon-Fri, noon-11pm Sat, noon-10pm Sun) This small, upmarket Midlands chain trades the chicken tikka masala clichés for the spicy flavours of Kerala. Menu highlights include delicious dosas (lentil-flour pancakes) and zingy crab and kingfish curries.

Good Earth VEGETARIAN £
(☎0116-262 6260; 19 Free Lane; mains £3.50-6.50; ⊙noon-3pm Mon-Fri, 10am-4pm Sat; ✍) Justifiably popular for its wholesome veggie bakes, huge, fresh salads and homemade cakes.

DON'T MISS

STEAMING AROUND LEICESTER

A fun jaunt rather than a serious way to get from A to B, the classic **Great Central Railway** (☎01509-632323; www.gcrailway.co.uk; return adult/child £14/9) operates steam locomotives from Leicester North station on Redhill Circle to Loughborough Central, following the 8-mile route along which Thomas Cook ran the original package tour in 1841. The locos chug several days a week from June to August and weekends for the rest of the year – check timetables online. To reach Leicester North station, take bus 25 from the Haymarket bus station on Charles St (bus 26 to return).

DON'T MISS

THE GOLDEN MILE

Lined with sari stores, jewellery emporiums, and pure-veg curry houses, Belgrave Rd – aka the Golden Mile – is *the* place to come for authentic Indian vegetarian food. Menus are built around the spicy flavours of the south, with delicious staples such as dosas (lentil-flour pancakes), *idli* (steamed rice cakes) and huge thalis (plate meals), with a mix of vegetable curries, flatbreads, rice and condiments.

There are more top-notch eateries on the Golden Mile than you can shake a chapatti at. Our top pick is **Bobby's** (☎0116-266 0106; www.eatatbobbys.com; 154-156 Belgrave Rd; dishes £4.50-5.95;), famed for its *namkeen* – lentil-flour snacks that come in myriad shapes and sizes. After dining, stop in at numerous shops along the strip selling *mithai* (Indian sweets), sugary combinations of nuts, fruit and milk curds.

Belgrave Rd is about 1 mile northeast of the centre – follow Belgrave Gate and cross Burleys Flyover, or take bus 22 from Haymarket bus station.(map p474).

Drinking

The Maiyango (p476) hotel's Moroccan-style bar mixes Leicester's best cocktails.

The Globe PUB

(www.theglobeleicester.co.uk; 43 Silver St) In the atmospheric Lanes – a tangle of alleys south of the High St – this old-fashioned boozer offers fine draught ales and a crowd who rate their drinks by quality rather than quantity.

Firebug BAR

(www.firebugbar.co.uk; 1 Millstone Lane; noon-2am Mon & Tue, noon-4am Wed-Sat, 1pm-2am Sun) A lava lounge for the student crowd, the Firebug has a great selection of beers on tap, as well as theme nights, stage shows and gigs.

Entertainment

Leicester's new Cultural Quarter development centres on Rutland St. Mainstream clubs cluster around Churchgate and Gravel St.

Curve Theatre THEATRE

(☎0116-242 3595; www.curveonline.co.uk; Rutland St) A sleek artistic space with big-name shows and some innovative modern theatre. Call the ticket office to book backstage tours (adult/child £3/2). The bar is a sophisticated place for lunch or a sundowner.

Phoenix Square CINEMA

(☎0116-242 2803; www.phoenix.org.uk; Midland St) Leicester's premier venue for art-house films and digital media.

De Montfort Hall LIVE MUSIC

(☎0116-233 3111; www.demontforthall.co.uk; Granville Rd) Big orchestras and big song-and-dance performances are on the bill at this huge venue near Leicester University.

Mosh NIGHTCLUB

(www.moshleicester.com; 37 St Nicholas Pl; 11pm-3am Tue, Fri & Sat) Unleash your inner indie kid at this loud and lively rock joint.

Superfly NIGHTCLUB

(www.superfly-city.com; 2 King St) Behind a towering mock-Tudor facade, Superfly serves up four floors of diverse beats, with guest DJs and gigs.

Shopping

Leicester Market MARKET

(www.leicestermarket.co.uk; Market Pl; outdoor market 7am-6pm Mon-Sat, indoor market 8am-5pm Tue-Sat) Over three hundred stalls at Leicester's indoor and outdoor markets sell everything from organic vegetables to aromatic spices, fish and shellfish, new and secondhand clothes and homewares, electronic goods, cosmetics, jewellery, flowers and fabrics.

Information

Post Office (39 Gallowtree Gate) On the ground floor of WH Smith bookshop; has a currency exchange service.

Tourist Office (☎0844 888 5181; www.goleicestershire.com; 7-9 Every St; 10am-5.30pm Mon-Fri, 10am-5pm Sat) Helpful office with reams of city and county info.

Getting There & Away

BUS Buses operate from St Margaret's bus station (map p474), north of the centre. The useful Skylink bus runs to East Midlands airport 24 hours a day (£6.20, 50 minutes, every 30 minutes). Bus 440 runs to Derby (£7, one hour, 10 daily); one bus a day continues to Buxton (£13.40, 2¼ hours).

WORTH A TRIP

TWYCROSS ZOO

England's largest collection of primates – from pygmy marmosets and lemurs to gibbons and mighty lowland gorillas – roam **Twycross Zoo** (☎0844 474 1777; www.twycrosszoo.org; adult/child £16.50/11; ⏰10am-5.30pm), one of the best zoos in the country, with a successful breeding program and loads of activities for kids. It's about 8 miles south of Ashby; bus 7 runs here from Ashby-de-la-Zouch (every 1½ hours, Monday to Saturday).

National Express services:

Coventry £6.50, 45 minutes, four daily

London £6.50, 2¾ hours, one or two hourly

Nottingham £3.80, 45 minutes, two hourly

TRAIN East Midlands trains run to London St Pancras (£45, 1¼ hours, two to four hourly) and Birmingham (£11.70, one hour, twice hourly).

Getting Around

The centre is cut off from the suburbs by a tangle of underpasses and flyovers, but downtown Leicester is easy to get around on foot. For unlimited transport on local buses, buy a £5 Flexi Day Ticket.

Around Leicester

Belvoir Castle (p468) is technically in Leicestershire, but the closest town is Grantham, Lincolnshire.

BOSWORTH BATTLEFIELD

Given a few hundred years, every battlefield ends up simply a field, but the site of the Battle of Bosworth – where Richard III met his maker in 1485 – is enlivened by an entertaining **Heritage Centre** (☎01455-290429; www.bosworthbattlefield.com; adult/child £7.50/4.50; ⏰10am-5pm Apr-Oct, to 4pm Nov-Mar) full of skeletons and musket balls. The best time to visit is in August, when the battle is re-enacted by enthusiasts in period costume.

Although it lasted just a few hours, the Battle of Bosworth saw the end of the Plantagenet dynasty and marked the dawn of the Tudor era. This was where the mortally wounded Richard III famously proclaimed 'A horse, a horse, my kingdom for a horse'...actually, he didn't. The quote was invented by that great Tudor propagandist William Shakespeare, who also painted the able-bodied Richard as a cruel, calculating hunchback with a withered arm.

The battlefield is 16 miles southwest of Leicester at Sutton Cheny, off the A447. Arriva bus 153 runs hourly from Leicester to Market Bosworth, a 3-mile walk from the battlefield. Alternatively, book a taxi with **Bosworth Gold Cars** (☎01455-291999).

ASHBY-DE-LA-ZOUCH

POP 12,758

Named for a family of Norman nobles, sleepy Ashby-de-la-Zouch is worth a quick stop for its ruined **castle** (EH; adult/child £4.50/2.70; ⏰10am-5pm Thu-Mon Apr-Jun, daily Jul & Aug, reduced hours Sep-Mar), made famous by Sir Walter Scott in his classic *Ivanhoe*. You can stroll around the sundered towers and battlements in the company of an engaging audioguide – bring a torch (flashlight) to explore the underground passageway connecting the tower with the kitchen. There are displays on the rise and fall of the castle in the pocket-size **Ashby Museum** (☎01530-560090; www.ashbydelazouchmuseum.org.uk; North St; adult/child £1/50p; ⏰11am-1pm & 2-4pm Mon-Fri, 10am-4pm Sat).

The town is also a handy base for visits to the National Forest – the **tourist office** (☎01530-411767; North St; ⏰9.30am-5pm Mon, Tue, Thu & Fri, 9.30am-4pm Sat), based at the town library, has more information. Ashby is on the A511 about 15 miles northwest of Leicester; Arriva buses 9 and 9A run hourly from St Margaret's bus station in Leicester.

CONKERS & THE NATIONAL FOREST

The **National Forest** (www.nationalforest.org) is an ambitious project to generate new areas of sustainable woodland by planting 30 million trees in Leicestershire, Derbyshire and Staffordshire. More than seven million saplings have already taken root, and all sorts of visitor attractions are springing up in the forest, including **Conkers** (☎01283-216633; www.visitconkers.com; Rawdon Rd; adult/child £8.95/6.95; ⏰10am-6pm Easter–mid-Oct, to 5pm mid-Oct–Easter), a family-oriented nature centre, with interactive displays, indoor and outdoor playgrounds and lots of hands-on activities. Conkers is 20 miles northwest of Leicester off the A444; bus 23 from Ashby-de-la-Zouch to Moira passes this way.

Nearby, bike trails run through the forest, including a flat 2km path around the lake, from the brand-new cycle centre **Hicks Lodge** (☎01751-460011; www.purplemountain.co.uk; Willesley Wood Side; bike rental per day adult/child £30/15; ⌚trails 8am-dusk, bike hire 10am-4pm Mon-Fri, 9am-5pm Sat & Sun), which rents wheels, has a cafe, and organises guided tours and night rides.

National Forest YHA hostel (☎0845 371 9672; www.yha.org.uk; dm £10-18, d £38-58; P@🛜), about 300m west of Conkers' entrance along Bath Lane, has loads of eco-friendly features (grey water and solar biomass boiler usage among them), en-suite rooms, and a restaurant serving local produce and organic wines.

Rutland

England's smallest county centres on **Rutland Water**, a vast artificial reservoir created by the damming of the Gwash Valley in 1976. Covering 1255 hectares, the reservoir attracts numerous bird species, including ospreys, best viewed from the hides at the **Rutland Water Nature Reserve** (www.rutlandwater.org.uk; adult/child £5.50/3.20; ⌚9am-5pm) near Oakham.

At Skyes Lane near Empingham, the **Rutland Water tourist office** (☎01780-686800; www.anglianwater.co.uk; ⌚10am-4pm) has a snack kiosk, access to walking and cycling trails, and information on the area.

A mile down the road, the **Whitwell Centre** (☎01780-460060; www.rutlandactivities.co.uk; ⌚9am-6pm) has a high-ropes course, an outdoor climbing wall and bikes for hire (from £16.99/9.99 per adult/child per day) for a gentle pedal around the lake shore. In the same compound, **Rutland Watersports** (☎01780-460154; www.anglianwater.co.uk/leisure) offers aquatic activities, including sailing and windsurfing. You can rent gear, take lessons or enrol in governing-body-approved certification courses.

The **Rutland Belle** (☎01572-787630; www.rutlandwatercruises.com; adult/child £8/5; ⌚Sat & Sun Apr & Oct, daily May-Sep, closed Nov-Mar) offers afternoon cruises from Whitwell to Normanton on the southern shore of the reservoir, where a stone causeway leads out across the water to **Normanton Church** (☎01780-686800; www.anglianwater.co.uk; adult/child £3/2; ⌚tours 12.30pm, 1.30pm & 2.30pm Sun-Wed Apr-Sep, 12.30pm, 1.30pm & 2.30pm Sun Oct, closed Nov-Mar), saved from inundation by a limestone barrier wall. Inside are displays on the history of the reservoir.

Close to the boat jetty, the **Normanton Centre** (☎01780-720888; www.rutlandactivities.co.uk) offers bike hire at the same rates as the Whitwell Centre. Just down the road at Edith Weston, **Rutland Sailing School** (☎01780-721999; www.rutlandsailingschool.co.uk) rents out boats and runs sailing courses.

The nearest places to stay are in and around Oakham, and Stamford, Lincolnshire.

OAKHAM & AROUND

POP 9975

Historic buildings line the winding streets of Rutland's county town, Oakham. Behind the market place, a path leads to **Oakham Castle** (www.rutland.gov.uk; admission free; ⌚10am-4pm Mon & Wed-Sat), whose unfortified Great Hall was constructed in around 1190; inside you can see a curious collection of commemorative horseshoes donated by peers of the realm. Nearby, an original set of **stocks** is displayed beneath the stone-tiled pavilion of the Buttermarket. The **tourist office** (☎01572-722577; www.discover-rutland.co.uk; museum admission free; ⌚10am-4pm Mon, Wed, Fri & Sat) doubles as the **Rutland County Museum**, and has information on the medieval bishops' palace-turned-almshouse, **Lyddington Bede House** (EH; ☎01572-822438;

WORTH A TRIP

WYMESWOLD

The cute village of Wymeswold, 16 miles north of Leicester via the A46, warrants a detour for a sensational meal. **Hammer & Pincers** (☎01509-880735; 5 East Rd; mains £13.95-31; ⌚lunch Tue-Sun, dinner Tue-Sat; 🖉) is set in bucolic gardens at the edge of the village. Everything – down to the breads and condiments – is homemade and steaks are a speciality. There are also gourmet menus (six/eight courses for £37.50/45), and cookery demonstrations by arrangement.

Wymeswold is best reached by your own wheels; buses from Leicester require changing at Loughborough or Ashfordby.

adult/child £4.30/2.60; ⏲10am-5pm Thu-Mon), 7 miles to the south.

One of England's finest country hotels, **Hambleton Hall** (☎01572-756991; www.hambletonhall.com; s/d incl breakfast from £215/270, mains £33-39; P), surveys the countryside from a peninsula jutting out into Rutland Water 3 miles east of Oakham. Its luxurious floral rooms and Michelin-starred restaurant are surrounded by gorgeous gardens. The restaurant is open to nonguests by reservation.

Trains run hourly to Oakham from Leicester (£13.10, 25 minutes), Peterborough (£10.80, 30 minutes) and Birmingham (£23.50, 1½ hours). Bus 19 runs from Nottingham (1¼ hours, hourly) and bus 9 runs from Stamford (30 minutes, 9 daily), passing along the north shore of Rutland Water.

DERBYSHIRE

The Derbyshire countryside is painted in two distinct tones – the lush green of rolling valleys, criss-crossed by dry stone walls, and the barren mottled brown hilltops of the high moorlands. The big attraction here is the Peak District National Park, which preserves some of England's most evocative scenery, attracting legions of hikers, climbers, cyclists and cave enthusiasts.

Getting There & Around

East Midlands Airport, near Derby, is the nearest air hub, and Derby is well served by trains, but connecting services to smaller towns are few. In the Peak District, the Derwent Valley Line runs from Derby to Matlock. Edale and Hope lie on the Hope Valley Line from Sheffield to Manchester. For a comprehensive list of Derbyshire bus routes, visit the 'Transport & roads' pages at www.derbyshire.gov.uk.

Derby & Around

POP 229,407

Derby was one of the crucibles of the Industrial Revolution. Almost overnight, a sleepy market town was transformed into a major manufacturing centre, producing everything from silk to bone china and, later, locomotives and Rolls-Royce aircraft engines. The city suffered the ravages of industrial decline in the 1980s, but has bounced back with some impressive cultural developments and a rejuvenated riverfront.

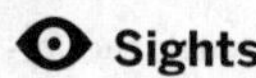

Sights

FREE **Derby Cathedral** CHURCH

(www.derbycathedral.org; 18 Irongate; ⏲9.30am-4.30pm Mon-Sat & services Sun) Founded in AD 943, but extensively reconstructed in the 18th century, Derby Cathedral's vaulted ceiling towers over a fine collection of medieval tombs, including the opulent grave of the oft-married Bess of Hardwick, who at various times held court at **Hardwick Hall** (NT; house & garden adult/child £11.50/5.80, garden only £5.80/free; ⏲house noon-4.30pm Wed-Sun, garden 9am-6pm daily), Chatsworth House (p497) and Bolsover Castle (p486). Peregrine falcolns nest in the tower – follow their progress at www.derbyperegrines.blogspot.co.uk.

FREE **Derby Museum & Art Gallery** MUSEUM

(www.derby.gov.uk; The Strand; ⏲10am-5pm Tue-Sat, 1-4pm Sun) Displays on local history and industry include fine ceramics produced by Royal Crown Derby and an archaeology gallery.

Quad GALLERY, CINEMA

(☎01332-290606; www.derbyquad.co.uk; Market Pl; gallery & BFI Mediatheque free; ⏲gallery 11am-6pm, from noon Sun, BFI Mediatheque 11am-8pm, from noon Sun) A striking modernist cube on Market Pl, Quad contains a futuristic art gallery, cinema and BFI Mediatheque – an archive of films and TV covering decades of broadcasting, run by the British Film Institute.

Royal Crown Derby Factory HISTORIC BUILDING

(☎01332-712833; www.royalcrownderby.co.uk; Osmaston Rd; tour & museum adult/child £5/4.75; ⏲10am-5pm Mon-Sat, tours 11am & 1.30pm Tue-Fri by reservation) Derby's historic pottery works still turns out some of the finest bone china in England, from edgy Asian-inspired designs to the kind of stuff your grandma used to collect. Children must be aged over 10 to join tours.

Sleeping

Chuckles B&B £

(☎01332-367193; www.chucklesguesthouse.co.uk; 48 Crompton St; s/d incl breakfast £32/54;) The friendliest of several cosy B&Bs just south of the centre, Chuckles is run by an arty couple and is renowned for its bountiful breakfasts. Take Green Lanes and turn onto Crompton St by the church.

Cathedral Quarter Hotel HOTEL ££
(☎01332-546080; www.thefinessecollection.com/cathedralquarter; 16 St Mary's Gate; s/d incl breakfast from £90/110; @📶) A bell's peal from the cathedral, this grand Georgian edifice houses Derby's finest digs. The service is as polished as the grand marble staircase and there's an on-site spa and fine-dining restaurant.

Eating

For atmospheric and inexpensive dining, also try Derby's pubs.

TOP CHOICE **Jack Rabbits** CAFE, DELI £
(☎01332-349966; www.jackrabbitskitchen.co.uk; 50 Queen St; mains £4.95-8.95; ⏰9.30am-3pm Mon, 9.30am-6pm Tue-Fri, 9am-5pm Sat; 🥗) Jack Rabbits' gourmet sandwiches, quiches and ready-to-eat meals (perfect for a riverside picnic) and its deli goods (including homemade jams and chutneys) have proved so popular that it's opened an adjoining sunlit cafe for lazy grazing on platters, cheeseboards and scrumptious cakes and slices.

European Restaurant & Bistro MODERN EUROPEAN ££
(☎01332-368732; www.theeuropeanrestaurant.co.uk; 22 Irongate; mains £9.50-19.90; ⏰lunch Tue-Sat, dinner Mon-Sat) 'European' generally translates to 'Italian' on the menu of this smart restaurant and bistro opposite the cathedral, which serves top-quality fare with pride.

Darleys MODERN BRITISH £££
(☎01332-364987; www.darleys.com; Waterfront, Darley Abbey; mains £19.20-21.50; ⏰lunch daily, dinner Mon-Sat) Two miles north of the centre, this upmarket restaurant has a gorgeous setting in a bright converted mill overlooking the river. Darleys' classy fare includes warm fig tart, goat's cheese mousse and toasted hazelnuts.

Drinking & Entertainment

Derby has a wonderful selection of historic real-ale pubs, many of which have live music.

Catch art-house films at Quad (p480) or, for theatre, check out Derby Live's productions at the Assembly Rooms, or **Guildhall Theatre** (Theatre Walk, Eagle Market).

Ye Olde Dolphin PUB
(☎01332-267711; 5a Queen St) Dating from 1530, Derby's oldest pub has a hearty menu, live music in the beer garden on weekends, and ghost tours.

Brunswick Inn PUB
(www.brunswickinn.co.uk; 1 Railway Tce) Set at the end of a working-class terrace near the station, this award-winning inn is a warren of cosy rooms where you can enjoy the nut-brown ales fermented by the house brewery.

The Brewery Tap PUB
(www.brewerytap-dbc.co.uk; 1 Derwent St) Serves its own brews and guest ales in elegant Victorian surrounds.

Old Silk Mill PUB
(19 Full St) Live music several times a week, including Sunday afternoon jazz.

Information

Tourist Office (☎01332-255802; www.visitderby.co.uk; Market Pl; ⏰9.30am-5pm Mon-Thu, to 5.30pm Fri & Sat) Under the **Assembly Rooms** (☎01332-255800; www.derbylive.co.uk; Market Pl) in the main square.

Getting There & Away

Air

About 8 miles northwest of Derby, East Midlands Airport (p459) is served by regular Skylink buses (30 minutes, at least hourly), which leave from Derby Bus Station.

Bus

Local and long-distance buses run from Derby's bus station, immediately east of the Westfield shopping mall. From Monday to Saturday, Transpeak has hourly buses between Derby and Buxton (2½ hours), via Matlock (1½ hours) and Bakewell (two hours). Five buses per day continue to Manchester (3½ hours).

Other services:

Leicester National Express; £7.40, one hour, seven daily

Nottingham Red Arrow; 30 minutes, half-hourly

Train

The train station is about half a mile southeast of the centre on Railway Tce. Services:

Birmingham £12.20, 45 minutes, four hourly

Leeds £20, 1½ hours, every 30 minutes

London St Pancras £53.30, 1¾ hours, two hourly

Sheffield £10.10, 30 minutes, every 15 minutes

Around Derby

CALKE ABBEY

Like an enormous, long-neglected cabinet of wonders, **Calke Abbey** (NT; ☎01332-863822; Ticknall; house & park adult/child £11/5.50, park only £6.80/3.40; ⌚house 12.30-5pm Sat-Wed, park 7.30am-7.30pm daily) is not your average stately home. Built around 1703, the house was occupied by a dynasty of eccentric and reclusive baronets. The result is a ramshackle maze of rooms crammed with ancient furniture, mounted animal heads, dusty books, stuffed birds and bric-a-brac spanning three centuries. Some rooms are in fabulous condition, while others are left much as they were found, with crumbling plaster and peeling wallpaper.

Other highlights include the chilly brewhouse tunnels and the ancient oak forests of Calke Park, preserved as a National Nature Reserve.

Calke is 10 miles south of Derby off the A514, close to the village of Ticknall. Arriva bus 61 from Derby to Swadlincote stops at Ticknall, a mile-and-a-half walk from the house.

KEDLESTON HALL

Sitting pretty in vast landscaped grounds, the neoclassical mansion **Kedleston Hall** (NT; house & gardens adult/child £9.90/4.90, gardens only £4.40/2.20; ⌚house noon-5pm Sat-Wed Feb-Nov, gardens 10am-6pm Feb-Nov, house & gardens closed Dec & Jan) is a must for fans of stately homes. The Curzon family has lived here since the 12th century but the current wonder was built by Sir Nathaniel Curzon in 1758. Meanwhile, the poor old peasants in Kedleston village had their humble dwellings moved a mile down the road, as they interfered with the view. Ah, the good old days...

Entering the house through a grand portico, you'll reach the breathtaking Marble Hall with massive alabaster columns and statues of Greek deities. Other highlights include Indian treasures amassed by Viceroy George Curzon and a domed, circular saloon modelled on the Pantheon in Rome, as well as 18th-century-style pleasure gardens.

Kedleston Hall is 5 miles northwest of Derby, off the A52. Arriva bus 109 between Derby and Ashbourne passes the Smithy, about 1 mile from Kedleston (25 minutes, every two hours Monday to Saturday). On summer Saturdays, the bus goes right to the hall.

ASHBOURNE

POP 7600

Perched at the southern edge of the Peak District National Park, Ashbourne is a pretty spread of steeply slanting stone streets lined with cafes, pubs and antique shops. The main attraction, however, is the chance to walk or cycle along the **Tissington Trail**, part of NCN Route 68, which runs north for 13 miles to Parsley Hay, connecting with the **Pennine Cycleway** (also NCN Route 68) and the **High Peak Trail** towards Buxton or Matlock. The track climbs gently along the tunnels, viaducts and cuttings of the disused railway line which once transported local milk to London.

Sleeping & Eating

Compton House B&B ££
(☎01335-343100; 27-31 Compton; s/d/f incl breakfast from £40/60/85; ⌚www.comptonhouse.co.uk; P 📶) Fresh, clean, frilly rooms, a warm welcome and central location make this the pick of Ashbourne's B&Bs.

Bramhalls CAFE £
(☎01335-342631; 22 Market Pl; dishes £3.25-7.95; ⌚8am-5pm Mon-Sat) This great little deli and

ROYAL SHROVETIDE FOOTBALL

Some people celebrate Shrove Tuesday (the last day before Lent) by eating pancakes or dressing up in carnival finery, but Ashbourne marks the occasion with a riotous game of football where the ball is wrestled as much as kicked from one end of town to the other by crowds of revellers. Following 12th-century rules, villagers are split into two teams – those from north of the river and those living to the south – and the 'goals' are two millstones, set 3 miles apart. Participants are free to kick, carry or throw the ball, though it's usually squeezed through the crowds like a rugby scrum. Sooner or later, both players and ball end up in the river.

Local shops board up their windows and the whole town comes out to watch or play. Fearless visitors are welcome to participate in the melee but under a quirk of the rules, only locals are allowed to score goals.

cafe serves posh light meals and sandwiches, excellent homemade pastries and breads, cold meats and 70 varieties of cheese.

Drinking

Smith's Tavern PUB

(36 St John's St) A tiny pub on the main shopping street, with a big selection of real ales and food and an old piano at the back.

Information

Tourist Office (☎01335-343666; www.visitashbourne.co.uk; Market Pl; ⏰10am-5pm daily Mar-Oct, 10.30am-4pm Mon-Sat Nov-Feb)

Getting There & Away

Useful bus services:

Buxton High Peak bus 42 (35 minutes) or 442 (one hour and 20 minutes, every one to two hours)

Derby Arriva 109/Trent Barton One Swift; 40 minutes, hourly

Leek Clowes bus 108; 50 minutes, six daily

Getting Around

About a mile above town along Mapleton Lane, the **Cycle Hire Centre** (☎01335-343156; half-day/day from £12.50/15.50; ⏰9am-5.30pm Mar-Oct, reduced hours Nov-Feb) is right on the Tissington Trail, at the end of a huge and atmospheric old railway tunnel leading under Ashbourne. You can also rent children's bikes, bikes with baby seats, trailers for buggies and tandems.

DOVEDALE

About 3 miles northwest of Ashbourne, the River Dove winds through the steep-sided valley of Dovedale; Ashbourne's tourist office has walking information.

Dovedale was a popular haunt for Izaak Walton, the 17th-century fisherman and author of *The Compleat Angler*.

The ivy-covered **Izaak Walton Hotel** (☎01335-350555; www.izaakwaltonhotel.com; d incl breakfast from £75, 3-course menu £35; 📶) arranges fly-fishing on the River Dove, and has upmarket evening meals and comfortable beds.

Matlock Bath & Around

POP 2202

Unashamedly tacky, Matlock Bath (not to be confused with the larger, workaday town of Matlock, 2 miles to the north) looks like a seaside resort that somehow lost its way and ended up at the foot of the Peak District National Park. Following the River Derwent through a sheer-walled gorge, the main promenade is lined with amusement arcades, tearooms, fish-and-chippies, pubs and shops catering to the bikers who congregate here on summer weekends. Outside summer, the town is considerably quieter and many lodgings and eateries shut.

Sights & Activities

Steep paths climb the eastern side of the gorge, reached by pedestrian bridges from the A6. The tourist office has details of longer, more challenging walks in the hills. Note that many of the lanes up the side of the valley are too narrow for cars, with no space for turning.

Peak District Mining Museum & Temple Mine MUSEUM

(www.peakmines.co.uk; The Pavilion; museum adult/child £3.50/2.50, mine £3.50/2.50; ⏰10am-5pm daily Apr-Oct, 11am-3pm Wed-Sat Nov-Mar) An educational introduction to the mining history of Matlock is provided by this enthusiast-run museum. Set in an old Victorian dancehall, kids can wriggle through its maze of tunnels and shafts, while adults browse historical displays. At noon and 2pm daily (weekends only November to March), you can go into the workings of the **Temple Mine** and pan for 'gold' (well, shiny minerals). Combined museum and mine tickets cost £6/4 per adult/child.

Gulliver's Kingdom AMUSEMENT PARK

(☎01925-444888; www.gulliversfun.co.uk; admission £13.95; 👪) This old-fashioned amusement park offers plenty of splashing, churning and looping attractions for anyone as tall as the signs at the start of the rides. Call for opening days and times or check the seasonal schedule online.

Heights of Abraham AMUSEMENT PARK

(☎01629-582365; www.heightsofabraham.com; adult/child £13/9; ⏰10am-5pm daily mid–late Feb, Sat & Sun late Feb–mid-Mar, daily mid-Mar–early Nov, closed rest of year) A spectacular **cable-car** ride (included in admission; no cable-car-only tickets) from the bottom of the gorge brings you to this hilltop leisure park, whose atmospheric cave and mine tours, and fossil exhibitions are a winner with kids.

Peak Rail HERITAGE RAILWAY

(www.peakrail.co.uk; adult/child £7.50/4) From a tiny platform just north of Sainsbury's supermarket on the outskirts of Matlock village, nostalgic steam trains trundle along a

4-mile length of track to the nearby village of Rowsley, home to Caudwell's Mill. Tickets include unlimited travel on the day of purchase. Services run five times a day Saturday and Sunday (and some weekdays) from May to October, and some weekends at other times of the year; check the timetables online for full details.

Festivals & Events

Matlock Bath Illuminations FESTIVAL
(www.derbyshiredales.gov.uk; Derwent Gardens; adult/child £4.50/free; from dusk Sat & Sun Sep & Oct) Long chains of twinkling lights, firework displays and a flotilla of outrageously decorated Venetian boats light up the river during Matlock Bath's festival of lights.

Sleeping & Eating

Despite its inland location, the official breakfast, lunch and dinner of Matlock is fish and chips, served at dozens of cafes, tearooms and pubs along the strip.

Hodgkinson's Hotel & Restaurant HOTEL ££
(01629-582170; www.hodgkinsons-hotel.co.uk; 150 South Pde; s/d incl breakfast from £41/77, 2-/3-course meals £29.50/34; restaurant dinner; P) Right in the thick of things on the parade, rooms at this hotel conjure up Matlock's golden age with antique furnishings, flowery wallpaper and cast-iron fireplaces.

Ashdale Guest House B&B ££
(01629-57826; www.ashdaleguesthouse.co.uk; 92 North Pde; s/d from £35/60; P) A tall stone house just beyond the tacky part of the promenade, with smart, tasteful rooms and organic breakfasts.

Temple Hotel HOTEL ££
(01629-583911; www.templehotel.co.uk; Temple Walk; s/d incl breakfast from £65/80, mains £7.95-9.50; P) The views from this hillside inn are so lovely that Lord Byron once felt inspired to etch a poem on the restaurant window. The hotel is a little dated, but the rooms are comfy and the Chatsworth Bar turns out filling meals and real ales.

Shopping

For arts, crafts and discounted clothing brands, check out the **Derwent Valley mills**.

Scarthin Books BOOKS
(www.scarthinbooks.com; The Promenade, Cromford; 9am-6pm Mon-Sat, noon-6pm Sun) Over 100,000 new and secondhand books are crammed into 12 rooms in this bibliophile's paradise, which hosts regular literary events. Wedged in amoungst the clutter, its vegetarian cafe serves organic pizza.

DERWENT VALLEY MILLS

Unlikely as it may sound, the industrial mills that line the Derwent Valley are ranked up there with the Taj Mahal on the Unesco World Heritage list. Founded in the 1770s by Richard Arkwright, the **Cromford Mill** (01629-825995; www.arkwrightsociety.org.uk; Mill Lane, Cromford; tour adult/child £3.50/2.50; 9am-5pm, tours by reservation), 3 miles south of Matlock Bath, was the first modern factory, producing cotton on automated machines, powered by a series of waterwheels along the River Derwent. This prototype inspired a succession of mills, ushering in the industrial age. The Arkwright Society runs atmospheric tours; buses 140 and 141 run here hourly from Matlock Bath (15 minutes, no Sunday service).

Other fascinating industrial relics include **Strutt's North Mill** (www.belpernorthmill.org; adult/child £3.50/2; 1-5pm Wed-Sun Mar-Oct, 1-5pm Sat & Sun Nov-Feb) at Belper, accessible on the Transpeak bus between Derby and Matlock; **Masson Mills** (01629-581001; www.massonmills.co.uk; Derby Rd; adult/child £3/2; 10am-4pm Mon-Fri, 11am-5pm Sat, to 4pm Sun, closed Dec), 1 mile south of Matlock Bath, where a museum tells the story of the valley's textile mills and an attached shopping village is full of outlet stores for big clothing brands; and **Caudwell's Mill** (01629-734374; www.caudwellsmillcraftcentre.co.uk; admission free, mill tours adult/child £4.50/2; 9.30am-4.30pm), near Rowsley, a chugging, grinding, water-powered mill that still produces flour the old-fashioned way, with various craft workshops and a tearoom. You can get to Rowsley direct from Matlock Bath by bus on the route to Bakewell, or take the Peak Rail (p483) steam train and follow the riverside path from the station.

WORTH A TRIP

CARSINGTON WATER

Less famous than the Derwent reservoirs to the north, but also less crowded, Carsington Water is a pretty spot to stroll, cycle or mess about on boats. The reservoir was built to store water from the River Derwent in the 1990s, but almost looks like a natural lake, with abundant bird life, and peaceful waterside walking and cycling trails.

Just off the B5035, **Carsington Water Sports & Cycle Hire Centre** (☎01629-540478; www.carsingtonwater.com; ⏲10am-5.30pm) rents mountain bikes (£17 per day), sailboats (from £22 per 1½ hours) and windsurfing equipment (£16 per 1½ hours); bus 110 from Ashbourne to Matlock passes by several times daily.

ℹ Information

Tourist Office (☎01629-761103; www.visitpeakdistrict.com; The Pavilion; ⏲10am-5pm Apr-Oct, 11am-3pm Nov-Mar) Visitor information point at the mining museum (p483).

ℹ Getting There & Away

Trains run hourly between Matlock Bath and Derby (£5, 30 minutes, hourly). Matlock is also a hub for buses around the Peak District.

Bakewell Bus 172; one hour, hourly Monday to Saturday

Chesterfield Bus 17; 35 minutes, two daily

Derby Transpeak; 1½ hours, hourly

Sheffield Bus 214; 1¼ hours, hourly

Chesterfield

POP 100,879

The eastern gateway to the Peaks, Chesterfield is worth a visit to see the astonishing **crooked spire** that rises atop **St Mary & All Saints Church** (☎01246-206506; www.chesterfieldparishchurch.org.uk; admission free, spire tours adult/child £3.50/1.50; ⏲spire tours 11.30am & 2pm Tue & Thu, 11.30am & 2.30pm Mon, Wed, Fri & Sat). Dating from 1360, the 68m-high spire is twisted in a right-handed corkscrew and it leans several metres southwest – not a result of warping green timbers, but buckling of the south-facing side of spire's lead casing in the sun. Learn more at the engaging **Chesterfield Museum & Art Gallery** (☎01246-345727; www.chesterfield.gov.uk; St Mary's Gate; ⏲10am-4pm Mon-Tue & Thu-Sat).

The Chesterfield **tourist office** (☎012246-345777; www.visitchesterfield.info; Rykneld Sq; ⏲9am-5.30pm Mon-Sat Easter-early Nov, to 5pm Mon-Sat early Nov-Easter) is directly opposite the crooked spire.

Chesterfield lies on the main rail line between Nottingham/Derby (30 minutes) and Sheffield (10 minutes), with hourly services in both directions. The station is just east of the centre. The Chesterfield Coach Station is on Beetwell St – useful local services include bus 170 to Bakewell (45 minutes, hourly) and bus 66 to Buxton (45 minutes, five daily, four Sunday services).

Around Chesterfield

HARDWICK HALL

One of the most complete Elizabethan mansions in the country, Hardwick Hall (p480) was home to the 16th century's second-most powerful woman, Elizabeth, Countess of Shrewsbury – known to all as Bess of Hardwick – who amassed a staggering fortune by marrying wealthy noblemen with one foot in the grave. Hardwick Hall was constructed using her inheritance from hubby number four, who shuffled off this mortal coil in 1590.

Designed by eminent architect Robert Smythson, the hall featured all the latest mod cons of the time, including fully glazed windows – a massive luxury in the 16th century. The atmospheric interiors are decked out with magnificent tapestries and oil paintings of forgotten dignitaries. Set aside some time to explore the formal gardens or longer walking trails of Hardwick Park.

Next door to the manor is Bess' first house, **Hardwick Old Hall** (EH; adult/child £5/3, joint ticket £14/7; ⏲10am-5pm Wed-Sun Apr-early Nov, 10am-5pm Sat & Sun early Nov-Mar), now a romantic ruin administered by English Heritage.

Hardwick Hall is 10 miles southeast of Chesterfield, just off the M1. Stagecoach Chesterfield–Nottingham buses stop at Glapwell, from where it's a 1½-mile walk to Hardwick Hall.

WORTH A TRIP

BOLSOVER CASTLE

About 6 miles east of Chesterfield on the A632, partly ruined **Bolsover Castle** (EH; adult/child £8/4.80; ⏲10am-5pm Apr–early Nov, 10am-4pm Sat & Sun early Nov–Mar) was founded in 1612 by Sir Charles Cavendish. Famous former residents include the inimitable Bess of Hardwick, whose extravagance can be seen in the surviving frescos and carved fireplaces.

Take Stagecoach bus 83 from Chesterfield.

PEAK DISTRICT

Rolling across the southernmost hills of the Pennines, the Peak District is one of the most beautiful parts of the country. Ancient stone villages are folded into creases in the landscape and the hillsides are littered with famous stately homes and rocky outcrops that attract hordes of walkers, climbers and cavers. No one knows how the Peak District got its name – certainly not from the landscape, which has hills and valleys, gorges and lakes, wild moorland and gritstone escarpments, but no peaks. The most popular theory is that the region was named for the Pecsaetan, the Anglo-Saxon tribe who once populated this part of England.

Founded in 1951, the Peak District National Park was England's first national park and is Europe's busiest. But escaping the crowds is easy if you avoid summer weekends. Even at the busiest times, there are 555 sq miles of open English countryside in which to find your own viewpoint to soak up the glorious scenery.

Locals divide the Peak District into the Dark Peak – dominated by exposed moorland and gritstone 'edges' – and the White Peak, made up of the limestone dales to the south.

PEAK DISTRICT TRANSPORT PASSES

Handy bus passes covering travel in the Peak District include the **Zigzag Plus** ticket, offering all-day travel on Trent Barton buses, including the Transpeak between Derby and Buxton, for £10 (one child travels free with each adult). The one-day **Derbyshire Wayfarer** (adult/child £11.10/5.55) covers buses and trains throughout the county and as far afield as Manchester and Sheffield.

Although there are several **YHA hostels** (p813) in the Peak District, they're often booked out in advance by groups, so contact them before turning up.

Activities

Caving & Climbing

The limestone sections of the Peak District are riddled with caves and caverns, including a series of 'show caves' in Castleton, Buxton and Matlock Bath. For serious caving (or potholing) trips, the first port of call should be the website www.peakdistrictcaving.info, run by the caving store **Hitch n Hike** (www.hitchnhike.co.uk; Mytham Bridge, Bamford), near Castleton, which has gear and advice for **climbing** (p488).

Walking

The Peak District is one of the most popular walking areas in England, with awe-inspiring vistas of hills, dales and sky that attract legions of hikers in summer. The White Peak is perfect for leisurely strolls, which can start from pretty much anywhere (be sure to close gates behind you). When exploring the rugged territory of the Dark Peak, make sure your boots are waterproof and beware of slipping into rivulets and marshes.

The Peak's most famous walking trail is the **Pennine Way** (http://penninewayassociation.co.uk), which runs north from Edale for more than 250 miles, finishing in the Scottish Borders. If you don't have three weeks to spare, you can reach the pretty town of Hebden Bridge in Yorkshire in three comfortable days.

The 46-mile **Limestone Way** winds through the Derbyshire countryside from Castleton to Rocester in Staffordshire, following footpaths, tracks and quiet lanes. Many people walk the 26-mile section between Castleton and Matlock in one long, tiring day, but two days is better. Tourist offices have a detailed leaflet.

Other popular routes include the **High Peak Trail**, **Tissington Trail**, and **Monsal Trail & Tunnels**, described under **Cycling**. Numerous short walks are available. If you want more info, see a local tourist office.

Cycling

The plunging dales and soaring scarps are a perfect testing ground for cyclists and local tourist offices are piled high with cycling maps and pamphlets. For easy traffic-free riding, head for the 17.5-mile **High Peak Trail**, which follows the old railway line

Peak District National Park

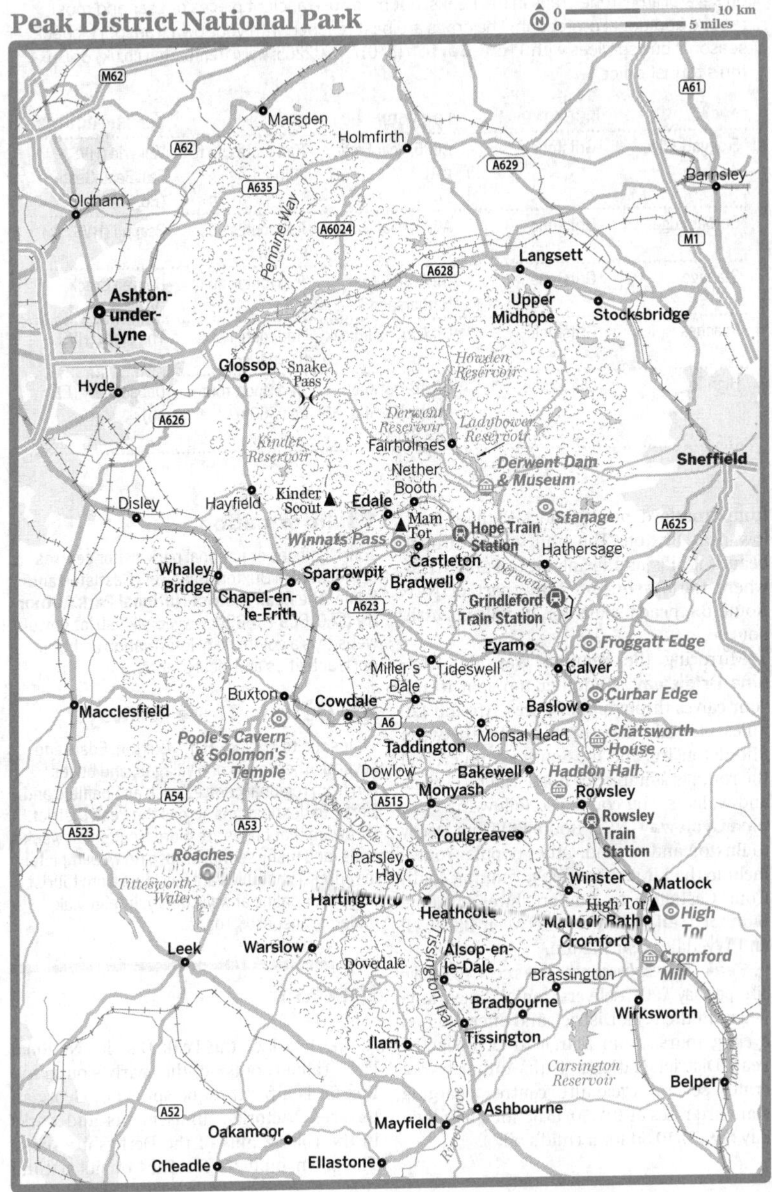

CLIMBING THE PEAKS

The Peak District has long been a training ground for England's top mountaineers. In place of looming mountains, it offers glorious technical climbing on a series of limestone gorges, exposed tors (crags) and gritstone 'edges' that extend south into the Staffordshire Moorlands. Gritstone climbing in the Peaks is predominantly on old-school trad routes, requiring a decent rack of friends, nuts and hexes. Bolted sport routes are found on several limestone crags in the Peaks, but many use ancient pieces of gear and most require additional protection. The crags are best reached with your own transport; check seasonal bus services with **Trent Barton** (☎01773-712265; www.trentbarton.co.uk) or Buxton's tourist office.

AREA	ROCK TYPE	LOCATION	ROUTES	CLASSIC ROUTES
Froggatt Edge	Gritstone	A625, near Froggatt	Trad routes up to 20m	Valkyrie (HVS, 5a), Beau Geste (E6, 6c)
Curbar Edge	Gritstone	A625, near Calver	Trad routes up to 23m	Peapod (HVS, 5b)
Stanage	Gritstone	Off A6187, near Hathersage	Trad routes up to 30m	Heaven Crack (VDiff)
Roaches	Gritstone	Off A53, near Leek	Trad routes & bouldering	The Sloth (HVS, 5a)
High Tor	Limestone	Off A6, between Matlock & Matlock Bath	Trad/sport routes up to 60m	Debauchery (E1, 5b)

from Cromford, near Matlock Bath, to Dowlow near Buxton. The trail winds through beautiful hills and farmland to Parsley Hay, where the **Tissington Trail**, part of NCN Route 68, heads south for 13 miles to Ashbourne.

Mirroring the Pennine Way, the **Pennine Bridleway** is another top spot to put your calves through their paces. Around 120 miles of trails have been created between Middleton Top and the South Pennines, and the route is suitable for horse riders, cyclists and walkers. You could also follow the **Pennine Cycleway** (NCN Route 68) from Derby to Buxton and beyond. Other popular routes include the **Limestone Way**, running south from Castleton to Staffordshire, and the **Monsal Trail & Tunnels** between Bakewell and Wyedale, near Buxton.

Peak Tours (www.peak-tours.com; mountain bike per day £20) delivers rental bikes anywhere in the Peak District, and offers guided cycling tours. From March to October, the Peak District National Park Authority operates several cycle-hire centres charging standard rates of £12.50/15.50 for a half-day/day (£8.50/10.50 for a child's bike).

Information

Tourist offices or national park visitor centres are located in Buxton, Bakewell, Castleton and Edale. The **Peak District National Park Authority** (☎01629-816200; www.peakdistrict.gov.uk) website is a goldmine of information on transport, activities and local events.

Getting There & Away

Trains run to Matlock Bath, Buxton, Edale and several other towns and villages, and buses run from regional centres such as Sheffield and Derby to destinations across the Peak District. Be aware that buses are more frequent at weekends, and many services close down completely in winter. Timetables are available from tourist offices, or online at www.derbyshire.gov.uk under 'Transport & roads'.

Buxton

POP 24,112

At the heart of the Peak District National Park (albeit outside the park boundary) Buxton is a picturesque sprawl of Georgian terraces, Victorian amusements and parks in the rolling hills of the Derbyshire dales. The town built its fortunes on its natural warm-water springs, which attracted health tourists in Buxton's heyday. Today, visitors are drawn here by the flamboyant Regency architecture and the natural wonders of the surrounding countryside. Tuesday and Saturday are market days, bringing colour to the grey limestone market place.

Sights

Buxton's historic centre is a riot of Victorian pavilions, concert halls and glasshouse domes.

Opera House HISTORIC BUILDING, OPERA
(Water St) Buxton's flamboyant, turreted Victorian Opera House is the town's most famous building. It hosts an impressive variety of stage shows.

Pavilion Gardens GARDENS
(www.paviliongardens.co.uk; ⊙9.30am-5pm) Next to the Opera House is the equally flamboyant Pavilion Gardens, dotted with domed pavilions. The main building contains a tropical greenhouse, a nostalgic cafe and the tourist office (p492). Beware of getting lost in the unlit gardens after dark.

Devonshire Dome HISTORIC BUILDING
A glorious piece of Victoriana, the Devonshire Dome contains part of the campus of the University of Derby and an opulent **spa** (☎01332-594408; www.devonshire-spa.co.uk; 1 Devonshire Rd; treatments include one-hour body spa £38, ocean wrap £49, day package from £65) offering a full range of pampering treatments.

Buxton Baths HISTORIC BUILDING
In Victorian times, spa activities centred on the extravagant Buxton Baths complex, built in grand Regency style in 1854. The various bath buildings are fronted by a grand, curving facade, known as the Crescent, inspired by the Royal Crescent in Bath. It's expected to re-open in 2014 as a five star hotel and spa.

Pump Room HISTORIC BUILDING
At the base of the Slopes is the Pump Room (to be turned into tearooms in 2014), which dispensed Buxton's spring water for nearly a century.

St Ann's Well FOUNTAIN
Modern day health tourists queue up to fill plastic bottles from a small spout known as St Ann's Well. Climbing the green terraces of the Slopes provides the definitive view over Buxton's grand Victorian rooftops.

FREE **Buxton Museum & Art Gallery** MUSEUM, GALLERY
(Terrace Rd; ⊙9.30am-5.30pm Tue-Fri, to 5pm Sat year-round, 10.30am-5pm Sun Easter-Sep) Just downhill from the town hall in a handsome Victorian building, the town museum displays local historical bric-a-brac and curiosities from Castleton's Victorian-era 'House of Wonders', including Harry Houdini's handcuffs.

Activities

Poole's Cavern CAVE
(www.poolescavern.co.uk; adult/child £8/4.75; ⊙9.30am-5pm) A pleasant mile stroll southwest from the centre will take you to Poole's Cavern, a magnificent natural limestone cavern. Few steps mean it's suitable for wheelchairs and prams/buggies.

From the cavern's car park, a 20-minute walk leads up through Grin Low Wood to Solomon's Temple, a ruined tower with fine views over the town.

Parsley Hay Cycle Hire BICYCLE RENTAL
(☎01298-84493) Rent bikes from the Peak District National Park Authority's Parsley Hay Cycle Hire, about 8 miles south of Buxton at the junction of the High Peak and Tissington Trails.

Festivals & Events

Buxton's big events revolve around the beautifully restored **Opera House** (www.buxtonoperahouse.org.uk; Water St).

Four Four Time MUSIC
(⊙Feb) Features a medley of jazz, blues, folk and world-music acts.

Buxton Festival CULTURE
(www.buxtonfestival.co.uk; ⊙Jul) One of the largest cultural festivals in the country, attracting top names in literature, music and opera.

Buxton Fringe CULTURE
(www.buxtonfringe.org.uk; ⊙Jul) Contemporary Buxton Festival spin-off, spanning film, music, dance, theatre and comedy.

International Gilbert & Sullivan Festival MUSICAL THEATRE
(www.gsfestivals.org; ⊙late Jul-early Aug) Hugely popular festival; Gilbert and Sullivan productions are also staged in Buxton throughout the year.

Buxton

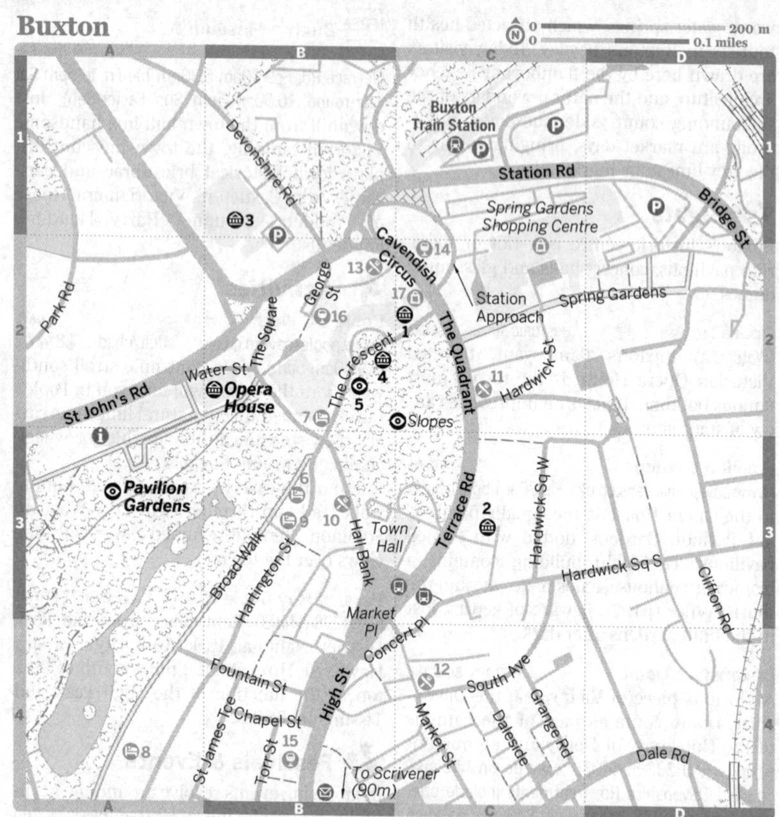

Sleeping

TOP CHOICE **Old Hall Hotel** HISTORIC HOTEL ££

(☎01298-22841; www.oldhallhotelbuxton.co.uk; The Square; s/d incl breakfast from £65/85; @☎) There is a tale to go with every creak of the floorboards at this history-soaked establishment, supposedly the oldest hotel in England. Among other esteemed residents, Mary, Queen of Scots, stayed here from 1576 to 1578, albeit against her will. The rooms are still the grandest in town, and there are several bars, lounges and dining options.

Roseleigh Hotel B&B ££

(☎01298-24904; www.roseleighhotel.co.uk; 19 Broad Walk; d incl breakfast from £78; P@☎) This gorgeous family-run B&B in a roomy old Victorian house has lovingly decorated rooms, many with fine views out over the Pavilion Gardens. The owners are a welcoming couple, both seasoned travellers, with plenty of interesting tales to tell.

Victorian Guest House B&B ££

(☎01298-78759; www.buxtonvictorian.co.uk; 3a Broad Walk; d incl breakfast from £82; P☎) Overlooking the park, this elegant house has eight individually decorated bedrooms furnished with Victorian and Edwardian antiques. The home-cooked breakfasts are renowned.

Grosvenor House B&B ££

(☎01298-72439; www.grosvenorbuxton.co.uk; 1 Broad Walk; s/d incl breakfast from £50/65; P☎) Overlooking the Pavilion Gardens, the Grosvenor is a venerable Victorian guesthouse with a huge parlour overlooking the park. Rooms have flowery upholstery, flowery drapes and, well, flowery everything else, really. There's a minimum two-night stay at peak times.

Buxton

Top Sights

Sights

Sleeping

Eating

Drinking

Shopping

Eating

Many of Buxton's drinking and entertainment venues also offer decent dining.

Columbine Restaurant MODERN BRITISH ££
(☎01298-78752; 7 Hall Bank; mains £12.25-17.80; ⊙dinner Mon-Sat, closed Tue Nov-Apr) On the lane leading down beside the town hall, this understated restaurant is the top choice among in-the-know Buxtonites. The chef conjures up imaginative dishes using mainly local produce, as well as wonderful puddings. Bookings recommended.

Green Pavilion CAFE £
(☎01298-77480; www.greenpavilion.co.uk; 6 Terrace Rd; dishes £3.50-8.95; ⊙8am-5pm;) A contemporary alternative to the Pavilion Gardens' old-fashioned tearooms, this funky little cafe brews Illy coffee and whips up gourmet burgers and wraps and packs picnic hampers (including blankets for loan).

Nat's Kitchen MODERN BRITISH £££
(☎01298-214642; www.natskitchen.co.uk; 9-11 Market St; 2-/3-course menus £21/27.50; ⊙9am-11pm) A relaxing dining room full of natural wood tones provides the backdrop to some inventive Modern British cooking. Ingredients are sourced from local suppliers and there are some smart B&B rooms upstairs. Bookings recommended.

Simply Thai THAI £
(☎01298-24471; www.simplythaibuxton.co.uk; 2-3 Cavendish Circus; mains £7.25-12.95; ⊙noon-11pm) Polished wood floors, Siamese sculptures and silk-attired staff make this an elegant place to enjoy refined Thai afternoon tea (2.30pm to 5pm, £15.95).

Drinking & Entertainment

Buxton's gorgeously restored Victorian Opera House (p489) hosts a full program of drama, dance, concerts and comedy.

Nightlife in Buxton centres on the pubs and restaurants around Market Pl and along the High St.

Barbarella's WINE BAR
(www.barbarellaswinebar.co.uk; 7 The Quadrant;) Black-and-white paisley wallpaper, chandeliers and glossy timber tables make this sleek retro wine bar the hottest new drinking den in Buxton.

Project X BAR
(www.project-x-cafe.com; The Old Court House, George St; ⊙8am-midnight;) Moroccan tables, hanging lanterns and deep violet walls create a kasbah vibe at this sultry cafe and bar, which hosts regular live music.

Old Sun Inn PUB
(33 High St) The cosiest of the High St pubs, with a warren of rooms full of original features, a lively crowd that spans the generations, and jam sessions on Tuesday nights.

Shopping

Retaining its original eggshell-blue art-deco tiles, the **Cavendish Arcade** (Cavendish Circus) houses boutiques selling upmarket gifts.

Scrivener's Books & Bookbinding BOOKS
(☎01298-73100; www.scrivenersbooks.co.uk; 42 High St; ⊙9am-5pm Mon-Sat, noon-4pm Sun) In

this delightfully chaotic bookshop sprawling over five floors, books are filed in piles and the Dewey system has yet to be discovered.

Information

Grove Movie Centre (01298-78087; 2 Eagle Pde; per 30min £2; 11am-9pm) DVD shop with several internet terminals.

Post Office (High St) With a currency exchange service.

Tourist Office (www.visitpeakdistrict.com; Pavilion Gardens; 9.30am-5pm;) Has useful leaflets on walks in the area. Free hour-long Roman Buxton town walks depart at 11am and 2pm Saturday.

Getting There & Away

Northern Rail has trains to and from Manchester (£9, one hour, hourly).

Buses stop on both sides of the road at Market Pl. The hourly Transpeak runs to Derby (2½ hours), via Bakewell (one hour) and Matlock Bath (1½ hours). To reach Manchester by bus, take Skyline bus 199 (1½ hours, every 30 minutes Monday to Saturday), run by High Peak Buses. Other bus services:

Chesterfield Bus 66; 1¼ hours, five daily Monday to Saturday (four services Sunday)

Nottingham National Express; £18, 2½ hours, one daily

Sheffield Bus 65; 1½ hours, five daily (three services Sunday)

Castleton

POP 1200

The charming village of Castleton guards the entrance to the forbidding Winnats Pass gorge. It's a magnet for visitors on summer weekends; consider visiting midweek to enjoy the sights in relative peace and quiet. The village's streets are lined with leaning stone houses, walking trails criss-cross the surrounding hills, a wonderfully atmospheric castle crowns the ridge above, and the bedrock below is riddled with facsinating caves.

Sights

The limestone caves around town have been mined for lead, silver and the semi-precious Blue John Stone (a vivid violet form of fluorspar) for centuries and four are open to the public on guided tours.

Peveril Castle CASTLE

(EH; adult/child £4.50/2.70; 10am-5pm Apr-Oct, 10am-4pm Sat & Sun Nov-Mar) Topping the ridge to the south of Castleton, this evocative castle has been so ravaged by the centuries that it almost looks like a crag itself. Constructed by William Peveril, son of William the Conqueror, the castle was used as a hunting lodge by Henry II, King John and Henry III, and the crumbling ruins offer swooping views over the Hope Valley.

FREE **Castleton Museum** MUSEUM

(01433-620679; Buxton Rd; 9.30am-5.30pm) Attached to the tourist office, the cute town museum has displays on everything from mining and geology to rock climbing, hang-gliding and the curious **Garland Festival**.

Peak Cavern CAVE

(01433-620285; http://devilsarse.com; adult/child £8.75/6.75; 10am-4pm daily Apr-Oct, Sat & Sun Nov-Mar) Castleton's most convenient cave is is easily reached by a pretty stream-side walk from the village centre. It has the largest natural cave entrance in England, known (not so prettily) as the Devil's Arse. Dramatic limestone formations are lit with fibre-optic cables.

Speedwell Cavern CAVE

(01433-621888; www.speedwellcavern.co.uk; adult/child £9.25/7.25; 9.30am-4pm) About half a mile west of Castleton at the mouth of Winnats Pass, this claustrophobe's nightmare is reached via an eerie boat ride through flooded tunnels that emerges by a huge subterranean lake called the Bottomless Pit. New chambers are discovered here all the time by potholing expeditions.

Treak Cliff Cavern CAVE

(01433-620571; www.bluejohnstone.com; adult/child £8.50/4.50; 10am-5pm, last tour 4.20pm) A short walk across the fields from Speedwell Cavern, Treak Cliff is notable for its forest of stalactites and exposed seams of colourful Blue John Stone, which is still mined to supply the jewellery trade. Tours focus on the history of mining; kids can polish their own Blue John Stone during school holidays.

Blue John Cavern CAVE

(01433-620638; www.bluejohn-cavern.co.uk; adult/child £9/4.50; 10am-5.30pm) Up the side of Mam Tor, Blue John is a maze of natural caverns with rich seams of Blue John Stone that are still mined every winter. You can get here on foot up the closed section of the Mam Tor road.

FLOWERY KINGS & QUEENS

Every 29 May – or on the 28th if the 29th is a Sunday – Castleton celebrates **Oak Apple Day** with a flamboyant village festival that can trace its origins back to at least the 17th century, and possibly all the way back to Celtic times. Every year, two residents of the village are chosen to be the Garland King and Queen and are then paraded through the village on horseback, with the Garland King buried under an enormous headdress woven with flowers. Even more interesting is the very strange behaviour of the Nettle Man, who whips anyone not wearing a sprig of oak leaves with a bunch of stinging nettles, which definitely adds to the surreal mood.

The tradition of wearing oak leaves dates back to the English Civil War, when it served as a badge of identification for supporters of Charles II, who escaped capture at the Battle of Worcester by hiding in an oak tree. However, scholars believe the festival may have its ultimate roots in the worship of the pagan fertility goddess Brigantia.

Activities

At the base of 517m Mam Tor, Castleton is the northern terminus of the **Limestone Way**, which follows narrow, rocky Cave Dale, far below the east wall of the castle. At the tourist office you can find maps and leaflets, including details of numerous easier walks.

Sleeping

Prices are often higher at weekends, for which booking ahead is advised.

Ye Olde Nag's Head Hotel PUB ££
(☎01433-620248; www.yeoldenagshead.co.uk; Cross St; d from £50; 🛜) The cosiest of the 'residential' pubs along the main road has comfortable, well-appointed rooms (some with four-poster beds and Jacuzzis), ale tasting trays and a popular restaurant, plus regular live music.

Causeway House B&B ££
(☎01433-623921; www.causewayhouse.co.uk; Back St; s/d from £33/65) The floors within this ancient character-soaked stone cottage are worn and warped with age, but the quaint bedrooms are bright and welcoming. Doubles have en-suite bathrooms but the two single rooms (one of which can be used as a twin) share a bathroom.

Rowter Farm CAMPSITE £
(☎01433-620271; sites per person £5; ⏲Easter-Oct; Ⓟ) This simple campsite, about 1 mile west of Castleton, has a stunning location up in the hills. Drivers should approach via Winnats Pass; on foot, follow the Cave Dale path.

Eating & Drinking

Teashops abound in Castleton. The village shop has limited stocks of provisions for walkers and is open seven days.

1530 ITALIAN ££
(☎01433-621870; www.1530therestaurant.co.uk; Cross St; mains £9-21.95; ⏲lunch & dinner Wed-Mon; 🖉) Crispy thin-crust pizzas and fresh pastas, like king prawn, crab, crayfish and calamari linguine, are the specialty of Castleton's swish new Italian flag bearer.

Ye Olde Cheshire Cheese Inn PUB ££
(☎01433-620330; www.cheshirecheeseinn.co.uk; How Lane; mains £7.95-10.95; 🛜🖉) Tradition is everything at this well-known alehouse, set in a fine old timbered building on the main road. The pub menu is more exotic than most (try the wild-boar casserole) and there are also comfy guest rooms.

Three Roofs Cafe CAFE £
(The Island; dishes £5.80-8.95; ⏲10am-5pm; 🛜) The most popular purveyor of cream teas, opposite the turn-off to the tourist office.

Information

Tourist Office (Buxton Rd; ⏲9.30am-5.30pm Mar-Oct, 10am-5pm Nov-Feb) With a snack kiosk, museum and lots of leaflets on local walks.

Getting There & Away

BUS Bus 272 runs to Sheffield (1¼ hours, hourly) and bus 173 to Bakewell (50 minutes, three daily) via Hope (10 minutes) and Tideswell (25 minutes). From Monday to Saturday, buses 68 and 173 travel from Castleton to Buxton (one hour) in the morning, returning in the afternoon. On Sundays only, bus 260 runs between Castleton and Edale (25 minutes, six services).

TRAIN The nearest train station is at Hope, about 3 miles east of Castleton on the line between Sheffield and Manchester. On summer weekends, a bus runs between Hope station and Castleton to meet the trains, but it's an easy walk.

Around Castleton

DERWENT RESERVOIRS

North of the Hope Valley, the upper reaches of the Derwent Valley were flooded between 1916 and 1935 to create three huge reservoirs to supply Sheffield, Leicester, Nottingham and Derby with water. These man-made lakes soon proved their worth – the **Dambusters** squadron carried out practice runs over Derwent Reservoir before unleashing their 'bouncing bombs' on the Ruhr Valley in Germany in WWII. Their exploits are detailed in the **Derwent Dam Museum** (www.derwentdammuseum.org; admission free; ⏲10am-4pm Sun) in a tower atop the dam.

These days, the Ladybower, Derwent and Howden Reservoirs are popular destinations for walkers, cyclists and mountain bikers – and lots of ducks, so drive slowly! **Fairholmes**, near the Derwent Dam, has a **tourist office** (⏲9.30am-5.30pm) dispensing walking and cycling advice; a car park; a snack bar; and a good **cycle hire centre** (☎01433-651261; ⏲9.30am-5.30pm), charging the standard Peak rates.

Fairholmes is 2 miles north of the A57, the main road between Sheffield and Manchester. Bus 273 from Sheffield Interchange runs to Fairholmes in the morning, returning in the afternoon.

Edale

POP 316

Surrounded by majestic Peak District countryside, this cluster of stone houses set around a pretty parish church is an enchanting place to pass the time. Edale lies between the White and Dark Peak areas, and is the southern terminus of the Pennine Way. Despite the remote location, the Manchester–Sheffield line passes through the village, bringing throngs of weekend visitors.

Activities

Predictably, walking is the number one drawcard, and there are plenty of diverting strolls for less committed hill walkers.

As well as trips to **Hollins Cross** and **Mam Tor**, on the ridge dividing Edale from Castleton, you can walk north onto the **Kinder Plateau**, dark and brooding when cloaked in mist, gloriously high and open when the sun's out. This was the setting for a famous act of civil disobedience by ramblers in 1932 that paved the way for the legal 'right to roam' and the creation of England's national parks.

Weather permitting, a fine circular walk starts by following a part of the **Pennine Way** through fields to Upper Booth, then up a path called Jacob's Ladder and along the southern edge of Kinder, before dropping down to Edale via the steep rocky valley of Grindsbrook Clough, or the ridge of Ringing Roger.

About 1.5 miles east of Edale, **Ladybooth Equestrian Centre** (☎01433-670205; www.ladybooth.co.uk; Nether Booth) offers horseback trips around the Peaks, lasting anything from one hour to a full day, plus pony farm rides for kids.

Sleeping

Upper Booth Farm CAMPSITE £
(☎01433-670250; www.upperboothcamping.co.uk; sites per person/car £5/3; ⏲Easter-Nov; P) Located along the Pennine Way about a mile from Edale, this peaceful campsite is set on a working farm and is surrounded by spectacular scenery. For hikers, there's a camping barn (per person £7) and small shop.

Edale YHA HOSTEL £
(☎0870 770 5808; www.yha.org.uk; dm from £18.40; @ 📶) Spectacular views across to Back Tor unfold from this country-house hostel 1.5 miles east of Edale. The attached **activity centre** is very popular with student groups. Follow the signed road from the road to Hope.

Stonecroft B&B ££
(☎01433-670262; www.stonecroftguesthouse.co.uk; Grindsbrook; d from £80; P 📶) This handsomely fitted-out stone house, built in the 1900s, has two comfortable bedrooms. Vegetarians and vegans are well catered for – host Julia is an award-winning chef and the organic breakfast is excellent.

Fieldhead Campsite CAMPSITE £
(☎01433-670386; www.fieldhead-campsite.co.uk; sites per person/car from £5/2.50; P) Right next to the Moorland Centre, this pretty and

well-equipped campsite spreads over six fields, with some pitches right by the river.

Eating & Drinking

Old Nag's Head PUB ££

(Grindsbrook; mains £7.55-12.95) Refurbished warm and welcoming walker-friendly pub.

Rambler Inn PUB ££

(☎01433-670268; www.theramblerinn.com; Grindsbrook; mains £9.25-10.95; 📶👪) Cosy stone pub with real ales, hearty steaks, pies and casseroles, B&B rooms and occasional live music.

Cooper's Cafe CAFE

(☎01433-670401; Cooper's Camp; dishes £2.50-4.50; ⏲8am-4pm; 📶) Load up on carbs at this cheerful cafe close to the village school.

Information

Moorland Tourist Office (☎01433-670207; www.edale-valley.co.uk; Grindsbrook; ⏲9.30am-5pm Mon-Fri, to 5.30pm Sat & Sun Apr-Sep, shorter hours in low season) Visitor centre with maps, displays on the moors, a kiosk and a campsite.

Getting There & Away

Trains run from Edale to Manchester (£10, 45 minutes, hourly) and Sheffield (£6.40, 40 minutes, every two hours) via Hope. From Monday to Friday on school days, bus 200 runs between Edale and Castleton (20 minutes, three daily) via Hope.

Eyam

POP 926

Quaint little Eyam (pronounced 'ee-em'), a former lead-mining village, has a poignant history. In 1665, the town was infected by the dreaded Black Death plague, carried here by fleas on a consignment of cloth from London, and the village rector, William Mompesson, convinced villagers to quarantine themselves. Some 270 of the village's 800 inhabitants succumbed, while surrounding villages remained relatively unscathed. Today, Eyam's sloping streets of old cottages backed by rows of green hills are delightful to wander.

Sights

Eyam Parish Church CHURCH

(⏲9am-6pm Mon-Sat) Many of the plague victims were buried at Eyam's church. You can view stained-glass panels and moving displays telling the story of the outbreak. The churchyard contains a Celtic cross carved in the 8th century.

Eyam Hall ARTS CENTRE

(www.eyamhall.co.uk; house & garden adult/child £7.50/4, craft centre admission free; ⏲house & garden noon-4pm Wed, Thu & Sun Easter-early May & late Jul-Aug, craft centre 10.30am-5pm Tue-Sun Mar-Oct, to 4pm Nov-Feb) This solid-looking 17th-century manor house with stone windows and doorframes is home to a craft centre and several eateries, surrounding a traditional English walled garden.

Eyam Museum MUSEUM

(www.eyammuseum.demon.co.uk; Hawkhill Rd; adult/child £2.50/2; ⏲10am-4.30pm Tue-Sun late Mar-early Nov, closed early Nov-late Mar) The town's engaging museum has vivid displays on the Eyam plague, plus exhibits on the village's history of lead mining and silk weaving.

Activities

Eyam makes a great base for walking and cycling in the White Peak area.

Mompesson's Well WALKING

For an interesting short walk, follow Water Lane out of the village from the main square, then turn right and climb the hill to reach Mompesson's Well, where supplies were left during the plague time for Eyam folk by friends from other villages. The goods were paid for using coins sterilised in vinegar. To return to Eyam, retrace your steps down the lane, then take a path which leads directly to the church. This 2-mile circuit takes about 1½ hours.

Sleeping & Eating

Miner's Arms PUB ££

(☎01433-630853; Water Lane; s £45, d £70-85, mains £8.45-14.95) Although its age isn't immediately obvious, this traditional village inn was built shortly before the plague hit Eyam. Inside you'll find beamed ceilings, affable staff, a cosy stone fireplace, comfy en-suite rooms and good-value pub food.

Crown Cottage B&B ££

(☎01433-630858; www.crown-cottage.co.uk; Main Rd; s/d from £50/70; P) Opposite the post office, this walker- and cyclist-friendly stone house full of pottery ornaments is crammed to the rafters most weekends, when there's a minimum two-night stay.

Eyam Tea Rooms TEAHOUSE £
(The Square; dishes $1.25-4.95; ⌚9.30am-4pm Wed-Mon) All chintz and doilies, this cute tearoom serves delicious homemade cakes and pastries, as well as hearty lunches.

Peak Pantry TEAHOUSE £
(The Square; dishes £2.10-3.50; ⌚9am-5pm Mon-Sat, 10am-5pm Sun) This unpretentious place on the village square has a mouth-watering array of slices and decent coffee.

Getting There & Away

Bus services:

Buxton Bus 65/66; 40 minutes, five daily (four Sunday)

Chesterfield Bus 66/66A; 40 minutes, five daily (four Sunday)

Sheffield Bus 65; 40 minutes, five daily (three Sunday)

Bakewell

POP 3979

The second-largest town in the Peak District, pretty Bakewell is a great base for exploring the White Peak. The town is ringed by famous walking trails and stately homes, but it's probably best known for its famous pudding (of which the Bakewell tart is just a poor imitation). Like other Peak towns, Bakewell is mobbed during the summer months – expect traffic jams and cut-throat competition for accommodation at weekends. The centre of town is Rutland Sq, the meeting point of the roads from Matlock, Buxton and Chesterfield.

Sights

All Saints Church CHURCH
(⌚9am-4.45pm Apr-Oct, to 3.45pm Nov-Mar) Up on the hill above Rutland Sq, All Saints Church is packed with ancient features, including a 14th-century font, a pair of Norman arches, some fine heraldic tombs and a collection of crude stone gravestones and crosses dating back to the 12th century.

Old House Museum MUSEUM
(www.oldhousemuseum.org.uk; Cunningham Pl; adult/child £3.50/2; ⌚11am-4pm Apr-early Nov, closed early Nov-Mar) Set in a time-worn stone house near All Saints Church, the Old House Museum explores local history. Check out the Tudor loo and the displays on wattle and daub, a traditional technique for building walls using woven twigs and cow dung.

Spirit of the 1940s MUSEUM
(www.oldhousemuseum.org.uk; Matlock St; adult/child £2/50p, joint ticket with Old House Museum £5/2; ⌚10.30am-4pm Fri-Mon Apr-early Nov, closed early Nov-Mar) Near the Old House Museum, its 2012-opened Spirit of the 1940s museum incorporates an evocative '40s street scene, letters and photographs, and wartime memorabilia.

Activities

Walking and cycling are, of course, the main activities. In addition to the Monsal Trail, walking routes go to the stately homes Haddon Hall and Chatsworth House.

Monsal Trail WALKING
The scenic Monsal Trail follows the path of a disused railway line from Combs Viaduct on the outskirts of Bakewell to Topley Pike in Wye Dale, about 3 miles east of Buxton, including a number of reopened old railway tunnels, covering 8½ miles in all.

For a rewarding shorter walk, follow the Monsal Trail for 3 miles to the dramatic viewpoint at Monsal Head, where you can pause for refreshment at the **Monsal Head Hotel** (☎01629-640250; www.monsalhead.com; s/d incl breakfast from £65/90, mains £11.20-16; Ⓟ), serving real ales and outstanding Modern British cuisine. With more time to kill, continue to Miller's Dale, where viaducts give a spectacular vista across the steep-sided valley. The tourist offices at Bakewell and Buxton have full details.

Sleeping

Rutland Arms Hotel HOTEL £££
(☎01629-812812; www.rutlandarmsbakewell.co.uk; The Square; s £88-118, d £140-165; Ⓟ) Jane Austen is said to have stayed in room 2 of this aristocratic, recently refurbished stone coaching inn while working on *Pride and Prejudice*. The more expensive of its 35 rooms have lots of flowery Victorian flourishes.

Melbourne House B&B ££
(☎01629-815357; www.bakewell-accommodation.co.uk; Buxton Rd; d incl breakfast from £60; Ⓟ) In a picturesque, creeper-covered building dating back more than three centuries, this inviting B&B is handily situated on the main road leading to Buxton.

Eating & Drinking

Bakewell's streets are lined with sweet tearooms and bakeries.

PUDDING OF CHAMPIONS

The Peak District's most famous dessert is – as any Bakewell resident will tell you – a pudding, not a tart. Invented following an accidental misreading of a recipe in around 1820, the Bakewell pudding is a pastry shell, spread with jam and topped with frangipane, a mixture of egg and ground almonds. If you've only ever seen the glazed version produced by commercial bakeries, the Bakewell original may look crude and misshapen, but is delicious. **The Old Original Bakewell Pudding Shop** (☎01629-812193; www.bakewellpuddingshop.co.uk; The Square; dishes £2.25-9.25; ⊙9am-5.30pm) and **Bloomers Original Bakewell Puddings** (☎01629-814844; Water St) both claim to be the 'original' creator of the Bakewell Pudding – decide for yourself.

TOP CHOICE **Piedaniel's** FRENCH ££
(☎01629-812687; www.piedaniels-restaurant.com; Bath St; mains £16; ⊙Tue-Sat) Chefs Eric and Christiana Piedaniel's modern French cuisine is the toast of the local restaurants. A whitewashed dining room is the exquisite setting for dining on the likes of lobster bisque with quenelles (feather-light flour, egg and cream dumplings) followed by monkfish in salmon mousse. Weekday lunch set menus (two/three courses for £13/15) are exceptional value. Ask about cooking classes and demonstrations.

Castle Inn PUB
(☎01629-812103; www.castle-inn-bakewell.co.uk; Bridge St; mains £7.39-16.99;) The ivy-draped Castle Inn is one of the better pubs in Bakewell, with four centuries' practice in rejuvenating hamstrung hikers. Gourmet burgers are a menu highlight; it also has four adjacent guest rooms.

Information

Tourist Office (☎01629-813227; Bridge St; ⊙9.30am-5pm Apr-Oct, from 10am Nov-Mar) Located in the old Market Hall, this helpful place with racks of leaflets and books can help arrange accommodation.

Getting There & Away

Bakewell lies on the Transpeak bus route. Buses run hourly to Nottingham (1¾ hours), Derby (1¼ hours), Matlock Bath (30 minutes) and Buxton (50 minutes). Five services a day continue to Manchester (1¾ hours).

Around Bakewell

HADDON HALL

Glorious **Haddon Hall** (www.haddonhall.co.uk; adult/child £9.50/5.50; ⊙noon-5pm daily May-Sep & early-late Dec, noon-5pm Sat, Sun & Mon Apr & Oct, closed Nov-early Dec & late Dec-Mar) looks exactly like a medieval manor house should – all stone turrets, time-worn timbers and walled gardens. The house was founded in the 12th century, and expanded and remodelled throughout medieval times. The 'modernisation' stopped when the house was abandoned in the 18th century, saving Haddon Hall from the more florid excesses of the Victorian period. It was used as a location for the period blockbusters *Jane Eyre* (1996 and 2011), *Elizabeth* (1998) and *Pride and Prejudice* (2005).

The house is 2 miles south of Bakewell on the A6. You can get here on the Transpeak bus from Bakewell to Matlock and Derby (hourly) or walk along the footpath through the fields, mostly on the east side of the river.

CHATSWORTH HOUSE

Known as the 'Palace of the Peak', the vast edifice of **Chatsworth House** (☎01246-582204; www.chatsworth.org; house & gardens adult/child £15/9, gardens only £10/6, playground £5, park free; ⊙11am-5.30pm mid-Mar–late Dec, closed late Dec–mid-Mar) has been occupied by the earls and dukes of Devonshire for centuries. The manor was founded in 1552 by the formidable Bess of Hardwick and her second husband, William Cavendish, who earned grace and favour by helping Henry VIII dissolve the English monasteries. Mary, Queen of Scots, was imprisoned at Chatsworth on the orders of Elizabeth I in 1569.

While the core of the house dates from the 16th century, Chatsworth was altered and enlarged over the centuries. The current building has a Georgian feel, dating back to the last overhaul in 1820. Inside, the lavish apartments and mural-painted staterooms are packed with priceless paintings and period furniture. Look out for the portraits of the current generation of Devonshires by Lucian Freud.

The house sits in 25 sq miles of grounds and ornamental gardens, some landscaped by Lancelot 'Capability' Brown. Kids will love the farmyard adventure playground with loads of ropes, swings and slides, and farmyard critters.

Chatsworth is 3 miles northeast of Bakewell. Bus 214 from Sheffield Interchange to Matlock goes right to Chatsworth (hourly, 50 minutes) and bus 215 runs from Bakewell (20 minutes, hourly) on Sunday. On other days, take bus 214.

From Bakewell, walkers can take footpaths through Chatsworth park via the mock-Venetian village of Edensor (pronounced 'en-sor').

Birmingham, the West Midlands & the Marches

Includes »

Best Places to Eat

- Grameen Khana (p509)
- Simpsons (p509)
- Church Street Townhouse (p523)
- Drapers Hall (p546)
- Richard Booth's Bookshop Cafe (p538)

Best Places to Stay

- Hotel du Vin (p508)
- Castle House (p536)
- Silken Strand (p529)
- Old House Suites (p546)

Why Go?

Few other places in the country come so close to the dream of England. If you are searching for chocolate-box villages of wonky timbered houses and ancient stone churches, or stately homes that look like the last lord of the manor just clip-clopped out of the stables, or the chance to walk in the footsteps of William Shakespeare, you'll find it here.

You'll also find the dust and grime of centuries of industrial history – exemplified by the World Heritage–listed mills of Ironbridge – and tumbling hills where the air is so clean you can taste it. Walkers and cyclists flock to the Marches, the long line of hills that marks out the border between England and Wales, only to vanish into the vastness of the landscape. Then there's the city of Birmingham, an industrial crucible reinvented as cultural melting pot, with the best food and nightlife in the Midlands.

When to Go

Literary buffs take note: Shakespeare takes a back seat to contemporary wordsmiths at Stratford's Literary Festival in April/May, and in May/June bookworms descend on Hay-on-Wye for the annual book festival. If you're up for a belt-loosening, belly-stretching good time, head to Ludlow's famous food and drink festival in September.

On weekends from April to September, shuttle buses provide access to wonderful walking trails on the Long Mynd and the Shropshire Hills.

Birmingham, the West Midlands & the Marches Highlights

1 Enjoying England's great contribution to the world of curry in the balti restaurants of **Birmingham** (p509)

2 Walking in the footsteps of the Bard in Shakespeare-obsessed **Stratford-upon-Avon** (p518)

3 Forging a path across the Shropshire Hills at the Long Mynd and Stiperstones near **Church Stretton** (p554)

4 Gazing out over the bewitching night-time panorama of **Bridgnorth** (p552)

5 Leafing through worthy tomes in the eccentric secondhand bookstores of **Hay-on-Wye** (p537)

6 Admiring the dragon-infested medieval map of the world in gorgeous **Hereford Cathedral** (p535)

7 Strolling around lovely **Lichfield** (p526), home to a fine cathedral, Dr Johnson and Darwin's grandad

8 Stepping into the magnificent interior of **St Giles Church** (p529) in Cheadle

History

This region has seen its share of action over the centuries, much of it centred on the Marches – the English counties in the West Midlands lying close to the border with Wales – where a succession of kingdoms and empires struggled to gain a foothold in the homelands of the Welsh tribes. Cross-border skirmishes became so problematic that 8th-century Anglo-Saxon king Offa of Mercia built an earthwork barricade along the border to keep the warring factions apart, and this border is now the route of a popular walking trail.

In an effort to subdue the Welsh and secure his new kingdom, William the Conqueror installed powerful, feudal barons – called Lords Marcher, from the Anglo-Saxon word *mearc* (meaning 'boundary') – in castles all along the border. Over the following centuries, these warlords staged repeated raids into Wales, taking as much territory as possible under their control.

Things continued in a similar vein until the 18th century, when the inventive locals discovered that industry was an easier way of making money than squabbling over land. The invention of modern iron-smelting in the Shropshire village of Ironbridge in 1709 gave birth to the Industrial Revolution, while the visionary Birmingham-based Lunar Society spawned factory owners, canal builders, scientists and engineers who transformed the world.

Activities

Outdoorsy types make for the lush green hills of the **Marches**. The tumbling landscape is scattered with ruined castles, and the exposed summits of the highest hills offer views equal to anything in the Peak and Lake Districts. As well as the famous **Offa's Dyke Path** (p535), there are numerous waymarked trails and long-distance paths. Top spots for walking and cycling include the **Long Mynd** and **Stiperstones** in Shropshire, the **Malvern Hills** in Worcestershire and the area around **Symonds Yat** in Herefordshire.

Canoeing and **kayaking** are popular diversions at Hereford, Hay-on-Wye, and Symonds Yat in Herefordshire and Ironbridge Gorge in Shropshire, and **hang-gliders** and **paragliders** launch from the hills above Church Stretton in Shropshire.

Information

Heart of England Tourist Board (☎01905-761100; www.visitheartofengland.com)

Getting There & Around

Birmingham has frequent services to nearby cities and to London Euston, though the Snow Hill station connects with London Marlyebone.

Excellent rail connections exist to towns across the West Midlands, and **National Express** (p819) and local bus companies connect larger towns and villages, though services are reduced in the low season. Ask locally about discounted all-day tickets. **Birmingham Airport** is the main air hub. For general route information, visit **Traveline Midlands** (www.travelinemidlands.co.uk) or www.networkwestmidlands.com.

BIRMINGHAM

POP 977,087

Once a byword for bad town planning, England's second-largest city – known locally as 'Brum' – is shaking off the legacy of industrial decline, and spending some serious money replacing its 1960s concrete architecture with gleaming glass and steel. The town centre looks better than it has done in decades, helped in no small part by the revitalised Bullring centre, and the iconic Selfridges building, which looks out over the city like the compound eye of a giant robot insect.

With its industrial legacy and chaotic road network, Birmingham might not leap out as a tourist attraction, but there's a lot to see, including some fine museums and galleries, and the Midland's finest nightlife and dining scene. Sleek Modern British restaurants dominate the centre, while the 'burbs were the birthplace of the balti (p509) – England's unique contribution to the world of curry, invented by Pakistani workers who moved here in the 1970s.

History

Described as a small village in the *Domesday Book* of 1086 and home to a handful of villagers and two ploughs (with a total value of £1), Brum later exploded into a bustling industrial and mercantile hub, building its fortunes first on the wool trade, and then on metal-working from the 16th century.

In the mid-18th century, the Lunar Society brought together the leading geologists, chemists, scientists, engineers and theorists of the age and Birmingham became the world's first industrialised town, attracting workers from across the nation.

BIRMINGHAM IN...

Two Days

Start off in the centre, dropping into Victoria Sq and the eclectic **Birmingham Museum & Art Gallery**. Go west through Centenary Sq to reach the **Birmingham Canals**, where you can while away an afternoon at the **National Sea Life Centre** or **Ikon gallery**, before dining at **Simpsons**. On day two, indulge your inner shopaholic at the gleaming malls of the **Bullring** and **Mailbox**, which both have good options for lunch. In the afternoon, catch up on some social history at the **Birmingham Back to Backs**. After dark, roam south to the **Balti Triangle** to sample Birmingham's unique contribution to the world of curry.

Four Days

Follow the two-day itinerary, but add a **canal cruise**. On day three, head north from the centre to **Aston Hall** and **Soho House**, or south to the famous **Barber Institute of Fine Arts**, then take in a show at the **Repertory Theatre** or a concert at **Symphony Hall**. Use day four to explore the fascinating **Jewellery Quarter**, with an upmarket Indian lunch at **Lasan**, and spend the afternoon reliving *Charlie and the Chocolate Factory* fantasies at **Cadbury World**.

Overcrowding, poverty and pollution soon became major social ills.

A degree of salvation came in the mid-1800s, when enlightened mayors such as Joseph Chamberlain (1836–1914) cleaned out the slums and filled the centre with grand civic buildings. Sadly, little evidence of this golden age remains today thanks to WWII bombers and overzealous town planning. Vast swaths of the centre were demolished in a bid to transform Birmingham into 'Britain's Motor City'.

Whatever the mistakes of the past, recent years have seen a series of successful regeneration projects as part of the 'Big City Plan', with 21st-century landmarks dotting the city.

One thing that has endured through all this is the distinctive Brummie accent – in a controversial nationwide survey in 2008, it was rated worse than silence, to the outrage of locals.

Sights & Activities

For information on all of Birmingham's museums, visit www.bmag.org.uk.

City Centre

Victoria Square SQUARE

Birmingham's grandest civic buildings cluster around pedestrianised Victoria Sq, at the western end of New St, dominated by the stately facade of **Council House**, erected in 1874–79. A facelift in the 1990s gave the square modernist sphinxes and a **fountain** topped by a naked female figure, 'the floozie in the jacuzzi' by locals, overlooked by a disapproving **statue of Queen Victoria**.

Town Hall HISTORIC BUILDING

(☎0121-780 3333; www.thsh.co.uk) The west side of Victoria Sq is marked out by the neoclassical Town Hall, constructed in 1834 and styled after the Temple of Castor and Pollux in Rome, and now used as a venue for classical concerts and stage performances.

Centenary Square SQUARE

Centenary Sq is book-ended by the art-deco **Hall of Memory War Memorial** and the **International Convention Centre** (ICC) and **Symphony Hall**. Across the road is a gilded **statue of Boulton, Watt and Murdoch**, three of the brightest lights of the Lunar Society. The impressive and inventively-designed new £189-million **Birmingham Library** building will open on the north side of the square in 2013.

FREE **Birmingham Museum & Art Gallery** MUSEUM

(☎0121-303 2834; www.bmag.org.uk; Chamberlain Sq; ⏲10am-5pm Mon-Thu & Sat, 10.30am-5pm Fri, 12.30-5pm Sun) Housed in the annexe at the back of Council House, the outstanding Birmingham Museum & Art Gallery displays a breathtaking selection of ancient treasures and Victorian art, including an excellent collection of major Pre-Raphaelite works by Rossetti, Edward Burne-Jones and others. The museum's other standout draw is part of the Staffordshire Hoard, a

Birmingham

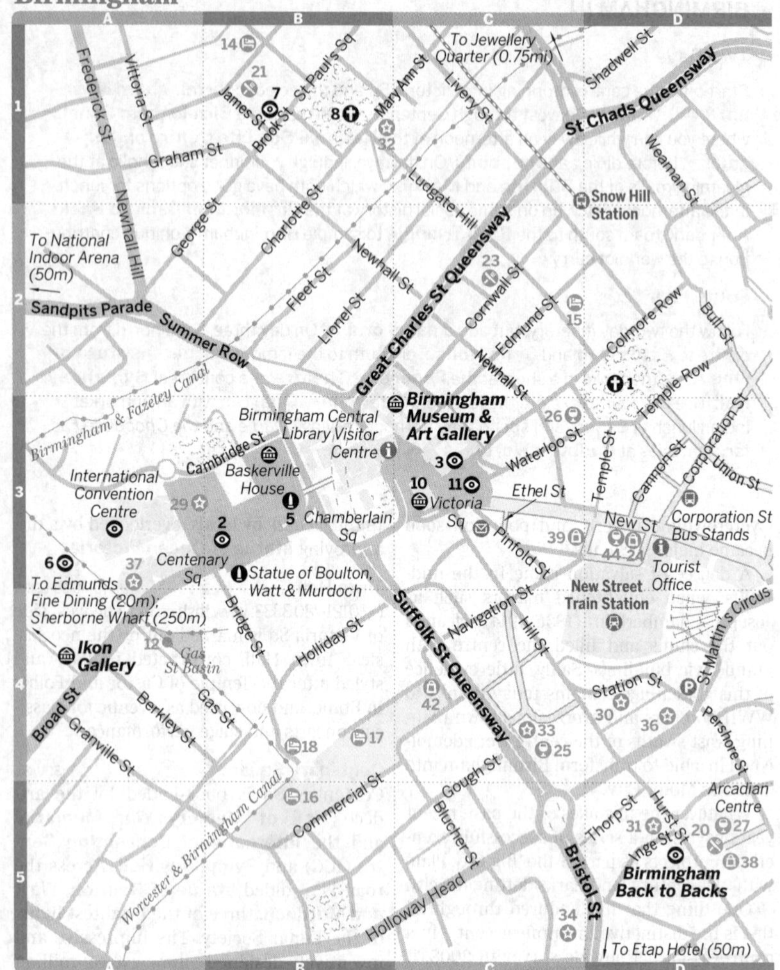

treasure trove of 7th-century Anglo-Saxon gold, unearthed near Lichfield in 2009.

Cathedral Church of St Philip CATHEDRAL
(☎0121-262 1840; Colmore Row; entry by donation; ⏲7.30am-6.30pm Mon-Fri, 8.30am-5pm Sat & Sun) One of England's smallest cathedrals, this striking church was constructed in a neoclassical style between 1709 and 1715. The Pre-Raphaelite artist Edward Burne-Jones was responsible for the magnificent stained-glass windows: the *Last Judgement*, which can be seen at the western end, and *Nativity*, *Crucifixion* and *Ascension* at the eastern end.

Birmingham Back to Backs NEIGHBOURHOOD
(NT; ☎0121-666 7671; 55-63 Hurst St; tour adult/child £6.30/3.20; ⏲10am-5pm Tue-Sun) This cluster of restored back-to-back terraced houses can be visited by a popular tour that takes you through four working-class homes, revealing the stories of those who lived here between the 1840s and the 1970s.

Birmingham Canals

During the industrial age, Birmingham was a major hub on the English canal network

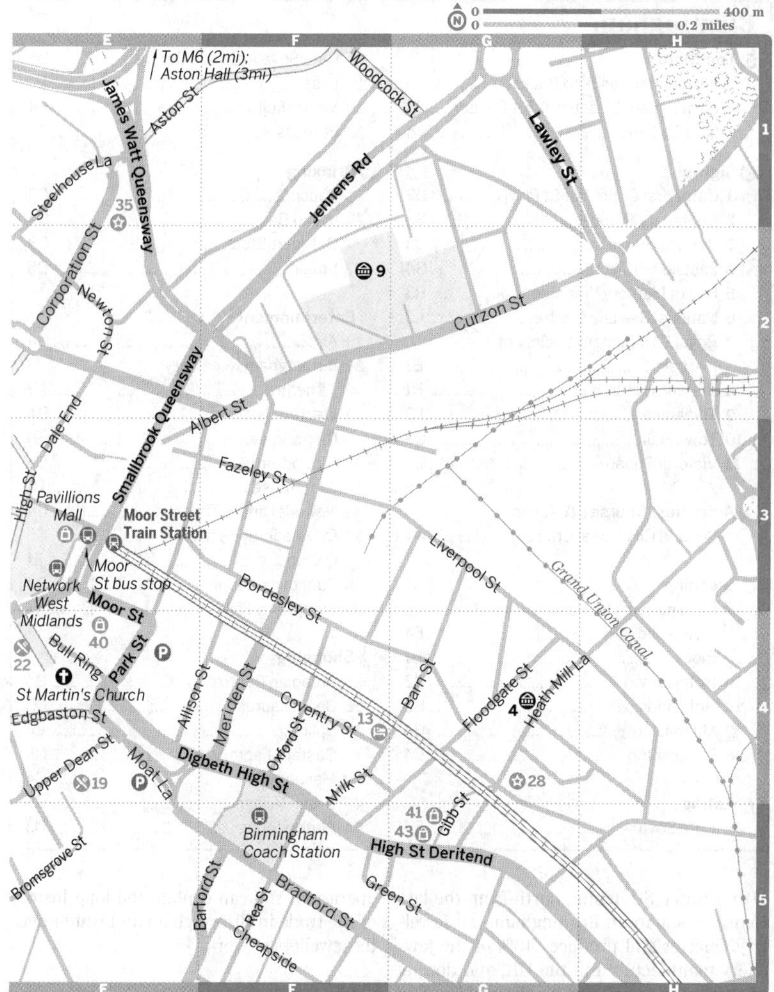

(with technically more miles of canals than Venice), and visiting narrow boats still float into Gas St Basin in the heart of the city.

The Brindley Pl development contains banking offices, designer restaurants and the sleek **Ikon Gallery** (☎0121-248 0708; www.ikon-gallery.co.uk; 1 Oozells Sq; admission free; ⏲11am-6pm Tue-Sun). Prepare to be thrilled, bemused or outraged, depending on your take on conceptual art.

National Sea Life Centre AQUARIUM
(☎0121-643 6777; www.visitsealife.com; 3a Brindley Pl; adult/child £18/14.40; ⏲10am-5pm Mon-Fri, to 6pm Sat & Sun) The Sir Norman Foster–designed National Sea Life Centre is the largest inland aquarium in England, its tanks teeming with exotic marine life including razor-jawed hammerhead sharks, turtles and otters. Buy tickets online ahead of time for fast-track entry (school holidays see long queues).

Jewellery Quarter

Birmingham has been a major player on the British jewellery scene ever since Charles II brought back a taste for fancy buckles and sparkly brocade from France in the

Birmingham

Top Sights
Birmingham Back to Backs ... D5
Birmingham Museum & Art Gallery ... C3
Ikon Gallery ... A4

Sights
1 Cathedral Church of St Philip ... D2
2 Centenary Square ... B3
3 Council House ... C3
4 Eastside Projects ... G4
5 Hall of Memory War Memorial ... B3
6 National Sea Life Centre ... A3
7 Royal Birmingham Society of Artists ... B1
8 St Paul's Church ... B1
9 Thinktank ... F2
10 Town Hall ... C3
11 Victoria Square ... C3

Activities, Courses & Tours
12 Second City Canal Cruises ... A4

Sleeping
13 Birmingham Central Backpackers ... F4
14 Bloc ... B1
15 Hotel du Vin ... C2
16 Hotel Indigo ... B5
17 Malmaison ... B4
18 Premier Inn ... B4

Eating
19 Cafe Soya ... E4
20 Cafe Soya Arcadian Centre ... D5
21 Lasan ... B1
22 Mount Fuji ... E4
23 Purnells ... C2

Drinking
24 Bacchus ... D3
25 Island Bar ... C4
26 Old Joint Stock ... C3
27 Sobar ... D5

Entertainment
28 Air ... G4
29 Birmingham Repertory Theatre ... A3
30 Electric Cinema ... D4
Giant Screen ... (see 9)
31 Hippodrome ... D5
32 Jam House ... B1
33 New Alexandra Theatre ... C4
34 O2 Academy ... C5
35 Q Club ... E1
36 Sunflower Lounge ... D4
37 Symphony Hall ... A3

Shopping
38 Arcadian Centre ... D5
39 Beadesaurus ... C3
40 Bullring ... E4
41 Custard Factory ... G5
42 Mailbox ... C4
43 Urban Village ... G5
44 Waterstones ... D3

17th century. Stretching north from the last Georgian square in Birmingham, the Jewellery Quarter still produces 40% of the jewellery manufactured in the UK, and dozens of workshops are open to the public. The tourist office (p512) provides a free booklet, *Jewellery Quarter: The Essential Guide*, or you can take a virtual tour at www.jewelleryquarter.net.

The Jewellery Quarter is three-quarters of a mile northwest of the centre; take bus 101 or ride the metro from Snow Hill or the train from Moor St to Jewellery Quarter station.

FREE Museum of the Jewellery Quarter MUSEUM
(0121-554 3598; 75-79 Vyse St; 10.30am-4pm Tue-Sun) In this museum, the Smith & Pepper jewellery factory is preserved as it was on its closing day in 1981, after 80 years of operation. You can explore the long history of the trade in Birmingham and watch master jewellers at work.

FREE Soho House HISTORIC BUILDING
(0121-554 9122; Soho Ave, Handsworth; 11.30am-4pm Tue-Sun Apr-Oct) About 1.5 miles northwest of the Jewellery Quarter, Soho House is where industrialist Matthew Boulton lived from 1766 to 1809. Among the restored 18th-century chambers is the dining room where Boulton and members of the Lunar Society met to discuss their world-changing ideas. Take bus 74 or 79.

FREE Royal Birmingham Society of Artists ARTS CENTRE
(0121-236 4353; www.rbsa.org.uk; 10.30am-5.30pm Mon-Fri, 10.30am-5pm Sat, 1-5pm Sun) At the northwest corner of the pretty Georgian

St Paul's Sq, the Royal Birmingham Society of Artists has been exhibiting the work of local artists and artisans since 1814.

St Paul's Church CHURCH
St Paul's Sq is dominated by this 18th-century church, where Luna Society members Matthew Boulton and James Watt came to pray.

Outlying Areas

Thinktank MUSEUM
(☎0121-202 2222; www.thinktank.ac; Millennium Point, Curzon St; adult/child £12.25/8.40; ⏲10am-5pm, last admission 4pm) A 10-minute walk northeast of the centre, surrounded by the footprints of vanished factories, the Millennium Point development contains this entertaining and ambitious attempt to make science accessible to children. There's also a digital Planetarium, covered by the same ticket, and a giant cinema screen (p510).

FREE **Barber Institute of Fine Arts** GALLERY
(☎0121-414 7333; www.barber.org.uk; ⏲10am-5pm Mon-Fri, 11am-5pm Sat & Sun) Around 2.5 miles south of the centre at the University of Birmingham, the Barber Institute of Fine Arts displays Renaissance masterpieces; European masters such as Rubens and Van Dyck; British greats including Gainsborough, Reynolds and Turner; and classics from modern titans Picasso, Magritte and others. Take the train to University station, or buses 61, 62 or 63.

Birmingham Botanical Gardens & Glasshouses GARDENS
(www.birminghambotanicalgardens.org.uk; Westbourne Rd; adult/child £7.50/4.75; ⏲9am-7pm Mon-Sat, from 10am Sun Apr-Sep, to dusk Oct-Mar) In Edgbaston, these are the Midlands' answer to Kew Gardens, with grand Victorian glasshouses full of flowers, cacti, palms and a collection of bonsai. Take bus 10, 22 or 23.

Cadbury World MUSEUM
(☎0844 880 7667; www.cadburyworld.co.uk; Linden Rd; adult/child £14.75/10.75, under 3yr free) Cadbury World, about 4 miles south of Birmingham in the village of Bournville, sets out to educate visitors about the history of cocoa and the Cadbury family, but sweetens the deal with free samples, chocolate-making machines, and chocolate-themed rides. Opening hours vary through the year (bookings essential in July and August), so check the website before you visit.

Surrounding the chocolate works, pretty **Bournville Village** was built by the philanthropic Cadbury family to accommodate early-20th-century factory workers. In the centre of the village, **Selly Manor** (☎0121-472 0199; www.bvt.org.uk/sellymanor; Maple Rd; adult/child £3.50/1.50; ⏲10am-5pm Tue-Fri year-round, plus 2-5pm Sat & Sun Apr-Sep) is a bona fide 14th-century manor house, shifted brick and mortar from its original location by George Cadbury to save it from destruction. Trains run to Bournville from Birmingham New St station.

Aston Hall HISTORIC BUILDING
(☎0121-675 4722; Trinity Rd; house adult/child £4/free, grounds free; ⏲noon-4pm Tue-Sun Apr-Oct) About 3 miles north of the centre in Aston (of Aston Villa fame), this well-preserved hall was built in extravagant Jacobean style between 1618 and 1635. To get to Aston Hall, take bus 65 or a train to Aston station from New St station.

Tours

The tourist office (p512) has a number of free themed walking tour pamphlets.

Birmingham Tours WALKING TOUR
(☎0121-427 2555; www.birmingham-tours.co.uk) Runs popular walking tours and the

BIRMINGHAM BRAINS

The Industrial Revolution was a great time for entrepreneurs, and nowhere more so than in Birmingham, where the industrialists, philosophers and intellectuals of the Lunar Society came together to swap ideas for the greatest technological leap forward since the invention of the wheel. As well as engineers such as Matthew Boulton, James Watt and gaslight mogul William Murdoch, the society drew in such great thinkers as philosopher and naturalist Erasmus Darwin, oxygen-discoverer Joseph Priestley, pottery boss Josiah Wedgwood, botanist Joseph Banks and founding father Benjamin Franklin.

Between 1765 and 1813, this esteemed company held regular meetings at Soho House (now an engaging museum) to thrash out their ground-breaking ideas. If you don't feel like dragging yourself out to the 'burbs, there's a gleaming golden statue of Boulton, Watt and Murdoch near Centenary Sq.

hop-on/hop-off **Big Brum Buz** (day ticket adult/child £12/5; ⏱Sat & Sun May-Sep).

Second City Canal Cruises BOAT TOUR
(☎0121-236 9811; www.secondcityboats.co.uk) Narrow-boat tours of Birmingham's canals lasting anything from one hour to two days, leaving from the Gas St Basin.

Sherborne Wharf BOAT TOUR
(☎0121-455 6163; www.sherbornewharf.co.uk; Sherborne St; adult/child £6.50/5; ⏱11.30am, 1pm, 2.30pm & 4pm daily mid-Apr–Oct, Sat & Sun Nov–mid-Apr) Nostalgic narrow-boat cruises from the quayside by the International Convention Centre.

Festivals & Events

Crufts Dog Show DOG SHOW
(www.crufts.org.uk) The world's greatest collection of pooches on parade, held every March at the National Exhibition Centre.

Birmingham Pride GAY FESTIVAL
(www.birminghampride.com) One of the largest and most colourful celebrations of gay and lesbian culture in the country, held in May.

Artsfest ARTS FESTIVAL
(www.artsfest.org.uk)

Sleeping

Most Birmingham hotels target business travellers, ensuring high weekday prices. Look out for cheap weekend deals or deals for longer stays. B&Bs are concentrated outside the centre in Acocks Green (to the southeast) and Edgbaston and Selly Oak (to the southwest).

TOP CHOICE **Hotel du Vin** HOTEL ££
(☎0121-200 0600; www.hotelduvin.com; Church St; s/d from £99; P@) Housed in the handsome Victorian precincts of the former Birmingham Eye Hospital, this spiffing red-brick hotel has real class, with wrought-iron balustrades, classical murals and seasoned charms. Art-deco-inspired rooms have spectacular bathrooms, there's a pampering spa, and a bistro with shabby-chic worn floorboards and a stellar wine list, plus a lounge bar with comfy leather furniture. There's a charge for parking.

Malmaison HOTEL ££
(☎0121-246 5000; www.malmaison-birmingham.com; 1 Wharfside St; d from £99; P@) Within tickling distance of Harvey Nichols and the smart eateries of the Mailbox, mood lighting and Regency tones set the scene in the stylish rooms, which offer floor-to-ceiling views. Indulgences include a brasserie, Champagne bar and miniature spa. Wheelchair accessible.

Birmingham Central Backpackers HOSTEL £
(☎0121-643 0033; www.birminghamcentralbackpackers.com; 58 Coventry St; dm from £13; @) Despite the railway-bridge-right-next-door setting in down-at-heel Digbeth, Birmingham's purple and turquoise backpacker hostel is handy for the bus station, and guests have a choice of clean, multicoloured dorms or funky Japanese-style pods. The excellent facilities include a lounge with DVD movies and a PlayStation, a guest kitchen and a bar.

Hotel Indigo HOTEL ££
(☎0121-643 2010; www.hotelindigo.com; The Cube, Wharfside St; d £100; P) A stylish and zesty core operation on the 23rd and 24th floors of standout The Cube, Hotel Indigo marries a handy location with chic boutique exuberance and great views from neat and trendy rooms. Panoramic vistas continue on the floor above with the Marco Pierre White Steakhouse Bar & Grill. Parking costs extra; there's a small swimming pool.

Bloc BOUTIQUE HOTEL £
(☎0121-212 1223; www.blochotels.com; St Paul's, Caroline St; r from £45;) Aesthetically doing what it says on the packet, this grey-brick block-like Jewellery Quarter 'boutique budget' hotel has sharp geometric looks and tiny rooms with monsoon showers, wet rooms, flat-screen TVs built into the wall and under-bed storage for your bag. Rooms come with a window or no window. Discount parking nearby.

Premier Inn BUSINESS HOTEL £
(☎0871 527 8078; www.premierinn.com; 20 Bridge St; r from £39; P) A room at a Premier Inn won't offer many surprises (basic utilitarian comfort is standard), but the highly central, canal-side location is excellent for shopping and sightseeing and gives it a measure of individuality. Staff are pleasant and helpful and the breakfasts are a great way to kick off your day in Brum.

Westbourne Lodge B&B ££
(☎0121-429 1003; www.westbournelodge.co.uk; Fountain Rd; s/d from £49.50/69; P@) This popular B&B is conveniently located about 2 miles southwest in the suburb of Edgbaston (follow the A456). Rooms are a little chintzy

but spacious, and there's a pleasant terrace to enjoy in summer.

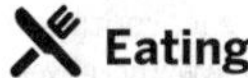

Eating

Birmingham is best known for its brilliant baltis (see the boxed text) but the city has a flourishing reputation for fine dining. For cheap eats, look to the myriad Asian eateries in Chinatown, just south of the centre.

Simpsons MODERN BRITISH, HOTEL £££
(☎0121-454 3434; www.simpsonsrestaurant.co.uk; 20 Highfield Rd; 3-course set lunch £38; r £180-225; ⊙closed dinner Sun) Simpsons is far from the centre in a gorgeous Victorian house in Edgbaston, but it's worth making the journey for the imaginative creations sliced and diced by Michelin-starred chef Andreas Antona. You could even stay the night in one of the four luxurious bedrooms upstairs (Tuesday to Saturday only). Reservations recommended.

Lasan INDIAN ££
(☎0121-212 3664; www.lasangroup.com; 3-4 Dakota Buildings, James St; mains £16-20; ⊙lunch Sun-Fri, dinner daily) Expletive-loving chef Gordon Ramsay gave his endorsement to this elegant and upscale Indian as Britain's best local restaurant. From our experience, the service and style are spot on and the North and South Indian dishes are effin' masterpieces.

Purnells MODERN BRITISH £££
(☎0121-212 9799; www.purnellsrestaurant.com; 55 Cornwall St; 2-/3-course lunch £22/27, dinner £36/42; ⊙lunch Tue-Fri, dinner Tue-Sat) Exquisite, inventive dishes (such as ox cheek with lentils cooked in toffee) are served in an airy Victorian redbrick building with a striking modern interior. Run by celebrated chef Glynn Purnell.

Edmunds Fine Dining MODERN BRITISH £££
(☎0121-633 4944; www.edmundsbirmingham.com; 6 Brindley Pl; 2-/3-course lunch/preconcert dinner from £19.50/24.50; ⊙lunch Tue-Fri, dinner Tue-Sat) Michelin-starred chef Andy Waters' sleek place is where traders from the surrounding banking houses come to spend their bonuses. Expect lots of locally sourced meats, fish and farm-fresh produce balanced with an enticing vegatarian menu. The restaurant is just back from the river in the Brindley Pl precinct.

Grameen Khana BALTI £
(☎0121-449 9994; www.grameenkhana.com; 310-312 Ladypool Rd; meals £15) In the Balti Triangle area, multicoloured lights and Bollywood movies provide a backdrop to one of the city's best baltis.

Saleem's Restaurant & Sweet House BALTI £
(☎0121-449 1861; 256-258 Ladypool Rd) This long-established Balti Triangle restaurant is understandably popular for its tasty milk-based Indian sweets and generous portions of balti.

Al Faisal's BALTI £
(☎0121-449 5695; www.alfaisal.co.uk; 136-140 Stoney Lane; mains from £6.50) Come to this Balti Triangle favourite for delicious dishes from the mountains of Kashmir, as well as for classic Birmingham baltis.

Mount Fuji JAPANESE ££
(☎0121-633 9853; www.mountfuji.co.uk; Bullring; mains £7-14) Put retail therapy on hold and sashay to this minimalist Japanese sushi cafe for raw fish, bento boxes and sake.

Cafe Soya ASIAN £
(☎0121-622 3888; Upper Dean St; mains £6.50-9) Excellent cafe dishing up tasty dim sum, rice dishes and filling bowls of noodles

THE BEAUTIFUL BALTI

If curry is the unofficial national dish of England, then the balti is its finest interpretation. First cooked up in the curry-houses of Sparkbrook in southern Birmingham, this one-pot curry is prepared in a cast-iron wok with plenty of onion and chilli. Tracing its origins back to Baltistan in northern Pakistan, the balti is traditionally served with a giant *karack* naan bread that's big enough to feed the whole table.

The best place to sample this Brummie delicacy is in the so-called **Balti Triangle** about 2.5 miles southeast of the centre, which includes Ladypool Rd, Stoney Lane and Stratford Rd. Reflecting the religious sensibilities of local residents, restaurants serve soft drinks, fruit juices and lassis (yoghurt shakes) instead of alcohol, but diners are welcome to bring their own beer and wine. To get here, take bus 2, 5, 5A or 6 from the Corporation St bus stands (p513) and ask the driver for Ladypool Rd.

GAY & LESBIAN BIRMINGHAM

Birmingham's loud and lively gay scene is centred on the streets south of the Bullring, which throng with the bold, bright and beautiful on weekend nights. For up-to-the-minute information on the Brummie scene, check out www.visitgaybrum.com, or ask the crowds during the bustling Pride march (www.birminghampride.com) in May.

(vermicelli, wheat noodles or *ho fun* thick rice noodles). There's also a branch in the **Arcadian Centre** (closed Wed).

Drinking

The pub scene in the centre is sadly dominated by bland commercial chains, but some diamonds glint in the Birmingham rough.

Old Joint Stock PUB
(0121-200 1892; www.oldjointstocktheatre.co.uk; 4 Temple Row West; 11am-10.30pm Mon-Sat, noon-5pm Sun;) A vast, high-ceilinged temple of a pub, housed in a former bank and appealing to a high-spirited after-work crowd. There's an 80-seat theatre upstairs that puts on plays and comedy shows.

Island Bar BAR
(0121-632 5296; www.bar-island.co.uk; 14-16 Suffolk St Queensway; 5pm-late Mon-Sat) Locals rave about the cocktails at this funky nightspot, where you can sit in perspex chairs in front of giant blow-ups of Hawaiian beaches and groove to rock and roll.

Sobar BAR
(0121-693 5084; www.sobar.co.uk; Arcadian Centre, Hurst St; 5pm-late Tue & Wed, noon-2am Thu, noon-3am Fri & Sat) A glammed-up, shirted and booted crowd packs out this black-and-red bar to the strains of mainstream dance and house.

Bacchus BAR
(0121 632-5445; Burlington Arcade, New St; 11am-11.30 Mon-Thu, 11am-midnight Fri & Sat, 11am-11pm Sun) Astonishing basement setting of Roman, Greek, Egyptian and medieval magnificence plus high-backed chairs meets a strong range of fine ales and food beneath the Burlington Hotel.

Entertainment

Tickets for most events can be purchased via the entertainment megacorporation **TicketWeb** (0870 060 0100; www.ticketweb.co.uk) Also check the free Birmingham listings mags for what's going on.

Nightclubs

The main party district is south of New St station, where a series of defunct pubs and warehouses have found new life as bars and clubs. Chinatown's **Arcadian Centre** (www.thearcadian.co.uk; Hurst St) is the gateway to this hedonistic quarter, with numerous party bars and dancing spots.

Air CLUB
(www.airbirmingham.com; Heath Mill Lane) Don't be put off by the grungy Digbeth location; this superclub is home to the renowned Godskitchen night (www.godskitchen.com), where some of the country's top DJs whip the crowd into a frenzy.

Q Club CLUB
(www.qclub.co.uk; 212 Corporation St; from 8.30pm or 10pm) The old brick Central Hall that houses this legendary club is on its last legs, but the Q is still going strong. DJs pump out boisterous electro, house, jungle and old-school club classics.

Cinema & Theatre

Birmingham Repertory Theatre THEATRE
(www.birmingham-rep.co.uk; Centenary Sq, Broad St) Due to reopen in September 2013 after a two-year redesign, the 'Rep' will have three performance spaces – the Main House, the more experimental Door and a new 300-seat studio theatre (as part of the new library development next door), presenting edgy drama and musicals, with an emphasis on contemporary work.

Electric Cinema CINEMA
(www.theelectric.co.uk; 47-49 Station St; deluxe seats £12) Topped with its art-deco sign, this is the oldest working cinema in the UK (screening since 1909). Enjoy a mix of mainstream and art-house cinema, waited upon in plush two-seater sofas, or have a drink in the small bar.

Giant Screen CINEMA
(0121-202 2222; www.thinktank.ac; Millennium Point, Curzon St; tickets from adult/child £9.60/7.60) Coming into its own in the age of the 3-D blockbuster, Birmingham's Giant

Screen is housed in the same building as the Thinktank (p507).

Hippodrome THEATRE
(☎0844 338 5000; www.birminghamhippodrome.com; Hurst St) The place to come to see stars off the telly, plus highbrow entertainment from the Birmingham Royal Ballet.

New Alexandra Theatre THEATRE
(www.alexandratheatre.org.uk; Suffolk St Queensway) This Brummie institution has been around even longer than the veteran comedians and touring stage shows walking its boards.

Live Music

The **National Indoor Arena** (☎0121-780 4141; www.thenia.co.uk; King Edwards Rd), north of Brindley Pl, and the giant **National Exhibition Centre Arena** (☎0121-780 4141; www.thenec.co.uk; off the M42), near Birmingham International Airport, host stadium fillers from the world of rock and pop.

Sunflower Lounge LIVE MUSIC
(☎0121-632 6756; www.thesunflowerlounge.co.uk; 76 Smallbrook Queensway; ⌚to 2am Fri & Sat) Tucked away on the dual carriageway near New St train station, this quirky little mod bar matches a magnificent alternative soundtrack with a regular program of live gigs and DJ nights.

Jam House BAR
(www.thejamhouse.com; 3-5 St Paul's Sq; ⌚6pm-midnight Tue & Wed, 6pm-1am Thu, 6pm-2am Fri & Sat) Pianist Jools Holland was the brains behind this moody smart-casual venue in posh St Paul's Sq. Acts range from jazz big bands to famous soul crooners. Friday and Saturday has a quite strict over-21s-only ruling.

Symphony Hall ARTS CENTRE
(www.symphonyhall.co.uk; Broad St) For top talent from the classical music world, head to the ultramodern Symphony Hall, the official home of the City of Birmingham Symphony Orchestra. Shows also take place in the handsome auditorium at the Town Hall.

O2 Academy LIVE MUSIC
(www.o2academybirmingham.co.uk; 16-18 Horsefair, Bristol St) Birmingham's leading venue for big-name rockers and tribute bands.

Shopping

The workshops of the Jewellery Quarter are well worth a browse and there are several bustling markets selling cheap imported clothes in the pedestrian precincts surrounding the Bullring. Downtown Birmingham is mall central.

Bullring MALL
(www.bullring.co.uk; St Martin's Circus; ⌚10am-8pm Mon-Fri, 9am-8pm Sat, 11am-5pm Sun) Split into two vast retail spaces – the East Mall and West Mall – the Bullring has all the international brands and chain cafes you could ask for, plus the standout architectural wonder of **Selfridges**.

Mailbox MALL
(www.mailboxlife.com; Wharfside St; ⌚10am-6pm Mon-Wed, to 7pm Thu-Sat, 11am-5pm Sun) Birmingham's stylish waterside shopping experience and development of the former Royal Mail sorting office comes complete with designer hotels, a fleet of upmarket restaurants, luxury department store **Harvey Nichols**, designer names and a super snazzy metallic extension called **The Cube**.

Urban Village VINTAGE
(☎0121-224 7367; www.urban-village.co.uk; shop 7, Custard Factory, Gibb St; ⌚10.30am-6pm Mon-Fri, 10.30am-5.30pm Sat) Parka-clad mods and modettes park their scooters outside this emporium of vintage 1960s narrow-lapel jackets, coats, blouses, button-down collar shirts, winkle-pickers and other classic togs from the glory days of Motown, Small Faces, Sam & Dave and Desmond Dekker.

Beadesaurus FASHION
(www.beadesaurus.co.uk; 8 Piccadilly Arcade, New St) Tucked away along Birmingham's Victorian **Piccadilly Arcade**, this fantastic boutique has an eye-catching line in retro-style

WORTH A TRIP

THE CUSTARD FACTORY

Drop by Digbeth to the **Custard Factory** (☎0121-224 7777; www.custardfactory.co.uk; Gibb St), a trendy art and design enclave set in the converted buildings of the factory that once churned out Britain's favourite custard. It's full of small galleries, quirky design boutiques, offbeat cafes, skateboard shops and vintage-clothing outlets. Adding to the neighbourhood's artistic frisson is nearby **Eastside Projects** (www.eastsideprojects.org; 86 Heath Mill Lane; ⌚noon-6.30pm Thu, noon-5pm Fri & Sat). Take bus 13, 17 or 57.

dresses, vintage-look clothing, colourful handbags and jewel-encrusted bling-bling.

Waterstones BOOKS
(☎0121-631 4333; 128 New St) This branch of the bookworm's favourite store occupies an ornate space – a former Victorian bank with a beautiful skylight and other period highlights. Look out for evening lectures and talks.

Information

Emergency

Police Station (☎0845 113 5000; Steelhouse Lane)

Media

Numerous free listings magazines are available in hotel lobbies, bars and restaurants, including the fortnightly *What's On* and the two-monthly *Live 24-Seven* and *Touchbase* magazines.

Medical Services

Birmingham Children's Hospital (☎0121-333 9999; www.bch.nhs.uk; Steelhouse Lane)

Heartlands Hospital (☎0121-424 2000; www.heartofengland.nhs.uk; Bordesley Green East) East of the city: catch bus 15, 17, 97 or 97A.

Money

You can't walk more than a block in the town centre without coming across a bank or an ATM, particularly around Brindley Pl and New St.

Thomas Cook (☎0121-643 5057; Middle Mall, Bullring; ⏲10am-8pm Mon-Fri, 9am-8pm Sat, 11am-5pm Sun) Currency exchange.

Post

Central Post Office (1 Pinfold St; ⏲9am-5.30pm Mon-Sat) Has a currency-exchange service.

Tourist Information

Tourist Office (☎0121-202 5115; www.visitbirmingham.com; cnr Corporation & New Sts; ⏲9am-5pm Mon-Sat, 10am-4pm Sun) With racks of brochures, maps and info on activities, transport and sights. There's also a branch in the **Birmingham Central Library** (Chamberlain Sq; ⏲10am-6pm Mon-Fri, 9am-5pm Sat).

Getting There & Away

Air

Birmingham international airport (☎0871 222 0072; www.birminghamairport.co.uk) is about 8 miles east of the centre, with flights to destinations around the UK and Europe, plus a few long-haul connections to America and Dubai.

Bus

Most intercity buses run from the **Birmingham Coach Station** (Digbeth High St), but the X20 to Stratford-upon-Avon (1¼ hours, hourly Monday to Friday, every two hours at weekends) leaves from a stop on Moor St, just north of the Pavilions mall. **National Express** (☎08718 81 81 81; www.nationalexpress.com) runs coaches between Birmingham and major cities across the country, including the following:

London £15.70, 2¾ hours, every 30 minutes
Manchester £12.60, 2½ hours, 12 daily
Oxford £11.60, 1½ to two hours, five daily

Train

Most long-distance trains leave from New St station, beneath the Pallasades shopping centre, but Chiltern Railways runs to **London Marylebone** (£31.90, 2½ hours, half-hourly) from Birmingham Snow Hill, and London Midland runs to **Stratford-upon-Avon** (£6.30, one hour, hourly) from Snow Hill and Moor St stations.

Useful services from New St:

Derby £13.80, 45 minutes, every 15 minutes
Leicester £13.10, one hour, half-hourly
London Euston £40.90, 1½ hours, half-hourly
Manchester £30.50, 1¾ hours, every 15 minutes
Shrewsbury £11.70, one hour, half-hourly

Getting Around

To/From the Airport

Fast and convenient trains run regularly between New St and Birmingham International station (20 minutes, every 10 minutes), or take bus 58 or 900 (45 minutes, every 20 minutes) from Moor St Queensway. A taxi from the airport to the centre costs about £20.

Car

All the big car-hire companies have town offices:

Avis (☎0844 544 6038; www.avis.co.uk; 17 Horse Fair)

Enterprise Rent-a-Car (☎0121-782 5158; www.enterprise.co.uk; 9-10 Suffolk St Queensway)

BIRMINGHAM'S HISTORY BUS

Every Sunday from May to October, a free bus runs around Birmingham's museums, stopping at the **Birmingham Museum & Art Gallery** (p503), **Soho House** (p506), **Aston Hall** (p507) and **Sarehole Mill**, as well as several smaller museums. Contact any of the museums for details.

WORTH A TRIP

THE BLACK COUNTRY

The industrial region west of Birmingham is known as the Black Country, after the soot that once rained down on the landscape from the factory chimneys of Dudley, Walsall and Wolverhampton. The heavy industry is now a distant memory, but it's worth swinging by to see the **Black Country Living Museum** (☎0121-557 9643; www.bclm.co.uk; Tipton Rd; adult/child £14.95/7.95; ⏲10am-5pm Mar-Oct, to 4pm Nov-Feb) in Dudley, a perfect recreation of a 19th-century mining village, inhabited by a complete cast of characters in period costume. Trams and trolleybuses run between the various buildings, where kids and history buffs can enjoy mine trips, narrow-boat rides, silent movie shows and recreations of crafts and industries of the time (the confectioners making traditional sweets always draw in a crowd).

Public Transport

Local buses run from a convenient hub on Corporation St, just north of the New St junction. For routes, pick up a free copy of the *Network Birmingham Map & Guide* from the tourist office. Commuter trains to destinations in the north of Birmingham (including Aston) operate from Moor St station, close to Selfridges. Birmingham's single tram line, the **Metro** (www.travelmetro.co.uk), runs from Snow Hill to Wolverhampton via the Jewellery Quarter, West Bromwich and Dudley.

Special saver tickets covering all the buses and trains are available from **Network West Midlands** (☎0121-214 7214; www.networkwestmidlands.com; ⏲9am-5.30pm Mon-Fri, to 5pm Sat) on the lower ground floor of the Pavilions mall.

TOA Taxis (☎0121-427 8888; www.toataxis.net) are a reliable black-cab taxi firm.

WARWICKSHIRE

Warwickshire could have been just another picturesque English county of rolling hills and market towns were it not for the birth of a rather talented wordsmith. William Shakespeare was born and died in, Stratford-upon-Avon, and the sights linked to his life are a tourist magnet. Famous Warwick Castle attracts similar crowds. Visitor numbers dwindle away from these tourist hubs, but Kenilworth boasts atmospheric castle ruins and Coventry has two fine cathedrals and a riveting transport museum.

Information

Shakespeare Country (www.shakespeare-country.co.uk)

Getting There & Around

The Warwickshire transport site (www.warwickshire.gov.uk/roadsandtravel) covers all aspects of travel in the county, including bus and train timetables. Coventry is the main transport hub, with frequent rail connections to London Euston and Birmingham New St.

Coventry

POP 300,848

Dominated today by its twin spires and identikit tower blocks, Coventry was once a bustling hub for the production of cloth, clocks, bicycles, automobiles and munitions. It was this last industry that drew the German Luftwaffe in WWII: on the night of 14 November 1940, the city was so badly blitzed that the Nazis coined a new verb, 'coventrieren', meaning 'to flatten'. Postwar planners filled in the gaps with dull concrete developments, and the city faced a further setback with the collapse of the British motor industry in the 1980s.

A handful of medieval streets escaped the bombers, offering a taste of old Coventry. Must-sees are the outstanding motoring museum (especially if you have kids in tow), and the dramatic modernist cathedral, rising alongside the poignant ruins of its bombed-out predecessor.

Sights

TOP CHOICE **Coventry Transport Museum** MUSEUM
(☎024-7623 4270; www.transport-museum.com; Hales St; admission free; ⏲10am-5pm) This stupendous museum has hundreds of cars from through the ages, from 'horseless carriages' to jet-powered, land speed record breakers. There's a brushed-stainless-steel, gull-wing-doors DeLorean DMC-12 (of *Back to the Future* fame) alongside a gorgeous Jaguar E-Type, a Daimler armoured car and, for specialists of 1970s British design oddities, a

Triumph TR7 and an Austin Allegro 'Special'. View the ThrustSCC, the current holder of the world land speed record and the Thrust 2, the previous record holder. Kids will love the atmospheric 'Coventry Blitz Experience' and the Thrust speed simulator (£1).

Coventry Cathedral CATHEDRAL
(024-7652 1200; www.coventrycathedral.org.uk; Priory Row; adult/child under 7 £7/5; 9am-5pm Mon-Sat, noon-3.45pm Sun) Symbolically adjoining the old cathedral's sandstone walls is the Sir Basil Spence–designed Coventry Cathedral, a modernist architectural masterpiece, with a futuristic organ, stained glass and a Jacob Epstein statue of the devil and St Michael.

Next door, the evocative ruins of old **St Michael's Cathedral** (spire adult/child £2.50/1), built around 1300 but destroyed by Nazi incendiary bombs in the blitz, stand as a permanent memorial to Coventry's darkest hour and as a symbol of peace and reconciliation. Climb the 180 steps of its Gothic spire for panoramic views.

FREE **Herbert Art Gallery & Museum** GALLERY
(024-7683 2386; www.theherbert.org.uk; 10am-4pm Mon-Sat, noon-4pm Sun) Behind the Coventry Cathedral, the Herbert has an eclectic collection of paintings and sculptures (including work by LS Lowry and Stanley Spencer), a delightful cafe, and lots of exhibitions and activities aimed at kids. The intriguing gallery on peace and reconciliation and the history gallery are worth a look-in.

FREE **Holy Trinity Church** CHURCH
(024-7622 0418; www.holytrinitycoventry.org.uk; Priory Row; 9.30am-4pm Mon-Sat) Near the Coventry Transport Museum, Holy Trinity Church has an astonishing 15th century Doom painting on an arch. The graveyard backs onto the ruins of the Benedictine priory of St Mary's, whose history is explored at the **Priory Visitor Centre** (024-7655 2242; www.prioryvisitorcentre.org; Priory Row; 10am-4pm Mon-Sat) right next to a branch of Nando's; tours of the undercrofts leave at 12.30pm (£1 per person).

FREE **St Mary's Guildhall** HISTORIC BUILDING
(024-7683 3328; Bayley Lane; 10am-4pm) Near the ruins of St Michael's Cathedral is St Mary's Guildhall, one of the country's finest medieval guildhalls. Inside rooms that once imprisoned Mary, Queen of Scots, you can view arms and armour, ancient oil paintings and 15th-century tapestries.

Spon Street HISTORIC BUILDINGS
Overlooked by a vast branch of Ikea on the other side of town (past the ghastly shopping precincts), Medieval Spon St is lined with wonky, drunkenly leaning Tudor buildings, some dating to the 14th century.

Coventry Canal Basin ARCHITECTURE
For canal-side walks and cycle rides, head up to Coventry Canal Basin and some fine industrial heritage architecture along the Greenway towpath. Along the route, converted Electric Wharf was the city's first power station, and you'll pass part of the old Daimler factory.

Sleeping

Ramada Coventry HOTEL ££
(024-7623 8110; www.ramadacoventry.co.uk; The Butts; r incl breakfast from £81;) Chain hotels have limited appeal, but this tall tower overlooking the city from just outside the ring road has cosier rooms than most. Views and stylish bathrooms add to the appeal. Wheelchair accessible.

Spire View Guest House B&B £
(024-7625 1602; www.spireviewguesthouse.co.uk; 36 Park Rd; s/tw from £25/51;) Rooms are a bit tired here but the location in a quiet residential street (with several other guesthouses nearby) a few minutes' walk from the train station is handy and the hosts are eager to please.

Eating & Drinking

Playwrights CAFE ££
(024-7623 1441; www.playwrightsrestaurant.co.uk; 4-6 Hay Lane; mains £6-20; 9am to late) On the lovely cobbled lane leading from Earl St to the Coventry Cathedral, this bright, inviting cafe, bar and bistro is as good for breakfast as it is for a working lunch or an intimate dinner, with tables flung out on the cobbles in warmer weather.

Golden Cross PUB
(8 Hay Lane) The beer is warm and so is the atmosphere at this historic alehouse near the Coventry Cathedral, set in a jettied timber-framed gem of a building from 1583.

Information

Tourist Office (024-7622 5616; www.visitcoventry.co.uk; 9.30am-4.30pm Mon-Fri,

10am-4.30pm Sat, 10am-noon & 1-4.30pm Sun) Housed in the restored tower of St Michael's Cathedral.

Getting There & Away

Trains go south to **London Euston** (£42.60; 1¼ hours, every 10 to 20 minutes) and you will rarely have to wait for a train to **Birmingham** (30 minutes, every 10 minutes).

From the main bus station, National Express buses serve most parts of the country. Bus X17 (every 20 minutes) goes to **Kenilworth** (25 minutes), **Leamington Spa** (40 minutes) and **Warwick** (1¼ hours).

Warwick

POP 25,434

Regularly namechecked by Shakespeare, Warwick was the ancestral seat of the Earls of Warwick, who played a pivotal role in the Wars of the Roses. Despite a devastating fire in 1694, Warwick remains a treasure house of medieval architecture, with rich veins of history and charming streets, dominated by the soaring turrets of magnificent Warwick Castle.

Sights

Warwick Castle CASTLE

(☎0870 442 2000; www.warwick-castle.co.uk; castle adult/child £19.95/11.95, castle & dungeon adult/child £27.45/19.45; ⏰10am-6pm Apr-Sep, to 5pm Oct-Mar; P) Founded in 1068 by William the Conqueror, the stunningly preserved Warwick Castle is the biggest show in town. The ancestral home of the Earls of Warwick, the castle remains impressively intact, and The Tussauds Group has filled the interior with noisy attractions that bring the castle's rich history to life in a flamboyant but undeniably family-friendly way.

The castle throbs with kid-centred activities and waxworks populate the private apartments. As well as sumptuous interiors, landscaped gardens and towering ramparts, there are jousting tournaments, daily trebuchet firings, themed evenings, a dungeon and loads to keep families agog. Tickets discounted if you buy online.

FREE **Collegiate Church of St Mary** CHURCH

(☎01926-492909; Old Sq; church entry by £2 donation, clock tower adult/child £2.50/1; ⏰10am-6pm Apr-Oct, to 4.30pm Nov-Mar) Founded in 1123, this magnificent Norman church was badly damaged in the Great Fire of Warwick and is packed with 16th- and 17th-century tombs. Highlights include the **Norman crypt** with a 14th century extension, the impressive **Beauchamp Chapel** (built between 1442 and 1464 to enshrine the mortal remains of the Earls of Warwick), and the **clock tower**, for supreme views over town.

Lord Leycester Hospital HISTORIC BUILDING

(☎01926-491422; www.lordleycester.com; High St; adult/child £4.90/3.90, garden only £2; ⏰10am-5pm Tue-Sun Apr-Sep, to 4pm Oct-Mar) Charmingly leaning against the Westgate and a survivor of the 1694 fire, the wonderfully wonky Lord Leycester Hospital has been used as a retirement home for soldiers (but not as a hospital) since 1571. Visitors can wander round the chapel, guildhall, regimental museum and restored walled garden, which includes a knot garden and a Norman arch.

FREE **Warwickshire Museum** MUSEUM

(☎01926-412501; Market Pl; ⏰10am-5pm Tue-Sat year-round, 11.30am-5pm Sun Apr-Sep) Housed in Warwick's striking 17th-century market hall, the Warwickshire Museum has some entertaining displays on local history and the Warwick Sea Dragons (ancient dinosaurs that once roamed the Jurassic seas).

Mill Garden GARDENS

(☎01926-492877; 55 Mill St; admission £3; ⏰9am-6pm Apr-Oct) For a fragrant perspective of the castle, head for the Mill Garden, an explosion of flowers and plants within splashing distance of the weir that powered the castle mill.

FREE **St John's House** MUSEUM

(☎01926-412132; St John's; ⏰10am-5pm Tue-Sat year-round, 2.30-5pm Sun Apr-Sep) Handsome St John's House has displays of Victoriana downstairs and a **regimental museum** upstairs.

Sleeping

The nearest YHA hostel is in Stratford-upon-Avon, but reasonably priced B&Bs line Emscote Rd, which runs northeast towards Leamington Spa.

Rose & Crown PUB ££

(☎01926-411117; www.roseandcrownwarwick.co.uk; 30 Market Pl; mains from £10.75; r incl breakfast from £75; P@) This convivial gastropub enjoys a congenial location on the

Warwick

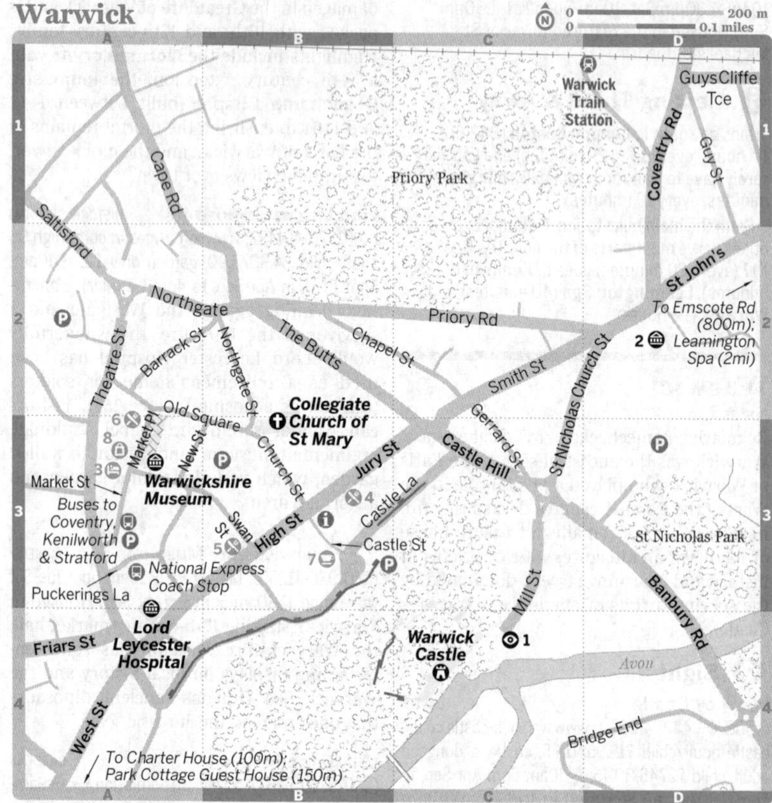

town square, and has five lovely, spacious and tastefully decorated rooms, as well as great beer and superior food. Breakfast is included.

Charter House B&B ££
(☎01926-496965; sheila@penon.gotadsl.co.uk; 87-91 West St; s/d incl breakfast from £65/85; P@) Southwest of the centre, this cute little wonky-fronted, 15th-century timbered cottage has a lovely antique air, low doors and a seriously twee dining room. Compare rooms and book well ahead.

Park Cottage Guest House B&B ££
(☎01926-410319; www.parkcottagewarwick.co.uk; 113 West St; s/d £52.50/70; P) This standalone, 16th-century, wattle-and-daub building to the southwest of the centre once served as the dairy for the castle. It has seven pretty rooms, each with a teddy bear, original floors and a courtyard garden.

Eating

A handful of pleasant small cafes can be found along Old Square near the Collegiate Church of St Mary.

Tailors MODERN BRITISH £££
(☎01926-410590; www.tailorsrestaurant.co.uk; 22 Market Pl; 2-/3-course dinner £28/32.50; ⊙Tue-Sat) Set in a former gentlemen's tailor shop, this elegant eatery serves prime ingredients – guinea fowl, pork belly and lamb from named farms – presented delicately in neat little towers.

Merchants BRASSERIE £
(☎01926-403833; www.merchantswarwick.co.uk; Swan St; mains from £5; ⊙lunch & dinner Mon-Sat) With an appealing layout and trendy leather furniture, this black-fronted chalkboard-intensive restaurant and wine bar offers a fab selection of £5 main courses.

Warwick

Catalan TAPAS ££
(☎01926-498930; www.cafecatalan.com; 6 Jury St; tapas £2.95-7.95, mains from £11.25; ⊙lunch & dinner Mon-Sat) East down Jury St from the tourist office, this bright and neatly presented tapas restaurant is trendy, cool and hits the spot. Tapas served till 7.30pm.

Drinking

Thomas Oken Tea Rooms TEAHOUSE
(☎01926-499307; 20 Castle St; snacks from £3; ⊙10am-6pm) Just an arrow's flight away from the castle, this tearoom is set in the former home of a local nobleman who became famous for his charitable works in the 16th century.

Shopping

Warwick Books BOOKS
(www.warwickbooks.net; 24 Market Pl) Helpful and friendly small bookshop with great recommendations and first-rate service.

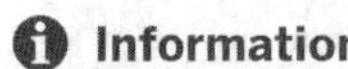

Information

Tourist Office (☎01926-492212; www.warwick-uk.co.uk; Court House, Jury St; ⊙9.30am-4.30pm Mon-Fri, from 10am Sat, 10am-4pm Sun) Found near the junction with Castle St, the tourist office is within the flagstone-floored Court House (1725) and sells the informative *Warwick Town Trail* leaflet (45 pages).

Getting There & Away

BUS National Express (p819) coaches operate from Puckerings Lane. **Stagecoach** (www.stagecoachbus.com) X17 runs to **Coventry** (1¼ hours, every 15 minutes Monday to Saturday), via **Kenilworth** (30 minutes). Stagecoach bus 16 goes to **Stratford-upon-Avon** (40 minutes, hourly) in one direction, and Coventry in the other. The main bus stops are on Market St.

TRAIN Trains run to **Birmingham** (£7, 45 minutes, half-hourly), **Stratford-upon-Avon** (£5.20, 30 minutes, hourly) and **London Marlyebone** (£25, 1¾ hours, every 20 minutes) from the station, northeast of the centre.

Around Warwick

LEAMINGTON SPA

Trading on the alleged healing qualities of its natural saline mineral waters, this very good-looking and genteel spa town is almost a suburb of Warwick, 2 miles to the east. A favourite destination for Victorian health tourists, the town (Royal Leamington Spa in full) was also the birthplace of lawn tennis.

Today, the **Royal Pump Rooms** (☎01926-742700; www.warwickdc.gov.uk/royalpumprooms; The Parade; admission free; ⊙10.30am-5pm Tue, Wed, Fri & Sat, 1.30-8pm Thu, 11am-4pm Sun) contains tearooms, a small gallery, a diverting museum on the history of the spa and a visitor information centre. To get here, jump on bus X17 from Warwick (five minutes, every 15 minutes Monday to Saturday).

BADDESLEY CLINTON

Boasting Elizabethan interiors that have barely changed since the 17th century, **Baddesley Clinton** (NT; ☎01564-783294; www.nationaltrust.org.uk/baddesley-clinton; house & gardens adult/child £9/4.50, gardens only £5.90/2.95; ⊙11am-5pm daily Mar-Oct, Wed-Sun Nov-Feb; P) is a beguiling medieval moated house with gorgeous gardens. It was a haven for persecuted Catholics in the 16th century, as demonstrated by the three cramped priest's holes.

Baddesley Clinton is 7.5 miles northwest of Warwick, just off the A4141. It is a pleasant 2-mile walk from Lapworth train station, served by hourly trains from Warwick (15 minutes) and Birmingham (30 minutes).

Kenilworth

POP 23,219

It's well worth deviating from the A46 between Warwick and Coventry to visit the spine-tingling, atmospheric ruins of Kenilworth Castle. The castle was the inspiration for Walter Scott's *Kenilworth*, and remains pretty inspiring today.

Sights & Activities

Kenilworth Castle CASTLE
(EH; ☎01926-852078; adult/child £8/4.80; ⏲10am-5pm Mar-Oct, to 4pm Nov-Feb; P) This sublime ruin sprawls among fields and hedges on the outskirts of Kenilworth. Built in the 1120s, the castle survived the longest siege in English history in 1266, when the forces of Lord Edward (later Edward I) threw themselves at the moat and battlements for six solid months. The fortress was dramatically extended in Tudor times, but it fell in the English Civil War and its walls were breached and water defences drained.

The excellent audioguide will tell you all about the relationship between former owner Robert Dudley and the 'Virgin Queen', who was wined and dined here at tremendous expense, almost bankrupting the castle. Don't miss the magnificent and recently restored Elizabethan gardens.

Stoneleigh Abbey HISTORIC HOME
(☎01926-858535; www.stoneleighabbey.org; adult/child £8/3.50; ⏲tours noon & 2pm Tue-Thu, 11am, 1pm & 3pm Sun Easter-Oct, garden open 11am-5pm same days; P) The kind of stately home that makes movie directors go weak at the knees, this 850-year-old country house by the River Avon name-drops Charles I and Jane Austen among its roll-call of visiting celebrities. The original abbey was founded by Cistercian monks in 1154, but the house was massively expanded by the wealthy Leigh family (distant cousins of the Austens) in the 16th century. Completed in 1726 and only viewable on tours (included in admission), the splendid Palladian west wing contains richly detailed plasterwork ceilings and wood-panelled rooms, and the landscaped grounds are fine picnic territory. Stoneleigh is 2 miles east of Kenilworth, off the B4115.

Sleeping & Eating

There are numerous pubs and eateries along the High St (east of the castle) and Warwick Rd (south).

The Old Bakery B&B ££
(☎01926-864111; www.theoldbakery.eu; 12 High St; s/d from £75/95; P 📶) Located down the High St east of the castle, this quiet and popular B&B has attractively fitted-out modern rooms and a cosy and welcoming bar serving real ales on the ground floor.

Loweridge Guest House B&B ££
(☎01926-859522; www.loweridgeguesthouse.co.uk; Hawkesworth Dr; s/d from £75/90; P @) This handsome Victorian house has a grand staircase and elegant guest lounge straight out of *Country Life* magazine. There are four huge rooms with swish, modern bathrooms, and three have their own private sun-trap patio. The guesthouse is a short walk northeast from the High St, off Coventry Rd.

Clarendon Arms PUB £
(☎01926-852017; www.clarendonarmspub.co.uk; 44 Castle Hill; mains £8-13) Almost opposite the castle, this bright and homely alehouse has home-cooked food, a warm ambience and a cosy little beer garden.

Information

For tourist information, browse the brochures at the **library** (☎01926-852595; 11 Smalley Pl; ⏲9am-7pm Mon & Thu, to 5.30pm Tue & Fri, 10.30am-5.30pm Wed, 9.30am-4pm Sat).

Getting There & Away

From Monday to Saturday, bus X17 runs every 15 minutes from Coventry to **Kenilworth** (25 minutes) and on to **Leamington Spa** (from Kenilworth, 15 minutes) and **Warwick** (20 minutes). On Sunday, take bus U17 (half-hourly) for Coventry or bus 18A (hourly) for Warwick.

Stratford-upon-Avon

POP 22,187

It's hard to believe that one man could spark so much interest – and so much merchandise – as Stratford's most famous son. The author of some of the most quoted lines ever written in the English language, William Shakespeare was born in Stratford in 1564 and died here in 1616, and the five houses linked to his life form the centrepiece of a tourist attraction that verges on a personality cult.

If you can leave without buying at least a Shakespeare novelty pencil, you'll have resisted one of the most keenly honed marketing machines in the nation.

Sights & Activities

Shakespeare Houses MUSEUM
(☎01789-204016; www.shakespeare.org.uk; all 5 properties adult/child £19/12, 3 in-town houses

£12.50/8; ⏱9am-5pm Apr-Oct, hours vary Nov-Mar) Five of the most important buildings associated with Shakespeare, all run by the **Shakespeare Birthplace Trust**, contain museums that form the core of the visitor experience at Stratford. You can buy individual tickets, but it's more cost-effective to buy a combination ticket, either covering the three houses in town, or all five properties. Expect long queues throughout the summer.

Shakespeare's Birthplace

(Henley St) Start your Shakespeare adventure at the house where the world's most popular playwright supposedly spent his childhood days. In fact, the jury is still out on whether this really was Shakespeare's birthplace, but devotees of the Bard have been dropping in since at least the 19th century, leaving their signatures scratched onto the windows. Set behind a modern facade, the house contains restored Tudor rooms, live presentations from famous Shakespearean characters, and an engaging exhibition on Stratford's favourite son.

Nash's House & New Place

(☎01789-292325; cnr Chapel St & Chapel Lane) When Shakespeare retired, he swapped the bright lights of London for a comfortable town house at New Pl, where he died of unknown causes in April 1616. The house was demolished in 1759, but an attractive Elizabethan **knot garden** occupies part of the grounds. Archaeologists are digging beneath the plot in search of Shakespearean treasures (see www.digforshakespeare.com for details). Recent finds are displayed in adjacent **Nash's House** – where Shakespeare's granddaughter Elizabeth lived – along with other displays describing the town's history and a collection of 17th-century furniture and tapestries.

Hall's Croft

(☎01789-292107; Old Town) Shakespeare's daughter Susanna married respected doctor John Hall, and their handsome Jacobean town house stands south of the centre en route to Holy Trinity Church. Deviating from the usual Shakespearean theme, the exhibition offers fascinating insights into medicine in the 16th and 17th centuries. The lovely walled garden sprouts with aromatic herbs employed in medicinal preparations.

Anne Hathaway's Cottage

(☎01789-292100; Cottage La, Shottery) Before tying the knot with Shakespeare, Anne Hathaway lived in Shottery, a mile west of the centre, in this delightful thatched farmhouse. As well as period furniture, there's the gorgeous gardens and an orchard and arboretum, with examples of all the trees mentioned in Shakespeare's plays. A footpath (no bikes allowed) leads to Shottery from Evesham Pl.

Mary Arden's Farm

(☎01789-293455; Station Rd, Wilmcote) Shakespeare genealogists can trace the family tree to the childhood home of the Bard's mum at Wilmcote, 3 miles west of Stratford. Aimed squarely at families, the working farm has exhibits tracing country life over the centuries, with nature trails, falconry displays and a collection of rare-breed farm animals. You can get here on the City Sightseeing bus, or cycle via Anne Hathaway's Cottage, following the Stratford-upon-Avon canal's towpath.

Holy Trinity Church CHURCH

(☎01789-266316; www.stratford-upon-avon.org; Old Town; church admission free, Shakespeare's grave adult/child £1.50/50p; ⏱8.30am-6pm Mon-Sat, 12.30-5pm Sun Apr-Sep, shorter hours Oct-Mar) The final resting place of the Bard is said to be the most visited parish church in England. Inside are handsome 16th- and 17th-century tombs (particularly in the Clopton Chapel), some fabulous carvings on the choir stalls and, of course, the **grave of William Shakespeare**, with its ominous epitaph: 'cursed be he that moves my bones'.

Harvard House HISTORIC HOME

(☎01789-204507; High St; adult/child £3.50/free) Tucked in beside the lavishly carved Garrick Inn pub, Harvard House was home to the mother of John Harvard, who lent his name to Boston's Harvard University. It now houses a **museum of British pewter** (open May to October). Call for opening times; admission free with Shakespeare Houses ticket.

Stratford-upon-Avon Butterfly Farm FARM, SANCTUARY

(☎01789-299288; www.butterflyfarm.co.uk; Swan's Nest Lane; adult/child £6.25/5.25; ⏱10am-6pm Apr-Sep, 10am-dusk Oct-Mar) The Stratford-upon-Avon Butterfly Farm is a large walk-through greenhouse by the river with hundreds of species of exotic butterflies, plus giant scorpions and a few iguanas. The spiders of 'Arachnoland' add the shudder factor.

Stratford-upon-Avon

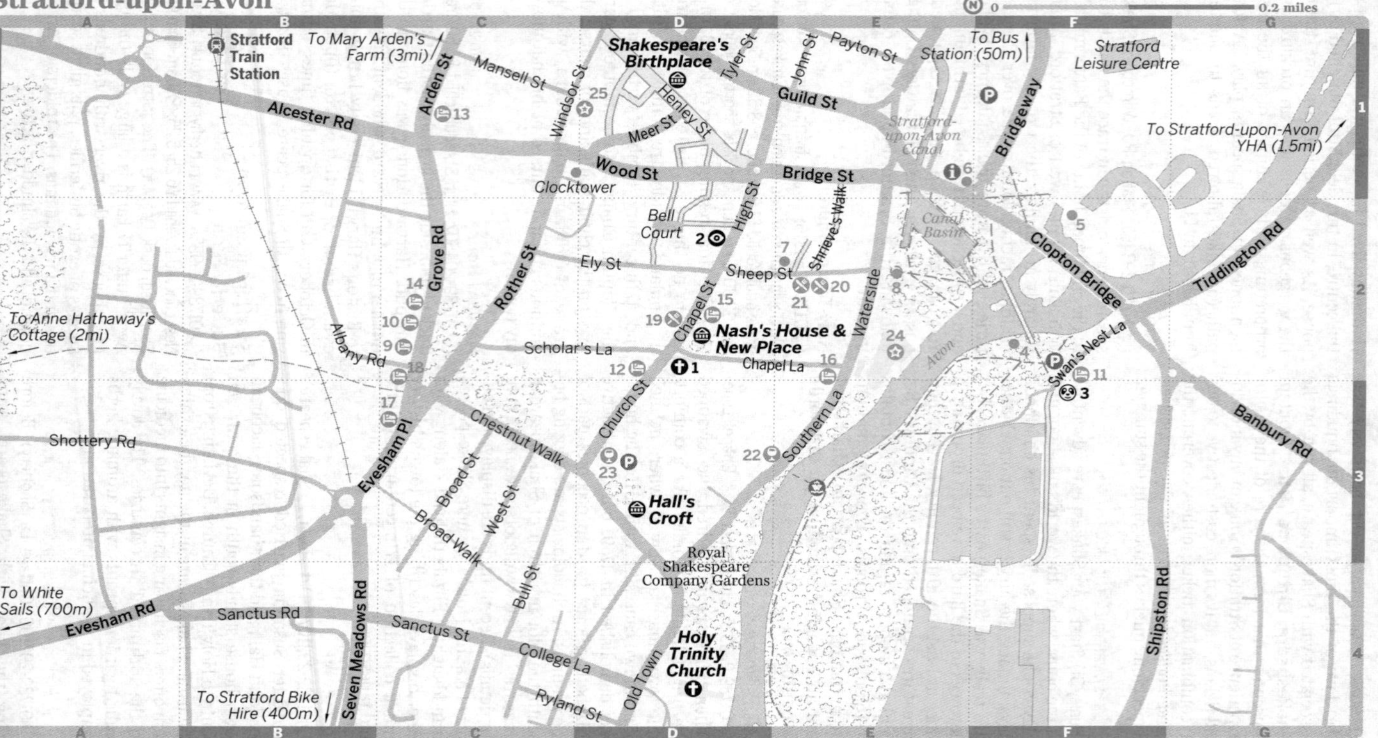

Stratford-upon-Avon

Top Sights
Hall's Croft ... D3
Holy Trinity Church ... D4
Nash's House & New Place ... D2
Shakespeare's Birthplace ... D1

Sights
1 Guild Chapel ... D2
2 Harvard House ... D2
3 Stratford-upon-Avon Butterfly Farm ... F3

Activities, Courses & Tours
4 Avon Boating ... F2
5 Bancroft Cruisers ... F2
6 City Sightseeing ... E1
7 Falstaff's Experience ... E2
8 Stratford Town Ghost Walk ... E2

Sleeping
9 Adelphi Guesthouse ... C2
10 Ambleside Guest House ... C2
11 Cherry Trees ... F2
12 Church Street Townhouse ... D2
13 Emsley Guesthouse ... C1
14 Salamander Guest House ... C2
15 Shakespeare Hotel ... D2
16 Arden Hotel ... E2
17 Twelfth Night ... C3
18 Woodstock House ... C2

Eating
Church Street Townhouse ... (see 12)
19 Edward Moon's ... D2
20 The Oppo ... E2
21 Lambs ... E2

Drinking
22 Dirty Duck ... D3
23 Windmill Inn ... D3

Entertainment
24 Royal Shakespeare Company ... E2
25 Stratford Picture House ... D1

Guild Chapel CHURCH
(cnr Chapel Lane & Church St) The Guild Chapel was founded in 1269 and is painted with motivational frescos showing the fate of the damned in the 15th century. It's only open to the public for services (10am Wednesday and noon on the first Saturday of the month April to September).

Next door is **King Edward VI School**, which Shakespeare almost certainly attended, housed in a vast timbered building that used to be the guildhall.

Tours

Popular and informative two-hour **guided town walks** (01789-292478; adult/child £5/2; 11am Mon-Wed, 2pm Thu-Sun), run by **Stratford Town Walk** (www.stratfordtownwalk.co.uk) depart from Waterside, opposite Sheep St, which is also the starting point for the company's spooky **Ghost Walk** (adult/child £6/3; 7.30pm Mon, Thu, Fri & Sat).

City Sightseeing BUS TOUR
(01789-412680; www.citysightseeing-stratford.com; adult/child £11.75/6; every 30min Apr-Sep, less frequently Oct-Mar) Open-top, hop-on/hop-off bus tours leave from the tourist office on Bridge St, rolling to each of the Shakespeare properties. Tickets are valid for 24 hours (48-hour tickets also exist) and can be bought from the driver; on-board commentary is in seven languages.

Falstaff's Experience GHOST TRAIN
(01789-298070; www.falstaffsexperience.co.uk; 40 Sheep St; adult/child £5/2.50; 10.30am-5.30pm) Set in an old timbered building, Falstaff's Experience offers a ghost-train take on Shakespeare's tales, with olde-worlde walk-throughs, mannequins of Tudor celebs and live actors hamming it up like Olivier. Night-time **ghost tours** (adults only) and haunted Stratford pub walks explore Stratford's paranormal dimension.

Avon Boating BOAT TOURS
(01789-267073; www.avon-boating.co.uk; The Boathouse, Swan's Nest Lane; 30min river cruises adult/child £4.50/3) Runs **river cruises** that depart every 20 minutes from either side of the main bridge.

Bancroft Cruisers BOAT TOUR
(01789-269669; www.bancroftcruisers.co.uk; 45min river cruise adult/child £5.50/3.50; daily Apr-Oct) These fun trips leave from the riverbank by the Holiday Inn, off Bridgeway.

Sleeping

B&Bs are plentiful, particularly along Grove Rd and Evesham Pl, but vacancies can be hard to find during the high season – the tourist office can help with bookings for a fee.

Church Street Townhouse BOUTIQUE HOTEL ££
(☎01789-262222; www.churchstreettownhouse.com; 16 Church St; r £110-180; 📶) The 12 rather decadent rooms at this exquisite boutique hotel are divine and very plush, some with free-standing bath and all with iPod dock, flatscreen TVs and luxurious furnishings. The building itself is a centrally located, 400-year old gem, with a first-rate restaurant (p523) and bar rounding out an excellent stay. Rooms are pricier at weekends.

Stratford-upon-Avon YHA HOSTEL £
(☎0845 371 9661; www.yha.org.uk; Hemmingford House, Alveston; dm from £16; P@) Set in a large, 200-year-old mansion 1.5 miles east of the town centre along Tiddington Rd, this superior hostel attracts travellers of all ages. There's a canteen, bar and kitchen, and buses 18 and 18a arrive here from Bridge St.

Shakespeare Hotel HOTEL £££
(☎01789-294997; www.mercure.com; Chapel St; s/d £135/150; P@) With rooms named after the Bard's plays or characters and a hearty fire crackling in the hearth, the gorgeous Shakespeare offers the full Tudor inn experience in a timbered medieval charmer on the main street. Rooms – some with four-poster beds and wood panels – are tasteful but a wee tired at this Mercure property, but staff are helpful and there's an undeniable historic appeal. Car parking is £10 per guest.

Arden Hotel HOTEL £££
(☎01789-298682; www.theardenhotelstratford.com; Waterside; r incl breakfast from £125; P@) Formerly the Thistle, this elegant property facing the Swan Theatre has been stylishly revamped, with a sleek brasserie and Champagne bar, and rooms featuring designer fabrics and bathrooms full of polished stone.

White Sails GUESTHOUSE ££
(☎01789-264326; www.white-sails.co.uk; 85 Evesham Rd; r from £95) Plush fabrics, framed prints, brass bedsteads and shabby-chic tables and lamps set the scene at this gorgeous, intimate guesthouse on the edge of the countryside. The five individually furnished rooms come with flatscreen TVs, climate control and glamorous bathrooms.

Cherry Trees B&B ££
(☎01789-292989; www.cherrytrees-stratford.co.uk; Swan's Nest Lane; d incl breakfast £105-125; P📶) It may lack character on the outside, but rooms are excellent and very clean at this quietly tucked-away B&B by the butterfly farm near the river. All three rooms come with a fridge, one has a four-poster bed, and two have conservatories backing onto a sweet garden. There's usually a two-day minimum stay.

Emsley Guesthouse B&B ££
(☎01789-299557; www.theemsley.co.uk; 4 Arden St; d from £64; P📶) This lovely five-bedroom Victorian property has a personable owner, sparkling and attractive accommodation and a large, pretty family room at the top with an exposed beam ceiling.

STRATFORD BED & BREAKFASTS

Stratford is well stocked with old-fashioned B&Bs, offering almost identical facilities at almost identical prices. With so much choice, it's helpful to have recommendations. Here is a top selection:

Ambleside Guest House (☎01789-297239; www.amblesideguesthouse.co.uk; 41 Grove Rd; s/d from £25/50; P@) Lovely, nonfrilly B&B, with spotless rooms, amiable, well-informed hosts and big organic breakfasts.

Adelphi Guesthouse (☎01789-204469; www.adelphi-guesthouse.com; 39 Grove Rd; r £35-45; P📶) Very good-looking accommodation, much hardwood furniture and a stunner of a top-floor room with a four-poster bed.

Salamander Guesthouse (☎01789-205728; www.salamanderguesthouse.co.uk; 40 Grove Rd; s/d incl breakfast from £20/40; P@📶) Comfortable and homely, with the added appeal of wi-fi.

Woodstock House (☎01789-299881; www.woodstock-house.co.uk; 30 Grove Rd; s/d from £30/55; P) Bright rooms and a friendly, warm welcome in a house with a tidy garden and wi-fi.

Twelfth Night B&B ££

(☎01789-414595; www.twelfthnight.co.uk; 13 Evesham Pl; s £40-50, d £60-110; P 📶) With a lovely tiled lobby, seven spotless rooms and showers (with bathrobes), plus delightful top-floor rooms and a charming breakfast room, this pretty place is run by a friendly, enthusiastic owner.

Eating

Sheep St is clustered with upmarket eating options, mostly aimed at theatregoers (look out for good-value pre-theatre menus). Brace for theatrical names in profusion – even Indian restaurants have names like 'Thespians'.

Church Street Townhouse BISTRO ££

(☎01789-262222; www.churchstreettownhouse.com; 16 Church St; mains from £11.50; ⏰8am-10pm; 📶) Open all day, this lovely restaurant is a fantastic place for immersing yourself in Stratford's historic charms, whether for breakfast, lunch or dinner. The food is delightful and the ambience congenial. Music students from Shakespeare's old grammar school across the way tinkle the piano ivories daily at 5.30pm.

Lambs MODERN EUROPEAN ££

(☎01789-292554; www.lambsrestaurant.co.uk; 12 Sheep St; mains £10.25-18.75; ⏰lunch Wed-Sun, dinner daily) Lambs swaps Shakespeare chintz in favour of Venetian blinds and modern elegance, but throws in authentic 16th-century ceiling beams for good measure. The menu embraces Gressingham duck, deep-fried goat's cheese and slow-roasted lamb shank, backed up by a strong wine list

The Oppo BISTRO ££

(☎01789-269980; www.theoppo.co.uk; 13 Sheep St; mains £11.50-24.50; ⏰closed lunch Sun) Inviting, charming and atmospheric Sheep St bistro with well-prepared and tasty dishes, perfect for putting paid to pre-theatre munchies.

Edward Moon's MODERN BRITISH ££

(☎01789-267069; www.edwardmoon.com; 9 Chapel St; mains £10-15) Named after a famous travelling chef who cooked up the flavours of home for the British colonial service, this snug and just-refurbished eatery serves delicious, hearty English dishes, many livened up with herbs and spices from the East.

Drinking

Dirty Duck PUB

(Waterside) Officially called the 'Black Swan', this enchanting riverside alehouse is a favourite thespian watering hole, boasting a roll-call of former regulars (Olivier, Attenborough etc) that reads like a *Who's Who* of actors.

Windmill Inn TRADITIONAL PUB

(Church St) Ale was flowing here at the same time as rhyming couplets gushed from Shakespeare's quill – this pub with low ceilings has been around a while.

Entertainment

Royal Shakespeare Company THEATRE

(RSC; ☎0844 800 1110; www.rsc.org.uk; tickets £8-38) Coming to Stratford without seeing a production of Shakespeare would be like going to Beijing and bypassing the Great Wall. The two theatre spaces run by the world-renowned Royal Shakespeare Company have witnessed performances by such legends as Lawrence Olivier, Richard Burton, Judi Dench, Helen Mirren, Ian McKellen and Patrick Stewart.

There are two grand stages in Stratford: **Royal Shakespeare Theatre** and **Swan Theatre** on Waterside, both extensively redeveloped between 2007 and 2010.

The redevelopment of the earlier 1932 Royal Shakespeare Theatre added a new thrust stage auditorium and an **observation tower** (admission £2.50; open 10am daily) for views over town. **Backstage tours** (adult/child £7.50/3), **front of house tours** (adult/child £5/2.50) and other tours throw light on the workings of the theatre; book ahead. For pre-theatre dining, the rooftop restaurant and bar offers both fine food and views.

Contact the RSC for the latest news on performance times at the two venues. There are often special deals for under 25-year-olds, students and seniors and a few tickets are held back for sale on the day of the performance, but eager backpackers tend to

---

DON'T MISS

STRATFORD LITERARY FESTIVAL

Although Shakespeare is the biggest show in town, the top event on the cultural calendar is the **Stratford Literary Festival** (☎01789-207100; www.stratfordliteraryfestival.co.uk) in April/May, which attracts literary big hitters of the calibre of John Simpson and Jonathan Miller.

ASK A LOCAL

For local information, turn to the helpful town hosts, who stroll around Stratford in yellow shirts helping confused tourists find their way to sights, hotels and restaurants.

snap these up fast. Wise theatregoers book well ahead.

Stratford Picture House CINEMA (www.picturehouses.co.uk; Windsor St) Theatre overload? Come here for popcorn-fare blockbusters and art-house cinema.

Information

Tourist Office (☎0870 160 7930; www.shakespeare-country.co.uk) Just west of Clopton Bridge on the corner with Bridgeway. Call for opening times.

Getting There & Away

BUS National Express coaches and other bus companies run from Stratford's Riverside bus station (behind the Stratford Leisure Centre on Bridgeway). Destinations served:

Birmingham National Express; £8.80, one hour, twice daily

London Victoria National Express; £17.60, three to four hours, five daily

Moreton-in-Marsh Bus 21/22; one hour, hourly

Oxford National Express; £11.20, one hour, twice daily

Warwick Bus 16, 40 minutes, hourly

CAR & MOTORCYCLE If you drive to Stratford, be warned that town car parks charge high fees, 24 hours a day.

TRAIN From Stratford train station, London Midland runs to **Birmingham** (£6.80, one hour, hourly), Chiltern Railways runs to **London Marylebone** (£25, 2¼ hours, four daily).

Getting Around

BICYCLE A bicycle is handy for getting out to the outlying Shakespeare properties, and **Stratford Bike Hire** (☎07711-776340; www.stratfordbikehire.com; 7 Seven Meadows Rd; per half-day/day from £7/13) will deliver to your accommodation.

BOAT Punts, canoes and rowing boats are available for hire from Avon Boating (p521) near Clopton Bridge.

Around Stratford-upon-Avon

A youthful Shakespeare is said to have poached deer in the grounds of **Charlecote Park** (NT; ☎01789-470277; adult/child £8.90/4.45; ⏲noon-5pm Fri-Tue Mar-Oct, noon-4pm Sat & Sun Dec), a lavish Elizabethan pile backing onto the River Avon. Fallow deer still roam the grounds today, and the interiors were restored from Georgian chintz to Tudor splendour in 1823. Highlights include culinary-mould-filled Victorian kitchens and an original Tudor gatehouse, unaltered since 1551. Charlecote is about 5 miles northeast of Stratford-upon-Avon. Bus 18 (18A on Sunday) runs to Charlecote hourly from Stratford (30 minutes), continuing to Leamington Spa (30 minutes).

STAFFORDSHIRE

Despite being wedged between the ever-expanding conurbations of Birmingham and Manchester, Staffordshire is surprisingly green and pleasant, and the northern half of the county rises to meet the rugged hills of the Peak District. Highlights of this under-explored neck of the woods include cathedral-crowned Lichfield, the famous theme parks at Drayton Manor and Alton Towers, and the outstanding walking country around Cannock Chase and the Roaches.

Information

Staffordshire Tourism (www.enjoystaffordshire.co.uk)

Getting There & Around

Regular trains and National Express buses serve Stafford and other major towns. The main local bus operator is **First Group** (☎0870 850 0868; www.firstgroup.com). For details of services, browse the public transport pages at www.staffordshire.gov.uk/transport.

STEAMING TO BIRMINGHAM

Offering a chance to relive the golden age of rail travel, the **Shakespeare Express steam train** (☎0121-708 4960; www.shakespeareexpress.com) runs twice every Sunday in July and August between Stratford and Birmingham Snow Hill.

THEME PARK SHENANIGANS

Staffordshire is rightly famous for its theme parks, which resound with the screams of adrenaline junkies lured here by fast and furious thrill rides such as Thirteen, the world's first vertical-drop roller coaster. As with anywhere, the rattle-and-shake rides are bundled together with costume parades, gentle merry-go-rounds for youngsters, and lots of junk food, and the queues can be horrendous, particularly during school holidays.

Alton Towers

The phenomenally popular **Alton Towers** (☎0870 444 4455; www.altontowers.com; adult/under 12yr £45/36; ⏰main hours 10am-5.30pm, open later for school holidays, weekends & high season, closed Nov-Mar) offers maximum g-forces for your buck. Roller-coaster fans are well catered for – as well as Thirteen, you can ride lying down, sitting down or suspended from the rails on the Nemesis, Oblivion, Air and Rita. Gentler thrills include log flumes, carousels, stage shows, a pirate-themed aquarium and a 'splashtastic' **water park** (adult/child £16.50/11.75, open year-round). For discounted entry fees, book online.

The attached resort has two hotels, but many people prefer to retreat from the action to one of the surrounding villages. The **Dimmingsdale YHA** (☎0845 371 9513; www.yha.org.uk; dm from £14) is a miniature hostel 2 miles northwest of the park, set in pleasant walking country.

Alton Towers is east of Cheadle off the B5032. Most large towns in the area offer package coach tours (inquire at tourist offices), or you can ride the Alton Towers bus from Leek, Stoke-on-Trent, Uttoxeter, Nottingham and Derby (see the Alton Towers website for details).

Drayton Manor

Alton Towers' closest rival, **Drayton Manor** (☎0844 472 1950; www.draytonmanor.co.uk; adult/child £36/25; ⏰10.30am-5pm Easter-Oct, longer hours May-Sep) has been serving up screams since 1949. Crowd-pleasers include the Apocalypse free-fall tower, voted Britain's scariest ride, and Shockwave, Europe's only stand-up roller coaster. Younger kids will be just as thrilled by **Thomas Land**, dedicated to the animated steam-train character.Book online for discount tickets.

The park currently has no on-site accommodation, but Tamworth is just 2 miles away, with plenty of B&Bs and hotels – contact **Tamworth Tourist Information** (☎01827-709581; Market St) for recommendations. Drayton Manor is on the A4091, between junctions 9 and 10 of the M42. Package coach tours run from Birmingham, or you can take bus 110 from Birmingham Bull St to Fazeley (one hour, every 20 minutes), and walk the last 15 minutes.

Stafford

POP 63,681

The capital of Staffordshire is a quiet little place that seems somewhat overshadowed by Lichfield and other towns around the county. The main shopping street has some handsome Georgian and medieval buildings, but little evidence remains that this was once the capital of the Anglo-Saxon kingdom of Mercia. For local info, drop into the **tourist office** (☎01785-619619; www.visitstafford.org; Eastgate St; ⏰9.30am-5pm Mon-Fri, 9am-4pm Sat) at the Stafford Gatehouse Theatre.

Surrounded by high-street shops, the **Ancient High House** (☎01785-619131; Greengate St; admission free; ⏰10am-4pm Tue-Sat) is the largest timber-framed town house in the country, artistically assembled in 1595. Creaking stairways lead to carefully restored rooms, and to displays on the history of the town and medieval construction techniques.

The hilltop remains of **Stafford Castle** (☎01785-257698; Newport Rd; admission free; ⏰visitor centre 11am-4pm Wed-Sun Apr-Oct, 11am-4pm Sat & Sun Nov-Mar), a classic Norman moat and bailey, sit romantically in a forest glade about 1 mile southwest of town, just off the A518. The castle was destroyed by parliamentarians during the Civil War, after royalists fled the bastion, leaving their ale and 'Popish books'.

Buses X1 (£2.20, 1¼ hours, hourly) and 101 (£3.30, 1¼ hours, hourly) run between Stafford and Hanley (Stoke-on-Trent). Trains run to Birmingham (£9.60, 40 minutes, every 20 minutes), Manchester (£20, one hour, every 30 minutes) and London Euston (£55, 1½ hours, hourly).

Around Stafford

SHUGBOROUGH

The regal, neoclassical mansion of **Shugborough** (01889-881388; www.shugborough.org.uk; adult/child £12/7, parking £3; 11am-5pm Tue-Sun Mar-Oct) is the ancestral home of renowned royal photographer Lord Lichfield and, accordingly, a good proportion of the wall space is devoted to his work. Unless you're an ardent monarchist, a more compelling reason to visit is the collection of exquisite Louis XV and XVI furniture in the state rooms.

Shugborough is 6 miles east of Stafford on the A513; bus 825 from Stafford to Lichfield runs nearby (20 minutes, half-hourly Monday to Saturday).

Lichfield

POP 27,900

Even without its magnificent Gothic cathedral – one of the most spectacular in the country – this quaintly cobbled market town would be worth a visit to tread in the footsteps of lexicographer and wit Samuel Johnson, and natural philosopher Erasmus Darwin, grandfather of Charles.

Sights & Activities

Lichfield Cathedral CATHEDRAL

(01543-306100; www.lichfield-cathedral.org; entry by donation; 7.30am-6.15pm daily, to 5pm Sun low season) Crowned by three dramatic towers, Lichfield Cathedral is a stunning Gothic fantasy, constructed in stages from 1200 to 1350. The enormous vaulted nave is set slightly off line from the choir, creating a bizarre perspective when viewed from the west door, and carvings inside the cathedral still bear signs of damage caused by Civil War soldiers sharpening their swords.

In the octagonal Chapter House, you can view the illuminated *Chad Gospels*, created around AD 730, an ornate Anglo-Saxon bas-relief known as the *Lichfield Angel*, and a faded but glorious medieval wall painting above the door.

At the time of writing, the seven splendid 1530s Flemish stained glass windows – the **Herkenrode Windows** – of the stunning Lady Chapel had been removed for conservation for the time being. Along the north and south aisles are memorials to generations of Lichfield bishops.

On the exterior, the grand west facade positively bows under the weight of 113 statues of bishops, saints and kings of England. Stroll around the delightful, once-fortified **Cathedral Close**, ringed with imposing 17th- and 18th-century houses.

Erasmus Darwin House MUSEUM

(01543-306260; www.erasmusdarwin.org; Beacon St; adult/child £3/1; noon-5pm Tue-Sun, last admission 4.15pm) After turning down the job of royal physician to King George III – perhaps a lucky escape, considering the monarch's descent into madness – Erasmus Darwin became a leading light in the Lunar Society, debating the origins of life with such luminaries as Wedgwood, Boulton and Watt, decades before his grandson Charles came up with the theory of evolution. The former house of the 'Grandfather of Evolution' contains some intriguing personal effects, and at the back is a fragrant herb garden leading to Cathedral Close.

FREE **Samuel Johnson Birthplace Museum** MUSEUM

(01543-264972; www.samueljohnsonbirthplace.org.uk; Breadmarket St; 10.30am-4.30pm Apr-Sep, 11am-3.30pm Oct-Mar) A short walk south of Erasmus Darwin House, this absorbing museum charts the life of the pioneering lexicographer, wit, poet and critic Samuel Johnson, who moved to London from his native Lichfield and devoted nine years to producing the first dictionary of the English language. Johnson was later immortalised in James Boswell's famous biography *The Life of Samuel Johnson*. Ten years in the making, Johnson's first dictionary helped define the word 'dull' with this example: 'to make dictionaries is dull work'. It's a lovely property to explore and a short dramatised film on a flatscreen TV upstairs narrates Johnson's life story.

Lichfield Heritage Centre MUSEUM

(01543-256611; www.lichfieldheritage.org.uk; Market Sq; adult/child £2.50/1, tower adult/child £2.75/1.25; 9.30am-4pm Mon-Fri, 9.30am-5pm

DON'T MISS

THE STAFFORDSHIRE HOARD

Discovered in July 2009 by a metal detector enthusiast in Hammerwich near Lichfield, the Staffordshire Hoard constitutes the largest collection of Anglo-Saxon gold ever found.

Unearthed in the ancient Anglo-Saxon kingdom of Mercia, the hoard presents a magnificent, but baffling, find. The intricate quality of the work is astonishing in its filigree gold-wire patterns, mounted garnets and animal patterns, while the metalwork is entirely martial and masculine in nature, yet torn and damaged. The ripped and split condition of much of the hoard has allowed experts to appreciate the interior structure of the metalwork, a perspective hidden by intact specimens.

Why the hoard was buried in the first place and in such a state is unknown – experts are set to puzzle over these conundrums until further evidence comes to light. You can see part of the hoard at the Birmingham Museum & Art Gallery (p503) and the Potteries Museum & Art Gallery (p528) in Stoke-on-Trent.

Sat, 10am-4pm Sun) A nicely presented series of exhibits covering 1300 years of Lichfield history, set in the old St Mary's Church. Climb the **tower** for sweeping city views.

Sleeping

The Bogey Hole B&B ££
(01543-264303; www.thebogeyhole.co.uk; 23 Dam St; s/d £40/60) This sweet little place near the cathedral has bright and rather feminine en-suite rooms, a lounge with a TV, and a kitchen at the top and laundry room below. With no sign, it's the cream-coloured quaint house at No 23.

George Hotel HOTEL ££
(01543-414822; www.thegeorgelichfield.co.uk; 12-14 Bird St; s/d £89/99; P@) Part of the Best Western chain, this old Georgian pub has been upgraded into a comfortable midrange hotel, scoring points for location rather than atmosphere.

Eating & Drinking

Chandlers' Grande Brasserie MODERN EUROPEAN ££
(01543-416688; www.chandlersrestaurant.co.uk; Bore St; mains £11-24; closed dinner Sun;) Set in the old Corn Exchange and decked out with natural wood and polished brass, this is where locals go for a big night out, as much for the ambience as for the Mediterranean-inspired main courses.

Chapters Cathedral Coffee Shop CAFE £
(01543-306125; 19 The Close; sandwiches & salads £3-6; breakfast & lunch) This fine 18th-century house has a lovely big window looking out onto the cathedral and views of a 13th-century walled garden. It serves morning and afternoon tea and Sunday lunches.

Damn Fine Cafe CAFE £
(16 Bird St; mains £6; 9am-4pm Tue, Thu & Fri, 9am-3.30pm Wed, 9am-5pm Sat, 10am-4pm Sun) Popular and teeming with locals, this cafe (order and pay at the counter) is a handy place to load up on sandwiches, soup, filling-and-full-on porky bacon and sausage breakfast, or vegetarian toad-in-the-hole.

Information

The **tourist office** (01543-412112; www.visitlichfield.co.uk; Lichfield Garrick; 10am-4pm Mon-Sat) doubles as the box office for the Lichfield Garrick theatre.

Getting There & Away

BUS The bus station is opposite the main train station on Birmingham Rd. Bus 112 runs to **Birmingham** (1¼ hours, hourly), while the 825 serves **Stafford** (1¼ hours, hourly).

TRAIN Lichfield has two train stations. Trains to **Birmingham** (40 minutes, every 20 minutes) leave from Lichfield City station in the centre. Trains to **London Euston** (£19.90, 2¼ hours) run from Lichfield Trent Valley station.

Stoke-on-Trent

POP 240,636

At the heart of the Potteries, the famous pottery-producing region of Staffordshire, Stoke-on-Trent is famed for its ceramics, but don't expect cute little artisanal producers. This was where pottery shifted to mass production during the Industrial Revolution, and Stoke is a sprawl of industrial townships bound together by flyovers and bypasses. There are dozens of active potteries that you can visit, including the famous Wedgwood factory, but the town museum presents a good overview for less-ceramic-obsessed visitors.

Hanley is the official 'city centre' with the main bus station, surrounded by the suburbs of Tunstall, Burslem, Fenton, Longton and Stoke (with the train station).

Sights & Activities

Wedgwood Visitor Centre INTERPRETATION CENTRE
(☎0870 606 1759; www.wedgwoodvisitorcentre.com; adult/child £10/8; ⏰10am-5pm Mon-Fri, 10am-4pm Sat & Sun) Set in attractive parkland, the modern production centre for Josiah Wedgwood's porcelain empire displays an extensive collection of historic pieces, including plenty of Wedgwood's delicate, neoclassical blue-and-white Jasperware. The fascinating industrial process is revealed and there's an interesting film on Josiah's life, his work, canal-building and the abolition of slavery.

FREE **Potteries Museum & Art Gallery** MUSEUM
(☎01782-232323; Bethesda St; ⏰10am-5pm Mon-Sat & 2-5pm Sun) This museum houses an extensive ceramics display, from Toby jugs and Jasperware to outrageous ornamental pieces, like the Minton Peacock. You can also see treasures from the outstanding **Staffordshire Hoard**, displays on the WWII Spitfire (created by the Stoke-born aviator Reginald Mitchell) and artworks by LS Lowry and Sir Henry Moore.

Sleeping & Eating

Hanley is well stocked with chain eateries and pubs.

Verdon Guest House B&B £
(☎01782-264244; www.verdonguesthouse.co.uk; 44 Charles St; s/d from £28/44; P@☎) The area's not an oil painting, but this central and lovingly kept Victorian B&B has comfy rooms a few short steps from the bus station. Breakfast £5 extra.

Kenwood Guest House B&B £
(☎01782-765787; www.kenwoodguesthousestoke.co.uk; 14 Stoke Rd; P☎) There's a warm welcome, very clean and well-equipped rooms, and filling breakfasts at this well-located family-run B&B.

Information

Tourist office (☎01782-236000; www.visitstoke.co.uk; Victoria Hall, Bagnall St; ⏰9am-5pm Mon-Fri, 10am-2pm Sat) Ask for a map with the locations of the various potteries.

Getting There & Away

From Stoke-on-Trent station in Stoke, trains run to **Stafford** (20 minutes, half-hourly) and **London Euston** (£53.50, 1½ hours, two hourly). The following bus services run from Hanley bus station on Lichfield St:

Alton Towers Bus 32A; one hour, every two hours

POTTER AROUND THE POTTERIES

Stoke-on-Trent lies at the hub of England's ceramic heartland, thanks to the pioneering work of the famous Wedgwood pottery, established by Josiah Wedgwood in 1759.

The Wedgwood factory moved from its original location in 1950, but the visitor centre still offers a fascinating insight into porcelain production techniques. The tourist office in Stoke-on-Trent has leaflets on other historic potteries that are open to the public, including the following:

Gladstone Pottery Museum (☎01782-237777; www.stokemuseums.org.uk/gpm; Uttoxeter Rd; adult/child £6.95/4.75; ⏰10am-5pm) One of the more traditional potteries; an atmospheric sprawl of brick buildings and bottle kilns, with an unusual display on ceramic toilets.

Dudson Museum (☎01782-285286; Hope St; admission free; ⏰10am-3pm Mon-Fri) Set inside one of the aptly named bottle kilns, with displays on all the famous styles of Stoke porcelain.

Moorcroft Heritage Visitor Centre (☎01782-820515; www.moorcroft.com; Sandbach Rd; tours adult/child £4.50/3.50; ⏰10am-5pm Mon-Fri, 9.30am-4.30pm Sat) This historic factory looks like a giant milk-bottle holder. Book ahead for tours, held at 11am and 2pm (11am only on Friday).

WORTH A TRIP

PUGIN'S MASTERPIECE

About 11 miles from Stoke-on-Trent, the sleepy market town of **Cheadle** is well worth a detour for the simply astonishing **St Giles Church** (☎01538-753130; www.stgilescatholicchurch.co.uk; 18 Charles St; ⊙8am-3pm), fashioned by the Gothic-revivalist Augustus Welby Pugin (1812–52). Famous for adding the Gothic flourishes to London's Houses of Parliament, Pugin filled St Giles with extravagant gilded murals of angels and medieval motifs that cover every square inch of walls, ceiling and pillars. Despite its 200-foot spire, the less flamboyant exterior hardly prepares you for the church interior, which is exactly like stepping into an illuminated manuscript. With its riot of gold, green, red and blue paintwork and splendid tiled floor, the church is quite simply a work of art. Note: to admire the interior in all its glory, there's a box for switching on the lights (£1 for 15 minutes).

It's a 10-minute walk south from Cheadle High St. Buses 32 and 32a run to Cheadle every 20 minutes from the Hanley bus stand in Stoke-on-Trent (30 minutes).

London National Express; £23.80, four hours, seven daily

Manchester National Express; £6.50, 1½ hours, eight daily

Stafford First Bus 101; 1¼ hours, hourly

Around Stoke-on-Trent

LITTLE MORETON HALL

About 10 miles north of Stoke-on-Trent, wonderfully wonky **Little Moreton Hall** (NT; ☎01260-272018; adult/child £6.40/3.20; ⊙11am-5pm Wed-Sun late Mar-Oct, Sat & Sun only Feb & Nov-mid Dec) is a gem of medieval architecture. A stack of time-worn timbers, warped gables and leaded windows, dating back to the 16th century, this moated mansion is a bona-fide museum piece, with original frescos and a charming knot garden. Little Moreton is off the A34 south of Congleton but you'll need your own transport to get here.

Leek

POP 18,768

Northeast of Stoke-on-Trent, the attractive market town of Leek is the gateway to the rugged Staffordshire Moorlands, which form part of the Peak District National Park. Topped by a line of gritstone crags known as the **Roaches**, this is prime walking and climbing country and the crags are home to curlews, peregrine falcons, buzzards and owls – and supposedly, a colony of wallabies who escaped from a private zoo in the 1940s.

Sights & Activities

Leek was a major centre for the production of textiles during the Industrial Revolution, littering the town with several interesting sights.

St Edward's Church CHURCH
(☎01538-388134; Church St; ⊙10am-3pm) The 14th-century St Edward's Church has drop-dead gorgeous Pre-Raphaelite stained-glass windows designed by Edward Burne-Jones, as well as the remains of a 7th-century Saxon preaching cross in the churchyard.

All Saints Church CHURCH
(☎01538-382588; ⊙9-11am Mon-Thu & Sat) Walk down St Edward St and Compton to reach the squat Victorian All Saints Church, decorated inside with winsome Pre-Raphaelite murals and more Edward Burne-Jones stained glass.

Brindley Mill HISTORIC BUILDING
(www.brindleymill.net; Mill St; adult/child £2/1.50; ⊙2-5pm Mon-Wed mid-Jul–Aug, 2-5pm Sat & Sun Easter-Sep) Downhill from St Edward's on the road to Macclesfield, historic Brindley Mill was built in 1752.

Peak Pursuits OUTDOORS
(☎01782-722226; www.peakpursuits.co.uk; ⊙10am-7pm Mar-Nov) About 3 miles north of Leek at Tittesworth Water, Peak Pursuits offers family-friendly outdoor activities, like kayaking and rock climbing on the Roaches. It's off the A53 near Meerbrook.

Sleeping & Eating

Silken Strand BOUTIQUE HOTEL ££
(☎01538-371022; www.thesilkenstrandhotel.co.uk; 64 St Edward St; tapas from £3.95; d/ste £95/105; 📶) With a lovely tiled floor, medieval stained glass in the reception area, gorgeous stonework, a fine tapas bar in the vaulted

cellar, films on the big screen in the restaurant, an attractive garden and trendy boutique rooms, this place has both historical charm and modern facilities in one attractive bundle.

Peak Weavers GUESTHOUSE ££
(☎01538-383729; www.peakweavershotel.co.uk; 21 King St; s/d incl breakfast from £35/85; P @) Peak Weavers is a delightfully restored former convent, with lovely rooms and attractive period touches. Hidden by evergreens, it's raised on a bank above the street, backing onto St Mary's church.

Information

Tourist Office (☎01538-483741; tourism.services@staffsmoorlands.gov.uk; 1 Market Pl; ⏱10am-5pm Mon, 9.30am-5pm Tue-Fri, 10am-4pm Sat) The tourist office is full of information on walks in the area, including the useful *The Roaches* and *Leek to Peak* booklets. Ask about shuttle buses to Alton Towers.

Getting There & Away

The following services depart from Leek's bus station on Haywood St:

Alton Towers Bus 10/10A; 25 minutes, six daily

Ashbourne Bus 108; 40 minutes, six daily (no Sunday service)

Buxton Bus 118; 30 minutes, four daily (three on Sunday)

Hanley (Stoke-on-Trent) Bus 18/118; 45 minutes, every 20 minutes

WORCESTERSHIRE

Perhaps best known for its sharp-tasting condiment, concocted by two Worcester chemists in 1837, Worcestershire marks the transition from the industrial heart of the Midlands to the peaceful countryside of the Welsh Marches.

The southern and western fringes of the county burst with lush countryside and sleepy market towns, while the capital is a classic English county town, whose magnificent cathedral inspired the composer Edward Elgar to write some of his greatest works. Further south, the elegant Victorian resort of Great Malvern sits regally at the heart of the rumpled Malvern Hills, one of England's great 'edges' and a mecca for walkers.

Activities

The longest riverside walk in the UK, the 210-mile **Severn Way** winds its way through Worcestershire en route from Plynlimon in Wales to the sea at Bristol. A shorter challenge is the 100-mile **Three Choirs Way**, linking Worcester to Hereford and Gloucester. The Malvern Hills are also prime country for walking, cycling and paragliding, though there are no official cycling routes.

Information

Visit Worcestershire (www.visitworcestershire.org)

Getting Around

Worcester is a convenient rail hub, and Kidderminster is the southern railhead of the quaint Severn Valley Railway (p553). Buses connect larger towns, but services to rural areas can be frustratingly infrequent – search the transport pages at www.worcestershire.gov.uk for bus companies and timetables.

Worcester

POP 94,029

Handsome Worcester – pronounced '*wooster*', as in 'Jeeves and Wooster' – has more than enough historic treasures to forgive the architectural bloopers of its postwar fling with concrete. The home of Lea & Perrins and that famous sauce (an unlikely combination of fermented tamarinds and anchovies), this ancient cathedral city was the site of the last battle of the Civil War.

Sights

Worcester Cathedral CATHEDRAL
(☎01905-732900; www.worcestercathedral.org.uk; entry by £5 donation, tower adult/child £4/2, tours £3/free; ⏱7.30am-6pm, tower 11am-5pm Sat & school holidays Apr-Oct, tours 11am & 2.30pm Mon-Sat Apr-Sep, Sat Oct-Mar, evensong 5.30pm Mon-Wed, Fri & Sat, 4pm Sun) Rising beautifully above the River Severn, Worcester's majestic cathedral is best known as the final resting place of Magna Carta signatory King John.

With its colossal Gothic arches, stained glass creating a kaleidoscope of colour and the exquisitely painted vaulted ceiling of the choir, the cathedral interior is magnificent. John's tomb is just one of many grand memorials dotted around, from the ostentatious mausoleums of bishops and earls to the worn graves of forgotten Crusader knights. Beneath it all is an atmospheric Norman crypt, constructed in 1084 by St

Wulfstan, the only Saxon bishop to hang on to his seat after the Norman invasion. Other highlights include a charming cloister and a 12th-century circular chapter house.

The strong-legged can tackle the 249 steps to the top of the **tower** where Charles II surveyed his troops during the disastrous Battle of Worcester. Hour-long **cathedral tours** run from the gift shop. Composer Edward Elgar was a local lad, and several of his works had their first public outings at the cathedral – to appreciate the acoustics, come for **evensong**.

Commandery MUSEUM
(☎01905-361821; www.worcestercitymuseums.org.uk; College St; adult/child £5.40/2.30; ⏰10am-5pm Mon-Sat, 1.30-5pm Sun) The town's history museum is housed in a splendid Tudor building that served as King Charles II's headquarters during the Battle of Worcester. Engaging audioguides and interactive exhibits tell the story of Worcester during key periods in its history. Be sure to visit the 'painted chamber', covered with intriguing 15th-century religious frescos.

Royal Worcester Porcelain Works MUSEUM
(☎01905-21247; www.worcesterporcelainmuseum.org.uk; Severn St; adult/concession £6/5; ⏰10am-5pm Mon-Sat Easter-Oct, 10.30am-4pm Tue-Sat Nov-Easter) Up there with Crown Derby and Wedgwood, the Royal Worcester porcelain factory gained an edge over its rivals by picking up the contract to provide fine crockery to the English monarchy. An entertaining audio tour reveals some quirkier sides to the Royal Worcester story, including its brief foray into porcelain dentures and 'portable fonts' designed for cholera outbreaks. The shop has some splendid pieces, from monk-shaped candle snuffers to decorated thimbles and pill boxes.

Greyfriars HISTORIC BUILDING
(NT; ☎01905-23571; Friar St; adult/child £4.15/2.05; ⏰1-5pm Wed-Sun Mar-Dec) Friar St was largely chock-a-block with historic architecture, until the iconoclastic 1960s when much was demolished, including the lovely medieval Lich Gate. Some creaky old almshouses survive and Greyfriars was saved in the nick of time by the National Trust, offering the chance to poke around a timber-framed merchant's house from 1480. It's full of atmospheric wood-panelled rooms and is backed by a pretty walled garden.

Tudor House HISTORIC BUILDING
(☎01905-426402; www.tudorhouse.org.uk; ⏰10am-4pm Wed & Sat year-round, 1-4pm Thu Jun-Sep) Once a weaver's house and then a brewery, the mid-16th-century Tudor House is wonderfully warped and contains a lovely Tudor ceiling upstairs (revealed when the plaster came down).

FREE **Guildhall** HISTORIC BUILDING
(High St; ⏰8.30am-4.30pm Mon-Sat) Peek into the flamboyant Georgian Guildhall. Note the two semi-gilded statues of Charles I and II either side of the door, plus the sculpted head of a man, said to be Cromwell, pinned by his ears to the top of the arch.

Tours

Worcester Walks WALKING TOUR
(☎01905-726311; www.worcesterwalks.co.uk; adult £5; ⏰11am Mon-Fri Apr-Sep) Offers popular half-hour walking tours.

Worcester River Cruises BOAT TOUR
(☎01905-611060; www.worcesterrivercruises.co.uk; adult/child £5.50/3.50; ⏰hourly 11am-5pm) Runs 45-minute cruises on the Severn.

Discover History Walking Tours WALKING TOUR
(☎07949 222137; www.discover-history.co.uk; adult £5) Offers a variety of themed historic tours with costumed guides.

Sleeping

Barrington House B&B ££
(☎01905-422965; www.barringtonhouse.eu; 204 Henwick Rd; r £80-90; P@) A lovely Georgian house by the river with wonderful views, a pretty walled garden, three plush bedrooms full of brocade and trim, and hearty breakfasts served with eggs from the owners' hens.

Diglis House Hotel HOTEL ££
(☎01905-353518; www.diglishousehotel.co.uk; Severn St; s/d from £70/105; P) This rambling and cosy 28-room Georgian house next to the new boathouse enjoys a lovely setting by the water, a short stroll from the cathedral. The best rooms have four poster beds, deluxe bathrooms and river views.

Ye Olde Talbot Hotel PUB, HOTEL ££
(☎01905-235730; www.oldenglishinns.co.uk; Friar St; s/d from £40/69) Attached to a popular bar and bistro right in the centre, this tasteful inn dates back to the 13th century, but many of the rooms are housed in a modern

WORTH A TRIP

ELGAR BIRTHPLACE MUSEUM

England's most popular classical composer is celebrated with appropriate pomp and circumstance at **Elgar Birthplace Museum** (☎01905-333224; www.elgarmuseum.org; Lower Broadheath; adult/child £7.50/3.50; ⌚11am-5pm Feb-late Dec), housed in the humble cottage where Edward Elgar was born in 1857. Admission includes an audio tour with musical interludes so that you can appreciate what all the fuss is about.

Buses 308 and 310 go from Worcester to Broadheath Common (15 minutes, three daily Monday to Saturday), a short walk from the museum.

extension. Discounted parking in multistorey carpark.

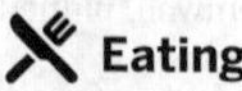

Eating

Phat Nancy's CAFE £

(☎01905-612658; www.phatnancys.co.uk; 16 New St; sandwiches from £3; ⌚9am-4pm Mon-Sat) Nancy's has a punk diner vibe and 'custom-built' sandwiches (gluten-free bread available). It's takeaway only and busy, busy at lunchtime.

Little Ginger Pig BISTRO £

(☎01905-338913; www.littlegingerpig.co.uk; 9-11 Copenhagen St; dishes from £6; ⌚9.30am-4pm Mon-Thu, 9.30am-5pm Fri, 8.30am-5pm Sat) The focus is on local produce and independent labels at this pleasant and frequently busy cafe, bistro and bar.

Mac & Jacks DELI £

(44 Friar St; mains from £4.95; ⌚Tue-Thu 10am-4pm, Fri & Sat 10am-5pm) This Friar St outfit has a lovely deli downstairs for quality titbits and a relaxing cafe upstairs for caffeine, sandwiches and a wholesome menu of hot dishes.

Bindles Brasserie BRASSERIE ££

(Sidbury; mains from £10.95; ⌚lunch & dinner Mon-Sat, brunch 10am-3pm Sun) Presentable restaurant with a satisfying and well-prepared menu featuring locally sourced produce.

Drinking & Entertainment

Cardinal's Hat PUB

(31 Friar St) Despite looking as English as Tudor ruffs and claiming a resident ghost, this atmospheric Worcester institution sells Austrian beers in traditional steins and serves authentic Austrian delicacies at lunchtime.

Marr's Bar LIVE MUSIC

(☎01905-613336; www.marrsbar.co.uk; 12 Pierpoint St; ⌚from 8pm) The best live-music venue for miles around, Marr's still has its original sprung dance floors from its days as a dance studio. There's a lively schedule of local and national bands, comedy shows, acoustic and jamming evenings most nights.

Information

The **tourist office** (☎01905-726311; www.visitworcester.com; Guildhall, High St; ⌚9.30am-5pm Mon-Sat) has stacks of brochures.

Getting There & Around

BUS The bus station is inside the Crowngate Centre on Friary Walk. Services:

Birmingham Bus 144; 1¾ hours, every 20 minutes (hourly Sunday)

Great Malvern Bus 44; 30 minutes, twice hourly

Ledbury Bus 417; 50 minutes, five daily Monday to Saturday

London National Express; £20.60, four hours, three daily

Upton-upon-Severn Bus 363; 30 minutes, hourly

TRAIN Worcester Foregate is the main rail hub, but services also run from Worcester Shrub Hill. Regular trains run to **London Paddington** (£28.60, 2½ hours, twice hourly) and **Hereford** (£8.30, 50 minutes, hourly).

Around Worcester

KIDDERMINSTER

Divided from Birmingham's urban sprawl by open fields, Kidderminster was a busy carpet-weaving centre during the Industrial Revolution. However, the main reason to visit today is to jump aboard the Severn Valley Railway (p553), a restored steam loco that chugs and puffs along 32 miles of track between Kidderminster and Bridgnorth in Shropshire. One-way/return tickets cost £11.50/16.50 (£6/8.50 for children) and the journey takes one hour.

Bus 192 runs between Birmingham and Kidderminster (one hour, hourly Monday to Saturday, every two hours Sunday); from Worcester, take bus 303 (40 minutes, hourly Monday to Saturday) or bus 300 on Sundays.

Great Malvern

POP 35,558

Tumbling down the side of a forested ridge about 7 miles southwest of Worcester, the picturesque spa town of Great Malvern is the gateway to the Malverns, a soaring range of volcanic hills that rise unexpectedly from the surrounding meadows. In Victorian times, the medicinal waters were prescribed as a panacea for everything from gout to sore eyes – should you wish to test the theory, you can sample Malvern water straight from the ground at a series of public wells dotted around the town.

In June, classical musicians flock to town for the biannual Elgar Festival, celebrating the life and works of great English composer Edward Elgar, who lived nearby at Malvern Link.

Sights & Activities

Great Malvern Priory MONASTERY

(☎01684-561020; www.greatmalvernpriory.org.uk; Church St; entry by £3 donation; ⊙9am-5pm Apr-Oct, reduced hours Nov-Mar) The 11th-century Great Malvern Priory is packed with remarkable features, from original Norman pillars to surreal modernist stained glass. The choir is enclosed by a screen of 15th-century tiles and the monks' stalls are decorated with delightfully irreverent 14th-century misericords, depicting everything from three rats hanging a cat to the mythological basilisk.

Malvern Museum of Local History MUSEUM

(☎01684-567811; www.malvernmuseum.co.uk; Priory Gatehouse, Abbey Rd; adult/child £2/50p; ⊙10.30am-5pm daily Mar-Oct, closed Wed during school terms) Straddling Abbey Rd in the grand Priory Gatehouse (from 1470), the town museum offers a thorough exploration of the things for which Great Malvern is renowned, including spring waters, medieval monasteries, the Malvern Hills and Morgan Motors.

FREE **Morgan Motor Company** MUSEUM

(☎01684-584580; www.morgan-motor.co.uk; Pickersleigh Rd; museum admission free, tours £10; ⊙8.30am-3pm Mon-Thu, to noon Fri) The Morgan Motor Company has been handcrafting elegant and beautiful sports cars since 1909, and you can still see the mechanics at work on guided tours of the factory (pre-booking essential). The museum has a fine fleet of vintage classics. Bus 44 from Church St runs past the factory.

Tours

Walking tours (adult/child £3/1.50) leave from the tourist office (p534) at 10.30am Saturday and 2.30pm Sunday, exploring the town's medieval and Victorian history.

Sleeping

Bredon House HOTEL ££

(☎01684-566990; www.bredonhouse.co.uk; 34 Worcester Rd; s/d from £45/70; P@) A short saunter from the centre, this genteel family and pet-friendly Victorian hotel backs onto a stunning vista. Rooms are decorated in a quirky but tasteful mix of new and old, and the books, magazines and family photographs dotted around the place make it feel like staying with family.

Como House B&B ££

(☎01684-561486; www.comohouse.co.uk; Como Rd; s/d £42/65; P@) This handsome Malvern-stone house benefits from a quiet location away from the central bustle. Rooms are snug, the garden is a delight and the mood is restoratively calm. The owners will

WALKING IN THE MALVERN HILLS

The jack-in-the-box Malvern Hills, which dramatically pop up out of the Severn plains on the boundary between Worcestershire and Herefordshire, rise to the lofty peak of the **Worcester Beacon** (419m), reached by a steep 3-mile climb above **Great Malvern**. More than 100 miles of trails traipse over the various summits, which are mostly capped by exposed grassland, offering the kind of views that inspire orchestral movements.

The tourist office (p534) has racks of pamphlets covering popular hikes, including a map of the mineral water springs, wells and fountains dotted around the town and the surrounding hills. The enthusiast-run website www.malverntrail.co.uk is also a goldmine of useful walking information.

pick you up from the station and drop you off by the walking trails.

Abbey Hotel HOTEL £££
(☎01684-892332; www.sarova.co.uk; Abbey Rd; s/d from £170/180; P@) Tangled in vines like a Brothers Grimm fairy-tale castle, this stately property offers decent enough rooms in a prime location by the museum and priory. Rooms are generally around £50 cheaper than rack rate much of the year.

Eating

St Ann's Well Cafe CAFE £
(☎01684-560285; www.stannswell.co.uk; snacks from £2; ⊙10am-4pm daily Easter-Sep, Fri-Sun Oct-Easter) A steep climb above St Ann's Rd, this quaint cafe is set in a handsome early-19th-century villa. You can wash back its cakes and vegetarian snacks with mountain-fresh spring water that bubbles into a carved basin by the door. Phone for the latest opening times before you start the climb.

Anupam INDIAN ££
(☎01684-573814; www.anupam.co.uk; 85 Church St; mains £9-15) Hidden in an arcade just off the main road, this stylish place has a menu that roams the subcontinent, from hearty Mughlai curries to Keralan treats such as tandoori kingfish.

Priors Croft MODERN BRITISH ££
(☎01684-891369; www.priorscroft.com; Grange Rd; mains £7.50-16) A grand folly opposite the theatre with quality pub-style food for enjoying inside or outside in the sunny garden.

Entertainment

Malvern Theatres THEATRE
(www.malvern-theatres.co.uk; Grange Rd) One of the country's best provincial theatres, this long-established cultural hub packs in a lively program of classical music, dance, comedy, drama and cinema. Several nearby restaurants offer good value pre-theatre menus.

Theatre of Small Convenience THEATRE
(www.wctheatre.co.uk; Edith Walk) Set in a converted Victorian public lavatory decked out with theatrical Italianate flourishes, this unusual place has just 12 seats and a program running from puppet shows to poetry and opera.

Information

The **tourist office** (☎01684-892289; www.malvernhills.gov.uk; 21 Church St; ⊙10am-5pm) is a mine of walking and cycling information. The post office on the square has a currency-exchange service. The **library** (☎01684-566553; Graham Rd; ⊙9.30am-5.30pm Mon, Fri & Sat, to 8pm Tue-Thu) has free internet access.

Getting There & Away

BUS National Express runs one bus daily to **London** (£20.40, 3½ to four hours). For **Worcester** (30 minutes, twice hourly), take bus 44 or 362/363 (the Malvern Link).

TRAIN The train station is east of the centre, off Ave Rd. Trains run to **Hereford** (£7, 35 minutes, hourly), **Worcester** (15 to 20 minutes, two or three hourly) and **Ledbury** (13 minutes, hourly).

HEREFORDSHIRE

Slumbering quietly in the English countryside, Herefordshire is a patchwork of fields, hills and cute little black-and-white villages, many dating back to the Tudor era and beyond. Getting around is complicated by infrequent bus services and meandering country lanes, but taking the scenic route is part of the appeal. The scenic River Wye provides a watery highway for canoeists, and there's plenty to see, including Hereford's glorious cathedral and literature-mad Hay-on-Wye.

Activities

As well as the famous **Offa's Dyke Path**, walkers can follow the **Herefordshire Trail** (www.herefordshiretrail.com) on a 150-mile circular loop through Leominster, Ledbury, Ross-on-Wye and Kington. Only slightly less ambitious is the 136-mile **Wye Valley Walk** (www.wyevalleywalk.org), which runs from Chepstow in Wales through Herefordshire and back out again to Hafren Forest. Then there's the **Three Choirs Way**, a 100-mile route connecting the cathedrals of Hereford, Worcester and Gloucester. Cyclists can trace the **Six Castles Cycleway** (NCN Route 44) from Hereford to Leominster and Shrewsbury, or NCN Route 68 to Great Malvern and Worcester.

Information

Visit Herefordshire (www.visitherefordshire.co.uk)

Getting Around

Trains run frequently to Hereford, Leominster and Ledbury, with regular bus connections on to the rest of the county. For bus timetables, see www.herefordshire.gov.uk. Alternatively, pick

OFFA'S DYKE PATH

Tracing the route of the mighty earthworks raised by the Saxon king Offa in the 8th century to keep the Welsh tribes out of England, the **Offa's Dyke Path** runs for 177 miles through Wales, Herefordshire and Shropshire, creating one of England's most scenic coast-to-coast walks.

The route starts at Sedbury near Chepstow and runs north through Monmouth, Hay-on-Wye, Kington and Knighton on its way to Prestatyn in North Wales. Most hikers complete the walk in two weeks, staying at pubs, hotels and guesthouses all along the route. The **Offa's Dyke Association** (www.offasdyke.demon.co.uk) is an excellent source of information, or you can drop into the **Offa's Dyke Centre** (01547-528753; 10am-5pm daily Mar-Nov, to 4pm Mon-Sat Dec-Feb) in Knighton, 17 miles west of Ludlow (buses 738/740 run here five times daily, except Sunday).

up the chunky *Bus and Train Timetable* from any tourist office (50p).

Hereford

POP 56,353

Best known for prime steaks and cider, Hereford dozes in the midst of apple orchards and rolling cow pastures at the heart of the Marches. Straddling the River Wye, there are some interesting things to see, including a vast Norman cathedral whose organist, George Sinclair, was a mentor to the young Edward Elgar.

Sights & Activities

Hereford Cathedral CATHEDRAL

(01432-374200; www.herefordcathedral.org; 5 College Cloisters; cathedral entry by £5 donation, Mappa Mundi £6; 9.15am to evensong; Mappa Mundi 10am-5pm Mon-Sat May-Sep, to 4pm Mon-Sat Oct-Apr, evensong 5.30pm Mon-Sat, 3.30pm Sun) After Welsh marauders torched the original Saxon cathedral, the Norman rulers of Hereford erected a larger, grander cathedral on the same site, which was subsequently remodelled in a succession of medieval architectural styles.

The signature highlight is the magnificent **Mappa Mundi** (see p536), a single piece of calfskin vellum intricately painted with some rather fantastical assumptions about the layout of the globe in around 1290. The same wing contains the world's largest surviving chained library of rare manuscripts manacled to the shelves, kept in a moisture and temperature controlled room. The collection includes a first edition of Dr Johnson's *A Dictionary of the English Language,* a first edition of the King Jame's Bible, a polyglot Bible from the 16th century, a 1217 copy of the revised Magna Carta and the illuminated 8th-century Hereford Gospels.

Heated by four impressive Gurney stoves, the magnificent cathedral comes alive with **evensong** and every three years in August (last held in July 2012) it holds the famous **Three Choirs Festival** (www.3choirs.org), shared with Gloucester and Worcester Cathedrals.

FREE **Old House** MUSEUM

(01432-260694; 10am-5pm Tue-Sat year-round, to 4pm Sun Apr-Sep) This gloriously creaky black-and-white, three-storey wooden house was built in 1621. Climb upstairs for beautifully kept medieval rooms with period furniture (including 17th century cradles), carved wood panelling and antique cast-iron firebacks.

FREE **Hereford Museum & Art Gallery** MUSEUM

(01432-260692; Broad St; 10am-5pm Tue-Sat year-round, to 4pm Sun Apr-Sep) The quirky collection at the town museum has displays on just about everything from 19th-century witch's curses to Roman antiquities.

Cider Museum & King Offa Distillery BREWERY

(01432-354207; www.cidermuseum.co.uk; 21 Ryelands St; adult/child £5/3; 10am-5pm Tue-Sat Apr-Oct, 11am-3pm Tue-Sat Nov-Mar) The name is the giveaway at this brewery and museum. Displays cover cider-making history, and you can sample the delicious modern brews. Look for the fine *costrels* (minibarrels) used by agricultural workers to carry their wages, which were partially paid in cider. To reach the brewery, follow Eign St west from the centre and turn south along Ryelands St.

THE WORLD AS VIEWED FROM HEREFORD

There are many medieval *mappa mundi* (maps of the world) in existence, but the vellum map held by Hereford Cathedral is perhaps the most intricate. Created by a Lincolnshire monk named Richard de Bello in the 13th century, the map is a pictorial representation of the knowledge of the world from the most informed men in England at the time it was created. It was based partly on hearsay, rumours and the exaggerations of drunken seafarers. Consequently, the layout of the continents is initially confusing, and real map points, such as Hereford and Jerusalem (the latter in the middle), are joined by a host of Biblical references such as Gog and Magog and the Biblical Garden of Eden. Nevertheless, the artist was aware of such remote geographical features as the Nile, the Ganges and the Himalayas. As a guide, the Mediterranean Sea is in the middle, the British Isles are at the bottom left, Africa is on the right and China (with the Great Wall indicated) at the top left. A copy of the map with translated place names is also on view.

Even more artistic license was taken with the inhabitants of this remarkable globe. The oceans are populated by mermaids and sea serpents, and land masses play host to dragons, half-plant–half-human mandrakes and sciapods (mythical inhabitants of India, with one giant foot used to shelter their heads from the sun).

Ultimate Left Bank CANOEING
(☎01432-360057; www.leftbankcanoehire.com; Bridge St; canoe hire half-day/day £15/20) If you fancy guiding yourself along the River Wye, you can rent open canoes from this Left Bank centre.

Tours

Guided walks (adult/child £3.50/free; ⏰11am Mon-Sat, 3pm Sun May-Sep) start from the tourist office, exploring less-well-known historic sights in the centre.

Sleeping

TOP CHOICE **Castle House** HOTEL £££
(☎01432-356321; www.castlehse.co.uk; Castle St; s/d/ste from £130/150/195; P@) This award-winning boutique hotel is tranquilly set in a regal Georgian town house that was once the luxurious digs of the Bishop of Hereford. There's a highly sophisticated restaurant, the sun-kissed garden spills down to the river, and suites and rooms are magnificent (with eight new rooms a short walk away at No 25 Castle St). Wheelchair accessible.

Charades B&B ££
(☎01432-269444; www.charadeshereford.co.uk; 34 Southbank Rd; s/d £50/65; P@) This imposing Victorian house has five inviting rooms with high ceilings, big and bright windows and some with soothing countryside views. The house itself has character in spades – look for old service bells in the hall and the plentiful Titanic memorabilia. It's handy to the bus station, but a 1km walk from Hereford Cathedral.

Norfolk Guest House B&B ££
(☎01432-340900; www.norfolkhousehereford.co.uk; 23 St Martins St; s/d £50/70; P) Charming and welcoming guesthouse in a lovely Georgian house on the far side of the Old Bridge. On-road parking.

Alberta Guest House B&B £
(☎01432-270313; www.thealbertaguesthouse.co.uk; 5-13 Newtown Rd; s/d £35/50; P) Simple but warm and welcoming; in the north of town.

Eating

The Stewing Pot BRITISH ££
(☎01432-265233; www.stewingpot.co.uk; 17 Church St; mains £13.95-17; ⏰lunch & dinner Tue-Sat) This popular restaurant opposite the Mousetrap cheese shop has a decidedly simple ambience and refreshingly good service, but its forte is wholesome and appetising dishes using seasonal, locally produced ingredients, like roast pork loin in cider.

Cafe@All Saints CAFE £
(☎01432-370414; www.cafeatallsaints.co.uk; High St; mains £6-9; ⏰8am-5pm Mon-Sat) This neatly designed offering inside the renovated nave of **All Saint's Church** on the High St has wholesome and daily changing dishes, kicking off from 8am with bacon butties, eggy bread and breakfasts; you can even enjoy a beer, cider or a glass of wine. There's outside seating for warmer days.

Drinking & Entertainment

Black Lion TRADITIONAL PUB
(www.theblacklionhereford.co.uk; 31 Bridge St) The more real ales and local ciders you knock back in this traditional pub, the more you may believe the tales of resident ghosts from the site's history as a monastery, an orphanage, a brothel and even a Chinese restaurant.

Jailhouse CLUB
(http://thejailhouse.wordpress.com; Gaol St; ⏲to 3am Wed, Fri & Sat) Edgy, underground DJs and alternative sounds are constantly on the billing at Hereford's leading club. Look out for secret sets by big-name spinners.

Information

Tourist office (☎01432-268430; www.visitherefordshire.co.uk; 1 King St; ⏲9.30am-5pm Mon-Sat) Opposite the cathedral.

Library (Broad St; ⏲9.30am-7.30pm Tue, Wed & Fri, to 5.30pm Thu, to 4pm Sat) There's free internet access at the library, which is in the same building as the Hereford Museum & Art Gallery (p535).

Getting There & Around

BUS The bus station is on Commercial Rd, northeast of the town centre. National Express goes to **London** (£20.60, 4½ hours, four daily) and **Gloucester** (£6.90, 1¼ hours, five daily). Local services:

Hay-on-Wye Bus 39/39A; one hour, twice hourly (three Sunday services)

Ledbury Bus 476; 30 minutes, hourly (five Sunday services)

Ludlow Bus 492; 1¼ hours, twice hourly (three Sunday services)

Ross-on-Wye Bus 38; 45 minutes, hourly (six Sunday services)

Worcester Bus 420; one hour, twice hourly (four services Sunday)

TRAIN The train station is northeast of the centre, with hourly trains to **Birmingham** (£14.20, 1½ hours) and **London Paddington** (£46.50, three hours), either direct or with a change in Newport, South Wales.

Around Hereford

AYMESTREY

About 15 miles north of Hereford, off the B4362 near the village of Aymestrey, the fanciful 14th-century **Croft Castle** (NT; ☎01568-780246; adult/child £7.70/4; ⏲10am-5pm daily Mar-Oct, 10am-4.30pm Sat & Sun Nov & Dec) was just another country house until the owners adorned it with castlelike trim in the 18th century. Surrounded by groves of ancient oaks and chestnuts, it's worth the trip if you're turned on by flamboyant interiors and forest walks. Without a car, the only way to get here is to take bus 492 from Ludlow or Hereford and get off at Gorbett Bank, a 2.5 mile walk from the castle.

Riverside Inn (☎01568-708440; www.theriversideinn.org; s/d from £45/70; Ⓟ) is a classic 16th-century black-and-white coaching inn resting alongside the River Lugg in the diminutive village of Aymestrey. It isn't on the way to anywhere, but gourmands are lured here by the locally sourced Modern British food, cooked up by award-winning chefs. The **Mortimer Trail** passes close by.

KILPECK

Deep in the Herefordshire countryside, the tiny hamlet of Kilpeck is home to the beguiling Norman **Church of St Mary & St David**, encircled by pagan carvings, from cartoonlike pigs and bunnies to a celebrated Sheela-na-gig (Celtic fertility figure). It's an extraordinary sight, well worth the 9-mile trip south from Hereford; just follow the A465 and turn off at Kilpeck.

Hay-on-Wye

POP 1900

This tiny town that straddles the England–Wales border has totally submitted itself to the secondhand book trade, attracting idle browsers, eagle-eyed collectors, and professional bibliophiles from around the globe.

BLACK-AND-WHITE VILLAGES

A triangle of Tudor England survives almost untouched in northwest Herefordshire, where higgledy- piggledy black-and-white houses cluster round idyllic village greens. A delightful 40-mile circular drive follows the **Black-and-White-Village Trail**, meandering past the most handsome timber-framed buildings, starting at Leominster and looping round through Eardisland and Kington (the southern terminus of the Mortimer Trail from Ludlow). You can pick up guides to exploring the villages by car, bus or bicycle from any tourist office.

Book couriers buzz up and down the narrow streets, and locals and visitors spend their days leafing through well-thumbed tomes in cafes, restaurants, pubs and even on the edge of the pavement. It's an eccentric spot – locals even declared themselves independent from Britain in 1977, in a famous publicity stunt.

Sights & Activities

Books (one million of them in 50 bookshops), shops selling books and even alleyways lined with literature are the main thing to see in Hay-on-Wye, but take a peek at the crumbling remains of the 13th-century town **castle**, home to a succession of Lords Marcher...and also home to a bookshop. Unfortunately, heritage regulations mean nothing can be done to stabilise the ruin – it's 'a listed building that's listing,' as one local quipped.

Hay sits on the northeastern corner of Brecon Beacons National Park and makes an excellent base for rambles into the Welsh Black Mountains, or tramps along **Offa's Dyke Path** (see p535). The Offa's Dyke Flyer minibus runs three times on summer Sundays and bank holidays to help you along the way. Alternatively, just explore the local area – there are trails along both banks of the river, connecting with the **Wye Valley Walk**.

Paddles & Pedals CANOEING

(☎01497-820604; www.canoehire.co.uk; 15 Castle St; kayaks per half-day/day £17.50/25; ⏲Easter-Oct) For fun on the river, hire kayaks and Canadian canoes from Paddles & Pedals, which, despite the name, doesn't do bikes. Rental prices include transport to pick-up/drop-off points along the Wye.

Festivals

Hay Festival of Literature LITERATURE FESTIVAL

(www.hayfestival.com) Every year for a week in May/June, Hay-on-Wye becomes the centre of the literary universe for the Hay Festival of Literature. The festival – catchily described as 'Woodstock of the mind' by Bill Clinton – attracts luminaries from the worlds of literature, art and politics, from Salman Rushdie to Martin Amis, Desmond Tutu and many others. A concurrent festival for children – Hay Fever – is also held. The bookish occasion has also expanded abroad into a host of associated international festivals.

Sleeping

Don't bet on a bed *anywhere* nearby while the festival is on – simply everywhere will be 'booked' out.

TOP CHOICE **Start** B&B ££

(☎01497-821391; www.the-start.net; Bridge St; r from £70; P 🛜) Peacefully set on the fringes of town, this little three-bedroom place boasts an unbeatable riverside setting, homely rooms in a renovated 18th-century house and a flagstone-floored breakfast room. The hosts are very friendly and can advise on local activities and walks.

Old Black Lion HOTEL, PUB ££

(☎01497-820841; www.oldblacklion.co.uk; Lion St; s/d £45/90; P 🛜) An atmospheric charmer of a 17th-century inn, full of blackened oak beams and moody lighting. Sturdy country furniture and colourful fabrics fill the spacious rooms, each complete with resident teddy. Breakfast included.

York House B&B B&B ££

(☎01497-820705; www.york-house.eu; Cusop; s/d £35/80) A few minute's walk into England from Hay-on-Wye, this charming B&B has very comfy rooms and much-applauded breakfasts.

Eating & Drinking

TOP CHOICE **Richard Booth's Bookshop Cafe** CAFE £

(www.boothbooks.co.uk; 44 Lion St; mains from £4; ⏲9.30am-4.30pm Wed-Sat, 11am-4pm Sun) There's really nowhere better than this delightful cafe in Richard Booth's tremendous bookshop (p539) for a coffee and a chat. Also on offer are treats such as buttermilk pancakes with maple syrup and whipped yoghurt, and Welsh rarebit, with the culinary boat even being pushed out to Morrocan lentil soup. It's lovely, and a book lover's paradise.

Three Tuns PUB ££

(☎01497-821855; www.three-tuns.com; Broad St; mains £12-18; 🛜) Restored after a devastating fire, this 16th-century building and smart gastropub has a large garden area for alfresco dining and a fancier restaurant upstairs. The international menu follows that dependable mantra: local, organic and sustainable.

WORTH A TRIP

GOLDEN VALLEY

Nudging the foot of the Black Mountains, this lush valley was made famous by children's author CS Lewis, of Narnia fame. Following the meandering River Dore, the valley is peppered with historical relics, including **Arthur's Stone**, a 5000-year-old neolithic chamber-tomb near the village of Dorestone, and the handsome 12th-century **Dore Abbey** (www.doreabbey.org.uk; daylight hours) in the appropriately named village of Abbey Dore. Bus 39 between Hereford and Hay-on-Wye (five daily Monday to Saturday) follows the valley, stopping at Dorestone and Peterchurch. For accommodation and dining ideas, visit www.herefordholidays.co.uk.

Shopping

Ask at the tourist office for the handy *Booksellers* map and pamphlet, marking the town's three dozen bookshops. Beyond books, antique vendors, pottery shops, delis and outdoor clothing specialists adds to the picture, although many in the sleepy town are in an outcry over a proposed supermarket development.

Richard Booth's Bookshop BOOKS
(01497-820322; www.boothbooks.co.uk; 44 Lion St; 9am-5.30pm Mon-Sat, 11am-5pm Sun) With the words 'Books bought anywhere in the world' painted on its gorgeous shopfront, Richard Booth's Bookshop allegedly has the highest turnover of secondhand books of any bookshop across the planet and now houses a lovely cafe, with a cinema that's open Friday to Sundays. A smaller branch exists in the Jacobean mansion built into the walls of the battered 13th-century town castle.

Murder and Mayhem BOOKS
(01497-821613; 5 Lion St) Crime and horror fiction specialists.

Mostly Maps MAPS
(01497-820539; www.mostlymaps.com; 2 Castle St) Antique prints and cartography.

Information

Tourist Office (01497-820144; www.hay-on-wye.co.uk; Oxford Rd; 10am-1pm & 2-5pm Easter-Oct, 11am-1pm & 2-4pm Nov-Easter) Beside the main car park.

Getting There & Away

Bus 39/39A runs to Hay from Hereford (one hour, twice hourly Monday to Saturday, three Sunday services), continuing to Brecon (45 minutes).

Near the tourist office, **Drover Holidays** (01497-821134; www.droverholidays.co.uk; 3 Oxford Rd; bike hire per half-day/day from £17.50/25) rents out good-quality road and mountain bikes from £25 per day.

Ross-on-Wye

POP 10,085

Laid-back Ross-on-Wye, which sits pretty on a red sandstone bluff over a kink in the River Wye was propelled to fame in the 18th century by poets Alexander Pope and Samuel Taylor Coleridge, who penned tributes to philanthropist John Kyrle, 'Man of Ross', who dedicated his life and fortune to the poor of the parish.

Sights & Activities

Market House HISTORIC BUILDING
(01989-260675; 10am-5pm Mon-Sat, 10.30am-4pm Sun Apr-Oct, 10.30am-4pm Tue-Sun Nov-Mar) The 17th-century Market House sits atop weathered sandstone columns in the Market Pl; inside the salmon-pink building is an agreeably hand-crafted heritage centre with local history displays.

Wilton Castle RUINS, CASTLE
(01989-565759; www.wiltoncastle.co.uk; adult/child £4/2; 11am-5pm Wed & Sun Jun-Aug) About 1 mile west of town, beside the River Wye, Wilton Castle is a delightful 12th-century ruin, scattered through the pretty gardens of a vine-covered private home.

St Mary's Church CHURCH
(Church St; 9am-5pm) Crowning the hilltop, pin-straight St Mary's Church is a 13th-century construction with a fine east window and grand alabaster memorials, including the grave of John Kyrle and the outrageously ostentatious tombs of the noble Rudhall family. Behind the church, Royal Parade runs to the edge of the bluff, lined with realistic-looking but ersatz **castle ruins**, constructed in 1833.

Sleeping & Eating

White House Guest House B&B ££
(☎01989-763572; www.whitehouseross.com; Wye St; s/d £45/65; P@📶) This 18th-century stone house has a great location across the road from the River Wye. Vivid window boxes give it a splash of colour, and the rooms, decorated in shades of burgundy and crisp white, are quiet and comfortable.

Bridge at Wilton B&B ££
(☎01989-562655; www.bridge-house-hotel.com; s/d from £80/98; P) A distinguished Georgian country-house restaurant a mile west of Ross, with smart rooms and a highly praised menu of Modern British food.

Pots and Pieces CAFE £
(www.potsandpieces.com; 40 High St; mains from £5; ⏲breakfast & lunch) The best of the tearooms around the market place, with ceramics and crafts to browse while you sip a coffee or munch on a cupcake or sandwich.

Information

Tourist Office (☎01432-260675; tic-ross@herefordshire.gov.uk; Market House, Market Pl; ⏲10.30am-4.30pm Wed-Mon Apr-Sep, to 4pm Sun Oct-Mar) Has information on sights and walks – ask for the *Ross-on-Wye Heritage Trail* booklet (50p).

Getting There & Around

The bus stand is on Cantilupe Rd. From Monday to Saturday, bus 38 runs hourly to **Hereford** (45 minutes), and bus 33 runs hourly to **Gloucester** (40 minutes). For **Monmouth**, take bus 34 (45 minutes, every two hours Monday to Saturday).

Forest of Dean

An ancient woodland with an almost magical character, the Forest of Dean is the oldest oak forest in England and a wonderfully scenic place to walk, cycle or paddle. Its steep, wooded hills, winding, tree-lined roads and glimmering lakes make it a remarkably tranquil place and an excellent spot for outdoor pursuits.

The forest was formerly a royal hunting ground and a centre of iron and coal mining, and its mysterious depths were supposedly the inspiration for Tolkien's forest of Middle Earth in the *Lord of the Rings* and for JK Rowling's Forbidden Forest in the Harry Potter adventures. Numerous other writers, poets, artists and craftspeople have been inspired by the stunning scenery, designated England's first National Forest Park in 1938.

The Forest of Dean spills over the Gloucestershire border near the village of Goodrich, off the A40 between Ross-on-Wye and Monmouth. The River Wye skirts the forest edge, offering glorious views to canoeists paddling out from the delightful village of Symonds Yat. Covering 42 sq miles between Gloucester, Ross-on-Wye and Chepstow, the forest is in an isolated position, but Coleford, the main population centre, has good transport connections. You'll find information on the area at www.visitforestofdean.co.uk.

GOODRICH

Goodrich Castle CASTLE
(EH; ☎01600-890538; adult/child £6/3.60; ⏲10am-5pm Apr-Oct, to 6pm Jul & Aug, 10am-4pm Wed-Sun Nov-Mar) Goodrich Castle is a fabulously complete medieval castle, topped by a superb 12th-century keep affording spectacular views.

Goodrich is five miles south of Ross off the A40. Bus 34 stops here every two hours on its way between Ross (20 minutes) and Monmouth (20 minutes), except on Sundays.

Symonds Yat

On the forest's edge, squeezed between the River Wye and the towering limestone outcrop known as Symonds Yat Rock, Symonds Yat East is an endearing tangle of pubs and guesthouses, with great walks and an excellent canoeing centre and campsite right in the middle of the village. An ancient hand-hauled ferry (adult/child/bicycle £1/50p/50p) crosses the Wye to Symonds Yat West on the other side of the valley, where there's a riverside caravan park. Travelling between the two villages by road involves a convoluted detour via the A40.

The area is renowned for canoeing and rock climbing and there's also good hiking and cycling in the nearby Forest of Dean – the scenic Peregrine Path follows the riverbanks from Symonds Yat East to Monmouth.

The most popular walk from Symonds Yat East picks its way up the side of the 504m Symonds Yat Rock, with fabulous river and valley views. Try to spot peregrine falcons soaring by the drop-off in July and August. Peaceful walking trails continue east through the forest into Gloucestershire.

Rock climbers follow a series of mainly trad routes directly up the face of the cliff, but routes in the easier grades tend to be very polished, and rock falls are common – bring a varied rack and wear your helmet. *Symonds Yat* by John Willson, is the definitive guidebook.

There's no direct public transport, but bus 34 between Ross-on-Wye and Monmouth can drop you off on the main road 1.5 miles from the village (services every two hours).

Activities

Wyedean Canoe Centre CANOEING
(01594-833238; www.wyedean.co.uk; half-day hire from £28; 8.30am-8.30pm) Hires out canoes and kayaks, and also organises multiday kayaking trips, white-water trips, caving and climbing. Strong currents make the river dangerous for swimming.

Sleeping & Eating

Garth Cottage B&B £
(01600-890364; www.garthcottage-symondsyat.com; per person £40.50; mid-March–Oct; P) The pick of accommodation on the east side, this friendly, family-run B&B sits by the riverside near the ferry crossing, and has spotlessly maintained, bright rooms with river views. Good deals for longer stays.

Old Court Hotel HOTEL ££
(01600-890367; www.oldcourthotel.co.uk; r £85-155; P) A striking 16th-century manor house set in lovely gardens on the outskirts of Symonds Yat West, complete with Elizabethan dining room. Choose from spic-and-span contemporary rooms, timbered charmers with four-poster beds or a barn apartment.

Wyedean Canoe Centre Campsite CAMPSITE £
(01600-890238; www.wyedean.co.uk; sites per adult/child £10/6; Apr-Oct) This popular canoe centre has a lovely campsite with a clean bathroom block, set right by the river. Rates drop by 25% from Monday to Thursday.

Ledbury

POP 8491

An atmospheric little town creaking with history and dotted with antique shops, Ledbury is a favourite destination for day trippers. The best way to pass the time is to wander the crooked black-and-white streets, which zero in on a delightfully leggy medieval market house.

Sights

Almost impossibly cute Church Lane runs its cobbled way from the High St to the town church, crowded with tilting timber-framed buildings, like JK Rowling's Diagon Alley.

Market House HISTORIC BUILDING
Markets still take place in Ledbury's delicate black-and-white Market House, as they have since the 17th century. The timber-framed structure is precariously balanced atop a series of wooden posts supposedly taken from the wrecked ships of the Spanish Armada.

FREE **Painted Room** HISTORIC BUILDING
(11am-1pm & 2-4pm Mon-Fri Easter-Sep, plus 2-5pm Sun Jul-Sep) At the corner of Church St, the Painted Room is adorned with 16th-century floral frescos.

FREE **Butcher's Row House** HISTORIC BUILDING
(01531-632942; Church Lane; 11am-5pm Easter-Sep) This charming house contains a pocket-sized folk museum stuffed with local curios, including an 18th-century communal bath that used to be carted from door to door for the poor to scrub up in.

St Michael and All Angels CHURCH
(www.ledburyparishchurch.org.uk; 8.30am-6pm, to 4pm low season) At the top of the lane lies the 12th-century church of St Michael and All Angels with a splendid 18th-century spire and tower divided from its medieval nave.

FREE **Heritage Centre** MUSEUM
(01531-635680; 10.30am-4.30pm Easter-Oct) The Heritage Centre sits in a half-timbered treasure across the street, with displays on local history.

Sleeping & Eating

The town pubs offer reasonably priced meals, but budget travellers will struggle to find cheap accommodation.

Verzon House Hotel HOTEL £££
(01531-670381; www.verzonhouse.com; s/d from £110/185; P@) The ultimate country-chic retreat, this lovely Georgian farmhouse has eight luxuriously appointed rooms with tactile fabrics, free-standing baths, goose-down pillows, and toe-tickling deep-pile carpets,

SIPPING YOUR WAY AROUND CIDER COUNTRY

Crisp, dry ciders have been produced in Herefordshire since medieval times. The **Herefordshire Cider Route** (www.ciderroute.co.uk) drops in on numerous local cider producers, where you can try before you buy and then totter off to the next one. Putting road safety first, tourist offices have maps and guide booklets to help you explore by bus or bicycle.

If you only have time to visit one cider maker, make it **Westons Cider Mills** (☎01531-660233; www.westons-cider.co.uk; The Bounds; ⏰9am-4.30pm Mon-Fri, 10am-4pm Sat & Sun), whose house brew is even served in the Houses of Parliament. Informative hour-long **tours** (adult/child £7.50/4) start at 11am, 12.30pm and 2.30pm, with free cider and perry tastings for the grown-ups. Westons is just under a mile west of Much Marcle.

and a very smart brasserie. Verzon House is 3 miles west of Ledbury on the A438.

Feathers Hotel HOTEL £££
(☎01531-635266; www.feathers-ledbury.co.uk; High St; mains £10-17, s/d from £95/140; P) This charming black-and-white Tudor hotel looms over the main road in Ledbury. Rooms in the oldest part of the building come with slanting floorboards, painted beams, and much more character than the modern rooms. There's an atmospheric wood-panelled restaurant and a swimming pool.

Cameron & Swan CAFE £
(☎01531-636791; www.cameronandswan.co.uk; 15 The Homend; mains £6-7; ⏰breakfast & lunch Mon-Sat) A bustling cafe serving tasty deli sandwiches, giant meringues and other tasty homemade treats in a bright dining room.

ℹ Information

Tourist Office (☎01531-636147; www.visitledbury.co.uk; 3 The Homend; ⏰10am-5pm Mon-Sat Apr-Oct, to 4pm Nov-Mar) Just off the High St, behind St Katherine's Chapel, this helpful office has information on tours of the town.

ℹ Getting There & Away

Trains run to **Great Malvern** (15 minutes, hourly), **Hereford** (£5.70, 20 minutes, hourly), **Worcester** (£6, 30 minutes, hourly) and further afield. Bus 476 runs to **Hereford** hourly (40 minutes, hourly Monday to Saturday, every two hours Sunday); bus 132 runs to **Gloucester** (one hour, hourly Monday to Saturday).

Around Ledbury

EASTNOR CASTLE

Built more for fancy than fortification, the extravagant medieval-revival folly of Eastnor Castle remains the family home of the grandchildren of the first Earl Somers, who constructed this elaborate confection in 1810. The grounds – hosting big rock acts every August as part of the **Big Chill** (www.bigchill.net) – are delightful.

The castle is just over 2 miles east of Ledbury on the A438; a taxi from Ledbury station will cost around £10.

MUCH MARCLE

Not much more than a blip on the map, the tiny village of Much Marcle is home to one of England's oldest and most fascinating houses. Built in the 12th century, **Hellens** (☎01531-660504; www.hellensmanor.com; adult/child £6/3; ⏰tours 2pm, 3pm & 4pm Wed, Thu, Sun & bank holidays Apr-Sep) is crammed with priceless tapestries, heirlooms and oils, including pieces formerly owned by Mary, Queen of Scots, Charles I and Anne Boleyn. As this is still a family home, you can only enter on guided tours, but the sense of history is tangible, both inside, and outside in the restored medieval garden.

You can see the brightly painted tomb of the former owner, Walter de Helyon, nearby at **St Bartholomew's Church** (⏰9am-dusk), along with other fine alabaster memorials from the 14th and 17th centuries.

Bus 45 from Ledbury goes to Much Marcle (40 minutes, four daily Monday to Friday, five services Saturday).

SHROPSHIRE

Sleepy Shropshire is a glorious scattering of hills, castles and timber-framed villages tucked against the Welsh border. Highlights include food-obsessed Ludlow, industrial Ironbridge and the beautiful Shropshire

Hills, which offer the best walking and cycling in the Marches.

Activities

Walking

The towering Shropshire Hills call out to walkers like a siren. Between Shrewsbury and Ludlow, the landscape rucks up into dramatic folds, with spectacular trails climbing the flanks of **Wenlock Edge** and the **Long Mynd** near Church Stretton. The county is also crossed by long-distance trails, including the famous Offa's Dyke Path (p535) and the popular **Shropshire Way**, which meanders around Ludlow, Craven Arms and Church Stretton. For general information on walking in the county, visit www.shropshirewalking.co.uk.

Cycling

Mountain bikers head for the muddy tracks that scramble over the Long Mynd near Church Stretton, or the rugged forest trails of **Hopton Wood**, near Craven Arms, while road riders aim for the **Six Castles Cycleway** (NCN 44), which runs for 58 miles from Shrewsbury to Leominster.

Tourist offices sell copies of *Cycling for Pleasure in the Marches,* a pack of five maps and guides covering the entire county. Alternatively, you can download cycling pamphlets for free from www.shropshirecycling.co.uk.

Information

North Shropshire (www.northshropshire.co.uk)

Secret Shropshire (www.secretshropshire.org.uk)

Shropshire Tourism (www.shropshiretourism.co.uk)

Virtual Shropshire (www.virtual-shropshire.co.uk)

Visit South Shropshire (www.visitsouthshropshire.co.uk)

Getting There & Around

Shrewsbury is the local transport hub, and handy rail services go to Church Stretton, Craven Arms and Ludlow. For London Euston, you will have to change at Birmingham. National Express coaches link Shrewsbury with London Victoria Coach Station. The invaluable *Shropshire Bus & Train Map,* available free from tourist offices, shows useful routes. **Shropshire Hills Shuttles** (www.shropshirehillsshuttles.co.uk) runs useful bus services along popular hiking routes on weekends and bank holidays.

Shrewsbury

POP 67,126

A delightful jumble of winding medieval streets and timbered Tudor houses leaning at precarious angles, Shrewsbury (*shroos-bree*) was a crucial front in the conflict between the English and Welsh in medieval days. Even today, the road bridge running east towards London is known as the English Bridge to mark it out from the Welsh Bridge leading northwest towards Holyhead. It is also the birthplace of Charles Darwin (1809–82).

Sights

Shrewsbury is studded with two-tone timbered beauties, many dating back to the Tudor era and beyond. The most handsome buildings can be found on the narrow lanes surrounding **St Alkmond's Church**, particularly along **Fish St** and bawdily named **Grope Lane**. At the bottom of the High St

SHREWSBURY'S SHUTS

Known in other English towns as 'wiends', 'snickets', 'ginnels', 'snares', 'twittons' or 'chares', 'shuts' are the ancient narrow passageways linking roads together in Shrewsbury. Pinched between walls, some have steps, others are covered and you may find an arch here or there, alongside other historic features.

Some shuts have endured name changes over the centuries, others retain their original monickers. **Grope Lane** off Fish St points to more ribald days; **Compasses Passage** off Wyle Cop recalls the namesake pub that served ale here. **Barracks Passage**, also off Wyle Cop, was once called Elisha's Shut and contains an attractive span of timbered buildings. In **Coffee House Passage**, linking The Square and College Hill, look out for the ancient carved beam above the entrance.

Other shuts with notable historic features include **King's Head Passage**, **Drayton's Passage**, **Bear Steps**, **Gullet Shut** and **St Mary's Shut**, the latter tightening to a mere 22 inches!

Shrewsbury

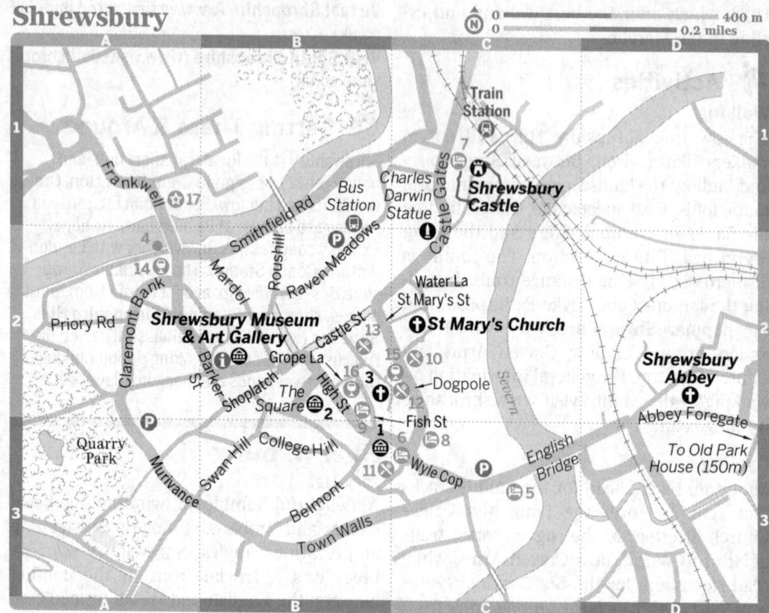

on Wyle Cop, the seriously overhanging **Henry Tudor House** was where Henry VII stayed before the Battle of Bosworth.

St Mary's Church CHURCH

(St Mary's St; ⏲10am-4pm Mon-Sat) The interior of this tall-spired medieval church contains a fabulous interior, graced with an impressive collection of stained glass, including a 1340 window depicting the Tree of Jesse, a Biblical representation of the lineage of Jesus, and a magnificent oak ceiling in the nave which largely collapsed in a huge gale in 1894 when the top of the spire blew off. Much of the glass in the church was sourced from the Continent, including some outstanding Dutch glass from 1500. There's a small cafe at the rear.

Shrewsbury Abbey CHURCH

(☎01743-232723; www.shrewsburyabbey.com; Abbey Foregate; entry by £2 donation; ⏲10.30am-3pm Mon-Sat, 11.30am-2.30pm Sun) Famous as the setting for Ellis Peters' *Chronicles of Brother Cadfael,* the lovely red-sandstone Shrewsbury Abbey is all that remains of a vast, cruciform Benedictine monastery founded in 1083. Twice the setting for meetings of the English parliament, the Abbey church lost its spire and two wings when the monastery was dissolved in 1540. It sustained further damage in 1826 when engineer Thomas Telford ran the London–Holyhead road right through the grounds. Nevertheless, you can still see some impressive Norman, Early English and Victorian features, including an exceptional 14th-century west window.

FREE **Shrewsbury Museum & Art Gallery** MUSEUM

(☎01743-281205; www.shrewsburymuseums.com; Barker St; ⏲10am-5pm Mon-Sat, to 4pm Sun May-Sep) The town museum is currently housed in the timbered Rowley's House from the 1590s (next to the lovely brick appendage of Rowley's Mansion from 1618), with exhibits ranging from Roman treasures to Shropshire gold, including the bronze age Perry Bracelet. The museum and tourist office are undergoing a slow move (due in 2013) to the Music Hall on the Square.

Shrewsbury Castle CASTLE

(☎01743-358516; adult/child £2.50/1.50; ⏲10am-5pm Mon-Sat, to 4pm Sun May-Sep, 10am-4pm Tue-Sat Feb-Apr) Hewn from flaking red Shropshire sandstone, the town castle contains the **Shropshire Regimental Museum,** plus fine views from **Laura's Tower** and the battlements. The lower level of the **Great Hall** dates from 1150.

Shrewsbury

Old Market Hall HISTORIC BUILDING
(www.oldmarkethall.co.uk) At the other end of the High St to St Alkmond's Church in cute cobbled The Square is Shrewsbury's good-looking 16th-century Old Market Hall, whose upper levels contain the town's pocket-sized cinema (p546) and a cafe.

Tours

Guided **walking tours** (adult/child £4/2) leave the tourist office (p547) at 2.30pm from Monday to Saturday, and at 11am on Sunday during high season. Tours only run on Saturday (2.30pm) from November to April.

Sabrina BOAT TOUR
(☎01743-369741; www.sabrinaboat.co.uk; from £3.50) Enjoy Shrewsbury from the water on board the Sabrina, which cruises the River Severn. Trips leave roughly hourly between 11am and 4pm (March to October) from Victoria Quay near the Welsh Bridge. **Ghost cruises** every Thursday evening.

Sleeping

Pretty Abbey Foregate is lined with B&Bs.

Lion Hotel HOTEL ££
(☎01753-353107; www.thelionhotelshrewsbury.co.uk; Wyle Cop; s/d from £80/98; P) A gilded wooden lion crowns the doorway of this famous 16th century coaching inn, decked out inside with portraits of lords and ladies in powdered wigs. Charles Dickens was a former guest and the lounge is warmed by a grand stone fireplace. Rooms are lovely, down to the period-pattern fabrics and ceramic water jugs. Breakfast is included.

Lion & Pheasant BOUTIQUE HOTEL ££
(☎01743-770345; www.lionandpheasant.co.uk; 50 Wyle Cop; d £95-175) There's more than a dash of pizazz at this stylish town house offering crisp, neat, bright and well-designed boutique accommodation in a former coaching inn, with 22 individually styled rooms. The hotel also owns two nearby cottages for nightly or weekly rates. Breakfast is included.

Tudor House B&B ££
(☎01743-351735; www.tudorhouseshrewsbury.com; 2 Fish St; s/d from £69/79; @ wi-fi) A bowing frontage festooned with hanging baskets and window boxes sets the scene at this delightful Tudor cottage. It's handy for everything in the centre, and rooms are adorned with shimmery fabrics and flowery trim. Not all rooms have an en suite.

Lucroft Hotel HOTEL ££
(☎01743-362421; www.lucrofthotel.com; Castle Gates; s/d from £29/45; wi-fi) Recently refurbished with pleasant, bright and charming rooms, this cheap and cheerful guesthouse is also great value for money and the location between the station and castle is faultless.

Albright Hussey Manor HOTEL ££
(☎01939-290523; www.albrighthussey.co.uk; Ellesmere Rd; s/d from £79/120; P@) This charmingly mismatched medieval manor has an excellent restaurant, and is surrounded by a moat. Found 2 miles north of town.

Eating

Drapers Hall FRENCH £££
(☎01743-344679; www.drapershallrestaurant.co.uk; St Mary's Pl; mains £12.50-24.50, s/d from £95/120; P) The sense of history is palpable in this beautifully preserved 16th-century hall, fronted by an elegant Elizabethan facade. Award-wining Anglo-French haute cuisine is served in rooms adorned with wood panelling and artwork. Upstairs are spectacular, heirloom-filled guest rooms.

No 4 Butcher Row CAFE £
(☎01743-366691; www.number-four.com; 4 Butcher Row; mains £4-8.50; ⊙8.30am-4pm Mon-Fri, 8.30am-5pm Sat, dinner from 6.30pm Fri only) Tucked away next to the Bull Inn near St Alkmond's Church, this neat, modern and very popular outfit is just the ticket for fantastic breakfasts, from eggs Benedict to bacon baguettes or a full English; lunch mains are excellent and affordable.

Mad Jack's MODERN EUROPEAN, HOTEL ££
(☎01743-358870; www.madjacks.uk.com; 15 St Mary's St; mains £11-16, s/d/ste from £70/80/90;) This classy place straddles the boundary between cafe, restaurant and bar, with an elegant dining room and a plant-filled courtyard. The menu features inventive Modern European cuisine prepared with locally sourced ingredients. There are four swish contemporary bedrooms upstairs.

DON'T MISS

SLEEP LIKE A QUEEN

Shrewsbury's most historic place to hang your tricorn hat, the **Old House Suites** (☎07974-099119; www.theoldhousesuites.com; The Old House, 20 Dogpole; ste £85-135; P@) are three lavish suites, all with views of the garden from a gloriously crooked timbered Tudor town house that was once owned by one of Catherine of Aragon's courtiers. Looking like a medieval oil painting brought to life, the main suite is glorious, with its own Tudor-styled loo that comes with a bathub, a shower in the passage and lounge (where breakfast is served). The owner conducts (voluntary) hour-long history tours of the property for guests. There's no sign, but it's up the steps from the Dogpole bus stop.

Good Life Wholefood Restaurant VEGETARIAN £
(☎01743-350455; Barracks Passage; mains £3.50-7; ⊙lunch Mon-Sat) Wholesome, freshly prepared vegetarian food is on the cards at this healthy refuge off Wyle Cop. Favourites include quiches, nut loaf, salads, soups, veggie lasagne and the lovely spinach moussaka.

Drinking

Armoury PUB
(www.armoury-shrewsbury.co.uk; Victoria Ave) Despite being a modern creation, the Armoury feels like it has been here for generations. It's cavernous, with long wooden tables, floor-to-ceiling bookshelves, assorted collectibles and the aromas of fine cooking.

Loggerheads PUB
(1 Church St; ⊙11am-11pm Mon-Sat, noon-10.30pm Sun) With its traditional charms, this pub in a 17th-century building has a crop of small, cosy corners including the Poet's Room, hung with portraits of Samuel Beckett, Ted Hughes and Sylvia Plath (in merrier days), and other luminaries of verse.

Three Fishes PUB
(4 Fish St) This quintessential creaky Tudor alehouse has a jolly publican, mellow regulars and hops hanging from the 15th-century beamed ceiling.

Entertainment

Theatre Severn THEATRE
(www.theatresevern.co.uk; Frankwell Quay) This much-acclaimed and expansive new riverside theatre and music venue hosts everything from pop gigs and comedy nights to plays and classical concerts.

Old Market Hall Film & Digital Media CINEMA
(☎01743-281 281; www.oldmarkethall.co.uk; The Square) View a selection of mainstream and art-house movies in a charming Elizabethan setting.

AN ABUNDANCE OF ABBEYS

Ravaged by Henry VIII's battle between church and state, Shropshire is dotted with ruined medieval monasteries, most bearing the scars of this tumultuous time in history. The Gothic wreck of **Wenlock Priory** (p551) in Much Wenlock and sandstone **Shrewsbury Abbey** (p544) are rightly famous. You'll find more atmospheric ruins dating back to the 12th century at delightful **Buildwas Abbey** (EH; ☎01952-433274; adult/child £3.40/2; ⊙10am-5pm Wed-Sun Apr-Sep) on the A1469, 2 miles west of Ironbridge, and peaceful **Haughmond Abbey** (☎01743-709661; EH; adult/child £3.40/2; ⊙10am-5pm Wed-Sun Apr-Sep), 3 miles northeast of Shrewsbury on the B5092.

Shopping

Appleyards Delicatessen DELI
(☎01743-240180; 85 Wyle Cop) Fantastic, traditional shop simply stuffed with a cornucopia of cheeses and beers.

Information

Reference Library (Castle Gates; ⊙9.30am-5pm Mon, Wed, Fri & Sat, to 8pm Tue & Thu, 1-4pm Sun) Free internet access.

Royal Shrewsbury Hospital (☎01743-261000; Mytton Oak Rd)

Tourist Office (☎01743-281200; www.visitshrewsbury.com; Barker St; ⊙10am-5pm Mon-Sat year-round, plus 10am-4pm Sun May-Sep) In the Shrewsbury Museum & Art Gallery (p544), the tourist office has walking tours and stacks of brochures.

Getting There & Away

BUS The bus station is beside the river on Smithfield Rd. Bus 435 runs to Ludlow (1½ hours, hourly Monday to Saturday), via Church Stretton. Other useful services:

Birmingham National Express; £6.70, 1½ hours, twice daily

Ironbridge Bus 96; 35 minutes, every two hours Monday to Saturday

London National Express; £19.80, 4½ hours, twice daily

TRAIN From the train station at the bottom of Castle Foregate, trains run half-hourly to **Ludlow** (£12.90, 30 minutes, hourly at weekends). For **London Euston** (£52, 2¾ hours) take one of the regular trains to Birmingham or Crewe and change.

If you're bound for Wales, **Arriva Trains Wales** (☎0845 900 0773; www.arrivatrainswales.co.uk) runs to **Swansea** (£33.80, 3¾ hours, hourly) and **Holyhead** (£39.80, three hours, hourly).

Getting Around

You can hire bikes at **Dave Mellor Cycles** (www.davemellorcycles.com; 9a New St, Frankwell; ⊙9am-6pm Mon-Sat).

Around Shrewsbury

ATTINGHAM PARK

The most impressive of Shropshire's stately homes, **Attingham Park** (NT; ☎01743-708123; house & grounds adult/child £9/5.25, grounds only £4.05/2.15; ⊙house 11am-5.30pm mid-Mar–early-Nov, grounds 9am-6am year-round) was built in imposing neoclassical style in 1785. With its grand columned facade, manicured lawns, and a stagecoach turning circle in the courtyard, the house could have been plucked straight from a bodice-ripping period drama. Home to some 300 fallow deer, the landscaped grounds swirl around an ornamental lake and the restored walled garden is a picture.

Attingham Park is 4 miles southeast of Shrewsbury at Atcham; take bus 81 or 96 (18 minutes, six daily Monday to Friday, less frequently at weekends).

Ironbridge Gorge

Strolling or cycling through the woods, hills and villages of this peaceful river gorge, it's hard to believe such a sleepy enclave could really have been the birthplace of the Industrial Revolution. Nevertheless, it was here that Abraham Darby perfected the art of smelting iron ore with coke in 1709, making it possible to mass-produce cast iron for the first time. Before long, the valley was dotted with factories churning out iron components for newly invented steam engines, pumps and turbines.

Abraham Darby's son, Abraham Darby II, invented a new forging process for producing single beams of iron, allowing Abraham Darby III to astound the world with the first-ever iron bridge, constructed in 1779. The bridge remains the focal point of this World Heritage Site, along with 10 very

Ironbridge Gorge

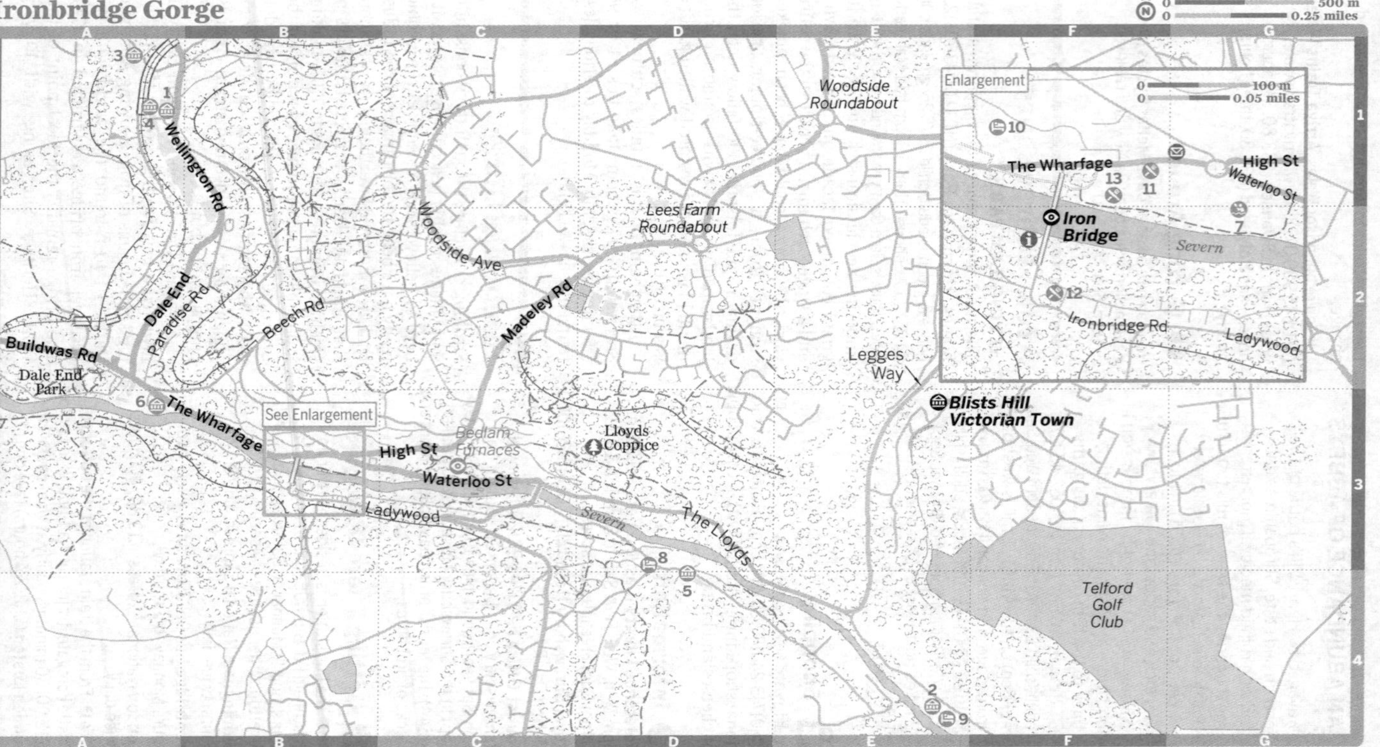

Ironbridge Gorge

Top Sights

Blists Hill Victorian Town E3
Iron Bridge F2

Sights

1 Coalbrookdale Museum of Iron A1
2 Coalport China Museum & Tar Tunnel E4
3 Darby Houses A1
4 Enginuity A1
5 Jackfield Tile Museum D4
6 Museum of the Gorge A3

Activities, Courses & Tours

7 Ironbridge Canoe Hire & Sales G2

Sleeping

8 Calcutts House D3
9 Coalport YHA E4
10 Library House F1

Eating

11 Da Vinci's F1
12 D'arcys at the Station F2
13 Restaurant Severn F1

different museums telling the story of the Industrial Revolution.

The Ironbridge museums are spread out along both sides of the River Severn near the village of Coalbrookdale, explorable on foot, by rented bicycle or on the special tourist bus.

Lloyds Coppice provides a backdrop to the northern slopes of the gorge.

Sights & Activities

The Ironbridge museums are administered by the **Ironbridge Gorge Museum Trust** (☎01952-884391; www.ironbridge.org.uk) and all are open from 10am to 5pm from late March to early November, unless stated otherwise. You can buy tickets as you go, but the good-value **passport ticket** (adult/child £21.95/14.25) allows year-round entry to all of the sites.

Museum of the Gorge MUSEUM
(☎01952-433424; The Wharfage; adult/child £3.60/2.35) Kick off your visit at the Museum of the Gorge, which offers an overview of the World Heritage Site using film, photos and 3-D models. Housed in a Gothic warehouse by the river, it's filled with entertaining, hands-on exhibits.

Iron Bridge BRIDGE
(toll-house admission free) The flamboyant, arching 384-tonne and gravel-strewn **Iron Bridge** that gives the area its name was constructed to flaunt the new technology invented by the Darby family. At the time of its construction in 1779, nobody could believe that anything so large could be built from cast iron without collapsing under its own weight. There's a small exhibition on the bridge's history at the former toll house.

Coalbrookdale Museum of Iron MUSEUM
(Wellington Rd; adult/child, £7.40/4.95) Set in the brooding buildings of Abraham Darby's original iron foundry, the museum contains some excellent interactive exhibits. As well as producing the girders for the iron bridge, the factory became famous for heavy machinery and extravagant ornamental castings, including the gates for London's Hyde Park. Combined tickets with Darby Houses also available.

Darby Houses MUSEUM
(☎01952-433522; adult/child £4.75/3.25; ⊙Apr-Oct) Just uphill from the Coalbrookdale Museum of Iron are these beautifully restored 18th-century homes, which housed generations of the Darby family in gracious but modest Quaker comfort.

Blists Hill Victorian Town MUSEUM
(☎01952-433424; Legges Way; adult/child £14.95/9.95) Set at the top of the Hay Inclined Plane (a cable lift that once transported coal barges uphill from the Shropshire Canal), Blists Hill is a lovingly restored Victorian village repopulated with townsfolk in period costume, busy with day-to-day chores. There's even a bank, where you can exchange your modern pounds for shillings to use at the village shops. In summer, a Victorian fair is an added fun attraction for young ones.

Coalport China Museum & Tar Tunnel MUSEUM
(museum adult/child £7.60/5.10, Tar Tunnel £2.60/2; ⊙ Tar Tunnel Apr-Sep) As iron making fell into decline, Ironbridge diversified into manufacturing china pots, using the fine clay mined around Blists Hill. Dominated by a pair of towering bottle kilns, the atmospheric old china works now contains

WORTH A TRIP

COSFORD ROYAL AIR FORCE MUSEUM

About 13 miles east of Ironbridge, this famous aerospace **museum** (☎01902-376200; www.rafmuseum.org.uk; Shifnal; ⏰10am-6pm Mar-Oct, 10am-5pm Nov-early Jan & mid-Jan–Feb) is run by the Royal Air Force, whose pilots once steered many of these winged wonders across the skies. Aircraft on display range from the Yokosuka MXY7 Model 11 – a rocket-powered and highly vulnerable Japanese kamikaze plane from WWII – and the gleaming, stainless-steel Bristol Type 188, known as the 'Flaming Pencil'. The museum is a half-mile walk from Cosford train station, on the Birmingham–Shrewsbury line. Visit in June for the annual **Cosford Air Show** (www.cosfordairshow.co.uk), when the Red Arrows stunt team paint the sky with coloured smoke.

an absorbing **museum** tracing the history of the industry, with demonstrations of traditional pottery techniques.

A short stroll along the canal brings you to the 200-year-old **Tar Tunnel**, an artificial watercourse that was abandoned when natural bitumen started trickling from its walls.

Jackfield Tile Museum MUSEUM
(☎01952-433424; adult/child £7.60/5.10) Once the largest tile factory in the world, Jackfield was famous for its encaustic tiles, with ornate designs produced using layers of different coloured clay (the tiles are still produced here today for period restorations). Gaslit galleries recreate ornately tiled rooms from past centuries, from Victorian public conveniences to fairy-tale friezes from children's hospital wards. The museum is on the south bank of the Severn, near the footbridge to the Coalport China Museum. **Tours** of the factory are held every Tuesday at 11.30am. To reach the museum, cross the footbridge at the bottom of the Hay Inclined Plane.

Enginuity MUSEUM
(Wellington Rd; adult/child £7.85/6.75) If the kids are starting to look glazed, recharge their batteries at this levers-and-pulleys science centre beside the Coalbrookdale Museum of Iron, where you can control robots, move a steam locomotive with your bare hands (and a little engineering know-how) and power up a vacuum cleaner with self-generated electricity.

Broseley Pipeworks MUSEUM
(adult/child £4.75/3.10; ⏰1-5pm mid-May–Sep) This was once the biggest clay tobacco-pipe maker in the country, but the industry took a nosedive after the introduction of pre-rolled cigarettes in the 1880s, and the factory was preserved much as the last worker left it when the last lights were turned off in 1957. The pipeworks is a 1-mile walk south of the river, on a winding lane that passes the old workers' cottages (ask at the tourist office (p551) for the *Jitties* leaflet). To reach the Broseley Pipeworks, cross the iron bridge and follow the signs.

Ironbridge Canoe Hire & Sales CANOEING
(☎01952-433518; www.ironbridgeleisure.co.uk; High St; canoe for 3 hrs from £30) In summer, when the river is at a safe level, you can rent canoes for fun trips along the Severn. Longer trips run upstream to Shrewsbury or downstream to Bridgnorth via the Jackfield rapids.

Sleeping

Rooms are everywhere in Ironbridge, even the **post office** can house you (£42 for a double room). There are two YHA hostels at Ironbridge, but the imposing and good-looking Coalbrookdale hostel is reserved for groups.

TOP CHOICE **Library House** B&B ££
(☎01952-432299; www.libraryhouse.com; 11 Severn Bank; s/d from £65/80; P@) Up an alley off the main street, this lovingly restored Georgian library building is hugged by vines, backed by a beautiful garden and decked out with stacks of vintage books, curios, prints and lithographs. There are three charmingly well-preserved, individually decorated rooms, named Milton, Chaucer and Eliot. The affable dog whipping around is Fizz.

Coalport YHA HOSTEL £
(☎0845 371 9325; www.yha.org.uk; High St; dm from £16, f from £50; P) This superior hostel is set in a converted china factory next to the Coalport China Museum and canal. Rooms are modern and functional; the big draw-cards are the facilities, including a laundry,

kitchen and licensed cafe, and its location in the quietest, prettiest corner of Ironbridge.

Calcutts House B&B ££
(☎01952-882631; www.calcuttshouse.co.uk; Calcutts Rd; s/tw/d from £50/70/55; P) This former ironmaster's pad, dating from the 18th century, is tucked away on the south bank around the corner from the Jackfield Tile Museum, about a mile east of the bridge. Its traditionally decorated rooms have heaps of character, one furnished with an outsize, 200-year-old four-poster bed.

Eating & Drinking

Most places to eat line the High St, but old-fashioned pubs dot both banks of the River Severn.

TOP CHOICE **Restaurant Severn** BRITISH, FRENCH £££
(☎01952-432233; www.restaurantseven.co.uk; 33 High St; 2-/3-course dinner from £23.95/25.95; dinner Wed-Sat, lunch Sun; P) The highly praised food at this small but busy riverside restaurant is a winning hybrid of English and French. The simple decor and laid-back service merely highlights the quality of the cooking, and the delectable, locally sourced menu changes weekly.

D'arcys at the Station MEDITERRANEAN ££
(☎01952-884499; www.darcysironbridge.co.uk; Ladywood; mains £11.25-13.50; dinner Tue-Sat) Just over the bridge and finely housed in the handsome old station building by the river, this restaurant has recently relocated to Ironbridge, bringing with it flavoursome Mediterranean dishes from Basque chicken to Cypriot kebabs and piri-piri trout.

Da Vinci's ITALIAN ££
(☎01952-432250; www.davinci-restaurant-ironbridge.co.uk; 26 High St; mains from £12.50; dinner Tue-Sat) Gourmet Italian food is served in a classy, narrow and wood-panelled dining room with oodles of charm.

Information

Tourist Office (☎01952-884391; www.visitironbridge.co.uk; The Wharfage; 10am-5pm) Located at the Museum of the Gorge.

Getting There & Away

The nearest train station is 6 miles away at Telford, but you can continue on to Ironbridge on bus 96 (20 minutes, every two hours Monday to Saturday). The same bus continues from the tourist office to **Shrewsbury** (40 minutes). Bus 9 runs from **Bridgnorth** (30 minutes, four daily Monday to Saturday) and bus 39 runs to **Much Wenlock** (30 minutes, four daily Monday to Saturday).

Getting Around

At weekends and on bank holidays from Easter to October, the **Gorge Connect bus** (free to museum passport ticket holders) runs from Telford bus station to all of the museums on the north bank of the Severn. A day pass costs £2.50/1.50 per adult/child.

Bikes can be rented from **Bicycle Hub** (☎01952-883249; rental per day from £15; 10am-5pm Mon-Sat) in the Fusion centre, behind the Jackfield Tile Museum.

Much Wenlock

POP 1959

With one of those quirky names that abound in the English countryside, Much Wenlock is as charming as it sounds. Surrounding the time-worn ruins of Wenlock Priory, the streets are studded with Tudor, Jacobean and Georgian houses, and locals say hello to everyone. As well as being a perfect English village, Much Wenlock also claims to have jump-started the modern Olympics.

Sights & Activities

Wenlock Priory RUINS
(EH; ☎01952-727466; adult/child incl audio tour £4/2.40; 10am-5pm daily May-Aug, 10am-5pm Wed-Sun Apr, Sep & Oct, 10am-4pm Sat & Sun Nov-Mar; P) The maudlin Cluniac ruins of Wenlock Priory rise up from vivid green lawns, sprinkled with animal-shaped topiary. Raised by Norman monks over the ruins of a Saxon monastery from AD680, the hallowed remains include a finely decorated chapter house and an unusual carved lavabo, where monks came to ceremonially wash before eating.

Guildhall HISTORIC BUILDING
(☎01952-727509; admission £1; 10.30am-1pm & 2-4.30pm Mon-Sat & 2-4.30pm Sun Apr-Oct) Across from the tourist office, the wonky Guildhall, built in classic Tudor style in 1540, features some splendidly ornate woodcarving. One of the pillars supporting it was used for public floggings in medieval times.

Holy Trinity Church CHURCH
(www.muchwenlockchurch.co.uk; 9am-5pm) A short walk north of the Guildhall, the ancient, eroded Holy Trinity Church was built

in 1150 over Saxon foundations. Note the Norman arch as you enter with the (as yet) undeciphered initials 'AB' and 'RI' on either side. Also look out for the old police station nearby, a good-looking building from 1864.

Sleeping & Eating

The closest hostel is Wilderhope Manor YHA (p552) on Wenlock Edge.

Raven Hotel HOTEL £££
(☎01952-727251; www.ravenhotel.com; Barrow St; mains £10-20; s/tw/d £85/120/130; P) Much Wenlock's finest, this 17th-century coaching inn and converted stables has oodles of historical charm and rich country-chic styling throughout. Overlooking a flowery courtyard, the excellent restaurant serves classic Mediterranean and British fare.

The Washhouse B&B ££
(☎01952-728334; 12 Back Lane; s/d £50/65) There's a grand total of two en-suite rooms in the detached cottage at this great B&B tucked away just off the High St. The upstairs room has more character, but both are pleasant.

Fox PUB ££
(☎01952-727292; www.the-fox-inn.co.uk; 46 High St; mains £13.50-23.50, s/d from £65/85; ⏲dinner Tue-Sat, lunch Tue-Sun ; @) Warm yourself by the massive fireplace, then settle down in the dining room to savour locally sourced venison, pheasant and beef, swished down with a pint of Shropshire ale. Candlelit dinners here are lovely. It also has five contemporary rooms.

Wenlock Deli DELI £
(11 High St; mains £8; ⏲10am-4pm Mon-Wed, 9am-5pm Thu-Sat) This quality spot next to the bookshop has some great surprises, from chorizo stew and Atlantic pie (pie with salmon, prawns and peas) to slices of 'fidget pie', a traditional Shropshire dish.

Information

Tourist Office (☎01952-727679; www.muchwenlockguide.info; The Square; museum admission free; ⏲10.30am-1pm & 1.30-5pm daily Apr-Oct, 10.30am-1pm & 1.30-5pm Tue & Fri, 10.30am-1pm Sat Nov-Mar) The tourist office has stacks of brochures on local sights and walks, and a modest museum of local history.

Getting There & Away

Buses 436 and 437 run from Shrewsbury to Much Wenlock (35 minutes, hourly Monday to Saturday, every two hours Sunday) and on to **Bridgnorth** (20 minutes). Bus 39 runs to **Ironbridge** (30 minutes, four daily Monday to Saturday).

Around Much Wenlock

WENLOCK EDGE

The spectacular limestone escarpment of Wenlock Edge swells up like an immense petrified wave, breaking over the Shropshire countryside. Formed from limestone that once lined the bottom of Silurian seas, the ridge sprawls for 15 miles from Much Wenlock to Craven Arms, providing a fantastic **hiking** back route from Ludlow and Ironbridge. The National Trust owns much of the ridge, and there are many marked trails starting from car parks dotted along the B4371. However, there are no convenient buses along this route.

For a bite, a beer or a bed, point your hiking boots towards the 17th-century **Wenlock Edge Inn** (☎01746-785678; www.wenlockedgeinn.co.uk; s/d £50/75, mains £8.95-17.95; P) perched atop the Edge about 4.5 miles southwest of Much Wenlock. It's a down-to-earth place with above-average pub grub, real ale and five chintzy but cosy rooms.

Alternatively, ramble out to the remote **Wilderhope Manor YHA** (☎0845 371 9149; www.yha.org.uk; Longville-in-the-Dale; dm £13.95, f £44.95; ⏲Fri, Sat & school holidays; P), a gloriously atmospheric gabled grey-stone Elizabethan manor, with spiral staircases, wood-panelled walls, an impressive stone-floored dining hall and spacious, oak-beamed rooms. This is hostelling for royalty! Bus 155 from Ludlow and buses 153 and 154 from Bridgnorth run infrequently to Shipton, a half-mile walk from Wilderhope – call the hostel for the latest timetable.

Bridgnorth & Around

POP 11,891

Cleaved into two by a dramatic sandstone bluff that tumbles down to the River Severn, Bridgnorth is one of Shropshire's finest-looking historic towns, with a wealth of architectural charm despite much of the high town succumbing to fire in 1646 during the Civil War.

The adorable **St Leonard's Close**, around its namesake church, contains some of the most attractive buildings and almshouses in

GRANDADDY OF THE MODERN OLYMPICS

All eyes were on London for the Olympic Games in 2012, but tiny Much Wenlock held its own Olympic Games in July the same year, as it has annually since 1850. The idea of holding a sporting tournament based on the games of ancient Greece was the brainchild of local doctor William Penny Brookes, who was looking for a healthy diversion for bored local youths. Accordingly, he created a tournament for 'every kind of man', with running races, high and long jumps, tilting, hammer throwing and wheelbarrow races – plus glee singing, knitting and sewing so every kind of woman wasn't left out!

The games soon piqued the interest of Baron Pierre Coubertin, who visited Much Wenlock in 1890 and consulted Brookes extensively before launching the modern Olympic Games in Athens in 1896. Unfortunately, Brookes was effectively airbrushed out of the Olympic story until 1994, when International Olympic Committee President Juan Antonio Samaranch visited Much Wenlock to pay his respects to 'the founder of the modern Olympic Games'.

The Much Wenlock Olympics are still held every July, with events that range from the triathlon to volleyball. You can find details at www.wenlock-olympian-society.org.uk.

town, including a splendid six-gabled house, once part of the grammar school.

Northgate HISTORIC BUILDING
On the High St, Northgate is the last surviving gate of five, and contains a small museum. Several narrow lanes drop down from the High Town to the Low Town, including the very steep pedestrian Cartway, at the bottom of which is Bishop Percy's House, dating from 1580.

Daniels Mill HISTORIC BUILDING
(☎01746-762753; www.danielsmill.co.uk; adult/child £4/3; ⏰11am-4pm Easter-Oct) Just south of town, Daniels Mill is the largest working water-powered mill in the country, and it still produces flour for local bakers. Visitors get a personal tour of the working machinery from the resident miller.

Severn Valley Railway HERITAGE RAILWAY
(☎01299-403816; www.svr.co.uk; adult one-way/return £11.50/16.50, child £5.75/8.25; ⏰daily May-Sep, Sat & Sun Oct-Apr) Bridgnorth is the northern terminus of the Severn Valley Railway, whose trains chug down the valley to Kidderminster (one hour), starting from the station on Hollybush Rd. Cyclists can follow a beautiful 20-mile section of the Mercian Way (NCN Route 45) beside the railway line towards the Wyre Forest.

Bridgnorth Cliff Railway HERITAGE RAILWAY
(☎01746-762052; www.bridgnorthcliffrailway.co.uk; return £1; ⏰8am-8pm Mon-Sat & noon-8pm Sun May-Sep, to 6.30pm Oct-Apr) Jump aboard the Bridgnorth Cliff Railway, the steepest inland railway in Britain, trundling up the cliff since 1892. At the top of the route, a pedestrian walkway (affording astonishing night-time panoramas) curves around the bluff to a pretty park dotted with scattered masonry, some leaning at an incredible angle (all that remains of **Bridgnorth Castle**), and passes the grand and imposing Thomas Telford–designed and cupola-topped **St Mary's Church**.

Sleeping

Severn Arms Hotel HOTEL ££
(☎01746-764616; www.thesevernarms.co.uk; Underhill St; s/tw/d £32/58/64; 📶) Standing at the bottom of the bluff next to the cliff railway, this riverside Georgian property has gorgeous views over the bridge and the Severn, with manifest charm and history, helpful owners and proximity to the centre of town. There's no parking, but a car park is a few minute's walk away over the bridge.

Eating

Cinnamon Cafe CAFE £
(☎01746-762944; Waterloo House, Cartway; mains £5-8; ⏰9am-6pm Mon-Wed & Fri, 10am-4pm Sat & Sun) Near the top of the Cartway, the licensed Cinnamon Cafe serves up savoury bakes (many vegetarian and vegan), plus quiches and homemade muesli and cakes, which you can munch indoors or out front with views from the terrace.

Shopping

Bridgnorth Delicatessen DELI
(45 High St; ⏰9am-5pm Mon-Sat, 11am-4pm Sun) Not far from the **Town Hall** on the High St,

the well-stocked Bridgnorth Delicatessen does business from a lovely old shop, full of gleaming jars.

Information

Based at the town library, the **tourist office** (☎01746-763257; www.visitbridgnorth.co.uk; ⌚9.30am-5pm Mon-Sat Apr-Oct, Mon-Wed, Fri & Sat Nov-Mar) can advise on local B&Bs.

Getting There & Away

Buses 436 and 437 run hourly Monday to Saturday from Shrewsbury to **Bridgnorth** (one hour, five Sunday services), via **Much Wenlock** (25 minutes). Bus 9 runs to **Ironbridge** (30 minutes, four daily Monday to Saturday, no Sunday service).

Church Stretton & Around

POP 3841

Set in a deep valley formed by the Long Mynd and the Caradoc Hills, Church Stretton is an ideal base for walks or cycle tours through the Shropshire Hills. Although black-and-white timbers are heavily in evidence, most of the buildings in town are 19th-century fakes, built by the Victorians who flocked here to take the country air. The surrounding hills are the main attraction, but the village is pleasant to explore.

Sights & Activities

The tourist office has maps of local walking and mountain-biking circuits and details of local riding stables.

St Laurence's Church CHURCH

The Norman-era St Laurence's Church features an exhibitionist Sheela-na-gig over its north door.

Snailbeach VILLAGE

Over the ridge from the Stiperstones is the village of Snailbeach, with its intriguing mining relics, passing the Bog cafe (p555) and information centre next to the ruins of an abandoned mining village.

Long Mynd WALKING

Church Stretton clings to the steeply sloping sides of the Long Mynd, Shropshire's most famous hill, which rises to 517m. Dubbed 'Little Switzerland' by the Victorians, this desolate but dramatic bluff is girdled by **walking trails** that offer soaring views over the surrounding countryside. Most people start walking from the National Trust car park at the end of the **Carding Mill Valley** (www.cardingmillvalley.org.uk), half a mile west of Shrewsbury Rd – a small tearoom (p555) provides refreshments. To escape the summer weekend crowds, head east across the A49 and climb the 459m summit of **Caer Caradoc**.

A maze of single-track roads climbs over the Long Mynd to the adjacent ridge of **Stiperstones**, which is crowned by a line of spooky-looking crags where Satan is said to hold court.

Plush Hill Cycles BICYCLE RENTAL

(☎01694-720133; www.plushhillcycles.co.uk; 8 The Square; per day from £20) A handy range of mountain bikes and electric bikes in a shop by the square. Rates include helmet, map and child seat.

Sleeping

Bridges Long Mynd YHA HOSTEL £

(☎01588-650656; www.yha.org.uk; Bridges; dm from £16; P) On the far side of the Long Mynd, this superior YHA property is housed in a former school in the tiny hamlet of Bridges near Ratlinghope. Popular with hikers, the hostel is wonderfully isolated, but meals and drinks are available at the nearby **Horseshoe Inn** pub. To get here, cross the Mynd to Ratlinghope, or take the Long Mynd shuttle bus (p555).

Jinlye Guest House B&B ££

(☎01694-723243; www.jinlye.co.uk; Castle Hill; s/d £70/95; P) High above the village of All Stretton atop the Mynd, Jinlye is a charmingly restored crofter's cottage. At the time of writing the new owners were refurbishing the property.

Mynd House B&B ££

(☎01694-722212; www.myndhouse.com; Ludlow Rd; s/d from £45/75; P@) South of Church Stretton in Little Stretton, this inviting, family-friendly guesthouse has splendid views across the valley, and backs directly onto the Mynd. The lovely rooms are named after local hills, and there's a small bar and lounge stocked with local books and a room for drying your boots.

Longmynd Hotel HOTEL ££

(☎01694-722244; www.longmynd.co.uk; Cunnery Rd; s £45-65, d £90-130; P@) Above town on the edge of the Mynd, this long-established Victorian hotel with excellent food has neoclassical airs. Rooms are cosy and facilities include a drying room for your hiking boots, a swimming pool and a sculpture trail.

Eating & Drinking

There are several cosy pubs along the High St.

Berry's Coffee House CAFE £

(☎01694-724452; www.berryscoffeehouse.co.uk; 17 High St; meals £6-8; ⏲9am-5pm, later Fri & Sat) A particularly homely and delightful cafe with loads of rooms in an 18th-century house, just off the main street, offering organic, free-range, fair-trade, home-cooked menu, Shropshire breakfasts and wicked desserts. No credit cards.

Studio MODERN EUROPEAN £££

(☎01694-722672; www.thestudiorestaurant.net; 59 High St; 2/3 courses £25.50/ 28.50; ⏲dinner Wed-Sat) A former artist's studio not far from the church sets the scene for the town's most intimate restaurant, featuring an award-winning menu of modern English and traditional French food.

Bog CAFE

(☎01743-792484; www.bogcentre.co.uk; ⏲10am-5pm Wed-Sun Easter-Oct) This former Victorian-era school is a cosy cafe and information centre next to the ruins of an abandoned Stiperstones mining village.

Carding Mill Valley Tea-Room CAFE

(⏲11am-5pm) Build up calories with afternoon teas and hot meals before tackling the Long Mynd.

Information

The **tourist office** (☎01694-723133; www.churchstretton.co.uk; Church St; ⏲9.30am-5pm Mon-Sat, closed 12.30-1.30pm in winter), adjoining the library, has abundant walking information, as well as free internet access.

Getting There & Around

Trains between Ludlow and Shrewsbury stop in Church Stretton every hour, taking 20 minutes from either end. Alternatively, take bus 435 from Shrewsbury or Ludlow (40 minutes, hourly Monday to Saturday).

The **Long Mynd & Stiperstones Shuttle** (www.shropshire hillsshuttles.co.uk; day ticket adult/child £7/2.50; ⏲seven daily Sat, Sun & bank-holiday Mon Apr-Sep) runs from the Carding Mill Valley in Church Stretton to the villages atop the Long Mynd, passing the YHA at Bridges, the Stiperstones and the Snailbeach mine.

Bishop's Castle

POP 1630

Set amid the blissfully peaceful Shropshire countryside, Bishop's Castle is a higgledy-piggledy tangle of timbered town houses and 'Old Mother Hubbard' cottages. No trace remains of the eponymous castle, but the village is a fine base for hiking or cycling, with several historic pubs where you can find liquid refreshment at the end of an energetic day.

Sights & Activities

High Street STREET

Lined with surprisingly posh boutiques, the High St climbs from the town church to the adorable Georgian town hall abutting the crooked 16th-century **House on Crutches** (☎01588-630075; admission free; ⏲2-5pm Sat & Sun Apr-Sep) which also houses the town museum.

Shropshire Way WALKING

Walkers can hike from north Bishops Castle along the **Shropshire Way** (www.shropshirewalking.co.uk), which joins up with the long-distance **Offa's Dyke Path** (p535) and **Kerry Ridgeway** to the west. The northern sections of the Shropshire Way climb to the high country of the Stiperstones and the Long Mynd near Church Stretton. The tourist office sells a series of *Walking for Pleasure* pamphlets covering local walks.

Six Castles Cycleway CYCLING

(www.shropshirecycling.co.uk; NCN Route 44) Bishops Castle also lies on the popular Six Castles Cycleway between Shrewsbury and Leominster.

Sleeping & Eating

Note that rooms are more expensive at weekends in Bishop's Castle.

Poppy House B&B ££

(☎01588-638443; www.poppyhouse.co.uk; 20 Market Sq; s/d from £40/70, dishes from £6; ⏲cafe 10am-5pm Wed-Fri & Sun, to 10pm Sat; 📶) This sweet guesthouse has lovely, individual rooms with latch doors (and all with bath) and loads of old beams. It's attached to a friendly cafe that upgrades to fine dining on Saturday nights.

Castle Hotel HOTEL ££

(☎01588-638403; www.thecastlehotelbishopscastle.co.uk; The Square; s/d/f £60/85/125; P📶) This solid-looking 18th-century coaching inn was built with stones from the vanished Bishop's Castle, which also contributed the gorgeous wood panelling in the dining room. All eight en-suite rooms are lovely, with modern fabrics meeting antique furniture. The pub-bar in the hotel is decidedly cosy and the garden delightful. Rates include breakfast.

Porch House B&B ££
(☎01588-638854; www.theporchhouse.com; High St; s from £50, d from £75; P@) Part of a terrace of timbered 16th-century buildings, this gem has two charming rooms with mod cons: one a suite with a vast bath, the other carrying a discernible list courtesy of the ancient timber work.

Yarborough House CAFE £
(www.yarboroughhouse.com; The Square; ⌚10am-5pm Tue & Thu-Sun) Just down from the Castle Hotel, this cafe has excellent coffee and cakes in a secondhand bookshop, with a vast collection of classical music CDs and records.

Drinking

Three Tuns PUB
(www.thethreetunsinn.co.uk; Salop St) Bishop's Castle's finest watering hole is attached to the tiny **Three Tuns Brewery** (www.threetunsbrewery.co.uk), which has been rolling barrels of nut-brown ale across the courtyard since 1642. It's a cosy local and the ales are delicious.

Six Bells Inn PUB
(Church St; mains £8-13; ⌚lunch Tue-Sun, dinner Wed-Sat) This historic 17th-century coaching inn is alive with loyal locals and ramblers who come to sample ales from its adjoining brewery.

Shopping

Decorative Antiques ANTIQUES
(www.decorative-antiques.co.uk; 47 Church St; ⌚9.30am-5.30pm Mon, Tue & Thu-Sat, to noon Wed) Small shop with a great collection of early-20th-century deco ceramics, antiques, glass jewellery and bakelite collectibles.

Information

Old Time (☎01588-638467; www.oldtime.co.uk; 29 High St; ⌚10am-6pm Mon-Sat, to 2pm Sun) The pleasingly potty Old Time is part furniture workshop and part tourist information office.

Getting There & Away

Bus 553 runs to and from Shrewsbury (one hour, six daily). On Saturdays and bank holiday weekends, you can jump on the **Secret Hills Shuttle** from **Craven Arms** (40 minutes, four per day).

Ludlow

POP 9548

Fanning out from the splendid ruins of its Norman castle, beautiful Ludlow's muddle of narrow streets are crammed with independent butchers, bakers, grocers, cheesemongers and exceptional restaurants. Chuck in bustling markets and a scattering of leaning Jacobean and Georgian buildings and it's easy to see the appeal.

Sights

Ludlow Castle CASTLE
(☎01584-873355; www.ludlowcastle.com; Castle Sq; adult/child £5/2.50; ⌚10am-7pm daily Aug, to 5pm Apr-Jul & Sep, to 4pm Oct, Nov, Feb & Mar, Sat & Sun only Dec & Jan) Perched in an ideal defensive location atop a cliff above a crook in the river, the town castle was built to ward off the marauding Welsh – or to enforce the English expansion into Wales, according to those west of the border. Founded after the Norman conquest, the castle was dramatically expanded in the 14th century.

The **Norman chapel** in the inner bailey is one of the few surviving round chapels in England, and the sturdy **keep** (built around 1090) offers wonderful views over the hills.

Church of St Laurence CHURCH
(www.stlaurences.org.uk; King St; entry by £2 donation; ⌚10am-5.30pm Apr-Sep, 11am-4pm Oct-Mar) One of the largest parish churches in Britain, the church of St Laurence contains grand **Elizabethan alabaster tombs** and some delightfully cheeky medieval misericords carved into its choir stalls, including a beer-swilling chap raiding his barrel. The Lady Chapel contains a marvelous **Jesse Window** originally dating from 1330 (although much of the glass is Victorian). Four windows in St John's Chapel date from the mid-15th century, including the honey-coloured **Golden Window**. Note the front pew at the front right, carved with sets of initials from vandals through history, including one William Payler (expertly chiselled) from 1783. Climb the **tower** (£3) for stunning views.

WALKING & CYCLING IN LUDLOW

Ludlow is ringed by wonderful landscapes for cyclists and walkers. Starting just outside the castle entrance, the waymarked **Mortimer Trail** runs for 30 miles through idyllic countryside to **Kington** in Herefordshire. The tourist office has various leaflets describing the route, or visit www.mortimercountry.co.uk.

Another fine walking or cycling route is the **Shropshire Way**, which runs northwest to **Craven Arms**, or northeast to **Wenlock Edge** over the dramatic summit of **Clee Hill** (540m), the highest point in the county. The hill affords awe-inspiring views south to Worcestershire's **Malvern Hills**.

For something more leisurely, just stroll around town. A scenic path drops behind Ludlow Castle and crosses the River Teme via the Dinham Bridge, following the south bank east to Ludford Bridge. Climbing the hill, duck through the narrow **Broadgate** (the sole survivor of seven medieval gates, with its slots for the portcullis still intact), marking the medieval town limits, and stroll past the **Georgian town houses** of Broad St to reach the **Buttercross**, Ludlow's medieval butter market.

Tours

Town Tours WALKING TOUR
(☎01584-874205; www.ludlowhistory.co.uk; adult/child £2.50/free; ⏲2.30pm Sat & Sun Apr-Oct) These popular town tours leave from the Cannon in Castle Sq.

Ghost Walk WALKING TOUR
(www.shropshireghostwalks.co.uk; per person £4; ⏲8pm Fri) Search for spooks on the ghost walk from outside the Church Inn on the Buttercross.

Festivals & Events

Ludlow Festival ARTS FESTIVAL
(www.ludlowfestival.co.uk) The town's busy calendar peaks with this fortnight of theatre and music in June and July that uses the castle as its dramatic backdrop.

Ludlow Food & Drink Festival FOOD
(www.foodfestival.co.uk) One of Britain's best foodie celebrations, spanning a long weekend in September.

Sleeping

TOP CHOICE **Feathers Hotel** HOTEL ££
(☎01584-875261; www.feathersatludlow.co.uk; Bull Ring; s/d from £85/105, 2/3 courses £32.50/39.95; P) Stepping through the almost impossibly ornate timbered Jacobean facade, it's all tapestries, creaky wood furniture, timber beams and stained glass: you can almost hear the Cavaliers toasting the health of King Charles. The best rooms are in the old building – rooms in the newer wing lack the character and romance. Prices creep up at weekends. The restaurant is also highly recommended.

De Grey's B&B ££
(☎01584-872764; www.degreys.co.uk; 5 Broad St; s/d from £95/110; P wi-fi) Above the tearooms of the same name, this smart B&B has nine comfy and twee rooms with low ceilings, beams, leaded windows, reassuringly solid oak beds and four-posters in the suites. Higher rates Friday and Saturday.

The Merchant House B&B ££
(☎01584-875438; www.merchanthouse.co.uk; Lower Corve St; s/d £55/85; wi-fi) With just two rooms, this quaint 15th-century house next to the Unicorn Inn features wonky timbers, low doorways, a log-burning stove, comfy beds, plenty of historic charm and a warm welcome.

Dinham Hall Hotel HOTEL ££
(☎01584-876464; www.dinhamhall.co.uk; s/d from £105/145; P) This resplendent 18th-century country manor has views of the castle and the river from gorgeous rooms full of heirloom furniture, plus a superb fine-dining restaurant and afternoon teas.

Eating

Almost every pub and restaurant in town has caught the local-produce-and-deli-ingredients bug.

La Bécasse MODERN FRENCH £££
(☎01584-872325; www.labecasse.co.uk; 17 Corve St; 2-/3-course lunch £26/30; ⏲lunch Wed-Sun, dinner Tue-Sat) Artistically presented Modern French cuisine bursting with inventive flavours is served in an oak-panelled,

brick-walled dining room in a 17th-century coach house where Michelin-starred chef Will Holland has created some remarkable dishes.

Mr Underhill's MODERN BRITISH, HOTEL £££
(☎01584-874431; www.mr-underhills.co.uk; Dinham Weir; 8-course set menu from £62.50, ste from £235; ⊙dinner Wed-Sun) This dignified and award-winning restaurant is set in a converted corn mill that dips its toes in the river, and the Modern British food is exquisitely prepared, using market-fresh ingredients in a daily-changing menu. Should you be too full to walk home, rest up in one of the four particularly elegant suites, which all overlook the garden and the river.

De Grey's TEAHOUSE £
(www.degreys.co.uk; 73 Broad St; light meals from £4; ⊙breakfast & lunch) A swooningly nostalgic tearoom that easily could be plucked from an Agatha Christie mystery, De Grey's serves excellent breakfasts, lunches and afternoon teas, and superior cakes and patisserie throughout the day.

Koo JAPANESE ££
(☎01584-878462; 127 Old St; mains £11-15, 4-course meal £26.95; ⊙dinner Tue-Sat) Cute and kooky, this simple and neatly presented restaurant is run by a friendly Japanese chef. It serves up traditional Japanese food: sushi, *yakisakana* (grilled fish) and shots of warm sake.

Drinking & Entertainment

Real ales are the order of the day in flavour-obsessed Ludlow.

Ludlow Brewing Company BREWERY
(www.theludlowbrewingcompany.co.uk; 105 Corve St; ⊙10am-5pm Mon-Fri, to 1pm Sun) The Ludlow Brewing Company produces award-winning brews, and sells directly from the brewery.

Church Inn PUB
(Buttercross) Of the many pubs, the hop-strewn Church Inn is a cosy little escape with a pulpit at the bar, tucked away on the narrow lane beside the old butter market.

Wheatsheaf Inn PUB
(Lower Broad St) The quiet little Wheatsheaf Inn, under the medieval Broadgate, has a good choice of local ales.

Ludlow Assembly Rooms CINEMA
(☎01584-878141; www.ludlowassemblyrooms.co.uk; adult/child £5/3) Overlooking the market square, Ludlow Assembly Rooms also double as the town cinema.

Shopping

The best of the delis, independent butchers and artisanal bakers are clustered around the market square and the surrounding lanes.

Ludlow Market MARKET
(⊙Mon, Wed, Fri & Sat) Ludlow Market takes place on the market square on the site of the old Victorian town hall, demolished overnight in 1986.

Deli on the Square DELI
(www.delionthesquare.co.uk; 4 Church St; ⊙9.30am-5pm Mon-Wed, 9.30am-1pm Thu, 9am-5pm Fri-Sat) Just the ticket if you can't resist a slice of the memorably named Stinking Bishop or another of their 140-plus cheese varieties.

G & D Ginger Antiques ANTIQUES
(www.gdgingerantiques.com; 5 Corve St; ⊙9am-5pm Mon-Fri, 10am-4pm Sat) Specialists in oak and country antique furniture, with a fine selection of dressers and some quite magnificent chairs and tables.

Myriad Organics FOOD
(☎01584-872665; 22 Corve St; ⊙8.30am-6pm Mon-Sat) If you can't wait till market day, try Myriad Organics.

Ludlow Food Centre FOOD
(☎01584-856000; www.ludlowfoodcentre.co.uk; Bromfield; ⊙9am-5.30pm Mon, Tue, Wed & Sat, 9am-6.30pm Thu & Fri, 10.30am-4.30pm Sun) A handy one-stop shop for wholefoods and gourmet ingredients, about 2 miles north-west of Ludlow on the A49.

Information

Tourist Office (☎01584-875053; www.ludlow.org.uk; Castle Sq; ⊙10am-5pm Mon-Sat, 10.30am-5pm Sun) This well-stocked office contains an inside-out **museum** (☎01584-813666; admission free; ⊙10am to 5pm Mon-Sat, plus Sun from Jun to Aug) featuring the town and surrounding area.

Library (☎01584-813600; 7-9 Parkway; ⊙9.30am-5pm Mon-Wed & Sat, to 7.30pm Fri) Free Internet access.

Getting There & Around

Trains run frequently from the station on the north edge of town to **Hereford** (£8.70, 25 minutes, half-hourly) and **Shrewsbury** (£11.20, 30 minutes, half-hourly) via **Church Stretton** (20 minutes). You can also reach **Shrewsbury** on bus 435 (1½ hours, hourly Monday to Saturday), which runs via **Craven Arms** (20 minutes) and **Church Stretton** (40 minutes).

You can hire bikes from **Wheely Wonderful** (01568-770755; www.wheelywonderfulcycling.co.uk; Petchfield Farm; adult bike per day from £18; 9am-5pm Mon-Sat Apr-Oct), 5 miles west of Ludlow.

Around Ludlow

CRAVEN ARMS

Just 7 miles northwest of Ludlow, Craven Arms bills itself as the gateway to the Shropshire Hills, by virtue of its train station and its position near the southern end of Wenlock Edge. It's worth deviating west along the B4368 to the quaint village of **Clun**, with its stone bridge and ruined **castle**, and **Clunton**, where a forest trail leads to the **Bury Ditches**, a huge Iron Age hill fort.

Craven Arms is also the central point on the **Shropshire Way** – from here, you can hike west to Bishop's Castle, north to the Long Mynd, or east to the summit of Clee Hill (540m) and Wenlock Edge. Eight miles west of Craven Arms, **Hopton Wood** is a favourite destination for mountain bikers, with some challenging waymarked trails.

Housed in a striking turf-roofed building on the A49, the **Shropshire Hills Discovery Centre** (01588-676000; adult/child £3.50/3; 10am-5pm all days, until 7pm Wed Apr-Oct, 10am-4.30pm all days, until 7pm Wed Nov-Mar) provides local information and has a great family-friendly **museum** on the geology and natural history of the Shropshire Hills. A reconstructed mammoth and simulated balloon flight are the highlights.

Trains on the Shrewsbury–Ludlow line pass through every 30 minutes; you can also get here on bus 435 from Shrewsbury or Ludlow (hourly Monday to Saturday). On weekends from April to September, the **Shropshire Hills Shuttles** (www.shropshirehillsshuttles.co.uk; day pass adult/child £7/2.50; Sat & Sun Apr-Sep) run to Clun, Bishop's Castle, Church Stretton and the villages of the Long Mynd.

Just 1 mile south of Craven Arms, Tolkeinesque **Stokesay Castle** (EH; 01588-672544; adult/child £5.80/3.50; 10am-5pm daily Apr-Sep, 10am-5pm Wed-Sun Oct, 10am-4pm Sat & Sun Nov-Mar) was built by Lawrence of Ludlow, Britain's most successful wool merchant, in 1291.

To really escape from it all, head to the secluded **Waterdine Inn** (01547-528214; http://waterdine.com; Llanfair Waterdine; s incl breakfast from £57.50, d per person inc breakfast & dinner £80; P), a timbered and ivy-clad 16th-century longhouse set right against the border with Wales. As well as offering comfortable cottage-style rooms, this foodie retreat serves some of the best Modern British food in Shropshire. Llanfair Waterdine is about 12 miles west of Ludlow.

THE CASTLES OF MARCH

The hills between Shrewsbury and Leominster are crowned by a series of dramatic castles, constructed by the Lords Marcher to protect their territory from the marauding Welsh. Some are impressively intact, while others, like Richard's Castle near Ludlow, have been almost entirely reclaimed by nature. Many of these time-worn fortresses can be visited on the **Shropshire Way** (www.shropshirecycling.co.uk) walking trail or the 58-mile **Six Castles Cycleway** (p555), which runs south from Shrewsbury to Leominster and Hereford, via Bishop's Castle, Craven Arms and Ludlow.

Top stops on the castle trail:

Shrewsbury Castle (p544) Russet-sandstone walls enclosing a military museum.

Bishop's Castle (p555) The castle is gone, but its stones prop up the hilltop pub.

Clun Castle (p559) A classic moat and bailey ruin overlooking the river in Clun.

Stokesay Castle (p559) A *Lord of the Rings* fantasy south of Craven Arms.

Ludlow Castle (p556) A ruin and round chapel in the middle of Shropshire's most charming town.

Croft Castle (p537) Not medieval, but suitably grand and turreted; near Aymestrey.

North Shropshire

North of Shrewsbury, the hills are lower and the landscape less dramatic, but several worthwhile diversions are set among the rolling green pastures. With a market dating back 750 years, **Market Drayton** was once home to Clive of India, founder of Britain's Indian Empire. The town church contains the medieval tomb of Thomas and Elizabeth Bulkley, distant ancestors of George W Bush. The **tourist office** (☎01584-653114; 49 Cheshire St; ⌚9.30am-4pm Mon-Sat) can point you towards the sights.

Five miles southwest of Market Drayton, **Wollerton Old Hall** (☎01630-685760; www.wollertonoldhallgarden.com; Wollerton; adult/child £6/1; ⌚Fri, Sun & bank holidays noon-5pm Apr-Aug, noon-5pm Fri Sep) is a treat for gardeners, with its beautifully manicured lawns and flowers surrounding a 16th-century house.

Heading 4 miles west of Wollerton Old Hall, **Hawkstone Park** (☎01939-200611; www.hawkstone.co.uk; adult/child £7/4.50; ⌚10am-4pm Apr-Aug, hours vary Sep-Mar) is a grand country house whose grounds contain the **Follies**, a magical complex of fantasy towers, deep ravines and spooky rock-hewn grottoes created in the 18th century. Check the website for winter opening hours.

So close to Wales you can almost hear the male-voice choirs, **Oswestry** is famous for its **Iron Age hill fort** and the community-owned **Whittington Castle** (☎01691-662397; admission free; ⌚10am-4pm Wed-Sun Mar-Oct, 10am-4pm Fri-Sun Nov-Feb).

About 3 miles northwest of Oswestry, the elegant **Pen-y-Dyffryn Hotel** (☎01691-653700; www.peny.co.uk; r from £63; P) offers calm comfort in a wonderful setting among steep green hills.

Yorkshire

Includes »

Best Places to Eat

» J Baker's Bistro Moderne (p575)

» Van Zeller (p582)

» Gusto (p620)

» Star Inn (p589)

Best Places to Stay

» Devonshire Fell (p599)

» Millgate House (p605)

» White Swan (p591)

» Hotel Helaina (p585)

Why Go?

With a population as big as Scotland's and an area half the size of Belgium, Yorkshire is almost a country in itself. It has its own flag, its own dialect and its own Yorkshire Day celebration (1 August). While local folk are proud to be English, they're even prouder to be natives of 'God's Own Country'.

What makes Yorkshire so special? First there's the landscape – from the brooding moors and green dales that roll their way to the dramatic coastline, Yorkshire has some of England's finest scenery. Second, there's the sheer breadth of history – every facet of the English experience is represented here, from Roman times to the 20th century.

But Yorkshire's greatest appeal is its people. Industrious and opinionated, they have a wry wit and a shrewd friendliness. Stay here for a while and you'll come away believing, like the locals, that God is indeed a Yorkshirewoman.

When to Go

In February the week-long Jorvik Festival sees York taken over by a Viking invasion.

In July, the Great Yorkshire Show happens in Harrogate, and Yorkshire's coastal sea-cliffs become a frenzy of nesting seabirds.

The ideal time for hiking in the Yorkshire Dales is September; the Walking Festival in Richmond also happens in September.

Yorkshire Highlights

1 Exploring the medieval streets of **York** (p566) and its awe-inspiring cathedral

2 Pulling on your hiking boots and striding out across the moors of the **Yorkshire Dales** (p597)

3 Wandering among the atmospheric medieval ruins of **Fountains Abbey** (p580)

4 Being beside the seaside at **Scarborough** (p583) with its traditional bucket-and-spade atmosphere

5 Riding on the **North Yorkshire Moors Railway** (p591), one of England's most scenic railway lines

6 Discovering the literary world of the Brontë sisters in the pretty village of **Haworth** (p616)

7 Understanding the development of the media at the National Media Museum in **Bradford** (p613)

0 40 km
0 20 miles
NORTH SEA
Billingham
Middlesbrough
Stockton-on-Tees
A174
A171
Whitby
Stokesley
Danby
Leven
Grosmont
Robin Hood's Bay
A171
A19
North York Moors National Park
5 North Yorkshire Moors Railway
Hambleton Hills
Seph
Hutton-le-Hole
4 Scarborough
Helmsley
Pickering
Thirsk
Seven
Derwent
Hertford
Rye
Bempton Cliffs Nature Reserve
A19
Cleveland Hills
Malton
Flamborough Head
Bridlington
Boroughbridge
B1363
A64
Great Driffield
A166
A59
1 York
Hull
A1079
EAST RIDING OF YORKSHIRE
A1
A19
Beverley
A164
Hull
Hull Ferry Terminal
Ouse
Patrington
Easington
Humber
Trent
AKEFIELD
NORTH LINCOLNSHIRE
A15
Kilnsea
Grimsby
Spurn Head
Scunthorpe
Cleethorpes
Doncaster
To Rotterdam & Zeebrugge
NORTHEAST LINCOLNSHIRE
A1031
A18
A15
Rotherham
Market Rasen
A631
Gainsborough
A46
LINCOLNSHIRE
Worksop
A153
A158
NOTTINGHAMSHIRE
A57
Lincoln
Chesterfield
DERBYSHIRE

History

As you drive through Yorkshire on the main A1 road, you're following in the footsteps of the Roman legions who conquered northern Britain in the 1st century AD. In fact, many Yorkshire towns – including York, Catterick and Malton – were founded by the Romans, and many modern roads (including the A1, A59, A166 and A1079) follow the lines of Roman roads.

When the Romans departed in the 5th century, native Britons battled for supremacy with invading Angles and, for a while, Yorkshire was part of the Kingdom of Northumbria. In the 9th century the Vikings arrived and conquered most of northern Britain. They divided the territory that is now Yorkshire into *thridings* (thirds), which all met at Jorvik (York), their thriving commercial capital. (The North, West and East Ridings of Yorkshire existed as English counties until 1974; today only the East Riding retains its ancient name.)

In 1066 Yorkshire was the scene of a pivotal showdown in the struggle for the English crown, when the Anglo-Saxon king Harold II rode north to defeat the forces of the Norwegian king Harold Hardrada at the Battle of Stamford Bridge, before returning south to meet William the Conqueror – and a fatal arrow – at the Battle of Hastings. The inhabitants of northern England did not take the subsequent Norman invasion lying down. The Norman nobles built a chain of formidable castles throughout Yorkshire, including those at York, Richmond, Scarborough, Pickering and Helmsley. They also oversaw the establishment of the great abbeys of Rievaulx, Fountains and Whitby.

The Norman land grab formed the basis of the great estates that supported England's medieval aristocrats. By the 15th century, the duchies of York and Lancaster had become so wealthy and powerful that they ended up battling for the English throne – the Wars of the Roses (1455–87) were recurring conflicts between the supporters of King Henry VI of the House of Lancaster (the red rose) and Richard, Duke of York (the white rose). They ended with the defeat of the Yorkist king Richard III by the earl of Richmond, Henry Tudor, at the Battle of Bosworth Field. The white rose remains the symbol of Yorkshire to this day.

Yorkshire prospered quietly, with fertile farms in the north and the cutlery business of Sheffield in the south, until the big bang of the Industrial Revolution transformed the landscape: south Yorkshire became a centre of coal mining and steel works, while west Yorkshire was home to a massive textile industry, and the cities of Leeds, Bradford, Sheffield and Rotherham flourished. By the late 20th century another revolution was taking place. The heavy industries had died out, and the cities of Yorkshire were re-inventing themselves as shiny, high-tech centres of finance, higher education and tourism.

Activities

Yorkshire's varied landscape of wild hills, tranquil valleys, high moors and spectacular coastline offers plenty of opportunities for outdoor activities. See www.outdooryorkshire.com for more details.

Cycling

Yorkshire has a vast network of country lanes, although the most scenic areas also attract lots of motorists so even minor roads can be busy at weekends. Options include:

North York Moors MOUNTAIN BIKING

(www.mtb-routes.co.uk/northyorkmoors) Off-road bikers can avail themselves of the networks of bridleways, former railways and disused mining tracks now converted to two-wheel use. **Dalby Forest** (www.forestry.gov.uk/forestry/INFD-6Y6EWY), near Pickering, boasts purpose-built mountain-biking trails of all grades from green to black.

Moor to Sea Cycle Route CYCLING

(www.moortoseacycle.net) Network of routes between Pickering, Danby and the coast, including a 20-mile traffic-free route that follows a disused railway line between Whitby and Scarborough.

White Rose Cycle Route CYCLING

(www.sustrans.org.uk; NCN route 65) A 120-mile cruise from Hull to York and on to Middlesbrough, via the rolling Yorkshire Wolds and the dramatic western scarp of the North York Moors, with a traffic-free section on the old railway between Selby and York.

Yorkshire Dales Cycleway CYCLING

(www.cyclethedales.org.uk) An exhilarating 130-mile loop, taking in the best of the national park. There's also lots of scope for off-road riding, with around 500 miles of bridleways and trails – check out www.mtbthedales.org.uk for inspiration.

Walking

For shorter walks and rambles the best area is the **Yorkshire Dales**, with a great selection of walks through scenic valleys or over wild hilltops, and a few higher summits thrown in for good measure. The East Riding's **Yorkshire Wolds** hold hidden delights, while the quiet valleys and dramatic coast of the **North York Moors** also have many good opportunities.

Long-distance trails include:

Cleveland Way WALKING
(www.nationaltrail.co.uk/clevelandway) A venerable moor-and-coast classic that circles the North York Moors National Park on its 109-mile, nine-day route from Helmsley to Filey.

Coast to Coast Walk WALKING
(www.wainwright.org.uk/coasttocoast.html) England's number one walk: 190 miles across northern England from the Lake District through the Yorkshire Dales and North York Moors national parks. The Yorkshire section takes a week to 10 days and offers some of the finest walking of its kind in England.

Dales Way WALKING
(www.dalesway.org.uk) A charming and not-too-strenuous amble from the Yorkshire Dales to the Lake District, following the River Wharfe through the heart of the Dales, and finishing at Bowness-on-Windermere.

Pennine Way WALKING
(www.nationaltrail.co.uk/pennineway) The Yorkshire section of England's most famous walk runs for over 100 miles via Hebden Bridge, Malham, Horton-in-Ribblesdale and Hawes, passing near Haworth and Skipton.

Wolds Way WALKING
(www.nationaltrail.co.uk/yorkshirewoldsway) A beautiful but oft-overlooked walk that winds through the scenic East Riding of Yorkshire.

White Rose Way WALKING
(www.whiteroseway.co.uk) A new long-distance trail that covers the 104 miles from Leeds city centre to Scarborough, taking in many remote and picturesque Yorkshire villages.

Information

Yorkshire Tourist Board (www.yorkshire.com; 312 Tadcaster Rd, York YO24 1GS) Has plenty of general leaflets and brochures (postal and email enquiries only). For more detailed information contact local tourist offices.

Getting There & Around

The major north–south road transport routes – the M1 and A1 motorways – run through the middle of Yorkshire, serving the key cities of Sheffield, Leeds and York. If you're arriving by sea from northern Europe, Hull (in the East Riding) is the region's main port.

Traveline Yorkshire (☎0871 200 22 33; www.yorkshiretravel.net) provides public transport information for the whole of Yorkshire.

BUS Long-distance coaches run by National Express (p577) serve most cities and large towns in Yorkshire from London, the south of England, the Midlands and Scotland.

Bus transport around Yorkshire is frequent and efficient, especially between major towns. Services are more sporadic in the national parks but still adequate for reaching most places, particularly in the summer months (June to September). Useful websites include:

Arriva (www.arrivabus.co.uk) From Scarborough and Whitby north to Middlesbrough

Coastliner (www.coastliner.co.uk) Links Leeds and York to Scarborough and Whitby.

DalesBus (p598) Local services in the Yorkshire Dales.

East Yorkshire (EYMS; www.eyms.co.uk) From Hull north to Scarborough.

Transdev Harrogate (www.harrogatebus.co.uk) Routes around Harrogate and Ripon.

West Yorkshire Metro (p606) Leeds, Bradford and around.

TRAIN The main line between London and Edinburgh runs through Yorkshire, with at least 10 trains per day calling at York and Doncaster, where you can change trains for other Yorkshire destinations. There are also direct services between the major towns and cities of Yorkshire and other northern cities such as Manchester and Newcastle. For timetable information contact National Rail Enquiries (p824).

NORTH YORKSHIRE

This, the largest of Yorkshire's four counties – and the largest county in England – is also the most beautiful. Unlike the rest of northern England, it has survived almost unscarred by the Industrial Revolution because, since the Middle Ages, North Yorkshire has been about sheep and the woolly wealth that they produce.

Instead of closed-down factories, mills and mines, the man-made monuments that dot the landscape round these parts are of the magnificent variety – the great houses and wealthy abbeys that sit ruined or restored, a reminder that there was plenty of money to be made off the sheep's back.

All the same, North Yorkshire's biggest attraction is an urban one. Sure, the genteel spa town of Harrogate and the bright and breezy seaside resorts of Scarborough and Whitby have many fans, but nothing compares to the unparalleled splendour of York, England's most-visited city outside London.

York

POP 181,100

Nowhere in northern England says 'medieval' quite like York, a city of extraordinary cultural and historical wealth that has lost little of its pre-industrial lustre. Its medieval spider's web of narrow streets is enclosed by a magnificent circuit of 13th-century walls. At the heart of the city lies the immense, awe-inspiring minster, one of the most beautiful Gothic cathedrals in the world. The city's long history and rich heritage is woven into virtually every brick and beam, and modern, tourist-oriented York – with its myriad museums, restaurants, cafes and traditional pubs – is a carefully maintained heir to that heritage.

Just to avoid the inevitable confusion, remember that round these parts *gate* means street and *bar* means gate.

History

In AD 71 the Romans built a garrison called Eboracum, and in time a civilian settlement grew up around what became a large fort. Hadrian used it as the base for his northern campaign, while Constantine the Great was proclaimed emperor here in AD 306. When the Roman Empire collapsed, the town was taken by the Anglo-Saxons who renamed it Eoforwic and made it the capital of the independent kingdom of Northumbria.

In 625 a Roman priest, Paulinus, arrived and managed to convert King Edwin and all his nobles. Two years later, they built the first wooden church here and for most of the next century the city was a major centre of learning, attracting students from all over Europe. In 866 the next wave of invaders arrived. This time it was the Vikings, who gave the town a more tongue-friendly name, Jorvik. It was to be their capital for most of the next 100 years, and during that time they turned the city into an important trading port.

King Eadred of Wessex drove out the last Viking ruler in 954 and reunited Danelaw with the south, but trouble quickly followed. In 1066 King Harold II fended off a Norwegian invasion at Stamford Bridge, east of York, but was defeated by William the Conqueror a few months later at the Battle of Hastings.

After William's two wooden castles were captured by an Anglo-Scandinavian army, he torched the whole city (and Durham) and the surrounding countryside. The Normans then set about rebuilding the city, including a grand new minster. Over the next 300 years York (a contraction of the Viking name Jorvik) prospered through royal patronage, textiles, trade and the church.

Throughout the 18th century the city was a fashionable social centre dominated by the aristocracy, who were drawn by its culture and new racecourse. When the railway was built in 1839 thousands of people were employed in the new industries that sprung up around it, such as confectionery. These industries went into decline in the latter half of the 20th century, but by then a new invader was asking for directions at the city gates, armed only with a guidebook.

Sights

York Minster CHURCH

(www.yorkminster.org; Deangate; adult/child £9/free, combined ticket incl Tower £14/3.50; 9am-5.30pm Mon-Sat Apr-Oct, 9.30am-5.30pm Mon-Sat Nov-Mar, noon-5.30pm Sun year-round) Not content with being Yorkshire's most important historic building, the awe-inspiring York Minster is also the largest medieval cathedral in all of Northern Europe. Seat of the archbishop of York, primate of England, it is second in importance only to Canterbury, home of the primate of *all* England – the separate titles were created to settle a debate over whether York or Canterbury was the true centre of the English church.

But that's where Canterbury's superiority ends, for York Minster is without doubt one of the world's most beautiful Gothic buildings. If this is the only cathedral you visit in England, you'll still walk away satisfied – so long as you have the patience to deal with the constant flow of school groups and organised tours that will inevitably clog up your camera's viewfinder.

The first church on this spot was a wooden chapel built for the baptism of King Edwin of Northumbria on Easter Day 627; its location is marked in the crypt. It was replaced with a stone church that was built on the site of a Roman basilica, parts of which can be seen in the foundations. The first Norman minster was built in the 11th century; again, you can see surviving fragments in the foundations and crypt.

The present minster, built mainly between 1220 and 1480, manages to encompass all the major stages of Gothic architectural development. The transepts (1220–55) were built in Early English style; the octagonal chapter house (1260–90) and the nave (1291–1340) in the Decorated style; and the west towers, west front and central (or lantern) tower (1470–72) in Perpendicular style.

Choir, Chapter House & Nave

Entrance is via the south transept, which was badly damaged by fire in 1984 but has now been fully restored. To your right is the 15th-century **choir screen** depicting the 15 kings from William I to Henry VI. Facing you is the magnificent **Five Sisters Window**, with five lancets over 15m high. This is the minster's oldest complete window; most of its tangle of coloured glass dates from around 1250. Just beyond it to the right is the 13th-century **chapter house**, a fine example of the Decorated style. Sinuous and intricately carved stonework (there are more than 200 expressive carved heads and figures) surrounds an airy, uninterrupted space.

Back in the main church, take note of the unusually tall and wide **nave**, the aisles of which (to the sides) are roofed in stone in contrast to the central roof, which is wood painted to look like stone. On both sides of the nave are painted stone shields of the nobles who met with Edward II at a parliament in York. Also note the **dragon's head** projecting from the gallery – it's a crane believed to have been used to lift a font cover. There are several fine windows dating from the early 14th century, but the most impressive is the **Great West Window** (1338), with its beautiful heart-shaped stone tracery.

Beyond the screen and the choir is the **lady chapel** and, behind it, the **high altar**, which is dominated by the huge **Great East Window** (1405). At 23.7m by 9.4m – roughly the size of a tennis court – it is the world's largest medieval stained-glass window and the cathedral's single most important treasure. Needless to say, its epic size matches the epic theme depicted within: the beginning and end of the world as described in *Genesis* and the *Book of Revelations*.

Undercroft, Treasury & Crypt

A set of stairs in the south transept leads down to the undercroft, where you'll also find the treasury and crypt – these should on no account be missed. In 1967 the foundations were shored up when the central tower threatened to collapse; while engineers worked frantically to save the building, archaeologists uncovered Roman and Norman remains that attest to the site's ancient history – one of the most extraordinary finds is a **Roman culvert**, still carrying water to the Ouse. The **treasury** houses 11th-century artefacts including relics from the graves of medieval archbishops.

The **crypt** contains fragments from the Norman cathedral, including the font showing King Edwin's baptism that also marks the site of the original wooden chapel. Look out for the **Doomstone**, a 12th-century carving showing a scene from the Last Judgement with demons casting doomed souls into Hell.

Improved access and new exhibitions are planned for the undercroft, scheduled to open sometime in 2013.

Tower

At the heart of the minster is the massive **tower** (adult/child £6/3.50, combined ticket incl Minster £14/3.50), which is well worth climbing for the unparalleled views of York. You'll have to tackle a fairly claustrophobic climb of 275 steps and, most probably, a queue of people with cameras in hand. Access to the tower is near the entrance in the south transept, dominated by the exquisite **Rose Window**, commemorating the union of the royal houses of Lancaster and York through the marriage of Henry VII and Elizabeth of York, which ended the Wars of the Roses and began the Tudor dynasty.

FREE **National Railway Museum** MUSEUM
(www.nrm.org.uk; Leeman Rd; ⏲10am-6pm) Many railway museums are the sole preserve of lone men in anoraks comparing dog-eared notebooks and getting high on the smell of machine oil, coal smoke and nostalgia. But this place is different. York's National Railway Museum – the biggest in the world, with more than 100 locomotives – is so well presented and full of fascinating stuff that it's interesting even to folk whose eyes don't mist over at the thought of a 4-6-2 A1 Pacific class chuffing into a tunnel.

Highlights for the trainspotters among us include a replica of George Stephenson's

York

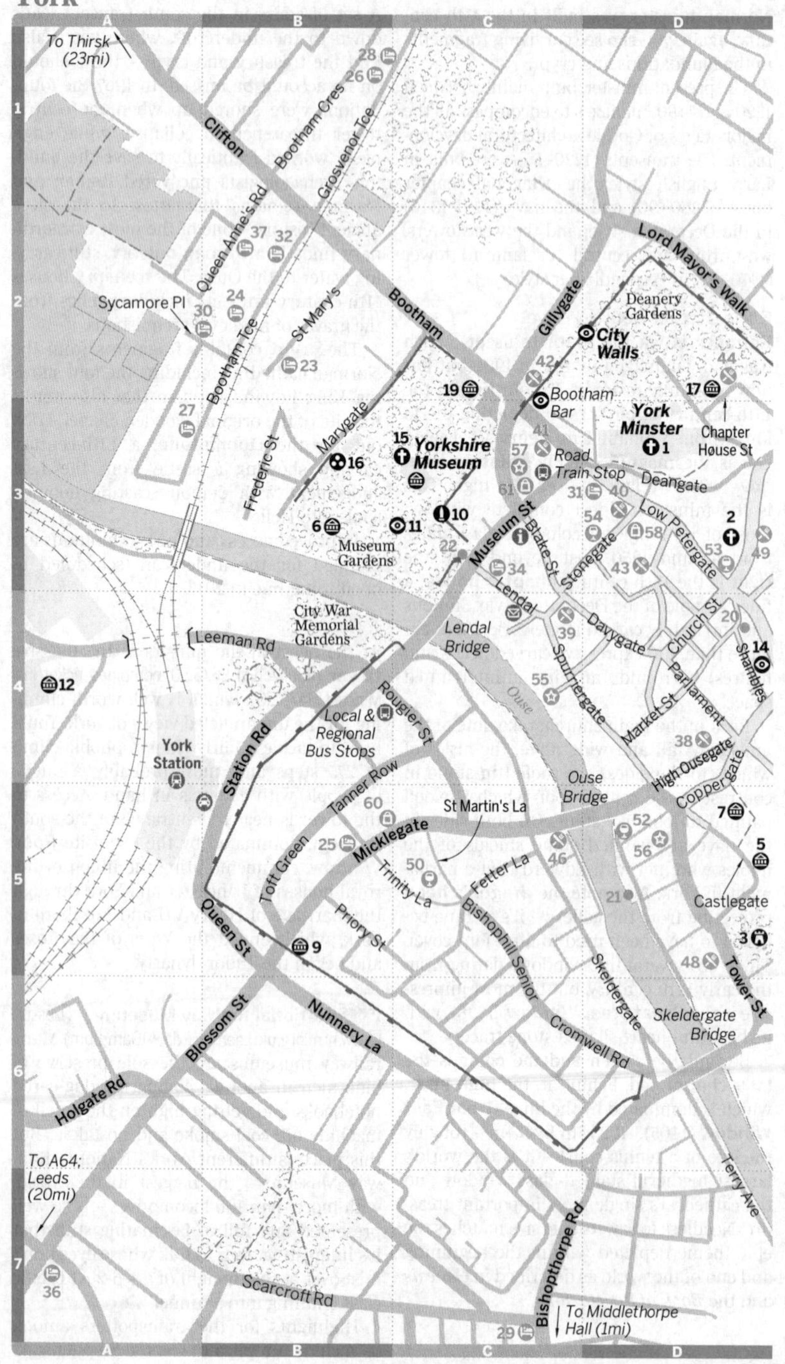
A
B
C
D
1
2
3
4
5
6
7
To Thirsk (23mi)
Clifton
Bootham Cres
Grosvenor Tce
Queen Anne's Rd
Bootham
Bootham Tce
St Mary's
Sycamore Pl
Marygate
Frederic St
Gillygate
Lord Mayor's Walk
Deanery Gardens
City Walls
Bootham Bar
York Minster
Chapter House St
Yorkshire Museum
Road Train Stop
Deangate
Low Petergate
Museum Gardens
Museum St
Blake St
Stonegate
Lendal
City War Memorial Gardens
Leeman Rd
Lendal Bridge
Davygate
Church St
Shambles
Spurriergate
Parliament
Market St
Ouse
York Station
Station Rd
Rougier St
Local & Regional Bus Stops
Tanner Row
Ouse Bridge
High Ousegate
Coppergate
St Martin's La
Micklegate
Toft Green
Trinity La
Fetter La
Castlegate
Queen St
Priory St
Bishophill Senior
Skeldergate
Tower St
Skeldergate Bridge
Blossom St
Nunnery La
Cromwell Rd
Holgate Rd
Terry Ave
To A64; Leeds (20mi)
Bishopthorpe Rd
Scarcroft Rd
To Middlethorpe Hall (1mi)

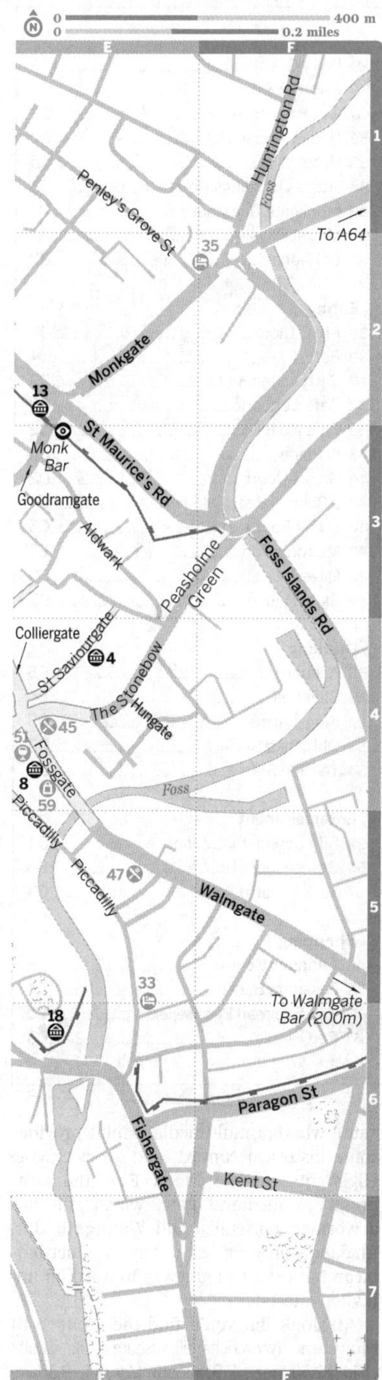

Rocket (1829), the world's first 'modern' steam locomotive; the sleek and streamlined *Mallard,* which set the world speed record for a steam locomotive in 1938 (126mph); a 1960s Japanese *Shinkansen* bullet train; and the world-famous *Flying Scotsman,* the first steam engine to break the 100mph barrier (restored to its former glory, and scheduled to return to the tracks in 2012). There's also a massive 4-6-2 loco from 1949 that's been cut in half so you can see how it works.

But even if you're not a rail nerd you'll enjoy looking around the gleaming, silk-lined carriages of the royal trains used by Queen Victoria and Edward VII, or having a *Brief Encounter* moment over tea and scones at the museum's station platform cafe called, erm, Brief Encounter. Allow at least two hours to do the museum justice.

The museum is about 400m west of the train station; if you don't fancy walking you can ride the **road train** (adult/child £2/1) that runs every 30 minutes from 11am to 4pm between the minster and the museum.

Jorvik Viking Centre MUSEUM

(www.jorvik-viking-centre.co.uk; Coppergate; adult/child £9.25/6.25; ⌚10am-5pm Apr-Oct, to 4pm Nov-Mar) Interactive multimedia exhibits aimed at 'bringing history to life' often achieve exactly the opposite, but the much-hyped Jorvik – the most visited attraction in town after the minster – manages to pull it off with admirable aplomb. It's a smells-and-all reconstruction of the Viking settlement that was unearthed here during excavations in the late 1970s, brought to you courtesy of a 'time-car' monorail that transports you through 9th-century Jorvik (the Viking name for York).

While some of the 'you will now travel back in time' malarkey is a bit naff, it's all done with a sense of humour tied to a historical authenticity that will leave you with a pretty good idea of what life must have been like in Viking-era York. In the exhibition at the end of the monorail, look out for the **Lloyds Bank Turd** – a fossilised human stool that measures an eye-watering nine inches long and half a pound in weight, and must be the only jobbie in the world to have its own Wikipedia entry.

You can cut time spent waiting in the queue by booking your tickets online and choosing the time you want to visit – it costs £1 extra.

York

Top Sights

City Walls D2
York Minster D3
Yorkshire Museum C3

Sights

1 Choir, Chapter House & Nave D3
2 Church of the Holy Trinity D3
3 Clifford's Tower D5
4 Dig E4
5 Fairfax House D5
6 Gatehall B3
Hospitium .... (see 6)
7 Jorvik Viking Centre D5
8 Merchant Adventurers' Hall E4
9 Micklegate Bar Museum B5
10 Multangular Tower C3
11 Museum Gardens C3
12 National Railway Museum A4
13 Richard III Museum E2
14 Shambles D4
15 St Mary's Abbey C3
16 St Mary's Lodge B3
Tower .... (see 1)
17 Treasurer's House D2
Undercroft, Treasury & Crypt .... (see 1)
18 York Castle Museum E6
19 York City Art Gallery C2

Activities, Courses & Tours

20 Ghost Hunt of York D4
21 YorkBoat D5
22 Yorkwalk C3

Sleeping

23 23 St Mary's B2
24 Abbeyfields B2
25 Ace Hotel B5
26 Arnot House B1
27 Briar Lea Guest House A3
28 Brontë House B1
29 Dairy Guesthouse C7
30 Elliotts B&B B2
31 Guy Fawkes Inn D3
32 Hedley House Hotel B2
33 Hotel 53 .... E5
34 Judges Lodgings Hotel C3
35 Monkgate Guesthouse F2
36 Mount Royale A7
37 St Raphael B2

Eating

38 Ate O'Clock D4
39 Bettys C4
40 Bettys Stonegate D3
41 Café Concerto C3
42 Cafe No 8 .... C2
43 El Piano D3
44 Gray's Court D2
45 J Baker's Bistro Moderne E4
46 Living Room C5
47 Melton's Too E5
48 Olive Tree D5
49 Siam House D3

Drinking

50 Ackhorne C5
51 Blue Bell E4
52 King's Arms D5
53 Old White Swan D3
54 Ye Olde Starre D3

Entertainment

55 City Screen Picturehouse C4
56 Grand Opera House D5
57 York Theatre Royal C3

Shopping

58 Antiques Centre D3
59 Fossgate Books E4
60 Ken Spelman Booksellers B5
61 Red House C3

FREE **City Walls** CITY WALLS

(8am-dusk) If the weather's good, don't miss the chance to walk the city walls, which follow the line of the original Roman walls – it gives a whole new perspective on the city. The full circuit is 4.5 miles (allow 1½ to two hours); if you're pushed for time, the short stretch from Bootham Bar to Monk Bar is worth doing for the views of the minster.

Start and finish in the Museum Gardens or at **Bootham Bar** (on the site of a Roman gate), where a multimedia exhibit provides some historical context, and go clockwise. Highlights include **Monk Bar**, the best-preserved medieval gate, which still has a working portcullis, and **Walmgate Bar**, England's only city gate with an intact barbican (an extended gateway to ward off uninvited guests).

At Monk Bar you'll find the **Richard III Museum** (www.richardiiimuseum.co.uk; adult/child £2.50/free; 9am-5pm Mar-Oct, 9.30am-

4pm Nov-Feb), which sets out the case of the murdered 'Princes in the Tower' and invites visitors to judge whether their uncle, Richard III, killed them. **Micklegate Bar Museum** (www.micklegatebar.com; Micklegate; adult/child £3.50/free; ⏲10am-4.30pm May-Sep, 11am-3.30pm Feb-Apr, Oct & Nov) charts the history of the city walls and the Battle of Towton, chief conflict in the Wars of the Roses.

You can download a free guide to the wall walk from www.visityork.org/explore/walls.html.

Yorkshire Museum MUSEUM

(www.yorkshiremuseum.org.uk; Museum St; adult/child £7.50/free; ⏲10am-5pm) Most of York's Roman archaeology is hidden beneath the medieval city, so the recently revamped displays in the Yorkshire Museum are invaluable if you want to get an idea of what Eboracum was like. There are maps and models of **Roman York**, funerary monuments, mosaic floors and wall paintings, and a 4th-century bust of Emperor Constantine.

There are excellent exhibits on Viking and medieval York too, including priceless artefacts such as the beautifully decorated 9th-century **York helmet**, and the exquisite 15th-century **Middleham Jewel**, an engraved gold pendant adorned with a giant sapphire. Kids will enjoy the **dinosaur exhibit**, centred around giant ichthyosaur fossils from Yorkshire's Jurassic coast.

In the grounds of the peaceful Museum Gardens (p573) you can see the **Multangular Tower** (Museum Gardens), a part of the city walls that was once the western tower of the Roman garrison's defensive ramparts. The Roman stonework at the base has been built over with 13th-century additions.

On the other side of the gardens are the ruins of **St Mary's Abbey** (founded 1089), which date from 1270–1294. The ruined **Gatehall** was its main entrance, providing access from the abbey to the river. The adjacent **Hospitium** dates from the 14th century, although the timber-framed upper storey is a much-restored survivor from the 15th century; it was used as the abbey guesthouse. **St Mary's Lodge** was built around 1470 to provide VIP accommodation.

Shambles MEDIEVAL STREET

(www.yorkshambles.com) The narrow, cobbled lane known as the Shambles, lined with 15th-century Tudor buildings that overhang so much they seem to meet above your head, is the most visited street in Europe. Quaint and picturesque it most certainly is, and it hints at what a medieval street may have looked like – even if it's now overrun with people told they have to buy a tacky souvenir and be back on the tour bus in 15 minutes. It takes its name from the Saxon word *shamel*, meaning 'slaughterhouse' – in 1862 there were 26 butcher shops on this one street.

York Castle Museum MUSEUM

(www.yorkcastlemuseum.org.uk; Tower St; adult/child £8.50/free; ⏲9.30am-5pm) This excellent museum contains displays of everyday life through the centuries, with reconstructed domestic interiors, a Victorian street, and a less-than-homely prison cell where you can try out a condemned man's bed – in this case the highwayman Dick Turpin (he was imprisoned here before being hanged in 1739). There's a bewildering array of evocative objects from the past 400 years, gathered together by a certain Dr Kirk from the 1920s onwards for fear that the items would become obsolete and disappear completely. He wasn't far wrong, which makes this place all the more interesting.

Treasurer's House HISTORIC BUILDING

(NT; www.nationaltrust.org.uk; Chapter House St; adult/child £6.30/3; ⏲11am-4.30pm Sat-Thu Apr-Oct, 11am-3pm Sat-Thu Nov) The Treasurer's House was home to the York Minster's medieval treasurers. Substantially rebuilt in the 17th and 18th centuries, the 13 rooms here house a fine collection of furniture and provide a good insight into 18th-century life. The house is also the setting for one of the city's most enduring ghost stories: during the 1950s a plumber working in the basement swore he saw a band of Roman soldiers walking *through* the walls. His story remains popular if unproven – but you can explore the cellar to find out.

Dig MUSEUM

(www.digyork.com; St Saviour's Church, St Saviourgate; adult/child £5.50/5, Dig & Jorvik combined £13.25/10; ⏲10am-5pm, closed 24-26 Dec; 👪) Under the same management as Jorvik, Dig cashes in on the popularity of archaeology programs on TV by giving you the chance to be an 'archaeological detective', unearthing the secrets of York's distant past as well as learning something of the archaeologist's world – what they do, how they do it and so on. Aimed mainly at kids, it's much more hands-on than Jorvik, and a lot depends on how good – and entertaining – your guide is. Last admission 4pm.

THE YORK PASS

If you plan on visiting a lot of sights, you can save yourself some money by using a **York Pass** (www.yorkpass.com; 1/2/3 days adult £34/48/58, child £18/22/26). It grants you free access to more than 30 pay-to-visit sights in York and around, including York Minster, Jorvik and Castle Howard. It's available at York tourist office, or you can buy online.

Clifford's Tower CASTLE

(EH; www.english-heritage.org.uk; Tower St; adult/child £4/2.40; ⊙10am-6pm Apr-Sep, to 5pm Oct) There's precious little left of York Castle except for this evocative stone tower, a highly unusual figure-of-eight design built into the castle's keep after the original one was destroyed in 1190 during anti-Jewish riots. An angry mob forced 150 Jews to be locked inside the tower and the hapless victims took their own lives rather than be killed. There's not much to see inside but the views over the city are excellent. Check website for winter opening hours.

FREE **Church of the Holy Trinity** CHURCH

(Goodramgate; ⊙10am-5pm Tue-Sat May-Sep, 10am-4pm Oct-Apr) Tucked away behind an inconspicuous gate and seemingly cut off from the rest of the town, the Church of the Holy Trinity is a fantastically atmospheric old building, having survived almost unchanged for the last 200 years. Inside are rare 17th- to 18th-century box pews, 15th-century stained glass, and wonky walls that seem to have been built without plumb line or spirit level.

FREE **York City Art Gallery** ART GALLERY

(www.yorkartgallery.org.uk; Exhibition Sq; ⊙10am-5pm) Includes works by Reynolds, Nash, Boudin, LS Lowry and controversial York artist William Etty, who (back in the 1820s) was the first major British artist to specialise in nude painting.

Merchant Adventurers' Hall HISTORIC BUILDING

(www.theyorkcompany.co.uk; Fossgate; adult/child £6/free; ⊙9am-5pm Mon-Thu, 9am-3.30pm Fri & Sat, 11am-4pm Sun Mar-Oct, 9am-4pm Mon-Fri, 9am-3.30pm Sat Nov-Feb) One of the most handsome timber-framed buildings in Europe, built between 1357 and 1361. Displays include oil paintings and antique silver, but the building itself is the star.

Fairfax House HISTORIC BUILDING

(www.fairfaxhouse.co.uk; Castlegate; adult/child £6/free; ⊙10am-5pm Tue-Sat, 12.30-4pm Sun, guided tours 11am & 2pm Mon) Built in 1762 by John Carr (of Harewood House fame), Fairfax House contains a superb collection of Georgian furniture.

Tours

There's a bewildering range of tours on offer, from historic walking tours to a host of ever more competitive night-time ghost tours (York is reputed to be England's most haunted city). For starters, check the tourist office's own suggestions for walking itineraries at www.visityork.org/explore.

Ghost Hunt of York WALKING TOUR

(www.ghosthunt.co.uk; adult/child £5/3; ⊙tours 7.30pm) An award-winning and highly entertaining 75-minute tour laced with authentic ghost stories; the kids will just love this one. It begins at the Shambles, whatever the weather (they never cancel). No need to book, just turn up.

Yorkwalk WALKING TOUR

(www.yorkwalk.co.uk; adult/child £5.50/3.50; ⊙tours 10.30am & 2.15pm Feb-Nov) Offers a series of two-hour themed walks on an ever-growing list of themes, from the classics – Roman York, the snickelways (alleys) and city walls – to specialised walks on chocolates and sweets, women in York, secret York and the inevitable graveyard, coffin and plague tour. Walks depart from Museum Gardens Gate on Museum St; no need to book.

YorkBoat BOAT TOUR

(www.yorkboat.co.uk; King's Staith; adult/child £7.50/3.50; ⊙10.30am, noon, 1.30pm & 3pm) Runs one-hour cruises on the River Ouse departing from King's Staith (and Lendal Bridge 10 minutes later). Also offers special lunch, dinner and evening cruises.

Original Ghost Walk of York WALKING TOUR

(www.theoriginalghostwalkofyork.co.uk; adult/child £4.50/3; ⊙tours 8pm) An evening of ghouls, ghosts, mystery and history courtesy of a well-established group departing from the King's Arms pub by Ouse Bridge.

York Citysightseeing BUS TOUR

(www.city-sightseeing.com; day tickets adult/child £10/4; ⊙9am-5pm) Hop-on/hop-off route with 16 stops, calling at all the main sights. Buses leave every 10 minutes from Exhibition Sq near York Minster.

FREE **Association of Voluntary Guides** WALKING TOUR
(avgyork.co.uk/; ⏲tours 10.15am & 2.15pm Apr-Oct, also 6.45pm Jun-Aug, 10.15am Nov-Mar) Two-hour walking tours of the city starting from Exhibition Sq in front of York City Art Gallery.

Festivals & Events

Check out a full calendar of events at www.yorkfestivals.com.

Jorvik Viking Festival HISTORY
(www.jorvik-viking-centre.co.uk/viking-festival) For a week in mid-February, York is invaded by Vikings once again as part of this festival, which features battle re-enactments, themed walks, markets and other bits of Viking-themed fun.

York Food Festival FOOD & DRINK
(www.yorkfoodfestival.com) Ten days in September of all that's good to eat and drink in Yorkshire – there are food stalls, tastings, a beer tent, cookery demonstrations and more.

York Christmas SHOPPING
(www.visityork.org/christmas) Kicking off with St Nicholas Fayre market in late November, the run-up to Christmas is an extravaganza of street decorations, market stalls, carol singers and mulled wine.

Sleeping

Beds are tough to find midsummer, even with the inflated prices of the high season. The tourist office's accommodation booking service charges £4, which might be the best four quid you spend if you arrive without a reservation.

Needless to say, prices get higher the closer to the city centre you are. However, there are plenty of decent B&Bs on the streets north and south of Bootham. Southwest of the town centre, there are B&Bs clustered around Scarcroft Rd, Southlands Rd and Bishopthorpe Rd.

It's also worth looking at serviced apartments if you're planning to stay two or three nights. **In York Holidays** (☎01904-632660; www.inyorkholidays.co.uk) offers a good selection of places from around £100 a night for a two-person apartment.

TOP CHOICE **Middlethorpe Hall** HOTEL £££
(☎01904-641241; www.middlethorpe.com; Bishopsthorpe Rd; s/d from £130/200; P 📶) York's top spot is this breathtaking 17th-century country house set in 20 acres of parkland that was once the home of diarist Lady Mary Wortley Montagu. The rooms are spread between the main house, the restored courtyard buildings and three cottage suites. Although we preferred the grandeur of the rooms in the main house, every room is beautifully decorated with original antiques and oil paintings, carefully collected so as to best reflect the period.

LOCAL KNOWLEDGE

ANDY DEXTROUS: GHOST TOUR GUIDE, YORK

Things I love about York include its outstanding architecture, the maze of 'snickelways' (narrow alleys), the array of small independent shops, the street entertainment and festivals, and central, green spaces like **Museum Gardens** (entrances on Museum St and Marygate; ⏲dawn-dusk). All year round the streets are full of appreciative visitors from all over the world enjoying the city, relaxing and adding to the atmosphere.

Yorkshire's Spookiest Spots Haunted pubs such as the Old White Swan (p576). Plus the Antiques Centre (p577) on Stonegate, which is also haunted. In the streets around the minster you're always within a breath of a ghost tale.

Best of York For beer and atmosphere, the Blue Bell (p576). For veggie and vegan food and a place that welcomes children, El Piano (p576). And for sheer ambience, Gray's Court (p575).

Best of Yorkshire The Forbidden Corner (p584) near Leyburn. Or take the North Yorkshire Moors Railway (p591) to Goathland, then walk to Mallyan Spout waterfall. Include a drink at the Birch Hall Inn at Beck Hole.

For a special meal there's the Star Inn (p589) at Harome or the Stone Trough Inn (p579) at Kirkham; stroll down to the abbey ruins before or after your meal.

Abbeyfields B&B ££
(☎01904-636471; www.abbeyfields.co.uk; 19 Bootham Tce; s/d from £49/79; 📶) Expect a warm welcome and thoughtfully arranged bedrooms here, with chairs and bedside lamps for comfortable reading. Breakfasts are among the best in town, with sausage and bacon from the local butcher, freshly laid eggs from a nearby farm, and the smell of newly baked bread.

Elliotts B&B B&B ££
(☎01904-623333; www.elliottshotel.co.uk; 2 Sycamore Pl; s/d from £55/80; P@📶) A beautifully converted 'gentleman's residence', Elliotts leans towards the boutique end of the guesthouse market with stylish and elegant rooms, and high-tech touches such as flatscreen TVs and free wi-fi. Excellent location, both quiet and central.

Hedley House Hotel HOTEL ££
(☎01904-637404; www.hedleyhouse.com; 3 Bootham Tce; s/d/f from £75/95/110; P📶) Run by a couple with young children, this smart red-brick terrace-house hotel could hardly be more family friendly – plus it has a spa bath on the outdoor terrace at the back, private parking, and is barely five minutes' walk from the city centre through the Museum Gardens.

Dairy Guesthouse B&B ££
(☎01904-639367; www.dairyguesthouse.co.uk; 3 Scarcroft Rd; s/d from £55/75; 📶) A lovely Victorian home that has retained many of its original features, including pine doors, stained glass and cast-iron fireplaces. But the real treat is the flower- and plant-filled courtyard that leads to the cottage-style rooms. Minimum two-night stay at weekends.

Guy Fawkes Inn INN ££
(☎01904-623716; www.gfyork.com; 25 High Petergate; s/d/ste from £65/90/200) Directly opposite the minster is this comfortable and atmospheric hotel complete with gas lamps and log fires. The premises include a cottage that is reputed to be the birthplace of Guy Fawkes himself. We're not convinced, but the cottage is still the handsomest option in the building, complete with a four-poster bed and lots of red velvet.

Mount Royale HOTEL £££
(☎01904-628856; www.mountroyale.co.uk; The Mount; s/d from £95/125; P📶🏊) A grand, early 19th-century listed building that has been converted into a superb luxury hotel, complete with a solarium, beauty spa and outdoor heated tub and swimming pool. The rooms in the main house are gorgeous, but the best of the lot are the open-plan garden suites, reached via a corridor of tropical fruit trees and bougainvillea.

Judges Lodgings Hotel HOTEL £££
(☎01904-638733; www.judgeslodgings.com; 9 Lendal; s/d from £90/150) Despite being housed in an elegant Georgian mansion that was built for a wealthy physician, this is really a place for the party crowd to crash – it's within easy reach of city centre pubs, and the hotel's own lively courtyard bar rocks late into the night.

Arnot House B&B ££
(☎01904-641966; www.arnothouseyork.co.uk; 17 Grosvenor Tce; r £80-88; P📶) With three beautifully decorated rooms (provided you're a fan of Victorian floral patterns), including two with impressive four-poster beds, Arnot House sports an authentically old-fashioned look that appeals to a more mature clientele. No children allowed.

Brontë House B&B ££
(☎01904-621066; www.bronte-guesthouse.com; 22 Grosvenor Tce; s/d/f from £45/80/100; P📶) The Brontë offers five homely en suite rooms, each decorated differently. Our favourite is the double with a carved, 19th-century canopied bed, William Morris wallpaper and assorted bits and pieces from another era.

23 St Mary's B&B ££
(☎01904-622738; www.23stmarys.co.uk; 23 St Mary's; s/d £55/90; P📶) A smart and stately town house with nine chintzy, country house-style rooms, some with hand-painted furniture for that rustic look, while others are decorated with antiques, lace and polished mahogany.

York YHA HOSTEL £
(☎0845 371 9051; www.yha.org.uk; 42 Water End, Clifton; dm £18-23; P@📶) Originally the Rowntree (Quaker confectioners) mansion, this handsome Victorian house makes a spacious and child-friendly youth hostel, with most of the rooms being four-bed dorms. It's about a mile northwest of the city centre; there's a riverside footpath from Lendal Bridge (poorly lit so avoid after dark). Alternatively, take bus 2 from Station Ave or Museum St.

Ace Hotel HOSTEL £

(☎01904-627720; www.acehotelyork.co.uk; 88-90 Micklegate; dm £18-30, tw £68; @📶) Housed in a Grade I Georgian building that was once home to the High Sheriff of Yorkshire, this is a large and well-equipped boutique hostel that is popular with school groups and stag and hen parties – don't come here looking for peace and quiet.

York Yurts YURT ££

(☎01759-380901; www.yorkyurts.com; Tadpole Cottage, Sutton Lane, Barmby Moor; d £70-80; P) Only a 15-minute drive from York, but half a world away in terms of ambience, York Yurts offers the chance to sleep under canvas without having to rough it. There are four yurts (circular, wood-framed tents originating from Mongolia) in a three-acre field, complete with double beds, candles (no electricity), wood-burning stoves, cooking tents and barbecues (though you can order breakfast brought to you in bed if you want). There's also a communal bathroom tent with rolltop bath and hot tub.

Briar Lea Guest House B&B ££

(☎01904-635061; www.briarlea.co.uk; 8 Longfield Tce; s/d from £37/62; 📶) Clean, simple rooms and a friendly welcome in a central location.

St Raphael B&B ££

(☎01904-645028; www.straphaelguesthouse.co.uk; 44 Queen Annes Rd; s/d from £65/78; P📶) Historic house with that half-timbered look, a great central location and home-baked bread for breakfast.

Monkgate Guesthouse B&B ££

(☎01904-655947; www.monkgateguesthouse.com; 65 Monkgate; s/d/f from £45/70/105; P📶) Attractive guesthouse with special family suite with separate bedroom for two kids.

Hotel 53 HOTEL ££

(☎01904-559000; www.hotel53.com; 53 Piccadilly; r from £95; P📶) Modern and minimalist, but very central with secure parking just across the street.

Eating

TOP CHOICE **J Baker's Bistro Moderne** MODERN BRITISH ££

(☎01904-622688; www.jbakers.co.uk; 7 Fossgate; 2-/3-course lunch £20/25, dinner £25/30; ⌚lunch & dinner Tue-Sat) Superstar chef Jeff Baker left a Michelin star in Leeds to pursue his own vision of Modern British cuisine here. The ironic '70s-style decor (think chocolate/oatmeal/tango) with moo-cow paintings is echoed in the unusual menu, which offers witty, gourmet interpretations of retro classics – try Olde York cheese and spinach pasties with dried grapes, capers and aged balsamic vinegar, or a Whitby crab cocktail with apple 'textures' and curry-spiced granola. Wicked desserts include a separate chocolate menu.

Cafe No 8 CAFE, BISTRO £

(☎01904-653074; www.cafeno8.co.uk; 8 Gillygate; mains £7-10, 2-course lunch £14; ⌚Mon–Fri 11am–10pm, Sat & Sun 10am–10pm; 📶👪) A cool little bistro with modern artwork mimicking the Edwardian stained glass at the front, No 8 offers a day-long menu of classic bistro dishes using fresh local produce, including smoked duck breast salad, and cassoulet of Yorkshire pork and chorizo; it also does Sunday brunch. Booking recommended.

Gray's Court CAFE ££

(www.grayscourtyork.com; Chapter House St; mains £6-10; ⌚lunch) An unexpected find right in the very heart of York, this 16th-century house has more of a country atmosphere. Enjoy gourmet coffee and cake in the sunny garden, or indulge in a light lunch in the historic setting of the oak-panelled Jacobean gallery (extra points if you grab the alcove table above the main door). The menu runs from smoked bacon with oatmeal pancakes and maple syrup to Yorkshire rarebit, and from lavender shortbread to lemon drizzle cake.

Ate O'Clock BISTRO ££

(☎01904-644080; www.ateoclock.co.uk; 13a High Ousegate; mains £14-17; ⌚lunch Tue-Sat, dinner Mon-Sat) A tempting menu of classic bistro dishes (sirloin steak, pork tenderloin, pan-fried duck breast) made with fresh Yorkshire produce has made this place hugely popular with locals – best book a table to avoid disappointment. Three-course dinner is £18 from 6pm to 7.55pm Tuesday to Thursday.

Bettys TEAHOUSE ££

(www.bettys.co.uk; St Helen's Sq; mains £6-13, afternoon tea £18; ⌚9am-9pm; 👪) Afternoon tea, old-school style, with white-aproned waitresses, linen tablecloths and a teapot collection ranged along the walls. House speciality is the Yorkshire Fat Rascal – a huge fruit scone smothered in melted butter – but the smoked haddock with poached egg and Hollandaise sauce is our favourite lunch dish. No bookings – queue for a table at busy times.

Betty's younger sister, **Betty's Stonegate** (www.bettys.co.uk; 46 Stonegate; mains £6-13; ⏲10am-5.30pm Sun-Fri, 9am-5.30pm Sat), is more demure and less crowded, but just as good.

Olive Tree MEDITERRANEAN ££

(☎01904-624433; www.theolivetreeyork.co.uk; 10 Tower St; mains £10-17; ⏲lunch & dinner) Local produce gets a Mediterranean makeover at this bright and breezy bistro with a view across the street to Clifford's Tower. Classic pizza and pasta dishes are complemented by more ambitious recipes such as seared scallops with chorizo, and sea bass with asparagus, cherry tomatoes and saffron cream sauce. The lunchtime and early evening menu offers two courses for £13.

Café Concerto CAFE, BISTRO ££

(☎01904-610478; www.cafeconcerto.biz; 21 High Petergate; snacks £5-10, mains £10-16; ⏲8.30am-10pm) Walls papered with sheet music, chilled jazz on the stereo and battered, mismatched tables and chairs set the bohemian tone in this comforting coffee shop-cum-bistro. During the day expect breakfasts, bagels and cappuccinos big enough to float a boat in, and a sophisticated bistro menu in the evening.

El Piano VEGAN £

(www.el-piano.com; 15 Grape Lane; meals £10-13; ⏲11am-11pm Mon-Sat, noon-5pm Sun; ✎) With a menu that is 100% vegan, nut-free and gluten-free, this colourful, Hispanic-style spot is a vegetarian haven. There's a lovely cafe downstairs and three themed rooms upstairs. The menu offers dishes such as falafel, onion bhaji, corn fritters and mushroom-and-basil salad, either in tapas-size portions or as mixed platters. There's also a takeaway counter.

Melton's Too BAR, BISTRO ££

(www.meltonstoo.co.uk; 25 Walmgate; mains £11-16; ⏲10.30am-midnight Mon-Sat, 10.30am-11pm Sun; 📶) A comfortable, chilled-out cafe-bar and bistro, Melton's Too serves everything from cake and cappuccino, to tapas-style snacks or a three-course dinner (early bird special offers three courses for £12).

Living Room INTERNATIONAL ££

(www.thelivingroom.co.uk; 1 Bridge St; mains £8-18; ⏲11am-midnight; 📶) Balcony tables overlooking the river and a menu focused on quality versions of classic dishes from around the world. Sunday brunch served noon to 6pm.

Siam House THAI ££

(www.yorksiamhouse.co.uk; 63a Goodramgate; mains £9-15; ⏲lunch Wed-Sat, dinner daily) Delicious, authentic Thai food in about as authentic an atmosphere as you can muster 6000km from Bangkok.

Drinking

With only a couple of exceptions, the best drinking holes in town are the older, traditional pubs. The area around Ousegate and Micklegate is popular with young drinkers and stag and hens parties, and can get a bit rowdy, especially at weekends.

TOP CHOICE **Blue Bell** PUB

(53 Fossgate) This is what a real English pub looks like – a tiny, wood-panelled room with a smouldering fireplace, decor (and beer and smoke stains) dating from c 1798. It also has a pile of ancient board games in the corner, friendly and efficient bar staff, and Timothy Taylor and Black Sheep ales on tap. Bliss, with froth on top.

Ye Olde Starre PUB

(40 Stonegate) Licensed since 1644, this is York's oldest pub – a warren of small rooms and a small beer garden, with a half-dozen real ales on tap. It was used as a morgue by the Roundheads during the Civil War, but the atmosphere's improved a lot since then.

Ackhorne PUB

(9 St Martin's Lane) Tucked away off beery, sloppy Micklegate, this locals' inn is as comfortable as old slippers – some of the old guys here look like they've merged with the furniture. There's a pleasant beer garden at the back, and an open-mic night for local musicians on the first Tuesday of the month.

Old White Swan PUB

(80 Goodramgate) Popular and atmospheric old pub with a small beer garden and a good range of guest real ales. And it's haunted...

King's Arms PUB

(King's Staith) York's best-known pub has a fabulous riverside location, with tables spilling out onto the quayside – a perfect spot on a summer evening, but be prepared to share it with a few hundred other people.

Entertainment

There are a couple of good theatres in York, and an interesting art-house cinema, but as far as clubs are concerned, forget it; historic York is best enjoyed without them anyway.

York Theatre Royal THEATRE
(www.yorktheatreroyal.co.uk; St Leonard's Pl) Stages well-regarded productions of theatre, opera and dance.

Grand Opera House MUSIC, COMEDY
(www.grandoperahouseyork.org.uk; Clifford St) Despite the name there's no opera here, but you can see a wide range of productions from live bands and popular musicals to stand-up comics and pantomime.

City Screen Picturehouse CINEMA
(www.picturehouses.co.uk; 13-17 Coney St) Appealing modern building in a converted printing works, screening both mainstream and art-house films. There's also a nice cafe-bar on the terrace overlooking the river.

Shopping

Coney St, Davygate and the adjoining streets are the hub of York's high-street shopping scene, but the real treat for visitors is the range of boutiques, jewellers, antique shops and second-hand book shops which are concentrated around Colliergate and Fossgate.

Ken Spelman Booksellers BOOKS
(www.kenspelman.com; 70 Micklegate) This fascinating shop has been selling rare, antiquarian and secondhand books since 1910. With an open fire crackling in the grate in winter, it's a browser's paradise.

Antiques Centre ANTIQUES
(www.antiquescentreyorkeshop.co.uk; 41 Stonegate) A Georgian town house with a veritable maze of rooms and corridors, showcasing the wares of around 120 dealers: everything from lapel pins and snuff boxes to oil paintings and longcase clocks. And the house is haunted, too…

Red House ANTIQUES
(www.redhouseyork.co.uk; Duncombe Pl) Has 10 showrooms spread over two floors, displaying the goods of around 60 antiques dealers, with items ranging from jewellery and porcelain to clocks and furniture.

Fossgate Books BOOKS
(36 Fossgate) Cheap paperbacks and unusual books.

Information

American Express (6 Stonegate; 9am-5.30pm Mon-Fri, 9am-5pm Sat) With foreign exchange service.

Post Office (22 Lendal; 8.30am-5.30pm Mon & Tue, 9am-5.30pm Wed-Sat)

York District Hospital (01904-631313; Wiggington Rd) A mile north of the centre.

York Tourist Office (01904-550099; www.visityork.org; 1 Museum St; 9am-6pm Mon-Sat, 10am-5pm Sun Apr-Sep, shorter hours Oct-Mar) Visitor and transport info for all of Yorkshire, accommodation booking, ticket sales and internet access.

Getting There & Away

BUS For timetable information call **Traveline Yorkshire** (0871 200 2233; www.yorkshiretravel.net), or check the computerised 24-hour information points at the train station and Rougier St. All local and regional buses stop on Rougier St, about 200m northeast of the train station.

There are **National Express** (08717 81 81 78; www.nationalexpress.com) coaches to London (£28, 5½ hours, four daily), Birmingham (£28, 3¼ hours, one daily) and Newcastle (£15, 2¾ hours, four daily).

CAR A car is more of a hindrance than a help in the city centre; use one of the Park & Ride car parks on the edge of the city. If you want to explore the surrounding area, rental options include **Europcar** (01904-654040; www.europcar.co.uk; Train Station, Station Rd; 8am-8.30pm Mon-Sat, 9am-8.30pm Sun), beside platform 1 in the train station (which also rents bicycles and stores luggage for £4 per bag); and **Hertz** (01904-612586; www.hertz.co.uk; Train Station, Station Rd) near platform 3 in the train station.

TRAIN York is a major railway hub with frequent direct services to Birmingham (£45, 2¼ hours), Newcastle (£15, one hour), Leeds (£11, 30 minutes), London's King's Cross (£80, two hours), Manchester (£15, 1½ hours) and Scarborough (£10, 50 minutes).

There are also trains to Cambridge (£60, 2¾ hours), changing at Peterborough.

Getting Around

York is easy to get around on foot – you're never more than 20 minutes from any of the major sights.

BICYCLE The tourist office has a useful free map showing York's cycle routes, or visit **Cycling City York** (www.cyclingcityyork.org.uk). Castle Howard (15 miles northeast of York via Haxby and Strensall) is a good destination, and there's also a section of the Trans-Pennine Trail cycle path from Bishopthorpe in York to Selby (15 miles) along the old railway line.

You can rent bikes from **Giant York** (www.giant-york.co.uk; 13 Lord Mayor's Walk; 9am-6pm Mon-Sat), outside Monk Bar; and Europcar, by platform 1 in the train station; both charge around £15 per day.

BUS Local bus services are operated by **First York** (www.firstgroup.com/ukbus/york); single fares range from £1.20 to £3, and a day pass valid on all local buses is £3.70 (available at Park & Ride car parks).

TAXI **Station Taxis** (01904-623332; Train Station, Station Rd) has a kiosk outside the train station.

Around York

Castle Howard CASTLE

(www.castlehoward.co.uk; adult/child house & grounds £13/7.50, grounds only £8.50/6; house 11am-4.30pm Apr-Oct, grounds 10am-5.30pm Mar-Oct & 1st 3 weeks Dec, 10am-4pm Nov-Feb) Stately homes may be two a penny in England, but you'll have to try pretty damn hard to find one as breathtakingly stately as Castle Howard (p578), a work of theatrical grandeur and audacity set in the rolling Howardian Hills. This is one of the world's most beautiful buildings, instantly recognisable from its starring role in the 1980s TV series *Brideshead Revisited* and more recently in the 2008 film of the same name (both based on Evelyn Waugh's 1945 novel of nostalgia for the English aristocracy).

When the earl of Carlisle hired his pal Sir John Vanbrugh to design his new home in 1699, he was hiring a bloke who had no formal training and was best known as a playwright. Luckily, Vanbrugh hired Nicholas Hawksmoor who had worked for Christopher Wren as his clerk of works – not only would Hawksmoor have a big part to play in the house's design but the two would later work wonders with Blenheim Palace. Today, the house is still home to the Hon Simon Howard and his family; he can often be seen around the place.

If you can, try to visit on a weekday, when it's easier to find the space to appreciate this hedonistic marriage of art, architecture, landscaping and natural beauty. As you wander about the peacock-haunted grounds, views open up over the hills, Vanbrugh's playful Temple of the Four Winds and Hawksmoor's stately mausoleum, but the great baroque house with its magnificent central cupola is an irresistible visual magnet. Inside, it is full of treasures – the breathtaking Great Hall with its soaring Corinthian pilasters, Pre-Raphaelite stained glass in the chapel, and corridors lined with classical antiquities.

The entrance courtyard has a good cafe, a gift shop and a farm shop filled with foodie delights from local producers.

Castle Howard is 15 miles northeast of York, off the A64. There are several organised tours from York – check with the tourist office for up-to-date schedules. **Stephenson's of Easingwold** (www.stephensonsofeasingwold.co.uk) operates a bus service (£7.50 return, 40 minutes, three daily Monday to Saturday) linking York to Castle Howard.

Thirsk

POP 9100

Monday and Saturday are market days in handsome Thirsk, which has been trading on its tidy, attractive streets and cobbled square since the Middle Ages. Thirsk's brisk business was always helped by its key position on two medieval trading routes: the old drove road between Scotland and York, and the route linking the Yorkshire Dales with the coast. That's all in the past, though; today, the town is all about the legacy of James Herriot, the wry Yorkshire vet adored by millions of fans of *All Creatures Great and Small*.

Thirsk does a good job as the real-life Darrowby of the books and TV series. And it should, as the real-life Herriot was in fact local vet Alf Wight, whose house and surgery has been dipped in 1940s aspic and turned into the incredibly popular **World of James Herriot** (www.worldofjamesherriot.org; 23 Kirkgate; adult/child £8.50/5; 10am-5pm Apr-Oct, 11am-4pm Nov-Mar, last entry 1hr before closing), an excellent museum full of Wight-related artefacts, a video documentary of his life and a re-creation of the TV-show set (the original set can be seen in the Richmondshire Museum in Richmond).

Thirsk is also a major horse-racing venue, and **Thirsk Racecourse** (www.thirskracecourse.net) hosts regular race meetings from April to September.

If you arrive in time for breakfast or just fancy a quick snack, head for the **Arabica Coffee Shop** (87 Market Pl; mains £3-7; 7.30am-5.30pm Mon-Sat, 10am-4.30pm Sun;) on the main square. This smart chrome-and-black diner is the opposite of chintz,

YORKSHIRE AROUND YORK

WORTH A TRIP

KIRKHAM PRIORY & STONE TROUGH INN

While the crowds queue up to get into Castle Howard, you could turn off on the other side of the A64 along the minor road to the hamlet of Kirkham. Here, the picturesque ruins of **Kirkham Priory** (EH; www.english-heritage.org.uk; adult/child £3.40/2; ⏲10am-5pm Thu-Mon Apr-Sep, daily Aug) rise gracefully above the banks of the River Derwent, sporting an impressive 13th-century gatehouse encrusted with heraldic symbols.

After a stroll by the river, head up the hill on the far side to the **Stone Trough Inn** (www.stonetroughinn.co.uk; mains £12-18; ⏲lunch & dinner;) for a spot of lunch. This traditional country inn serves gourmet-style pub grub, and has an outdoor terrace with a great view over the valley.

and serves excellent freshly ground coffee, croissants, fry-ups, and giant Yorkshire puddings filled with gravy.

Thirsk's **tourist office** (☎01845-522755; www.visitthirsk.org.uk; 49 Market Pl; ⏲10am-5pm Apr-Nov, 10am-4pm Dec-Mar) is located on the main square.

Thirsk is well served by trains on the line between York and Middlesbrough; however, the train station is a mile west of town and the only way to cover that distance is on foot or by **taxi** (☎07817 858077). There are also frequent daily buses from York (45 minutes).

Ripon

POP 16,468

Small town, huge cathedral: Ripon – with its winding streets and a broad, symmetrical marketplace lined with Georgian houses – is mostly about its elegant church, but tourists also seem quite taken by the **Ripon Hornblower**, who 'sets the watch' every evening at 9pm in a tradition that supposedly dates back to 886, when Alfred the Great gave the locals a horn to sound the changing of the guard.

Ripon Cathedral (www.riponcathedral.org.uk; admission free, suggested donation £3; ⏲8.30am-6pm) is well worth exploring. The first church on this site was built in 660 by St Wilfred, and its rough, humble crypt lies intact beneath today's soaring edifice. Above ground, this building was begun in the 11th century, with its harmonious Early English west front clocking in at 1220. Medieval additions have resulted in a medley of Gothic styles throughout, culminating in the rebuilding of the central tower – work that was never completed. It was not until 1836 that this impressive parish church got cathedral status. Look out for the fantastical creatures (including a pig playing bagpipes) decorating the medieval misericords, which are believed to have inspired Lewis Carroll – his father was canon here from 1852 to 1868.

Until 1888 Ripon was responsible for its own law enforcement, and this has resulted in a grand array of 'punishing attractions'. The **Law & Order Museums** (www.riponmuseums.co.uk; ⏲1-4pm Apr-Oct, 10am-4pm bank holidays) include the **Courthouse Museum** (Minster Rd; adult/child £2.50/free), a 19th-century courthouse (recognisable from TV series *Heartbeat*), the **Prison & Police Museum** (St Marygate; adult/child £4/2), which includes the medieval punishment yard and the clammy cells where no-good Victorians were banged up, and the **Workhouse Museum** (Allhallowgate; adult/child £4/2), which shows the grim treatment meted out to poor vagrants from the 19th century until WWII.

The pedestrianised Kirkgate leads from the cathedral to the town square, and has several good places to eat including the **Royal Oak** (www.royaloakripon.co.uk; 36 Kirkgate; mains £9-18, 3-course lunch or dinner £13;) gastropub and **Flô Café-Brasserie** (www.flocafebrasserie.com; 2 Kirkgate; 2-/3-course lunch £13/16; ⏲9am-11pm).

The **tourist office** (☎01765-604625; www.visitripon.org; Minster Rd; ⏲10am-1pm & 1.30-5pm Mon-Sat, 10am-1pm Sun Apr-Oct, 10am-4pm Thu & Sat Nov-Mar) is near the cathedral, has information on local walks and will book accommodation. Market day is Thursday.

Bus 36 runs from Leeds via Harrogate to Ripon (£5.50, one hour 20 minutes, every 20 minutes). From York, take the train to Harrogate (£8, 30 minutes, hourly), then bus 36 to Ripon (£4.80). Bus 159 runs between Ripon and Richmond (£6, 1½ hours, every two hours Monday to Saturday) via Masham and Middleham.

Fountains Abbey & Studley Royal

Nestled in the secluded valley of the River Skell lie two of Yorkshire's most beautiful attractions – an absolute must on any northern itinerary. The alluring and strangely obsessive water gardens of the **Studley Royal** estate were built in the 18th century to enhance the picturesque ruins of 12th-century **Fountains Abbey** (NT; www.fountainsabbey.org.uk; adult/child £9/4.85; ⌚10am-5pm Apr-Sep, to 4pm Oct-Mar). Together they present a breathtaking picture of pastoral elegance and tranquillity that have earned them a Unesco World Heritage listing, and made them the most visited of all the National Trust's pay-to-enter properties.

After falling out with the Benedictines of York in 1132, a band of rebel monks came here to establish their own monastery. Struggling to make it alone, they were formally adopted by the Cistercians in 1135; by the middle of the 13th century the new abbey had become the most successful Cistercian venture in the country. After the Dissolution the abbey's estate was sold into private hands, and between 1598 and 1611 **Fountains Hall** was built using stone from the abbey ruins. The hall and ruins were united with the Studley Royal estate in 1768.

Studley Royal was owned by John Aislabie (once Chancellor of the Exchequer), who dedicated his life to creating the park after a financial scandal saw him expelled from parliament. The main house of Studley Royal burnt down in 1946, but the superb landscaping, with its serene artificial lakes, survives almost unchanged from the 18th century.

The remains of the abbey are impressively grandiose, gathered around the sunny Romanesque **cloister** with a huge vaulted **cellarium** leading off the west end of the church – here the abbey's 200 lay brothers lived, and food and wool from the abbey's farms were stored. At the east end is the soaring **Chapel of Nine Altars**; on the outside of the northeast window is a Green Man carving (a pre-Christian fertility symbol).

A choice of scenic walking trails leads for one mile to the famous **water gardens**, designed to enhance the romantic views of the ruined abbey. Don't miss **St Mary's Church** above the gardens, a neogothic jewel designed by William Burgess; ask the attendant to point out the trademark mouse carved into the stone of the mausoleum.

Fountains Abbey is 4 miles west of Ripon off the B6265. Bus 139 goes from Ripon to Fountains Abbey visitor centre year-round (15 minutes, four daily Monday to Saturday).

Harrogate

POP 85,128

The quintessential Victorian spa town, prim and pretty Harrogate has long been associated with a certain kind of old-fashioned Englishness, the kind that seems to be the preserve of retired army chaps and formidable dowagers who always vote Tory. They come to Harrogate to enjoy the flower shows and gardens that fill the town with magnificent displays of colour, especially in spring and autumn. It is fitting that the town's most famous visitor was Agatha Christie, who fled here incognito in 1926 to escape her broken marriage.

Yet this picture of Victoriana redux is not quite complete. While it's undoubtedly true that Harrogate remains a firm favourite of visitors in their golden years, the town has plenty of smart hotels and trendy eateries catering to the boom in Harrogate's newest trade – conferences. All those dynamic young sales-and-marketing guns have to eat and sleep somewhere…

Sights & Activities

Royal Pump Room Museum MUSEUM
(www.harrogate.gov.uk/harrogate-987; Crown Pl; adult/child £3.75/2.20; ⌚10.30am-5pm Mon-Sat & 2-5pm Sun Apr-Oct, to 4pm Nov-Mar) The ritual of visiting a spa town to 'take the waters' as a health cure became fashionable in the 19th century and peaked during the Edwardian era in the years before WWI. Charles Dickens visited Harrogate in 1858 and described it as 'the queerest place, with the strangest people in it, leading the oddest lives of dancing, newspaper-reading and dining.' (Sounds quite pleasant, really.)

You can learn all about the history of Harrogate as a spa town in the ornate Royal Pump Room, built in 1842 over the most famous of the sulphur springs. It gives an insight into how the phenomenon shaped the town and records the illustrious visitors that it attracted; at the end you get the chance to sample the spa water, if you dare.

Turkish Baths SPA
(01423-556746; www.harrogate.gov.uk/harrogate-1100; Parliament St; admission £14.50-20.50; check website) Plunge into Harrogate's past at the town's fabulously tiled Turkish Baths. This mock-Moorish facility is gloriously Victorian and offers a range of watery delights – hot rooms, steam rooms, plunge pools and so on; a visit should last around 1½ hours. There's a complicated schedule of opening hours that are by turns ladies-only and mixed – call or check online for details. If you prefer to stay dry, there are also **guided tours** (per person £3.50; 9-10am Wed only) of the building.

Montpellier Quarter NEIGHBOURHOOD
(www.montpellierharrogate.com) The most attractive part of town is the Montpellier Quarter, overlooking Prospect Gardens between Crescent Rd and Montpellier Hill. It's an area of pedestrianised streets lined with restored 19th-century buildings that are now home to art galleries, antique shops, fashion boutiques, cafes and restaurants – an upmarket annex to the main shopping area around Oxford St and Cambridge St.

Harlow Carr Botanical Gardens GARDEN
(www.rhs.org.uk; Crag Lane, Beckwithshaw; adult/child £7.50/3.75; 9.30am-6pm Mar-Oct, to 4pm Nov-Feb) A huge green thumbs-up to Harrogate's gardeners; the town has some of the most beautiful public gardens in England. Flower fanatics should make for the Harlow Carr gardens, the northern showpiece of the Royal Horticultural Society, which are 1.5 miles southwest of town; take the B6162 Otley Rd, or walk through the Pine Woods southwest of the Valley Gardens.

Much closer to the town centre are the **Valley Gardens**, overlooked by the vast, glass-domed Sun Pavilion, built in 1933. The nearby bandstand houses concerts on Sunday afternoons from June to August.

BLACK SHEEP OF THE BREWING FAMILY

The village of Masham is a place of pilgrimage for connoisseurs of real ale – it's the frothing fountainhead of Theakston's beers, which have been brewed here since 1827. The company's most famous brew, Old Peculier, takes its name from the Peculier of Masham, a parish court established in medieval times to deal with religious offences, including drunkenness, brawling, and 'taking a skull from the churchyard and placing it under a person's head to charm them to sleep'. The court seal is used as the emblem of Theakston Ales.

To the horror of real-ale fans, and after much falling out among members of the Theakston family, the Theakston Brewery was taken over by much-hated megabrewer Scottish & Newcastle in 1987. Five years later, Paul Theakston – who had refused to go and work for S&N, and was determined to keep small-scale, artisan brewing alive – bought an old maltings building in Masham and set up his own brewery, which he called Black Sheep. He managed to salvage all kinds of traditional brewing equipment, including six Yorkshire 'stone square' brewing vessels, and was soon running a successful enterprise.

History came full circle in 2004 when Paul's four brothers took the Theakston brewery back into family ownership. Both the **Black Sheep Brewery** (01765-680101; www.blacksheepbrewery.com; tour £5.95; 10am-4.30pm Sun-Wed, 10am-11pm Thu-Sat) and **Theakston's Brewery** (01765-680000; www.theakstons.co.uk; tour £6.50; 10.30am-5.30pm Jul & Aug, to 4.30pm May, Jun, Sep & Oct) have information centres and offer guided tours (best booked in advance).

Seven miles north of Masham, on the road to Leyburn, is one of Yorkshire's best gastropubs. The **Blue Lion** (01969-624273; www.thebluelion.co.uk; East Witton; mains £16-26; lunch & dinner) combines rustic wooden settles, flagstone floors and a huge open fireplace with crisp linen napkins, impeccable service and an unpretentious menu of fine dining based on Yorkshire produce. They also have accommodation (single/double from £70/109).

Masham (pronounced 'Massam') is 9 miles northwest of Ripon on the A6108 to Leyburn. Bus 159 from Ripon to Richmond stops at Masham (30 minutes, every two hours Monday to Saturday).

FREE **Mercer Art Gallery** ART GALLERY

(Swan Rd; ⊙10am-5pm Tue-Sat, 2-5pm Sun) Another surviving spa building, the Promenade Room is now home to this elegant gallery, a stately space that hosts constantly changing exhibitions of visual arts.

Festivals & Events

All three of Harrogate's major events are held at the Great Yorkshire Showground, just off the A661 on the southeastern edge of town.

Spring Flower Show HORTICULTURE

(www.flowershow.org.uk; admission £14-15) The year's main event, held in late April. A colourful three-day extravaganza of blooms and blossoms, flower competitions, gardening demonstrations, market stalls, crafts and gardening shops.

Great Yorkshire Show AGRICULTURE

(www.greatyorkshireshow.co.uk; adult/child £23/11) Staged over three days in mid-July by the Yorkshire Agricultural Society. Expect all manner of primped and prettified farm animals competing for prizes, and entertainment ranging from show-jumping and falconry to cookery demonstrations and hot-air balloon rides.

Autumn Flower Show HORTICULTURE

(www.flowershow.org.uk; admission £14-15) Held in late September. Vegetable- and fruit-growing championships, a heaviest-onion competition, cookery demonstrations, children's events and more.

Sleeping

There are lots of excellent B&Bs and guesthouses just north of Harrogate town centre, on and around Franklin Rd and Ripon Rd.

Bijou B&B ££

(☎01423-567974; www.thebijou.co.uk; 17 Ripon Rd; s/d from £69/89; P@☜) Bijou by name and bijou by nature, this Victorian villa sits firmly at the boutique end of the B&B spectrum – you can tell that a lot of thought and care has gone into its design. The husband-and-wife team who own the place make fantastic hosts, warm and helpful but unobtrusive.

Hotel du Vin BOUTIQUE HOTEL ££

(☎01423-856800; www.hotelduvin.com; Prospect Pl; r/ste from £110/180; P@☜) An extremely stylish boutique hotel that has made the other lodgings in town sit up and take notice. The loft suites with their exposed oak beams, hardwood floors and designer bathrooms are among the nicest rooms we've seen in town, but even the standard rooms are spacious and very comfortable (though they can be noisy), each with a trademark huge bed draped in soft Egyptian cotton.

Acorn Lodge B&B ££

(☎01423-525630; www.acornlodgeharrogate.co.uk; 1 Studley Rd; s/d from £47/85; P☜) Attention to detail makes the difference between an average and an excellent B&B, and the details at Acorn Lodge are spot on – stylish decor, crisp cotton sheets, powerful showers, and perfect poached eggs for breakfast. The location is good too, just 10 minutes' walk from the town centre.

Harrogate Brasserie & Hotel BOUTIQUE HOTEL ££

(☎01423-505041; www.harrogatebrasserie.co.uk; 26-30 Cheltenham Pde; s/d/f from £60/80/100; P☜) Stripped pine, leather armchairs and subtle colour combinations make this one of Harrogate's most appealing places to stay. The cheerful and cosy accommodation is complemented by an excellent restaurant and bar, with live jazz every evening except Monday.

Arden House Hotel B&B ££

(☎01423-509224; www.ardenhousehotel.co.uk; 69-71 Franklin Rd; s/d from £50/80; P☜) This grand old Edwardian house has been given a modern makeover with stylish contemporary furniture, Egyptian cotton bed linen and posh toiletries, but still retains some lovely period details including tiled, cast-iron fireplaces. Attentive service, good breakfasts and a central location are the icing on the cake.

Eating

TOP CHOICE **Van Zeller** MODERN BRITISH £££

(☎01423-508762; www.vanzellerrestaurants.co.uk; 8 Montpellier St; 2-course lunch £18, 3-course dinner £40; ⊙lunch & dinner Tue-Sat) Michelin-trained Yorkshire chef Tom van Zeller offers exquisite interpretations of classic British dishes, such as Yorkshire lamb served with tarragon gnocchi, globe artichoke and smoked almonds, in a refreshingly relaxed atmosphere – 'fine food without the fuss' is his motto. Lunch and pre-theatre menu: five courses for £25.

Bettys TEAROOM ££

(www.bettys.co.uk; 1 Parliament St; mains £6-13, afternoon tea £18; ⏰9am-9pm) A classic tearoom in a classic location with views across the park, Bettys is a local institution. It was established in 1919 by a Swiss immigrant confectioner who took the wrong train, ended up in Yorkshire and decided to stay. It has exquisite home-baked breads, scones and cakes, quality tea and coffee, and a gallery lined with art nouveau marquetry designs of Yorkshire scenes commissioned by the founder in the 1930s.

Le D2 BISTRO ££

(www.led2.co.uk; 7 Bower Rd; 2-course lunch/dinner £13/18; ⏰Tue-Sat) This bright and airy bistro is always busy, with diners drawn back again and again by the relaxed atmosphere, warm and friendly service, and a hearty menu that takes fresh local produce and adds a twist of French sophistication.

Tannin Level BISTRO ££

(☎01423-560595; www.tanninlevel.co.uk; 5 Raglan St; mains £10-15; ⏰Tue-Sat) Old terracotta floor tiles, polished mahogany tables and gilt-framed mirrors and paintings create a relaxed yet elegant atmosphere at this popular neighbourhood bistro. A competitively priced menu based on seasonal British produce – think a herb-crusted rump of lamb, or pan-fried scallops – means that you'd best book a table or face being turned away.

Le Jardin BISTRO £

(☎01423-507323; www.lejardin-harrogate.com; 7 Montpellier Pde; lunch mains £5-9; ⏰lunch Tue-Fri & Sun, dinner Tue-Sat) This cool little bistro has a snug, intimate atmosphere, especially in the evening when candlelight adds a romantic glow. During the day locals throng to the tables, enjoying great salads, sandwiches and homemade ice cream. A two-/three-course dinner is £9/13.

Sasso ITALIAN £££

(☎01423-508838; www.sassorestaurant.co.uk; 8-10 Princes Sq; mains £15-21; ⏰lunch & dinner Mon-Sat) A top-class basement trattoria where homemade pasta is served in a variety of traditional and authentic ways, along with a host of other Italian specialties.

☆ Entertainment

Harrogate Theatre THEATRE

(www.harrogatetheatre.co.uk; Oxford St) An historic Victorian building that dates from 1900, staging variety, comedy, musicals and dancing.

Royal Hall MUSIC

(www.royalhall.co.uk; Ripon Rd) A gorgeous Edwardian theatre that is now part of the Harrogate International conference centre. The musical program covers orchestral and choral performances, piano recitals and jazz.

ℹ Information

Post Office (11 Cambridge Rd; ⏰9.30am-5.30pm Mon-Sat)

Tourist Office (☎0845 389 3223; www.harrogate.gov.uk/tourism; Crescent Rd; ⏰9am-5.30pm Mon-Sat & 10am-1pm Sun Apr-Oct, shorter hours and closed Sun Nov-Mar)

ℹ Getting There & Away

BUS National Express coaches run from Leeds (40 minutes, five daily). Bus 36 comes from Ripon (30 minutes, every 20 minutes), continuing to Leeds.

TRAIN Trains run to Harrogate from Leeds (£7.40, 40 minutes, about half-hourly) and York (£7.40, 45 minutes, hourly).

Scarborough

POP 57,649

Scarborough is where the whole tradition of English seaside holidays began. And it began earlier than you might think – in the 1660s a book promoting the medicinal properties of a local spring (now the site of Scarborough Spa) pulled in the first flood of visitors. A belief in the health-giving effects of sea-bathing saw wheeled bathing carriages appear on the beach in the 1730s, and with the arrival of the railway in 1845 Scarborough's fate was determined. By the time the 20th century rolled in, it was all donkey rides, fish and chips, seaside rock and boat trips round the bay, with saucy postcards, kiss-me-quick hats and blokes from Leeds with knotted hankies on their heads just a decade or two away.

Like all British seaside towns, Scarborough suffered a downturn in the last decades of the 20th century, when people jetted off to the Costa Blanca on newly affordable foreign holidays, but things are looking up again. The town retains all the trappings of the classic seaside resort, but is in the process of reinventing itself as a centre for the creative arts and digital industries – the Victorian spa is being redeveloped as a conference and entertainment centre, a former

WORTH A TRIP

DETOUR: FORBIDDEN CORNER

Hidden away in the eastern foothills of the Yorkshire Dales, 2 miles west of the village of Middleham, is one of Yorkshire's most bizarre tourist attractions. Built more than 20 years ago as a private 'folly' for a local landowner, the **Forbidden Corner** (☎01969-640638; www.theforbiddencorner.co.uk; Tupgill Park; adult/child/family £10.50/8.50/36; ⏰noon-6pm Mon-Sat, 10am-6pm Sun Apr-Oct, also 10am-6pm Sun Nov-Christmas) is a labyrinth of miniature castles, caves, temples and gardens decorated with all manner of weird and wonderful sculptures.

Enter through a gateway in the shape of a fanged mouth and follow the 'clues' in rhyming couplets to reach a 'temple of the underworld'. It's great fun for kids, and some of the jokes will make adults smile. Watch out for the sign *cave aquae* ('beware of the water'). Admission is through bookings only, either online or by phone.

museum has been converted into studio space for artists, and there's free, open-access wi-fi along the promenade beside the harbour – an area being developed as the town's bar, cafe and restaurant quarter.

As well as the usual seaside attractions, Scarborough offers excellent coastal walking, a geology museum, one of Yorkshire's most impressively sited castles, and a renowned theatre that is the home base of popular playwright Alan Ayckbourn, whose plays always premiere here.

Sights

Scarborough Castle CASTLE
(EH; www.english-heritage.org.uk; adult/child £4.90/2.90; ⏰10am-6pm Apr-Sep, 10am-4pm Thu-Mon Oct, 10am-4pm Sat & Sun Nov-Mar) Scarborough is not exclusively about sandcastles, seaside rock and walks along the prom. The massive medieval keep of Scarborough Castle occupies a commanding position atop its headland – legend has it that Richard I loved the views so much that his ghost just keeps coming back. The Romans appreciated this viewpoint too – take a walk out to the edge of the cliffs where you can see the 2000-year-old remains of a **Roman signal station**.

Rotunda Museum MUSEUM
(www.rotundamuseum.co.uk; Vernon Rd; adult/under-18s £4.50/free; ⏰10am-5pm Tue-Sun; 👪) The Rotunda Museum is dedicated to seaside rock of a different kind: the coastal geology of northeast Yorkshire, which has yielded many of Britain's most important dinosaur fossils. The strata in the local cliffs here were also important in deciphering the geological history of England. Founded by William Smith, the 'father of English geology', who lived in Scarborough in the 1820s, the museum displays original Victorian exhibits, as well as having a hands-on gallery for kids.

Sea Life Centre & Marine Sanctuary AQUARIUM
(www.sealife.co.uk; Scalby Mills; adult/child/family £15/11.40/46.80; ⏰10am-5pm) Of all the family-oriented attractions on the waterfront, the best of the lot is the Sea Life Centre overlooking North Bay. You can see coral reefs, turtles, octopuses, seahorses, otters and many other fascinating creatures, though the biggest draw is the **Seal Rescue Centre** (feeding times 11.30am and 2.30pm). It's at the far north end of North Beach; the miniature North Bay Railway runs the 0.75-mile route. Note that a lot of the attractions are outdoors, so it's not an ideal rainy-day refuge.

FREE **Peasholm Park** PARK
(www.peasholmpark.com; Columbus Ravine; ⏰24 hrs) Set back from the North Bay, Scarborough's beautiful Edwardian pleasure gardens are famous for their summer sessions of **Naval Warfare** (adult/child £3.70/2.10; ⏰3pm various days Jun-Aug), when large model ships re-enact famous naval battles on the boating lake (check website for dates).

FREE **St Mary's Church** CHURCH
(Castle Rd; ⏰10am-4pm Mon-Fri, 1-4pm Sun May-Sep) This church dates from 1180. In the little cemetery across the lane from the church is the **grave of Anne Brontë**.

Activities

There are some decent waves on England's northeast coast, which support a growing surfing scene. A top spot is **Cayton Bay**, 4 miles south of town, where you'll find

Scarborough Surf School (www.scarboroughsurfschool.co.uk; parking £2) offering full-day lessons for £45 per person, and equipment hire (surfboard £18 per day).

Back in town, you can get information and advice from the **Secretspot Surf Shop** (www.secretspot.co.uk; 4 Pavilion Tce) near the train station.

Sleeping

In Scarborough, if a house has four walls and a roof it'll offer B&B. Competition is intense, and in such a tough market multinight-stay special offers are two a penny, which means that single-night rates are the highest of all.

TOP CHOICE **Hotel Helaina** B&B ££
(01723-375191; www.hotelhelaina.co.uk; 14 Blenheim Tce; s/d from £59/79; daily Apr-Nov, closed Dec & Jan, Fri & Sat only Feb & Mar;) Location, location, location – you'd be hard pushed to find a place with a better sea view than this elegant guest house perched on the clifftop overlooking North Beach. And the view inside the rooms is pretty good too, with sharply styled contemporary furniture and cool colours. The standard rooms are a touch on the small side – it's well worth paying a bit extra for the deluxe sea-view room with the bay window.

Beiderbecke's Hotel HOTEL £££
(01723-365766; www.beiderbeckes.com; 1-3 The Crescent; s/d from £85/130; P) Set in an elegant Georgian terrace in the middle of town, on a quiet street overlooking gardens, this hotel combines stylish and spacious rooms with attentive but friendly and informal service. It's not quite boutique, but with intriguing modern art on the walls and snazzily coloured toilet seats it's heading in that direction.

Windmill B&B ££
(01723-372735; www.windmill-hotel.co.uk; Mill St; d £95; P) Quirky doesn't begin to describe this place – a beautifully converted 18th-century windmill in the middle of town. There are two self-catering cottages and three four-poster doubles around a cobbled courtyard, but try to get the balcony suite (£140 a night) in the upper floors of the windmill itself, with great views from the wrap-around balcony.

The Waves B&B ££
(01723-373658; www.scarboroughwaves.co.uk; 39 Esplanade Rd, South Cliff; per person £32-39; P) Crisp Egyptian cotton sheets and powerful showers make for comfortable accommodation at this B&B, but it's the second B that's the real star – vegetarian- and vegan-friendly breakfasts range from fruit salads and smoothies to fry-ups, kippers and kedgree. A unique selling point is the jukebox in the lounge, loaded with 1960s and 70s hits.

Interludes B&B ££
(01723-360513; www.interludeshotel.co.uk; 32 Princess St; s/d £45/68;) Owners Ian and Bob have a flair for the theatrical and have brought it to bear with visible success on this lovely, gay-friendly Georgian home plastered with old theatre posters, prints and other thespian mementos. The individually decorated rooms are given to colourful flights of fancy that can't but put a smile on your face. Children, alas, are not welcome.

Scarborough YHA HOSTEL £
(0845 371 9657; www.yha.org.uk; Burniston Rd; dm £19.50; P) An idyllic hostel set in a converted 17th-century water mill. It's 2 miles north of town along the A166 to Whitby; take bus 3, 12 or 21.

Crown Spa Hotel HOTEL ££
(01723-357400; www.crownspahotel.com; Esplanade; s/d from £64/88; P) This grand old hotel opened its doors in 1845 and has been going strong ever since, offering superb sea views and a luxurious modern spa.

Eating

Marmalade's BRASSERIE ££
(01723-365766; 1-3 The Crescent; 2-/3-course dinner £18/22; noon-9.30pm) This stylish brasserie in Beiderbecke's Hotel – cream and chocolate colours, art with a musical theme, and cool jazz in the background (live on Thursday and Saturday) – has a menu that adds a gourmet twist to traditional dishes such as roast pork, rack of lamb, and steak and chips.

Glass House CAFE £
(01723-368791; www.glasshousebistro.co.uk; Burniston Rd; mains £4-8; 10am-5pm;) Homemade lasagne, steak-and-ale pie, and filled baked potatoes pull in the lunchtime crowds at this appealing (and always busy) cafe beside the start of the North Bay Railway, while fried breakfasts, sandwiches, cakes and scones fill the menu for the rest of the day.

Scarborough

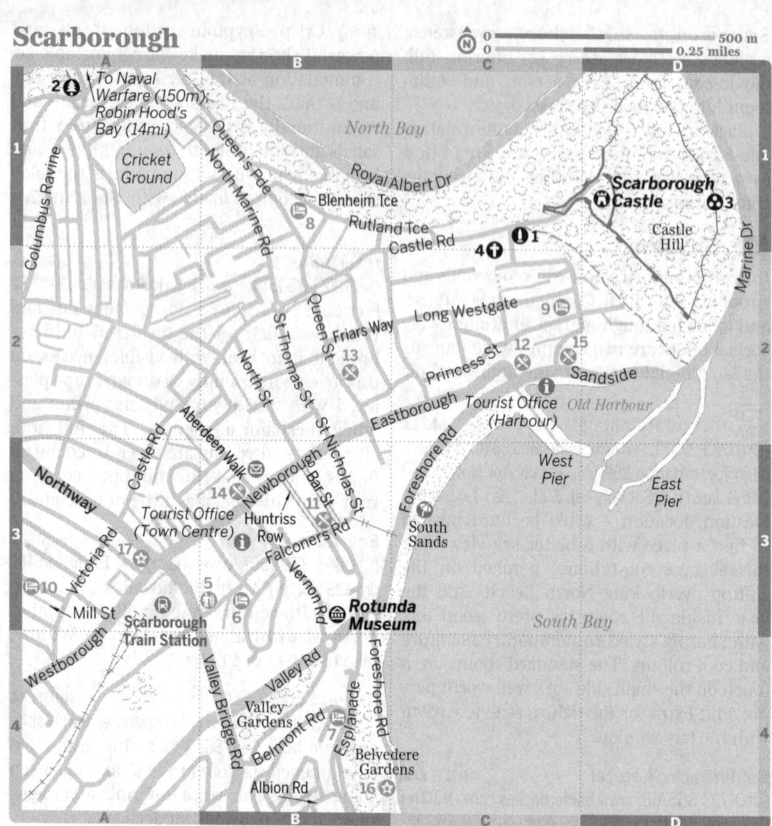

Lanterna ITALIAN £££
(☎01723-363616; www.lanterna-ristorante.co.uk; 33 Queen St; mains £15-21; ⊙dinner Mon-Sat) A snug, old-fashioned Italian trattoria that specialises in fresh local seafood (including lobster, from £32), and classic dishes from the old country such as *stufato de ceci* (old-style chickpea stew with oxtail) and white-truffle dishes in season (October to December, £30 to £45). As well as sourcing Yorkshire produce, the chef imports delicacies direct from Italy, including truffles, olive oil, prosciutto and a range of cheeses.

Golden Grid SEAFOOD ££
(www.goldengrid.co.uk; 4 Sandside; mains £8-18; ⊙11.30am-11pm) Whoever said fish and chips can't be eaten with dignity hasn't tried the Golden Grid, a sit-down fish restaurant that has been serving the best cod in Scarborough since 1883. It's staunchly traditional, with starched white tablecloths and starched white aprons, as is the menu – as well as fish and chips there's freshly landed crab, lobster, prawns and oysters, plus sausage and mash, liver and bacon, and steak and chips.

Roasters CAFE £
(www.roasterscoffee.co.uk; 8 Aberdeen Walk; mains £5-7; ⊙9am-5pm) A funky coffee shop with chunky pine tables, brown leather chairs, and an excellent range of freshly ground coffees. There's a juice and smoothie bar too, and the lunch menu includes ciabatta sandwiches, salads and jacket potatoes.

Bonnet's TEAROOM £
(38-40 Huntriss Row; mains £5-9; ⊙9am-5pm Mon-Sat, 11am-4pm Sun) One of the oldest cafes in town (open since 1880), Bonnet's serves delicious cakes and light meals in a quiet courtyard.

Scarborough

Top Sights

	Rotunda Museum	B3
	Scarborough Castle	D1

Sights

1	Grave of Anne Brontë	C1
2	Peasholm Park	A1
3	Roman Signal Station	D1
4	St Mary's Church	C1

Activities, Courses & Tours

5	Secretspot Surf Shop	B3

Sleeping

6	Beiderbecke's Hotel	B3
7	Crown Spa Hotel	B4
8	Hotel Helaina	B1
9	Interludes	C2
10	Windmill	A3

Eating

11	Bonnet's	B3
12	Golden Grid	C2
13	Lanterna	B2
	Marmalade's	(see 6)
14	Roasters	B3
15	Tunny Club	C2

Entertainment

16	Scarborough Spa	B4
17	Stephen Joseph Theatre	A3

Tunny Club FISH & CHIPS £

(1 Sandgate; mains £4-7; ⌚11am-11pm) A decent chippie where the upstairs dining room is a shrine to Scarborough's history of big-game fishing.

☆ Entertainment

Stephen Joseph Theatre THEATRE

(www.sjt.uk.com; Westborough) Stages a good range of drama. Renowned chronicler of middle-class mores Alan Ayckbourn premieres his plays here.

Scarborough Spa VARIETY

(www.scarboroughspa.co.uk; Foreshore Rd, South Bay) The revitalised spa complex stages a wide range of entertainment, especially in the summer months, including orchestral performances, variety shows, popular musicals and old-fashioned afternoon-tea dances.

Information

FreeBay Wifi (free) Free wi-fi internet access along harbourfront from West Pier to East Pier.

Post Office (11-15 Aberdeen Walk; ⌚9am-5.30pm Mon-Fri, to 12.30pm Sat)

Tourist Office (☎01723-383637; www.discoveryorkshirecoast.com) Scarborough Brunswick (Brunswick Shopping Centre, Westborough; ⌚9.30am-5.30pm daily Apr-Oct, 10am-4.30pm Mon-Sat Nov-Mar) Scarborough Harbour (Sandside; ⌚10am-5.30pm Apr-Oct, to 9pm Jul & Aug)

Getting There & Away

BUS Bus 128 goes along the A170 from Helmsley to Scarborough (1½ hours, hourly) via Pickering, while buses 93 and X93 come from Whitby (one hour, every 30 minutes) via Robin Hood's Bay (hourly).

THE TUNNY CLUB

Strange but true: in the 1930s Atlantic bluefin tuna (also known as tunny) started to follow the herring shoals into the North Sea, and Yorkshire became the hub of a US-style big-game fishery. Professional hunter Lorenzo Mitchell-Henry set the record for a rod-caught fish in British waters when he landed a 386kg monster in 1933, and Scarborough was soon home to the Tunny Club of Great Britain. Visiting millionaires and movie stars chartered local boats and vied with each other to smash the record.

Overfishing led to the disappearance of the herring shoals in the 1950s, and with them the tunny. However, in recent years the ocean giants have returned, attracted by warmer waters (attributed by many to be due to climate change) and recovering herring stocks. Meanwhile, all that remains in Scarborough is the former premises of the Tunny Club (p587), now a fish-and-chip shop; the upstairs dining room is filled with big-game fishing memorabilia.

Bus 843 goes to Scarborough from Leeds (£12, 2¾ hours, hourly) via York (£10, 1¾ hours, hourly).

TRAIN There are regular trains from Hull (£14, 1½ hours, hourly), Leeds (£26, one hour 20 minutes, hourly) and York (£18, 50 minutes, hourly).

Getting Around

Tiny, Victorian-era **funicular railways** (per person £0.75; Feb-Oct) rattle up and down Scarborough's steep cliffs between town and beach.

Local **buses** leave from the western end of Westborough and outside the train station.

For a taxi call **Station Taxis** (☎01723-366366); £5 should get you to most places in town.

NORTH YORK MOORS NATIONAL PARK

Inland from the north Yorkshire coast, the wild and windswept North York Moors rise in desolate splendour. Three-quarters of all the world's heather moorland is to be found in Britain, and this is the largest expanse in all of England. Ridge-top roads climb up from lush green valleys to the bleak open moors where weather-beaten stone crosses mark the line of ancient drove roads. In summer the heather blooms in billowing drifts of purple haze.

This is classic walking country, and the moors are criss-crossed with footpaths old and new, and dotted with pretty, flower-bedecked villages. The national park is also home to one of England's most picturesque steam railways.

The park produces the very useful *Moors & Coast* visitor guide, available at tourist offices, hotels etc, with information on things to see and do. See also www.northyorkmoors.org.uk.

Getting Around

The **Moorsbus** (www.northyorkmoors.org.uk/moorsbus) network covers all the main villages, operating on Sundays and bank holiday Mondays only from April to October. Pick up a timetable and route map from tourist offices or download one from the website. A standard day pass costs £6. (Note a new service will replace it in 2014.)

There's also a free public transport map, the *Moors Explorer Travel Guide*, available from tourist offices.

If you're planning to drive on the minor roads over the moors, beware of wandering sheep and lambs – hundreds are killed by drivers every year.

Helmsley

POP 1620

Helmsley is a classic North Yorkshire market town, a handsome place full of old houses, historic coaching inns and – inevitably – a cobbled market square (market day Friday), all basking under the watchful gaze of a sturdy Norman castle. Nearby are the romantic ruins of Rievaulx Abbey and a fistful of country walks.

Sights & Activities

The impressive ruins of 12th-century **Helmsley Castle** (EH; www.english-heritage.org.uk; adult/child £4.90/2.90; ⌚10am-6pm Apr-Sep, to 5pm Oct, to 4pm Sat & Sun only Nov-Mar) are defended by a striking series of deep ditches and banks to which later rulers added the thick stone walls and defensive towers – only one tooth-shaped tower survives today following the dismantling of the fortress by Sir Thomas Fairfax after the Civil War. The castle's tumultuous history is well explained in the tourist office.

Located just outside the castle, **Helmsley Walled Garden** (www.helmsleywalledgarden.org.uk; adult/child £5.50/free; ⌚9.30am-5pm Mar-Oct) would be just another plant-and-produce centre were it not for its dramatic position and fabulous selection of flowers, fruits and vegetables – some of which are rare – not to mention the herbs, including 40 varieties of mint. If you're into horticulture with a historical twist, this is Eden.

South of the castle stretches the superb landscape of **Duncombe Park Estate** (www.duncombepark.com; adult/child £5/free; ⌚11am-5.30pm Sun-Fri Jun-Aug) with the stately home of Duncombe Park House at its heart. From the house (no longer open to the public) and its formal gardens, wide grassy walkways and terraces lead through woodland to mock-classical temples, while longer walking trails are set out in the parkland, now protected as a nature reserve. The house is 1.5 miles south of town, an easy walk through the park.

You could easily spend a half-day here, especially if you take in one of the many walks. Cream of the crop is the 3.5-mile route to **Rievaulx Abbey** – the tourist office can provide route leaflets and advise on buses if you don't want to walk both ways. This route is also the opening section of the **Cleveland Way**.

North York Moors National Park

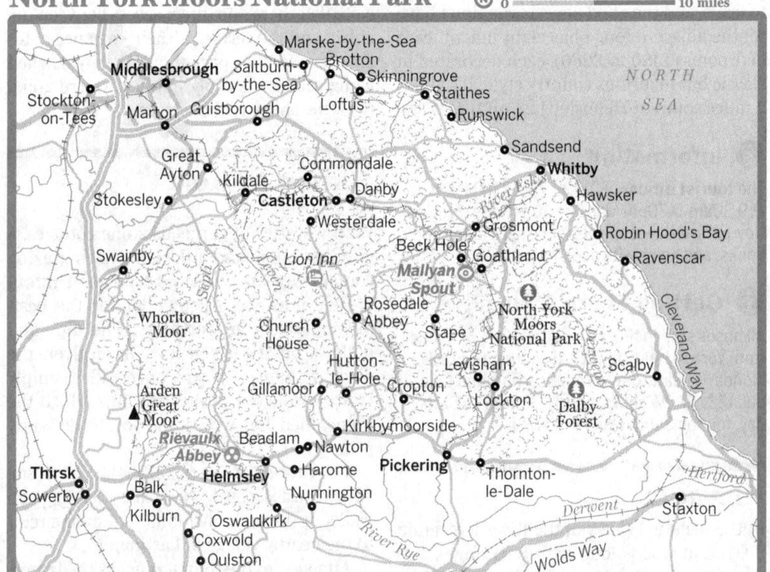

Sleeping

Feversham Arms HOTEL £££
(☎01439-770766; www.fevershamarms.com; High St; r from £130; P 📶 🏊) The Feversham Arms has recently had a designer makeover, creating a snug and sophisticated atmosphere where country charm meets boutique chic. Individually decorated bedrooms are complemented by an excellent restaurant, spa treatments, and a heated outdoor pool in the central courtyard.

Feathers Hotel INN ££
(☎01439-770275; www.feathershotelhelmsley.co.uk; Market Pl; s/d from £55/100) One of a number of old coaching inns on Market Pl that offer B&B accommodation, half-decent grub and a pint of hand-pumped real ale. There are four-poster beds in some rooms and historical trimmings are found throughout.

Helmsley YHA HOSTEL
(☎0845 371 9638; www.yha.org.uk; Carlton Lane; dm £19.50; P) Although it looks a bit like an ordinary suburban home, this hostel's location (400m east of the market square and at the start of the Cleveland Way) means that it's often busy, so book in advance.

Wrens of Ryedale CAMPSITE £
(☎01439-771260; www.wrensofryedale.co.uk; Gale Lane; tent & 2 adults £10, with car £17; ⊙Apr-Oct) Sheltered campsite with three acres of pristine parkland 3 miles east of Helmsley, just south of Beadlam.

Eating

Helmsley is a bit of a foodie town, sporting a couple of quality delicatessens on the main square. There's **Thomas of Helmsley** (18 Market Pl; ⊙7.30am-5.30pm Mon-Sat, 10am-4pm Sun), a butcher and deli specialising in local produce; and flower-bedecked **Hunters of Helmsley** (www.huntersofhelmsley.com; 13 Market Pl; ⊙8am-5.30pm daily), a cornucopia of locally made chutneys, jams, beers, cheeses, bacon, humbugs and ice cream – a great place to stock up for a gourmet picnic.

TOP CHOICE **Star Inn** GASTROPUB £££
(☎01439-770397; www.thestaratharome.co.uk; mains £18-26; ⊙lunch Tue-Sun, dinner Mon-Sat; 🖉) This thatch-roofed country gastropub is home to one of Yorkshire's best restaurants, with a menu that revels in top-quality produce from the surrounding countryside – Whitby cod with buttered marsh samphire, or Harome roe deer venison with wild mushrooms; there's also a gourmet vegetarian

menu. It's the sort of place you won't want to leave, and the good news is you don't have to: the adjacent lodge has eight magnificent bedrooms (£180 to £260), each decorated in classic but luxurious country style. It's about 2 miles south of Helmsley just off the A170.

Information

The **tourist office** (☎01439-770173; Castlegate; ⌚9.30am-5.30pm Mar-Oct, 10am-4pm Fri-Sun Nov-Feb) at the castle entrance sells maps and books, and helps with accommodation.

Getting There & Away

All buses stop in the main square. Bus 31X runs from York to Helmsley (£7, 1¼ hours, two daily Monday to Saturday). From Scarborough take bus 128 (£7, 1½ hours, hourly Monday to Saturday, four on Sunday) via Pickering.

Rievaulx

In the secluded valley of the River Rye, amid fields and woods loud with birdsong, stand the magnificent ruins of the EH-listed **Rievaulx Abbey** (www.english-heritage.org.uk; adult/child £5.80/3.50; ⌚10am-6pm Apr-Sep, to 5pm Thu-Mon Oct, to 4pm Sat & Sun Nov-Mar). This idyllic spot was chosen by Cistercian monks in 1132 as a base for missionary activity in northern Britain. St Aelred, the third abbot, famously described the abbey's setting as 'everywhere peace, everywhere serenity, and a marvellous freedom from the tumult of the world'. But the monks of Rievaulx (pronounced 'Ree-voh') were far from unworldly, and soon created a network of commercial interests ranging from sheep farms to lead mines that formed the backbone of the local economy. The extensive ruins give a wonderful feel for the size and complexity of the community that once lived here – their story is fleshed out in a series of fascinating exhibits in the neighbouring visitor centre.

In the 1750s landscape-gardening fashion favoured a Gothic look, and many aristocrats had mock ruins built in their parks. The Duncombe family went one better, as their lands contained a real medieval ruin – Rievaulx Abbey. They built National Trust–listed **Rievaulx Terrace & Temples** (www.nationaltrust.org.uk; adult/child £5.50/3.10; ⌚11am-5pm Mar-Oct) so that lords and ladies could stroll effortlessly in the 'wilderness' and admire the abbey in the valley below. Today, we can do the same, with views over Ryedale and the Hambleton Hills forming a perfect backdrop.

Rievaulx is about 3 miles west of Helmsley. Note that there's no direct access between the abbey and the terrace – their entrance gates are about a mile apart, though easily reached along a lane – steeply uphill if you're going from the abbey to the terrace.

Hutton-le-Hole

POP 210

With a scatter of gorgeous stone cottages, a gurgling brook and a flock of sheep grazing contentedly on the village green, Hutton-le-Hole must be a contender for the best-looking village in Yorkshire. The dips and hollows on the green may have given the place its name – it was once called simply Hutton Hole but posh Victorians added the Frenchified 'le', which the locals defiantly pronounce 'lee'.

The **tourist office** (☎01751-417367; ⌚10am-5.30pm mid-Mar–early Nov) has leaflets on walks in the area, including a 5-mile circuit to the nearby village of Lastingham.

Attached to the tourist office is the largely open-air **Ryedale Folk Museum** (☎01751-417367; www.ryedalefolkmuseum.co.uk; adult/child £7/6; ⌚10am-6pm Feb-Oct), a collection of North York Moors buildings from different eras, including a medieval manor house, simple farmers' houses, a blacksmith's forge and a row of 1930s village shops. Demonstrations and displays throughout the season give a fascinating insight into local life as it was in the past.

The **Daffodil Walk** is a 2½-mile circular walk following the banks of the River Dove. As the name suggests, the main draw is the daffs, usually at their best in the last couple of weeks in April.

Sleeping & Eating

Lion Inn PUB, B&B ££

(☎01751-417320; www.lionblakey.co.uk; Blakey Ridge; s/d from £48/80, mains £11-23; P) From Hutton, the Blakey Ridge road climbs over the moors to Danby and, after 6 miles, passes one of the highest and most remote pubs in England (altitude 404m). With its low-beamed ceilings and cosy fireplaces, hearty grub and range of real ales, the Lion is a firm favourite with hikers and bikers.

Burnley House B&B ££

(☎01751-417548; www.burnleyhouse.co.uk; per person £36-45; P wi-fi) This elegant Georgian home offers comfortable bedrooms and a hearty breakfast, but the best features are the lovely sitting room and garden where you can relax with a cup of tea and a book.

Getting There & Away

Hutton-le-Hole is 2½ miles north of the main A170 road, about halfway between Helmsley and Pickering. Sunday-only Moorsbus services to Hutton-le-Hole include the M3 between Helmsley and Danby via the Lion Inn (five per day). On Mondays and Fridays, bus 174 runs to Hutton from Pickering (30 minutes, once daily).

Pickering

POP 6600

Pickering is a lively market town with an imposing Norman castle, that advertises itself as the 'Gateway to the North York Moors'. That gateway is the terminus of the wonderful North Yorkshire Moors Railway, a picturesque survivor from the great days of steam.

The **tourist office** (☎01751-473791; The Ropery; ⌚9.30am-5.30pm Mon-Sat & 9.30am-4pm Sun Mar-Oct, 10am-4pm Mon-Sat Nov-Feb) has the usual details as well as plenty of NYMR-related info.

Sights

The privately owned **North Yorkshire Moors Railway** (NYMR; www.nymr.co.uk; Pickering-Whitby Day Rover ticket adult/child £22.50/11.30) runs for 18 miles from Pickering through beautiful countryside to the village of Grosmont, with connections to Whitby. Lovingly restored steam locomotives pull period carriages, resplendent in polished brass and bright paintwork. For visitors without wheels, it's ideal for reaching out-of-the-way villages in the middle of the moors. Grosmont is also on the main railway line between Middlesbrough and Whitby, opening up yet more possibilities for walking and sightseeing. Check the website for timetables.

Dating mostly from the 13th and 14th centuries, **Pickering Castle** (EH; www.english-heritage.org.uk; adult/child £3.60/2.30; ⌚10am-5pm Jul & Aug, 10am-5pm Thu-Mon Apr-Jun & Sep) is a lot like the castles we drew as kids: thick stone walls around a central keep, perched atop a high motte (mound) with great views of the surrounding countryside.

Four miles south of Pickering, off the A169 to Malton, is the family oriented **Flamingo Land** (flamingoland.co.uk; Kirkby Misperton; per person £28.50, family £95; ⌚9.30am-5pm Apr-Oct, to 6pm Jul & Aug), a vast, sprawling combination of amusement park, complete with rollercoasters, extreme rides, boating lake and a zoo inhabited by lions, giraffes, meerkats, chimps, and a flock of the eponymous pink birds.

Sleeping & Eating

TOP CHOICE **White Swan Hotel** PUB, HOTEL £££
(☎01751-472288; www.white-swan.co.uk; Market Pl; r from £139, mains £13-23; P 📶) The top spot in town successfully combines a smart pub, a superb restaurant serving local produce cooked with a Continental twist, and a luxurious boutique hotel. Nine modern rooms in the converted coach house up the ante with flatscreen TVs and other stylish paraphernalia that add to the luxury found throughout the hotel.

There's a strip of B&Bs on tree-lined Eastgate (the A170 to Scarborough), and a few more on Westgate (heading towards Helmsley). Decent options include **Eleven Westgate** (☎01751-475111; www.elevenwestgate.co.uk; 11 Westgate; s/d from £50/70; P 📶), a pretty house with patio and garden; and the elegant Georgian town house at **17 Burgate** (☎01751-473463; www.17burgate.co.uk; 17 Burgate; s/d £90/110; P @ 📶).

There are several cafes and teashops on Market Pl, but don't overlook the **tearoom** (Pickering Station, Park St; mains £6; ⌚8.30am-4pm) at Pickering station, which serves excellent home-baked goodies and does a tasty roast-pork roll with apple sauce, crackling and stuffing.

Getting There & Away

In addition to the NYMR trains, bus 128 between Helmsley (40 minutes) and Scarborough (50 minutes) runs hourly via Pickering. Bus 840 between Leeds and Whitby links Pickering with York (£8, 70 minutes, hourly).

Danby

POP 290

The Blakey Ridge road from Hutton-le-Hole swoops steeply down to Danby, a compact, stone-built village set deep amid the moors at the head of Eskdale. It's home to the **Moors Centre** (☎01439-772737; www.northyorkmoors.org.uk; Lodge Lane; ⌚10am-5pm Mar-Oct, 11am-4pm Nov-Feb), the national park's HQ, which has interesting exhibits on the natural history of the moors as well as a cafe, an accommodation booking service and a huge range of local guidebooks, maps and leaflets.

WORTH A TRIP

GOATHLAND

This picture-postcard halt on the North Yorkshire Moors Railway stars as Hogsmeade train station in the *Harry Potter* films, and the village appears as Aidensfield in the British TV series *Heartbeat*. It's also the starting point for lots of easy and enjoyable walks, often with the chuff-chuff-chuff of passing steam engines in the background.

One of the most popular hikes is to head northwest from the station (via a gate on the platform on the far side from the village) to the hamlet of Beck Hole, where you can stop for a pork pie and a pint of Black Sheep at the wonderfully atmospheric **Birch Hall Inn** (www.beckhole.info) – it's like stepping into the past. Return to Goathland via the waterfall at **Mallyan Spout**.

You can reach Danby on the delightful **Esk Valley Railway** (www.eskvalleyrailway.co.uk) – Whitby is 20 minutes east, Middlesbrough 45 minutes west (both fares £5.30). There are four departures daily Monday to Saturday, and two on Sunday.

Whitby

POP 13,600

Whitby is a town of two halves, split down the middle by the mouth of the River Esk. It's also a town with two personalities – on the one hand a busy commercial and fishing port with a bustling quayside fishmarket; on the other a traditional seaside resort, complete with sandy beach, amusement arcades and promenading holidaymakers slurping ice-cream cones in the sun.

It's the combination of these two aspects that makes Whitby more interesting than your average resort. The town has managed to retain much of its 18th-century character, recalling the time when James Cook – Whitby's most famous adopted son – was making his first forays at sea on his way towards becoming one of the best-known explorers in history. The narrow streets and alleys of the old town hug the riverside, now lined with restaurants, pubs and cute little shops, all with views across the handsome harbour where colourful fishing boats ply to and fro. Keeping a watchful eye over the whole scene is the atmospheric ruined abbey atop the East Cliff.

But Whitby also has a darker side. Most famously, it was the inspiration and setting

Whitby

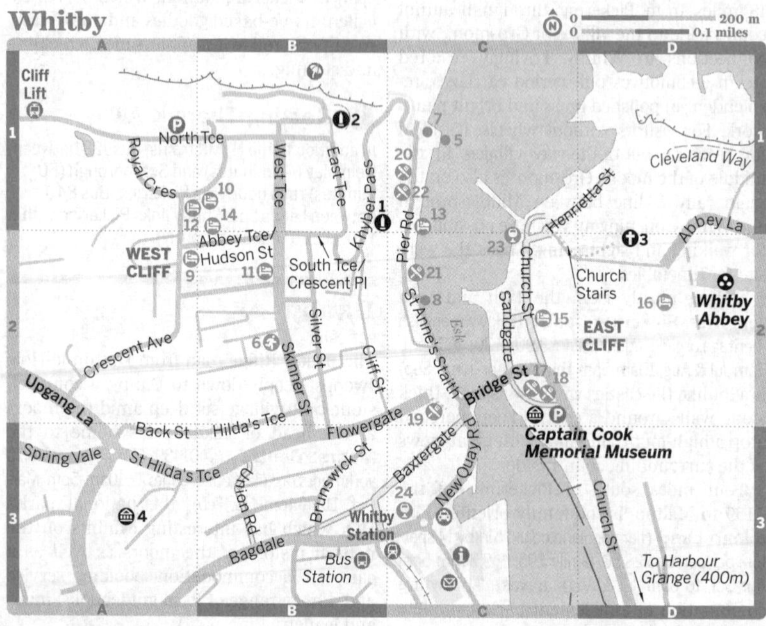

Whitby

Top Sights

Captain Cook Memorial Museum ... C2
Whitby Abbey ... D2

Sights

1 Bram Stoker memorial seat ... B1
2 Captain Cook Monument ... B1
3 St Mary's Church ... D2
Whalebone Arch ... (see 2)
4 Whitby Museum ... A3

Activities, Courses & Tours

5 Cook's Endeavour ... C1
6 Dr Crank's Bike Shack ... B2
7 Elizabeth the Steam Bus ... C1
8 Whitby Coastal Cruises ... C2

Sleeping

9 Argyle House ... A2
10 Avalon Hotel ... B1
11 Bramblewick ... B2
12 Langley Hotel ... A1
13 Marine Hotel ... C1
14 Rosslyn House ... B1
15 Shepherd's Purse ... C2
16 Whitby YHA ... D2

Eating

17 Green's ... C2
18 Humble Pie'n'Mash ... C2
19 Java Cafe-Bar ... C2
20 Magpie Cafe ... C1
21 Moon & Sixpence ... C2
22 Quayside ... C1

Drinking

23 Duke of York ... C2
24 Station Inn ... C3

for part of Bram Stoker's Gothic horror story *Dracula*. Less well known is the fact that Whitby is famous for the **jet** (fossilised wood) that has been mined from the local sea cliffs for centuries; this smooth, black substance was popularised in the 19th century when Queen Victoria took to wearing mourning jewellery made from Whitby jet. In recent years these morbid associations have seen the rise of a series of hugely popular Goth festivals.

Sights

Whitby Abbey RUINS

(EH; www.english-heritage.org.uk; adult/child £6.20/3.70; ⏲10am-6pm Apr-Sep, 10am-4pm Thu-Mon Oct, 10am-4pm Sat & Sun Nov-Mar) There are ruined abbeys and there are picturesque ruined abbeys, and then there's Whitby Abbey, dominating the skyline above the East Cliff like a great Gothic tombstone silhouetted against the sky. Looking more like it was built as an atmospheric film set than as a monastic establishment, it is hardly surprising that this medieval hulk inspired the Victorian novelist Bram Stoker – who holidayed in Whitby – to make it the setting for Count Dracula's dramatic landfall.

From the end of Church St, which has many shops selling jet jewellery, the 199 steps of **Church Stairs** lead steeply up to Whitby Abbey passing the equally atmospheric **St Mary's Church** (admission free; ⏲10am-5pm Apr-Oct, to 4pm Nov-Mar) and its spooky graveyard, a favourite haunt of courting Goth couples.

Captain Cook Memorial Museum MUSEUM

(www.cookmuseumwhitby.co.uk; Grape Lane; adult/child £4.50/3; ⏲9.45am-5pm Apr-Oct, 11am-3pm

CAPTAIN COOK – WHITBY'S ADOPTED SON

Although he was born in Marton (now a suburb of Middlesbrough), Whitby has adopted the famous explorer Captain James Cook, and ever since the first tourists got off the train in Victorian times local entrepreneurs have mercilessly cashed in on his memory, as endless 'Endeavour Cafes' and 'Captain Cook Chip Shops' testify.

Still, Whitby played a key role in Cook's eventual success as a world-famous explorer. It was here that he first went to sea, serving his apprenticeship with local ship owners, and the design of the ships used for his voyages of discovery – including the famous *Endeavour* – were based on the design of Whitby 'cats', flat-bottomed ships that carried coal from Newcastle to London.

DRACULA IN WHITBY

The famous story of *Dracula*, inspiration for a thousand lurid horror movies, was written by Bram Stoker while holidaying in Whitby in 1897 (a blue plaque at 6 Royal Cres marks the house where he stayed). Although most Hollywood versions of the tale concentrate on deepest, darkest Transylvania, a large part of the original book was set in Whitby, and many sites can still be seen today.

The tourist office sells a *Dracula Trail* leaflet (£1), which will direct you to the **Bram Stoker memorial seat** on Khyber Pass, from where you can see all the Whitby-based settings used in the novel.

Mar) This fascinating museum occupies the house of the ship owner with whom Cook began his seafaring career. Highlights include the attic where Cook lodged as a young apprentice, Cook's own maps and letters, etchings from the South Seas and a wonderful model of the *Endeavour*, with all the crew and stores laid out for inspection.

Whitby Sands BEACH

Whitby's days as a seaside resort continue with donkey rides, ice cream and bucket-and-spade escapades on Whitby Sands, stretching west from the harbour mouth. Atop the cliff on the harbour's west side, the **Captain Cook Monument** shows the great man looking out to sea, often with a seagull perched on his head. Nearby is the **Whalebone Arch**, which recalls Whitby's days as a whaling port. Whitby Sands can be reached from West Cliff via the **cliff lift**, a tram-elevator that has been running since 1931.

Whitby Museum MUSEUM

(www.whitbymuseum.org.uk; Pannett Park; adult/child £4/1; ⏲9.30am-4.30pm Tue-Sun) Set in a park to the west of the town centre is the wonderfully eclectic Whitby Museum with its displays of fossil plesiosaurs and dinosaur footprints, Captain Cook memorabilia, ships in bottles, jet jewellery and even the 'Hand of Glory' – a preserved human hand reputedly cut from the corpse of an executed criminal.

Activities

For a cracking day out, take a bus to Robin Hood's Bay, explore the village, have lunch, then hike the 6-mile **clifftop footpath** back to Whitby (allow three hours).

First choice for a bike ride is the excellent 20-mile Whitby-to-Scarborough **Coastal Cycle Trail**, which starts a mile south of the town centre and follows the route of an old railway line via Robin Hood's Bay. Bikes can be hired from **Dr Crank's Bike Shack** (☎01947 606 661; 20 Skinner St; ⏲10am-4.30pm Mon, Tue & Thu-Sat) in Whitby, or **Trailways** (www.trailways.info) at Hawsker for £15 to £22 a day.

Tours

Cook's Endeavour BOAT TOUR

(☎01723-364100; www.endeavourwhitby.com; Pier Rd; adult/child £3/2; ⏲Easter-Oct) Take a half-hour trip along the coast in a scaled down 2001 replica of Captain Cook's ship *Endeavour*, the star of numerous TV programs. Cruise times are weather and tide dependent – call ahead to check.

Elizabeth the Steam Bus BUS TOUR

(www.whitbysteambusandcharabanc.co.uk; Pier Rd; adult/child £4/2; ⏲Mar-Nov) Toot-toot! All aboard for a 20-minute spin around the town in this 1931 steam-powered bus.

Whitby Coastal Cruises BOAT TOUR

(www.whitbycoastalcruises.co.uk; Brewery Steps, St Anne's Staith; ⏲Apr-Oct) Offers trips around the harbour in the *Esk Belle II* (£2.50, 20 minutes, daily), as well as longer cruises along the coast to Staithes and back (£12, 3½ hours, twice a week). From August to October there are also whale-spotting cruises aboard the *Specksioneer* motor yacht.

Festivals & Events

Whitby Goth Weekends COUNTER CULTURE

(www.whitbygothweekend.co.uk; tickets £50) Goth heaven, with gigs, events and the Bizarre Bazaar – dozens of traders selling Goth gear, jewellery, art and music. Twice yearly on the last weekends of April and October.

Whitby Spring Session MUSIC & ARTS

(www.moorandcoast.co.uk; tickets from £35) Beards, sandals and real ale galore at this traditional festival of folk music, dance and dubious Celtic art; on the May Bank Holiday weekend.

Sleeping

B&Bs are concentrated in West Cliff in the streets to the south and east of Royal Cres; if a house here ain't offering B&B, chances are it's derelict. Accommodation can be tough to find at festival times; it's wise to book ahead.

TOP CHOICE **Marine Hotel** INN £££
(☎01947-605022; www.the-marine-hotel.co.uk; 13 Marine Pde; r £135-150; wi-fi) Feeling more like mini-suites than ordinary hotel accommodation, the four bedrooms at the Marine are quirky, stylish and comfortable – it's the sort of place that makes you want to stay in rather than go out. Ask for one of the two rooms that have a balcony – they have great views across the harbour.

Langley Hotel B&B ££
(☎01947-604250; www.langleyhotel.com; 16 Royal Cres; s/d from £70/105; P wi-fi) With a cream-and-crimson colour scheme, and a gilt four-poster bed in one room, this grand old guesthouse exudes a whiff of Victorian splendour. Go for room 1 or 2, if possible, to make the most of the panoramic views from West Cliff.

Avalon Hotel B&B ££
(☎01947-825315; www.avalonhotelwhitby.org.uk; 13-14 Royal Cres; d from £66) Just a few doors along from the house where Bram Stoker stayed during his holiday in 1897, the Avalon shares the same glorious sea views as those enjoyed by the author of *Dracula*. The rooms are clean and comfortable – many have recently been refurbished – and the owner is as friendly and helpful as you could hope for.

Shepherd's Purse GUESTHOUSE ££
(☎01947-820228; www.theshepherdspurse.com; 95 Church St; r £60-75) This place combines a beads-and-baubles boutique and wholefood shop with guest accommodation in the courtyard at the back. The plainer rooms share a bathroom and are perfectly adequate, but we recommend the rustic en suite bedrooms situated around the courtyard; the four-poster beds feel a bit like they've been shoehorned in, but the atmosphere is cute rather than cramped. Breakfast is not provided.

Whitby YHA HOSTEL £
(☎0845 371 9049; www.yha.org.uk; Church Lane; dm £18-22; P @ wi-fi) With an unbeatable position next to the abbey, this hostel doesn't have to try too hard, and it doesn't. You'll have to book well in advance to get your body into one of the basic bunks. Hike up the 199 steps from the town, or take bus 97 from the train station to Whitby Abbey (twice hourly Monday to Saturday).

Harbour Grange HOSTEL £
(☎01947-600817; www.whitbybackpackers.co.uk; Spital Bridge; dm from £17) Overlooking the harbour and less than 10 minutes' walk from the train station, this tidy hostel is conveniently located but has an 11.30pm curfew – good thing we're all teetotalling early-to-bedders, right?

Trailways SELF CATERING ££
(☎01947-820207; www.trailways.info; Hawsker; from £290 for 3 nights; P) If travelling on the North Yorkshire Moors Railway has given you a taste for trains, how about sleeping in one? Trailways has a beautifully converted InterCity125 coach parked at the old Hawsker train station on the Whitby–Scarborough cycle route, offering luxurious self-catering accommodation with all mod cons for two to seven people.

Rosslyn House B&B ££
(☎01947-604086; www.guesthousewhitby.co.uk; 11 Abbey Tce; s/d from £40/58) Bright and cheerful with a friendly welcome.

Bramblewick B&B ££
(☎01947-604504; www.bramblewickwhitby.com; 3 Havelock Pl; s/d £35/70; P wi-fi) Friendly owners, hearty breakfasts and abbey views from the top-floor room.

Argyle House B&B ££
(☎01947-602733; www.argyle-house.co.uk; 18 Hudson St; per person £28-35; wi-fi) Comfortable as old slippers, with kippers for breakfast.

Eating

Green's SEAFOOD ££
(☎01947-600284; www.greensofwhitby.com; 13 Bridge St; mains £13-20; ⊙lunch & dinner Mon-Fri, noon-10pm Sat & Sun) The classiest eatery in town is ideally situated to take its pick of the fish and shellfish freshly landed at the harbour. Grab a hearty lunch in the ground floor bistro (*moules-frites*, sausage and mash, fish and chips) or head to the upstairs restaurant for a sophisticated dinner date.

Moon & Sixpence BRASSERIE ££
(☎01947-604416; www.moon-and-sixpence.co.uk; 5 Marine Pde; mains £10-16; ⊙10am-midnight; wi-fi) This brasserie and cocktail bar has a prime

position, with views across the harbour to the abbey ruins. The seafood-dominated menu concentrates on hearty, straightforward dishes such as chunky vegetable soup, fish pie, homemade burgers, mussels and chips, and seafood chowder.

Magpie Cafe SEAFOOD ££
(www.magpiecafe.co.uk; 14 Pier Rd; mains £7-16; 11.30am-9pm) The Magpie flaunts its reputation for serving the 'World's Best Fish and Chips'. Damn fine they are too, but the world and his dog knows about it, and summertime queues can stretch along the street. Fish and chips from the takeaway counter cost £5; the sit-down restaurant is dearer, but offers a wide range of seafood dishes, from grilled sea bass to paella.

Humble Pie'n'Mash BRITISH £
(www.humblepienmash.com; 163 Church St; mains £5; 12.30-8.30pm Mon-Sat, 12.30-5pm Sun) Superb homemade pies with fillings ranging from lamb, leek and rosemary to roast veg and goat's cheese, served in a cosy, timber-framed cottage.

Java Cafe-Bar CAFE £
(2 Flowergate; mains £5-7; 8am-6pm;) A cool little diner with stainless-steel counters and retro decor, with music vids on the flatscreen and a menu of healthy salads, sandwiches and wraps washed down with excellent coffee.

Quayside FISH & CHIPS ££
(www.whitbyfishandchips.com; 7 Pier Rd; mains £7-14; 11am-10pm;) Top-notch fish and chips minus the 'World's Best' tag line – this place is your best bet if you want to avoid the queues at the Magpie (takeaway prices £5).

Drinking

Station Inn PUB
(New Quay Rd) Best place in town for atmosphere and real ale with an impressive range of cask-conditioned beers including Timothy Taylor's Golden Best and Ossett Silver King.

Duke of York PUB
(www.dukeofyork.co.uk; Church St) Popular watering hole at the bottom of the Church Stairs, with great views over the harbour. Serves Timothy Taylor ales.

Information

Post Office (Langbourne Rd; 8.30am-5.30pm Mon-Sat) Located inside the Co-op supermarket.

Tourist Office (01947-602674; www.visitwhitby.com; Langbourne Rd; 9.30am-6pm May-Sep, 10am-4.30pm Oct-Apr)

Getting There & Away

BUS Buses 93 and X93 run south to Scarborough (one hour, every 30 minutes) via Robin Hood's Bay (15 minutes, hourly), and north to Middlesbrough (hourly), with fewer services on Sunday. The Coastliner service 840 runs from Leeds to Whitby (£12.50, 3¼ hours, six daily Monday to Saturday) via York and Pickering.

TRAIN Coming from the north, you can get to Whitby by train along the Esk Valley Railway from Middlesbrough (£5.30, 1½ hours, four per day), with connections from Durham and Newcastle. From the south, it's easier to get a train from York to Scarborough, then a bus from Scarborough to Whitby.

Robin Hood's Bay

Picturesque Robin Hood's Bay (www.robin-hoods-bay.co.uk) is the end point of the famous Coast to Coast Walk (p565). It has nothing to do with the hero of Sherwood Forest – the origin of the name is a mystery, and the locals call it Bay Town, or just Bay. But there's no denying that this fishing village is one of the prettiest spots on the Yorkshire coast.

Leave your car at the parking area in the upper village (minimum £3 for four hours), where 19th-century ship's captains built comfortable Victorian villas, and walk downhill to **Old Bay**, the oldest part of the village (don't even think about driving down). This maze of narrow lanes and passages is dotted with tearooms, pubs, craft shops and artists' studios – there's even a tiny cinema – and at low tide you can go down onto the beach and fossick around in the rock pools. The NT-listed **Old Coastguard Station** (www.nationaltrust.org.uk; The Dock; admission free; 10am-5pm Apr-Oct, 10am-4pm Sat & Sun Nov-Mar) houses an exhibition on local geology and natural history.

There are several pubs and cafes – the best pub for ambience and real ale is **Ye Dolphin** (King St), while the **Swell Cafe** (www.swell.org.uk; Chapel St; mains £5-7; 10am-4pm Mon-Fri, 10am-4.30pm Sat & Sun) does great coffee and has a terrace with a view over the beach.

Robin Hood's Bay is 6 miles south of Whitby; you can walk here along the coastal path in two or three hours, or bike it along the cycle trail in 40 minutes. Also, bus 93 runs hourly between Whitby and Scarborough via Robin Hood's Bay – the bus stop is at the top of the hill, in the new part of town.

YORKSHIRE DALES NATIONAL PARK

The Yorkshire Dales – named from the old Norse word *dalr*, meaning 'valleys' – is the central jewel in the necklace of three national parks strung across the neck of northern England, with the dramatic fells of the Lake District to the west and the brooding heaths of the North Yorkshire Moors to the east.

From well-known names such as Wensleydale and Ribblesdale, to obscure and evocative Langstrothdale and Arkengarthdale, these glacial valleys are characterised by a distinctive landscape of high heather moorland, stepped skylines and flat-topped hills. Down in the green valleys, patchworked with drystone dykes, are picture-postcard towns and hamlets, where sheep and cattle still graze on village greens. And in the limestone country in the southern Dales you'll find England's best examples of karst scenery.

The Dales have been protected as a national park since the 1950s, assuring their status as a walker's and cyclist's paradise. But there's plenty for non-walkers as well, from exploring the legacy of literary vet James Herriot of *All Creatures Great and Small* fame, to sampling Wallace and Gromit's favourite teatime snack at the Wensleydale Creamery.

The *Visitor* newspaper, available from tourist offices, lists local events and walks guided by park rangers, as well as many places to stay and eat. The official park website (www.yorkshiredales.org.uk) is also useful.

Yorkshire Dales National Park

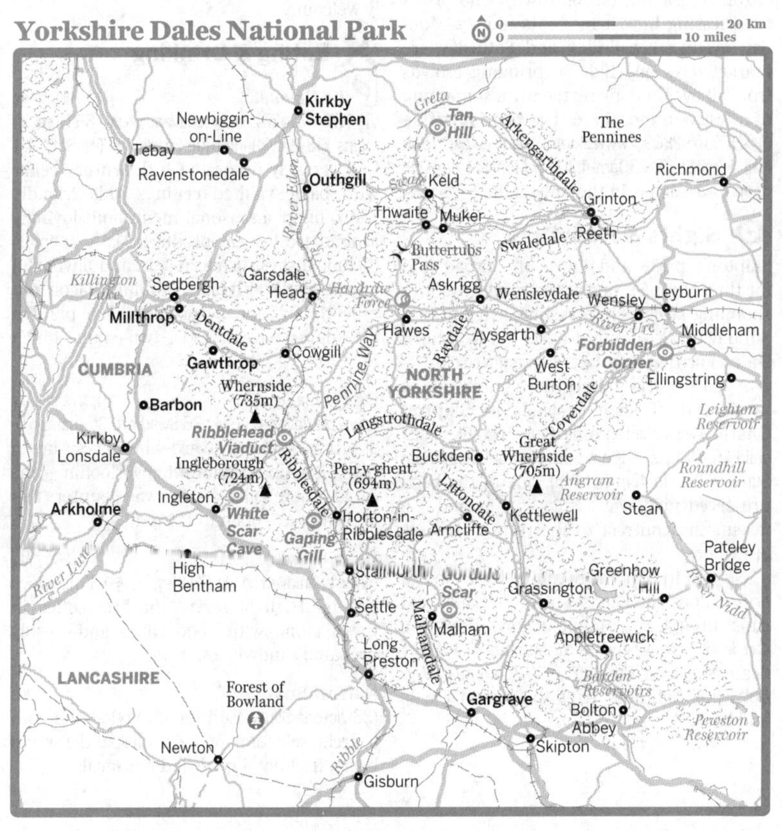

Getting There & Around

Around 90% of visitors to the park arrive by car, and the narrow roads can be extremely crowded in summer; parking can also be a serious problem. If you can, try to use public transport as much as possible.

Pick up a *Dales Bus Timetable* from tourist offices, or consult the **Dalesbus** (www.dalesbus.org) website.

By train, the best and most interesting access to the Dales is via the famous **Settle–Carlisle Line** (www.settle-carlisle.co.uk). Trains run between Leeds and Carlisle, stopping at Skipton, Settle, and numerous small villages, offering unrivalled access to the hills straight from the station platform.

Skipton

POP 14,300

This busy market town on the southern edge of the Dales takes its name from the Anglo-Saxon *sceape ton* (sheep town) – no prizes for guessing how it made its money. Monday, Wednesday, Friday and Saturday are market days on High St, bringing crowds from all over and giving the town something of a festive atmosphere. The **tourist office** (☎01756-792809; www.skiptononline.co.uk; Town Hall, High St; ⏲9.30am-4.30pm Mon-Sat Apr-Oct, to 4pm Nov-Mar) is in the town hall.

Sights & Activities

Skipton's pride and joy is the broad and bustling **High St**, one of the most attractive shopping streets in Yorkshire. On the first Sunday of the month it hosts the **Northern Dales Farmers Market** (www.ndfm.co.uk).

A gate to the side of the church at the north end of High St leads to **Skipton Castle** (www.skiptoncastle.co.uk; High St; adult/child £6.70/4.10; ⏲10am-6pm Mon-Sat, noon-6pm Sun Mar-Sep, to 4pm Oct-Feb), one of the best-preserved medieval castles in England – a fascinating contrast to the ruins you'll see elsewhere.

No trip to Skipton is complete without a cruise along the Leeds–Liverpool Canal that runs through the middle of town. **Pennine Cruisers** (www.penninecruisers.com; The Wharf, Coach St; adult/child £3/2; ⏲10.30am-dusk Mar-Oct) runs half-hour trips to Skipton Castle and back.

Sleeping

There's a strip of B&Bs just outside the centre on Keighley Rd. All those between Nos 46 and 57 are worth trying.

Park Hill B&B ££

(☎01756-792772; www.parkhillskipton.co.uk; 17 Grassington Rd; d £75; P@☎) From the complementary glass of sherry on arrival, to the hearty breakfasts based on local produce including farm-fresh eggs and homegrown tomatoes, this B&B provides a real Yorkshire welcome. It enjoys an attractive rural location half a mile north of the town centre, on the B6265 road towards Grassington.

Carlton House B&B ££

(☎01756-700921; www.carltonhouseskipton.co.uk; 46 Keighley Rd; s/d from £30/60) A handsome house with five pretty, comfortable rooms – no frills but lots of floral prints. The B&B is deservedly popular on account of the friendly welcome.

Eating & Drinking

Le Caveau FRENCH ££

(☎01756-794274; www.lecaveau.co.uk; 86 High St; mains £13-23; ⏲lunch Tue-Fri, dinner Tue-Sat) Set in a stylishly decorated 16th-century cellar with barrel-vaulted ceilings, this friendly bistro offers a seasonal menu built lovingly around fresh local produce. Daily specials include dishes such as a light and flavourful quiche made with black pudding, bacon and mushrooms, and a succulent fish pie. On weekdays you can get a two-course lunch for £10.

Bizzie Lizzies FISH & CHIPS £

(www.bizzielizzies.co.uk; 36 Swadford St; mains £6-9; ⏲11am-9pm) An award-winning, sit-down fish-and-chip restaurant overlooking the canal. There's also a takeaway counter (fish and chips £5, open to 11.15pm).

Bean Loved CAFE

(www.beanloved.co.uk; 17 Otley St; ☎) This place just off High St serves the best coffee in town, along with good cakes and freshly prepared sandwiches.

Narrow Boat PUB

(38 Victoria St) A traditionally styled pub with a great selection of local ales and foreign beers, friendly service and bar meals.

Getting There & Away

For Grassington, take bus 72 (30 minutes, hourly Monday to Saturday, no Sunday service) from Skipton train station, or 66A (hourly on Sunday) from the Market Place.

Skipton is the last stop on the Metro rail network from Leeds and Bradford (£8.40, 45 minutes, half-hourly, hourly on Sunday).

Bolton Abbey

The tiny village and country estate of Bolton Abbey, owned by the Duke of Devonshire, is about 5 miles east of Skipton. The big draw here is the ruined church of **Bolton Priory** (www.boltonabbey.com; admission free, parking £6; 9am-7pm Apr-Oct, last admission 5.30pm, shorter hours Nov-Mar), an evocative and beautiful 12th-century building. Its soaring arches and huge windows silhouetted against the sky have inspired artists such as Wordsworth and Turner. Part of the building is still used as a church today.

Apart from the priory ruins, the main attraction is the scenic **River Wharfe** which flows through the grounds – there's a network of walking trails beside the river and through the surrounding area. It's very popular with families (part of the riverbank looks like a beach at weekends); you can buy teas and ice creams in the **Cavendish Pavilion**, a short walk from the priory. Other highlights include the stepping stones – a large gap between stones in the middle of the river frequently forces faint-hearted walkers to turn around and use the bridge – and **The Strid**, a picturesque wooded gorge just upstream from the pavilion, carpeted with wild garlic and bluebells in spring.

The **Devonshire Arms Country House Hotel** (01756-718111; www.thedevonshirearms.co.uk; s/d from £215/275; P@) – also owned by the duke of Devonshire – is actually more like a 'stately home' hotel. The decoration of each bedroom was designed by the duchess herself, and while her tastes might not be everyone's cup of tea, there's no arguing with the quality and beauty of the furnishings; almost all of them were permanently borrowed from another of their properties, Chatsworth in Derbyshire. The hotel's **Burlington Restaurant** (3-course dinner £65) has a Michelin star, though the less formal **Devonshire Brasserie** (mains £12-23) is more to our taste.

There are half-hourly buses to Bolton Abbey from Skipton and Grassington Monday to Saturday; on Sunday there's only an hourly service from Skipton.

Grassington

POP 1120

The perfect base for jaunts around the south Dales, Grassington's handsome Georgian centre teems with walkers and visitors throughout the summer months, soaking up an atmosphere that – despite the odd touch of faux rusticity – is as attractive and traditional as you'll find in these parts.

The **tourist office** (01756-751690; Hebden Rd; 9.30am-5pm Apr-Oct, Fri-Sun only Nov-Mar) is beside the big car park on the edge of town.

Sleeping & Eating

There are several B&Bs along and just off Main St.

TOP CHOICE Devonshire Fell HOTEL £££

(01756-718111; www.devonshirefell.co.uk; Burnsall; s/d from £129/159; P@) A sister property to Bolton Abbey's Devonshire Arms Country House Hotel, this former gentleman's club for mill owners has a much more contemporary feel, with beautiful modern furnishings crafted by local experts. The Conservatory Restaurant (also used as a breakfast room) has a stunning view over the valley. It's 3 miles southeast of Grassington on the B6160.

Ashfield House B&B ££

(01756-752584; www.ashfieldhouse.co.uk; Summers Fold; r from £96; P@) A secluded 17th-century country house behind a walled garden with exposed stone walls, open fireplaces and an all-round cosy feel. It's just off the main square.

Cobblestones Café CAFE £

(3 The Square; mains £3-6; 9.30am-5pm;) A cute little cafe, dog-friendly and popular with locals as well as visitors. In addition to cakes, coffee and Yorkshire tea, the menu includes lunch dishes such as fish and chips and steak-and-ale pie, and a full English breakfast served till noon.

Malham

POP 120

Stretching west from Grassington to Ingleton is the largest area of limestone country in England, a distinctive landscape dotted with dry valleys, potholes, limestone pavements and gorges. Two of the most spectacular features – Malham Cove and Gordale Scar – lie near the pretty village of Malham.

The **national park centre** (☎01969-652380; www.yorkshiredales.org.uk; ⏰10am-5pm daily Apr-Oct, 10am-4pm Sat & Sun Nov-Mar) at the southern edge of the village has the usual wealth of information.

Sights & Activities

A 0.75 mile walk north from Malham village leads to **Malham Cove**, a huge rock amphitheatre lined with 80m-high vertical cliffs – peregrine falcons nest here in spring, when the Royal Society for the Protection of Birds (RSPB) sets up a birdwatching lookout. You can hike up the steep left-hand side of the cove (on the Pennine Way footpath) to see the extensive limestone pavement above the cliffs. Another 1.5 miles further north is **Malham Tarn**, a glacial lake and nature reserve.

A mile east of Malham along a narrow road (very limited parking) is spectacular **Gordale Scar**, a deep limestone canyon with scenic cascades and the remains of an Iron-Age settlement. The national park centre has a leaflet describing the **Malham Landscape Trail**, a 5-mile circular walk that takes in Malham Cove, Gordale Scar and the Janet's Foss waterfall.

The **Pennine Way** passes through Malham; Horton-in-Ribblesdale lies a day's hike away to the northwest.

Sleeping

Beck Hall HOTEL ££
(☎01729-830332; www.beckhallmalham.com; s/d from £45/65; P 📶) This rambling 17th-century country house on the edge of the village has 15 individually decorated rooms – we recommend the Green Room, with its old-style furnishings and four-poster bed. There's a gurgling stream flowing through the garden and a nice tearoom (open 11am to 6pm Tuesday to Sunday).

Malham YHA HOSTEL £
(☎0845 371 9529; www.yha.org.uk; dm £19.50; P) You'll find this purpose-built hostel in the village centre; the facilities are top-notch and young children are well catered for.

Getting There & Away

There are two to five buses a day from Skipton to Malham – check the Dalesbus (p598) website or ask at Skipton tourist office for details.

Note that Malham is reached via narrow roads that can be very congested in summer; leave your car at the national park centre and walk into the village.

Ribblesdale & the Three Peaks

Scenic Ribblesdale cuts through the south-western corner of the Yorkshire Dales National Park, where the skyline is dominated by a trio of distinctive hills known as the **Three Peaks** – Whernside (735m), Ingleborough (724m) and Pen-y-ghent (694m). Easily accessible via the Settle-Carlisle railway line, this is one of England's most popular areas for outdoor activities, attracting thousands of hikers, cyclists and cavers each weekend.

SETTLE

POP 3621

The busy market town of Settle, dominated by its grand neo-Gothic town hall, is the gateway to Ribblesdale and marks the beginning of the scenic part of the famous Settle–Carlisle railway line. Narrow cobbled streets lined with shops and pubs lead out from the central market square (Tuesday is market day), and the town offers plenty of accommodation options.

The **tourist office** (☎01729-825192; Town Hall, Cheapside; ⏰9.30am-4.30pm Apr-Oct, to 4pm Nov-Mar) has maps and guidebooks.

Around the main square there are several good cafes, including **Ye Olde Naked Man** (Market Pl; mains £4-7), formerly an undertakers (look for the 'naked man' on the outside wall, dated 1663); and the excellent **Shambles** (Market Pl; mains £6-8) fish and chip shop.

Trains from Leeds heading to Carlisle stop at Settle station near the town centre (£11, one hour, eight daily); those heading for Morecambe (on the west coast) stop at Giggleswick, about 1.5 miles outside town.

HORTON-IN-RIBBLESDALE

POP 560

A favourite with outdoor enthusiasts, the little village of Horton and its railway station is 5 miles north of Settle. Everything centres on the Pen-y-ghent Cafe, which acts as the village tourist office, wet-weather retreat and hikers' information centre.

Horton is the starting point for climbing Pen-y-ghent and for doing the **Three Peaks Walk**; it's also a stop on the Pennine Way. At the head of the valley, 5 miles north of Horton, is the spectacular **Ribblehead Viaduct**,

THREE PEAKS CHALLENGES

Since 1968 more than 200,000 hikers have taken up the challenge of climbing Yorkshire's Three Peaks in less than 12 hours. The circular 25-mile route begins and ends at the Pen-y-ghent Cafe (p601) in Horton-in-Ribblesdale – where you clock-in and clock-out to verify your time – and takes in the summits of Pen-y-ghent, Whernside and Ingleborough. Succeed, and you're a member of the cafe's Three Peaks of Yorkshire Club. You can find details of the route at www.merseyventure.com/yorks and download a guide (£4) at www.walkingworld.com (walk ID 4228 and 4229).

Fancy a more gruelling test of your endurance? Then join the fell-runners in the annual **Three Peaks Race** (www.threepeaksrace.org.uk) on the last Saturday in April, and run the route instead of walking it. First held in 1954 when six people competed, it now attracts around 900 entries; the course record is two hours, 43 minutes and three seconds.

In the last week of September, cyclists get their chance too in the **Three Peaks Cyclo-Cross** (www.3peakscyclocross.org.uk) which covers 38 miles of rough country and 1524m of ascent.

built in 1874 and the longest on the Settle-Carlisle Line – more than 30m high and 400m long. You can hike there along the Pennine Way and travel back by train from Ribblehead station.

Sleeping & Eating

Horton is popular, so it's wise to book accommodation in advance.

Golden Lion INN
(☎01729-860206; www.goldenlionhotel.co.uk; s/d from £40/65, bunkhouse per person £12) The Golden Lion is a lively pub that offers comfortable B&B bedrooms, a 40-bed bunkhouse, and three public bars where you can tuck into a bit of grub washed down with a pint of hand-pulled ale.

Holme Farm Campsite CAMPSITE £
(☎01729-860281; per person £2, per tent £2) Basic, no-frills campsite right next door to the Golden Lion pub, much used by Pennine Way hikers.

Pen-y-Ghent Cafe CAFE
(mains [illegible]; 9am-5.30pm Mon & Wed-Fri, 8.30am-5pm Sat & Sun) A traditional caff run by the same family since 1965, the Pen-y-ghent fills walkers' fuel tanks with fried egg and chips, homemade scones and pint-sized mugs of tea. It also sells maps, guidebooks and walking gear.

INGLETON

POP 2000

The village of Ingleton, perched precariously above a river gorge, is the caving capital of England. It sits at the foot of one of the country's most extensive areas of limestone upland, crowned by the dominating peak of Ingleborough and riddled with countless potholes and cave systems.

The **tourist office** (☎01524-241049; www.visitingleton.co.uk; 10am-4pm Apr-Sep) is beside the main car park, while **Bernie's Cafe** (4 Main St; 9am-4pm Mon, Wed & Thu, 9am-6pm Fri-Sun) is the centre of the local caving scene.

Ingleton is the starting point for two famous Dales hikes. The shorter and easier of the two is the circular, 4.5-mile **Waterfalls Walk** (www.ingletonwaterfallstrail.co.uk; adult/child £5/2), which passes through native oak woodland on its way past a series of spectacular waterfalls on the River Twiss and River Doe. The more strenuous option is **Ingleborough** (724m). Around 120,000 people climb this hill every year, but that doesn't make the 6-mile round trip any less of an effort; this is a proper hill walk, so pack waterproofs, food, water, a map and a compass.

Although most of the local caves are accessible only to experienced potholers, some are open to the general public. **White Scar Cave** (www.whitescarcave.co.uk; 80-min guided tour adult/child [illegible]; 10am-4.30pm Feb-Oct, Sat & Sun only Nov-Jan) is the longest show cave in England, with a series of underground waterfalls and impressive dripstone formations leading to the 100m-long **Battlefield Cavern**, one of the largest cave chambers in the country. The cave is 1.5 miles northeast of the village on the B6255 road.

Gaping Gill, on the southeastern flank of Ingleborough, is one of the most famous caves in England. A huge vertical pothole 105m deep, it was the largest known cave

THE SETTLE–CARLISLE LINE

The 72-mile Settle–Carlisle Line (SCL), built between 1869 and 1875, offers one of England's most scenic railway journeys. The line's construction was one of the great engineering achievements of the Victorian era: 5000 navvies armed with picks and shovels built 325 bridges, 21 viaducts and blasted 14 tunnels in horrific conditions – nearly 200 of them died in the process.

Trains run between Leeds and Carlisle via Settle about eight times per day. The first section of the journey from Leeds is along the Aire Valley, stopping at **Keighley**, where the Keighley & Worth Valley Railway branches off to **Haworth**, **Skipton** (gateway to the southern Dales) and **Settle**. The train then labours up the valley beside the River Ribble, through **Horton-in-Ribblesdale**, across the spectacular **Ribblehead Viaduct** and then through Blea Moor Tunnel to reach remote **Dent station**, at 350m the highest main-line station in the country.

The line reaches its highest point (356m) at Ais Gill where it leaves the Dales behind before easing down to **Kirkby Stephen**. The last halts are **Appleby** and **Langwathby**, just northeast of Penrith (a jumping-off point for the Lake District), before the train finally pulls into **Carlisle**.

The entire journey from Leeds to Carlisle takes two hours and 40 minutes and costs £26/32 for a single/day return. Various hop-on/hop-off passes for one or three days are also available. You can pick up a free SCL timetable – which includes a colour map of the line and brief details about places of interest – from most Yorkshire stations. For more information contact **National Rail Enquiries** (08457 48 49 50; www.nationalrail.co.uk) or see www.settle-carlisle.co.uk.

shaft in the UK until the discovery of Titan in Derbyshire in 1999. Gaping Gill is normally off-limits to non-cavers but, twice a year during the May and August bank holiday weekends, local caving clubs set up a winch so that members of the public can descend into the dark depths of the shaft in a special chair (£10 per person). For details see www.bpc-cave.org.uk and www.cravenpotholeclub.org, and click on the Gaping Gill link.

Ingleton is 10 miles northwest of Settle; take bus 581 from Settle train station (25 minutes, two daily).

Hawes

POP 700

Hawes is the beating heart of Wensleydale, a thriving and picturesque market town (market day is Tuesday) that has the added attraction of its own waterfall in the village centre. On busy summer weekends, however, Hawes' narrow arteries can get seriously clogged with traffic – leave the car in the parking area beside the **national park centre** (01969-666210; Station Yard; 10am-5pm year round) at the eastern entrance to the village.

Sights & Activities

Sharing a building with the park centre is the **Dales Countryside Museum** (01969-666210; Station Yard; adult/child £4/free; 10am-5pm, closed Jan), a beautifully presented social history of the area that explains the forces that shaped the landscape, from geology to lead mining to land enclosure.

At the other end of the village lies the **Wensleydale Creamery** (www.wensleydale.co.uk; tour £2.50; 9.30am-5pm Mon-Sat, 10am-4.30pm Sun), devoted to the production of Wallace and Gromit's favourite crumbly, white cheese. You can visit the cheese museum and then try-before-you-buy in the shop, which is free to enter. There are one-hour guided tours of the creamery between 10am and 3pm.

About 1.5 miles north of Hawes is 30m-high **Hardraw Force**, the highest unbroken waterfall in England, although by international standards it's not that impressive (except after heavy rain). Access is through the Green Dragon pub, which levies a £2 admission fee.

Sleeping & Eating

Herriot's Guest House B&B ££
(01969-667536; www.herriotsinhawes.co.uk; Main St; r per person from £40;) A delightful

guesthouse set in an old stone building close to the bridge by the waterfall, Herriot's has seven comfy, en suite bedrooms set above an art gallery and coffee shop.

Green Dragon Inn INN ££
(01969-667392; www.greendragonhardraw.co.uk; Hardraw; B&B per person £35-45, dm £15;) A fine old pub with flagstone floors, low timber beams, ancient oak furniture and Theakstons on draught, the Dragon serves up a tasty steak-and-ale pie and offers bunkhouse accommodation, or B&B in plain but adequate rooms, as well as a pair of larger, more comfortable suites.

Bainbridge Ings Caravan & Camp Site CAMPSITE £
(01969-667354; www.bainbridge-ings.co.uk; hikers & cyclists per person £5, car, tent & 2 adults £14;) An attractive site set in stone-walled fields around a spacious farmhouse about half a mile east of town. Gas, milk and eggs are sold on site.

Hawes YHA HOSTEL £
(0845 371 9120; www.yha.org.uk; Lancaster Tce; dm £19.50; P) A modern place on the western edge of town, at the junction of the main A684 (Aysgarth Rd) and B6255, this is a family friendly hostel with great views of Wensleydale.

Cart House TEAROOM £
(01969-667691; Hardraw; mains £6; Mar-Nov) Across the bridge from the Green Dragon, this craft shop and tearoom offers a healthier diet of homemade soup, organic bread, and a 'Fellman's Lunch' of Wensleydale cheese, pickle and salad. There's a basic campsite at the back (£11 for two adults, tent and car).

Getting There & Away

Buses 156 and 157 run from Hawes to Leyburn (50 minutes, four daily Monday to Saturday), where you can connect with buses to/from Richmond.

From Garsdale station on the Settle–Carlisle Line, bus 113 runs to Hawes (20 minutes, three daily Monday to Friday); on Sundays and bank holidays from April to October bus 831 goes to Hawes from Ribblehead station (25 minutes, one daily). Check bus times Traveline Yorkshire (p565) or a tourist office before using these routes.

Richmond

POP 8200

The handsome market town of Richmond is one of England's best-kept secrets, perched on a rocky outcrop overlooking the River Swale and guarded by the ruins of a massive castle. A maze of cobbled streets radiates from the broad, sloping market square (market day is Saturday), lined with elegant Georgian buildings and photogenic stone cottages, with glimpses of the surrounding hills and dales peeking through the gaps.

Sights

Top of the pile is the impressive heap that is EH-listed **Richmond Castle** (www.english-heritage.org.uk; Market Pl; adult/child £4.70/2.80; 10am-6pm Apr-Sep, 10am-4pm Oct, 10am-4pm Sat & Sun Nov-Mar), founded in 1070 and one of the first castles in England since Roman times to be built of stone. It's had many uses through the years, including a stint as a prison for conscientious objectors during WWI (there's a small and sobering exhibition about their part in the castle's history). The best part is the view from the top of the remarkably well-preserved 30m-high keep which towers over the River Swale.

WORTH A TRIP

WEST BURTON

Hidden away at the foot of a valley leading off Wensleydale, West Burton is easy to miss. But this picturesque hamlet is often voted 'Most beautiful Village in England', and beautiful it most certainly is. There are no real sights as such, just a necklace of sandstone cottages, including a pub, tearoom, village shop and butcher shop, strung around a vast village green complete with ancient market cross and punishment stocks. There's not much to do except soak up the view, or perhaps take a stroll to Cauldron Falls, the local beauty spot. By then, it'll be time for a pint...

To find West Burton, turn south off the A684 Leyburn to Hawes road, a few miles east of Aysgarth, on the B6160 (signposted West Burton, Kettlewell and Grassington).

Richmond

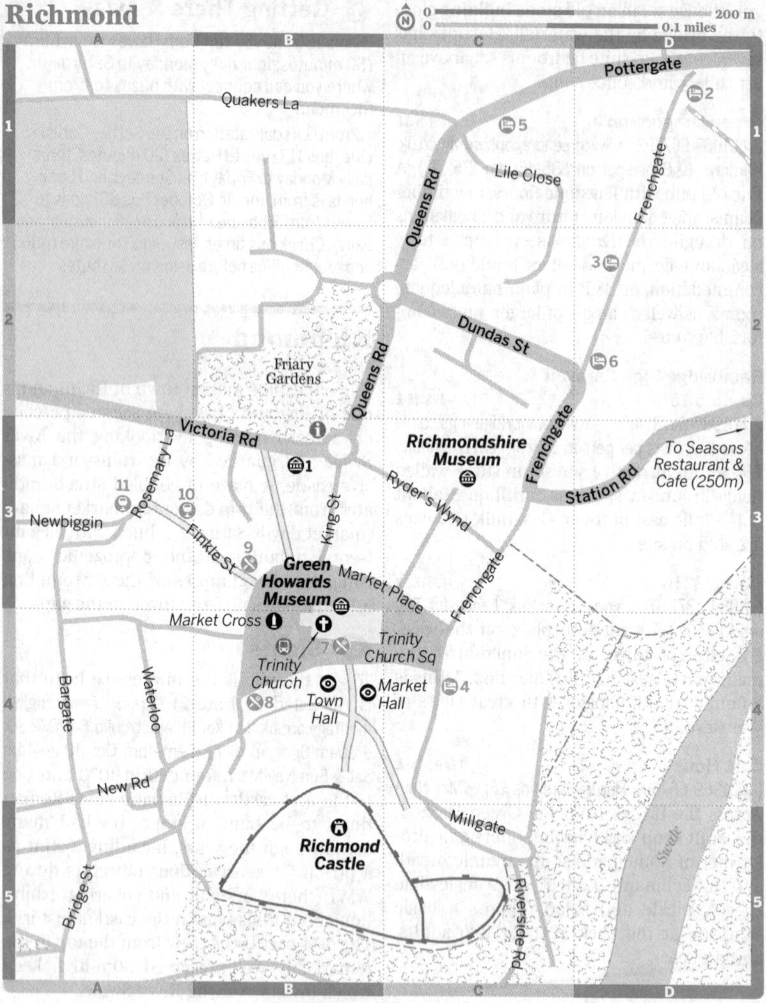

Military buffs will enjoy the **Green Howards Museum** (www.greenhowards.org.uk; Trinity Church Sq; adult/child £3.50/1; ⏲10am-4.30pm Mon-Sat, closed 24 Dec-31 Jan, also 12.30-4.30pm Sun Apr-Oct), which pays tribute to the famous Yorkshire regiment. In a different vein, the **Richmondshire Museum** (www.richmondshiremuseum.org.uk; Ryder's Wynd; adult/child £3/free; ⏲10.30am-4pm Apr-Oct) is a delight, with local history exhibits including an early Yorkshire cave-dwelling and displays on lead mining, which forever altered the Swaledale landscape a century ago. You can also see the original set that served as James Herriot's surgery in the TV series *All Creatures Great and Small.*

Built in 1788, the **Georgian Theatre Royal** (www.georgiantheatreroyal.co.uk; Victoria Rd; tours per person £3.50; ⏲tours hourly 10am-4pm Mon-Sat mid-Feb–mid-Dec) is the most complete Georgian playhouse in Britain. Tours include a look at the country's oldest surviving stage scenery, painted between 1818 and 1836.

Activities

Walkers can follow paths along the River Swale, both upstream and downstream from

Richmond

Top Sights

Sights

Sleeping

Eating

Drinking

the town. A longer option is to follow part of the famous long-distance Coast to Coast Walk (p565) all the way to Reeth (11 miles) and take the bus back (see www.dalesbus.info/richmond).

In September/October the town hosts the **Richmond Walking & Book Festival** (www.booksandboots.org), which includes 10 days of guided walks, talks, films and other events in its busy timetable.

Cyclists can also follow Swaledale – as far as Reeth may be enough, while a trip along Arkengarthdale and then over the high wild moors to Kirkby Stephen via the Tan Hill Inn is a more serious (but very rewarding) 40-mile undertaking.

Sleeping

TOP CHOICE Millgate House B&B £££
(☎01748-823571; www.millgatehouse.com; Market Pl; r £110-145; P@) Behind an unassuming grey door lies the unexpected pleasure of one of the most attractive guest houses in England. While the house itself is a Georgian gem crammed with period details, it is overshadowed by the multi-award-winning garden at the back, which has superb views over the River Swale and the Cleveland Hills. If possible, book the Garden Suite.

Frenchgate Hotel HOTEL ££
(☎01748-822087; www.thefrenchgate.co.uk; 59-61 Frenchgate; s/d from £88/118; P) Nine elegant bedrooms occupy the upper floors of this converted Georgian town house, now a boutique hotel decorated with local art. The rooms have cool designer fittings – a period fireplace here, a Victorian roll-top bath there. Downstairs there's an excellent restaurant (three-course dinner £34) and a hospitable lounge with oak beams and an open fire.

Willance House B&B ££
(☎01748-824467; www.willancehouse.com; 24 Frenchgate; s/d £55/71; wi-fi) This is an oak-beamed house, built in 1600, with three immaculate rooms (one with a four-poster bed) that combine old-fashioned charm and all mod cons.

There's also a batch of pleasant places to stay along Frenchgate, and a couple more on Pottergate (the road into town from the east). These include:

66 Frenchgate B&B ££
(☎01748-823421; www.66frenchgate.co.uk; 66 Frenchgate; s/d £70/94; wi-fi) Three of the six stylish bedrooms have superb river views.

Pottergate Guesthouse B&B ££
(☎01748-823826; 4 Pottergate; d from £60) Compact and chintzy, with a friendly and helpful landlady.

Eating & Drinking

Rustique FRENCH ££
(☎01748-821565; www.rustiqueyork.co.uk; Chantry Wynd, Finkle St; mains £10-16; ⊙10am-9pm Mon-Sat, noon-9pm Sun) Tucked away in an arcade, this cosy bistro has consistently impressed with its mastery of French country cooking, from *confit de canard* (duck slow roasted in its own fat) to *paupiette de poulet* (chicken breast stuffed with brie and sun-dried tomatoes). Booking recommended.

Cross View Tearoom CAFE £
(www.crossviewtearooms.co.uk; 38 Market Pl; mains £4-7; ⊙9am-5.30pm Mon-Sat) So popular with locals that you might have to queue for a table at lunchtime, the Cross View is the place to go for a hearty breakfast, homemade cakes, a hot lunch, or just a nice cup of tea.

Seasons Restaurant & Cafe INTERNATIONAL ££
(www.restaurant-seasons.co.uk; Richmond Station, Station Rd; mains £6-15; ⊙9am-9pm Mon-Sat, 9am-7pm Sun) Housed in the restored Victorian

station building, this attractive, open-plan eatery shares space with a boutique brewery, artisan bakery, ice-cream factory and cheesemonger – and yes, all this local produce is on the menu.

Barkers FISH & CHIPS £
(Trinity Church Sq; mains £7-10; ⊙11am-9.30pm) The best fish and chips in town, sit-down or takeaway.

Black Lion Hotel PUB
(Finkle St) Cosy bars, low beams and good beer and food.

Unicorn Inn PUB
(2 Newbiggin) A determinedly old-fashioned free house serving Theakstons and Old Speckled Hen.

Information

The tourist office (Friary Gardens, Victoria Rd) has maps and guides, plus leaflets showing walks in town and the surrounding countryside.

Getting There & Away

From Darlington (on the railway between London and Edinburgh) it's easy to reach Richmond on bus 27 or X27 (30 minutes, every 30 minutes, hourly on Sunday). All buses stop in Market Place.

On Sundays and bank holiday Mondays only, from May to October, the Northern Dalesman bus 830 runs from Richmond to Hawes (1½ hours, one daily) via Reeth, and continuing on to Ribblehead and Ingleton (2 hours, one daily).

Swaledale & Arkengarthdale

The quietest and least-visited of the Dales which stretch west from Richmond, the wild and rugged beauty of Swaledale and Arkengarthdale is in sharp contrast to the softer, greener dales to the south. It's hard to imagine that only a century ago this was a major lead-mining area. When the price of ore fell in the 19th century, many people left to find work in England's burgeoning industrial cities, while others emigrated – especially to Wisconsin in the USA – leaving the valley almost empty, with just a few lonely villages scattered along its length.

Where Swaledale meets the even wilder Arkengarthdale lies the pretty village of **Reeth**, home to some art-and-craft shops, cafes and a few good pubs dotted around a large sloping green (Friday is market day). There is a **national park centre** (☎01748-884059) and the dusty little **Swaledale Museum** (www.swaledalemuseum.org; adult/child £3/free; ⊙10.30am-5.30pm Mon-Fri, noon-5.30pm Sun Apr-Oct), which tells the fascinating history of the Dales.

The best way to explore the dales is by bike, which you can hire from the **Dales Bike Centre** (www.dalesbikecentre.co.uk; road bikes/full-suspension mountain bikes for £20/40 per day), just east of Reeth.

The excellent **Overton House Café** (www.overtonhousecafe.co.uk; High Row; mains £7-17; ⊙lunch Tue-Sat, dinner Thu-Sat) has menu offerings ranging from a simple bacon sandwich (on ciabatta with onion relish) to expertly prepared fish dishes.

WEST YORKSHIRE

It was the tough and unforgiving textile industry that drove West Yorkshire's economy from the 18th century on. The woollen mills, factories and canals that were built to transport raw materials and finished products defined much of the county's landscape. But that's all in the past, and recent years have seen the transformation of this once hard-bitten area into quite the picture postcard.

Leeds and Bradford, two adjoining cities so big that they've virtually become one, are the perfect case in point. Though both were founded amid the dark, satanic mills of the Industrial Revolution, both are undergoing radical redevelopment and reinvention, prettifying their town centres and trying to tempt the more adventurous tourist with a lot of new museums, galleries, restaurants and bars.

Beyond the cities, West Yorkshire is a landscape of bleak moorland dissected by deep valleys dotted with old mill towns and villages. The relics of the wool and cloth industries are still visible in the rows of weavers' cottages and workers' houses built along ridges overlooking the towering chimneys of the mills in the valleys – landscapes that were so vividly described by the Brontë sisters, West Yorkshire's most renowned literary export and biggest tourist draw.

Getting Around

The Metro is West Yorkshire's highly efficient train and bus network, centred on Leeds and Bradford – which are also the main gateways to the county. For transport information call **West Yorkshire Metro** (☎0113-245 7676; www.wymetro.com).

WORTH A TRIP

TAN HILL INN

From Reeth, a narrow, twisting road leads northwest through scenic Arkengarthdale before climbing up to the vast, bleak expanses of the north Pennine moors. About 11 miles from Reeth, sitting in the middle of nowhere at an elevation of 328m (1732ft) is Britain's highest pub.

Despite its isolation, the **Tan Hill Inn** (☎01833-628246; www.tanhillinn.com; Tan Hill; 📶🐾) is an unexpectedly comfortable and welcoming hostelry, with an ancient fireplace in the atmospheric, stone-flagged public bar and leather sofas in the lounge, as well as an assorted menagerie of dogs, cats and sheep wandering in and out of the building. An important watering hole on the Pennine Way, the inn offers real ale on tap, a decent pub-grub menu (mains £6 to £10), live music in the evenings, B&B accommodation (from £80 a double), a bunkhouse (£25 per person) and basic camping (£3 per person).

Day Rover (£7.10) tickets are good for unlimited travel on Metro buses and trains after 9.30am on weekdays and all day at weekends. There's a range of additional Rover tickets covering buses and/or trains, plus heaps of useful Metro maps and timetables, available from bus and train stations and most tourist offices in West Yorkshire.

Leeds

POP 750,200

One of the fastest growing cities in the UK, Leeds is the glitzy embodiment of rediscovered northern self-confidence. More than a decade of redevelopment has seen the city centre transform from near-derelict mill town into a vision of 21st-century urban chic, with skyscraping office blocks, glass-and-steel waterfront apartment complexes and renovated Victorian shopping arcades. The financial crisis that began in 2008 saw many flagship development projects grind to a halt, but tower cranes are beginning to sprout on the skyline again and the massive new entertainment venue, the **Leeds Arena** (www.leeds.gov.uk/arena; Clay Pit Lane), is scheduled to open in 2013.

Known as the 'Knightsbridge of the North', Leeds has made itself into a shopping mecca, its streets lined with bustling malls sporting the top names in fashion. And when you've shopped till you've dropped there's a plethora of pubs, clubs and excellent restaurants to relax in. From cutting-edge couture to contemporary cuisine, Leeds will serve it to you on a plate (or more likely in a stylishly designed bag). Amid all this cutting-edge style, it seems fitting that the network of city bus routes includes peach, mauve and magenta lines as well as the more humdrum red, orange and blue.

Sights

FREE Royal Armouries MUSEUM
(www.royalarmouries.org; Armouries Dr; ⏰10am-5pm) Leeds' most interesting museum is undoubtedly the Royal Armouries, beside the snazzy Clarence Dock residential development. It was originally built to house the armour and weapons from the Tower of London but was subsequently expanded to cover 3000-years of fighting and self-defence. It all sounds a bit macho, but the exhibits are as varied as they are fascinating: films, live-action demonstrations and hands-on technology can awaken interests you never thought you had, from jousting to Indian elephant armour – we dare you not to learn something! To get here, walk east along the river from Centenary Footbridge (10 minutes), or take bus 28 from Albion St.

Leeds Industrial Museum MUSEUM
(www.leeds.gov.uk/armleymills; Canal Rd; adult/child £3.30/1.20; ⏰10am-5pm Tue-Sat, 1-5pm Sun) One of the world's largest textile mills has been transformed into a museum telling the story of Leeds' industrial past, both glorious and ignominious. The city became rich off the sheep's back, but at some cost in human terms – working conditions were, well, Dickensian. As well as a selection of working machinery, there's a particularly informative display on how cloth is made. Take bus 5 from the train station to get here.

FREE Kirkstall Abbey CHURCH
(www.leeds.gov.uk/kirkstallabbey; Abbey Rd; ⏰10am-4pm Tue-Thu, Sat & Sun) Leeds' most impressive medieval structure is the beautiful Kirkstall Abbey, founded in 1152 by Cistercian monks from Fountains Abbey in North Yorkshire, and one of the best-preserved

Leeds

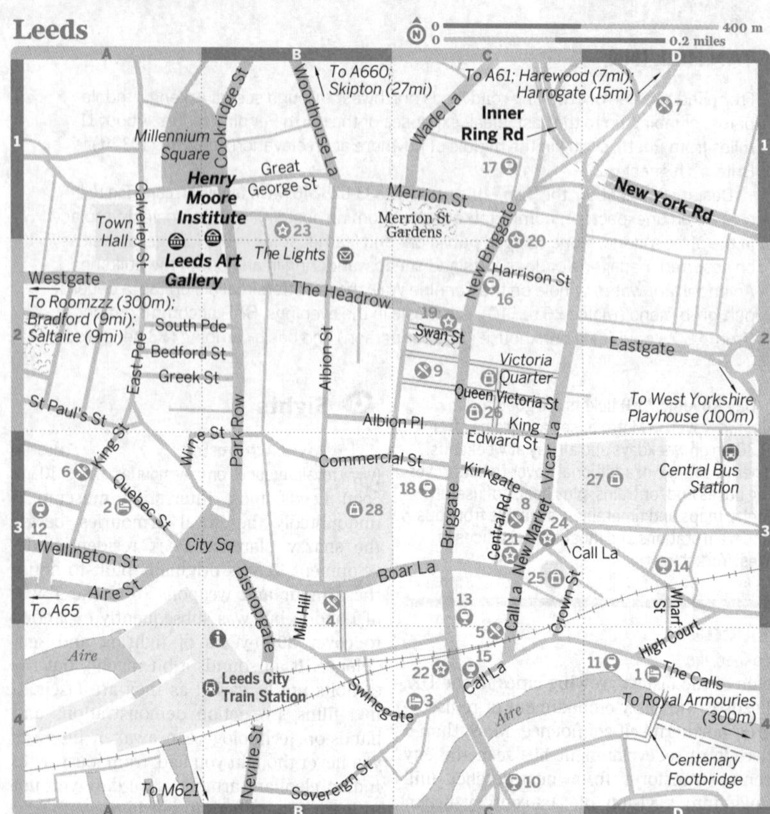

medieval abbeys in Britain. Across the road, the **Abbey House Museum** (www.leeds.gov.uk/abbeyhouse; Abbey Rd; adult/child £3.80/1.70; 10am-5pm Tue-Fri & Sun, noon-5pm Sat), once the Great Gate House to the abbey, contains meticulously reconstructed shops and houses that evoke Victorian Leeds, and displays that give an interesting insight into monastic life. The abbey and museum are off the A65, 3 miles northwest of the centre; take bus 33, 33A or 757.

FREE **Leeds Art Gallery** GALLERY
(www.leeds.gov.uk/artgallery; The Headrow; 10am-5pm Mon, Tue & Thu-Sat, noon-5pm Wed, 1-5pm Sun) The municipal gallery is packed with 19th- and 20th-century British heavyweights – Turner, Constable, Stanley Spencer, Wyndham Lewis et al – along with contemporary pieces by more recent arrivals such as Antony Gormley, sculptor of the *Angel of the North*.

FREE **Henry Moore Institute** GALLERY
(www.henry-moore.org; The Headrow; 11am-5.30pm Thu-Mon, 11am-8pm Wed) Housed in a converted Victorian warehouse in the city centre, this gallery showcases the work of 20th-century sculptors, but not, despite the name, anything by Henry Moore (1898–1986), who graduated from the Leeds School of Art. To see works by Moore, head to the Yorkshire Sculpture Park (p614).

Festivals

The August Bank Holiday (the weekend preceding the last Monday in August) sees 50,000-plus music fans converge on Bramham Park, 10 miles outside the city centre, for the **Leeds Festival** (www.leedsfestival.com), one of England's biggest music festivals.

Sleeping

There are no budget options in the city centre, and the midrange choices here are

Leeds

Top Sights

	Henry Moore Institute	B1
	Leeds Art Gallery	A2

Sleeping

1	42 The Calls	D4
2	Quebecs	A3
3	Roomzzz	C4

Eating

4	Anthony's	B3
5	Art's Cafe Bar & Restaurant	C4
6	Create	A3
7	Hansa's Gujarati	D1
8	Little Tokyo	C3
	Piazza by Anthony	(see 25)
9	Pickles & Potter	C2

Drinking

10	Adelphi	C4
11	Aire Bar	D4
12	Baby Jupiter	A3
13	Bar Fibre	C3
14	Duck & Drake	D3
15	Elbow Room	C4
16	Northbar	C2
17	Sandinista	C1
18	Whitelocks	C3

Entertainment

19	City Varieties	C2
	Cockpit	(see 3)
20	Grand Theatre & Opera House	C1
21	HiFi Club	C3
22	Mission	C4
23	Vue Cinema	B1
24	Wire	C3

Shopping

25	Corn Exchange	C3
26	Harvey Nichols	C2
27	Leeds City Market	D3
28	Trinity Leeds	B3

either chain hotels or places we wouldn't recommend. If you want somewhere cheapish you'll be forced to head for the 'burbs, where there are plenty of decent B&Bs and smallish hotels.

TOP CHOICE Quebecs BOUTIQUE HOTEL £££
(0113-244 8989; www.quebecshotel.co.uk; 9 Quebec St; d/ste from £180/300; @) Victorian grace at its opulent best is the theme of our favourite hotel in town, a conversion of the former Leeds & County Liberal Club. The elaborate wood panelling and heraldic stained-glass windows in the public areas are matched by the contemporary design of the bedrooms. Booking online can get you a room for as little as half the rack rate.

Roomzzz APARTMENTS ££
(0844 499 4888; www.roomzzz.co.uk; 10 Swinegate & 2 Burley Rd; 2-person apt from £79; @) This outfit offers bright and modern luxury apartments complete with fitted kitchen, with the advantage of a 24-hour hotel reception. Roomzzz Leeds City is at 10 Swinegate, right in the city centre; Roomzzz Leeds City West is half a mile west on Burley Rd.

42 The Calls BOUTIQUE HOTEL ££
(0113-244 0099; www.42thecalls.co.uk; 42 The Calls; r/ste from £110/170; @) This snazzy boutique hotel in what was once a 19th-century grain mill overlooking the river is a big hit with the trendy business crowd, who love its sharp, polished lines and designer aesthetic. The smaller 'study' rooms are pretty compact, and breakfast is not included; it'll cost you an extra £15 for the full English.

Bewleys Hotel HOTEL ££
(0113-234 2340; www.bewleyshotels.com/leeds; City Walk, Sweet St; r from £64; P@) Bewleys is super-convenient for motorists, sitting just off Junction 3 on the M621 but also just 10 minutes' walk from the city centre, and with secure basement parking. Rooms are stylish and well appointed, with soundproofed walls and windows. The flat rate accommodates up to two adults plus two kids under 12.

The following places outside the city centre are also recommended:

Moorlea B&B £
(0113-243 2653; www.moorleahotel.co.uk; 146 Woodsley Rd; s/d from £40/50;) Gay-friendly hotel northwest of the centre, near the University of Leeds.

Boundary Hotel Express HOTEL £
(0113-275 7700; www.boundaryhotel.co.uk; 42 Cardigan Rd; s/d £42/54; P@) Basic but

welcoming; 1.5 miles northwest of centre, near Headingley cricket ground.

Headingley Lodge HOTEL ££
(☎0844 858 2858; www.headingleylodge.co.uk; Headingley Stadium, St Michael's Lane; d/f £55/65; P@) Smart, comfortable rooms with views of Headingley cricket ground; part of the stadium complex.

Eating

The Leeds restaurant scene is constantly evolving, with new places springing up in the wake of new shopping and residential developments. The refurbished **Corn Exchange** (www.leedscornexchange.co.uk;), a beautiful Victorian building with a spectacular domed roof, houses a branch of Anthony's, while celebrity chef James Martin's new restaurant, Leeds Kitchen, is in the recently opened Alea Casino at Clarence Dock.

Brasserie Blanc FRENCH ££
(☎0113-220 6060; www.brasserieblanc.com; Victoria Mill, Sovereign St; mains £10-18; lunch & dinner Mon-Fri, noon-10.30pm Sat, noon-9pm Sun;) Raymond Blanc manages to create a surprisingly intimate and romantic space amid the cast-iron pillars and red brick of an old Victorian warehouse, with a scatter of outdoor tables for sunny lunchtimes beside the river. The menu is unerringly French, from *escargot* (edible snails) to Toulouse sausage. The lunch and pre-7pm menu (pre-6.30pm Saturday) offers three courses plus a glass of wine for £14.

Hansa's Gujarati INDIAN £
(www.hansasrestaurant.com; 72-74 North St; mains £6-8; lunch Sun, dinner Mon-Sat;) A Leeds institution, Hansa's has been dishing up wholesome Gujarati vegetarian cuisine for 20 years. The restaurant is plain and unassuming (save for a Hindu shrine), but the food is exquisite – specialities of the house include *samosa chaat*, a mix of spiced potato and chickpea samosas with a yogurt and tamarind sauce.

Piazza by Anthony INTERNATIONAL ££
(www.anthonysrestaurant.co.uk; Corn Exchange, Call Lane; mains £10-18; 10am-10pm Mon-Sat, 10am-9pm Sun;) Leeds' landmark development is the refurbished Corn Exchange, with this cool and contemporary restaurant taking pride of place beneath a spectacular cast-iron Victorian roof. The all-day menu ranges from gourmet salads and sandwiches to pasta, meat and fish dishes such as roast scallops with chorizo and butternut squash purée.

Pickles & Potter DELI, CAFE £
(www.picklesandpotter.co.uk; 18-20 Queens Arcade; mains £4-5; 9am-5pm Mon-Fri, 9am-6pm Sat, 10.30am-5pm Sun) This rustic cafe is famous for its superb sandwiches, especially the sumptuous roast-beef version compete with mustard, onion marmalade and fresh salad. There's also homemade soup, delicious cakes, and a meat or vegetarian main course of the day.

Art's Cafe Bar & Restaurant INTERNATIONAL ££
(www.artscafebar.co.uk; 42 Call Lane; mains £10-16; noon-11pm) Local art on the walls and a Bohemian vibe throughout make this a popular place for quiet reflection, a chat and a really good cup of coffee. The dinner menu offers a half-dozen classic dishes, such as slow-cooked shoulder of venison and black pudding wrapped in Parma ham.

Anthony's MODERN BRITISH £££
(☎0113-245 5922; www.anthonysrestaurant.co.uk; 19 Boar Lane; 2-/3-course dinner £36/45; Tue-Sat) Anthony's serves top-notch Modern British cuisine to a clientele so eager that they'll think nothing of booking a month in advance. If you go at any other time except Saturday evening, you'll get away with making your reservations a day or so in advance.

Little Tokyo JAPANESE ££
(www.littletokyo-leeds.co.uk; 24 Central Rd; mains £8-16; noon-10pm) Fans of genuine Japanese food should go no further than this superb restaurant, which serves a wide array of quality sushi and sashimi (including half-portions) and Bento boxes – those handy trays that contain the Japanese equivalent of a four-course meal.

Create MODERN BRITISH ££
(☎0113-242 0628; www.foodbycreate.co.uk/restaurant; 31 King St; 2-/3-course dinner £14/17; 11.30am-6pm Mon, 11.30am-10pm Tue-Sat) A new social enterprise restaurant that not only serves superb British cuisine, but also provides jobs and work experience for homeless and marginalised people.

Leeds Kitchen MODERN BRITISH ££
(☎0113-341 3266; www.theleedskitchen.co.uk; Alea Casino, Clarence Dock; mains £13-23; lunch Sun, dinner Mon-Sat) TV celebrity chef James Martin's new restaurant serves the best of British produce with a gourmet twist. Close to the Royal Armouries museum.

Drinking

Leeds is renowned for its selection of pubs and bars. Glammed-up hordes of party animals crawl the cluster of venues around Boar and Call Lanes, where bars are opening (and closing) all the time. Most bars open till 2am; many turn into clubs after 11pm or midnight, with an admission charge.

Northbar BAR
(www.northbar.com; 24 New Briggate) There's a continental feel to this long, narrow, minimalist bar that's enhanced by the unfamiliar beer labels, from Dortmunder and Duvel to Schneider and Snake Dog. In fact, Northbar is dedicated to the best of world beers, with more than a dozen ales on tap and dozens more in bottles.

Duck & Drake PUB
(www.duckndrake.co.uk; 43 Kirkgate) A down-to-earth, traditional boozer with a well-worn atmosphere, a cast of regular pub characters and no fewer than 15 hand-pulled real ales to choose from. The Duck also provides a stage for local rock and blues bands from Thursday to Sunday nights.

Whitelocks PUB
(6-8 Turk's Head Yard) There's lots of polished wood, gleaming brass and colourful stained glass in this popular, traditional pub dating from 1715. Theakstons, Deuchars IPA and several other real ales are on tap, and in summer the crowds spill out into the courtyard.

Baby Jupiter BAR
(www.babyjupiter.co.uk; 11 York Pl) A retro gem with lots of purple velvet, hanging fishbowls and images from old sci-fi films, this basement bar sports a cool soundtrack that ranges from indie, funk and soul to punk, new wave and electro.

Sandinista COCKTAIL BAR
(www.sandinistaleeds.co.uk; 5/5a Cross Belgrave St) This laid-back bar has a Latin look but a unifying theme, attracting an eclectic clientele with its mixed bag of music and unpretentious atmosphere. If you enjoy a well-mixed cocktail but aren't too fussed about looking glam, this is the spot for you.

Bar Fibre BAR
(www.barfibre.com; 168 Lower Briggate) Leeds' most popular gay bar, which spills out onto the aptly named Queen's Crt, is where the beautiful set congregates. There's another cluster of gay bars downhill at the junction of Lower Briggate and The Calls.

Adelphi PUB
(www.theadelphileeds.co.uk; 3-5 Hunslet Rd) Built in 1898 and hardly changed since.

Aire Bar BAR
(www.airebar.co.uk; 32 The Calls) Red-brick vaults, leather sofas, Timothy Taylor's Landlord real ale and a terrace overhanging the river.

Elbow Room BAR
(www.theelbowroom.co.uk/leeds; 64 Call Lane) Pop art, purple pool tables and laid-back music.

Entertainment

In order to make sense of the ever-evolving scene, get your hands on the fortnightly *Leeds Guide* (www.leedsguide.co.uk; £1.50).

Clubs

The tremendous Leeds club scene attracts people from miles around. In true northern tradition, people brave the cold wearing next to nothing, even in winter, which is a spectacle in itself. Clubs charge a variety of admission prices, ranging from as little as £1 on a slow weeknight to £10 or more on Saturday.

HiFi Club CLUB
(www.thehificlub.co.uk; 2 Central Rd) This intimate club is a good break from the hardcore sound of four-to-the-floor. If it's Tamla Motown or the percussive beats of dance-floor jazz that shake your booty, this is the spot for you.

Cockpit LIVE MUSIC
(www.thecockpit.co.uk; Swinegate) Snugly ensconced in a series of railway arches, the legendary Cockpit is the antidote to dance clubs. A live music venue of note (Coldplay, The White Stripes and The Flaming Lips have all played here), it also hosts The Session on Friday nights, a superb indie/electro/guitar club night.

Mission CLUB
(www.clubmission.com; 8-13 Heaton's Ct) A massive club that redefines the term 'up-for-it'. Thursday sees the 'Full Moon Thai Beach Party' student night, while Saturdays offer a range of house, dance and classic-anthem club nights, plus the 'Backdoor Disco' gay club.

Wire CLUB
(www.wireclub.co.uk; 2-8 Call Lane; ⏲Thu-Sat plus occ midweek nights) This small, atmospheric basement club, set in a forest of Victorian cast-iron pillars, throbs to a different beat every night, from rock 'n' roll to drum and bass. Popular with local students.

Theatre & Opera

City Varieties MUSIC HALL
(www.cityvarieties.co.uk; Swan St) Founded in 1865, the City Varieties is the world's longest-running music hall, where the likes of Harry Houdini, Charlie Chaplin and Lily Langtry once trod the boards. Reopened after a major revamp, the program now features standup comedy, live music, pantomime and old-fashioned variety shows.

Grand Theatre & Opera House MUSICALS, THEATRE
(www.leedsgrandtheatre.com; 46 New Briggate) Hosts musicals, plays and opera, including performances by the acclaimed **Opera North** (www.operanorth.co.uk).

West Yorkshire Playhouse THEATRE
(www.wyp.org.uk; Quarry Hill Mount) The Playhouse has a reputation for excellent live drama, from the classics to cutting-edge new writing.

Cinema

Hyde Park Picture House CINEMA
(www.hydeparkpicturehouse.co.uk; Brudenell Rd) This Edwardian cinema shows a meaty range of art-house and mainstream choices. Take bus 56 from the city centre to get here.

Vue Cinema MULTIPLEX
(www.myvue.com; 22 The Light, The Headrow) For mainstream, first-run films, head for the Vue on the 2nd floor of The Light entertainment complex.

Sport

Leeds United Football Club FOOTBALL
(www.leedsunited.com; Elland Rd) Leeds supporters know all about pain: the team was relegated from the Premiership in 2004, and then from the Championship to League One in 2007. Loyal fans were rewarded with promotion back to the Championship in 2010, and continue to pack the Elland Rd stadium in their masses. Take bus 93 or 96 from City Sq.

Yorkshire County Cricket Club CRICKET
(www.yorkshireccc.com; Headingley Carnegie Cricket Ground, St Michael's Lane) Headingley, the spiritual home of Yorkshire cricket, has been hosting cricket matches since 1890 and is still used for test matches. To get to the ground, take bus 18 or 56 from the city centre.

Shopping

Leeds' city centre has so many shopping arcades that they all seem to blend into one giant mall. The latest development – **Trinity Leeds** (www.trinityleeds.com), scheduled to open in 2013 – will be the city's biggest.

The mosaic-paved, stained-glass-roofed Victorian arcades of **Victoria Quarter**, between Briggate and Vicar Lane, are well worth visiting for aesthetic reasons alone. Dedicated shoppers can join the footballers' wives browsing boutiques by Louis Vuitton, Vivienne Westwood and Swarovski. The flagship store here, of course, is **Harvey Nichols** (www.harveynichols.com; 107-111 Briggate).

Just across the street to the east you'll find the opposite end of the retail spectrum in **Leeds City Market** (www.leedsmarket.com; Kirkgate; ⏲9am-5pm Mon-Sat, to 1pm Wed, open-air market Thu-Tue). Once the home of Michael Marks, who later joined Spencer, this is Britain's largest covered market, selling fresh meat, fish, fruit and vegetables, as well as household goods.

Information

Gateway Yorkshire & Leeds Visitor Centre (☎0113-242 5242; www.visitleeds.co.uk; The Arcade, Leeds City Train Station; ⏲9am-5.30pm Mon-Sat, 10am-4pm Sun)

Leeds General Infirmary (☎0113-243 2799; Great George St)

Post Office (St John's Centre, 116 Albion St; ⏲9am-5.30pm Mon-Sat)

Getting There & Away

AIR Eleven miles northwest of the city via the A65, **Leeds Bradford International Airport** (www.leedsbradfordairport.co.uk) offers flights to a range of domestic and international destinations. The **Metroconnect 757 bus** (£3.30, 40 minutes, every 30 minutes, hourly on Sunday) runs between Leeds bus station and the airport. A taxi costs about £20.

BUS National Express serves most major cities, including services from London (from £12, 4½ hours, hourly) and Manchester (from £5, 1¼ hours, every 30 minutes).

Yorkshire Coastliner (www.coastliner.co.uk) has useful services from Leeds to York, Pickering, Goathland and Whitby (840); to York and Scarborough (843); and to Bridlington (845 and

X45). A Freedom Ticket (£15) gives unlimited bus travel on this service for a day.

TRAIN Leeds City Station has hourly services from London King's Cross (£50, 2½ hours), Sheffield (£13, one hour), Manchester (£15, one hour) and York (£12, 30 minutes).

Leeds is also the starting point for services on the famous Settle–Carlisle railway line.

Getting Around

Leeds CityBus (www.wymetro.com; flat fare £0.50) runs every few minutes from 6.30am to 7.30pm Monday to Saturday, linking the bus and train stations to all the main shopping areas in the city centre.

The various Day Rover passes covering trains and/or buses are good for reaching Bradford, Haworth and Hebden Bridge.

Around Leeds

A day-trip from Leeds opens up a fascinating range of options: stately splendour at Harewood, dust and darkness at the National Coal Mining Museum for England, or technology and poppadums at Bradford, to name but a few. Places are listed roughly in order of distance from Leeds, first to the west and north, then to the south:

BRADFORD

POP 293,700

Their suburbs may have merged into one sprawling urban conurbation, but Bradford remains far removed from its much more glamorous neighbour, Leeds. Thanks to its role as a major player in the wool trade, Bradford attracted large numbers of Bangladeshi and Pakistani immigrants throughout the 20th century, who – despite occasional racial tensions – have helped reinvigorate the city and give it new energy (plus a reputation for superb curry restaurants). A high point of the year is the colourful **Bradford Mela** (www.bradfordmela.org.uk), a two-day celebration of Asian music, dance, arts, crafts and food in mid-June.

Bradford's top attraction is the **National Media Museum** (www.nationalmediamuseum.org.uk; off Little Horton Lane; admission free; ⊙10am-6pm, closed 25 Dec), an impressive, glass-fronted building that tells the story of photography, film, TV, radio and the web from 19th-century cameras and early animation to digital technology and the psychology of advertising. There's lots of hands-on stuff too; you can film yourself in a bedroom scene, pretend to be a TV newsreader, or play 1970s and 80s video games. The **IMAX cinema** (adult/child £11/8.50) here shows the usual combination of in-your-face nature films, space documentaries and 3-D animation.

The museum looks out over **City Park**, Bradford's brand new central square which is home to the Mirror Pool, the country's largest urban water feature.

Bradford is famous for its curries – it was voted the UK's Curry Capital in 2011 – so don't miss trying one of the city's hundred or so restaurants. A great help is the **Bradford Curry Guide** (www.visitbradford.com/food-and-drink/Bradford-Curry-Guide.aspx).

Top recommendations include Bradford's oldest curry house, the **Kashmir** (27 Morley St; mains £4-6; ⊙dinner), for good Asian tucker, served with no frills in very basic surroundings. At the opposite end of the spectrum is **Zouk Tea Bar** (www.zoukteabar.co.uk; 1312 Leeds Rd; mains £7-12; ⊙10am-midnight), a modern and stylish cafe-restaurant staffed by chefs from Lahore, and serving everything from *chana puri* (curried chickpeas) for breakfast to legendary *lamb Nihari* (slow cooked lamb with a thick and spicy sauce) for dinner.

Bradford is on the Metro train line from Leeds (£3.30, 20 minutes), with very frequent services every day.

SALTAIRE

A Victorian-era landmark, Saltaire was a model industrial village built in 1851 by philanthropic wool-baron and teetotaller Titus Salt. The rows of neat, honey-coloured cottages – now a Unesco World Heritage Site – overlook what was once the largest factory in the world.

The factory is now **Salt's Mill** (www.saltsmill.org.uk; admission free; ⊙10am-5.30pm Mon-Fri, 10am-6pm Sat & Sun), a splendidly bright and airy building where the main attraction is a permanent exhibition of 1970s and '80s artworks by local boy David Hockney (1937–). In a fitting metaphor for the shift in the British economy from making things to selling them, this former engine of industry is now a shrine to retail therapy, housing shops selling books, crafts and outdoor equipment, and a cafe and restaurant.

Saltaire's **tourist office** (☎01274-437942; www.saltairevillage.info; Salt's Mill, Victoria Rd; ⊙10am-5pm) has maps of the village and runs hour-long guided walks (adult/child £4/3) through the town throughout the year.

Saltaire is 9 miles west of Leeds centre, and 3 miles north of Bradford centre. It's easily reached by Metro rail from either.

HAREWOOD

The great park, sumptuous gardens and mighty edifice of **Harewood House** (www.harewood.org; adult/child £14/7; ⏲grounds 10am-6pm, house noon-3pm Apr-Oct) could easily fill an entire day-trip from Leeds, and also makes a good port of call on the way to Harrogate.

A classic example of a stately English pile, the house was built between 1759 and 1772 by the era's superstar designers: John Carr designed the exterior, Lancelot 'Capability' Brown laid out the grounds, Thomas Chippendale supplied the furniture (the largest commission he ever received, costing the unheard of amount of £10,000), Robert Adams designed the interior, and Italy was raided to create an appropriate art collection. The superb terrace was added 100 years later by yet another top name, Sir Charles Barry – he of the Houses of Parliament.

Many locals come to Harewood just to relax or saunter through the **grounds** (grounds-only ticket £10/6), without even thinking of going inside the house. Hours of entertainment can be had in the **Bird Garden**, with many exotic species including penguins (feeding time at 2pm is a highlight), and there's also a boating lake, cafe and adventure playground. For more activity, there's a network of walking trails around the lake or through the parkland.

Harewood is about 7 miles north of Leeds on the A61. Take bus 36 (20 minutes, at least half-hourly Monday to Saturday, hourly on Sunday) which continues to Harrogate. Visitors coming by bus get half-price admission, so hang on to your ticket. From the main gate, it's a 2-mile walk through the grounds to the house and gardens, or you can use the free shuttle service.

NATIONAL COAL MINING MUSEUM

For close to three centuries, West and South Yorkshire were synonymous with coal production; the collieries shaped and scarred the landscape, while entire villages grew up around the pits, each male inhabitant and their descendants destined to spend their working lives underground. The industry came to a shuddering halt in the 1980s, but the imprint of coal is still very much in evidence, even if there's only a handful of collieries left. One of these, at Claphouse, is now the **National Coal Mining Museum for England** (www.ncm.org.uk; Overton, near Wakefield; admission free; ⏲10am-5pm, last tour 3.15pm), a superb testament to the inner workings of a coal mine.

The highlight of a visit is the underground tour (departing every 10 minutes). Equipped with helmet and head-torch you descend 140m in the 'cage' then follow subterranean passages to the coal seam where massive drilling machines now stand idle. Former miners work as guides, and explain the details – sometimes with a suitably authentic and almost impenetrable mix of local dialect (known in Yorkshire as Tyke) and technical terminology.

Up on top, there are audiovisual displays, some fascinating memorabilia (including sketches by Henry Moore), and exhibits about trade unions, strikes and the wider mining communities – only a bit over-romanticised in parts. You can also stroll round the pit-pony stables (their equine inhabitants also now retired) or the slightly eerie bathhouse, unchanged since the miners scrubbed off the coal dust for the last time and emptied their lockers.

The museum is about 10 miles south of Leeds on the A642 between Wakefield and Huddersfield, which drivers can reach via Junction 40 on the M1. By public transport, take a train from Leeds to Wakefield (15 minutes, at least hourly), and then bus 232 towards Huddersfield (25 minutes, hourly).

YORKSHIRE SCULPTURE PARK

One of England's most impressive collections of sculpture is scattered across the formidable 18th-century estate of Bretton Park, 200-odd hectares of lawns, fields and trees. A bit like the art world's equivalent of a safari park, the **Yorkshire Sculpture Park** (www.ysp.co.uk; Bretton Park, near Wakefield; admission free, parking £4; ⏲10am-6pm Apr-Oct, to 5pm Nov-Mar) showcases the work of dozens of sculptors both national and international. But the main focus of this outdoor gallery is the work of local kids Barbara Hepworth (1903–75), who was born in nearby Wakefield, and Henry Moore (1898–1986).

The rural setting is especially fitting for Moore's work, as the artist was hugely influenced by the outdoors and preferred his art to be sited in the landscape rather than indoors. Other highlights include pieces by Andy Goldsworthy and Eduardo Paolozzi. There's also a program of temporary exhibitions and installations by visiting artists, plus a bookshop and cafe.

The park is 12 miles south of Leeds and 18 miles north of Sheffield, just off Junction 38 on the M1 motorway. If you're on public transport, take a train from Leeds to Wakefield (15 minutes, at least hourly), or from Sheffield to Barnsley (20 minutes, at least hourly); then take bus *96* which runs between Wakefield and Barnsley via Bretton Park (30 minutes, hourly Monday to Saturday).

HEPWORTH WAKEFIELD

West Yorkshire's standing on the international arts scene got a boost in 2011 when the Yorkshire Sculpture Park was joined by this award-winning gallery of modern art, housed in a stunningly angular building on the banks of the River Calder. The **Hepworth Wakefield** (☎01924-247360; www.hepworthwakefield.org; Gallery Walk; admission free, parking £4.50; ⊙10am-5pm Tue-Sun) has been built around the works of Wakefield-born sculptor Barbara Hepworth, perhaps best known for her work *Single Form*, which graces the United Nations Headquarters in New York. The gallery showcases more than a dozen Hepworth originals, as well as works by other 20th-century British artists including Ivon Hitchens, Paul Nash, Victor Pasmore, John Piper and Henry Moore. The Gott Collection of 19th-century art includes a 1793 painting of Wakefield Bridge and Chantry Chapel, which you can compare with the real thing by looking out the neighbouring window.

The gallery is near the centre of Wakefield, a 10-minute walk south of Wakefield Kirkgate train station.

Hebden Bridge

POP 4086

Tucked tightly into the fold of a steep-sided valley, Yorkshire's funkiest little town is a former mill town that refused to go gently with the dying of industry's light. Instead it raged a bit and then morphed into an attractive little tourist trap with a distinctly bohemian atmosphere. Besides the honest-to-God Yorkshire folk who have lived here for years, the town is home to university academics, artists, die-hard hippies and a substantial gay community (it allegedly boasts the highest proportion of lesbians per head of population in the UK) – all of which explains the abundance of craft shops, organic cafes and secondhand bookstores.

From the town centre, a short stroll along the attractive waterfront of the Rochdale Canal leads to the **Alternative Technology Centre** (www.alternativetechnology.org.uk; Hebble End Mill; admission free; ⊙10am-5pm Mon-Fri, noon-4pm Sat, 1-4pm Sun), which promotes renewable energy, recycling and sustainable lifestyles through a series of intriguing exhibits and workshops.

Above the town is the much older village of **Heptonstall**, its narrow cobbled street lined with 500-year-old cottages and the ruins of a beautiful 13th-century church. But it's the churchyard of the newer St Thomas' Church that draws literary pilgrims, for here is buried the poet **Sylvia Plath** (1932–63), wife of another famous poet, Ted Hughes (1930–98), who was born in nearby Mytholmroyd.

The **Hebden Bridge Tourist Office & Canal Centre** (☎01422-843831; www.hebdenbridge.co.uk; Butlers Wharf, New Rd; ⊙9.30am-5.30pm Mon-Fri, 10.30am-5pm Sat & Sun mid-Mar–mid-Oct, shorter hours rest of year) has a good stock of maps and leaflets on local walks, including a saunter to **Hardcastle Crags**, the local beauty spot, and nearby NT-listed **Gibson Mill** (www.nationaltrust.org.uk; adult/child £3.80/1.90; ⊙11am-4pm Tue-Thu, Sat & Sun Mar-Oct, 11am-3pm Sat & Sun Nov-Feb), a renovated 19th-century cotton mill. The mill houses a visitor centre with exhibitions covering the industrial and social history of the mill and its former workers.

Sleeping & Eating

Holme House B&B ££
(☎01422-847588; www.holmehousehebdenbridge.co.uk; New Rd; s/d from £62/78;) Holme House is an elegant Victorian villa right in the heart of town, with stylish and spacious bedrooms and fluffy robes and towels in the bathrooms. At breakfast you can choose from smoked haddock with poached egg, fresh fruit and yoghurt, or a fry-up prepared using local produce.

Mankinholes YHA HOSTEL £
(☎0845 371 9751; www.yha.org.uk; dm £19.40; P) A converted 17th-century manor house 4 miles southwest of Hebden Bridge, this hostel has limited facilities (no TV room) but is very popular with walkers (the Pennine Way passes only half a mile away). There are buses from New Rd in Hebden to Todmorden every 10 minutes; from there, bus T6/T8 goes to the hostel.

Green's Vegetarian Café VEGETARIAN ££
(☎01422-843587; www.greensvegetariancafe.co.uk; Old Oxford House, Albert St; mains £10; ⊙11am-3pm Wed-Sun, 6.30-9pm Fri & Sat) One of Yorkshire's best vegetarian restaurants, Green's adopts a gourmet attitude towards veggie and vegan cuisine, serving dishes

such as Sicilian *caponata* (aubergines, red pepper, celery, olives and capers) with spaghetti, and Thai green curry with chickpeas, squash and tofu. Best book a table to avoid disappointment, especially for dinner.

Mooch CAFE, BAR £
(24 Market St; mains £5-8; ⏲9am-8pm Mon & Wed-Sat, 10am-7pm Sun) This chilled-out little cafe-bar exemplifies Hebden's alternative atmosphere. The menu includes a full-vegan breakfast, brie-and-grape ciabatta, and Mediterranean lunch platters of olives, hummus, stuffed vine leaves, tabouleh and more. There's also Krombacher beer on draught, and excellent espresso.

Organic House CAFE £
(www.organic-house.co.uk; 2 Market St; mains £6-11; ⏲9am-5pm Mon-Sat, 10am-5pm Sun;) Practically everything on the menu at this busy local caff is organic, locally produced or fair-trade, from the veggie breakfast to the pâté *du jour* (served with toast and chutney). There are outdoor tables in the garden, and a shiatsu and reflexology studio upstairs.

Getting There & Away

Hebden Bridge is on the Leeds–Manchester train line (£4.80, 50 minutes, every 20 minutes Monday to Saturday, hourly on Sunday). Get off at Todmorden for the Mankinholes YHA.

Haworth

POP 6100

It seems that only Shakespeare himself is held in higher esteem than the beloved Brontë sisters, Emily, Anne and Charlotte – at least, judging by the 8 million visitors a year who trudge up the hill from the train station to pay their respects at the handsome parsonage where the literary classics *Jane Eyre* and *Wuthering Heights* were born.

Not surprisingly, the whole village is given over to Brontë-linked tourism, but even without the literary associations Haworth is still worth a visit, though you'll be hard pushed not to be overwhelmed by the cottage industry that has grown up around the Brontës and their wonderful creations.

STEAM ENGINES & RAILWAY CHILDREN

Haworth is on the **Keighley & Worth Valley Railway** (www.kwvr.co.uk; adult/child return £10/5, Day Rover £15/7.50), which runs steam and classic diesel engines between Keighley and Oxenhope. It was here, in 1969, that the classic movie The Railway Children was shot: Mr Perks was stationmaster at Oakworth, where the Edwardian look has been meticulously maintained. Trains operate about hourly at weekends all year; in holidayperiods they run hourly every day.

Sights

FREE **Haworth Parish Church** CHURCH
(Church St; ⏲9am-5.30pm) Your first stop should be Haworth Parish Church, a lovely old place of worship built in the late 19th century on the site of the older church that the Brontë sisters knew, which was demolished in 1879. In the surrounding churchyard, gravestones are covered in moss or thrust to one side by gnarled tree roots, giving the place a tremendous feeling of age.

Brontë Parsonage Museum MUSEUM
(www.bronte.info; Church St; adult/child £7/3.60; ⏲10am-5.30pm Apr-Sep, 11am-5pm Oct-Mar) Set in a pretty garden overlooking the church and graveyard, the house where the Brontë family lived from 1820 till 1861 is now a museum. The rooms are meticulously furnished and decorated exactly as they were in the Brontë era, including Charlotte's bedroom, her clothes and her writing paraphernalia. There's also an informative exhibition, which includes the fascinating miniature books the Brontës wrote as children.

Activities

Above Haworth stretch the bleak moors of the South Pennines – immediately familiar to Brontë fans – and the tourist office (p618) has leaflets on local **walks** to endless Brontë-related places. A 6.5-mile favourite leads to Top Withins, a ruined farm thought to have inspired *Wuthering Heights*, even though a plaque clearly states that the farmhouse bore no resemblance to the one Emily wrote about.

Other walks can be worked around the **Brontë Way**, a longer route linking Bradford and Colne via Haworth. Alternatively, you can walk or cycle the 8 miles south to Hebden Bridge via the scenic valley of Hardcastle Crags.

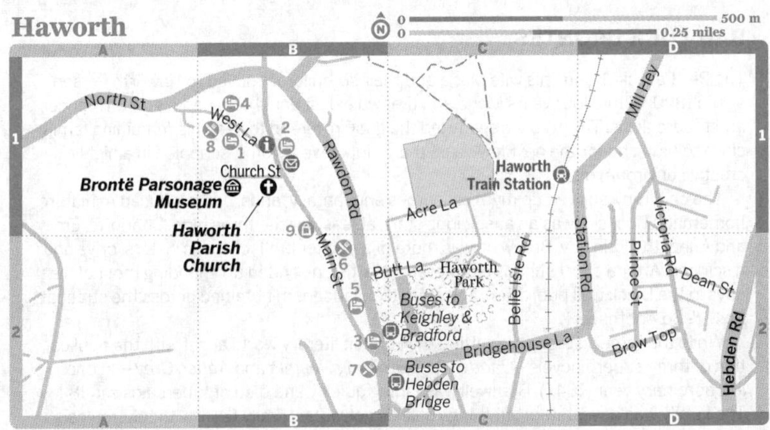

Sleeping & Eating

Virtually every second house on Main St offers B&B; they're mostly indistinguishable from each other but some are just that little bit cuter. There are a couple of good restaurants in town, and many of the B&Bs also have small cafes that are good for a spot of lunch.

Old Registry B&B ££
(☎01535-646503; www.theoldregistryhaworth.co.uk; 2-4 Main St; r £75-120;) This place is a bit special. It's an elegantly rustic guesthouse where each of the carefully themed rooms has a four-poster bed, whirlpool bath or valley view. The Blue Heaven room is just that – at least for fans of Laura Ashley's delphinium blue.

Ye Sleeping House B&B ££
(☎01535-546992; www.yesleepinghouse.co.uk; 8 Main St; s/d from £29/58) There's a cosy, country cottage atmosphere at this welcoming B&B, with just three small rooms and two friendly resident cats. Try to get the one en suite room, which can sleep a family of four and has great views over the valley.

Aitches B&B ££
(☎01535-642501; www.aitches.co.uk; 11 West Lane; s/d from £40/60) A classy, stone-built Victorian house with four en suite rooms, each differently decorated with a pleasantly olde-worlde atmosphere. There's a residents' dining room where a three-course meal will cost £16 (prebooked, minimum four persons).

Apothecary Guest House B&B £
(☎01535-643642; www.theapothecaryguesthouse.co.uk; 86 Main St; s/d £35/55;) Oak beams and narrow, slanted passageways lead to smallish rooms with cheerful decor.

Haworth

Top Sights
- Brontë Parsonage Museum B1
- Haworth Parish Church B1

Sleeping
1. Aitches B1
2. Apothecary Guest House B1
3. Old Registry B2
4. Old White Lion Hotel B1
5. Ye Sleeping House B2

Eating
6. Cobbles and Clay B2
7. Haworth Old Hall B2
8. Weaver's B1

Shopping
9. Venables & Bainbridge B1

Old White Lion Hotel INN ££
(☎01535-642313; www.oldwhitelionhotel.com; West Lane; s/d from £70/98;) Pub-style accommodation – comfortable if not spectacular – above an oak-panelled bar and highly rated restaurant.

Haworth YHA HOSTEL £
(☎0845 371 9520; www.yha.org.uk; Longlands Dr; dm £19.40; P@) A big old house with a games room, lounge, cycle store and laundry. It's on the northeastern edge of town, off Lees Lane.

Weaver's BRITISH ££
(☎01535-643822; www.weaversmallhotel.co.uk; 15 West Lane; mains £15-20; lunch Wed-Fri, dinner Tue-Sat) A stylish and atmospheric

BAD-LUCK BRONTËS

The Rev Patrick Brontë, his wife Maria and their six children moved to Haworth Parsonage in 1820. Within four years Maria and the two eldest daughters had died from cancer and tuberculosis. This treble tragedy led the good reverend to keep his remaining family close to him, and for the next few years the children were home-schooled in a highly creative environment.

The children conjured up mythical heroes and fantasy lands, and produced miniature homemade books. It was an auspicious start, at least for the three girls, Charlotte, Emily and Anne; the lone boy, Branwell, was more of a painter but lacked his sisters' drive and discipline. After a short stint as a professional artist, he ended up spending most of his days in the Black Bull pub, drunk and stoned on laudanum obtained across the street at Rose & Co Apothecary.

While the three sisters were setting the London literary world alight with the publication of three superb novels – *Jane Eyre*, *Wuthering Heights* and *Agnes Grey* – in one extraordinary year (1847), Branwell was fading quickly and died of tuberculosis in 1848. The family was devastated, but things quickly got worse. Emily fell ill with tuberculosis soon after her brother's funeral; she never left the house again and died on 19 December. Anne, who had also been sick, was next; Charlotte took her to Scarborough to seek a sea cure but she died on 28 May 1849.

The remaining family never recovered. Despite her growing fame, Charlotte struggled with depression and never quite adapted to her high position in literary society. Despite her misgivings she eventually married, but died in the early stages of pregnancy on 31 March 1855. All things considered, it's hardly surprising that poor old Patrick Brontë spent the remaining years of his life going increasingly insane.

restaurant, Weaver's offers a menu featuring local produce (such as slow-cooked shoulder of Pennine lamb with fennel seed and coriander stuffing), or simple lunches like an Ellison's pork pie with mushy peas and mint sauce (2-course lunch £16). Upstairs are three comfy bedrooms, two of which have views towards the moors.

Cobbles and Clay CAFE £
(www.cobblesandclay.co.uk; 60 Main St; mains £5-8; 9am-5pm;) This attractive, child-friendly cafe not only offers fair-trade coffee and healthy salads and snacks – Tuscan bean stew, or hummus with pita bread and raw veggie sticks – but also the opportunity to indulge in a bit of pottery painting.

Haworth Old Hall PUB ££
(01535-642709; www.hawortholdhall.co.uk; Sun St; mains £9-17) A 16th-century pub serving real ale and decent food. If you want to linger longer, two comfortable doubles cost £60 each.

Information

Post Office (98 Main St; 9am-5.30pm Mon-Fri, to 12.30pm Sat)

Tourist Office (01535-642329; www.aworth-village.org.uk; 2-4 West Lane; 9am-5.30pm Apr-Sep, to 5pm Oct-Mar)

Venables & Bainbridge (111 Main St; 11am-5pm) Secondhand books including many vintage Brontë volumes.

Getting There & Away

From Leeds, the easiest approach is via Keighley, which is on the Metro rail network. Bus 500 runs from Keighley bus station to Haworth (15 minutes, hourly) and continues to Todmorden and Hebden Bridge. However, the most interesting way to get from Keighley to Haworth is via the Keighley & Worth Valley Railway.

SOUTH YORKSHIRE

What wool was to West Yorkshire, so steel was to South Yorkshire. A confluence of natural resources – coal, iron ore and ample water – made the region a crucible of the British iron and steel industries. From the 18th century to the 20th, the region was the industrial powerhouse of northern England.

Sheffield and Rotherham's blast furnaces and the coal pits of Barnsley and Doncaster may have closed long ago, but the hulking reminders of that irrepressible Victorian dynamism remain, not only in the old steel works and pit-heads – some of which have been converted into museums and exhibition spaces – but also in the grand civic buildings that grace Sheffield's city centre, fitting testaments to the untrammelled ambitions of their 19th-century patrons.

Sheffield

POP 525,800

Steel is everywhere in Sheffield. Today, however, it's not the steel of the foundries, mills and forges that made the city's fortune, nor the canteens of cutlery that made 'Sheffield steel' a household name, but the steel of scaffolding and cranes, of modern sculptures and supertrams, and of new steel-framed buildings rising against the skyline.

The steel industry that made the city famous is long gone, but after many years of decline Sheffield is on the up again. Like many of northern England's cities it has grabbed the opportunities presented by urban renewal with both hands and is working hard to reinvent itself. The new economy is based on services, shopping and the 'knowledge industry' that flows from the city's universities.

This renaissance got off to a shaky start in 2000 when the city's signature millennium project, the National Centre for Popular Music, closed down due to lack of visitors only 15 months after it opened. An eye-catching and controversial piece of modern architecture shaped like four giant, stainless-steel kettles, it now houses Sheffield Hallam University's student union.

But the city's redevelopment seems to be hitting its stride now, with attractive new public spaces and a clutch of interesting museums and galleries. And there's a lively nightlife fuelled by the large student population – the city's two universities support around 24,000 potential pubbers and clubbers – and Sheffield's long-standing reputation as a top spot for music (the birthplace of Joe Cocker, Pulp and Arctic Monkeys).

The most interesting parts of Sheffield are clustered in the 'Heart of the City' district about 300m northwest of the train station (and immediately west of the bus station), a compact area outlined by Arundel Gate, Furnival St, Carver St, West St, Church St and High St. Stretching west from here, Division St and Devonshire St have hip clothes and record shops, popular restaurants and trendy bars.

Sights

Since 2000 the city centre has been in the throes of a massive redevelopment that will continue into 2020 and beyond, so expect building sites and road works for several years to come.

Of the parts that are already complete, pride of place goes to the **Winter Gardens** (Surrey St; admission free; 8am-6pm), a wonderfully ambitious public space with a soaring glass roof supported by graceful arches of laminated timber. The 21st-century architecture contrasts sharply with the Victorian **town hall** nearby, and is further enhanced by the **Peace Gardens** – complete with fountains, sculptures and lawns full of lunching office workers whenever there's a bit of sun.

Sheffield's cultural revival is spearheaded by the **Millennium Gallery** (www.museums-sheffield.org.uk; Arundel Gate; admission free; 10am-5pm Mon-Sat, 11am-4pm Sun), a collection of four galleries under one roof. Inside, the **Ruskin Gallery** houses an eclectic collection of paintings, drawings and manuscripts established and inspired by Victorian artist, writer, critic and philosopher John Ruskin, while the **Metalwork Gallery** charts the transformation of Sheffield's steel industry into craft and design – the 'Sheffield Steel' stamp on locally made cutlery and tableware now has the cachet of designer chic.

The nearby **Graves Gallery** (www.museums-sheffield.org.uk; Surrey St; admission free; 10am-5pm Mon-Sat) has a neat and accessible display of British and European modern art; the big names represented include Cézanne, Gauguin, Miró, Klee and Picasso.

In the days before steel mills, metalworking was a cottage industry (just like wool and cotton). For a glimpse of that earlier, more innocent era, explore the restored 18th-century forges, workshops and machines at the **Abbeydale Industrial Hamlet** (www.simt.co.uk; admission free; 10am-4pm Mon-Thu, 11am-4.45pm Sun, closed early Oct-early Apr), 4 miles southwest of the centre on the A621 (towards the Peak District).

Festivals & Events

The hugely popular **World Snooker Championship** (www.worldsnooker.com) is staged at the Crucible Theatre in April. During this time, accommodation is at a premium.

Sleeping & Eating

Tourism has not quite taken off yet in Sheffield, and most of the city-centre hotels cater primarily to business travellers. New restaurants are springing up – there are several in the Leopold Square development on Leopold St – but the main restaurant areas are outside the centre.

There's a mile-long strip of bars, restaurants, cafes and take-aways on **Ecclesall Rd**, a mile to the southwest of the city centre, while **London Rd**, a mile south of the city centre, has a concentration of good-value ethnic restaurants ranging from Turkish to Thai. To find student bars and eateries head along **Division St** and **Devonshire St** just west of the city centre.

Leopold Hotel BOUTIQUE HOTEL ££
(0845 078 0067; www.leopoldhotel.co.uk; 2 Leopold St; r from £89;) Housed in a former grammar school building, Sheffield's first boutique hotel brings some much-needed style and sophistication to the city's accommodation scene (but without a London-sized price tag). Can suffer late-night noise from the bars on Leopold Square – ask for a quiet room at the back.

Houseboat Hotels HOUSEBOAT ££
(01909-569393; www.houseboathotels.com; Victoria Quays, Wharfe St; d/q from £69/95; P) Here's something a bit different: kick off your shoes and relax on board your very own permanently moored houseboat, complete with self-catering kitchen and patio area. Guests are entitled to use the gym and pool facilities at the Hilton across the road.

TOP CHOICE **Gusto** ITALIAN ££
(0114-276 0004; www.gustosheffield.com; 12 Norfolk Row; mains £9-19; 9am-9pm Mon-Sat;) Gusto is a *real* Italian cafe-restaurant, from the Italian owners serving homemade Italian food to the genuine Italian coffee being enjoyed by Italian customers reading Italian newspapers…you get the idea. Coffee and homebaked Italian cakes and pastries served all day, plus a lunch and dinner menu of exquisite Italian cuisine. Best to book for dinner.

22A CAFE £
(22a Norfolk Row; mains £5-9; 8am-5pm Mon-Sat) Nice music, nice people, nice place – this homely cafe serves hearty breakfasts with a decent cup of java, and offers a range of inventive dishes at lunchtime – carrot, leek, cashew and orange stir-fry sounds intriguing...

Blue Moon Cafe VEGETARIAN £
(2 St James St; mains £6-7; 8am-8pm Mon-Sat) Tasty veggie and vegan creations, and other healthy dishes, all served with the ubiquitous salad, in a very pleasant atmosphere – perfect for Saturday afternoon lounging.

Drinking

Lots of bars in a relatively small area plus 24,000 students = a wild night out – a pretty straightforward formula, really! The main concentrations of bars are around Division St/Devonshire St and West St in the city centre, and Ecclesall Rd to the southwest. Virtually every bar does pub grub until about 7pm.

Showroom Bar CAFE, BAR
(www.showroomworkstation.org.uk; 7 Paternoster Row;) Originally aimed at film fans, this stylish bar with its arty, hip clientele is one of the best night-time destinations in town. The ambience is good, and so is the food (served from noon to 9pm), and Sunday afternoons have live jazz.

Fat Cat PUB
(www.thefatcat.co.uk; 23 Alma St) One of Sheffield's finest pubs, the Fat Cat serves a wide range of real ales (including Kelham Island, brewed nearby by the pub's owner) in a wonderfully unreconstructed interior. There are three bars, good pub grub, a roaring fire in winter and – in the men's toilets – a fascinating exhibit on local sanitation.

Frog & Parrot PUB
(94 Division St) Home to the world's strongest beer (allegedly), the 12% ABV 'Roger & Out'. Unsuspecting ale-heads saunter in looking to down a pint of something as strong as your average wine, which is why this particular brew is only served in half-pint glasses (...so that you have at least a 50/50 chance of walking out under your own steam).

Entertainment

Sheffield has a good selection of nightclubs, a couple of top-notch theatres, and venues that attract the big names in music. The weekly *Sheffield Telegraph* (out on Friday) has the lowdown on Sheffield's entertainment scene, as does the freebie *Exposed*, available almost everywhere, and the e-zine www.sheffieldmusic scene.info.

Clubs & Live Music

Leadmill LIVE MUSIC, CLUB
(www.leadmill.co.uk; 6-7 Leadmill Rd) Every touring band has played the dark and dingy Leadmill on the way up (or on the way down), and it remains the best place in town to hear live rock and alternative music. There are club nights too, but they tend to play cheesy 1970s and '80s disco classics.

University of Sheffield Student Union LIVE MUSIC, CLUB
(www.sheffieldunion.com; Western Bank) A varied and generally good program of rock gigs and club nights – including appearances by some pretty classy DJs – make this a good spot to spend an evening, plus there's the Last Laugh Comedy Club on Sunday nights. The Union is about a mile west of the city centre.

Theatre & Cinemas

The **Crucible Theatre** and **Lyceum Theatre** on Tudor Sq share the same **box office** (☎0114-249 6000; www.sheffieldtheatres.co.uk). Both are home to excellent regional drama as wells as Shakespeare, musicals and children's theatre.

The **Showroom Cinema** (www.showroomworkstation.org.uk; Paternoster Row) is the largest independent cinema in England, screening a great mix of art-house, off-beat and not-quite-mainstream films. For everything else, there's the **Odeon** (www.odeon.co.uk; 45-47 Arundel Gate).

Information

Post Office (Norfolk Row; ⏲8.30am-5.30pm Mon-Fri, to 3pm Sat)

Tourist Office (☎0114-221 1900; www.welcometosheffield.co.uk; Winter Garden, Surrey St; ⏲9.30am-5pm Mon-Fri, 9.30am-4pm Sat, closed 1-1.30pm)

Getting There & Away

For all travel-related info on Sheffield and South Yorkshire, contact **Travel South Yorkshire** (☎01709-515151; www.travelsouthyorkshire.com).

BUS The bus station – called the Interchange – is just east of the centre, about 250m north of the train station. National Express services link Sheffield with most major centres in the north; there are frequent buses to Leeds (£6, one hour, hourly), Manchester (£9, 1½ hours, four daily) and London (£10, 4½ hours, eight daily).

TRAIN Sheffield is served by trains from all directions: Leeds (£10, one hour, twice hourly); London St Pancras (£60, 2½ hours, hourly) via Derby or Nottingham; Manchester Piccadilly (£10, one hour, twice hourly); and York (£10, 1¼ hours, twice hourly).

Getting Around

For a day of sightseeing, a **South Yorkshire Day Tripper Pass** (£6.30) is valid for one day on all bus and tram services and some trains in South Yorkshire. Buy at the information centre in Sheffield bus station, from the bus driver or at a train station.

BUS City buses run every 10 minutes during the day (Monday to Saturday, less frequently on Sundays). The free **FreeBee** bus runs every seven minutes from 8am to 7pm Monday to Saturday, linking the bus station with popular city centre locations.

TRAM Sheffield also boasts a modern **Supertram** (www.supertram.com; tickets £1.50-2.70; ⏲6am-midnight Mon-Sat, 8am-midnight Sun) that links the train station to the city centre and outer suburbs.

Around Sheffield

Magna MUSEUM
(www.visitmagna.co.uk; Sheffield Rd; adult/child £10.95/8.95; ⏲10am-5pm, last entry 4pm) At its peak, the Templeborough steelworks was the world's most productive steel smelter, with six 3000°C, electric-arc furnaces producing 1.8 million tonnes of metal a year. The mile-long works, which once had a 10,000-strong workforce, is now a 'science adventure centre' called Magna.

An unashamed celebration of heavy industry, this vast, dimly lit shed smelling vaguely of machine oil, hot metal and past glory, is a hands-on paradise for kids of all ages, with a huge range of science and technology exhibits based around the themes of earth, air, water and fire. The latter section is especially impressive, with a towering tornado of flame as a centrepiece and the chance to use a real electric arc to create your own tiny puddle of molten steel (if only for a moment or two). The hourly 'Big Melt' re-enacts the firing up of one of the original arc furnaces.

Magna is 4 miles northeast of Sheffield, just off the M1 motorway near Rotherham. Take bus 69 from Sheffield bus station (30 minutes, every 20 minutes Monday to Friday, half-hourly Saturday, hourly Sunday) towards Rotherham; it'll drop you at the door.

EAST RIDING OF YORKSHIRE

In command of Yorkshire's East Riding – the only one of Yorkshire's three original Viking 'thirds' to retain its name – is the tough old sea dog known as Hull, a no-nonsense port that looks to the North Sea for its livelihood. Just to its north, and in complete contrast to Hull's salt and grit, is the East Riding's most attractive town, Beverley, with lots of Georgian character and one of England's finest churches.

Stretching north from Hull and Beverley are the Yorkshire Wolds, a swell of gently rolling, chalky hills that reach the coast in a splash of white sea cliffs at Flamborough Head. Close by there are some classic seaside towns – bucket-and-spade Bridlington and the rather more upmarket Filey – while further south the coastline tapers away into the strange and other-wordly landscape of sand dunes and tussock grass that is Spurn Head.

Hull

POP 256,200

Tough and uncompromising, Hull is a curmudgeonly English seaport with a proud seafaring tradition. It has long been the principal cargo port of England's east coast, with an economy that grew up around carrying wool out and bringing wine in. It was also a major whaling and fishing port until the trawling industry died out, but it remains a busy cargo terminal and departure point for ferries to the Continent.

Hull has climbed aboard the regeneration bandwagon, but the recession has called a halt to many projects including the East Bank and Fruit Market developments on the waterfront, though at the time of research a new footbridge was being built across the Hull River at Scale Lane.

Meanwhile, the city's attractions include a fine collection of Victorian and Edwardian architecture, several good museums and a world-class aquarium. It's also home to the famous Hull Truck Theatre company, and counts among its famous former residents William Wilberforce (1759–1833), the Yorkshire politician who led the movement to abolish the slave trade; and the quintessentially English poet Philip Larkin (1922–85), who presided over Hull's university library for many years.

A distinctive feature of the city and surrounding area is its old-fashioned telephone boxes, which are cream-coloured rather than red. Hull was the only place in the UK to retain its own municipal phone system after all others were taken over by the Post Office in 1913; the company, now known as Kingston Communications, still provides the local phone service independently of British Telecom.

The train and bus stations – collectively known as Hull Paragon Interchange – sit on the western edge of the city centre; all the main sights are within 20 minutes' walk from here.

Sights & Activities

The Deep AQUARIUM
(www.thedeep.co.uk; Tower St; adult/child £10.50/8.50; ⏲10am-6pm, last entry 5pm; 👪) Hull's biggest tourist attraction is The Deep, a vast aquarium housed in a colossal, angular building that appears to lunge above the muddy waters of the Humber like a giant shark's head. Inside it's just as dramatic, with echoing commentaries and computer-generated interactive displays that guide you through the formation of the oceans and the evolution of sea life. The largest aquarium is 10m deep, filled with sharks, stingrays and colourful coral fishes, with moray eels draped over rocks like scarves of iridescent slime. A glass elevator plies up and down inside the tank, though you'll get a better view by taking the stairs. Don't miss the cafe on the very top floor, which has a great view of the Humber estuary.

FREE **Museum Quarter** MUSEUMS
(www.hullcc.gov.uk/museums; 36 High St; ⏲10am-5pm Mon-Sat, 1.30-4.30pm Sun) Hull has several city-run museums concentrated in an area promoted as the Museum Quarter. All share the same contact details and opening hours, and all are free.

The fascinating **Streetlife Museum** contains re-created street scenes from Georgian and Victorian times and from the 1930s, with all sorts of historic vehicles to explore, from stagecoaches to bicycles to buses and trams. Behind the museum, marooned in the mud of the River Hull, is the *Arctic Corsair*. **Tours** (⏲tours 10am-4.30pm Wed & Sat, 1.30-4.30pm Sun) of this Atlantic trawler, a veteran of the 1970s 'Cod Wars', demonstrate the hardships of fishing north of the Arctic Circle.

Nearby you'll find the **Hull & East Riding Museum** (local history and archaeology), and **Wilberforce House** (the birthplace of William Wilberforce, now a museum about the slave trade and its abolition).

FREE **Old Town** NEIGHBOURHOOD

Hull's Old Town, whose grand public buildings retain a sense of the prosperity the town once knew, occupies the thumb of land between the River Hull to the east and Princes Quay to the west. The most impressive legacy is the **Guildhall** (☎01482-300300; Low Gate; ⌚8.30am-4.30pm Mon-Thu, to 3.30pm Fri), a huge neoclassical building that dates from 1916 and houses acres of polished marble, and oak and walnut panelling, plus a small collection of sculpture and art. Phone to arrange a free guided tour.

FREE **Spurn Lightship** MUSEUM

(Castle St; ⌚10am-4.30pm Mon-Sat, 1.30-4pm Sun) Built in 1927, Hull's lighthouse-ship once served as a navigation mark for ships entering the notorious Humber estuary. Now safely retired in the marina, it houses an interesting exhibition about its own history, and an interesting contrast between the former living quarters of captain and crew.

FREE **Larkin Trail** WALKING TOUR

(www.thelarkintrail.co.uk) Hull's most famous son, the poet Philip Larkin, is commemorated in this self-guided walking tour that begins beside a bronze statue of the man in the train station. It leads past places mentioned in his poetry, and on to some of his favourite pubs. Pick up a free leaflet in the tourist office.

FREE **Ferens Art Gallery** GALLERY

(Queen Victoria Sq; ⌚10am-5pm Mon-Sat, 1.30-4.30pm Sun) This gallery features works by Stanley Spencer and Peter Blake.

Maritime Museum MUSEUM

(Queen Victoria Sq; ⌚10am-5pm Mon-Sat, 1.30-4.30pm Sun) Housed in the former dock offices (1871), the Maritime Museum celebrates Hull's long association with the sea.

Festivals

Hull Literature Festival LITERATURE

(www.humbermouth.co.uk) Besides the Larkin connection, poets Andrew Marvell, Stevie Smith and playwright Alan Plater all hail from Hull. Last two weeks of June.

Hull Jazz Festival JAZZ

(www.hulljazz.org.uk) This week-long July festival brings an impressive line-up of jazz musicians to the city.

Sleeping & Eating

Good accommodation in the city centre is pretty thin on the ground – mostly business-oriented chain hotels and a few mediocre guesthouses. The tourist office will help book accommodation for free.

The best concentration of eating places is to be found along Princes Ave, from Welbeck St to Blenheim St, a mile northwest of the centre.

Kingston Theatre Hotel HOTEL ££

(☎01482-225828; www.kingstontheatrehotel.com; 1-2 Kingston Sq; s/d/ste from £50/65/90; 📶) Overlooking leafy Kingston Sq, close to the New Theatre, this hotel is one of the best options in the city centre, with elegant bedrooms, friendly service and an excellent breakfast.

Fudge CAFE, BRASSERIE ££

(www.fudgefood.com; 93 Princes Ave; mains £7-16; ⌚10.30am-2.30pm & 5.30-10pm Tue-Thu, 9.30am-4pm Fri-Sat, 9.30am-3.30pm Sun) This funky cafe serves hearty breakfasts, cakes and coffee all day, but also offers a tempting brasserie menu at lunch and dinner times, with dishes that include juicy burgers (beef or veggie), herby crab cakes and roast pork belly with leek and bacon suet pudding.

Hitchcock's Vegetarian Restaurant VEGETARIAN ££

(☎01482-320233; www.hitchcocksrestaurant.co.uk; 1 Bishop Lane, High St; per person £15; ⌚dinner Tue-Sat) The word 'quirky' could have been invented to describe this place – an atmospheric maze of small rooms, and an all-you-can-eat vegetarian buffet whose theme – Thai, Indian, Spanish, whatever – is chosen by the first person to book that evening. But hey – the food is excellent and the welcome is warm. Bookings necessary.

Drinking & Entertainment

Come nightfall – especially at weekends – Hull can be raucous and often rowdy, especially in the streets around Trinity Sq in the Old Town, and on the strip of pubs along Beverley Rd to the north of the city centre.

Minerva PUB

(Nelson St) If you're more into pubbing than clubbing, try a pint of Black Sheep at this lovely, 200-year-old pub down by the waterfront; on a sunny day you can sit outdoors and watch the ships go by.

Hull Truck Theatre THEATRE
(www.hulltruck.co.uk; Spring St) Home to acclaimed playwright John Godber, who made his name with gritty comedies *Bouncers* and *Up'n'Under* (he is one of the most-performed playwrights in the English-speaking world), Hull Truck presents a lively program of drama, comedy and Sunday jazz. It's just northwest of the Old Town.

Welly Club CLUB
(www.giveitsomewelly.com; 105-107 Beverley Rd; admission £5-12; ⏲10pm-3am Thu-Sat) The East Riding's top nightclub offers two venues – the mainstream Welly:One (which hosts Shuffle, the regular Saturday night dance club) and the more alternative Welly:Two (more house, techno, drum and bass).

Hull New Theatre THEATRE
(www.hullcc.gov.uk; Kingston Sq) A traditional regional theatre hosting popular drama, concerts and musicals.

Information

Post Office (63 Market Pl; ⏲9am-5.30pm Mon-Sat)

Tourist Office (☎0844 811 2070; www.visithullandeastyorkshire.com; 1 Paragon St; ⏲10am-5pm Mon-Sat, 11am-3pm Sun)

Getting There & Away

BOAT The ferry port is 3 miles east of the centre at King George Dock; a bus connects the train station with the ferries. There are ferry services to Zeebrugge and Rotterdam.

BUS There are buses direct from London (£26, 6½ hours, one daily), Leeds (£8, 1¾ hours, six daily Monday to Friday, eight Saturday, two Sunday) and York (£8, 1¾ hours, one daily).

TRAIN Hull has good rail links north and south to Newcastle (£30, 2½ hours, hourly, change at York or Doncaster) and London King's Cross (£60, 2¾ hours, every two hours), and west to York (£20, 1¼ hours, every two hours) and Leeds (£14, one hour, hourly).

Around Hull

Humber Bridge BRIDGE
(www.humberbridge.co.uk) Opened in 1981, the Humber Bridge swoops gracefully across the broad estuary of the River Humber. Its 1410m span made it the world's longest single-span suspension bridge – until 1998 when it lost the title to Japan's Akashi Kaikyo bridge. It links Yorkshire to Lincolnshire, opening up what was once an often-overlooked corner of the country.

The best way to appreciate the scale of the bridge, and the vastness of the estuary, is to walk or cycle out along the footway from the **Humber Bridge tourist office** (☎01482-640852; ⏲9am-5pm May-Sep, 10am-3pm Nov-Feb, to 4pm Mar, Apr & Oct, to 3pm Nov-Feb) at the north end of the bridge (follow road signs for Humber Bridge Country Park). The car park here hosts a popular **farmers market** on the first Sunday in the month.

The bridge is a mile west of the small riverside town of Hessle, about 4 miles west of Hull. Bus 350 runs from Hull Paragon Interchange to Ferriby Rd in Hessle (25 minutes, five daily), from where it's a 300m walk to the tourist office.

Spurn Head

About 3½ miles long and less than 100m wide, Spurn Head (also called Spurn Point) is the front line in a constant battle between the River Humber and the North Sea. A series of sand and shingle banks tenuously held together by tussocks of marram grass, this fragile and unusual environment is a paradise for birdwatchers and fossil hunters.

Most of the land is now part of the **Spurn National Nature Reserve** (www.ywt.org.uk; admission per car £3) which is managed by the Yorkshire Wildlife Trust; the tidal mud flats on the west side of the headland are a haven for wading birds and migrating water fowl. You can park for free at the **Blue Bell Tea Room & Tourist Office** (⏲11am-4.30pm Sat & 11am-5pm Sun Apr-Oct) and walk out along the Spurn Footpath to the tip of the headland (7 miles round trip), or pay the admission fee and drive along the very narrow road to a parking area at the old lighthouse. There are sandy beaches on either side, where the shingle is littered with fossil ammonites, and the very end of the headland is home to a remote community of lifeboat personnel and harbour pilots.

In 1804 gun batteries were built here to repel a possible French invasion, and during WWII guns of all sizes mounted in heavy concrete emplacements were added – the shattered concrete blocks and sandy scarps near the Blue Bell are a graphic illustration of how fast this coast is being lost to the sea.

There are a couple of pubs and tearooms in **Kilnsea**, the last village before the Blue Bell, and at **Easington**, two miles to the north.

Spurn Head is about 28 miles southeast of Hull city centre, on mostly minor roads – it's about an hour's drive. On Sundays and bank holidays from Easter to October, you can take bus 75 from Hull to Patrington (one hour, hourly), then the 73 Spurn Ranger to Spurn Head car park (45 minutes, four a day).

Beverley

POP 29,110

Handsome, unspoilt Beverley is one of the most attractive towns in Yorkshire, largely on account of its magnificent minster – a rival to any cathedral in England – and the tangle of streets that lie beneath it, each brimming with exquisite Georgian and Victorian buildings.

All the sights are a short walk from either train or bus station. There's a large market in the main square on Saturday, and a smaller one on Wednesday on the square called... Wednesday Market.

Sights

Beverley Minster CHURCH

(www.beverleyminster.org; admission by donation, treadwheel crane guided tours £5; 9am-4pm Mon-Sat & noon-4pm Sun, till 5pm Mon-Sat May-Aug, treadwheel crane 11.15am, 2.15pm & 3.30pm Mon-Sat) One of the great glories of English religious architecture, Beverley Minster is the most impressive church in the country that is not a cathedral. Construction began in 1220 – it was the third church to be built on this site, the first dating from the 7th century – and continued for two centuries, spanning the Early English, Decorated and Perpendicular periods of the Gothic style.

The soaring lines of the exterior are imposing, but it is inside that the charm and beauty lie. The 14th-century **north aisle** is lined with original stone carvings, mostly of musicians. Indeed, much of our knowledge of early British musical instruments comes from these images. You'll also see goblins, devils and grotesque figures. Look out for the bagpipe player.

Close to the altar, the elaborate and intricate **Percy Canopy** (1340), a decorative frill above the tomb of local aristocrat Lady Eleanor Percy, is a testament to the skill of the sculptor, and the finest example of Gothic stone carving in England. In complete contrast, in the nearby chancel, is the 10th-century Saxon **frith stool**, a plain and polished stone chair that once gave sanctuary to anyone escaping the law.

In the roof of the tower is a restored **treadwheel crane**, where workers ground around like hapless hamsters to lift the huge loads necessary to build a medieval church. Access to the roof is by guided tour only.

FREE **St Mary's Church** CHURCH

(9.30am-4.30pm Mon-Fri, 10am-4pm Sat & 2-4pm Sun Apr-Sep, shorter hours Oct-Mar) Doomed to play second fiddle to Beverley Minster, St Mary's Church at the other end of town was built between 1120 and 1530. The west front (early 15th century) is considered one of the finest of any parish church in England. In the north choir aisle there is a **carving** (c 1330) of a rabbit dressed as a pilgrim that is said to have inspired Lewis Carroll's White Rabbit.

Sleeping & Eating

Friary YHA HOSTEL £

(0845 371 9004; www.yha.org.uk; Friar's Lane; dm £19.40; P) In Beverley, the cheapest accommodation also has the best setting and location. This hostel is housed in a beautifully restored 14th-century Dominican friary mentioned in Chaucer's *The Canterbury Tales*, and is only 100m from the minster and a short walk from the train station.

Kings Head INN ££

(01482-868103; www.kingsheadpubbeverley.co.uk; 38 Saturday Market; s/d £70/80; @) A Georgian coaching inn that has been given a modern makeover, the Kings Head is a lively pub with 12 bright and cheerful rooms above the bar. The pub opens late on weekend nights, but earplugs are supplied for those who don't want to join the revelry.

Eastgate Guest House B&B ££

(01482-868464; www.eastgateguesthouse.com; 7 Eastgate; s/d from £60/80;) A red-brick Victorian town house with comfortable rooms in a central location.

Dine on the Rowe BRITISH ££

(01482-502269; www.dineontherowe.com; 12-14 Butcher Row; mains £15-25; noon-10pm Tue-Thu, 11am-10pm Fri-Sat, 11am-4.30pm Sun;) This friendly brasserie rivals Grant's Bistro in its dedication to local produce, but offers a less formal atmosphere. Try their signature dish – smoked haddock and salmon fishcake with curry cream – or aged Yorkshire sirloin with black pudding potato cake. Lunch dishes are available noon to 6pm, when a sharing platter for two, including two glasses of wine, costs £28.

Grant's Bistro MODERN BRITISH £££
(☎01482-887624; www.grantsbistro.co.uk; 22 North Bar Within; mains £15-24; ⏲lunch Fri & Sat, dinner Mon-Sat) Grant's is a great place for a romantic dinner *à deux*, with dark-wood tables, fresh flowers and candlelight. The menu makes the most of fresh local beef, game and especially seafood, with dishes such as pan-fried scallops with black pudding. From Monday to Thursday you can get a two-course dinner, including a glass of wine, for £15.

Café Lempicka CAFE £
(13 Wednesday Market; mains £5-7) Snug little cafe serves fair-trade coffee and tea, wicked hot chocolate, homemade cakes and daily lunch specials.

Information

Post Office (Register Sq; ⏲9am-5.30pm Mon-Fri, to 12.30pm Sat)

Tourist Office (☎01482-391672; www.beverley.gov.uk; 34 Butcher Row; ⏲9.30am-5.15pm Mon-Fri & 10am-4.45pm Sat year-round, 11am-3pm Sun Jul & Aug)

Getting There & Away

BUS There are frequent bus services from Hull including numbers 121, 122, 246 and X46/X47 (30 minutes, every 20 minutes). Bus X46/X47 links Beverley with York (£6.20, 1¼ hours, hourly).

TRAIN There are regular trains to Scarborough via Filey (£12.80, 1¼ hours, every two hours) and Hull (£6, 15 minutes, twice hourly).

Bridlington

POP 33,600

Bridlington is one of those sleepy seaside resorts that seems to have been bypassed by the 21st century, pulling in a crowd of contented regulars who return year after year to enjoy the neatly groomed beaches of golden sand, the minigolf and paddling pool, the deckchairs and donkey rides.

The reopening of **Bridlington Spa** (☎01262-401400; South Marine Dr) in 2007 provided the town with a bit of a shot in the arm. The renovated building, which retains its Edwardian theatre and 1930s art deco ballroom, stages a lively program of music and entertainment events that has livened things up down by the South Beach, and has a decent **cafe-bar** with a panoramic sea view.

Food wise, Bridlington is famous for **Audrey's Fish & Chips** (2 Queen St; mains £4-6; ⏲lunch), an old-school fish-and-chip restaurant that serves crisp, battered haddock fried in beef dripping – the real deal.

The **tourist office** (☎01262-673474; 25 Prince St; ⏲9.30am-5.30pm Mon-Sat, 11am-3pm Sun) is near the North Beach and has short-term parking at the front.

Bridlington is on the railway line between Hull (£11.40, 50 minutes, every 30 minutes) and Scarborough (£6.60, 40 minutes, every two hours).

WANT MORE?

Head to **Lonely Planet** (www.lonelyplanet.com/england/yorkshire/york) for planning advice, author recommendations, traveller reviews and insider tips.

Around Bridlington

Northeast of Bridlington, the 120m-high chalk cliffs of **Flamborough Head** thrust out into the North Sea, providing nesting sites for England's largest seabird colony. The headland is also home to the country's oldest-surviving **lighthouse tower**, dating from around 1670 – it stands in the golf course about 300m before the car park beside the modern lighthouse.

On the northern side of the headland, about 4 miles north of Bridlington, is the RSPB's **Bempton Cliffs Nature Reserve** (www.rspb.org.uk; parking £5 Mar-Oct; ⏲visitor centre 9.30am-5pm Mar-Oct, 9.30am-4pm Nov-Feb). From April to August these cliffs are home to more than 200,000 nesting seabirds, including guillemots, razorbills, fulmars, a rare colony of gannets, and those supermodels of the seagull world, the delicate and elegant kittiwakes, with their fat and fluffy chicks. Most popular though, are the comical and colourful puffins. There is a tourist office at the car park and the reserve has 3 miles of well-maintained paths along the cliffs. Binoculars can be rented for £3; there are helpful volunteers on hand to offer guidance.

To get here take a train from Bridlington to Bempton village (seven minutes, every 1½ hours), from where it's a 1½-mile walk to the reserve.

Manchester, Liverpool & the Northwest

Includes »

Best Places to Eat

» Australasia (p640)
» Monro (p660)
» Mark Addy (p640)
» Upstairs at the Grill (p650)
» Tanroagan (p671)

Best Places to Stay

» Stone Villa (p649)
» Great John Street Hotel (p638)
» Hope Street Hotel (p659)
» Malmaison (p659)

Why Go?

Hedonism – the kind only proper cities can provide. History – of the notable firsts kind. And music – think the Smiths, the Stone Roses and the Beatles. Just a taster of three good reasons to explore England's once-mighty industrial heartland, the birthplace of the first modern city, the cradle of capitalism and the Age of Englightenment. The industry is, for the most part, gone but among the hulking relics are two of the country's most exciting cities, as well as a Tudor postcard-town (Chester) and, in Blackpool, the *sine qua non* of traditional holidays-by-the-sea. And, if you fancy a bit of respite from the concrete paw-print of humankind, there's some of the most beautiful countryside in England.

Not content with defining the progress of the last two centuries, northwest England is dead set on making an imprint on the 21st. It's a tall order, but it's going about it the right way.

When to Go

The world's most famous steeplechase, the Aintree Grand National, is run just outside Liverpool over the first weekend in April. May and June are Tourist Trophy (TT) Festival season on the Isle of Man – beloved of motor enthusiasts the world over. The football (soccer) season runs from late August until May.

For the arts, the highlight is the the Manchester International Arts Festival, a biennial showstopper held in July. Music buffs should visit Liverpool in the last week of August for madness at Creamfields (dance) and the Mathew St Festival, an ode to all things Beatles.

Liverpool, Manchester & the Northwest Highlights

1. Learning a valuable history lesson at the outstanding **International Slavery Museum** (p656) in Liverpool
2. Having your insides churned and twisted at Blackpool's **Pleasure Beach** (p665)
3. Learning exactly what kind of hell war is in the **Imperial War Museum North** (p635) in Manchester
4. Sampling Manchester culinary delights at one (or more) of the city's superb **restaurants** (p640)

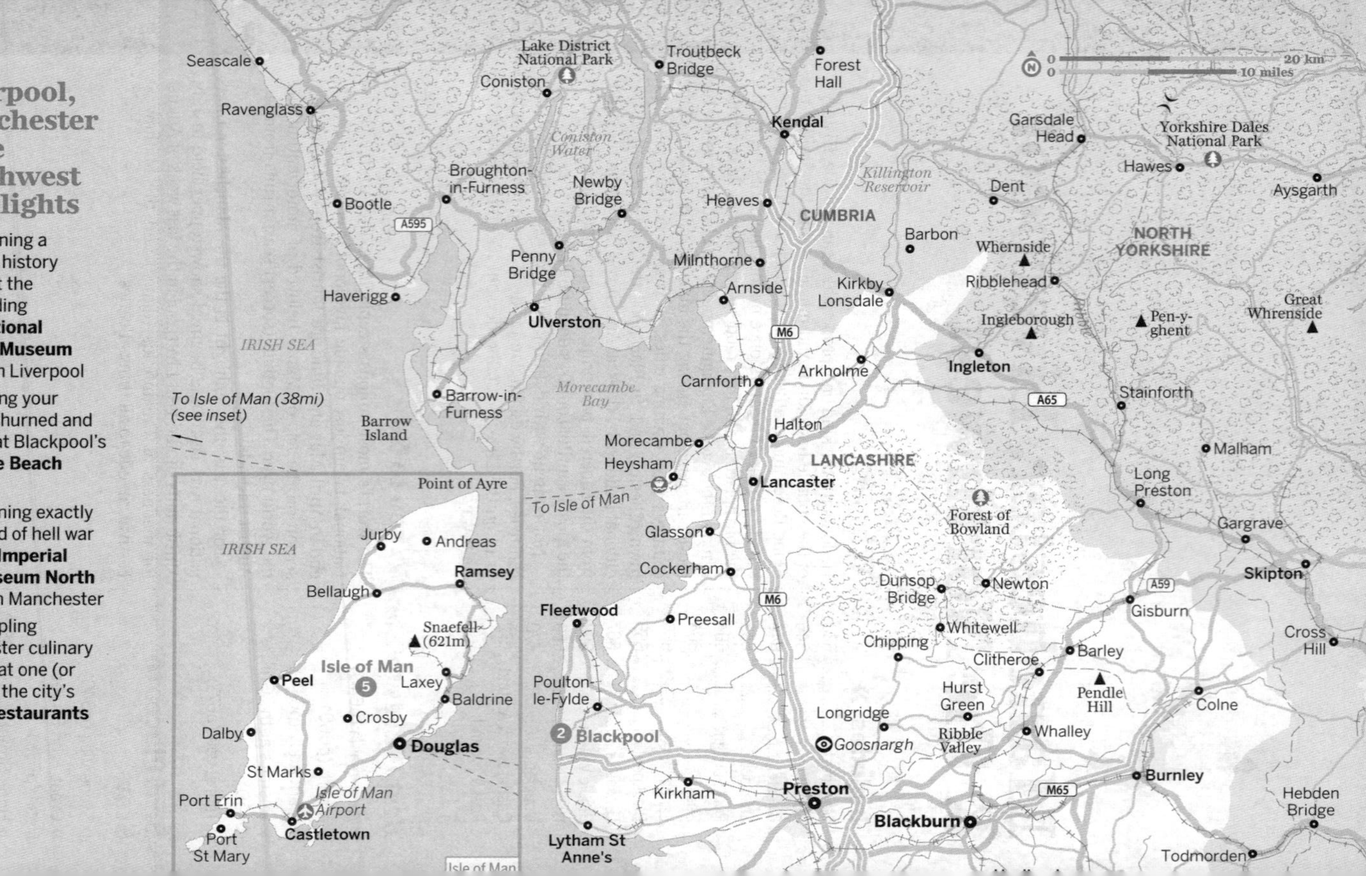

5 Getting to grips with the **Isle of Man** (p669) – about as exotic as England gets

6 Letting Liverpool tell you its story at **Museum of Liverpool** (p658)

7 Tramping Chester's **city walls** (p646), like the Romans did 2000 years ago

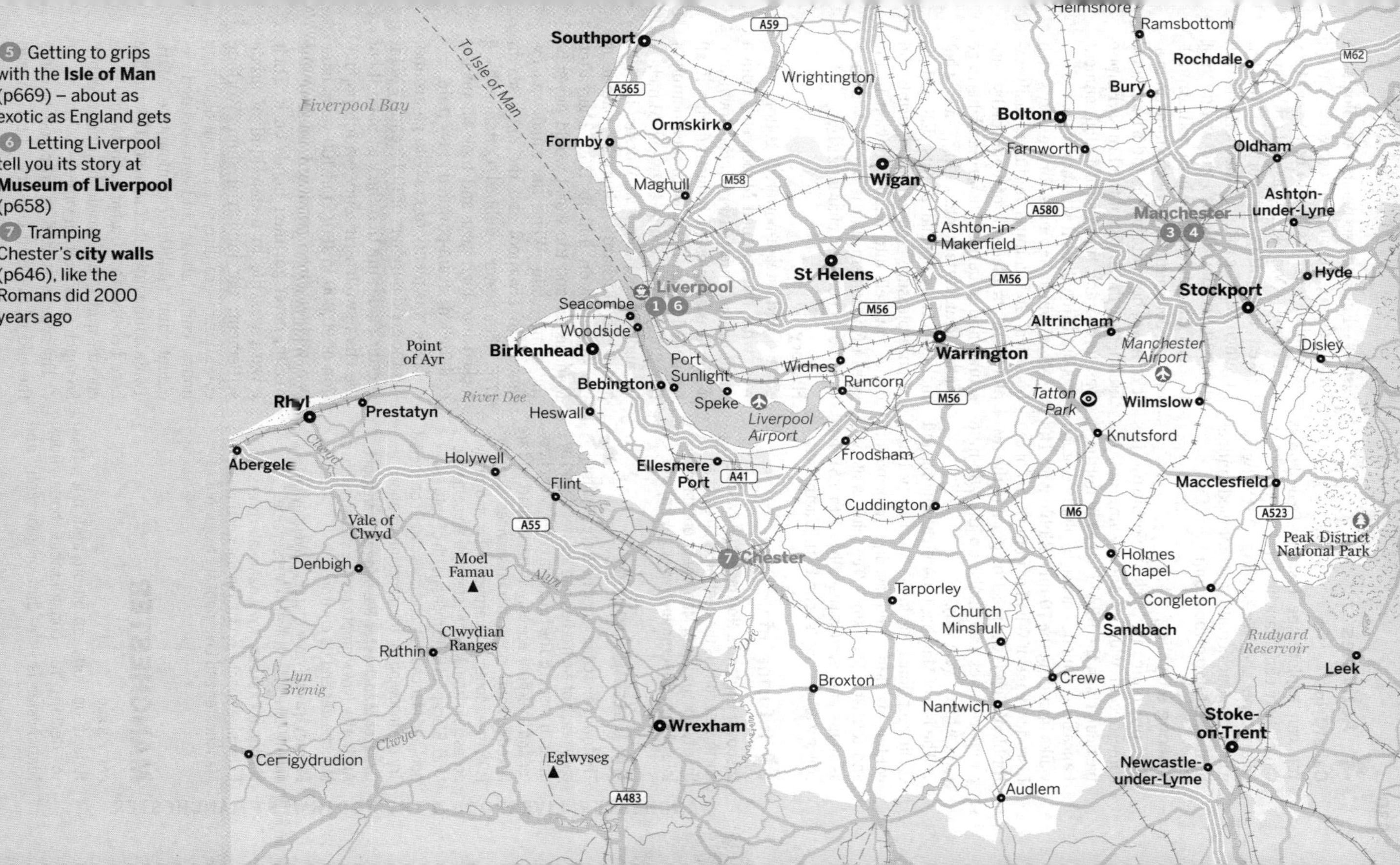

Activities

Canal Trips

You can explore the historic Peak Forest Canal between Manchester and the Peak District on the **Wandering Duck** (www.wanderingduck.co.uk) a combined budget hostel and narrowboat tour.

Walking & Cycling

The predominantly urban northwest has some decent walking and cycling options, particularly in the Ribble Valley in northern Lancashire, which is home to plenty of good walks including the 70-mile Ribble Way. The historic village of Whalley, in the heart of the Ribble Valley, is the meeting point of the two circular routes that make up the 260-mile Lancashire Cycle Way.

The Isle of Man has top-notch walking and cycling options. Regional tourism websites contain walking and cycling information, and tourist offices stock free leaflets as well as maps and guides (usually £1 to £5) that cover walking, cycling and other activities.

Information

Discover England's Northwest (www.visitnorthwest.com) is the centralised tourist authority; for the Isle of Man, check out the main **Isle of Man Government** (www.gov.im) site.

Getting Around

The towns and cities listed here are all within easy reach of each other, and are well linked by public transport. The two main cities, Manchester and Liverpool, are only 34 miles apart and are linked by hourly bus and train services. Chester is 18 miles south of Liverpool, but is also easily accessible from Manchester by train or via the M56. Blackpool is 50 miles north of both Liverpool and Manchester, and is also well connected. Try the following for transport information:

Greater Manchester Passenger Transport Authority (www.gmpte.com) Extensive info on Manchester and its environs.

Merseytravel (www.merseytravel.gov.uk) Taking care of all travel in Merseyside.

National Express (www.nationalexpress.com) Extensive coach services in the northwest; Manchester and Liverpool are major hubs.

MANCHESTER

POP 498,800

Raised on lofty ambition and not afraid to declare its considerable bona fides, Manchester is – by dint of geography and history – England's second city (apologies to Birmingham), although if you were to ask a Mancunian what it's like to be second they might reply: 'Don't know; ask a Londoner.'

Even accounting for northern bluster, the uncrowned capital of the north is well deserving of the title. It's the world's first modern city; the place where both capitalism and communism were given theoretical legs; it was here, during the Industrial Revolution, that the might of the British Empire was forged and the Age of Enlightenment was put through its first, tentative paces.

All of which accounts for the city's rich historical and cultural heritage, easily explored in its plethora of noteworthy museums and galleries. History and heritage make Manchester interesting, but what makes it truly special are its distractions of pure pleasure. You can dine, drink and dance yourself into happy oblivion in the swirl of hedonism that is one of Manchester's most cherished characteristics.

History

Canals and steam-powered cotton mills were what transformed Manchester from a small disease-infested provincial town into a big disease-infested industrial city. It all happened in the 1760s, with the opening of the Bridgewater Canal between Manchester and the coal mines at Worsley in 1763, and with Richard Arkwright patenting his super cotton mill in 1769. Thereafter, Manchester and the world would never be the same again. When the canal was extended to Liverpool and the open sea in 1776, Manchester – dubbed 'Cottonopolis' – kicked into high gear and took off on the coal-fuelled, steam-powered gravy train.

There was plenty of gravy to go around, but the good burghers of 19th-century Manchester made sure that the vast majority of the city's swollen citizenry (with a population of 90,000 in 1801, and 100 years later, two million), who produced most of the wealth, never got their hands on it. Their reward was life in a new kind of urban settlement: the industrial slum. Working conditions were dire, with impossibly long hours, child labour, and work-related accidents and fatalities commonplace. Mark Twain commented that he would like to live here because the 'transition between Manchester and Death would be unnoticeable'. So much for Victorian values.

The wheels started to come off towards the end of the 19th century. The USA had begun to flex its own industrial muscles and was taking over a sizeable chunk of the textile trade; production in Manchester's mills began to slow, and then it stopped altogether. By WWII there was hardly enough cotton produced in the city to make a tablecloth. The postwar years weren't much better: 150,000 manufacturing jobs were lost between 1961 and 1983 and the port – still the UK's third largest in 1963 – finally closed in 1982 due to declining traffic. The nadir came on 15 June 1996, when an IRA bomb wrecked a chunk of the city centre, but the subsequent reconstruction proved to be the beginning of the glass-and-chrome revolution so much in evidence today.

Sights & Activities

There's so much to see in the city centre and in the surrounding suburbs – from Salford Quays towards the west (across the River Irwell) to the museums and galleries of the University of Manchester (south of the city centre along and off Oxford Rd). Beyond the city centre, public transport – bus or tram – is the best way to travel.

CITY CENTRE

FREE Museum of Science & Industry MUSEUM
(MOSI; ☎0161-832 2244; www.msim.org.uk; Liverpool Rd; charges vary for special exhibitions; ⏲10am-5pm) The city's largest museum comprises 2.8 hectares in the heart of 19th-century industrial Manchester. It's in the landscape of enormous, weather-stained brick buildings and rusting cast-iron relics of canals, viaducts, bridges, warehouses and market buildings that makes up Castlefield, now deemed an 'urban heritage park'.

If there's anything you want to know about the Industrial (and post-Industrial) Revolution and Manchester's key role in it, you'll find the answers here, among the collection of steam engines and locomotives, factory machinery from the mills, and the excellent exhibition telling the story of Manchester from the sewers up.

It's an all-ages kind of museum, but the emphasis is on making sure the young 'uns don't get bored – they could easily spend a whole day poking about the place, testing early electric-shock machines here and trying out a printing press there. A unifying theme (besides the fact that science and industry were pretty handy for the development of society) is that Manchester and Mancunians were key to most industrial developments: did you know that Manchester was home to the world's first computer (a giant contraption called 'the baby') in 1948, or that the world's first submarine was built to the designs of local curate Reverend George Garrett in 1880? Nope, neither did we.

TOP CHOICE National Football Museum MUSEUM
(☎0161-605 8200; www.nationalfootballmuseum.com; Corporation St, Urbis, Cathedral Gardens;

MANCHESTER IN...

Two Days

Explore the **Museum of Science & Industry**, visit the **People's History Museum** and come to grips with the beautiful game at the **National Football Museum**. For food, try the **Oast House** before trying one of the bars in the Northern Quarter.

On day two, take the Metrolink to Salford and explore the **Imperial War Museum North**, the **Lowry** and the **Manchester United Museum** at Old Trafford. Take a tour of the BBC spread at **MediaCityUK**. Back in the city, indulge some retail chi at the high-end shops of **Spinningfields** or the offbeat boutiques of the **Northern Quarter**. Treat yourself with dinner at **Australasia**.

Four Days

Follow the two-day itinerary and tackle some of the city's lesser-known museums – the **John Rylands Library**, **Chetham's Library & School of Music** and the **Manchester Jewish Museum**. Go south and explore the **Manchester Museum** and **Whitworth Art Gallery**. Examine the riches of the **Manchester Art Gallery**. End the evening with a dance at **Factory 251**. The next day, take a walking tour – the tourist office has details of a whole host of themed ones – and if you're serious about clubbing, make the pilgrimage to Ancoats for the absolutely fabulous **Sankey's**.

Manchester

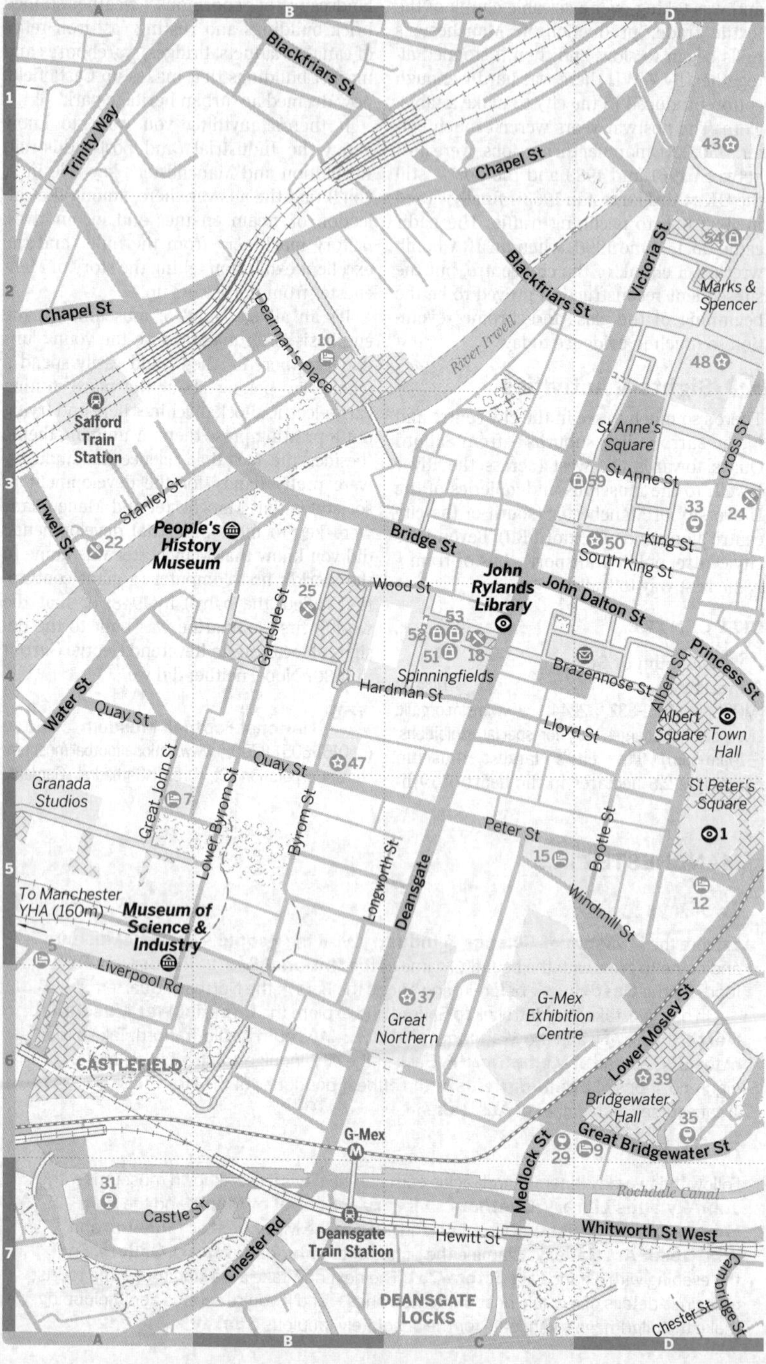
A
B
C
D
1
2
3
4
5
6
7
Blackfriars St
Trinity Way
Chapel St
43
54
Marks & Spencer
Victoria St
Chapel St
Blackfriars St
Dearman's Place
10
River Irwell
48
Salford Train Station
St Anne's Square
Cross St
St Anne St
59
Stanley St
Irwell St
24
33
People's History Museum
22
Bridge St
50
King St
South King St
John Rylands Library
Wood St
25
Gartside St
John Dalton St
53
52
51
18
Spinningfields
Brazennose St
Albert Sq
Princess St
Hardman St
Water St
Quay St
Lloyd St
Albert Square
Town Hall
Quay St
47
Granada Studios
Great John St
7
Lower Byrom St
Byrom St
St Peter's Square
Peter St
1
Bootle St
15
Longworth St
Deansgate
12
To Manchester YHA (160m)
Museum of Science & Industry
Windmill St
5
Liverpool Rd
37
Great Northern
G-Mex Exhibition Centre
Lower Mosley St
CASTLEFIELD
39
Bridgewater Hall
35
G-Mex
Great Bridgewater St
Medlock St
29
9
31
Rochdale Canal
Castle St
Chester Rd
Deansgate Train Station
Hewitt St
Whitworth St West
Cambridge St
DEANSGATE LOCKS
Chester St

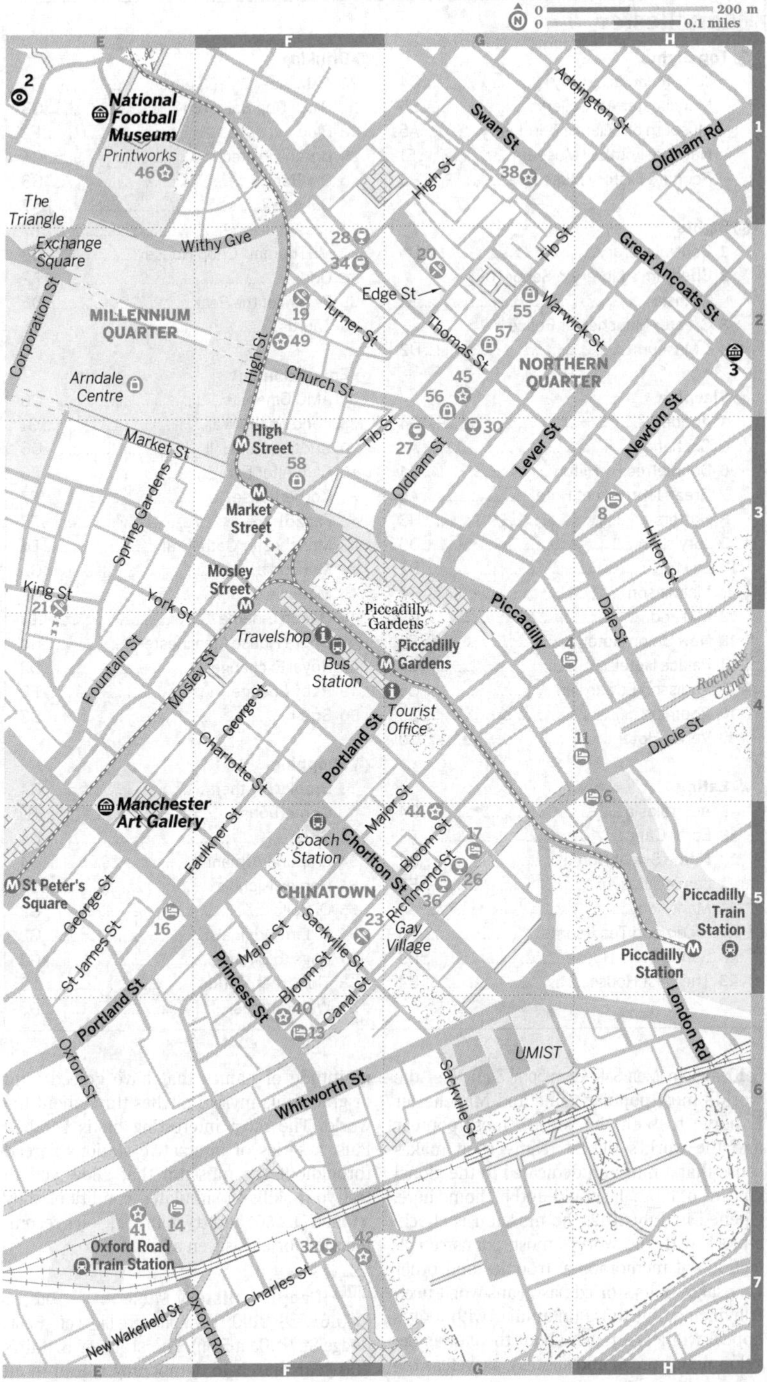

0
200 m
0
0.1 miles
E
F
G
H
1
2
3
4
5
6
7
National Football Museum
Printworks
46
2
The Triangle
Exchange Square
Withy Gve
Corporation St
MILLENNIUM QUARTER
Arndale Centre
Market St
High Street
Market Street
Mosley Street
Spring Gardens
King St
21
York St
Fountain St
Mosley St
George St
Charlotte St
Manchester Art Gallery
Faulkner St
St Peter's Square
George St
St James St
16
Portland St
Oxford St
Princess St
Major St
Bloom St
40
13
Canal St
Sackville St
23
CHINATOWN
Coach Station
Chorlton St
Portland St
Travelshop
Bus Station
Piccadilly Gardens
Tourist Office
Major St
44
Bloom St
17
Richmond St
26
36
Gay Village
Whitworth St
UMIST
Sackville St
41
14
Oxford Road Train Station
32
42
Charles St
New Wakefield St
Oxford Rd
High St
28
34
19
49
Turner St
Edge St
20
Church St
Tib St
27
58
Oldham St
Thomas St
45
56
30
57
55
Warwick St
Tib St
High St
Swan St
38
Addington St
Oldham Rd
Great Ancoats St
3
NORTHERN QUARTER
Newton St
Lever St
8
Hilton St
Piccadilly
Dale St
4
Rochdale Canal
Ducie St
11
6
Piccadilly Train Station
Piccadilly Station
London Rd

Manchester

Top Sights

John Rylands Library ... C4
Manchester Art Gallery ... E5
Museum of Science & Industry ... A5
National Football Museum ... E1
People's History Museum ... B3

Sights

1 Central Library ... D5
2 Chetham's Library & School of Music ... E1
3 Greater Manchester Police Museum ... H2

Sleeping

4 Abode ... G4
5 Castlefield ... A5
6 Doubletree By Hilton ... H4
7 Great John Street Hotel ... A5
8 Hatters ... H3
9 Jury's Inn ... D6
10 Lowry ... B2
11 Malmaison ... H4
12 Midland ... D5
13 New Union Hotel ... F6
14 Palace Hotel ... E7
15 Radisson Edwardian ... C5
16 Roomzzz ... E5
17 Velvet Hotel ... G5

Eating

18 Australasia ... C4
19 Earth Cafe ... F2
20 Home Sweet Home ... G2
21 Jamie's Italian ... E3
22 Mark Addy ... A3
23 Richmond Tea Rooms ... F5
24 Sam's Chop House ... D3
25 The Oast House ... B4

Drinking

26 AXM ... G5
27 Black Dog Ballroom ... G3
28 Bluu ... F2
29 Britons Protection ... C6
30 Dry Bar ... G3
31 Dukes 92 ... A7
32 Lass O'Gowrie ... F7
33 Mr Thomas' Chop House ... D3
34 Odd ... F2
35 Peveril of the Peak ... D6
36 Taurus ... G5

Entertainment

37 AMC Cinemas ... C6
38 Band on the Wall ... G1
39 Bridgewater Hall ... D6
40 Club Alter Ego ... F6
41 Cornerhouse ... E7
42 Fac251 ... F7
43 Manchester Cathedral ... D1
44 Mancunia ... G5
45 Moho Live ... G2
46 Odeon Cinema ... E1
47 Opera House Manchester ... B4
48 Royal Exchange ... D2
49 Ruby Lounge ... F2
50 South ... D3

Shopping

51 Brooks Brothers ... C4
Cornerhouse ... (see 41)
52 DKNY ... C4
53 Emporio Armani ... C4
54 Harvey Nichols ... D2
55 Oi Polloi ... G2
56 Oxfam Originals ... G2
57 Rags to Bitches ... G2
58 Tib Street Market ... F3
59 Waterstones ... D3

10am-5pm Mon-Sat, 11am-5pm Sun) It's the world's most popular game and Manchester is home to both the world's most popular and the world's richest teams, so it makes sense that a museum dedicated to the global charms of football should find its home here. Opened in July 2012, the museum is chock-a-block with the world's most extensive collections of memorabilia, trophies and other keepsakes of its storied past. Fans won't need convincing, but those unfamiliar with footy's appeal will learn much about the game's development, spread and success; as well as the multitude of names that have graced (and disgraced) its myriad pitches throughout the world. The most interesting bit is Football Plus, a series of interactive stations spread throughout the museum that allow you to test your skills in simulated conditions; buy a token (£2.50) and try your luck – it's recommended for kids seven and older.

FREE **People's History Museum** MUSEUM
(0161-838 9190; www.phm.org.uk; Left Bank, Bridge St; 10am-5pm) The story of Britain's 200-year march to democracy is told in all

its pain and pathos at this superb museum, housed in a refurbished Edwardian pumping station. Clock in on the 1st floor (you literally punch your card in an old mill clock, which managers would infamously fiddle so as to make employees work longer) and plunge into the heart of Britain's struggle for basic democratic rights, labour reform and fair pay. Amid displays like the (tiny) desk at which Thomas Paine (1737–1809) wrote *Rights of Man* (1791) and an array of beautifully made and colourful union banners are compelling interactive displays, including a screen where you can trace the effects of all the events covered in the museum on five generations of the same family. The 2nd floor takes up the struggle for equal rights from WWII to the current day, touching on gay rights, anti-racism initiatives and the defining British socio-political landmarks of the last 50 years, including the founding of the National Health Service (NHS), the Miners' Strike and the widespread protests against the Poll Tax. It's compelling stuff, and a marvellous example of a museum's relevance to our everyday lives.

FREE John Rylands Library LIBRARY
(☎0161-306 0555; www.library.manchester.ac.uk; 150 Deansgate; ⊙noon-5pm Mon & Sun, 10am-5pm Tue-Sat) Less a library and more a cathedral to books, Basil Champneys' stunning building is arguably the most beautiful library in Britain and one hell of a way for Rylands' widow to remember her husband, John. It's a breathtaking example of Victorian Gothic, no more so than the Reading Room, complete with high-vaulted ceilings and stained-glass windows. The collection of early printed books and rare manuscripts is equally impressive, and includes a Gutenberg Bible, the earliest extant of a New Testament text and the country's second largest assembly of works by Britain's first printer, William Caxton. A £16 million refit has resulted in the addition of a surprisingly tasteful modern annexe with a cafe and a bookshop.

FREE Manchester Art Gallery ART MUSEUM
(☎0161-235 8888; www.manchestergalleries.org; Mosley St; ⊙10am-5pm Tue-Sun) A superb collection of British art and a hefty number of European masters are on display at the city's top gallery. The older wing, designed by Charles Barry (of Houses of Parliament fame) in 1834, has an impressive collection that includes 37 Turner watercolours, as well as the country's best collection of Pre-Raphaelite art. The newer gallery features a permanent collection of 20th-century British art starring Lucien Freud, Francis Bacon, Stanley Spencer, Henry Moore and David Hockney. Finally, the Gallery of Craft & Design, in the Athenaeum, houses a permanent collection of pre-17th-century art, with works predominantly from the Dutch and early Renaissance masters.

FREE Greater Manchester Police Museum MUSEUM
(www.gmpmuseum.com/; 57a Newton St; ⊙10.30am-3.30pm Tue) One of the city's best-kept secrets is this superb museum housed within a former Victorian police station. The original building has been magnificently – if a little creepily – brought back to life, and you can wander in and out of 19th-century cells where prisoners rested their heads on wooden pillows; visit a restored magistrates' court from 1895; and examine the case histories (complete with mugshots and photos of weapons) of some of the more notorious names to have passed through its doors.

SALFORD QUAYS

Just west of the city centre and easily reached via Metrolink (£2) is Salford Quays, home to the city's big-ticket attractions and new hub of the BBC's northern HQ. Check out www.thequays.co.uk for more information.

FREE Imperial War Museum North MUSEUM
(☎0161-836 4000; www.iwm.org.uk/north; Trafford Wharf Rd; ⊙10am-5pm) War museums generally appeal to those with a fascination for military hardware and battle strategy (toy soldiers optional), but Daniel Libeskind's visually stunning Imperial War Museum North takes a radically different approach. War is hell, it tells us, but it's a hell we revisit with tragic regularity.

The exhibits cover the main conflicts of the 20th century through a broad selection of displays, but the really effective bit comes every half-hour when the entire exhibition hall goes dark and one of three 15-minute films *(Children and War, The War at Home* or *Weapons of War)* is projected throughout. Visitors are encouraged to walk around the darkened room so as to get the most out of the sensory bombardment.

Although the audiovisuals and displays are compelling, the extraordinary aluminium-clad building itself is a huge part of the attraction, and the exhibition spaces are genuinely breathtaking. Libeskind's building is meant to look like a cup, dropped and broken into three shards, each representing a distinct theatre of war: air, land and sea. Take the Metrolink to Harbour City.

Old Trafford (Manchester United Museum & Tour) STADIUM
(☎0161 868 8000; www.manutd.com; Sir Matt Busby Way; ⊙9.30am-5pm) Home of the world's most famous club, the Old Trafford stadium is both a theatre and a temple for millions of fans worldwide, many of whom come in pilgrimage to the ground to pay tribute to the minor deities (disguised as highly paid footballers) who play there. Since 1986 they have been managed by Sir Alex Ferguson, who has brought them unprecedented success, including 12 league titles, five FA Cup titles and two UEFA Champions' League trophies – in 2011 they renamed one of the stands in his honour. Yet all that glory doesn't impress at least half the local population, who prefer their less-famous rivals Manchester City. Still, a visit to the stadium is one of the more memorable things you'll do here. We strongly recommend that you take the **tour** (adult/child £15/10; ⊙9.40am-4.30pm every 10 min except match days), which includes a seat in the stands, a stop in the changing rooms, a peek at the players' lounge (from which the manager is banned unless invited by the players) and a walk down the tunnel to the pitchside dugout, which is as close to ecstasy as many of the club's fans will ever get. It's pretty impressive stuff. The **museum** (adult/child £10.50/8.50; ⊙9.30am-5pm), which is part of the tour but can be visited independently, has a comprehensive history of the club, and a state-of-the-art call-up system that means you can view your favourite goals – as well as a holographic 'chat' with Sir Alex Ferguson. Take the Metrolink to Old Trafford.

NOTABLE BUILDINGS

Manchester has no shortage of eye-catching architecture, especially from the Victorian Age. Most notable of all is the impressive **Town Hall** (☎0161-234 5000; www.manchester.gov.uk; Albert Sq), crowned by an 85m-high tower and featuring an especially ornate interior. More recent additions to the cityscape include the neoclassical **Central Library** (☎0161-234 1900; St Peter's Sq), built in 1934 to resemble the Roman Pantheon. It is Britain's largest municipal library and is currently undergoing a major facelift; it'll reopen sometime in late 2013. 1935 saw the opening of Edwin Lutyens' stunning Art Deco Midlands Bank, now home to a branch of Jamie's Italian (p640) – even if you don't eat there it's well worth having a look inside; be sure to go downstairs and peek in at the deposit vaults.

Lowry ARTS CENTRE
(☎0161-876 2020; www.thelowry.com; Pier 8, Salford Quays; ⊙11am-8pm Tue-Fri, 10am-8pm Sat, 11am-6pm Sun & Mon) Looking more like a shiny steel ship than an arts centre, the Lowry is the quays' most notable success. It attracts more than one million visitors a year to its myriad functions, which include everything from art exhibits and performances to bars, restaurants and, inevitably, shops. You can even get married here.

The complex is home to more than 300 paintings and drawings by northern England's favourite artist, LS Lowry (1887–1976), who was born in nearby Stretford. He became famous for his humanistic depictions of industrial landscapes and northern towns, and gave his name to the complex.

MediaCityUK ARTS CENTRE
(☎0161-886 5300; www.mediacityuk.co.uk; Salford Quays; adult £8.50, students £7.25, children £5.25 ; ⊙Tours 10.30am, 12.30 & 3pm Mon-Wed) The BBC's new northern home is but one significant element of this vast, 81-hectare site. Besides hosting six departments of the national broadcaster (BBC Breakfast, Children's, Sport, Radio 5Live, Learning and Future Media & Technology), it will also be home to a bespoke set for the world's longest-running soap opera, the perennially popular *Coronation Street* (which broadcasts on ITV). There are no plans as yet to offer tours of the Corrie set, but you can visit the BBC's impressive set-up and see the (new) sets of some of TV's most iconic programs on a guided 90-minute tour that also includes a chance for kids to 'make' a programme in an interactive studio.

South of the City

University of Manchester UNIVERSITY
About a mile south of the city, the University of Manchester is one of England's most

TOP FIVE MANCHESTER ALBUMS

» *Stone Roses* The Stone Roses

» *The Queen is Dead* The Smiths

» *Unknown Pleasures* Joy Division

» *Urban Hymns* The Verve

» *Ninety* 808 State

extraordinary institutions, and not just because it is a top-class university with a remarkable academic pedigree and a great place to party. It is also home to a world-class museum and a superb art gallery. Take bus 11, 16, 41 or 42 from Piccadilly Gardens or bus 47, 190 or 191 from Victoria station.

Manchester Museum

If you're into natural history and social science, this extraordinary **museum** (www.museum.manchester.ac.uk; University of Manchester, Oxford Rd; ⌚10am-5pm Tue-Sat, 11am-4pm Sun & Mon) is the place for you. It has galleries devoted to archaeology, archery, botany, ethnology, geology, numismatics and zoology. The real treat here, though, is the Egyptology section and its collection of mummies. One particularly interesting part is devoted to the work of Dr Richard Neave, who has rebuilt faces of people who have been dead for more than 3000 years; his pioneering techniques are now used in criminal forensics.

Whitworth Art Gallery

Manchester's second most important **art gallery** (☎0161-275 7450; www.whitworth.manchester.ac.uk; Oxford Rd, University of Manchester; ⌚10am-5pm Mon-Sat, noon-4pm Sun) has a wonderful collection of British watercolours. It also houses the best selection of historic textiles outside London, and has a number of galleries devoted to the work of artists from Dürer and Rembrandt to Lucien Freud and David Hockney. All this high art aside, you may find that the most interesting part of the gallery is the group of rooms dedicated to wallpaper – proof that bland pastels and horrible flowery patterns are not the final word in home decoration.

Tours

The tourist office sells tickets for guided walks on all aspects of the city, from architecture to radical history, which operate almost daily year-round and cost £6/5 per adult/child.

Festivals & Events

Screenfields FILM

(www.spinningfieldsonline.com; Spinningfields; £2, season ticket £9.99; ⌚8pm Thu, Apr-Jul) Season of outdoor films, complete with deckchairs and picnics.

FutureEverything CONTEMPORARY ARTS

(www.futureeverything.org) Superb electronic music and media arts festival that takes place in a number of venues over a week in mid-May.

Manchester Day PARADE

(www.themanchesterdayparade.co.uk) Inaugurated in 2010, a parade to celebrate all things Manchester, with music, performances and fireworks. Occurs in June.

Manchester International Festival ARTS

(☎0161-238 7300; www.mif.co.uk) A three-week-long biennial arts festival of new work across visual arts, performance and popular culture. The next festival is scheduled for July 2013.

Manchester Jazz Festival MUSIC

(www.manchesterjazz.com) Takes place in 50 venues throughout the city over a week in July.

Manchester Pride GAY/LESBIAN

(☎0161-831 7700; www.manchesterpride.com) One of England's biggest celebrations of gay, bisexual and transgender life, held over 10 days in late August.

Manchester Food & Drink Festival FOOD

(www.foodanddrinkfestival.com) Manchester's superb foodie scene shows off its wares over 10 days in mid-October; farmers' markets, pop-up restaurants and gourmet events are just part of the program.

Manchester International Film Festival FILM

(www.kinofilm.org.uk) A biennial late-October film festival that was launched in 2007.

Sleeping

Manchester's hotels recognise that the business traveller is their best bet, but in keeping with their capital of cool status, they like to throw in more than a bit of style, so you'll find plenty of designer digs around town. The popularity of serviced apartments has spread, offering a little more versatility than the standard hotel room. Remember that during the football season (August to May),

MORE MUSEUMS

If you can't get enough of annotated exhibits, Manchester has a number of other museums worth checking out.

The **Manchester Jewish Museum** (www.manchesterjewishmuseum.com; 190 Cheetham Hill Rd; adult/child £3.95/2.95; ⌚10.30am-4pm Mon-Thu, 1-5pm Sun), in a Moorish-style former synagogue, tells the story of the city's Jewish community in fascinating detail, including the story of Polish refugee Michael Marks, who opened his first shop with partner Tom Spencer at 20 Cheetham Hill Rd in 1894. From Piccadilly Gardens, take bus 59, 89, 135 or 167.

Transport buffs will enjoy the wonderful **Museum of Transport** (www.gmts.co.uk; Boyle St; adult/child £4/free; ⌚10am-4.30pm Wed, Sat & Sun), packed with old buses, fire engines and lorries (trucks) built in the last 100 years.

Chetham's Library & School of Music (☎0161-834 7861; www.chethams.org.uk; Long Millgate; ⌚9am-12.30pm & 1.30-4.30pm Mon-Fri), built in 1421, is the city's oldest structure that's still completely intact – and was where Messrs Marx and Engels used to study (by the big bay window in the main reading room). It is only open by prearranged visit, as it is part of a national school for young musicians.

Pankhurst Centre (www.thepankhurstcentre.org.uk; 60-62 Nelson St; ⌚10am-4pm Mon-Fri) is the converted childhood home of Emmeline Pankhurst (1858–1928), a leading light of the British suffragette movement. It has displays on her remarkable life and political struggles.

Immensely popular with plane spotters, the **Runway Visitor Park** (www.manchester airport.co.uk; Sunbank Lane; admission free, Concorde tour £13; ⌚8am-dusk) is also the only place in Britain where you can climb aboard Concorde (by separate tour) and explore the inside of a DC-10, an Avro RJX-100 (the last civilian airliner built in the UK) and an RAF Nimrod, which was in active service in Afghanistan as recently as 2010. The park is sign-posted off the A538 between Junction 6 of the M56 and the airport tunnels, but can also be reached via bus transfer from the airport itself.

rooms are tough to find if either of the city's football clubs are playing at home (especially United). If you are having difficulty finding a bed, the tourist office's free accommodation service can help.

Great John Street Hotel HOTEL £££
(☎0161-831 3211; www.greatjohnstreet.co.uk; Great John St; r £85-345; @📶) Elegant, designer luxury? Present. Fabulous rooms with all the usual delights (Egyptian cotton sheets, fabulous toiletries, free-standing baths and lots of high-tech electronics)? Present. A butler to run your bath in the Opus Grand Suite? Present. This former schoolhouse (ah, now you get it) is small but sumptuous. Beyond the Moderne-style lobby are the fabulous bedrooms, each an example of style and luxury. If only every school left such warm, comfortable memories.

Velvet Hotel BOUTIQUE HOTEL ££
(☎0161-236 9003; www.velvetmanchester.com; 2 Canal St; r from £99; 📶) Nineteen beautiful bespoke rooms, each oozing style. There's the sleigh bed in Room 24, the double bath in Room 34, and the saucy framed photographs of a stripped-down David Beckham (this is Gay Village, after all). But there's substance, too: iPod docking stations in every room, free wi-fi and a well-stocked DVD library. Despite the tantalising decor and location, this is not an exclusive hotel and is as popular with straight visitors as it is with the same-sex crowd.

Abode HOTEL ££
(☎0161-247 7744; www.abodehotels.co.uk; 107 Piccadilly St; r from £75; @📶) Modern British style is the catchphrase at this converted textile factory. The original fittings have been combined successfully with 61 bedrooms divided into four categories of ever-increasing luxury: Comfortable, Desirable, Enviable and Fabulous, the latter being five seriously swanky top-floor suites. Vi-Spring beds, Monsoon showers, LCD-screen TVs and stacks of Aqua Sulis toiletries are standard throughout. In the basement, star chef Michael Caines has a champagne and cocktail bar adjacent to his very own restaurant.

Lowry HOTEL £££
(☎0161-827 4000; www.roccofortecollection.com; 50 Dearman's Pl; r £120-950; P@🛜) Simply dripping with designer luxury and five-star comfort, Manchester's top hotel (not to be confused with the arts centre in the Salford Quays) has fabulous rooms with enormous beds, ergonomically designed furniture, walk-in wardrobes, and bathrooms finished with Italian porcelain tiles and glass mosaic. You can soothe yourself with a skin-brightening treatment or an aromatherapy head-massage at the health spa.

Roomzzz SERVICED ACCOMMODATION ££
(☎0161-236 2121; www.roomzzz.co.uk; 36 Princess St; r £59-169; @🛜) The inelegant name belies the designer digs inside this beautifully restored Grade II building, which features serviced apartments equipped with a kitchen and the latest connectivity gadgetry, including sleek iMac computers and free wi-fi throughout. There's a small pantry with food for sale downstairs. Highly recommended if you're planning a longer stay.

Malmaison HOTEL £££
(☎0161-278 1000; www.malmaison.com; Piccadilly St; r from £109; 🚆Piccadilly Station, Piccadilly Station) Drop-dead trendy and full of crushed-red velvet, deep purples, art deco ironwork and signature black-and-white tiles, Malmaison Manchester follows the chain's quirky design style and passion for cool, although rarely at the expense of comfort; the rooms are terrific. The **Smoak Grill** (☎0161-278-1000; www.smoak-grill.com; Malmaison, Piccadilly St; mains £13-25) downstairs is hugely popular.

Radisson Edwardian HOTEL ££
(☎0161-835 9929; www.radissonedwardian.com/manchester; Peter St; r from £90; P@🛜) Gladstone, Dickens and Fitzgerald...just some of the names associated with the historic Free Trade Hall, now a sumptuous five-star hotel, all minimalist Zen and luxury (bespoke furnishings, Bang & Olufsen televisions). 'Sacrilege!' scream the purists, but the hotel has done its best to preserve the memories of the building's most famous visitors: suites are named after Bob Dylan and Shirley Bassey, while meeting rooms carry the names of Disraeli, Thackeray and Pankhurst.

Hatters HOSTEL £
(☎0161-236 9500; www.hattersgroup.com; 50 Newton St; dm/s/d/tr from £15.50/28/52/65; P@🛜) The old-style lift and porcelain sinks are the only leftovers of this former milliner's factory, now one of the best hostels in town, with location to boot – smack in the heart of the Northern Quarter, you won't have to go far to get the best of alternative Manchester.

Doubletree By Hilton HOTEL ££
(☎0161-242 1001; www.doubletree.hilton.com; One Piccadilly Place, 1 Auburn St; From £79; 🛜) A bright, comfortable business hotel only a few yards from the train station, the Doubletree's rooms are perfect if all you need is a modern, functional spot to lay your head. There's free wi-fi and the restaurant downstairs is excellent.

Manchester YHA HOSTEL £
(☎0845 371 9647; www.yha.org.uk; Potato Wharf; dm incl breakfast from £16; P@🛜) This purpose-built canalside hostel in the Castlefield area is one of the best in the country. It's a top-class option with four- and six-bed dorms, all with bathroom, as well as three doubles and a host of good facilities. Potato Wharf is just left off Liverpool Rd.

Palace Hotel BOUTIQUE HOTEL ££
(☎0161-288 1111; www.principal-hotels.com; Oxford St; s/d from £85/105; 🛜) An elegant refurbishment of one of Manchester's most magnificent Victorian palaces resulted in a special boutique hotel, combining grand public areas with modern bedrooms.

Castlefield HOTEL ££
(☎0161-832 7073; www.castlefield-hotel.co.uk; 3 Liverpool Rd; s/d from £60/90; P🛜🏊) This is another successful warehouse conversion that has resulted in a thoroughly modern business hotel. Overlooking the canal basin, it has spacious, comfortable rooms and excellent amenities, including a fitness centre and pool that are free to guests.

Jury's Inn HOTEL ££
(☎0161-953 8888; www.jurysdoyle.com; 56 Great Bridgewater St; r from £55) Comfortable Irish chain hotel with large, clean, bland rooms. Convenient location though.

Park Inn Hotel HOTEL ££
(☎0161-832 6565; www.sasparkinn.com; 4 Cheetham Hill Rd; r from £79; 🛜🏊) Spacious, modern rooms (with floor-to-ceiling windows) in a massive hotel overlooking the MEN Arena; perfect if you're going to a gig. It's directly north of the MEN Arena.

New Union Hotel HOTEL £
(☎0161-228 1492; www.newunionhotel.com; 111 Princess St; r from £40) Affordable fun in the heart

of the Gay Village, a smart hotel that isn't exclusively pink. It is a good place for partiers: not recommended for a quiet layover.

Midland HOTEL ££
(☎0161-236 3333; www.themidland.co.uk; Peter St; r from £104; @) Mr Rolls and Mr Royce sealed the deal in the elegant lobby of this fancy business hotel.

Eating

With a choice of restaurants unrivalled outside London, Manchester has something for every palate and budget. The Northern Quarter is all about hipster cafes serving locally sourced, organic grub, but there are plenty of good choices throughout the centre. Following is but a small starter course:

TOP CHOICE **Australasia** PAN-ASIAN ££
(☎0161-831 0288; www.australasia.uk.com; 1 The Avenue, Spinningfields; mains £13-30, 2-/3-/4-course lunch £11/15/20) What should you do with the dusty old basement archive of the Manchester Evening News? Convert it into the city centre's best new restaurant, of course. Descend through an IM-Pei-inspired glass triangle into a stunning, beautifully-lit space lined with comfortable booths. The menu combines Pacific Rim cuisine with southeast Asian flavours – the lunchtime selection of fresh sushi is particularly good, as are the specials. A late license sees it turn into a very cool bar with DJs and dancing in the evenings.

The Oast House INTERNATIONAL ££
(☎0161-829 3830; www.theoasthouse.uk.com; Crown Square, Spinningfields; mains £9-15) An oast house is a 16th-century kiln used to dry out hops as part of the beer-making process. In Manchester, the Oast House is Tim Bacon's exciting new BBQ restaurant, a slice of medieval charm in the heart of (slightly) po-faced Spinningfields' contemporary designer chic. The kitchen is an outdoor covered grill, so staff have to shuttle the grilled delights (nothing fancy: burgers, kebabs, steaks and rotisserie chickens) to diners inside, but it works – brilliantly. The deli boards (lots of cold cuts and cheeses) are equally delicious.

Sam's Chop House BRITISH £
(☎0161-834 3210; www.samschophouse.co.uk; Back Pool Fold, Chapel Walks, off Cross St; mains £6-8) Arguably the city's top gastropub, Sam's is a Victorian classic that serves dishes straight out of a Dickens novel. The highlight is the crispy corned beef hash cake, which is salt-cured for 10 days on the premises. 'There is no such passion in human nature as the passion for gravy among commercial gentlemen,' declared Mrs Todgers in *Martin Chuzzlewit*; she would certainly approve of Sam's. The owners also run Mr Thomas' Chop House (p641).

Richmond Tea Rooms CAFE £
(☎0161-237 9667; www.richmondtearooms.com; Richmond St; mains £5-8) You've never seen Victorian tearooms like this. Or maybe you have – in Tim Burton's *Alice in Wonderland*. Bold, clashing colours, a potpourri of period furniture and a counter painted to resemble the icing on a cake are just some of the features that make the Richmond one of the city's best new additions. Sandwiches and light meals (rarebit, quiche) are the menu's mainstay, but the real treat is the selection of afternoon teas, complete with four-fingered sandwiches, scones, cakes and, of course, your choice of teas.

Mark Addy MODERN BRITISH ££
(☎0161-832 4080; www.markaddy.co.uk; Stanley St; mains £8.90-12.50; ⊙lunch & dinner Wed-Fri, dinner Sat) Another contender for best pub grub in town, the Mark Addy owes its culinary success to Robert Owen Brown, whose loving interpretations of standard British classics – pork chop with honey-roasted bramley, pan-fried dab with cockles and spring onion et al (all locally sourced) – has them queuing at the door for a taste. It recently opened a riverside deck, so you can eat by the river where, during the 19th century, local publican Mark Addy rescued 50 people from drowning.

Jamie's Italian ITALIAN ££
(☎0161-241 3901; www.jamieoliver.com; 100 King St; mains £8-14) The magnificent banking hall of Edwin Lutyens' castle-like Art Deco Midland Bank (1935) is now home to a branch of Jamie Oliver's fast-expanding gourmet empire. And while the food is perfectly adequate – it's an appealing blend of British staples given the Italian treatment (braised British shin of beef with Parmesan polenta; a south coast fritto misto of crispy fried fresh fish and shellfish with Italian tartare sauce) – the real treat is the building itself. In the basement, the old deposit vaults have been converted into private dining rooms.

Home Sweet Home

CAFE £

(☎0161-833 1248; www.cheesburgertoastie.co.uk; 49-51 Edge St) In 2012 the cupcake craze swept hipster Manchester, and the Northern Quarter responded in kind. Best of the area's cake cafes is this spot, where the cupcakes (fairy cakes in England) are divine, the service is haphazard but the friendliness is genuine. They also serve sandwiches, a variety of breakfast egg combos (for late-risers) and more substantial, diner-like cuisine: mac & cheese, chilli dogs and chowder.

Earth Cafe

VEGETARIAN £

(☎0161-834 1996; www.earthcafe.co.uk; 16-20 Turner St; chef's special £3.20; ⊙lunch only;) Below the Manchester Buddhist Centre, this gourmet vegetarian café's motto is 'right food, right place, right time', which is reflected in its overriding commitment to ensuring that it serves as much local seasonable produce as possible. The result is wonderful: here you'll eat well in the knowledge that you're eating right. The chef's special – a main dish, side and two salad portions – is generally excellent and always filling.

Drinking

There's every kind of drinking hole in Manchester, from the really grungy ones that smell but have plenty of character to the ones that were designed by a team of architects but have the atmosphere of a freezer. Every neighbourhood in town has its favourites; here's a few to get you going.

Bluu

BAR

(☎0161-839 7740; www.bluu.co.uk; Smithfield Market Buildings, Thomas St; ⊙noon-midnight Sun-Mon, to 1am Tue-Thu, to 2am Fri & Sat) Our favourite of the Northern Quarter's collection of great bars. Bluu is cool, comfortable and comes with a great terrace on which to enjoy a pint and listen to music selected by folks with really good taste.

Black Dog Ballroom

BAR

(www.blackdogballroom.co.uk; 52 Church St) A basement bar with a speakeasy vibe, there's nothing illicit about drinking here: the cocktails are terrific, the atmosphere is always buzzing and the music always good and loud.

Britons Protection

PUB

(☎0161-236 5895; 50 Great Bridgewater St) Whisky – 200 different kinds of it – is the beverage of choice at this liver-threatening, proper English pub that also does Tudor-style meals (boar, venison and the like; mains £8). An old-fashioned boozer with open fires in the back rooms, a cosy atmosphere...perfect on a cold evening.

TOP FOUR PUBS FOR A PINT IN THE NORTHWEST

» Philharmonic (p661), Liverpool

» Britons Protection (p641), Manchester

» Albion (p650), Chester

» Magnet (p661), Liverpool

Lass O'Gowrie

PUB

(☎0161-273 6932; 36 Charles S) A Victorian classic, off Princess St, that brews its own beer in the basement. It's a favourite with students, old-timers and a clique of BBC employees who work just across the street in the Beeb's Manchester HQ. It also does good-value bar meals (£6).

Odd

BAR

(☎0161-833 0070; www.oddbar.co.uk; 30-32 Thomas St; ⊙11am-11pm Mon-Sat, to 10.30pm Sun) This eclectic little bar – with its oddball furnishings, wacky tunes and anti-establishment crew of customers – is the perfect antidote to the increasingly uniform look of so many modern bars. A slice of Mancuniana to be treasured.

Dry Bar

BAR

(28-30 Oldham St; ⊙noon-midnight Mon-Wed, noon-2am Thu-Sat, 6pm-midnight Sun) The former HQ of Madchester's maddest protagonists (legend has it Shaun Ryder once pulled a gun on Tony Wilson here), Dry has remained cool long after the scene froze over, and it's still one of the best bars in the Northern Quarter.

Dukes 92

PUB

(www.dukes92.com; 2 Castle St) Castlefield's best pub, housed in converted stables that once belonged to the duke of Bridgewater, has comfy, deep sofas inside and plenty of seating outside, overlooking Lock 92 of the Rochdale Canal – hence the name. If it's sunny, there's no better spot to enjoy a pint of ale.

Mr Thomas' Chop House

PUB

(52 Cross St) An old-style boozer that is very popular for a pint as well as food (mains £10).

Peveril of the Peak

PUB

(☎0161-236 6364; 127 Great Bridgewater St) An unpretentious pub with wonderful Victorian glazed tilework outside.

☆ Entertainment

Nightclubs

A handy tip: if you want to thrive in Manchester's excellent nightlife, drop all mention of Madchester (a legendary era; p644) and keep talk of being 'up for it' to strict irony. Otherwise, you'll risk being labelled a saddo nostalgic or, worse, someone who should have gone home and grown up a decade ago. But fear not; there is still a terrific club scene and Manchester remains at the vanguard of dance-floor culture. There's a constantly changing mixture of club nights, so check the *Manchester Evening News* for details of what's on. Following are our favourite places:

TOP CHOICE Sankey's CLUB
(☎0161-950 4201; www.sankeys.info; Radium St, Ancoats; admission free-£12; ⊙10pm-3am Thu & Fri, to 4am Sat) If you're a fan of techno, electro or any kind of non-mainstream house music, then a pilgrimage to Manchester's best nightclub should on no account be missed. Sankey's has earned itself legendary status for being at the vanguard of dance music (Chemical Brothers, Daft Punk and others got their start here) and its commitment to top-class DJs is unwavering. These days, you'll hear the likes of Timo Maas, Seb Leger and Thomas Schumacher mix it up with the absolutely superb residents. Choon! Sankey's is about a mile east of the Northern Quarter. The best way to get here is to board the free Disco Bus that picks up at locations throughout the city from 10.30pm to 2am Friday and Saturday, and between 10.10pm and 1am the rest of the week. See the website for details.

Fac251 CLUB
(☎0161-272 7251; www.factorymanchester.com; 112-118 Princess St; admission £1-6; ⊙9.30pm-3am Mon-Sat) It might be a paeon to days of yore, but Fac251, located in Tony Wilson's former Factory Records HQ, stands on its own two feet as one of the best venues in town. Three rooms, all with a broad musical appeal, from Monday's Hit & Run (drum 'n' bass, hip hop and dubstep) to Stoned Love on Saturday, which has indie rock, Motown and techno across three rooms. Something for everybody.

South CLUB
(☎0161-831 7756; 4a South King St; admission £5-8; ⊙10pm-3am Fri & Sat) An excellent basement club to kick off the weekend: Friday night is CWord with Strangerways, featuring everything from Ibrahim Ferrer to Northern Soul, and Saturday is the always excellent Disco Rescue with Clint Boon (once of the Inspiral Carpets), which is more of the same eclectic mix of alternative and dance.

Cinemas

Cornerhouse ART HOUSE
(www.cornerhouse.org; 70 Oxford St) Your only destination for good art-house releases; also has a gallery, bookshop and cafe.

Odeon Cinema MULTIPLEX
(www.odeon.co.uk; The Printworks, Exchange Sq) A 20-screen complex in the middle of the Printworks centre.

AMC Cinemas MULTIPLEX
(www.amccinemas.co.uk; The Great Northern, 235 Deansgate) A 16-screen multiplex in a retail centre that was formerly a goods warehouse for the Northern Railway Company.

Theatre

Opera House Manchester MUSIC VENUE
(☎0161-242 2509; www.atgv.co.uk; 3 Quay St) West End shows and lavish musicals make up the bulk of the program.

LOCAL KNOWLEDGE

JOHN RYAN: RADIO PRODUCER & GUIDE

John Ryan is the chair of Gaydio 88.4FM, an accredited tour guide and an all-round bon vivant.

Favourite neighbourhood? I love the Northern Quarter, so I based myself there. But Spinningfields is worth a look, for its upscale shopping and its wonderful choice of eateries – favourites are Australasia (p640) and The Oast House (p640).

Secret to getting the most of a night out? Mix up the city's offerings for a proper night out. Town is compact, so there really is something for everyone.

John Ryan's ideal night out? I'd start off with a bit of food – in either Home Sweet Home (p641) or Sam's Chop House (p640). If I'm feeling cultural, I'd take in a play at the Royal Exchange (p643), Manchester's most striking theatre. Afterwards, a drink – or a reading – at Taurus (p645), in the Gay Village.

Royal Exchange THEATRE
(☎0161-833 9833; www.royalexchange.co.uk; St Anne's Sq) Interesting contemporary plays are standard at this magnificent, modern theatre-in-the-round.

Live Music

ROCK MUSIC

Band on the Wall BAR, LIVE MUSIC
(☎0161-834 1786; www.bandonthewall.org; 25 Swan St) A top-notch venue that hosts everything from rock to world music, with splashes of jazz, blues and folk thrown in for good measure.

MEN Arena VENUE
(www.men-arena.com; Great Ducie St) A giant arena north of the centre that hosts large-scale rock concerts (as well as being the home of the city's ice-hockey and basketball teams). It's about 300m north of Victoria Station.

Moho Live VENUE
(www.moholive.com; 21-31 Oldham St) A 500-capacity live-music venue that has already proven incredibly popular with its line-up of live music and club nights.

Ruby Lounge BAR, LIVE MUSIC
(☎0161-834 1392; 26-28 High St) Terrific live-music venue in the Northern Quarter that features mostly rock bands.

CLASSICAL MUSIC

Bridgewater Hall CONCERT HALL
(☎0161-907 9000; www.bridgewater-hall.co.uk; Lower Mosley St) The world-renowned Hallé Orchestra has its home at this enormous and impressive concert hall, which hosts up to 250 concerts and events a year. It has a widespread program that includes opera, folk music, children's shows, comedy and contemporary music.

Manchester Cathedral CATHEDRAL
(☎0161-833 2220; www.manchestercathedral.org; Victoria St) Hosts a summer season of concerts by the Cantata Choir and ensemble groups.

Royal Northern College of Music COLLEGE
(☎0161-907 5555; www.rncm.ac.uk; 124 Oxford Rd) Presents a full program of extremely high-quality classical music and other contemporary offerings.

Sport

Sport in Manchester is primarily about football. There are two clubs: the mega-successful Manchester United, with fans the world over; and Manchester City, perennial understudies until the injection of Midas-like money saw them catapulted to the top of the league in 2012 for the first time since 1968, narrowly fending off the predictable challenge of their crosstown nemesis.

Manchester City FOOTBALL
Perennial underdogs turned 2012 league champions, Manchester City owe their new-found success to Sheikh Mansour of Abu Dhabi, who bought the club in 2008 and in doing so transformed it into the world's wealthiest football team. Out went the mediocre players, in came global (highly-paid) stars like David Silva, Ya Ya Touré and Sergio Agüero, who delivered the ultimate prize to the club's success-starved fans for the first time since 1968. A new era of glory has now begun, so long as the money keeps flowing and the club is able to manage the more mercenary tendencies of some of its biggest stars. In the meantime, you can enjoy the **Manchester City Stadium Tour** (☎0161-444 1894; www.mcfc.co.uk; tours adult/child £8.50/6; ⏰tours 11am, 1.30pm & 3.30pm Mon-Sat, 11.45am, 1.45pm & 3.30pm Sun except match days) – a tour of the ground, dressing rooms and museum before the inevitable steer into the kit shop. Tours must be booked in advance. Take bus 53, 54, 185 or 186 from Piccadilly Gardens.

Lancashire County Cricket Club CRICKET
(☎0161-282 4000; www.lccc.co.uk; Warwick Rd) Cricket is a big deal here, and Lancashire, founded in 1816 as the Aurora before changing its name in 1864, is one of the most beloved of England's county teams, despite the fact that it hasn't won the county championship since 1934. Matches are played at Old Trafford (same name, different but adjacent

THE FOLK TRAIN

One of the more offbeat ways to enjoy live music is to ride the **Folk Train** (☎0161-244 1880; www.hvhptp.org.uk/folktran.htm; ticket £9; ⏰11.45am Sat Jul-Sep), a one-hour journey between Manchester and Hathersage in the Peak District. On-board entertainment is blues, folk, Irish and old-style country music, played by a rotating list of terrific local bands. There's nothing formal about it: just get on board and enjoy the music. The train departs from Manchester Piccadilly.

THE MADCHESTER SOUND

It is often claimed that Manchester is the engine room of British pop. If this is indeed the case, then the chief engineer was TV presenter and music impresario Tony Wilson (1950–2007), founder of Factory Records. This is the label that in 1983 released New Order's ground-breaking 'Blue Monday', to this day the best-selling 12in in British history, which successfully fused the guitar-driven sound of punk with a pulsating dance beat.

When the money started pouring in, Wilson took the next, all-important step: he opened his own nightclub that would provide a platform for local bands to perform. The Hacienda opened its doors with plenty of fanfare but just wouldn't take off. Things started to turn around when the club embraced a brand new sound coming out of Chicago and Detroit: house. DJs Mike Pickering, Graeme Park and Jon Da Silva were the music's most important apostles, and when ecstasy hit the scene late in the decade, it seemed that every kid in town was 'mad for it'.

Heavily influenced by these new arrivals, the city's guitar bands took notice and began shaping their sounds to suit the clubbers' needs. The most successful was the Stone Roses, who in 1989 released 'Fools Gold', a pulsating hit with the rapid shuffle of James Brown's 'Funky Drummer' and a druggie guitar sound that drove dancers wild. Around the same time, Happy Mondays, fronted by the laddish Shaun Ryder and the wacked-out Bez (whose only job was to lead the dancing from the stage), hit the scene with the infectious 'Hallelujah'. The other big anthems of the day were 'The One I Love' by the Charlatans, 'Voodoo Ray' by A Guy Called Gerald, and 'Pacific' by 808 State – all local bands and producers. The party known as Madchester was officially opened and the music they danced to became known as 'baggy' – named after the loose-fitting clothes that everybody in the scene was wearing.

The party ended in 1992. Overdanced and overdrugged, the city woke up with a terrible hangover. The Haçienda went bust, Shaun Ryder's legendary drug intake stymied his musical creativity and the Stone Roses withdrew in a haze of postparty depression. The latter were not to be heard of again until 1994 when they released *Second Coming*, which just couldn't match their eponymous debut album. They lasted another two years before breaking up. The fertile crossover scene, which had seen clubbers go mad at rock gigs, and rock bands play the kind of dance sounds that kept the floor thumping until the early hours, virtually disappeared and the two genres withdrew into a more familiar isolation.

Madchester is legendary precisely because it is no more, but it was exciting. If you missed the party, you can get a terrific sense of what it was like by watching Michael Winterbottom's *24-Hour Party People* (2002), which captures the hedonism, extravagance and genius of Madchester's cast of characters; and the superb *Control* (2007) by Anton Corbijn, which tells the tragic story of Ian Curtis, Joy Division's lead singer.

ground to the football stadium) and the key fixture in Lancashire's calendar is the Roses match against Yorkshire, but if you're not around for that, the other games in the county season (admission £11 to £17) are a great day out. The season runs throughout the summer. International test matches are also played here occasionally. Take the Metrolink to Old Trafford.

Shopping

From the boho boutiques of the Northern Quarter to Spinningfields' swanky stores – **Armani** (☎0161-220 2980; Unit G1 & 2, The Avenue, Spinningfields), **Brooks Brothers** (☎0161-834 6649; Unit G19, The Avenue, Spinningfields), **DKNY** (☎0161-833 3277; Unit G18, The Avenue, Spinningfields) etc – Manchester's retail credentials are assured. New Cathedral St and King St also have fancy shops, while the Arndale Centre is the city's equivalent of the English high street.

Oi Polloi BOUTIQUE

(www.oipolloi.com; 70 Tib St) Besides the impressive range of casual footwear, this trendy boutique also stocks a range of designers including APC, Lyle & Scott, Nudie Jeans and Fjallraven.

Harvey Nichols DEPARTMENT STORE

(21 New Cathedral St; restaurant mains £8-16; ⊙restaurant lunch daily, dinner Tue-Sat) The king of British department stores has an elegant presence on fashionista row. The 2nd-floor

restaurant is excellent and even has a wine list of more than 400 different wines.

Tib Street Market MARKET
(☎0161-234 7357; Tib St; ⏲10am-5pm Sat) Up-and-coming local designers get a chance to display their wares at this newish weekly market where you can pick up everything from purses to lingerie and hats to jewellery.

Oxfam Originals VINTAGE
(Unit 8, Smithfield Bldg, Oldham St) If you're into retro, this terrific store has high-quality gear from the 1960s and '70s. Shop in the knowledge that it's for a good cause.

Rags to Bitches VINTAGE
(www.rags-to-bitches.co.uk; 60 Tib St) Award-winning vintage boutique with fashions from the 1930s to the '80s. This is the place to go to pick up unusual, individual pieces or that outfit for the fancy-dress ball.

Cornerhouse BOOKS
(www.cornerhouse.org; 70 Oxford St) Art and film books, specialist magazines and kitschy cards.

Waterstones BOOKS
(www.waterstones.com; St Anne's Sq) Biggest bookstore in town; also has a Deansgate branch.

Information

Emergency

Ambulance (☎0161-436 3999)
Police Station (☎0161-872 5050; Bootle St)
Rape Crisis Centre (☎0161-273 4500)
Samaritans (☎0161-236 8000) A confidential emotional support service for people suffering despair, distress and suicidal feelings.

Internet Access

L2K Internet Gaming Cafe (32 Princess St; per 30min £2; ⏲9am-10pm Mon-Fri, 9am-9pm Sat & Sun)

Internet Resources

Manchester After Dark (www.manchesterad.com) Reviews and descriptions of the best places to be when the sun goes down.
Manchester City Council (www.manchester.gov.uk) The council's official website, which includes a visitors' section.
Manchester Evening News (www.menmedia.co.uk) The city's evening paper in electronic form.
Manchester Online (www.manchesteronline.co.uk) Local online newspaper.
Real Manchester (www.realmanchester.com) Online guide to nightlife.
Restaurants of Manchester (www.restaurantsofmanchester.com) Thorough, up-to-date reviews of restaurants in the city and suburbs.
Virtual Manchester (www.manchester.com) Restaurants, pubs, clubs and where to sleep.
Visit Manchester (www.visitmanchester.com) The official website for Greater Manchester.

Medical Services

Cameolord Chemist (St Peter's Sq; ⏲10am-10pm)
Manchester Royal Infirmary (Oxford Rd)

GAY & LESBIAN MANCHESTER

The city's gay scene is unrivalled outside London, and caters to every taste. Its healthy heart beats loudest in the Gay Village, centred on handsome Canal St. Here you'll find bars, clubs, restaurants and – crucially – karaoke joints that cater almost exclusively to the pink pound.

Manchester Pride (p637) is a 10-day festival from the middle of August each year that attracts more than 500,000 people.

There are bars to suit every taste, but you won't go far wrong in **AXM** (www.axm-bar.co.uk; 10 Canal St), which is more of a cocktail lounge for the city's flash crowd, or **Taurus** (www.taurus-bar.co.uk; 1 Canal St), which is a little shabbier but equally good fun.

For your clubbing needs, look no further than **Club Alter Ego** (www.clubalterego.co.uk; 105-107 Princess St; ⏲11pm-5am Thu-Sat) and **Mancunia** (8 Minshull St; ⏲11pm-5am Thu-Sat), which is just as popular.

And then there's karaoke, the ultimate choice for midweek fun. The best of the lot is at the New Union Hotel (p639), where you can find your inner Madonna and Cyndi Lauper every Tuesday and Thursday – for a top prize of £50.

For more information, check with the **Lesbian & Gay Foundation** (☎0161-235 8035; www.lgf.org.uk; 105-107 Princess St; ⏲4-10pm). The city's best pink website is www.visitgaymanchester.co.uk.

Post

Post Office (Brazennose St; ⊙9am-5.30pm Mon-Fri)

Tourist Information

Tourist Office (www.visitmanchester.com; Piccadilly Plaza, Portland St; ⊙10am-5.15pm Mon-Sat, 10am-4.30pm Sun)

 Getting There & Away

Air

Manchester Airport (☎0161-489 3000; www.manchesterairport.co.uk), south of the city, is the largest airport outside London and is served by 13 locations throughout Britain, as well as more than 50 international destinations.

Bus

National Express (☎08717 81 81 81; www.nationalexpress.com) serves most major cities almost hourly from Chorlton St coach station in the city centre. Sample destinations:

Leeds £8.40, one hour, hourly.

Liverpool £6.80, 1¼ hours, hourly.

London £25, 3¾ hours, hourly.

Train

Manchester Piccadilly (east of the Gay Village) is the main station for trains to and from the rest of the country, although Victoria station (north of the National Football Museum) serves Halifax and Bradford. The two stations are linked by Metrolink. Off-peak fares are considerably cheaper.

Blackpool £15.20, 1¼ hours, half-hourly.

Liverpool Lime St £11, 45 minutes, half-hourly.

London Euston £73.20, three hours, seven daily.

Newcastle £54.20, three hours, six daily.

 Getting Around

To/From the Airport

The airport is 12 miles south of the city. A train to or from Victoria station costs £3.80; a coach is £3. A taxi is nearly four times as much in light traffic.

Public Transport

The excellent public transport system can be used with a variety of **Day Saver tickets** (bus £4.80, train £4.60, Metrolink £4.50, bus, train and Metrolink £10). For inquiries about local transport, including night buses, contact **Travelshop** (☎0161-228 7811; www.gmpte.com; 9 Portland St, Piccadilly Gardens; ⊙8am-8pm).

Centreline bus 4 provides a free service around the heart of Manchester every 10 minutes. Pick up a route map from the tourist office. Most local buses start from Piccadilly Gardens.

There are frequent **Metrolink** (www.metrolink.co.uk) trams between Victoria and Piccadilly train stations and G-Mex (for Castlefield) as well as further afield to Salford Quays. Buy your tickets from the platform machine.

Castlefield is served by Deansgate station with rail links to Piccadilly, Oxford Rd and Salford stations.

CHESHIRE

Generally overshadowed by the loud, busy conurbations of Liverpool and Manchester, Cheshire gets on with life in a quiet, usually bucolic kind of way, happy enough with its reputation as a contemporary version of ye olde Englande – complete with fields of Friesian cows and half-timbered Tudor houses. Interspersed throughout this idyll are the high-walled estates of the region's richest burghers (including many soccer millionaires looking to add a little class to their immense wealth), but for the hoi polloi Cheshire is really just about Chester.

Chester

POP 80,130

Marvellous Chester is one of English history's greatest gifts to the contemporary visitor. Its red-sandstone wall, which today gift-wraps a tidy collection of Tudor and Victorian buildings, was built during Roman times. The town was then called Castra Devana, and was the largest Roman fortress in Britain.

Though it's hard to believe today, during the Middle Ages Chester made its money as the most important port in the northwest. However, the River Dee silted up over time and Liverpool became more importance.

Besides its obvious elegance and grace, Chester earns a fairly substantial living as a major retail centre and tourist hot spot; visitors come, see and shop.

⊙ Sights & Activities

FREE City Walls LANDMARK

A good way to get a sense of Chester's unique character is to walk the 2-mile circuit along the walls that surround the historic centre. Originally built by the Romans around AD 70, the walls were altered substantially over the following centuries but have retained their current position since around 1200. The tourist office's *Walk Around Chester Walls* leaflet is an excellent guide.

Of the many features along the walls, the most eye-catching is the prominent **Eastgate**, where you can see the most famous **clock** in England after London's Big Ben, built for Queen Victoria's Diamond Jubilee in 1897.

At the southeastern corner of the walls are the **wishing steps**, added in 1785; local legend claims that if you can run up and down these uneven steps while holding your breath your wish will come true. We question the veracity of this claim because our wish was not to twist an ankle.

Just inside Southgate, known here as **Bridgegate** (as it's located at the northern end of the Old Dee Bridge), is the **Bear & Billet** (http://bearandbillet.com; Southgate) pub. Built in 1664, it is Chester's oldest timber-framed building and once a tollgate into the city.

Rows ARCHITECTURE

Chester's other great draw is the Rows, a series of two-level galleried arcades along the four streets that fan out in each direction from the **Central Cross**. The architecture is a handsome mix of Victorian and Tudor (original and mock) buildings that house a fantastic collection of individually owned shops. The origin of the Rows is a little unclear, but it is believed that as the Roman walls slowly crumbled, medieval traders built their shops against the resulting rubble banks, while later arrivals built theirs on top.

Chester Cathedral CATHEDRAL

(☎01244-324 756; www.chestercathedral.com; 12 Abbey Square; adult/child £6/2.50; ⊙9am-5pm Mon-Sat, 1-4pm Sun) Originally a Benedictine abbey built on the remains of an earlier Saxon church dedicated to St Werburgh (the city's patron saint), it was shut down in 1540 as part of Henry VIII's dissolution frenzy but reconsecrated as a cathedral the following year. Although the cathedral itself was given a substantial Victorian facelift, the 12th-century cloister and its surrounding buildings are essentially unaltered and retain much of the structure from the early monastic years. Your admission price includes a 45-minute audio tour of the building.

FREE **Grosvenor Museum** MUSEUM

(☎01244-972 197; www.grosvenormuseum.co.uk; 27 Grosvenor St; ⊙10.30am-5pm Mon-Sat, 2-5pm Sun) An excellent museum with the country's most comprehensive collection of Roman tombstones. At the back of the museum is a preserved Georgian house, complete with kitchen, drawing room, bedroom and bathroom.

Dewa Roman Experience MUSEUM

(☎01244-343 407; www.dewaromanexperience.co.uk; Pierpoint Lane; adult/child £4.95/3.25; ⊙9am-5pm Mon-Sat, 10am-5pm Sun) Walk through a reconstructed Roman street to reveal what Roman life was like. It's just off Bridge St.

FREE **Roman Amphitheatre** RUINS

(Little St John St) Just outside the city walls is what was once an arena that seated 7000 spectators (making it the country's largest). Some historians have suggested that it may also have been the site of King Arthur's Camelot and that his knights' Round Table was really just this circular construction. Excavations continue; during summer months there are occasional shows held here.

St John the Baptist Church CHURCH

(Vicar's Lane; ⊙9.15am-6pm) Built on the site of an older Saxon church in 1075, it's been a peaceful ruin since 1581. It includes the remains of a Norman choir and medieval chapels.

Tours

Chester Visitors' Centre (www.visitchester.com; Vicar's Lane; ⊙9.30am-5.30pm Mon-Sat & 10am-4pm Sun) offers a broad range of walking tours departing from the town hall. Each tour lasts between 1½ and two hours.

Chester Heritage Tours BUS TOURS

(☎0844-585 4144; www.chesterheritagetours.co.uk; adult/child £6.50/3.50; ⊙every 15-20min) A 30-minute tour of Chester's main attractions aboard a vintage 1924 bus.

Chester Boat BOAT TOURS

(☎01244-325394; www.chesterboat.co.uk) Runs 30-minute and hour-long cruises up and down the Dee, including a foray into the gorgeous Eaton Estate, home of the duke and duchess of Westminster. All departures are from the riverside along the promenade known as the Groves and trips cost from £6.50 to £14.

Walking Tours WALKING TOURS

The Chester Visitors' Centre offers a broad range of walking tours departing from the town hall. Each tour lasts between 1½ and two hours. Tours include **Chester Rows: The Inside Story** (adult/child £5/4; ⊙2pm), which tells the fascinating history of

Chester

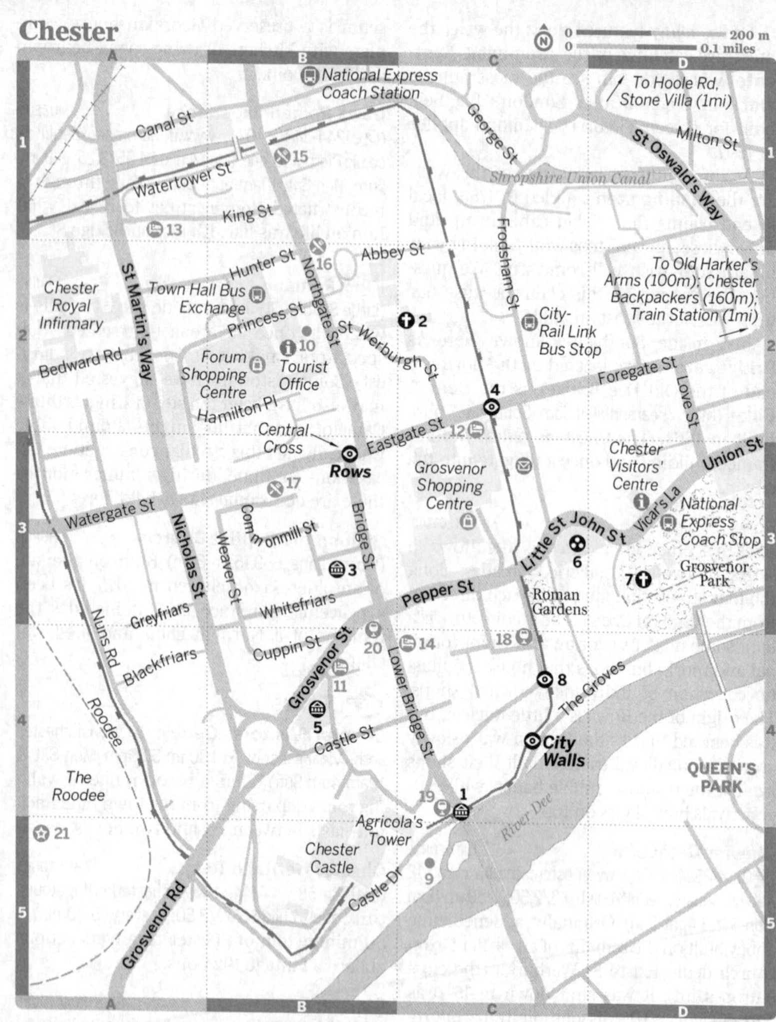

Chester's most outstanding architectural feature, and **Secret Chester** (adult/child £6/5; ⌚2pm & 3.30pm Mon, Tue & Sun May-Oct), about Chester's historical secrets.

Chester Revealed AUDIO TOUR

(www.walktalktour.com; £5) Downloadable MP3 tour of the city and its history – includes the sound of a town crier in full voice.

Festivals & Events

Chestival ARTS & MUSIC

(www.chesterfestivals.co.uk) The festival season kicks off with this multi-disciplinary festival that runs from June to mid-July, featuring everything from open-air film screenings and music gigs to show jumping and bike riding.

Summer Music Festival MUSIC

(www.chesterfestivals.co.uk) A season highlight is this two-week classical festival (early August) featuring performances by all manner of stars both big and small.

Chester County Jazz Festival MUSIC

(www.chestercountyjazz.com; admission free-£12) A two-week showcase of national and international jazz talent held in August/September.

Chester

Top Sights

Sights

Activities, Courses & Tours

Sleeping

Eating

Drinking

Entertainment

Sleeping

Rooms are at a premium between Easter and September so book early to avoid disappointment or a forced upgrade into a higher price bracket. Except for a handful of options most of the accommodation is outside the city walls but within easy walking distance of the centre. Hoole Rd, just under a mile's walk northeast from the centre and leading beyond the railway tracks to the M53/M56, is lined with budget to midrange B&Bs.

TOP CHOICE Stone Villa B&B ££
(01244-345014; www.stonevillachester.co.uk; 3 Stone Pl, Hoole Rd; s/d from £45/75; P Wi-Fi) Twice winner of Chester's B&B of the Year in the last 10 years, this beautiful villa has everything you need for a memorable stay. Elegant bedrooms (from standard to executive, which have flatscreen TVs), a fabulous breakfast and welcoming, friendly owners all add up to one of the best lodgings in town.

Green Bough BOUTIQUE HOTEL £££
(01244-326241; www.chestergreenboughhotel.co.uk; 60 Hoole Rd; r from £175; P @ Wi-Fi) The epitome of the boutique hotel, this exclusive, award-winning Victorian town house has individually styled rooms dressed in the best Italian fabrics. The rooms come adorned with wall coverings, superb antique furniture and period cast-iron and wooden beds, including a handful of elegant four-posters. Modern touches include plasma-screen TVs, mini stereos and a range of fancy toiletries. It is 1 mi northeast of town along Hoole Rd.

ABode Chester HOTEL £££
(01244-347000; www.abodehotels.co.uk; Grosvenor Rd; r from £135) Ultra-modern, trendy and slavishy 'designer', ABode hotel rooms are all about bright colours, glass and lots of light, and it's no different in the latest addition to their growing empire, located on the site of the old Cheshire Constabulary HQ. The 5th-floor Michael Caines restaurant has already won awards for its delicious grub.

Chester Grosvenor Hotel & Spa HOTEL £££
(01244-324024; www.chestergrosvenor.com; 58 Eastgate St; r from £170; P @ Wi-Fi) This hotel is perfectly located and has huge, sprawling rooms with exquisite period furnishings and all mod cons. The spa (which is open to nonguests) offers a range of body treatments, including reiki, LaStone therapy, Indian head massage and four-handed massage. There's also a Michelin-starred restaurant downstairs.

Oddfellows BOUTIQUE HOTEL £££
(01244-895 700; www.oddfellowschester.com; 20 Lwr Bridge St; r from £170) Taking its name from a 17th-century tradesmens' society (read: Masonic lodge), Oddfellows is a superb 18-bedroom hotel (14 rooms are brand new) where each room is an exploration of old style and good taste. Downstairs is a very trendy bar and restaurant run by Simon Bradley.

Chester Townhouse B&B ££
(☎01244-350021; www.chestertownhouse.co.uk; 23 King St; s/d £45/75; P) Five beautifully decorated rooms in a handsome 17th-century house within the city walls make Chester Townhouse a terrific option – you're close to the action and you'll sleep in relative luxury.

Chester Backpackers HOSTEL £
(☎01244-400185; www.chesterbackpackers.co.uk; 67 Boughton; dm from £15.50; 📶) Comfortable dorm rooms with nice pine beds in a typically Tudor white-and-black building. It's just a short walk from the city walls and there's also a pleasant garden.

Eating

Chester has great food – it's just not in any of the tourist-oriented restaurants that line the Rows. Besides the better restaurants, you'll find the best grub in some of the pubs.

Joseph Benjamin MODERN BRITISH ££
(☎01244-344295; www.josephbenjamin.co.uk; 134-140 Northgate St; mains £13-17; ⊙9am-5pm Tue-Wed, 9am-midnight Thu-Fri, 10am-5pm Sun) A bright star in Chester's culinary firmament is this combo restaurant, bar and deli that delivers carefully prepared local produce to take out or sit-in. Excellent sandwiches and gorgeous salads are the mainstay of the takeout menu, while the more formal dinner menu features fine examples of modern British cuisine – the Cajun spiced fillet of rainbow trout with cuttlefish, cous cous, and mint and lime yoghurt was especially good.

Upstairs at the Grill STEAKHOUSE £££
(☎01244-344883; www.upstairsatthegrill.co.uk; 70 Watergate St; mains £15-28; ⊙dinner Mon-Sat, lunch & dinner Sun) A Manhattan-style steakhouse almost hidden on the 2nd floor, this is the place to devour every cut of meat from American-style porterhouse to a sauce-sodden chateaubriand. All of the cuts are locally sourced and dry aged five weeks to guarantee succulence; most cuts are available in 225g or 340g except for the bone-in rib eye, which comes as a daunting 680g, racket-sized hunk of meat.

Old Harker's Arms PUB ££
(☎01244-344525; www.harkersarms-chester.co.uk; 1 Russell St; mains £9-14; ⊙lunch & dinner) An old-style boozer with a gourmet kitchen, this is the perfect place to tuck into Cumberland sausages or a Creole rice salad with sweet potatoes, and then rinse your palate with a pint of local ale, such as Cheshire Cat. It also serves bar snacks and sandwiches.

The Cheese Shop CHEESE
(www.chestercheeseshop.co.uk; 116 Northgate St; ⊙8.30am-5.30pm Mon-Sat, 10.30am-5.30pm Sun) Cows, goats and ewes provide the basics for the 200 different types of cheese sold in this family owned local institution, including eight kinds of Cheshire cheese. You can't but be tempted by the likes of Sandham's Butterton Organic Crumbly Lancashire or Muldoon's Picnic, a Lancashire cheese made on Saddleworth Moor. Blessed are the cheesemakers.

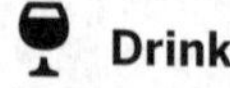

Drinking

Albion PUB
(4 Albion St) No children, no music, and no machines or big screens (but plenty of Union Jacks). This 'family hostile' Edwardian classic pub is a throwback to a time when ale drinking still had its own rituals. Still, this is one of the finest pubs in northwest England precisely because it doggedly refuses to modernise.

Falcon PUB
(Lower Bridge St) This is an old-fashioned boozer with a lovely atmosphere; the surprisingly adventurous menu offers up dishes such as Jamaican peppered beef or spicy Italian sausage casserole. Great for both a pint and a bite (mains from £5.50).

Entertainment

Roodee HORSE RACING
(www.chester-races.co.uk; The Racecoarse; ⊙May-Sep) Chester's ancient and very beautiful racetrack, which has been hosting races since the 16th century, is on the western side of the walls. Highlights of the summer flat season include the two-day July Festival and the August equivalent.

Information

Cheshire Constabulary (☎01244-350000; Town Hall, Northgate St)

Countess of Chester Hospital (☎01244-365000; Health Park, Liverpool Rd)

Post Office (2 St John St; ⊙9am-5.30pm Mon-Sat)

Tourist Office (☎01244-402111; www.visitchester.com; Town Hall, Northgate St; ⊙9am-5.30pm Mon-Sat, 10am-4pm Sun May-Oct, 10am-5pm Mon-Sat Nov-Apr)

Getting There & Away

Bus

National Express (☎08717 81 81 81; www.nationalexpress.com) coaches stop on Vicar's Lane, just opposite the tourist office by the Roman amphitheatre. Destinations include the following:

Birmingham £14, 2¼ hours, four daily.

Liverpool £7.90, one hour, four daily.

London £23, 5½ hours, three daily.

Manchester £7.40, 1¼ hours, three daily.

For information on local bus services, ring the **Cheshire Bus Line** (☎01244-602666). Local buses leave from the Town Hall Bus Exchange on Princess St.

Train

The train station is about a mile from the city centre via Foregate St and City Rd, or Brook St. City-Rail Link buses are free for people with rail tickets, and operate between the station and Bus Stop A on Frodsham St. Destinations include:

Liverpool £6.20, 45 minutes, hourly.

London Euston £73.20, 2½ hours, hourly.

Manchester £11.30, one hour, hourly.

Getting Around

Much of the city centre is closed to traffic from 10.30am to 4.30pm, so a car is likely to be a hindrance. Anyway, the city is easy to walk around and most places of interest are close to the wall.

City buses depart from the Town Hall Bus Exchange.

Around Chester

Chester Zoo ZOO

(www.chesterzoo.org; Upton-by-Chester; adult/child £16.30/12.60, monorail adult/child £2/1.50, waterbus adult/child £2/1.50; ⏲10am-dusk, last admission 4pm Mon-Fri, till 5pm Sat & Sun) The largest of its kind in the country, Chester Zoo is about as pleasant a place as caged animals in artificial renditions of their natural habitats could ever expect to live. It's so big that there's even a **monorail** and a **waterbus** for getting around. The zoo is on the A41, three miles north of Chester's city centre. First Group Service No 1 (every 15 minutes Monday to Saturday, half-hourly Sunday) runs between Chester's Town Hall Bus Exchange and the zoo.

Blue Planet Aquarium AQUARIUM

(www.blueplanetaquarium.com; adult/child £15.50/11.25; ⏲10am-5pm Mon-Fri, 10am-6pm Sat & Sun) Things aren't done by halves around Chester, where you'll also find the country's largest aquarium, Blue Planet. It's home to 10 different kinds of shark, which can be viewed from a 70m-long moving walkway that lets you eye them up close. It's nine miles north of Chester at junction 10 of the M53 to Liverpool. Buses 1 and 4 run there every half-hour from Chester Town Hall Bus Exchange.

Ellesmere Port Boat Museum MUSEUM

(www.nwm.org.uk; South Pier Rd; adult/child £6.50/5.50; ⏲10am-5pm) Near the aquarium, on the Shropshire Union Canal about 8 miles north of Chester, is the superb Ellesmere Port Boat Museum, which has a large collection of canal boats as well as indoor exhibits. Take bus 4 from the Town Hall Bus Exchange in Chester, or it's a 10-minute walk from Ellesmere Port train station.

Knutsford

POP 12,660

A popular commuter town for Manchester's middle classes, Knutsford's appeal is largely the result of the eccentric philanthropy of Richard Watt (1842–1913), a millionaire glove manufacturer whose love of Mediterranean architecture resulted in the commissioning of a group of weird and wonderful buildings that make the town centre one of the most interesting places in Cheshire.

Knutsford's other celebrity link is with author Elizabeth Cleghorn Gaskell (1810–65), who used it as the model for the fictional town of Cranford in her most noteworthy novel (*Cranford* 1853). Gaskell wrote it in her home in the Manchester suburb of Ardwick, which has been converted into a **museum** (www.elizabethgaskellhouse.org; 84 Plymouth Grove; admission free; ⏲noon-4pm 1st Sun of month Mar-Dec), closed at the time of research for major refurbishment.

Knutsford Heritage Centre (www.knutsfordheritage.com; 90a King St; admission free; ⏲11am-4pm Tue-Sat, 2-5pm Sun Apr-Sep, 11am-4pm Tue-Sat Oct-Mar) is a reconstructed former smithy that has plenty of information on Gaskell; the most interesting displays, though, are on Watt and his quirky contributions to English architecture. The centre also organises a variety of walking tours around the town.

The best examples of the town's quirky buildings are along King St, which is a fine example of the haphazard harmony of English urban architecture. See in particular the **Ruskin Reading Room** (Drury Lane).

ROYAL MAY DAY

Since 1864 Knutsford has liked to go a bit wild on Royal May Day. The main festivities take place on the heath, a large area of common land, and include Morris dancing, brass bands and a pageant of historical characters from fiction and fact. Perhaps the most interesting tradition is that of 'sanding', whereby the streets are covered in colourful messages written in sand. Legend has it that the Danish King Knut, while crossing the marsh between Over and Nether Knutsford, scrawled a message in the sand wishing happiness to a young couple who were on the way to their wedding. The custom is also practised at weddings and on feast days.

The **Gaskell Memorial Tower** incorporates the swanky **Belle Epoque Brasserie** (☎01565-633060; www.thebelleepoque.com; 60 King St; mains £9-16, s/d £95/110; ⏰Mon-Sat), a *fin-de-siècle*-style restaurant that Oscar Wilde would look perfectly at home in. Upstairs the rooms are styled in accordance with the late-19th-century theme of the building.

Information

Tourist Office (Toft Rd; ⏰9am-5pm Mon-Fri, 9am-1pm Sat) In the council offices opposite the train station.

Getting There & Away

Knutsford is 15 miles southwest of Manchester and is on the Manchester–Chester train line (Chester £10, 45 minutes, hourly; Manchester £5.20, 30 minutes, hourly). The train station is on Adams Hill, at the southern end of King St.

Around Knutsford

At the northern end of King St is the entrance to the 400-hectare **Tatton Park** (NT; www.tattonpark.org.uk; admission free, individual attractions adult/child £5/2.50; ⏰10am-7pm, last entry 6pm). At its heart is a Regency **mansion**; a Tudor **Old Hall** that's open only on select days (see the website); a 1930s-style **working farm** (⏰noon-5pm Tue-Sun); and a series of superb Victorian **gardens** (⏰10am-6pm Tue-Sun). The **Totally Tatton Ticket** (adult/child £10/5) allows entry to all attractions over two days. Car admission to the park costs £5.

On Sunday bus X2 links Tatton Park with Chester (one hour). At other times you'll need your own wheels.

Nantwich

POP 13,450

If it wasn't for salt, Cheshire's second-best example of black-and-white Tudor architecture might never have been rebuilt after a devastating fire in 1583. The town produced the stuff, and Elizabeth I thought it so important that she interceded and donated £1000 of her (well, England's) money for the reconstruction. The town thanked her for her largesse with a handsome plaque on the appropriately named **Queen's Aid House** (High St; ⏰9am-5pm), itself a striking Tudor building.

The rest of the largely pedestrianised centre has plenty of fine examples of the black-and-white style, although it's a wonder so many of them stay standing, such is their off-kilter shape and design.

Very few buildings survived the fire; the most important of those that did is the 14th-century **Church of St Mary** (Church Lane; ⏰9am-5pm), a fine example of medieval architecture.

Apart from salt, the town grew up around the production of cheese and leather, and all three are depicted in the **Nantwich Museum** (☎01270-627104; www.nantwichmuseum.org.uk; Pillory St; admission free; ⏰10am-4.30pm Tue-Sat).

Sleeping & Eating

Crown Hotel HOTEL ££
(☎01565-625283; www.crownhotelnantwich.com; High St; rs/d from £76/86) There is barely a straight line in the place, but this gorgeous Tudor half-timbered hotel (part of the Best Western group) is easily top choice in town. The ground-floor **Casa Brasserie** (mains £8.25-14.95; ⏰lunch & dinner Mon-Sat, dinner only Sun) is a decent and popular restaurant with an unsurprising but generally tasty selection of Italian dishes.

Pillory House & Coffee Shop TEAROOM £
(18 Pillory St; sandwiches £3.50-5) An old-style tearoom that serves sandwiches and inexpensive hot dishes – perfect for that quick lunch.

Information

Tourist Office (Church Walk; ⏰9.30am-5pm Mon-Fri, 10am-4pm Sat, 11am-3pm Sun) Near the main square.

Getting There & Away

The **bus station** (Beam St) is 300m north of the tourist office; Arriva bus 84 serves the town from Chester (£5.90, one hour).

To get to Manchester, Chester or Liverpool by train, you'll have to change in Crewe (15 minutes, half-hourly). The train station is about half a mile south of the centre.

LIVERPOOL

POP 469,020

Few English cities are as shackled by reputation as Liverpool, and none has worked so hard to outgrow the clichés that for so long have been used to define it.

Yes, the city has had a hardscrabble history beset by chronic misfortune and a myriad of social ills. Yes, those tough times have helped forge the city's famous sense of humour, which is really just a coping mechanism for getting through difficulty. Yes, they love football here. And yes, the Beatles occupy a huge chunk of the city's cultural heritage.

All these things are true, but they do little justice to a city that has more listed buildings than any other outside London, has transformed its centre via a breathtaking program of urban regeneration and is home to some of the best museums and galleries north of the Watford Gap.

Of course they still cherish the Beatles around here. But not because they're stuck in the past and haven't gotten over the fact that they're long gone – it's because their worldwide popularity would make it crazy *not* to do so.

The main attractions are Albert Dock (west of the city centre), and the trendy Ropewalks area (south of Hanover St and west of the two cathedrals). Lime St station, the bus station and the Cavern Quarter – a mecca for Beatles fans – lie just to the north.

History

Liverpool grew wealthy on the back of the triangular trading of slaves, raw materials and finished goods. From 1700, ships carried cotton goods and hardware from Liverpool to West Africa, where they were exchanged for slaves, who in turn were carried to the West Indies and Virginia, where they were exchanged for sugar, rum, tobacco and raw cotton.

As a great port, the city drew thousands of Irish and Scottish immigrants, and its Celtic influences are still apparent. However, between 1830 and 1930 nine million emigrants – mainly English, Scots and Irish, but also Swedes, Norwegians and Russian Jews – sailed from here for the New World.

The start of WWII led to a resurgence of Liverpool's importance. More than one million American GIs disembarked here before D-Day and the port was, once again, hugely important as the western gateway for transatlantic supplies. The GIs brought with them the latest American records, and Liverpool was thus the first European port of call for the new rhythm and blues that would eventually become rock and roll. Within 20

LIVERPOOL IN...

Two Days

Start at the waterfront's collection of superb museums. Visit the new **Museum of Liverpool** and, just south, the **International Slavery Museum** in Albert Dock.

Pay the Fab Four their due at the **Beatles Story** before heading into town to the Cavern Quarter around Mathew St. The **Monro** is worth a visit for lunch and the **Marco Pierre White Steakhouse & Grill** for dinner. Round off the day with a pint at the marvellous **Philharmonic**, and wrap yourself in the crisp sheets of the **Hotel Indigo**. Night hawks can tear it up in the bars and clubs of the hip **Ropewalks** area. The next day, explore the city's two **cathedrals** and check out the twin delights of the **World Museum Liverpool** and the **Walker Art Gallery**.

Four Days

Follow the two-day itinerary and make a pilgrimage to **Mendips** and **20 Forthlin Rd**, the childhood homes of John Lennon and Paul McCartney respectively. For dinner, try the **Italian Club**. The next day, walk on holy ground at Anfield, home of **Liverpool Football Club**. Race junkies can head to the visitor centre at **Aintree racecourse**, which hosts England's beloved race, the Grand National.

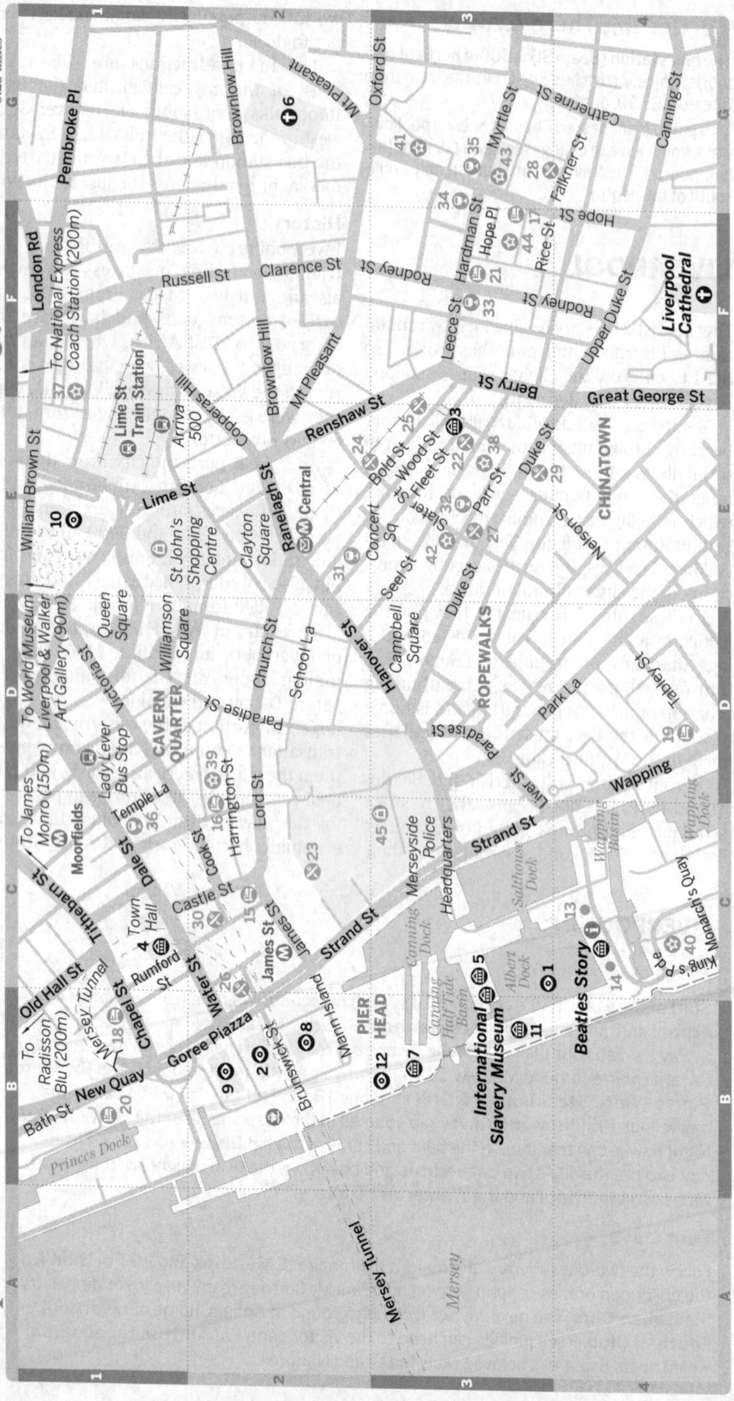

Liverpool

0 500 m
0 0.25 miles

To Radisson Blu (200m)
To James Monro (150m)
Moorfields
To World Museum Liverpool & Walker Art Gallery (90m)
William Brown St
10
London Rd
To National Express Coach Station (200m)
37
Pembroke Pl
Bath St
New Quay
Old Hall St
Tithebarn St
Princes Dock
20
Mersey Tunnel
18
Chapel St
Rumford St
4
Town Hall
Dale St
36
Temple La
Lady Lever Bus Stop
Victoria St
Queen Square
Lime St Train Station
Arriva 500
CAVERN QUARTER
Williamson Square
St John's Shopping Centre
Lime St
Copperas Hill
Russell St
Goree Piazza
Water St
30
Castle St
Cook St
16
39
Harrington St
Paradise St
Clayton Square
Brownlow Hill
9
26
15
Lord St
Church St
Ranelagh St
2
Brunswick St
James St
Central
Mt Pleasant
6
8
Mann Island
23
School La
Renshaw St
Clarence St
Strand St
31
24
Mersey Tunnel
PIER HEAD
12
45
Hanover St
Concert Sq
Bold St
Rodney St
Oxford St
41
7
Canning Dock
Merseyside Police Headquarters
Campbell Square
Seel St
Slater St
Wood St
Fleet St
25
Mersey
Canning Half Tide Basin
42
32
22
3
Leece St
Hardman St
34
35
Duke St
Parr St
38
33
21
Hope Pl
43
Myrtle St
International Slavery Museum
5
ROPEWALKS
27
Berry St
44
17
28
11
Albert Dock
Salthouse Dock
Liver St
Paradise St
Rice St
Falkner St
1
Park La
29
Rodney St
Hope St
Catherine St
Beatles Story
13
Nelson St
CHINATOWN
Upper Duke St
14
Wapping Basin
Wapping
King's Pde
40
Monarch's Quay
Wapping Dock
19
Tabley St
Great George St
Liverpool Cathedral
Canning St

Liverpool

Top Sights
Beatles Story ... C4
International Slavery Museum ... C3
Liverpool Cathedral ... F4

Sights
1 Albert Dock ... C3
2 Cunard Building ... B2
3 FACT ... E3
4 Liverpool War Museum ... C1
5 Merseyside Maritime Museum ... C3
6 Metropolitan Cathedral of Christ the King ... G2
7 Museum of Liverpool ... B3
8 Port of Liverpool Building ... B2
9 Royal Liver Building ... B2
10 St George's Hall ... E1
11 Tate Liverpool ... B3
12 The Beatles Story: Elvis & Us ... B3

Activities, Courses & Tours
13 Magical Mystery Tour ... C4
14 Yellow Duckmarine Tour ... C4

Sleeping
15 62 Castle St ... C2
16 Hard Days Night Hotel ... C2
17 Hope Street Hotel ... F3
18 Hotel Indigo ... B1
19 Liverpool YHA ... D4
20 Malmaison ... B1
21 Roscoe House ... F3

Eating
22 Alma de Cuba ... E3
23 Chaophraya ... C2
24 Italian Club ... E2
25 Italian Club Fish ... E3
London Carriage Works ... (see 17)
Marco Pierre White Steakhouse & Grill ... (see 18)
26 Meet Argentinean ... C2
27 Monro ... E3
28 Quarter ... G3
29 Sapporo Teppanyaki ... E3
30 The Noble House ... C2

Drinking
31 Bar Ça Va ... E2
32 Brink ... E3
33 Hannah's ... F3
34 Magnet ... G3
35 Philharmonic ... G3
36 Rigby's ... C1

Entertainment
37 Academy ... F1
38 Masque ... E3
39 Cavern Club ... D2
40 ECHO Arena ... C4
41 Everyman Theatre ... G3
42 Nation ... E3
43 Philharmonic Hall ... G3
44 Unity Theatre ... F3

Shopping
45 Liverpool ONE ... C3

years, the Mersey Beat was *the* sound of British pop, and four mop-topped Scousers had formed a skiffle band...

Sights

The wonderful Albert Dock is the city's biggest tourist attraction, and the key to understanding the city's history, but the city centre is where you'll find most of Liverpool's real day-to-day life.

CITY CENTRE

FREE World Museum MUSEUM
(☎0151-478 4399; www.liverpoolmuseums.org.uk/wml; William Brown St; ⏲10am-5pm) Natural history, science and technology are the themes of this sprawling museum, whose exhibits range from birds of prey to space exploration. It also includes the country's only free planetarium. This vastly entertaining and educational museum is divided into four major sections: the Human World, one of the top anthropological collections in the country; the Natural World, which includes a new aquarium as well as live insect colonies; Earth, a geological treasure trove; and Space & Time, which includes the planetarium. Highly recommended.

FREE Walker Art Gallery ART MUSEUM
(☎0151-478 4199; www.liverpoolmuseums.org.uk/walker; William Brown St; ⏲10am-5pm) The city's foremost gallery is the national gallery for northern England, housing an outstanding collection of art from the 14th to the 21st centuries. Its strong suits are Pre-Raphaelite art, modern British art and sculpture – not to mention the rotating

exhibits of contemporary expression. It's a family friendly place, too: the ground-floor Big Art for Little People gallery is designed especially for under-eights and features interactive exhibits and games that will (hopefully) result in a life-long love affair with art.

Liverpool Cathedral CATHEDRAL
(☎0151-709 6271; www.liverpoolcathedral.org.uk; Upper Duke St; ⊙8am-6pm) Liverpool's Anglican cathedral is a building of superlatives. Not only is it Britain's largest church, it's also the world's largest Anglican cathedral, and it's all thanks to Sir Giles Gilbert Scott, who made its construction his life's work. Sir Scott also gave us the red telephone box and the Southwark Power Station in London, now Tate Modern. The central bell is the world's third-largest (with the world's highest and heaviest peal), while the organ, with its 9765 pipes, is likely the world's largest operational model.

The **visitor centre** (£5; ⊙8am-6pm) features the **Great Space**, a 10-minute, panoramic high-definition movie about the history of the cathedral. It's followed by your own audiovisual tour, courtesy of a headset. Your ticket also gives you access to the cathedral's 101m tower, from which there are terrific views of the city and beyond – on a clear day you can see Blackpool Tower.

FREE **St George's Hall** CULTURAL CENTRE
(☎0151-707 2391; www.stgeorgesliverpool.co.uk; William Brown St; ⊙10am-5pm Tue-Sat, 1-5pm Sun) Arguably Liverpool's most impressive building is the Grade I–listed St George's Hall, a magnificent example of neoclassical architecture that is as imposing today as it was when it was completed in 1854. Curiously, it was built as law courts *and* a concert hall – presumably a judge could pass sentence and then relax to a string quartet. Today it serves as an all-purpose cultural and civic centre, hosting concerts, corporate gigs and a host of other civic get-togethers; it is also the focal point of any city-wide celebration. **Tours** (☎0151-225 6909; £3.50; ⊙2pm Wed, 11am & 2pm Sat & Sun) of the hall are run in conjunction with the tourist office; the tour route can vary depending on what's going on in the building.

Metropolitan Cathedral of Christ the King CHURCH
(☎0151-709 9222; www.liverpoolmetrocathedral.org.uk; Brownlow Hill; ⊙8am-6pm Mon-Sat, to 5pm Sun Oct-Mar) Known colloquially as Paddy's Wigwam, Liverpool's Catholic cathedral is a mightily impressive modern building that looks like a soaring concrete teepee, hence its nickname. It was completed in 1967 according to the design of Sir Frederick Gibberd and after the original plans by Sir Edwin Lutyens, whose crypt is inside. The central tower frames the world's largest stained-glass window, created by John Piper and Patrick Reyntiens.

Liverpool War Museum MUSEUM
(www.liverpoolwarmuseum.co.uk; 1 Rumford St; adult/child £6/4; ⊙10.30am-4.30pm Mon-Thu & Sat Mar-Oct) The secret command centre for the Battle of the Atlantic, the Western Approaches, was abandoned at the end of the war with virtually everything left intact. You can get a good glimpse of the labyrinthine nerve centre of Allied operations, including the all-important map room, where you can imagine playing a real-life, full-scale version of Risk.

FACT GALLERY
(Foundation for Art & Creative Technology; www.fact.co.uk; 88 Wood St; ⊙galleries 11am-6pm Tue & Wed, 11am-8pm Thu-Sat, noon-5pm Sun, cinemas noon-10pm) This well-established media centre has two galleries that feature constantly changing exhibitions, usually to do with new media and digital art. Three screens show a mix of art-house films, old classics and mainstream releases. The bar and cafe are popular daytime hangouts for the city's creative types.

ALBERT DOCK

Liverpool's biggest tourist attraction is **Albert Dock** (☎0151-708 8854; www.albertdock.com; admission free), 2.75 hectares of water ringed by enormous cast-iron columns and impressive five-storey warehouses; these make up the country's largest collection of protected buildings and are a Unesco World Heritage Site. Here you'll find some of the city's best museums and the northern extension of the Tate Gallery – as well as the city's most visited attraction.

TOP CHOICE **International Slavery Museum** MUSEUM
(☎0151-478 4499; www.liverpoolmuseums.org.uk/ism; Albert Dock; admission free; ⊙10am-5pm) Museums are, by their very nature, like a still of the past, but the extraordinary International Slavery Museum resonates very much in the present. It reveals slavery's unimaginable horrors – including Liverpool's own role in the triangular slave

LIVERPOOL FOR CHILDREN

The waterfront museums are extremely popular with kids, especially the brand-new Museum of Liverpool (p658) and the Merseyside Maritime Museum (p657) – which has a couple of boats for kids to mess about on. The Yellow Duckmarine Tour (p658) is a sure-fire winner, while a visit to Anfield Rd (p663) is a must if they have any kind of interest in football. The Big Art for Little People gallery at the Walker Art Gallery (p655) is perfect for kids who want to find out that art is more than just something adults stare at.

trade – in a clear and uncompromising manner. It does this through a remarkable series of multimedia and other displays, and it doesn't baulk at confronting racism, slavery's shadowy ideological justification for this inhumane practice.

The history of slavery is made real through a series of personal experiences, including a carefully kept ship's log and captain's diary. These tell the story of one slaver's experience on a typical trip, departing Liverpool for West Africa. The ship then purchased or captured as many slaves as it could carry before embarking on the gruesome 'middle passage' across the Atlantic to the West Indies. The slaves that survived the torturous journey were sold for sugar, rum and molasses, which were then brought back to England for profit. Exhibits include original shackles, chains and instruments used to punish rebellious slaves – each piece of metal is more horrendous than the next.

It's potent, disturbing stuff, but as well as providing an insightful history lesson, we are reminded of our own obligations to humanity and justice throughout the museum, not least in the Legacies of Slavery exhibit, which explores the continuing fight for freedom and equality. A visit to this magnificent museum is unmissable.

Beatles Story MUSEUM

(☎0151-709 1963; www.beatlesstory.com; Albert Dock; adult/student/child £12.95/9/7, including Elvis & Us £15.95/12/7; ⏲9am-7pm, last admission 5pm) Liverpool's most popular museum won't illuminate any dark, juicy corners in the turbulent history of the world's most famous foursome – there's ne'er a mention of internal discord, drugs or Yoko Ono – but there's plenty of genuine memorabilia to keep a Beatles fan happy. Particularly impressive is the full-size replica Cavern Club (which was actually tiny) and the Abbey Rd studio where the lads recorded their first singles, while George Harrison's crappy first guitar (now worth half a million quid) should inspire budding, penniless musicians to keep the faith. The museum is also the departure point for the Yellow Duckmarine Tour. You can also get a combo ticket for the Elvis & Us (p658) exhibit at the new Beatles Story extension on Pier Head.

FREE **Merseyside Maritime Museum** MUSEUM

(☎0151-478 4499; www.liverpoolmuseums.org.uk/maritime; Albert Dock; ⏲10am-5pm) The story of one of the world's great ports is the theme of this excellent museum and, believe us, it's a graphic and compelling page-turner. One of the many great exhibits is Emigration to a New World, which tells the story of nine million emigrants and their efforts to get to North America and Australia; the walk-through model of a typical ship shows just how tough conditions on board really were.

FREE **Tate Liverpool** ART MUSEUM

(☎0151-702 7400; www.tate.org.uk/liverpool; Albert Dock; special exhibitions adult/child from £5/4; ⏲10am-5.50pm Jun-Aug, 10am-5.50pm Tue-Sun Sep-May) Touted as the home of modern art in the north, this gallery features a substantial checklist of 20th-century artists across its four floors, as well as touring exhibitions from the mother ship on London's Bankside. But it's all a little sparse, with none of the energy we'd expect from the world-famous Tate.

NORTH OF ALBERT DOCK

The area to the north of Albert Dock is known as **Pier Head**, after a stone pier built in the 1760s. This is still the departure point for ferries across the River Mersey, and was, for millions of migrants, their final contact with European soil.

The new Museum of Liverpool is an impressive architectural interloper, but pride of place in this part of the dock still goes to the trio of Edwardian buildings known as the 'Three Graces', dating from the days when Liverpool's star was still ascending. The southernmost, with the dome mimicking St Paul's Cathedral, is the **Port of Liverpool Building**, completed in 1907. Next to it is the **Cunard Building**, in the style of an Italian palazzo, once HQ to the Cunard Steamship Line. Finally, the **Royal Liver Building** (pronounced *lie*-ver) was opened in 1911 as the head office of the Royal Liver Friendly Society. It's crowned by Liverpool's symbol, the famous 5.5m copper Liver Bird.

FREE Museum of Liverpool MUSEUM
(0151-478 4545; www.liverpoolmuseums.org.uk; Pier Head; 10am-5pm) Liverpool's storied past is explored within the confines of an eye-catching futuristic building designed in typical Scandinavian verve by Danish firm 3XN. Inside, it's all fizz-bang-wallop as you wend your way through an interactive exploration of the cultural and historical milestones of Liverpool – the railroad, poverty, wealth, *Brookside* (a popular 80s TV soap opera set in the city), the Beatles and football (the film on the meaning of the game to the city is worth the 15 minutes). The desire to tell all of the city's rich story means there isn't a huge amount of depth, but the kids will love it, as will anyone who doesn't want a doctoral dissertation on urban development and population growth.

Beatles Story: Elvis & Us EXHIBITION
(0151-709 1963; www.elvisandus.com; Mersey Ferries Terminal, Pier Head; £6; 9am-7pm Apr-Sep, 10am-6pm Oct-Mar) In a near perfect rock 'n' roll symbiosis, the Beatles met Elvis on 27 August, 1965 at his home in Bel Air, California. The meeting of pop music's most iconic figures forms the basis of this exhibit atop the Pier Head ferry terminal. Want to gawk at the white Fender bass Paul played at the meeting? Stare lovingly at the shirt Elvis wore in *Jailhouse Rock*? Look at rare footage and examine a ticket to the '68 comeback special? Then this is the place to do it.

Tours

Beatles Fab Four Taxi Tour MUSIC TOURS
(0151-601 2111; www.thebeatlesfabfourtaxitour.co.uk; 3/2-hour £50/40) Themed tours of the city's mop-top landmarks – there's the three-hour original Lennon tour or the two-hour Epstein express tour. Pick-ups arranged when booking. Up to five people per tour.

Liverpool Beatles Tour MUSIC TOURS
(0151-281 7738; www.beatlestours.co.uk; tours from £50) Your own personalised tour of every bit of Beatles minutiae, from cradle to grave. Tours range from the two-hour Helter Skelter excursion to the all-day There Are Places I Remember, by the end of which, presumably, you'll be convinced you were actually in the band. Pick-ups are arranged upon booking.

Magical Mystery Tour MUSIC TOURS
(0151-709 3285; www.beatlestour.org; per person £15.95; 2.30pm year-round, plus noon Sat Jul & Aug) Two-hour tour that takes in all Beatles-related landmarks – their birthplaces, childhood homes, schools and places such as Penny Lane and Strawberry Field – before finishing up in the Cavern Club (which isn't the original). Departs from outside the tourist office on Albert Dock.

River Explorer Cruise BOAT TOURS
(0151-639 0609; www.merseyferries.co.uk; adult/child return £8/4.50; hourly 10am-3pm Mon-Fri, 10am-5pm Sat & Sun) Liverpool is at its very best when viewed from the water, so take a ferry 'cross the Mersey (as Gerry & the Pacemakers said), exploring the bay and all its attractions as you go. Departs from Pier Head ferry terminal.

Yellow Duckmarine Tour WATER TOURS
(0151-708 7799; www.theyellowduckmarine.co.uk; adult/child £14.95/9.95; from 11am) Take to the dock waters in a WWII amphibious vehicle after a quickie tour of the city centre's main points of interest. It's not especially educational, but it is a bit of fun. Departs from Albert Dock, near the Beatles Story.

Festivals & Events

Aintree Festival HORSE RACING
(www.aintree.co.uk) A three-day race meeting culminating in the world-famous Grand National steeplechase, held on the first Saturday in April.

Africa Oye MUSIC
(www.africaoye.com) The UK's largest free festival celebrating African music and culture takes place in the suburb of Sefton Park in the second half of June.

Creamfields MUSIC
(www.cream.co.uk) An alfresco dance-fest that brings together some of the world's best DJs and dance acts during the last weekend in August. It takes place at the Daresbury Estate near Halton, Cheshire.

Mathew St Festival MUSIC
(0151-239 9091; www.mathewstreetfestival.org) The world's biggest tribute to the Beatles features six days of music, a convention and

a memorabilia auction during the last week of August.

Liverpool Comedy Festival COMEDY
(☎0870 787 1866; www.liverpoolcomedyfestival.com) A fortnight of comedy, with the best of local and international talent in venues throughout the city, over 10 days at the end of September and the first week in October.

Liverpool Music Week MUSIC
(www.liverpoolmusicweek.com) Two weeks, 250 bands, 26 venues – early October sees Liverpool showcase the best of local and emerging national talent. Most gigs are free.

Sleeping

There are some pretty fancy pillows on which to lay your head in Liverpool, from sexy boutique hotels to stylish upmarket properties. For the rest, it's all about standard business hotels and midrange chains. Beds are rarer than hen's teeth when Liverpool FC are playing at home (it's less of an issue with Everton) and during the mobbed out Beatles convention in the last week of August. If you fancy self-catering options, the tourist office has all the information you'll need.

CITY CENTRE

Hope Street Hotel BOUTIQUE £££
(☎0151-709 3000; www.hopestreethotel.co.uk; 40 Hope St; r/ste from £125/170; @☎) Luxurious Liverpool's pre-eminent flag-waver is this stunning boutique hotel, on the city's most elegant street. King-sized beds draped in Egyptian cotton, oak floors with underfloor heating, LCD wide-screen TVs and sleek modern bathrooms (with REN bath and beauty products) are but the most obvious touches of class at this supremely cool address. Breakfast, taken in the marvellous London Carriage Works, is not included.

Hotel Indigo HOTEL ££
(☎0151-559 0111; www.hotelindigoliverpool.co.uk; 10 Chapel St; r from £65; @☎) It's labeled a boutique hotel, but the 151-room Indigo is just too big and part of a franchise, so the feel is more corporate swish than bespoke boutique. Still, the rooms are bright, extremely well-appointed and distinctly modern; downstairs, the **Marco Pierre White Steakhouse & Grill** (www.mpwsteakhouseliverpool.co.uk; Hotel Indigo, 10 Chapel St; mains £16-25; ⊙lunch & dinner) is full of diners looking for a good night out. An excellent midrange choice.

Radisson Blu HOTEL ££
(☎0151-966 1500; www.radissonblu.co.uk; 107 Old Hall St; r from £89; @☎) Ergonomic designer furniture in the lobby – funky red couches and the like – beneath a soaring nine-storey atrium...there's something so appealing about Scandinavian corporate style, at least if you're a fan of contemporary decor. The rooms are divided into 'Ocean', a blue-coloured, wave-themed look with views of the docks and the Mersey; and 'Urban', all luscious reds and other deep colours, with views of the city centre. Each comes with all the designer gadgetry you'd expect: flat-screen TVs, funky see-through mini-bars and super-hip bathrooms. They're not especially huge, but they're very cool, baby.

62 Castle St BOUTIQUE HOTEL ££
(☎0151-702 7898; www.62castlest.com; 62 Castle St; r from £69; P@☎) This elegant property on (arguably) the city's most handsome street successfully blends the traditional Victorian features of the neoclassical building with a sleek, contemporary style. The 20 fabulously different suites come with HD plasma screen TVs, drench showers and Elemis toiletries as standard.

Hard Days Night Hotel HOTEL £££
(☎0151-236 1964; www.harddaysnighthotel.com; Central Bldgs, North John St; r £95-160, ste £750; @☎) You don't have to be a fan to stay here, but it helps. Unquestionably luxurious, the 110 ultramodern, fully equipped rooms are decorated with specially commissioned drawings of the Beatles. And if you opt for one of the suites, named after Lennon and McCartney, you'll get a white baby grand piano in the style of 'Imagine' and a bottle of fancy bubbly on arrival.

Roscoe House BOUTIQUE HOTEL ££
(☎0151-709 0286; www.hotelliverpool.net; 27 Rodney St; r from £50; ☎) A handsome Georgian home once owned by Liverpool-born writer and historian William Roscoe (1753–1831) has been given the once-over and is now a chic boutique hotel. The elegant rooms combine period touches (original coving, fireplaces and furnishings) with contemporary comforts such as flatscreen TVs and fancy Egyptian cotton linen.

AROUND ALBERT DOCK

Malmaison HOTEL £
(☎0151-229 5000; www.malmaison.com; 7 William Jessop Way, Princes Dock; r from £69; P@☎) The Malmaison's preferred colour scheme of plum

and black is everywhere in this purpose-built hotel, which gives it an air of contemporary sophistication but sort of makes it hard to see anything very clearly. But you don't really *see* plush – you experience it, and everything about the Liverpool Mal is plush, from the huge beds and the deep baths to the heavy velvet curtains and the excellent buffet breakfast. And, just in case you were ever in doubt as to which Malmaison property you were in, the sound of the Beatles is heard throughout the bedroom corridors (but thankfully not the bedrooms).

Liverpool YHA HOSTEL £
(0845 371 9527; www.yha.org.uk; 25 Tabley St; dm from £16; P) It may have the look of an Eastern European apartment complex, but this award-winning hostel, adorned with plenty of Beatles memorabilia, is one of the most comfortable you'll find anywhere in the country. The dorms with attached bathroom even have heated towel rails.

Eating

Top grade international cuisine, the best of British and the greasy spoon...you'll find plenty of choices to satisfy every taste. Best spots include Ropewalks, along Hardman St and Hope St or along Nelson St in the heart of Chinatown.

Monro GASTROPUB ££
(0151-707 9933; www.themonro.com; 92 Duke St; 2-course lunch £11.95, dinner mains £14-20; lunch and dinner) The Monro has fast become one of the city's favourite spots for lunch, dinner and, especially, weekend brunch – the constantly changing menu of classic British dishes made with ingredients sourced as locally as possible has transformed this handsome old pub into a superb dining experience. Tough to find pub grub this good elsewhere, unless you go to its sister pub, the **James Monro** (0151-236 9700; www.thejamesmonro.com; 69 Tithebarn St; lunch & dinner Tue-Sun).

Italian Club ITALIAN £
(0151-708 5508; www.theitalianclubliverpool.co.uk; 85 Bold St; mains £6-11; 10am-7pm Mon-Sat) The Crolla family must have been homesick for southern Italy, so they opened this fabulous spot, adorned it with family pictures and began serving the kind of food relatives visiting from the home country would be glad to tuck into. They've been so successful that they recently opened **Italian Club Fish** (0151-707 2110; 128 Bold St; mains £8-14; Tue-Sun) just down the street, specialising in, erm, fish.

The Noble House INTERNATIONAL ££
(0151-236 5346; www.thenoblehouse.co.uk; Heywood Building, 5 Brunswick St; mains £10-16) The handsome Heywood Building (1799) was once the city's oldest bank – now it's a classy restaurant with a vaguely Manhattanite feel (if it weren't for the occasional groups of football fans you could imagine yourself surrounded by Wall Streeters tucking into a menu of steaks, burgers and salads). The menu has expanded recently to include North African dishes as well as a handful of Mediterranean options. It's owned by the same crowd that run the Alma de Cuba (p660).

London Carriage Works MODERN BRITISH £££
(0151-705 2222; www.thelondoncarriageworks.co.uk; 40 Hope St; 2-/3-course meals £15/20, mains £15-27) Liverpool's dining revolution is being led by Paul Askew's award-winning restaurant, which successfully blends ethnic influences from around the globe with staunch British favourites and serves up the result in a beautiful dining room – actually more of a bright glass box divided only by a series of sculpted glass shards. Reservations are recommended.

Alma de Cuba CUBAN ££
(0151-709 7097; www.alma-de-cuba.com; St Peter's Church, Seel St; mains £13-25; lunch & dinner) This extraordinary venture has seen the transformation of a Polish church into a Miami-style Cuban extravaganza, a bar and restaurant where you can feast on a suckling pig (the menu heavily favours meat) or clink a perfectly made mojito at the long bar. *¡Salud!*

Meet Argentinean STEAKHOUSE ££
(0151-258 1816; www.meetrestaurant.co.uk; 2 Brunswick St; mains £11-26; lunch & dinner) Liverpool's first Argentine restaurant is really an elegant tribute to grilled beef served the size of a small wheel – just as any self-respecting gaucho would demand. Thankfully, there are some cuts that are smaller but just as good; the 450g grilled fillet steak was plenty for us.

Sapporo Teppanyaki JAPANESE £££
(0151-705 3005; www.sapporo.co.uk; 134 Duke St; teppanyaki sets £25-40, mains £15-25) As good a teppan-yaki (food that is grilled on a hot plate in front of you) experience as you'll have outside of Japan. Also decent sushi and sashimi.

Quarter WINE BAR, BISTRO ££
(☎0151-707 1965; 7-11 Falkner St; mains £9-13; ⊙lunch & dinner) A gorgeous little wine bar and bistro with outdoor seating for that elusive summer's day.

Chaophraya THAI ££
(☎0151-707 6323; www.chaophraya.co.uk; Liverpool ONE; mains £9-17; ⊙11am-late) Excellent Thai restaurant on the upper deck of Liverpool ONE with an exhaustive menu of fabulous dishes from the Land of Smiles and a commanding view of the city centre.

Drinking

From the party bars of Ropewalks to the traditional pubs embracing a cask ale renaissance, Liverpool has boozers for every sensibility – including those who want to forego all sense on a night out. Unless specified, all bars included here open 11am until 2am Monday to Saturday, although most have a nominal entry charge after 11pm.

Philharmonic PUB
(36 Hope St; ⊙to 11.30pm) This extraordinary bar, designed by the shipwrights who built the *Lusitania,* is one of the most beautiful bars in all of England. The interior is resplendent with etched and stained glass, wrought iron, mosaics and ceramic tiling – and if you think that's good, just wait until you see inside the marble men's toilets, the only heritage-listed lav in the country.

Magnet BAR
(www.magnetliverpool.co.uk; 39 Hardman St) Red leather booths, plenty of velvet and a suitably seedy New York–dive atmosphere where Iggy Pop or Tom Waits would feel right at home. The upstairs bar is very cool but totally chilled out, while downstairs the dance floor shakes to the best music in town, spun by up-and-comers and supported with guest slots by some of England's most established DJs.

Rigby's PUB
(21 Dale St) A traditional boozer that serves 'real ale' (ie a traditional brew with no extraneous carbon dioxide), Rigby's looks, feels and smells like an old-school pub. The perfect antidote to the noise of newer bars.

Bar Ça Va BAR
(4a Wood St; ⊙11am-2am Mon-Sat) Our favourite of the Ropewalks bars, this place has more of an indie vibe than the others that surround it. You can still get coloured jello shots and cheap bottles of alcopops, but the crowd here is a little more discerning, meaning it takes a lot more booze than usual to start a conga line.

Hannah's BAR
(☎0151-708 5959; 2 Leece St) One of the top student bars in town. Try to land yourself a table on the outdoor patio, which is covered in the event of rain. Staying open late, a friendly, easygoing crowd and some pretty decent music make this one of the better places in which to have a drink.

DRINKING THE DRY BAR

Brink (☎0151-703 0582; www.thebrinkliverpool.com; 15-21 Parr St) is Liverpool's first 'dry' bar – opened to give non-drinkers (or indeed anyone looking for a night out without alcohol) a nightlife option after all the cafes have closed. Inevitably, it is patronised by (and set up for) recovering addicts and alcoholics, but not exclusively – nor is the atmosphere lessened by the lack of booze; there's a broad range of entertainment on offer, from live mics to gigs.

Entertainment

The schedule is pretty full these days, whether it's excellent fringe theatre, a performance by the superb Philharmonic or an all-day rock concert. And then there's the constant backbeat provided by the city's club scene, which pulses and throbs to the wee hours, six nights out of seven. For all information, consult the *Liverpool Echo.*

Nightclubs

Most of the city's clubs are concentrated in Ropewalks, where they compete for customers with a ton of late-night bars; considering the number of punters in the area on a Friday or Saturday night, we're guessing there's plenty of business for everyone.

Masque CLUB
(☎0151-707 6171; www.chibuku.com; 90 Seel St; admission £4-11; ⊙Mon-Sat) This converted theatre is home to our favourite club in town. The fortnightly Saturday **Chibuku** is one of the best club nights in all of England, led by a mix of superb DJs including Yousef (formerly of Cream nightclub) and superstars such as Dmitri from Paris and Gilles Peterson. The music ranges from hip hop to deep house – if you're in town, get in line.

Other nights feature a superb mixed bag of music, from trash to techno.

Nation CLUB

(☎0151-709 1693; 40 Slater St, Wolstenholme Sq; admission £4-13) It looks like an air-raid shelter, but it's the big-name DJs dropping the bombs at the city's premier dance club, formerly the home of Cream. These days, it also hosts live bands as well as pumping techno nights.

Theatre

Most of Liverpool's theatres feature a mixed bag of revues, musicals and stage successes that are as easy on the eye as they are on the mind, but there is also more interesting work on offer.

The city's most famous repertory theatre (and also one of the best-known in England), the **Everyman** (☎0151-709 4776; www.everymanplayhouse.com), is currently being rebuilt and should reopen in 2013.

Unity Theatre THEATRE

(☎0151-709 4988; Hope Pl) Fringe theatre for those keen on the unusual and challenging. There's also a great bar on the premises.

Music

Philharmonic Hall CLASSICAL MUSIC

(☎0151-709 3789; Hope St) One of Liverpool's most beautiful buildings, the art deco Phil is home to the city's main classical orchestra, but it also stages the work of avant-garde musicians such as John Cage and Nick Cave.

Cavern Club LIVE MUSIC

(☎0151-236 1965; www.cavernclub.org; 8-10 Mathew St) It's a reconstruction, and not even on the same spot, but the 'world's most famous club' is still a great spot to see local bands.

Academy LIVE MUSIC

(☎0151-794 6868; Liverpool University, 11-13 Hotham St) Good spot to see midsize bands on tour.

ECHO Arena LIVE MUSIC

(☎0844 800 0400; Monarch's Quay) Brand new mega venue that hosts the city's pop shows, from top artists to Broadway extravaganzas.

Sport

Are you red or blue? There's no question of you *not* being a football fan in Liverpool, merely your choice of team – the reds of Liverpool FC or the blues of Everton. There is no city in England where the fortunes of its home football clubs are so inextricably linked with those of its inhabitants, which makes attendance at a game a heap of fun but also generates never-ending sport-as-metaphor-for-life conversations.

It's almost easy to forget Liverpool is also home to the Grand National – the world's most famous steeplechase event – which is run on the first weekend in April at Aintree, north of the city.

Liverpool FC FOOTBALL

(☎0151-263 9199, ticket office 0151-220 2345; www.liverpoolfc.tv; Anfield Rd) Doff o' the cap

(NEVER) LET IT BE

They broke up more than 40 years ago and two of their members are dead, but the Beatles are bigger business than ever in Liverpool.

Most of it centres around tiny Mathew St, site of the original Cavern Club, which is now the main thoroughfare of the 'Cavern Quarter.' Here you can shuck oysters in the Rubber Soul Oyster Bar, buy a George pillowcase in the From Me to You shop and put it on the pillows of the Hard Day's Night Hotel. Ringo may have dissed the city in 2008 by declaring that he missed nothing about it, but the city's tourist authorities continue to exploit Liverpool's ties to the world's most famous group and have done so with enormous success – the Mathew St Festival (p658) attracts over 350,000 fans and generates revenue for the city in excess of £17m per annum.

Wandering around Mathew St is plenty of fun – and the Beatles Shop is best for memorabilia – but if you really want a bit of Beatles lore, you'll have to visit the National Trust–owned **Mendips**, the home where John lived with his Aunt Mimi from 1945 to 1963 (which is also the time period covered by Sam Taylor-Wood's superb 2009 biopic of the young Lennon, *Nowhere Boy*) and **20 Forthlin Road**, the plain terraced home where Paul grew up; you can only do so by prebooked **tour** (☎0151-427 7231; www.nationaltrust.org.uk; 31 Keel Wharf; adult/child £20/5; ⏱Wed-Sun Easter-Oct) from outside Jurys Inn in Wapping Dock. Visitors to Speke Hall can also visit both from there.

If you'd rather do it yourself, the tourist offices stock the *Discover Lennon's Liverpool* guide and map, and *Robin Jones' Beatles Liverpool*.

to Evertonians and Beatle-maniacs, but no single institution represents the Mersey spirit and strong sense of identity more powerfully than **Liverpool FC**, who won everything in the '70s and '80s but have struggled ever since. They last won the league title in 1990 and in 2011 their bitter rivals Manchester United won it for the 19th time – one more than Liverpool.

In 2010 the club was bought by US sports investment company Fenway Sports Group, who know a thing or two about turning long-standing disappointment around – it also owns the Boston Red Sox baseball team – and Liverpool fans have pinned their hopes on also being delivered to the promised land (although they'd rather not wait the 86 years it took the Red Sox to win the championship).

There are vague plans to redevelop the utterly marvellous **Anfield Road** (☎0151-260 6677; www.liverpoolfc.tv; Anfield Rd; tour & museum adult/child £15/9, museum only adult/child £6/4; ⏱hourly 10am-3pm except match days), where the experience of a live match is one of the sporting highlights of an English visit, especially the sound of 40,000 fans singing the club's anthem, 'You'll Never Walk Alone'. Take bus 26 or 27 from **Paradise St Interchange** or 17 or 217 from the Queen St Bus Station.

Everton Football Club FOOTBALL
(☎0151-330 2400, ticket office 0151-330 2300; www.evertonfc.com; Goodison Park) Liverpool's blue half consoles itself for existing in the shadow of its more successful neighbour with the historical truth that 'we were there first' – founded in 1878, **Everton FC** was the city's first club.

Tours (☎0151-530 5212; www.evertonfc.com; adult/child £8.50/5; ⏱11am & 1pm Sun-Mon, Wed & Fri) of Goodison Park run throughout the year, except on the Friday before home matches. Take bus 19, 20 or 21 from Paradise St Interchange or Queen St Bus Station.

Shopping

In between the Albert Dock, the Cavern Quarter and Ropewalks is the enormous **Liverpool ONE** (www.liverpool-one.com) shopping district ('centre' just feels too small), 17 hectares of retail and restaurant pleasure aimed primarily at the under-30s market but also addressing the needs of the older shopper.

Information

Emergency

Merseyside Police Headquarters (☎0151-709 6010; Canning Pl) Opposite Albert Dock.

Internet Access

CafeLatte.net (4 South Hunter St; per 30min £2; ⏱9am-6pm)

Internet Resources

A Night in Liverpool (www.anightinliverpool.com) One-stop guide to city nightlife.

Itchy Liverpool (www.itchyliverpool.co.uk) Irreverent guide to the city.

Liverpool Magazine (www.liverpool.com) Insiders' guide to the city, including lots of great recommendations for food and nights out.

Mersey Guide (www.merseyguide.co.uk) Guide to the Greater Mersey area.

Tourist Office (www.visitliverpool.com)

Medical Services

Mars Pharmacy (68 London Rd) Open until 10pm every night.

Royal Liverpool University Hospital (☎0151-706 2000; Prescot St)

Post

Post Office (Ranelagh St; ⏱9am-5.30pm Mon-Sat)

Tourist Information

Liverpool's tourist business is mostly done online, but there is an **accommodation hotline** (☎0845 601 1125; ⏱9am-5.30pm Mon-Fri, 10am-4pm Sat), and a small tourist office in Albert Dock.

Tourist Office (☎www.visitliverpool.com 0151-707 0729; Anchor Courtyard; ⏱10am-6pm) Leaflets, maps and information are provided in the small tourist office.

Getting There & Away

Air

Liverpool John Lennon Airport (☎0870 750 8484; www.liverpoolairport.com; Speke Hall Ave) serves a variety of international destinations as well as destinations in the UK (Belfast, London and the Isle of Man).

Bus

The **National Express Coach Station** (Norton St) is 300m north of Lime St station. There are services to/from most major towns:

Birmingham £13.80, 2¾ hours, five daily.

London £28, five to six hours, six daily.

Manchester £6.80, 1¼ hours, hourly.

Newcastle £24.50, 6½ hours, three daily.

Train

Liverpool's main station is Lime St. It has hourly services to almost everywhere, including the following:

Chester £6.20, 45 minutes.

London Euston £73.20, 3¼ hours.

Manchester £11, 45 minutes.

THE GRAND NATIONAL

The world's most famous steeplechase – and one of England's most cherished events – takes place on the first Saturday in April across 4.5 miles, over the most difficult fences in world racing. Its protagonists are 40-odd veteran stalwarts of the jumps, ageing bruisers full of the oh-so-English qualities of grit and derring-do.

You can book **tickets** (☎0151-522 2929; www.aintree.co.uk) for the Grand National, or visit the **Grand National Experience** (☎0151-523 2600; www.aintree.co.uk; adult/child with tour £11/6, without tour £6/4), a visitor centre that includes a race simulator – those jumps are very steep indeed. Redevelopment work on the centre means you have to book the tour in advance – call to make sure.

ℹ Getting Around

To/From the Airport

The airport is 8 miles south of the centre. **Arriva Airlink** (www.arriva.co.uk; £2; ⏲6am-11pm) buses 80A and 180 depart from Paradise St bus station, and **Arriva 500** (www.arriva.co.uk; £2.50; ⏲5.15am-12.15am) buses leave from outside Lime St station. Buses from both stations take half an hour and run every 20 minutes. A taxi to the city centre should cost no more than £18.

Boat

The famous cross-Mersey **ferry** (www.merseyferries.co.uk; adult/child £2.10/1.50) for Woodside and Seacombe departs from Pier Head Ferry Terminal, next to the Royal Liver Building (to the north of Albert Dock).

Car & Motorcycle

You won't really have much use for a car in Liverpool, and it'll no doubt end up costing you plenty in parking fees. If you have to drive, there are parking meters around the city and a number of open and sheltered car parks. Car break-ins are a significant problem, so leave absolutely nothing of value in the car.

Public Transport

Local public transport is coordinated by **Merseytravel** (www.merseytravel.gov.uk). If you arrive by train, you can purchase **Plusbus** (adult/child £3/1.50), which allows for unlimited bus travel within the city; otherwise **Saveaway** (adult/child £5/2.50) allows for one day's off-peak (after 9.30am) travel on all bus, train and ferry services throughout Merseyside. Tickets are available at shops and post offices throughout the city. Paradise St bus station is in the city centre.

Train **Merseyrail** (www.merseyrail.org) is an extensive suburban rail service linking Liverpool with the Greater Merseyside area. There are four stops in the city centre: Lime St, Central (handy for Ropewalks), James St (close to Albert Dock) and Moorfields (for the Liverpool War Museum).

Taxi

Mersey Cabs (☎0151-298 2222) operates tourist taxi services and also has some wheelchair-accessible cabs.

AROUND LIVERPOOL

Port Sunlight

Southwest of Liverpool, across the River Mersey on the Wirral Peninsula, picturesque Port Sunlight is a 19th-century village created by the philanthropic Lever family to house workers from their soap factory. The main reason to come here is the wonderful **Lady Lever Art Gallery** (www.liverpoolmuseums.org.uk/ladylever; admission free; ⏲10am-5pm), off Greendale Rd, where you can see some of the greatest works of the Pre-Raphaelite Brotherhood, as well as some fine Wedgwood pottery.

Take the Merseyrail to Bebington on the Wirral line; the gallery is a five-minute walk from the station. Alternatively, Arriva bus 464 from the Sir Thomas St **bus stop**, off Dale St in Liverpool, will get you here.

Speke

A marvellous example of a black-and-white half-timbered hall can be visited at **Speke Hall** (NT; www.nationaltrust.org.uk; house & gardens adult/child £8.10/4, gardens only adult/child £4.95/2.60; ⏲11am-5pm Wed-Sun), 6 miles south of Liverpool in the plain suburb of Speke. It contains several priests' holes where 16th-century Roman Catholic priests could hide when they were forbidden to hold Masses. Any airport bus from Paradise St will drop you within a half-mile of the entrance. Speke Hall can also be combined with a National Trust 1½-hour **tour** (☎0151-486 4006; with Speke Hall adult/child £20/5) to the childhood homes of both Lennon and McCartney – you can book at Speke Hall or at the tourist offices in Liverpool.

LANCASHIRE

No part of England may be so heavily urbanised as Lancashire, but as you travel north the concrete conurbations break up and bits of green begin to appear. North of Blackpool – the faded queen of beachside holidays – the landscape truly reveals itself in all its undulating, bucolic glory. The Ribble Valley is a gentle and beautiful warm-up for the Lake District that lies beyond the county's northern border. North of the Ribble Valley is the county's handsome Georgian capital, Lancaster.

Blackpool

POP 142,290

The queen bee of England's fun-by-the-sea-type resorts is unquestionably Blackpool. It's bold and brazen in its efforts to cement its position as the country's second-most-visited town after London. Tacky, trashy and, in recent years, just a little bit tawdry, Blackpool doesn't care because 16 million annual visitors don't either.

Blackpool works so well because it has mastered the time-tested, traditional British holiday-by-the-sea formula with high-tech, 21st-century amusements that thrill even the most cynical observer.

The town is famous for its tower, its three piers, its Pleasure Beach and its Illuminations, the latter being a successful ploy to extend the brief summer holiday season. From early September to early November, 5 miles of the Promenade are illuminated with thousands of electric and neon lights.

Sights

Pleasure Beach AMUSEMENT PARK
(www.blackpoolpleasurebeach.com; Central Promenade; Pleasure Beach Pass £5, wristband 1-day adult/child £27/22, 2-day £45/40, Speedy Pass £7.50 per person; from 10am Feb-Oct, Sat & Sun only Nov) The main reason for Blackpool's immense popularity is the Pleasure Beach, a 16-hectare collection of more than 145 rides that attracts some seven million visitors annually and, as amusement parks go, is easily the best in Britain.

The park's major rides include the Big One, the tallest and fastest roller coaster in Europe, reaching a top speed of 85mph before hitting a near-vertical descent of 75m; the Ice Blast, which delivers you up a 65m steel tower before returning to earth at 80mph; and the vertiginous Infusion, which features five loops, a double-line twist and a suspended looping coaster – which should help bring up that lunch just nicely.

The high-tech, modern rides draw the biggest queues, but spare a moment to check out the marvellous collection of old-style wooden roller coasters, known as 'woodies'. You can see the world's first Big Dipper (1923), but be sure to have a go on the Grand National (1935), whose carriages trundle along a 1½-mile track in an experience that is typically Blackpool – complete with riders waving their hands (despite the sombre-toned announcement not to).

Rides are divided into categories, and once you've gained entry to the park with your Freedom Ticket you can buy tickets for individual categories or for a mixture of them all. Alternatively, an **Unlimited Ride wristband** includes the £5 entrance fee; there are great discounts if you book your tickets online in advance. A new addition is the **Speedy Pass**, which saves you the hassle of queuing for rides by allocating you a specific ride time; rent it (£5) and add as many people to it as you want.

There are no set times for closing; it depends how busy it is.

Blackpool Tower ENTERTAINMENT COMPLEX
(0844-856 1000; www.theblackpooltower.com; tower admission free, Tower Eye & 4D Experience £12.60/7.20; 10.30am-4pm) Built in 1894, this 154m-high tower is Blackpool's most recognisable landmark. In 2011 it reopened after a major refurbishment, which saw the addition of the **Blackpool Tower Eye and 4D Experience**, where you watch a film on the town's history (and feel the spray of the sea and the smell of the donkeys) before taking the elevator 154m up to the new observation deck, which has splendid views and only a (thick) glass floor between you and the ant-sized people below.

Back at ground level, a new **dungeon** exhibit has opened to sit alongside the old Moorish circus and the magnificent rococo **ballroom**, with extraordinary sculptured and gilded plasterwork, murals, chandeliers and couples gliding across the beautifully polished wooden floor to the melodramatic tones of a huge Wurlitzer organ.

Sandcastle Waterpark WATERPARK
(www.sandcastle-waterpark.co.uk; adult/child £12.50/10.50, Hyperzone £5/2.50; from 10am May-Oct, from 10am Sat & Sun Nov-Feb) Across from the Pleasure Beach is this indoor

water complex with 15 different slides and rides, including the Hyperzone, which has the complex's most popular slides – Aztec Falls, Montezooma, the Sidewinder and Master Blaster, the world's largest indoor waterslide.

FREE **North Pier** ARCHITECTURAL LANDMARK
(Promenade) Built in 1862 and opening a year later, the most famous of the three Victorian piers once charged a penny for admission; its plethora of unexciting rides are now free.

Sleeping

With so many visitors, it's hardly surprising that every second building in town seems to be a hotel, B&B or self-catering unit. Most of them are fairly unremarkable, and you're advised to book ahead if you want to get a decent room between July and September. If you want to stay close to the waterfront, prepare for a noisy, boisterous night; accommodation along Albert and Hornby Rds, 300m back from the sea, is that little bit quieter. The tourist office will assist you in finding a bed.

Number One BOUTIQUE HOTEL ££
(01253-343901; www.numberoneblackpool.com; 1 St Lukes Rd; s/d from £70/120; P) Far fancier than anything else around, this stunning boutique guesthouse is all luxury and contemporary style. Everything exudes a kind of discreet elegance, from the dark-wood furniture and high-end mod cons to the top-notch breakfast. It's on a quiet road just set back from the South Promenade near the Pleasure Beach.

Big Blue Hotel HOTEL ££
(01253-400 045; www.bigbluehotel.com; Blackpool Pleasure Beach; r from £95; P@) A handsome family hotel with smartly kitted-out rooms. Kids' needs are met with DVD players and computer games, while its location at the southern entrance to the Pleasure Beach should ensure that everyone has something to do.

STAYING IN THE BLACK

A visit to all of Blackpool's attractions – including those dreaded words 'Again, Daddy, again!' – can put a strain on the budget. Consider booking all of your tickets online. Try www.blackpoolpleasurebeach.com, where you can benefit from substantial discounts on standard prices. It all adds up!

New President Hotel HOTEL ££
(01253-624460; www.thepresidenthotel.co.uk; 320-324 North Promenade; r from £70; P) Distinctive seafront hotel with 65 comfortable rooms. Also serves meals (£8 to £12) in the fancy-ish **Atlanta** restaurant.

Eating

Forget gourmet meals – the Blackpool experience is all about stuffing your face with burgers, doughnuts, and fish and chips. Most people eat at their hotels, where roast and three vegetables often costs just £5 per head.

There are a few restaurants around Talbot Sq (near the tourist office) on Queen St, Talbot Rd and Clifton St. Our favourite meal in town is at the Mediterranean **Kwizeen** (www.kwizeenrestaurant.co.uk; 49 King St; mains £13), which specialises in excellent Mediterranean fare using locally sourced produce.

Information

Tourist Office (01253-478222; www.visitblackpool.com; 1 Clifton St; 9am-5pm Mon-Sat)

Getting There & Away

Bus

The central coach station is on Talbot Rd, near the town centre.

Liverpool £9.90, 3 hours, four daily.

Manchester £8.20, 1¾ hours, four daily.

Train

The main train station is Blackpool North, about five blocks east of the North Pier on Talbot Rd. There is a direct service from Manchester (£15.20, 1¼ hours, half-hourly) and Liverpool (£16.40, 1½ hours, seven daily), but most other arrivals change in Preston (£7, 30 minutes, half-hourly).

Getting Around

A host of travel-card options for trams and buses ranging from one day to a week are available at the tourist office and most newsagents. With more than 14,000 car-parking spaces in Blackpool, you'll have no problem parking. The **land train service** (one way/return £2/3; from 10.30am Apr-Oct) shuttles funsters between the central corridor car parks and the main entrance to the Pleasure Beach every five minutes or so throughout the day. Otherwise, the town has recently introduced a **bike hire**

scheme (www.hourbike.com/blackpool; 3hr for £6) with bikes available for hire from stations along the Promenade and in Stanley Park.

Lancaster

POP 45,960

Lancashire's county seat is genteel, austere and much, much quieter than it was in its 18th-century heyday, when it served as an important trading port for all manner of goods, including people. The city's handsome Georgian architecture was one of the slave trade's ancillary benefits.

Sights

Lancaster Castle & Priory CASTLE

(☎01524-64998; www.lancastercastle.com; Castle Park; adult/child £5/4; ⊙10am-5pm, guided tour every 30min 10.30am-4pm) Lancaster's imposing castle was originally built in 1150. Later additions include the **Well Tower** – more commonly known as the Witches' Tower because it was used to incarcerate the accused of the famous Pendle Witches Trial of 1612 – and the impressive twin-towered **gatehouse**, both of which were added in the 14th century. However, most of what you see today dates from the 18th and 19th centuries, when the castle was substantially altered to suit its new, and still current, role as a prison. Consequently, you can only visit the castle as part of a 45-minute **guided tour**, but you do get a chance to experience what it was like to be locked up in the dungeon.

Immediately next to the castle is the equally fine **priory church** (Priory Cl; admission free; ⊙9.30am-5pm), founded in 1094 but extensively remodelled in the Middle Ages.

Judges' Lodgings MUSEUM

(Church St; adult/child £3/2; ⊙10am-4pm Jun-Jul, 1-4pm Easter-May & Aug-Oct) Once the home of witch-hunter Thomas Covell (he who 'caught' the poor Pendle women), Lancaster's oldest town house, a Grade I-listed Georgian building, is now home to a **Museum of Furnishings** by master builders Gillows of Lancaster, whose work graces the Houses of Parliament. It also houses a **Museum of Childhood**, which has memorabilia from the turn of the 20th century.

Williamson Park & Tropical Butterfly House GARDENS

(Tropical Butterfly House adult/child £3.60/2.60; ⊙10am-5pm Apr-Sep, 10am-4pm Oct-Mar) Lancaster's highest point is the 22-hectare spread of this elegant park, from which there are great views of the town, Morecambe Bay and the Cumbrian fells to the north. In the middle is the **Ashton Memorial**, a 67m-high baroque folly built by Lord Ashton (the son of the park's founder, James Williamson) for his wife.

More beautiful, however, is the Edwardian Palm House, now the **Tropical Butterfly House**, full of exotic and stunning species. Take bus 25 or 25A from the station, or else it's a steep short walk up Moor Lane.

Maritime Museum MUSEUM

(St George's Quay; adult/child £3/2; ⊙11am-5pm) The 18th-century Custom House recalls the days when Lancaster was a flourishing port at the centre of the slave trade.

Cottage Museum MUSEUM

(15 Castle Hill; adult/child £1/75p; ⊙2-5pm Easter-Sep) Gives us a peep into life in early Victorian times.

Sleeping & Eating

Sun Hotel & Bar HOTEL ££

(☎01524-66006; www.thesunhotelandbar.co.uk; 63 Church St; s/d from £75/85; P) An excellent hotel in a 300-year-old building with a rustic, old-world look that stops at the bedroom door; a recent renovation has resulted in 16 pretty snazzy rooms. The pub downstairs is one of the best in town and a top spot for a bit of grub; the two-course roast of the day (£9.95) is excellent.

Royal King's Arms Hotel HOTEL ££

(☎01524-32451; www.oxfordhotelsandinns.com; Market St; r from £75; P) Lancaster's swankiest hotel is a period house with modern, comfortable rooms and an all-round businesslike interior. Look out for the beautiful stained-glass windows, one of the only leftovers from the mid-19th century when Charles Dickens frequented the place. The hotel restaurant is an excellent dining choice, with mains around £11.

Whale Tail Cafe VEGETARIAN £

(www.whaletailcafe.co.uk; 78a Penny St; mains £7-10; ⊙10am-4pm Mon-Fri, to 5pm Sat, to 3pm Sun;) This gorgeous 1st-floor veggie restaurant has an elegant dining room and a more informal plant-filled yard for lunch on a sunny day. The spicy bean burger (£6.50) is particularly good. Food here is locally produced and, when possible, organic.

WORTH A TRIP

HELMSHORE MILLS TEXTILE MUSEUM

If you're on your way to the Ribble Valley from Manchester or if, like us, you have an insatiable curiosity about the Industrial Revolution's early years, then a visit to this **museum** (Holcombe Rd; adult/child £4/free; ⌚noon-4pm Mon-Fri, noon-5pm Sat & Sun Mar-Oct) is a must. Two of Lancashire's original textile mills – Higher Mill and Whitaker's Mill – house exhibits which tell the story of how cotton and wool became cloth, including a version of Richard Arkwright's Water Frame and a working water wheel. These fabrics made the fortunes of many an 18th-century industrialist, and helped determine the course of human history, which is no mean boast. The museum is in Helmshore (on the outskirts of Haslingden), about 16 miles north of Manchester.

Information

Post Office (85 Market St; ⌚9am-5.30pm Mon-Fri, 9am-12.30pm Sat)

Tourist Office (☎01524-582394; www.citycoastcountryside.co.uk; Storey Creative Industries Centre, Meeting House Lane; ⌚9am-5pm Mon-Sat)

Getting There & Away

Lancaster is on the main west-coast railway line and on the Cumbrian coast line. Destinations include Carlisle (£19.50, one hour, hourly) and Manchester (£9.50, one hour, hourly).

Ribble Valley

Known locally as 'Little Switzerland,' Lancashire's most attractive landscapes lie east of the brash tackiness of Blackpool and north of the sprawling urban areas of Preston and Blackburn.

The northern half of the valley is dominated by the sparsely populated moorland of the Forest of Bowland, which is a fantastic place for walks, while the southern half features rolling hills, attractive market towns and ruins, with the River Ribble flowing between them.

Activities

Walking & Cycling

The **Ribble Way**, a 70-mile footpath that follows the River Ribble from its source at Ribblehead (in the Yorkshire Dales) to the estuary at Preston, is one of the more popular walks in the area and passes through Clitheroe. For online information check out www.visitlancashire.com or www.ribblevalley.co.uk.

The valley is also well covered by the northern loop of the **Lancashire Cycle Way**; for more information about routes, safety and so on contact **Blazing Saddles** (☎01442-844435; www.blazingsaddles.co.uk; 35 West End, Hebden Bridge, West Yorkshire), a Yorkshire-based bike store.

The Ribble Valley Tourist Authority has a bunch of downloadable walking and cycling routes, including *Bowlands by Bike*, *Mountain Bike Ribble Valley Circular Routes* and *Mountain Bike Rides in Gisburn Forest*, which you can pick up at the Tourist Office (p668) in Clitheroe.

CLITHEROE

POP 14,700

Located northeast of Preston, the Ribble Valley's largest market town is best known for its impressive **Norman keep** (admission free; ⌚dawn-dusk), built in the 12th century and now, sadly, standing empty; there are great views from it of the river valley below.

The extensive grounds are home to the newly refurbished **castle museum** (Castle Hill; adult/child £3.75/free; ⌚11am-4pm Mar-Oct, noon-4pm Mon-Tue & Fri-Sun Nov-Feb), which explores just the short matter of 350 *million* years of local history.

Sleeping & Eating

Old Post House Hotel HOTEL ££
(☎01200-422025; www.posthousehotel.co.uk; 44-48 King St; s/d from £48/65; P 📶) A former post office is now Clitheroe's most handsome hotel, with 11 superbly decorated rooms.

Halpenny's of Clitheroe TEAROOM £
(Old Toll House, 1-5 Parson Lane; mains £6) A traditional teashop that serves sandwiches, and dishes such as Lancashire hotpot.

Information

Tourist Office (☎01200-425566; www.visitribblevalley.co.uk; Church Walk; ⌚9am-5pm Mon-Sat) Information on the town and surrounding area.

PENDLE HILL

A lovely walk brings you to the top of Pendle Hill (558m) from where there are marvelous views of the surrounding countryside.

In 1612, however, Pendle Hill was the stomping ground of the Pendle Witches, subjects of the most famous witch trial in British history. Basically, 12 women – some of whom were known locally as 'cunning folk' (ie they practiced a bit of healing) – found themselves branded as malevolent sorceresses and were sentenced to death. Every Halloween a pseudomystical ceremony is performed here to commemorate their 'activities'. If that wasn't enough, in 1652 George Fox had the vision here that led him to found the Quakers.

FOREST OF BOWLAND

This vast, grouse-ridden moorland is somewhat of a misnomer. The use of 'forest' is a throwback to an earlier definition, when it served as a royal hunting ground. Today it is an Area of Outstanding Natural Beauty (AONB), which makes for good walking and cycling. The **Pendle Witch Way**, a 45-mile walk from Pendle Hill to northeast of Lancaster, cuts right through the area, and the **Lancashire Cycle Way** runs along the eastern border. The forest's main town is **Slaidburn**, about 9 miles north of Clitheroe on the B6478.

Other villages worth exploring are **Newton**, **Whitewell** and **Dunsop Bridge**.

Sleeping & Eating

Inn at Whitewell INN ££
(☎01200-448222; www.innatwhitewell.com; s/d from £88/120) Once the home of Bowland's forest keeper, this is now a superb guesthouse with antique furniture, peat fires and Victorian claw-foot baths. The restaurant (mains £10 to £18) specialises in traditional English game dishes.

Hark to Bounty Inn INN ££
(☎01200-446246; www.harktobounty.co.uk; s/d from £42.50/65) This marvellous 13th-century inn has atmospheric rooms with exposed oak beams. An excellent restaurant (mains £9 to £15) downstairs specialises in homemade herb breads.

Slaidburn YHA HOSTEL £
(☎0845 371 9343; www.yha.org.uk; King's House; dm £17; ⊙Apr-Oct) A converted 17th-century village inn that is especially popular with walkers and cyclists.

Getting There & Away

Clitheroe is served by regular buses from Preston and Blackburn as well as by hourly train from Manchester (£9.80, 75 minutes) and Preston (£6.60, 50 minutes). Once here, you're better off if you have your own transport, as there is only a Sunday bus service between Clitheroe and the rest of the valley villages.

ISLE OF MAN

Deliberately different and not-so-ferociously independent, the Isle of Man (Ellan Vannin in Manx, the local lingo) has doggedly held onto its semi-autonomous status (it is home to the world's oldest continuous parliament, the Tynwald) so as to continue doing its own thing, which really means operating as a popular tax haven.

The islanders' rejection of England's warm embrace has led to an oft-quoted prejudice that there's something odd about them, but the only thing that's odd here is the local tail-less cat.

Crass commercialism and mass tourism have no place here, except of course for the world-famous summer season of Tourist Trophy (TT) motorbike racing, which attracts around 50,000 punters and bike freaks every May and June, bringing noise and mayhem to the otherwise lush valleys, barren hills and rugged coastlines of this beautiful island. Needless to say, if you want a slice of silence, be sure to avoid the high-rev bike fest.

Activities

Walking & Cycling

With plenty of great marked trails, the Isle of Man is a firm favourite with walkers and is regularly voted one of the best walking destinations in Britain. Ordnance Survey (OS) *Landranger Map 95* (£6.99) covers the whole island, while the free *Walks on the Isle of Man* is available from the tourist office in Douglas. The **Millennium Way** is a walking path that runs the length of the island amid some spectacular scenery. The most demanding of all the island's walks is the 95-mile **Raad ny Foillan** (Road of the Gull), a well-marked path that makes a complete circuit of the island and normally takes about five days to complete. The **Isle of Man Walking Festival** (www.isleofmanwalking.com; ⊙mid-May) takes place over five days in May.

A WALK THROUGH MIDDLE EARTH

Ever wondered what it would be like to walk in Frodo Baggins' beloved Shire... without the aid of hallucinogens? JRR Tolkien's descriptions of Hobbiton and the Shire in *The Lord of the Rings* were inspired by the countryside around Hurst Green, about 5 miles southwest of Clitheroe. Tolkien was a regular guest in the grounds of Stonyhurst College during the years in which he wrote the epic novel.

A 5.5-mile circular walk has been created, following Tolkien's own footsteps – it begins at Shireburn Arms (where he was partial to the ale) and includes the crossing of the Rivers Ribble and Hodder (Rivers Shirebourne and Brandywine in the book). The Ribble Valley official website (www.ribblevalley.gov.uk) has details of the walk. Hurst Green is on the Clitheroe–Preston bus line (the bus trip takes about 10 minutes).

There are six off-road mountain-biking trails on the island, each with varying ranges of difficulty. See www.visitisleofman.com for details.

 Information

Most of the island's historic sites are operated by **Manx National Heritage** (MH; www.gov.im/mnh), which offers free admission for National Trust or English Heritage members. Unless otherwise indicated, Manx Heritage sites are open 10am to 5pm daily, from Easter to October. The **Manx Heritage Explorer Pass** (www.manxheritageshop.com; adult/child/family £18/9/44) grants you entry into all heritage sites over 10 days; pick it up at any of the tourist offices or online.

You can also check out www.iomevents.com for listings of what's on in the Isle of Man, along with accommodation and other tourist information.

 Getting There & Away

Air

Ronaldsway Airport (www.iom-airport.com) is 10 miles south of Douglas near Castletown.

Airline contacts include:

Aer Lingus Regional (www.aerlingus.com; from £25) From Dublin.

Blue Islands (www.blueislands.com; from £167) From Guernsey and Jersey.

Easyjet (www.easyjet.com; from £16) From Liverpool and London Gatwick.

Flybe (www.flybe.com; from £21) From Birmingham, Bristol, Jersey, London Gatwick, Luton, Liverpool, Manchester, Glasgow and Edinburgh.

Manx2 (www.manx2.com; from £20) From Belfast, Blackpool, Leeds-Bradford, Gloucester M5, Newcastle and East Midlands.

BOAT **Isle of Man Steam Packet** (www.steam-packet.com; foot passenger single/return £19/32.50, car & 2 passengers return from £106) is a car ferry and high-speed catamaran service from Liverpool and Heysham to Douglas. There is also a summer service (mid-April to mid-September) to Dublin (three hours) and Belfast (three hours). It's usually cheaper to buy a return ticket than to pay the single fare.

 Getting Around

Buses link the airport with Douglas every 30 minutes between 7am and 11pm; a taxi should cost you no more than £18.

The island has a comprehensive **bus service** (www.iombusandrail.info); the tourist office in Douglas has timetables and sells tickets. It also sells the **Island Explorer** (1-day adult/child £16/8, 3-day £32/16), which gives you free rides on all public transport, including the tram to Snaefell and Douglas' horse-trams.

Bikes can be hired from **Eurocycles** (www.eurocycles.co.im; 8 Victoria Rd; per day £14-20; ⏲Mon-Sat).

Petrol-heads will love the scenic, sweeping bends that make for some exciting driving – and the fact that outside of Douglas town there's no speed limit. Naturally, the most popular drive is along the TT route. Car-hire operators have desks at the airport, and charge from around £38 per day.

The 19th-century electric and steam **rail services** (☎01624-663366; www.iombusandrail.info; ⏲Mar-Oct) are a thoroughly satisfying way of getting from A to B:

Douglas–Castletown–Port Erin Steam Train (return £11.60)

Douglas–Laxey–Ramsey Electric Tramway (return £11.60)

Laxey–Summit Snaefell Mountain Railway (return £10)

Douglas

POP 26,218

Much like Blackpool across the water, Douglas' heyday was in the middle of the 19th century, when it was a favourite destination for Victorian mass tourism. It's not nearly as popular – or as pretty – today, but it still has the best of the island's hotels and restaurants – as well as the bulk of the finance houses that are frequented so regularly by tax-allergic Brits.

The **Manx Museum** (www.gov.im/mnh; Kingswood Grove; admission free; 10am-5pm Mon-Sat) gives an introduction to everything from the island's prehistoric past to the latest TT race winners.

Sleeping

The seafront promenade is crammed with B&Bs. Unless you booked back at the beginning of the millennium, however, there's little chance of finding accommodation during TT week and the weeks either side of it. The tourist office's camping information sheet lists sites all around the island.

Other decent options:

Claremont Hotel HOTEL ££
(01624-617068; www.theclaremont.im; 18-22 Loch Promenade; r from £100; P@) Within the classic Victorian shell is a thoroughly modern hotel with comfortable, well-appointed rooms aimed primarily at the business traveller. Aveda products in the bathrooms, iPod docking facilities and free wi-fi are luxuries that will also draw in the leisure visitor.

Sefton Hotel HOTEL ££
(01624-645500; www.seftonhotel.co.im; Harris Promenade; r from £90; P) Douglas' best hotel is an upmarket oasis with its own indoor water garden and rooms that range from plain and comfy to elegant and very luxurious. The rooms overlooking the water garden are superb, even better than the ones with sea views. You save up to 10% if you book online.

Admiral House B&B ££
(01624-629551; www.admiralhouse.com; Loch Promenade; r from £75; P) This elegant guesthouse overlooks the harbour near the ferry port. The 23 spotless and modern rooms are a cheerful alternative to the worn look of a lot of other seafront B&Bs.

Hilton Hotel HOTEL ££
(01624-662662; www.hilton.co.uk/isleofman; Central Promenade; r from £75; P@) Tidy, modern rooms, a small gym and a casino – the Hilton takes care of your every need.

Eating & Drinking

Tanroagan SEAFOOD ££
(01624-472411; www.tanroagan.co.uk; 9 Ridgeway St; mains £16-21; lunch & dinner Tue-Fri, dinner Sat) The place for all things from the sea, this elegant eatery is Douglas' smartest. It serves fresh fish straight off the boats, giving them the merest of Continental twists or just a spell on the hot grill. Reservations are recommended.

14North MEDITERRANEAN ££
(01624-664414; www.14north.im; mains £9-19; lunch & dinner Mon-Sat, lunch Sun) An old timber merchant's house is now home to this smart eatery serving North African–style flatbreads (basically gourmet pizzas with a variety of toppings) and a selection of fish and meat dishes. The monkfish, with saffron and mussel chowder, is particularly tasty.

There are a few good pubs around, including the trendy **Bar George** (St George's Chambers, 3 Hill St), and **Rover's Return** (11 Church St), which specialises in the local brew, Bushy Ales.

Information

Tourist Office (01624-686766; www.visitisleofman.com; Sea Terminal Bldg; 9.15am-7pm) Makes accommodation bookings for free.

Around Douglas

You can follow the TT circuit up and over the mountain or wind around the coast. The mountain route goes close to the summit of **Snaefell** (621m), the island's highest point. It's an easy walk up to the summit, or you can take the electric tram from Laxey, near the coast.

On the edge of Ramsey, on the north of the island, is the **Grove Museum of Victorian Life** (MH; Andreas Rd; admission £4.50; 10am-5pm Apr-Oct). The church in the small village of **Maughold** is on the site of an ancient monastery; a small shelter houses quite a good selection of stone crosses and ancient inscriptions.

It's no exaggeration to describe the **Lady Isabella Laxey Wheel** (MH; Mines Rd; admission £4.50; 10am-5pm Apr-Oct), built in 1854 to pump water from a mine, as a 'great' wheel; it measures 22m across and can draw 1140L of water per minute from a depth of 550m. It is named after the wife of the then lieutenant-governor and is the largest wheel of its kind in the world.

The wheel-headed cross at **Lonan Old Church**, just north of Douglas, is the island's most impressive early Christian cross.

Castletown & Around

At the southern end of the island is Castletown, a quiet harbour town that was originally the capital of the Isle of Man. The town is dominated by the impressive 13th-century **Castle Rushen** (MH; Castletown Sq; admission £5.80; ⏲10am-5pm Apr-Oct). The flag tower affords fine views of the town and coast.

You can role play as 19th-century parliamentarians in the lower house of the Tynwald, the **Old House of Keys** (MH; ☎01624-648017; Parliament Square; admission £4.50), as well as learn about the island's struggle for self-determination.

There's also a small **Nautical Museum** (MH; Bridge St; admission £4.50; ⏲10am-5pm Easter-Oct) displaying, among other things, its pride and joy, a boat called *Peggy*, built in 1791 and still housed in its original boathouse. There is an old grammar school dating back to 1570 in **St Mary's church** (MH; admission free; ⏲10am-5pm, Mar-Nov), behind the castle.

Between Castletown and Cregneash, the Iron Age hillfort at **Chapel Hill** encloses a Viking ship burial site.

On the southern tip of the island, the **Cregneash Village Folk Museum** (MH; admission £4.50; ⏲10am-5pm Apr-Oct) recalls traditional Manx rural life. The **Calf of Man**, the small island just off Cregneash, is a bird sanctuary. **Calf Island Cruises** (☎01624-832339; adult/child £12/6; ⏲10.15am, 11.30am & 1.30pm Apr-Oct, weather permitting) run between Port Erin and the island.

PORT ERIN & PORT ST MARY

Port Erin, another Victorian seaside resort, plays host to the small **Railway Museum** (Station Rd; adult/child £1/50p; ⏲10am-5pm Apr-Oct), which reveals the history of steam railway on the island.

Port Erin has a good range of accommodation, as does Port St Mary, across the headland and linked by steam train.

Our Port Erin accommodation choice would be the Victorian **Falcon's Nest Hotel** (☎01624-834077; www.falconsnesthotel.co.uk; Station Rd; r from £42.50; 📶), once supremely elegant, now just handsome in a nostalgic sort of way. The rooms are not particularly special, but the views over the water are superb.

The slightly more splendid Victorian-style **Aaron House** (☎01624-835702; www.aaronhouse.co.uk; The Promenade; s/d from £35/70) is a B&B that has fussed over every detail, from the gorgeous brass beds and claw-foot baths to the old-fashioned photographs on the walls. The sea views are also sensational.

MOTOR MUSEUMS

As befits an island seemingly obsessed with motorised vehicles, the island is home to two vintage motor museums. The largest of them is the collection of old buses and trucks at the **Jurby Transport Museum** (☎07624-490093; www.jtmiom.im; Hangar 230, Jurby Industrial Estate; Admission free; ⏲10am-4pm Sat-Sun), housed in a WWII hangar on the old Jurby airfield, on the coast road in the northwest of the island. Kirk Michael is home to a **Motorcycle Collection** (☎01624-878242; www.aremuseum.com; The Old Vicarage, Main Road, Kirk Michael; ⏲2-5.30pm Sun Easter-Oct, daily during TT and Manx Grand Prix season) of 100 vintage bikes by Triumph, AMC, BSA, Vincent and Moto Guzzi.

Peel & Around

The west coast's most appealing town, Peel has a fine sandy beach, but its real attraction is the 11th-century **Peel Castle** (MH; admission £4.50; ⏲10am-5pm Apr-Oct), stunningly positioned atop St Patrick's Island and joined to Peel by a causeway.

The excellent **House of Manannan** (MH; admission £6; ⏲10am-5pm Apr-Oct) museum uses interactive displays to explain Manx history and its seafaring traditions. A combined ticket for both the castle and museum costs £7.70.

Three miles east of Peel is **Tynwald Hill** at St John's, where the annual parliamentary ceremony takes place on 5 July.

Peel has several B&Bs, including the **Fernleigh Hotel** (☎01624-842435; www.isleofman.com/Business/f/fernleigh; Marine Pde; r per person incl breakfast from £26; ⏲Feb-Nov), which has 12 decent bedrooms. For a better-than-average bite, head for the **Creek Inn** (☎01624-842216; www.thecreekinn.co.uk/; East Quay; mains around £8), opposite the House of Manannan, which serves Manx queenies (scallops served with white cheese sauce) and has self-catering rooms from £35.

The Lake District & Cumbria

Includes »

Best Places to Eat

- » L'Enclume (p710)
- » Drunken Duck (p695)
- » Punch Bowl Inn (p709)
- » Mason's Arms (p683)
- » Yanwath Gate Inn (p710)

Best Places to Stay

- » The Boundary (p680)
- » Wasdale Head Inn (p697)
- » Moss Grove Organic (p689)
- » Old Dungeon Ghyll (p696)
- » Eltermere Inn (p696)

Why Go?

For knockout natural splendour, nowhere in England can compare to Cumbria. This green, grand, glorious county is a place of nonstop superlatives – home to the nation's longest lake, smallest church, steepest road, highest town and tallest peak. At the heart of the county is the breathtaking Lake District, one of England's oldest and best-loved national parks, still considered by many to be the spiritual heartland of English hiking.

But there is so much more to this region than just fell-walking and fine views. There's a wealth of historic pubs, literary landmarks, tumbledown castles and stately homes to enjoy, and the little-explored coastline is ideal if you're looking to escape the crowds. And whether it's cruising across a lake at twilight or surveying the scene from the top of a cloud-capped fell, one thing's for certain – this is one corner of England that definitely knows how to inspire.

When to Go

Cumbria's largest mountain festival is held in Keswick in mid-May, followed by the town's lively Beer Festival in June. The Kendal Calling Music festival kicks into action at Lowther Park in late July, while Grasmere's annual sports day takes place on the August Bank Holiday.

In November, the world's greatest liars congregate on Santon Bridge for their annual fibbing contest. Crowds can be a problem at Easter and in July and August, so try to visit in late spring or early autumn when the weather is also usually at its most settled.

The Lake District & Cumbria Highlights

1. Conquer the top of England's highest mountain, **Scafell Pike** (p697)
2. Take a cruise in an antique steam launch on **Coniston Water** (p693)
3. Wander round WIlliam Wordsworth's homes at **Dove Cottage** (p688) and **Rydal Mount** (p688)
4. Feel the whiff of wildness around the dramatic valley of **Wasdale** (p697)
5. Cycle round the wooded trails of **Grizedale Forest** (p692)
6. Tackle the iconic fell-tops around **Great Langdale** (p696)
7. Delve the depths of the slate mines around **Honister Pass** (p705)
8. Catch the miniature steam trains of **La'al Ratty** (p713) into Eskdale

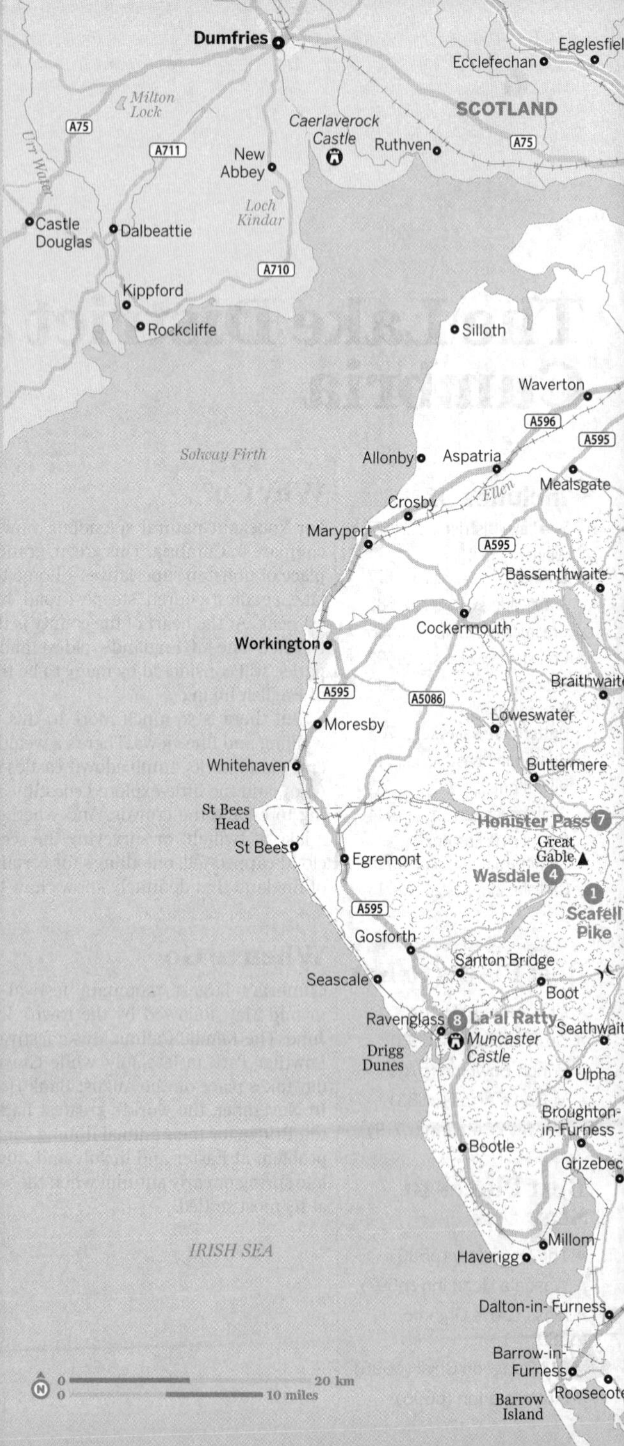

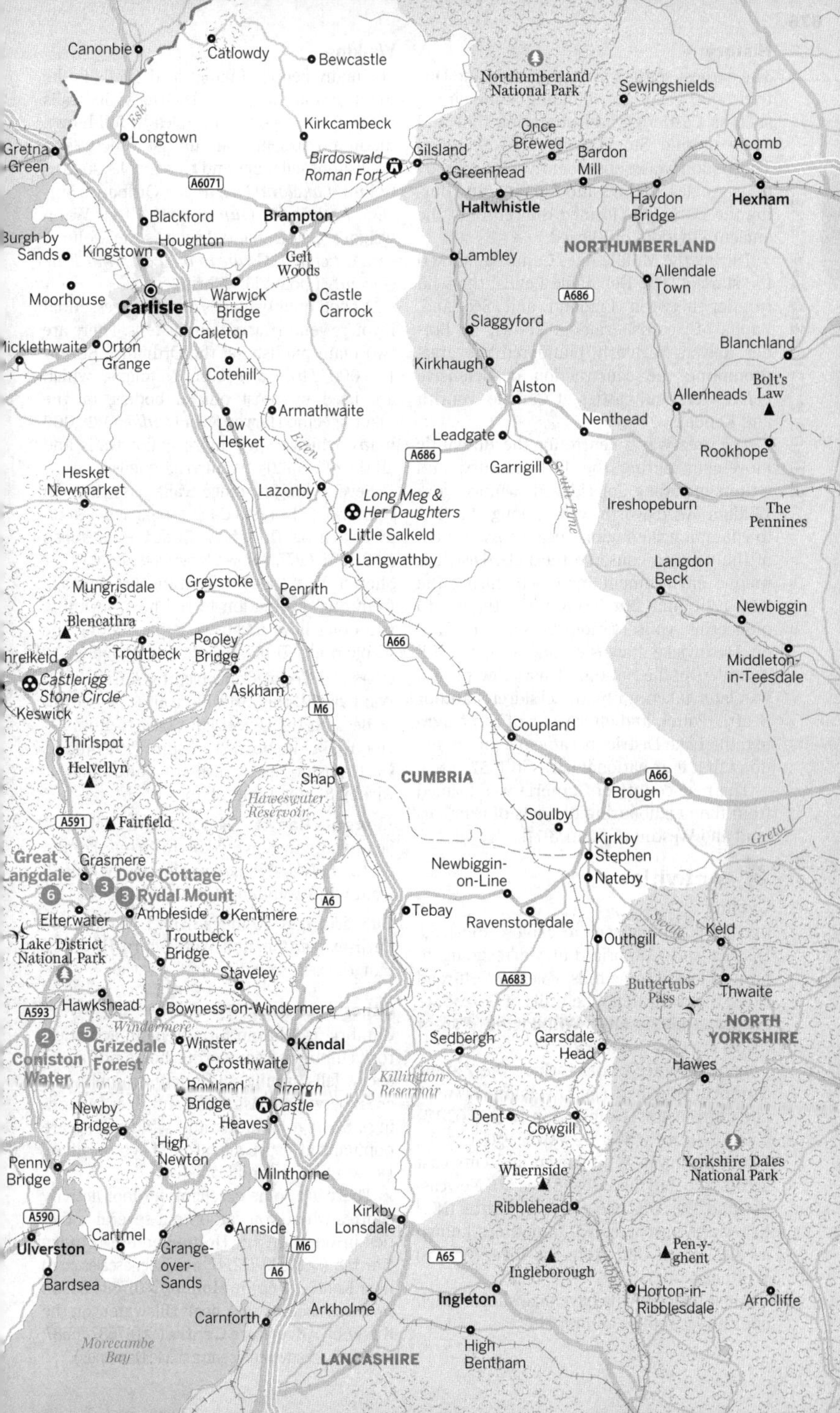

Canonbie
Catlowdy
Bewcastle
Northumberland National Park
Sewingshields
Esk
Kirkcambeck
Once Brewed
Longtown
Gretna Green
Gilsland
Bardon Mill
Acomb
Birdoswald Roman Fort
Greenhead
A6071
Haltwhistle
Haydon Bridge
Hexham
Blackford
Brampton
Burgh by Sands
Kingstown
Houghton
Gelt Woods
NORTHUMBERLAND
Lambley
Moorhouse
Warwick Bridge
Castle Carrock
Allendale Town
Carlisle
A686
Carleton
Slaggyford
Micklethwaite
Orton Grange
Blanchland
Cotehill
Kirkhaugh
Bolt's Law
Alston
Allenheads
Armathwaite
Low Hesket
Nenthead
Eden
Leadgate
A686
Rookhope
Garrigill
Hesket Newmarket
South Tyne
Lazonby
Long Meg & Her Daughters
Ireshopeburn
The Pennines
Little Salkeld
Langwathby
Langdon Beck
Mungrisdale
Greystoke
Penrith
Newbiggin
Blencathra
Threlkeld
Troutbeck
Pooley Bridge
A66
Middleton-in-Teesdale
Castlerigg Stone Circle
Askham
Keswick
M6
Coupland
Thirlspot
Helvellyn
Shap
CUMBRIA
A66
Brough
Haweswater Reservoir
A591
Fairfield
Soulby
Kirkby Stephen
Greta
Great Langdale
Grasmere
Dove Cottage
Newbiggin-on-Line
Nateby
6
3
3
Rydal Mount
Ambleside
Kentmere
A6
Tebay
Ravenstonedale
Elterwater
Swale
Keld
Lake District National Park
Troutbeck Bridge
Outhgill
Staveley
A683
Buttertubs Pass
Thwaite
Hawkshead
A593
Bowness-on-Windermere
NORTH YORKSHIRE
Windermere
2
5
Winster
Kendal
Sedbergh
Garsdale Head
Coniston Water
Grizedale Forest
Crosthwaite
Hawes
Killington Reservoir
Bowland Bridge
Sizergh Castle
Newby Bridge
Heaves
Dent
Cowgill
High Newton
Yorkshire Dales National Park
Penny Bridge
Milnthorpe
Whernside
A590
Kirkby Lonsdale
Ribblehead
Cartmel
Arnside
Ulverston
Grange-over-Sands
M6
A65
Pen-y-ghent
Bardsea
A6
Ingleborough
Ribble
Horton-in-Ribblesdale
Ingleton
Arncliffe
Carnforth
Arkholme
Morecambe Bay
High Bentham
LANCASHIRE

History

The earliest settlers arrived in the Lake District 5000 years ago, building stone circles such as Castlerigg and quarrying flint and stone around Stonethwaite and Seatoller. The region was subsequently occupied by Celts, Angles, Vikings and Romans, and during the Dark Ages formed the centre of the ancient kingdom of Rheged.

During the Middle Ages Cumbria marked the start of 'The Debatable Lands', the wild frontier between England and Scotland. Bands of Scottish raiders known as Border Reivers regularly plundered the area, prompting the construction of defensive *pele* towers and castles at Carlisle, Penrith and Kendal.

The area was a centre for the Romantic movement during the 19th century, and writers including Coleridge, de Quincey and William Wordsworth were among the first to champion the region's beauty. Awareness of the need to conserve the Lake District's unique environment increased during the late 19th and 20th centuries, thanks to pioneering conservationists such as Canon Hardwicke Rawnsley and Octavia Hill (founders of the National Trust). Their cause was later taken up by the children's author Beatrix Potter, and after years of campaigning, the Lake District became one of the nation's first four national parks in 1951.

The new county of Cumbria was formed from the neighbouring districts of Cumberland and Westmorland in 1974.

Activities

Cycling

Cycling is a great way to explore the Lake District and Cumbria, but you're going to have to tackle some hills. For short off-road rides, the dedicated bike trails of **Grizedale Forest** (p692) and **Whinlatter Forest** (p701) are very popular.

Long-distance routes include the 72-mile **Cumbria Way** between Ulverston, Keswick and Carlisle, the 140-mile **Sea To Sea (C2C) Cycle Route** (NCN 7; www.c2c-guide.co.uk), which begins in Whitehaven and cuts east across the northern Pennines to Newcastle, and the 173-mile **Reivers Route** (NCN 10; www.reivers-route.co.uk), sometimes known as the Return C2C, from the River Tyne to Whitehaven.

Most major towns have bike shops which offer hire, supplies and repair.

Walking

For many people, hiking on the fells is the main reason for a Lake District visit. Trails range from low-level rambles to full-blown mountain ascents; all tourist offices and bookshops sell maps and guidebooks, such as Collins' *Lakeland Fellranger*, Ordnance Survey's *Pathfinder Guides*, and Alfred Wainwright's classic hand-drawn, seven-volume set, *A Pictorial Guide to the Lakeland Fells* (recently updated by Chris Jesty).

A good-quality map is absolutely essential if you're venturing out on the fells. There are two main publishers: the Ordnance Survey 1:25,000 *Landranger* series maps, which are used by most official bodies, or the hiker-specific Harvey *Superwalker* 1:25,000 maps, which clearly mark major trails and all the official 214 'Wainwright' fells.

Several long distance trails pass through Cumbria. Door-to-door baggage services such as **Coast to Coast Packhorse** (☎017683-71777; www.c2cpackhorse.co.uk) or Sherpa Van (p40) will transport luggage from one destination to the next, meaning you don't have to lug your pack along the whole route. Trails include the following:

Coast to Coast Conceived by Alfred Wainwright, this 191-mile trail travels from St Bees on the Cumbrian Coast to Robin Hood's Bay in North Yorkshire (191 miles), via Honister Pass, Grasmere, Patterdale, Kirkby Stephen and Shap.

Allerdale Ramble 54-mile route from Seathwaite in Borrowdale to Grune Point on the Solway Firth, covering everything from windswept coast to wild hills.

Cumbria Way 70 miles from Ulverston to Carlisle, via Coniston Water, Tarn Hows, Langdale, Borrowdale and Keswick.

Other Activities

Cumbria is a haven for adrenalin activities: rock climbing, orienteering, horse riding, archery, fell-running and ghyll scrambling (a cross between coasteering and river canyoning). Sailing, kayaking and windsurfing are popular too, especially around Windermere, Derwent Water and Coniston.

There are some excellent outdoor activity centres where you can try out several activities in one day: try **Holmescales Activity Centre** (☎01539-722147; www.holmescales.com) near Kendal, **Rookin House** (☎017684-83561; www.rookinhouse.co.uk) near Ullswater, or the **Keswick Adventure Centre** (☎017687-75687; www.keswickadventurecentre.co.uk; Newlands).

TRAVEL PASSES

There are several useful travel passes covering Cumbria. The Lakes Day Ranger ticket is available from main train stations; bus-only passes can be purchased from drivers.

Lakes Day Ranger (£20.50) is the best-value multitransport ticket, allowing unlimited travel for one day on all trains and buses in Cumbria. Also includes a boat cruise on Windermere, 10% discount on the two steam railways, and 20% discount on cruise services on Derwent Water, Ullswater and Coniston.

Cumbria Day Ranger (£38.50) provides one day's train travel anywhere in Cumbria, and parts of Lancashire, North Yorkshire, Northumberland and Dumfries & Galloway.

North West Explorer (one day £10, three days £20) offers unlimited bus travel for up to three days in Cumbria and Lancashire. The seven-day version is called the Northwest Megarider Gold (£25).

Central Lakes Dayrider (£7) covers Bowness, Ambleside, Grasmere, Langdale and Coniston; includes the 599, 505 and 516.

There are also two vintage steam railways: the Lakeside & Haverthwaite Railway (p678) from Haverthwaite to Newby Bridge, near Windermere, and the miniature Ravenglass & Eskdale Railway (p713) through the Eskdale valley.

Getting There & Away

TRAIN Carlisle is on the main West Coast line from London Euston to Manchester to Glasgow. To get to the Lake District, you need to change at Oxenholme, where regular trains travel west to Kendal and Windermere. The lines around the Cumbrian Coast and between Settle and Carlisle are particularly scenic.

National Express (p819) coaches run direct from London Victoria and Glasgow to Windermere, Carlisle and Kendal.

Getting Around

Traveline Northeast (☎0871-200 22 33; www.travelinenortheast.info) provides comprehensive travel information for the whole of Cumbria and the Lake District. Bus timetables are available from TICs.

THE LAKE DISTRICT

If you're a lover of the great outdoors, the Lake District is one corner of England where you'll want to linger. This sweeping panorama of slate-capped fells, craggy hilltops, misty mountain tarns and glittering lakes has been pulling in the crowds ever since the Romantics pitched up in the early 19th century, and it remains one of the country's most popular beauty spots. Literary sights abound, from Wordsworth's boyhood school to the lavish country estate of John Ruskin at Brantwood, and there are enough hilltop trails, hidden pubs and country hotels to fill a lifetime of visits.

Information

The national park's main visitor centre is at Brockhole (p683), just outside Windermere, and there are efficient tourist offices in Windermere Town, Bowness, Ambleside, Keswick, Carlisle and several other towns. All carry a wealth of information on local sights, activities, accommodation and public transport, and can help with accommodation bookings.

Windermere & Bowness

POP 8432

Of all England's lakes, none carries the cachet of Windermere. Stretching for 10.5 silvery miles from Ambleside to Newby Bridge, it's a classic Lake District vista, and has been a centre for tourism since the first steam trains chugged into town in 1847.

The town itself is split between Windermere, 1.5 miles uphill from the lake, and bustling Bowness-on-Windermere (usually shortened to Bowness), with its touristy collection of teashops, ice-cream stalls and cruise boats. On summer days it can feel uncomfortably crowded, but even then it's usually possibly to find some serenity, either by venturing out on the lake itself, or drinking in the views form the surrounding hills.

The two areas of town are linked by Lake Road, lined with hotels and B&Bs. The train and bus stations are both in Windermere town.

Lake District

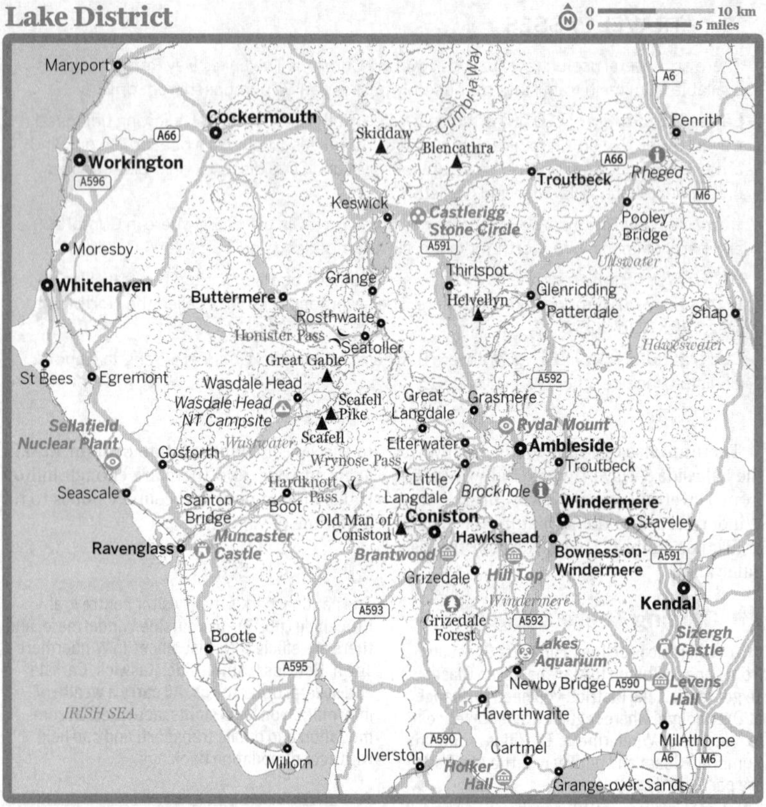

Sights & Activities

Windermere Lake Cruises BOAT TOURS
(☎015395-31188; www.windermere-lakecruises.co.uk) Top on the list of things to do in Windermere is to take a lake cruise. The first passenger ferry was launched back in 1845, and cruising on the lake is still a popular pastime. Some of the vessels are modern, but there are a couple of period beauties dating back to the 1930s.

All cruises allow you to jump off at one of the ferry landings (Waterhead/Ambleside, Wray Castle, Brockhole, Bowness, Ferry Landing, Fell Foot Ferry and Lakeside) and catch a later boat back.

Freedom of the Lake Ticket (adult/child/family £17.75/8.90/48.50) One day's unlimited travel on all routes.

Blue Cruise (adult/child/family £7.20/3.60/19.80) 45-minute cruise around Windermere's islands and bays.

Green Cruise (adult/child/family £7.20/3.60/19.80) 45-minute cruise from Waterhead/Ambleside via Wray Castle and Brockhole Visitor Centre.

Red Cruise (adult/child/family £9.75/5.85/28.25) North lake cruise from Bowness to Ambleside.

Yellow Cruise (adult/child/family £10/6/29) South cruise from Bowness to Lakeside and the Lakes Aquarium.

Bowness to Ferry House (single adult/child/family £2.55/1.50/7.35) Shuttle service to Ferry House, from where you can catch a bus to Hill Top and Hawkshead.

From April to October rowing boats can be hired from the lake jetty for £12. Motorboats coast from £18 to £22 for two adults; children under 16 go free. There's a 10mph speed limit on Windermere.

World of Beatrix Potter CHILDREN'S MUSEUM
(www.hop-skip-jump.com; adult/child £6.75/3.50; ⏲10am-5.30pm Apr-Sep, 10am-4.30pm Oct-Mar) This attraction brings to life various scenes from the author's books using a combination of life-size models and decorated rooms. Among the scenes on show are Peter Rabbit's garden, Mr McGregor's greenhouse, Mrs Tiggywinkle's kitchen, Jemima Puddleduck's glade; there's even a themed tearoom. Be prepared for long queues in summer.

Lakes Aquarium AQUARIUM
(☎015395-30153; www.lakesaquarium.co.uk; Lakeside; adult/child £8.95/5.95; ⏲9am-6pm Apr-Oct) At the southern end of the lake near Newby Bridge, this aquarium explores a range of underwater habitats from tropical Africa through to Morecambe Bay. Highlights include a simulated diving bell and an underwater tunnel beneath Windermere's lake bed, complete with pike, char and diving ducks. Various talks are held throughout the day; otter feeding takes place at 10.30am and 3pm.

Windermere Lake Cruises (p678) and the Lakeside & Haverthwaite Railway (p678) both stop right beside the aquarium, or you could catch Bus 618 from Bowness.

Discounts are available for buying tickets online or buying a combination ticket (p681).

Lakeside & Haverthwaite Railway HERITAGE RAILWAY
(☎015395-31594; www.lakesiderailway.co.uk; adult/child/family return £6.30/3.20/16.90; ⏲mid-Mar–Oct) Originally built to carry ore, timber and other industrial goods to the ports at Ulverston and Barrow, these vintage steam trains now puff their way between Haverthwaite, near Ulverston, to Newby Bridge and Lakeside. There are between five and seven trains a day depending on the season, handily timed to correspond with the Windermere cruise boats.

FREE **Fell Foot Park** GARDEN
(www.nationaltrust.org.uk/fell-foot-park; ⏲8am-8pm summer, 9am-5pm winter) At the southern end of Windermere, 7 miles south of Bowness, this 18-acre lakeside estate originally belonged to a manor house. It's now owned by the National Trust, and its shoreline paths and grassy lawns are ideal for a sunny-day picnic. There's also a small cafe (open 10am to 5pm), and rowing boats are available for hire.

NATIONAL TRUST CAMPSITE BOOKINGS

The **National Trust** (☎015394-63862; www.nationaltrust.org.uk; ⏲10am-noon & 2-4pm Mon-Fri) has four Lake District campsites at Low Wray (near Ambleside), Wasdale, Great Langdale and Hoathwaite (near Coniston). All accept advance reservations up to 24 hours before your arrival; there's a fee of £5 for booking online, or £7.50 by telephone and email, and stays must be for a minimum of 2 nights.

Blackwell House HISTORIC BUILDING, CRAFTS
(www.blackwell.org.uk; adult/child £7.95/4.40; ⏲10.30am-5pm Apr-Oct, to 4pm Feb-Mar & Nov-Dec) Two miles south of Bowness on the B5360, Blackwell House is one of the finest examples of the 19th-century Arts and Crafts Movement, which championed the importance of humane design, handmade goods and high-quality craftsmanship over the mass-produced mentality of the Industrial Revolution.

Designed by Mackay Hugh Baillie Scott for a wealthy brewer, the house has many hallmarks of Arts and Crafts design: light, airy rooms, detailed decor and lots of bespoke craftwork (including wood panelling, stained glass and Delft tiles). Of particular note is the huge wood-panelled Great Hall and the serene White Drawing Room.

Lakeland Motor Museum CAR MUSEUM
(www.lakelandmotormuseum.co.uk; Backbarrow; adult/child £7.80/5; ⏲9.30am-5.30pm Apr-Sep, to 4.30pm Oct-Mar) Now installed in a purpose-built home two miles south of Newby Bridge, this car museum houses a wonderful collection of antique cars: classic (Minis, Austin Healeys, MGs), sporty (DeLoreans, Audi Quattros, Aston Martins) and downright odd (Scootacars, Amphicars).

A separate building explores the history of Donald and Malcolm Campbell's record attempts on Coniston Water, with replicas of the original 1935 *Bluebird* car and the 1967 boat, *Bluebird K7*.

The museum is on the A590 from Newby Bridge towards Kendal. The X35 (hourly Monday to Saturday, thee on Sunday) from Newby Bridge to Ulverston and Kendal stops nearby.

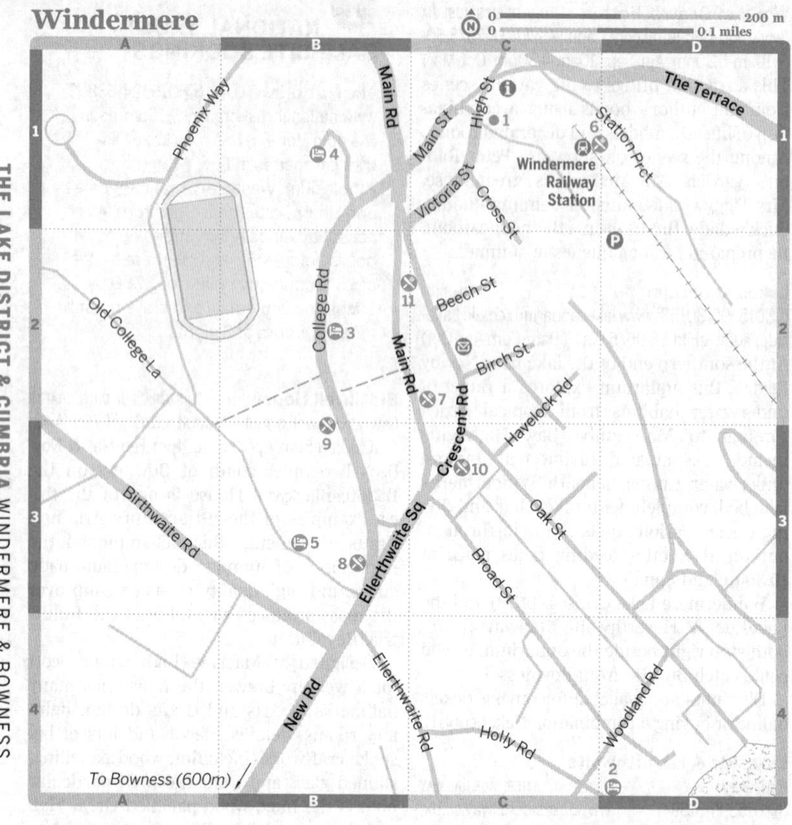

Sleeping

Windermere's accommodation tends to be substantially pricier than elsewhere around the Lakes (in some cases, B&B prices have started to hit hotel levels).

TOP CHOICE The Boundary B&B ££

(015394-48978; www.theboundaryonline.co.uk; Lake Rd; d £100-180; P wi-fi) Certainly not the cheapest sleep in Windermere, but definitely one of the sexiest. Owners Steve and Helen have a sharp eye for modern design, and they've given this Victorian house a sleek, boutique makeover: chic decor, monochrome colours, quirky furniture and all. Steve's a cricket obsessive, and all the rooms are named after famous batsmen; you can browse old copies of *Wisden* over breakfast.

Wheatlands Lodge B&B ££

(015394-43789; www.wheatlandslodge-windermere.co.uk; Old College Lane; d £80-150; P wi-fi) Between Bowness and Windermere, this detached house looks venerably Victorian, but inside you'll find eight elegant, contemporary rooms with either a power shower or sit-down jacuzzi. It's set back from the road so it feels serene, and owner Sarah knows how to spoil her guests – from the welcome coffee-and-cake to the slap-up, locally sourced breakfast.

Cranleigh HOTEL ££

(015394-43293; www.thecranleigh.com; Kendal Rd; d £75-180, ste £250-400; P wi-fi) This heavily refurbed guesthouse is minutes from the Bowness waterfront, and offers a pick-and-mix of rooms each with their own distinctive decor; it's worth bumping up to 'Superior' for space and snazzy bathrooms. The two Suites are fabulously over-the-top – check out the Sanctuary with its Bose stereo, glass bath and picture-fireplace.

Windermere

1 Park Road B&B ££
(www.1parkroad.com; 1 Park Road; £76-104; P) It's the little treats that keep this cosy guesthouse a cut above: bath goodies from Pure Lakes and The White Company, iPod docks in every room, and home-made baked beans and marmalade on the breakfast table. Rooms are comfortable, and the rates stay reasonable even in season.

Rosemount B&B ££
(015394-43739; www.lakedistrictguesthouse.com; Lake Rd; s £41-55, d £80-120; P) Lodged inside a solid stone house and run by a friendly husband and wife, this is a refreshing find in Windermere: a simple, no-fuss B&B providing sweet rooms at sensible rates. There is a choice of standard or superior, as well as a big four-poster. All rooms have quirky wallpapers and lovely modern bathrooms, but the superior rooms are larger.

Archway B&B £
(015394-45613; www.the-archway.com; 13 College Rd; d £60-55) A no-nonsense, great-value, old-fashioned B&B, worth a mention for its fell views, knock-down rates and absurdly generous breakfast (choices include Manx kippers, smoked haddock, parma ham omelettes and American-style pancakes).

Number 80 Bed Then Breakfast B&B ££
(015394-43584; www.number80bed.co.uk; 80 Craig Walk; d £80-90;) This cute Bowness refuge is still off the radar, so keep it under your hats. Just four rooms, but all are up-to-date; Room 1 has a pine four-poster, the other three feel more modern.

Lake District Backpackers Lodge HOSTEL £
(015394-46374; www.lakedistrictbackpackers.co.uk; High St; dm £15; @) Windermere's indie hostel is handy for the station, but it's cramped and showing its age. Dorms and kitchen are small, but rates include bed linen and breakfast.

Gilpin Lodge HOTEL £££
(015394-88818; www.gilpinlodge.co.uk; Crook Rd; r £310-580; P) Windermere's B&Bs might be pushing up their rates to silly levels, but this famously posh country-house retreat shows them how it should be done. The fabulously fancy rooms are named after fells, garden suites even have their own decks and outdoor hot tubs, and the new Lake House comes with its own chauffeur. A superb restaurant, spa and acres of grounds complete the package.

Eating

TOP CHOICE **Hooked** SEAFOOD ££
(015394-48443; www.hookedwindermere.co.uk; Ellerthwaite Sq; mains £16.95-19.95; dinner Tue-Sun) It's only been open since 2011, but this admirably simple seafood restaurant (owned by Melbourne-born Michael Gould)

WINDERMERE COMBO TICKETS

Combination tickets cover several of Windermere's attractions provide substantial discounts.

Boat & Train (adult/child/family £14.75/8.30/41.25) Includes a Windermere Lake Cruise and a trip on the Lakeside & Haverthwaite Steam Railway.

Boat & Aquarium (adult/child/family £16.45/9.45/40.00) Cruise and admission to the Lakes Aquarium.

Boat, Train & Aquarium (adult/child/family £20.95/11.45/59.80)

Boat, Bus, Train & Motor Museum (adult/child/family £20.45/12.10/57.25) Includes a cruise from Bowness, a return trip on the railway to/from Newby Bridge, admission to the Lakeland Motor Museum and a bus back to Bowness.

Bowness

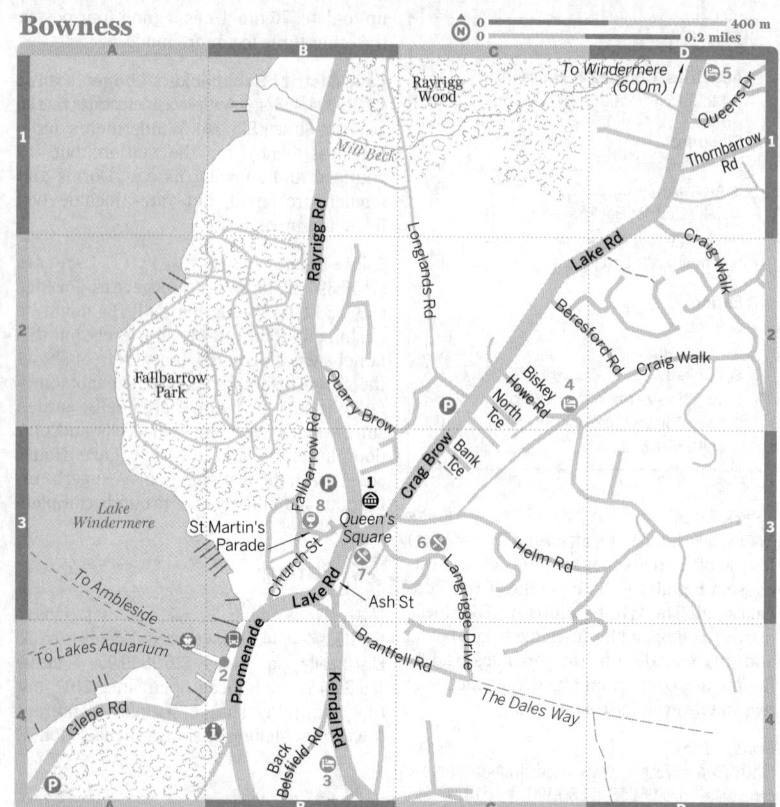

already has a loyal following. Fish arrives daily from the Fleetwood docks, and is dished up with Mediterranean-meets-Asian flair: turbot with basil pesto, snapper with saffron pasta, curried monkfish in a creamy sauce. The uncluttered interior keep the focus on the dishes – and quite right too.

TOP CHOICE Brown Horse Inn PUB ££
(☎015394-43443; www.thebrownhorseinn.co.uk; Winster; mains £11.95-17.95) Three miles from Windermere in Winster, the whitewashed Brown Horse is one of the area's top dining pubs. Produce is sourced from the nearby Brown Horse Estate, furnishing the chefs with copious local meat and game: Winster venison, spring lamb, roast pigeon. Beams and stone fireplaces give the pub plenty of rustic atmosphere, and there are two home-brewed ales on tap (Old School and Best Bitter). Definitely worth the trip.

Jericho's at the Waverley Hotel BRITISH £££
(☎015394-42522; www.jerichos.co.uk; College Rd; dinner mains £15-25; ⊙dinner Tue-Sun) This townhouse restaurant is run by renowned local chef Chris Blaydes, who's previously worked at some of the Lake District's top hotels. The dining room feels chic with its tall windows and gloss-wood floors, an ideal counterpoint to the modern British food: stacks of spring lamb, or ruby-pink Scotch beef in a cabernet sauce. Smart rooms are available upstairs (£75-125).

Francine's BISTRO ££
(☎015394-44088; www.francinesrestaurantwindermere.co.uk; 27 Main Rd; 2-/3-course dinner menu £15.95/18.95, dinner mains £9.95-15.95; ⊙lunch & dinner Tue-Sat) A buzzy little place that's as popular with the Windermere locals as with the tourists (always a good sign). Tiny tables, potted plants and flowers-in-jugs lend it a cosy neighbourhood vibe, and the menu offers an eclectic choice; taking

Bowness

Sights

1 World of Beatrix Potter B3

Activities, Courses & Tours

2 Windermere Lake Cruises B4

Sleeping

3 Cranleigh B4
4 Number 80 Bed Then Breakfast C2
5 The Boundary D1

Eating

6 Angel Inn C3
7 Postilion B3

Drinking

8 Hole in T' Wall B3

in everything from garlicky mussels to pot roast lamb and daube of venison.

Angel Inn GASTROPUB ££
(☎015394-44080; www.the-angelinn.com; Helm Rd; mains £10.95-16.50) This attractive pub is set on top of a grassy hummock behind the Bowness shoreline. It's more big-city-modern than backcountry-cosy, festuring leather sofas, wooden floors and blackboards, plus a gastropub menu of pork belly ballontine and honey-roasted chicken.

Lazy Daisy's Lakeland Kitchen CAFE £
(☎015394-43877; 31-33 Crescent Rd; lunch £4-10, dinner £10-16; ⊙Mon-Sat 10am-9pm) Filling comfort food is the order of the day at this trad cafe: Cumberland sausages served with a giant Yorkshire pudding, or steak-and-Guinness pie doused in lashings of gravy. Look out for the regular pudding clubs.

Postilion BISTRO ££
(☎015394-45852; www.postilionrestaurant.co.uk; Ash St; mains £12-16, set menu £18.95; ⊙lunch & dinner) Reliable bistro tucked away off Ash St with a decent French-Mediterranean menu.

Lighthouse CAFE £
(Main Rd; mains £8-15; ⊙breakfast, lunch & dinner) This three-floored cafe just downhill from the station offers a continental-style menu, quality coffee and fresh-baked pastries.

Booth's SUPERMARKET £
Windermere's main supermarket is next to the station.

Drinking

Hole in T' Wall PUB
(Falbarrow Rd) Bowness' best-loved boozer is also the town's oldest, dating back to 1612, and offering lashings of rough-beamed, low-ceilinged atmosphere.

Hawkshead Brewery BREWERY
(☎01539-822644; www.hawksheadbrewery.co.uk; Mill Yard, Staveley) This award-winning craft brewery now has its own brewhall in Staveley, 3 miles east of Windermere. Core beers include Hawkshead Bitter, dark Brodie's Prime and fruity Red. Guided tours of the vats can be arranged in advance.

Information

Bowness Tourist Office (☎015394-42895; bownesstic@lake-district.gov.uk; Glebe Rd; ⊙9.30am-5.30pm Easter-Oct, 10am-4pm Fri-Sun Nov-Easter) Beside the waterfront.

Brockhole National Park Visitor Centre (☎015394-46601; www.lake-district.gov.uk; ⊙10am-5pm Easter-Oct) Installed inside a 19th-century mansion 3 miles north of Windermere on the A591, this is the Lake District's flagship visitor centre, and also has a teashop, adventure playground and gardens.

Windermere Tourist Office (☎015394-46499; windermeretic@southlakeland.gov.uk; Victoria St; ⊙9am-5.30pm Mon-Sat, 9.30am-5.30pm Sun Apr-Oct, shorter hours in winter) Opposite NatWest Bank.

WORTH A TRIP

THE MASON'S ARMS

Teetering on a steep fellside 3 miles east of the lake, not far from Bowlands Bridge, the marvellous **Mason's Arms** (☎015395-68486; www.masonsarmsstrawberrybank.co.uk; Winster; mains £13-20, d £75-105) is a proper locals' secret. The rafters, flagstones and cast-iron range haven't changed in centuries, but the food's bang up-to-date: Cartmel lamb with creamy fondant potatoes, or roast guineafowl slathered in red-wine gravy. The front patio has to-die-for views across green fields and distant fells, as do the pick of the rooms and self-contained cottages. In short, it's an absolute cracker – but keep it under your hat,OK?

THE CROSS-LAKES EXPERIENCE

The **Cross Lakes Experience** (http://www.lakedistrict.gov.uk/visiting/planningyourvisit/travelandtransport/crosslakes; ⏲Mar-Oct) is an integrated boat, bus and minibus service that enables travel from Windermere to Coniston without a car.

Tickets include travel on the Windermere Ferry from Bowness to Ferry House, from where the Mountain Goat minibus runs to Hill Top and Hawkshead. From Hawkshead, you can catch the X30 bus to Grizedale Forest, or the 505 bus to Coniston, and then travel across the lake on the Coniston Launch. For info and timetables, contact **Mountain Goat** (☎015394-45161; www.mountain-goat.com; Victoria Rd) or local tourist offices.

Bikes can be carried on boats and buses for £1 per bike, although space is limited and you can't prebook.

A return from Bowness to Coniston costs adult/child £19.10/10.90. Single fares:

Ferry House (£2.55/1.50)

Hill Top (£5.35/3.05)

Hawkshead (£6.35/3.50)

Coniston (adult/child £11.25/6.20)

Post Office (21 Crescent Rd; ⏲9am-17.30pm Mon-Sat)

Getting There & Away

BOAT Windermere Ferry (car/bike/pedestrian £4.30/1/50p; ⏲6.50am-9.50pm Mon-Fri, 9.10am-9.50pm Sat & Sun Mar-Oct, last ferry one hour earlier in winter) carries vehicles and pedestrians from Ferry Nab, just south of Bowness, across to Ferry House on the lake's west side. There's a ferry roughly every 20 minutes, although queues can be horrendous in summer.

BUS There's one daily National Express coach from London (£30, eight hours) via Lancaster and Kendal. Local buses:

555/556 Lakeslink (half-hourly Monday to Saturday, hourly at weekends) Starts at the train station, stopping at Troutbeck Bridge (5 minutes), Brockhole Visitor Centre (7 minutes), Ambleside (15 minutes), Grasmere (30 minutes) and Keswick (1 hour). In the opposite direction it continues to Kendal (25 minutes) and Lancaster (1 hour 40 minutes).

505 Coniston Rambler (eight daily Monday to Saturday, six on Sunday) Travels from Windermere to Coniston (50 minutes) via Troutbeck, Brockhole, Ambleside, Skelwith Fold, Hawkshead and Hawkshead Hill. Two buses a day serve Kendal.

599 Lakes Rider (three times hourly Monday to Saturday, hourly on Sunday in summer) Open-top bus between Bowness, Troutbeck, Brockhole, Rydal Church (for Rydal Mount), Dove Cottage and Grasmere. Some buses stop at Windermere train station.

TRAIN Windermere is the only town in the national park accessible by train. It's on the branch line to Kendal (£4.20, 15 minutes) and on to Oxenholme (£4.90, 20 minutes), which has frequent connections north and south as shown following.

Edinburgh £55, 2½ hours

Glasgow £43.40, 2¾ hours

London Euston £92.10, 3¼ hours

Manchester Piccadilly £32.40, 1½ to 2 hours via **Lancaster** £12.60, 45 minutes

Troutbeck

Nestled amongst the fells to the north of Windermere on the road towards the Kirkstone Pass, this rural hamlet feels a world away from the Bowness bustle.

Apart from the countryside, it's worth a stop for the historic National Trust–owned farmhouse of **Townend** (NT; ☎01539-432628; www.nationaltrust.org.uk/townend; adult/child £4.70/2.35; ⏲1-5pm Wed-Sun Mar-Oct, open daily during school holidays), which contains a collection of vintage farming tools and furniture that belonged to the Browne family, who owned the house until 1943. Public visiting hours are from 1pm to 5pm, but you can join hourly guided tours from 11am to 1pm.

Sleeping & Eating

Queen's Head INN, PUB ££

(☎015394-32174; www.queensheadhotel.com; d £99-110, mains £12.95-16.95; P) This 17th-century coaching inn and pub in Troutbeck is a winning blend of old and new: it's been given a modern makeover, but still has all the essentials (oak bar, big fire, whitewashed facade). The bedrooms are surprisingly fancy, with bright bedspreads, flatscreen TVs and teddy bears, but it's the solid food and ale that keeps the place busy. There's a three-course menu (£20) chalked up over the fireplace.

Windermere YHA HOSTEL £
(☎0845-371 9352; www.yha.org.uk/hostel/windermere; Bridge Lane; dm £19.65; ⏲reception 7.30-11.30am & 1-11pm; P@) This sprawling period house is the closest YHA to Windermere. The rooms are modern, and facilities include a well-stocked shop, canteen and gear-drying room. Buses stop at Troutbeck Bridge, a mile-long walk uphill to the hostel.

Mortal Man PUB, INN ££
(☎015394-33193; www.themortalmaninn.co.uk; mains £8.95-14.95, r £90-150) Troutbeck's other inn gets its name from a medieval proverb (you can read it on the sign outside). The gabled inn dates from 1689 and feels atmospherically antique, all dark oak and hidden snugs. But the real sell is the beer garden, offering grand views stretching all the way to Windermere.

Getting There & Away

Bus 517 (the Kirkstone Rambler) travels through Troutbeck en route across the Kirkstone Pass to Ullswater (1 hour, three daily mid-July to August, weekends only other times).

Ambleside

POP 3382

Tucked at the northern head of Windermere and surrounded by a cluster of towering fells, Ambleside feels less commercialised than its sister towns further to the south, but that doesn't stop it getting jammed throughout the summer. It's a favourite base for hikers, with plenty of quality outdoor shops dotted round town, and it marks the start of several classic hikes.

It's also handily positioned for forays west towards Grasmere and the lakes beyond, and cruise boats from Bowness dock regularly down at the Waterhead dock, just south of town.

Sights

Ambleside has few must-see sights, but its slate streets are made for wandering.

In previous centuries, the town was a hive of industry, with a network of spinning water-wheels providing power for its many breweries, tanneries, blacksmiths and bobbin-mills. You can still see an original waterwheel on the side of the Old Mill Tea Room, uphill from the Hub tourist office.

The town's best-known landmark is **Bridge House**, a tiny cottage that spans the clattering brook of Stock Ghyll; now occupied by a National Trust shop, it's thought to have originally been used as an apple store.

On Church St, a plaque marks the old **Stamp House**, where William Wordsworth worked following his appointment as Distributor of Stamps for Westmorland in 1813.

Armitt Museum MUSEUM
(www.armitt.com; Rydal Rd; adult £2.50; ⏲10am-5pm) Artefacts at Ambleside's modest town museum include a lock of John Ruskin's hair, a collection of botanical watercolours by Beatrix Potter, and prints by the pharmacist-turned-photographer Herbert Bell.

FREE **Galava Roman Fort** RUINS
(NT) The foundations of Ambleside's ruined roman fort, built c AD79, can be seen just west of the Waterhead jetties. The land is now owned by the National Trust; it's possible to make out the fort's general layout and the shape of some of its grain stores and internal rooms.

Activities

Fell Hikes WALKING
Ambleside makes a great base for hikes; the tourist office has a good selection of trail leaflets and guidebooks.

The most popular walk is the half-hour stroll up to the 60ft waterfall of **Stock Ghyll Force**; the trail is signposted behind the old Market Hall at the bottom of Stock Ghyll Lane.

From the falls, you can hike on across the top of **Wansfell** (487m/1597ft), which affords a stunning panorama across Windermere, before looping back via Troutbeck, Skelghyll Wood, and the Jenkin's Crag viewpoint. In total, it's a walk of around 6 miles.

A more formidable proposition is the 10-mile **Fairfield Horseshoe**, via the summits of Nab Scar, Heron Pike, Fairfield and Dove Crag. It's a full-blown mountain walk, so you'll need boots, map and supplies.

Low Wood Watersports BOATING
(☎015394-39441; www.englishlakes.co.uk/watersports) An experienced and well-equipped watersports centre that offers waterskiing, sailing and kayaking. Rowboats and motorboats are also available for hire.

Festivals & Events

Ambleside Rushbearing FOLK FESTIVAL
(1st Sat in July) Rushes and wreaths are carried through the streets of Ambleside in this traditional folk festival.

Sleeping

Regent Hotel HOTEL ££
(015394-32254; www.regentlakes.co.uk; Waterhead Bay; d £119-149; P) Recently refurbished and looking much the better for it, this hotel has a near-the-lake location without the sky-high price tag. The rooms offer different settings: some have balconies overlooking the garden, others have bunk-beds for the kids, and a few sneak in views over Windermere. All are spankingly modern; couples should choose the romantic Sail Loft with its private decked patio.

Lakes Lodge B&B ££
(015394-33240; www.lakeslodge.co.uk; Lake Rd; r £79-129; P) Run by the same team behind the Regent Hotel, this modish minihotel offers a touch more luxury than Ambleside's other guesthouses. The 16 rooms are all clean lines, stark walls and zero clutter, and most feature a full-size wall mural featuring a local beauty spot. Some rooms are in an annexe next to the main building. Breakfast is self-serve.

The Gables B&B ££
(015394-33272; www.thegables-ambleside.co.uk; Church Walk; s £45-50, d £90-120; P) One of the best of Ambleside's B&Bs, in a quiet spot overlooking the recreation ground. Spotty cushions and colourful prints keep things cheery, but room sizes are very variable (in this instance, bigger is definitely better). Guests receive discounts at the owner's restaurant, Sheila's Cottage.

The Waterwheel B&B ££
(015394-33286; www.waterwheelambleside.co.uk; 3 Bridge St; d £85-100) You'll be lulled to sleep by the sound of the river at this tiny B&B, tucked off the main street. The three rooms are tiny but sweet: Rattleghyll is cosily Victorian, Loughrigg squeezes in under the rafters and Stockghyll features a brass bed and clawfoot bath. The only parking is in a public car park 250m away.

Riverside B&B ££
(015394-32395; www.riverside-at-ambleside.co.uk; Under Loughrigg; d £102-122; P) Lodged beside the River Rothay, half a mile from town, this detached Victorian villa is distinguished by its luxuries, including walking guides, ethical bath products, chutneys from the Hawkshead Relish Company. Two rooms have spa baths, one a pine four-poster.

Waterhead Hotel HOTEL £££
(08458-504503; www.elh.co.uk/hotels/waterhead; r £125-165; P) Ambleside's main hotel has a super position down beside the lakeshore. The exterior is classic Lakeland, all solid stone and bay windows, but inside it's very much a modern hotel, with spacious rooms stocked with heritage furniture and designer fabrics, and a sophisticated restaurant, the Mountain View.

Compston House Hotel B&B ££
(015394-32305; www.compstonhouse.co.uk; Compston Rd; d from £80;) All the rooms here are themed after a different American state – sunny Hawaii, bright Florida, maritime Maine – perhaps unsurprising, since the owners are ex–New Yorkers. Breakfast includes blueberry muffins and proper maple pancakes.

Cote How B&B £££
(015394-32765; www.bedbreakfastlakedistrict.com; Rydal, near Ambleside; d £120-160; P) Approved by the Soil Association, this detached house makes a virtue of its sustainable credentials. Food is 100% local and organic, power's sourced from a green supplier, and there's a discount if you don't bring a car. The three rooms are olde Edwardian, with cast-iron beds, roll-top baths and fireplaces. It's in Rydal, 1.5 miles from Ambleside.

Low Wray CAMPSITE £
(NT; bookings 015394-63862; www.ntlakescampsites.org.uk; tents £8.25-12.50 plus £5.50 per extra adult, eco-pods £30-50; campsite arrivals 3-7pm Sat-Thu, 3-9pm Fri, Mar-Oct) Lakeside camping courtesy of the National Trust, although waterside pitches are extra (£7.50 for a lake view, £10 for the lakeshore). It's 3 miles from town along the B5286; bus 505 stops nearby. Luxury yurts can be booked through **Long Valley** (01539-731089; www.luxury-yurt-holidays.co.uk; per week £335-490) and **Wild in Style** (07909-446381; www.wildinstyle.co.uk; per week £325-495), while **4Winds Lakeland Tipis** (01539-821227; www.4windslakelandtipis.co.uk; tipis per week £290-465) offers 12 Native American–style teepees.

Ambleside YHA HOSTEL £
(☎0845 371 9620; ambleside@yha.org.uk; Windermere Rd; dm/d £23/40, f £99-149; P) One of the YHA's flagship Lake District hostels, this huge lakeside house organises activity holidays (everything from kayaking to ghyll-scrambling). Great facilities (kitchen, bike rental, boat jetty and bar) mean it's heavily subscribed, so book well ahead.

Eating

Glass House MEDITERRANEAN ££
(☎015394-32137; www.theglasshouserestaurant.co.uk; Rydal Rd; mains £10.25-14.75) Classy dining in a converted fulling mill (with original millwheels and machinery still in place). It's known for its accomplished Med and French food, so expect plenty of zingy flavours underpinned by Lakeland ingredients.

Zeffirelli's ITALIAN £
(☎015394-33845; www.zeffirellis.com; Compston Rd; pizzas & mains £8-12; until 10pm) If it's pizza and pasta you want, Zeff's is the place. The cellar dining room is buzzy, with glass sculptures, spotlights and curvy seats, and the menu has copious Italian dishes. The owners also run Ambleside's main cinema; ask about the £17.95 'Double Feature' deal, which includes two courses and a ticket to the flicks. There's a jazz club upstairs.

Fellini's VEGETARIAN ££
(☎015394-32487; www.fellinisambleside.com; Church St; mains £11.95; dinner, closed Mon in winter) Fear not, veggies, you might be in the land of the Cumberland sausage and the tattie hotpot, but that doesn't mean you can't indulge. Fellini's turns out fancy 'vegeterranean' food – squash-and-cabbage hotpot, leek-and-brie filo parcels – that would tempt even the hardiest of carnivores. It's run by Zeff's owners; a small upstairs screen shows arthouse and opera performances.

Lucy's on a Plate CAFE, BISTRO ££
(☎015394-31191; www.lucysofambleside.co.uk; Church St; mains £12-20; breakfast, lunch & dinner) This longstanding bistro has been through turbulent times (original owner Lucy Nicholson went bust in 2011), but it's been rescued from the brink and is back to doing what it does best: quirky bistro food and generous puddings laced with a dash of offbeat imagination. Cooking lessons are available at **Lucy Cooks** (☎015394-32288; www.lucycooks.co.uk; Mill Yard, Staveley) in nearby Staveley, 3 miles from Windermere.

Sheila's Cottage BISTRO ££
(☎015394-33079; The Slack; mains £9.90-19.95; lunch & dinner) Rough walls and cottagey furnishings make this a snug place to dine. It serves a mix-and-match menu: chunky sandwiches and salads for lunch, big plates of lamb chump, salmon fillet or squash risotto for dinner. It's on alley off the main street.

Tarantella RESTAURANT ££
(10 Lake Rd; mains £9.95-15.95; lunch & dinner) Reliable Italian food, with wood-fired pizzas and authentic pastas partnered by unusual regional fare such as duck-and-chilli sausage and roast tuna.

Doi Intanon THAI
(☎015394-32119; Market Pl; mains £8.50-15.50; dinner) Tasty Thai cuisine, with fiery green, red and yellow curries served in the surrounds of Ambleside's old market hall.

Lucy 4 TAPAS £
(2 St Mary's Lane; tapas £4-10; 5-10.30pm Mon-Fri, noon-10.30pm Sat & Sun) Cosy wine-bar offshoot of Lucy's that also does good tapas.

Apple Pie CAFE £
(Rydal Rd; lunches £4-10; breakfast & lunch) Sunny cafe popular for its sandwiches, buns and hearty pies.

Drinking & Entertainment

Ambleside has plenty of pubs. Locals favour the **Golden Rule** (Smithy Brow) and **The Unicorn** (North Rd) for their real ale selection, while the **Royal Oak** (Market Pl) has a nice patio terrace.

Ambleside's two-screen **Zeffirelli's Cinema** (☎015394-33100; Compston Rd) is next to Zeff's, with extra screens in a converted church down the road.

Shopping

Compston Rd has enough outdoor equipment shops to launch an assault on Everest.

Gaynor Sports OUTDOOR EQUIPMENT
(☎01524-734938; www.gaynors.co.uk; Market Cross) The best (and biggest) outdoors store in Ambleside, with three floors of gear from major brands including The North Face, Berghaus, Mountain Equipment and Jack Wolfskin.

Mountain Factor OUTDOOR EQUIPMENT
(☎015394-32752; www.themountainfactor.com; 5 Lake Rd) High-end gear from Paramo, Icebreaker, Patagonia and Fjällraven.

Climber's Shop OUTDOOR EQUIPMENT
(☎015394-30122; www.climbers-shop.com; Compston Rd) Offers local knowlege and great gear.

Information

The Hub (☎015394-32582; tic@thehubofambleside.com; Central Buildings, Market Cross; ⏲9am-5pm) The tourist office and the post office are both here.

Getting There & Around

BUS

555 (hourly, 10 buses on Sunday) To Grasmere and Windermere.

505 (eight daily Monday to Saturday, six on Sunday) Stops in Ambleside en route from Windermere to Hawkshead and Coniston.

516 (six daily, five on Sunday) Elterwater and Langdale.

BICYCLE Bikes and gear can be hired from **Biketreks** (☎015394-31505; www.biketreks.net; Compston Rd; per day £20) and **Ghyllside Cycles** (☎015394-33592; www.ghyllside.co.uk; The Slack; per day £18).

Around Ambleside

TOP CHOICE **Rydal Mount** HISTORIC BUILDING
(www.rydalmount.co.uk; adult/child £6/2.50, gardens only adults £4; ⏲9.30am-5pm Mar-Oct, 11am-4pm Wed-Mon Nov & Feb) William Wordsworth's best-known Lakeland residence is definitely Dove Cottage, but he actually spent much more time at Rydal Mount, a far grander house halfway between Ambleside and Grasmere. This was the Wordsworth family's home from 1813 until the poet's death in 1850, and it's still owned by his descendants.

The house is a treasure trove of Wordsworth memorabilia. Downstairs you can wander around the library, dining room and drawing room (look out in the cabinets for William's pen, inkstand and picnic box, and a famous portrait of the poet by the American painter Henry Inman hangs above the fireplace). Upstairs are the family bedrooms and Wordsworth's attic study, containing his encyclopedia and a sword belonging to his brother John, who was lost in a shipwreck in 1805.

Most of the gardens around the house were laid out according to Wordsworth's own designs. Below the house is **Dora's Field**, which Wordsworth planted with daffodils in memory of his eldest daughter, who died from tuberculosis in 1847.

The house is 1.5 miles northwest of Ambleside, off the A591. Bus 555 (and bus 599 from April to October) both stop at the end of the drive.

Grasmere

POP 1458

Even without its Romantic connections, Grasmere would still be one of the Lakes' biggest draws. It's one of the prettiest of the Lakeland hamlets, huddled at the base of a sweeping valley dotted with woods, pastures and slate-coloured hills, but most of the thousands of trippers come in search of its famous former residents: opium-eating Thomas de Quincey, unruly Coleridge and grand old man William Wordsworth. With such a rich literary heritage, Grasmere unsurprisingly gets crammed; avoid high summer if you can.

Sights

Dove Cottage HISTORIC BUILDING
(☎015394-35544; www.wordsworth.org.uk; adult/child £7.50/4.50; ⏲9.30am-5.30pm) This tiny, creeper-clad cottage on the edge of the village famously belonged to William Wordsworth. He arrived here with his sister Dorothy in 1799 before being joined in 1802 by his new wife, Mary, and soon after, three children – John, Dora and Thomas – who were born here in 1803, 1804 and 1806.

The tiny cottage was a cramped but happy home for the growing family until 1808, when it was subsequently rented by Thomas de Quincey (author of *Confessions of an English Opium Eater*).

Like nearby Rydal Mount, the cottage's small rooms are full of artefacts: keep your eyes peeled for the poet's passport, a pair of his spectacles and a portrait of his favourite dog Pepper, given to him by Sir Walter Scott. One upstairs bedroom was lined with newspaper by Wordsworth's sister Dorothy to try and keep out the draughts.

Entry is by timed ticket to avoid overcrowding, and includes an informative guided tour.

Next door to the cottage, the **Wordsworth Museum & Art Gallery** (☎015394-35544; www.wordsworth.org.uk; A591; adult £7.50, child £4.50, family £17.20; ⏲9.30am-5.30pm), houses one of the nation's main collections relating to the Romantic movement, including many original manuscripts.

Grasmere Lake & Rydal Water LAKE

Quiet paths lead along the shorelines of Grasmere's twin-set lakes. Rowing boats can be hired at the northern end of Grasmere Lake from the **Faeryland Tea Garden** (⏲10.30am-4pm), a five-minute walk from the village centre.

St Oswald's Church CHURCH

In the churchyard of this tiny chapel in the centre of Grasmere are the graves of many of the Wordsworths, including William, his wife Mary, sister Dorothy, and children Dora, Catherine and Thomas. Samuel Taylor Coleridge's son Hartley is also buried here.

Activities

The most popular walk from Grasmere is the steep slog to the summit of **Helm Crag** (1328ft), known locally as the 'Lion and the Lamb'. The trail is signed from Easedale Road. It's about 3 miles there and back, but it is quite steep, so allow a couple of hours.

Other options include the trail to the waterfall at **Sour Milk Ghyll**, also signed off Easedale Rd, and the hike to the top of **Loughrigg Fell** (1099ft) from the shores of Grasmere Lake.

For an easier walk, the **Old Coffin Trail** between Ambleside and Grasmere gets its name from the days when coffins had to be carried along here to be buried at the parish church, St Oswald's. You can pick up the path behind Dove Cottage.

Festivals & Events

Grasmere Sports TRADITIONAL SPORTS

(www.grasmeresports.com; ⏲Sun, August bank holiday weekend) Traditional sports such as hound-trailing, Cumbrian wrestling and guides racing, held on Grasmere's village green since 1882.

Sleeping

TOP CHOICE **Moss Grove Organic** HOTEL £££

(☎015394-35251; www.mossgrove.com; r Sun-Thu £114-209, Fri & Sat £129-259; P 📶) This eco-chic hotel champions its green credentials: sheep-wool insulation, organic paints, reclaimed timber beds – but for once eco also equals elegance. Rooms are enormous, and bathrooms sparkle with sexy showers and underfloor heating. Breakfast is served buffet-style in the kitchen-diner downstairs. Lovely.

How Foot Lodge B&B ££

(☎015394-35366; www.howfoot.co.uk; Town End; d £72-8; P) Just a stroll from Dove Cottage, this stone house has six rooms finished in fawn and beige; the nicest are the deluxe doubles, one with sun terrace and the other with private sitting room. Rates are an absolute bargain considering the location.

Heidi's Grasmere Lodge B&B ££

(☎015394-35248; www.heidisgrasmerelodge.co.uk; Red Lion Square; d £99-135; 📶) A plush B&B plonked above Heidi's cafe, offering six super-feminine rooms full of frilly cushions and Cath Kidston–style patterns. They're quite small but very comfy; Room 6 has its own sun patio, reached via a spiral staircase.

Raise View House B&B ££

(☎015394-35215; www.raiseviewhouse.co.uk; White Bridge; s/d £90/106; P 📶) All the rooms are named after fells here, and boast hill views to match; Helm Crag, Easedale and Stone Arthur are particularly impressive. On the edge of Grasmere, the house is smartly appointed, with Farrow & Ball paints, Gilchrist & Soames bathstuffs and Wedgwood china on the breakfast table.

Lancrigg B&B £££

(☎015394-35317; www.lancrigg.co.uk; Easedale; r £130-218; P) Unashamedly old-fashioned, this fine old house half a mile along Easedale Rd once belonged to Arctic adventurer John Richardson. Rooms are heavy on the swags and flock wallpapers, but the views across the Easedale fells are top-drawer. Tea is served on the terrace on sunny days.

Butharlyp How YHA HOSTEL £

(☎0845-371 9319; www.yha.org.uk; Easedale Rd; dm £15.50; ⏲reception 7am-10pm Feb-Nov, weekends only Dec & Jan; P @) Grasmere's only remaining YHA (since Thorney How was sold off due to cost-cutting) is in a large Victorian house set amongst grassy grounds. There's a good range of different-sized dorms and an unusually good cafe-bar.

Thorney How HOSTEL £

(☎015394-35597; www.thorneyhow.co.uk; Easedale Rd; dm £21-5) Now independent, this former YHA is in a Grade-II listed farmhouse off Easedale Rd, 15 minutes from Grasmere. Accommodation is in six- to 10-bed dorms, although there are a few doubles, all with fresh carpets and pine furniture. Facilities include a kitchen, cafe and a bike shelter, but the showers need renovating.

Grasmere Hostel HOSTEL £
(☎015394-35055; www.grasmerehostel.co.uk; Broadrayne Farm; dm £19.50; P@) This independent hostel is in a converted farmhouse on the A591, near the Traveller's Rest pub. There are two kitchens, and each dorm has its own en suite bathroom. There's even a Nordic-style sauna.

Eating & Drinking

TOP CHOICE **Jumble Room** RESTAURANT £££
(☎015394-35188; Langdale Rd; dinner mains £14.50-26.50; ⊙lunch Fri-Sun, dinner Wed-Sun) Husband-and-wife team Andy and Crissy Hill have turned this village bistro into a much-loved dining landmark. Mixing Lakeland produce with pan-global influences, it's a really fun and friendly place to dine out. Spotty crockery, cow murals and primary colours set the boho tone, matched by a magpie menu taking in everything from honeyed chicken to cauliflower fritters. Bookings essential.

Sara's Bistro BISTRO ££
(Broadgate; mains £10-16) Hearty homespun cooking is Sarah's raison d'être – big portions of roast chicken, lamb shanks and apple crumble, served without the faintest hint of fuss.

Heidi's of Grasmere CAFE £
(Red Lion Sq; mains £4-8; ⊙9am-5.30pm) This cute pine-clad cafe makes a welcome refuge if the weather turns. Thick-cut sandwiches and hot soups are its mainstay, but the house special 'cheese smokeys' are the choice if you're hungry.

Baldry's Tea Room CAFE
(Red Lion Sq; lunch £3-8; ⊙10am-5pm) This lacy cafe is the spot for a classic cream tea, served in a bone-china pot and accompanied by buttery scones or Victoria sponges.

Greens CAFE £
(Green St; mains £5-12) Friendly caff offering paninis, baked potatoes and salads with a Fair Trade ethos.

Rowan Tree CAFE £
(Stocks Lane; mains £3-10, pizzas £6-9) Riverside cafe serving basic pasta and pizzas.

Miller Howe Cafe CAFE ££
(Red Lion Sq; mains £5-14) Smart chrome cafe on the main square.

Traveller's Rest PUB
With its sputtering fires and inglenook bar, this 16th-century coaching inn on the A591 makes a fine place for a pint and a simple pie supper.

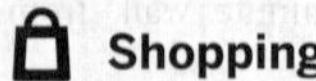

Shopping

Sarah Nelson's Gingerbread Shop FOOD
(www.grasmeregingerbread.co.uk; Church Stile; 12 pieces of gingerbread £4.95; ⊙9.15am-5.30pm Mon-Sat, 12.30-5pm Sun) In business since 1854, this famous sweet shop makes Grasmere's essential souvenir: traditional gingerbread with a half-biscuity, half-cakey texture, cooked according to a top-secret recipe by ladies in frilly pinnies and starched bonnets.

Getting There & Away

The 555 runs from Windermere to Grasmere (15 minutes), via Ambleside, Rydal Church and Dove Cottage.

The open-top 599 (two or three per hour in summer) runs from Grasmere via Ambleside, Troutbeck Bridge, Windermere and Bowness.

Hawkshead

POP 1640

Lakeland villages don't come much more postcard-perfect than Hawkshead, a muddle of whitewashed cottages, cobbled lanes and old pubs lost among bottle-green countryside between Ambleside and Coniston. Chuck in connections to both Wordsworth and Beatrix Potter, and you won't be surprised to find Hawkshead awash with visitors.

Sights

Hawkshead Grammar School HISTORIC BUILDING
(www.hawksheadgrammar.org.uk; admission £2; ⊙10am-1pm & 2-5pm Mon-Sat, 1-5pm Sun Apr-Sep, closed Nov-Mar) In centuries past, promising young gentleman were sent to Hawkshead's village school for their educational foundation. Among the former pupils was a certain William Wordsworth, who attended the school from 1779 to 1787. The curriculum was punishing: 10 hours' study a day, covering weighty subjects such as Latin, Greek, geometry, science and rhetoric. Hardly surprising young Willie (among others) felt the urge to carve his name into one of the desks.

Upstairs is a small exhibition exploring the history of the school.

Beatrix Potter Gallery GALLERY

(NT; www.nationaltrust.org.uk/beatrix-potter-gallery; Red Lion Sq; adult/child £4.80/2.40; ⏲11am-5pm Sat-Thu mid-Mar–Oct) As well as being a bestselling children's author, Beatrix Potter was also a talented botanical painter and amateur naturalist. This small gallery (housed in the offices of Potter's husband, solicitor William Heelis) contains a collection of delicate watercolours depicting local flora and fauna. She seems to have been particularly fascinated by mushrooms.

There's discounted admission if you show show your ticket from Hill Top (p691).

Sleeping

Yewfield B&B ££

(☎015394-36765; www.yewfield.co.uk; Hawkshead Hill; s £49-65, d £98-130; P 📶) This detached house occupies a commanding hilltop spot near Tarn Hows, halfway between Coniston and Hawkshead. It's run by the owners of Zeff's, and though the building itself is Victorian, it's operated along eco-alternative lines: breakfast is veggie and organic, power comes from a wood-mass boiler, and much of the produce comes from the kitchen garden. There are extensive grounds, too.

Summer Hill Country House HOTEL ££

(☎015394-36180; www.summerhillcountryhouse.com; Hawkshead Hill; d £96-116; P @ 📶) Also on Hawkshead Hill, this 1700s house has a wonderfully out-of-the-way setting, 3 miles from both Coniston & Hawkshead. The five rooms vary in shape and size, but all feature posh bath products and net-connected Mac Minis for getting online or watching DVDs. The garden boasts sculptures and a summerhouse that belonged to John Ruskin.

Hawkshead YHA HOSTEL £

(☎0845-371 9321; hawkshead@yha.org.uk; dm from £14; P @) This hostel occupies a Regency house a mile along the Newby Bridge road. Like many Lakeland YHAs, the period architecture is impressive – corniçing, panelled doors, a verandah – and the big dorms boast big views. There's bike rental and a kitchen, and buses stop outside the door.

Queen's Head B&B, PUB ££

(☎015394-36271; www.queensheadhawkshead.co.uk; Main St; s £70, d £100-130, mains £14-22) Hawkshead has several decent pubs, but our pick is the old Queen's Head, which brims with oak-panelled appeal. Hale and hearty country food (Esthwaite trout, Winster pork, Gressingham duck) in the hugger-mugger bar, partnered by small, prim rooms upstairs. Avoid the lodge annexe if you're staying.

Eating

Hawkshead Relish Company DELI £

(☎015394-36614; www.hawksheadrelish.com; The Square; ⏲9.30am-5pm winter, 9am-5.30pm summer) This renowned chutney company sells an enormous choice of relishes and jams. Go for fig and cinnamon or damson chutney if you're after something fruity, or 'Chillililli' (their version of picallilli) if you prefer things fiery.

The Honeypot DELI £

(The Square) Excellent deli stocking hams, cheeses, jams and other goodies, as well as made-to-order sandwiches.

Poppi Red CAFE, SHOP £

(The Square) This girly giftshop-cum-tearoom sells frilly souvenirs and serves tea and cake in its teeny cafe.

Getting There & Away

Hawkshead is linked with Windermere, Ambleside and Coniston by bus 505 (eight daily Monday to Saturday, six on Sunday).

Around Hawkshead

CLAIFE HEIGHTS & WRAY CASTLE

Windermere's quiet western shores are a world away from the tourist-thronged quays of Bowness.

To the north of the ferry landings at Ferry House, a network of peaceful paths winds through the woods of **Claife Heights**. Further north, the National Trust–owned estate of **Wray Castle** (NT; www.nationaltrust.org.uk/wray-castle; adult/child £6/3; ⏲10.30am-5pm) encompasses 25 hectares of lakeside grounds and a turreted mansion, built in mock-Gothic style during the mid-19th century for retired Liverpudlian surgeon James Dawson. The house was used as a holiday home by Beatrix Potter's family, but it's had a somewhat chequered history since: it's been unoccupied for many years, and though the original furniture is long-gone, you can still wander round the house's opulent, empty rooms.

HILL TOP

The button-cute farmhouse of **Hill Top** (NT; ☎015394-36269; www.nationaltrust.org.uk/hill-top; adult/child £8/4; ⏲10am-5pm Sat-Thu

DON'T MISS

TARN HOWS

The Lake District has beauty spots aplenty, but the idyllic lake of **Tarn Hows** (NT; www.nationaltrust.org.uk/coniston-and-tarn-hows) is up there with the best.

Set among the fells between Hawkshead and Coniston, and surrounded by pines, firs and colourful conifers, it's one of the national park's classic postcard images – but in reality it's not the work of Mother Nature at all. The present-day tarn is actually an artificial creation, dreamt up by the landowner James Marshall in 1862, who joined three separate pools, rejigged the shoreline and replanted the trees to enhance the area's aesthetic appeal.

Regardless of its origins, it's a fantastically photogenic spot. Shady trails wind their way around the tarn and surrounding woodland and you might well spot a red squirrel or two frolicking around in the treetops.

There's a small National Trust car park beside the tarn, but it fills quickly. Several buses, including the 505 and the X30, stop nearby; alternatively, you can follow trails up from nearby Hawkshead and Coniston.

mid-Feb–Oct, shorter hours outside summer) is a must for Beatrix Potter buffs; it was her first house in the Lake District, and is also where she wrote and illustrated many of her famous tales.

Beatrix Potter purchased the house in 1905 on the proceeds of her first bestseller, *The Tale of Peter Rabbit*. Nearly every room has decorative details from the author's illustrations. The house itself featured extensively in *Samuel Whiskers*, *Tom Kitten*, *Jemima Puddleduck*, and *Pigling Bland*, and the cottage garden outside is a dead ringer for the one explored by Peter Rabbit. The house still contains much of Potter's own furniture and belongings, including her writing desk, kitchen dresser and doll collection.

There's no electric light inside the house, so it can be dark on dull days; note also that photos are only permitted in the gardens, not inside the house itself.

Thanks to its worldwide fame – especially since the 2006 biopic *Miss Potter* starring Renée Zellwegger – Hill Top is one of the Lakes' busiest attractions. Entry is by timed ticket to avoid overcrowding, but the queues can still be daunting. Arrive early or late to avoid the worst crowds.

The cottage is in Near Sawrey, 2 miles from Hawkshead and Ferry House. The Cross Lakes Experience (p684) stops en route from Ferry House to Hawkshead.

GRIZEDALE FOREST

Sprawling across the hills between Coniston Water and Esthwaite Water, **Grizedale Forest** (from the Old Norse for 'wild boar') is one of the Lake District's most beautiful woodlands – not to mention its largest outdoor art project. More than 90 large-scale artworks and sculptures are sprinkled throughout the forest, from an enormous xylophone to a Tolkienesque 'man of the forest'.

It's also a great place to explore on two wheels; the **Grizedale Visitors Centre** (☎01229-860010; www.forestry.gov.uk/grizedaleforestpark; ⏲10am-5pm, 11am-4pm winter) provides guide leaflets and forest maps detailing the forest's maintained mountain bike trails. You can bring your own bike, or rent one from **Grizedale Mountain Bikes** (☎01229-860369; www.grizedalemountainbikes.co.uk; per day adult/child from £26/16; ⏲9am-5pm, last hire 3pm) next to the visitor centre.

And if all that's not tiring enough, you could test your nerve at **Go Ape** (www.goape.co.uk; adult/child £30/25; ⏲9-5pm Mar-Oct, weekends only Nov-Feb), a gravity defying treetop assault course with a wealth of rope ladders, bridges, platforms and zip-slides to tackle.

ℹ Getting There & Away

Grizedale Visitor Centre is 3 miles south of Hawkshead. It has a large pay-and-display car park; there are several other smaller car parks around the forest's edges.

The X30 bus stops at the visitor centre on its circular route between Ferry House, Hawkshead, Tarn Hows and Satterthwaite.

Coniston

POP 1948

Hunkered beneath the pockmarked peak of the Old Man (803m), the lakeside village of Coniston was established as a centre for the copper-mining industry, but the only remnants of the industry are the many abandoned quarries and mine shafts that now litter the surrounding hilltops.

Coniston's main claim to fame is as the location for a string of world-record speed attempts made here by Sir Malcolm Campbell and his son, Donald, between the 1930s and 1960s. Tragically, after beating the record several times, Donald was killed during an attempt in 1967, when his futuristic jet-boat *Bluebird K7* flipped at around 320mph. The boat and its pilot were recovered in 2001, and Campbell was buried in the cemetery near St Andrew's church. A long labour of love to restore the boat to its former glory is ongoing.

Coniston is a fairly quiet village these days, mainly worth a visit for its lovely lake cruises and a trip to the former house of John Ruskin at Brantwood – as well as the chance to conquer the Old Man, one of the Lake District's 'must-do' hikes.

Sights

Brantwood HISTORIC BUILDING
(015394-41396; www.brantwood.org.uk; adult/child £6.30/1.35, gardens only £4.50/1.35; 10.30am-5pm mid-Mar-mid-Nov, 10.30am-4pm Wed-Sun mid-Novmid-Mar) John Ruskin (1819–1900), the great Victorian polymath, philosopher and critic, was one of the formeost thinkers of 19th-century British society, expounding views on everything from Venetian architecture to the finer points of traditional lace-making.

In 1871 he purchased this impressive house overlooking Coniston, and spent the next 20 years expanding and modifying it. The house is a monument to Ruskin's belief in the value of traditional 'Arts and Crafts' over factory-made materials: he helped design everything from the furniture to the garden terraces, and even dreamt up some of the wallpaper designs. Look out for his enormous shell collection in the downstairs study, and works by JMW Turner (one of Ruskin's favourite artists) in an upstairs bedroom.

The best way to arrive is by boat from Coniston. While you wait for the boat back you can have lunch at **Jumping Jenny** (lunches £4-8) in the house's former stables.

If you'd prefer to drive, take the B5285 towards Coniston from Hawkshead and follow the signs.

Ruskin Museum MUSEUM
(www.ruskinmuseum.com; adult/child £5.25/2.50; 10am-5.30pm Easter–mid-Nov, 10.30am-3.30pm Wed-Sun at other times) Coniston's museum explores the village's history, touching on copper mining, Arthur Ransome and the Campbell story. There's also an extensive section on John Ruskin, with displays of his writings, watercolours and sketchbooks.

The new Bluebird Wing currently houses the recovered engine from Donald Campbell's *Bluebird K7* boat, but it's eventually hoped that the whole boat will be displayed here when (and if) it's finally restored.

Coniston Water LAKE
Coniston's gleaming 5-mile lake – the third largest in the Lake District after Windermere and Ullswater – is a half-mile walk from town along Lake Rd.

Along with its connections to the Campbells, the lake is famous for inspiring Arthur Ransome's classic children's tale *Swallows & Amazons*. Peel Island, towards the southern end of Coniston Water, supposedly provided the model for Wild Cat Island in the book. Both of Coniston's launch boats provide special cruises exploring Ransome's links with Coniston.

The best way to explore the lake is by paddling. Dinghies, row boats, canoes and kayaks can be hired from the **Coniston Boating Centre** (015394-41366; Coniston Jetty), or you can cheat and hire a motorboat instead.

Activities

Steam Yacht Gondola BOAT TOUR
(NT; 015394-63850; www.nationaltrust.org.uk/gondola; standard cruise adult/child £9.90/4.90) Built in 1859 and restored in the 1980s by the National Trust, this wonderful steam yacht looks like a cross between a Venetian *vaporetto* and an English houseboat, complete with cushioned saloons and polished wood seats. It's a stately way of seeing the lake, especially if you're visiting Brantwood, and it's even ecofriendly: since 2008 it's been powered by waste wood.

There are five trips daily from mid March to October. Longer 'Explorer' cruises covering Ransome, the Campbells and Ruskin run at 2pm on Mondays and Thursdays (adult/child £19.90/9.90). There's also a 'Wild Cat Island' cruise on Mondays at 2pm (£19.90/9.90). There's a 10% discount for online bookings.

Coniston Launch BOAT TOUR
(015394-36216; www.conistonlaunch.co.uk; Northern service adult/child return £9.50/4.95,

Southern service adult/child return £14.50/7.25) A more contemporary way to get around the lake is aboard Coniston's two modern launches, which have been solar-powered since 2005.

There are two routes: the 45-minute **Northern service** calls at the Waterhead Hotel, Torver and Brantwood, while the 105-minute **Southern service** sails to the jetties at Torver, Water Park, Lake Bank, Sunny Bank and Brantwood via Peel Island. You can break your journey and walk to the next jetty. There are between five and nine daily trips depending on the time of year.

As with the gondola, there are commentated cruises focussing on the Campbell story (adult/child £12/6; 4.40pm Tuesday) and *Swallows & Amazons* (£12.90/6.45; 4.40pm Wednesday). These cruises usually run from May to September depending on demand.

Sleeping

Yew Tree Farm B&B ££
(☎015394-41433; www.yewtree-farm.com; d £90-124; P) This delightful farmhouse a couple of miles from Coniston has real star quality – it was owned by Beatrix Potter and doubled as Hill Top in the Renée Zellwegger biopic *Miss Potter*. It's still a working farm, but offers three rustic-chic rooms: Wetherlam and Tarn Hows feature antique furniture and four-posters, while little Holme Fell has valley views.

Bank Ground Farm B&B ££
(☎015394-41264; www.bankground.com; East of the Lake; d from £90 wiith 2-night minimum; P) This lakeside farmhouse has literary cachet: Arthur Ransome used it as the model for Holly Howe Farm in *Swallows & Amazons*. Parts of the house date back to the 15th century, so the rooms are snug. Some have sleigh beds, others with exposed beams. The **tearoom** is a beauty, too, and there are cottages for longer stays.

Lakeland House B&B ££
(☎015394-41303; www.lakelandhouse.co.uk; Tilberthwaite Ave; s £40-50, d £78-120) Perched above the village's internet cafe is this bare-bones, no-fuss B&B. Budget doubles border on the ultilitarian – a bed, tea-tray, and wardrobe is all you get – so it's worth stretching to Superior for space and comfort. The Lookout Suite has its own sitting room.

Crown Inn Coniston B&B ££
(☎015394-41243; www.crowninnconiston.com; Tilberthwaite Ave; d £70-90, f £120-140; P) Pleasant rooms in magnolia shades above this popular town-centre pub.

Coniston Holly How YHA HOSTEL £
(☎0845-371 9511; conistonhh@yha.org.uk; Far End; dm from £16; ⊙reception 7.30-10am & 5-10pm) Another fine period house offering the usual YHA standards: decent dorms, well-equipped kitchens, organised walks, in-house cafe. It's a favourite with groups, so book ahead.

Coppermines YHA HOSTEL £
(☎0845-371 9630; coppermines@yha.org.uk; dm from £16; ⊙reception 7-11am & 5-10pm, open Easter-Oct) This high-altitude hostel is set among the old copper-workings, along a rough unsealed road 1.2 miles from Coniston. Facilities are surprisingly good considering the location, and include kitchen, showers, a licensed bar and a guests' lounge. It's ideal if you want to get an early start on the Old Man.

CONQUERING THE OLD MAN

There's one summit every visitor wants to reach, and that's the one belonging to the **Old Man of Coniston** (803m). This slate-capped giant dominates the skyline to the west of Coniston, except when the Lakeland weather rolls in and he disappears behind a mantle of mist and cloud.

As always, there are various ways to reach the summit. The standard trail climbs the mountain's east side, winding sharply upwards via abandoned copper-mines, slate staircases and rocky paths to the top. A better (but longer) route swings west over the peaks of Brown Pike, Buck Pike and Dow Crag before ascending the Old Man's western flank.

Count on around 5 miles return for the first route, 8 miles for the one via Dow Crag. Either way, the views are stellar: if the weather's really clear, you can see all the way to the Cumbrian Coast.

The tourist office has leaflets detailing both routes. As usual, wear proper footwear, and take plenty of food and water along for the climb, as well as the all-essential map.

DON'T MISS

THE DRUNKEN DUCK

Inns are ten-a-penny in the Lakes, but few command the culinary cachet of the **Drunken Duck** (015394-36347; www.drunkenduckinn.co.uk; Barngates; mains £13-25, r £95-275; P). Run by the same family since the 1970s, it's established itself as one of the region's most renowned dining pubs. The inn's 400 years old, but the interior has been tastefully modernised, with vintage signs, hunting prints and a smart slate bar. The menu is seriously classy – whole-roasted duck, lamb rump with champ potatoes, beetroot tarte tatin – and ales come straight from the Barngates Brewery behind the pub. Stylish rooms upstairs feature spoils such as DAB radios and rolltop baths. It's very popular – you'll need to book well ahead for dinner, although lunch is served on a first-come, first-served basis.

It's a bit tricky to find: follow the B5286 from Hawkshead towards Ambleside, and look out for the brown signs.

Hoathwaite Campsite CAMPSITE £
(NT; bookings 015394-63862; www.ntlakescampsites.org.uk; sites from £6 for 1 adult, tent & car; Easter-Nov) This simple National Trust-owned campsite is on the A5394 between Coniston and Torver. It's basic – there's a toilet block, mains water taps and not much else – but the views over Coniston Water are super.

Eating & Drinking

Sun Hotel PUB ££
(www.thesunconiston.com; mains £12-20) Dine under solid rafters or in a fell-view conservatory at the Sun, perched on a hill just behind the village, and famously used as an HQ by Donald Campbell during his final fateful campaign.

Harry's CAFE £
(4 Yewdale Rd; mains £6-14) Part wine bar, part cafe, part bistro – serving steaks, pizzas, pastas and club sandwiches, along with the prodigious Harry's Big Breakfast.

Bluebird Cafe CAFE £
(Lake Rd; mains £4-8; breakfast & lunch) This lakeside cafe does a brisk trade from people waiting for the Coniston launches. The usual salads and sandwiches are on offer, and there are lots of outside tables.

Black Bull PUB
(www.conistonbrewery.com/black-bull-coniston.htm; Yewdale Rd) Coniston's main meeting spot, the old Black Bull offers a warren of rooms and a popular outside terrace. The grub's good, but it's mainly known for its home-brewed ales: Bluebird Bitter and Old Man Ale are always on tap, and there are seasonal ones too.

Information

Coniston Tourist Office (015394-41533; www.conistontic.org; Ruskin Ave; 9.30am-5.30pm Easter-Oct, till 4pm Nov-Easter) Sells the Coniston Loyalty Card (£3) offering local discounts.

Hollands Cafe (Tilberthwaite Ave; per hr £5; 9am-5pm)

Getting There & Away

Bus 505 runs from Windermere (eight daily Monday to Saturday, six on Sunday), via Ambleside, with a couple of daily connections to Kendal (1¼ hours).

The Langdale Valleys

A few miles northwest of Coniston and west of Ambleside, civilisation peters out and barren hilltops loom on every horizon. West of the small tarn of Elterwater is **Great Langdale**, one of the national park's most iconic valleys, while to the north, the neighbouring valley of **Little Langdale** leads over the formidably steep passes of Wrynose and Hardknott into Eskdale and the Cumbrian Coast.

Getting There & Away

Bus 516 (the Langdale Rambler, six daily, five on Sunday) is the only bus, with stops at Ambleside, Skelwith Bridge, Elterwater, and the Old Dungeon Ghyll Hotel in Great Langdale.

ELTERWATER

Ringed by trees and fields, the small, charming lake of Elterwater derives its name from the Old Norse for 'swan', after the colonies of whooper swans that winter here. With its maple-shaded village green, it's a popular base for exploring the Langdale fells.

The village has two excellent pubs: the old-fashioned **Britannia Inn** (☎015394-37210; www.britinn.net; d £90-125, mains £13.50-17.50), which does a mean Sunday roast and hosts its own annual beer festival, and the extremely smart **Eltermere Inn** (☎015394-37207; www.eltermere.co.uk; r £125-225, mains £14-19.50), which offers classy gastropub food and country-house style rooms.

There are also two hostels nearby: the **Elterwater YHA** (☎0845-371 9017; elterwater@yha.org.uk; dm £14; ⏲reception 7.30am-10am & 5-10.30pm Easter-Oct; @), in a low-ceilinged farmhouse near the village green, and the larger **Langdale YHA** (☎0845-371 9748; langdale@yha.org.uk; High Close, Loughrigg; dm £14; ⏲reception 7.30-10am & 5-11pm Mar-Oct; P@), in a Victorian house on the road towards Grasmere.

GREAT LANGDALE

Hemmed in by hills, this is one of the Lake District's classic hiking valleys. It's surrounded by high fells including the spiky **Langdale Pikes**: Pike O'Stickle (709m), Loft Crag (682m), Harrison Stickle (736m) and Pavey Ark (700m), collectively one of the national park's most rewarding day hikes.

If you don't fancy taking on the whole thing, you could just walk up to the impressive waterfall of **Dungeon Ghyll** instead.

Sleeping & Eating

TOP CHOICE **Old Dungeon Ghyll** HOTEL ££
(☎015394-37272; www.odg.co.uk; d from £106, half-board £156; P) A historic gem awash with Lakeland heritage. Countless famous walkers have stayed here, including Prince Charles and Chris Bonington. It's endearingly olde-worlde, with well-worn furniture and furnishings, plus views from every window. The beamed Hiker's Bar is a must for a post-hike pint.

New Dungeon Ghyll INN, HOTEL ££
(☎015394-37213; www.dungeon-ghyll.co.uk; d £104-128; P) Rooms at the valley's second inn-hotel tend towards the chintzy, but it makes a useful fallback if the ODG is full.

Great Langdale Campsite CAMPSITE £
(NT; ☎015394-63862; www.ntlakescampsites.org.uk; tent sites £8.25-12.50, extra adult £5.50, pods £30-50; ⏲arrivals 3-7pm Sat-Thu, 3-9pm Fri; P) Quite possibly the most spectacularly positioned campsite in the Lake District, spread out over grassy meadows overlooked by Langdale's fells. Onsite facitilies include a laundry and shop, but the site gets crowded in season. Most of the sites (around three quarters) are pre-bookable; the remainder are first-come, first-served. Camping pods and yurts can be hired.

Stickle Barn PUB £
(☎015394-37356; mains £6-12) A walkers' fave, with a lively pub serving filling food such as curries, chillies and hotpots.

LITTLE LANGDALE

Separated from Great Langdale by Lingmoor Fell (459m), the valley of Little Langdale is on the road to Wrynose Pass. There are many little-known walks nearby, including to the windswept lake of **Blea Tarn**. At the head of the valley is the **Three Shire Stone**, marking the traditional meeting point of Cumberland, Westmoreland and Lancashire.

En route towards the pass is the **Three Shires Inn** (☎015394-37215; www.threeshiresinn.co.uk; mains £11.95-18.95, r £88-120; P), a cosy inn serving good grub and beer.

Eskdale

Strap yourself in – the road west from Little Langdale into the Eskdale Valley is a roller coaster, snaking and twisting across empty hills all the way to the Cumbrian coast.

En route, the road traverses two of the country's steepest stretches of tarmac – **Wrynose Pass** (with a gradient of 1 in 4) and **Hardknott Pass** (1 in 3). Passing places are few and far between, so it's definitely not for nervous drivers, and it's probably worth avoiding altogether on summer weekends, when the road becomes one long traffic snarl-up.

On the way down into Eskdale Valley, look out for the remains of **Hardknott Roman Fort**, which guarded the old pack route from the Roman harbour at Ravenglass. You can still just about make out the foundations of the commandant's house, watchtowers and parade ground.

Three miles further down the valley is the hamlet of **Boot**, which hosts a hearty beer festival every June, and **Dalegarth**, the eastern terminus of the Ravenglass & Eskdale Railway (p713).

Sleeping & Eating

Stanley House B&B ££
(☎019467-23327; www.stanleyghyll-eskdale.co.uk; Eskdale; s £64, d £100-120, f £140-160; P📶🐾) This turn-of-the-century house is halfway down the Eskdale valley, near Beckfoot station. It's a real home-from-home; guests are given the run of the place, with cosy lounges, rhododendron-filled gardens and an 'open larder' stocked with help-yourself beans, bread and spaghetti hoops. First-floor rooms are dog-friendly, and the house's hot water and heating comes from an ecofriendly biomass boiler.

Eskdale YHA HOSTEL £
(☎0845-371 9317; eskdale@yha.org.uk; Boot; dm from £16; ⏰reception 7.30-10am & 5-10.30pm Easter-Oct) Clad in stone and commanding a panoramic view, this hostel is ideal for hikers and passengers on La'al Ratty. Dorms are small, but there's a nice communal lounge and generous daily dinners (£9.95 for two courses, £11.95 for three courses).

Woolpack Inn PUB ££
(☎019467-23230; www.woolpack.co.uk; Boot; 2-/3-course menu £20/27; P) Recently taken over by new owners, this old Eskdale inn has been given the full gastropub makeover. Half the pub is now taken up by a contemporary cafe, and there's a small shop where you can get Cumbrian goodies and craftwork. Best of all, the front garden has great views of the Eskdale hills. **Rooms** (s £50-80, d £60-80) are plain, but decent value.

Boot Inn PUB ££
(☎019467-23224; www.bootinn.co.uk; Boot; mains £10-18; P) As the venue for the annual Boot Beer Festival, this whitewashed pub still has one main priority: ale, and plenty of it. There's a comprehensive choice, with a regularly changing line-up of guest brews on tap. The food is basic pub grub, but it's filling enough after a day on the fells.

Wasdale

Carving its way for 5 miles from the Cumbrian coast, the craggy, windlashed valley of Wasdale is where the Lake District scenery takes a turn on the wild side. Ground out by a long-extinct glacier, it's home to the Lake District's highest and wildest peaks, including the slate-capped summits of Scafell Pike, Great Gable and Yewbarrow, as well as the steely grey expanse of Wastwater, England's deepest and coldest lake. Wasdale's plentiful fells also makes it an irresistible draw for hikers, especially those who are planning to tackle the slog to the top of England's tallest mountain.

Windswept, rain-lashed and frequently cloaked in mist, this remote valley is a real eye-opener, so it's little wonder that it's frequently been voted one of the nation's favourite views. It's also home to one of England's tiniest chapels, the 16th-century **St Olaf's Church** (a local legend claims the roof-beams were salvaged from a Viking longboat).

The **Barn Door Shop** (☎019467-26384; www.wasdaleweb.com), next door to the Wasdale Head Inn, sells camping and walking supplies.

Sleeping & Eating

TOP CHOICE **Wasdale Head Inn** B&B, PUB ££
(☎019467-26229; www.wasdale.com; s £59, d £118-130, tr £177, mains £9.95-16.95; P) If you're looking for the quintessential Lakeland inn,

CLIMBING THE ROOF OF ENGLAND

In Scotland it's Ben Nevis (1344m/4409ft), in Wales it's Snowdon (1085m/3560ft), and in England it's **Scafell Pike** (978m/3210ft), collectively they're the three highest peaks in mainland Britain. This trio of summits represents the ultimate goal for peak-baggers, especially those attempting the Three Peaks Challenge, in which all three mountains are conquered in 24 hours.

The classic route to the top of Scafell Pike starts from Wasdale Head and is well within the reach of most walkers, although it's long, steep and hard to navigate in bad weather. You're looking at around six to seven hours out on the mountain, and you'll need to be properly equipped with wet-weather gear, rucksack, map, compass, food and water, and decent hiking boots.

A favourable weather forecast won't go amiss either – it'd be a bit of a shame to make all that effort and not be able to enjoy the views.

WORTH A TRIP

ENNERDALE

Crowds can be a constant headache in the Lakes, but there are some corners of the national park which remain people-free.

The remote valley and lake of **Ennerdale** just to the north of Wasdale are slowly being returned to nature as part of the innovative Wild Ennerdale project (www.wildennerdale.co.uk). All signs of artifice are slowly being removed, and 1930s conifer plantations are gradually being replaced with native broadleaf species to encourage local wildlife.

Needless to say, the valley is paradise if you prefer your trails quiet, and is also home to one of the Lake District's most isolated hostels, the **Black Sail YHA** (☎0845 371 9680; www.yha.org.uk/hostel/black-sail; dm £19.40), housed in a shepherd's bothy halfway between Ennerdale and Buttermere.

look no longer; the Wasdale Head is the real McCoy, a 19th-century hostelry full of period furniture, sepia-tinted photos and hillwalking heritage galore. Dog-eared photos and climbing memorabilia are dotted around the inn, and the upstairs rooms are full of times-past charm. Hearty dinners are served up in the restaurant, and the slate-floored bar is packed with hikers drinking pints of home-brewed Wasd'ale and Great Gable. Don't forget to check out the guests' books before you leave: they have entries dating back to the early 1800s.

Wasdale Head Campsite CAMPSITE £
(NT; ☎bookings 015394-63862; www.ntlakescampsites.org.uk; sites £8.25-12.50, extra adult £5.50, camping pods £30-50; ⏰arrivals 8-11am & 5-8pm, open year-round) This National Trust campsite is in a fantastically wild spot, nestled beneath the Scafell range. Facilities are basic (laundry room, showers), but the views are out of this world.

Low Wood Hall HOTEL ££
(☎019467-26100; www.lowwoodhall.co.uk; Nether Wasdale; d £80-90; P) Prim, plush rooms in a country house in Nether Wasdale, a few miles drive from Wasdale Head. The six superior ones are in the main house and have the best views; the rest are in a lodge annexe. Dinner is available.

Wastwater YHA HOSTEL £
(☎0845-371 9350; wasdale@yha.org.uk; Wasdale Hall, Nether Wasdale; dm from £14; ⏰reception 8-10am & 5-10.30pm) This lakeside hostel on the shores of Wastwater has the kind of location you'd normally pay through the nose for. It's in a 19th-century mansion that still boasts most of its period architecture, including original roof trusses and latticed windows. There's a library full of books to browse, a restaurant serving Cumbrian nosh and ale, and some dorms have lake views.

Lingmell House B&B ££
(☎019467-26261; www.lingmellhouse.co.uk; Wasdale Head; s/d £35/70; P) Sparsely decorated rooms inside an isolated farmhouse near the Wasdale Head Inn.

Getting There & Away

The **Wasdale Taxibus** (☎019467-25308; £3) runs between Gosforth and Wasdale twice daily on Thursday, Saturday and Sunday, but you need to ring and book a seat the day before.

Cockermouth

POP 8225

Just beyond the northerly Lakeland fells, the Georgian town of Cockermouth was hitherto best known as the birthplace of William Wordsworth – but in November 2009 the town hit the national headlines after it was hit by devastating flash floods, causing millions of pounds of damage and forcing the evacuation of many residents.

The town centre has since been thoroughly spruced up, although look closely and you might still spot highwater marks on some of the buildings along Main St. Top things to do include a visit to Wordsworth's birthplace and a tour of the famous Jenning's brewery.

Sights

TOP CHOICE **Wordsworth House** HISTORIC BUILDING
(NT; ☎01900-824805; Main St; adult/child £6.15/3.10; ⏰11am-5pm Sat-Thu Mar-Oct) William Wordsworth was born on 7 April 1770 at this handsome Georgian house at the end of Main St. He spent most of his early life here with his four siblings, until he was packed off to boarding school at Hawkshead.

Built around 1745, the house had been painstakingly restored based on accounts from the Wordsworth archive. The decor is as close to original as possible, with authentic paints, period furniture and wallpapers; among the rooms on display are the drawing room, kitchen and several family bedrooms, including William's own. Costumed guides are on hand to help bring the house to life.

The kitchen garden (mentioned in Wordsworth's autobiographical poem *The Prelude*) was badly damaged during the floods, but has since been carefully replanted.

Jenning's Brewery BREWERY

(☎01900-821011; www.jenningsbrewery.co.uk; adult/child £8/4; ⊙guided tours 11am & 2pm Mon-Sat Apr-Oct, extra tours during July & August) The town's historic brewer has been in business since 1874 (bar a brief interruption during the 2009 floods). Guided tours include a visit to see the main brewing vats and include a tasting session in the Old Cooperage Bar. Take your pick from golden Cocker Hoop, classic Bitter and the strong, dark, superbly named Sneck Lifter.

Sleeping

Old Homestead B&B ££

(☎01900-822223; www.byresteads.co.uk; Byresteads Farm; s £60, d £80-100; P) A sweet farm conversion 2 miles west of Cockermouth, with a stone exterior concealing lavish rooms gleaming with wood floors, restored rafters, leather sofas and rendered walls. The Cruck Rooms and Master's Loft have the most space and luxury.

Six Castlegate B&B ££

(☎01900-826749; www.sixcastlegate.co.uk; 6 Castlegate; s £42, d £65-75; 📶) A Grade II-listed town house combining Georgian heritage with a modern twist. Feathery pillows, lofty ceilings and shiny showers make this one of Cockermouth's most attractive B&Bs.

Croft House B&B ££

(☎01900-827533; www.croftguesthouse.com; 6/8 Challoner St; s £45, d £60-80) Gutted by the floods but now fully restored, this swish lemon-yellow B&B is a real winner; rooms are delightfully finished with exposed stone, reclaimed maple-wood floors and just-so colour schemes.

Cockermouth YHA HOSTEL £

(☎0845-371 9313; cockermouth@yha.org.uk; Double Mills; dm from £14; ⊙reception 7.30-10am & 5-10pm Apr-Oct) A simple hostel in a converted 17th-century watermill, about half a mile from town. Camping space and cycle storage are available.

Eating & Drinking

Quince & Medlar VEGETARIAN ££

(www.quinceandmedlar.co.uk; 13 Castlegate; mains £12-16; ⊙dinner Tue-Sat; 🖉) Imaginative veggie food served in the refined surrounds of one of Castlegate's Georgian houses. Dishes are rich and filling – think spinach and Wensleydale gateau, or caramelised red onion in a polenta nest.

Bitter End PUB

(☎01900-828993; www.bitterend.co.uk; 15 Kirkgate; mains £9.50-12.55; ⊙lunch & dinner) This brewpub produces award-winning beers such as Cockermouth Pride, Lakeland Honey Beer and Cuddy Lugs. You can watch the vats at work through a glass partition in the main bar, which still feels like a traditional pub should with its booth seats and monochrome photos. The food's not at all bad, either.

Merienda CAFE £

(7a Station St; mains £4-8; ⊙breakfast & lunch) The town's best bet for lunch, this is a bright cafe that serves fresh soups and open-face sandwiches.

Information

There's an online guide to Cockermouth (www.cockermouth.org.uk).

Tourist Office (☎01900-822634; cockermouthtic@co-net.com; ⊙10am-4pm Mon-Fri, 10am-2pm Sat, closed for lunch 12.30-1pm) Inside the town hall.

Getting There & Away

The X5 (half-hourly Monday to Saturday, six on Sunday) travels from Workington via Cockermouth, and continues to Keswick (35 minutes) and Penrith (1¼ hours).

Keswick

POP 5257

The sturdy slate town of Keswick is nestled alongside one of the region's most idyllic lakes, Derwentwater, a silvery curve studded with wooded islands and criss-crossed by puttering cruise boats. Keswick makes a less frantic Lakeland base than Ambleside or Windermere, but there's plenty around town to keep you occupied.

Keswick

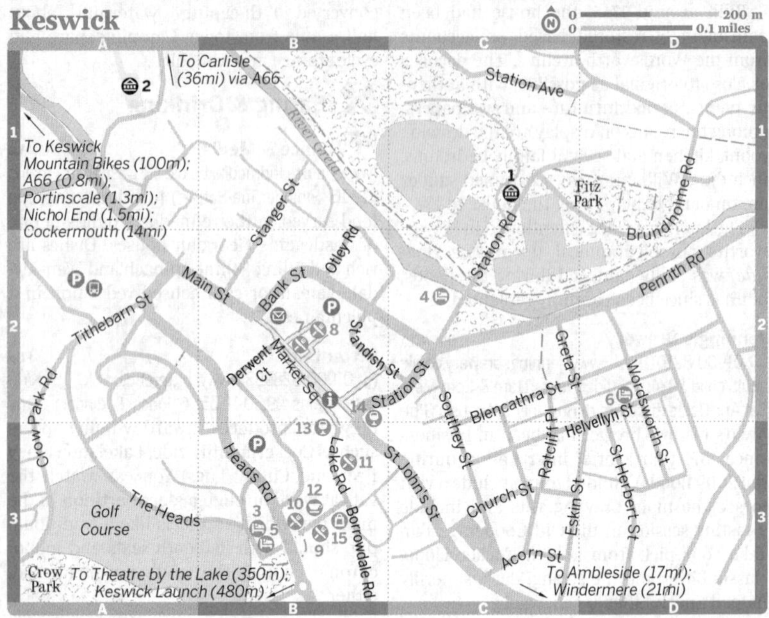

Sights

The heart of Keswick is the old Market Pl at the old **Moot Hall** (now occupied by the tourist office).

Keswick's quirky **town museum** (017687-73263; www.keswickmuseum.webs.com; Station Rd) closed in mid-2012 for a £2m refurbishment, and is expected to reopen late in 2013.

Keswick Launch BOAT TOUR
(017687-72263; www.keswick-launch.co.uk; round-the-lake ticket adult/child £9.25/4.50) Derwentwater is undoubtedly one of the Lake District's most attractive lakes, and remained a lifelong favourite of Beatrix Potter. The lake jetties are a short stroll south of town, next to the fields of Crow Park. Boats putter out to landing stages at Ashness Gate, Lodore Falls, High Brandlehow, Low Brandlehow, Hawse End, Nichol End. Departures run clockwise and anticlockwise; you can get off and walk to the next stage if you wish. Single fares to each jetty are also available

There are six daily boats from March to November, with a couple of extra afternoon sailings and a twilight cruise in summer. There are only two sailings a day in winter.

Rowboats (£12 per hour) and motorboats (£27 per hour) can be hired next to the launch jetties.

FREE **Castlerigg Stone Circle** MONUMENT
Set on a hilltop a mile east of town, this jaw-dropping stone circle consists of 48 stones between 3000 and 4000 years old, surrounded by a dramatic ring of mountain peaks.

Pencil Museum MUSEUM
(www.pencilmuseum.co.uk; Southy Works; adult/child £4/3; 9.30am-5pm) In the mid 17th-century, graphite was discovered in the Borrowdale fells, and Keswick became a centre for of pencil production. The old Cumberland Pencil Factory now houses this rather odd pencil-themed museum, whose exhibits include the world's longest pencil (measuring 8m end to end) and a replica of a Borrowdale slate mine. You can buy luxury Derwent colouring pencils in the shop.

Activities

Fell Walks HIKING
Keswick has a wealth of local walks. The most popular is the family friendly fell of **Catbells** (451m), on the lake's west side; the

Keswick

Sights

1 Keswick Museum C1
2 Pencil Museum A1

Sleeping

3 Howe Keld B3
4 Keswick YHA C2
5 Lakeside House B3
6 Oakthwaite House D2

Eating

Abraham's Tea Rooms .... (see 15)
7 Bryson's B2
8 Lakeland Pedlar Wholefood Cafe B2
9 Mayson's B3
10 Morrel's B3
11 Pumpkin B3

Drinking

12 Cafe-Bar 26 .... B3
13 Dog & Gun B3
14 George Hotel B2

Shopping

15 George Fisher B3

trailhead starts next to the jetty at Hawse End, served by the Keswick Launch.

Hardcore hikers will prefer the more challenging slog up **Skiddaw** (931m), the huge mountain that looms on Keswick's northern skyline. To the north east of town near Threlkeld, **Blencathra** (868m) is an equally challenging proposition.

Whinlatter Forest Park FOREST
(www.forestry.gov.uk/whinlatterforestpark) Encompassing 1200 hectares of pine, larch and spruce, Whinlatter is England's only true mountain forest, rising sharply to 790m about 5 miles from Keswick. The forest is a designated red squirrel reserve; you can check out live video feeds from squirrel cams at the visitor centre.

It's also home to two exciting mountain-bike trails and the **Go Ape** (www.goape.co.uk/days-out/whinlatter; adult/child £30/25; 9am-5pm mid-Mar–Oct) tree-top assault course. Bikes can be hired from **Cyclewise** (017687-78711; www.cyclewise.co.uk; 10am-5pm), next to the visitor centre, which also runs regular skills sessions and training courses.

Mountain bikes can be also hired from **Keswick Mountain Bikes** (017687-75202; www.keswickmountainbikes.co.uk; 133 Main St; adult bikes £15-40 per day; 9.30am-5.30pm). Their road-specific shop is above the Lakeland Pedlar Cafe in Keswick.

Bus 77 (four daily) runs to the visitor centre from Keswick. If you're driving, head towards Cockermouth on the A66 and look out for the brown signs near the turn-off at Braithwaite.

Festivals & Events

Keswick Mountain Festival OUTDOOR ACTIVITIES
(www.keswickmountainfestival.co.uk) This May festival celebrates all things mountainous.

Keswick Beer Festival BEER
(www.keswickbeerfestival.co.uk) Lots and lots of beer is drunk during Keswick's real ale fest in June.

Sleeping

TOP CHOICE **Howe Keld** B&B ££
(017687-72417; www.howekeld.co.uk; 5-7 The Heads; s £55-58, d £90-130;) This Gold standard B&B pulls out all the stops with goose-down duvets, slate-floored bathrooms, chic colours and furniture made by a local carpenter. The best rooms have views across Crow Park and the golf course, and the breakfast is a pick-and-mix delight: fresh smoothies, vegetarian rissoles, French pancakes and make-your-own muesli. Free parking is available on the Heads if there's space.

The Lookout B&B ££
(017687-80407; www.thelookoutkeswick.co.uk; Chestnut Hill; d £90-110;) It's out of town, but as the name suggests, you can glimpse Keswick's fells from every window at the Lookout. The house is modern with rooms to match: soothing coffee-and-cream colour schemes, blonde wood beds and minimalist Kudos glass showers. Take Penrith Rd west and turn right onto Chestnut Hill; the B&B is on the left.

Oakthwaite House B&B ££
(017687-72398; www.oakthwaite-keswick.co.uk; 35 Helvellyn St; d £66-80) One of the top choices in the B&B-heavy neighbourhood round Helvellyn Rt. There are just four rooms (so not too crowded), all with power showers, white linen and soothingly neutral tones.

Lakeside House B&B ££
(017687-72868; www.lakesidehouse.co.uk; 40 Lake Rd; d £135-140;) On the corner of Lake Rd, this Victorian house has a top location; the town centre and Derwentwater are

both just a couple of minutes away. It looks much fresher thanks to a recent revamp, but rooms are variable; try to get one with a bay window for park views.

Powe House B&B ££
(017687-73611; www.powehouse.com; Portinscale; s £60, d £80-4;) Pleasantly removed from the Keswick crush about a mile from town in Portinscale, this detached house has six great-value rooms: ask for No 3 or 5 if you're after space, or No 2 if you'd like a view of Skiddaw from bed.

Keswick YHA HOSTEL £
(0845-371 9746; keswick@yha.org.uk; Station Rd; dm £23.40; @) Keswick's YHA is a beauty, lodged inside a converted woollen mill by the clattering River Rothay, and renovated thanks to the benevolence of a generous doctor. Dorms are cosy, there's an excellent cafe and some rooms even have balconies over Fitz Park.

Eating

Morrel's BRITISH ££
(017687-72666; www.morrels.co.uk; Lake Rd; 3-course menu £19.95, mains £10.50-16; dinner Tue-Sun) This reliable restaurant is the address for bistro food in Keswick. The feel inside is suitably sleek and shiny, with tall windows, leather chairs, spotlights and wood floors, providing the perfect setting for plates of guinea fowl with celeriac puree or pork belly on black mash. There are two **self-catering apartments** (£400-700 per week) upstairs.

The Pheasant Inn PUB ££
(017687-72219; www.the-pheasant.co.uk; Bassenthwaite; mains £14-18) If you've got a car, you won't regret taking a spin along Bassenthwaite to find this hidden-away pub, which boasts one of Lakeland's most convincingly antique interiors. Hunting prints and pewter tankards cover the old bar, stocked with vintage whiskies and Lakeland ales, and the two restaurants serve great country food – as well as a fine afternoon tea, served in the proper fashion on tiered cake towers.

Mayson's INTERNATIONAL £
(017687-74104; 33 Lake Rd; dishes £7-10) Buffet-style dining, cheap prices and generous portions are the modus operandi at this no-fuss diner. Each of the counter-top woks has a different fusion theme (Thai, Chinese, Mexican etc); take your pick, buy a drink, and wait for it to be brought to your table.

Abraham's Tea Rooms CAFE £
(2 Borrowdale Rd; mains £6-10; 10am-5pm Mon-Sat, 10.30am-4.30pm Sun) Squeezed into an attic on the top floor of George Fishers, this old-timey cafe is great for a country lunch. Go for a hot rarebit (toasted-cheese-on-toast) or mackerel paté, and chase it down with a glass of fresh-made lemonade or a classic cream tea.

Lakeland Pedlar Wholefood Cafe CAFE £
(www.lakelandpedlar.co.uk; Hendersons Yard; mains £4-10; 9am-5pm) This emporium offering organic veggies and wholefoods has been going for donkey's years, but there's nowhere better in town if you fancy a chunky sandwich or a bowl of soup. There's a bike shop upstairs.

Bryson's CAFE £
(42 Main St; cakes £2-5) Keswick's renowned bakery is known for its fruit cakes, Battenburgs and chocolately florentines.

Pumpkin CAFE £
(19 Lake Rd; lunches £3-6; 8.30am-5pm Mon-Sat) Deli sandwiches are made to order at this streetside cafe, but it's the counter of cakes and pastries that'll catch your eye. There's seating upstairs or you can order to go – and the coffee's the best in Keswick.

Drinking

Dog & Gun PUB
(2 Lake Rd) Wooden benches, low ceilings, hearths – the old Dog is the picture of a Lakeland pub. You even get to drink with a conscience: for each pint of 'Thirst Rescue' ale you down, the pub makes a donation to the Keswick Mountain Rescue Team.

George Hotel PUB
(St John's St) Keswick's most venerable drinking hole, this well-worn pub is a locals' lair, and serves Jenning's ales and runs a popular quiz night on Tuesday.

Cafe-Bar 26 CAFE
(26 Lake Rd; tapas £4-10) An attractive corner wine-bar that also serves good plates of tapas.

Entertainment

Theatre by the Lake THEATRE
(www.theatrebythelake.com; Lakeside) Keswick's theatre shows new and classic dramas, as well as occasional live gigs and events.

THE BASSENTHWAITE OSPREYS

In 2001 the first wild **ospreys** to breed in England for 150 years set up home at Bassenthwaite Lake, near Keswick. These magnificent birds of prey (known elsewhere as fish eagles or sea hawks) were once widespread, but were driven to extinction by hunting, environmental damage and egg collectors.

Their return to Bassenthwaite is a source of enormous local pride. The birds usually arrive around April or May, spending the summer here before heading for Africa in late August or early September. If you want to see them, there are two official **viewpoints** (10am-5pm) in Dodd Wood on the lake's west side, about 3 miles north of Keswick on the A591. There's a large car park near the stately home of Mirehouse, or you can catch the 73/73A bus from Keswick.

If you have trouble spotting them, you can see an osprey display and live-video feeds from the birds' nests at the **Whinlatter Forest Park visitor centre** (☎01768-778469; ⌚10am-5pm).

For all the latest news, check out the informative website at www.ospreywatch.co.uk.

Shopping

George Fisher OUTDOOR EQUIPMENT

(2 Borrowdale Rd) There are countless outdoor shops dotted along the Main St, but none can match George Fisher for heritage. This three-floored store has been here for nigh on a century and stocks everything you could possibly need for a day on the hills – and the boot-fitting service is legendary.

Information

There is a Keswick online town guide (www.keswick.org).

Tourist Office (☎017687-72645; keswicktic@lake-district.gov.uk; Moot Hall, Market Pl; ⌚9.30am-5.30pm Apr-Oct, to 4.30pm Nov-Mar) Sells discounted tickets for the Keswick Launch.

Getting There & Away

There's a ticket called the Borrowdale Day Rider (adult/child £7/5), valid on buses 77/77A and 78 between Keswick and the Borrowdale Valley.

Buses from Keswick:

555/556 Lakeslink Hourly to Ambleside (40 minutes), Windermere (50 minutes) and Kendal (1½ hours).

X4/X5 Penrith to Workington via Keswick (hourly Monday to Friday, six on Sunday).

73 Caldbeck Rambler (two daily April to November, weekends only in winter) Stops at Mirehouse and Bassenthwaite Lake before continuing to Caldbeck.

77/77A Honister Rambler (four daily) Circular route from Keswick via Portinscale, Catbells, Grange, Seatoller, Honister Pass, Buttermere, Lorton and Whinlatter.

78 Borrowdale Rambler (hourly Monday to Saturday, seven on Sunday) The main Borrowdale bus, with stops at Lodore, Grange, Rosthwaite and Seatoller.

Borrowdale & Buttermere Valleys

These side-by-side valleys are many people's idea of the quintessential Lakeland landscape – an impossibly pretty patchwork of craggy hills, broad fields, tinkling streams, and winding drystone walls. Once a centre for mineral mining (especially for slate, coal and graphite), these days this is walkers' country, and apart from the odd rickety barn or puttering tractor, there's precious little to spoil the view.

BORROWDALE

Of the two valleys, Borrowdale is the gentler (and greener). The B5289 road runs south along the eastern shore of Derwentwater and meanders through a landscape of bottle-coloured meadows and tiny hamlets, including **Grange-in-Borrowdale**, **Rosthwaite** and **Seathwaite**. About 5 miles southwest of Keswick, the road reaches a cluster of whitewashed cottages at Seatoller and then snakes up and over the Honister Pass into Buttermere.

Sights

Watendlath Tarn LAKE

This National Trust–owned tarn is reached via a turn-off on the B5285 south of Keswick. On the way, the road passes over one of the Lake District's most photographed packhorse crossings at **Ashness Bridge**. Parking at the tarn is free for NT members, but the road is narrow and has few passing places, so it's more pleasant to walk up in summer.

Lodore Falls WATERFALL

At the southern end of Derwentwater, this famous waterfall featured in a poem by Robert Southey, but it's only worth visiting after a good spell of rain. It's in the grounds of the Lodore Hotel; there's an honesty box for donations.

Castle Crag HIKE

Once a slate mine, this scree-strewn hillock (985m) provides knockout views across Borrowdale. It's reached via a mainly level trail from Grange, but gets steep towards the end, and the heaps of slate on the hillside make the going slippery in the wet. There are several side junctions on the way; bring a map to avoid getting lost.

Bowder Stone NATURAL FEATURE

A mile or so south from Grange, a turn-off leads up to the geological curiosity known as the Bowder Stone, a 1870-ton lump of rock thought to have been left behind by a retreating glacier. A small stepladder leads up to the top of the rock.

Activities

Platty+ BOATING

(017687-76572; www.plattyplus.co.uk; kayaks & canoes £6-13 per hour) Based at the Lodore Boat Landings, this experienced company hires out kayaks, canoes and sailing dinghies, and also runs instruction courses.

Sleeping & Eating

TOP CHOICE **Langstrath Inn** B&B ££

(017687-77239; www.thelangstrath.com; Stonethwaite; d £100-128, mains from £11.30; P) Borrowdale's country hotels are expensive, so you'll be better off basing yourself at this deliciously out-of-the-way inn in Stonethwaite. The eight lovely rooms feature white walls, crimson throws and pleasant en suites, and the countryside views are to die for. Hearty food and beers from Hawkshead Brewery and Jenning's are served in the restaurant downstairs.

Seatoller House B&B ££

(017687-77218; www.seatollerhouse.co.uk; s/d £55/122; P) This tiny hideaway in Seatoller feels like a Beatrix Potter burrow. It's tucked beneath Honister Pass and all the rooms are named after animals: attic Osprey has skylight views, Rabbit is pleasantly pine-filled and Badger looks over the garden.

Yew Tree Farm B&B ££

(017687-77675; www.borrowdaleherdwick.co.uk; Rosthwaite; d £75; P) There are floral patterns galore at this sturdy Cumbrian farmhouse in rural Rosthwaite, with three rooms snuggled amongst cob walls and tiny windows. It's run by working sheep farmers, and you'll be able to spot Herdwicks in the nearby fields. Breakfast is huge, and the Flock-In tearoom serves a cracking sticky toffee pudding.

Scafell Hotel HOTEL £££

(017687-77208; www.scafell.co.uk; Rosthwaite; d £120-150, mains £8.95-15.95; P) Whitewashed and slate-roofed, this coaching inn has benefited from a recent refit, which has made its 23 rooms much more modern (LCD TVs, colourful fabrics, H2K bathstuffs). They're split between the main inn and a modern annexe. Good food and local beers are served at the Riverside Bar, an ever-popular haunt for weary walkers.

Hazel Bank HOTEL ££

(017687-77248; www.hazelbankhotel.co.uk; Rosthwaite; d incl dinner £160-198; P) A country hotel par excellence, this place is surrounded by acres of grounds and reached via its own humpback bridge. Minimal it isn't; expect drapes, swooshy curtains and canopied beds. Rates include a four-course dinner for two.

Derwentwater Hostel HOSTEL £

(017687-77246; www.derwentwater.org; Barrow House; dm £18.40-20.40, r from £60; P@) With its 7-hectare grounds and private waterfall, this listed 19th-century mansion makes a princely location for a hostel – which makes the YHA's decision to sell it all the more baffling. It's now independently run, and offers clean, basic dorms (most are four- to eight-bed, but there's one huge 22-bed). There's also a kitchen, a cafe and plenty of lounge space, but it's the aristocratic architecture that makes it.

Borrowdale YHA HOSTEL £

(0845-371 9624; borrowdale@yha.org.uk; Longthwaite; dm from £16; Feb-Dec) Purpose-built chalet hostel, specialising in walking and activity trips.

Getting There & Away

The regular 78 bus (Borrowdale Rambler, at least hourly Monday to Saturday, seven on Sunday) travels from Keswick and stops at all of Borrowdale's villages. The Borrowdale Day Rider ticket (adult £7, child £5) is valid on buses 77/77A and 78 between Keswick and the Borrowdale Valley.

HONISTER PASS

Perched high on a rocky saddle between Borrowdale and Buttermere, the windswept **Honister Pass** has been one of the Lake District's most productive areas for slate quarrying since the 1700s. Much of the grey-green slate that features so prominently in many of local buildings comes from here, but the **Honister Slate Mine** (☎017687-77230; www.honister-slate-mine.co.uk; mine tour adult/child £9.95/4.95, via ferrata £20/15, all-day pass £34/25; ⏲tours 10.30am, 12.30pm & 3.30pm Mar-Oct) has now been transformed into an award-winning visitor attraction, thanks almost entirely to the vision and dedication of one man, local entrepreneur Mark Weir (who was sadly killed in a helicopter accident in 2011).

Among the activities are the chance to take an unforgettable guided tour into one of the site's three **slate mines**. Tours of the Kimberley and Honister Mines run at least three times daily, but you'll need to book ahead if you want to visit the working Cathedral Mine, which is still being used to extract slate. Tours (£19.75) run on Friday evenings, but only if there are sufficient numbers.

Honister is also the location of the UK's first **Via Ferrata**, a system of fixed ropes and iron ladders which enables you to traverse sheer cliffs with no climbing experience. Plans to install a zip-line from the top of nearby Fleetwith Pike have been scuppered due to local opposition, but planning permission has recently been granted to upgrade the site's Via Ferrata routes – check the website to see which routes are open.

You can also buy handmade signs, placemats, flagstones and other slate souvenirs in the onsite shop, or just 'fill ya boot' with as much slate as your car can carry for a flat-rate £20 – but remember to make sure your brakes are in good working order before you set off down the pass!

Car parking at the mine is free for visitors, otherwise it's £5 per day.

BUTTERMERE

From the high point of Honister, the road drops sharply into the deep bowl of Buttermere, which feels much starker and wilder than nearby Borrowdale. It's a textbook glacial valley, with sharp arêtes and sheer, U-shaped walls carved out by ice floes over the course of thousands of years. The melting glacier also created the valley's twin lakes (Buttermere and Crummock Water) and left behind lofty fells which provide an irresistible attraction for fellwalkers.

The circuit along the tops of Red Pike (755m), High Stile (807m), High Crag (744m) and Haystacks (597m) was one of Alfred Wainwright's favourite hikes; in fact, he liked it so much he decided to stay here for good, and asked for his ashes to be scattered over the top of Haystacks following his death in 1991.

Sleeping & Eating

Bridge Hotel HOTEL £££
(☎017687-70252; www.bridge-hotel.com; r £130-150; P) Unashamedly frilly rooms and an antique ambience define the old Bridge. As the name suggests, it's right beside Buttermere's village bridge. There's standard pub food in the bar, or more upmarket fare in the smart-casual restaurant. Half-board is good value.

Buttermere YHA HOSTEL £
(☎0845-371 9508; buttermere@yha.org.uk; dm from £16; ⏲reception 8.30-10am & 5-10.30pm) Another excellent Lakeland YHA, with a lake-view location halfway between Honiston and Buttermere village. Front dorms have an amazing outlook, and the restaurant-bar is a beauty.

TOP CHOICE **Kirkstile Inn** PUB, INN ££
(☎01900-85219; www.kirkstile Inn; mains £12-16, s £61.50-90, d £93-107) A finer country pub you simply could not hope to find. Hidden away on a lane near the little lake of Loweswater, a mile or so north of Buttermere, the Kirkstile is a joy, crackling fires, oak beams, worn carpets, wooden bar and all. It's known right across the Lakes for its high-quality food and award-winning ales. Rooms are quaint; some have views across Lorton Vale.

Fish Inn PUB ££
(☎017687-70253; www.fishinnbuttermere.co.uk; mains £8-14; P) This whitewashed inn once employed the 18th-century beauty known as the 'Maid of Buttermere', but these days it's just a welcoming local's pub, serving basic staples such as lasagne and battered haddock, washed down with ales from several local breweries.

Getting There & Away

North of Crummock Water, the B5289 winds past the little lake of Loweswater into the valley of Lorton, before looping over Whinlatter Pass. A second minor road from Buttermere village cuts east across the fells to Keswick, travelling via the little-visited Newlands Valley.

TOP 5 LAKE DISTRICT CAMPSITES

With its unspoilt countryside, majestic scenery and (with a bit of luck) starry skies, the Lake District makes a wonderful place to experience a night under canvas.

In addition to the four great campsites run by the National Trust (near Ambleside, Great Langdale, Wasdale and Coniston), There are five more favourites:

The Quiet Site (01768-727016; www.thequietsite.co.uk; sites £15-30, pods £35-50; year-round;) Spacious site spread across the fells above Ullswater, which has won awards for its ecofriendliness.

Syke Farm (01768-770222; sites adult/child £7/3.50; Easter-Oct) Back-to-basics camping beside the river in Buttermere. Fresh milk and homemade ice cream are available from the farm shop.

Bowkerstead Farm (01229-860208; www.grizedale-camping.co.uk; Satterthwaite; adult/child £7/3, camping pods £30 per night, yurts £50-60 per night Mon-Fri, £60-70 per night Sat-Sun) Pitch beside the trees of Grizedale Forest, either in your own tent, a luxury yurt or a timber eco-pod.

Seatoller Farm (017687-77232; www.seatollerfarm.co.uk; £6/3; Easter-Oct) A tucked-away site on a 500 year-old farm near Seatoller in Borrowdale, with a choice of either riverside or woodland pitches.

Fisherground Farm (019467-23349; www.fishergroundcampsite.co.uk; adult/child £6/3, cars £2.50; Mar-Oct) Family friendly camping in idyllic Eskdale.

The valley is served by the 77/77A bus (four times daily), which runs on a circular route from Keswick via Honister, Buttermere, Lorton and Whinlatter Pass.

Ullswater & Around

Second only in stature to Windermere, Ullswater cuts a silvery 7.5 mile slash through a dramatic panorama of fells, most notably the razor ridge of **Helvellyn** (950m), Cumbria's third-highest mountain.

Historic steamers have been puttering around the lake since the mid-19th century, and there are woods and gardens to explore nearby – including the daffodil-filled grounds which inspired one of Wordsworth's most famous poems.

There are three small hamlets dotted along Ullswater's west side (Pooley Bridge, Glenridding and Patterdale). Most of the pubs, hotels and B&Bs, as well as the main tourist office, are in Glenridding.

Sights

Gowbarrow Park & Aira Force PARK, WATERFALL

(NT) This rolling park stretches out across the lakeshore halfway between Pooley Bridge and Glenridding. Well-marked paths lead up to the impressive waterfall of **Aira Force**, a 66ft casacde that tumbles down a wooded ravine. Another waterfall, **High Force**, can be seen further up the hillside. Apart from the charge for the car park, the park is free to visit.

A little south of Gowbarrow Park is the inlet of **Glencoyne Bay**, where the prodigious springtime displays of daffodils inspired Wordsworth to pen the immortal lines: 'I wandered lonely as a cloud/That floats on high over hills and dales/When all at once I saw a crowd/A host, of golden daffodils...'

February and March are usually the best months to visit, but note that picking flowers is strictly prohibited.

Activities

Ullswater 'Steamers' CRUISE

(017684-82229; www.ullswater-steamers.co.uk; round-the-lake ticket adult/child £12.70/6.35) Ullswater's historic steamer service has been running since 1855. There are now four boats, all dressed in the company's distinctive livery; the stately *Lady of the Lake* was launched in 1888, making it the oldest passenger boat still working in the world.

The boats run east–west from Pooley Bridge, stopping at the titchy village of Howtown on the southern shore en route to Glenridding. There's a round-the-lake ticket (adult £12.70, child £6.35), or you can buy single fares in each direction.

There are up to 11 sailings a day in summer, dropping to four in winter.

Helvellyn WALKING

Along with Scafell Pike, this challenging hike is the one everyone wants to do. The classic ascent takes in the twin ridges of Striding and Swirral Edge, which are spectacular but very exposed, and involve some scrambling with dizzyingly steep drops on either side – if you're at all nervous of heights, Helvellyn in probably not the fell for you.

The usual routes climb up through Glenridding or Patterdale. As usual, check the weather forecast and take all the necessary supplies.

Glenridding Sailing Centre BOATING

(☎017684-82541; www.glenriddingsailingcentre.co.uk) The lake's main sailing centre hires out canoes (£15/40 for 1/3 hours, £65 for full-day), kayaks (£10/25 for 1/3 hours) and a range of sailboats and dinghies (£70 to £110 per day).

Rookin House ACTIVITY CENTRE

(☎017684-83561; www.rookinhouse.co.uk) This excellent outdoors centre offers unusual activities such as archery, clay-pigeon shooting, climbing, horse riding and off-road driving. You can even turn yourself into a human bowling ball.

The centre is 3 miles north of Ullswater on the A5091.

Sleeping

Lowthwaite Farm B&B ££

(☎017684-82343; www.lowthwaiteullswater.com; Matterdale; d £80-86, 2-night minimum at weekends) Lost in the hills around Matterdale, a couple of miles from the lake, this sweet farmhouse is run by a pair of globe-trotters who have filled the place with souvenirs collected on their journeys. Rooms are all different; Blencathra is the best, split over two levels in an old tractor shed. Ring ahead for directions, as it's tricky to find.

Waternook B&B ££

(☎017684-86839; www.waternookonullswater.com; nr Howtown; d £90-110) If you really feel like getting away from it all, this is the spot: a fantastically remote house on Ullswater's isolated southern side. The four rooms all have White Company linen, duck-down pillows and stonking lake views, but they're quite small; deluxe 'Fusedale' has space to spare. You can even borrow binoculars to spot local wildlife.

Cherry Holme B&B ££

(☎017684-82512; www.cherryholme.co.uk; Glenridding; s £90-130, d £120-160; P 📶) There are plenty of luxury extras at this roomy house, including a Nordic-style sauna that makes a perfect place to soothe those bones post-Helvellyn – although the fairly standard rooms are underwhelming considering the price.

Old Water View B&B ££

(☎017684-82175; www.oldwaterview.co.uk; Patterdale; d £84) Simple B&B with rooms to cover all needs; split-level 'Bothy' is ideal for families with attic beds for the kids, 'Little Gem' overlooks a stream and 'Place Fell' is said to have been a favourite of Alfred Wainwright.

Inn on the Lake HOTEL £££

(☎017684-82444; http://lakedistricthotels.net/innonthelake; Patterdale; d £170-274; P @) This enormous Patterdale hotel has tons of rooms, but it feels corporate rather than charming. Still, rooms have magnificent mountain or lake views, and facilities include tennis courts, sauna and gym.

Patterdale YHA HOSTEL £

(☎0845-371 9337; patterdale@yha.org.uk; Patterdale; dm £18.40; ⏲reception 7.30-10am & 5-10.30pm Easter-Oct) This purpose-built hostel lacks the heritage of some Lakeland hostels and has a definite whiff of the 70s about it, but boasts the usual YHA trappings (kitchen, cafe, TV lounge) and the lake's a stone's throw away. Shame the dorm block looks so much like a prison wing.

Helvellyn YHA HOSTEL £

(☎0845-371 9742; helvellyn@yha.org.uk; Greenside; dm £20; ⏲Easter-Oct) Saved from the YHA cost-cutting axe, this high-level hostel makes the perfect start or Helvellyn hikers. It's in a converted cottage 274m above the valley at the end of a rough, stony track on the main Helvellyn trail. Dorms are small, clean and cosy, and filling meals are provided by the hostel staff – handy, since the nearest cafe or shop is three-quarters of a mile away.

Eating

Fellbites CAFE ££

(Glenridding; lunch mains £8-12; evening menus £17.50-23.50; ⏲lunch daily, dinner Thu-Sat) This popular Glenridding cafe serves a good selection of spuds, sarnies and all-day breakfasts, plus a daily roast. It stays open for dinner at weekends.

Traveller's Rest PUB ££

(Glenridding; mains £5.50-15) Down a pint with a grandstand view of the fells at this top-of-Glenridding stalwart. Food is plain (steaks, pies, prawn cocktails) but the portions are huge.

Information

Ullswater Information Centre (017684-82414; ullswatertic@lake-district.gov.uk; Glenridding; 9am-5.30pm Apr-Oct)

Getting There & Away

The Ullswater Bus-and-Boat Combo ticket (adult/child £14.30/7.75) includes a day's travel on the 108 with a return trip on an Ullswater Steamer; buy the ticket on the bus.

108 Penrith to Patterdale via Pooley Bridge and Glenridding (five daily Monday to Friday, four on weekends).

517 Runs via Glenridding and Patterdale, then crosses the Kirkstone Pass to Troutbeck and Bowness (Kirkstone Rambler; three daily July and August, otherwise weekends only).

Kendal

POP 28,398

Technically Kendal isn't in the Lake District, but it's a major gateway for the national park. Known as the 'Auld Grey Town' thanks to the sombre grey stone used in its buildings, Kendal is a bustling shopping centre with some good restaurants, a funky arts centre and intriguing museums. But it'll forever be synonymous in many people's minds with its famous mint cake, a staple item in the nation's hiking packs ever since Edmund Hillary and Tensing Norgay munched it during their ascent of Everest in 1953.

Sights

FREE **Kendal Museum** MUSEUM
(www.kendalmuseum.org.uk; Station Rd; 10.30am-5pm Wed-Sat) Founded in 1796 by the inveterate Victorian collector William Todhunter, this mixed-bag museum features everything from stuffed beasts and transfixed butterflies to medieval coin hoards. There's also a reconstruction of the office of Alfred Wainwright, who served as honorary curator at the museum from 1945 to 1974; look out for his pipe and knapsack.

Abbot Hall Art Gallery GALLERY
(www.abbothall.org.uk; adult/child £6.85/free; 10.30am-5pm Mon-Sat Apr-Oct, to 4pm Nov-Mar) Kendal's fine art gallery houses one of the northwest's best collections of 18th- and 19th-century art, and recently celebrated its 50-year birthday. It's especially strong on portraiture and Lakeland landscapes; look out for works by Constable, Varley and Turner, as well as portraits by John Ruskin and local boy George Romney, born in Dalton-in-Furness in 1734, and a key figure in the 'Kendal School'.

A joint ticket with the Museum of Lakeland Life & Industry costs £8.30.

Museum of Lakeland Life & Industry MUSEUM
(www.lakelandmuseum.org.uk; adult/child £5/free; 10.30am-5pm Mon-Sat Mar-Oct, to 4pm Nov-Feb) Directly opposite Abbot Hall, this museum recreates various scenes from Lakeland life from centuries past, including a farmhouse parlour, a Lakeland kitchen, an apothecary and the study of Arthur Ransome, author of *Swallows and Amazons*.

Festivals & Events

Kendal Mountain Festival OUTDOOR ACTIVITIES
(www.mountainfest.co.uk) Annual mountain-themed celebration encompassing films, books and talks in November.

Sleeping

Crosthwaite House B&B ££
(015395-68264; www.crosthwaitehouse.co.uk; d £70-80; P) Zingy and zesty, this bright number has lots of imagination; the six rooms are colourfully decorated with swirly wallpapers, funky fabrics and retro furniture, and all are named after a type of damson fruit. Breakfast is cooked on an aga, and includes tasty options including blueberry pancakes and huevos rancheros.

Beech House B&B ££
(01539-720385; www.beechhouse-kendal.co.uk; 40 Greenside; s £60-75, d £80-100; P) Top Kendal honours go to this extremely elegant B&B at the top of the steep hill of Beast Banks. Rooms are a prim-and-proper treat; some feature sleigh beds and fluffy cushions, others freestanding baths and comfy sofas.

Riverside Hotel HOTEL
(01539-734861; www.riversidekendal.co.uk; Beezon Rd; d £98-118; P) The decor at this mid-sized hotel is disappointingly generic, but as its name suggests, it sits in a great water-front spot along the River Kent.

Eating

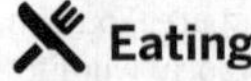

Hare & Hounds PUB ££
(015395-68333; www.hareandhoundsbowlandbridge.co.uk; Bowland Bridge; mains £10.95-15.95) It's a drive from Kendal – 3 miles away in

WORTH A TRIP

THE PUNCH BOWL INN

It's far from a secret these days, but the **Punch Bowl** (015395-68237; www.the-punchbowl.co.uk; Crosthwaite; mains £14-28; r £160-310; P) is still an essential stop for gastropub connoisseurs. You're a long way from steak-and-ale pie here – the menu indulges in sophisticated stuff such as pork tenderloin with damson purée, or sea-bass with vanilla beurre blanc – and while the old pub interior's been attractively updated, the building has still clung to its rustic essence. Upstairs rooms are straight out of a coffee-table glossy: reclaimed beams, Roberts Revival radios, underfloor heating. All in all, it's one of Lakeland's poshest pub packages.

You'll find it in Crosthwaite in the little-visited Lyth Valley, 6 miles from both Kendal and Bowness.

fact, in the village of Bowland Bridge – but the old Hare justifies the journey. There's not a patch of fancy fabric or stripped wood – it's just a real Lakeland pub, with logs stacked by the fire, flagstones on the floor and old lamps in the window. Rich food and a renowned Sunday lunch pull in the locals, and the house's special ale, 'Hare of the Dog', goes down nice and smooth.

New Moon BISTRO ££
(01539-729254; www.newmoonrestaurant.co.uk; 129 Highgate; 2-course lunch £9.95, mains £11.95-17; Tue-Sat) Flavoursome fusion food is the mainstay at this town-centre bistro – pork loin with dates, chilli-spiced tiger prawns, or confit duck served with ginger, chilli and honey. The dining room is light and contemporary, and the two-course pre-7pm dinner menu is great value at £12.95.

1657 Chocolate House CAFE £
(54 Branthwaite Brow; lunches £3-8) One for chocaholics. You'll find handmade chocolates and mintcake in the basement shop and in the frippy upstairs cafe, waitresses in starchy aprons serve umpteen varieties of hot chocolate, flavoured with almond, violet, mint and bitter orange.

Waterside Wholefoods CAFE £
(Kent View; light meals £4-10; 8.30am-4.30pm Mon-Sat) Kendal's veggies make a beeline for this riverside cafe, a long-standing staple for filling sandwiches, flapjacks and naughty-but-nice cakes.

Grain Store BISTRO ££
(pizzas £6.50-10, mains £10-16.50; 10am-11pm Mon-Sat) The Brewery Arts Centre's eatery does a decent line in bistro grub and stonebaked pizzas.

Staff of Life BAKERY £
(01539-738606; http://www.artisanbreadmakers.co.uk; 27 Finkle St) Kendal's renowned artisan bread maker.

☆ Entertainment

Brewery Arts Centre THEATRE, CINEMA
(01539-725133; www.breweryarts.co.uk; Highgate) Lively arts complex with a gallery, cafe, theatre and a brace of cinemas.

Getting There & Around

BUS Kendal is well-served by buses.

106 To Penrith (80 minutes, six daily Monday to Saturday).

555/556 Regular bus (half-hourly Monday to Saturday, hourly at weekends) to Windermere (30 minutes), Ambleside (40 minutes) and Grasmere (1¼ hours).

505 To Windermere, Ambleside, Hawkshead and Coniston (eight daily Monday to Saturday, six on Sunday).

X35 South to Grange, then westwards via Newby Bridge, Haverthwaite, Ulverston and Barrow (hourly Monday to Saturday, four on Sunday) .

TRAIN Kendal is on the branch line between Oxenholme and Windermere.

Around Kendal

Sizergh Castle CASTLE
(NT; 015395-60070; www.nationaltrust.org.uk/sizergh-castle; adult/child £8.15/4.05, gardens only £5.45/2.70; house 1-5pm Sun-Thu, gardens 11am-5pm daily) Three and a half miles south of Kendal along the A591, this castle is the feudal seat of the Strickland family. Set around a *pele* tower, its finest asset is the lavish wood panelling on display in the Great Hall.

Levens Hall HISTORIC HOME

(015395-60321; www.levenshall.co.uk; adult/child £12/5; house noon-5pm, gardens 10am-5pm Sun-Thu Mar-Oct) Two miles further south along the A6 is another Elizabethan manor built around a mid-13th-century *pele* tower. Fine Jacobean furniture is on display throughout the house, but the real drawcard is the 17th-century topiary garden: a surreal riot of pyramids, swirls, curls, pom-poms and peacocks straight out of *Alice in Wonderland*.

The *555/556* bus runs past the castle gates.

TOP CHOICE **Low Sizergh Barn** FARM SHOP

(015395-60426; www.lowsizerghbarn.co.uk; shop 9am-5.30pm, tearoom 9.30am-5.30pm) A prodigious selection of Lakeland goodies are available at this beamed farm shop, one of the Lake District's very best. Breads from Grange Bakery, meats from Mansergh Hall, cheeses from Thornby Moor Dairy and beers from the Coniston Brewery Co are just some of the gourmet treats in store. There's also a farm trail and woodland walk to follow if the weather's nice.

Look out for the signs just outside Kendal on the A590.

CUMBRIAN COAST

While it might not quite compare to the wild cliffs and craggy grandeur of Scotland or Northumberland, Cumbria's bleakly beautiful coastline is still worth exploring. Dotted with sandy bays and seaside towns, as well as a renowned bird reserve at St Bees Head and a historic steam railway near Ravenglass, it's a little-visited corner of Cumbria that always stays much less crowded than the national park. Somewhat less attractive is the nuclear power plant of Sellafield, still stirring up controversy some 50 years after its construction.

Getting Around

The Furness Railway and Cumbrian Coast lines follow a 120-mile loop from Lancaster all the way to Carlisle, stopping at towns including Grange-over-Sands, Barrow-in-Furness, Ravenglass and Whitehaven.

The Cumbrian Coast Day Ranger ticket (adult/child £18/8.50) covers a day's travel.

Grange-over-Sands

POP 4098

Established as an Edwardian seaside resort, stately Grange still has a distinct feel of bygone days. Lined with teashops, well-kept gardens and impressive period villas, it's a pleasant place to stroll the seafront and drink in the coastal views out over Morecambe Bay.

While you're here, don't miss the chance for afternoon tea at the wonderful Grade-II listed **Hazelmere Cafe** (www.hazelmerecafe.co.uk; 1-2 Yewbarrow Tce; sandwiches £4-6, mains £6-10; 10am-5pm Mon-Sat), a delightful doily-clad tearoom built in 1897 that serves sponge cakes, sticky buns, potted shrimps and meat pies made in the old-fashioned way – washed down, of course, with a choice of 30-odd different teas.

The X35 bus (hourly Monday to Saturday) stops in Grange on its way from Kendal to Newby Bridge, Ulverston and Barrow. Trains run to Cark-in-Cartmel and along the coast to Barrow and on to Whitehaven.

Cartmel

POP 1798

Tucked away in the countryside near Grange, tiny Cartmel is known for three things: its 12th-century priory, its miniature racecourse and its world-famous sticky toffee pudding, on sale at the **Cartmel Village Shop** (015395-36280; www.stickytoffeepudding.co.uk; 9am-5pm Mon-Sat, 10am-4.30pm Sun).

The heart of the village is the medieval market square, from where a winding lane leads to **Cartmel Priory** (9am-5.30pm May-Oct, to 3.30pm Nov-Apr), one of the few priories to escape demolition during the Dissolution. Light pours in through the 15th-century **east window**, illuminating the tombs set into the flagstoned floor; note the *memento mori* of skulls and hourglasses, intended to remind the pious of their own inescapable mortality.

Sleeping & Eating

TOP CHOICE **L'Enclume** GASTRONOMIC £££

(015395-36362; www.lenclume.co.uk; Cavendish St; 8-/12-course tasting menu £69/89, d £99-159, ste £179-199; lunch Wed-Sun, dinner daily) Recently featured in BBC2's *The Trip*, Simon Rogan's Michelin-starred flagship is one of

MORECAMBE BAY & THE QUEEN'S GUIDE

The vast expanse of **Morecambe Bay** sprawls for more than 310 sq km between the Cumbrian and Lancashire coastlines. It's one of the UK's largest areas of tidal mudflats, providing a unique marine habitat and some of the country's richest cockle-beds.

The bay is also notorious for its fast-rising tide and quicksands, which have caused countless strandings and drownings down the centuries – most notably in 2004, when a group of Chinese cockle-pickers were caught out by the tide and tragically drowned.

Due to the dangers, it's only possible to walk across the flats at low tide in the company of the official **Queen's Guide to the Sands**, a prestigious role established by the monarch in 1536. The present incumbent is local man Cedric Robinson, who has been leading walks across the bay since 1963.

The 8-mile crossing from Arnside to Kents Bank Station (near Grange-over-Sands) takes around 3½ hours. Walks usually take place between May and September, and you need to register at least a fortnight in advance.

Ask at the **Grange Tourist Office** (☎015395-34026; grangetic@southlakeland.gov.uk; Victoria Hall, Main St; ⊙10am-5pm Mon-Sat Easter-Oct) for details of the next crossing.

Cumbria's most adventurous restaurants. Seriously sophisticated dishes showcase Rogan's fondness for ingredients foraged from Cumbria's coast and countryside, as well as his flair for artful presentation. There's no à la carte menu; you just choose from an 8-course or (gulp) 12-course tasting menu. Needless to say, reservations are absolutely essential, and the restaurant offers a selection of plush rooms across several buildings.

Rogan & Company BRITISH ££
(☎015395-35917; www.roganandcompany.co.uk; The Square; mains £14.50-21; ⊙Wed-Sun) Simon Rogan's Cartmel bistro showcases his culinary flair with a recent refocus on more serious gourmet British dishes. The restaurant mixes old architecture with trendy touches, and there's even a sweet garden for alfresco dining.

Cavendish Arms PUB ££
(☎015395-36240; www.thecavendisharms.co.uk; mains £11-18; d from £90) A local trend towards fine dining has rippled out to this lemon-coloured Cartmel pub, which now serves surprisingly upmarket food among solid beams and burnished wood. There's also a delightful beer garden, and if you feel like sleeping over, you can choose from quaint pub rooms or three modern suites above a shop in the village square.

King's Arms PUB £
(The Square; mains £8-14) This olde-worlde pub has a whitewashed exterior, plenty of country knick-knacks and outside tables on the market square.

Getting There & Away

Bus 530/532 (hourly Monday to Saturday) travels from Cartmel to Grange (40 minutes), stopping at the train station at Cark-in-Cartmel.

Holker Hall

This **house** (☎015395-58328; www.holker-hall.co.uk; adult/child £11.50/6, grounds only £7.50/4; ⊙house 11am-4pm Sun-Fri, grounds 10.30am-5pm Mar-Oct) has been the seat of the Cavendish family for about 400 years. Though parts of it date from the 16th century, it was almost entirely rebuilt following a fire in 1871.

It's a typically Victorian affair, covered with mullioned windows, gables and copper-topped turrets. Among its wealth of grand rooms are the drawing room, the library and the lavish Long Gallery (renowned for its elaborate plasterwork).

Outside, Holker's grounds sprawl for more than 10 hectares, encompassing a rose garden, woodland, ornamental fountains and a 22m-high lime tree. There's also a fantastic **food hall** (☎015395-59084; www.holkerfoodhall.co.uk) stocking produce from the estate, including venison and saltmarsh lamb.

Ulverston

POP 11,670

It might not have the looks of some of Cumbria's prettier towns, but in many ways Ulverston is a more authentic place. Set around a market square, it's been a trading town since the Middle Ages, and later grew wealthy on the leather, copper and iron-mining trades. The town's Georgian houses provide a hint of its former wealth, but these days Ulverston's a quiet, workaday place, and a useful base for exploring the Cumbrian coast and the western Lakes.

Ulverston's most famous son is Stan Laurel, the spindlier half of Laurel & Hardy. A new statue of the duo was unveiled outside Coronation Hall in 2009, designed by artist Graham Ibbeson.

Sights

Laurel & Hardy Museum MUSEUM
(01229-582292; www.laurel-and-hardy.co.uk; Brogden St, Ulverston; adult/child £4/2; 10am-5pm Feb-Dec) Founded by avid Laurel & Hardy collector Bill Cubin back in 1983, this eclectic museum has new premises inside the town's old Roxy cinema. It's crammed floor-to-ceiling with a cornucopia of cinematic memorabilia, from original posters to film props – and there's a shoebox-sized cinema showing back-to-back Laurel & Hardy classics.

Hoad Monument VIEWPOINT
(Hoad Hill) Standing high on a hill above town, this tower commemorates the explorer Sir John Barrow (1764–1848), who helped map the Northwest Passage. The views of the fells and the coast are wonderful.

Sleeping

Candlewyck Farm B&B ££
(01229-580432; www.candlewyck.co.uk; Old Hall Rd; s £55-65, d £75-95) Ulverston's town-centre B&Bs are shabby, so it's worth travelling out to this rural farmhouse – especially if you can bag the self-contained barn suite, which has oodles of space and its own wet-room shower. The two rooms in the main house are smaller and decorated in farmhouse style.

Bay Horse Hotel HOTEL ££
(01229-583972; www.thebayhorsehotel.co.uk; Canal Foot; d £95-120; P) Plonked at the end of Ulverston's old canal, this hotel offers pleasant waterfront rooms, most of which have balconies overlooking the pebbly sands of the Levens Estuary. The decor's a bit behind the times, but it's very comfy and has a good country restaurant. Follow signs to Canal Foot from the A590.

Eden Lodge B&B ££
(01229-587067; www.eden-lodge.com; Bardsea; s £80, d £110-135; P) Modern and minimalist, this gabled guesthouse is in nearby Bardsea, a few miles drive south of Ulverston. It's crisply decorated and extremely handy for the coast.

Eating & Drinking

Ulverston's lively **market** fills the town's streets every Thursday, with a smaller market on Saturday and a local **food fair** every third Saturday of the month.

Gillams CAFE £
(64 Market St; lunches £3-10; Mon-Sat) With a century of grocery service behind it, Gillams knows how to pour a decent cuppa. It was built c 1892 and feels antique, but the delicious veggie-organic food is very much of the moment – hot quiches, savoury tarts, fresh soups, quinoa salads. Luxury biscuits, jams and other foodie souvenirs are sold in the old grocer's shop next door.

Rustique BISTRO ££
(01229-587373; www.eatatrustique.co.uk; Brogden St; mains £16.50-22.50; Tue-Sat) Jason Bright's bistro looks bland and boxy, but it dishes up a mix of classic British and zingy fusion flavours, such as classic chicken breast with fondant potatoes, or spicy Thai seafood broth with pak choi, coconut and mussels. He also runs a good **deli** (9.30am-4pm Mon-Sat, to 1pm Wed) along the street.

Farmer's Arms PUB ££
(www.thefarmers-ulverston.co.uk; 3 Market Place; mains £9.95-12.95) For sit-down grub, this central pub is always a good option, with bistro-style food served beneath its raftered interior. The deli-boards are great for sharing, and come in charcuterie, seafood and tortilla versions.

World Peace Cafe CAFE £
(www.worldpeacecafe.org; 5 Cavendish St; mains £4-8; 10am-4.30pm Tue-Sat;) Co-run by the Conishead Priory, this all-organic cafe is ideal for chilling; Fair Trade food and herbal teas downstairs, meditation sessions upstairs.

Information

The town has a website (www.ulverston.net).

Tourist Office (01229-587120; ulverstontic@southlakeland.gov.uk; County Sq; 9am-5pm Mon-Sat, 10am-4pm winter)

Getting There & Away

BUS The X35 bus (hourly Monday to Saturday) stops in Ulverston en route from Kendal to Haverthwaite and Newby Bridge.

TRAIN Destinations include Ravenglass (£8.30, 1¼ hours), Whitehaven (£11.10, 1¾ hours) and Carlisle (£28 1¾ to 2 hours).

Around Ulverston

CONISHEAD PRIORY

Two miles south of Ulverston, **Conishead Priory** (www.conisheadpriory.org; admission free, guided tours weekends £3; ⏲2-5pm Mon-Fri, noon-5pm weekends Easter-Oct, 2-4pm Nov-Easter) has variously served as a stately home, military hospital and miners' hostel, but it now houses a Kadampa Buddhist Temple and Europe's largest bronze buddha.

FURNESS ABBEY

Eight and a half miles southwest of Ulverston, the rosy ruins of **Furness Abbey** (EH; adult/child £12.30/3.90; ⏲10am-5pm Thu-Mon) are all that remains of one of northern England's largest and most powerful monasteries.

Founded in the 12th century, the abbey's lands and properties once stretched right across southern Cumbria, but like many of England's monasteries, it met an ignominious end in 1537 during the dissolution.

You can still make out the abbey's basic footprint; various arches, windows and the north and south transept walls are still standing, alongside the remains of the abbey bell tower. An informative audioguide is included in the admission price.

During recent excavations of a medieval abbot's grave, archaeologists discovered treasures including a gold crozier and an ornate gemstone ring, both now displayed in the abbey museum.

Several buses including the X35 stop nearby.

SOUTH LAKES WILD ANIMAL PARK

Animals from five continents populate this **wildlife park** (www.wildanimalpark.co.uk; adult/child £13.50/8; ⏲10am-5pm), from big cats (jaguars, Amur and Sumatran tigers) to tiny lemurs (red-ruffed, ring-tailed) and everything in between. You can watch the tigers being fed, and even give the keepers a hand with feeding the penguins and giraffes twice a day.

The park is half a mile outside Dalton-in-Furness off the A590 – follow the brown elephant signs.

Ravenglass & Around

Between Ravenglass & Whitehaven, the coastline curves past seaside towns and the gloomy chimney stacks of Sellafield en route to the dramatic promontory and RSPB bird reserve on St Bees Head.

MUNCASTER CASTLE

Like many Cumbrian castles, **Muncaster** (www.muncaster.co.uk; adult/child £13/7.50; ⏲gardens & owl centre 10.30am-5pm, castle noon-4.30pm Sun-Fri) was originally built around a 14th-century *pele* tower, constructed to resist Reiver raids from across the Scottish border. Home to the Pennington family for the last seven centuries, the castle's features include its majestic great hall and octagonal library, and in its grounds you'll find an ornamental maze and an owl centre.

DON'T MISS

LA'AL RATTY

The pocket-size choo-choos of the **Ravenglass & Eskdale Railway** (☎01229-717171; www.ravenglass-railway.co.uk; single fares adult/child £6.60/3.30, day tickets £11.20/5.60) – affectionately known to all as La'al Ratty – were originally built in 1876 to ferry iron ore from the Eskdale mines to the coast. Lovingly restored, they're now one of Cumbria's most popular visitor attractions.

The tiny steam trains chug for 7 miles from Ravenglass into the Eskdale Valley, terminating at Dalegarth Station, near Boot. The trip is enormous fun and the scenery is fabulous, but as the carriages are fairly open to the elements, you might be wise to leave your trip for fine weather (or pack a decent raincoat).

There are up to 14 trips daily between March and October. At other times of year, the trains generally only run on weekends and bank holidays. Bikes can be carried on most trains, but you need to book at least 24 hours ahead.

There's a large car park and a small visitor museum next to Ravenglass Station.

The castle is also known for its copious ghosts: keep your eyes peeled for the Muncaster Boggle and a malevolent jester known as Tom Fool (hence 'tomfoolery').

ST BEES HEAD

This wind-battered **headland** (RSPB; stbees.head@rspb.org.uk), 5.5 miles south of Whitehaven and 1.5 miles north of the tiny town of St Bees, is one of Cumbria's most important reserves for nesting seabirds.

Depending on the season, species nesting here include fulmars, kittiwakes and razorbills, as well as Britain's only population of resident black guillemots.

There are more than 2 miles of cliff-paths to explore, so make sure you remember to bring some binoculars.

Whitehaven

POP 23,795

Tall Georgian townhouses and orderly streets provide the only hint that, three centuries ago, Whitehaven was England's third largest port, with a roaring trade in coal, iron, spices and slaves. Much of the maritime trade disappeared following the arrival of the railway, and these days Whitehaven is a sleepy, salty coastal town, worth visiting for its breezy views and battered seaside charm.

Sights

Like most English ports, Whitehaven was once a jumble of alleys and harbourside slips, but during the 1700s it became the first town in England to be redeveloped according to a grid system, with squares and straight streets replacing the old medieval tangle.

The Beacon MUSEUM

(www.thebeacon-whitehaven.co.uk; West Strand; adult/child £5.50/free; 10am-4.30pm Tue-Sun) This intriguing museum is housed in Whitehaven's old lighthouse and explores the town's maritime history. It's split into four levels: Work and Play on the 2nd floor, Time and Tides on the 3rd, and the Viewing Gallery and Weather Zone on the 4th, where you can gaze across the harbour with a high-powered telescope and present your own weather forecast.

There are a few displays on the infamous raid of John Paul Jones, a US naval captain (actually born in Scotland) who attacked the town during the American War of Independence, hoping to strike a decisive blow against a key British port. Unfortunately for Jones, the raid was a flop; of the 200-odd ships in Whitehaven's harbour, he sank just a single coal barge.

The Rum Story WAXWORK MUSEUM

(www.rumstory.co.uk; Lowther St; adult/child £5.45/3.45; 10am-4.30pm) This rather budget museum explores Whitehaven's rum-running history through a mix of waxwork models and dioramas, including an 18th-century sugar workshop and a debauched 'punch tavern'. It's fun, if tacky.

St Nicholas Church CHURCH

(Lowther St) Ulverston's redbrick Victorian church was burned to the ground during a huge fire in 1971. Only the clock tower remains, but the nave is now a pleasant public garden, with a memorial commemorating miners killed in Ulverston's coal pits.

Sleeping & Eating

Lowther House B&B £

(01946-63169; www.lowtherhouse-whitehaven.com; s/d £70/90;) The top B&B in town, with a carefully-designed interior evoking Whitehaven's seafaring past, featuring nautical knick-knacks, wooden shutters and rooms named after prominent ships once stationed in Whitehaven's harbour.

Georgian House Hotel HOTEL ££

(01946-696611; www.thegeorgianhousehotel.net; 9-11 Church St; s/d from £79/89;) Comfy and central, this former merchant's house has unremarkable rooms decked out in shipshape fashion with a mix of modern and Georgian features.

Moresby Hall HOTEL ££

(01946-696317; www.moresbyhall.co.uk; Moresby; s £90-105, d £120-150;) This Grade I-listed house is straight out of an Evelyn Waugh novel, with orderly lawns, antique-filled rooms, enormous staircase and a wonderfully ornate 17th-century frontage. It's 2 miles north along the A595.

Glenfield B&B ££

(01946-691911; www.glenfield-whitehaven.co.uk; Back Corkickle; s £35, d £55-65;) Heritage B&B with six Victoriana-stocked rooms.

Zest BISTRO ££

(harbourside cafe 01946-66981, restaurant 01946-692848; www.zestwhitehaven.com; harbourside cafe 11am-9pm, restaurant 6-11pm Wed-Sun) A zippy modern bistro with two branches: a relaxed cafe by the harbour and a more upmarket restaurant a mile or so from town along Low Road. Choose the harbourside for ciabattas and 'blinding butties', or book a table at the restaurant for a smart bistro supper.

Getting There & Away

Whitehaven is on the Cumbrian Coast Line with hourly trains in each direction. Bus 6/X6 travels to Ravenglass and Muncaster Castle (one hour, four daily).

NORTHERN & EASTERN CUMBRIA

Many visitors speed through the northern and eastern reaches of Cumbria in a headlong dash for the Lake District, but it's worth taking the time to delve into the little-explored countryside inland from the national park.

It might not have the big-name fells and chocolate-box villages, but it's still full of interest, with traditional towns, crumbling castles, abandoned abbeys and sweeping moors, all set alongside the magnificent Roman engineering project of Hadrian's Wall.

Carlisle

POP 69,527

Carlisle isn't Britain's prettiest city, but it has history and heritage aplenty. Precariously perched on the frontier between England and Scotland, in the area once ominously dubbed the 'Debatable Lands', Cumbria's capital is a city with a notoriously stormy past; sacked by the Vikings, pillaged by the Scots, and plundered by the Border Reivers, the city has been on the frontline of England's defences for more than 1000 years.

Reminders of the city's past are still evident in its great crimson castle and cathedral, built from the same rosy red sandstone as most of the city's houses. It might not have the wow factor of some of northern England's other regenerated conurbations, but Carlisle certainly has enough to justify at least a couple of days of investigation.

History

A Celtic camp (or *caer*) provided an early military station for the Romans, and Carlisle became a major strategic centre following the construction of Hadrian's Wall.

After centuries of intermittent conflict between Picts, Saxons and Viking raiders, the Normans seized Carlisle from the Scots in 1092. The English subsequently developed Carlisle as a military stronghold throughout the Middle Ages, enlarging the walls, citadels and the great gates. The city was also an important garrison for Royalist forces during the Civil War.

Peace came to the city with the Restoration, and the city developed as an industrial centre for cotton and textiles after the arrival of the railway in the mid-19th century.

Sights & Activities

TOP CHOICE **Carlisle Castle** CASTLE

(EH; www.english-heritage.org.uk/daysout/properties/carlisle-castle; adult/child £5.50/3.30; 9.30am-5pm Apr-Sep, 10am-4pm Oct-Mar) Carlisle's brooding, rust-red castle lurks dramatically on the north side of the city. Founded around a Celtic and Roman stronghold, the Norman keep was added in 1092 by William Rufus, followed by successive refortifications by Henry II, Edward I and Henry VIII (who added the supposedly cannon-proof towers).

The castle has witnessed some dramatic events over the centuries. Mary, Queen of Scots was imprisoned here in 1568, and the castle was the site of a notorious eight-month siege during the English Civil War, when the Royalist garrison survived by eating rats, mice and the castle dogs before finally surrendering in 1645. Look out for the 'licking stones' in the dungeon, which Jacobite prisoners supposedly lapped for moisture.

Admission includes entry to the **Kings Own Royal Border Regiment Museum**, which details the history of Cumbria's Infantry Regiment. There are guided tours from April to September.

Carlisle Cathedral CHURCH

(www.carlislecathedral.org.uk; 7 The Abbey; suggested donation £5, photography permit £1; 7.30am-6.15pm Mon-Sat, to 5pm Sun;) Built from the same scarlet sandstone as the castle, Carlisle's cathedral began life as a priory church in 1122, and became a cathedral when its first abbot, Athelwold, became the first Bishop of Carlisle.

Among its notable features are the 15th-century choir stalls, the impressive barrel-vaulted roof and the wonderful 14th-century East Window, one of the largest Gothic

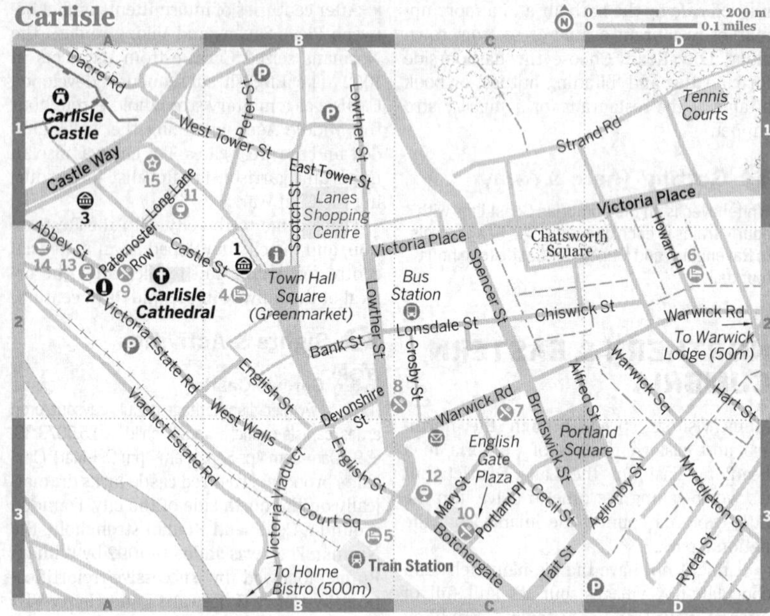

Carlisle

Top Sights

Carlisle Castle	A1
Carlisle Cathedral	A2

Sights

Fratry	(see 9)
1 Guildhall Museum	B2
2 Prior's Tower	A2
3 Tullie House Museum	A1

Sleeping

4 Crown & Mitre	B2
5 Hallmark Hotel	B3
6 Langleigh Guest House	D2

Eating

7 David's	C2
8 Gilded Lily	C2
9 Prior's Kitchen Restaurant	A2
10 Teza	C3

Drinking

11 Alcoves Cafe Bar	A1
12 Cafe Solo	C3
13 Fats	A2
14 Foxes Cafe Lounge	A2

Entertainment

15 Brickyard	A1

windows in England. Surrounding the cathedral are other priory relics, including the 16th-century **Fratry** and the **Prior's Tower**.

Tullie House Museum MUSEUM
(www.tulliehouse.co.uk; Castle St; adult/child £5.20/50p; ⏲10am-5pm Mon-Sat, 11am-4pm Sun) This museum ranges through the city's past, from its Celtic foundation through to the development of modern Carlisle. The highlight is the new **Roman Frontier Gallery**, which was opened in 2011 and uses a mix of archaeological exhibits and interactive displays to tell the story of the Roman occupation of Carlisle. There are some particularly fine busts and decorative headstones, as well as a showpiece bronze face-mask dating from the 1st century AD.

Upstairs, the **Border Galleries** cover the rest of the city's history, from the Bronze Age through to the Border Reivers, the Jacobite Rebellion and the Industrial Revolution. The **Carlisle Life Gallery** details the city's social history through photos, films and recorded stories, and **Old Tullie House** has a collection of fine arts, sculpture and porcelain.

Guildhall Museum MUSEUM
(Greenmarket) This tiny museum occupies one of Carlisle's oldest buildings, built for the city's trade guilds during the 15th century. It's currently closed for restoration, but you can still admire the impressive galleried exterior.

Tours

Open Book Visitor Guiding TOUR
(01228-670578; www.greatguidedtours.co.uk) Tours of Carlisle and the surrounding area (including Hadrian's Wall) can be arranged through the tourist office.

Sleeping

Carlisle's accommodation leaves a lot to be desired. Apart from a few chain hotels, the choice in the centre is disappointing. You'll be better off heading to the outskirts.

Willowbeck Lodge B&B ££
(01228-513607; www.willowbeck-lodge.com; Lambley Bank, Scotby; d £100-130; P) Escape the city hustle at this uncompromisingly modern house, 3 miles from the centre. Six deluxe rooms are closer to hotel standard than B&B, offering tasteful shades of beige and taupe, luxurious bathrooms and a gabled lounge overlooking a private pond.

Warwick Hall B&B ££
(01228-561546; www.warwickhall.org; Warwick-on-Eden; s £84-98, d/ste £120/180) This fine country house 2 miles from the centre along Warwick Rd is a real country retreat. With its huge rooms, high ceilings and antique decor, it feels a bit like staying on an aristocratic friend's estate. There are acres of grounds and it even has its own stretch of river for fishing.

Crown & Mitre HISTORIC HOTEL ££
(01228-525491; www.peelhotels.co.uk/hotels/crown-and-mitre-hotel-carlisle-cumbria-england; English St; d £85-105) This redbrick pile commands a super spot over the main market square, and in its heyday must have offered Edwardian splendour aplenty. It's been modernised in standard chain-hotel style, so the rooms are well-equipped but disappointingly dull – although the reception area and central staircase still look rather grand.

Langleigh Guest House B&B ££
(01228-530440; www.langleighhouse.co.uk; 6 Howard Pl; s/d £40/75; P) Chaotic, yes, but full of period charm, this B&B is decorated in Edwardian fashion – think brass lamps, antique clocks and watercolour prints.

Hallmark Hotel HOTEL ££
(01228-531951; carlisle.reception@hallmarkhotels.co.uk; Court Sq; d from £75; P) If you're stuck for somewhere to sleep (or if you're catching an early train), this railway hotel offers plenty of rooms, but the decor is looking extremely tired in places.

Eating

Holme Bistro BRITISH ££
(01228-534343; www.holmebistro.co.uk; 56-58 Denton St; mains £10.95-17.95; Tue-Sat) The top place to eat in Carlisle, this slick bistro is run by brother-and-sister team Rob Don and Kirsty Robson, and has earned a loyal clientele for its unpretentious cuisine. Tuck into chunky steaks or pancetta-wrapped chicken, followed by a choice selection of Cumbrian cheeses. The two- or three-course pre-7.30pm menu is a steal. To get here, head southwest along Victoria Viaduct.

David's BISTRO ££
(01228-523578; www.davidsrestaurant.co.uk; 62 Warwick Rd; 2-/3-course lunch £12.95/15.95, dinner mains £14.95-23.95; Tue-Sat) Town-house dining with a gentlemanly air. David's has been a name on the Carlisle scene for some years, and it's still up there with the best. Expect original mantelpieces and overhead chandeliers in the dining rooms, and a menu of suave dishes such as 'best-end' of herb-encrusted lamb, or salmon and crayfish millefeuille.

Teza INDIAN ££
(01228-525111; www.tezacarlisle.co.uk; 4a English Gate Plaza; mains £7.95-12.95) Carlisle has plenty of curry houses, but Teza is worth mentioning for its metro-modern design (glass, chrome, minimalist furniture) and refreshing lack of piped sitars. All the usual classics are on the menu, alongside specials such as 'steamroller chicken' (flattened chicken marinated in coriander, chili and red onion).

Gilded Lily GASTROPUB ££
(01228-593600; www.gildedlily.info; 6 Lowther St; mains £9-15; 9am-midnight Mon-Thu, 9am-1am Fri & Sat, noon-midnight Sun) Carlisle's answer to the city gastropub turns out reliable food; there's a good choice of seafood

WORTH A TRIP

BIRDOSWALD ROMAN FORT

Though most of the forts along Hadrian's Wall have long since been plundered for building materials, you can still visit **Birdoswald Roman Fort** (EH; 01697-747602; www.birdoswaldromanfort.org; adult/child £5.20/3.10; 10am-5.30pm, shorter hours in winter), about 20 miles east of Carlisle, near Bampton.

Built to replace an earlier timber-and-turf fort, Birdoswald would have been the operating base for around 1000 Roman soldiers. Excavations have revealed three of the four gateways, as well as granary stores, workshops, exterior walls and a military drill hall. A visitor centre explores the fort's history and the background behind the construction of Hadrian's Wall.

The AD 122 bus from Carlisle to Hexham passes by the fort.

and steaks, and the Sunday roast is always good. The fireplaces and overhead skylight are original, left over from the building's former incarnation as a bank, but much of the furnishings are metropolitan-modern.

Prior's Kitchen Restaurant CAFE £
(Carlisle Cathedral; lunches £4-6; 9.45am-4pm Mon-Sat) Carlisle's best place for traditional afternoon tea is in the cathedral's fratry, once used as a monk's mess hall. The cream teas are cracking, and there are quiches, cakes and rounds of sandwiches if you feel like something more filling.

Drinking & Entertainment

If you want to find out what the phenomenon of British binge-drinking is all about, Botchergate on a weekend night is a pretty good place to start. If you prefer to drink in peace, try these alternatives.

Foxes Cafe Lounge CAFE
(www.foxescafelounge.co.uk; 18 Abbey St; mains £4-10; 10am-7pm Tue-Thu, to 11pm Fri, to 4.30pm Sat) This cool cafe-gallery provides a venue for all kinds of creative happenings, from open mic nights and live gigs to photo exhibitions. Count on continental cafe food and excellent coffee.

Fats PUB
(48 Abbey St; 11am-11pm) An open-plan layout and a tucked-away location ensures Fats usually feels less hectic than many of Carlisle's pubs. DJs and comedy nights are held regularly.

Alcoves Cafe Bar BAR
(Up Long Lane, 18 Fisher St; 6pm-late Tue-Sat) Easy to miss, but this alleyway hang-out off Fisher St is a popular spot for late-night drinks and DJs when you want to evade the Botchergate hullabaloo.

Cafe Solo BAR
(1 Botchergate) Spanish cocktails, tapas and Sol beers at a tiny corner-bar on the edge of Botchergate.

Brickyard CONCERT VENUE
(www.thebrickyardonline.com; 14 Fisher St) Carlisle's grungy gig venue, housed in the former Memorial Hall.

Information

Cumberland Infirmary (01228-523444; Newtown Rd) Half a mile west of the city centre.

Police Station (0845-330 0247; English St; 8am-midnight)

Tourist Office (01228-625600; www.historic-carlisle.org.uk; Greenmarket; 9.30am-5pm Mon-Sat, 10.30am-4pm Sun)

Getting There & Away

BUS Carlisle is Cumbria's main transport hub. National Express coaches depart from the bus station on Lonsdale St for destinations including London (£34.80, 7½ hours, three direct daily), Manchester (£25.30 to £27.70, 3 to 3½ hours, five daily) and Glasgow (£18.70 to £19.10, 2 hours, four to six daily).

Useful local bus routes:

104 To Penrith (40 minutes, hourly Monday to Saturday, every 2 hours on Sunday).

554 To Keswick (70 minutes, four daily).

AD 122 (Hadrian's Wall Bus; three daily April to September) Runs along the wall, with stops including Brampton, Birdoswald Roman Fort, Haltwhistle, Vindolanda Roman Fort, Housesteads Roman Fort and Hexham. Three extra buses a day only run as far as Haltwhistle station.

TRAIN Carlisle is on the main west coast line from London to Glasgow. It's also the terminus for the scenic Cumbrian Coast and Tyne Valley Lines, as well as the historic **Settle to Carlisle Railway** (www.settle-carlisle.co.uk; single to

Settle £18.90, anytime return £24.40) across the Yorkshire Dales. Main destinations:

Glasgow £21.80, 1¼ hours

Lancaster £19.50, 45 minutes

London Euston £102.10, 3½ hours

Manchester £50, 2 hours

Newcastle-upon-Tyne £13, 1½ hours

Getting Around

To book a taxi, call **Radio Taxis** (01228-527575), **Citadel Station Taxis** (01228-523971) or **County Cabs** (01228-596789).

Alston

POP 2227

Surrounded by the bleak hilltops of the Pennines, isolated Alston's main claim to fame is its elevation; at 305m above sea level, it's thought to be the highest market town in England (despite no longer having a market).

It's also famous among steam enthusiasts thanks to the **South Tynedale Railway** (01434-381696, timetable 01434-382828; www.strps.org.uk; adult/child return £7.50/3; Apr-Oct), which puffs through the hilly country between Alston and Kirkhaugh, along a route that originally operated from 1852 to 1976. The return trip takes about an hour; there are up to five daily trains in midsummer.

Penrith

POP 14,882

Once the region's capital, stout, redbrick Penrith is a busy market town with a centuries-old market square. Alongside the usual high street chains, its streets are dotted with traditional greengrocers and whitewashed pubs, and the town makes a useful base for forays into the nearby Eden Valley and eastern Cumbria.

Penrith Castle RUINS

(7.30am-9pm Easter-Oct, to 4.30pm other times) Opposite the train station are the remains of Penrith's 14th-century castle, built by William Strickland (later Bishop of Carlisle and Archbishop of Canterbury) and expanded by Richard III to resist Scottish raids, one of which razed the town in 1345. It's now largely ruined, although some of the original walls are still standing.

St Andrews Church CHURCH

Penrith's name derives from an old Celtic word meaning 'red fell', and the area's crimson sandstone is clear to see in many of the town's buildings, including its parish church. Legend has it that a great giant (the 'rightful king of all Cumbria') is buried in the churchyard, but the stone pillars marking his grave are actually the weathered remains of Celtic crosses.

Rheged VISITOR CENTRE

(www.rheged.com; 10am-6pm) Cunningly disguised as a Lakeland hill 2 miles west of Penrith, this visitor centre houses a large-screen Imax cinema and an exhibition on the history and geology of Cumbria. There's also a large retail hall selling Cumbrian foodstuffs and souvenirs, and local celeb chef Peter Sidwell has recently reinvented the menu at the centre's cafe.

The frequent X4/X5 bus stops at the centre.

Sleeping

Brooklands B&B ££

(01768-863395; www.brooklandsguesthouse.com; 2 Portland Pl; s £40, d £78-88;) The town's most elegant B&B is this Victorian redbrick on Portland Place. Rich furnishings and posh extras (such as fridges, chocolates on the tea tray and White Company toiletries) keep it a cut above the competition.

Brandelhow B&B ££

(01768-864470; www.brandelhowguesthouse.co.uk; 1 Portland Pl; s/d £35/70;) This family-run establishment is a useful option. The rooms are bog-standard B&B, but the little treats make it worth considering – especially the welcome tea, with chunks of Bootle Gingerbread or Lanie's Expedition Flapjack.

George Hotel HOTEL £££

(01768-862696; www.lakedistricthotels.net/georgehotel; d £134-204; P) Penrith's venerable redbrick coaching inn offers classically decorated rooms in prim stripes and country patterns, plus a quaint bar and restaurant. It's right in the heart of town, but pricey.

Eating

TOP CHOICE **Yanwath Gate Inn** GASTROPUB ££

(01768-862886; Yanwath; mains £16-19) Pubs simply don't get any better than the utterly excellent 'Yat', 2 miles south of town. It's been named Cumbria's Top Dining Pub for the last thee years running In *Good Pub Guide*, and the grub puts many of the county's

WORTH A TRIP

LOWTHER PARK

Encompassing huge tracts of woodland, park and pasture to the south of Penrith and the east of Ullswater, **Lowther Park** (☎01931-712192; www.lowthercastle.org; adult/child £8/free) was once the greatest of Cumbria's great estates. For centuries it has been the ancestral seat of the Earl of Lonsdale, whose dominion once encompassed much of eastern Cumbria. The estate's most impressive asset is undoubtedly **Lowther Castle**, a crenellated mansion designed by the Victorian architect Robert Smirke (whose other credits include the British Museum and Covent Garden Theatre).

Sadly, over the last century or so, the estate has steadily fallen into disrepair – largely due to the profligacy of the 5th Earl of Lonsdale, who bankrupted the family's coal mines, squandered its fortune and literally sold off most of the silver. But thanks to a £9 million grant from the Regional Development Agency, long-held plans to restore the grounds and its once-lavish landscaped gardens are coming to fruition.

It's expected that renovations to the house and visitor centre will be completed by 2014, but in the meantime, the estate is open to visitors as a 'work-in-progress'. It's thought it'll be a couple of decades before the gardens will be back to their full Victorian glory.

The grounds also contain the **Lakeland Birds of Prey Centre** (adult/child £6/3; 11am-5pm Apr-Oct), and host the popular **Kendal Calling** (www.kendalcalling.co.uk) music festival every July.

gastronomic restaurants to shame. It's big on rich, generous dishes that showcase the region's quality meats and wild game: venison, saltmarsh lamb, rare-breed pork, locally reared goose. The setting is a treat, too, with original A-frame beams, wood panelling and country curios galore.

No 15 CAFE £
(15 Victoria Rd; lunches £6-10; 9am-5pm Mon-Sat) Fifteen reasons to visit this cafe-bar-gallery are chalked on the blackboard, but you won't need persuading. It's Penrith's best place for lunch, cakes and coffee, with a light dining room and a gallery annexe displaying local photography and artwork. Lunch options include homemade burgers, spicy falafel salads and great veggie quiches.

Lounge BISTRO, BAR ££
(☎01768-866395; www.theloungehotelandbar.co.uk; King St; meze dishes £3.50-5) This snazzy new addition to the Penrith dining scene has proved popular. There's a strong Mediterranean feel to the menu with a large choice of meze platters. Bold colours and pattern prints in the dining room keep the sunny vibe going. Upstairs rooms (from £55) are plain but comfy.

JJ Graham DELI £
(6-7 Market Sq) Wonderful old-world grocer selling crusty breads, cakes, jams, biscuits, cheeses, meats and practically every other Cumbrian treat you can think of.

Magic Bean CAFE ££
(Poet's Walk; mains £6-14; lunch & dinner Mon-Sat) This lacy cafe has a split personality: standard cakes, sandwiches and cream teas by day, curry specials after dark. It's along a narrow alleyway off Castlegate.

Information

Tourist Office (☎01768-867466; pen.tic@eden.gov.uk; Middlegate; 9.30am-5pm Mon-Sat, 1-4.45pm Sun) Also houses Penrith's tiny museum.

Getting There & Away

BUS The bus station is northeast of the centre, off Sandgate.

104 To Carlisle (40 minutes, hourly Monday to Saturday, every 2 hours on Sunday).

X4/X5 Via Rheged, Keswick and Cockermouth to the Cumbrian coast (half-hourly Monday to Saturday, six on Sunday).

TRAIN There are frequent connections to Carlisle (£6.70, 15 minutes) and Lancaster (£15.40, one hour).

Newcastle & the Northeast

Includes »

Best Places to Eat

» Oldfields (p729)
» Jesmond Dene House (p730)
» Bouchon Bistrot (p749)
» Blackfriars (p729)
» The Broad Chare (p730)

Best Places to Stay

» Ashcroft (p750)
» No 1 Sallyport (p760)
» Gadds Townhouse (p737)
» Chillingham (p754)
» Alnwick Lodge (p755)

Why Go?

Ask a Kentish farmer or Cornish fisherman about northeast England and they may describe a forbidding industrial wasteland inhabited by football-mad folk with impenetrable accents. What they mightn't mention are the untamed landscapes, Newcastle's cultural renaissance, the wealth of Roman sites and the no-nonsense likeability of the locals. Some post-industrial gloom remains, but there's so much more to this frontier country than slag heaps and silenced steelworks.

In fact, if it's silence you are looking for, the northeast is ideal for flits into unpopulated backcountry – the rounded Cheviot Hills, the brooding Northumberland National Park, the harsh remoteness of the North Pennines...you're spoilt for choice if you need to flee the urban hullabaloo. Spectacular Hadrian's Wall cuts a lonely path through this wild landscape dotted with dramatic castle ruins, haunting reminders of a long and bloody struggle with the Picts and Celts to the north.

When to Go

The best time to discover Northumberland's miles of wide sandy beaches is during the June to August season. September through October is great for losing yourself in the autumnal landscapes of the North Pennines. A good place to celebrate New Year's Eve is in Allendale at the Baal Fire procession.

Newcastle & the Northeast Highlights
1 Getting down and dirty in the Killhope Lead Mining Museum (p742)
2 Enjoying a thumping night out on the tiles in the raucous city centre of Newcastle (p725)
3 Hugging the XXL ankles of the Angel of the North (p734)
4 Gazing in awe at Durham Cathedral (p735), a spectacular Unesco World Heritage Site
5 Getting all hands-on with the northeast's industrial past at Beamish Open-Air Museum (p738)
6 Walking like a Roman – by taking a hike along Hadrian's Wall (p744)
0
40 km
0
20 miles
EAST LOTHIAN
SCOTLAND
Cockburnspath
Grantshouse
Coldingham
St Abbs
Eyemouth
B6355
A1
Chirnside
Duns
BERWICKSHIRE
Berwick-upon-Tweed
Tweed
A698
Holy Island
Norham Castle
Etal
Ford
Crookham
Coldstream
Farne Islands
Earlston
Kelso
Melrose
A698
St Boswell's
Kirk Yetholm
Town Yetholm
Bowmont Water
Bamburgh
Belford
Seahouses
Wooler
Low Newton-by-the-Sea
Embleton
Dunstanburgh Castle
Craster
NORTH SEA
A68
Teviot
Ale Water
Jedburgh
A68
Cheviot
Kale Water
ROXBURGHSHIRE
Till
A697
A1
Alnwick
Bonchester Bridge
Northumberland National Park
Alnmouth
Warkworth
Amble
Danger Area (MOD Live Firing Range)
Coquet
Rothbury
A68
Liddel Water
Kielder Burn
Border Forest Park
Otterburn
NORTHUMBERLAND
A696
Ashington
Kielder Water
North Tyne
Morpeth
Bellingham
Kirkharle

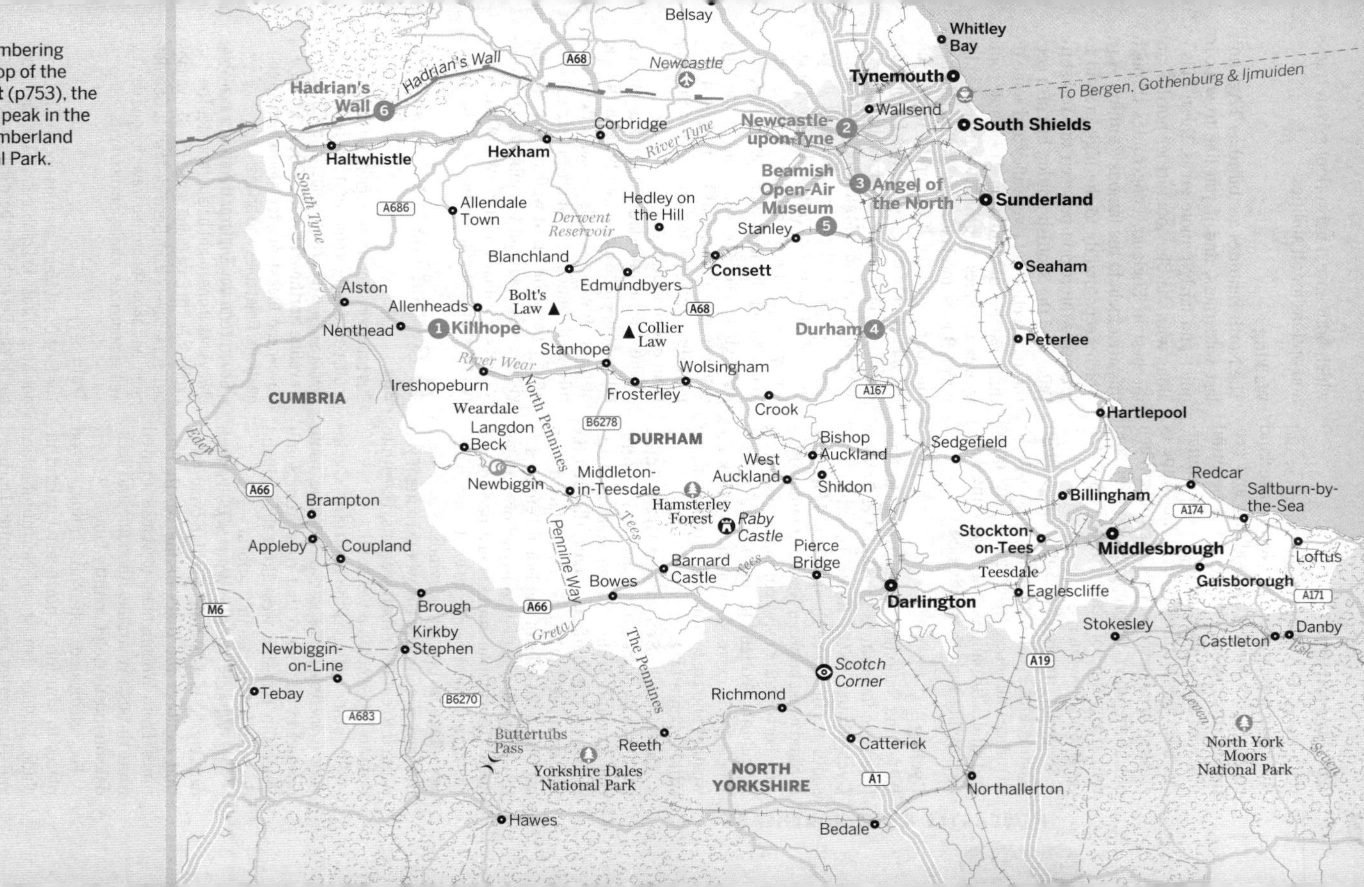

7 Clambering to the top of the **Cheviot** (p753), the highest peak in the Northumberland National Park.

Activities

With the rugged moors of the Pennines and stunning seascape of the Northumberland coast, there's some good walking and cycling in this region. The scenery is beautiful in a wild and untouched way – quite different from the picture-postcard landscape of areas such as Devon or the Cotswolds. When out in the open, be prepared for wind and rain at any time of year and for very harsh conditions in winter.

Regional tourism websites all contain walking and cycling information, and tourist offices all stock free leaflets plus maps and guides (usually £1 to £5) covering walking, cycling and other activities.

Cycling

Part of the National Cycle Network (NCN), a long-time favourite is the **Coast & Castles Cycle Route** (NCN Route 1), which runs south–north along the glorious Northumberland coast between Newcastle-upon-Tyne and Berwick-upon-Tweed, before swinging inland into Scotland to finish at Edinburgh. The coast is exposed, though, so check the weather and try to time your ride so that the wind is behind you.

The 140-mile **Sea to Sea Cycle Route** (C2C; www.c2c-guide.co.uk) runs across northern England from Whitehaven or Workington on the Cumbrian coast, through the northern part of the Lake District, and then over the wild hills of the North Pennines to finish at Newcastle-upon-Tyne or Sunderland. This popular route is fast becoming a classic, and most people go west–east to take advantage of prevailing winds. You'll need five days to complete the whole route; if you wanted to cut the urban sections, Penrith to Consett is perfect in a weekend.

The other option is the **Hadrian's Cycleway** (www.cycle-routes.org), a 191-mile route opened in July 2006 that runs from South Shields in Tyneside, west along the wall and down to Ravenglass in Cumbria.

The **Wheels to the Wild** (www.northpennines.org.uk) is a 70-mile circular cycle route that explores the dales of the North Pennines. From Wolsingham, it weaves a paved route through Weardale, Allendale and Teesdale on mostly quiet country lanes.

For dedicated off-road riding, good places to aim for in northeast England include Kielder Forest in Northumberland and Hamsterley Forest in County Durham, which both have a network of sylvan tracks and options for all abilities.

Walking

The North Pennines are billed as 'England's last wilderness', and if you like to walk in quiet and fairly remote areas, these hills – along with the Cheviots further north – are the best in England. Long routes through this area include the famous **Pennine Way**, which keeps mainly to the high ground as it crosses the region between the Yorkshire Dales and the Scottish border, but also goes through sections of river valley and some tedious patches of plantation. The whole route is over 250 miles, but the 70-mile section between Bowes and Hadrian's Wall would be a fine four-day taster. If you prefer to go walking just for the day, good bases for circular walks in the North Pennines include the towns of Alston and Middleton-in-Teesdale.

Elsewhere in the area, the great Roman ruin of **Hadrian's Wall** is an ideal focus for walking. There's a huge range of easy loops taking in forts and other historical highlights. A very popular walk is the long-distance route from end to end (84 miles), providing good section options for anything from one to four days.

The Northumberland coast has endless miles of open beaches, and little in the way of resort towns, so walkers can often enjoy this wild, windswept shore in virtual solitude. One of the finest walks is between the villages of Craster and Bamburgh via Dunstanburgh, which includes two of the county's most spectacular castles.

Getting There & Around

Bus

Bus transport around the region can be difficult, particularly around the more remote reaches of western Northumberland. Contact **Traveline Northeast** (☎0871-2002233; www.travelinenortheast.info) for information on connections, timetables and prices.

Several one-day Explorer tickets are available; always ask if one might be appropriate. The Explorer North East (adult/child £9/8), available on buses, covers from Berwick down to Scarborough, and allows unlimited travel for one day, as well as numerous admission discounts.

Train

The East Coast Main Line runs north from London King's Cross to Edinburgh via Durham, Newcastle and Berwick; Northern Rail operates local and interurban services in the north, including west to Carlisle.

There are numerous Rover tickets for single-day travel and longer periods, so ask if one might be worthwhile. For example, the North Country Rover (adult/child £82/41) allows unlimited travel throughout the north (not including Northumberland) any four days out of eight.

NEWCASTLE-UPON-TYNE

POP 189,863

Of all of northern England's cities, Newcastle is perhaps the most surprising to the first-time visitor, especially if they come armed with the preconceived notions that have dogged the city's reputation since, well, always. Think it's a sooty, industrial wasteland for salt-of-the-earth toughies whose favourite hobby is drinking and braving the elements bare-chested? Coal slags and cold slags? You may be in for a pleasant surprise.

Welcome to the hipster capital of the northeast, a cool urban centre that knows how to take care of itself and anyone else who comes to visit with an unexpected mix of culture, heritage and sophistication, exemplified by its excellent new art galleries and magnificent concert hall, and also by its growing number of fine restaurants, choice hotels and interesting bars. It's not just about the Tyne bridges – although the eclectic, cluttered array of Newcastle's most recognisable feature is pretty impressive.

Thankfully, Newcastle's hip reputation is built on a set of deep-rooted traditions embodied by the city's greatest strength: the locals. Raised and subsequently abandoned by coal and steel, Geordies are a fiercely independent bunch, tied together by history, adversity and that impenetrable dialect, the closest language to 1500-year-old Anglo-Saxon left in England.

And then of course there's the nightlife, source of so many of the city's most brazen stereotypes. Of course you can go mad here – there's an irrepressible energy that borders on the irresponsible – but you don't have to, and there are plenty of options that don't involve draining blue-coloured vodka or running unclad through the streets.

Sights

City Centre

Newcastle's supremely elegant Victorian centre is a compact area bordered roughly by Grainger St to the west and Pilgrim St to the east. At its heart is the extraordinarily handsome Grey St, lined with fine classical buildings – undoubtedly one of the country's finest thoroughfares: in 2010 it was voted the UK's 3rd prettiest street in the Google Street View Awards.

FREE Great North Museum MUSEUM
(www.greatnorthmuseum.org; Barras Bridge; 10am-5pm Mon-Sat, 1-5pm Sun) This outstanding museum has been created by bringing together the contents of Newcastle University's museums and adding them to the natural history exhibits of the prestigious Hancock Museum in the latter's renovated neoclassical building. The result is a fascinating jumble of dinosaurs, Roman altar stones, Egyptian mummies, Samurai warriors and some impressive taxidermy, all presented in an engaging and easily digestible way. The indisputable highlights are a life-size model of a Tyrannosaurus rex and an interactive model of Hadrian's Wall showing every milecastle and fortress. There's also lots of hands-on stuff for the kids, a planetarium with screenings throughout the day and a decent snack bar.

Life Science Centre SCIENCE VILLAGE
(www.life.org.uk; Times Sq; adult/child £9.95/6.95; 10am-6pm Mon-Sat, 11am-6pm Sun) This excellent science village, part of the sober-minded complex of institutes devoted to the study of genetic science, is one of the more interesting attractions in town. Through a series of hands-on exhibits and the latest technology you (or your kids) can discover the incredible secrets of life. The highlight is the Motion Ride, a motion simulator that lets you 'feel' what it's like to experience things like bungee jumping and other extreme sports (the 3-D film changes every year). There's lots of thought-provoking arcade-style games, and if the information sometimes gets lost on the way, never mind, kids will love it.

FREE Discovery Museum MUSEUM
(www.twmuseums.org.uk; Blandford Sq; 10am-5pm Mon-Sat, 2-5pm Sun) Tyneside's rich history is uncovered through a fascinating series of exhibits at this unmissable museum. The exhibitions, spread across three floors of the former Co-operative Wholesale Society building, surround the mightily impressive 30m-long *Turbinia,* the fastest ship in the world in 1897. There's an absorbing section dedicated to shipbuilding on the Tyne including a scale model of the river as

Newcastle-Upon-Tyne

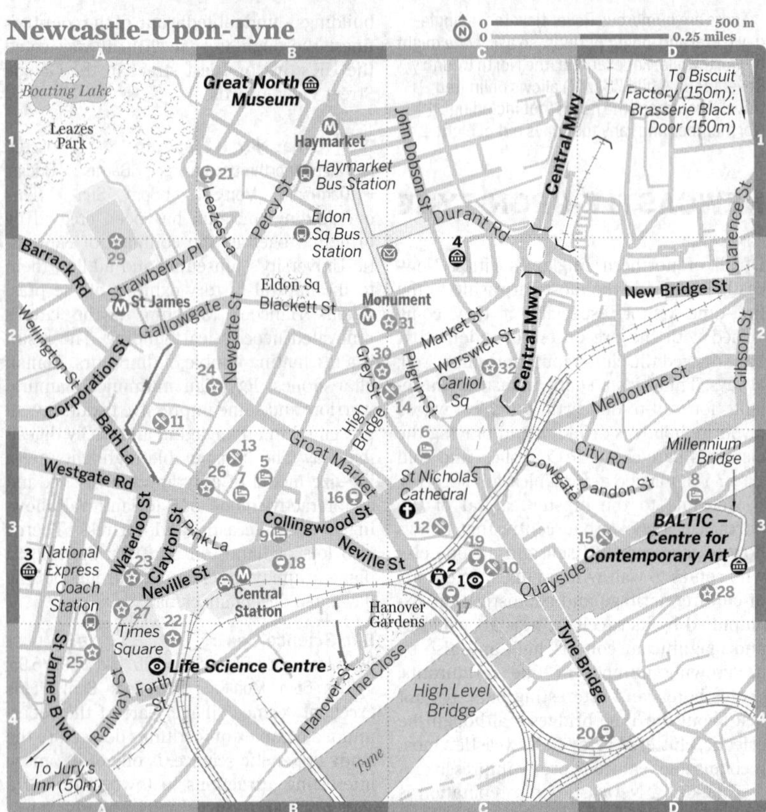

it was in 1929, a buzzers-and-bells science maze for the kids and a 'Story of Newcastle' section giving the lowdown on the city's history from Pons Aelius (Newcastle's Roman name) to Cheryl Cole.

Castle Garth Keep CASTLE

(www.castlekeep-newcastle.org.uk; adult/child £4/free; ⏲10am-4.15pm Mon-Sat, from noon Sun) The stronghold that put both the 'new' and 'castle' into Newcastle has been largely swallowed up by the train station, leaving the square Norman keep as one of the few remaining fragments. Inside you'll discover a fine chevron-covered chapel and an exhibition of architectural models ranging from Hadrian's Wall to 20th-century eyesores. The 360-degree city views from the rooftop are much better than from the BALTIC's 'Viewing Box' across the water.

FREE **Laing Art Gallery** GALLERY

(www.twmuseums.org.uk; New Bridge St; ⏲10am-5pm Mon-Sat, 2-5pm Sun) The exceptional collection at the Laing includes works by Gainsborough, Gauguin and Henry Moore, and an important collection of paintings by Northumberland-born artist John Martin (1789–1854). Free guided tours run Saturdays at 11am.

FREE **Bessie Surtee's House** HISTORIC HOME

(EH; 41-44 Sandhill; ⏲10am-4pm Mon-Fri) The Tyne's northern bank was the hub of commercial Newcastle in the 16th century and on Sandhill a row of leaning merchant houses has survived from that era. One of them is the Bessie Surtee's House, where three rooms are open to the public. The daughter of a wealthy banker, feisty Bessie annoyed daddy by falling in love with John Scott (1751–1838), a pauper. It all ended in smiles as John went on to become Lord Chancellor.

Newcastle-Upon-Tyne

Top Sights

	BALTIC – Centre for Contemporary Art	D3
	Great North Museum	B1
	Life Science Centre	A4

Sights

1	Bessie Surtee's House	C3
2	Castle Garth Keep	C3
3	Discovery Museum	A3
4	Laing Art Gallery	C2

Sleeping

5	Albatross Backpackers In!	B3
6	Greystreethotel	C3
7	Hotel Indigo	B3
8	Malmaison	D3
9	Sleeperz	B3

Eating

10	Big Mussel	C3
11	Blackfriars	A2
12	Oldfields	C3
13	Scrumpy Willow & the Singing Kettle	B3
14	Starters & Puds	C2
15	The Broad Chare	D3

Drinking

16	Blackie Boy	B3
17	Bridge Hotel	C3
18	Centurion Bar	B3
19	Crown Posada	C3
20	The Central	D4
21	Trent House	B1

Entertainment

22	Digital	A4
23	Eazy Street	A3
24	Gate	B2
25	Loft	A4
26	O2 Academy	B3
27	Powerhouse Nightclub	A3
28	Sage Gateshead	D3
29	St James' Park	A2
30	Theatre Royal	B2
31	Tyneside Cinema	C2
32	World Headquarters	C2

Ouseburn Valley

About a mile east of the city centre is the much-touted Ouseburn Valley, the 19th-century industrial heartland of Newcastle and now an up-and-coming, semi-regenerated district, dotted with potteries, glass-blowing studios and other skilled craftspeople, as well as a handful of great bars, clubs and a superb cinema (though much of the area is still an unsightly industrial estate). The yellow Quayside Q2 bus loops through the valley from the city centre. For more info, check out www.ouseburntrust.org.uk.

Biscuit Factory COMMERCIAL GALLERY

(www.thebiscuitfactory.com; 16 Stoddart St; ⊙10am-5pm Mon-Fri, 10am-6pm Sat, 11am-5pm Sun) No prizes for guessing what this commercial art gallery used to be. What it is now, though, is the country's biggest art shop, where you can peruse and buy work by artists from near and far in a variety of mediums, including painting, sculpture, glassware and furniture, much of which has a northeast theme. Even if you don't buy, the art is excellent and there's a top-class restaurant too (Brasserie Black Door).

Seven Stories – The Centre For Children's Books LITERATURE MUSEUM

(www.sevenstories.org.uk; 30 Lime St; adult/child £6.50/5.50; ⊙10am-5pm Mon-Sat, to 4pm Sun) A marvellous conversion of a handsome Victorian mill has resulted in Seven Stories, a very hands-on museum dedicated to the wondrous world of children's literature. Across the seven floors you'll find original manuscripts, a growing collection of artwork from the 1930s onwards, and a constantly changing program of exhibitions, activities and events designed to encourage the AA Milnes of the new millennium.

36 Lime Street ARTISTS COOPERATIVE

(www.36limestreet.co.uk; Ouseburn Warehouse, 36 Lime St) The artistic, independent spirit of Ouseburn is particularly well represented in this artists cooperative, the largest of its kind in the northeast, featuring an interesting mix of artists, performers, designers and musicians. They all share a historic building designed by Newcastle's most important architect, John Dobson (1787–1865), who also designed Grey St and Central Station in the neoclassical style. As it's a working studio you can't just wander in, but there are

BRIDGING THE TYNE

The most famous view in Newcastle is the cluster of Tyne bridges, the most famous of these being the **Tyne Bridge** (1925–28). Its resemblance to Australia's Sydney Harbour Bridge is no coincidence as both were built by the same company (Dorman Long of Middlesbrough) around the same time. The quaint little **Swing Bridge** pivots in the middle to let ships through. Nearby, **High Level Bridge**, designed by Robert Stephenson, was the world's first combined road and railway bridge (1849). The most recent addition is the multiple-award-winning **Millennium Bridge** (aka Blinking Bridge; 2002), which opens like an eyelid to let ships pass. A really great way of experiencing the river and its sights is by boat (p728).

regular exhibitions and open days; check the website for details.

Gateshead

As you cross the Tyne to its southern side you've technically left Newcastle and entered the town of Gateshead, a fact local authorities have tried to make us aware of by promoting the whole kit-and-caboodle-on-Tyne as 'NewcastleGateshead', a clumsy piece of marketing that is moot to all but the most pedantic of visitors. Indeed, the main reason to venture south is to explore the impressive developments along the Tyne but there's little else beyond the river's edge save a residential sprawl.

FREE **BALTIC – Centre for Contemporary Art** ART MUSEUM
(www.balticmill.com; Gateshead Quays; ⏲10am-6pm Wed-Mon, from 10.30am Tue) Once a huge, dirty, yellow grain store overlooking the Tyne, BALTIC is now a huge, dirty, yellow art gallery to rival London's Tate Modern. Unlike the Tate, there are no permanent exhibitions here, but the constantly rotating shows feature the work and installations of some of contemporary art's biggest show stoppers. The complex has artists in residence, a performance space, a cinema, a bar, a spectacular rooftop restaurant (you'll need to book) and a ground-floor restaurant with riverside tables. There's also a viewing box for a fine Tyne vista.

Tours

Newcastle City Tours WALKING TOURS
(☎07780-958679; www.newcastlecitytours.co.uk; per tour from £40) Tailored tours of the city as well as heritage tours of the surrounding region.

River Escapes RIVER CRUISES
(☎01670-785 666; www.riverescapes.co.uk; adult/child £6/4; ⏲noon, 1.30pm & 3.30pm Sat & Sun Jun-Sep) One-hour river cruises departing from Quayside pier at the Millennium Bridge, opposite BALTIC.

Tom Keating Tours WALKING TOURS
(☎0191-488 5115; www.tomkeating.net) Expert, tailor-made tours of the city by a well-respected blue-badge guide. Tours of surrounding region also available.

Sleeping

Budget chains and midrange corporate hotels dominate the city centre. Most of the other accommodation options are in the handsome northern suburb of Jesmond, which is also a popular student hangout. Weekend arrivals will find that most places drop their prices for Friday and Saturday nights.

City Centre

Hotel Indigo HOTEL ££
(☎0191-300 9222; www.hotelindigonewcastle.co.uk; 2-8 Fenkle St; r from £99) Brand new for summer 2012 is this edition of the excellent boutique chain, offering clean lines and pristine rooms equipped with all mod cons, including rainfall showers and a 'media station' (which really means somewhere to charge and play your iGear). Downstairs is the chain's partner restaurant, Marco Pierre White Steakhouse & Grill.

Greystreethotel HOTEL ££
(☎0191-230 6777; www.greystreethotel.com; 2-12 Grey St; r from £99; P) A bit of designer touch along the classiest street in the city centre has been long overdue. The rooms here are gorgeous if a touch poky, all cluttered up with flatscreen TVs, big beds and handsome modern furnishings.

Malmaison HOTEL £££
(☎0191-245 5000; www.malmaison.com; Quayside; r from £99, ste from £189; P@☜) The deliberately stylish Malmaison touch has been

applied to this former warehouse with considerable success, even down to the French-speaking lifts. Big beds, sleek lighting and designer furniture embellish the bouncy boudoirs and slick chambers.

Backpackers Newcastle HOSTEL £
(☎0191-340 7334; www.backpackersnewcastle.com; 262 Westgate Rd; dm from £17.95;) This clean, well-run budget flophouse has just 26 beds, lending it a bit more of a backpacker vibe than its competitors in the city. Bike storage, a kitchen, a big games room, power-showers and a mildly designer feel make this a great option on the Tyne.

Sleeperz HOTEL ££
(☎0191-261 6171; www.sleeperz.com; 15 Westgate St; r from £67) A good location makes this new hotel a good choice for revellers, who won't care that the tidy rooms are on the smallish side.

Jury's Inn HOTEL ££
(☎0191-201 4400; www.jurysinn.com; St James' Gate, Scotswood Rd; r from £49) This edition of the popular Irish chain has rooms, a restaurant, and a bar best described as big, bland and absolutely inoffensive. And at these prices, who cares?

Albatross Backpackers In! HOSTEL £
(☎0191-233 1330; www.albatrossnewcastle.com; 51 Grainger St; dm/d from £17.50/49;) Clean, fully equipped hostel with decent-sized dorms and a self-catering kitchen. There's even a small car park.

Jesmond

The shabby-chic suburb of Jesmond is the place to head for budget and midrange accommodation. Catch the Metro to Jesmond or West Jesmond, bus 80A from near Central Station, or the 38 from Westgate Rd.

Jesmond Dene House HOTEL £££
(☎0191-212 3000; www.jesmonddenehouse.co.uk; Jesmond Dene Rd; s/d/ste from £85/120/180;) This exquisite property is the perfect marriage between traditional styles and modern luxury. The large, gorgeous bedrooms are furnished in a modern interpretation of the Arts and Crafts style and are bedecked with all manner of technological goodies (flatscreen digital TVs, digital radios) and wonderful bathrooms complete with underfloor heating. The restaurant is not bad either.

Newcastle YHA HOSTEL £
(☎0845 371 9335; www.yha.org.uk; 107 Jesmond Rd; dm from £18.50) This nice, rambling place has small dorms that are generally full, so book in advance. It's close to the Jesmond Metro stop.

Eating

The Geordie palate is pretty refined these days and there are a host of fine dining options in all price categories that make their mark. Of course for many locals, Geordies plus food equals the legendary **Greggs** (15 locations throughout the city centre; 8am-5pm), a fast-food chain that started in Newcastle. It has been serving cheap and filling cakes, sandwiches, pastries and drinks since 1951.

City Centre

TOP CHOICE **Blackfriars** BRITISH ££
(☎0191-261 5945; www.blackfriarsrestaurant.co.uk; Friars St; mains £12-21; Lunch & dinner Mon-Sat, lunch Sun) The city centre's top eatery is housed in a 12th-century friary, where chef Troy Terrington serves up a cuisine described as 'modern medieval': beautifully presented, hearty fare sourced locally (check the table-mat map for the provenance of your bream, woodpigeon or roast suckling pygge). Everything else is made from scratch on site, including breads, pastries, ice creams and sausage. Bookings are recommended.

Oldfields BRITISH ££
(www.oldfieldsrealfood.co.uk; Milburn House, Dean St; mains around £16; Mon-Sat, lunch Sun)

NEWCASTLE FOR CHILDREN

The utterly wonderful Seven Stories (p727) is the perfect destination for any kid who has an imagination, while closer to the centre the Centre for Life (p725) and the Discovery Museum (p725) are brilliant and should keep the kids busy for the guts of a day. The most popular park in town is **Leazes Park**, just north of St James' Park, which has a rowing lake, but the nicest of all is **Saltwell Park** (dawn-dusk), an elegant Victorian space behind Gateshead College and easily accessible by buses 53 and 54 from the Gateshead Interchange. Pedestrians can get in through entrances on East Park Rd, West Rd, Saltwell Rd South, Saltwell View and Joicey Rd.

Top-notch, no-nonsense British gourmet fare, using locally sourced ingredients wherever possible, is Oldfields' tasty trade. Tuck into rich and satisfying dishes such as Durham rabbit and crayfish pie, mutton hotpot and Eccles cake with custard in the circular, wood-panelled dining room, before finishing off with a shot of Wylam gin or a locally microbrewed ale.

The Broad Chare GASTROPUB
(☎0191-211 2144; www.thebroadchare.co.uk; 25 Broad Chare; mains £11; ⊙Lunch & dinner Mon-Sat, lunch Sun) Classic English pub grub – the grilled pork chop with black pudding and cider sauce is divine – and superb cask ales make this gastropub one of the best spots in town for a bite to eat. The Michelin people agreed, and stuck it into their Good Pub Guide. Recommended.

Starters & Puds RESTAURANT ££
(☎0191-233 2515; 2-6 Shakespeare St; starters £3.50-7, puddings £5; ⊙Mon-Sat) Situated in a low-lit cellar opposite the Theatre Royal, the idea here is to come for a pretheatre starter, cross the road for a thespian main course then head back for a postperformance dessert (and drink). However, word has got round about the award-winning fare served up here, so now there's also a lunch menu (£10).

Scrumpy Willow & the Singing Kettle ORGANIC RESTAURANT ££
(☎0191-221 2323; www.scrumpywillowandthesingingkettle.co.uk; 89 Clayton St; mains £5-11; ⊙Mon-Sat, lunch Sun; 🖉) Voted one of the UK's top organic eateries by *Guardian* readers, this incredibly popular place bursts at the seams at mealtimes, and one mouthful is enough to understand why. Vegans, veggies and gluten-free eaters are all catered for with an eclectic menu featuring everything from peanut butter sandwiches to Irish stew. All the art on the walls is for sale. Booking recommended.

Big Mussel BELGIAN DINER ££
(www.bigmussel.co.uk; 15 The Side; mains £12-19) This informal diner specialises in one of Europe's oddest national dishes – mussels and chips – the favourite nosh of the Belgians, ideally washed down with a fruity Flemish ale. There are ample pasta and vegetarian options and live jazz on weekday evenings (from 7pm).

Ouseburn Valley

Brasserie Black Door BRASSERIE ££
(Biscuit Factory, 16 Stoddard St; mains £10-16; ⊙Mon-Sat, lunch Sun) Less a gallery restaurant and more a restaurant in a gallery, the Black Door serves up excellent modern English fare – which generally involves a twist from pretty much any other part of the world – in a bright, elegant dining space. A great spot for lunch even if you're not visiting the gallery.

Jesmond

Jesmond Dene House REGIONAL CUISINE £££
(☎0191-212 5555; www.jesmonddenehouse.co.uk; Jesmond Dene Rd; mains £14-40) Head chef Pierre Rigothier is the architect of an exquisite menu heavily influenced by the northeast – venison from County Durham, oysters from Lindisfarne and the freshest herbs plucked straight from the garden – all infused with a touch of French sophistication. The result is a gourmet delight and one of the best dining experiences in the northeast.

Pizzeria Francesca PIZZERIA ££
(134 Manor House Rd; pizzas & pastas £5, other mains £7-15; ⊙Mon-Sat) One of the northeast's best pizza and pasta joints, this chaotic, friendly place is how all Italian restaurants should be. Excitable, happy waiters and huge portions of pizza and pasta keep them queuing at the door – get in line and wait because you can't book in advance.

Drinking

(In)famous for its no-holds barred, alco-fuelled nightlife, a night on the Toon doesn't necessarily need to be about coloured cocktails and ear-popping music. There are plenty of pubs – especially in Ouseburn – that attract a mellower crowd.

City Centre

Centurion Bar BAR
(Central Station) Voted Newcastle's best bar in 2008, the former first-class waiting room at Central Station is ideal for a pre-club drink in style or a pre-train brew on the hop. The exquisitely ornate Victorian tile decoration reaching from floor to ceiling is said to be worth four million pounds. There's an adjoining cafe and deli platform-side.

Crown Posada PUB
(31 The Side) An unspoilt, real-ale pub that is a favourite with more seasoned drinkers, be they the after-work or instead-of-work crowd.

Trent House PUB
(1-2 Leazes Lane) The wall has a simple message: 'Drink Beer. Be Sincere.' This simply unique place is one of the best bars in town because it is all about an ethos rather than a look. Totally relaxed and utterly devoid of pretentiousness, it is an old-school boozer that out-cools every other bar because it isn't trying to. Run by the same folks behind the superb World Headquarters.

Bridge Hotel PUB
(Castle Sq) Next to the High-Level Bridge, this is one of the city centre's more traditional taverns with dark-wood Victorian snugs, kaleidoscope stained glass and a very long bar of real ales.

Blackie Boy PUB
(11 Groat Market) Locals grumble that this darkened boozer, one of the city's original taverns, has gone too upmarket, but it's still a popular place to drink even if the decor has gone all weird. Visitors from the US may have trouble deciphering the novel toilet door signage.

Ouseburn Valley

Ship Inn PUB
(Stepney Bank) A firm fixture on the valley's pub crawl, the Ouseburn's oldest surviving pub (early 19th century) is a traditional boozer popular with locals and incoming fun seekers. On busy days the elbow-bending spills out onto the small green in front.

Cumberland Arms PUB
(off Byker Bank, Ouseburn) Sitting on a hill at the top of the Ouseburn, this 19th-century bar has a sensational selection of ales and ciders as well as a range of Northumberland meads. There's a terrace outside, where you can read a book from the Bring One, Borrow One library inside.

Cluny BAR, MUSIC VENUE
(36 Lime St) Cool bar by day, even cooler music venue by night, this superpopular spot defines the independent spirit of the Ouseburn Valley.

Gateshead

The Central PUB
(Half Moon La) Owned by the same crowd as the Cluny, the Central is one reason to cross the Tyne into Gateshead. This popular boozer has a quirky main bar and live music upstairs.

Jesmond

Mr Lynch BAR
(Archbold Tce) Newcastle goes shabby chic with this '60s-style retro bar at the southernmost edge of Jesmond. Ignore the appearance and focus on the crowd, a knowledgeable mix of students and local trendies. There's live music Friday and Saturday.

☆ Entertainment

Are you up for it? You'd better be, because Newcastle's nightlife doesn't mess about. There is action beyond the club scene – you'll just have to wade through a sea of staggering, glassy-eyed clubbers to get to it.

The large, loud entertainment complex that is the **Gate** (www.thegatenewcastle.co.uk; Newgate St) adds another tier to Newcastle's entertainment scene, albeit one that smells of new plastic and pizza. Behind the shimmering glass edifice there are countless chain eateries, a nightclub, bars, a casino and a 12-screen cinema.

The Crack (www.thecrackmagazine.com) is a free monthly magazine available from clubs, tourist offices and some hotels containing comprehensive club, theatre, music and cinema listings for the northeast's nightlife hotspots.

Cinema

Tyneside Cinema CINEMA
(www.tynesidecinema.co.uk; Pilgrim St) Opened in 1937 as Newcastle's first newsreel cinema, this period picture house is all plush red-velvet seats and swish art deco design. It screens a blend of mainstream and offbeat movies as well as archive British Pathé films (11.30am; free). Free guided tours of the building (one hour) run on Tuesday, Wednesday, Friday and Saturday at 11.15am.

Star and Shadow CINEMA
(www.starandshadow.org.uk; Stepney Bank; membership £1, admission £4) This unlikely looking cine-club is based in an old warehouse once used to store props for Tyne-Tees TV. It is the best movie experience in town, and the place to go for your art-house, cult, black-and-white, and gay and lesbian film needs. Asylum seekers get in free.

Live Music

Sage Gateshead MUSIC VENUE
(☎0191-443 4666; www.thesagegateshead.org; Gateshead Quays) Few contemporary pieces of architecture will stand the test of time, but Norman Foster's magnificent

chrome-and-glass horizontal bottle might just be one that does. Most come to gape and wander, some to hear live music, from folk to classical orchestras, or engage in educational or research activities. It is the home of the Northern Sinfonia and Folkworks.

Head of Steam@The Cluny MUSIC VENUE
(☎0191-230 4474; www.headofsteam.co.uk; 36 Lime St) This is one of the best-known spots in town to hear live music, attracting all kinds of performers, from experimental prog-rock heads to up-and-coming pop goddesses. Touring acts and local talent fill the bill every night of the week.

Newcastle Arena MUSIC VENUE
(☎0844-493 6666; www.metroradioarena.co.uk; Arena Way, off Scotswood Rd) The biggest concert venue in the northeast attracts some of the most glitter-sprinkled names of the international pop and rock world as well as musical productions and TV talent show spin-offs. Gigs share the multipurpose auditorium with basketball, ice-hockey and other events. The arena is near the waterfront west of the city centre.

Nightclubs

Digital NIGHTCLUB
(www.yourfutureisdigital.com; Times Sq) A two-floored cathedral to dance music, this mega-club was voted one of the top 20 clubs in the world by *DJ Magazine* – thanks to the best sound system you're ever likely to hear. Mondays are 'Born in the '80s' nights, Thursdays 'Stonelove' Indie nights are unmissable and Saturdays are pure 'Love'.

World Headquarters NIGHTCLUB
(www.welovewhq.com; Curtis Mayfield House, Carliol Sq) Dedicated to the genius of black music in all its guises – funk, rare groove, dance-floor jazz, northern soul, genuine R&B, lush disco, proper house and reggae – this fabulous club is strictly for true believers, and judging from the numbers, there are thousands of them.

O2 Academy NIGHTCLUB
(www.o2academynewcastle.co.uk; Westgate Rd; admission £4) Every Saturday, 25,000 people cram into the Academy for Propaganda, probably the country's biggest indie club night. Guest DJs are the norm, generally well-known musicians playing their favourite records.

Theatre

Northern Stage THEATRE
(☎0191-230 5151; www.northernstage.co.uk; Barras Bridge, Haymarket) The original Newcastle Playhouse has been transformed into this marvellous performance space (three stages and a high-tech, movable acoustic wall) that attracts touring international and national shows.

Theatre Royal THEATRE
(☎08448-112121; www.theatreroyal.co.uk; 100 Grey St) The winter home of the Royal Shakespeare Company is full of Victorian splendour and has an excellent program of drama.

Sport

Newcastle United Football Club FOOTBALL
(www.nufc.co.uk) NUFC is more than just a football team: it is the collective expression of Geordie hope and pride as well as the release for decades of economic, social and sporting frustration. The club's fabulous ground, **St James' Park** (Strawberry Pl), is always packed, but you can get a **stadium tour** (☎0844-372 1892; adult/child £10/7; ⏱11am, 1.30pm daily & 4hr before kick-off on match days) of the place, including the dugout and changing rooms. Match tickets go on public sale about two weeks before a game or you

GAY & LESBIAN NEWCASTLE

Newcastle's gay scene is pretty dynamic, with its hub at the 'Pink Triangle' formed by Waterloo, Neville and Collingwood Sts, but stretching as far south as Scotswood Rd. There are plenty of gay bars in the area and a few great clubs.

» A welcoming mixed crowd make up the numbers at **Eazy Street** (8-10 Westmorland Rd) – the cabaret nights are especially good.

» **Loft** (10a Scotswood Rd) Loud, proud and completely cheesy, this 1st-floor club is open seven nights a week from 11pm.

» **Powerhouse Nightclub** (www.clubph.co.uk; 9-19 Westmorland Rd) Newcastle's brashest queer nightclub, with flashing lights, video screens and lots of suggestive posing.

THE GREAT NORTH RUN

First held in 1981, the world's biggest half-marathon sees over 50,000 runners grunt and sweat a gruelling 13.1 miles from just north of the city centre, along the central motorway, across the Tyne Bridge and east along the Tyne to slump on the seafront at South Shields. Held in early autumn, it's one of the largest annual occasions in the city's sporting calendar and brings out the Geordie crowds, who line the route egging on the athletes with applause and, less appropriately, plastic cups of Newkie Brown beer. Bands pump out Geordie anthems at strategic points, adding to the festival atmosphere.

can try the stadium on the day, but there's no chance for big matches, such as those against arch-rivals Sunderland.

Information

City Library (33 New Bridge St W; ⌚8.30am-8pm Mon-Thu, to 5.30 Fri & Sat) Free internet access at Newcastle's stomping new library building. Bring ID.

Police Station (☎03456-043043; cnr Pilgrim & Market Sts)

Post Office (36 Northumberland St; ⌚9am-5.30pm Mon-Sat) On the 2nd floor of WH Smith. Has a bureau de change.

Newcastle General Hospital (☎0191-233 6161; Westgate Rd) Has an Accident and Emergency unit.

Tourist Office (☎0191-277 8000; www.visitnewcastlegateshead.com; Central Arcade, Market St; ⌚9.30am-5.30pm Mon-Sat, 10am-4pm Sun) Information and a booking service.

Getting There & Away

Air

Newcastle International Airport (☎0871-882 1121; www.newcastleairport.com) Seven miles north of the city off the A696. It has direct services to many UK and European cities as well as long-haul flights to Dubai. Tour operators fly charters to the Americas and Africa.

Boat

DFDS Seaways (☎0870-522 9955; www.dfdsseaways.co.uk) Operates ferries to Newcastle from the Dutch port of Ijmuiden, near Amsterdam. No-frills flights have put an end to all the ferries to and from Norway and Sweden.

Bus

Local and regional buses leave from Haymarket or Eldon Sq bus stations. National Express buses arrive and depart from the coach station on St James Blvd. For local buses around the northeast, the excellent-value Explorer North East ticket (£9) is valid on most services.

Berwick-upon-Tweed Bus 501/505; two hours, five daily.

Edinburgh National Express; £17.50, three hours, two daily.

London National Express/Megabus; £12 to £35, seven hours, nine daily.

Manchester National Express; £21, five hours, five daily.

Train

Newcastle is on the main rail line between London and Edinburgh and is the starting point of the scenic Tyne Valley Line west to Carlisle.

Alnmouth (for bus connections to Alnwick) £9, 25 minutes, hourly.

Berwick £23.50, 45 minutes, hourly.

Carlisle £14.40, 1½ hours, hourly.

London King's Cross £116.20, three hours, half-hourly.

York £33.50, one hour, every 20 minutes.

Getting Around

To/From the Airport

The airport is linked to town by the Metro (£3.50, 25 minutes, every 15 minutes).

Car

Driving around Newcastle isn't fun thanks to the web of roads, bridges and one-way systems, but there are plenty of car parks in town and around the outskirts.

Public Transport

There's a large bus network, but the best means of getting around is the excellent Metro, with fares from £1.50. Several saver passes are also available. The tourist office can supply you with route plans for the bus and Metro networks.

The DaySaver (£5, £4.20 after 9am) gives unlimited Metro travel for one day, and the DayRover (adult/child £6.80/3.70) gives unlimited travel on all modes of transport in Tyne and Wear for one day.

Taxi

On weekend nights taxis can be as rare as covered flesh; try **Noda Taxis** (☎0191-222 1888), which has a kiosk outside the entrance to Central Station.

NORTHUMBERLANDIA

Surely set to become one of the northeast's most bizarre attractions, and a rival to the *Angel of the North*, **Northumberlandia** (www.northumberlandia.com) between the A1 and the town of Cramlington, around 7 miles north of Newcastle city centre, will be the world's largest human form sculpted into the landscape. Using 1.5 million tons of slag (nicknames already abound) from Shotton surface mine, artist Charles Jencks (or more like a gang of Geordies with excavators) have fashioned a 400m-long female nude, whose breasts will reach a perky height of 34m. The sculpture is scheduled for completion by the end of 2012.

AROUND NEWCASTLE

Angel of the North LANDMARK

Nicknamed the Gateshead Flasher, this extraordinary 200-tonne, rust-coloured human frame with wings, more soberly known as the *Angel of the North*, has been looming over the A1 (M) about 5 miles south of Newcastle since 1998. At 20m high and with a wingspan wider than a Boeing 767, Antony Gormley's most successful work is the UK's largest sculpture and the most viewed piece of public art in the country, though Mark Wallinger's *White Horse* in Kent may pinch both titles over the next decade. Buses 21 and 22 from Eldon Sq in Newcastle will take you there.

Tynemouth

One of the most popular Geordie days out is to this handsome seaside resort 6 miles east of Newcastle. Besides being the mouth of the Tyne, this is one of the best surf spots in all England, with great all-year breaks off the immense, crescent-shaped Blue Flag beach. The town even occasionally hosts the **National Surfing Championships.** (www.britishsurfchamps.co.uk)

For all your surfing needs, including lessons, call into the **Tynemouth Surf Company** (☎0191-258 2496; www.tynemouthsurf.co.uk; Grand Pde), which provides two-hour group lessons for £25 or one-hour individual lessons for the same price.

If riding nippy surf is not your thing, the town's other main draw is the 11th-century ruins of **Tynemouth Priory** (EH; adult/child £5/2.50; ⊙10am-5pm Apr-Sep), built by Benedictine monks on a strategic bluff above the mouth of the Tyne, but ransacked during the Dissolution in 1539. The military took over for four centuries, only leaving in 1960, and today the skeletal remains of the priory church sit alongside old military installations, their guns aimed out to sea at an enemy that never came.

Every weekend Tynemouth's beautiful Victorian Metro station hosts **Tynemouth Market** (www.tynemouthmarket.co.uk), one of Tyneside's best secondhand bazaars.

From Newcastle city centre take the Metro to Tynemouth or bus 306 from the Haymarket.

Segedunum HISTORIC SITE, TOWER

(www.twmuseums.org.uk; adult/child £4.95/free; ⊙10am-5pm Apr-Oct) The last strong post of Hadrian's Wall was the fort of **Segedunum**, 6 miles east of Newcastle at Wallsend. Beneath the 35m-high tower, which you can climb for some terrific views, is an absorbing site that includes a reconstructed Roman bathhouse (with steaming pools and frescoes) and a fascinating museum that gives visitors a well-rounded picture of life during Roman times.

Segedeunum is in Wallsend, which is on the Metro line from Newcastle.

COUNTY DURHAM

Spread out across the lonely, rabbit-inhabited North Pennines and the gentle ochre hills of Teesdale, County Durham's star attraction is its county town – home to a magnificent cathedral that is easily one of England's finest.

The cathedral and the adjoining castle were the seat of the once-powerful prince bishops, rulers since 1081 of the Palatinate of Durham, a political entity created by William the Conqueror as a bulwark against rowdy Saxons and uppity Scots.

In more recent times, the county was at the heart of the region's coal mining industry, a brutal business that ended with the last pit closing in 1984, leaving the landscape with some fast-dissolving yet evocative scarring.

Information

Durham's tourist information services have been centralised under the **Visit Durham** (☎03000-262626; www.thisisdurham.com) banner and are now available online or on the phone. Tourist offices have been replaced with visitor contact points, which offer town maps and leaflets but nothing more.

Durham

POP 42,940

Consider the setting: England's most beautiful Romanesque cathedral, a masterpiece of Norman architecture and a resplendent monument to the country's ecclesiastical history; a huge castle; and, surrounding them both, a cobweb of cobbled streets usually full of upper-crust students attending Durham's other big pull, England's third university of choice (after Oxford and Cambridge). Welcome to Durham.

Durham is unquestionably beautiful, but once you've visited the cathedral and walked the old town looking for the best views there isn't much else to do; a day-trip from Newcastle or an overnight stop on your way to explore the rest of the county is the best way to see the city of the Prince Bishops.

Sights

Durham Cathedral CATHEDRAL

(www.durhamcathedral.co.uk; donation requested, guided tours adult/child £4/free; ⌚7.30am-6pm, to 5.30pm Sun, guided tours 10.30am, 11am & 2pm Mon-Sat, Evensong 5.15pm Mon-Sat, 3.30pm Sun) This exquisite cathedral is the definitive structure of the Anglo-Norman Romanesque style, one of the world's greatest places of worship and, since 1986, a Unesco World Heritage Site.

It's an overwhelming building with an unusually solid, fortified appearance. It may have been built to pay tribute to God and to house the bones of local St Cuthbert, but it needed to be strong enough to withstand attack by Scots and Saxons unimpressed with the arrival of the Normans some years earlier.

Beyond the main door – and the famous (and much-reproduced) **Sanctuary Knocker**, which medieval felons would strike to gain 37 days asylum within the cathedral before standing trial or leaving the country – is a spectacular interior. This is the first European cathedral to be roofed with stone-ribbed vaulting, which upheld the heavy stone roof and made it possible to build pointed transverse arches – the first in England, and a great architectural achievement. The central tower dates from 1262, but was damaged in a fire caused by lightning in 1429, and was unsatisfactorily patched up until it was entirely rebuilt in 1470. The western towers were added in 1217–26.

One of the cathedral's most beautiful parts is the **Galilee Chapel**, which dates from 1175 and whose northern side features rare examples of 12th-century wall painting (thought to feature portraits of Sts Cuthbert and Oswald). The chapel also contains the **tomb of the Venerable Bede**, the 8th-century Northumbrian monk turned historian: his *Ecclesiastical History of the English People* is still the prime source of information on the development of early Christian Britain. Among other things, he introduced the numbering of years from the birth of Jesus. He was first buried at Jarrow, but in 1022 a miscreant monk stole his remains and brought them here.

Other highlights include the 14th-century **Bishop's Throne** and the beautiful stone Neville Screen (1372-80), which separates the high altar from **St Cuthbert's tomb**.

The mostly 19th-century **Cloisters** is where you'll find the **Monk's Domitory**, now a library of 30,000 books and displaying Anglo-Saxon carved stones. There are also **audiovisual displays** on the building of the cathedral and the life of St Cuthbert. Also worthwhile are the **guided tours** and **Evensong** services.

The **tower** (£5) provides show-stopping vistas, but you've got to climb 325 steps to enjoy them.

Durham Castle CASTLE

(www.dur.ac.uk; admission by guided tour only, adult/child £5/3.50; ⌚tours 2pm, 3pm & 4pm term time, 10am, 11am & noon during university vacations) Built as a standard motte-and-bailey fort in 1072, Durham Castle was the prince bishops' home until 1837, when it became the first college of the new university. It remains a university hall, and you can stay here.

The castle has been much altered over the centuries, as each successive prince bishop sought to put his particular imprint on the place, but heavy restoration and reconstruction were necessary anyway as the castle is

Durham

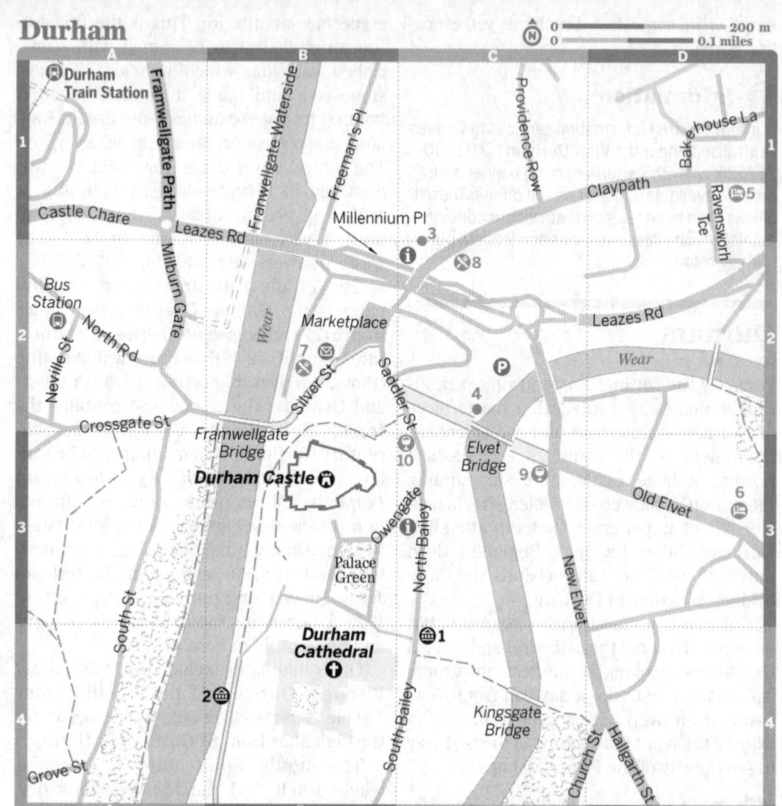

built of soft stone on soft ground. Highlights of the 45-minute tour include the groaning 17th-century **Black Staircase**, the 16th-century **chapel** and the beautifully preserved **Norman chapel** (1080).

Durham Heritage Centre MUSEUM
(www.durhamheritagecentre.org.uk; admission £2.50; ⏲2pm-4.30pm Easter-Oct) A pretty crowded collection of displays on Durham's history from the Middle Ages to mining.

Museum of Archaeology MUSEUM
(Old Fulling Mill, Prebend's Walk; admission £1; ⏲11am-4pm Apr-Oct) A university museum with a collection dating back to prehistoric times.

Oriental Museum MUSEUM
(Elvet Hill; admission £1.50; ⏲10am-5pm Mon-Fri, noon-5pm Sat & Sun) Egyptian artefacts and a giant Chinese bed are highlights of this excellent museum 3 miles south of the city centre. Take bus 5 or 5A.

Crook Hall GARDENS
(www.crookhallgardens.co.uk; Frankland Lane; adult/child £6/5.50; ⏲11am-5pm Sun-Thu Apr-Sep) This medieval hall with 1.6 hectares of charming small gardens is about 200m north of the city centre.

Durham Light Infantry Museum MUSEUM
(Aykley Heads; adult/child £3.60/1.60; ⏲10am-5pm Apr-Oct, to 4pm Nov-Mar) The history of Durham's County Regiment is brought to life at this museum, 500m northwest of city centre.

Activities

There are superb views back to the cathedral and castle from the leafy riverbanks; walk around the bend between Elvet and Framwellgate Bridges, or hire a boat at Elvet Bridge.

Durham

Top Sights

Durham Castle B3
Durham Cathedral B4

Sights

1 Durham Heritage Centre C4
2 Museum of Archaeology B4

Activities, Courses & Tours

Browns Boathouse (see 4)
3 Guided Walks C1
4 Prince Bishop River Cruiser C2

Sleeping

5 Cathedral View D1
6 Gadds Townhouse D3

Eating

7 Cottons B2
8 Oldfields C2

Drinking

9 Half Moon Inn C3
10 Shakespeare C3

Prince Bishop River Cruiser BOAT TOUR
(☎0191-386 9525; www.princebishoprc.co.uk; Elvet Bridge; adult/child £7/4; ⏲cruises 12.30, 2 & 3pm Jun-Sep) One-hour cruises on the Wear.

Browns Boathouse BOAT HIRE
(☎0191-386 3779; per hr per person £5) Rowing boats can be hired from below Elvet Bridge.

Guided Walks WALKING TOUR
(adult/child £3.50/free; ⏲2pm Sat & Sun May-Sep) Walks lasting 1½ hours leave from Millennium Pl. Contact the tourist office for details.

Ghost Walks THEMED WALKS
(adult/child £4/1; ⏲7.30pm Mon Jul-Sep) Ghost walks also drift around town. Contact the tourist office for details.

Cycle Force 2000 MOUNTAIN BIKING
(29 Claypath) Charges £10/16 per half-/full day for mountain-bike hire.

Sleeping

The **tourist office** makes local bookings free of charge, which is a good thing considering that Durham is always busy with visitors; graduation week in late June results in accommodation gridlock.

TOP CHOICE **Gadds Townhouse** BOUTIQUE HOTEL £££
(☎0191-384 1037; www.gaddstownhouse.com; 34 Old Elvet; d from £90) Possibly the northeast's most bizarre digs, the 11 rooms at this fun place leave few indifferent. Each room has a theme with the 'Le Jardin' featuring a shed and garden furniture, the 'Premiere' boasting a huge projection screen and popcorn machine, while the 'Edwardian Express' recreates a night in a yesteryear sleeper compartment. The most 'normal' room is the Garden Lodge, complete with outdoor tub and underfloor heating. The restaurant is superb and some rooms have cathedral views.

Cathedral View B&B ££
(☎0191-386 9566; www.cathedralview.com; 212 Gilesgate; s/d from £70/85) This anonymous Georgian house has no sign, but inside it does exactly what it says on the tin. Six large rooms decorated with lots of cushions and coordinated bed linen and window dressings make up the numbers, but it's the two at the back that are worth the fuss: the views of the cathedral are fantastic. Breakfast is cooked to order and served out on the vista-rich terrace or in the dining room lined with prints by Beryl Cook, the amateur painter who became a national sensation with her colourful paintings of larger-than-life figures.

Farnley Tower B&B ££
(☎0191-375 0011; www.farnley-tower.co.uk; The Ave; s/d from £65/75; P) A beautiful Victorian stone building that looks more like a small manor house than a family-run B&B, this place has 13 large rooms, none better than the superior class, which are not just spacious but have excellent views of the cathedral and castle. The service is impeccable. It's situated around 1km southwest of the train station.

Victorian Town House B&B ££
(☎05601-459168; www.durhambedandbreakfast.co.uk; 2 Victoria Tce; s/d £60/80; Wi-Fi) This three-room B&B occupying an 1850s townhouse near the train station comfortably combines period fireplaces and fancy ceiling roses with flatscreen TVs and DVD libraries. Two rooms have cathedral views and there's a peaceful terraced garden out the back.

Eating

Cheap eats aren't a problem in Durham thanks to the students, but quality is a little thin on the ground. Some pubs do good bar food.

BEDE'S WORLD

The fairly grim southeastern suburb of Jarrow is embedded in labour history for the 1936 Jarrow Crusade, when 200 men walked from here to London to protest against the appalling conditions brought about by unemployment.

But it is also famous as the home of the Venerable Bede, author of the *Ecclesiastical History of the English People*. **Bede's World** (www.bedesworld.co.uk; Church Bank; adult/child £5.50/3.50; ⏲10am-5.30pm) comprises St Paul's Church, which dates back to the 7th century; a museum; and many reconstructed medieval buildings. It's accessible via the Metro.

Oldfields BRITISH ££
(18 Claypath; mains £12-19) With its strictly seasonal menus that use only local or organic ingredients sourced within a 60-mile radius of Durham, this award-winning restaurant is one of the county's finest, though it's not quite as good as its Newcastle sister. With dishes such as smoked haddock pan haggerty and wild boar pie on the menu, all served in the old boardroom of the former HQ of the Durham Gas Company (1881), it's the best meal in town.

Cottons CAFE £
(32 Silver St; snacks £2.50-5; ⏲9.30am-5.30pm Mon-Sat, 11am-4.30 Sun) Down an inconspicuous flight of steps two doors along from the post office, this junk shop/art gallery/tearoom hides in a brick-and-stone cellar where a range of teas plus sandwiches, jacket potatoes and cakes are served to in-the-know punters.

Drinking

Durham may be a big student town, but most scholars seem to take the whole study thing really seriously, and the nightlife here isn't as boisterous as you might expect from a university town. There is, however, a fistful of lovely old bars.

Half Moon Inn PUB
(New Elvet) Sports fans love this old-style bar for its devotion to the mixed pleasures of Sky Sports; we like it for its wonderful collection of whiskies and ales. There's a summer beer garden if you want to avoid the whoops and hollers of the armchair jocks.

Shakespeare PUB
(63 Saddler St) As authentic a traditional bar as you're likely to find in these parts, this is the perfect locals' boozer, complete with dartboard and cosy snugs. Needless to say, the selection of beers and spirits is terrific. Not surprisingly, students love it too.

Information

Post Office (Silver St)

Public Library (Millennium Pl; ⏲9.30am-7pm Mon-Fri, 9am-5pm Sat, 10.30am-4pm Sun) Bring ID to surf the web.

Visitor Contact Point (www.thisisdurham.com; Owen Gate; ⏲9.30am-5.30pm Mon-Sat, 11am-4pm Sun) Small but helpful, with all the usual tourist information.

Getting There & Away

Bus

Darlington Buses 5 and 7; one hour, four hourly.

Leeds National Express; £18.20, 2½ hours, four daily.

London National Express; £36.90, 6½ hours, four daily.

Newcastle Buses 21, 44, X41, X2; one hour to 1¾ hours, several per hour.

Train

The East Coast mainline arches over Durham for speedy connections to many destinations across the country:

Edinburgh £54.50, two hours, hourly.

London (King's Cross) £150.50, three hours, hourly.

Newcastle £4.70, 15 minutes, five hourly.

York £25, one hour, four hourly.

Getting Around

Pratt's (☎0191-386 0700) A trustworthy taxi company.

Around Durham

Beamish Open-Air Museum INDUSTRIAL MUSEUM
(www.beamish.org.uk; adult/child £17.50/10; ⏲10am-5pm Apr-Oct) County Durham's greatest attraction is **Beamish**, a living, breathing, working museum that offers a fabulous, warts-and-all portrait of industrial life in the

northeast during the 19th and 20th centuries. Instructive and lots of fun to boot, this huge museum spread over 121 hectares will appeal to all ages.

You can go underground, explore mine heads, a working farm, a school, a dentist and a pub, and marvel at how every cramped pit cottage seemed to find room for a piano. Don't miss a ride behind an 1815 Steam Elephant locomotive or a replica of Stephenson's *Locomotion No 1*.

Allow at least three hours to do the place justice. Many elements (such as the railway) aren't open in the winter (when the admission price is lower); check the website for details.

Beamish is about 8 miles northwest of Durham. Buses 28 from Newcastle (one hour, half hourly) and 720 from Durham (30 minutes, hourly) operate to the museum.

Bishop Auckland

The name's a giveaway, but this friendly, midsized market town 11 miles southwest of Durham has been the country residence of the bishops of Durham since the 12th century and their official home for over 100 years. The castle is just next to the large, attractive market square; leading off it are small-town streets lined with shops and a sense that anything exciting is happening elsewhere.

The imposing gates of **Auckland Castle** (www.auckland-castle.co.uk; adult/child £4/free; ⏲2-5pm Sun-Mon Easter-Jul & Sep, plus Wed Aug), just off Market Pl behind the town hall, lead to the official home of the bishop of Durham. It's palatial – each successive bishop extended the building. Underneath the spiky Restoration Gothic exterior, the buildings are mainly medieval. The outstanding attraction of the castle is the striking 17th-century chapel, which thrusts up into the sky. It has a remarkable interior, some of which dates from the 12th century, which was converted from the former great hall. Admission is by guided tour only.

Around the castle is a hilly and wooded 324-hectare **deer park** (admission free; ⏲7am-sunset) with an 18th-century deer shelter.

Ever noticed that Stan Laurel had a bit of a north country accent? He spent much of his childhood in Bishop Auckland where ma and pa ran the Theatre Royal. The tourist office has free maps of the **Stan Laurel walk** for fans.

The **visitor contact point** (Market Pl; ⏲10am-5pm Mon-Fri, 9am-4pm Sat) is in the town hall on the main square.

Bus 1/1B (three hourly) run to Darlington, Durham is served hourly by bus X24 and to and from Newcastle take bus 21 (half hourly). Change at Darlington for regular trains to Bishop Auckland.

Binchester Roman Fort HISTORIC SITE

(www.durham.gov.uk/binchester; admission £2.50; ⏲11am-5pm Easter-Jun & Sep, 10am-5pm Jul & Aug) One and a half miles north of Bishop Auckland are the ruins of Binchester Roman Fort, or Vinovia as it was originally called. The fort, first built in wood around AD 80 and refashioned in stone early in the 2nd century, was the largest in County Durham, covering 4 hectares. Excavations show the remains of Dere St, the main high road from York to Hadrian's Wall, and the best-preserved example of a heating system in the country – part of the commandant's private bath suite. Findings from the site are displayed at the Bowes Museum in Barnard Castle.

FREE **Escomb Church** CHURCH

(www.escombsaxonchurch.com; Saxon Green; admission free; ⏲9am-8pm Apr-Sep) The stones of the abandoned Binchester Fort were often reused, and Roman inscriptions can be spotted in the walls of the hauntingly beautiful Escomb Church. The church dates from the 7th century – it's one of only three complete

LOCOMOTION

If steam gets you and your kids hot under the collar, then a half-day trip to the National Railway Museum at Shildon, now known as **Locomotion** (www.nrm.org.uk; admission free; ⏲10am-5pm Apr-Oct), is a must. Shildon is best known as the starting point for Stephenson's *No 1 Locomotion* in 1825, which finished up in Stockton-on-Tees. Less museum and more hands-on experience, this regional extension of the National Railway Museum in York has all manner of railway paraphernalia spread out over a half-mile area that all leads to a huge hanger containing 70-odd locomotives from all eras. Shildon is on the Darlington to Bishop Auckland rail line; alternatively take buses 1 and 1B from Darlington.

WORTH A TRIP

MIDDLESBROUGH INSTITUTE OF MODERN ART

Teeside's largest town is Middlesbrough, which is something of a post-industrial mess, an unattractive urban centre that does little to entice visitors. However the town's one redeeming attraction is the boldly modern **Middlesbrough Institute of Modern Art** (MIMA; www.visitmima.com; Centre Sq; admission free; ⌚10am-5pm Tue, Wed, Fri & Sat, 10am-7pm Thu, noon-4pm Sun), which has gathered the city's municipal art collections under one impressive roof. The 1500 or so pieces include work by some of Britain's most important 20th-century artists, including Duncan Grant, Vanessa Bell (sister of Virginia Woolf), Henri Gaudier-Brzeska and Frank Auerbach. There's also a good collection of ceramics and jewellery.

Middlesbrough is served by hourly buses from Newcastle (£6.80, 90 minutes). The bus station is about 500m from MIMA. Arriva X1 between Middlesbrough and Newcastle stops at Durham (every 30 minutes, one hour).

surviving Saxon churches in Britain. The whitewashed cell, striking and moving in its simplicity, is incongruously encircled by 20th-century housing. If no one's about, the keys sometimes hang on a hook outside a nearby house. Escomb is 3 miles west of Bishop Auckland (bus 86, hourly).

Barnard Castle

POP 6720

Barnard Castle, or just plain Barney, is a charming market town full of antiquarian shops and atmospheric old pubs that serve as a wonderful setting for the town's twin-starred attractions, a daunting ruined castle at its edge and an extraordinary French chateau on its outskirts. If you can drag yourself away, it is also a terrific base for exploring Teesdale and the North Pennines.

Sights

Barnard Castle CASTLE RUINS

(EH; adult/child £4.40/2.60; ⌚10am-6pm Easter-Sep) Partly dismantled during the 16th century, one of northern England's largest castles, built on a cliff above the Tees, still manages to cover more than two very impressive hectares. Founded by Guy de Bailleul and rebuilt around 1150, its occupants spent their time suppressing the locals and fighting off the Scots – on their days off they sat around enjoying the wonderful river views.

Bowes Museum MUSEUM

(www.thebowesmuseum.org.uk; adult/child £9/free; ⌚10am-5pm) About half a mile east of town stands a Louvre-inspired French chateau containing an extraordinary and wholly unexpected museum. Funded by 19th-century industrialist John Bowes, but largely the brainchild of his Parisienne actress wife Josephine, the museum was built by French architect Jules Pellechet to display a collection the Bowes had travelled the world to assemble. Opened in 1892, this spectacular museum has lavish furniture and paintings by Canaletto, El Greco and Goya as well as 15,000 other *objets d'art*, including 55 paintings by Josephine herself. A new section examines textiles through the ages, with some incredible dresses from the 17th century to the 1970s, while the precious metals exhibition displays clocks, watches and tableware in gold and silver. The museum's star attraction, however, is the marvellous mechanical swan, which performs every day at 2pm. If you miss it or arrive too early, there's now a film showing it in action.

Sleeping & Eating

Marwood House B&B ££

(☎01833-637493; www.marwoodhouse.co.uk; 98 Galgate; s/d from £30/60) A handsome Victorian property with tastefully appointed rooms (the owner's tapestries feature in the decor and her homemade biscuits sit on a tray), Marwood House's standout feature is the small fitness room in the basement, complete with a sauna that fits up to four people.

Old Well Inn HOTEL ££

(☎01833-690130; www.theoldwellinn.co.uk; 21 The Bank; r from £69; 📶) You won't find larger bedrooms in town than at this old coaching inn, which is built over a huge well (not visible). Of the 10 rooms, No 9 is the most impressive with its own private entrance, flagstone floors and a bath. The pub has a reputation for excellent, filling pub grub and real ales from Darlington and Yorkshire. The amateur Castle Players, who perform a different Shakespeare play at the castle every summer, were formed here during an early '80s power cut.

Information

Visitor Contact Point (☎03000-262626; www.thisisdurham.com; Woodleigh, Flatts Rd; ⏱9.30am-5pm Mon-Sat, 10am-4pm Sun Easter-Oct) Has information on all the sights.

Getting There & Away

Buses 95 and 96 run hourly between Barnard Castle and Middleton-in-Teesdale.

Around Barnard Castle

Raby Castle CASTLE
(www.rabycastle.com; adult/child £10/4.50; ⏱1-5pm Sun-Wed May, Jun & Sep, Sun-Fri Jul & Aug) About 7 miles northeast of Barnard Castle is the sprawling, romantic Raby Castle, a stronghold of the Catholic Neville family until it engaged in some ill-judged plotting (the 'Rising of the North') against the oh-so Protestant Queen Elizabeth in 1569. Most of the interior dates from the 18th and 19th centuries, but the exterior remains true to the original design, built around a courtyard and surrounded by a moat. There are beautiful formal gardens and a deer park. Bus 8 zips between Barnard Castle and Raby (15 minutes, eight daily).

Egglestone Abbey RUIN
(EH; ⏱dawn-dusk) The ransacked, spectral ruins of Egglestone Abbey, dating from the 1190s, overlook a lovely bend of the Tees. You can envisage the abbey's one-time grandeur despite the gaunt remains. They're a pleasant 1.5-mile-long walk southeast of Barnard Castle.

North Pennines

The North Pennines stretch from western Durham to just short of Hadrian's Wall in the north. In the south is Teesdale, the gently undulating valley of the River Tees; to the north is the much wilder Weardale, carved through by the River Wear. Both dales are marked by ancient quarries and mines – industries that date back to Roman times. The wilds of the North Pennines are also home to the picturesque Derwent and Allen Valleys, north of Weardale.

For online information, check out www.northpennines.org.uk and www.exploreteesdale.co.uk.

TEESDALE

A patchwork quilt of sheep-dotted green, sewn with dry-stone thread, Teesdale, stretching from the confluence of the Rivers Greta and Tees to Caldron Snout waterfall at the eastern end of Cow Green Reservoir (the source of the Tees), is a relaxing introduction to the North Pennines. The landscapes get wilder as you travel northward into the Pennines; the Pennine Way snakes along the dale.

MIDDLETON-IN-TEESDALE

This tranquil, pretty village of white and stone houses among soft green hills was from 1753 a 'company town', the entire kit and caboodle being the property of the London Lead Company, a Quaker concern. The upshot was that the lead miners worked the same hours in the same appalling conditions as everyone else, but couldn't benefit from a Sunday pint to let off steam.

For information on local walks, go to the volunteer-run **tourist office** (☎01833-641001; 10 Market Sq; ⏱10am-1pm).

MIDDLETON TO LANGDON BECK

As you travel up the valley past Middleton towards Langdon Beck, you'll find the newly opened **Bowlees Visitor Centre** (☎01388-528801; www.aonb.org.uk; ⏱10.30am-5pm) 3 miles on, run by the North Pennine's AONB, with plenty of walking and wildlife leaflets, a small natural-history display and a decent cafe. A number of easygoing trails spread out from here, including a five-minute stroll to **Low Force**, a series of tumbling rapids and steps urging the otherwise slow-moving waters of the Tees along a scenic stretch of river. Around 1.5 miles further on (along the B2677) is the much more compelling **High Force** (adult/child £1.50/1, car park £2), England's largest waterfall – 21m of almighty roar that shatters the general tranquillity of the surroundings. If you follow the Pennine Way along the south bank of the Tees you'll hear High Force a long time before it comes into sight (and there's no admission fee if you approach the falls from the Pennine Way).

The B6277 leaves the River Tees at High Force and continues up to the hamlet of Langdon Beck, where the scenery quickly turns from green rounded hills to the lonely landscape of the North Pennines. You can either continue on the B6277 over the Pennines to Alston and Cumbria or turn right and take an amazingly scenic minor road over the moors to St John's Chapel in Weardale.

Sleeping & Eating

Langdon Beck YHA YOUTH HOSTEL £
(☎0845-371 9027; www.yha.org.uk; Forest-in-Teesdale; dm £17) Walkers on the Pennine Way are avid fans of this remote hostel between High Force and Langdon Beck. With its own wind turbine, recycling bins and lots of other green facilities, you'll not find a more ecofriendly hostel in the UK. The food is good too.

Brunswick House B&B ££
(☎01833-640393; www.brunswickhouse.net; 55 Market Pl, Middleton-in-Teesdale; s/d £50/80) This pretty Georgian house has smart en suite rooms, real coal fires heating a cosy lounge and a scrumptious optional dinner – just the ticket after a day in the Pennine's bracing, appetite-inducing air.

High Force Hotel HOTEL ££
(☎01833-622222; www.highforcehotel.com; Forest-in-Teesdale; s/d £45/80) This former brewery by the High Force waterfall has six decent enough bedrooms and the bar serves food.

Getting There & Away

Bus 73 connects Middleton and Langdon Beck, via Bowlees and High Force three times a day. Bus 95 serves Middleton from Barnard Castle at least three times daily.

WEARDALE

A one-time hunting ground of the prince bishops, Weardale's 19th-century legacy as a lead-mining centre has left rust- and olive-coloured patchwork moors pitted with mining scars. Mining relics notwithstanding, there are some splendid walks in and around the surrounding valley, which is sheltered by the Pennines.

STANHOPE & IRESHOPEBURN

Peaceful Stanhope is a honey-coloured town with a cobbled marketplace – a good base for windswept walks across the moors. Its interesting church is Norman at the base, but mostly dates from the 12th century. There's a great farmers market on the last Saturday of every month.

In Ireshopeburn, 8 miles west of Stanhope, the **Weardale Museum** (☎01388-537433; www.weardalemuseum.co.uk; adult/child £3/50p; ⊙2-5pm Wed-Sun May-Jul & Sep, daily Aug) allows a glimpse into local history, including a spotless lead-mining family kitchen and information on preacher John Wesley. It's next to **High House Chapel** (1760), the oldest Methodist chapel in the country to have held weekly services since it was established and one of Wesley's old stomping grounds.

Sleeping & Eating

Fossil Tree B&B ££
(☎01388-527851; www.weardale-accommodation.co.uk; 2 Market Pl, Stanhope; s/d £35/70) This B&B near the tourist office has three modern, fresh, light rooms, but you may have to queue for your morning shower as facilities are shared. Two-wheelers stay free of charge (the town is the last stop on the C2C route before cyclists push on to Sunderland).

Queen's Head PUB £
(89 Front St; mains £6-10) This handsome pub in the middle of Stanhope is a good spot for hearty pub grub.

KILLHOPE

At the top of the valley, about 13 miles from Stanhope, is a good example of just how bleak miners' lives really were. At the **Killhope Lead Mining Museum** (☎01388-537505; www.killhope.org.uk; adult/child £7.15/4.10; ⊙10.30am-5pm Apr-Oct), the blackened machinery of the old works is dominated by an imposing 10m-high water wheel that drove a crushing mechanism (most northeasterners still refer to the museum as the 'Killhope Wheel').

In one of those unfortunate linguistic ironies, 'hope' actually means 'side valley', but once you get a look inside the place you'll understand the miners' black humour about the name. An absorbing exhibition demonstrates the backbreaking work involved in lead mining – a job that made coal mining seem simple in comparison.

The mine closed in 1910 but you can still visit its atmospheric underground network as it was in 1878, on a fascinating hour-long guided tour, the highlight of any visit; wear warm clothes. There's also a visitors centre housing a collection of miners' 'spar boxes' blinged up with local minerals.

Information

Tourist Office (☎01388-527650; www.durhamdalescentre.co.uk; Market Pl; ⊙10am-5pm Apr-Oct) Has lots of information on walks in the area, and there's a large tearoom.

Getting There & Away

Bus 101 makes the regular trip up the valley from Bishop Auckland to Stanhope (11 daily). If you

LOCAL KNOWLEDGE

GEOFF LEE: EXPERT GUIDE AT KILLHOPE LEAD MINING MUSEUM

I've lived and worked in this beautiful area for most of my life but I still see new and wonderful things. That's why I always carry a camera with me – I never know when I'll spot something amazing to snap. Here are my reasons why you should head into the wild and remote North Pennines, with or without your camera:

Must See Killhope Lead Mining Museum (p742) is an opportunity to see what life was like here over a century ago. Try your hand at a washer boy's work and take home a small piece of galena or rare green Weardale fluorspar. Our red squirrels are also a big draw.

Top Tip The Weardale Museum (p742) at Ireshopeburn adds more to the social history of the area and is particularly interesting for anyone researching family history. As the mines closed in Weardale in the late 19th century many emigrated to Australasia and America, so visitors hail from all over the world.

Off the Beaten Track The North Pennines Area of Outstanding Natural Beauty (AONB) is a stunning landscape of open heather moors, dramatic dales, and close-knit communities. Get out there to discover glorious waterfalls, rare plant life, stone-built villages and reminders of our mining and industrial past, as well as many species of bird and insect inhabiting the heather-carpeted moors.

ring ahead, it will go on to Killhope midmorning and pick you up in the afternoon. Call **Wearhead Motor Services** (☎01388-528235) to arrange the service.

DERWENT VALLEY

The cute little villages of Blanchland and Edmundbyers lie south of the drinkably pure expanse of **Derwent Reservoir**, surrounded by wind-tussled moorland and forests. The 3.5-mile-long reservoir has been here since 1967, and the county border separating Durham and Northumberland runs right through it. The valley's a good spot for walking and cycling, as well as sailing, which can be arranged through the **Derwent Reservoir Sailing Club** (☎01434-675033; www.drsc.co.uk).

Nestling among trees, and surrounded by wild mauve-and-mustard moors, **Blanchland** is a surprise. It's a charming, golden-stoned grouping of small cottages arranged around an L-shaped square, framed by a medieval gateway. The village was named after the white cassocks of local monks – there was a Premonstratensian abbey here from the 12th century. Around 1721 the prince bishop of the time, Lord Crewe, seeing the village and abbey falling into disrepair, bequeathed the buildings to trustees on the condition that they be protected and looked after.

Another inviting, quiet village, **Edmundbyers** is 4 miles east of Blanchland on the B6306 along the southern edge of Derwent Reservoir.

Edmundbyers is 12 miles north of Stanhope and 10 miles south of Hexham on the B6306. Bus 773 runs from Consett to Townfield via Blanchland and Edmundbyers four times a day, Monday to Saturday.

Sleeping & Eating

Edmundbyers YHA YOUTH HOSTEL £
(☎0845-371 9633; www.yha.org.uk; Low House; dm £15.50) This beautiful hostel is in a converted 17th-century former inn. The hostel is a welcome halt for walkers in the area and cyclists on the C2C route.

Lord Crewe Arms Hotel HOTEL ££
(☎01434-675251; www.lordcrewehotel.co.uk; Blanchland; r from £75) This glorious hotel was built as the abbot's lodge. It's a mainly 17th-century building, with a 12th-century crypt that makes a cosy bar. If you're looking for a bit of atmosphere – open fires, hidden corners, tall windows and superb food (lunch £6 to £12) – you won't find better, but make sure to ask for a garden room, which has its own sitting room.

ALLEN VALLEY

The Allen Valley is in the heart of the North Pennines, with individual, remote villages huddled high up, surrounded by bumpy hills and heather- and gorse-covered moors. It's fantastic walking country, speckled with the legacy of the lead-mining industry.

Tiny **Allendale** is a hamlet around a big open square. The quiet rural community hots up on New Year's Eve when the distinctly pagan and magical 'Tar Barrels' ceremony is performed. It's 7 miles from Hexham on the B6295.

Four miles further south towards the Wear Valley is **Allenheads**, England's highest village nestled at the head of Allen Valley. No more than a few houses and a marvellously eccentric hotel, it's also a major stop on the C2C cycling route. There's a tiny **heritage centre** (admission £1; ⏲9am-5pm Apr-Oct) with some displays on the history of the village and surroundings, occasional access to a blacksmith's cottage, and a cafe.

An attraction in its own right, **Allenheads Inn** (☎01434-685200; www.theallenheadsinn.co.uk; Allenheads; s/d £39/60), an 18th-century low-beamed pub, has a quite extraordinary and bizarre collection of assorted bric-a-brac and ephemera, from ancient skis to Queen Mum plates. However, the one-star rooms above are the haunt of sweaty cyclists and the service here isn't always as friendly as you might like.

Bus 688 runs up and down the Allen Valley from Hexham to Allenheads (stopping at Allendale town; 45 minutes, five daily).

HADRIAN'S WALL

What exactly have the Romans ever done for us? The aqueducts. Law and order. And this enormous wall, built between AD 122 and 128 to keep 'us' (Romans, subdued Brits) in and 'them' (hairy Pictish barbarians from Scotland) out. Or so the story goes. Hadrian's Wall, named in honour of the emperor who ordered it built, was one of Rome's greatest engineering projects, a spectacular 73-mile testament to ambition and the practical Roman mind.

Building it wasn't easy. When completed, the mammoth structure ran across the narrow neck of the island, from the Solway Firth in the west almost to the mouth of the Tyne in the east. Every Roman mile

Hadrian's Wall & Northumberland National Park

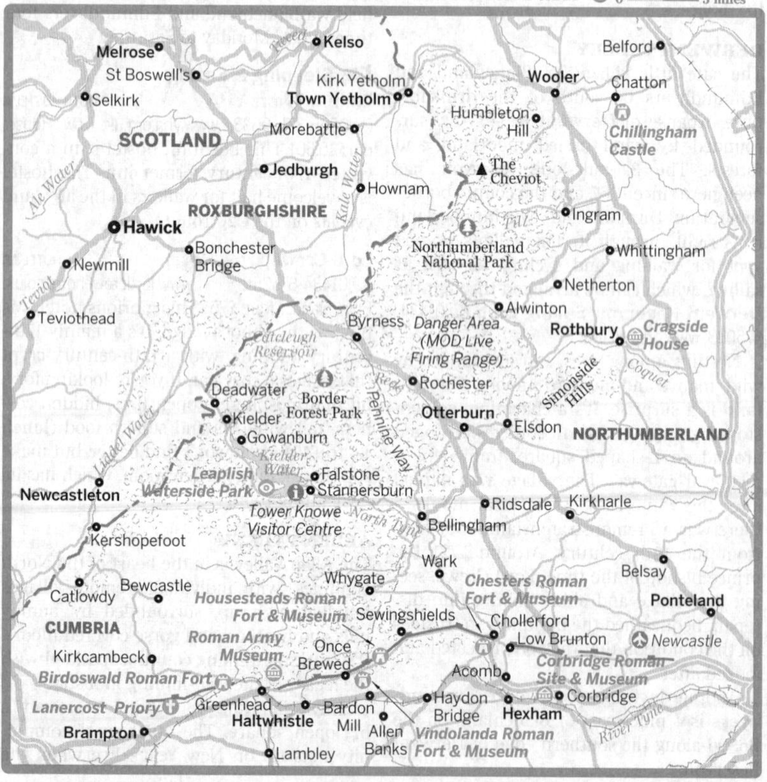

(0.95 miles) there was a gateway guarded by a small fort (milecastle) and between each milecastle were two observation turrets. Milecastles are numbered right across the country, starting with Milecastle 0 at Wallsend and ending with Milecastle 80 at Bowness-on-Solway.

A series of forts were developed as bases some distance south (and may predate the wall), and 16 lie astride it. The prime remaining forts on the wall are Cilurnum (Chesters), Vercovicium (Housesteads) and Banna (Birdoswald). The best forts behind the wall are Corstopitum at Corbridge, and Vindolanda, north of Bardon Mill.

Carlisle in the west, and Newcastle in the east, are obviously good starting points, but Brampton, Haltwhistle, Hexham and Corbridge all make good bases. The B6318 follows the course of the wall from the outskirts of Newcastle to Birdoswald; from Birdoswald to Carlisle it pays to have a detailed map. The main A69 road and the railway line follow 3 or 4 miles to the south.

History

Hadrian's Wall wasn't built to stop invasion – a concentrated attack would have breached any part of it – but to mark the empire's northernmost border. By drawing a physical boundary, the Romans were also tightening their grip on the population to the south – for the first time in history, passports were issued to citizens of the Empire, marking them out not just as citizens but, more importantly, as taxpayers.

But all good things come to an end. It's likely that around 409, as the Roman administration collapsed, the frontier garrisons ceased receiving Roman pay. The wall communities had to then rely on their own resources and were gradually reabsorbed into the local population. Most of the foreign soldiers posted to Hadrian's Wall at the zenith of the Roman Empire had long since returned home.

Activities

The **Hadrian's Wall Path** (www.nationaltrail.co.uk/hadrianswall) is an 84-mile National Trail that runs the length of the wall from Wallsend in the east to Bowness-on-Solway in the west. The entire route should take about seven days on foot, giving plenty of time to explore the rich archaeological heritage along the way. Anthony Burton's *Hadrian's Wall Path – National Trail Guide* (Aurum Press, £12.99) available at most bookshops and tourist offices in the region, is good for history, archaeology and the like, while the *Essential Guide to Hadrian's Wall Path National Trail* (Hadrian's Wall Heritage Ltd, £3.95) by David McGlade is a guide to everyday facilities and services along the walk.

If you're planning to cycle along the wall, tourist offices sell the *Hadrian's Wall Country Cycle Map* (£3.95); you'll be cycling along part of **Hadrian's Cycleway** (www.cycle-routes.org/hadrianscycleway).

Information

Carlisle and Newcastle tourist offices are good places to start gathering information, but there are also tourist offices in Hexham, Haltwhistle, Corbridge and Brampton.

May sees a **spring festival**, with lots of re-creations of Roman life along the wall (contact tourist offices for details).

A great resource is the website of **Hadrian's Wall Country** (www.hadrians-wall.org). It's the official portal for the whole wall, and it's an excellent, easily navigable site.

Hadrian's Wall Information Line (☎01434-322002)

Northumberland National Park Visitor Centre (☎01434-344396; www.northumberlandnationalpark.org.uk; Once Brewed; ⊙9.30am-5.30pm Apr-Oct) Off the B6318.

Getting There & Around

Bus

The AD 122 Hadrian's Wall bus (eight daily, April to October) is a hail-and-ride service that runs between Hexham and Carlisle, with one bus a day starting and ending at Newcastle's Central Station and not all services covering the entire route. Bus 185 zips along the wall the rest of the year (Monday to Saturday only).

West of Hexham the wall runs parallel to the A69, which connects Carlisle and Newcastle. Bus 685 runs along the A69 hourly, passing near the YHA hostels and 2 miles to 3 miles south of the main sites throughout the year.

All these services can be used with the Hadrian's Wall Rover ticket (adult/child one-day £9/4.50, three-day £18/9), available from bus drivers and tourist offices, where you can also get timetables.

Car & Motorcycle

This is obviously the most convenient method of transport with one fort or garrison usually just a short hop from the next. Parking costs £4 and the ticket is valid at all other sites along the wall.

Hadrian's Wall

ROME'S FINAL FRONTIER

Of all Britain's Roman ruins, Emperor Hadrian's 2nd-century wall, cutting across northern England from the Irish Sea to the North Sea, is by far the most spectacular; Unesco awarded it world cultural heritage status in 1987.

We've picked out the highlights, one of which is the prime remaining Roman fort on the wall, Housesteads, which we've reconstructed here.

Housesteads' granaries
Nothing like the clever underground ventilation system, which kept vital supplies of grain dry in Northumberland's damp and drizzly climate, would be seen again in these parts for 1500 years.

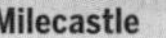

Birdoswald Roman Fort
Explore the longest intact stretch of the wall, scramble over the remains of a large fort then head indoors to wonder at a full-scale model of the wall at its zenith. Great fun for the kids.

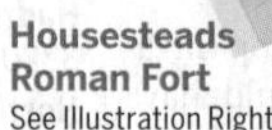

Housesteads Roman Fort
See Illustration Right

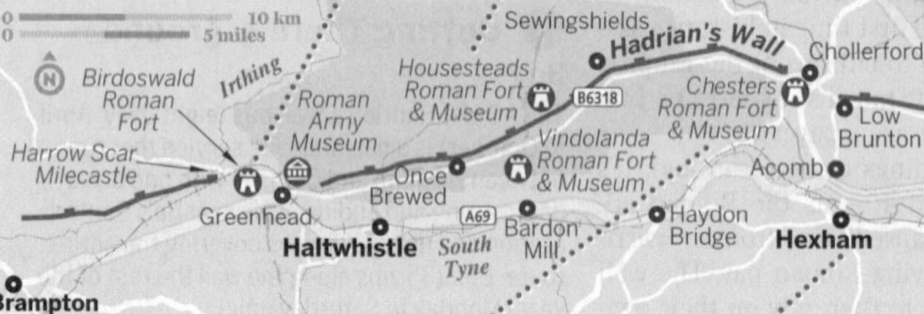

Chesters Roman Fort
Built to keep watch over a bridge spanning the River North Tyne, Britain's best-preserved Roman cavalry fort has a terrific bathhouse, essential if you have months of nippy northern winter ahead.

Hexham Abbey
This may be the finest non-Roman sight near Hadrian's Wall, but the 7th-century parts of this magnificent church were built with stone quarried by the Romans for use in their forts.

Housesteads' hospital
Operations performed at the hospital would have been surprisingly effective, even without anaesthetics; religious rituals and prayers to Aesculapius, the Roman god of healing, were possibly less helpful for a hernia or appendicitis.

ousesteads' latrines
ımmunal toilets were the norm in Roman ıes and Housesteads' are remarkably well eserved – fortunately no traces remain of the ıegar-soaked sponges that were used instead toilet paper.

QUICK WALL FACTS & FIGURES

» **Latin name** Vallum Aelium

» **Length** 73.5 miles (80 Roman miles)

» **Construction date** AD 122–128

» **Manpower for construction** Three legions (around 16,000 men)

» **Features** at least 16 forts, 80 milecastles, 160 turrets

» **Did you know** Hadrian's wasn't the only wall in Britain – the Antonine Wall was built across what is now central Scotland in the AD 140s, but it was abandoned soon after

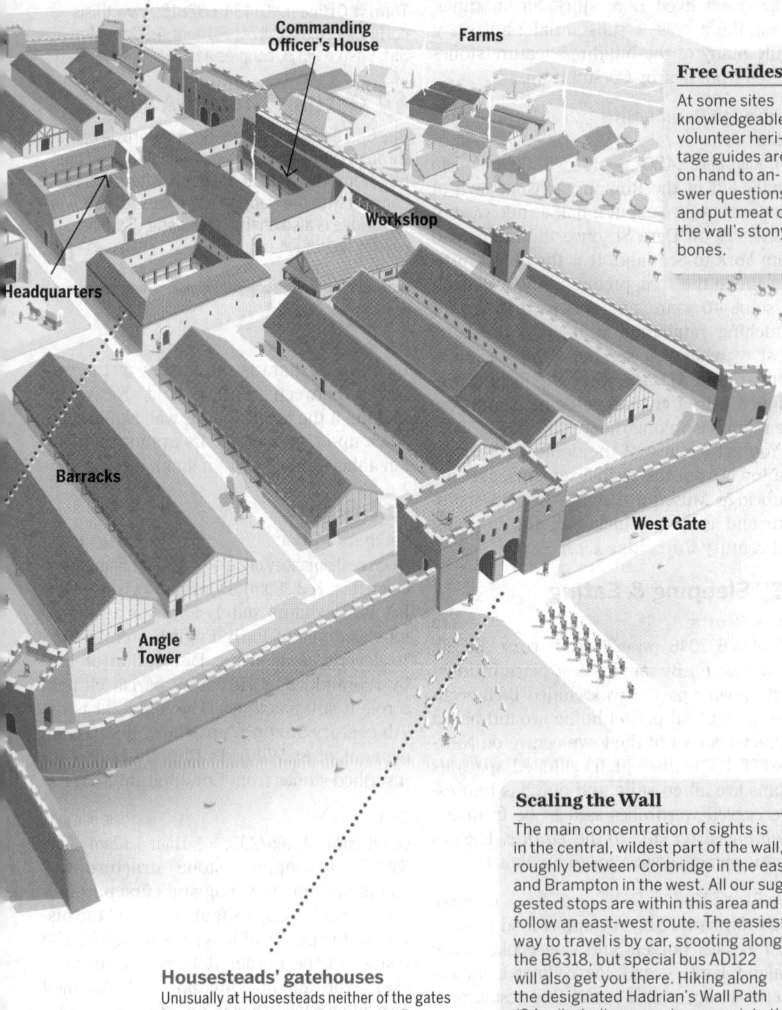

Commanding Officer's House

Farms

Workshop

Headquarters

Barracks

West Gate

Angle Tower

Free Guides

At some sites knowledgeable volunteer heritage guides are on hand to answer questions and put meat on the wall's stony bones.

Scaling the Wall

The main concentration of sights is in the central, wildest part of the wall, roughly between Corbridge in the east and Brampton in the west. All our suggested stops are within this area and follow an east-west route. The easiest way to travel is by car, scooting along the B6318, but special bus AD122 will also get you there. Hiking along the designated Hadrian's Wall Path (84 miles) allows you to appreciate the achievement up close.

Housesteads' gatehouses
Unusually at Housesteads neither of the gates faces the enemy, as was the norm at a Roman fort – builders aligned them east-west. Ruts worn by cart wheels are still visible in the stone.

Train

The railway line between Newcastle and Carlisle (Tyne Valley Line) has stations at Corbridge, Hexham, Haydon Bridge, Bardon Mill, Haltwhistle and Brampton. Trains run hourly but not all services stop at all stations.

Corbridge

POP 2800

The mellow commuter town of Corbridge is a handsome spot above a green-banked curve in the Tyne, and its shady, cobbled streets are lined with old-fashioned shops. Folks have lived here since Saxon times, when there was a substantial monastery, while many of the buildings feature stones nicked from nearby Corstopitum.

Corbridge Roman Site & Museum ROMAN GARRISON

(EH; adult/child £4.50/3; 10am-5.30pm Apr-Sep) What's left of the Roman garrison town of Corstopitum lies about a half a mile west of Market Pl on Dere St, once the main road from York to Scotland. It is the oldest fortified site in the area, predating the wall itself by some 40 years, and was used by troops launching retaliation raids into Scotland. Most of what you see here, though, dates from around AD 200, when the fort had developed into a civilian settlement and was the main base along the wall.

You get a sense of the domestic heart of the town from the visible remains, and the Corbridge Museum displays Roman sculpture and carvings, including the amazing 3rd-century **Corbridge Lion**.

Sleeping & Eating

2 The Crofts B&B ££

(01434-633046; www.2thecrofts.co.uk; B6530; r from £65; P) By far the best place in town to drop your pack, this secluded B&B occupies a beautiful period home around half a mile's walk east of the town centre on Newcastle Rd. The three high-ceilinged, spacious rooms are all en suite and one has impressive carved wardrobes said to be from the *Olympic,* sister ship to the *Titanic*. The energetic owners cook a mean breakfast.

The Black Bull BRITISH ££

(Middle St; mains £8-16) A comfort-food menu – such as beef burgers and slow-cooked New Zealand lamb – and low-ceilinged, atmospheric dining rooms make this restaurant/tavern a fine spot to fill the hole.

Valley Restaurant INDIAN ££

(Station Rd; mains £8-12; dinner Mon-Sat) Taking up the entire train station building, this temple to spice was declared 'best Indian in the north' by the Curry Club, and they're a bunch who know good subcontinental grub when they taste it. Diners from Newcastle can catch the 'Passage to India' train (£36.50) to Corbridge accompanied by a waiter, who will supply snacks and phone ahead to have the meal ready when the train arrives.

Information

Tourist Office (01434-632815; www.thisiscorbridge.co.uk; Hill St; 10am-4.30pm Mon-Sat, Easter-Oct) Occupies a corner of the library.

Getting There & Away

Bus 685 between Newcastle and Carlisle comes through Corbridge, as does the half-hourly bus 602 from Newcastle to Hexham, where you can connect with the Hadrian's Wall bus AD 122. Corbridge is also on the Newcastle–Carlisle railway line.

Hexham

POP 10,690

Bustling Hexham is the busiest of the wall towns between Carlisle and Newcastle, making it the ideal stop for wall explorers to stock up on provisions. Its grand Augustinian abbey is also worth a look.

Sights

Hexham Abbey MONASTERY

(www.hexhamabbey.org.uk; 9.30am-5pm, Saxon crypt 11am & 3.30pm) Dominating tiny Market Pl, Hexham's stately abbey is a marvellous example of Early English architecture. It cleverly escaped the Dissolution of 1537 by rebranding as Hexham's parish church, a role it still has today. The highlight is the 7th-century **Saxon crypt**, the only surviving element of St Wilifrid's Church, built with inscribed stones from Corstopitum in 674.

Old Gaol HISTORIC BUILDING

(adult/child £3.95/2.10; 11am-4.30pm Tue-Sat) This strapping stone structure was completed in 1333 as England's first purpose-built prison; today its four floors tell the history of the jail in all its gruesome glory. The history of the Border Reivers – a group of clans who fought, kidnapped, blackmailed and killed each other in an effort to exercise control over a lawless tract of land along the

Anglo-Scottish border throughout the 16th century – is also retold, along with tales of the punishments handed out in the prison.

Chesters Roman Fort & Museum ROMAN GARRISON

(EH; ☎01434-681379; Chollerford; adult/child £4.80/2.40; ⏰10am-6pm Apr-Sep) Set among idyllic green woods and meadows near the village of Chollerford, these Roman cavalry fort remains were originally constructed to house a unit of troops from Asturias in northern Spain. They include part of a bridge (beautifully constructed and best appreciated from the eastern bank) across the River North Tyne, four well-preserved gatehouses, an extraordinary bathhouse and an underfloor heating system. The museum has a large collection of Roman sculpture. Take bus 880 or 882 from Hexham (5.5 miles away); it is also on the route of Hadrian's Wall bus AD 122.

Sleeping & Eating

Hexham has few accommodation options and some of the tourist office's recommendations are unashamedly grotty.

Hallbank Guest House B&B ££

(☎01434-605567; www.hallbankguesthouse.com; Hallgate; s/d from £60/80; P 📶) Behind the Old Gaol is this fine Edwardian house with eight stylishly furnished rooms, which combine period elegance with flatscreen TVs and huge beds. Very popular so book ahead.

TOP CHOICE **Bouchon Bistrot** FRENCH ££

(www.bouchonbistrot.co.uk; 4-6 Gilesgate; mains £12-19; ⏰Tue-Sat) Hexham may be an unlikely setting for fine dining, but this Gallic affair has such an enviable reputation and was voted the UK's best local French restaurant in 2010 by Channel 4 viewers of Gordon Ramsey's *The F Word*. Country-style menus are reassuringly brief, ingredients as fresh as nature can provide and the wine list an elite selection of champagnes, reds and whites. The owners have also created a cosy, understated interior in which to enjoy all of the above.

Dipton Mill PUB £

(Dipton Mill Rd; mains around £6-10) This superb country pub is 2 miles out on the road to Blanchland, in woodland and by a river. It offers real ploughman's lunches and real ale by real fires – really.

Information

Tourist Office (☎01434-652220; Wentworth Car Park; ⏰9am-6pm Mon-Sat, 10am-5pm Sun) Northeast of the town centre.

Getting There & Away

Bus 685 between Newcastle and Carlisle comes through Hexham hourly. The AD 122 and the winter-service bus 185 connect with other towns along the wall, and the town is on the scenic railway line between Newcastle (twice hourly) and Carlisle (hourly).

Haltwhistle & Around

POP 3810

It's one of the more important debates in contemporary Britain: where exactly is the centre of the country? The residents of Haltwhistle, basically one long street just north of the A69, claim that they're in it. But then so do the folks in Dunsop Bridge, 71 miles to the south. Will we ever know the truth? In the meantime, Haltwhistle is the spot to get some cash and load up on gear and groceries. Thursday is market day.

Sights

Vindolanda Roman Fort & Museum ROMAN FORT, MUSEUM

(www.vindolanda.com; adult/child £6.25/3.75, with Roman Army Museum £9.50/5.25; ⏰10am-6pm Apr-Sep, to 5pm Feb, Mar & Oct) The extensive site of Vindolanda offers a fascinating glimpse into the daily life of a Roman garrison town. The time-capsule museum displays leather sandals, signature Roman toothbrush-flourish helmet decorations, and numerous writing tablets recently returned from the British Library. These include a student's marked work ('sloppy'), and a parent's note with a present of socks and underpants (things haven't changed – in this climate you can never have too many).

The museum is just one part of this large, extensively excavated site, which includes impressive parts of the fort and town (excavations continue) and reconstructed turrets and temple. It's 1.5 miles north of Bardon Mill between the A69 and B6318 and a mile from Once Brewed.

Housesteads Roman Fort & Museum ROMAN FORT, MUSEUM

(EH; adult/child £6/3.60; ⏰10am-6pm Apr-Sep) The wall's most dramatic site – and the best-preserved Roman fort in the whole country – is at Housesteads. From here, high on a ridge and covering 2 hectares, you can survey the moors of Northumberland National Park and the snaking wall, with a sense of awe at the landscape and the aura of the Roman lookouts.

The substantial foundations bring fort life alive. The remains include an impressive hospital, granaries with a carefully worked-out ventilation system and barrack blocks. Most memorable are the spectacularly situated communal flushable latrines, which summon up Romans at their most mundane. Information boards show what the individual buildings would have looked like in their heyday and there's a scale model of the entire fort in the small museum at the ticket office.

Housesteads is 2.5 miles north of Bardon Mill on the B6318, and about 6 miles from Haltwhistle.

Roman Army Museum MUSEUM
(www.vindolanda.com; adult/child £5/2.75, with Vindolanda £9.50/5.25; ⏲10am-6pm) A mile northwest of Greenhead, near Walltown Crags, this kid-pleasing museum provides lots of colourful background detail to wall life, such as how the soldiers spent their R&R time in this lonely outpost of the empire.

Birdoswald Roman Fort ROMAN FORT
(EH; ☎016977-47602; adult/child £5.20/3.10; ⏲10am-5.30pm Mar-Oct) *Technically* in Cumbria, the remains of this once-formidable fort on an escarpment overlooking the beautiful Irthing Gorge are on a minor road off the B6318, about 3 miles west of Greenhead. A fine stretch of wall extends from here to Harrow's Scar Milecastle.

Lanercost Priory PRIORY
(EH; adult/child £3.40/2; ⏲10am-5pm) About 3 miles further west along the A69 from Birdoswald, these peaceful raspberry-coloured ruins are all that remain of a priory founded in 1166 by Augustinian canons. Post-dissolution it became a private house and a priory church was created from the Early English nave. The AD 122 bus drops off at the gate.

Sleeping

TOP CHOICE Ashcroft B&B ££
(☎01434-320213; www.ashcroftguesthouse.co.uk; Lanty's Lonnen, Haltwhistle; s/d from £55/85; wi-fi) In the world of British B&Bs, things don't get better than this. Picture a large, elegant Edwardian vicarage surrounded by 2 acres of beautifully manicured, layered lawns and gardens from which there are stunning views. Inside, the nine rooms – some with private balconies and terraces – hoist preposterously high ceilings and are fitted out in an understated style but also contain every gadget 21st-century humankind needs for survival. The dining room is grander than some snooty hotels and the welcome certainly more genuine. Highly recommended.

Centre of Britain HOTEL ££
(☎01434-322422; www.centre-of-britain.org.uk; Haltwhistle; s/d from £64/80) Just across from where locals claim the 'Centre of Britain' to be, this Norwegian-owned hotel (hence the slightly Scandinavian feel) incorporates a sturdy 15th-century *pele* (fortified) tower, one of the oldest chunks of architecture in town. The most spacious rooms (two have their own full-blown sauna) are located in the historical main building. There are smaller, quite oddly designed two-level rooms in the courtyard, and a separate annex almost next door takes the spill-over. Ask staff to see the smuggler's tunnel and secret staircase if you dare.

Holmhead Guest House B&B ££
(☎01697-747402; www.bandbhadrianswall.com; Greenhead Brampton; dm/s/d from £12.50/46/65) Built using recycled bits of the wall on whose foundations its stands, this superb farmhouse B&B offers everything from comfy rooms to a basic bunk barn to camping pitches. Both the Pennine Way and the Hadrian's Wall Path pass through the grounds and the jagged ruins of Thirwall Castle loom above the scene. The owners will gladly show you their piece of 3rd-century Roman graffiti. Half a mile north of Greenhead.

Hadrian's Wall Camp Site CAMPSITE £
(☎01434-320495; www.romanwallcamping.co.uk; Melkridge Tilery, near Haltwhistle; pitch/dm from £10/15) Small, secluded camping ground with a bunk barn for when the weather turns particularly cruel. Signposted just south of the B6318.

Once Brewed YHA YOUTH HOSTEL £
(☎0845-371 9753; www.yha.org.uk; Military Rd, Bardon Mill; dm £14; ⏲Feb-Nov) This modern and well-equipped hostel is central for visiting both Housesteads Fort, 3 miles away, and Vindolanda, 1 mile away. The Hadrian's Wall bus drops you at the door.

Greenhead YOUTH HOSTEL £

(☎016977-47411; Greenhead; dm from £15) No longer affiliated to the YHA, this hostel occupies a converted Methodist chapel by a trickling stream and a pleasant garden, 3 miles west of Haltwhistle. Served by bus AD 122 or 685.

Birdoswald YHA YOUTH HOSTEL £

(☎0845-371 9551; www.yha.org.uk; dm £15; ⏱Jul-Sep, call to check other times) Within the grounds of the Birdoswald complex, this hostel has basic facilities, including a self-service kitchen and laundry. The price includes a visit to the fort.

Information

Tourist Office (☎01434-322002; Mechanics Institute, Westgate; ⏱9.30am-1pm & 2-5.30pm Mon-Sat, 1-5pm Sun) Haltwhistle's tourist office has all the usual info.

NORTHUMBERLAND NATIONAL PARK

England's last great wilderness is the 405 sq miles of natural wonderland that make up Northumberland National Park, spread about the soft swells of the Cheviot Hills, the spiky moors of autumn-coloured heather and gorse, and the endless acres of forest guarding the deep, colossal Kielder Water. Even the negligible human influence (this is England's least populated national park with only 2000 inhabitants) has been benevolent: the finest sections of Hadrian's Wall run along the park's southern edge and the landscape is dotted with prehistoric remains and fortified houses – the thick-walled *peles* were the only solid buildings built here until the mid-18th century.

Activities

The most spectacular stretch of the Hadrian's Wall Path is between Sewingshields and Greenhead in the south of the park.

There are many fine walks through the Cheviots, frequently passing by prehistoric remnants; the towns of Ingram, Wooler and Rothbury make good bases, and their tourist offices can provide maps, guides and route information.

Though at times strenuous, cycling in the park is a pleasure; the roads are good and the traffic is light. There's off-road cycling in Border Forest Park.

Information

For information, contact **Northumberland National Park** (☎01434-605555; www.northumberlandnationalpark.org.uk; Eastburn, South Park, Hexham), or visit the national park offices in **Once Brewed** (☎01434-344396; Military Rd; ⏱9.30am-5pm Apr-Oct) and **Ingram** (☎01665-578890; ⏱10am- 5pm Apr-Oct). There are tourist offices listed in each town, all handle accommodation bookings.

Getting There & Around

Public transport options are limited, aside from buses on the A69. Bus 808 (55 minutes, two daily Monday to Saturday) runs between Otterburn and Newcastle. Bus 880 (50 minutes, twice daily Tuesday, Friday & Saturday) run between Hexham and Bellingham (and on to Kielder). A National Express service calls at Otterburn (£6.20, 50 minutes, daily) on its way from Newcastle to Edinburgh.

Rothbury

POP 1740

The one-time prosperous Victorian resort of Rothbury is an attractive, restful market town on the River Coquet that makes a convenient base for the Cheviots.

Visitors flock to Rothbury to see **Cragside House, Garden and Estate** (NT; ☎01669-620333; admission £13.90, gardens & estate only £9; ⏱house 1-5pm or 11am-5pm Tue-Sun depending on the month, gardens 10.30am-5pm Tue-Sun mid-Mar–Oct), the quite incredible country retreat of the first Lord Armstrong. In the 1880s the house had hot and cold running water, a telephone and alarm system, and was the first in the world to be lit by electricity, generated through hydropower – the original system has been restored and can be observed in the Power House. The Victorian gardens are also well worth exploring: huge and remarkably varied, they feature lakes, moors and one of Europe's largest rock gardens. Visit late May to mid-June to see Cragside's famous rhododendrons in bloom.

The estate is 1 mile northeast of town just off the B6341; there's no public transport to the front gates from Rothbury; try **Rothbury Motors** (☎01669-620516) if you need a taxi.

High St is a good area to look for a place to stay. Beamed ceilings, stone fireplaces and canopied four-poster beds make **Katerina's Guest House** (☎01669-620691; www.katerinasguesthouse.co.uk; Sun Buildings, High St; r £74; 📶) one of the town's better choices, though the three rooms are a little small for the price. Alternatively, the **Haven** (☎01669-620577; www.thehavenrothbury.co.uk; Back Crofts; s/d/ste £40/80/130; P) is a beautiful Edwardian home up on a hill with six comfy bedrooms and one elegant suite.

There's plenty of pub grub available along High St or you could try **Sun Kitchen** (High St; snacks & meals £3.60-6.50) where they've been serving up sandwiches, jacket potatoes and other snacks for four decades. **Rothbury Bakery** (High St) does great takeaway pies and sandwiches.

The **tourist office** (☎01669-620887; Church St; ⏲10am-5pm Apr-Oct) has a free exhibition on the Northumberland National Park.

Bus 144 runs hourly to and from Morpeth (30 minutes) Monday to Saturday.

Bellingham

The small, remote village of Bellingham (bellin-*jum*) is a pleasant enough spot on the banks of the North Tyne, surrounded by beautiful, deserted countryside on all sides. It's an excellent launch pad for trips into the national park and a welcome refuelling halt on the Pennine Way.

The **Bellingham Heritage Centre** (www.bellingham-heritage.org.uk; Station Yard, Woodburn Rd; adult/child £4/2.50; ⏲9.30am-4.30pm Mon-Sat, 10.30am-3.30pm Apr-Oct) houses a new **museum** with heaps of railway paraphernalia, an interesting section on the Border Reivers and mock-ups of old village shops. The heritage centre shares its premises with the tourist office.

The **Hareshaw Linn Walk** passes through a wooded valley and over six bridges, leading to a 9m-high waterfall 2.5 miles north of Bellingham (*linn* is an Old English name for waterfall).

Bellingham is popular with hikers so book ahead for accommodation in summer. Most of the B&Bs cluster around the village green.

Demesne Farm (☎01434-220107; www.demesnefarmcampsite.co.uk; Woodburn Rd; dm/pitch £17/14) is a working smallholding in the middle of the village but with a very comfortable 15-bed bunkhouse and lots of soft green grass for tents. There's also cycle storage, a drying room and kitchen. It's affiliated with the YHA.

The **tourist office** (☎01434-220616; Station Yard, Woodburn Rd; ⏲9.30am-4.30pm Mon-Sat Apr-Sep) handles visitor inquiries (and is the same building as the heritage centre).

Kielder Water

Taken a shower or had a cup of tea while in the northeast? Chances are the water you used came from Kielder Water, Europe's largest artificial lake holding 200,000 million litres. Surrounding its 27-mile-long shoreline is England's largest forest, 150 million spruce and pine trees growing in nice, orderly fashion.

Besides being busy supplying H2O and O2 for this part of the world, the lake and forest are the setting for one of England's largest outdoor-adventure playgrounds, with water parks, cycle trails, walking routes and plenty of birdwatching sites. It's also a great place to escape humanity: you are often as much as 10 miles from the nearest village. In summer, however, your constant companion will be the insistent midge (mosquito-like insect), so bring strong repellent.

Sights & Activities

Bike Place (☎01434-250457; www.thebikeplace.co.uk; Station Garage, Kielder; hire per day adult/child £20/15; ⏲9.30am-5.30pm Easter-Sep) supplies detailed cycle trail maps for the entire Kielder area and they'll even pick you up in Newcastle.

Leaplish Waterside Park ACTIVITY CENTRE
(☎01434-251000) Most of the lake's activities are focused on this centre located a few miles northwest of Tower Knowe. It is a purpose-built complex with a heated outdoor pool, sauna, fishing and other water sports as well as restaurants, cafes and accommodation.

Birds of Prey Centre BIRD CENTRE
(www.discoverit.co.uk/falconry; Leaplish Waterside Park; admission £5; ⏲10.30am-late afternoon) Come and see flapping owls, falcons and hawks, which are shown to the public three times daily.

FREE **Kielder Castle** CASTLE
(Kielder; ⏲10am-5pm Apr-Oct) At the lake's northern end, a couple of miles from the Scottish border, is the drowsy village of Kielder and its castle, built in 1775 as a hunting lodge by the Duke of Northumberland. The building is now a Forestry Commission information centre with exhibitions on

LAKESIDE GALLERY

The Kielder area claims to be the world's largest open-air gallery, with 20 award-winning works of contemporary art and architecture dotting the surrounding landscape. Arguably the most striking and intriguing pieces are the **Minotaur Maze** in Kielder, James Turnell's **Skyspace** on the southern shore and the **Silvas Capitalis** (forest head), a giant decapitated larch wood bonce located in woodland on the northern shore, around 3 miles from Kielder. For more information and images of the pieces, log on to www.visitkielder.com.

renewable energy, forestry, Kielder's birdlife and local architecture.

Sleeping

Leaplish Waterside Park CARAVAN PARK £
(☎01434-251000; site per person £28.50, 3-night stay in 4-person cabin £599; ⌚Apr-Oct) The water park has a caravan park set among the trees and a group of fully self-contained log cabins offering a bit of waterside luxury, complete with TVs and DVD players. The catch is that the cabins can only be rented for a minimum of three nights. Prices change throughout the limited season.

No 27 B&B ££
(☎01434-250366; www.staykielder.co.uk; 27 Castle Dr, Kielder; s/d £40/80) This cosy B&B near Kielder Castle has only one room but the flexible owners are willing to house out-of-the-blue nomads in their self-catering property when there's space. Cycle storage, no-need-for-lunch breakfasts and a friendly send-off come as standard.

Kielder YHA YOUTH HOSTEL £
(☎0845-371 9126; www.yha.org.uk; Butteryhaugh; dm £17) This well-equipped, activities-based hostel on the lake's northern shore has small dorms and a couple of four-bed rooms. Open year round.

Falstone Tea Rooms CAFE £
(Old School House, Falstone; mains £5-7) This characterful place serves tasty, home-cooked food in the old school house.

Information

Tower Knowe Visitor Centre (☎01434-240436; www.visitkielder.com; parking £3; ⌚10am-5pm Jun & Sep, to 6pm Jul & Aug, to 4pm Oct-May) Near the southeastern end of the lake, this visitor centre has plenty of information on the area, with lots of walking leaflets and maps, a cafe and a small exhibition on the history of the valley and lake. *Cycling at Kielder* and *Walking at Kielder* are useful leaflets (£3 each). They describe trails in and around the forest, their length and difficulty.

Getting There & Around

From Newcastle, bus 714 (two hours) goes directly to Kielder on Sundays and bank holidays, June to October. The bus leaves in the morning, turns into a shuttle between the various lake attractions and returns in the afternoon. Mondays and Thursdays a dial-a-ride service (01434-606156) operates between Bellingham and Kielder. A day's notice is required. Bus 880 (twice daily Tuesday, Friday and Saturday) runs from Hexham via Bellingham.

If driving, be aware that there is no petrol station in Kielder – the nearest fuel is in Bellingham, 18 miles away.

The **Osprey Ferry** (adult/child £6.95/4.35) navigates the lake (four per day Easter to October plus additional service June to August) between Tower Knowe, Leaplish and Belvedere on the northern shore. It is the best way to get a sense of the huge size of the lake.

Wooler

POP 1860

A harmonious, stone-terraced town, Wooler owes its sense of unified design to a devastating fire in 1863, which resulted in an almost complete rebuild. It is an excellent spot in which to catch your breath, especially as it is surrounded by some fantastic forays into the nearby Cheviots (including a clamber to the top of the Cheviot, the highest peak in the range). It's also the midway point for the 65-mile St Cuthbert's Way, which runs from Melrose in Scotland to Holy Island on the coast.

Activities

A popular walk from Wooler takes in **Humbleton Hill**, the site of an Iron Age hill fort and the location of yet another battle (1402) between the Scots and the English. It's immortalised in 'The Ballad of Chevy

Chase' and Shakespeare's *Henry IV*. There are great views of the wild Cheviot Hills to the south and plains to the north, merging into the horizon. The well-posted 4-mile trail starts and ends at the bus station (follow the signs to Wooler Common). It takes approximately two hours. Alternatively, the yearly **Chevy Chase** (www.woolerrunningclub.co.uk) is a classic 20-mile fell run with over 4000ft of accumulated climb, run at the beginning of July.

A more arduous hike leads to the top of the **Cheviot** (815m), 6 miles southeast. The top is barren and wild, but on a clear day you can see the castle at Bamburgh and as far out as Holy Island. It takes around four hours to reach the top from Wooler. Check with the tourist office for information before setting out.

Cycle hire is available at **Haugh Head Garage** (☎01668-281316; per day from £18) in Haugh Head, 1 mile south of Wooler on the A697.

Sleeping & Eating

Tilldale House B&B ££
(☎01668-281450; www.tilldalehouse.co.uk; 34-40 High St; s/d from £44/64) One of the houses to survive the fire of 1863 now contains comfortable, spacious rooms that radiate a welcoming golden hue. The five-star breakfast includes veggie and gluten-free options.

Wooler YHA YOUTH HOSTEL £
(☎01668-281365; www.yha.org.uk; 30 Cheviot St; dm £16) In a low, red-brick building above the town, the northernmost YHA hostel (at least until the new Berwick hostel opens) contains 46 beds in a variety of rooms, a modern lounge and a small cafe.

Spice Village INDIAN RESTAURANT £
(3 Peth Head; mains from £7; ⊙dinner) There's bog-standard pub grub galore in Wooler, but for a bit more flavour, head for this small takeaway/restaurant that does spicy Indian and Bangladeshi dishes.

Information

Tourist Office (☎01668-282123; www.wooler.org.uk; Cheviot Centre, 12 Padgepool Pl; ⊙10am-4.30pm Easter-Oct) A mine of information on walks in the hills.

Getting There & Around

Wooler has good bus connections to the major towns in Northumberland. To reach Wooler from Newcastle change at Alnwick.

Alnwick Buses 470 and 473; nine daily Monday to Saturday.

Berwick Buses 464 and 267; 50 minutes, nine daily Monday to Saturday.

Around Wooler

Recently voted best castle in Europe by readers of the *Independent*, **Chillingham** (☎01668-215359; www.chillingham-castle.com; adult/child £8.50/4; ⊙noon-5pm Sun-Fri Easter-Sep) is steeped in history, warfare, torture and ghosts. It is said to be one of the country's most haunted places, with ghostly clientele ranging from a phantom funeral to Lady Mary Berkeley in search of her errant husband.

Today's visitor is in for a real treat, from the extravagant medieval staterooms that have hosted a handful of kings in their day to the stone-flagged banquet halls to the torture chamber in the basement, complete with a polished rack and an especially grisly iron maiden. There's also a museum with a fantastically jumbled collection of objects – it's like stepping into the attic of a compulsive and well-travelled hoarder.

It's possible to stay at the medieval fortress in the seven apartments designed for guests, where the likes of Henry III and Edward I once snoozed. Prices vary depending on the luxury of the apartment; the **Grey Apartment** (£170) is the most expensive – it has a dining table to seat 12 – or there's the **Tower Apartment** (£130), in the Northwest Tower. All of the apartments are self-catering.

Chillingham is 6 miles southeast of Wooler. Bus 470 running between Alnwick and Wooler (three daily Monday to Saturday) stops at Chillingham.

NORTHUMBERLAND COAST

The utterly wild and stunningly beautiful landscapes of Northumberland don't stop with the national park. It's hard to imagine an undiscovered wilderness in a country so modern and populated, but as you cast your eye across the rugged interior you will see ne'er a trace of habitation save the fortified houses and lonely villages that dot the horizon.

While the west is covered by the national park, the magnificent and pale sweeping coast to the east is the scene of long, stunning beaches, bookmarked by dramatic wind-worn castles and tiny islands offshore that really do have an air of magic about them. Hadrian's Wall emerges from the national park and slices through the south.

Alnwick

POP 7770

Northumberland's historic ducal town, Alnwick (no tongue gymnastics: just say 'annick') is an elegant maze of narrow cobbled streets spread out beneath the watchful gaze of a colossal medieval castle. England's most perfect bookshop, the northeast's most visited attraction at Alnwick Garden and some olde-worlde emporiums attract secondhand book worms, antique fans, castle junkies and the green-fingered in equal measure, and there's even a little something for *Harry Potter* nerds.

Most of the action takes place around Bondgate Within, Bondgate Without and Clayport St with the castle to the north overlooking the River Aln.

Sights

Alnwick Castle CASTLE

(www.alnwickcastle.com; adult/child £14/7, with Alnwick Garden £24/10; ⌚10am-6pm Apr-Oct) The outwardly imposing ancestral home of the Duke of Northumberland and a favourite set for film-makers (it was Hogwarts for the first couple of *Harry Potter* films) has changed little since the 14th century. The interior is sumptuous and extravagant; the six rooms open to the public – staterooms, dining room, guard chamber and library – have an incredible display of Italian paintings, including Titian's *Ecce Homo* and many Canalettos.

A free *Harry Potter* tour runs every day at 2.30pm and includes details of other productions – period drama *Elizabeth* and the British comedy series *Blackadder* to name but two – to have used the castle as a backdrop.

The castle is set in parklands designed by Lancelot 'Capability' Brown. The woodland walk offers some great aspects of the castle, or for a view looking up the River Aln, take the B1340 towards the coast.

Alnwick Garden GARDENS

(www.alnwickgarden.com; adult/child £12/4; ⌚10am-6pm Apr-Oct) As spectacular a bit of green-thumb artistry as you'll see in England, this is one of the northeast's great success stories. Since the project began in 2000, the 4.8-hectare walled garden has been transformed from a derelict site into a spectacle that easily exceeds the grandeur of the castle's 19th-century gardens, a series of magnificent green spaces surrounding the breathtaking Grand Cascade – 120 separate jets spurting over 30,000L of water down 21 weirs for everyone to marvel at and kids to splash around in.

There are a half-dozen other gardens, including the Franco-Italian-influenced **Ornamental Garden** (with more than 15,000 plants), the **Rose Garden** and the particularly fascinating **Poison Garden**, home to some of the deadliest – and most illegal – plants in the world, including cannabis, magic mushrooms, belladonna and even tobacco.

Bailiffgate Museum MUSEUM

(www.bailiffgatemuseum.co.uk; 14 Bailiffgate; adult/child £2.50/free; ⌚10am-4pm Easter-Oct) The three floors at this often overlooked museum near the castle are taken up with interesting exhibitions on coal mining, the history of Alnwick, Border Reivers and the railways as well as locally themed temporary shows.

Sleeping

Alnwick packs them in at weekends from Easter onwards so book ahead. B&Bs cluster near the castle.

TOP CHOICE **Alnwick Lodge** B&B ££

(☎01665-604363; www.alnwicklodge.com; West Cawledge Park, 2 miles S off the A1; s/d from £55/100; P 📶) Is it a B&B, is it a lonely Victorian farmstead, is it an antiques gallery? The answer is it's all of these and more. The never-ending jumble of rooms, each one different and all containing restored antiques; the quirky touches such as free-standing baths with lids; the roaring fire in the Victorian guest lounge; the friendly, flexible owners and the cooked breakfasts around a huge circular banqueting table – all its features make this a truly unique place to stay. The catch – you'll need a car or taxi to get here.

White Swan Hotel HOTEL ££

(☎01665-602109; www.classiclodges.co.uk; Bondgate Within; r from £90; P 📶) Alnwick's top address is this 300-year-old coaching inn right in the heart of town. Its rooms are all of a pretty good standard (LCD screen TVs, DVD players and free wi-fi), but this spot stands out for its dining room, filched in its entirety from the *Olympic,* sister ship to the *Titanic,* elaborate panelling, ceiling and stained-glass windows included.

Blackmore's BOUTIQUE HOTEL ££
(☎01665-602395; www.blackmoresofalnwick.com; Bondgate Without; r £100; P 📶) Trendy Blackmore's motto of 'Eat well, sleep well and party hard' may be a touch incongruous in slow-paced Alnwick, but this takes nothing away from the 14 very comfortable rooms with boutique elements and up-to-the-minute bathrooms. The timber and leather bar-restaurant downstairs is where Alnwick's suited and booted come to booze and get hitched.

Eating & Drinking

Art House INTERNATIONAL ££
(www.arthouserestaurant.com; 14 Bondgate Within; mains £9-16; ⊙Thu-Mon) Located partially within the 15th-century Hotspur Tower (known locally as the Bondgate Tower), this bright, sharp-edged restaurant/art gallery offers simple but flavoursome combos such as salmon in white wine and pesto sauce, and chicken breast with wild mushrooms and tarragon. Ingredients are locally picked, caught and reared wherever possible. All the art on the walls is for sale.

Market Tavern PUB
(7 Fenkle St; stottie £6) Near Market Sq, this is the place to go for a traditional giant beef stottie (round loaf) sluiced down with a yard of real ale. B&B available (£30).

Ye Old Cross PUB
Known as 'Bottles', after the dusty bottles in the window, this is another atmospheric stottie-and-pint halt. Legend has it that 150 years ago the owner collapsed and died while trying to move the bottles and no one's dared attempt it since; the irony is that the old window is now behind plexiglass to stop revellers stealing them!

Shopping

TOP CHOICE **Barter Books** SECONDHAND BOOKS
(☎01665-604888; www.barterbooks.co.uk; Alnwick Station; ⊙9am-7pm) If you're familiar with the renaissance of the WWII 'Keep Calm and Carry On' slogan, it's thanks to Barter Books, one of the country's largest and most beautiful second-hand bookshops. When converting the old Victorian railway station, the owner came across a set of posters – and turned the discovery into a successful cottage industry. Coal fires, velvet ottomans and reading rooms make this a place you could spend days in, the silence interrupted only by the tiny rumble of the toy train that runs along the track above your head.

Information

Tourist Office (☎01665-511333; www.visitalnwick.org.uk; 2 The Shambles; ⊙9am-5pm Mon-Sat, 10am-4pm Sun) Located by the marketplace; staff can help find accommodation.

Getting There & Away

Alnwick's nearest train station is at Alnmouth, connected to Alnwick by bus every 15 minutes.

Berwick-upon-Tweed Buses 501 & 505; 50 minutes, 10 daily.

Newcastle Buses 501, 505, 518; one hour, two to three hourly.

Warkworth Buses 518 & 472; 25 minutes, twice hourly.

Warkworth

Biscuit-coloured Warkworth is little more than a cluster of houses around a loop in the River Coquet, but it makes for an impressive sight – especially if you arrive on the A1068 from Alnwick, when the village literally unfolds before you to reveal the craggy ruin of an enormous 14th-century castle.

A 'worm-eaten hold of ragged stone', **Warkworth Castle** (EH; adult/child £4.90/2.90; ⊙10am-5pm Apr-Sep) features in Shakespeare's *Henry IV* Parts I and II, and it will not disappoint modern visitors. Yes, it is still pretty worm-eaten and ragged, but it crowns an imposing site, high above the gentle, twisting river. *Elizabeth* (1998), starring Cate Blanchett, was filmed here.

Tiny, mystical, 14th-century **Warkworth Hermitage** (EH; adult/child £3.30/2; ⊙11am-5pm Wed & Sun Apr-Sep), carved into the rock, is a few hundred yards upriver. Follow the signs along the path, then take possibly the world's shortest ferry ride. It's a lovely stretch of water and you can hire a **rowing boat** (adult/child per 45min £5.50/3; ⊙Sat & Sun May-Sep).

Bus 518 links Newcastle (1½ hours, hourly), Warkworth, Alnmouth and Alnwick.

Craster

Sandy, salty Craster is a small sheltered fishing village about 6 miles north of Alnwick, and it is famous for its kippers. In the early

20th century, 2500 herring were smoked here daily; these days, it's mostly cigarettes that are smoked, but the kippers they do produce often grace the Queen's breakfast table no less.

The place to buy them is **Robson & Sons** (www.kipper.co.uk; 2 for around £8), which has been stoking oak-sawdust fires since 1865.

You can also sample the day's catch – crab and kipper pâté are particularly good – and contemplate the splendid views at the **Jolly Fisherman** (sandwiches £3-6).

For fishy facts and other local info, call into the **tourist office** (01665-576007; Quarry Car Park; 10am-4.30pm Easter-Oct).

Bus 411 or 501 from Alnwick calls at Craster (30 minutes, around eight daily). A pay-and-display car park is the only place in Craster where it's possible to park your car.

Dunstanburgh Castle CASTLE, RUINS
(EH & NT; adult/child £4/2.40; 10am-5pm Apr-Sep) The dramatic 1.5-mile walk along the coast from Craster (not accessible by car) is the most scenic path to the moody, weather-beaten ruins of yet another atmospheric castle. The haunting sight of the ruins, high on a basalt outcrop famous for its sea birds, can be seen for miles along this exhilarating stretch of tide-thrashed shoreline.

Dunstanburgh was once one of the largest border castles. Its construction began in 1314, it was strengthened during the Wars of the Roses, but then left to crumble. Only parts of the original wall and gatehouse keep are still standing; it was already a ruin by 1550, so it's a tribute to its builders that so much is left today.

You can also reach the castle on foot from Embleton (1.5 miles).

Embleton Bay

From Dunstanburgh, beautiful Embleton Bay, a pale wide arc of sand, stretches around to the endearing, sloping village of **Embleton**. The village is home to a cluster of houses and the stunning seaside **Dunstanburgh Castle Golf Club** (www.dunstanburgh.com; green fee weekday/weekend £26/30), first laid out in 1900 and improved upon by golf legend and 'inventor' of the dogleg, James Braid (1870–1950) in 1922. Buses 401 and 501 from Alnwick call here.

Past Embleton, the broad vanilla-coloured strand curves around to end at **Low-Newton-by-the-Sea**, a tiny whitewashed, National Trust–preserved village with a fine pub. Behind the bay is a path leading to the **Newton Pool Nature Reserve**, an important spot for breeding and migrating birds such as black-headed gulls and grasshopper warblers. There are a couple of hides where you can peer out at them. You can continue walking along the headland beyond Low Newton, where you'll find **Football Hole**, a delightful hidden beach between headlands.

Sleeping & Eating

Sportsman HOTEL ££
(01665-576588; www.sportsmanhotel.co.uk; 6 Sea lane; r from £80) This large, relaxed place set up from the bay has a wide deck out the front and a spacious, plain wooden bar that serves award-winning local nosh (mains £12 to £17). Upstairs are 12 beautifully appointed rooms – nine of which look over the bay and golf course – and all have sturdy oak beds and handsome pine furniture.

Ship Inn PUB ££
(www.shipinnnewton.co.uk; Low-Newton-by-the-Sea; mains £7-17) This wonderfully traditional ale house has a large open yard for fine weather, although it would take a real dose of sunshine to tear yourself away from the cosy interior. Local lobster (caught 50m away), Craster kippers and the superb ploughman's lunch made with cheddar from a local dairy are the highlights of the locally themed menu.

Farne Islands

One of England's most incredible seabird conventions is found on a rocky archipelago of islands about 3 miles offshore from the undistinguished fishing village of **Seahouses**.

The best time to visit the **Farne Islands** (NT; admission £6; depending on island & time of year) is during breeding season (roughly May to July), when you can see feeding chicks of 20 species of seabird, including puffin, kittiwake, Arctic tern, eider duck, cormorant and gull. This is a quite extraordinary experience, for there are few places in the world where you can get so close to nesting seabirds. The islands are also home to a colony of grey seals.

There are various tours, from 1½-hour cruises to all-day specials, and they get going from 10am April to October. Crossings can be rough, and may be impossible in bad weather. Some of the boats have no proper cabin, so make sure you've got warm, waterproof clothing if there's a chance of rain. Also recommended is an old hat – those birds sure can ruin a head of hair.

Of the four operators that sail from the dock in Seahouses, **Billy Shiel** (☎01665-720308; www.farne-islands.com; 3hr tour adult/child £13/9, all-day tour with landing £30/18) is probably the best known – he even got an MBE for his troubles.

To protect the islands from environmental damage, only two are accessible to the public: Inner Farne and Staple Island. Inner Farne is the more interesting of the two, as it is also the site of a tiny **chapel** (1370, restored 1848) to the memory of St Cuthbert, who lived here for a spell and died here in 687.

Information

The **tourist office** (☎01665-720884; Seafield car park; ⊙10am-5pm Apr-Oct) near the harbour in Seahouses and a **National Trust Shop** (16 Main St; ⊙10am-5pm Apr-Oct) are on hand to provide island-specific information.

Getting There & Away

Alnwick Bus 501 or 505; six daily, one hour.

Berwick Bus 501 or 505; six daily, 50 minutes.

Bamburgh

POP 450

Cute little Bamburgh is dominated by its castle, a massive, imposing structure roosting high up on a basalt crag and a solid contender for England's best. The village itself – a tidy fist of houses around a pleasant green – will be forever associated with the valiant achievements of local lass, Grace Darling.

Bamburgh Castle CASTLE
(www.bamburghcastle.com; adult/child £9/4; ⊙10am-5pm Mar-Oct, 11am-4pm Nov-Mar) Northumberland's most dramatic castle was built around a powerful 11th-century Norman keep by Henry II, although its name is a derivative of Bebbanburgh, after the wife of Anglo-Saxon ruler Aedelfrip, whose fortified home occupied this basalt outcrop 500 years earlier. The castle played a key role in the border wars of the 13th and 14th centuries, and in 1464 was the first English castle to fall as the result of a sustained artillery attack, by Richard Neville, Earl of Warwick, during the Wars of the Roses. It was restored in the 19th century by the great industrialist Lord Armstrong, who died before work was completed. The castle is still home to the Armstrong family.

Once through the gates, head for the **museum** to view scraps of WWII German bombers washed up on Northumberland's beaches, plus exhibits illustrating just how the Armstrongs raked in their millions (ships, weapons, locomotives), before entering the castle proper. The 12 rooms and chambers inside are crammed with antique furniture, suits of armour, priceless ceramics and works of art, but top billing must go to the **King's Hall**, a stunning piece of 19th-century neo-Gothic fakery, all wood panelling, leaded windows and hefty beams supporting the roof.

The Bamburgh Castle app (£1.99) is a downloadable audio guide to the castle (available from the app store).

RNLI Grace Darling Museum MUSEUM
(1 Radcliffe Rd; admission free; ⊙10am-5pm) Born in Bamburgh, Grace Darling was the lighthouse keeper's daughter on Outer Farne who rowed out to the grounded, flailing SS *Forfarshire* in 1838 and saved its crew in the middle of a dreadful storm. This recently refurbished museum is dedicated to the plucky Victorian heroine and even has the actual coble (rowboat) in which she braved the churning North Sea, as well as a film on the events of that stormy night. Grace was born just three houses down from the museum and is buried in the churchyard opposite, her ornate wrought-iron and sandstone tomb built tall so as to be visible to passing ships.

Sleeping & Eating

Bamburgh has some fine places to snooze.

You can stock up for a picnic at the **Pantry** (13 Front St; sandwiches £2.20-4.50); the **Copper Kettle** (22 Front St; afternoon tea £5-7) is a gift shop with a terrific tearoom.

Bamburgh Hall Farm B&B ££
(☎01668-214230; www.bamburghhallfarm.com; s/d £45/70; P) This magnificent minimansion built in 1697 and wedged between the castle and the golf course comes highly recommended for the sheer pleasure of the views, right down to the sea, and the huge breakfast, served in the very dining room where Jacobite officers met during the rebellion of 1715. Studies in understated elegance, the four rooms are a superb deal.

Victoria Hotel HOTEL ££
(☎01668-214431; www.victoriahotel.net; Front St; r from £80; P) Overlooking the village green is this handsome hotel with bedrooms decorated with quality antiques and – in the superior rooms – handcrafted four-posters and castle views. Here you'll also find the best restaurant in the village, with a surprisingly adventurous menu (mains £11 to £17) that blends local fare with exotic flavours.

Getting There & Away

Alnwick Bus 401 or 501; one hour, four to six daily.

Newcastle Bus 501; 2½ hours, three daily Monday to Saturday, two Sunday. Stops at Alnwick and Seahouses.

Holy Island (Lindisfarne)

Holy Island is often referred to as an unearthly place, and while a lot of this talk is just that (and a little bit of bring-'em-in tourist bluster), there *is* something almost other-worldly about this small island (it's only 2 sq miles). It's slightly tricky to reach, as it's connected to the mainland by a narrow causeway that only appears at low tide. It's also fiercely desolate and isolated, barely any different from when St Aidan arrived to found a monastery in 635. As you cross the empty flats to get here, it's not difficult to imagine the marauding Vikings who repeatedly sacked the settlement between 793 and 875, when the monks finally took the hint and left. They carried with them the illuminated *Lindisfarne Gospels* (now in the British Library in London) and the miraculously preserved body of St Cuthbert, who lived here for a couple of years but preferred the hermit's life on Inner Farne. A priory was re-established in the 11th century but didn't survive the Dissolution in 1537.

Holy Island is a strange mix of magic and menace that attracts the pious and the curious; during summer weekends the tiny fishing village, built around the red-sandstone remains of the medieval priory, swarms with visitors. The island's peculiar isolation is best appreciated at high tide or out of season, when the wind-lashed, marram-covered dunes offer the same bleak existence as that taken on by St Aidan and his band of hardy monks.

Pay attention to the crossing-time information, posted at tourist offices and on notice boards throughout the area. Every year a handful of go-it-alone fools are caught midway by the incoming tide and have to abandon their cars.

Sights

Lindisfarne Priory PRIORY
(EH; adult/child £4.90/2.90; ⏲9.30am-5pm Apr-Sep) The skeletal, red and grey ruins of the priory are an eerie sight and give a fleeting impression of the isolated life lead by the Lindisfarne monks. The later 13th-century St Mary the Virgin Church is built on the site of the first church between the Tees and the Firth of Forth, and the adjacent museum displays the remains of the first monastery and tells the story of the monastic community before and after the Dissolution.

Lindisfarne Heritage Centre MUSEUM
(www.lindisfarne.org.uk; Marygate; adult/child £3/1; ⏲10am-5pm Apr-Oct, according to tides Nov-Mar) Twenty pages of the luminescent *Lindisfarne Gospels* can be flicked through on touch-screens here, though there's normally a queue for the two terminals. While you wait your turn there are fascinating exhibitions on the Vikings and the sacking of Lindisfarne in 793.

Lindisfarne Castle CASTLE
(NT; adult/child £6/3; ⏲10.30am-3pm or noon-4.30pm Tue-Sun Mar-Oct) Half a mile from the village stands this tiny, storybook castle, moulded onto a hunk of rock in 1550, and extended and converted by Sir Edwin Lutyens from 1902 to 1910 for Mr Hudson, the owner of *Country Life* magazine. You can imagine some decadent parties have graced its alluring rooms – Jay Gatsby would have been proud. Its opening times may be extended depending on the tide.

Sleeping & Eating

It's possible to stay on the island, but you'll need to book well in advance. Two recommended options are **Open Gate** (☎01289-389222; www.aidanandhilda.org; Marygate; s/d £55/70), which is geared primarily at those looking to exploit the island's more spiritual aspects; and the **Manor House Hotel** (☎01289-389207; www.manorhouselindisfarne.com; s/d £55/95), which has decent rooms and a good restaurant (mains £8-12).

Shopping

St Aidan's Winery WINERY
(www.lindisfarne-mead.co.uk) Sample and buy deliciously sweet Lindisfarne Mead, said to

be a potent aphrodisiac, at the island's winery housed in a new modern complex.

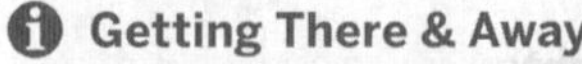

Getting There & Away

Holy Island can be reached by bus 477 from Berwick (Wednesday and Saturday only, Monday to Saturday July and August). People taking cars across are requested to park in one of the signposted car parks (£5 per day). The sea covers the causeway and cuts the island off from the mainland for about five hours each day. Tide times are listed at tourist offices, in local newspapers and at each side of the crossing.

If arriving by car, a **shuttle bus** (£2; every 20min) runs from the car park to the castle.

Berwick-upon-Tweed

POP 11,665

England's northernmost city is a salt-encrusted fortress with a history of conflict: it changed hands 14 times between the Scots and the English between 1174 and 1482, which has resulted in a strong local identity. Locals speak English with a noticeable Scottish burr and its football team, Berwick Rangers, are the only English team to play in the Scottish leagues.

Sights & Activities

FREE Berwick's Walls WALLS

(EH) You can walk almost the entire length of Berwick's hefty Elizabethan walls, begun in 1558 to reinforce an earlier set built during the reign of Edward II. The mile-long walk is a must, with wonderful, wide-open views. Only a small fragment remains of the once mighty **border castle**, most of the building having been replaced by the train station.

Berwick Barracks MUSEUM, GALLERY

(EH; The Parade; adult/child £3.90/2.30; 10am-5pm Mon-Fri) Designed by Nicholas Hawksmoor, the oldest purpose-built barracks (1717) in Britain now house an assortment of museums and art galleries, covering a history of the town and British soldiery since the 17th century. The **Gymnasium Gallery** hosts big-name contemporary art exhibitions.

Cell Block Museum MUSEUM

(Marygate; adult/child £3/1; tours 10.30am & 2pm Mon-Fri Apr-Sep) The original jail cells in the upper floor of the town hall (1750–61) have been preserved as a museum devoted to crime and punishment. Tours take in the public rooms, museum, jail and belfry.

FREE Lowry Trail WALKING TOUR

Some of LS Lowry's finest works are actually the result of his many visits over 40 years to Berwick. The artist is known primarily for his drawings and paintings that populate the northwest's industrial landscapes with matchstick figures. Most of the trail's information boards stand on the town's walls, but the route also crosses the 17th-century Old Bridge into the aptly grim suburbs of Tweedmouth and Spittal. Ask for a free map from the tourist office.

Wilson Cycles CYCLING

(01289-331476; 17a Bridge St) Hire a bike for £15 a day.

Sleeping

There's a cluster of fairly basic B&Bs in Church St.

TOP CHOICE No 1 Sallyport BOUTIQUE B&B £££

(01289-308827; www.sallyport.co.uk; 1 Sallyport, off Bridge St; r £150) Not just the best in town, but one of the best B&Bs in England, No 1 Sallyport has only six suites – each carefully appointed to fit a theme. The Manhattan Loft, crammed into the attic, makes the minimalist most of the confined space; the Lowry Room is a country-style Georgian classic; the Smuggler's Suite has a separate sitting room complete with widescreen TV, DVD players and plenty of space to lounge around. The Tiffany Suite has a grand fireplace and the attic Mulberry Suite has a sexy freestanding bath. The downstairs **restaurant** (mains £8.95 to £12.95) is Berwick's finest-serving Cheviot lamb, North Sea fish and homemade cakes and pastries.

YHA Berwick HOSTEL ££

(0845-371 9676; www.yha.org.uk; Dewars La; dm/d from £15/48) A 240-year-old granary with a distinct 'lean' has been converted into a smart hostel with all the usual facilties: comfortable dorms, a handful of doubles, a TV room, laundry and internet. The staff are terrifically friendly and helpful.

Eating & Drinking

Good dining is a little thin on the ground, but there are a few exceptions.

Foxton's CONTINENTAL ££

(26 Hide Hill; mains £9-15; Mon-Sat) This decent brasserie-style restaurant has Continental dishes to complement the local fare, which means there's something for everyone.

Reivers Tryst BRITISH £

(119 Marygate; mains £5.20-9; ⏲Mon-Sat) From the hearty all-day brekkie to homemade pies for lunch and the likes of gammon and pineapple in the evening, this place specialises in English cuisine – nothing fancy, but very good.

Barrels Alehouse PUB

(56 Bridge St) Berwick's best watering hole attracts a mixed, laid-back crowd who can be found supping real ales and microdistilled gins and whiskies at all hours. There's regular live music in the atmospherically dingy basement bar.

 Information

Berwick Library (Walkergate; ⏲closed Thu & Sun) Bring ID to access the internet.

Tourist Office (☎01289-330733; www.visitnorthumberland.com; 106 Marygate; ⏲10am-5pm Mon-Sat, 11am-3pm Sun Easter-Oct) Can help find accommodation and runs one-hour guided walks at 10am, 11.45am & 2pm on weekdays (£5).

 Getting There & Away

Bus

Buses stop on Golden Sq (where Marygate becomes Castlegate).

Edinburgh National Express; £15.10, one hour 20 minutes, twice daily.

Holy Island Bus 477; 35 minutes, two services on Wednesday and Saturday, Monday to Saturday in August.

London National Express; £44.60, eight hours, twice daily.

Newcastle Buses 505, 501 (via Alnwick); 2½ hours, nine daily.

Train

Berwick is almost exactly halfway between **Edinburgh** (£27.50, 50 minutes, half hourly) and **Newcastle** (£23.50, 50 minutes, half hourly) on the main east-coast London–Edinburgh line.

Getting Around

The best tool for getting around Berwick is at the end of your legs, but if you're feeling lazy try **Berwick Taxis** (☎01289-307771).

Around Berwick-upon-Tweed

Norham Castle CASTLE, RUINS

(EH; admission free; ⏲10am-5pm Apr-Sep) Once considered the most dangerous place in the country, the pinkish ruins of **Norham Castle** are quiet these days, but during the border wars it was besieged no less than 13 times, including a year-long siege by Robert the Bruce in 1318. The last attack came just three weeks before the Battle of Flodden and the castle was once again restored to the prince bishops of Durham, for whom it was originally built in 1160 to guard a swerving bend in the River Tweed.

The castle ruins are 6.5 miles southwest of Berwick on a minor road off the A698; bus 67 regularly passes Norham Castle from Berwick train station on its way to Galashiels in Scotland (six daily Monday to Saturday).

ETAL & FORD

The pretty villages of Etal and Ford are part of a 23.45-sq-mile working rural estate set between the coast and the Cheviots, a lush and ordered landscape that belies its ferocious, bloody history.

Etal (*eet*-le) perches at the estate's northern end, and its main attraction is the roofless 14th-century **Etal Castle** (EH; adult/child £3.90/2.30; ⏲11am-4.30pm Apr-Oct). It was captured by the Scots just before the ferocious Battle of Flodden and has a striking border-warfare exhibition. It is 12 miles south of Berwick on the B6354.

About 1.5 miles southeast of here is Ford, home to the **Lady Waterford Hall** (adult/child £2.50/2; ⏲11am-5pm Mar-Oct, other times by appointment), a fine Victorian schoolhouse decorated with biblical murals and pictures by Louisa Anna, Marchioness of Waterford. The imposing 14th-century **Ford Castle** is closed to the public.

If you're travelling with kids, take a spin on the toy-town **Heatherslaw Light Railway** (www.heatherslawlightrailway.co.uk; adult/child £6.50/2; ⏲hourly 10am-3pm Apr-Oct), which chugs from the Heatherslaw Corn Mill (about halfway between the two villages) to Etal Castle. The 3.5-mile return journey follows the river through pretty countryside.

Sleeping & Eating

Estate House B&B ££

(☎01890-820668; www.theestatehouse.info; s/d £55/75) This fine house near Lady Waterford Hall has three lovely bedrooms (all with handsome brass beds) overlooking a colourful, mature garden. An excellent choice – the owners have a plethora of local information.

Black Bull PUB

This whitewashed, popular place is Northumberland's only thatched pub. It serves great pub food (mains £7 to £10, no food Tuesday) and pours a variety of well-kept ales.

Getting There & Away

Bus 267 between Berwick and Wooler stops at both Etal and Ford (four daily, Monday to Saturday).

CROOKHAM & AROUND

Unless you're a Scot or a historian, chances are you won't have heard of the Battle of Flodden, but this 1513 encounter between the Scots and the English – which left the English victorious and the Scots to count 10,000 dead, including James IV of Scotland and most of his nobles – was a watershed in the centuries-old scrap between the two. A large stone cross, a monument 'to the brave of both nations', surmounts an innocuous hill overlooking the battlefield and is the only memorial to the thousands used as arrow fodder.

Sleeping & Eating

TOP CHOICE **Coach House** B&B ££

(01890-820293; www.coachhousecrookham.com; s/d £85/105) This exquisite guesthouse spread about a 17th-century cottage, an old smithy and other outbuildings has a variety of rooms, from the traditional (with rare chestnut beams and country-style furniture) to contemporary layouts flavoured with Mediterranean and Indian touches. The food (dinner £23), beginning with an organic breakfast, is absolutely delicious and the equal of any restaurant around.

Getting There & Away

The battlefield is 1.5 miles west of Crookham, on a minor road off the A697; Crookham itself is 3 miles west of Ford. Bus 267, between Berwick-upon-Tweed and Wooler stops outside Crookham post office (six daily, 36 minutes).

Understand England

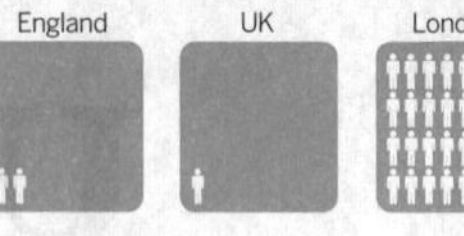

England Today

For England and the English, the first dozen years of the 21st century have been a time of change, crisis, controversy and national soul-searching. And it doesn't look like settling down any time soon...

Change at the Top

In May 2010 a general election resulted in the Labour government being ousted after 13 years of rule when an agreement between the Conservatives and Liberal Democrats created the first UK coalition government in modern history. The 'Con-Lib' alignment was predicted by very few political pundits, but the new government got down to work and initially impressed most observers with displays of collaboration, despite the two parties coming from opposite sides of centre ground.

Home & Away

» Population: 51 million

» Size: 50,000 sq miles (130,000 sq km)

» Inflation: 3%

Cracks appeared in 2011, and were further strained in 2012, but the new government forged on under the helm of Prime Minister David Cameron (the Conservative leader) and Deputy PM Nick Clegg (the Lib-Dem leader), with several new – and often controversial – policies introduced. Most notable were changes to the education system allowing parents to set up their own schools, a major overhaul of the police service, and a reform of the National Health Service, long regarded by politicians and the public alike as a national treasure.

The biggest current issue for most people is the impact of the global financial crisis and the country's own levels of debt, addressed by the coalition government with an austerity package that included tax increases and public spending cuts. The Labour opposition has espoused increased public spending, pointing to slow economic growth and rising unemployment (especially for young adults) as failures of government policies.

Books

» **Notes from a Small Island** (Bill Bryson) It's dated, but this American's fond take on British behaviour is still spot-on today.

» **Icons of England** (Bill Bryson) That man again, still in love with his adopted home.

» **Watching the English** (Kate Fox) A fascinating field guide to the nation's peculiar habits.

» **I Never Knew That About England** (Christopher Winn) A treasure trove of bizarre facts.

» **The English** (Jeremy Paxman) A perceptive look at the national character.

belief systems
(% of population)

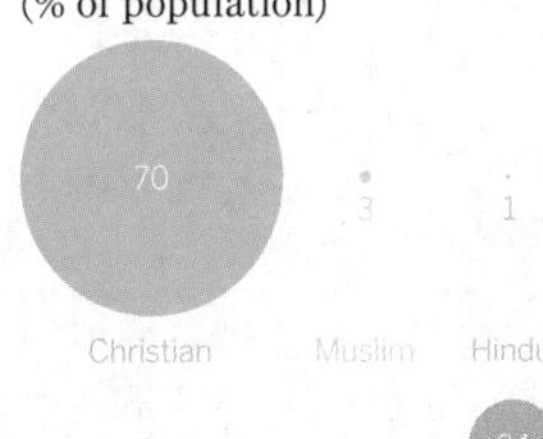

if England were 100 people

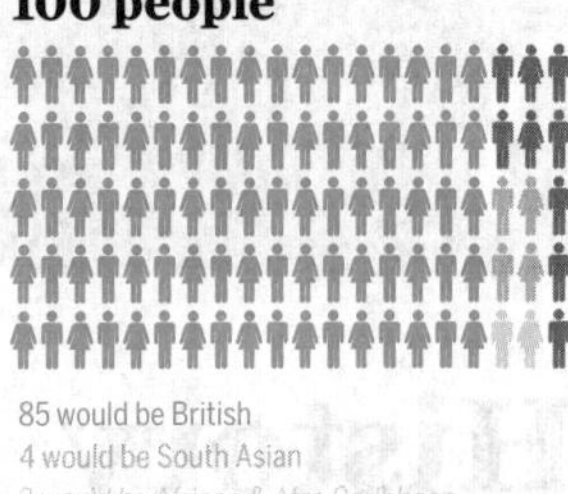

85 would be British
4 would be South Asian
2 would be African & Afro Caribbean
9 would be other

Greece is the Word

The global financial crisis has also exposed weaknesses in the Euro zone countries, especially Greece, with the Governor of the Bank of England stating in May 2012 that the UK's recovery was hampered by the poor health of Europe's single currency. On the upside, the Bank of England also predicted that London's hosting of the Olympic and Paralympic Games would benefit the national economy – so the English have at least one reason to thank the Greeks.

Whither Albion?

Meanwhile, away from political and economic battles, deeper schisms are evident. For most English people, the difference between being British and being English is pretty hazy. However, in the wake of continuing UK devolution and the rise of regional assemblies in Scotland and Wales, the very identity of England has become a subject of fierce debate and the people of England are being forced to reflect on the values, beliefs and institutions that bind the country together.

Yet if there's one thing this plucky little nation has proven down the centuries, it is its resilience (so long as there's a nice hot mug of tea to hand). No matter what the future may hold, the true jewels in England's crown – its grand castles and chocolate-box villages, its landmark monuments and buzzing music scene, its sweeping countryside and revitalised cities – remain as bright and untarnished as ever.

The politicians aren't trusted, the economy's looking dicey and national identity is under the glass, but England's days are far from over.

» Proportion of population using social networking sites: 51%

» Text messages sent per person per month: 150

» Cups of tea consumed per person per day: 3

Top Tunes

» *A New England* Billy Bragg

» *England My Home* The Levellers

» *I was Made in England* Elton John

» *Old England* The Waterboys

» *This is England* The Clash

» *Waterloo Sunset* The Kinks

» *England My Lionheart* Kate Bush

» *Village Green Preservation Society* Kate Rusby

» *London* The Smiths

Movies

» *Brief Encounter* (1945)

» *This Sporting Life* (1961)

» *My Beautiful Laundrette* (1985)

» *Sense and Sensibility* (1996)

» *The Full Monty* (1997)

» *Elizabeth: The Golden Age* (2007)

» *War Horse* (2011)

History

England may be a small country on the edge of Europe, but it's never been on the sidelines of history. For thousands of years, invaders and incomers have arrived, settled and made their mark. The result is England's fascinating mix of landscape, culture and language – a dynamic pattern that shaped the nation and continues to evolve today.

Among the earliest migrants were Neolithic peoples. Much later the Celts arrived, then the Romans left a legacy of spectacular ruins that can still be seen. After the Romans, the Anglo-Saxon migration was a key period; thanks to kings such as Alfred the Great, the foundations were laid for the modern state we now call England.

Then came 1066, a pivotal date in English history, when the country was invaded by the French Norman army of William the Conqueror, which in turn led to the great castles and cathedrals of the medieval period. By the 18th century, aristocrats were building the great 'stately homes' which dot the English landscape and feature on tourist itineraries today.

For many visitors, this rich historic legacy – everything from Stonehenge and Hadrian's Wall to Canterbury Cathedral and the Tower of London – is England's main attraction. In this chapter, we concentrate on high-profile events but also mention some historic locations you may see on your travels.

The country of England is part of the island of Great Britain (along with Wales and Scotland). The words 'England' and 'Britain' are not synonymous, and getting to grips with this basic principle will ease your understanding of English history and culture.

Stone Age & Iron Age

Stone tools discovered near Lowestoft in Suffolk show that human habitation in England stretches back at least 700,000 years, although exact dates depend somewhat on your definition of 'human'. These early peoples were nomadic hunter-gatherers, but by around 4000 BC, most had settled down, notably in open areas such as Salisbury Plain in southern England. Alongside fields they built burial mounds (today called barrows), but their most enduring legacies are the great stone circles of Avebury and Stonehenge, still clearly visible today.

TIMELINE

4000 BC

Neolithic peoples migrate from continental Europe. They differ significantly from previous arrivals: instead of hunting and moving on, they settle in one place and start farming.

c 55 BC

Relatively small groups of Roman invaders under the command of Emperor Julius Caesar make forays into southern England from the northern coast of Gaul (today's France).

AD 43

Emperor Claudius leads the first proper Roman invasion of England. His army wages a ruthless campaign, and the Romans control most of southern England by AD 50.

Move on a millennium or two and it's the Iron Age. Better tools meant trees could be felled and more land turned over to farming. As landscapes altered, this was also a time of cultural change: a new wave of migrants – the Celts – arrived in Britain. It's not clear if the new arrivals absorbed the indigenous people, or vice versa, but the end result was the widespread adoption of Celtic language and culture, and the creation of a Celtic-British population – today often known as the Britons (or Ancient Britons to distinguish them from today's natives).

By around 100BC, the Ancient Britons had separated into about 20 different tribes, including the Cantiaci (in today's county of Kent), the Iceni (today's Norfolk) and the Brigantes (northwest England). Did you notice the Latin-sounding names? That's because the tribal tags were handed out by the next arrivals on England's shores...

The Romans

Although there had been some earlier expeditionary campaigns, the main Roman invasion of England was in AD 43. They called their newly won province Britannia, and within a decade most of southern England was under Roman control. It wasn't a walkover though: some locals fought back, most famously the warrior-queen Boudica, who led a rebel army against Londinium, the Roman port on the present site of London.

Opposition was mostly sporadic, however, and no real threat to Roman military might. By around AD 80 Britannia comprised much of today's England and Wales. Though it's tempting to imagine noble natives battling courageously against occupying forces, Roman control and stability may well have been welcomed by the general population, tired of feuding chiefs and insecure tribal territories.

Roman settlement in England continued for almost four centuries, and intermarriage was common between locals and incomers (many from other parts of the empire – including modern-day Belgium, Spain and Syria – rather than Rome itself). A Romano-British population thus evolved, particularly in the towns, while indigenous Celtic-British culture remained in rural areas.

Along with stability and wealth, the Romans introduced another cultural facet: a new religion called Christianity, after it was recognised by Emperor Constantine in the 4th century. (Recent research, however, indicates that Celtic Christians may have brought the religion to Britain even earlier.) But although Romano-British culture was thriving in Britannia, back in its Mediterranean heartland the Empire was already in decline.

It was an untidy finale. The Romans were not driven out by the ancient Britons (after more than 300 years, Romano-British culture was so established there was nowhere for many to go 'home' to). In reality,

STONEHENGE

Probably built around 3000 BC, Stonehenge has stood on Salisbury Plain for more than 5000 years, making it older than the Great Pyramids of Egypt.

60

The Iceni warrior queen Boudica (also known as Boadicea) leads a rebel army against the Romans, destroys the Roman town of Colchester and gets as far as their port at Londinium (now London).

200

The Romans build a defensive wall around the city of London with four main entrance gates, still remembered today by the districts of Aldgate, Ludgate, Newgate and Bishopsgate.

c 410

As the classical world's greatest empire declines after more than three centuries of relative peace and prosperity, Roman rule ends in Britain with more of a whimper than a bang.

5th century

Teutonic tribes – known today as the Anglo-Saxons – from the area now called Germany migrate to England, and quickly spread across much of the country.

Britannia was simply dumped by the rulers in Rome, and the colony slowly fizzled out. But historians are neat folk, and the end of Roman power in England is generally dated at AD 410.

A History of England in 100 Places by John Julius Norwich is a fascinating handbook mixing history with geography, and covering a range of locations 'from Stonehenge to the Gherkin'.

Fledgling England

When Roman power faded, the province of Britannia went downhill. Romano-British towns were abandoned and rural areas became no-go zones as local warlords fought over fiefdoms. The vacuum didn't go unnoticed, and once again invaders crossed from the European mainland – this time Germanic tribes called Angles and Saxons.

Historians disagree on what happened next; either the Anglo-Saxons largely overcame or absorbed the Romano-British and Celts, or the indigenous tribes simply adopted Anglo-Saxon language and culture. Either way, by the late 6th century much of England was predominantly Anglo-Saxon, divided into separate kingdoms dominated by Wessex (in southern England), Mercia (today's Midlands) and Northumbria (northern England).

Some areas remained unaffected by the incomers, but the overall impact was immense. Today, the core of the English language is Anglo-Saxon, many place names have Anglo-Saxon roots, and the very term 'Anglo-Saxon' has become a (much abused and factually incorrect) byword for 'pure English'.

The Vikings & Alfred the Great

In the 9th century England was yet again invaded by a bunch of pesky Continentals. This time it was the Vikings from today's Scandinavia. They quickly conquered the eastern and northeastern areas of England, then started to expand into central England. Blocking their route were

LEGACY OF THE LEGIONS

To control their new territory, the Romans built garrisons across England. Many developed into towns, later called 'chesters', today remembered by names like Winchester, Manchester and, of course, Chester. The Romans also built roads, initially so soldiers could march quickly from place to place, and later so that trade could develop. Wherever possible the roads were straight lines (because it was efficient, not – as the old joke goes – to stop Ancient Britons hiding round corners) and included Ermine Street between London and York, Watling Street between Kent and Wales, and the Fosse Way between Exeter and Lincoln. As you travel around England, you'll notice that many modern highways still follow Roman roads. In a country better known for old lanes and turnpike routes winding through the landscape, these ruler-straight highways clearly stand out on the map.

8th century
King Offa of Mercia orders the construction of a clear border between his kingdom and Wales – a defensive ditch called Offa's Dyke that is still visible today.

850
Vikings come from what is today Denmark and conquer east and northeast England. They establish their capital at Yorvik, today's city of York.

927
Athelstan, grandson of Alfred the Great and son of Edward the Elder, is the first monarch to be crowned King of England, building on his ancestors' success in regaining Viking territory.

1066
Incumbent King Harold is defeated by an invading Norman army at the Battle of Hastings, and England finds itself with a new monarch: William the Conqueror.

the Anglo-Saxon armies heading north, led by Alfred the Great, the king of Wessex and one of English history's best-known characters.

Thus England was divided in two: north and east was the Viking land, known as 'Danelaw', while south and west was Anglo-Saxon territory. Alfred was hailed as king of the English – the first time the Anglo-Saxons regarded themselves as a truly united people. His capital was Winchester; if you come to visit the famous cathedral, look out for the nearby statue of Alfred in the city centre.

Alfred's son and successor was Edward, known as Edward the Elder. After more battles, he gained control of Danelaw, and thus became the first king to rule the whole country – a major milestone in English history.

But it was hardly cause for celebration. Later in the 10th century, more raids from Scandinavia threatened the fledgling English unity, and as the 1st millennium AD came to an end, the future was anything but certain.

1066 & All That

When King Edward the Confessor died, the crown passed to Harold, his brother-in-law. That should have settled things, but Edward had a cousin in Normandy (in northern France) called William, who thought *he* should have succeeded to the throne of England.

The end result was the Battle of Hastings in 1066, the most memorable of dates for anyone who has studied English history. William sailed from Normandy with an army, the Saxons were defeated, and King Harold was killed – by an arrow in the eye, according to legend. William became king of England, earning himself the prestigious epithet Conqueror.

In the years after the invasion, the French-speaking Normans and the English-speaking Anglo-Saxons kept pretty much to themselves. At the top of the feudal system came the monarch, and below that came the nobles: barons and baronesses, dukes and duchesses, plus the bishops. Then came earls, knights and lords – and their ladies. At the bottom were peasants or 'serfs', and this strict hierarchy became the basis of a class system that, to a certain extent, still exists in England today.

CELTS VS ANGLO-SAXONS

Despite Anglo-Saxon dominance from around AD 500, the Celtic language was still being spoken in parts of southern England when the Normans invaded in the 11th century.

Royal & Holy Squabbling

William's successor, William II, was assassinated during a hunting trip and succeeded by Henry I, Stephen of Blois, then Henry II, establishing the House of Plantagenet. This period also established the long-standing English tradition of competition for the throne, and introduced an equally enduring tendency of bickering between royalty and the Church. Things came to a head in 1170 when Henry II had 'turbulent priest' Thomas Becket murdered in Canterbury Cathedral, one of England's finest medieval cathedrals.

Perhaps the next king, Richard I, wanted to make amends for his forebears' unholy sentiments by fighting against Muslim 'infidels' in the Holy

1085–86

The Norman invaders compile the Domesday Book – a thorough census of England's stock and future potential; it's still a vital historical document today.

1095

The start of the First Crusade – a campaign of Christian European armies against the Muslim occupation of Jerusalem and the 'Holy Land'. A series of crusades continues until 1272.

12th century

Oxford University founded. There's evidence of teaching in the area since 1096, but King Henry II's 1167 ban on students attending the University of Paris solidifies Oxford's importance.

DAVID C TOMLINSON / GETTY IMAGES ©

»Magdalen College, Oxford

Land (today known as Israel and the Palestinian territories, plus parts of Syria, Jordan and Lebanon). Unfortunately, he was too busy crusading to bother about governing England – although his bravery earned Richard the sobriquet 'Lionheart' – and in his absence the country fell into disarray.

Richard was succeeded by his brother John. According to legend, it was during this time that a noble named Robert of Loxley, better known as Robin Hood, hid in Sherwood Forest and engaged in a spot of wealth redistribution.

Plantagenet Progress

By the early 13th century King John's erratic rule was too much for the powerful barons, and they forced him to sign a document called the Magna Carta ('Great Charter') at Runnymede, near Windsor; you can still visit the site today.

The next king was Henry III, followed in 1272 by Edward I – a skilled ruler and ambitious general. During a busy 35-year reign, he was unashamedly expansionist, leading campaigns into Wales and Scotland, where his ruthless activities earned him the title 'Hammer of the Scots'.

Edward I was succeeded by Edward II, who lacked his forebear's military success. He failed in the marriage department, too, and came to a grisly end when his wife, Isabella, and her lover, Roger Mortimer, had him murdered in Berkeley Castle. Today, fans of ghoulish ends can visit the very spot where it happened.

MEDIEVAL WOMEN

Medieval Women by Henrietta Leyser looks through a female lens at the period of English history from AD 500 to 1500; a life of work, marriage, sex and children – not necessarily in that order.

Houses of Lancaster & York

In 1399 Richard II was ousted by a powerful baron called Henry Bolingbroke, who became Henry IV – the first monarch of the House of Lancaster. He was followed, neatly, by Henry V, who decided it was time to finally end the Hundred Years' War, a long-standing conflict between England and France. Henry's victory at the Battle of Agincourt and the patriotic speech he was given by Shakespeare in his namesake play ('cry God for Harry, England and St George') ensured his position among the most famous English monarchs.

Still keeping things neat, Henry V was followed by Henry VI. His main claims to fame were overseeing the building of great places of worship – King's College Chapel, in Cambridge, Eton Chapel, near Windsor – and suffering from great bouts of insanity.

The Hundred Years' War finally ground to a halt in 1453, but just a few years later England was plunged into a civil conflict dubbed the Wars of the Roses. Briefly it went like this: Henry VI of the House of Lancaster (emblem: a red rose) was challenged by Richard, Duke of York (emblem: a white rose). Henry was weak and it was almost a walkover for Richard,

1215

King John signs the Magna Carta, limiting the monarch's power for the first time in English history: an early step on the path towards constitutional rule.

1337–1453

England battles France in a long conflict known as the Hundred Years' War. It was actually a series of small conflicts. And it lasted for more than a century.

1348

The arrival of the Black Death. Commonly attributed to bubonic plague, the pandemic killed more than 1.5 million people, over a third of the country's population.

1415

The invading English army under Henry V defeats the French army at the Battle of Agincourt – a crucial battle in the Hundred Years' War. (The war itself continues for almost another 40 years).

but Henry's wife, Margaret of Anjou, was made of sterner mettle and her forces defeated the challenger. Then Richard's son Edward entered with an army, turned the tables, drove out Henry, and became King Edward IV – the first monarch of the House of York.

Today, 600 years after the Wars of the Roses, Yorkshire's symbol is still a white rose, while Lancashire's is still a red rose. Rivalry between these two counties remains strong – especially when it comes to cricket and football.

Dark Deeds in the Tower

Edward IV hardly had time to catch his breath before facing a challenge from the Earl of Warwick, who teamed up with the energetic Margaret of Anjou to shuttle Edward into exile and bring Henry VI to the throne. A year later Edward IV came bouncing back, killed Warwick, captured Margaret and had Henry executed in the Tower of London.

Edward IV was succeeded by his 12-year-old son, Edward V. But in 1483 the boy-king was mysteriously murdered, along with his brother, and once again the Tower of London was the scene of the crime

With the 'little princes' dispatched, the throne was open for their Uncle Richard. Whether he was the princes' killer remains the subject of debate, but his rule as Richard III was short-lived: in 1485 he was tumbled from the top job (thus concluding the House of Plantagenet) by a Welsh nobleman named Henry Tudor, who became King Henry VII.

Peace & Dissolution

With the Wars of the Roses only recently ended, Henry VII's Tudor neutrality was important. He also mended fences with his northern neighbours by marrying off his daughter to James IV of Scotland. The result was a much-welcomed period of peace for England.

The next king, Henry VIII, is one of England's best-known monarchs, mainly thanks to his six wives – the result of a desperate quest for a male heir. He also had a profound impact on England's history; his excommunication from the Roman Catholic Church was followed by the

RULING THE ROOST

The gallop through the story of England's ruling dynasties clearly shows that life is never dull for the person at the top. Despite immense power and privilege, the position of monarch (or, perhaps worse, *potential* monarch) probably ranks as one of history's least safe occupations. English kings to meet an untimely end include Harold (killed in battle), William II (assassinated), Charles I (beheaded by Republicans), Edward V (murdered by an uncle), Richard II (probably starved to death), John (too much eating and drinking), James II (deposed), Edward II (dispatched by his queen and her lover) and William III (died after his horse tripped over a molehill). As you visit the castles and battlefields of England, you may feel a touch of sympathy – but only a touch – for those all-powerful figures continually looking over their shoulders.

1459–71

The Wars of the Roses: a conflict between two competing dynasties – the Houses of Lancaster and York. The Yorkists are successful, and King Edward IV gains the throne.

1485

Henry Tudor defeats Richard III at the Battle of Bosworth to become King Henry VII, establishing the Tudor dynasty and ending York-Lancaster rivalry for the throne.

1509–47

Reign of King Henry VIII. The Pope's disapproval of Henry's serial marriage and divorce results in the English Reformation and the founding of the Church of England.

1558–1603

Reign of Queen Elizabeth I, a period of boundless English optimism. Enter stage right playwright William Shakespeare. Exit due west navigators Walter Raleigh and Francis Drake.

'Dissolution' – the infamous closure of many monasteries – the ruins of which can still be seen today at places such as Fountains Abbey and Rievaulx Abbey in Yorkshire.

The 1955 film version of Shakespeare's *Richard III*, staring Laurence Olivier and John Gielgud, was the award-winning drama of its time, and is well worth watching for a view on this turbulent period in English history.

The Elizabethan Age

Henry VIII was succeeded by his son Edward VI, then his daughter Mary I, but their reigns were short. And so Elizabeth, his third child, unexpectedly came to the throne.

As Elizabeth I, she inherited a nasty mess of religious strife and divided loyalties, but after an uncertain start she gained confidence and turned the country around. Refusing marriage, she borrowed biblical motifs and became known as the Virgin Queen – perhaps the first English monarch to create a cult image.

Highlights of her 45-year reign included the naval defeat of the Spanish Armada, the far-flung explorations of English seafarers Walter Raleigh and Francis Drake and the expansion of England's trading network (including newly established colonies on the east coast of America) – not to mention a cultural flourishing, thanks to writers such as William Shakespeare and Christopher Marlowe.

Meanwhile, Elizabeth's cousin Mary (daughter of Scottish King James V, and a Catholic) had become Queen of Scotland. She'd spent her childhood in France and had married the French dauphin (crown prince), thereby becoming queen of France as well. Why stop at two? After her husband's death and so no longer France's queen, Mary returned to Scotland, and from there ambitiously claimed the English throne as well, on the grounds that Elizabeth was illegitimate.

Shakespeare's *Henry V* was filmed most recently in 1989 – a superb epic, starring Kenneth Branagh as the eponymous king. Also worth catching is the earlier movie of the same name starring Laurence Olivier, made in 1944 as a patriotic rallying cry.

Mary's plans failed; she was imprisoned and forced to abdicate, but escaped to England and appealed to Elizabeth for help. This could have been a rookie error, or she might have been advised by courtiers with their own agenda. Either way, it was a bad move. Mary was, not surprisingly, seen as a security risk and imprisoned once again. In an uncharacteristic display of indecision, before finally ordering her execution Elizabeth held Mary under arrest for 19 years, moving her frequently from house to house. As you travel around England today, you can visit many stately homes (and even a few pubs) that proudly claim, 'Mary Queen of Scots slept here'.

United & Disunited Britain

Elizabeth died in 1603, but despite a bountiful reign the Virgin Queen had failed to provide an heir. She was succeeded by her closest relative, the Scottish King James, the safely Protestant son of the murdered Mary. Thus, he became James I of England and VI of Scotland, the first English monarch of the House of Stuart. James did his best to soothe

1605

King James' attempts to smooth religious relations are set back by an anti-Catholic outcry following the Gunpowder Plot, a terrorist attempt to blow up Parliament led by Guy Fawkes.

1644–49

English Civil War Royalist forces supporting the king are pitted against Oliver Cromwell's army of 'parliamentarians'. Cromwell is victorious, and England becomes a republic.

» Houses of Parliament (p57), London

Catholic-Protestant tensions and united England, Wales and Scotland into one kingdom for the first time – another step towards British unity, at least on paper.

But the divide between king and Parliament continued to smoulder, and the power struggle worsened during the reign of Charles I, eventually degenerating into the English Civil War. The antiroyalist (or 'parliamentarian') forces were led by Oliver Cromwell, a Puritan who preached against the excesses of the monarchy and established Church. His army (known as the Roundheads) was pitched against the king's forces (the Cavaliers) in a conflict that tore England apart, although it was the final civil war in English history. It ended with victory for the Roundheads; the king was executed, and England declared a republic, with Cromwell hailed as 'Protector'.

The Return of the King

By 1653 Cromwell was finding Parliament too restricting and assumed dictatorial powers, much to his supporters' dismay. On his death in 1658, he was followed half-heartedly by his son, but in 1660 Parliament decided to re-establish the monarchy, as republican alternatives were proving far worse.

Charles II (the exiled son of Charles I) came to the throne, and his rule – known as 'the Restoration' – saw scientific and cultural activity bursting forth after the strait-laced ethics of Cromwell's time. Exploration and expansion were also on the agenda. Backed by the army and navy (which had been modernised by Cromwell), colonies stretched down the American coast, while the East India Company set up headquarters in Bombay, laying foundations for what was to become the British Empire.

The next king, James II, had a harder time. Attempts to ease restrictive laws on Catholics ended with his defeat at the Battle of the Boyne by William III, the Protestant king of Holland, aka William of Orange, who was married to James' daughter Mary. William and Mary had equal rights to the throne, and their joint accession in 1688 was known as the Glorious Revolution. Luckily they were married or there might have been another civil war.

Empire Building

In 1694 Mary died, leaving William as monarch. He died a few years later and was succeeded by his sister-in-law, Anne. During her reign, in 1707, the Act of Union was passed, linking the countries of England, Wales and Scotland under one Parliament – based in London – for the first time.

Queen Anne died without an heir in 1714, marking the end of the Stuart line. The throne passed to distant (but still safely Protestant) German relatives, the House of Hanover.

ELIZABETH

The movie *Elizabeth*, directed by Shekhar Kapur (1998) and starring Cate Blanchett, covers the early years of the Virgin Queen's rule, as she graduates from princess to commanding monarch – a time of forbidden love, unwanted suitors, intrigue and death.

1749
Author and magistrate Henry Fielding founds the Bow Street Runners, London's first professional police force. A 1792 Act of Parliament allows the Bow Street model to spread across England.

1776–83
The American War of Independence is the British Empire's first major reversal, forcing England to withdraw from the world stage, a fact not missed by French military leader Napoleon.

1799–1815
The Napoleonic Wars see a weakened Britain threatened with invasion by Napoleon, whose ambitions are curtailed at the famous battles of Trafalgar (1805) and Waterloo (1815).

1837–1901
Reign of Queen Victoria. The British Empire – 'the Empire where the sun never sets' – expands from Canada through Africa and India to Australia and New Zealand.

Meanwhile, the British Empire, which despite its title was predominantly an English entity, continued to grow in the Americas, as well as in Asia, while claims were made to Australia after James Cook's epic voyage in 1768.

The Industrial Era

While the Empire expanded abroad, at home Britain had become the crucible of the Industrial Revolution. Steam power (patented by James Watt in 1781) and steam trains (launched by George Stephenson in 1830) transformed methods of production and transport, and the towns of the English Midlands became the first industrial cities.

A History of England in a Nutshell by John Mathew provides exactly what it says: a quick overview of the nation's key events in less than 200 pages.

The industrial growth led to Britain's first major period of internal migration, as vast numbers of people from the countryside came to the cities in search of work. At the same time, medical advances improved life expectancy, creating a sharp population increase, so for many ordinary people the effects of Britain's economic blossoming were dislocation and poverty.

But despite the social turmoil of the early 19th century, by the time Queen Victoria took the throne in 1837 Britain's factories and fleets dominated world trade. The rest of the 19th century was seen as Britain's Golden Age – a period of patriotic confidence not seen since the days of the last great queen, Elizabeth I.

The times were optimistic, but it wasn't all tub-thumping jingoism. Prime Minister Disraeli and his successor, William Gladstone, also introduced social reforms to address the worst exploitive excesses of the Industrial Revolution. Education became universal, trade unions were legalised and the right to vote was extended to male commoners – women didn't get the vote for another few decades.

World War I

When Queen Victoria died in 1901, it seemed that all of Britain's energy fizzled out, too, and the country entered a period of decline. Meanwhile, in continental Europe, the military powers of Russia, Austro-Hungary, Turkey and Germany were sabre-rattling in the Balkan states, a dispute that eventually started the 'Great War' (now known as WWI). By the war's weary end in 1918, millions had died, with hardly a street or village untouched, as the sobering lists of names on war memorials all over England still show

The Isles: A History, by Norman Davies, provides much-acclaimed and highly readable coverage of the past 10,000 years in England, within the broader history of the British Isles.

For the soldiers who did return from WWI, a disillusion with the social order helped make the Labour Party – which represented the working class – a political force, upsetting the balance long enjoyed by the Liberal and Conservative parties.

The Labour Party came to power for the first time, in coalition with the Liberals, in the 1923 election, but by the mid-1920s the Conservatives

1914

Archduke Franz Ferdinand of Austria is assassinated in the Balkan city of Sarajevo – the final spark in a decade-long crisis that starts the Great War, now called WWI.

1926

Increasing mistrust of the government, fuelled by soaring unemployment, leads to the General Strike. Millions of workers – train drivers, miners, shipbuilders – down tools and bring the country to a halt.

1939–45

WWII rages across Europe, and much of Africa and Asia. Britain and her Allies, including America, Russia, Australia, India and New Zealand, eventually defeat the armies of Germany, Japan and Italy.

1946–48

The Labour Party nationalises key industries such as shipyards, coalmines and steel foundries. Britain's 'big four' train companies are combined into British Railways.

were back. The world economy was now in decline and industrial unrest had become widespread

The situation worsened in the 1930s as the Great Depression meant another decade of misery and political upheaval, and even the royal family took a knock when Edward VIII abdicated in 1936 so he could marry Wallis Simpson, a woman who was twice divorced and – horror of horrors – American.

One of the finest novels about WWI is *Birdsong* by Sebastian Faulks. Understated, perfectly paced and intensely moving, it tells of passion, fear, waste, incompetent generals and the poor bloody infantry.

World War II

The next monarch was Edward's less-than-charismatic brother, George VI, and Britain dithered through the rest of the decade, with mediocre government failing to confront the country's deep-set problems.

Adolf Hitler came to power in Germany and in 1939 invaded Poland. Two days later Britain was once again at war. The German army swept through Europe and pushed back British forces to the beaches of Dunkirk, in northern France. In June 1940 an extraordinary flotilla of rescue vessels turned total disaster into a brave defeat, and Dunkirk Day is still remembered with pride and sadness in Britain every year.

By mid-1940, most of Europe was controlled by Germany. Russia had negotiated a peace agreement and the USA was neutral, leaving Britain virtually isolated. Into this arena came a new prime minister called Winston Churchill (p776).

Between September 1940 and May 1941, the German air force launched 'The Blitz', a series of (mainly night-time) bombing raids on London and other cities. But morale in Britain remained strong, thanks partly to Churchill's regular radio broadcasts. The USA entered the war after the Japanese bombing of Pearl Harbor, and in late 1941 the tide began to turn.

By 1944 Germany was in retreat. Russia pushed back from the east, and Britain, USA and other Allies were again on the beaches of France. The Normandy landings (D-Day, as it's remembered) marked the start of the liberation of Europe's western side. By 1945 Hitler was dead and the war finally over.

London is an epic novel by Edward Rutherford – or rather around 50 separate mini-novels – each set in a key historical era; from the Roman invasion to the Blitz of WWII. Exhaustive, exhausting and great for a sense of each period.

Swinging & Sliding

In Britain, despite the WWII victory, there was an unexpected swing on the political front. An electorate tired of war tumbled Churchill's Conservatives from power in favour of the Labour Party. There was change abroad too, as parts of the British Empire became independent, including India and Pakistan in 1947 and Malaya in 1957, followed by much of Africa and the Caribbean.

But while the Empire's sun may have been setting, Britain's royal family was still going strong. In 1952 George VI was succeeded by his daughter, Elizabeth II.

1948

Aneurin Bevan, the Health Minister in the Labour government, launches the National Health Service – free medical care for all – the core of Britain as a 'welfare state'.

1952

Princess Elizabeth becomes Queen Elizabeth II when her father, George VI, dies. Her coronation takes place in Westminster Abbey in June 1953.

1960–66

The era of African and Caribbean independence brings the freedom of Nigeria, Tanzania, Jamaica, Trinidad & Tobago, Kenya, Malawi, Gambia and Barbados.

1971

Britain adopts the 'decimal' currency (1 pound equals 100 pence) and drops the ancient system of 20 shillings or 240 pennies per pound, the centuries-old bane of school maths lessons.

WINSTON CHURCHILL

More than a century after he became part of the British government, Winston Churchill is still one of the country's best-known political figures. He was born in 1874 and, although from an aristocratic family, his early years were not auspicious; he was famously a 'dunce' at school – an image he actively cultivated in later life.

As a young man Churchill joined the British Army and also acted as a war correspondent for various newspapers and wrote several books about his exploits. In 1901 he was elected to Parliament as a Conservative MP. In 1904 he defected to the Liberals, the main opposition party at the time. A year later, after a Liberal election victory, he became a government minister. Churchill rejoined the Conservatives in 1922, and held various ministerial positions through the rest of the 1920s. Notable statements during this period included calling Mussolini a 'genius' and Gandhi 'a half-naked fakir'.

Churchill criticised Prime Minister Neville Chamberlain's 1938 'appeasement' of Hitler and called for British rearmament to face a growing German threat, but his political life was generally quiet – so he concentrated on writing. His multivolume *History of the English-Speaking Peoples* was drafted during this period; although biased and flawed, it remains his best-known work.

In 1939 Britain entered WWII, and by 1940 Churchill was prime minister, taking additional responsibility as Minister of Defence. Hitler had expected an easy victory in the war, but Churchill's extraordinary dedication (not to mention his radio speeches, most famously offering 'nothing but blood, toil, sweat and tears' and promising to 'fight on the beaches...') inspired the British people to resist.

Between July and October 1940 the Royal Air Force withstood Germany's aerial raids to win what became known as the Battle of Britain – a major turning point in the war, and a chance for land forces to rebuild their strength. It was an audacious strategy, but it paid off and Churchill was lauded as a national hero – praise that continued to the end of the war, beyond his death in 1965, and which continues today.

By the late 1950s, postwar recovery was strong enough for Prime Minister Harold Macmillan to famously remind the British people they had 'never had it so good'. Some saw this as a boast for a confident future, others as a warning about difficult times ahead. But many people didn't care either way, as the 1960s had arrived and grey old England was suddenly more fun and lively than it had been for generations – especially if you were over 10 and under 30.

The '60s may have been swinging, but by the 1970s decline had set in, thanks to a combination of inflation, an oil crisis and international competition revealing the weaknesses of Britain's economy.

The rest of the decade was marked by strikes, disputes and general all-round gloom, but neither the Conservatives (also known as the Tories)

1979

A Conservative government led by Margaret Thatcher wins the general election, ushering in a decade of dramatic political and social change.

1990

Mrs Thatcher ousted as leader, and the Conservative party enters a period of decline, but remains in power largely due to inept Labour opposition.

1997

The general election sees Tony Blair lead 'New' Labour to victory, with a record-breaking parliamentary majority, ending more than 20 years of Conservative rule.

2003

Britain joins the USA in the invasion of Iraq, initially with some support from Parliament and the public – despite large anti-war demonstrations held in London and other cities.

under Prime Minister Edward Heath, nor Labour, under Prime Ministers Harold Wilson and Jim Callaghan, proved capable of controlling the strife. The British public had had enough, and the elections of May 1979 saw the arrival of a new Prime Minister: a little-known politician named Margaret Thatcher.

The Thatcher Years

Soon everyone had heard of Margaret Thatcher. Love her or hate her, no one could argue that her methods weren't dramatic, and many policies had a lasting impact, one of the most prominent being the sale of former state-run industries nationalised in the late 1940s.

Looking back from a 21st-century vantage point, most commentators agree that by economic measures the Thatcher government's policies were largely successful, but by social measures they were a failure and created a polarised Britain: on one side were the people who gained from the prosperous wave of opportunities in the 'new' industries, while on the other side were the unemployed and dispossessed as the 'old' industries such as coal-mining and steel production became an increasingly small part of the country's economic picture.

Despite policies that were frequently described as uncompromising, by 1988 Margaret Thatcher was the longest-serving British prime minister of the 20th century, although her repeated electoral victories were helped considerably by the Labour Party's ineffective campaigns and destructive internal struggles.

Handy Historic Websites

» www.royal.gov.uk

» www.bbc.co.uk/history

» www.victorianweb.org

New Labour, New Millennium, New Government

The pendulum started to swing in the early 1990s. Margaret Thatcher was replaced as leader by John Major, but the voters still regarded Labour with suspicion, allowing the Conservatives to unexpectedly win the 1992 election. It all came to a head in the 1997 election, when 'New' Labour swept to power under a new fresh-faced leader called Tony Blair.

Tony Blair and the Labour Party enjoyed an extended honeymoon period, and the next election (in 2001) was another walkover. The Conservative party continued to struggle, allowing Labour to win a historic third term in 2005, and a year later Blair became the longest-serving Labour prime minister in British history.

In May 2010, a record 13 years of Labour rule came to an end, and a new coalition between the Conservative and Liberal-Democrat parties became the new government (p764).

BARBARA VAN ZANTEN / GETTY IMAGES ©

» Palace of Westminster (p57), London

2010

Labour is defeated in the general election as the minority Liberal-Democrats align with the Conservatives to form the first coalition government in Britain's postwar history.

2012

London hosts the Olympic and Paralympic Games, hailed by the British public and most international observers as a great success.

2

RICHARD TAYLOR / 4CORNERS ©

3

AMOS CHAPPLE / GETTY IMAGES ©

Royal London

Along with Stonehenge and Big Ben, the greatest symbols of England include the current monarch, Queen Elizabeth II, while pretty much anything else connected to the country's royal heritage is a guaranteed attraction – especially the capital's fine collection of palaces and castles.

The Tower of London

1 The Tower of London has a 1000-year-old history and foundations that date back to Roman times. Over the centuries it's been a royal residence, treasury, mint, prison and arsenal. Today it's home to the spectacular Crown Jewels, as well as red-coated Beefeaters and ravens attributed with mythical power.

Windsor Castle

2 Although not actually in London, Windsor Castle is near enough to visit on a day-trip. This is the largest and oldest occupied fortress in the world, an astounding edifice of walls, towers and battlements, used for state occasions and as the Queen's weekend retreat.

Buckingham Palace

3 Buckingham Palace has been the royal city residence since 1837, and the current Queen divides her time between here, Windsor Castle and Balmoral in Scotland. If she's in, the 'royal standard' flag flies on the roof. If she's out, you can take a tour to see inside. Either way, don't miss the famous changing of the guard.

Hampton Court Palace

4 Hampton Court Palace is England's largest and grandest Tudor structure, used by King Henry VIII as a riverside hideaway. After admiring the grand interior, you can relax in the extensive gardens, but don't get lost in the 300-year-old maze.

Clockwise from top left

1 Tower of London **2** Windsor Castle **3** Changing of the guard at Buckingham Palace **4** Hampton Court Palace

Flavour of England

Food-lovers will be delighted to learn that England has shaken off its reputation for bland food. Today, wherever you go in the country it's easy to find good-quality dishes, which focus on locally sourced or seasonally grown ingredients wherever possible. There's still no English equivalent of *'bon appetit'* but at least the term can be genuinely used these days – instead of with a dash of irony.

For many visitors to England, the culinary day begins in a hotel or B&B with the phenomenon known as the 'Full English' – a large plateful of mainly fried food that may be a shock if you usually have just a bowl of cereal. But perseverance is recommended, as there's enough fuel here to see you through several hours of energetic sight-seeing.

For lunch or an evening meal, England has an astounding range of options to suit all budgets, but during your trip you should definitely sample two quintessentially English eateries: the cafe and the pub.

In cities, cafes are a good cheaper option, while in country areas they're often called teashops – perfect for a traditional afternoon tea with scones, jam and cream. Wherever you go, pubs are the obvious place to sample traditional English beer, as well as being a reliable option for good-value meals – the very best are now called 'gastropubs'.

ENGLISH CLASSICS

» **Fish & chips** Long-standing favourite, best sampled in coastal towns.

» **Sandwich** Global snack today, but an English 'invention' from the 18th century.

» **Ploughman's lunch** Bread and cheese, a pub menu regular, perfect with a pint.

» **Roast beef & Yorkshire pudding** Traditional English Sunday lunch.

» **Cumberland sausage** Northern speciality, so big it's coiled to fit on your plate.

» **Cornish pasty** Once restricted to the southwest, now available country-wide.

1

3

Clockwise from top left

1 Chef preparing food **2** Traditional fish and chips meal
3 Classic pub grub: a Sunday roast

2

SIMON REDDY / ALAMY ©

G FLETCHER / GETTY IMAGES ©

The English Table

Wherever you travel in England, for every greasy spoon or fast-food joint, there's a local pub or speciality restaurant serving up enticing home-made meals. London is now regarded as a global gastronomic capital, and it's increasingly easy to find decent food options in other cities, towns and villages across the country, where epicures can splash out big bucks on fine dining, while shoestringers can also enjoy tasty eating that definitely won't break the bank.

The Full English

For the locals, the English culinary day is punctuated by the three traditional main meals of breakfast, lunch and dinner. And just to keep you on your toes, those latter two meals are also called dinner and tea, or lunch and supper – depending on social class and location.

Breakfast

Many people in England make do with toast or a bowl of cereal before dashing to work, but visitors staying in hotels and B&Bs will undoubtedly encounter a phenomenon called the 'Full English Breakfast'. This usually consists of bacon, sausages, eggs, tomatoes, mushrooms, baked beans and fried bread. If you don't feel like eating half a farmyard first thing in the morning it's OK to ask for just the egg and tomatoes, for example. Some B&Bs offer other alternatives such as kippers (smoked fish) or a 'continental breakfast' – which completely omits the cooked stuff and may even add something exotic such as croissants.

Rick Stein is a TV chef, energetic restaurateur and good-food evangelist. His books *Food Heroes* and *Food Heroes - Another Helping* extol small-scale producers and top-notch local food, from organic veg to wild boar sausages.

Lunch

One of the many great inventions that England gave the world is the sandwich, often eaten as a midday meal. Slapping a slice of cheese or ham between two bits of bread may seem a simple concept, but no one apparently thought of it until the 18th century, when the Earl of Sandwich (his title comes from a town in southeast England that originally got its name from the Viking word for 'sandy beach') ordered his servants to bring cold meat between bread so he could keep working at his desk or, as some historians claim, keep playing cards late at night.

Another English classic – served especially in pubs – is the ploughman's lunch. Basically it's bread and cheese, and although hearty yokels

EATING PRICE BANDS

In restaurant reviews throughout this book, we indicate an approximate price-band.

» **£** means a budget place; a main dish is less then £9

» **££** means midrange; mains are £9 to £18

» **£££** means top end; mains are more than £18

NAME THAT PASTY

A favourite speciality in southwest England is the Cornish pasty. Originally a mix of cooked vegetables wrapped in pastry, it's often available in meat varieties (much to the scorn of the Cornish people) and is now sold everywhere in England. Invented long before Tupperware, the pasty was an all-in-one lunch pack that tin miners carried underground and left on a ledge ready for mealtime. So pasties weren't mixed up, they were marked with their owners' initials – always at one end, so the miner could eat half and safely leave the rest to snack on later without it mistakenly disappearing into the mouth of a workmate. Before going back to the surface, the miners traditionally left the last few crumbs of the pasty as a gift for the spirits of the mine, known as 'knockers', to ensure a safe shift the next day.

probably did carry such food to the fields in the days of yore, the meal was actually invented in the 1960s by the national cheesemakers' organisation to boost consumption, neatly cashing in on public nostalgia and fondness for tradition.

Dinner

For generations, a typical English dinner has been 'meat and two veg'. Dressed up as 'evening meal' or dressed down as 'cooked tea', there was little variation: the meat would be pork, beef or lamb, one of the vegetables would be potatoes and the other would inevitably be carrots, cabbage or cauliflower – just as inevitably cooked long and hard. Although tastes and diets are changing, this classic combination still graces the tables of many English families several times a week.

Traditionally, the beef is roast beef (always roast, never 'roasted') and with the beef – especially at Sunday lunches – comes Yorkshire pudding. It's simply roast batter, but very tasty when properly cooked. Another classic English dish brings Yorkshire pudding and sausages together, with the delightful name of 'toad-in-the-hole'.

Yorkshire pudding also turns up in another guise, especially in pubs and cafes in northern England, where a big bowl-shaped pudding is filled with stew, beans or vegetables. You can even find multicultural crossover Yorkshire puddings filled with curry.

Perhaps the best-known classic English meal is fish and chips, often bought from the 'chippie' as a takeaway wrapped in paper to eat on the spot or enjoy at home. For visitors, English fish and chips can be an acquired taste. Sometimes the chips can be limp and the fish tasteless, especially once you get away from the sea, but in towns with salt in the air this classic deep-fried delight is always worth trying.

In Yorkshire, the eponymous pudding is traditionally a *starter*, a reminder of days when food was scarce and the pudding was a premeal stomach-filler.

Dessert

After the main course – usually at an evening meal, or if you're enjoying a hearty lunch – comes dessert or 'pudding'. A classic English pudding is rhubarb crumble, the juicy stem of a large-leafed garden plant, stewed and sweetened, then topped with a crunchy mix of flour, butter and more sugar – and served with custard or ice cream. Other favourites include treacle sponge, bread-and-butter pudding and plum pudding, a dome-shaped cake with fruit, nuts and brandy or rum, traditionally eaten at Christmas.

Regional Specialities

With the country's large coastline, it's no surprise that seafood is a speciality in many English regions. Yorkshire's seaside resorts are particularly famous for huge servings of cod – despite it becoming an endangered species thanks to overfishing – while restaurants in Devon and Cornwall regularly conjure up prawns, oysters, mussels and scallops. Other local seafood you may encounter elsewhere on your travels includes Norfolk crab and Northumberland kippers.

In northern and central England you'll find Cumberland sausage – a tasty mix of minced pork and herbs, so large it has to be spiralled to fit on your plate. Look out too for Melton Mowbray pork pies – cooked ham in a casing of pastry and eaten cold. A legal victory in 2005 ensured that only pies from the eponymous Midlands town could carry the Melton Mowbray moniker, in the same way that only fizzy wine from the Champagne region of France can carry that name. Another English speciality that enjoys the same protection is Stilton – a strong white cheese, either plain or in a blue vein variety. Only five dairies in all of England are allowed to produce cheese with this name.

Perhaps less appealing is black pudding, a large sausage made from ground meat, offal, fat and blood, and traditionally served for breakfast in northern England.

CAGE FREE

Like meat, but not battery pens? Go to the Royal Society for the Prevention of Cruelty to Animals (www.rspca.org.uk) and follow links to Freedom Food.

Eating Out

In England, 'eating out' means simply going to a restaurant or cafe – anywhere away from home. There's a huge choice across the country.

Picnics & Self-Catering

When shopping for food, as well as the more obvious chain stores and corner shops, markets can be a great place for bargains – everything from dented tins of tomatoes to home-baked cakes and organic goat's cheese. Farmers markets are always worth a visit; they're a great way for producers to sell good food direct to consumers, with both sides avoiding the grip of the supermarkets.

Cafes & Teashops

The traditional English cafe is nothing like its continental European namesake. For a start, asking for a brandy with your coffee may cause confusion, as cafes in England rarely serve alcohol. Most are simple places serving simple meals such as meat pie, beans on toast, baked potato or omelette with chips (costing around £3 to £4) and stuff like sandwiches, cakes and other snacks (£1 to £2). Quality varies enormously: some cafes definitely earn their 'greasy spoon' handle, while others are neat and clean.

In London and some other cities, a rearguard of classic cafes – with formica tables, seats in booths, and decor unchanged from the their 1950s glory days – stand against the onslaught of the international chains. In rural areas, many market towns and villages have cafes catering for tourists, walkers, cyclists and other outdoor types, and in summer they're open every day. Whether you're in town or country, good English cafes are a wonderful institution and always worth a stop during your travels.

THE PIG, THE WHOLE SHEEP & NOTHING BUT THE COW

One of the many trends enjoyed by modern British cuisine is the revival of 'nose to tail' cooking – that is, using the whole animal, not just the more obvious cuts such as chops and fillet steaks. This does not mean boiling or grilling a pig or sheep all in one go – although spit-roasts are popular. It means utilising the parts that may at first seem unappetising or, frankly, inedible. So as well as dishes involving liver, heart, chitterlings (intestines) and other offal, traditional delights such as bone marrow on toast, or tripe (stomach) and onions once again grace the menus of fashionable restaurants.

The movement has been spearheaded by chef Fergus Henderson at his St John restaurant in London and via his influential recipe books *Nose to Tail Eating: A Kind of British Cooking* and *Beyond Nose To Tail*.

CAFES & RESTAURANTS - STANDARD HOURS

» Standard hours for cafes are 9am to 5pm. Most cafes are open daily.

» Where we specify 'breakfast & lunch' we mean open 9am to 5pm.

» In cities, some cafes open 7am for breakfast, then shut at 6pm or later.

» In country areas, some cafes open until 7pm or later in the summer.

» In winter months, country cafe hours are reduced; some close completely from October to Easter.

» Standard hours for restaurants are: Lunch – noon to 3pm. Dinner – 6pm to 11pm (to midnight or later in cities). Most restaurants are open daily; some are closed Sunday evening or all day Monday.

» Some restaurants are open only for lunch, or only for dinner.

» A few restaurants are open for breakfast (usually 9am), but mainly cafes do this.

Smarter cafes are called teashops – also more often found in country areas – where you might pay a bit more for extras such as neat decor and table service.

As well as the traditional establishments, in most cities and towns you'll also find coffee shops – independents and and international chains – and a growing number of Euro-style cafe-bars, serving decent lattes and espressos and offering bagels or ciabattas rather than beans on toast (you'll probably be able to get that brandy too). Some of these modern places even have outdoor chairs and tables – rather brave considering the narrow pavements and inclement weather much of England enjoys.

Restaurants

London has scores of excellent restaurants that could hold their own in major cities worldwide, while places in Bath, Leeds and Manchester can give the capital a fair run for its money (actually, often for rather less money). We've taken great pleasure in seeking out some of the finest and best-value restaurants in England.

Prices vary considerably across the country, with a main course in a straightforward restaurant costing around £9 or less, and anywhere between £10 and £18 at midrange places. Utterly excellent food, service and surroundings can be enjoyed for £20 to £50 – although in London you can, if you want, pay double this.

For vegetarians, England is not too bad. Many restaurants and pubs have at least one token vegetarian dish, while better places offer much more imaginative choices. Vegans will find the going trickier, except of course at dedicated veggie/vegan restaurants.

Many towns and cities in England hold regular farmers markets – a chance for food producers large and small to sell direct to the public. For more info and a list, see www.farmersmarkets.net.

Pubs & Gastropubs

Not so many years ago, a pub was the place to go for a drink. And that was it. If you felt peckish, your choice might be ham or cheese roll, with pickled onions if you were lucky. Today many pubs sell a wide range of food, and it's usually a good-value option, whether you want a toasted sandwich between museum visits in London, or a three-course meal in the evening after touring castles and stately homes in Yorkshire.

While the food in many pubs is good quality and good value, some places raised the bar to such a degree that a whole new genre of eatery – the gastropub – was born. The finest gastropubs are almost restaurants in style (with smart decor, neat menus and uniformed table service), while others have gone for a more relaxed atmosphere, with mismatched cutlery, waiters in T-shirts, and today's choices chalked up on a blackboard.

The key for all, though, is top-notch no-frills food and drink. For visitors relaxing after a hard day's sight-seeing, nothing beats the luxury of a wholesome shepherd's pie washed down with a decent ale, without the worry of guessing which fork to use.

Drinking in England

The two drinks most associated with England are probably tea and beer. Both are unlike drinks of the same name found elsewhere in the world, and well worth trying on your travels around the country.

Tea & Coffee

In England, if a local asks 'Would you like a drink?' don't automatically expect a gin and tonic. They may well mean a 'cuppa' – cup of tea – England's best-known beverage. It's usually made with dark tea leaves to produce a strong brown drink, more bitter in taste than tea served in some other Western countries, which is partly why it's usually served with a dash of milk.

Although tea is sometimes billed as the national drink, coffee is equally popular these days. The Brits consume 165 million cups a day and the British coffee market is worth almost £700 million a year – but with the prices some coffee shops charge, maybe that's not surprising. A final word of warning: when you're ordering a coffee and the server asks 'white or black?', don't panic. It simply means, 'Do you want milk in it?'.

Beer & Wine

Among alcoholic drinks, England is probably best known for its beer, and as you travel around the country, you should try some local brews. English beer typically ranges from dark brown to bright orange in colour, and is often served at room temperature. Technically it's ale but it's often called 'bitter'. This is to distinguish it from lager – the drink that most of the rest of the word calls 'beer' – which is generally yellow and served cold.

Bitter that is traditionally brewed and served is called 'real ale', to distinguish it from mass-produced brands, and there are many different varieties around England. But be ready: a local English brew may come as a shock – a warm, flat and expensive shock. This is partly to do with England's climate, and partly because the beer is being served by hand pump rather than gas pressure. But it's mainly due to integral flavour. Traditional English beer doesn't need to be chilled or fizzed to make it palatable.

On hot summer days, you could go for a shandy – beer and lemonade mixed in equal quantities. You'll usually need to specify 'lager shandy' or 'bitter shandy'. It may seem an astonishing combination for outsiders, but it's very refreshing and of course not very strong.

Another option is cider – available in sweet and dry varieties. In western and southwestern counties, you could try 'scrumpy', a very strong dry cider traditionally made from local apples.

Many visitors are surprised to learn that wine is produced in England, and has been since the time of the Romans. Today, more than 400 vineyards and wineries produce around two million bottles a year, many win-

REAL ALE

The Campaign for Real Ale promotes the understanding of traditional British beer. Look for endorsement stickers on pub windows, and for more info see www.camra.org.uk.

WHERE THERE'S SMOKE

All restaurants and cafes in England are nonsmoking throughout. Virtually all pubs have the same rule, which is why there's often a small crowd of smokers standing on the pavement outside. Some pubs provide specific outdoor smoking areas, ranging from a simple yard to elaborate gazebos with canvas walls and the full complement of lighting, heating, piped music and TV screens – where you'd never need to know you were 'outside' at all, apart from the pungent clouds of burning tobacco.

THE OLDEST PUB IN ENGLAND?

Many drinkers are surprised to learn that the word 'pub' (short for 'public house'), although apparently steeped in history, dates only from the 19th century. But places selling beer have been around for much longer, and the 'oldest pub in England' is a hotly contested title.

One of the country's oldest pubs, with the paperwork to prove it, is Ye Olde Trip to Jerusalem in Nottingham, which was serving ale to departing crusaders in the 12th century.

Other contenders sniff that Ye Olde Trip is a mere newcomer. A fine old inn called the Royalist Hotel in Stow-on-the-Wold, Gloucestershire claims to have been selling beer since AD 947, while another pub called Ye Olde Fighting Cocks in St Albans (Hertfordshire) claims to date back to the 8th century – although the 13th is more likely.

But then back comes Ye Olde Trip with a counterclaim: one of its bars is a cave hollowed out of living rock, and that's more than a million years old.

ning major awards. English white sparkling wines have been a particular success story, especially those produced in the southeast, where the growing conditions are similar to those of the Champagne region in France.

Bars & Pubs

In England, the difference between a bar and a pub is sometimes vague, but generally bars are smarter and louder than pubs, possibly with a younger crowd. Drinks are more expensive, too, unless there's a gallon-of-vodka-and-Red-Bull-for-a-fiver promotion – which there often is.

As well as beer and wine, bars and pubs offer the usual choice of spirits, often served with a 'mixer', producing English favourites such as gin and tonic, rum and coke, and vodka and lime. These drinks are served in measures called 'singles' and 'doubles'. A single is 35ml – just over one US fluid ounce. Only more upmarket city bars have a large array of cocktail options.

And finally, two tips: First, if you see a pub called a 'free house', it means it doesn't belong to a brewery or pub company, and thus is 'free' to sell any brand of beer. It doesn't mean the booze is free of charge. Second, remember that drinks in English pubs are ordered and paid for at the bar. You can always spot the freshly arrived tourists – they're the ones sitting forlornly at a empty table hoping to spot a server.

In the 16th century, Queen Elizabeth I decreed that mutton could only be served with bitter herbs – intended to stop people eating sheep in order to help the wool trade – but her subjects discovered mint sauce, and it's been a favourite condiment ever since.

Food & Drink Glossary

aubergine	large purple-skinned vegetable; 'eggplant' in the USA and Australia
bangers	sausages (colloquial)
bap	a large, wide, flat, soft bread roll
bevvy	drink (slang; originally from northern England)
bill	the total you need to pay after eating in a restaurant ('check' to Americans)
bitter	ale; a type of beer
black pudding	type of sausage made from dried blood and other ingredients
bun	bread roll, usually sweet, eg currant bun, cream bun
BYO	bring your own (usually in the context of bringing your own drink to a restaurant)
caff	abbreviated form of cafe
candy floss	light sugar-based confectionary; called 'cotton candy' in the USA, 'fairy floss' in Australia

chips	sliced, deep-fried potatoes, eaten hot (what Americans call 'fries')
cider	beer made from apples
clotted cream	cream so heavy or rich that it's become almost solid (but not sour)
corkage	a small charge levied by the restaurant when you BYO (bring your own)
courgette	green vegetable ('zucchini' to Americans)
cream cracker	white unsalted savoury biscuit
cream tea	cup of tea and a scone loaded with jam and cream
crisps	thin slices of fried potato bought in a packet, eaten cold; called 'chips' or 'potato chips' in the USA and Australia
crumpet	circular piece of doughy bread, toasted before eating, usually covered with butter
double cream	heavy or thick cream
dram	whisky measure
fish fingers	strips of fish pieces covered in breadcrumbs, usually bought frozen and cooked by frying or grilling
greasy spoon	cheap cafe (colloquial)
ice lolly	flavoured ice on a stick; called 'popsicle' in the USA, 'icy pole' in Australia
icing	thick, sweet and solid covering on a cake
jam	fruit conserve often spread on bread
jelly	sweet dessert of flavoured gelatine; called jello in the US
joint	cut of meat used for roasting
kippers	salted and smoked fish, traditionally herring
pickle	a thick, vinegary vegetable-based condiment
Pimms	popular English spirit mixed with lemonade, mint and fresh fruit
pint	beer (as in 'let me buy you a pint')
pop	fizzy drink
salad cream	creamy, vinegary salad dressing, much sharper than mayonnaise
scrumpy	a type of strong dry cider
shandy	beer and lemonade mixed together in equal quantities
shep-herd's pie	two-layered dish with a ground beef and onion mixture on the bottom and mashed potato on the top, cooked in an oven
shout	to buy a group of people drinks, usually reciprocated (colloquial)
single cream	light cream (to distinguish from *double cream* and *clotted cream*)
snug	usually a small separate room in a pub
squash	fruit drink concentrate mixed with water
stout	dark, full-bodied beer made from malt; Guinness is the most famous variety
swede	large root vegetable; sometimes called 'yellow turnip' or 'rutabaga' in the USA
sweets	what Americans call 'candy' and Australians call 'lollies'
treacle	molasses or dark syrup

Architecture in England

With an architectural heritage that stretches back four millennia or more, the many different buildings of England – from simple cottages to grand cathedrals – are an obvious highlight of any visit.

The construction of Stonehenge pushed the limits of technology in the Neolithic era. Some giant menhirs (standing stones) were brought from a great distance, and many were shaped slightly wider at the top to take account of perspective – a trick used by the Greeks many centuries later.

Early Foundations

The oldest buildings in the country are the grass-covered mounds of earth called 'tumuli' or 'barrows', used as burial sites by England's prehistoric residents. These mounds – measuring anything from a rough semisphere just 2m high to much larger, elongated semi-ovoids 5m high and 10m long – are dotted across the countryside from Cornwall to Cumbria, and are especially common in chalk areas such as Salisbury Plain and the Wiltshire Downs in southern England.

Perhaps the most famous barrow – and certainly the largest and most mysterious – is Silbury Hill, near Marlborough. Historians are not sure exactly why this huge conical mound was built – there's no evidence of it actually being used for burial. Theories suggest it was used at cultural ceremonies or as part of the worship of deities in the style of the South American pyramids, but whatever its original purpose, it's still very impressive today, many centuries after being built.

Even more impressive than giant tumuli are another legacy of the Neolithic era: menhirs, or standing stones, especially well known when they're set out in rings. These include the iconic stone circle of Stonehenge and the even larger Avebury Stone Circle, both in Wiltshire.

Bronze Age & Iron Age

There are more than a thousand Iron Age hill forts in England. Impressive examples include Danebury Ring, Hampshire; Barbury Castle, Wiltshire; Uffington Castle, Oxfordshire; Carl Wark, Derbyshire and Cadbury Castle, Somerset.

Compared with the large stone circles of the Neolithic era, the architecture of the Bronze Age that we can see today is on a more domestic scale. Hut circles from this period can still be seen in several parts of England, most notably on Dartmoor.

By the time we reach the Iron Age, the early peoples of England were organising themselves into clans or tribes. Their legacy includes the forts they built to defend territory and protect themselves from rival tribes or other invaders. Most forts consisted of a large circular or oval ditch, with a steep mound of earth behind. A famous example is Maiden Castle in Dorset.

The Roman Era

Roman remains are found in many English towns and cities, including Chester, Exeter and St Albans – as well as the lavish Roman spa and bathing complex in Bath. But England's largest and most impressive Roman relic is the 73-mile sweep of Hadrian's Wall (p744), built in the 2nd century AD as a defensive line stretching coast to coast across the country.

Originally built to separate marauding Pictish warriors to the north of the wall (in modern Scotland) from the Empire's territories to the south, it later became as much a symbol of Roman power as a necessary defence mechanism.

Medieval Masterpieces

In the centuries following the Norman Invasion of 1066, England saw an explosion of architecture inspired by the two most pressing concerns of the day: worship and defence. Churches, abbeys, monasteries and minsters sprang up during the early Middle Ages, as did many awe-inspiring cathedrals, such as those at Salisbury, Canterbury, Winchester and York.

As for castles, you're spoilt for choice: England's spectacular strongholds range from the atmospheric ruins of Tintagel and Dunstanburgh and the feudal keeps of Lancaster and Bamburgh to the sturdy fortresses of Warwick and Windsor. And then there's the most impressive of them all – the Tower of London (p69), guardian of the capital for more than 1000 years.

England's Top Castles

- Alnwick Castle
- Bamburgh Castle
- Berkeley Castle
- Carlisle Castle
- Corfe Castle
- Ludlow Castle
- Richmond Castle
- Skipton Castle
- Tintagel Castle
- Tower of London
- Warwick Castle
- Windsor Castle

Stately Homes of England

The medieval period was tumultuous, but by around 1600 life became more settled, and the nobility started to have less need for their castles. While they were excellent for keeping out rivals or the common riff-raff, they were often too dark, cold and draughty to be comfortable. So many castles saw the home improvements of the day – the installation of larger windows, wider staircases and better drainage. Others were simply abandoned for a brand new dwelling next door; an example of this is Hardwick Hall in Derbyshire.

Following the Civil War, the trend away from castles gathered pace, as through the 17th century the landed gentry developed a taste for fine 'country houses' designed by the most famous architects of the day. Many became the 'stately homes' that are a major feature of the English landscape, celebrated by Noel Coward's famous song, and a major attraction for visitors. Among the most extravagant are Holkham Hall in Norfolk, Chatsworth House in Derbyshire, and Blenheim Palace in Oxfordshire.

The great stately homes all display the proportion, symmetry and architectural harmony so in vogue during the 17th and 18th centuries, styles later reflected in the fashionable town houses of the Georgian era – most notably in the city of Bath, where the stunning Royal Crescent is the epitome of the genre.

Victoriana

The Victorian era was a time of great building. A style called Victorian-Gothic developed, echoing the towers and spires that were such a feature of the original Gothic cathedrals. The most famous example of this style is the Palace of Westminster (better known as the Houses of Parliament) and Elizabeth Tower (home to Big Ben), in London. Other highlights include London's Natural History Museum and St Pancras train station.

CHALK FIGURES

As you travel around England, look out for the chalk figures gracing many of the country's hilltops. They're made by cutting through the turf to reveal the white chalk soil below, so they're obviously found in chalk areas – most notably in southwestern England, especially the counties of Dorset and Wiltshire. Some figures, such as the Uffington White Horse, date from the Bronze Age, but most are more recent; the formidably endowed Cerne Abbas Giant is often thought to be an ancient pagan figure, although recent research suggests it was etched sometime in the 17th century.

HOUSE & HOME

It's not all about big houses. Alongside the stately homes, ordinary domestic architecture from the 16th century onwards can also still be seen in rural areas: black-and-white 'half-timbered' houses still characterise counties such as Worcestershire, while brick-and-flint cottages pepper Suffolk and Sussex, and hardy centuries-old farms built with slate or local gritstone are a feature of areas such as Derbyshire and the Lake District.

Through the early 20th century, as England's cities grew in size and stature, the newly moneyed middle classes built streets and squares of smart town houses. Meanwhile, in other suburbs the first town planners oversaw the construction of endless terraces of red-brick two-up-two-down houses to accommodate the massive influx of workers required to fuel the country's factories – not especially scenic but perhaps the most enduring mark of all on the English architectural landscape today.

Postwar Pains & Pride

During WWII many of England's cities were damaged by bombing, and the rebuilding that followed showed scant regard for the overall aesthetic of the cities, or for the lives of the people who lived in them. The rows of terraces were swept away in favour of high-rise tower blocks, while the 'brutalist' architects of the 1950s and '60s employed the modern and efficient materials of steel and concrete, leaving legacies such as London's South Bank Centre.

Perhaps this is why, on the whole, the English are conservative in their architectural tastes, and often resent ambitious or experimental designs, especially when they're applied to public buildings, or when form appears more important than function. But a familiar pattern often unfolds: after a few years of resentment, first comes a nickname, then grudging acceptance, and finally – once the locals have got used to it – comes pride and affection for the new building. The English just don't like to be rushed, that's all.

With this attitude in mind, over the last few decades, English architecture has started to redeem itself, and many big cities now have contemporary buildings their residents can be proud of and enjoy. Highlights in London's financial district include the bulging cone with the official address of 30 St Mary Axe (but widely known by its nickname, the Gherkin), and the former Millennium Dome (now rebranded as simply the O2) which has been transformed from a source of national embarrassment into one of the capital's leading live-music venues.

England's Finest Stately Homes

- Audley End House
- Blickling Hall
- Burghley House
- Blenheim Palace
- Castle Howard
- Chastleton House
- Chatsworth House
- Cotehele
- Harewood House
- Leeds Castle
- Snowshill Manor
- Waddesdon Manor

21st Century

Through the first decade of the 21st century, many areas of England placed a new importance on progressive, popular architecture as a part of wider regeneration. Top examples include Manchester's Imperial War Museum North, The Deep aquarium in Hull, Cornwall's futuristic Eden Project, and the Sage concert hall in Gateshead, near Newcastle.

From around 2010, development slowed and some plans were shelved, thanks to the global slowdown, but several significant projects continued, including the Turner Contemporary Gallery in Margate (opened 2011) and the futuristic Library of Birmingham (due to open 2013).

But England's largest and most high-profile architectural project of recent times was of course the Olympic Park, the centrepiece of the 2012 Games, in the London suburb of Stratford. As well as the main Olympic Stadium, other arenas include the Velodrome and the Aquatics Centre – all dramatic structures in their own right, using cutting-edge construction techniques. The velodrome also won the prestigious Prime Minister's Better Public Buildings Award in 2011.

Meanwhile, in the centre of the capital, the London Bridge Tower (its tall and jagged shape means it was quickly nicknamed the Shard) was officially opened in July 2012; at 306m, it's one of Europe's tallest buildings. On the other side of the River Thames, two more giant skyscrapers are already underway: 20 Fenchurch St (yes, already with a nickname: the Walkie-Talkie) and the Leadenhall Building (the Cheese-grater) both due for completion in 2014.

So London continues to grow upwards, and English architecture continues to push new boundaries of style and technology. The buildings may look a little different, but it's great to see the spirit of Stonehenge alive and well after all these years.

Glossary of English Architecture

bailey	outermost wall of a castle
bar	fortified gate (York, and some other northern cities)
barrel vault	semicircular arched roof
brass	memorial consisting of a brass plate, set into the side or lid of a tomb, or into the floor of a church to indicate a burial place below
buttress	vertical support for a wall; see also *flying buttress*
campanile	free-standing belfry or bell tower
chancel	eastern end of the church, usually reserved for choir and clergy
choir	area in the church where the choir is seated
cloister	covered walkway linking the church with adjacent monastic buildings
close	buildings grouped around a cathedral
cob	mixture of mud and straw for building
corbel	stone or wooden projection from a wall supporting a beam or arch
flying buttress	supporting *buttress* in the form of one side of an open arch
lancet	pointed window in Early English style
lierne vault	*vault* containing many tertiary ribs
Martello tower	small, circular tower used for coastal defence
minster	church connected to a monastery
nave	main body of the church at the western end, where the congregation gather
oast house	building containing a kiln for drying hops
pargeting	decorative stucco plasterwork
pele	fortified house
precincts	see *close*
priory	religious house governed by a prior
quire	medieval term for *choir*
rood	archaic word for cross (in churches)
transepts	north–south projections from a church's *nave*, giving church a cruciform (cross-shaped plan)
undercroft	vaulted underground room or cellar
vault	roof with arched ribs, usually in a decorative pattern

The English Landscape

England may be small, but even a relatively short journey can take you through a surprising mix of landscapes. Seeing the change – subtle in some areas, dramatic in others – is one of this country's great drawcards.

Southern England's countryside is gently undulating, with a few hilly areas such as the Cotswolds, and farmland between the towns and cities. East Anglia is mainly low and flat, while the Southwest Peninsula has wild moors and rich pastures – hence Devon's world-famous cream – with a rugged coast and sheltered beaches, making it a popular holiday destination.

In England's north, farmland remains interspersed with towns and cities, but the landscape is bumpier. A line of large hills called the Pennines (fondly tagged 'the backbone of England') runs from Derbyshire to the Scottish border, and includes the peaty plateaus of the Peak District, the delightful valleys of the Yorkshire Dales and the frequently windswept but ruggedly beautiful moors of Northumberland.

Perhaps England's best-known landscape is the Lake District, a small but spectacular cluster of hills and mountains in the northwest, where Scafell Pike (a towering 978m) is England's highest peak.

Landscape Online

» www.wildaboutbritain.co.uk

» www.environment-agency.gov.uk

» www.nationalparks.gov.uk

» www.landscapesforlife.org.uk

Beaches

England has a great many beaches – from tiny hidden coves in Cornwall to vast neon-lined strands such as Brighton or Blackpool. Other great beaches can be found in Devon, Somerset and along the south coast, in Suffolk, Norfolk, Lancashire, Yorkshire and Northumberland – each with their own distinct character. The best resort beaches earn the coveted international Blue Flag (www.blueflag.org) award, meaning sand and water are clean and unpolluted. Other parameters include the presence of lifeguards, litter bins and recycling facilities – meaning some wild beaches may not earn the award, but are stunning nonetheless.

Wildlife of Britain, by George McGavin et al, is subtitled 'the definitive visual guide'. Although too heavy to carry around during your travels, this beautiful photographic book is great for pre-trip inspiration or post-trip memories.

National Parks

Back in 1810, English poet William Wordsworth suggested that the wild landscape of the Lake District in Cumbria should be 'a sort of national property, in which every man has a right'. More than a century later, the Lake District did indeed become a national park, along with Dartmoor, Exmoor, the New Forest, Norfolk and Suffolk Broads, Northumberland, the North York Moors, the Peak District, the South Downs and the Yorkshire Dales.

But the term 'national park' can cause confusion. First, in England the parks are not state-owned: nearly all land is private, belonging to farmers, private estates and conservation organisations. Second, they are *not* areas of wilderness as in many other countries.

In England's national parks you'll see crop fields in lower areas and grazing sheep on the uplands, as well as roads, railways and villages, and even towns, quarries and factories in some parks. It's a reminder of the balance that is struck in this crowded country between protecting the natural environment and catering for the people who live in it.

Despite these anomalies, England's national parks still contain mountains, hills, downs, moors, woods, river valleys and other areas of quiet countryside, all ideal for enjoying nature however you like to experience it.

Protected Areas

As well as national parks, other parts of the England are designated as Areas of Outstanding Natural Beauty (AONBs), the second tier of protected landscape after national parks. Some of the finest AONBs in England include: the Chilterns, Cornwall, the Cotswolds, the Isles of Scilly, the North Pennines, the Northumberland Coast, the Suffolk Coast and the Wye Valley.

Around England there are also Conservation Areas, Sites of Special Scientific Interest and many other types of protected landscape that you can enjoy as you travel around.

Wildlife

For a small country, England has a diverse range of plants and animals. Many native species are hidden away, but there are some undoubted gems – from lowland woods carpeted in shimmering bluebells to stately herds of deer on the high moors. Having a closer look will enhance your trip enormously, especially if you have the inclination to enjoy some walking through the English landscape.

Animals

Farmland

In rural areas, rabbits are everywhere, but if you're hiking through the countryside be on the lookout for the much larger brown hares, an increasingly rare species. Males who battle for territory by boxing on their hind legs in early spring are, of course, as 'mad as a March hare'.

ENGLAND'S NATIONAL PARKS

NATIONAL PARK	FEATURES
Dartmoor	rolling hills, rocky outcrops, serene valleys; Iron Age relics; wild ponies, deer, peregrine falcons
Exmoor	sweeping moors, craggy sea cliffs; red deer, wild ponies, horned sheep
Lake District	majestic fells, rugged mountains, shimmering lakes; literary heritage; ospreys, red squirrels, golden eagles
New Forest	woodlands, heath; wild ponies, otters, Dartford warbler, southern damselfly
Norfolk & Suffolk Broads	expansive shallow lakes, rivers, marshlands; windmills; water lilies, wildfowl, otters
North York Moors	heather-clad hills, deep-green valleys, isolated villages; merlins, curlews, golden plovers
Northumberland	wild rolling moors, heather, gorse; Hadrian's Wall; black grouse, red squirrels
Peak District	high moors, tranquil dales, limestone caves; kestrels, badgers, grouse
South Downs	rolling grassy chalky hills, chalky sea-cliffs, gorse, heather; Adonis blue butterfly
Yorkshire Dales	rugged hills, lush valleys, limestone pavements; red squirrels, hares, curlews, lapwings, buzzards

Common birds of farmland areas (and urban gardens) include the robin, with its instantly recognisable red breast and cheerful whistle; the wren, whose loud trilling song belies its tiny size; and the yellowhammer, with a song that sounds like (if you use your imagination) 'a-little-bit-of-bread-and-no-cheese'. In open fields, the warbling cry of a skylark is another classic, but now threatened, sound of the English outdoors. You're more likely to see a pheasant, a large bird originally introduced from Russia to the nobility's shooting estates, but now considered naturalised.

Alongside rivers, the once-rare otter is making a comeback. Elsewhere, the black-and-white striped badger is under threat from farmers who believe they transmit bovine tuberculosis to cattle, although conservationists say the case is far from proven. Also at the centre of controversy is the fox; this animal is widespread in the countryside and well adapted to a scavenging life in rural towns, and even city suburbs.

Woodland

In woodland areas, mammals include the small white-spotted fallow deer and the even smaller roe deer. Woodland is full of birds, too, but you'll hear them more than see them. Listen out for willow warblers (which have a warbling song with a descending cadence) and chiffchaffs (which make a repetitive 'chiff chaff' noise).

If you hear rustling among the fallen leaves it might be a hedgehog – a spiny-backed insect eater – but it's an increasingly rare sound these days; conservationists say they'll be extinct in Britain by 2025, thanks to farming insecticides, decreasing habitat and their inability to safely cross roads.

Grey squirrels (introduced from North America) have proved very adaptable, to the extent that England's native red squirrels are severely endangered because the greys eat all the food.

Perhaps unexpectedly, England is home to herds of 'wild' ponies, notably in the New Forest, Exmoor and Dartmoor, but although these animals roam free they are privately owned and regularly managed. There's

Perhaps surprisingly, England's most wooded county is Surrey, despite its proximity to London. The soil is too poor for agriculture, so while woodland areas elsewhere in England were cleared, Surrey's trees were spared.

ACTIVITIES	BEST TIME TO VISIT
walking, mountain biking, horse riding	May-Jun (wildflowers bloom)
horse riding, walking	Sep (heather flowering)
water sports, walking, mountaineering, rock climbing	Sep-Oct (summer crowds departed, autumn colours abound)
walking, cycling, horse riding	Apr-Sep (lush vegetation)
walking, cycling, boating	Apr-May (birds most active)
walking, mountain biking	Aug-Sep (heather flowering)
walking, cycling, mountain biking, climbing	Apr-May (lambs) & Sep (heather flowering)
walking, cycling, mountain biking, hang-gliding, climbing	Apr-May (even more lambs)
walking, mountain biking	Aug (heather flowering)
walking, cycling, mountain biking, climbing	Apr-May (visitors outnumbered by, you guessed it, lambs)

even a pocket of wild goats near Lynmouth in Devon, where they've apparently gambolled merrily for almost 1000 years.

Mountains & High Moors

On mountains and high moors the most visible mammal is the red deer. Males of the species grow their famous large antlers between April and July, and shed them again in February. Also on the high ground, well-known and easily recognised birds include the red grouse, which often hides in the heather until almost stepped on then flies away with a loud warning call, and the curlew, with its stately long legs and elegant curved bill. Look hard, and you may see beautifully camouflaged golden plovers, while the spectacular aerial displays of lapwings are impossible to miss.

Landscape Facts

Here's an idea of how England fits into wider geographic areas (all in sq miles):

» **England** 50,000

» **Britain** (England, Scotland, Wales) 88,500

» **UK** (Britain & Northern Ireland) 95,000

» **British Isles** (UK, Ireland & other smaller islands) 123,000

By comparison, France is about 212,000 sq miles, Australia 2.7 million sq miles and the USA about 3.5 million sq miles.

Coastal Areas

By the sea, two seal species frequent English coasts: the larger grey seal, which is more often seen, and the misnamed common seal. In areas such as Norfolk and Northumberland, boat trips to see seal colonies are a popular attraction. Dolphins, porpoises, minke whales and basking sharks can also be seen off the western coasts, especially from about May to September when viewing conditions are better. Boat trips are available from many coastal holiday resorts.

England's estuaries and mudflats are feeding grounds for numerous migrant wading birds; easily spotted are black-and-white oystercatchers with their long red bills, while flocks of ringed plovers skitter along the sand. On the coastal cliffs in early summer, particularly in Cornwall and Yorkshire, countless thousands of guillemots, razorbills, kittiwakes and other breeding seabirds fight for space on crowded rock ledges, and the air is thick with their sound. It is one of England's finest wildlife spectacles.

Plants

In the hill country of southern England and the limestone areas further north (such as the Peak District and Yorkshire Dales), the best place to see wildflowers are the fields that evade large-scale farming – many erupt with great profusions of cowslips and primroses in April and May.

For woodland flowers, the best time is also April and May, before the leaf canopy is fully developed so sunlight can reach plants such as bluebells. Another classic English plant is gorse: you can't miss this spiky bush in heath areas such as the New Forest. Its vivid yellow flowers show year-round.

In contrast, the blooming season for heather is quite short, but no less dramatic; through August and September areas such as the North York Moors and Dartmoor are covered in a riot of purple.

WILDLIFE IN YOUR POCKET

Is it a rabbit or a hare? A gull or a tern? Buttercup or cowslip? If you need to know a bit more about England's plant and animal kingdoms the following field guides are ideal for entry-level naturalists:

» *Complete Guide to British Wildlife*, by Paul Sterry, is portable and highly recommended, covering mammals, birds, fish, plants, snakes, insects and even fungi, with brief descriptions and excellent photos.

» If feathered friends are enough, the *Complete Guide to British Birds*, by Paul Sterry, has clear photos and descriptions, plus info on when and where each species may be seen.

» *Wildlife of the North Atlantic*, by film-maker Tony Soper, beautifully covers the animals seen from beach, boat and clifftop in the British Isles and beyond.

» The Collins GEM series includes handy little books on wildlife topics such as *Birds*, *Trees*, *Fish* and *Wild Flowers*.

'THE UNSPEAKABLE IN PURSUIT OF THE INEDIBLE'

The red fox, with its characteristic bushy tail and an anthropomorphic reputation for cunning, is a controversial creature in England. The controversy focuses on hunting foxes with the use of hounds. Supporters say it's been a traditional English rural activity for centuries, and helps control the fox population; opponents say it's a savage blood sport that has virtually no impact on overall numbers. Distaste for this type of hunting is not a new phenomenon, the activity was famously described as 'the unspeakable in pursuit of the inedible' by Oscar Wilde more than a century ago. Today, many observers say the hunting debate has come to represent much bigger issues: town versus country, or the relative limits of privilege, state control and individual freedom. Either way, fox hunting with dogs was banned in 2005 by law. And opinion is still very strongly divided.

Environmental Issues

With England's long history of human occupation, it's not surprising that the country's appearance is almost totally the result of people's interaction with the environment. Since the earliest times, trees have been chopped down and fields created for crops or animals, but the biggest changes to rural areas came after WWII, continuing into the '50s and '60s, when a drive to be self-reliant in food meant new – intensive and large-scale – farming methods. The result was dramatic: an ancient patchwork of small meadows became a landscape of vast prairie-like fields, as walls were demolished, woodlands felled, ponds filled, wetlands drained and, most notably, hedgerows ripped out.

In most cases the hedgerows were lines of dense bushes, shrubs and trees forming a network that stretched across the countryside, protecting fields from erosion, supporting a varied range of flowers, and providing shelter for numerous insects, birds and small mammals. But in the rush to improve farm yields, thousands of miles of hedgerows were destroyed in the postwar decades, and between the mid-1980s and the early 2000s another 25% disappeared.

Although the hedgerows around fields have been reduced, new 'hedgerows' have appeared in the landscape: the long strips of grass and bushes alongside motorways and major roads. These areas support thousands of insect species, plus mice and shrews, so kestrels are often seen – unconcerned by traffic.

Hedgerows have come to symbolise many other environmental issues in rural areas, and in recent years the destruction has abated, partly because farmers recognise their anti-erosion qualities, and partly because they're encouraged – with financial incentives from UK or European agencies – to 'set aside' such areas as wildlife havens.

In addition to hedgerow clearance, other farming techniques remain hot environmental issues. Studies have shown that the use of pesticides and intensive irrigation results in rivers being poisoned or simply running dry. Meanwhile, monocropping means the fields have one type of grass and not another plant to be seen. These 'green deserts' support no insects, so in turn wild bird populations have plummeted. This picture is not a case of wizened old peasants recalling the idyllic days of their forbears; you only have to be aged about 40 in England to remember a countryside where birds such as skylarks or lapwings were visibly much more numerous.

But all is not lost. In the face of apparently overwhelming odds, England still boasts great biodiversity, and some of the best wildlife habitats are protected (to a greater or lesser extent) by the creation of national parks and similar areas, or private reserves owned by conservation campaign groups such as the Wildlife Trusts (www.wildlifetrusts.org), National Trust (www.nationaltrust.org.uk), Woodland Trust (www.woodland-trust.org) and the Royal Society for the Protection of Birds (www.rspb.org.uk). Many of these areas are open to the public – ideal spots for walking, birdwatching or simply enjoying the peace and beauty of the countryside – and well worth a visit.

England's Great Outdoors

What's the best way to slow down, meet the locals and get off the beaten track as you travel around England? Simple: go for a walk, get on a bike or enjoy any other kind of outdoor activity. Whatever your budget, enjoying England's great outdoors could be a highlight of your trip.

Walking

1 England can seem crowded, but away from the cities there are many beautiful areas, perfect for walking. You can go for a short riverside stroll or a major hike over mountain ranges – or anything in between. The best places include the Cotswolds, Lake District and Yorkshire Dales.

Cycling

2 A bike is perfect for exploring England's countryside. Areas such as Suffolk and Wiltshire offer a vast network of quiet country roads ideal for cycle-touring. For off-road fun, mountain-bikers can go further into the wilds in places such as the Peak District and South Downs.

Horse Riding

3 If walking or cycling is too much of a sweat, exploring the wilder parts of England on horseback is highly recommended. In rural areas and national parks such as Dartmoor and Northumberland, riding centres cater to all levels of proficiency.

Surfing

4 England is not an obvious place for surfing, but conditions are surprisingly good at key locations. Top of the list is the west coast of Cornwall and Devon, and there are smaller scenes on the east coast, notably Norfolk and Yorkshire.

Clockwise from top left
1 Hiking in the hills 2 Mountain biking in the Peak District (p486) 3 Horse riding in Northumberland (p751)

JOHN HAY / GETTY IMAGES ©

2

JONATHAN BARTON / GETTY IMAGES ©

The Arts

England's contributions to the worlds of literature, drama, cinema and pop are celebrated around the world, thanks in no small part to the global dominance of the English language. As you travel around England today you'll see landscapes made famous as movie sets and literary locations, or by links to your favourite songs, so in this chapter we've picked out some major milestones and focused on works with a connection to real places where you can experience something of famous figures or even walk in the footsteps of their characters.

English Literature

The roots of England's poetic and story-telling heritage stretch back to Nordic sagas and Early English epics such as *Beowulf,* but modern English literature starts around 1387 (yes, that is 'modern' in history-soaked England) when Geoffrey Chaucer (p143) produced *The Canterbury Tales*. This mammoth poem is a collection of fables, stories and morality tales using travelling pilgrims – the Knight, the Wife of Bath and so on – as a narrative hook.

LITERARY LANDSCAPE

For extra insight while travelling, the *Oxford Literary Guide to Great Britain & Ireland,* edited by Daniel Hahn and Nicholas Robins, gives details of towns, villages and countryside immortalised by writers, from Geoffrey Chaucer's Canterbury to Jane Austen's Bath.

William Shakespeare

The next big name in English literature came in the 16th century, when William Shakespeare entered the scene. Best known for his plays (see also Theatre, p806) he was also a remarkably prolific and influential poet. 'Shall I compare thee to a summers day?' is just one of his famous lines still widely quoted today.

The Romantic Era

During the late 18th and early 19th century, a new generation of writers drew inspiration from human imagination and the natural world (in many cases helped along by a healthy dose of laudanum). Leading lights of the movement were William Blake, John Keats, Percy Bysshe Shelley, Lord Byron and Samuel Taylor Coleridge, and perhaps the best known English poet of all, William Wordsworth. His famous line 'I wandered lonely as a cloud', from 'Daffodils', was inspired by a hike in the hills of the Lake District in northern England.

Victoriana

As industrialisation expanded during the reign of Queen Victoria, so key novels of the time explored social themes. Charles Dickens tackled many prevailing issues of his day: in *Oliver Twist,* he captures the lives of young thieves in the London slums; *Bleak House* is a critique of the English legal system; and *Hard Times* criticises the excesses of capitalism. At around the same time, but choosing a rural setting, George Eliot (the pen-name of Mary Anne Evans) wrote *The Mill on the Floss,* where the central character struggles against society's expectations.

JANE AUSTEN & THE BRONTËS

The beginning of the 19th century saw the emergence of some of English literature's best known and beloved writers: Jane Austen and the Brontë sisters.

Austen's fame stems from her exquisite observations of love, friendship, intrigues and passions boiling under the stilted preserve of middle-class social convention – and from the endless stream of movies and TV costume dramas based on her works, such as *Pride and Prejudice* and *Sense and Sensibility*. For visitors today, the location most associated with Jane Austen is the city of Bath, a beautiful place even without the literary link. As one of her heroines said, 'who can ever be tired of Bath?'.

Of the Brontë sisters' prodigious output, Emily Brontë's *Wuthering Heights* is the best known – it's an epic tale of obsession and revenge, where the dark and moody landscape plays a role as great as any human character. Charlotte Brontë's *Jane Eyre* and Anne Brontë's *The Tenant of Wildfell Hall* are classics of passion, mystery and love. Fans still flock to their former home in the Yorkshire town of Haworth, perched on the edge of the wild Pennine moors, which inspired so many of their books.

Thomas Hardy's classic *Tess of the D'Urbervilles* deals with the peasantry's decline, and *The Trumpet Major* paints a picture of idyllic English country life interrupted by war and encroaching modernity. Many of Hardy's works are based in the fictionalised county of Wessex (today's Dorset and surrounding counties), where towns such as Dorchester are popular stops on tourist itineraries.

The 20th Century

The end of WWI and the ensuing social disruption fed into the modernist movement, with DH Lawrence perhaps its finest exponent; *Sons and Lovers* follows the lives and loves of generations in the English Midlands as the country changes from rural idyll to an increasingly industrial landscape, while his controversial exploration of sexuality in *Lady Chatterley's Lover* was originally banned as 'obscene'. Other highlights of this period included Daphne du Maurier's romantic suspense novel *Rebecca*, set on the Cornish coast, and Evelyn Waugh's *Brideshead Revisited*, an exploration of moral and social disintegration among the English aristocracy.

The 1970s saw the arrival of two novelists who became prolific through the rest of the century and beyond. Martin Amis published *The Rachel Papers* then produced a string of novels where common themes include the absurdity and unappealing nature of modern life, including *London Fields* (1989) and *Lionel Asbo: State of England* (2012). Meanwhile, Ian McEwan debuted with *The Cement Garden*, and earned critical acclaim for finely observed studies of the English character such as *The Child in Time* (1987), *Atonement* (2001) and *On Chesil Beach* (2007).

Helen Fielding's book *Bridget Jones's Diary*, originally a series of newspaper articles, is a fond look at the heartache of a modern single woman's blundering search for love, and the epitome of the late-1990s 'chick-lit' genre. It's also (very loosely) based on *Pride and Prejudice* by Jane Austen.

New Millennium

As the 20th century drew to a close, the nation's multicultural landscape proved a rich inspiration for contemporary novelists: Hanif Kureishi sowed the seeds with his groundbreaking *The Buddha of Suburbia*, about a group of Anglo-Asians in suburban London; Zadie Smith published her acclaimed debut *White Teeth* in 2000, followed by a string of best sellers including *The Autograph Man* and 2012's *NW;* Andrea Levy published *Small Island*, about a Jamaican couple settled in postwar London; and Monica Ali's *Brick Lane* was shortlisted for the high-profile Man Booker Prize in 2003.

Other contemporary writers include Will Self, known for his surreal, satirical novels including *The Book of Dave;* Nick Hornby, best known for novels like *Fever Pitch*, a study of the insecurities of English blokishness; Julian Barnes, whose books include *England, England*, a darkly ironic study of nationalism and tourism among other themes, and *The Sense of an Ending,* winner of the 2011 Man Booker Prize; and Hilary Mantel, author of many novels on an astoundingly wide range of themes and subjects, including *Wolf Hall* (another Man Booker Prize winner) about Henry VIII and his ruthless adviser Thomas Cromwell, followed by the sequels *Bring Up the Bodies* (published in 2012) and *The Mirror and the Light.*

For other worlds and other-worldly humour, try two of England's funniest – and most successful – writers: Douglas Adams (*The Hitchhiker's Guide to the Galaxy* and several sequels) and Terry Pratchett (the *Discworld* series).

A new name on the literary scene is Stephen Kelman, whose debut novel *Pidgin English,* about gang culture and multicultural tensions, was nominated ('gatecrashed' in the words of the author) for the Man Booker Prize in 2011. Other names and books to look out for include David Mitchell *(Black Swan Green),* Kazuo Ishiguro (*Remains of the Day*) and Alan Hollinghurst *(Line of Beauty).*

Cinema

England had a number of successful directors in the early days of cinema. Many cut their teeth in the silent-film industry – including Alfred Hitchcock, who directed *Blackmail,* one of the first English 'talkies' in 1929, before migrating to America in the early 1940s.

War & Postwar

During WWII, films such as *In Which We Serve* (1942) were designed to raise morale, while a young director called David Lean produced the classic tale of buttoned-up English passion, *Brief Encounter* (1945), before graduating to Hollywood epics including *Lawrence of Arabia.* After the war, English audiences were in the mood for escape and entertainment, so the domestic film industry specialised in eccentric English comedies epitomised by the work of Ealing Studios: such as *Passport to Pimlico* (1949) and *The Ladykillers* (1955).

The Ladykillers (1955) is a classic Ealing comedy about a band of hapless bank robbers holed up in a London guesthouse, and features Alec Guinness sporting the most outrageous set of false teeth ever committed to celluloid.

Swinging Sixties

In the late 1950s 'British New Wave' and 'Free Cinema' explored the gritty realities of British life in semi-documentary style, with directors Lindsay Anderson and Tony Richardson crystallising the movement in films such as *This Sporting Life* (1961) and *A Taste of Honey* (1961). At the other end of the spectrum were the *Carry On* films, the cinematic equivalent of the smutty seaside postcard, packed with bawdy gags and double entendres. The 1960s also saw the birth of another classic English genre: the James Bond films, starring Sean Connery (who is actually Scottish).

Brit Flicks

The 1970s was a tough decade for the British film industry, but the 1980s saw recovery, thanks partly to David Puttnam's Oscar success with *Chariots of Fire,* and the newly established Channel Four investing in edgy films such as *My Beautiful Laundrette* (1985).

A GRAND SUCCESS

One of the great success stories of English TV and cinema has been Bristol-based animator Nick Park and the production company Aardman Animations, best known for the award-winning man-and-dog duo Wallace and Gromit. This lovable pair first appeared in Park's graduation film, *A Grand Day Out* (1989), and went on to star in *The Wrong Trousers* (1993), *A Close Shave* (1995) and their full-length feature debut, *The Curse of the Were-Rabbit* (2005). Known for their intricate plots, film homages and amazingly realistic animation, the Wallace and Gromit films have scooped Nick Park four Oscars. Other Aardman features include *Chicken Run* (2000), *Flushed Away* (2006) and *The Pirates! – In an Adventure with Scientists* (2012).

MAKING MOVIES

There's nothing wrong with enhancing your travels in England with the occasional flights of fancy through the imaginary world of the cinema. Real-life locations for films made in England range from the busy London streets that feature in movies such as *Notting Hill* and *Bridget Jones,* to remote rural spots such as Sycamore Gap on Hadrian's Wall in Northumberland, used in the 1991 version of *Robin Hood* (despite supposedly being on the route from Dover to London). But perhaps the most popular locations for visitors feature in the various *Harry Potter* films. These include: Alnwick Castle (Northumberland), Durham Cathedral, the Bodleian Library and several colleges at Oxford University, Gloucester Cathedral, and Lacock Abbey in Wiltshire. London features in several *Harry Potter* films, with key locations including Leadenhall Market, St Pancras Station and King's Cross Station, where you really can see a sign for Platform 9¾ ....

Another minor renaissance occurred in the 1990s, ushered in by the massively successful *Four Weddings and a Funeral* (1994), which introduced Hugh Grant in his trademark role as a self-deprecating Englishman, a character type he reprised in subsequent hits, including *Notting Hill, About a Boy* and *Love Actually*.

The 'Brit Flick' genre – characterised by themes such as irony, social realism and humour in the face of adversity – included: *Brassed Off* (1996) about a struggling colliery band; *The Full Monty* (1997) following a troupe of laid-off steel workers turned male strippers; and *Billy Elliott* (2000), the story of an aspiring young ballet dancer striving to escape the slag heaps and boarded-up factories of the industrial north.

The British Film Institute (BFI; www.bfi.org.uk) is dedicated to promoting film and cinema in Britain, and publishes the monthly academic journal *Sight & Sound*.

Meanwhile, films such as *East Is East* (1999) and *Bend it like Beckham* (2002) explored the tensions of modern multicultural Britain, while veteran director Mike Leigh, known for his heavily improvised style, found success with *Life Is Sweet* (1991), *Naked* (1993) and the Palme d'Or winning *Secrets and Lies* (1996).

21st-Century Box

In the first decade or so of the new millennium, literary adaptations have continued to provide the richest seam of success in the English film industry, including 2012's *Anna Karenina,* directed by Joe Wright and staring Keira Knightley, and of course the blockbuster *Harry Potter* franchise. Biopics are also a perennial favourite: recent big-screen subjects include Joy Division's Ian Curtis (*Control,* 2007), Elizabeth I (*Elizabeth: The Golden Age,* 2007) and Elizabeth II (*The Queen,* 2006).

Meanwhile the oldest of English film franchises trundled on: a tough, toned 21st-century James Bond appeared in 2006 courtesy of Daniel Craig and the blockbuster *Casino Royal,* followed by *Quantum of Solace* (2008) and *Skyfall* (2012).

The UK's biggest film magazine is *Empire* (www.empireonline.co.uk). For less mainstream opinion check out *Little White Lies* (www.littlewhitelies.co.uk).

Pop & Rock Music

England has been putting the world through its musical paces ever since some mop-haired lads from Liverpool created The Beatles. And while Elvis may have invented rock' n' roll, it was the Fab Four that transformed it into a global phenomenon, backed by other bands of the 1960s 'British Invasion' – The Rolling Stones, The Who, Cream and The Kinks.

Glam to Punk

Glam rock arrived in the 1970s, fronted by artists such as chameleonlike David Bowie and the anthemic Queen, while Led Zeppelin laid down the blueprint for heavy metal, and the psychedelia of the previous decade morphed into the prog rock of Pink Floyd and Yes.

At the end of the decade it was all swept aside as punk exploded onto the scene, most famously with The Sex Pistols, ably assisted by The Clash, The Damned, The Buzzcocks and The Stranglers. Then punk begat New Wave, with acts including The Jam and Elvis Costello blending spiky tunes and sharp lyrics into a more radio-friendly sound.

Movies on the English music scene include: *Backbeat* (1994), about The Beatles' early days; *Sid & Nancy* (1986), Sex Pistols' bassist and girlfriend; *Quadrophenia* (1979), mods and rockers; *Velvet Goldmine* (1998), glam rock; *24 Hour Party People* (2002), Manchester scene; and *Nowhere Boy* (2009), John Lennon pre-Beatles.

The '80s

The conspicuous consumption of the early 1980s influenced the era's pop scene. Big hair and shoulder pads became the uniform of the day, with big names including Wham! (a boyish duo headed by an up-and-coming popster called George Michael) and New Romantic bands such as Spandau Ballet and Duran Duran. Away from the glitz, fans enjoyed the doom-laden lyrics of The Cure, the heavy-metal of Iron Maiden and Black Sabbath, and the 'miserabilism' of The Smiths.

Indie & Brit Pop

The 1990s saw the rise of synthesised sounds and ecstasy-fuelled rave culture, centred on famous clubs like Manchester's Haçienda and London's Ministry of Sound. Manchester was also a focus for the burgeoning British 'indie' scene, driven by guitar-based bands such The Stone Roses, James, Happy Mondays and Oasis. Then indie grew up and became Britpop, with Oasis still at the forefront, and now including the likes of Pulp, Supergrass and Blur, whose distinctively British music chimed with the country's reborn sense of optimism after the landslide election of New Labour in 1997.

New Millennium Sounds

The first decade of the new millennium saw no let-up in the music scene's continual shifting and reinventing. Jazz, soul, R&B and hip-hop fused into a new 'urban' sound epitomised by artists like Dizzee Rascal, Tinie Tempah and Plan B. Meanwhile, singer-songwriters – such as Katie Melua, Ed Sheeran and the all-conquering Adele – have made a comeback, and the spirit of British punk and indie stays alive thanks to the likes of Florence & the Machine, Coldplay, Muse, Kasabian, Radiohead and The Horrors.

One thing's for sure, the English music scene has never stood still. By the time you read this, half of the 'great new bands' of last year will have sunk without trace, and a fresh batch of unknowns will have risen to dominate the airwaves and download sites.

Sound & Vision

Some classic English pop songs are listed in the England Today chapter, while venues for live music are listed throughout this book.

ROCK 'N' ROLL LOCATIONS...

Fans buy the single, then the T-shirt. But true fans visit the locations featured on album covers. Here are a few favourites:

» Abbey Road, St John's Wood, London – *Abbey Road*, The Beatles

» Battersea Power Station, London – *Animals*, Pink Floyd (the inflatable pig has gone)

» Berwick St, Soho, London – *(What's the Story) Morning Glory*, Oasis

» Big Ben plus a corner of plinth under Boudica's statue, London – *My Generation* (US version), The Who

» Durdle Door, Dorset – *North Atlantic Drift*, Ocean Colour Scene

» Salford Boys Club, Manchester – *The Queen is Dead*, The Smiths

» Thor's Cave, Manifold Valley, near Ashbourne, Peak District National Park – *A Storm In Heaven*, The Verve

» Yes Tor, Dartmoor, Devon – *Tomato*, by prog-rockers Yes

Painting & Sculpture

For many centuries, continental Europe – especially Holland, Spain, France and Italy – set the visual arts agenda. The first artist with a truly English style and sensibility was arguably William Hogarth, whose riotous canvases exposed the vice and corruption of 18th-century London. His most celebrated work is *A Rake's Progress,* displayed today at Sir John Soane's Museum in London, which kick-started a long tradition of caricatures continued by modern-day cartoonists such as Gerald Scarfe and Steve Bell.

Portraits

While Hogarth was busy satirising society, other artists were hard at work showing it in its best light. The leading figures of 18th-century English portraiture were Sir Joshua Reynolds, Thomas Gainsborough and George Romney, while George Stubbs is best known for his intricate studies of animals (particularly horses). Most of these artists are represented at Tate Britain or the National Gallery in London.

Landscape & Fables

In the 19th century, leading painters favoured the English landscape. John Constable's best known works include *Salisbury Cathedral* and *The Haywain,* depicting a mill in Suffolk (National Gallery), while JMW Turner was fascinated by the effects of light and colour on English scenes, with his works becoming almost entirely abstract by the 1840s.

In contrast, the Pre-Raphaelite painters of the late 19th century preferred a figurative style reflecting the Victorian taste for English fables and fairy tales. Key members of the movement included Dante Gabriel Rossetti, John Everett Millais and William Holman Hunt, all represented at London's Tate Britain or Victoria & Albert Museum.

Stones & Sticks

In the tumultuous 20th century, English art became increasingly experimental. Francis Bacon placed Freudian psychoanalysis on the canvas in his portraits, while pioneering sculptors such as Henry Moore and Barbara Hepworth experimented with natural forms in stone and new materials. At about the same time, the painter LS Lowry was setting his 'matchstick men' among the smokestacks of northern England, and is today remembered by the major art centre that bears his name in Manchester.

HENRY MOORE

Some of Henry Moore's work can be seen at the Yorkshire Sculpture Park. Barbara Hepworth is celebrated at the new eponymous gallery in Wakefield and is also associated with St Ives, Cornwall.

Pop Art

The mid-1950s and early '60s saw an explosion of English 'pop art', as artists plundered popular culture for inspiration. Leaders of this new movement included David Hockney. His bold colours and simple lines were ground-breaking, and are still used to great effect half a century later; his exhibition at the Royal Academy in 2012 was a sell-out. A contemporary, Peter Blake, designed the cut-up collage cover for The Beatles' landmark album *Sgt Pepper's Lonely Hearts Club Band.* The 1960s also saw the rise of sculptor Anthony Caro; creating large abstract works in steel and bronze, he remains one of England's most influential sculptors.

Britart & Beyond

Thanks partly to the support (and money) of advertising tycoon Charles Saatchi, a new wave of British artists came to the fore in the 1990s. The movement was dubbed, inevitably, 'Britart'; its leading members included Damien Hirst, famous (or infamous) initially for works involving pickled sharks, semi-dissected human figures and more recently for a diamond-encrusted skull entitled *For the Love of God.* A contemporary is Tracey Emin, once an *enfant terrible* who incurred the wrath

ANISH KAPOOR

The sculptor Anish Kapoor has been working in London since the 1970s. He is best known for his large outdoor installations, which often feature curved shapes and reflective materials, such as highly polished steel. His recent works include a major new installation in London, called *Arcelor Mittal Orbit*, to celebrate the 2012 Olympic Games. At over 110m high, this is the largest piece of public art in Britain.

of the tabloids for works such as *My Bed*, a messed-up bedroom scene, but now a respected figure and patron of the new Turner Gallery in Margate.

JMW Turner also gives his name to the Turner Prize, a high-profile, and frequently controversial, annual award for British visual artists. As well as Hirst, other winners have included Martin Creed (his work was a room with lights going on and off), Mark Wallinger (a collection of anti-war objects), Simon Starling (a shed converted to a boat and back again), Rachel Whiteread (a plaster cast of a house) and Antony Gormley (best known in England for his gigantic *Angel of the North*).

The winner of the Turner prize in 2011 was Martin Boyce, for his *Do Words Have Voices*, a room with angular installations representing an urban park in autumn. Thousands of people came to see the work when it was on display at the BALTIC Centre, proving that contemporary art can be popular, even if it remains controversial.

Theatre

English theatre can trace its roots back to medieval morality plays, court jesters and travelling storytellers, and possibly even to dramas during Roman times in amphitheatres – a few of which still remain, such as at Chester and Cirencester. But most scholars agree that the key milestone in the story was the opening of England's first theatre – called simply The Theatre – in London in 1576. A few years later, the Rose and the Globe Theatres appeared, and the stage was set for the entrance of England's best-known playwright.

You can enjoy Shakespeare plays at the rebuilt Globe Theatre in London or at the Royal Shakespeare Company's own theatre in Stratford-upon-Avon.

THE GLOBE

William Shakespeare

For most visitors to England (and for most locals) English drama means just one name: William Shakespeare. Born in 1564, in the Midlands town of Stratford-upon-Avon, Shakespeare made his mark in London between around 1590 and 1610, where most of his plays were performed at the Globe Theatre. His brilliant plots and spectacular use of language, plus the sheer size of his canon of work (including classics such as *Hamlet, Romeo and Juliet, Henry V* and *A Midsummer Night's Dream*), have turned him into a national – and international – icon, so that today, almost 400 years after shuffling off his mortal coil, The Bard's plays still pull in big crowds.

English Theatre Today

However you budget your time and money during your visit to England, make sure that you see some English theatre as part of your travels. It easily lives up to its reputation as the finest in the world, especially in London, while other big cities around the country boast their own top-class venues, such as the Birmingham Repertory Theatre, the Bristol Old Vic, Chichester Festival Theatre, and the Playhouse in Nottingham.

Many accomplished English actors, including Judi Dench, Ralph Fiennes, Brenda Blethyn, Toby Stephens and Simon Callow, juggle high-paying Hollywood roles with appearances on the English stage, while several stars have taken hefty pay cuts to tread the London boards, including Glenn Close, Gwyneth Paltrow, Macaulay Culkin, Christian Slater and Danny DeVito, as well as Australia's Nicole Kidman. Kevin Spacey liked it so much he decided to stay; since 2004 he's been in charge at one of London's famous theatres, the Old Vic.

Other options in London include the Donmar Warehouse and Royal Court Theatre, best known for new and experimental works. Meanwhile, for big names, most people head to the West End, where famous spots include the Shaftsbury, Adelphi and Theatre Royal at Drury Lane. These venues are mostly the preserve of classic plays, with top shows in 2012 including *War Horse,* the play that inspired the Spielberg movie of the same name, and *39 Steps,* also well-known as an Alfred Hitchcock movie in the 1930s, plus *The Mousetrap,* the legendary whodunit and world's longest-running play; 2012 was its 60th year.

West End Musicals

London's West End also means big musicals, with a long history of crowd-pullers such as *Cats, Wizard of Oz, Les Miserables, Sweeny Todd, Phantom of the Opera* and *The Lion King,* with many of today's shows raiding the pop world for material, such as *We Will Rock You,* inspired by the music of Queen. In 2012, the massively successful musical *Matilda,* based on the novel by Roald Dahl, broke all records by winning seven Olivier Awards, the most prestigious prize in English theatre.

For details of other top shows and venues, and how to buy tickets, see the Entertainment section of the London chapter. Details of major theatres in other cities around England are also given in the relevant chapters.

Sporting England

The English invented – or at least codified the modern rules – of many of the world's favourite sports, including cricket, tennis, rugby and football, and ever since then the national teams have enjoyed mixed results. Despite some standout success stories from the last decade – including victory at the Rugby World Cup in 2004, a long-awaited win against Australia in the 2005 Ashes cricket series, followed by another win against the Aussies in the Twenty20 Cricket World Cup in 2010 and retaining the Ashes in 2011 – it says something about the nation's football prowess, and something about the nation itself, when the most revered date in the brain of every self-respecting fan is still England's victory in the Football World Cup, way back in 1966.

But even when England isn't winning, it doesn't dull the enthusiasm of the fans. Every weekend thousands of people turn out to cheer their favourite team, and sporting highlights such as the FA Cup, Wimbledon or the Derby keep the entire nation enthralled. Admiration for the nation's sports stars reached new heights in 2012, when English athletes were part of the British team that won 65 medals (including 29 golds) at the London Olympics, and many more at the Paralympics a few weeks later. Fans and spectators now look towards the 2014 Commonwealth Games in Scotland, and hope the Olympian performances will once again be repeated.

For the dates and details of major football and cricket matches, horse racing and other sporting fixtures across the country, a great place to start is the sports pages of www.britevents.com.

Cricket

Along with Big Ben and cups of tea, cricket is an icon of England. Dating from the 18th century – although its roots are much older – this quintessentially English sport spread through the Commonwealth during Britain's colonial era. Australia, the Caribbean and the Indian subcontinent took to the game with gusto, and today the former colonies delight in giving the old country a good spanking on the cricket pitch.

While many English people follow cricket like a religion, to the uninitiated it's an impenetrable spectacle. Spread over one-day games or

SPORTING HISTORY

England's enthralling sports have equally fascinating histories. No one can say when football was invented, but the word 'soccer' (the favoured term in countries where 'football' means another game) is reputedly derived from 'sock'. In medieval times this was a tough leather foot-cover worn by peasants – ideal for kicking around a pig's bladder in the park on a Saturday afternoon.

In contrast, rugby can trace its roots to a football match in 1823 at Rugby School, in Warwickshire. A player called William Webb Ellis, frustrated at the limitations of mere kicking, reputedly picked up the ball and ran with it towards the goal. True to the sense of English fair play, rather than Ellis being dismissed from the game, a whole new sport was developed around his tactic, and the Rugby Football Union was formally inaugurated in 1871. The Rugby World Cup is named the Webb Ellis Trophy after this enterprising young tearaway.

THE ASHES

The historic test cricket series between England and Australia known as the Ashes has been played every other year since 1882 (bar a few interruptions during the World Wars). It is played alternately in England and Australia with each of the five matches in the series held at a different cricket ground, always in the summer in the host location.

The contest's name dates back to the landmark test match of 1882, won (for the very first time) by the Australians. Defeat of the mother country by the colonial upstarts was a source of profound national shock: a mock-obituary in the *Sporting Times* lamented the death of English cricket and referred to the sport's ashes being taken to Australia.

Later the name was given to a terracotta urn presented the following year to the English captain Ivo Bligh (later Lord Darnley), purportedly containing the cremated ashes of a stump or bail used in this landmark match. Since 1953 this hallowed relic has resided at the Marylebone Cricket Club (MCC) Museum at Lord's. Despite the vast importance given to winning the series, the urn itself is a diminutive six inches high (150cm).

The recent history of the Ashes is not without drama. After eight straight defeats, England won the series in 2005, then handed the prize straight back to the Aussies after a thrashing in 2007, before 'regaining the Ashes' in 2009 and winning again in 2011.

five-day 'test matches', progress seems so *slow*, and dominated by arcane terminology like 'innings, overs, googlies, outswinger, leg-bye and silly-mid-off'. Nonetheless, at least one cricket match should feature in your travels around England. If you're patient and learn the intricacies, you might find cricket as enriching and enticing as all the Brits who remain glued to their radio or computer all summer 'just to see how England's getting on'.

Causing ructions is Twenty20 cricket, a new format which limits the time each team has to play, putting the emphasis on fast big-batting scores. Traditionalists see it changing the character of the game, though there's no doubting its popularity – most Twenty20 matches sell out.

International tests and one-day games are played at grounds including Lords in London, Edgbaston in Birmingham and Headingley in Leeds. Tickets cost from £30 to well over £200. The County Championship pits together the best teams from around the country. Tickets cost £15 to £25, and only the most crucial games tend to sell out.

Easiest option of all – and often the most enjoyable – is stumbling across a local game on a village green. There's no charge for spectators, and no one will mind if you nip into the pub during a quiet period.

GRAND NATIONAL

Queen Elizabeth II is a great horse-racing fan, and the royal stables have produced many winners. The 2005 Grand National famously clashed with the marriage of Prince Charles: rumours abound that the start was delayed so the Queen could attend the nuptials *and* see the race.

Football (Soccer)

The English Premier League (www.premierleague.com) has some of the finest teams in the world, dominated in recent years by four top teams – Arsenal, Liverpool, Chelsea and Manchester United – joined in 2012 by a fifth big player in the shape of Manchester City. Down in quality from the Premiership, 72 other teams play in the English divisions called the Championship, League One and League Two.

The football season is the same for all divisions (August to May), so seeing a match can easily be tied into most visitors' itineraries, but tickets for the Premier League are like gold dust – your chances of bagging one are low unless you're a club member, or know someone who is. You're better off buying a ticket at one of the lower-division games – they're cheaper and more easily available. Tickets can often be bought on the spot, or at online agencies like www.ticketmaster.co.uk and www.myticketmarket.com.

Horse Racing

The tradition of horse racing in England stretches back centuries, with a 'meeting' somewhere in England pretty much every day. For all but the

THE SWEET FA CUP

The Football Association held its first interclub knockout tournament in 1871. Fifteen clubs took part, playing for a nice piece of silverware called the FA Cup – then worth about £20.

Nowadays, around 600 clubs compete for this legendary and priceless trophy. It differs from many other competitions in that every team – from the lowest-ranking part-timers to the stars of the Premier League – is in with a chance. The preliminary rounds begin in August, and the final is held in May at the iconic Wembley Stadium in London.

Manchester United has the most FA Cup victories, but public attention – and affection – is invariably focussed on the 'giant-killers': minor clubs that claw their way up through the rounds, unexpectedly beating higher-ranking competitors. The best-known giant-killing event occurred in 1992, when Wrexham, then ranked 24th in Division 3, famously beat league champions Arsenal. Other shock wins include nonleague Kidderminster Harriers' 1994 defeat of Birmingham City, and Oldham Athletic beating premier leaguers Manchester City in 2005.

In recent years, the FA Cup has become one football competition among many. The Premier League and Champion's League (against European teams) have higher profiles, bigger kudos, and simply more money to play with. But – just as the country gets behind the English national side – nothing raises community spirit more than a town team doing better than expected.

major events you should be able to get a ticket on the day - or buy in advance from the official site www.gotothe races.com.

The top event in the calendar is Royal Ascot (www.royalascot.co.uk) in mid-June, where the rich and famous come to see and be seen, and the fashion is almost as important as the horses. Other highlights include the Grand National steeplechase at Aintree in early April, and the Derby, run at Epsom on the first Saturday in June.

Rugby

A wit once said that football was a gentlemen's game played by hooligans, while rugby was the other way around. That may be true, but it's worth catching a game for the skill (OK, and brawn) and the fun atmosphere.

A highlight of the international rugby calendar is the annual Six Nations Championship, in which England battles against teams from Wales, Scotland, Ireland, France and Italy.

There are two versions of the game: Rugby Union (www.rfu.com) is played more in southern England, Wales and Scotland, and is traditionally thought of as the game of the middle and upper classes. Rugby League (www.therfl.com) is played predominantly in northern England, traditionally by the working classes. Today, leading rugby union clubs include Leicester, Bath and Gloucester, while London has a host of good-quality teams (including Wasps and Saracens). In rugby league, teams to watch include the Wigan Warriors, Bradford Bulls and Leeds Rhinos. Tickets for games cost around £15 to £40 depending on the club's status and fortunes.

Major events on the horizon are the Rugby League World Cup, with matches to be held at various venues around England and Wales in 2013 (plus some neighbouring countries, with the final played in Manchester), and the Rugby Union World Cup to be hosted by England in 2015, with the final played at Twickenham. For details see www.rugbyworldcup.com.

Tennis

Over 27 tonnes of strawberries and 7000L of cream are consumed every year during the two weeks of the Wimbledon Tennis Championships.

Tennis is widely played at club and regional level, but the best-known tournament is the All England Championships - known to all as Wimbledon (www.wimbledon.org) - when tennis fever sweeps through the country in the last week of June and first week of July. There's something quintessentially English about the combination of grass courts, polite applause and umpires in boaters, with strawberries and cream devoured by the truckload.

Demand for seats at Wimbledon always outstrips supply, but to give everyone an equal chance the tickets are sold through a public ballot. You can also take your chance on the spot; about 6000 tickets are sold each day (but not the last four days), but you'll need to be an early riser.

Survival Guide

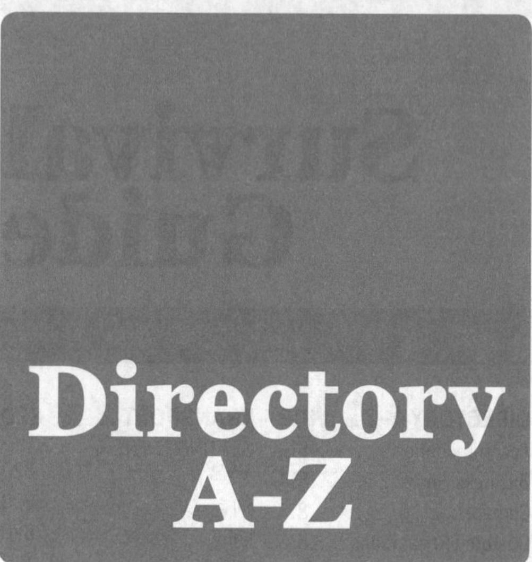

Directory A-Z

Accommodation

B&Bs & Guesthouses

The B&B (bed and breakfast) is a great British institution. At smaller places it's pretty much a room in somebody's house; larger places may be called a guesthouse – ie halfway between a B&B and a full hotel. Prices range from around £20 per person for a simple bedroom and shared bathroom, to around £25 to £30 when you get a private bathroom – either down the hall or en suite.

B&B prices are usually quoted per person, based on two people sharing a room. Single rooms are harder to find, and attract a 20% to 50% premium. Some B&Bs won't take singles (unless you pay the full double-room price), especially in summer.

» In country areas, B&Bs might be in a village or an isolated farm; in cities they're usually a suburban house.

» Advance reservations are preferred at B&Bs, and are essential during popular periods.

» You can book many B&Bs via online agencies, but rates may be cheaper if you book directly. If you haven't booked in advance, most towns have a main drag of B&Bs; those with spare rooms hang up a 'Vacancies' sign.

» Many B&Bs require a minimum two-night stay at weekends. Some places reduce rates for longer stays (two or three nights) midweek.

» Some smaller country B&Bs don't take credit/debit cards, so you'll need to pay with cash.

» If a B&B is full, owners may recommend another place nearby (possibly a private house taking occasional guests).

» In cities, some B&Bs are for long-term residents; they don't take passing tourists.

» In country areas most B&Bs cater for walkers and cyclists, but some don't, so let them know if you'll be turning up with dirty boots or wheels.

» Most B&Bs serve enormous breakfasts; some offer packed lunches (around £5) and evening meals (around £12 to £15).

» When booking, check where your B&B actually is. In country areas, postal addresses include the nearest town, which may be 20 miles away. Some B&B owners will pick you up by car for a small charge.

BOOK YOUR STAY ONLINE

For more accommodation reviews by Lonely Planet authors, check out http://hotels.lonelyplanet.com. You'll find independent reviews, as well as recommendations on the best places to stay. Best of all, you can book online.

Bunkhouses & Camping Barns

A bunkhouse in England is a simple place, usually in country areas, with a communal sleeping area and bathroom, plus stoves for self-catering. You provide sleeping bag and possibly cooking gear. Most charge around £10 per person per night.

Camping barns are even more basic: usually converted farm buildings. Take everything you'd need to camp except the tent. Charges are from around £5 per person.

Camping

The opportunities for camping in England are numerous, ranging from farmers' fields with a tap and a basic toilet, costing from £3 per person per night, to smarter affairs with hot showers and many other facilities, charging up to £10. You usually need all your own kit.

England doesn't have huge sites of permanent tents, as found in France and some other countries, but a few campsites in England also offer self-catering accommodation in chalets, caravans, tepees and yurts. Some options are very stylish – dubbed 'glamping'.

ACCOMMODATION PRICE RANGES

The following price ranges have been used in our reviews of places to stay. Prices are all based on double room with private bathroom, in high season.

BUDGET	LONDON	ELSEWHERE
budget (£)	<£90	<£60
midrange (££)	£90-180	£60–130
top end (£££)	>£180	>£130

Hostels

There are two types of hostel in England: those run by the **Youth Hostel Association** (YHA; www.yha.org.uk) and independent hostels – most listed with **Independent Hostels** (www.independenthostelguide.co.uk). Hostels are widespread and are aimed at all types of travellers, young and old.

Some hostels in England are converted cottages, country houses and even castles – often in wonderful locations. Sleeping is usually in dorms; some hostels also have twin or four-bed rooms.

INDEPENDENT HOSTELS

In rural areas, independent hostels can be little more than a bunkhouse (charging about £7), or up to B&B standard (£15 or more). In cities, independent backpacker hostels are usually aimed at young budget travellers. Most are open 24-hours, with a lively atmosphere, range of rooms (doubles or dorms), bar, cafe, internet, wi-fi and laundry. Prices go from about £15 for a dorm bed to £35 for a bed in a private room.

YHA HOSTELS

A bed in a simple YHA hostel costs from £10. Hostels with more facilities are £15 to £20. London's YHA hostels cost from £25 (add £3 if you're not a YHA member). Payments with credit card are usually possible.

You don't *have* to be a member of the YHA (or another Hostelling International organisation) to stay at YHA hostels, but it's usually worth joining. Annual YHA membership costs £16; under-26s and families get discounts.

YHA prices vary according to demand and season. Book early for a Tuesday night in May and you'll get the best rate. Book late for a weekend in August and you'll pay top price – if there's space at all. We have generally quoted the cheaper rates (in line with those listed on the YHA's website); you may find yourself paying more.

YHA hostels tend to have complicated opening times and days, especially in remote locations or out of tourist season, so check before turning up.

Hotels

There's a massive choice of hotels in England, from small townhouses to grand country mansions, from no-frills locations to boutique hideaways. At the bargain end, singles/double rooms cost from £30/40. Move up the scale and you'll pay £100/150 or beyond.

If all you want is a place to get your head down, budget chain hotels can be a good option. Most are lacking in ambience, but who cares? You'll only be there for eight hours, and six of them you'll be asleep. Prices vary on demand: at quiet times twin-bed rooms start from £20; at the height of the tourist season you'll pay £45 or more. Budget chain options include the following:

Etap Hotels (www.etaphotel.com)

Hotel Formule 1 (www.hotelformule1.com)

Premier Inn (www.premierinn.com)

Travelodge (www.travelodge.co.uk)

Houseboats

A popular English holiday option is renting a houseboat on one of the country's picturesque waterways, combining accommodation and transport for a few days or a week. For information, websites include **UK Boat Hire** (www.ukboathire.com) and **Hoseasons**

NO SUCH THING AS A 'STANDARD' HOTEL RATE

It's worth noting that there's often no such thing as a 'standard' hotel rate in England. Many hotels, especially larger places or chains, vary their prices according to demand – or have different rates for online, phone or walk-in bookings – just like airlines and train operators. So if you book early for a night during low season, rates are cheap. Book late for a public holiday weekend and you'll pay a lot. However, if you're prepared to be flexible and leave booking to the very last minute you can sometimes get a bargain as rates may drop. The end result is you can pay anything from £19 to £190 for the very same hotel room. With that in mind, the hotel rates we quote are often guide prices only. B&B prices tend to much more consistent.

(www.hoseasons.co.uk). For budget travellers, 'floating hostels' include **Wandering Duck** (www.wanderingduck.co.uk).

Pubs & Inns

As well as selling drinks, many pubs and inns offer lodging, particularly in country areas. For bed and breakfast, you'll pay around £20 per person for a basic room, around £35 for something better. An advantage for solo tourists: pubs are more likely to have single rooms.

Rental Accommodation

If you want to stay put for a bit, renting for a week can be ideal. Choose from neat apartments in cities, or quaint old houses (always called 'cottages', whatever the size) in country areas. Cottages for four people cost between £200 and £600 in high season. Rates fall at quieter times, and you may be able to rent for a long weekend. Handy websites:

Bed & Breakfast Nationwide (www.bedandbreakfastnationwide.com)

Cottages4U (www.cottages4u.co.uk)

Hoseasons (www.hoseasons.co.uk)

National Trust (www.nationaltrust.org.uk/holidays)

Stilwell's (www.stilwell.co.uk)

University Accommodation

During vacations, many universities offer **accommodation** to visitors. You usually get a functional single bedroom, and self-catering flats are also available. Prices range from £20 to £50 per person.

Business Hours

Banks

» Monday to Friday, 9.30am until 4pm or 5pm.

» Saturday, main branches 9.30am to 1pm.

» Sunday closed.

Climate

London

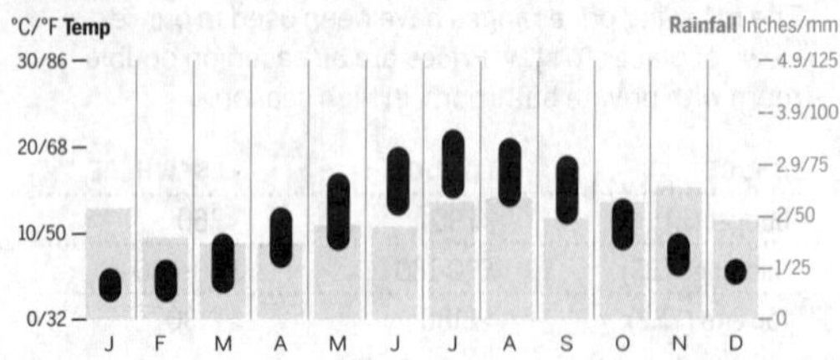

Bath

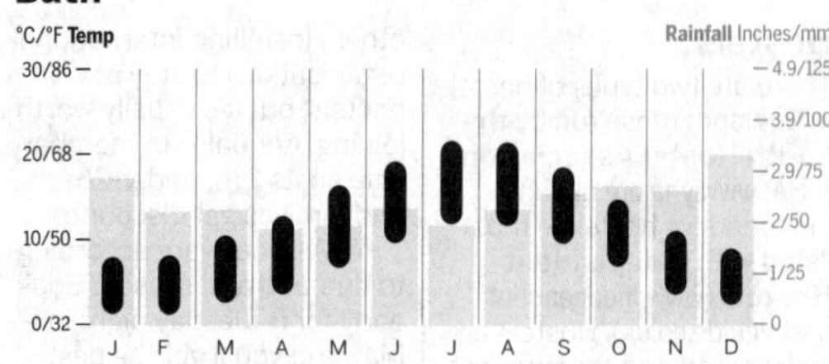

York

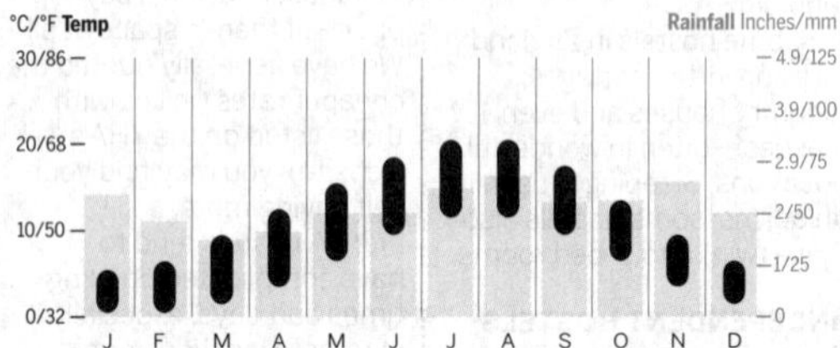

Bars, Pubs & Clubs

» Standard hours for pubs: 11am to 11pm Monday to Sunday. Some pubs shut 3pm to 6pm. Some pubs open to midnight or 1am Friday and Saturday.

» Standard hours for bars: 11am until midnight, often later, especially at weekends.

» Clubs open any time from 8pm to 10pm, until 2am or beyond.

Cafes & Restaurants

In this book, we work on the basis that most restaurants and cafes are open for lunch or dinner or both, so precise opening times and days are given only if they differ markedly from the patterns outlined here.

» Standard hours for cafes are 9am to 5pm. Most cafes open daily.

» In this book, where we specify 'breakfast & lunch' we mean open 9am to 5pm.

» In cities, some cafes open 7am for breakfast, then shut at 6pm or later.

» In country areas, some cafes open until 7pm or later in the summer. In winter months, country cafe hours are reduced; some close completely October to Easter.

» Standard hours for restaurants: lunch served from noon to 3pm; dinner served from 6pm to 11pm (to midnight or later in cities). Most restaurants open daily; some close Sunday evening or all day Monday.

» A few restaurants open for breakfast (usually 9am), but mainly cafes do this.

Museums & Sights

» Large museums and sights usually open daily.

» Some smaller places open Saturday and Sunday but close Monday and/or Tuesday.
» Smaller places open daily in high season; weekends only or completely closed in low season.

Post Offices

» Monday to Friday, same hours as shops.
» Saturday, 9am to 12.30pm. Main branches to 5pm.
» Sunday closed.

Shops

» Monday to Friday, 9am to 5pm (6pm in cities).
» Saturday, 9am to 5pm.
» Sunday, larger shops open 10am to 4pm.
» London and other cities have convenience stores open 24/7.
» In smaller towns and country areas, shops often shut for lunch (normally 1pm to 2pm) and on Wednesday or Thursday afternoon.

Customs Regulations

The UK has a two-tier customs system: one for goods bought duty-free outside the EU; the other for goods bought in another EU country where tax and duty is paid. For more information go to www.hmce.gov.uk and search for 'Customs Allowances'.

Duty Free

The duty-free limit for goods from *outside* the EU, include 200 cigarettes or equivalent in cigars, 4L of wine, 1L of spirits, 60cc of perfume, and other goods worth up to £390.

Tax & Duty Paid

There is no limit on goods from *within* the EU (if taxes have been paid), but customs officials use the following guidelines to distinguish personal use from commercial imports: 800 cigarettes, 200 cigars, 10L of spirits, 90L of wine and 110L of beer.

PRACTICALITIES

Newspapers & Magazines Leading tabloids include the *Sun* and *Mirror*; quality papers (from right to left, politically) include the *Telegraph, Times, Independent* and *Guardian*.

TV All TV in the UK is digital. Leading free-to-air options include BBC 1 and 2, and Channel 4. Satellite and cable broadcasters offer about 800 other channels.

DVD PAL format (incompatible with NTSC/Secam).

Weights & Measures England uses metric and imperial units. For length and distance, most people still use inches, feet, yards and miles, although mountain heights on maps are given in metres (m). For weight, goods in shops are measured in kilograms (kg), but Brits weigh themselves in stones, an archaic unit of 14lb. Most liquids are sold in litres (L), except milk and beer – available in pints. Garages sell petrol priced in pence per litre, but car performance is measured in miles per gallon. In this book we have reflected this wacky system of mixed measurements. Heights are given in metres and distances in miles and metres.

Electricity

230V/50Hz

Embassies & Consulates

The table (p816) gives a selection of embassies, consulates and high commissions in London. For a complete list of embassies in the UK, see the website of the **Foreign & Commonwealth Office** (www.fco.gov.uk), which also lists Britain's diplomatic missions overseas.

Gay & Lesbian Travellers

England is generally a tolerant place for gays and lesbians. London, Manchester and Brighton have flourishing gay scenes, and in other sizeable cities you'll find communities not entirely in the closet. That said, you'll still find pockets of homophobic hostility in some areas. Resources include the following:

Diva (www.divamag.co.uk)

Gay Times (www.gaytimes.co.uk)

London Lesbian & Gay Switchboard (☎0300 330 0630; www.llgs.org.uk)

Health

No immunisations are mandatory for visiting England or the rest of the UK.

EMBASSIES & CONSULATES IN LONDON

COUNTRY	PHONE	WEBSITE	ADDRESS
Australia	020-7887 5776	www.uk.embassy.gov.au	The Strand, WC2B 4LA
Canada	020-7258 6600	www.canada.org.uk	1 Grosvenor Sq, W1X 4AB
China	020-7299 4049	www.chinese-embassy.org.uk	Portland Pl, W1B 1QD
France	020-7073 1000	www.ambafrance-uk.org	58 Knightsbridge, SW1X 7JT
Germany	020-7824 1300	www.london.diplo.de	23 Belgrave Sq, SW1X 8PX
Ireland	020-7235 2171	www.embassyofireland.co.uk	17 Grosvenor Pl, SW1X 7HR
Japan	020-7465 6500	www.uk.emb-japan.go.jp	101 Piccadilly, W1J 7JT
Netherlands	020-7590 3200	www.netherlands-embassy.org.uk	38 Hyde Park Gate, SW7 5DP
New Zealand	020-7930 8422	www.nzembassy.com/uk	80 Haymarket, SW1Y 4TQ
Poland	020-7291 3520	www.londyn.polemb.net	47 Portland Pl, W1B 1HQ
USA	020-7499 9000	www.usembassy.org.uk	24 Grosvenor Sq, W1A 1AE

Regardless of nationality, everyone receives free emergency treatment at accident and emergency (A&E) departments of state-run NHS hospitals.

European Economic Area (EEA) nationals get free non-emergency treatment (ie the same service British citizens receive) with a European Health Insurance Card (EHIC) validated in their home country.

Reciprocal arrangements between the UK and some other countries (including Australia) allow free medical treatment at hospitals and surgeries, and subsidised dental care.

Chemists (pharmacies) can advise on minor ailments such as sore throats and earaches. In large cities, there's always at least one 24/7 chemist.

For more details see **Department of Health** (www.doh.gov.uk) – follow links to 'Health care', 'Entitlements' and 'Overseas Visitors'.

Heritage Organisations

A highlight of a journey through England is visiting the numerous castles and historic sites that pepper the country, many managed by the **National Trust** (NT; www.nationaltrust.org.uk) and **English Heritage** (EH; www.english-heritage.org.uk). Joining one or both of these organisations gets you free admission (a good saving, as individual entry to NT sites can be around £5, while EH sites range from free to about £6), as well as reciprocal arrangements with other heritage organisations (in Wales, Scotland and beyond), information handbooks and so on. You can join at the first NT or EH site you visit.

The National Trust is a charity protecting historic buildings and land with scenic importance. Annual membership costs £53 (with discounts for under-26s and families). A Touring Pass allows free entry to NT properties for one/two weeks (£23/28 per person); families and couples get cheaper rates.

English Heritage is a state-funded organisation responsible for numerous historic sites. Annual membership costs £47 (couples and seniors get discounts). An Overseas Visitors Pass allows free entry to most sites for nine/16 days for £23/27 (with cheaper rates for couples and families).

Insurance

Although everyone receives free emergency treatment, regardless of nationality, travel insurance is still highly recommended. It will usually cover medical and dental consultation and treatment at private clinics, which can be quicker than NHS places, as well as the cost of any emergency flights home – plus all the usual stuff such as loss of baggage. Worldwide travel insurance is available at www.lonelyplanet.com/travel_services. You can buy, extend and claim online any time – even if you're already on the road.

Internet Access

Internet cafes are surprisingly rare in England, especially away from big cities and tourist spots. Most charge from £1 per hour, and out in the sticks you can pay up to £5 per hour.

Public libraries often have computers with free internet access, but only for 30-minute slots, and demand is high. All the usual warnings apply about keystroke-capturing software and other security risks.

If you'll be using your laptop to get online, an increasing number of hotels, hostels, stations and coffee shops (even some trains) have wi-fi access, charging anything from nothing to £5 per hour.

Legal Matters

You must be over 18 to buy alcohol and cigarettes. You usually have to be 18 to enter a pub or bar, although rules are different if you have a meal. Some bars and clubs are over-21 only.

Illegal drugs are widely available, especially in clubs. Cannabis possession is a criminal offence; punishment for carrying a small amount may be a warning, a fine or imprisonment. Dealers face stiffer penalties, as do people caught with other drugs.

On buses and trains (including the London Underground), people without a valid ticket are fined on the spot – usually around £20.

Money

The currency of England (and the rest of the UK) is the pound sterling (£). Paper money comes in £5, £10, £20 and £50 denominations. Some shops don't accept £50 notes because fakes circulate.

For information on exchange rates, see p19.

GOVERNMENT TRAVEL ADVICE

The following government websites offer travel advisories and information on current hot spots.

Australian Department of Foreign Affairs (www.smarttraveller.gov.au)

Canadian Department of Foreign Affairs (www.voyage.gc.ca)

US State Department (http://travel.state.gov)

ATMs

ATMs (usually called 'cash machines' in England) are common in cities and even small towns. Watch out for tampered ATMs; a common ruse is to attach a card-reader or mini-camera.

Credit & Debit Cards

Visa and MasterCard credit and debit cards are widely accepted in England. Most businesses will assume your card is 'Chip and PIN' enabled (using a PIN instead of signing). If it isn't, you should be able to sign in the usual way, but some places may not accept your card. Some smaller country B&Bs don't take cards, so you'll need to pay with cash.

Moneychangers

Cities and larger towns have banks and bureaus for changing money. Rates and commissions are higher at airports; independent change bureaus may move a little on rates for larger transactions. You can also change money at some post offices in England; very handy in country areas, and exchange rates are fair.

Tipping

In England, you're not obliged to tip if the service or food was unsatisfactory (even if it's been automatically added to your bill as a 'service charge').

Restaurants Around 10%. Also teashops and cafes with full table service. At smarter restaurants waiters expect tips nearer 12% or 15%.

Taxis Around 10%, or rounded up to the nearest pound. It's less usual to tip minicab drivers.

Toilet attendants Around 50p.

Pubs Around 10% if you order food at the table and your meal is brought to you. If you order and pay at the bar (food or drinks), tips are not expected.

Public Holidays

In England and Wales, most businesses and banks close on these official public holidays (hence the term 'bank holiday'):

New Year's Day 1 January

Easter March/April (Good Friday to Easter Monday inclusive)

TRAVEL HEALTH WEBSITES

Before visiting England from overseas, consult your government's travel health website:

Australia (www.smarttraveller.gov.au)

Canada (www.publichealth.gc.ca/travel)

USA (www.cdc.gov/travel/)

May Day First Monday in May

Spring Bank Holiday Last Monday in May

Summer Bank Holiday Last Monday in August

Christmas Day 25 December

Boxing Day 26 December

If a public holiday falls on a weekend, the nearest Monday is usually taken instead.

On public holidays, some small museums and places of interest close, but larger attractions have their busiest times.

If a place closes on Sunday, it'll probably be shut on bank holidays as well.

Virtually everything – attractions, shops, banks, offices – closes on Christmas Day, although pubs are open at lunchtime. There's usually no public transport on Christmas Day, and a minimal service on Boxing Day.

Roads get busy and hotel prices go up during school holidays. Exact dates vary from year to year and region to region, but are roughly:

Easter Holiday Week before and week after Easter.

Summer Holiday Third week of July to first week of September.

Christmas Holiday Mid-December to first week of January.

There are also three week-long 'half-term' school holidays: usually late February (or early March), late May and late October.

Safe Travel

England is a remarkably safe country, but crime is not unknown in London and other cities. Watch out for pickpockets and hustlers in crowded tourist areas, such as around Westminster Bridge in London. When travelling by tube, tram or urban train service at night, choose a carriage containing other people.

Unlicensed minicabs – a bloke with a car earning money on the side – operate in large cities, but these are worth avoiding unless you know what you're doing. Annoyances include being driven around in circles, then charged an enormous fare. Dangers include being driven to a remote location then robbed or raped. To avoid this, use a metered taxi or phone a reputable minicab company and get an upfront quote for the ride.

Telephone Codes

Area codes

Area codes in Britain do not have a standard format or length, eg 020 for London, 0161 for Manchester, 01225 for Bath, 015394 for Ambleside, followed as usual by the individual number.

National codes

- 0500 or 0800 – free calls
- 0845 – calls at local rate, wherever you're dialling from within the UK
- 087 – national rate
- 089 or 09 – premium rate
- 07 – mobile phones, more expensive than calling a landline

International codes

To call outside the UK dial 00, then the country code (1 for USA, 61 for Australia etc), the area code (you usually drop the initial zero) and the number.

The international code for England (and the rest of the UK) is +44.

Operator

For help and reverse-charge (collect) calls:

- National operator 100
- International operator 155

Directory

For directory inquiries, a host of agencies compete for your business and charge from 10p to 40p; numbers include 118 192, 118 118, 118 500 and 118 811.

Time

In the winter, the country is on GMT/UTC 0. England and the rest of the UK uses daylight saving in summer (from late March to late October) so the time is GMT/UTC +1.

In summer, if it's noon in London, it's:

- 9pm in Melbourne, Australia.
- 7am in New York, USA.

Tourist Offices

All English cities and towns, and some villages, have a tourist information centre or visitor welcome centre. (We use the term 'tourist office' in this book to cover them all.) These places have helpful staff, books and maps for sale, leaflets to give away, and advice on things to see or do. Some can also assist with booking accommodation. Some tourist offices are run by national parks and also have small exhibits about the area.

TOURISM SITES

Before leaving home, check the informative, comprehensive and wide-ranging websites **Visit Britain** (www.visitbritain.com) and **Visit England** (www.visitengland.com), covering all angles of national tourism, with links to numerous other sites.

Most tourist offices keep regular business hours; in quiet areas they close from October to March, while in popular areas they open daily year-round.

Travellers with Disabilities

All new buildings have wheelchair access, and even hotels in grand old country houses often have lifts, ramps and other facilities. Smaller B&Bs are often harder to adapt, so you'll have less choice there.

In cities, new buses have low floors for easy access, but few have conductors who can lend a hand when you're getting on or off. Many taxis take wheelchairs, or just have more room in the back.

For long-distance travel, coaches may present problems if you can't walk, but the main operator, **National Express** (www.nationalexpress.com) has wheelchair-friendly coaches on many routes. For details, ring their dedicated Disabled Passenger Travel Helpline on ☎0121-423 8479 or try the main website.

On intercity trains there's more room and better facilities, and usually station staff around; just have a word and they'll be happy to help out. A **Disabled Person's Railcard** (www.disabledpersons-railcard.co.uk) costs £20 and gets you 33% off most train fares.

Useful organisations:

Disability Rights UK (www.disabilityrightsuk.org) Published titles include a *Holiday Guide*. Other services include a key for 7000 public disabled toilets across the UK.

Good Access Guide (www.goodaccessguide.co.uk)

Tourism For All (www.tourismforall.org.uk)

Visas

If you're a European Economic Area (EEA) national, you don't need a visa to visit (or work in) England or any other part of the UK. Citizens of Australia, Canada, New Zealand, South Africa and the USA are given leave to enter the UK at their point of arrival for up to six months (three months for some nationalities), but are prohibited from working. For more info see www.ukba.homeoffice.gov.uk.

Work

Nationals of most European countries don't need a permit to work in England, but everyone else does. Exceptions include most Commonwealth citizens with a UK-born parent; the 'Right of Abode' allows you to live and work in England and the rest of the UK.

Commonwealth citizens under 31 are usually eligible for a Working Holidaymaker Visa – valid for two years, you can work for a total of 12 months, and it must be obtained in advance.

Useful websites include www.ukba.homeoffice.gov.uk and www.workpermit.com. Also very handy is the 'Living & Working Abroad' thread on the Thorntree forum at www.lonelyplanet.com.

Transport

GETTING THERE & AWAY

London is a global transport hub, so you can easily fly to England from just about anywhere. In recent years, the massive growth of budget ('no-frills') airlines has increased the number of routes – and reduced the fares – between England and other countries in Europe.

Your other main option between England and mainland Europe is ferry, either port-to-port or combined with a long-distance bus trip, although journeys can be long and financial savings not huge compared with budget airfares.

International trains are comfortable (and a 'greener' option); the Channel Tunnel allows direct rail services between England, France and Belgium, with onward connections to other European destinations.

Getting from England to Scotland and Wales is easy. The bus and train systems are fully integrated and in most cases you won't even know you've crossed the border.

Flights, tours and rail tickets can be booked online at www.lonelyplanet.com/bookings.

Air

Airports

London's main airports are listed here. For details of getting from the airport into the city, see Getting Around in the London chapter (p134).

Heathrow (LHR; www.heathrowairport.com) The UK's main airport for international flights; often chaotic and crowded. About 15 miles west of central London.

Gatwick (LGW; www.gatwickairport.com) Britain's number-two airport, mainly for international flights, 30 miles south of central London.

Stansted (STN; www.stanstedairport.com) About 35 miles northeast of central London, mainly handling charter and budget European flights.

Luton (LTN; www.london-luton.co.uk) Some 35 miles north of central London, well-known as a holiday-flight airport.

London City (LCY; www.londoncityairport.com) A few miles east of central London, specialising in flights to/from European and other UK airports.

Regional Airports

Major regional airports in England include Manchester (with European and long-haul routes), while smaller regional airports such as Southampton and Birmingham are served by flights to/from continental Europe and Ireland.

Land

Bus & Coach

You can easily get between England and other European countries via long-distance

CLIMATE CHANGE & TRAVEL

Every form of transport that relies on carbon-based fuel generates CO_2, the main cause of human-induced climate change. Modern travel is dependent on aeroplanes, which might use less fuel per kilometre per person than most cars but travel much greater distances. The altitude at which aircraft emit gases (including CO_2) and particles also contributes to their climate change impact. Many websites offer 'carbon calculators' that allow people to estimate the carbon emissions generated by their journey and, for those who wish to do so, to offset the impact of the greenhouse gases emitted with contributions to portfolios of climate-friendly initiatives throughout the world. Lonely Planet offsets the carbon footprint of all staff and author travel.

bus or coach. The international network **Eurolines** (www.eurolines.com) connects a huge number of destinations; buy tickets online via one of the national operators.

Services to/from England are operated by **National Express** (www.nationalexpress.com). Some sample journey times to/from London:

Amsterdam 12 hours.
Barcelona 24 hours.
Dublin 12 hours.
Paris Eight hours.

Long-Distance Bus Fares

If you book early, and can be flexible with timings (ie travel when few other people want to) you can get some very good deals, for example, London to Paris or Amsterdam from about £10 one way (although paying nearer £30 is more usual).

Channel Tunnel Train Services

PASSENGER SERVICE

High-speed **Eurostar** (www.eurostar.com) passenger services hurtle at least 10 times daily between London and Paris (2½ hours) or Brussels (two hours). Buy tickets from travel agencies, major train stations or direct from the Eurostar website. The normal one-way fare between London and Paris/Brussels is around £150 to £180; advance booking and off-peak travel gets you cheaper fares as low as £40 one-way.

CAR SERVICE

Drivers use **Eurotunnel** (www.eurotunnel.com). At Folkestone in England or Calais in France, you drive onto a train, get carried through the tunnel, and then drive off at the other end. The trains run about four times an hour from 6am to 10pm, then hourly. Loading and unloading is an hour; the journey takes 35 minutes. Book in advance online or pay on the spot. The one-way cost for a car and passengers is around £70 to £150 depending on time of day (less busy times are cheaper); promotional fares often bring it nearer to £50.

TRAIN & FERRY CONNECTIONS

As well as Eurostar, many 'normal' trains run between England and mainland Europe. You buy one ticket, but get off the train at the port, walk onto a ferry, then get another train on the other side. Main routes include Amsterdam to London (via Hook of Holland and Harwich). Between Ireland and England, the main train-ferry-train route is Dublin to London, via Dun Laoghaire and Holyhead. Ferries also run from Rosslare to Fishguard in Wales, with train connections on either side.

Sea

The main ferry routes between England and other European countries include:

- Dover to Calais (France)
- Dover to Boulogne (France)
- Harwich to Hook of Holland (Netherlands)
- Hull to Zeebrugge (Belgium)
- Hull to Rotterdam (Netherlands)
- Portsmouth to Santander (Spain)
- Portsmouth to Bilbao (Spain)
- Holyhead (Wales) to Dun Laoghaire (Ireland)
- Fishguard (Wales) to Rosslare (Ireland)

Ferry Fares

Most ferry operators offer flexible fares, meaning there are great bargains at quiet times of the day or year. For example, short cross-channel routes such as Dover to Calais or Boulogne can be as low as £20 for a car plus up to five passengers, although around £50 is more likely. If you're a foot passenger, or cycling, there's less need to book ahead; cheap fares on short crossings start from about £10 each way.

Ferry Booking

You can book direct with one of the ferry operators listed below, or use the very handy www.ferrybooker.com, a single site covering all sea-ferry routes, plus Eurotunnel.

Brittany Ferries (www.brittany-ferries.com)
DFDS Seaways (www.dfdseaways.co.uk)
Irish Ferries (www.irishferries.com)
LD Lines (www.ldlines.co.uk)
P&O Ferries (www.poferries.com)
Stena Line (www.stenaline.com)

GETTING AROUND

For getting around England, your first decision is whether to go by car or public transport. Having your own car makes the best use of time, and helps reach remote places, but rental and fuel costs can be expensive for budget travellers, while the trials of traffic jams in major cities hit everyone – so public transport is often the better way to go.

Your main public transport options are train and long-distance bus (called coach in England). Services between major towns and cities are generally good, although at 'peak' (busy) times you must book in advance to be sure of getting a ticket. Also, if you book ahead early and/or travel at 'off-peak' periods, tickets can be very cheap.

As long as you have time, by using a mix of train, coach, local bus, the odd taxi, walking and occasionally hiring a bike, you can get almost anywhere without having to drive. You'll certainly see more of the countryside than you might slogging along grey motorways.

Air

Airlines serving domestic routes in England include British Airways, easyJet and Ryanair, but flights aren't really necessary for tourists; even if you're going from one end of the country to the other (eg London to Newcastle, or Manchester to Newquay) trains compare favourably with planes, once airport down-time is factored in. On costs, you might get a bargain airfare, but with advance planning trains can still be cheaper.

Bicycle

Renting a bike for an hour or two, or a week or longer, is a great way to see the country if you've time to spare.

London

London is famous for its Barclays Cycle Hire Scheme (known as 'Boris bikes' after the mayor that introduced them to the city). Bikes can be hired on the spot from automatic docking stations. For info see p135, or go to Transport for London (www.tfl.gov.uk) and follow the links to Cycling. Other rental options in the capital are listed at www.lcc.org.uk.

Around the Country

Tourist towns such as Oxford and Cambridge have plentiful bike rental options, and bikes can also be hired in national parks or forestry sites now primarily used for leisure activities, such as Grizedale Forest in the Lake District. In some areas, disused railway lines are now bike routes, notably the Peak District in Derbyshire. Rates start at about £10 per day, or £20 for something half decent.

HOW MUCH TO...?

When travelling long-distance by train or bus/coach in England, it's important to realise there's no such thing as a standard fare. Prices vary according to demand and when you buy your ticket. Book well in advance and travel on Tuesday mid-morning, and it's cheap. Buy your ticket on the spot late Friday afternoon, and it will be a lot more expensive. Ferries use similar systems. We have generally quoted *sample* fares somewhere in between the very cheapest and most expensive options. The price you pay will almost certainly be different.

Bus & Coach

If you're on a tight budget, long-distance buses (called coaches in England) are nearly always the cheapest way to get around, although they're also the slowest – sometimes by a considerable margin. Many towns have separate bus and coach stations; make sure you go to the right place.

National Express (www.nationalexpress.com) is the main coach operator, with a wide network and frequent services between main centres. Fares are cheaper if you book in advance and travel at quieter times, and more expensive if you buy your ticket on the spot and it's Friday afternoon. As a guide, a 200-mile trip (eg London to York) will cost around £15 to £20 if you book a few days in advance.

Megabus (www.megabus.com) operates a budget-airline-style coach service between about 30 destinations around the country. Go at a quiet time, book early, and your ticket will be very cheap. Book later, for a busy time and...you get the picture.

Short-distance and local bus services are covered under Local Transport in this chapter.

Passes & Discounts

National Express offers discount passes to full-time students and under-26s, called Young Persons Coachcards. They cost £10 and get you 30% off standard adult fares. Also available are coachcards for people over 60, families and disabled travellers.

For touring the country, National Express offers Brit Xplorer passes, allowing unlimited travel for seven days (£79), 14 days (£139) and 28 days (£219). You don't need to book journeys in advance; if the coach has a spare seat, you can take it.

Car & Motorcycle

Travelling by car or motorbike around England means you can be independent and flexible, and reach remote places. Downsides for drivers include traffic jams and high parking costs in cities.

Car Rental

Compared with many countries (especially the USA), rental rates are expensive in England; the smallest cars start from about £120 per week, and around £250 per week for a medium car. All rates include unlimited mileage, and can rise at busy times (or drop at quiet times).

Some main players:

Avis (www.avis.co.uk)

Budget (www.budget.co.uk)

Europcar (www.europcar.co.uk)

Sixt (www.sixt.co.uk)
Thrifty (www.thrifty.co.uk)

Another option is to look online for small local car-hire companies in England that undercut the international franchises. Generally those in cities are cheaper than in rural areas. See a rental-broker site such as **UK Car Hire** (www.ukcarhire.net).

Drinking & Driving

Drinking and driving is taken very seriously in England; you're allowed a maximum blood-alcohol level of 80mg/100mL (0.08%).

Insurance

It's illegal to drive a car or motorbike in England without (at least) third-party insurance. This will be included with all rental cars. If you're bringing your own car, you will need to arrange this.

Motorhome Rental

Hiring a motorhome or campervan is more expensive than hiring a car, but saves on accommodation costs, and gives almost unlimited freedom. Sites to check include:

Just Go (www.justgo.uk.com)
Wild Horizon (www.wildhorizon.co.uk)

Parking

Many cities in England have short-stay and long-stay car parks; the latter are cheaper though may be less convenient. 'Park & Ride' systems allow you to park on the edge of the city then ride to the centre on regular nonstop buses for an all-in-one price.

Yellow lines along the edge of the road indicate parking restrictions. Find the nearby sign that spells out when you can and can't park. In London and other big cities, traffic wardens operate with efficiency; if you park on yellow lines at the wrong time, your car will be clamped or towed away, and it'll cost you £100 or more to get driving again. In some cities there are also red lines, which mean no stopping at all. Ever.

Roads

Motorways and main A-roads deliver you quickly from one end of the country to another. Lesser A-roads, B-roads and minor roads are much more scenic, ideal for car or motorcycle touring. You can't travel fast, but you won't care.

Rules

A foreign driving licence is valid in England for up to 12 months. Some other important rules include:

» drive on the left
» wear fitted seat belts in cars
» wear crash helmets on motorcycles
» give way to your right at junctions and roundabouts
» always use the left-side lane on motorways and dual-carriageways, unless overtaking (so many people ignore this rule, you'd think it didn't exist)
» don't use a mobile phone while driving unless it's fully hands-free (another rule frequently flouted)

Speed limits

The speed limits in England are:

» 30mph (48km/h) in built-up areas
» 60mph (96km/h) on main roads
» 70mph (112km/h) on motorways and most (but not all) dual carriageways

MOTORING ORGANISATIONS

Organisations include the **Automobile Association** (www.theaa.com) and the **Royal Automobile Club** (www.rac.co.uk); annual membership starts at around £30, including 24-hour roadside breakdown assistance. A greener alternative is the **Environmental Transport Association** (www.eta.co.uk); it provides all the usual services (breakdown assistance, roadside rescue, vehicle inspections etc) but doesn't campaign for more roads.

Hitching

Hitchhiking is not as common as it used to be, maybe because more people have cars or because few drivers stop. It's a perfectly feasible way to get around though, if you don't mind long waits, although travellers should understand that they're taking a small but potentially serious risk, and we don't recommend it. If you decide to hitch, note that it's illegal on motorways; you must use approach roads or service stations.

Local Transport

English cities usually have good local public transport systems – a combination of bus, train and tram – often run by a confusing number of separate companies. Tourist offices can provide maps and information.

Local Bus

There are good local bus networks in cities and towns. Buses also run in some rural areas year-round, although timetables are designed to serve schools and businesses, so services are limited around midday and at weekends (and may stop completely during school holidays), or may link local villages to a market town on only one day each week.

In tourist areas (especially national parks) there are frequent services from Easter to September. It's always worth double-checking at a tourist office before planning your day's activities around a bus that may not actually be running.

In this book, we give local bus route numbers, frequency and duration, and provide indicative prices if the fare is over £5. If it's less than this, we have generally omitted the fare.

LOCAL BUS PASSES

If you're taking several local bus rides in one area, one-day or three-day passes (with names like Rover, Wayfarer or Explorer) are cheaper than buying several single tickets. Often they can be bought on your first bus, and may also include local rail services. It's always worth asking ticket clerks or bus drivers about your options.

Taxi

There are two sorts of taxi in England: those which have meters and can be hailed in the street; and minicabs, which are cheaper but can only be called by phone. Unlicensed minicabs operate in some cities; see the advice under Safe Travel.

In London, most taxis are the famous 'black cabs' (some with advertising livery in other colours) which charge by distance and time. Depending on the time of day, a 1-mile journey takes five to 10 minutes and costs £5 to £9. Longer journeys are proportionally cheaper. Taxis are best flagged down in the street; a 'for hire' light on the roof indicates availability.

In rural areas, taxis need to be phoned. Fares are around £2 to £3 per mile. The best place to find the local taxi's phone number is the local pub.

Handy resources include:

National Cabline (☎0800 123444) Call from a landline phone; the service pinpoints your location and transfers you to an approved local taxi company.

Train-Taxi (www.traintaxi.co.uk) Portal site to help 'bridge the final gap' between the train station and your hotel or other final destination.

Train

For long-distance travel around England, trains are generally faster and more comfortable than coaches but can be more expensive, although with discount tickets they're competitive – and often take you through beautiful countryside. The English like to moan about their trains, but around 85% run on time. The other 15% that get delayed or cancelled mostly affect commuter services rather than long-distance journeys.

Train Operators

About 20 different companies operate train services in Britain (for example: First Great Western trains run from London to Bristol, Cornwall and South Wales; Virgin Trains run from London to Birmingham, Liverpool, Carlisle and Scotland), while Network Rail operates track and stations. For some passengers this system can be confusing at first, but information and ticket-buying services are mostly centralised. If you have to change trains, or use two or more train operators, you still buy one ticket that's valid for the whole of your journey. The main railcards are also accepted by all operators.

Information

Your first stop should be **National Rail Enquiries** (☎08457 48 49 50; www.nationalrail.co.uk), the nationwide timetable and fare information service. This site also advertises special offers, and has real-time links to station departure boards.

For planning your trip, some very handy maps of the UK's rail network can be downloaded from the National Rail Enquiries website.

Buying Train Tickets

Once you've found the journey you need, links take you to the relevant train opera-

BIKES ON TRAINS

Bicycles can be taken free of charge on most local urban trains (although they may not be allowed at peak times when the trains are too crowded with commuters) and on shorter trips in rural areas, on a first-come, first-served basis. Bikes can be carried on long-distance train journeys free of charge as well, but advance booking is required for most conventional bikes. (Folding bikes can be carried on pretty much any train at any time.) In theory, this shouldn't be too much trouble as most long-distance rail trips are best bought in advance anyway, but you have to go a long way down the path of booking your seat, before you start booking your bike – only to find space for it isn't available. A better course of action is to buy in advance at a major rail station, where the booking clerk can help you through the options, or phone the relevant operator's Customer Service department. Have a large cup of coffee and a stress-reliever handy. And a final warning: when railways are being repaired, cancelled trains are replaced by buses – and they won't take bikes.

A very useful leaflet called '*Cycling by Train*' is available at major stations or downloadable from www.nationalrail.co.uk (from the homepage follow links to 'Stations & On-train' then 'Cyclists').

STATION NAMES

London has several mainline train stations, such as Victoria, Paddington, King's Cross, Waterloo, Charing Cross and Liverpool St, positioned in a rough circle around the city's central area (and mostly linked by the Circle underground line). The stations' proper names are London Victoria, London Paddington, London King's Cross and so on, and this is how you'll see them on official timetables, information boards and booking websites, although the English never use the full names in everyday speech.

In this book, we have used the full name for London stations. This is to help distinguish the London stations from stations in some other British cities that also share names such as Victoria and Charing Cross.

tor to buy the ticket. If you buy online, you can have the ticket posted (UK addresses only), or collect it at the station on the day of travel from automatic machines. There's usually no booking fee on top of the ticket price.

You can also use a centralised ticketing service to buy your train ticket. These cover all train services in a single site, and make a small booking fee on top of every ticket price. The main players:

QJump (www.qjump.co.uk)
Rail Easy (www.raileasy.co.uk)
Train Line (www.thetrainline.com)

To use operator or centralised ticketing websites you always have to state a preferred time and day of travel, even if you don't mind when you go, but you can change it as you go through the process, and with a little delving around you can find some real bargains.

You can also buy train tickets on the spot at stations, which is fine for short journeys (under about 50 miles), but discount tickets for longer trips are usually not available and must be bought in advance by phone or online.

Ticket Costs & Reservations

For longer journeys, on-the-spot fares are always available, but tickets are much cheaper if bought in advance. The earlier you book, the cheaper it gets. You also save if you travel 'off-peak' (ie the days and times that aren't busy). Buying online usually gets a reserved seat too.

Whichever operator you travel with and wherever you buy tickets, these are the three main fare types:

Anytime Buy ticket any time, travel any time.
Off-peak Buy ticket any time, travel off-peak.
Advance Buy ticket in advance, travel only on specific trains.

For an idea of the price difference, an Anytime single ticket from London to York will cost around £100, an Off-peak around £80, while an Advance is around £20, and even less if you book early enough or don't mind arriving at midnight. The cheapest fares are non-refundable; if you miss your train you'll need a new ticket.

Classes

There are two classes of rail travel: 1st and standard. First class costs around 50% more than standard and, except on very crowded trains, is not really worth it. At weekends some train operators offer 'upgrades' for an extra £10 to £15 on top of your standard class fare.

Onward Travel

If trains don't get you all the way to your destination, get a **PlusBus** (www.plusbus.info) supplement to validate your train ticket for onward travel. This is more convenient, and usually cheaper, than buying a separate bus ticket.

Train Passes

LOCAL & REGIONAL PASSES

Local train passes usually cover rail networks around a city (many include bus travel too), and are detailed in the relevant sections throughout this book.

If you're concentrating on travels in southeast England (eg London to Dover, Weymouth, Cambridge or Oxford), a **Network Railcard** (www.railcard.co.uk/network; per year £28) covers up to four adults and up to four children travelling together, and gets good discounts on train travel outside peak times.

DISCOUNT PASSES

If you're staying in England awhile, **Railcard** (www.railcard.co.uk) passes are available:

16-25 Railcard For those aged 16 to 25, or a full-time UK student.
Family & Friends Railcard Covers up to four adults and four children.
Senior Railcard For anyone over 60.

Railcards cost £28 (valid for one year, available from major stations or online) and get you a 33% discount on most train fares, except those already heavily discounted. With the Family card, adults get 33% and children get 60% discounts, so the fee is easily repaid in a couple of journeys.

NATIONAL PASSES

For countrywide travel, a **BritRail Pass** (www.britrail.com) is available to overseas visitors. It must be bought in your country of origin from a travel agency. Available in three versions (England only; all Britain; UK and Ireland) for periods from four to 30 days.

almshouse – accommodation for the aged or needy

bloke – man (colloquial)
bridleway – path or track that can be used by walkers, horse riders and cyclists
Brummie – native of Birmingham

chemist – pharmacist
circus – junction of several city streets, usually circular, and usually with a green or other feature at the centre
coasteering – adventurous activity that involves making your way around a rocky coastline by climbing, scrambling, jumping or swimming

downs – rolling hills, characterised by lack of trees
duvet – quilt replacing sheets and blankets ('doona' to Australians)

evensong – daily evening service (Church of England)

fell race – tough running race through hills or moors
fen – drained or marshy low-lying flat land
fiver – five-pound note (colloquial)
flat – apartment (colloquial)
flip-flops – plastic sandals with a single strap over toes ('thongs' to Australians)
footpath – path through countryside or between houses in towns and cities, not beside a road (that's called a 'pavement')

guv, **guvner** – from governor, a colloquial but respectful term of address for owner or boss; can sometimes be used ironically

inn – pub with accommodation

lift – machine for carrying people up and down in large buildings ('elevator' to Americans)
lock – part of a canal or river that can be closed off and the water levels changed to raise or lower boats

mad – insane (not angry, as in American English)
Marches –borderlands between England and Wales, after the Anglo-Saxon word *mearc*, meaning 'boundary'
motorway – major road linking cities (equivalent to 'interstate' or 'freeway')
motte – mound on which a castle was built

naff – inferior, in poor taste (colloquial)

p (pronounced 'pee') – pence (ie 2p is 'two p' not 'two pence' or 'tuppence')
postbus – minibus delivering the mail, also carrying passengers – found in remote areas
punter – customer (colloquial)

quid – pound (colloquial)

ramble – short easy walk

RSPB – Royal Society for the Protection of Birds

sarsen – boulder, a geological remnant usually found in chalky areas (sometimes used in neolithic constructions eg Stonehenge and Avebury)

tenner – £10 note (colloquial)
tor – pointed hill
Tory – Conservative (political party)
towpath – path running beside a river or canal, where horses once towed barges
twitcher – obsessive birdwatcher
Tube, the – London's underground railway system (colloquial)

Underground, the – London's underground railway system

verderer – officer upholding law and order in the royal forests

wolds – open, rolling countryside

YHA – Youth Hostels Association

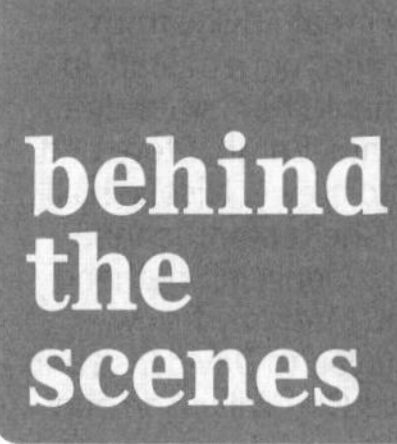

SEND US YOUR FEEDBACK

We love to hear from travellers – your comments keep us on our toes and help make our books better. Our well-travelled team reads every word on what you loved or loathed about this book. Although we cannot reply individually to postal submissions, we always guarantee that your feedback goes straight to the appropriate authors, in time for the next edition. Each person who sends us information is thanked in the next edition – the most useful submissions are rewarded with a selection of digital PDF chapters.

Visit **lonelyplanet.com/contact** to submit your updates and suggestions or to ask for help. Our award-winning website also features inspirational travel stories, news and discussions.

Note: We may edit, reproduce and incorporate your comments in Lonely Planet products such as guidebooks, websites and digital products, so let us know if you don't want your comments reproduced or your name acknowledged. For a copy of our privacy policy visit lonelyplanet.com/privacy.

OUR READERS

Many thanks to the travellers who used the last edition and wrote to us with helpful hints, useful advice and interesting anecdotes:

A Liam Allerton, Joanne Ashby, Andrew Askins B Pete Badham, William Ballantine, Yana Bey, Martin Brewin C Tim Corke, Bill Cranston D Owen Davies, Alastair Dimech, Eean Doleman E Simon Eaton F Matthew Fuller G Dr David Gibson, Dara Gilroy, Lee Griffin H Alice Haigh, Jason Hollingsworth J Dave Jackson, Kenneth Jefferies, Andy Joyce K Matt Kane L Mike Laity, Hayley Lewis, Annie Liggins, Matthew Lombardi M Lucinda Macpherson, Stefan R Mailvaganam, Shomi Malik, Trevor Mazzucchelli, Curtis Miller, Caroline Molenaar, Valentin Monn O Bertrand Olivier P Olivier Pirard, Peter the Pirate, Gemma Purves R Annette Rees, Lisa Roberts, David Robinson, Harris Rothschild, Graham Rutter S Marli Sadzinski, Arran Scott, Thomas Shingler, Richie Smith-Gore, Sue Spivey, Nicolae Stegozu, Michael Stock T Gemma Taylor, Susie Thornhill W Simon Wardle, Nigel Westwood, Kelly Widley, Valerie Wood, Carol Wright

AUTHOR THANKS

David Else

As always, massive appreciation goes to my wife Corinne, for joining me on many of my research trips around England, and for not minding when I locked myself away for 12 hours at a time to write this book – and for bringing coffee when it gets nearer 16 hours. Thanks also to the co-authors of this book; my name goes down as coordinating author, but I couldn't have done it without this team. Finally, thanks to Cliff Wilkinson, my commissioning editor at Lonely Planet London, and to all the friendly faces in the production department at Lonely Planet Melbourne who helped bring this book to final fruition.

Oliver Berry

Thanks to Cliff Wilkinson for the England gig, David Else for keeping us on course, Belinda Dixon for co-authoring and moral support, and David Carroll, Dan Corbett and the rest of the SPP team for being there whenever we needed you! Special thanks to Susie, Molly and Gracie Berry, and to all the people I met out on the road.

Fionn Davenport

A huge thanks to John Ryan, Emma Fox, Andy Parkinson, Louise Latham, Andrew Stokes, Erica Dillon, Sylvia O'Malley, Tina Snowball and

Andy Hook. As always, thanks to Caroline for putting up with me.

Marc Di Duca

A huge 'ta' goes to all the staff at tourist offices across the Southeast (those that haven't been axed, that is) but especially the helpful guys in Brighton, Hastings, Canterbury and Rye. Also thanks to David Else for his guidance throughout, Therese at Canterbury Cathedral and my Kyiv parents-in-law Mykola and Vira for looking after our son Taras while I was on the road. And last, but certainly not least, heartfelt gratitude must go to my wife Tanya, for all those long days we spend apart.

Belinda Dixon

Huge thanks go to Lonely Planet's behind-the-scenes team who magic the words from my battered notebooks onto the shelves (technical wizards, take an oh-so-hard-earned bow); Cliff for the gig; everyone encountered on the road for tips, facts and countless kindnesses; and JL for (still) making me smile.

Damian Harper

My hat is off to a long list of helpful people, including Daniel Hands, Bill Moran, Matthew Scudamore, Daisy Harper, George Whitman, Jane Egginton, Richard Samuels and the helpful staff at Waterstone's (Piccadilly). A slap on the back for the folk of the West Midlands and London for unflagging chirpiness in the face of driving rain would not go amiss, while big thanks are further extended to the staff at Lonely Planet for helping in the production of this book.

Anna Kaminski

I'm grateful for all the great advice from friends, family, locals and tourism staff. In particular, I'd like to thank the Cambridge crew – Subo, Dawn, Sara, Sarah, Steve and my parents; the Oxford crew – Nicolas, Bill and Georgia; Colin in Cheltenam; Joanna and Gabriel Dick in Ely; Genie in Southend-on-Sea; and Sonia and Matt, my fellow gourmets. A big thank you to David Else and commissioning editors Cliff Wilkinson and Katie O'Connell.

Catherine Le Nevez

Cheers first and foremost to Julian, and to all of the locals, tourism professionals and fellow travellers who provided insights, inspiration and good times throughout Nottingham and the East Midlands. Thanks especially to Ade Andrews (and Erin Huckle) for the interview, and to Becca and crew for the castle adventure. Thanks also to David Else, Cliff Wilkinson, Katie O'Connell, Angela Tinson, Mandy Sierp and everyone at Lonely Planet. As ever, *merci encore* to my parents, brother and *belle-soeur*.

Neil Wilson

Thanks to the many Yorkshire folk who freely offered advice and recommendations, to the tourist office staff for answering dumb questions, and to the eerie Andy Dextrous in York. Thanks also to Lonely Planet's editors and cartographers, and to Carol for her company in York and Harrogate's restaurants.

THIS BOOK

This 7th edition of *England* was researched and written by David Else (coordinating author), Oliver Berry, Fionn Davenport, Marc Di Duca, Belinda Dixon, Damian Harper, Anna Kaminski, Catherine Le Nevez and Neil Wilson. The book was commissioned in Lonely Planet's London office, and produced by the following people:

Commissioning Editor Katie O'Connell, Clifton Wilkinson
Coordinating Editors Evan Jones, Ross Taylor
Coordinating Cartographer Eve Kelly
Coordinating Layout Designer Nicholas Colicchia
Managing Editors Brigitte Ellemor, Angela Tinson
Senior Editor Andi Jones
Managing Cartographers Shahara Ahmed, Amanda Sierp
Managing Layout Designer Chris Girdler
Assisting Editors Alice Barker, Laura Gibb, Kate Kiely, Pat Kinsella, Helen Koehne, Robyn Loughnane, Kate Mathews, Lucy Monie, Anne Mulvaney, Luna Soo, Tracy Whitmey
Assisting Cartographers Anita Banh, Xavier Di Toro, Julie Dodkins, Heinz von Eckartsberg, Joelene Kowalski, Robert Townsend, Samantha Tyson
Cover Research Naomi Parker
Internal Image Research Kylie McLaughlin
Illustrator Javier Zarracina
Thanks to Dan Austin, Kate Chapman, Daniel Corbett, Barbara Delissen, Ryan Evans, Jennifer Fernández, Samantha Forge, Larissa Frost, Jouve India, Asha Ioculari, Kate McDonnell, Darren O'Connell, Mardi O'Connor, Silvia Rosas, Danny Williams, Alison Ridgway, Averil Robertson, Dianne Schallmeiner, Fiona Siseman, Branislava Vladisavljevic, Diana Von Holdt, Gerard Walker

ACKNOWLEDGMENTS

Climate map data adapted from Peel MC, Finlayson BL & McMahon TA (2007) 'Updated World Map of the Köppen-Geiger Climate Classification', *Hydrology and Earth System Sciences*, 11, 163344.

Illustrations pp70-1, pp80-1, pp746-7 byJavier Zarracina.
Cover photograph:Bamburgh Castle on the Northumberland coast, Rainer Mirau / 4Corners©.

Index

Map Pages **000**
Photo Pages 000

D

E

Map Pages **000**
Photo Pages 000

M

Map Pages **000**
Photo Pages **000**

Map Pages **000**
Photo Pages **000**

O

P

Q

R

Map Pages **000**
Photo Pages **000**

T

Map Pages **000**
Photo Pages **000**

how to use this book

These symbols will help you find the listings you want:

- Sights
- Beaches
- Activities
- Courses
- Tours
- Festivals & Events
- Sleeping
- Eating
- Drinking
- Entertainment
- Shopping
- Information/ Transport

These symbols give you the vital information for each listing:

- Telephone Numbers
- Opening Hours
- Parking
- Nonsmoking
- Air-Conditioning
- Internet Access
- Wi-Fi Access
- Swimming Pool
- Vegetarian Selection
- English-Language Menu
- Family-Friendly
- Pet-Friendly
- Bus
- Ferry
- Metro
- Subway
- London Tube
- Tram
- Train

Reviews are organised by author preference.

Look out for these icons:

- TOP CHOICE — Our author's recommendation
- FREE — No payment required
- A green or sustainable option

Our authors have nominated these places as demonstrating a strong commitment to sustainability – for example by supporting local communities and producers, operating in an environmentally friendly way, or supporting conservation projects.

Map Legend

Sights
Beach
Buddhist
Castle
Christian
Hindu
Islamic
Jewish
Monument
Museum/Gallery
Ruin
Winery/Vineyard
Zoo
Other Sight

Activities, Courses & Tours
Diving/Snorkelling
Canoeing/Kayaking
Skiing
Surfing
Swimming/Pool
Walking
Windsurfing
Other Activity/ Course/Tour

Sleeping
Sleeping
Camping

Eating
Eating

Drinking
Drinking
Cafe

Entertainment
Entertainment

Shopping
Shopping

Information
Post Office
Tourist Information

Transport
Airport
Border Crossing
Bus
Cable Car/ Funicular
Cycling
Ferry
Monorail
Parking
S-Bahn
Taxi
Train/Railway
Tram
Tube Station
U-Bahn
Underground Train Station
Other Transport

Routes
Tollway
Freeway
Primary
Secondary
Tertiary
Lane
Unsealed Road
Plaza/Mall
Steps
Tunnel
Pedestrian Overpass
Walking Tour
Walking Tour Detour
Path

Boundaries
International
State/Province
Disputed
Regional/Suburb
Marine Park
Cliff
Wall

Population
Capital (National)
Capital (State/Province)
City/Large Town
Town/Village

Geographic
Hut/Shelter
Lighthouse
Lookout
Mountain/Volcano
Oasis
Park
Pass
Picnic Area
Waterfall

Hydrography
River/Creek
Intermittent River
Swamp/Mangrove
Reef
Canal
Water
Dry/Salt/ Intermittent Lake
Glacier

Areas
Beach/Desert
Cemetery (Christian)
Cemetery (Other)
Park/Forest
Sportsground
Sight (Building)
Top Sight (Building)

Marc Di Duca

Canterbury & the Southeast Originally from Darlington, County Durham, Marc has been a northerner-gone-south since 2000 and covered his adopted corner of weald and down for the past two editions of Lonely Planet's *England* and *Great Britain*. A travel author for eight years, Marc has updated and written the Lonely Planet guides of *Ukraine, Russia, Trans-Siberian Railway, Poland* and *Germany*, though he can usually be found in Sandwich, Kent, where he lives with his Kievite wife Tanya and their two sons.

Read more about Marc at: lonelyplanet.com/memebers/madidu

Belinda Dixon

Part of Wessex; Devon Belinda made a gleeful bolt for the sunny southwest for her post-grad, having been drawn there by the palm trees on campus. Like the best Westcountry limpets she's proved hard to shift since and now writes and broadcasts in the region. Research highlights for this book included kayaking up (and riding the tide down) the River Dart, hugging sarsen stones at Avebury, taking time out in Ilfracombe and oh-so-diligently testing the pick of Plymouth's newest eateries.

Damian Harper

London; Birmingham, the West Midlands & the Marches Born in London and growing up in Notting Hill, Damian went to school in Hampshire for a decade, cultivating a sense of affection for both city and country. Writing for Lonely Planet for more than 15 years, Damian recently turned his attention from far-flung cultures to his lush and well-watered homeland, revelling in England's diversity, good looks, insular charms, awe-inspiring sense of history and entirely intelligible local tongue (in the main).

Anna Kaminski

Oxford, Cotswolds & Around; Cambridge & East Anglia Anna's love affair with England began in 1991 once she got over the shock of moving from the Soviet Union to Cambridge – her home for the next 20 years. Since budget flights hadn't been invented at the time, her parents tirelessly tried to instil some culture in her by taking her to every museum, castle, church and stately home in a 250-mile radius, most of which she revisited with great pleasure during this research trip. Memorable moments from her most recent trip include slurping fresh oysters in Aldeburgh, driving along some impossibly narrow country lanes in the Cotswolds and getting acquainted with Oxford's ghosts.

Catherine Le Nevez

Nottingham & the East Midlands Catherine first roadtripped around England aged four and she's been roadtripping here at every opportunity since, completing her Doctorate of Creative Arts in Writing, Masters in Professional Writing, and post-grad qualifications in Editing and Publishing along the way, as well as dozens of Lonely Planet guidebooks and newspaper, magazine and online articles throughout the UK, Europe and beyond. Roaming castle ruins and corridors of stately homes were the highlights of researching this book, as was discovering idyllic countryside pubs.

Neil Wilson

Yorkshire From rock climbing trips to Yorkshire gritstone, to weekend getaways in York and Whitby, Neil has made many cross-border forays into 'God's own country' from his home in Scotland. Whether hiking across the high tops of the Yorkshire Dales, savouring Britain's best fish and chips on the Whitby waterfront or worshipping at the fountainhead of Theakston's Ales in Masham, he's never short of an excuse for yet another visit. Neil is a full-time travel writer based in Edinburgh, and has written more than 40 guidebooks for various publishers, including previous Lonely Planet editions of *England*.

OUR STORY

A beat-up old car, a few dollars in the pocket and a sense of adventure. In 1972 that's all Tony and Maureen Wheeler needed for the trip of a lifetime – across Europe and Asia overland to Australia. It took several months, and at the end – broke but inspired – they sat at their kitchen table writing and stapling together their first travel guide, *Across Asia on the Cheap*. Within a week they'd sold 1500 copies. Lonely Planet was born.

Today, Lonely Planet has offices in Melbourne, London and Oakland, with more than 600 staff and writers. We share Tony's belief that 'a great guidebook should do three things: inform, educate and amuse'.

OUR WRITERS

David Else

Coordinating Author As a professional writer, David has authored more than 40 books, including several editions of Lonely Planet's *England* and *Great Britain* guides. His knowledge comes from a lifetime of travel around the country – often on foot or by bike – a passion dating from university years, when heading for the hills was always more attractive than visiting the library. Originally from London, David has lived in Yorkshire and Derbyshire, and is now a resident of the Cotswolds. For this current edition of *England*, David's research took him from the Isle of Wight in the south, to Hadrian's Wall in the north – via most of the bits in between.

Read more about David at:
lonelyplanet.com/memebers/davidelse

Oliver Berry

Part of Wessex; Cornwall; the Lake District Oliver is a writer and photographer based in Cornwall. Among many other projects for Lonely Planet, Oliver has written the first editions of *Devon, Cornwall & Southwest England* and *The Lake District*, and worked on several previous editions of the *England* and *Great Britain* guides. You can see some of his latest work at www.oliverberry.com and follow him at www.twitter.com/olivertomberry.

Read more about Oliver at:
lonelyplanet.com/memebers/oliverberry

Fionn Davenport

Manchester, Liverpool & the Northwest; Newcastle & the Northeast Fionn has been traipsing about Northern England's bigger burgs for over a decade and has found that the cities of the north are simply fantastic; a rich repository of culture, fine museums, terrific restaurants and – most importantly – peopled by a few million lovable gruffs that exude a no-nonsense warmth. Working on recent editions of *England* has afforded him the opportunity to watch these regions find a myriad interesting ways to reinvent themselves in the face of constant economic challenges. And, when he needs a little bit of greenery, he just skips out to northern Lancashire or the Northumberland coast for a bit of bucolic R&R. Fionn is a full-time travel writer and broadcaster based in Dublin, Ireland – you can catch him on Newstalk 106-108 (www.newstalk.ie).

OVER PAGE MORE WRITERS

Published by Lonely Planet Publications Pty Ltd
ABN 36 005 607 983
7th edition – Mar 2013
ISBN 978 1 74220 050 7

10 9 8 7 6 5 4 3 2
Printed in China